A User's Guide to Trade Marks and Passing Off

Other titles in the 'A User's Guide' series:

A User's Guide to Intellectual Property in Life Sciences
March 2021
9781526511751
£125

A User's Guide to Data Protection, Fourth Edition
August 2020
9781526515704
£115

A User's Guide to Patents, Fifth Edition
June 2019
9781526508683
£125

A User's Guide to Copyright, Seventh Edition
December 2017
9781847666857
£135

www.bloomsburyprofessional.com/usersguide

A User's Guide to Trade Marks and Passing Off

Fifth edition

Nicholas Caddick QC
Barrister of Hogarth Chambers

Ben Longstaff
Barrister of Hogarth Chambers

Jamie Muir Wood
Barrister of Hogarth Chambers

Charlotte Duly
Chartered Trade Mark Attorney, Head of Brand Protection at Charles Russell Speechlys LLP

Bloomsbury Professional

LONDON • DUBLIN • EDINBURGH • NEW YORK • NEW DELHI • SYDNEY

BLOOMSBURY PROFESSIONAL
Bloomsbury Publishing Plc
50 Bedford Square, London, WC1B 3DP, UK
1385 Broadway, New York, NY 10018, USA
29 Earlsfort Terrace, Dublin 2, Ireland

British Library Cataloguing-in-Publication Data

A catalogue record for this book is available from the British Library.

ISBN: PB: 978 1 52651 155 3
Epdf: 978 1 52651 157 7
Epub: 978 1 52651 156 0

Typeset by Evolution Design & Digital Ltd (Kent)

Preface

This is the fifth edition of the *User's Guide to Trade Marks and Passing Off*, one of Bloomsbury Professional's series of User's Guides. Like the other Guides, this book provides practical guidance as to both the law and practice in relation to its subject matter

Previous editions of this work reflected the extent to which, as a result of the UK's membership of the European Union, modern trade mark law in the UK has been shaped by European legislation and decisions of the European Court. This present edition is being published in the aftermath of the ending of that membership and seeks to provide assistance as to the state of trade mark law as a result of Brexit. Most significant is the ending of protection in the UK for European Union trade marks and the automatic replacement of such marks in existence as at 31 December 2020 with corresponding rights in the UK. Otherwise, for the time being at least, UK trade mark law is likely to remain on a parallel track to EU trade mark law given that the UK's Trade Marks Act 1994 was enacted and amended to implement various EU directives intended to harmonise trade mark law across the EU, and the provisions of those directives are mirrored in the European Union Trade Marks Regulation (2017/1001) which governs EU trade marks. Also, European decisions made and European legislation enacted prior to 31 December 2020 will remain in effect in the UK as part of 'EU retained law', although subsequent decisions and legislation will not be binding on UK courts but merely matters to which UK courts can have regard.

Whilst EU trade marks are no longer effective in the UK and the UK courts will no longer sit as EU trade mark courts, this edition continues to address the law with regard to both UK and EU trade marks as practitioners are likely to continue to need to deal with both types of right.

This edition reflects the law as at August 2021. In addition to dealing with the fallout of Brexit, it deals with the coming into effect of the EU Trade Marks Regulation 2017. Other areas updated include:

- Chapter 2 – changes to the definition of a sign capable of registration (the removal of the requirement that it be capable of graphical representation) and a consideration of decisions as regards the significance of colours with regard to registrability.

- Chapter 3 – the introduction of European Union certification marks.
- Chapter 4 – the impact of the *London Taxi* and *Jaguar Land Rover* cases as regards the issue of distinctiveness and, in relation to the law on bad faith, the significant guidance provided by the CJEU in the *Koton* and *Skykick* cases.
- Chapter 5 – the effect of the Court of Appeal's decision in *Comic Enterprises* as regards the relative grounds of opposition to registrability.
- Chapters 7, 8 and 10 – the latest practice of the UKIPO and the EUIPO as regards the registration of trade marks and rights of representation.
- Chapter 13 – changes in the law as regards licensees and their right to sue for infringement.
- Chapter 17 – the impact of Brexit on remedies, changes in the law as regards notifications to the Customs authorities and with important guidance as to the law of search orders and imaging orders given by the Court of Appeal in the *TBD* case.
- Chapter 18 – rewritten to reflect changes made in the law by the Intellectual Property (Unjustified Threats) Act 2017.

For this edition, we are pleased to welcome Jamie Muir Wood (a fellow barrister at Hogarth Chambers) and Charlotte Duly (Head of Brand Protection at Charles Russell Speechlys LLP) to the editorial team and, as always, we are grateful to all our colleagues for their input on issues of interest to trade mark lawyers – particularly Brexit – and to our publishers for their patience and support.

Nicholas Caddick QC
Ben Longstaff
Jamie Muir Wood
Charlotte Duly

London, 2021

Contents

Preface *v*
Table of Cases *xxi*
Table of Statutes *xlv*
Table of Statutory Instruments *li*
Table of EC and International Material *lv*

Chapter 1 Introduction
Registered trade marks 1.02
Well-known trade marks 1.09
Certification and collective marks 1.10
Geographical indications, designations of origin, traditional speciality guarantees 1.11
International conventions 1.12
Passing off 1.13
Olympic symbols 1.14

Chapter 2 What is a trade mark?
Trade mark: the statutory definition 2.01
A 'sign' 2.03
Capable of being represented clearly and precisely 2.04
Capable of distinguishing goods or services of one undertaking from those of other undertakings 2.10
Registration in respect of goods or services 2.11
Undertakings 2.12
Unregistered trade marks 2.13
Passing off, s 2(2) 2.14
Impediment to registration 2.15
Defence to infringement, s 11(3) 2.16
Well-known trade marks 2.17
Well-known trade marks 2.18
Who is entitled to protection—meaning of 'Convention country' 2.19
Meaning of 'well known' 2.20
Well-known marks—basis for opposing registration of later marks 2.23

Well-known marks—defence to infringement of later marks? 2.24
Well-known marks—remedies for infringement 2.26
Company names, business names and internet domain names 2.27
Company names 2.28
Choice of name 2.29
Changing a company's name—voluntary 2.30
Changing a company's name—compulsory 2.31
Publicity to be given to a company name 2.32
Passing off and trade mark infringement 2.33
Unincorporated businesses and partnerships 2.35
Domain names 2.36

Chapter 3 Other kinds of mark—collective and certification marks, and protected descriptions

Introduction 3.01
Collective and certification marks 3.02
Protected descriptions 3.05
UK—applications for registration of certification and collective marks 3.06
UK—who is the 'applicant' 3.08
UK—registration process for certification and collective marks 3.12
UK—absolute grounds for refusal 3.13
UK—applicant for a certification mark must not carry on a business in the goods or services 3.16
UK—misleading marks 3.17
UK—regulations relating to certification/collective marks 3.19
UK—time for filing the regulations 3.21
UK—regulations relating to collective marks 3.22
UK—regulations relating to certification marks 3.23
UK—post-registration amendment of regulations 3.24
UK—post-registration transfer of ownership 3.25
UK—revocation and invalidity of certification and collective marks 3.27
UK—infringement of collective and certification marks 3.30
European Union collective and certification marks 3.31
EU—collective and certification marks—the application process 3.32
EU—collective and certification marks—requirement to submit regulations 3.33
EU—collective and certification marks—examination 3.34
EU—collective and certification marks—amendment of regulations 3.35
EU—collective and certification marks—revocation and invalidity 3.36
EU—collective and certification marks—infringement 3.37

Protected geographical indications and designations of origin 3.38
Protected Descriptions—the subject matter of protection 3.39
Protected Descriptions—descriptors ineligible for protection 3.43
Protected Descriptions—formal requirements for protection 3.47
Protected Descriptions—use of the protected description 3.50
Protected Descriptions—scope of protection 3.52
Protected Descriptions—relationships with trade marks 3.53
Traditional Speciality Guarantees 3.54

Chapter 4 Absolute grounds for refusal
The absolute grounds for a refusal of registration 4.01
Signs that do not satisfy the definition of a trade mark—s 3(1)(a); Art 7(1)(b) 4.06
Marks devoid of distinctive character—s 3(1)(b); Art 7(1)(b) 4.07
Descriptive marks—s 3(1)(c); Art 7(1)(c) 4.19
Generic marks—s 3(1)(d); Art 7(1)(d) 4.30
Acquired distinctiveness—s 3(1); Art 7(3) 4.34
Marks for the shape of the goods—s 3(2); Art 7(1)(e) 4.40
Marks contrary to policy or morality—s 3(3)(a); Art 7(1)(f) 4.45
Deceptive trade marks—s 3(3)(b); Art 7(1)(g) 4.49
Contrary to law—s 3(4) 4.52
Emblems—ss 3(5), 4, 57 and 58; Art 7(1)(h) and 7(1)(i) 4.53
Bad faith—s 3(6); Art 52(1)(b) 4.55

Chapter 5 Relative grounds for refusal of registration; trade mark functions; honest concurrent use
Introduction 5.01
Overlap with infringement provisions 5.03
References to legislation 5.04
Conflicts with earlier registered trade marks 5.05
Grounds for opposing registration 5.05
Harm to the trade mark function 5.06
Applications for registration of an earlier mark 5.07
Issues arising 5.08
Earlier trade mark 5.10
Identity of marks 5.13
Similarity of marks 5.17
Identity of goods or services 5.28
Similarity of goods and services 5.32
Likelihood of confusion 5.37
Interdependence of assessments of similarity 5.53
Distinctiveness of the earlier trade mark through use 5.56
To what extent are the common elements of the marks used by various parties? 5.59

Marks with a reputation 5.63
Taking unfair advantage of the distinctive character or repute of the mark 5.75
Detriment to distinctive character or repute 5.79
Use of the later mark without due cause 5.87
Conflicts with other earlier rights 5.90
UK: rights protecting unregistered trade marks used in the course of trade 5.91
UK: protection for other unregistered rights (copyright, design right, etc) 5.93
Unregistered rights applicable to EUTMs 5.94
Trade mark 'functions' 5.97
The essential function—origin 5.98
Other functions—the advertising and investment functions 5.100
Current status of 'honest concurrent use' 5.106

Chapter 6 Classification
The requirement for a classification system 6.01
Nice Classification System 6.02
The requirement for an applicant to specify class(es) and the goods, and/or services 6.03
Points for the applicant to consider when applying 6.04
Requirement for clarity and precision in specifying goods or services 6.04
Use of the Class headings to specify goods and services 6.05
Specification should cover goods/services in both existing and anticipated future areas of activity 6.06
Difficulties arising when the specification is too broadly stated 6.07
Exclusions from protection—practice since *Postkantoor* 6.12
Retail, wholesale and shopping-centre services 6.14
Amendments to applications—restrictions on widening the scope of an application post-filing 6.16

Chapter 7 UK procedure for the registration of a trade mark
Introduction 7.01
The application 7.03
The application form and fees payable 7.03
Requirements for the filing of an application 7.08
Requirements in order to obtain a filing date 7.09
Requirements not necessary to obtain a filing date 7.10
Deficient applications 7.11
Further requirements 7.12
Examination of the application 7.14
Publication of the application 7.17
Opposition to the application 7.18

The time for filing opposition to the registration 7.19
The need to contact the applicant for the trade mark before opposing—impact on costs 7.21
Formalities in the filing of opposition 7.23
Notification of opposition to applicant 7.27
The cooling-off period 7.28
Extension of the cooling-off period 7.29
Termination of the cooling-off period 7.30
The applicant's Form TM8 incorporating the counterstatement 7.31
The request for the opponent to prove use 7.32
The counterstatement 7.33
Preliminary indications 7.36
Implications of a preliminary indication 7.37
Procedural consequences of a preliminary indication 7.39
Notice to proceed with the opposition 7.43
The filing of evidence 7.44
Time limits for the filing of evidence 7.47
Extension of time for filing evidence 7.48
The form of evidence in opposition proceedings 7.50
Who should give the witness statement 7.51
Evidence by the opponent regarding the likelihood of confusion—the distinctiveness of the earlier mark 7.53
Evidence by the applicant regarding the likelihood of confusion—the distinctiveness of the earlier mark 7.58
Evidence regarding the goods and services 7.64
Challenging evidence 7.66
Cross-examination 7.68
Hearings 7.73
Skeleton arguments 7.74
Costs 7.75
Fast track oppositions 7.77
Fast track procedure 7.78
Appeals 7.81
Observations 7.82

Chapter 8 Application procedure before EUIPO
Introduction—EU trade marks 8.01
EUIPO and its procedures 8.02
The filing of an application for a EUTM 8.04
The requirements if the application is to be given a filing date 8.05
Representation of the mark 8.06
Further formal requirements 8.07
Claiming priority 8.09
Claiming seniority 8.10
Withdrawal or amendment of application 8.11

Examination of the application 8.12
The search 8.13
Publication 8.14
The opposition procedure 8.15
Opposition—the basis for opposing registration 8.16
Opposition—procedural requirements 8.18
Opposition—admissibility of the notice of opposition 8.23
Opposition—the absolute requirements for admissibility 8.25
Opposition—payment of the fees 8.26
Opposition—more on the absolute requirements for admissibility 8.27
Opposition—relative admissibility requirements 8.31
Opposition—further elements to consider 8.37
Opposition—two-month cooling-off period 8.41
Opposition—filing of evidence 8.42
Opposition—proving existence and validity of earlier trade mark applications/registrations 8.44
Opposition—documents to be in the language of the proceedings or translated 8.47
Opposition—applicant's evidence and observations in reply 8.49
Opposition—applicant's request that opponent proves use 8.52
Opposition—opponent's proof of 'genuine use' 8.54
Opposition—the evidence to prove genuine use 8.56
Opposition—further evidence and arguments 8.59
Opposition—formalities for filing evidence 8.60
Opposition—costs 8.63
Appeals 8.64

Chapter 9 International conventions—the Madrid System
Introduction 9.01
The Madrid System 9.02
The Madrid System in outline 9.04
The basic application/registration 9.08
The application form for an international registration 9.12
Consideration by WIPO—notification of formal irregularities (irregularities other than as to the classification of goods and services or their indication) 9.20
Consideration by WIPO—irregularities as the specification of goods and services 9.25
Designations with additional requirements 9.30
International registration, notification of the office of origin 9.31

Chapter 10 Representation
Introduction 10.01
Representation before UKIPO 10.02

Need for an address in the UK, EEA or Channel Islands 10.02
Appointment of a representative before the UKIPO 10.03
Cancellation of representation 10.04
Representation before EUIPO 10.05
Meaning of 'legal practitioner' 10.06
Meaning of 'professional representative' 10.07
Representation before WIPO 10.09
Appointment of a representative 10.10
Cancellation of appointment 10.11

Chapter 11 Invalidity
Introduction 11.01
A Invalidity under the TMA 1994—s 47 11.02
The grounds for declaring a trade mark invalid 11.02
Invalidity due to breach of s 3 (absolute grounds for refusal) 11.03
Invalidity due to existence of an earlier trade mark or earlier right (relative grounds for refusal) 11.04
The procedure for invalidation of UK trade marks under s 47 11.12
The procedure before UKIPO 11.13
B Invalidation proceedings at EUIPO 11.18
The basis for invalidation proceedings at EUIPO 11.18
Procedure for an application for invalidity before EUIPO 11.24
Next steps—procedure following an admissible application for a declaration of invalidity 11.32
Proof of use 11.33
Costs and appeals before EUIPO 11.35

Chapter 12 Revocation
Introduction 12.01
The action for revocation 12.02
The legislative provisions 12.03
A Revocation for non-use: s 46(1)(a)–(b); Art 58(1)(a) 12.04
The date to be considered 12.05
The meaning of 'genuine use' 12.06
The level of use required 12.07
Nature of activities 12.08
Use of the mark as registered 12.10
Whether a mark differs in elements that affect its distinctive character 12.11
Use for the goods or services of the registration 12.15
Use in the relevant time period 12.16
Use in the relevant territory 12.18
Partial revocation 12.19
The UK approach to partial revocation on the basis of non-use 12.20

The approach to partial revocation on the basis of non-use before EUIPO 12.23
Proper reasons for non-use 12.25
Cases where proper reasons have been found 12.26
B Revocation where trade mark has become the common name in the trade for a product or service for which it is registered: s 46(1)(c); Art 58(1)(b) 12.28
'The common name' and 'in the trade' 12.29
For the product or service for which it is registered 12.30
Resulting from the acts or inactivity of the registered proprietor 12.34
C Revocation where trade mark has become misleading: s 46(1)(d); Art 58(1)(c) 12.37
Practice and procedure 12.38

Chapter 13 Ownership of and dealings with trade marks
Introduction 13.01
UK registered trade marks 13.02
UK trade mark—a property right; legal and beneficial ownership 13.02
UK trade mark—co-ownership 13.03
UK trade marks—assignments and other transfers 13.04
UK trade marks—registration of assignments and of other transfers 13.08
UK trade marks—title to and dealings with applications for registration 13.10
UK trade marks—licence and mere 'consents' 13.11
UK trade marks—the terms of a licence 13.15
UK trade mark—right of licensees to bring infringement proceedings 13.38
UK trade mark—recordal of licences 13.43
UK trade mark—consequences of failure to register a registrable transaction 13.47
European Community trade marks 13.49
EUTM—property right to be dealt with in its entirety 13.49
EUTM—applications for an EUTM 13.50
EUTM—transfers 13.51
EUTM—effect vis-à-vis third parties 13.54
EUTM—recordal of transfers 13.55
EUTM—licences 13.58
EUTM—recording of licences at EUIPO 13.65
International registrations 13.69
International registrations—recordal of assignments at WIPO 13.69
International registrations—recordal of licences at WIPO 13.71

Chapter 14 Infringement and parties to infringement actions

Introduction 14.01
A Summary of the infringement provisions 14.03
Relevant legislation 14.03
The infringement provisions 14.04
Overlap with relative grounds for a refusal to register a mark 14.05
B Exclusive rights 14.06
C Identical marks, identical goods or services ('double identity')—Directive Art 10(2)(a); TMA 1994 s 10(1); EUTMR Art 9(2)(a) 14.09
Condition (i)—use of a sign by a third party 14.12
Condition (ii)—the use must be use in the course of trade 14.20
Condition (iii)—the use must be without the consent of the trade mark proprietor 14.22
Condition (iv)—the use must be of a sign that is identical to the mark 14.23
Condition (v)—the use in relation to identical goods or services 14.24
Condition (vi)—the use must affect or be liable to affect the functions of the trade mark 14.30
D Likelihood of confusion—Directive Art 10(2)(b); TMA 1994 s 10(2); EUTMR Art 9(2)(b) 14.39
Conditions (i), (ii) and (iii) 14.41
Condition (iv)—use of a sign that is identical or similar to the mark 14.42
Condition (v)—use in relation to identical or similar goods or services 14.43
Condition (vi)—likelihood of confusion 14.44
E Unfair advantage of or detriment to the distinctive character or repute of a mark—Directive Art 10(2)(c), TMA 1994 s 10(3), EUTMR Art 9(2)(c) 14.45
Condition (i)—mark must have a reputation 14.47
Conditions (ii)–(v) 14.48
Condition (vi) 14.49
Condition (vii)—link with the mark 14.50
Condition (viii)—injury: causing detriment to or taking unfair advantage of distinctive character or repute 14.51
Condition (ix)—use was without due cause 14.53
F Who may be sued for infringement 14.54
Those using the mark 14.55
Joint tortfeasors 14.56
Affixing a sign to materials—Directive Art 11; TMA 1994 s 10(3B); EUTMR Art 10 14.59
G Who may sue for infringement? 14.61

Proprietors 14.61
Co-proprietors 14.62
Licensees 14.63

Chapter 15 Defences, disclaimers and limitations
Introduction 15.01
Defences under s 11/Arts 14, 16 and 138 15.05
Use of a registered trade mark where that mark is not liable to be declared invalid—s 11(1)/Art 16 15.06
Descriptive use—s 11(2)/Art 14 15.09
Use of one's own name—s 11(2)(a)/Art 14(1)(a) 15.10
Use of indications of characteristics—s 11(2)(b)/Art 14(1)(b) 15.13
Use to indicate intended purpose—s 11(2)(c)/Art 14(1)(c) 15.19
The 'honest practices' proviso to s 11(2)/Art 14 15.23
Use of earlier rights in a particular locality—s 11(3)/Art 138 15.26
Acquiescence—s 48/Art 61 15.27
Exhaustion of rights—s 12/Art 15 15.31
Exhaustion in Europe and beyond 15.34
Acts amounting to first marketing 15.37
By or with the consent of the proprietor 15.39
Demonstrating consent 15.40
Legitimate reasons to oppose the further dealings in the goods 15.43
The meaning of artificial partitioning 15.46
Adversely affecting the original condition of the product 15.48
Presentation not to affect the reputation of the trade mark or of its owner 15.49
Requirement to label, provide notice and provide samples 15.51
Disclaimers—s 13(1)(a) 15.52
Limitations—s 13(1)(b) 15.57
The rights of co-proprietors under UK law 15.58

Chapter 16 Comparative and misleading advertising, and malicious falsehood
Introduction 16.01
General scheme of the CAD 16.07
The definitions in Article 2 16.08
Misleading advertising—Article 3 16.11
Allowance comparative advertising—Article 4 16.13
Malicious falsehood 16.22
Definition of malice 16.24
The meaning of the statement 16.26
Damage 16.28
Hyperbole and puffery 16.29
Malicious falsehood and comparative advertising 16.31
Relief 16.32

Chapter 17 Remedies
Introduction 17.01
Remedies for infringement of registered trade marks 17.02
Remedies—UK trade marks 17.02
Remedies—the effect of Brexit; comparable trade marks (EU) 17.03
Remedies—EUTMs 17.04
Pecuniary remedies—election between damages or an account of profits 17.05
Damages 17.08
Accounts of profits, s 14(2) 17.17
Injunctions, s 14(2) 17.20
Any other relief, s 14(2) 17.28
Remedies in respect of infringing goods, material and articles 17.34
Regulation (EU) No 608/2013 (as amended) 17.54
TMA 1994 s 89 17.62
Remedies for infringement of well-known marks 17.65
Unauthorised application for registration by an agent or representative 17.73
Unauthorised use of royal arms 17.76
Co-proprietors 17.80
Licensees 17.82
Jurisdiction of the courts 17.86

Chapter 18 Groundless threats
Introduction 18.01
Threats of infringement proceedings 18.03
Form of 'threat' 18.04
Excluded threats 18.05
The permitted communications exclusion 18.06
Not an 'express threat' 18.07
A permitted communication 18.08
Information that is 'necessary' 18.09
A permitted purpose 18.10
Purposes that are not permitted 18.11
Person aggrieved 18.12
Person liable in respect of an actionable threat 18.13
Threats by professional adviser 18.14
Professional adviser 18.15
The conditions to be satisfied 18.16
Defences 18.17
Remedies 18.18

Chapter 19 Criminal offences
Introduction 19.01

Unauthorised use of a trade mark: counterfeiting	19.02
The mental element	19.04
Without consent	19.08
Infringing signs	19.10
Section 92(1)—goods bearing the sign	19.16
Section 92(2)—materials bearing the sign	19.20
Section 92(3)—articles for making signs	19.23
Section 92(5) defence—reasonable belief of non-infringement	19.26
Partnerships and bodies corporate	19.30
Enforcement	19.31
Penalties	19.32
Offences relating to the register	19.34
Section 94—Falsification of the register	19.35
Section 95—Falsely representing a mark as registered	19.38
Other offences	19.42
Section 99—Unauthorised use of royal arms	19.42

Chapter 20 Passing off

Introduction	20.01
The boundaries of passing off—need for deception and goodwill	20.03
Contrast with trade mark law	20.06
Who can sue	20.07
'Extended' and 'reverse' passing off	20.08
Significance of case law	20.09
Elements of the classic form of passing off	20.10
Structure of this chapter	20.17
A Nature of goodwill	20.18
Definition of goodwill	20.19
Ownership of goodwill	20.20
Scope and extent of goodwill	20.24
Time of assessment	20.26
Goodwill in 'extended' passing off	20.27
International goodwill	20.29
'Anticipatory' goodwill	20.32
Residual goodwill	20.33
An alternative to goodwill—s 56(2) of the Trade Marks Act 1994	20.34
B Embodiment of goodwill	20.35
Inherently distinctive trade marks	20.36
Other signs, get-ups, images and features	20.38
Descriptive names—secondary meaning	20.41
C The subject matter of the misrepresentation	20.44
Misrepresentation as to origin	20.45

Misrepresentation as to association, sponsorship, endorsement or other trade connection 20.46
Other misrepresentations: the key element of deception, and the notion of 'initial interest' confusion 20.49
Who must be deceived by the misrepresentation? 20.51
D Factors which may negate a 'misrepresentation' 20.53
Does intent matter? 20.54
Use of own name 20.56
Acts outside the United Kingdom 20.57
Descriptive use of terms or names 20.59
Use of other distinguishing material, including disclaimers 20.61
Comparative advertising, spares and accessories 20.63
E Common field of activity 20.64
Relevance to deception or likelihood of deception 20.65
Relationship with damage 20.67
F Damage to or loss of goodwill 20.68
Loss of sales, damage by substitution 20.69
Dilution of the value of the goodwill 20.70
G Evidence 20.71
Evidence of reputation/goodwill 20.72
Evidence of misrepresentation 20.74
Evidence of damage to goodwill 20.82
Methods of obtaining evidence 20.88
H Defences 20.96
I Remedies 20.100
Damages 20.101
Account of profits 20.103
Injunctions 20.105
Interim injunctions 20.106
Comment on interim injunctions 20.107
Delivery up 20.109
Order to change name 20.110
J Practical matters 20.111
Pre-emptive measures to consider 20.111
Other matters 20.113

Chapter 21 Olympic symbols
Introduction 21.01
The Olympics Association Right 21.03
Infringement 21.05
Relevant representations 21.07
Suggesting an association 21.09
Use in course of trade, in the UK, without consent 21.12
Defences 21.13
Remedies 21.16

Appendices

Appendix 1 Trade Marks Act 1994 421
Appendix 2 Regulation (EU) 2017/1001 of the European Parliament and of the Council of 14 June 2017 on the European Union trade mark (codification) 559
Appendix 3 Directive (EU) 2015/2436 of the European Parliament and of the Council of 16 December 2015 to approximate the laws of the Member States relating to trade marks 681

Index *713*

Table of Cases

32Red Plc v WHG (International) Ltd [2011] EWHC 62 (Ch), [2011] ETMR 21, [2011] All ER (D) 210 (Jan) 4.58, 12.28, 12.37, 17.14

A

AS v Deutsches Patent und Markenamt (Case C-541/18) [2019] Bus LR 2248, [2019] 9 WLUK 121, [2019] ETMR 59 .... 2.09
AS Watson v Boots Co (Patents County Court, 8 September 211)........... 4.10
Abba Case *see* Lyngstad v Anabas Products Ltd
Adam Opel AG v Autec AG (Case C-48/05) [2007] ECR I-01017, [2007] ETMR 33, [2007] All ER (D) 193 (Jan) 5.06, 14.10, 15.15
Adidas-Salomon AG and Adidas Benelux v Fitnessworld Trading Ltd (Case C-408/01) [2004] Ch 120, [2003] ECR I-12537, [2003] ETMR 91 .... 5.21, 5.65, 5.75, 5.86, 14.50
Ad-Lib Club v Granville [1971] 2 All ER 300, [1972] RPC 673, [1971] FSR 1 .... 20.33
Adobe Systems Inc v Netcom Distributors Ltd [2012] 5 WLUK 822...... 12.02
Advocaat Case *see* Erven Warnink BV v J Townend & Sons (Hull) Ltd (No 1)
Ajinomoto Sweeteners Europe SAS v Asda Stores Ltd [2010] FSR 30... 16.27
Akhtar v Grout (1998) 162 JP 714, (1998) 162 JPN 786 .... 19.09
ALADIN trade mark *see* Reckitt Benckiser (España) v OHIM
Alain Bernardin et Cie v Pavilion Properties Ltd (Crazy Horse) [1967] RPC 581, [1967] FSR 341... 20.29
Alcon Inc v OHIM (Case C-412/05) [2007] ETMR 68, [2007] All ER (D) 238 (Apr) 5.46
American Clothing Associates NV v OHIM (Case C-202/08) [2010] ETMR 3 .... 4.54
American Cyanamid Co v Ethicon Ltd [1975] AC 396, [1975] 2 WLR 316, [1975] 1 All ER 504, [1975] RPC 513, [1975] FSR 101.. 16.33, 17.23, 17.24, 20.106, 20.107
Anciens Établissements Panhard et Levassor SA v Panhard-Levassor Motor Co Ltd [1901] 2 Ch 513, 85 LT 20, [1900–3] All ER Rep 477... 20.29
Andrex/Nouvelle *see* Kimberly-Clark Ltd v Fort Sterling Ltd
Anheuser-Busch Inc v Budejovicky Budvar NP [1984] FSR 413, (1984) 128 SJ 398, (1984) 81 LS Gaz 1369 .... 20.29

Anheuser-Busch Inc v Budejovicky Budvar Národni Podnik (Case C-245/02) [2004] ECR I-10989, [2005] ETMR 27, [2004] All ER (D) 271 (Nov)........ 5.101, 14.10, 15.24, 15.25
Annabel's (Berkeley Square) Ltd v G Schock (t/a Annabel's Escort Agency) [1972] RPC 838, [1972] FSR 261........ 20.65
Ansul BV v Ajax Brandbeveiliging BV (Case C-40/01) [2005] Ch 97, [2003] ECR I-2439, [2003] ETMR 45, [2003] RPC 40 .. 8.54, 12.06, 12.08, 12.15
Antec International Ltd v South Western Chicks (Warren) Ltd (Interlocutory Injunction) [1997] FSR 278........ 20.106
Antec International Ltd v South Western Chicks (Warren) Ltd [1998] FSR 738, (1998) 21(6) IPD 21062, (1998) 95(18) LSG 32........ 20.41
Anton Piller KG v Manufacturing Processes Ltd [1976] Ch 55, [1976] 2 WLR 162, [1976] 1 All ER 779, [1976] RPC 719, [1976] FSR 129........ 17.28
Apple Inc v Deutsches Patent und Markenamt (Case C-421/13) [2014] Bus LR 962, [2015] CEC 120, [2014] ETMR 48........ 2.03, 2.08
Argos Ltd v Argos Systems Inc [2017] EWHC 231 (Ch); *aff'd* [2018] EWCA Civ 2211, [2019] Bus LR 1728, [2019] FSR 3........ 5.79, 14.18
Arsenal Football Club v Reed (Case C-206/01) [2003] Ch 454, [2002] ECR I-10273, [2003] ETMR 19, [2003] 1 CMLR 12, [2003] RPC 9........ 5.06, 5.49, 5.101, 5.105, 14.10, 14.31
Artistic Upholstery Ltd v Art Forma (Furniture) Ltd [1999] 4 All ER 277, [2000] FSR 311........ 20.23
Ashworth Hospital Authority v MGN Ltd [2002] UKHL 29, [2002] 1 WLR 2033, [2002] 4 All ER 193........ 17.31
Asprey & Garrard Ltd v WRA (Guns) Ltd (t/a William R Asprey Esq) [2001] EWCA Civ 1499, [2002] FSR 31, [2002] ETMR 47, [2002] IP&T 38........ 15.12, 20.56
Associated Newspapers Ltd v Express Newspapers [2003] FSR 51........ 20.41
Ate My Heart Inc v Mind Candy Ltd (Lady Ga Ga Case) [2011] EWHC 2741 (Ch)........ 17.26
ATURION *see* Sanofi-Aventis
Audi AG v OHIM (Case C-398/08) [2010] ETMR 18, [2010] FSR 24........ 2.09, 4.17

B

BBC v Talksport Ltd (No 1) [2001] FSR 6........ 20.106
BABY-DRY *see* Procter & Gamble Co v OHIM
Backaldrin Osterreich The Kornspitz Co GmbH v Pfahnl Backmittel GmbH (Case C-409/12) [2014] Bus LR 320, [2014] ETMR 30........ 12.29, 12.34
Balden v Shorter [1933] Ch 427, [1933] All ER Rep 249, 102 LJ 191, 148 LT 471........ 16.24
Barnsley Brewery Co Ltd v RBNB [1997] FSR 462........ 20.106
Basic Trademark SA's Trade Mark Application [2005] RPC 25, [2006] ETMR 24........ 4.48
Bayerische Motorenwerke AG v Deenik (Case C-63/97) [1999] ECR I-905, [1999] 1 CMLR 1099, [1999] ETMR 339........ 15.20

Bayerische Motorenwerke AG v Round & Metal Ltd [2012] EWHC 2099 (Pat), [2012] ECC 28, [2013] FSR 18 .... 15.25
Bayerische Motorenwerke AG v Shaun Coley (t/a BMW Mini Gearbox Centre) [2014] EWHC 3053 (IPEC) 20.50
Baywatch Productions Co Inc v Home Video Channel [1997] FSR 22, [1997] EMLR 102, (1997) 20(1) IPD 20010 .... 20.47, 20.48
Belgian Electronic Sorting Technology v Peelaers (Case C-657/11) [2013] Bus LR 1265, [2013] ETMR 45 .... 16.08
Ben & Jerry's Case 19 January 1995, IPD 18051 .... 20.32
Bentley 1962 Ltd v Bentley Motors Ltd [2019] EWHC 2925 (Ch), [2019] 11 WLUK 2, [2020] ETMR 8 .... 5.110
BergSpechte Outdoor Reisen und Alpinschule Edi Koblmuller GmbH v Guni (Case C-278/08) [2010] ECR I-2517, [2010] All ER (D) 280 (Mar) 14.21, 14.27
Best Buy Co Inc v Worldwide Sales Corpn Espana SL [2011] EWCA Civ 618, [2011] Bus LR 1166, [2011] FSR 30 ... 18.02, 18.03, 18.04, 18.12
Bignell (t/a Just Employment) v Just Employment Law Ltd [2007] EWHC 2203 (Ch), [2008] FSR 6 .... 20.24
Bimbo SA v OHIM (Case C-519/12P) [2014] ETMR 41 .... 5.38
BIOMILD *see* Campina Melkunie BV v Benelux-Merkenbureau
Björnekulla Fruktindustrier AB v Procordia Food AB (BOSTONGURKA) (Case C-371/02) [2004] ECR I-5791, [2004] RPC 912, [2002] ETMR 42, [2005] IP & T 112 .... 12.29
Blayney v Clogau St David's Gold Mines Ltd [2002] EWCA Civ 1007, [2003] FSR 19, [2002] All ER (D) 242 (Jul) 17.13, 17.14
Blomqvist v Rolex SA (Case C-98/13) [2014] Bus LR 356, [2014] ETMR 25, [2014] ECDR 10 .... 14.19, 17.60
Blu-Tack *see* Bostik Ltd v Sellotape GB Ltd
Boegli-Gravures SA v Darsail-ASP Ltd [2009] EWHC 2690 (Pat), [2009] All ER (D) 238 (Nov) 14.57
Boehringer Ingelheim KG v Swingward Ltd (Case C-348/04) [2007] ETMR 71, [2007] All ER (D) 240 (Apr) 15.50, 15.51
Boehringer Ingelheim Ltd v Vetplus Ltd [2007] EWCA Civ 583, [2007] FSR 29, [2007] All ER (D) 221 (Jun) 16.33
Bollinger (J) v Costa Brava Wine Co Ltd (No 3) [1960] Ch 262, [1959] 3 WLR 966, [1959] 3 All ER 800, [1960] RPC 16 .... 20.27
Bollinger (J) v Costa Brava Wine Co Ltd (No 4) [1961] 1 WLR 277, [1961] 1 All ER 561, [1961] RPC 116 .... 20.27
Bonnard v Perryman [1891] 2 Ch 269, 60 LJ Ch 617, 65 LT 506, 39 WR 435, 7 TLR 453 .... 16.33
Bostik Ltd v Sellotape GB Ltd (Blu-Tack) [1994] RPC 556, (1994) The Times, January 11 .... 20.61
BOSTONGURKA *see* Björnekulla Fruktindustrier AB v Procordia Food AB
Bovemij Verzekeringen NV v Benelux-Merkenbureau (EUROPOLIS) (Case C-108/05) [2007] ETMR 29, [2006] All ER (D) 46 (Sep) 4.37
Boxing Brands Ltd v Sports Direct International plc [2013] EWHC 2200 .... 15.26
Brain v Ingeldew Brown Bennington & Garrett (No 3); Brain v Riso National Laboratory [1997] FSR 511, (1997) 20(5) IPD 20047 . 18.03, 18.12

Bravado Merchandising Services Ltd v Mainstream Publishing (Edinburgh) Ltd (WET WET WET) [1996] FSR 205, 1996 SLT 597, 1996 SCLR 1, Ct of Sess (OH) 15.17
Bristol Conservatories Ltd v Conservatories Custom Built Ltd [1989] RPC 455 .... 20.49
Bristol-Myers Squibb v Paranova (Case C-427/93, C-429/93 & C-436/93) [2003] Ch 75, [1996] ECR I-3457, [1997] 1 CMLR 1151, [1997] FSR 102, [1996] ETMR 1 .... 15.45, 15.46, 15.47, 15.51
British Airways Plc v Ryanair Ltd [2001] FSR 32, [2001] ETMR 24, [2001] IP & T 373, [2008] All ER (D) 2118 .... 16.04
British Amateur Gymnastics Association v UK Gymanstics Ltd [2020] EWHC 1678 (IPEC), [2020] 6 WLUK 486 .... 5.84
British Diabetic Association v Diabetic Society Ltd [1995] 4 All ER 812, [1996] FSR 1, (1995) The Times, October 23 .... 20.42
British Shorinji Kempo Federation's Trade Mark Application (No 2569771) [2014] EWHC 285 (Ch) 4.28
British Sky Broadcasting Group v Microsoft Corpn [2013] EWHC 1826 (Ch) 5.54
British Sugar plc v James Robertson & Sons Ltd (TREAT) [1996] RPC 281, [1997] ETMR 118, (1996) 19(3) IPD 13 .... 5.32, 5.38, 7.62, 15.15
British Telecommunications v One in a Million Ltd [1999] 1 WLR 903, [1998] 4 All ER 476, [1999] FSR 1, [1998] ETMR 61, [1998] FSR 265, [1997] Info TLR 316, (1997) 16 Tr LR 554 .... 20.42, 20.50, 20.55, 20.78, 20.110
BUD and BUDWEISER BUDGRAU Trade Marks *see* Budejovicky Budvar Narodni Podnik v Anheuser Busch Inc
Budejovicky Budvar Narodni Podnik v Anheuser Busch Inc [2002] EWCA Civ 1534, [2003] IP & T 667; *sub nom* BUD and BUDWEISER BUDGRAU Trade Marks [2003] RPC 477 .... 12.11
Budejovicky Budvar Narodni Podnik v Anheuser Busch Inc [2008] EWHC 263 (Ch), [2008] RPC 21, [2008] All ER (D) 274 (Feb) 15.28
Budějovickí Budvar Národní Podnik v Anheuser-Busch Inc [2009] EWCA Civ 1022, [2010] RPC 7, [2009] All ER (D) 196 (Oct) 15.29
Budějovickí Budvar v OHIM – AnheuserBusch (BUDWEISER) T-225/06 and T-309/06 [2009] All ER (D) 250 (Feb), CFI 5.94
Budějovickí Budvar, národní podnik v Anheuser-Busch Inc (BUDWEISER), (Case C-482/09) [2011] WLR (D) 279, (2011) 22 September, CJEU, (2011) 3 February, AGO 5.108, 5.109, 5.110, 11.08, 11.09, 11.22, 15.30
Burberrys v Cording & Co Ltd (1909) 26 RPC 693, 100 LT 985, 25 TLR 576 .... 20.42
Burdon v Steel O-369-13 .... 20.33
Burge v Haycock [2001] EWCA Civ 900, [2002] RPC 28 .... 20.19

C

C v T BC [2014] EWHC 2482 (QB), [2015] ELR 1 .... 16.22

C & A Modes v C & A (Waterford) Ltd [1976] IR 148, [1978] FSR 126, Eire Sup Ct 20.31
C & P Development Co (London) Ltd v Sisabro Novelty Co Ltd [1953] 1 WLUK 57, (1953) 70 RPC 277 .... 18.03
CBS Songs Ltd v Amstrad Consumer Electronics plc [1988] AC 1013, [1988] 2 WLR 1191, [1988] 2 All ER 484, [1988] 2 FTLR 168, (1988) 132 SJ 789 .... 14.56
CPS v Morgan; *sub nom* R v Morgan (Prosecution Appeal under s 58 of the Criminal Justice Act 2003) [2006] EWCA Crim 1742, [2008] All ER (D) 120 (Mar) (Crim) 19.11
Cadbury Schweppes Pty Ltd v Pub Squash Co Pty Ltd [1981] 1 All ER 213, [1981] 1 WLR 193, [1981] RPC 429, PC 20.06, 20.38, 20.43
Cadbury Ltd v Ulmer GmbH [1988] FSR 385 .... 20.50
Calvin Klein Inc v International Apparel Syndicate [1995] FSR 515, [1995] IPLR 83 .... 20.31
Calvin Klein Trademark Trust v OHIM (Case C-254/09P) [2011] ETMR 5, [2010] All ER (D) 29 (Sep) 5.37
Camel Hair Belting Case *see* Reddaway (Frank) & Co Ltd v George Banham & Co Ltd
Campina Melkunie BV v Benelux-Merkenbureau (BIOMILD) (Case C-265/00) [2004] ECR I-1699, [2004] ETMR 58, [2004] IP & T 959 .... 4.26, 4.28
Canary Wharf Group plc v Comptroller General of Patents, Designs & Trade Marks [2015] EWHC 1588 (Ch), [2015] 6 WLUK 212, [2015] FSR 34 .... 4.28
Canon Kabushiki Kaisha v Metro-Golden-Mayer (Case C-39/97) [1998] ECR I-5507, [1998] All ER (EC) 934, [1999] FSR 332, [1999] RPC 117, [1999] 1 CMLR 77 .... 5.21, 5.32, 5.38, 5.53, 5.54, 5.56, 5.99
Carflow Products (UK) Ltd v Linwood Securities (Birmingham) Ltd [1996] 3 WLUK 80, [1996] FSR 424, (1996) 19 (6) IPD 19048 .... 18.12
Cartier International AG v British Sky Broadcasting Ltd [2014] EWHC 3765 (Ch) 17.21
Cartier International AG v British Sky Broadcasting Ltd [2014] EWHC 3354 (Ch), [2015] ETMR 1 .... 14.10, 14.32
Caspian Pizza Ltd v Shah [2017] EWCA Civ 1874, [2017] 11 WLUK 570, [2018] ECC 18 .... 20.24
Céline Sarl v Céline Ltd (Case C-17/06) [2007] ECR I-7041, [2007] ETMR 80, [2007] AR ER (D) 55 (Sept) 5.101, 14.10, 14.16, 15.11, 15.12, 15.24
Celltech R&D Ltd v OHIM (Case C-273/05) [2007] ETMR 52, [2007] All ER (D) 135 (Apr) 4.28
Cellular Clothing Co Ltd v G White & Co Ltd (1952) 70 RPC 9 .... 20.94
Centrotherm Systemtechnik GmbH v Centrotherm Clean Solutions GmbH & Co KG (OHIM) (Case C-610/11/P) [2013] 9 WLUK 544, [2014] ETMR 7 .... 12.06
CERNIVET O/475/01 [2002] RPC 30 .... 12.27
Chartered Institute of Patent Attorneys v Registrar of Trade Marks (IP TRANSLATOR) (Case C-307/10) [2013] Bus LR 740, [2013] CEC 361, [2013] RPC 11 .... 5.28, 6.04, 6.05, 6.07

Chartered Institute of Patent Attorneys Trade Mark Application, Re [2013] ETMR 42, [2013] RPC 20 .... 6.16
Children's Television Workshop Inc v Woolworths (NSW) Ltd [1981] 1 NSWLR 273 .... 20.65
Chocoladenfabriken Lindt & Sprüngli AG v Franz Haüswirth GmbH ('Chocolate Bunnies') (Case C-529/07) [2009] ETMR 56, [2010] Bus LR 443, [2009] All ER (D) 114 (Jun) 4.56, 4.57, 6.10
Chocolate Bunnies *see* Chocoladenfabriken Lindt & Sprüngli AG v Franz Haüswirth GmbH
Chocosuisse Union Des Fabricants Suisses de Chocolat v Cadbury Ltd (SWISS CHALET) [1999] RPC 826, [1999] ETMR 1020, (1999) 22(8) IPD 22079 , [1998] RPC 117, [1998] ETMR 205, (1998) 21(1) IPD 21007, (1997) Times, 25 November 20.27, 20.70, 20.76, 20.85, 20.89, 20.90, 20.106
Ciba-Geigy v Parke Davis & Co Ltd [1994] FSR 8, 14 BMLR 64, (1993) IP & T Dig 7 .... 16.30
City Link Travel Holdings Ltd v Lakin [1979] FSR 653 .... 20.79
Class International BV v Colgate Palmolive Co (Case C-405/03) [2006] Ch 154, [2006] 2 WLR 507, [2006] IP & T 178; *sub nom* Class International BV v Unilever NV [2005] ECR I-8735 .... 14.19
Class International BV v Unilever NV *see* Class International BV v Colgate Palmolive Co
Cnl-Sucal NV (SA) v Hag GF AG (Hag II) (Case C-10/89) [1990] ECR I-3711, [1990] 3 CMLR 571 .... 5.100, 5.105
Coca-Cola Co v OHIM T-175/06 [2008] ECR II-1055, CFI 5.35
Coca-Cola Co v OHIM (Trade Marks and Designs) (T-411/14) [2016] 2 WLUK 650, [2016] ETMR 25 .... 4.15
Colloseum Holding AG v Levi Strauss & Co [2013] Bus LR 768, [2013] ETMR 34 .... 12.14
Combe International Ltd v Scholl (UK) Ltd [1980] RPC 1, [1977] FSR 464 .... 20.49
Comic Enterprises Ltd v Twentieth Century Fox Film Corpn [2014] EWHC 185 (Ch), [2014] ETMR 46, [2014] FSR 35 .... 12.06, 12.22, 15.17, 20.69
Comic Enterprises Ltd v Twentieth Century Fox Film Corpn [2014] EWHC 2286 (Ch), [2014] ETMR 51 .... 17.27, 17.45
Comic Enterprises Ltd v Twentieth Century Fox Film Corpn [2016] EWCA Civ 41, [2016] 2 WLUK 217, [2016] ETMR 22 .... 5.22, 5.42, 5.49, 5.52, 5.80, 14.46
Commercy AG v OHIM (EASYHOTEL) T-316/07 [2009] ECR II-43, [2009] All ER (D) 193 (Jan), CFI 5.33
Consorzio del Prosciutto di Parma v Marks & Spencer plc (Parma Ham Case) [1991] RPC 351 & ChD 20.10
Copad SA v Christian Dior Couture SA (Case C-59/08) [2009] FSR 22, [2009] Bus LR 1571, [2009] All ER (D) 193 (Apr) 15.42, 15.49
Coreix v Coretx Holdings plc [2017] EWHC 1695 (IPEC), [2017] 7 WLUK 205, [2018] FSR 6 .... 5.66
Cosmetic Warriors Ltd v Amazon.co.uk [2013] EWHC 2470 (Ch), [2014] FSR 15 .... 20.89

Cosmetic Warriors Ltd v Amazon.co.uk [2014] EWHC 1316 (Ch) 17.27
Cosmetic Warriors Ltd v Amazon.co.uk [2014] EWHC 181 (Ch), [2014] FSR 31 .... 5.104, 5.105, 14.10, 14.17, 14.21, 14.34, 14.38, 14.57
Coty Prestige Lancaster Group GmbH v Simex Trading AG (Case C-127/09) [2010] FSR 38 .... 15.38
Cowshed Products Ltd v Island Origins Ltd [2010] EWHC 3357 (Ch), [2011] ETMR 42, [2010] All ER (D) 229 (Dec) 20.106
County Sound plc v Ocean Sound Ltd [1991] FSR 367, (1989) The Times, November 7 .... 20.60
Cranford Community College v Cranford College Ltd [2014] EWHC 2999 (IPEC), [2015] ETMR 7 .... 20.42
Crazy Horse *see* Alain Bernardin et Cie v Pavilion Properties Ltd
Crescent Tool Co v Kilborn & Bishop Co 247 F 299 (2 Cir 1917), USA 20.40
Cruddas v Calvert [2013] EWHC 2298 (QB) 16.25, 16.27

D

D Green & Co (Stoke Newington) Ltd and Plastico Ltd v Regalzone Ltd (SPORK) [2001] EWCA Civ 639, [2002] ETMR 22, [2001] IP & T 1071, [2001] All ER (D) 62 (Aug) 4.33
DHL Express France SAS v Chronopost SA (Case C-235/09) [2011] IP & T 403 [2011] All ER (D) 105 (Apr), Grand Chamber of the ECJ 11 April 2011 .... 8.01
DKV v OHIM *see* Deutsche Krankenversicherung AG (DKV) v OHIM
Daimler Chrysler AG v Javid Alavi (t/a Merc) [2001] RPC 42, [2001] ETMR 98, [2001] All ER (D) 189 (Jan), (2001) The Times, February 16 .... 20.26, 20.98
Daimler Chrysler (PICASSO/PICARRO) (Case C-361/04P) [2006] ECR I-643, [2006] ETMR 29 .... 5.45
Dalgety Spillers Foods Ltd v Food Brokers Ltd (Pot Noodle) [1994] FSR 504, (1993) The Times, December 2 .... 20.90, 20.106
Dalsouple Societe Samuroise du Caoutchouc v Dalsouple Direct Ltd [2014] EWHC 3963 (Ch), [2015] Bus LR 464, [2015] ETMR 8 ..... 11.05
Datacard Corpnoration v Eagle Technologies Ltd [2011] EWHC 244 (Pat), [2011] RPC 17, [2011] All ER (D) 199 (Feb) 5.40, 5.49, 5.103, 14.10, 14.32, 14.47, 14.50, 15.20
Data Marketing & Secretarial Ltd v S & S Enterprises Ltd [2014] EWHC 1499 (IPEC), [2014] ECC 22, [2015] FSR 1 .... 18.12
Davidoff & Cie v Gofkid Ltd (Case C-292/00) [2003] ECR I-389, [2003] 1 WLR 1714, [2003] ETMR 42 .... 5.65
De Landtsheer Emmanuel SA v Comite Interprofessionel du Vin de Champagne (Case C-381/05) [2008] ECR I-3115, [2008] All ER (EC) 1068, [2007] ETMR 69, [2007] All ER (D) 144 (Apr) 16.09, 16.13, 16.15
Dent v Turpin 70 ER 1003, (1861) 2 John & H 139 .... 20.22
Deutsche Krankenversicherung AG (DKV) v OHIM (Case C-104/00P) [2002] ECR I-7561, [2002] All ER (D) 100 (Sep) 4.12
Devonshire Pine v Day [2013] EWHC 2619 (Ch) 20.08

Diageo North America Inc v Intercontinental Brands (ICB) Ltd (Vodkat Case) [2010] EWCA Civ 920, [2011] 1 All ER 242, [2010] ETMR 57, [2011] RPC 2, [2010] All ER (D) 360 (Jul), [2010] EWHC 17 (Ch), [2010] 3 All ER 147, [2010] ETMR 17, [2010] RPC 12............20.08, 20.27, 20.28, 20.52, 20.70, 20.89, 20.94, 20.95
Diageo North America Inc v Intercontinental Brands (ICB) Ltd [2010] EWHC 173 (Pat) (2010) 2 February 20.105
Dick Lexic Ltd's Application (Case R-111/2002) [2005] ETMR 99........ 4.48
Dimplex (UK) Ltd v De Longhi Ltd [1996] FSR 622, (1996) 19(5) IPD 8.. 18.12
Direct Line Group Ltd v Direct Line Estate Agency Ltd [1997] FSR 374.. 20.108
Direct Line Insurance plc v Esure Insurance Ltd [2008] EWCA Civ 842, [2008] RPC 34, [2009] Bus LR 438, [2008] ETMR 77.................5.09, 5.20
Dormeuil Frères v Feraglow Ltd [1990] RPC 449 .... 20.84
Durferrit GmbH v OHIM, Kolene Corpn Intervening (Case T-224/01) [2003] ECR II-1589, CFI.. 4.48
Dyson Ltd v Registrar of Trade Marks (Case C-321/03) [2007] ETMR 34, [2007] RPC 27, [2007] All ER (D) 201 (Jan) 2.03

E

EC Medica Group UK Ltd v Dearnley-Davison [2018] EWHC 1952, [2018] 7 WLUK 687... 18.03
Easygroup Ltd v Easylife Ltd [2021] EWHC 1705 (Ch), [2021] 6 WLUK 311...5.110, 20.90
EASYHOTEL *see* Commercy AG v OHIM
Elderflower Champagne *see* Taittinger SA v Allbev Ltd
Eli Lilly & Co v 8PM Chemists Ltd [2008] EWCA Civ 24, [2008] FSR 12, [2008] IP & T 730, 100 BMLR 53 .... 14.19
Elvis Presley Trade Marks [1997] RPC 543, (1997) 20(5) IPD 20044, (1997) The Times, March 25..20.21, 20.47
Emanuel (Elizabeth Florence) v Continental Shelf 128 Ltd (Case C-259/04) [2006] ECR I-3089, [2006] ETMR 56, [2006] IUP & T 887, [2006] All ER (D) 444 (Mar) 4.50
Enterprise Holdings Inc v Europcar Group UK Ltd [2015] EWHC 17 (Ch), [2015] 1 WLUK 118, [2015] FSR 22.................................... 5.75
Erven Warnink BV v J Townend & Sons (Hull) Ltd (No 1) (Advocaat Case) [1979] AC 731, [1979] 3 WLR 68, [1979] 2 All ER 927, [1980] RPC 31, [1979] FSR 397............. 20.08, 20.12, 20.27, 20.49, 20.68
Essex Trading Standards v Singh [2009] EWHC 520 (Admin) (2009) March 3, DC... 19.27
Eurim-Pharm v Beiersdorf (Case C-71/94) [1997] 1 CMLR 1222 .... 15.48
Eurohypo AG v OHIM (Case C-304/06P) [2008] ECR I-3297, [2008] ETMR 59 .... 4.13
EUROPOLIS *see* Bovemij Verzekeringen NV v Benelux-Merkenbureau
Evans (t/a Firecraft) v Focal Point Fires [2009] EWHC 2784 (Ch), [2010] RPC 15, [2010] ETMR 29, [2009] All ER (D) 130 (Nov).........5.62, 11.13, 15.07

Evegate Publishiing Ltd v Newsquest Media (Southern) Ltd [2013] EWHC 1975 (Ch) 15.25, 20.42
Ewing (t/a Buttercup Dairy Co) v Buttercup Margarine Co Ltd [1917] 2 Ch 1, 86 LJ Ch 441, 117 LT 67, 33 TLR 321, 61 Sol Jo 443, (1917) 34 RPC 232 .... 20.47
Experience Hendrix LLC v Times Newspapers Ltd [2010] EWHC 1986 (Ch), [2010] All ER (D) 16 (Aug) 17.11, 17.13
Extreme Trade Mark; Pan World Brands Ltd v Tripp Ltd [2008] RPC 2, Appointed Person 7.66

F

Fabio Perini SPA v LPC Group plc [2010] EWCA Civ 525, [2010] All ER (D) 138 (May) 14.56
Fage UK v Chobani UK [2013] EWHC 630 (Ch), [2013] ETMR 28, [2013] FSR 32 .... 20.08, 20.27, 20.89, 20.106
Fenty v Arcadia Group Brands (t/a Topshop) [2013] EWHC 2310 (Ch), [2014] ECDR 3, [2014] FSR 5; *on appeal* [2015] EWCA Civ 3 .... 20.47
Fenty v Arcadia Group Brands (t/a Topshop) [2013] EWHC 1945 (Ch), [2013] Bus LR 1165 .... 20.93
Fido Dido Inc v Venture Stores (Retailers) Pty Ltd (1988) 16 IPR 365, Australia 20.65
Films Rover International Ltd v Cannon Film Sales Ltd [1987] 1 WLR 670, [1986] 3 All ER 772, (1987) 131 SJ 743 .... 20.106
Financial Times Ltd v Evening Standard Ltd [1991] FSR 7, (1990) IP & T Dig 39 .... 20.89
Fine & Country Ltd v Okotoks Ltd (formerly Spicerhaart Ltd) [2013] EWCA Civ 672, [2014] FSR 11 .... 4.28, 15.15, 20.23
Fletcher Challenge v Fletcher Challenge Pty Ltd [1981] 1 NSWLR 196, [1982] FSR 1 .... 20.31, 20.32
Fortnum & Mason plc v Fortnam Ltd [1994] FSR 438 .... 20.03, 20.57, 20.61, 20.65, 20.79
Francotype-Postalia v Mailing Room (unreported, 8 December 2014) 16.33
Fromageries Bel SA v J Sainsbury plc [2019] EWHC 3454 (Ch), [2020] Bus LR 440, [2020] ETMR 14 .... 2.04, 15.57

G

GE Trade Mark; General Electric Co (of USA) v General Electric Co [1972] 1 WLR 729, [1972] 2 All ER 507, [1973] RPC 297 .... 20.09
General Motors Corpn v Yplon SA (Case C-375/97) [1999] ECR I-5421, [1999] ETMR 950, [2000] RPC 572 .... 2.22, 5.67, 5.69, 5.70, 5.72, 14.47
General Tire & Rubber Co v Firestone Tyre & Rubber Co Ltd [1975] 1 WLR 819, [1975] 2 All ER 173, [1976] RPC 197, [1975] FSR 273 .... 17.12, 17.13
Generics (UK) Ltd v Warner-Lambert Co LLC [2015] EWHC 2548 (Pat), [2015] 9 WLUK 205, [2016] RPC 3 .... 18.12
Gerber Garment Technology Inc v Lectra Systems Ltd [1997] RPC 443, [1997] Masons CLR 13, (1997) 20(5) IPD 20046 .... 17.12, 17.13, 17.15, 17.16

Gerolsteiner Brunnen GmbH & Co v Putsch GmbH (Case C-100/02) [2004] ECR I-691, [2004] RPC 761, [2004] ETMR 40 .... 15.15, 15.25
Ghazilian's Trade Mark Application [2002] RPC 33 .... 4.48
Gillette Co v LA Laboratories Ltd Oy (Case C-228/03) [2005] ECR I-2337, [2005] ETMR 67, [2005] All ER (EC) 940, [2005] IP & T 1003 .... 15.20, 15.21, 15.24
Gillette UK Ltd v Edenwest Ltd [1994] RPC 279, (1994) The Times, March 9 .... 20.55, 20.102
Giorgio Armani SpA v Sunrich Clothing Ltd [2010] EWHC 2939 (Ch), [2011] RPC 15, [2010] All ER (D) 222 (Nov) 12.22
Glaverbel SA v OHIM (Case C-445/02P) [2004] ECR I-6267, [2005] ETMR 70, CFI 4.10
Glaxo plc and Wellcome plc v Glaxo Wellcome Ltd [1996] FSR 388 .... 20.32, 20.110
Glen Catrine Bonded Warehouse Ltd's Application for Revocation *see* INVERMONT Trade Mark
Google France SARL v Louis Vuitton Malletier SA Google France SARL v Viaticum SA Google France SARL v Centre National de Recherche en Relations Humaines (CNRRH) SARL (Joined cases (Cases C-236–238/08) [2010] ECR I-2417 [2011] All ER (EC) 411, [2010] ETMR 30 .... 5.06, 5.102, 14.21, 14.32
Granuband v OHIM, T-534/08 30 September 2010, General Court 5.95
Greers Ltd v Pearman and Corder Ltd (1922) 39 RPC 406, KBD & CA. 16.24
Grimme Landmaschinenfabrik GmbH & Co KG v Scott [2009] EWHC 2691 (Pat), [2010] FSR 11, [2009] All ER (D) 63 (Nov) 18.03
Gromax Plasticulture Ltd v Don & Low Nonwovens Ltd [1999] RPC 367, (1998) 21(9) IPD 21098 .... 20.22
Gut Springenheide and Tusky (Case C-210/96) [1998] ECR I-4657, [1999] 1 CMLR 1383 .... 4.36, 5.47

H

HFC Bank plc v HSBC Bank plc; *sub nom* HFC Bank v Midland Bank [2000] FSR 176 .... 20.44
HUP Uslugi Polska (IT@MANPOWER) (Case C-520/08) (2009) (2008) 24 September, CFI 4.51
Hag II *see* Cnl-Sucal NV (SA) v Hag GF AG
Halliwell v Panini (Spice Girls Case) (1997) 6 June, (unreported) .. 20.21, 20.47, 20.65
Harrods Ltd v Harrodian School Ltd [1996] RPC 697, (1996) 19(10) IPD 4 .... 20.09, 20.47, 20.51, 20.54, 20.64, 20.65, 20.70, 20.79
Harrods Ltd v UK Network Services Ltd, Ch 1996 No 5453, (unreported) 20.110
Harte-Hanks Data Technologies Inc v Trillium Digital Systems Inc (TRILLIUM Trade Mark) (Case C-53447/1) (28 March 2000) 6.09
Hasbro Inc v 123 Nahrmittel GmbH [2011] EWHC 199 (Ch), [2011] ETMR 25, [2011] All ER (D) 131 (Feb) 15.18, 15.24
Hasbro Inc v 123 Nahrmittel GmbH [2011] FSR 21 .... 16.20

HAVE A BREAK *see* Société des Produits Nestlé SA v Mars UK Ltd
Hearst Holdings v Avela [2014] EWHC 439 (Ch), [2014] ETMR 34, [2014] FSR 36 .... 15.17, 15.25, 20.47
Heidelberger Bauchemie GmbH's Trade Mark Application (Case C-49/02) [2004] ECR I-6129, [2004] ETMR 99, [2004] All ER (D) 268 (Jun) 2.05
Henderson v All Around the World Recording Ltd [2014] EWHC 3087 (IPEC), [2014] 10 WLUK 97 .... 17.11
Henderson v Radio Corpn Pty Ltd [1969] RPC 218, NSW SC 20.86
Henkel KGaA v OHIM (Case C-456/01P & C-457/01P) [2004] ECR I-5089, [2005] ETMR 44, [2005] IP & T 1 .... 4.15
Hit Factory *see* Pete Waterman Ltd v CBS United Kingdom Ltd
Hodge Clemco Ltd v Airblast Ltd [1995] FSR 806 .... 20.27, 20.49
Hodgkinson and Corby Ltd v Wards Mobility Services Ltd (Roho Case) [1994] 1 WLR 1564, [1995] FSR 169, (1995) 14 Tr LR 79 .... 20.04, 20.39, 20.40, 20.49, 20.61, 20.66, 20.73
Hoffmann-La Roche & Co; AG & Hoffmann-La Roche AG v Centrafarm Vertriebsgesellschaft Pharmazeutischer Erzeugnisse mbH (Case 102/77) [1978] ECR 1139, [1978] 3 CMLR 217, [1978] FSR 598 .... 5.98
Hollister Inc v Medik Ostomy Supplies Ltd [2012] EWCA Civ 1419, [2013] FSR 24 .... 15.51, 17.08, 17.19
Honda Motor Co Ltd v David Silver Spares Ltd [2010] EWHC 1973 (Ch), [2010] FSR 40, [2010] All ER (D) 290 (Jul) 15.36
Hormel Foods Corpn v Antilles Landscape Investments NV (SPAMBUSTER) [2005] EWHC 13 (Ch), [2005] RPC 28, [2005] ETMR 54, [2005] All ER (D) 206 (Jan) 4.33, 12.29
Hotel Cipriani Srl v Cipriani (Grosvenor Street) Ltd [2010] EWCA Civ 110, [2010] RPC 16, [2010] All ER (D) 267 (Feb), [2008] EWHC 3032 (Ch), [2009] RPC 9, [2009] Bus LR D81, [2008] All ER (D) 94 (Dec) 2.20, 4.56, 15.12, 15.24, 20.30, 20.56

I

IA Sheimer (M) Sdn Bhd's Trade Mark Application (VISA) [2000] RPC 484 .... 5.84
ILG Ltd v Crunch International Fitness Inc [2008] ETMR 17, OHIM 12.08
IPC Media Ltd v Media 10 Ltd [2014] EWCA Civ 1439 .... 5.110
IRC v Muller & Co's Margarine Ltd [1901] AC 217, [1900–3] All ER Rep 413, 70 LJKB 677, 84 LT 729, 49 WR 603, 17 TLR 530 .... 20.19
Imagination Technologies Ltd v OHIM (PURE DIGITAL) (Case C-542/07) [2010] ETMR 19 .... 4.38
Imperial Group plc v Philip Morris Ltd [1984] RPC 293 .... 20.89
IN Newman Ltd v Adlem [2005] EWCA Civ 741, [2006] FSR 16, [2005] All ER (D) 228 (Jun) 20.56
Indichii Salus Ltd (in reivership) v Chandrasekaran [2006] EWHC 521 (Ch) (2006) February 15 .... 17.29
Intel Corpn Inc v CPM United Kingdom Ltd (Case C-252/07) [2008] ECR I-8823, [2009] RPC 15, [2009] ETMR 13 .... 5.79, 5.80, 5.81, 5.86, 14.50, 14.52

Interflora Inc v Marks & Spencer plc (Case C-323/09) [2011] All ER (D) 169 (Oct), (2011) 22 September, CJEU, (2011) 24 March, AGO..........5.06, 5.77, 5.82, 5.88, 5.102, 5.103, 5.104, 5.105, 14.21, 14.22, 14.27, 14.31, 14.32, 14.33, 14.34, 14.36, 14.37, 14.38
Interflora v Marks & Spencer [2012] EWCA Civ 1501, [2013] 2 All ER 663, [2013] FSR 21 .... 5.47
Interflora v Marks & Spencer [2013] EWCA Civ 319, [2013] FSR 26.... 20.89
Interflora v Marks & Spencer [2014] EWCA Civ 1403, [2015] ETMR 5, [2015] FSR 10..........14.04, 14.32
Internetportal und Marketing GmbH v Schlicht (Case C-569/08) [2011] Bus LR 726, [2010] ETMR 48, CJEU (Second chamber), 3 June 2010.......... 4.59
INTERTOPS *see* Sportwetten GmbH Gera v OHIM
INVERMONT Trade Mark [1997] RPC 125; *sub nom* Glen Catrine Bonded Warehouse Ltd's Application for Revocation [1996–97] ETMR 56, TMR.......... 12.27
IP TRANSLATOR *see* Chartered Institute of Patent Attorneys v Registrar of Trade Marks
Iron & Smith Kft v Unilever NV (Case C-125/14) [2015] Bus LR 1025, [2015] 9 WLUK 45, [2015] ETMR 45 .... 5.74
Irvine v Talksport Ltd [2002] 1 WLR 2355, [2002] 2 All ER 414, [2002] FSR 60, [2002] EMLR 32 , (2002) 25 (6) IPD 25, 039.......... 20.47
Irvine v Talksport Ltd [2003] EWCA Civ 423, [2003] 2 All ER 881, [2003] EMLR 2, [2003] FSR 35, (2003) 147 SJLB 421, (2003) 26(5) IPD 26029 .... 20.101
Island Records Ltd v Tring International plc [1995] 3 All ER 444, [1995] FSR 560, (1995) The Times, April 28.......... 17.07
IT@MANPOWER *see* HUP Uslugi Polska

J

J Portugal Ramos Vinhos SA v Adega Cooperative de Borba CRL (Case C-629/17) [2019] Bus LR 353, [2018] 12 WLUK 53, [2019] ETMR 14.......... 4.28
JW Spear & Sons Ltd v Zynga (No 2) [2012] EWHC 3345 (Ch), [2013] FSR 28; *aff'd* [2013] EWCA Civ 1175, [2014] 1 All ER 1093....2.03, 2.04, 4.14, 12.29
Jack Wills v House of Fraser (Stores) [2014] EWHC 110 (Ch), [2014] ETMR 28, [2014] FSR 39..........5.47, 5.78
Jacobson (D) & Sons Ltd v Globe (GB) Ltd [2008] EWHC 88 (Ch), [2008] FSR 21, [2008] All ER (D) 197 (Jan).......... 20.38
Jaguar Land Rover Ltd v Bombardier Recreational Products Inc [2016] EWHC 3266 (Ch), [2016] 11 WLUK 225, [2017] FSR 20 .... 4.59
Jaguar Land Rover Ltd v Ineos Industries Holdings Ltd [2020] EWHC 2130 (Ch), [2020] 8 WLUK 7, [2020] ETMR 56.......... 4.11
Jean Christian Perfumes Ltd v Thakrar [2011] EWHC 1383 (Ch), [2011] FSR 813, [2011] All ER (D) 06 (Jun).......... 13.60
Jian Tools for Sales Inc v Roderick Manhattan Group Ltd [1995] FSR 924.......... 20.29

Jif Lemon Case *see* Reckitt & Colman Products Ltd v Borden Inc
Joseph Rodgers & Sons v W N Rodgers & Co (1924) 41 RPC 277......... 20.56
Julius Sämann Ltd v Tetrosyl Ltd (MAGIC TREE) [2006] EWHC 529 (Ch), [2006] ETMR 75, [2006] FSR 849, [2006] All ER (D) 274 (Mar) 4.44, 5.52, 12.28

K

Kampol v OHIM (Case T-382/12) 5.35
Kaye v Robertson [1991] FSR 62, (1990) IP & T Dig 17 .... 16.22, 16.25
Kenneth (trading as Screw You)'s Application (SCREW YOU) R 495/2005-G [2007] ETMR 7, OHIM Grand Board of Appeal...... 4.47
Khader v Aziz [2009] EWHC 2027 (QB), [2009] All ER (D) 41 (Aug), QBD 16.24
Khodaparast v Shad [2000] 1 All ER 545, [2000] 1 WLR 618, [2000] 2 WLR 566, [2000] EMLR 265 .... 16.32
Kimberly-Clark Ltd v Fort Sterling Ltd (Andrex/Nouvelle) [1997] FSR 877, (1997) 20(7) IPD 20066........................ 20.81, 20.90
Kingspan Group Plc v Rockwool Ltd [2011] EWHC 250 (Ch), [2011] All ER (D) 242 (Feb) 16.21, 16.31
Koninklijke KPN Nederland NV v Benelux-Merkenbureau (POSTKANTOOR) (Case C-363/99) [2006] Ch 1, [2004] ECR I-1619, [2004] ETMR 57, [2005] All ER (EC) 19.............. 4.13, 4.26, 4.27, 4.28, 4.29, 6.03, 6.07, 6.12
Koninklijke Philips Electronics v Remington Consumer Products (Case C-299/99) [2003] Ch 159, [2002] ETMR 81, [2003] RPC 2........ 4.09, 4.36, 4.39, 4.41, 4.42, 4.44
Koninklijke Philips Electronics v Lucheng Meijing Industrial Co Ltd (Case C-446/09) [2012] Bus LR 1850, [2012] ETMR 13 .... 17.60
Koton Magazacilik Tekstil Sanayi ve Ticaret v EUIPO (Case C-104/18P) (12 September 2019)........................ 4.57

L

LB Europe Ltd (t/a DuPont Liquid Packaging Systems) v Smurfit Bag in Box SA [2008] EWHC 1231 (Ch), [2008] All ER (D) 55 (Jun)....... 18.18
LEEC Ltd v Morquip Ltd (unreported, noted in [1996] 6 EIPR D-176).. 20.49
LTJ Diffusion SA v Sadas Vertbaudet SA (Case C-291/00) [2003] ECR I-2799, [2003] ETMR 83, [2003] IP & T 994 .... 5.15
La Mer Technology Inc v Laboratoires Goemar SA (Case C-259/02) [2004] CR I-1159, [2004] FSR 38 .... 12.06, 12.07
Lady Ga Ga Case *see* Ate My Heart Inc v Mind Candy Ltd
Land Securities plc v The Registrar of Trade Marks [2008] EWHC 1744 (Pat), [2009] RPC 5, [2008] ETMR 67........................ 6.15
Law Society of England and Wales v Griffiths [1995] RPC 16......... 20.49, 20.54
Law Society of England and Wales v Society of Lawyers [1996] FSR 739, (1996) 19(6) IPD 8........................ 20.38, 20.47, 20.110
Lego Juris A/S v OHIM (Case C-48/09P) [2010] ETMR 63, [2010] IP &T 1160........................ 4.43
Lego System A/S v Lego M Lemelstritch Ltd [1983] FSR 155 .... 20.65, 20.70, 20.86

Leidseplein Beheer BV v Red Bull GmbH (Case C-65/12) [2014] Bus LR 280, [2014] 2 WLUK 206, [2014] ETMR 24 .... 5.88
Leno Merken BV v Hagelkruis Beheer BV [2013] Bus LR 928, [2013] ETMR 16 .... 12.06, 12.18
Libertel Groep BV v Benelux-Merkenbureau (Case C-104/01) [2004] Ch 83, [2003] ECR I-3793, [2003] ETMR 63, [2004] FSR 4.. 2.05, 4.11, 4.12
Liberty X Case *see* Sutherland v V2 Music Ltd
Lidl Belgium GmbH & Co KG v Etablissementen Franz Colruyt NV (Case C-356/04) [2007] ETMR 28 .... 16.16
Lidl SNC v Vierzon Distribution SA (Case C-159/09) [2011] ETMR 6, [2011] IP & T 141 .... 16.14
Lifestyle Equities CV v Amazon UK Services Ltd [2021] EWHC 118 (Ch), [2021] 1 WLUK 313, [2021] ETMR 27............... 14.18, 14.19, 14.21, 14.57, 18.03
Linde AG, Winward Industries Inc and Rado Uhren AG (Case C-53/01,C-55/01) [2003] ECR I3161, [2003] RPC 803, [2004] IP & T 172.. 4.11, 4.12
LIQUID FORCE Trade Mark [1999] RPC 429, Appointed Person 7.49
Lloyd Schuhfabrik Meyer v Klijsen Handel BV (Case C-342/97) [1999] ECR I-3819, [1999] 2 CMLR 1343, [1999] ETMR 690... 5.23, 5.27, 5.56
London Taxi Corpn Ltd (t/a London Taxi Co) v Fraser-Nash Research Ltd [2016] EWHC 52 (Ch), [2016] 1 WLUK 321, [2016] ETMR 18.. 4.11, 4.44, 5.56
L'Oréal v Bellure (Case C-487/07) [2009] ECR I-5185, [2010] All ER (EC) 28, [2009] ETMR 55....................... 2.20, 5.75, 5.76, 5.78, 5.88, 5.89, 5.102, 14.31, 16.18, 16.19, 16.20
L'Oréal SA v Bellure NV [2007] EWCA Civ 968, [2008] RPC 9, [2008] IP & T 526.. 20.50
L'Oreal SA v Bellure NV [2010] EWCA Civ 535, [2010] RPC 23, [2010] All ER (D) 205 (May) 20.50
L'Oreal SA v eBay [2009] EWHC 1094 (Ch), [2009] All ER (D) 169 (Jun), [2009] RPC 21, [2009] 32(7) IPD 32050 .... 14.56, 14.58, 15.38
L'Oréal v eBay International (Case C-324/09) [2011] ETMR 52, (2011) The Times, July 19, CJEU 5.82, 5.85, 14.16, 14.17, 14.18, 14.20, 14.21, 14.28, 14.37, 15.38
L'Oreal (UK) Ltd v Johnson & Johnson [2000] ETMR 691, [2000] FSR 686, (2000) 23 (6) IPD 23045....................................... 18.02, 18.03, 18.04
Louboutin v Van Haren Schoenen BV (Case C-163/16) [2018] Bus LR 1411, [2018] 6 WLUK 178, [2018] ETMR 31 .... 4.41
Lyngstad v Anabas Products Ltd (Abba Case) [1977] FSR 62......... 20.47, 20.64, 20.65

M

MCA Records Inc v Charly Records Ltd [2001] EWCA Civ 1441, [2002] FSR 26, [2002] EMLR 1, [2002] ECDR 37 .... 14.57
McCain International v Country Fayre Foods [1981] RPC 69 .... 20.60

McCulloch v Lewis A May (Produce Distributors) Ltd (Uncle Mac) [1947] 2 All ER 845, (1948) 65 RPC 58, 92 SJ 54 .... 20.64
MAGIC BALL Trade Mark O/084/99 [2000] RPC 439, [2000] ETMR 226 .... 12.26
MAGIC TREE *see* Julius Sämann Ltd v Tetrosyl Ltd
Maier v Asos plc [2013] EWHC 2831 (Ch), [2014] ETMR 35, [2014] FSR 16 .... 5.86, 20.67
Maier v Asos plc [2015] EWCA Civ 220, [2016] 2 All ER 738, [2015] ETMR 26 .... 12.20, 15.24, 15.25
Malaysia Dairy Industries Pte Ltd v Ankenaevnet for Patenter og Varemaerker (Case C-320/12) [2013] Bus LR 1106, [2013] ETMR 36 .... 4.55
Marca Mode (Case C-425/98) [2000] ECR I 4861, [2000] All ER (EC) 694, [2000] 2 CMLR 1061 .... 5.22
Marengo v Daily Sketch and Sunday Graphic Ltd [1948] 1 All ER 406, (1948) 65 RPC 242, [1948] LJR 787 .... 20.56
Marks & Spencer plc v One in a Million [1999] 1 WLR 903, [1998] 4 All ER 476, [1998] FSR 265, (1997) 16 Tr LR 554, (1998) 21(2) IPD 21016 .... 14.21
Mary Wilson Enterprises Inc's Trade Mark Application (The Supremes) [2003] EMLR 14, Appointed Person 20.33
Maslyukov v Diageo Distilling Ltd [2010] EWHC 443 (Ch), [2010] RPC 21, [2010] All ER (D) 64 (May) 20.33
Masterman 's Design [1991] RPC 89, (1990) The Times, December 19 . 4.48
Matratzen Concord AG v Hukla Germany SA (Case C-421/04) [2006] ETMR 48, [2006] IP & T 483, [2006] All ER (D) 154 (Mar) 4.10
Mecklermedia Corpn v DC Congress GmbH [1998] Ch 40, [1997] 3 WLR 479, [1998] 1 All ER 148, [1997] FSR 627, [1997] ETMR 265 ...... 20.58
Media Agency Group Ltd v Space Media Agency Ltd [2019] EWCA Civ 712, [2019] 3 WLUK 690, [2019] FSR 27 .... 20.24
Merck, Sharp & Dohme GmbH v Paranova Pharmazeutika Handels GmbH (Case C-443/99) [2002] ETMR 80 .... 15.47
Merz & Krell GmbH & Co v Deutsches Patent- und Markehamt (Case C-517/99) [2001] ECR I-6959, [2002] All ER (EC) 441, [2002] ETMR 21 .... 4.32
Michael Hölterhoff v Ulrich Freiesleben (Case C-2/00) [2002] ECR I-4187, [2002] All ER (EC) 665, [2002] IP & T 163 .... 5.06
Microsoft Corpn v Plato Technology Ltd [1999] FSR 834, [1999] Masons CLR 87, (1999) 22(5) IPD 22047 .... 20.105
Miller Brewing Co v Ruhi Enterprises Ltd [2003] EWHC 1606 (Ch), [2004] FSR 5, [2004] IP & T 542 .... 17.49
Minsterstone Ltd v Be Modern Ltd [2002] FSR 53, PCC 17.90
Mirage Studios v Counter-Feat Clothing Co Ltd (Teenage Mutant Ninja Turtles) [1991] FSR 145, (1990) IP & T Dig 22 .... 20.47, 20.65
Mitsui & Co Ltd v Nexen Petroleum UK Ltd [2005] EWHC 625 (Ch), [2005] 3 All ER 511 .... 17.31
Mondelez UK Holdings & Services Ltd v EUIPO / Société des produits Nestlé SA (Case T-112/13) [2016] 12 WLUK 398, [2017] ETMR 13 .... 4.11

Mont Blanc Simplo GmbH v Sepia Products Inc (2000) 23(3) IPD 23021, The Times, 2 February 2000 ... 20.52
Moroccanoil Israel Ltd v Aldi Stores Ltd [2014] EWHC 1686 (IPEC), [2014] ETMR 55, [2015] FSR 4 ... 20.48, 20.49, 20.61
Mothercare UK Ltd v Penguin Books Ltd [1988] RPC 113 ... 20.89
Mülhens v OHIM T-150/04 [2007] ECR II-2353, CFI ... 5.35
Music Choice Ltd v Target Brands Inc [2005] EWHC 3323 (Ch), [2006] RPC 13, [2005] All ER (D) 197 (Dec) ... 11.15
My Kinda Town Ltd v Soll and Grunts Investments [1983] RPC 407, [1983] RPC 15, [1982] FSR 147, [1981] Com LR 194 ... 20.60, 20.103

N

NAD Electronics Inc v NAD Computer Systems Ltd [1997] FSR 380, (1997) 20(7) IPD 20068 ... 20.56, 20.65
NASA *see* Nice and Safe Attitude Ltd v Piers Flook (T/A 'Slaam! Clothing Co')
Nanjing Automobile (Group) Corpn v MG Sports and Racing Europe [2010] EWHC 270 (Ch), [2010] All ER (D) 37 (Jun) ... 12.37
National Guild of Removers & Storers Ltd v Silveria [2010] EWPCC 015, [2011] FSR 9 ... 17.13, 17.14
National Guild of Removers & Storers v Statham [2014] EWHC 3572 (IPEC) ... 20.101
Nationwide Building Society v Nationwide Estate Agents [1987] FSR 579, DC ... 20.89
Nestlé v OHIM, (Case C-193/06P) [2007] ECR I-114, 20 September 2007 ... 5.22
Nestlé (UK) Ltd v Trustin the Food Finders Ltd (Polo) (1996) 22 August, (unreported) ... 20.47, 20.48, 20.61, 20.89
Neutralia/Neutrogena *see* Neutrogena Corpn v Golden Ltd (t/a Garnier)
Neutrogena Corpn v Golden Ltd (t/a Garnier) (Neutralia/Neutrogena) [1996] RPC 473, (1996) 19(4) IPD 5 ... 20.80, 20.90, 20.92
New Look Ltd v OHIM T-117/03 to T-119/03 and T-171/03 [2004] ECR II-3471, [2005] ETMR 35, [2004] All ER (D) 62 (Oct), CFI ... 5.50
Nice and Safe Attitude Ltd v Piers Flook (T/A 'Slaam! Clothing Co') (NASA) [1997] FSR 14, (1996) 19(4) IPD 8, HC ... 20.31, 20.49, 20.65
Niche Products Ltd v MacDermid Offshore Solutions LLC [2013] EWHC 3540 (IPEC), [2014] EMLR 9, [2014] FSR 24 ... 16.23, 16.25
Nike (Ireland) Ltd v Network Management Ltd (1994) 22 July, (unreported) ... 20.65
NIRVANA Trade Mark Case O/262/06, Appointed Person ... 12.12, 12.13
Northern & Shell plc v Conde Nast and National Magazines Distributers Ltd [1995] RPC 117, [1995] Tr LR 263 ... 17.83, 17.84
Norwich Pharmacal Co v Customs and Excise Commissioners [1974] AC 133, [1973] 3 WLR 164, [1973] 2 All ER 943, [1974] RPC 101, [1973] FSR 365 ... 17.31
Numatic International Ltd v Qualtex UK Ltd [2010] EWHC 1237 (Ch), [2010] RPC 25, [2010] All ER (D) 290 (May) ... 20.40

O

O2 Holdings Ltd v Hutchison 3G UK Ltd [2006] EWCA Civ 1656, [2007] RPC 16, [2007] 2 CMLR 332 .... 16.04, 16.05
O2 Holdings Ltd v Hutchison 3G UK Ltd (Case C-533/06) [2008] ECR I-4231, [2008] RPC 33, [2008] ETMR 55, [2008] All ER (D) 155 (Jun) 5.38, 5.40, 5.52, 16.20
OAO Alpha-Bank v Alpha Bank AE [2011] EWHC 2021 (Ch), [2011] 7 WLUK 861 .... 12.13
OHIM v Erpo Mobelwerk GmbH (Case C-64/02P) [2005] ETMR 58 .... 2.09
Och-Ziff Management Europe Ltd and Oz Management LP v Och Capital LLP, Union Investment Management Ltd and Ochocki [2010] EWHC 2599 (Ch), [2011] FSR 11, [2011] ECC 5, [2011] ETMR 1, [2011] Bus LR 632 .... 4.56, 5.14, 5.16, 5.42, 5.49, 5.66, 15.24, 20.49, 20.56, 20.65, 20.70
Oertli (T) AG v EJ Bowman (London) Ltd (No 3) [1959] RPC 1 .... 20.20
Office Cleaning Services Ltd v Westminster Office Cleaning Association (Note) [1946] 1 All ER 320, (1946) 63 RPC 39, 174 LT 229 .... 20.42
Oracle America Inc (formerly Sun Microsystems Inc) v M-Tech Data Ltd [2012] UKSC 27, [2010] ETMR 64 .... 15.04, 15.37
Orifarm A/S v Merck Sharp & Dohme Corpn (Case C-400/09) [2012] 1 CMLR 10, [2011] ETMR 59 .... 15.51

P

PAGO International GmbH v Tirolmilch registrierte Genossenschaft mbH (Case C-301/07) [2009] ECR I-9429, [2010] ETMR 5 .... 5.74, 14.47
Parfums Christian Dior SA and Another v Evora BV (Case C-337/95) [1998] RPC 166, [1998] ETMR 26, [1998] 1 CMLR 737 .... 5.101, 15.49
Parker-Knoll Ltd v Knoll International Ltd [1962] RPC 265 .... 20.89
Parma Ham Case *see* Consorzio del Prosciutto di Parma v Marks & Spencer plc
Peak Holdings AB v Axolin-Elinor AB (Case C-16/03) [2005] Ch 261, [2004] ECR I-11313, [2005] ETMR 28 .... 15.37
Penguin / Puffin Case *see* United Biscuits (UK) Ltd v Asda Stores Ltd
Permanent Secretary of the Ministry of Energy, Commerce & Tourism, Republic of Cyprus v John & Pascalis Ltd [2018] EWHC 3226 (Ch), [2018] 11 WLUK 498 .... 11.15
Pete Waterman Ltd v CBS United Kingdom Ltd (The Hit Factory) [1993] EMLR 27 .... 20.30
Philosophy Inc v Ferretti Studio Srl [2002] EWCA Civ 921, [2003] RPC 15, [2002] All ER (D) 72 (Jun) 12.17, 12.25
Phones 4U Ltd v Phone4u.co.uk Internet Ltd [2006] EWCA Civ 244, [2007] RPC 5, [2006] All ER (D) 286 (May) 20.41
PICARRO See Daimler Chrysler (PICASSO/PICARRO)
PICASSO See Daimler Chrysler (PICASSO/PICARRO)
Picasso v OHIM *see* Daimler Chrysler (PICASSO/PICARRO)
Pie Optiek SPRL v Burean Gevers SA, European Registry for Internet Domains ASBL (Case C-376/11), [2013] CEC 478, [2012] ETMR 46 .... 2.38

Pippig Augenoptik GmbH & Co KG v Hartlauer Hendelsgesellschaft mbH (Case C-44/01) [2003] ECR I-3095, [2004] All ER (EC) 1156, [2004] ETMR 5 .... 16.10, 16.12, 16.14
Pirie's Application (1932) 49 RPC 195 .... 5.106
Planetart LLC v Photobox Ltd [2020] EWHC 713 (Ch), [2020] Bus LR 2048, [2020] 3 WLUK 417 .... 5.54, 5.88, 20.60
Polo *see* Nestlé (UK) Ltd v Trustin the Food Finders Ltd
Postkantoor *see* Koninklijke KPN Nederland NV v Benelux Merkenbureau
Pot Noodle *see* Dalgety Spillers Foods Ltd v Food Brokers Ltd
Powell v Birmingham Vinegar Brewery Co [1897] AC 710, 14 RPC 720, 66 LJ Ch 763, 76 LT 792 .... 20.19
Praktiker Bau- und Heimwerkermarkte AG v Deutsches Patent- und Markenamt (Case C-418/02) [2006] Ch 144, [2005] ECR I–5873, [2006] 3 CMLR 830 .... 6.14
Premier Luggage & Bags Ltd v Premier Co (UK) Ltd [2002] EWCA Civ 387, [2003] FSR 5 .... 15.11, 20.56
Primark Stores Ltd v Lollypop Clothing Ltd [2001] FSR 37, [2001] ETMR 30 .... 20.47
Procea Products Ltd v Evans & Sons Ltd (1951) 68 RPC 210 .... 20.94
Procter & Gamble Co v OHIM (BABY-DRY) (Case C-383/99) [2002] Ch 82, [2001] ECR I-6251,[2002] RPC 369, [2002] ETMR 3 .... 4.08, 4.12, 4.22, 4.23, 4.25
Procter & Gamble Company v OHIM (Joined Cases C-468/01 & C-472/01) [2004] ECR I-5141, [2004] ETMR 88, [2005] I P & T 1 .... 4.12, 4.16
PURE DIGITAL *see* Imagination Technologies Ltd v OHIM

Q

Quads 4 Kids Ltd v Campbell [2006] EWHC 2482 (Ch), [2006] Info TLR 338, [2006] All ER (D) 162 (Oct) 18.03, 18.04

R

R v Beazley (Rosemary) [2013] EWCA Crim 567, [2013] 1 WLR 3331 19.33
R v Boulter [2008] EWCA Crim 2375, [2009] ETMR 6 .... 19.12
R v Drain [2018] EWCA Crim 19.31
R v Ghori (Kamran Hamreed) [2012] EWCA Crim 1115 .... 19.33
R v Johnstone [2003] UKHL 28, [2003] 3 All ER 884, [2003] 1 WLR 1736 [2003] FSR 42, [2004] ETMR 2 .... 19.11, 19.27
R v Kousar [2009] EWCA Crim 139, [2009] 2 Cr App R 5, [2009] All ER (D) 289 (Mar) 19.18
R v M, R v C [2017] UKSC 58, [2017] 1 WLR 3006, [2018] 1 All ER 304 .... 19.02, 19.16
R v Malik (Ashok Kumar) [2011] EWCA Crim 1107 .... 19.27, 19.28
R v McCrudden [2005] EWCA Crim 466 .... 19.27
R v Morgan *see* CPS v Morgan
R v Pettit [2009] EWCA Crim 2573 .... 19.27
R v Rhodes [2002] EWCA Crim 1390, [2003] FSR 9 .... 19.28, 19.29
R v Wakefield [2004] EWCA Crim 2278, (2004) 168 JP 505, (2004) 168 JPN 780 .... 19.30

R v Woolin (Stephen Leslie) [1999] 1 AC 82, [1998] 3 WLR 382, [1998] 4 All ER 103, [1999] 1 Cr App R 8 .... 19.07
R v Zaman [2002] EWCA Crim 1862, [2003] FSR 13, [2002] All ER (D) 22 (Jul) 19.06, 19.19
R (on the application of British American Tobacco UK Ltd) v Secretary of State for Health [2016] EWCA Civ 1182, [2018] QB 149, [2017] RPC 16 .... 5.103
RHM Foods v Bovril [1982] 1 All ER 673, [1983] RPC 275 .... 20.38
Radio Taxicabs v Owner Drivers Radio Taxi Services [2004] RPC 19 .... 20.42, 20.55
Ralf Sieckmann v Deutches Patent und Markenamt (Case C-273/00) [2003] Ch 487, [2003] ETMR 37, [2003] RPC 38 .... 2.07
Reber Holding & Co KG v OHIM (Case C-141/13P) (17 July 2014) 12.06
Reckitt & Colman Products Ltd v Borden Inc (Jif Lemon Case) [1990] 1 All ER 873, [1990] RPC 341, (1990) 134 SJ 784 .... 20.10, 20.11, 20.38, 20.41, 20.52, 20.60, 20.61, 20.76
Reckitt Benckiser (España) v OHIM (ALADIN trade mark) (Case T-126/03) [2005] ECR II-2861, [2006] ETMR 50, [2005] All ER (D) 198 (Jul), CFI 12.23
Red Bull GmbH v European Intellectual Property Office (Case C-124/18P) [2019] 7 WLUK 455, [2019] ETMR 57, [2019] FSR 37 .... 2.05
Red Bull v Sun Mark [2012] EWHC 1929 (Ch), [2012] 7 WLUK 525, [2013] ETMR 53 .... 5.67, 5.78
Reddaway (Frank) & Co Ltd v George Banham & Co Ltd (Camel Hair Belting case) [1896] AC 199, (1896) 13 RPC 218, 74 LT 289 .... 20.01, 20.39, 20.41
Redd Solicitors LLP v Red Legal Ltd [2012] EWPCC 54, [2013] ETMR 13 .... 12.22, 15.26
REMUS Trade Mark Case O-061–08, Appointed Person 12.12, 12.13
Rivella International AG v OHIM (Case C-445/12P) [2013] ETMR 4; *appeal rejected* [2014] Bus LR 298, [2014] ETMR 20 .... 12.18
Roho Case *see* Hodgkinson and Corby Ltd v Wards Mobility Services Ltd
Rousselon Freres et Cie v Horwood Homewares Ltd [2008] EWHC 881 (Ch), [2008] All ER (D) 337 (Apr) 12.28
Rugby Football Union v Consolidated Information Services, Rugby Football Union v Viagogo Ltd [2012] UKSC 55, [2012] 1 WLR 3333, [2013] 1 All ER 928 .... 17.31
Rugby Football Union v Cotton Traders Ltd [2002] EWHC 467, [2002] ETMR 76, [2002] All ER (D) 417 (Mar) 20.23
Ruiz Picasso v OHIM *see* Daimler Chrysler (PICASSO/PICARRO)

S

SAT 1 Satellitenfernsehen GmbH v OHIM (SAT 2) (Case C-329/02P) [2004] ECR I-8317, [2005] ETMR 20, [2005] IP & T 943 .... 4.14
Sabaf SPA v MFI Furniture Centres [2002] EWCA Civ 976, [2003] RPC 14 .... 14.56
Sabel BV v Puma AG, Rudolf Dassler Sport (Case C-251/95) [1997] ECR I-6191, [1998] RPC 199, [1998] ETMR 1 .... 5.22, 5.27, 5.38, 5.41, 5.54

Samsung Electronics (UK) Ltd v Apple Inc [2012] EWHC 889 (Ch), [2012] 4 WLUK 98, [2013] FSR 7 .... 18.03, 18.04
Samuel Smith Old Brewery (Tadcaster) v Philip Lee [2011] EWHC 1879 (Ch), [2011] All ER (D) 229 (Jul) 5.14, 5.22, 5.23, 5.39, 5.42, 5.52, 5.54, 15.17, 15.24, 18.12
Sanofi-Aventis (ATURION) T-146/06 [2008] ECR II-17, CFI 5.25
Scandecor Development AB v Scandecor Marketing AV [1999] FSR 26, (1999) 22(1) IPD 22009, [1998] FSR 500, (1998) 21(7) IPD 21071, (1998) 95(12) LSG 28 .... 20.22
Scotch Whisky Association v Glen Kella Distillers Ltd (No 2) [1997] EuLR 455, (1997) 20(7) IPD 20067, (1997) 141 SJLB 91 .... 20.28
Scotch Whisky Association v JD Vintners Ltd [1997] EuLR 446 .... 20.27
Scranage's Trade Mark Application (O/182/05) 4.48
SCREW YOU *see* Kenneth (trading as Screw You)'s Application
Sebago Inc and Ancienne Maison Dubois et Fils SA v GB-Unic SA (Case C-173/98) [1999] All ER (EC) 575, [1999] 2 CMLR 1317, [1999] CEC 273, [1999] ETMR 681 .... 15.39
Second Sight Ltd v Novell UK Ltd [1995] RPC 423 .... 19.40
Sergio Rossi SpA v OHIM T-169/03 [2005] ECR II-685, CFI 5.35
Series 5 Software Ltd v Clarke [1996] 1 All ER 853, [1996] FSR 273, [1996] CLC 631, (1996) 19(3) IPD 16 .... 17.24
Sheraton Corpn of America v Sheraton Motels Ltd [1964] RPC 202 .... 20.29
Shield Mark BV v Kist (t/a Memex) (Case C-283/01) [2004] Ch 97, [2003] ECR I-14313, [2004] ETMR 33, [2004] RPC 17 .... 2.06
Siemens AG v VIPA Gesellschaft für Visualisierung und Prozessautomatisierung mbH (Case C-59/05) [2006] ECR I-2147, [2006] ETMR 47, [2007] IP & T 292, [2006] All ER (D) 339 (Feb) 5.76, 16.17
Silberquelle GmbH v Maselli-Strickmode GmbH (WELLNESS) (Case C-495/07) [2009] ETMR 28, [2009] All ER (D) 72 (Jan) 12.06, 12.08
Silhouette International Schmied GmbH & Co KG v Hartlauer Handelsgesellschaft mbH (Case C-355/96) [1998] 3 WLR 1218, [1998] All ER (EC) 769, [1998] ETMR 539 .... 15.35
Singer Manufacturing Co v Loog (1880) 18 Ch D 395, 44 LT 888, 29 WR 699 .... 20.39
Singer Manufacturing Co v Wilson (1876) 2 Ch D 434, 34 LT 858 .... 20.09
Sir Robert McAlpine Ltd v Alfred McAlpine Plc [2004] EWHC 630 (Ch), [2004] RPC 36, [2004] All ER (D) 579 (Mar) 20.22
Skinner v Perry (1893) 10 RPC 1 .... 18.04
Sky plc v SkyKick UK Ltd (Case C-371/18) [2020] Bus LR 1550, [2020] 1 WLUK 242, [2020] ETMR 24 .... 4.46, 6.09, 6.10
Sky plc v SkyKick UK Ltd [2018] EWHC 943 (Ch), [2018] 4 WLUK 535, [2018] RPC 12 .... 4.59, 6.09, 6.10
Slazenger & Sons v Feltham & Co (1889) 6 RPC 531 .... 20.54
Slater v Anglo Atlantic Media Ltd [2020] EWHC 710 (Ch), [2020] 4 WLUK 114, [2020] FSR 32 .... 5.62, 15.07
Smart Technologies ULC v OHIM (Case C-311/11P) [2012] ETMR 49. 2.09

Société des Produits Nestlé SA v Cadbury UK Ltd [2013] EWCA Civ 1174, [2014] 1 All ER 1079, [2014] Bus LR 134................ 2.01, 2.03, 2.04, 2.05
Société des Produits Nestlé SA v Cadbury UK Ltd [2014] EWHC 16 (Ch), [2014] ETMR 17, [2014] FSR 17.............................. 4.15, 4.36, 4.39, 4.43, 5.15
Société des Produits Nestlé SA v Cadbury UK Ltd [2016] EWHC 50 (Ch), [2016] 4 All ER 1081; *aff'd* [2017] EWCA Civ 358, [2018] 2 All ER 39 .... 4.39
Société des Produits Nestlé SA v Cadbury UK Ltd (Case C-215/14) [2015] ETMR 50, [2016] FSR 8.. 4.43
Société des Produits Nestlé SA v Mars UK Ltd (HAVE A BREAK) (Case C-353/03) [2005] ECR I-6135, [2006] All ER (EC) 348, [2005] ETMR 96... 4.36
Sodastream Ltd v Thorn Cascade Co Ltd [1982] RPC 459, [1982] Com LR 64 .... 20.54, 20.61, 20.75, 20.78
Spalding (AG) & Bros v AW Gamage Ltd (1915) 32 RPC 273, 84 LJ Ch 449.. 20.49, 20.74
Spalding (AG) & Bros v AW Gamage Ltd (No 2) (1918) 35 RPC 101.... 20.83
SPAMBUSTER *see* Hormel Foods Corpn v Antilles Landscape Investments NV
Special Effects Ltd v L'Oréal SA [2007] EWCA Civ 1, [2007] RPC 15, [2007] IP & T 617, [2007] All ER (D) 29 (Jan).............................. 11.13
Speciality European Pharma Ltd v Doncaster Pharmaceuticals Group Ltd [2013] EWHC 3624 (Ch), [2014] ETMR 11, [2014] RPC 11 ... 15.50
Specsavers International Healthcare Ltd v Asda Stores Ltd (No 2) [2010] EWHC 2035 (Ch), [2011] FSR 1; *revs'd in part* [2012] EWCA Civ 24, [2012] ETMR 17, [2012] FSR 19; *preliminary ruling given* [2013] Bus LR 1277, [2013] ETMR 46, [2014] FSR 4 .... 5.22, 5.24, 5.42, 5.52, 5.86, 5.89, 7.09, 12.14, 14.50, 20.61, 20.62
Spice Girls Case *see* Halliwell v Panini
SPORK *see* D Green & Co (Stoke Newington) Ltd and Plastico Ltd v Regalzone Ltd
Sportwetten GmbH Gera v OHIM (INTERTOPS) T-140/02 [2006] ETMR 15, [2005] All ER (D) 72 (Sep), CFI 4.46, 4.48
Starbucks (HK) Ltd v British Sky Broadcasting Group plc [2012] EWHC 3074 (Ch), [2013] FSR 29; *aff'd* [2013] EWCA Civ 1465, [2014] ECC 4, [2014] FSR 20... 4.27, 17.66, 20.29, 20.32
Star Industrial Co Ltd v Yap Kwee Kor (t/a New Star Industrial Co Ltd) [1976] FSR 256, PC... 20.77
Stephens v Avery [1988] Ch 449, [1988] 2 WLR 1280, [1988] 2 All ER 477, [1988] FSR 510.. 4.48
Stichting BDO v BDO Unibank Inc [2013] EWHC 418 (Ch), [2013] ETMR 31, [2013] FSR 35.. 12.22
Stockton-on-Tees Borough Concil v Frost [2010] EWHC 1304 (Admin), [2010] All ER (D) 07 (Jun) 19.27

Storck v OHIM (Case C-25/05) [2006] ECR I-5719, [2006] All ER (D) 276 (Jun) 4.16
Stringfellow v McCain Foods (GB) Ltd [1984] RPC 501 & CA 20.65, 20.67, 20.70, 20.87
Sunrider Corpnoration v Vitasoy International Holdings Ltd [2007] EWHC 37 (Ch), [2007] RPC 641, [2007] All ER (D) 139 (Jan), (2007) The Times, February 27.......... 12.06
Supremes *see* Mary Wilson Enterprises Inc's Trade Mark Application
Sutherland v V2 Music Ltd (Liberty X) [2002] EWHC 14 (Ch), [2002] EMLR 28, [2002] All ER (D) 156 (Jan).......... 20.33
SWISS CHALET *see* Chocosuisse Union Des Fabricants Suisses de Chocolat v Cadbury Ltd
Sykes v Sykes (1824) 3 B & C 541, 5 Dow & Ry KB 292, 3 LJOSKB 46, 107 ER 834 .... 20.50

T

TBD (Owen Holland) Ltd v Simons [2020] EWCA Civ 1182, [2021] 1 WLR 992, [2020] 9 WLUK 47 .... 17.29, 17.30
TFC Croydon Ltd v Foodland UK Ltd O-443-14.......... 20.22
Taittinger SA v Allbev Ltd (Elderflower Champagne) [1994] 4 All ER 75, [1993] FSR 641, [1993] 2 CMLR 741, [1992] FSR 647 .... 20.27, 20.70
Tan-Ichi Co v Jancar Ltd [1990] FSR 151, (1989) IP & T Dig 29, Sup Ct Hong Kong.......... 20.31
Tavener Rutledge Ltd v Trexapalm Ltd (Kojak) [1977] RPC 275, [1975] FSR 479 .... 20.47, 20.65
Tech 21 UK Ltd v Logitech Europe SA [2015] EWHC 2614 (Ch), [2015] Bus LR 1276, [2015] 9 WLUK 273.......... 18.03
Teenage Mutant Ninja Turtles *see* Mirage Studios v Counter-Feat Clothing Co Ltd
Terrapin (Overseas) Ltd v Terranova Industrie CA Kapferer & Co (Case C-119/75) [1976] ECR 1039, [1975] 2 CMLR 482.......... 5.98
Tesla Motors Ltd v BBC [2011] EWHC 2760 (QB) 16.25
Thermawear Ltd v Vedonis Ltd [1982] RPC 44 .... 20.33
Thomas Pink v Victoria's Secret UK [2014] EWHC 2631 (Ch), [2014] ETMR 57, [2014] FSR 40.......... 5.56, 5.75
Thomson Holidays Ltd v Norwegian Cruise Line Ltd [2002] EWCA Civ 1828, [2003] RPC 586, [2003] IP & T 299, [2002] All ER (D) 249 (Dec) 12.20, 12.22
Torbay District Council v Singh (Satnam) [2000] FSR 158, [1999] 2 Cr App R 451, (1999) 163 JP 744, (1999) 22(9) IPD 22086, QBD 19.28
Toshiba Europe GmbH v Katun Germany GmbH (Case C-112/99) [2002] FSR 39.......... 16.08, 16.13, 16.17
TREAT *see* British Sugar plc v James Robertson & Sons Ltd
Trebor Bassett Ltd v Football Association [1997] FSR 211 .... 14.15, 14.26
Trump International Ltd v DTTM Operations LLC [2019] EWHC 769 (Ch), [2019] Bus LR 2048, [2019] FSR 28 .... 4.58

U

Ukelele Orchestra of Great Britain (a firm) v Clausen [2014] EWHC 3789 (IPEC) 20.106

Uncle Mac *see* McCulloch v Lewis A May (Produce Distributors) Ltd
Unilever plc v Gillette (UK) Ltd [1989] RPC 583, (1989) Financial Times, June 29 .... 14.56
Unilever plc v Griffin [2010] EWHC 899 (Ch), [2010] 4 WLUK 343, [2010] FSR 33 .... 14.16
Unilever plc v Proctor & Gamble Co [2000] 1 WLR 2436, [2001] 1 All ER 783, [1999] 10 WLUK 900 .... 18.04
United Biscuits (UK) Ltd v Asda Stores Ltd (Penguin / Puffin Case) [1997] RPC 513, (1997) 20(5) IPD 20043 .... 20.21, 20.36, 20.38, 20.47, 20.54, 20.55, 20.61, 20.62

V

Van Doren +Q GmbH v Lifestyle sports + sportswear Handelsgesellschaft mbH (Case C-244/00) [2003] ECR I-3051, [2003] 2 CMLR 203, [2003] ETMR 75 .... 15.36
Verein Radetzky-Orden v Bundesvereinigung Kameradschaft Feldmarschall Radetzky (Case C-442/07) [2009] ETMR 14 .... 12.06, 12.08
Vertical Leisure Ltd v Poleplus Ltd [2014] EWHC 2077 (IPEC) 20.50
Victoria Plum Ltd v Victorian Plumbing [2016] EWHC 2911 (Ch), [2017] Bus LR 363, [2017] FSR 17 .... 5.110
Vine Products Ltd v MacKenzie & Co Ltd (No 2) [1969] RPC 1, [1967] FSR 402 .... 20.27
VISA *see* IA Sheimer (M) Sdn Bhd's Trade Mark Application
Vodafone Group plc v Orange Personal Communications Services Ltd [1997] FSR 34, [1997] EMLR 84, [1997] Info TLR 8 .... 16.27, 16.29, 16.30
Vodkat Case *see* Diageo North America Inc v Intercontinental Brands (ICB) Ltd

W

WF Gozze Frottierweberei GmbH v Baumwollborse (Case C-689/15) [2017] Bus LR 1795, [2017] 6 WLUK 124 .... 4.50, 12.06
WS Foster & Son Ltd v Brooks Bros UK Ltd [2013] EWPCC 18 .... 20.22, 20.33
Wagamama v City Centre Restaurants [1995] FSR 713 .... 5.38
Walker (John) & Sons Ltd v Henry Ost & Co Ltd [1970] 1 WLR 917, [1970] 2 All ER 106, [1970] RPC 489, [1970] FSR 63 .... 20.27
Walton International v Verweij Fashions [2018] EWHC 1608 (Ch), [2018] 6 WLUK 592, [2018] ETMR 34 .... 4.56, 12.06
Wasabi Frog v Gulk 2014 WL 4423396 .... 5.35
WELLNESS *see* Silberquelle GmbH v Maselli-Strickmode GmbH
West Sussex County Council v Kahraman [2006] EWHC 1703 (Admin), [2006] All ER (D) 104 Jun, 2006 WL 1546643 .... 19.27
West (trading as Eastenders) v Fuller Smith & Turner plc (ESB) [2003] EWCA Civ 48, [2003] FSR 44, [2003] IP & T 768, 147 SJLB 179 .... 12.22
WET WET WET *see* Bravado Merchandising Services Ltd v Mainstream Publishing (Edinburgh) Ltd
Whirlpool Corpnoration v Kenwood Ltd [2008] EWHC 1930 (Ch), [2009] RPC 19, [2008] All ER (D) 38 (Aug) 15.16, 15.56
William Stephens Ltd v Cassell (1913) 30 RPC 199 .... 20.41

Wilts UDL v Thomas Robinson Sons & Co Ltd [1957] RPC 220, [1957] CLY 1988 .... 16.23, 16.24
Windsurfing Chiemsee Produktions- und Vertriebs GmbH v Boots- und Segelzubehor Walter Huber (Case C-108/97) [1999] ETMR 585 .... 4.21, 4.22, 4.36, 4.39, 4.42
Wombles Ltd v Womble Skips Ltd [1977] RPC 99, [1975] FSR 488 .... 20.47, 20.65
Woodman v French Connection Ltd [2007] ETMR 8, [2007] RPC 1, Appointed Person 4.48
Wooley v UP Global Sourcing UK Ltd [2014] EWHC 493 (Ch), [2014] FSR 37 .... 17.19, 20.103
Woolley v Ultimate Products [2012] EWCA Civ 1038, [2012] 7 WLUK 869 .... 20.49
WORTH Trade Marks O/286/98 [1998] RPC 875, TMR 12.26
Wm Wrigley Jr Co v OHIM (DOUBLEMINT) (Case C-191/01P) [2003] ECR I-12447, [2004] RPC 327, [2004] ETMR 9 .... 4.24, 4.25
Wright, Layman & Umney Ltd v Wright (1949) 66 RPC 149 .... 20.56

Z

Zee Entertainment Enterprises Ltd v Zeebox Ltd [2014] EWCA Civ 82, [2014] FSR 26 .... 20.89
Zino Davidoff SA v A&G Imports Ltd (Case C-414/99) [2002] Ch 109, [2001] ECR I-8691, [2002] RPC 20, [2002] ETMR 9 .. 11.05, 14.19, 15.33, 15.41

Table of Statutes

C

Companies Act 2006 .. 2.29, 2.34; 7.20
  Pt 5 (ss 53–85) 2.28
  s 53–55, 60, 66 .... 2.29
    67 .... 2.31
    69–74 .... 2.34
    75, 76 .... 2.31
    77–81 .... 2.30
Copyright, Designs and Patents Act 1988
  s 253B(2) 18.11
County Courts Act 1984
  s 15 .... 17.88, 17.89, 17.90

D

Defamation Act 1952
  s 3(1) 16.22
Defamation Act 1996
  s 5 .... 16.22

E

European Communities Act 1972 .... 1.05
  s 2(1) 1.05
European Union (Withdrawal) Act 2018 .... 1.05; 14.03
  s 6, 7 .... 14.03
European Union (Withdrawal Agreement) Act 2020 ..... 1.05

I

Insolvency Act 1986
  s 306 .... 13.07
Intellectual Property (Unjustified Threats) Act 2017 .... 18.02

L

Limitation Act 1980
  s 4A, 32A 16.22
London Olympic Games and Paralympic Games Act 2006 .... 1.14; 21.01, 21.02, 21.04
  s 40(8) 21.04
  Sch 4
    para 3 .... 21.07
      10(2)(b) 21.04

M

Magistrates' Courts Act 1980
  s 32(9) 19.33

O

Olympic Symbol etc (Protection) Act 1995 .... 1.14; 21.01, 21.02, 21.03, 21.06, 21.07, 21.08, 21.10, 21.12, 21.13
  s 1(1), (2) 21.03
    2(2) 21.12
      (b) 21.12
    3(1) 21.05, 21.07, 21.12
      (2) 21.06
    4(1) 21.13
      (3) 21.05, 21.09
        (a) 21.10
        (b) 21.14
      (5), (11)–(14) 21.13
    5A 21.03
    6, 7 .... 21.16
    18(1) 21.05
      (2)(a), (b) 21.07

P

Patents Act 1977 .... 17.15
s 61 .... 17.15
Proceeds of Crime Act 2002 .. 19.33

T

Trade Descriptions Act 1968 .. 4.52
Trade Marks Act 1938 ...... 1.03; 5.106, 5.107; 14.15; 15.54
Trade Marks Act 1994 .... 1.02, 1.03, 1.04, 1.05, 1.09, 1.10; 2.04, 2.07, 2.09, 2.18, 2.21, 2.26, 2.27; 3.04, 3.29, 3.30; 5.04, 5.11, 5.88; 6.07, 6.16; 7.14, 7.68; 10.03; 11.01, 11.22; 12.04, 12.05, 12.29, 12.30; 13.02, 13.03, 13.05, 13.10, 13.13, 13.14, 13.15, 13.28, 13.37, 13.41, 13.43, 13.51, 13.53, 13.62, 13.63, 13.64; 14.03, 14.04, 14.07, 14.08, 14.14, 14.15; 15.02, 15.03, 15.08, 15.13, 15.27, 15.55; 17.03, 17.27, 17.76, 17.77, 17.87; 18.02, 18.03, 18.04, 18.09, 18.12; 19.01; 20.06, 20.61
s 1 .... 2.08
(1) 2.01; 4.06, 4.40, 4.41; 17.79
(b) 3.01
(2) 15.08
2(1) 13.02; 15.08; 17.02
(2) 1.13; 2.13, 2.14
2A 1.02
3 .... 3.12; 4.02; 11.02, 11.03
(1) 4.04, 4.34, 4.35, 4.38; 12.31, 12.33
(a) 4.06
(b) 4.07, 4.16; 11.02

Trade Marks Act 1994 – *contd*
3(1)(c) 4.19, 4.20, 4.44; 11.02
(d) 4.30; 11.02
(2) 4.40
(3)(a) 4.45, 4.46, 4.48
(b) 4.49
(4) 4.52
(5) 4.53
(6) 4.55
4 .... 4.02, 4.53
5 .... 2.15, 2.23; 3.12; 11.13
(1) 5.05, 5.31; 7.23, 7.35, 7.36, 7.41, 7.42, 7.77; 11.02, 11.16
(2) 5.21; 7.23, 7.35, 7.36, 7.41, 7.42, 7.77; 11.02, 11.16
(a) 5.05, 5.31, 5.37
(b) 5.05, 5.40
(3) 5.05, 5.21, 5.63, 5.65, 5.79
(4) 11.02
(a) 5.91, 5.93; 11.13
(b) 5.93
6 .... 2.15; 5.11, 5.93
(1)(c) 2.23; 11.06, 11.16
(2) 5.07
7 .... 5.107
9 .... 14.03, 14.04, 14.20
(1) 13.14; 14.08
(3) 14.07; 19.15
(a) 14.07
10 .... 2.26; 5.65; 14.03; 17.66
(1) 14.04, 14.09; 17.68
(2) 2.21; 5.40; 12.20; 14.04, 14.39, 14.48; 16.20; 17.68, 17.69
(3) 2.21, 2.22; 5.63, 5.65; 14.04, 14.45; 17.06

Trade Marks Act 1994 – *contd*
s 10(3A) 14.04, 14.49
(3B) 14.04, 14.59
(4) 14.15
(5) 14.54, 14.59, 14.60
(6) 16.04
10A 14.03, 14.04
10B 14.04; 17.73, 17.74, 17.75
(2) 17.74
11 .... 2.24; 15.02, 15.05, 15.08
(1) 15.06; 17.71
(1A) 15.08
(2) 15.09, 15.23
(a) 15.10
(b) 15.13, 15.15, 15.17; 16.05
(c) 15.19
(3) 2.16, 2.24, 2.25; 15.26; 17.70
11A 15.02
12 .... 11.05; 15.02, 15.31, 15.43
(2) 15.43
13 .... 15.02, 15.03
(1)(a) 15.52
(b) 15.57
14 .... 17.02, 17.35, 17.90
(2) 17.02, 17.05, 17.17, 17.20, 17.27
15 .... 17.35, 17.39, 17.40, 17.88, 17.90
(1) 17.02, 17.34, 17.45
(a) 17.39
(b) 17.41
(2) 17.02, 17.34, 17.40, 17.41
16 .... 17.02, 17.34, 17.35, 17.43, 17.46, 17.49, 17.88, 17.90
(1) 17.43, 17.45
(2) 17.43

Trade Marks Act 1994 – *contd*
s 16(3) 17.45
17 .... 17.35
(2) 17.36
(4) 17.37
(5) 17.38
18 .... 17.35, 17.43
(1)(a)–(c) 17.46
(2), (3) 17.47
19 .... 17.35, 17.43, 17.45, 17.49, 17.51, 17.88
(1) 17.02, 17.34, 17.48, 17.49, 17.50
(3) 17.51
(4) 17.52
(5) 17.50
21 .... 18.02
(1) 18.03
(2) 18.04
21A 18.02
(1) 18.12
(2) 18.05
(a) 18.17
(3)–(6) 18.05
21B 18.02, 18.05
(1) 18.06, 18.11
(b) 18.11
(2) 18.10
(a)–(c) 18.10
(3), (4) 18.11
(6) 18.06
21C 18.02
(1) 18.13, 18.18
(2), (3) 18.17
21D 18.02
(1) 18.14
(2) 18.15
(3) 18.16
(4) 18.14
(5) 18.14
21E, 21F 18.02
22 .... 13.02
23 .... 15.02, 15.58; 17.80
(1), (3), (4) 13.03
(5) 14.62; 17.81, 17.88

Trade Marks Act 1994 – *contd*
s 23(6) 14.62
24(1) 13.04, 13.06, 13.53
(1A) 13.05
(2) 13.04
(a) 13.53
(3) 13.04, 13.05, 13.06, 13.52
(4) 13.04, 13.05
(5) 13.05
25 .... 13.43, 13.47, 13.48
(1) 13.08
(2) 13.08
(b) 13.13
(3) 13.13, 13.61
(a), (b) 13.47
(4) 13.47
(b) 17.88
26 .... 13.02
27 .... 13.02, 13.08, 13.10
(1) 13.13
28(2), (3) 13.13
(4) 13.28
(5) 13.37, 13.64
29(1) 17.83
30 .... 13.40, 13.42, 13.47; 17.16, 17.82, 17.84
(1A) 13.41, 13.63; 17.84
(2), (3) 13.41, 13.63; 17.84
(4) 13.41; 17.84
(5) 13.41
(6) 13.41; 17.85
(6A) 13.41
(7) 17.85
31 .... 13.38, 13.42, 13.47; 17.16, 17.82
(1) 17.02, 17.83, 17.85
(2) 13.39; 17.02, 17.83
(4) 13.39; 17.83
(5) 13.39

Trade Marks Act 1994 – *contd*
s 31(6) 13.39; 17.85
(a)–(c) 17.83
(8) 13.39; 17.83
32 .... 7.03
(2)(c) 6.03
(3) 4.59; 6.09
34(1) 6.01
37 .... 7.14
(3), (4) 7.15
38(1), (2) 7.18
(3) 7.82
39 .... 3.18
(1), (2) 6.16
46 .... 3.27; 12.03, 12.04; 17.88
(1) 12.25
(a) 11.06; 12.03
(b) 12.03, 12.04
(c) 12.03, 12.28; 13.15
(d) 12.03, 12.37; 13.15
(2) 12.10, 12.18
(3) 12.17
(5) 12.19, 12.30
(6) 12.48
47 .... 3.27; 11.02, 11.12; 15.06; 17.88
(1) 11.03
(2) 2.23; 11.04, 11.05
(2A) 11.02, 11.06; 15.05, 15.06
(2B) 11.06
(2C)–(2F) 11.06
(2G) 11.02; 15.05, 15.06
(3) 11.12
48 .... 2.26; 11.08, 11.09, 11.11; 15.02, 15.27; 17.70, 17.71
(1) 11.07, 11.10, 11.11; 15.05, 15.06, 15.28
(b) 15.27
49 .... 3.06

Trade Marks Act 1994 – *contd*
s 49(1) 3.02, 3.09
(1A) 3.09
50 .... 3.06
(1) 3.03
54A 1.02
55(1)(b) 2.19; 17.70
56 .... 2.18, 2.19, 2.24; 17.70
(1) 2.25; 17.66
(2) 2.21, 2.26; 17.01, 17.66, 17.67, 17.68, 17.69, 17.70, 17.71, 17.72; 20.34
(3) 17.71
57, 58 .... 4.53
60 .... 2.26; 17.01, 17.74
64 .... 17.88
69 .... 7.68
72 .... 5.55
73, 74 .... 17.88
75 .... 17.87, 17.90
76 .... 7.81
(2)–(4) 11.17
77 .... 11.17
80(2) 7.19
82, 83 .... 10.03
89 .... 17.02, 17.34, 17.53, 17.62, 17.64; 19.31
(1) 17.62
(2) 17.63
(3) 17.53, 17.62
90 .... 17.64; 19.31
91 .... 19.31
92 .... 19.02, 19.03, 19.04, 19.05, 19.08, 19.10, 19.11, 19.14, 19.18, 19.19, 19.23, 19.32
(1) 19.02, 19.16, 19.17, 19.18, 19.21, 19.22, 19.26
(b) 19.22

Trade Marks Act 1994 – *contd*
s 92(2) 19.02, 19.20, 19.21, 19.25, 19.26
(a)–(c) 19.22
(3) 19.02, 19.23, 19.24, 19.25, 19.26
(4) 19.13, 19.14
(5) 19.02, 19.26, 19.28, 19.29
(6) 19.32
92A 19.31
93 .... 19.31
94 .... 19.34, 19.35, 19.37
(1), (2) 19.36
(3) 19.37
95 .... 12.35; 19.34
(1) 19.38
(2) 19.39, 19.40
97 .... 19.31
(1) 19.31
(2), (3) 19.31
99 .... 17.79; 19.42
(1) 17.76
(2) 17.76; 19.42
(3) 17.76
(4) 17.01, 17.77, 17.79
(5) 17.79
100 .... 12.06
101 .... 19.30
(4), (5) 19.30
103(2) 14.15
104 .... 15.08
Sch 1 .... 3.04, 3.12, 3.30
para 3 .... 3.15
(1) 3.04
(2) 3.15
4 .... 3.17
5 .... 3.07, 3.19, 3.22
10 .... 3.24
11 .... 3.30
12 .... 3.30; 17.88
13 .... 3.29
14 .... 3.28
Sch 2 .... 3.04, 3.12, 3.30
para 3 .... 3.15

Trade Marks Act 1994 – *contd*
para 3(1) 3.04
(2) 3.15
4 .... 3.16
5 .... 3.17
6 .... 3.07, 3.19, 3.23
11 .... 3.24
12 .... 3.25
13 .... 3.30
14 .... 3.30; 17.88

Trade Marks Act 1994 – *contd*
para 15 .... 3.29
16 .... 3.28
Sch 2A 1.02; 2.01; 5.11; 17.03
para 1(3) 18.02
20(1)–(4) 17.03
25 .... 5.11
Sch 2B 1.02; 5.11
para 28, 29, 33 .... 5.11

Table of Statutory Instruments

A

Agricultural Products, Food and Drink (Amendment etc) (EU Exit) Regulations 2020, SI 2020/1637 .... 3.38

B

Business Protection from Misleading Marketing Regulations 2008, SI 2008/1276 ... 16.01, 16.02, 16.08
- reg 2 .... 16.08
- 3(2) 16.08
- (3)–(5) 16.11
- 4 .... 16.13

C

Civil Procedure (Amendment No 7) Rules 2013, SI 2013/1974
- r 26 .... 17.86, 17.87

Civil Procedure Rules 1998, SI 1998/3132 .... 7.50; 17.20, 17.86; 18.07
- Pt 32 (rr 32.1–32.20) 7.71
- PD 25A 17.30
- Pt 63 .... 17.86
- r 63.13 .... 17.86, 17.89, 17.90
- 63.17A(1) 17.88
- 63.27(4) 17.88
- PD 63 .... 17.86, 17.89

Community Trade Mark Regulations 2006, SI 2006/1027 .... 17.62; 18.02
- reg 5(3) 17.35
- 12(1) 17.88, 17.89
- (2) 17.89

Company, Limited Liability Partnership and Business (Names and Trading Disclosures) Regulations 2015, SI 2015/17 .... 2.32

Company, Limited Liability Partnership and Business Names (Sensitive Words and Expressions) Regulations 2009, SI 2009/2615 .... 2.29

Company, Limited Liability Partnership and Business Names (Sensitive Words and Expressions) Regulations 2014, SI 2014/3140 .... 2.29

Consumer Protection from Unfair Trading Regulations 2008, SI 2008/1277 .... 16.01

Control of Misleading Advertising Regulations 1988, SI 1988/915 .... 16.01

Customs (Enforcement of Intellectual Property Rights) (Amendment) (EU Exit) Regulations 2019, SI 2019/514 .. 17.02, 17.34, 17.53

D

Designs and International Trade Marks (Amendment etc) (EU Exit) Regulations 2019, SI 2019/638
- reg 6 .... 1.02

H

High Court and County Court Jurisdiction Order 1991, SI 1991/1222
art 2(1)(l) 17.89

I

Intellectual Property (Amendment etc) (EU Exit) Regulations 2020, SI 2020/1050 .... 17.03
Pt 4 (regs 7–12) 1.02
Pt 5 (regs 13–25) 1.02
Intellectual Property (Enforcement etc) Regulations 2006, SI 2006/1028 .... 17.10
reg 3(1)–(3) 17.10

P

Patents County Court (Financial Limits) (No 2) Order 2011, SI 2011/2222
art 3 .... 17.88

T

Trade Mark Rules 2008, SI 2008/1797 .... 7.14; 10.02
r 2(1)7.77
3(2) 7.03
5 .... 7.03
7 .... 6.01
8 .... 7.12
(2) 6.03
(2A), (2B) 6.05
9(1)–(4) 7.12
11 .... 10.02
(1)(a) 7.13
(4) 7.13
12 .... 7.13
13(3)(a), (b) 7.11
16 .... 7.17
17(1) 7.18
(2) 7.19
(3) 7.19, 7.20
(4) 7.19
(5)(d) 7.24
(8) 7.27
(9) 7.20

Trade Mark Rules 2008 – *contd*
17A 7.78
18(2), (3) 7.27
(4) 7.28
(b) 7.28
(c) 7.30
(5) 7.29
19 .... 7.36, 7.80
(4) 7.39
(5) 7.40
(6) 7.43
(7) 7.37, 7.38
20 .... 7.80
(1) 7.47
(4) 7.44
38(1) 12.38
(4) 12.38, 12.39
(6) 12.39
(8) 12.39
39(1) 12.38
(3) 12.38, 12.39
40(1), (4) 12.39
41(1)–(4) 11.13
(5) 11.14
(6) 11.14, 11.15
(7) 11.14
42(1)–(5) 11.16
48(1)(a) 13.09
(b) 13.45
(c)–(e) 13.09
(f) 13.46
49(1)(a) 13.09
(b) 13.44
(c) 13.09, 13.46
(d), (e) 13.09
(2) 13.09, 13.44
(a), (b) 13.09
55(2) 7.68
60(1)–(3), (5) 10.03
61 .... 10.03
62 .... 11.17
(1) 11.13
(g), (j) 7.80
(2) 7.68
(5), (6) 7.80
63 .... 7.73; 11.17
64 .... 7.32; 11.16, 11.17
(1), (2) 7.50

Trade Mark Rules 2008 – *contd*
r 64(3) 7.50; 12.39
(5), (6) 7.50
65 .... 7.68; 11.17
67, 68 .... 7.75; 11.17
69 .... 11.17
70 .... 7.81; 11.17
71–73 .... 11.17
77 .... 7.48
Trade Marks (Amendment etc) (EU Exit) Regulations 2019, SI 2019/269 .... 17.03
reg 2 .... 1.02
Trade Marks and Registered Designs (Amendment) Rules 2013, SI 2013/444 .... 7.13
Trade Marks (Customs) Regulations 1994, SI 1994/2625 .... 17.62, 17.64
reg 2 .... 17.62, 17.64
3–5 .... 17.64
Trade Marks (Fast Track Opposition) (Amendment) Rules 2013, SI 2013/2235 .... 7.77
Trade Marks (International Registration) Order 2008, SI 2008/2206 .... 18.02
reg 3(3) 18.02
Sch 1 .... 18.02
Trade Marks (International Registration) Order 1996, SI 1996/714 .... 18.02
art 4(6) 18.02
Trade Marks Regulations 2018, SI 2018/825 .... 13.41
reg 11 .... 17.74
14 .... 13.05
16 .... 13.37
17 .... 13.63
(6) 13.41
28, 53, 54 .... 17.74

Table of European Legislation

TREATIES AND CONVENTIONS

Convention for the Protection of Industrial Property (Paris, 20 March 1883)........ 2.18; 5.11; 6.02; 9.01; 11.16
art 6*bis*.................. 2.17, 2.18; 5.12; 8.16; 17.69
6(1)(a) 4.54

Treaty establishing the European Community (Rome, 13 March 1957)
Annex I.............................. 3.39

Treaty on the Functioning of the European Union (Lisbon, 13 December 2007)
art 34–36 .... 15.04

REGULATIONS

Council Regulation (EC) No 40/94 of 20 December 1994 on the Community trade mark
art 7(1)(c) 4.22, 4.24

Commission Regulation (EC) No 874/2004 of 28 April 2004 laying down public policy rules concerning the implementation and functions of the .eu Top Level Domain and the principles governing registration 2.38

Council Regulation (EC) No 510/2006 of 20 March 2006 on the protection of geographical indications and designations of origin for agricultural products and foodstuffs
art 5(9)............................... 3.38

Council Regulation (EC) No 207/2009 on the Community trade mark 1.04; 5.04, 5.10, 5.88
Recital 8 .... 5.06
art 4 .... 4.40, 4.41
7(1)(e) 4.40
8(1)(a) 5.05
(b)..................... 5.05, 5.21, 5.37, 5.40
(2)............................... 5.12
(b).......................... 5.07
(c) 2.18
(4)............................... 5.94
(5).......................... 5.05, 5.21, 5.63, 5.65, 5.79
9(1)(a) 4.56
(b)....................... 4.56; 5.41
(c) 5.63
52(1)(b) 4.55
99(1)............................. 5.55
107 .... 4.56

Commission Regulation (EC) No 607/2009 of 14 July 2009 laying down certain detailed rules for the implementation of Council Regulation (EC) No 479/2008 as regards protected designations of origin and geographical indications, traditional terms, labelling and presentation of certain wine sector products 3.40
Regulation (EC) No 1151/2012 of the European Parliament and of the Council of 21 November 2012 on quality schemes for agricultural products and foodstuffs.... 3.05, 3.38, 3.39, 3.40, 3.54, 3.55
art 2 ...... 3.40
3 ...... 3.55
5 ...... 3.47
(1), (2) 3.42
6 ...... 3.43
7 ...... 3.48
8 ...... 3.47
12 ...... 3.50
13 ...... 3.52, 3.53
14 ...... 3.53
(2) 3.53
18 ...... 3.56
36 ...... 3.52
37 ...... 3.50
52(3) 3.56
53 ...... 3.48
54 ...... 3.46
Regulation (EU) No 608/2013 of the European Parliament and of the Council of 12 June 2013 concerning customs enforcement of intellectual property rights and repealing Council Regulation (EC) No 1383/2003......... 17.02, 17.34, 17.53, 17.54, 17.56, 17.62; 19.31
Regulation(EU)No608/2013–*contd*
art 1(1) 17.54
(3)–(5) 17.55
2(1)(a) 17.55
(2) 17.55, 17.62
(7) 17.55
(19) 17.60
3 ...... 17.56
6 ...... 17.57
7 ...... 17.62
11, 12 ...... 17.58
15 ...... 17.57
17(1)–(4) 17.58
18(1)–(4) 17.59
19(2) 17.61
23(1), (3)–(5) 17.60
26 ...... 17.57, 17.60
(1), (3)–(9) 17.60
27 ...... 17.61
28, 29 ...... 17.57, 17.61
Regulation 2013/0088 (COD) of the European Parliament and of the Council amending Council Regulation (EC) No 207/2009 on the Community trade mark (proposal) 5.05; 15.11
Commission Delegated Regulation (EU) No 664/2014 of 18 December 2013 supplementing Regulation (EU) No 1151/2012 of the European Parliament and of the Council with regard to the establishment of the Union symbols for protected designations of origin, protected geographical indications and traditional specialities guaranteed and with regard to certain rules on sourcing, certain procedural rules and certain additional transitional rules 3.48
Annex 1 ...... 3.51

Regulation (EU) 2015/2424 of the European Parliament and of the Council of 16 December 2015 amending Council Regulation (EC) No 207/2009 on the Community trade mark and Commission Regulation (EC) No 2868/95 implementing Council Regulation (EC) No 40/94 on the Community trade mark, and repealing Commission Regulation (EC) No 2869/95 on the fees payable to the Office for Harmonization in the Internal Market (Trade Marks and Designs) ... 1.04; 14.03
art 3(1)(e) 4.42
7 .... 4.03
(1)(a) 4.06, 4.09
(b) 4.07, 4.08, 4.09, 4.18, 4.20, 4.21, 4.28, 4.29, 4.31
(c) 4.07, 4.08, 4.09, 4.19, 4.20, 4.21, 4.22, 4.23, 4.24, 4.29, 4.31
(d) 4.09, 4.30, 4.31, 4.32
(f) 4.45, 4.46
(g) 4.03, 4.49
(h) 4.53, 4.54
(i) 4.53
(j), (k) 4.52
(2) 4.05
(3) 4.04, 4.34, 4.35
Regulation (EU) 2017/1001 of the European Parliament and of the Council of 14 June 2017 on the European Union trade mark. 1.02, 1.04, 1.05, 1.09, 1.10; 2.04, 2.06, 2.07, 2.10; 3.37; 5.04; 6.16; 8.01, 8.06; 10.05; 11.01, 11.20, 11.21; 12.29, 12.30; 13.37, 13.49, 13.51, 13.53, 13.60, 13.62; 14.03, 14.14, 14.49; 15.03; 17.03

Regulation (EU) 2017/1001 – *contd*
Recital 8 .... 14.30
Recital 16 .... 14.30
art 1(2) 14.08
4 .... 2.01
(a) 3.01
5(1) 14.23
(a) 14.41
(b) 14.48
(2) 14.50
7 .... 11.19; 12.31
(1)(b)–(d) 11.19
(3) 4.38; 12.33
8 .... 11.20
(2)(a)(i)–(iv) 8.16
(b), (c) 8.16
(3) 8.29
(4) 2.15; 8.16; 11.25
9 .... 14.03, 14.58
(1) 14.04
(2) 14.20
(2)(a) 14.04, 14.09
(b) 14.04, 14.39
(c) 14.04, 14.45
(3) 14.15
(4) 14.04
9a 14.04
10 .... 14.58, 14.59
11 .... 14.04, 14.58
12, 13 .... 14.58
14 .... 15.03, 15.05, 15.09, 15.23
(1)(a) 15.10
(b) 15.13
(c) 15.19
15 .... 15.03, 15.31
(2) 15.43
16 .... 13.52; 15.03, 15.05, 15.06, 15.08
17 .... 14.58; 17.04
18(1)(a) 12.10
19(1), (2) 13.49
20(1) 13.53
(3) 13.52
(4) 13.55
(5) 13.56
22 .... 13.05, 13.51
25 .... 8.18; 13.58

Regulation (EU) 2017/1001 – *contd*
t 25(2).......................... 13.37, 13.64
(3).......................... 3.37; 13.62, 13.63
(4).......................... 3.37
(5).......................... 13.65
26(1).......................... 13.65
27.......................... 13.61
(1), (2).......................... 13.54
28.......................... 13.50
31(1).......................... 8.05
(2).......................... 8.07
32.......................... 8.07, 8.12
33.......................... 6.01, 6.03
34, 35.......................... 8.09
36.......................... 8.09, 8.12
37.......................... 15.03
39.......................... 8.10
(2), (3).......................... 8.10
41(3).......................... 8.25
43.......................... 8.11
(1), (2).......................... 8.13
44.......................... 8.14
45.......................... 3.34
46.......................... 8.25
(1).......................... 8.15, 8.16; 11.25
(a)–(c).......................... 8.18
(3).......................... 8.25
47(2).......................... 8.52
49(1), (2).......................... 6.16
52.......................... 11.19
58.......................... 3.36; 12.03
(1).......................... 12.25
(a).......................... 12.03, 12.04
(b).......................... 12.03, 12.28
(c).......................... 12.03, 12.37
(2).......................... 12.19, 12.23, 12.30
59.......................... 3.36; 11.18, 11.19
(1)(a), (b).......................... 11.19
(2), (3).......................... 11.19
60.......................... 3.36; 11.18, 11.20
(1).......................... 11.25
(2).......................... 11.20, 11.25
(3), (4).......................... 11.21
61.......................... 15.03, 15.27, 15.28

Regulation (EU) 2017/1001 – *contd*
art 61(1), (3).......................... 11.22
62(1).......................... 12.48
(3).......................... 11.23
63(1).......................... 11.24
(a)–(c).......................... 11.25
(2).......................... 11.24
64(1).......................... 11.32; 12.46
(2), (3).......................... 11.33
66(1).......................... 11.36
68.......................... 8.64
(1).......................... 11.36
69(1).......................... 11.36
70(2).......................... 11.36
72(1).......................... 11.36
74.......................... 3.31, 3.34, 3.38
(1).......................... 3.02
75.......................... 3.33
(2).......................... 3.33
76(1), (2).......................... 3.34
77.......................... 3.34
79(2).......................... 3.36
80.......................... 3.37
81.......................... 3.36
Ch VIII (arts 83–93).......................... 3.31
art 83.......................... 3.34, 3.37
(1).......................... 3.03, 3.04
84.......................... 3.33
85(1), (2).......................... 3.34
86.......................... 3.34
88(2).......................... 3.36
91.......................... 3.36
109.......................... 8.63; 11.35
(1), (2).......................... 8.63
119(1).......................... 10.05
(2), (3).......................... 8.19; 10.05
120(2).......................... 10.07
(a), (b).......................... 10.08
(3).......................... 10.08
Ch X (arts 122–135).... 17.03, 17.04
art 122–127.......................... 17.03
128.......................... 17.03
(2), (4), (6), (7).......................... 17.03
129–131.......................... 17.03, 17.04
132.......................... 17.03
133–135.......................... 17.03
138.......................... 15.03, 15.05, 15.26
146.......................... 8.08

Regulation (EU) 2017/1001 – *contd*
art 146(1), (2) 11.31; 12.42
(5)–(8) 11.31; 12.42
(7) 8.32
180 .... 8.26
Annex 1
para 20 .... 11.24; 12.43
21 .... 11.36
Commission Delegated Regulation (EU) 2018/625 of 5 March 2018 supplementing Regulation (EU) 2017/1001 of the European Parliament and of the Council on the European Union trade mark, and repealing Delegated Regulation (EU) 2017/1430 .... 8.25, 8.31, 8.33, 8.34, 8.35
art 2 .... 8.25
(1)(e) 11.29
(2) 8.25
(a) 8.27
(b) 8.28
(i)–(iv) 8.29
(c) 8.29, 8.30
(d) 8.33
(g) 8.35
(i) 8.38
(4) 8.25
5 .... 8.23, 8.25, 8.32, 8.36
(5) 8.34
6(1) 8.41
7(1) 8.42
(2) 8.42, 8.44
(4) 8.43, 8.47
8(1) 8.42
(2) 8.49
(c) 8.44
(3), (4) 8.44, 8.49
(5) 8.44
10 .... 8.52
(3) 8.57
(4) 8.56
(5) 8.53; 11.34
12 .... 11.24, 11.26, 11.30; 12.41
Commission Delegated Regulation (EU) 2018/625 – *contd*
art 12(1)(a) 11.27
(b) 11.28
(c)(i), (ii) 11.29
(d) 11.28
(2), (4) 11.28
15(1) 12.43
(4) 11.30
17(1), (2) 11.32; 12.44
19(1) 11.34; 12.44
23 .... 11.36
65(1)(e) 13.56
Commission Implementing Regulation (EU) 2018/626 of 5 March 2018 laying down detailed rules for implementing certain provisions of Regulation (EU) 2017/1001 of the European Parliament and of the Council on the European trade mark, and repealing implementing Regulation (EU) 2017/1431 .... 3.33; 8.01, 8.27, 8.28, 8.30, 8.32, 8.56, 8.57, 8.58; 13.60
art 1 .... 8.05
2(1)(b) 11.29
(c) 8.05
(d) 8.06
3 .... 8.06
4 .... 8.09
6 .... 8.10
7 .... 6.03
(d) 6.01
8(1)–(5) 8.30
9 .... 8.12
13 .... 13.65
(1) 13.56
(d) 13.65
(3) 13.56
16, 17 .... 3.33
18 .... 8.63
24 .... 8.47
32 .... 8.10
109(1) 11.35

Regulation (EU) 2019/517 of the European Parliament and of the Council of 19 March 2019 on the implementation and functioning of the .eu top-level domain name and amending and repealing Regulation (EC) No 733/2002 and repealing Commission Regulation (EC) No 874/2004 .... 2.38

DIRECTIVES

Council Directive 84/450/EEC of 10 September 1984 relating to the approximation of the laws, regulations and administrative provisions of the Member States concerning misleading advertising 16.01

First Council Directive 89/104/EEC of 21 December 1988 to approximate the laws of the Member States relating to trade marks 1.03; 14.03
art 9(1) 11.08

Directive 2004/48/EC of the European Parliament and of the Council of 29 April 2004 on the enforcement of intellectual property rights 17.09, 17.27, 17.28, 17.33
art 7 .... 17.28
8 .... 17.28
(1) 17.32
(2), (3) 17.33
9 .... 17.20, 17.22
11 .... 17.20, 17.27
13 .... 17.09
(1) 17.06, 17.09, 17.10, 17.11, 17.12
(2) 17.09

Directive 2005/29/EC of the European Parliament and of the Council of 11 May 2005 concerning unfair business-to-consumer commercial practices in the internal market and amending Council Directive 84/450/EEC, Directives 97/7/EC, 98/27/EC and 2002/65/EC of the European Parliament and of the Council and Regulation (EC) No 2006/2004 of the European Parliament and of the Council (Unfair Commercial Practices Directive) 16.13

Directive 2006/114/EC of the European Parliament and of the Council of 12 December 2006 concerning misleading and comparative advertising 16.01, 16.02, 16.04, 16.05, 16.06, 16.07, 16.08, 16.09, 16.10, 16.14, 16.31
art 2 .... 16.07, 16.08
(b) 16.13
3 .... 16.07, 16.11, 16.13
4 .... 16.07, 16.13, 16.19
(d) 16.14
(e) 16.15
(f), (g) 16.18, 16.19
(h) 16.20
5(1)(a) 16.19
6(1) 16.05
8(1) 16.13

Directive 2008/95/EC of the European Parliament and of the Council of 22 October 2008 to approximate laws of the Member States relating to trade marks 1.03; 2.01; 5.04, 5.101; 14.03

Directive 2008/95/EC – *contd*
Recital 11 .... 5.06; 14.30
art 3(1)
(c) 4.26
(d) 4.32, 4.33
4(3).............................. 5.65
5(1)(b) 16.20
9 .... 11.09
(1).............................. 11.08
Directive (EU) 2015/2436 of the European Parliament and of the Council of 16 December 2015 to approximate the laws of the Member States relating to trade marks 1.03; 2.04, 2.06, 2.07, 2.10; 5.04; 14.03; 15.05, 15.11, 15.28, 15.30
Recital 11 .... 5.99
art 1 .... 2.01
4(1)(b) 5.37
5(1)(a) 5.05
(b) 5.05, 5.21, 5.40
(2).............................. 5.85
(c) 5.07
(3).............................. 5.05
(a) 5.21, 5.63
9 .... 15.29
(1).............................. 11.22
10 .... 14.03, 14.16, 14.17
(1)............................ 14.04
(a) 5.101, 5.102
(2)..................... 14.04, 14.17, 14.59
(a) 14.04, 14.09, 14.17, 14.23, 14.30, 14.31
(b) 5.40; 14.04, 14.31, 14.39
(c) 5.63; 14.04, 14.45
(3)..................... 14.04, 14.14, 14.59
(4)............................ 14.04
11 .... 14.03, 14.04
13 .... 14.04
16(1)............................ 12.05
Directive 2013/0089 (COD) of the European Parliament and of the Council to approximate the laws of the Member States relating to trade marks (Recast) (*draft*) 5.05; 15.11
art 4(2)(b) 4.10

AGREEMENTS

Agreement on the European Economic Area (1 January 1994)................ 2.12
Agreement on the withdrawal of the United Kingdom of Great Britain and Northern Ireland from the European Union and the European Atomic Energy Community (Doc 2019/C 384 I/01)
art 54 .... 3.38
Agreement on Trade-related Aspects of Intellectual Property Rights (TRIPS) (15 April 1994) 9.01
Madrid Agreement concerning the International Registration of Marks (Madrid, 14 April 1891) 8.16; 9.01, 9.02, 9.03, 9.04
art 2(1).......................... 9.08
3(1).......................... 9.12
(4).......................... 9.32
5(1).......................... 9.32
(2)(a)–(c)................ 9.33
(3)....................... 9.34, 9.36
(5).......................... 9.35
(6).......................... 9.34
6(1).......................... 9.40
(2)–(4) 9.41
7 .... 9.40
9 .... 13.69
9quinquies............. 9.42, 9.43
9ter 13.70
Protocol 1.12; 6.03; 7.59; 8.16; 9.01, 9.02, 9.03, 9.04

Protocol relating to the Madrid Agreement concerning the international registration of marks (Madrid, 1989)
r 3(1) 10.09
(2)(a), (b) 10.10
(6)(a) 10.11
(b)–(d) 10.12
9 .... 9.12
11(2) 9.23
(b) 9.23
(3) 9.22
(b) 9.23
(4) 9.21
(b) 9.23
(5) 9.23
12(1)(a), (b) 9.26
(2), (4)–(6) 9.26
(7), (8) 9.27
13(1) 9.28
(2)(a), (b) 9.29
14(1), (2) 9.31
17 .... 9.37

Protocol (Madrid, 1989) – *contd*
(3) 9.37
18 .... 9.37
18*ter*(1) 9.35
ter(2)–(4) 9.36
20*bis* 13.72
Nice Agreement concerning the International Classification of Goods and Services for the Purposes of the Registration of Marks (Nice, 15 June 1957) ... 1.05; 6.02
art 2(3) 6.02
Trade and Cooperation Agreement between the European Union and the European Atomic Energy Community and the United Kingdom of Great Britain and Northern Ireland (Doc 22020A1231(01)) 1.05
Pt 2 Title V Ch 2 .... 1.05
WTO Agreement 11.16

Chapter 1

Introduction

1.01 This book focuses on the current law relating to the protection of registered trade marks and certain related rights both in the UK and, notwithstanding the UK's withdrawal from the EU, in the EU.[1] It covers:

(a) Registered trade marks.
(b) Well-known trade marks.
(c) Certification marks.
(d) Collective marks.
(e) Protected geographical origin indicators.
(f) International conventions.
(g) Passing off.
(h) Olympic symbols.

1 For the history of trade mark law, see Morcom, Roughton and St Quintin *The Modern Law of Trade Marks* (sixth edn, 2021, LexisNexis) and *Kerly's Law of Trade Marks and Trade Names* (sixteenth edn, 2017, Sweet & Maxwell).

REGISTERED TRADE MARKS

1.02 Certain signs are capable of being registered as trade marks:

(a) **UK**—in the UK at the UK Intellectual Property Office ('UKIPO') under the Trade Marks Act 1994 ('TMA 1994'). The protection of UK trade marks ('UKTMs') is unaffected by the UK's withdrawal from the EU;
(b) **EU**—in the EU at the European Union Intellectual Property Office ('EUIPO') under the European Union Trade Marks Regulation[1] ('EUTMR'). Since the UK's withdrawal from the EU became effective at 11pm on 31 December 2020, EU trade marks ('EUTMs') have ceased to be protected as such in the UK;[2] and/or
(c) **International**—internationally at the World Intellectual Property Organisation ('WIPO') under the Madrid System.[3]

1 Regulation (EU) 2017/1001 of the European Parliament and of the Council on the European Union trade mark.

2 However, EUTMs that were in existence as at 31 December 2020 remain protected in the UK after that date because they are treated as having been registered under the TMA 1994 and, unless otherwise provided in Sch 2A of the TMA 1994, the provisions of the TMA 1994 will apply to them. See s 2A and Sch 2A of the TMA 1994 (added by SI 2019/269, reg 2, as amended by SI 2020/1050, Pt 4). Such marks are referred to as comparable trade marks (EU).

3 For the Madrid System, see Ch 9 below. International trade marks protected in the EU as at 31 December 2020 also remain protected in the UK after that date because they are also treated as having been registered under the TMA 1994. See s 54A and Sch 2B of the TMA 1994 (added by SI 2019/638, reg 6, as amended by SI 2020/1050, Pt 5).

1.03 *UK Trade Marks Act 1994* — UK trade marks ('UKTMs') are protected under the Trade Marks Act 1994 ('TMA 1994'). The TMA 1994 replaces the earlier Trade Marks Act 1938, which is for the most part no longer relevant.

Prior to the UK's withdrawal from the EU, the TMA 1994 had been amended several times to give effect to various European Trade Mark Directives[1] intended to 'approximate' the laws of Member States of the European Union relating to trade marks.

1 Chronologically, Directive 89/104/EEC, Directive 2008/95/EC and, most recently, Directive (EU) 2015/2436. Unless otherwise stated, references in this Guide to 'The Directive' are to Directive (EU) 2015/2436.

1.04 *European Union Trade Mark Regulation (EU) 2017/1001*— European Union Trade Marks ('EUTMs') (formerly known as Community Trade Marks ('CTMs')) are protected under the Regulation (EU) 2017/1001 of the European Parliament and of the Council on the European Union trade mark (the 'EUTMR').[1]

Since the UK's withdrawal from the EU became effective at 11pm on 31 December 2020, EUTMs have not been protected in the UK. However, EUTMs that were in existence as at that date will continue to qualify for protection in the UK as they are treated as having been registered as trade marks under the TMA 1994.[2]

1 Regulation (EU) 2017/1001 is a codifying regulation replacing Council Regulation (EC) No 207/2009 of 26 February 2009 on the Community Trade Mark (as amended by Regulation (EU) 2015/2424). Unless otherwise stated, references in this Guide to 'The Regulation' are to Regulation 2017/1001. Under the Regulation, the Office for Harmonisation in the Internal Market ('OHIM') was renamed the EUIPO and Community trade marks ('CTMs') were renamed European Union trade marks ('EUTMs').

2 The same applies to International trade marks protected in the EU as at 31 December 2020. See footnotes 2 and 3 to para.1-02 above.

1.05 *Common principles and the effect of Brexit*—Currently much of the substantive law governing the protection of UKTMs under the TMA 1994 is the same as that which governs the protection of EUTMs under the EUTMR. This is because, before the UK's withdrawal from the EU, the TMA 1994 was amended to give effect to the various EU Directives referred to above and those Directives formed the basis for the provisions of the EUTMR (and its predecessors) regarding registrability and the scope of the rights conferred on an EUTM.

Further, in the years leading up to the UK's withdrawal from the EU, issues of interpretation of trade mark law, whether in respect of UKTMs or EUTMs were determined in accordance with guidance provided by the Court of Justice of the European Union (the 'CJEU')[1] regarding the provisions and objectives of the relevant EU Directives and Regulations. That guidance was given in decisions on cases referred to the CJEU by the courts of EU Member States (either in relation to national trade marks or to EUTMs) or decisions on appeals from the EUIPO and the General Court.[2]

However, by reason of the UK's withdrawal from the EU, there have been very significant changes. In particular, under the UK's European Union (Withdrawal) Act 2018 and European Union (Withdrawal Agreement) Act 2020:

(a) The European Communities Act 1972 has been repealed.
(b) As a result, UK courts and tribunals are not bound by decisions of the CJEU given after 31 December 2020 although they can, where relevant, have regard to such decisions.
(c) Certain aspects of EU law that were part of UK law as at 11pm on 31 December 2020 have been retained and incorporated into UK law. These aspects are referred to as 'EU retained law' and include:
    (i) all EU derived domestic (UK) legislation that was effective in the UK as at 11pm on 31 December 2020;
    (ii) all operative EU legislation of direct effect as at that date; and
    (iii) all rights, powers, liabilities, obligations, restrictions, remedies and procedures recognised in domestic law under s 2(1) of the European Communities Act 1972.

    Such law (including decisions of the CJEU prior to 31 December 2020) is binding on UK courts and tribunals (except the Supreme Court and the Court of Appeal).

On this basis, whilst in the short term at least, the law as regards UKTMs is likely to remain very similar to that as regards EUTMs, it is possible that the two areas of protection will diverge as and when the Supreme Court or Court of Appeal (or Parliament) decides to depart from principles of retained EU law or if UK courts decide not to follow the lead of EU law given in CJEU judgments or EU legislation post-31 December 2020. In this regard, it is worth bearing in mind the provisions contained in the withdrawal agreement reached between the UK and the EU on 24 December 2020 relating to trade marks.[3]

1 The European Court of Justice (ECJ) was renamed the Court of Justice of the European Union (CJEU) as of 1 December 2009 by the Lisbon Treaty. For convenience, in this User's Guide, it will be referred to as the 'CJEU'.

2 For EUIPO procedure and appeals, see **Chapter 8**. The EUIPO also acts as the registry for registered Community designs, an entirely different intellectual property right—see Thorne and Bennett, *A User's Guide to Design Law* (Bloomsbury Professional, 2010).

3 The Trade and Cooperation Agreement between the European Union and the European Atomic Energy Community, of the one part, and the United Kingdom of Great Britain and Northern Ireland, of the other part. The provisions relating to trade marks are contained in Pt Two, Title V, Ch 2. They include, in section 1, an affirmation of the parties' commitment to various international agreements and, in section 2, an agreement to retain a classification system consistent with the Nice Agreement and as to what may constitute a sign capable of registration, the nature of the rights conferred by registration and the exceptions thereto.

1.06 As regards the acquisition of trade mark rights, this User's Guide will consider the following:

(a) Definition of a trade mark—see **Chapter 2**;
(b) Absolute grounds for a refusal to register a mark—**Chapter 4**;
(c) Relative grounds for a refusal to register a mark—**Chapter 5**;
(d) Classification of marks—**Chapter 6**; and
(e) Procedure and representation in UKIPO and in the EUIPO—**Chapters 7–8** and **Chapter 10**.

1.07 As regards the loss of trade mark rights, this User's Guide will deal with:

(a) Invalidation – see **Chapter 11**; and
(b) Revocation – see **Chapter 12**.

1.08 This User's Guide will then deal with the exploitation and enforcement of trade mark rights as follows:

(a) Licensing and assignment—**Chapter 13**;
(b) Infringement—**Chapter 14**;
(c) Defences to infringement actions—**Chapter 15**;
(d) Comparative and misleading advertising—**Chapter 16**;
(e) Remedies—**Chapter 17**;
(f) Threats actions—**Chapter 18**; and
(g) Criminal offences—**Chapter 19**.

WELL-KNOWN TRADE MARKS

1.09 The TMA 1994 and the EUTMR also provide for the protection of certain well-known trade marks even if not registered. This protection is considered at **2.17–2.26** below.

CERTIFICATION AND COLLECTIVE MARKS

1.10 The TMA 1994 and the EUTMR also provide for the protection of:

(a) registered certification marks (ie, marks that guarantee that goods or services bearing those marks meet a certain defined standard or possess a particular characteristic); and
(b) registered collective marks (ie, marks which indicate that goods and services bearing those marks originate from members of the relevant trade associations).

Certification and collective marks are considered in **Chapter 3**.

GEOGRAPHICAL INDICATIONS, DESIGNATIONS OF ORIGIN, TRADITIONAL SPECIALITY GUARANTEES

1.11 Separate European regulations have created registration systems designed to protect geographical indications, designations of origin and traditional speciality guarantees for certain types of foodstuff and agricultural products intended for human consumption. These forms of protection are also considered in **Chapter 3**.

INTERNATIONAL CONVENTIONS

1.12 The only international convention considered in detail in this guide is the Protocol to the Madrid Agreement[1]—of which both the UK and the EUIPO are members. Under this Protocol, a person with a UKTM or an EUTM can apply for an international registration providing protection for that mark in other designated members of the Protocol. Such protection is considered in **Chapter 9**.

1 Concluded in 1989 and intended to provide a more flexible, and attractive system of protection.

PASSING OFF

1.13 Passing off is a common law tort providing a remedy where, typically, a trader causes damage to the goodwill of another by means of a misrepresentation. It is not based on any registered right, and although section 2(2) of the TMA 1994 states that no proceedings lie to prevent or recover damages for the infringement of an unregistered trade mark as such, it goes on expressly to provide that *'nothing in this Act affects the law relating to passing off'*.

Passing-off claims are frequently made where the claimant is also relying on a registered trade mark. However, even in such cases, a passing-off claim may succeed where a trade mark claim fails. Passing off is considered in **Chapter 20**.

OLYMPIC SYMBOLS

1.14 **Chapter 21** considers the protection provided by the Olympic Symbol, etc. (Protection) Act 1995. This Act creates rights, known as the 'Olympics Association Right' and the 'Paralympics Association Right' that can be infringed by the use of the Olympic symbol, or motto, or the use of certain 'representations' that are likely to suggest to the public an association with the Olympics or Paralympics, which can constitute infringements. The London Olympic Games and Paralympic Games Act 2006 created a similar right known as the 'London Olympics Association Right'. However, that right ceased to have effect at the end of 31 December 2012.

Chapter 2

What is a trade mark?

TRADE MARK: THE STATUTORY DEFINITION

2.01 Section 1(1) of the Trade Marks Act 1994 ('TMA 1994') provides that a trade mark is any sign which is capable:

> '(a) of being represented in the register in a manner which enables the registrar and other competent authorities and the public to determine the clear and precise subject matter of the protection afforded to the proprietor, and
> '(b) of distinguishing goods or services of one undertaking from those of other undertakings.'

And it further provides:

> 'A trade mark may, in particular, consist of words (including personal names), designs, letters, numerals, colours, sounds or the shape of goods or their packaging.'

This definition is substantively the same as that in Art 1 of the European Trade Mark Directive (EU) 2015/2436 ('the Directive') which replaced the earlier European Trade Mark Directive (2008/95/EC). Thus, the statutory definition in the UK reflects the harmonised position across the EU as it stood prior to Brexit. It also mirrors the definition in Art 4 of the European Trade Mark Regulation (EU) 2017/1001 ('EUTMR'), which governs EU trade marks or 'EUTMs'.[1]

By reason of this definition, an application to register a trade mark must satisfy three conditions:

(1) there must be a sign;
(2) the sign must be capable of being represented in a sufficiently well-defined manner; and
(3) the sign must be capable of distinguishing goods or services of one undertaking, from those of other undertakings. (This quality is

what is usually meant when referring to 'distinctiveness' of trade marks. 'Distinctive' in trade mark parlance does not refer to the more general sense of something standing out or being noticeable.)

As will be seen, a trade mark registration affords its proprietor a 'negative right' to prevent others using confusingly similar marks (subject to certain conditions). The purpose of the requirements set out in the definition is to ensure that marks on the register are sufficiently clear and capable of performing their intended function, and to prevent traders abusing trade mark law by seeking to obtain an unfair competitive advantage over other traders.[2]

1 Unlike national trade marks, EUTMs have effect across the EU. Following Brexit (which for these purposes occurred at 11pm on 31 December 2020), EUTMs are no longer in force in the UK, but have instead been automatically replaced by 'comparable trade marks (EU)' on the national register – see Sch 2A of the TMA 1994.

2 *Société Des Produits Nestlé SA v Cadbury UK Ltd* [2013] EWCA Civ 1174 at [15] (1)–(2).

2.02 Apart from the requirements of clear and precise representation and a capacity to distinguish, there is no statutory limit to the type of sign that may qualify as a 'trade mark'. In other words, the list of possible signs referred to in the legislation ('words … designs …', etc) is not an exhaustive list. On the other hand, signs included in that list do not automatically qualify as trade marks; they must still satisfy the other limbs of the definition.

This chapter first looks as what constitutes a 'sign' and then considers the further requirements—ie, that the sign must be capable of representation and capable of distinguishing goods or services. A sign that satisfies these three limbs may still be unregistrable if any of the absolute or relative grounds for a refusal of registration apply. Those grounds are considered in **Chapter 4** and **Chapter 5**.

A 'sign'

2.03 The word 'sign' is not defined in the legislation. However, the fact that the non-exhaustive list of what a sign may consist now includes sounds, shapes and colours confirms that the word has a wide meaning and is somewhat open-ended in its possibilities, provided that the other requirements of section 1 are met.

The European Court of Justice ('CJEU') considered the meaning of 'sign' in *Dyson Ltd v Registrar of Trade Marks*.[1] In that case, the application was to register a trade mark which was said to consist of 'a transparent bin or collecting chamber forming part of the external surface of a vacuum cleaner …' but which was not restricted to any particular external shape. The Court ruled that such an application related in essence to an idea and was not a 'sign' even though it was something that could be perceived visually. The application was, therefore, rejected. Since the application was not for 'specific subject-matter' it would, if granted, have given Dyson an unfair monopoly over all transparent bins or collecting chambers rather than only those with a specific shape. To be registrable, a sign must be defined with sufficient precision.

The reasoning in *Dyson* was applied in *JW Spear & Sons Ltd v Zynga (No 2)*[2] where the Court of Appeal found that the proprietors of the word game 'Scrabble' were not entitled to register their 'Tile Mark' described as 'a three-dimensional ivory-coloured tile on the top surface of which was shown a letter of the roman alphabet and a numeral in the range 1 to 10'. The Court ruled that this was not a 'sign'. Instead it potentially covered many signs achievable by numerous permutations, presentations, and combinations of the subject matter of the registrations. On the other hand, the CJEU has held that the layout of a retail store may in principle be registered as a trade mark: *Apple Inc v Deutsches Patent und Markenamt*.[3]

The essential issue is whether the registration authorities and actual or potential competitors would be able to ascertain the scope of the mark for which protection is claimed. It is not enough for an applicant to describe the mark; other people have to be able to tell whether or not other signs are or are not covered by that description.[4] The same issue underlies the requirement that a mark must be capable of clear and precise representation. It also underlies the decisions of the CJEU relating to unusual types of sign; such as smells, sounds and colours (see below).

1 C-321/03; *Dyson Ltd v Registrar of Trade Marks* [2007] ETMR 34; [2007] RPC 27.
2 *JW Spear & Sons Ltd v Zynga (No 2)* [2013] EWCA Civ 1175.
3 C-421/13; *Apple Inc v Deutsches Patent und Markenamt* [2014] ETMR 48.
4 *Société Des Produits Nestlé SA v Cadbury UK Ltd* [2013] EWCA Civ 1174 at [62].

Capable of being represented clearly and precisely

2.04 The definition of 'trade mark' in EU and UK law formerly required that the sign be capable of graphical representation. Essentially, the reason for this requirement was that a mark has to be recorded and published, and needs to be capable of being searched for in the Register. However, this requirement was also criticised as being unduly rigid, and for creating difficulties in relation to non-standard marks such as colours or sounds.

Accordingly, the EUTMR and Directive (and thus the TMA 1994) no longer include this stipulation, in order to permit greater flexibility as to the mode of representation. Recital 9 to the amending Regulation (EU) 2015/2424 stated the rationale as follows:

> 'A sign should be permitted to be represented in any appropriate form using generally available technology, and thus not necessarily by graphic means, as long as the representation is clear, precise, self-contained, easily accessible, intelligible, durable and objective.'

The wording of that recital reflects the form of words frequently used by the CJEU, and remains consistent with authorities in which the 'graphical' requirement was not met on the basis of lack of precision. For example, the Court of Appeal in *Nestle*[1] commented that a mark that could take on a multitude of different appearances was not capable of being represented graphically. This was also one reason why the same Court of Appeal found the claimant's 'Tile Mark' in *JW Spear & Sons Ltd v Zynga*[2] to be unregistrable. Likewise, in *Fromageries Bel SA v J Sainsbury Plc* 'the colour red' was too imprecise to specify a sign as part of a 3D mark for cheeses.,[3]

1 *Societe Des Produits Nestle SA v Cadbury UK Ltd* [2013] EWCA Civ 1174 at [15](4).
2 *JW Spear & Sons Ltd v Zynga (No 2)* [2013] EWCA Civ 1175. The case concerned the tiles used in the 'Scrabble' word game. The mark was also refused registration on the basis that it was not 'a sign' (see para **2.03** above).
3 *Fromageries Bel SA v J Sainsbury Plc* [2019] EWHC 3454 (Ch); [2020] ETMR 14.

Colours

2.05 A device mark or a work mark can be depicted in black and white or in a particular colour or combination of colours.[1] Here the requirement that a mark be capable of clear and precise representation should present no difficulty in that the colour is part of the device or word and is easily depicted. However, one must still clearly define both the colour and the way in which it is to be used to form the sign (eg, shape, spatial extent, combination, etc). Historically, applicants for trade marks have run into difficulties where the sign sought to be registered is a mere colour (eg, the colour orange) or a combination of colours (orange and blue) designated in the abstract, and without shape or contours (referred to by the EUIPO as 'colour *per se*'). The authorities show that, in principle, such marks are capable of registration, but will be very carefully examined to ensure that they meet the requirements both that there be a sign, and that that sign be capable of graphical representation.[2]

In *Libertel*[3] the applicant sought to register a single colour; a particular shade of orange. The application contained a sample of the colour but no colour code. The CJEU held that a colour was capable of being a sign where used in relation to goods or services. As to whether the sign was capable of graphical representation, the need for the registration to be precise, and durable meant that merely providing a sample of the colour was not sufficient. The colour would have to be accurately described, for example, by using one of the internationally accepted colour code schemes such as Pantone.

In *Heidelberger*[4] the applicant sought to register its corporate colours of blue and yellow which, it stated were used 'in every conceivable form, in particular on packaging and labels' and whose colour codes were set out in the application.[5] The Court held that a combination of colours without any other parameters such as shape was capable of being a sign where the evidence was that the combination of colours as used did represent a sign and where the colours were specified according to an internationally recognised colour classification system. However, since the colours were claimed in the abstract without any particular arrangement, and the application specifically claimed 'every conceivable' combination, the requirement that the sign be capable of graphical representation was not satisfied. The same principles were applied to refuse marks consisting of specified shades of blue and silver juxtaposed in equal proportion in *Red Bull GmbH v European Union Intellectual Property Office*.[6]

In *Nestle*[7] the confectioner Cadbury applied to register the colour purple for its products. Whilst the particular shade of purple was adequately identified by reference to an accepted colour code (Pantone 2685C) the application was rejected because the mark sought to be registered was not limited to the use of that colour. Instead, it sought to cover any use where that colour purple was the 'predominant colour'. It would, therefore, have covered not just that colour purple as a sign, but also other signs in which that colour purple predominated over other colours and other matters. The use of the word 'predominant' made the description of the mark too subjective, too imprecise, and insufficiently clear and intelligible, to be capable of registration. It meant that people looking at the Register would not be able to tell the full scope and extent of the registration and, in particular, would not be able to tell whether or not a given sign was or was not within the scope of the mark.[8] As a result, the mark (covering as it did multiple signs with different permutations, presentations and appearances) was not 'a sign'. Nor was it capable of being represented graphically. It was not for an unchanging application of a single colour as in *Libertel*.

1 See para **7.04** (for procedure in UKIPO) and para **8.06** (EUIPO; Representation of the mark).

2 *Société Des Produits Nestlé SA v Cadbury UK Ltd* [2013] EWCA Civ 1174 at [62]. As mentioned above, the requirement that a mark be capable of graphic representation has been replaced with a requirement that it be capable of being represented in a manner which enables the competent authorities and the public to determine the precise subject of the protection afforded to its proprietor. On this basis, the reasoning of the courts in the cases considered in this paragraph is unlikely to be much altered.

3 C-104/01 *Liberate Groep BV v Benelux-Merkenbureau* [2004] Ch 83; [2003] ETMR 63; [2004] FSR 4.

4 C-49/02 *Heidelberger Bauchemie GmbH's Trade Mark Application* [2004] ETMR 99.
5 RAL 5015/HKS 47—blue; RAL 1016/HKS 3—yellow.
6 *Red Bull GmbH v European Union Intellectual Property Office* (C-124/18 P) EU:C:2019:641; [2019] ETMR 57.
7 *Société Des Produits Nestlé SA v Cadbury UK Ltd* [2013] EWCA Civ 1174.
8 See [52].

Sounds

2.06 The express inclusion of sounds in the legislation as an example of a 'sign' is a recent change.[1] As with colours, the CJEU had already accepted that a sound *could* act as a sign. The only remaining issue now is whether the sound is clearly and precisely represented.[2] In *Shield Mark*[3] the court gave guidance as to what kind of representation would be sufficient. It held that identifying standard musical notation[4] would be acceptable but that descriptions in words (eg, 'the first nine notes of *Für Elise*') or onomatopoeic formulations (eg, a word depicting the sound of a cockerel) would not be.[5]

1 See para **2.01** above – the list of examples of signs was updated in the Directive and the EUTMR.
2 As mentioned above, the new would, if adopted, remove any requirement that the sound be capable of graphic representation and open the door to representation of a soundmark by any means (eg, by a sound file) provided it permits a more precise identification of the mark and thereby serves the aim of enhanced legal certainty. (See para **2.04**, and para **2.01**, fn 1 above.)
3 C-283/01 *Shield Mark BV v Kist (t/a Memex)* [2004] Ch 97; [2004] ETMR 33; [2004] RPC 17.
4 A stave with clef, measures, rests, etc. The court specifically disapproved a simple list of notes (eg, A, C, D# …).
5 See the EUIPO's *Guidelines for Examination in the Office*, Part B, Section 2 at para 9.3.7, which also allows for a sound mark to be represented by an MP3 file of less than 2MB.

Smells

2.07 The definition of a trade mark makes no reference to smells.[1] On the current wording of the legislation there is, as a matter of principle, nothing to preclude a smell mark being considered for registration provided it could be represented graphically. Indeed, in 2003, the CJEU in *Sieckmann*[2] recognised that even the old requirement of graphical representation did not require a sign necessarily to be visual provided it could be represented graphically and could act to distinguish goods or services. The Court commented that a precise description might satisfy the requirement of graphical representation, but a sample of the smell or a description of the smell in general terms would not.

Although *Sieckmann* suggests that a smell *could* in theory fulfil the requirement, in practice it will be next to impossible to provide such a description without an accepted standard (such as those which exist for colours). In this regard, the Court rejected the idea of graphically representing a smell by reference to its chemical formula, since the formula represented the chemical and not the smell.

Accordingly, whilst 'smellmarks' were formerly accepted under the TMA 1994, in the light of *Sieckmann* those marks must now be considered of dubious validity. Indeed, the EUIPO's *Guidelines for Examination State* (Part B, Section 2, at para 9.3.11.2) that smell, olfactory and taste marks are not currently acceptable whilst UKIPO's *Trade Marks Manual* is equally sceptical about the registrability of smell marks.[3]

1 Interestingly, although the EUTMR and Directive added both colour and sounds to the list of example signs, smells or fragrances remained absent.

2 C-273/00 *Ralf Sieckmann v Deutches Patent und Markenamt* [2003] Ch 487; [2003] ETMR 37; [2003] RPC 38.

3 See the Examination Guide section under Part B: Alphabetical list of examination practice.

Designs and the shape of goods or their packaging

2.08 The legislation makes clear that both 'designs' and the 'shape of goods or of their packaging' may be signs and may therefore be registrable as trade marks. For the most part, the case law in relation to such marks focuses on their ability to distinguish goods or services since the requirement that they be represented on the register can, for the most part, easily be achieved pictorially.

The CJEU has ruled that a representation that depicts the layout of a retail store is a design for these purposes and may, therefore, constitute a trade mark—even if it contains no indication as to the size and proportions of the store in question. The only other issue arising under s 1 of TMA 1994, therefore, is whether such a representation is capable of distinguishing the products or services of one undertaking from those of another.[1]

There are a number of specific exclusions relating to the shape of goods that are considered in **Chapter 4**.

1 C-421/13 *Apple Inc v Deutsches Patent und Markenamt* [2014] ETMR 48.

Phrases and slogans

2.09 Phrases and slogans are of course normally capable of clear and precise representation so their registrability is more a matter of distinctiveness (see para **2.10** below and also **Chapter 4**). After the 1994 Act came into force it was for a time doubtful whether such marks could be registered, as the CJEU's decision in *Erpo*[1] was generally understood to mean that slogans generally were not sufficiently distinctive. However, in *Audi*[2] the CJEU explained that *Erpo* had been misunderstood. The registrability of a slogan in the Audi case—'Vorsprung durch Technik'—depended on the same criteria (particularly distinctiveness) as other types of marks.[3] More recently the same questions arose in respect of the hashtag #darferdas ['Can he do that?'] in *AS v Deutsches Patent und Markenamt*.[4]

1 C-64/02 *OHIM v Erpo Mobelwerk* [2005] ETMR 58.
2 C-398/08 *Audi AG v OHIM* [2010] ETMR 18; [2010] FSR 24.
3 See also C-311/11 P *Smart Technologies ULC v OHIM* where the slogan was 'WIR MACHEN DAS BESONDERE EINFACH' ('WE MAKE SPECIAL THINGS SIMPLE'). The CJEU held that the criteria for assessing whether the slogan had distinctive character were no stricter than those that applied to other types of sign.
4 C-541/18 *AS v Deutsches Patent und Markenamt* [2019] ETMR 59.

Capable of distinguishing goods or services of one undertaking from those of other undertakings

2.10 The third limb of the definition of 'trade mark' is of fundamental importance because it embodies the principle that a trade mark must serve to distinguish the goods or services to which it is applied from those of other undertakings. On numerous occasions, the CJEU has identified this characteristic as the *essential function* of a trade mark. The characteristic is discussed in detail in relation to trade mark use in **Chapter 14**. See also the discussion of trade mark 'functions' at para **5.97** et seq.

This limb of the definition of a trade mark (which was retained unaltered in the updated Directive and EUTMR[1]) ties in closely with the absolute grounds for refusal of registration of a trade mark (eg, the prohibition on marks that are descriptive of the goods or services for which registration is sought), as to which see **Chapter 4**.

1 See para **2.01** above.

REGISTRATION IN RESPECT OF GOODS OR SERVICES

2.11 Trade marks must be registered by reference to the particular goods and/or services to which they are to relate. This helps define and circumscribe the protection afforded by the mark. For convenience, goods and services are grouped in *classes*. UKIPO and EUIPO both use the Nice classification system, currently in its eleventh edition (2017), with an updated version published each year. It comprises 34 classes of goods and 11 classes of services. The classification system is described in **Chapter 6**.

UNDERTAKINGS

2.12 The definition of a trade mark does not refer to the applicant's goods or services: it refers to the goods or services of 'undertakings'. The word 'undertakings' is not defined in the legislation. A definition in the

EEA Treaty refers to 'any entity carrying out activities of a commercial or economic nature'. A full analysis may be found in *European Community Law of Competition*[1] but in essence any natural or legal person carrying out commercial or economic activities, whether or not for profit, is an undertaking and is therefore eligible to acquire trade mark rights.

1 *Bellamy & Child*, 2018 (eighth edn, Oxford University Press).

UNREGISTERED TRADE MARKS

2.13 Although s 2(2) of the TMA 1994 provides that no proceedings lie either to prevent or recover damages for the infringement of an unregistered trade mark, unregistered trade marks can be important for a number of reasons:

Passing off, s 2(2)

2.14 First, s 2(2) of the TMA 1994 expressly provides that nothing in the Act affects the law relating to passing off (as to which, see **Chapter 20**).

Impediment to registration

2.15 Second, in the context of registrability, s 5 of the TMA 1994 provides that an application to register a trade mark may be refused on either of the following bases:

(a) if it conflicts with an 'earlier trade mark' which, pursuant to s 6, includes an unregistered trade mark which is either:
   (i) well known; or
   (ii) the subject of an earlier filed application; or
(b) if the use of the mark applied for is liable to be prevented in the United Kingdom by virtue of any rule of law protecting unregistered trade marks or signs used in the course of trade (in particular, the law of passing off – see **Chapter 20**).

A mark that is registered contrary to s 5 is liable to be declared invalid (see **Chapter 11**).

A similar limit on registration based on conflicts with earlier unregistered marks is found in Art 8(4) of the EUTMR.

Defence to infringement, s 11(3)

2.16 Third, in the context of defences to an infringement action, the use of an 'earlier right' in a particular locality, which applies only in that locality, does not infringe a later registered trade mark.

For the purpose of this defence, 'an earlier right' means an unregistered trade mark or other sign that has been continuously used since before both the use and registration of the registered trade mark. Accordingly, the proprietor of the unregistered trade mark which is an 'earlier right' for the purpose of s 11(3) of the TMA 1994 can continue to use that trade mark notwithstanding that such use would otherwise infringe the registered trade mark. See further **Chapters 14–15**.

Well-known trade marks

2.17 Finally, an unregistered trade mark may also be so well known that it is entitled to the special protection that the legislation confers on such marks in accordance with Art 6*bis* of the Paris Convention. Such protection for well-known marks is considered below.

WELL-KNOWN TRADE MARKS

2.18 In accordance with Article 6*bis* of the Paris Convention, s 56 of the TMA 1994 and Art 8(2)(c) of the EUTMR confer certain rights and remedies on the proprietor of a 'well known' trade mark.

Section 56 provides that, for the purposes of the TMA 1994, a reference to a trade mark that is entitled to protection under the Paris Convention as a well-known trade mark is to be construed as a reference to a mark which is:

> '… well known in the United Kingdom as being the mark of a person who:
> (a) is a national of a Convention country; or
> (b) is domiciled in, or has a real and effective industrial or commercial establishment in a Convention country,
>
> whether or not that person carries on business, or has any goodwill, in the United Kingdom.'

A number of points arise in relation to this definition of a well-known mark.

Who is entitled to protection—meaning of 'Convention country'

2.19 The definition of 'Convention country' in s 55(1)(b) of the TMA 1994 limits the category of relevant well-known trade marks for the purposes of s 56 to those which are owned by persons who are: (a) nationals of; or (b) domiciled in, or have a real and effective industrial or commercial establishment in a Convention country. Such persons are entitled to protection under s 56 whether or not they carry on business, or possess any goodwill in the United Kingdom.

Importantly, the United Kingdom is not a Convention country for the purposes of s 56. Accordingly, proprietors of well-known marks who are nationals of or domiciled in the United Kingdom will either have to register their marks or rely upon the tort of passing off.

Meaning of 'well known'

2.20 The law as to well-known marks in the United Kingdom and in many of the important jurisdictions of the world is considered in detail in *Famous and Well-Known Marks* by Frederick Mostert.[1]

Mostert's analysis was referred to with approval by Arnold J in *Hotel Cipriani.*[2] Arnold J also referred to the 1999 WIPO *Joint Recommendation Concerning Provision on the Protection of Well-Known Marks* which lists, at art 2(b), the following six factors as the most important considerations in determining whether or not a mark is well-known:

(1) the degree of knowledge or recognition of the mark in the relevant sector of the public;
(2) the duration, extent and geographical area of any use of the mark;
(3) the duration, extent and geographical area of any promotion of the mark, including advertising or publicity and the presentation, at fairs or exhibitions, of the goods and/or services to which the mark applies;
(4) the duration and geographical area of any registration, and/or any applications for registration, of the mark, to the extent that they reflect use or recognition of the mark;
(5) the record of successful enforcement of rights in the mark, in particular, the extent to which the mark was recognised as well known by competent authorities; and
(6) the value associated with the mark.

1 Published by the International Trade mark Association, 2004.
2 *Hotel Cipriani Srl v Cipriani (Grosvenor Street) Ltd* [2008] EWHC 3032 (Ch); [2009] RPC 9, approved by the Court of Appeal [2010] EWCA Civ 110; [2010] RPC 16. Mostert's work was also referred to by the CJEU in C-487/07 *L'Oréal SA and others v Bellure NV and others* [2009] ETMR 55.

2.21 Whether a mark is well known is essentially a question of fact. The problem is to assess in advance the extent to which a mark must be known before it can be said to be 'well known'. In addition to the factors set out above, further light may be thrown on this issue by looking at those sections of the TMA 1994 where well-known trade marks are or may be relevant.

To start with, s 56(2) provides that the proprietor of a well-known trade mark can obtain an injunction to restrain the use of that well-known mark by third parties in the United Kingdom. However, an injunction will only be available:

(a) if that well-known mark has been used by a third party in relation to goods or services which are identical with or similar to the goods or services for which the mark is well known; and
(b) where such use by the third party is likely to deceive or cause confusion.

Accordingly, the injunction available to the proprietor of a well-known mark under s 56(2) is no broader (and arguably is narrower) than the injunction which would be available to the proprietor of a registered trade mark pursuant to s 10(2) (see **Chapter 14**). Further, the injunction under s 56(2) will never be available in the circumstances described in s 10(3) (where infringement may occur without confusion). The fact that an injunction is only available in limited circumstances (limited when compared with s 10(2)–(3)), might suggest that the level of notoriety required to show that a mark is well known should not be set too high.

2.22 Against this, in *General Motors*[1] A-G Jacob suggested that a well-known mark should be subject to a higher threshold of recognition than a mark with a reputation under s 10(3). After all, well-known marks are provided with protection even though they are not registered in the relevant territory. This view may well be preferable in that it accords better with the principle that, since trade marks are proprietary territorial rights, they should receive protection outside the relevant territory only in unusual circumstances.

1 C-375/97 *General Motors Corp v Yplon SA* [1999] ETMR 950; [2000] RPC 572.

Well-known marks—basis for opposing registration of later marks

2.23 As mentioned in paragraph **2.15** above, a well-known trade mark is deemed to be an 'earlier trade mark' for the purposes of s 5 of the TMA 1994 (see s 6(1)(c)). It can, therefore, be the basis on which an application to register a later conflicting identical or similar trade mark is refused, provided that the well-known mark was well known as at the date of that application. A mark registered contrary to this provision can be declared invalid (see s 47(2) of the TMA 1994 and **Chapter 11**).

Well-known marks—defence to infringement of later marks?

2.24 Section 11 of the TMA 1994, which sets out various limits on the effect of a registered mark (see **Chapter 15**), does not provide expressly that a registered trade mark will not be infringed by the use of an earlier well-known mark. It might nonetheless be thought that a mark which is well known in the Paris Convention sense, and which thereby enjoys protection under s 56 of the TMA 1994, would also come within the meaning of the phrase 'earlier right' for the purposes of the defence set out in s 11(3). However, the s 11(3) defence is only available where the earlier right is used in a 'particular locality' and where the earlier right 'applies only in that locality'. For this to include well-known marks would require the whole of the United Kingdom to be considered a 'locality' for the purposes of s 11(3), which it is suggested is beyond the limits of the provision.

2.25 There is perhaps a second difficulty in that the s 11(3) defence is only available where the use of the earlier right is 'protected by virtue of any rule of law (in particular the law of passing off)'. A well-known mark need not necessarily be protected by virtue of any rule of law (whether passing off or otherwise) because the definition in s 56(1) is wide enough to include well-known marks of proprietors who do not have any goodwill in the United Kingdom: certainly, the law of passing off would not provide such protection (see **Chapter 20**). This is perhaps rather theoretical, however; in reality the proprietor of a well-known mark is likely to have sufficient goodwill to act as a deterrent to any action for infringement by the holder of a later registered mark, since that goodwill could be used to invalidate the later mark (see para **2.23** above).

Well-known marks—remedies for infringement

2.26 Under s 56(2) of the TMA 1994, the proprietor of a well-known mark is entitled to an injunction to restrain the use in the UK of a trade mark which is identical with or similar to his well-known mark, provided that the mark is being used in relation to identical or similar goods or services and where such use is likely to cause confusion. This right is subject to the acquiescence provisions set out in s 48 of the TMA, as to which see **Chapter 15**.

Until the repeal of s 60 of the TMA 1994 on 14 January 2019 the proprietor of a well-known mark was also entitled to the benefit of the special rights and remedies set out in that section *vis-à-vis* the acts of their agents and representatives, provided they were the proprietor of the well-known mark in a Convention country. Essentially, if the agent or representative attempted to register the mark, the proprietor could call either for its invalidation or its assignment to themselves. The repeal of s 60 does not affect the proprietor's right to prevent the unauthorised use of a well-known mark by a third party either as infringement under s 10 (if the well-known mark is registered under the TMA 1994) or as passing off where the elements of that tort are satisfied (as to which, see **Chapter 20**). The remedies available for each of these causes of action are discussed in **Chapters 14**, **17** and **20**.

COMPANY NAMES, BUSINESS NAMES AND INTERNET DOMAIN NAMES

2.27 Such names can operate as trade marks for the purposes of the TMA 1994, whether as registered or unregistered trade marks. However, the purpose of the following paragraphs is to describe their function and purpose in the context of their status as company, business or domain names (as the case may be) and to distinguish them from registrable trade marks.

Company names

2.28 A company carrying on business in Great Britain must comply with the requirements of Part 5 of the Companies Act 2006 ('CA 2006') concerning the choice and use of company names.

Choice of name

2.29 Under the CA 2006, a company cannot register a name:

(a) which is the same as a name already on the index of company names maintained by the Registrar of Companies;[1] or
(b) if its use would constitute an offence or is offensive in the opinion of the Secretary of State.[2]

Further, the approval of the Secretary of State is required to use a name which:

(a) suggests a connection with the government or a local authority;[3] or
(b) contains sensitive words specified in the Company, Limited Liability Partnership and Business Names (Sensitive Words and Expressions) Regulations 2014.[4]

Subject to limited exemptions found in s 60 CA 2006 (such as being a charity), the final words of the name of a registered company must be either 'limited' (or its abbreviation 'ltd'), or if it is a public company 'public limited company' (or its abbreviation 'plc').

1 CA 2006 s 66.
2 CA 2006 s 53.
3 CA 2006 s 54.
4 SI 2014/3140 made under CA 2006 s 55 (revoking the 2009 Regulations of the same name, SI 2009/2615).

Changing a company's name—voluntary

2.30 A company may change its name at any time by a special resolution of its shareholders provided the new name complies with all the requirements specified above for the selection of the original name.

On the payment of a small fee, the Registrar of Companies will issue an altered certificate of incorporation, and notice of this issue must be published in the *London Gazette*. The new name will only be effective from the date of issue of the altered certificate of incorporation on change of name.[1]

1 CA 2006 ss 77–81.

Changing a company's name—compulsory

2.31 The Registrar may require a company to change its name if it is too similar to a name appearing on the index or that should have appeared on the index.[1]

Changes may also be required by the Registrar if misleading information was provided for the purposes of registration, or if the name gives such a misleading indication of the nature of the goods or services provided that it is likely to cause harm to the public.[2]

1 CA 2006 s 67.
2 CA 2006 ss 75–76.

Publicity to be given to a company name

2.32 A company must comply with the following requirements for the disclosure and publicity of the company name, to ensure that it is apparent to those dealing with the company that it is a limited liability company.[1] In brief:

(a) The company name must be fixed in a conspicuous position and in easily legible letters outside its registered office and every location where the company does business (unless primarily used for living accommodation), in characters that can be read with the naked eye and so that it may easily seen by any visitor.
(b) The company's name must be mentioned in legible characters in all of the company's:
   (i) business letters, notices and other official publications;
   (ii) websites;
   (iii) bills of exchange, promissory notes, endorsements, cheques and orders for money or goods purporting to be signed on behalf of the company; and
   (iv) bills of parcels, invoices, receipts and letters of credit.
(c) Failure to comply with the requirements is an offence on the part of the company and officers responsible, each of whom is liable, on conviction, to a fine and a daily default fine for continued breach.

1 Company, Limited Liability Partnership and Business (Names and Trading Disclosures) Regulations 2015, 2015/17.

Passing off and trade mark infringement

2.33 A company name must be registered on the Companies Registry index and this should prevent another company being registered with the same name. Of itself, registration of a company name as required by the Companies Act confers no proprietary rights on the company (or its directors or shareholders) that can be enforced against a third party who uses a similar or identical name. However, depending on the facts, use of a company name by a third party may constitute either:

(a) infringement of a UK registered trade mark or a EUTM; and/or
(b) passing off.

Thus, when choosing a company name, it is advisable to check both the Companies Registry index and the Trade Marks Register to ensure that a name has not already been registered and to minimise the risk of potential infringement.

2.34 The CA 2006 introduced, in ss 69–74, a procedure for a person with goodwill in a name to object to registration of a company name that is sufficiently similar to the name in which there is goodwill that its use would be likely to mislead by suggesting a connection between the two undertakings. Company Names Adjudicators have the power to determine these disputes.

Unincorporated businesses and partnerships

2.35 There is no provision for the registration of the name of an unincorporated business or partnership. The name of such a business or partnership may need to be recorded with a professional or trade association, but such record or registration does not give the owner of the name any proprietary rights in the name. To be protected, the owner must obtain a trade mark registration of its name and/or rely on its unregistered rights.

Domain names

2.36 On the internet, each device is assigned a unique identifying number known as its internet protocol address or 'IP address', analogous to a telephone number. Historically, internet users had to key in these numbers in order to communicate. However, in the 1980s the Domain Name System (DNS) was devised. This allowed users to remember unique addresses much more easily, by assigning each computer a unique IP Address (consisting of numbers) and a domain name made up of a series of alphanumeric characters followed by suffixes such as '.com', '.co.uk', '.org', etc. The domain name is translated into the numerical

IP Address by the DNS. Since 2010, non-Latin alphabet characters have also been used.

The network is divided into a series of top-level domains ('TLDs'). Some of the most popular generic TLDs are:

- 'com'—which identifies the user as commercial;
- 'org'—which is for non-commercial or non-profit entities; and
- 'net'—which is for network service providers.

These are the domains predominantly used in the USA; however, as they have no geographic reference, international companies have also sought to register domain names with these suffixes.

Each country has its own domain registries to allocate TLDs, which in general have a geographic reference (for example, '.uk', '.jp', '.us') followed by a second-level domain which identifies the entity. For example, in the UK there is '.co.uk', and also '.org.uk'. The number of TLDs available is ever increasing. From a mere 22, the website of ICANN (the International Corporation for Assigned Names and Numbers) currently lists many hundreds of TLDs (eg, '.flowers', '.sexy', '.lego' and '.meme')[1] and states that a further 1,300 TLDs could become available over the next few years.[1]

The official register for domain names with the '.uk' suffix is managed by Nominet (a not-for-profit membership company established by the UK internet community in 1996). The international domain name registrar dealing with TLDs is ICANN. Other relevant global bodies are the United Nations Internet Governance Forum (IGF) and the Council of European National Top-Level Domain Registries (CENTR).

1 See the full database at https://www.iana.org/domains/root/db
2 http://newgtlds.icann.org/en/

2.37 With multiple TLDs it is possible for 'ABC.com' and 'ABC.co.uk' to be registered by two completely unconnected organisations. Also, registration of a domain name for, say, 'Apple' will not preclude registrations for 'Apples', 'the apples', etc. Currently there is no easy way of monitoring registration of domain names with different geographical suffixes throughout the world. With the growth of the internet and the importance of commercial organisations being connected to the internet as part of their global marketing strategy, there is a huge potential for disputes arising when an organisation discovers that its preferred domain name has already been allocated to another entity.

2.38 Registration of domain names has historically been done on a 'first-come-first-served' basis. Applying to register a domain name is a relatively simple procedure. In the United Kingdom applications for domain names for either a website or an e-mail address can be made directly to Nominet or via a service provider. Public policy rules concerning the implementation and functions of the .eu TLD and the public policy principles on registration of such domain names are laid down by Commission Regulation.[1]

1 Commission Regulation (EC) No 874/2004 of 28 April 2004 (due to be repealed and superseded by Regulation (EU) 2019/517 as of 13 October 2022). For a decision of the CJEU in relation to the entitlement to apply to register a .eu TLD, see Case C-376/11 *Pie Optiek SPRL v Bureau Gevers SA, European Registry for Internet Domains ASBL* [2012] ETMR 46.

2.39 Despite their increasing importance, allocation of a domain name, like a company name:

(a) confers no proprietary rights in the name which can be enforced against a third party who uses an identical or similar name (although over time it may provide a basis for accruing goodwill); but
(b) the use of the domain name may constitute an infringement of a third party's registered trade mark and/or passing off.

Due to problems with 'cyber-squatting', most domain name registrars (including Nominet and ICANN) run a dispute resolution service under which a request to transfer a domain name may be made. If the dispute cannot be resolved between the parties, an arbitration ensues and 'ownership' of the domain name is resolved. For the most part, it is necessary to show that the respondent registered the domain name sought by the complainant in bad faith and not merely that the complainant has rights to that name.

Chapter 3

Other kinds of mark – collective and certification marks, and protected descriptions

INTRODUCTION

3.01 The type of trade marks that are most commonly registered (referred to in this book as 'ordinary' trade marks) are marks that are intended to distinguish the goods or services of one undertaking from those of other undertakings.[1]

This chapter deals with certain other types of mark, namely collective and certification marks and certain protected descriptions of goods.

1 Trade Marks Act 1994 ('TMA 1994') s 1(1)(b) and European Union Trade Marks Regulation ('EUTMR') Art 4(a).

COLLECTIVE AND CERTIFICATION MARKS

3.02 *Collective mark*—a collective mark is one that indicates that the goods and services bearing that mark originate from members of a trade association. It is defined as a mark which distinguishes the goods or services of members of the association which is the proprietor of the mark from those of other undertakings.[1] An example is 'Chartered Certified Accountant'. Protection for such marks is available in the UK by registration at the UKIPO and also in Europe by registration at the EUIPO[2]—an example being 'Parma ham'.

1 TMA 1994 s 49(1).
2 EUTMR Art 74(1).

3.03 *Certification mark*—a certification mark is a mark that guarantees that goods or services bearing that mark meet a certain defined standard or possess a particular characteristic. It is defined as a mark which indicates that the goods or services in connection with which that mark is used are certified by the proprietor of the mark in respect of origin, material, mode of manufacture of goods or performance of services, quality, accuracy or other characteristic.[1] Examples of such marks would be 'Woolmark' or 'WiFi'. Protection for such marks is, again, available in the UK by registration at the UKIPO and also since European certification marks were introduced in 2017 is also available in Europe by registration at the EUIPO – an example being the 'Global Organic Textile Standard GOTS' logo.

1 TMA 1994 s 50(1) and EUTMR Art 83(1).

3.04 In the UK, the provisions of the TMA 1994 apply to collective and certification marks subject to, respectively, Sch 1 and Sch 2 to the TMA 1994. The major difference is that in theory ordinary trade marks indicate a single source of origin, whereas certification and collective marks do not. Instead, they indicate characteristics of the goods or services, or of their users. Thus, whilst a mark that consists of an indication of geographical origin is not registrable as an ordinary trade mark, it may be registrable as a collective or certification mark in the UK.[1] It is not possible to register an indication of geographical origin as an EU certification mark.[2]

1 TMA 1994 Sch 1 para 3(1), and Sch 2 para 3(1).
2 EUTMR Art 83(1).

PROTECTED DESCRIPTIONS

3.05 European law also gives protection to three further types of mark:

- geographical indications ('PGIs');
- designations of origin ('PDOs') for foodstuffs and agricultural products; and
- traditional speciality guarantees ('TSGs').

These marks are governed by Council Regulation (EC) 1151/2012 and are specific to certain types of foodstuffs and the like. They are dealt with in outline at the end of this chapter.

UK—APPLICATIONS FOR REGISTRATION OF CERTIFICATION AND COLLECTIVE MARKS

3.06 Collective and certification marks may be registered at UKIPO in accordance with ss 49–50 of the TMA 1994 respectively. An application for registration is made by filing Form TM3 at UKIPO (as with ordinary trade marks) and by paying the appropriate fee.

3.07 Much of what is set out in this book in relation to applications for the registration of ordinary trade marks—including the comments regarding the specification of goods and services—applies equally to collective and certification marks.[1] However, one significant difference is that the applicant for registration of a collective or certification mark must also file regulations governing the use of the mark.[2]

1 See **Chapters 4–7** below.
2 TMA 1994 Sch 1 para 5 and Sch 2 para 6. See further paras **3.19–3.24** below.

UK—who is the 'applicant'

3.08 In the case of a collective mark, the applicant must act as an association. Thus, the registered proprietor of the collective marks 'Chartered Certified Accountant' and 'Parma ham' are, respectively, The Association of Chartered Certified Accountants and Consorzio del Prosciutto di Parma.

3.09 Whilst s 49(1)–(1A) of the TMA 1994 refers to an 'association', this is not defined and the term is given a wide meaning by UKIPO. What matters in this context is the manner in which the applicant acts—the applicant must demonstrate that it 'has a form of membership'.[1] Evidence of this is not always required but where it is required, it may include evidence demonstrating that the applicant has membership meetings, that there are conditions of membership, payment of membership fees and the like.

1 UKIPO *Trade Marks Manual*, Certification and collective marks, section 3.3.1.

3.10 In the case of a certification mark, the applicant should be the proprietor who will be certifying the goods or services and must, therefore, be competent to certify the goods or services involved. UKIPO has indicated that established trade bodies or Government departments are unlikely to need to provide evidence of their capability to certify the goods or services, but in other situations the applicant will need to prove evidence of such capability. This will often require evidence and supporting proof as to the history of the applicant in the field involved.

3.11 It should be borne in mind that an unincorporated association may not have the legal capacity to own property. If so, it cannot apply for a proprietary right in its own name. In such cases the organisation will need to act through an individual. UKIPO will not examine the applicant's ability to hold property, but if it is clear that the applicant named on the application form is unlikely to be able to hold property then an objection may be raised by UKIPO.

UK—registration process for certification and collective marks

3.12 As set out below, the registration process for collective and certification marks involves two stages:

- First, the mark is examined to see whether registration should be refused by reason of the absolute and/or, in the case of certification marks, relative grounds. These are the grounds set out in ss 3 and 5 of the TMA 1994 as modified and extended by Schs 1 and 2 to reflect the particular nature of certification and collective marks. Unlike ordinary trade mark applications[1] in certain circumstances relative grounds can lead to a refusal of an application for a certification mark.[2]
- Second, the regulations that the applicant must file governing use of the mark are considered.

1 See para **7.16**.
2 See para **3.16**.

UK—absolute grounds for refusal

3.13 As with ordinary trade marks, certification and collective marks are examined to see if any of the absolute grounds for refusal apply.[1] This process is designed to verify whether or not the mark in question fulfils its function as a trade mark. In carrying out this examination, the matters taken into account are the same as those which apply in relation to ordinary trade marks, namely that the mark should:

- be capable of distinguishing the relevant goods or services;
- not seek to monopolise terms which are legitimately required for use by other traders; and
- not seek to monopolise terms which are customary in the current language or bona fide practices of the trade.

1 See **Chapter 4**.

3.14 The manner of overcoming objections is the same for collective and certification marks as it is for ordinary trade marks. The difference is, of course, that where an objection is raised due to alleged descriptiveness of the mark, evidence is simply required that the mark in question has come to indicate goods or services which are provided by the members of the association to which the collective mark applies or which are identified by the proposed certification mark.

3.15 In relation to collective and certification marks, the absolute grounds of refusal are modified in that (in contrast to the position as regards ordinary trade marks) a mark which consists of signs or indications serving to indicate the geographical origin of the goods or services may be registered[1]—provided, of course, that in the case of a collective mark they help distinguish goods or services of members of the association from the goods or services of others and, in the case of certification marks, that they help differentiate the certified goods from uncertified goods.

1 TMA 1994 Sch 1 para 3 (collective marks) and Sch 2 para 3 (certification marks). The proprietor of such a mark cannot complain about use of the signs or indications in accordance with honest practices in industrial or commercial matters (in particular, by a person who is entitled to use a geographical name)—see Sch 1 para 3(2) and Sch 2 para 3(2).

UK—applicant for a certification mark must not carry on a business in the goods or services

3.16 A certification mark cannot be registered if the proprietor carries on a business involving the supply of goods or services of the kind certified.[1] To this end, the examination of a certification mark will include a check that the applicant does not own an ordinary trade mark in respect of the same goods or services. In practice, an objection made on this basis can be overcome by a statement from the applicant that no trade is carried on in the goods or services certified. If this proves to be untrue, a third party may successfully challenge the validity of the resulting registration in invalidation proceedings (if it carried on such a trade at the time of the application) or by way of revocation (if trade commenced subsequent to the registration of the mark).

1 TMA 1994 Sch 2 para 4.

UK—misleading marks

3.17 A collective or a certification mark will not be registered if it is likely to mislead the public as regards its character or significance—in particular if the mark is likely to be taken as something other than a collective or certification mark.[1]

1 TMA 1994 Sch 1 para 4 (collective marks) and Sch 2 para 5 (certification marks).

3.18 Whilst the wording of some marks may make it clear that the mark is intended to identify the goods or services provided by the member of the relevant association (for example, by including the word 'Association' in the mark) or to identify goods or services conforming to certain characteristics, other marks may simply be seen as ordinary trade marks. Where this is the case, the examiner will require that the mark includes some indication that it is a collective or certification mark—by for example, adding the words 'certification mark' or 'collective mark' (as appropriate) to the mark[1], or by including a clause in the regulations filed with the mark in which its nature is made clear. An example of such a requirement is:

> 'It is a condition of use that the mark shall not be used without indicating that is a collective/certification mark.'[2]

1 Such an amendment is permitted irrespective of TMA 1994 s 39.
2 UKIPO *Trade Marks Manual*, Certification and collective marks, section 2.5.2.

UK—regulations relating to certification/collective marks

3.19 The second phase of the registration process is the examination of the regulations that the applicant for a certification or a collective mark is required to file. Such regulations set out how appropriate persons will be able to use the mark.[1] Their purpose is to enable the mark to be used only by those persons intended to use it.

1 TMA 1994 Sch 1 para 5, and Sch 2 para 6.

3.20 UKIPO has emphasised the importance of such regulations and, in particular, the fact that as a certification mark may become an industry standard, overly onerous regulations, including charging excessively high fees, may be anti-competitive.

UK—time for filing the regulations

3.21 The regulations should be filed within a period specified by the registrar of not less than three months from the filing of the application for registration.[1] However, this period can be extended to a date after the registrability of the mark itself has been established.[2] The regulations when filed must be accompanied by Form TM35 and payment of the requisite fee (£200).

1 Trade Mark Rules 2008 ('TMR 2008') r 29.
2 TMR, r 77 and UKIPO *Trade Marks Manual*, Certification and collective marks, section 3.2. See **Chapter 7** for more details of UKIPO procedure.

UK—regulations relating to collective marks

3.22 The regulations filed by the applicant relating to collective marks must deal with the following matters[1]:

- *Who is authorised*—the regulations must designate the persons authorised to use the mark. This does not have to be by way of an actual list of the persons so authorised; it may simply be by reference to a class of users. Where the authorised users must fulfil requirements beyond those for membership of the association, those requirements must be set out in detail, as must the conditions for membership of the association. Where the collective mark consists of the geographical origin of the goods/services, the regulations must authorise any person whose goods/services originate in the geographical area concerned to become a member of the association, provided that the person also meets the other conditions of the regulations.

- *Conditions and limitations in the manner of use*—the regulations must deal with any limitations on the manner of use of the collective mark by authorised users. The applicant may also need to include a condition regarding the use of additional wording where the mark itself does not immediately make it clear that it is a collective mark.[2]
- *Sanctions for misuse*—the regulations must set out any sanctions that the applicant intends to impose against members for misuse of the mark (including use other than in accordance with the limitations as to the manner of use, or use of a particular mark where the member does not fulfil the requirements of the regulations).

1 TMA 1994 Sch 1 para 5.
2 See para **3.18** above.

UK—regulations relating to certification marks

3.23 In the case of certification marks, the regulations must deal with the following matters[1]:

- *Authorisation to use a certification mark*—the regulations should set out what requirements must be fulfilled for a party to use the certification mark. The nature of certification marks is that where an undertaking fulfils those requirements, it will able to use the mark. However, where the use of the certification is restricted to a class of individuals (perhaps by virtue of their qualifications or membership of certain bodies) this should be specified.
- *The characteristic or characteristics being certified*—the regulations must set out in sufficient detail what characteristics are being certified so that any people or undertakings will know exactly whether their goods or services fall within the requirements. The use of a certification mark is potentially open to all who comply with the regulations and so these must be clear.
- *How those characteristics will be tested/supervised by the applicant*—as one would expect, the grant of permission to use the certification mark should be subject to an approval procedure. In addition, the ongoing use of the mark should be subject to some level of supervision or ongoing testing. The conditions surrounding the first grant of approval to use the certification mark and the ongoing use of the mark must therefore be provided. There is no

requirement that the proprietor of the mark conducts the testing to ensure that the proposed user fulfils the conditions for use. However, if the proprietor is to conduct tests, the regulations will need to include an explanation of who will conduct that testing on their behalf. Where a certification mark becomes misleading it may be revoked, and so an ongoing compliance scheme is important to ensure that the certification mark does not become vulnerable to challenge.

- *The fees to be paid (if any)*—if any fees are to be paid in relation to the use of the certification mark then this should be made clear in the regulations. There is no requirement that the proprietor conducts the activities on a not-for-profit basis but UKIPO guidelines state that these should be 'be proportionate to the nature of certification necessary'.[2]
- *Procedure in case of disputes*—lastly, the regulations should provide for procedures to be followed in the case of a dispute. The most obvious example of such a dispute would be the refusal to provide authorisation to use the certification mark (or the withdrawal of authorisation) for users who believe that they have fulfilled the conditions for use. The appeal mechanism should provide for impartiality, fairness and equality in the resolution of the dispute.

1 TMA 1994 Sch 2 para 6.
2 UKIPO *Trade Mark Manual*, chapter 4, section 3.4.2.

UK—post-registration amendment of regulations

3.24 Regulations that have been accepted may subsequently be amended.[1] This might be required where, for example, there is a change of the organisation responsible for testing that the goods or services involved fulfil the relevant conditions.

Any application to amend the regulations must be accompanied by the relevant Form (TM36) and fee. The amended regulations will be re-examined to ensure that they are acceptable. If the amendment is refused then the regulations will remain unamended and the proprietor will be left with the choice of amending the proposal and re-applying, or (potentially) surrendering the certification mark.

If the amendment is permitted then the registrar has the power to request that the amended regulations be republished for opposition purposes. In practice, UKIPO has indicated that all but the most minor amendments (such as the address details of the proprietor) will lead to the regulations being republished. Third parties may then oppose, or file observations relating to the proposed amendment.

1 TMA 1994 Sch 1 para 10, and Sch 2 para 11.

UK—post-registration transfer of ownership

3.25 Certification and collective marks may be assigned in the same way as ordinary trade marks. With regard to certification marks, any new owner should be in a position to continue the certification activities if the registration is to remain valid and the Registrar must consent to such assignment in order for it to be effective.[1] Without such consent, the certification mark is deemed not to have been transferred.

1 TMA 1994 Sch 2 para 12.

3.26 Where a transfer has occurred, the regulations will generally need to be amended to reflect any changes in the details. As mentioned above, it is likely that these changes will need to be published for opposition purposes. Further, any changes will be subject to the payment of fees relating to the filing of the Form TM36 (application to amend regulations).

UK—revocation and invalidity of certification and collective marks

3.27 As well as the grounds for objection contained in ss 46 and 47 of the TMA 1994 which apply to ordinary trade marks,[1] there are further grounds for invalidating or revoking the registration of a certification or collective mark.

1 As to which, see **Chapters 11–12**.

3.28 In relation to both certification and collective marks, the registration may be declared invalid if it is shown that the public is likely to be misled as to the nature of the mark or if the regulations do not contain the relevant information.[1] A certification mark may also be invalidated if the proprietor carries on a trade in the goods or services in question or is no longer capable of certifying the goods or services in question.[2] A collective mark may be declared invalid if the owner does not meet the requirements.[3]

1 TMA 1994 Sch 1 para 14, and Sch 2 para 16.
2 TMA 1994 Sch 2 para 16.
3 TMA 1994 Sch 1 para 14.

3.29 There are also specific grounds for revocation which apply in the case of certification and collective marks[1] namely (amongst other things) where:

- the manner of use of the mark has led to its nature becoming misleading as regards its character or significance;
- the proprietor has not taken reasonable steps to prevent the mark being used in a manner incompatible with the regulations; or

- an amendment to the regulations has meant that they no longer comply with the relevant provisions of the TMA 1994.

1 TMA 1994 Sch 1 para 13 and Sch 2 para 15.

UK—infringement of collective and certification marks

3.30 As mentioned above, the provisions of the TMA 1994 apply to collective and certification marks subject to the provisions of Schs 1 and 2. Neither Schedule contains provisions relating to infringement. The normal rules therefore apply.[1]

Authorised users of collective marks have the right to call on the proprietor of the mark to take action and may otherwise bring proceedings in their own name.[2] Furthermore, certain provisions of the TMA 1994 regarding licensees apply to an authorised user of a registered certification or collective mark.[3]

1 As to which see **Chapter 14**.
2 TMA 1994 Sch 1 para 12.
3 TMA 1994 Sch 1 paras 11–12, and Sch 2 paras 13–14.

EUROPEAN UNION COLLECTIVE AND CERTIFICATION MARKS

3.31 It is possible to obtain an EU-wide collective mark.[1] The requirements for these are set out in Chapter VIII of the EUTMR (Arts 74–82). As has been noted, an EU-wide certification mark was introduced in 2017 and the requirements are also found in Chapter VIII of the EUTMR (Arts 83–93). As with ordinary EUTMs that had achieved registration by 31 December 2020, EU collective and certification marks in existence at that date were cloned into national UK comparable registrations on 1 January 2021 following Brexit. EUTM applications that were pending on 31 December 2020 (and those filed subsequently) are of no effect in the UK and must be the subject of a separate national application in the UK.

As with UK collective marks, EU collective marks are intended to distinguish the goods and services provided by members of the association from others. The grounds for refusal of an EU collective mark are the same as those for an ordinary EUTM, except that it may be possible to obtain an EU collective mark in respect of a mark that, if it were an ordinary trade mark, would be liable to objection on the basis that it is an indicator of geographical origin.

An EU collective mark may also be objected to on the basis that it is misleading as to its nature. In that regard, EUIPO has given the example of a collective mark that gives the impression that it is available for use by anyone who meets certain objective criteria, when in reality it is only available to members of a particular association.[2]

As with the UK, EU certification marks distinguish goods or services which are certified by the proprietor of the mark from those which are not certified. An EU certification mark cannot be owned by a person carrying out a business involving the goods or services of the kind certified. Further, an EU certification mark cannot be used for distinguishing goods or services in respect of geographical origin.[3]

1 EUTMR, Art 74.
2 EUIPO *Trade Mark Guidelines*, Part B, section 4, Chapter 15, 3.1.
3 EUIPO *Trade Mark Guidelines*, Part B, section 4, Chapter 16.

EU—collective and certification marks—the application process

3.32 The application for an EU collective or certification mark is made by way of the standard application form (or a self-designed form which contains the same information). As with an application for an ordinary EU trade mark, the application must include the relevant information relating to the mark, the applicant and the specification. The basic fees for an EU collective or certification mark are greater than for a standard EUTM—currently €1,500 as against €850 for a standard EUTM filed online in one class.

An application will be subject to examination on absolute grounds in the same way as an ordinary EUTM, albeit that the examination will also verify that the mark does not mislead as to its nature (see above). As with a UK collective or certification mark, the applicant must submit regulations relating to the mark.

EU—collective and certification marks—requirement to submit regulations

3.33 Under Arts 75 and 84 respectively of the EUTMR, an applicant for an EU collective or certification mark must file regulations relating to the use of that mark. These must be submitted within a period of two months from the filing of the application if they are not filed at the same time as the application.

The EU Trade Mark Implementing Regulation ('EUTMIR') contains a list of the information that must be contained within the regulations. In the case of both collective and certification marks the following are required:[1]

(a) the name of the applicant;
(b) a representation of the mark;
(c) the persons authorised to use the mark;
(d) conditions for use of the mark (including sanctions); and
(e) goods or services covered by the mark.

In addition, for collective marks the following are required:

(f) the object of the organisation;
(g) the bodies authorised to represent the organisation;
(h) in the case of an association, conditions for membership; and
(i) where the mark designates the geographical origin of goods or services, authorisation for any person whose goods or service originate in the geographical area to become a member of the organisation.[2]

For certification marks the following are required:

(j) a declaration that the applicant does not carry on a business in the supply of goods or services of the kind certified;
(k) the characteristics of the goods or services to be certified, such as the material, mode of manufacture of goods or performance of services, quality or accuracy;
(l) how the characteristics are tested and use of the certification mark is supervised.

The substantive examination of the applications begins once the regulations have been received. The EUIPO provides a template to guide applicants through the drafting of the regulations.[3]

1 Commission Implementing Regulation (EU) No 2018/626 of 5 March 2018 (EUTMIR); see Arts 16–17. See also EUTMR, Arts 75 and 84.
2 EUTMIR Art 16 and EUTMR Art 75(2).
3 EUIPO *Trade Mark Guidelines*, Part B, section 4, Chapter 15, 3.2 and Chapter 16, 3.4 and https://euipo.europa.eu/ohimportal/en/certification-and-collective-marks#23

EU—collective and certification marks—examination

3.34 Applications for EU collective and certification marks are examined to assess whether, in particular, the mark satisfies the conditions of Arts 74 and 83 respectively and whether regulations have been submitted which are not contrary to public policy or morality.[1] They are also examined to ensure that they are not misleading and that they would not be taken to be something other than a collective or certification mark by the public.[2] As for an ordinary application, third parties may submit observations under Art 45[3] and additionally on particular grounds that relate only to collective or certification marks.[4]

Regulations for collective marks that conflict with geographical indications, traditional terms for wine or traditional specialities guaranteed should detail any limitation to overcome such conflicts.[5]

1 EUTMR Arts 76(1) and 85(1).
2 EUTMR Arts 76(2) and 85(2).
3 See **Chapter 8**.
4 EUTMR Arts 77 and 86.
5 EUIPO *Trade Mark Guidelines*, Part B, section 4, Chapter 15, 1.4.

EU—collective and certification marks—amendment of regulations

3.35 As with UK collective and certification marks, the regulations for use of a mark may be amended. EUIPO has the power to reject such amendments if they fall foul of the main provisions governing the regulations.

EU—collective and certification marks—revocation and invalidity

3.36 The grounds for revocation and invalidity of ordinary EUTMs found in Arts 58–60 of EUTMR[1] apply equally to EU collective and certification marks.

However, in addition to these usual grounds for revocation and invalidation, the following additional grounds for revocation for collective and certification marks are set out in Arts 81 and 91 of the EUTMR:

(a) the proprietor has failed to take reasonable steps to prevent the mark being used in a manner incompatible with its status as a collective or certification mark;
(b) the manner in which the mark has been used has caused it to become liable to mislead the public;
(c) the regulations for use of the mark have been amended in breach of Arts 79(2) or 88(2) unless the regulations are further amended so as to be compliant; or
(d) the regulations governing use are contrary to public policy or to accepted principles of morality, or if the public is liable to be misled as to the character or significance of the mark—particularly it is likely to be taken for something other than a collective or certification mark.

A further ground exists for certification marks under Art 91 where the proprietor carries on a business involving the supply of goods or services of the kind certified.

1 As to which, see **Chapters 11–12**.

EU—collective and certification marks—infringement

3.37 Articles 74 and 83 provide that the other provisions of the EUTMR apply to EU collective and certification marks respectively unless the Articles under Title VIII specify otherwise. Thus the usual provisions as to infringement apply.[1] However, Arts 80 and 90 provide that the proprietor of the mark shall be entitled to claim compensation on behalf of those entitled to use the mark where damage has been caused by unauthorised use. This is in effect a kind of representative action. Further, Art 80 also states that the provisions of the EUTMR governing actions by licensees (Art 25(3)–(4)) apply to all persons authorised to use the EU collective mark. This does not apply to certification marks.

1 As to which, see **Chapter 14**.

PROTECTED GEOGRAPHICAL INDICATIONS AND DESIGNATIONS OF ORIGIN

3.38 As mentioned above, European law also gives protection to:

- geographical indications ('PGIs'); and
- designations of origin ('PDOs') for foodstuffs and agricultural products.

These two rights ('Protected Descriptions') are specific to certain foodstuffs and agricultural products intended for human consumption. Though governed by Regulation 1151/2012, similar rights exist in other jurisdictions by virtue of their inclusion in the international TRIPS agreement.[1] Regulation 1151/2012 provides that the protected indications of 'third countries' (ie, non-EU countries) may be protected under the Regulation 1151/2012 if they fulfil the necessary conditions and are registered in their country of origin.[2]

Protection for Protected Descriptions is available in the EU by registration at the EUIPO. In the UK, EU Protected Descriptions coming into existence after the end of the Brexit transition period (31 December 2020) are not protected. However, Protected Descriptions in existence before then continue to be protected[3] under the UK geographical indication schemes.[4] If such a Protected Description loses its protection in the EU after the end of the transition period, it will also cease to be protected in the UK.

1 Agreement on Trade-Related Aspects of Intellectual Property Rights, 15 April 1994.
2 Regulation 510/2006 Art 5(9).
3 Agreement on the withdrawal of the United Kingdom of Great Britain and Northern Ireland from the European Union 2019/C 384 I/01 Art 54.
4 The Agricultural Products, Food and Drink (Amendment etc) (EU Exit) Regulations 2020, SI 2020/1637. The Department for Environment, Food and Rural Affairs (Defra) is the competent authority for the GI schemes in the UK (including Northern Ireland).

Protected Descriptions—the subject matter of protection

3.39 The purpose of Protected Descriptions is not to distinguish or protect the goods of particular undertakings but rather to protect the identity and 'genuine' nature of food products that have traditionally been produced in a particular geographical location or region. A list of the foodstuffs to which Regulation 1151/2012 relates are to be found in Annex I to the Treaty Establishing the European Community.

3.40 The foodstuffs to which Regulation 1151/2012 applies include many cheeses (such as Wensleydale), meat products (such as Parma ham) and other processed foodstuffs (such as Melton Mowbray pork pies). However, Regulation 1151/2012 does not apply to wines since their designations of origin are subject to international agreements with other wine-producing countries such as South Africa and Australia.[1]

1 Art 2 of Regulation 1151/2012. See also particularly Council Regulation (EC) 607/2009 and related legislation.

3.41 What is protected is the name of a place or region that is used as a descriptor for a foodstuff or agricultural product. The substantive criteria for protection are that the descriptor is a geographical name used in relation to products, and that the products must: (i) originate in that region; (ii) be produced, prepared and/or processed in that region; and (iii) possess a quality attributable to the environment (designations of origin) or possess a reputation attributable to the geographical region (geographical indicators).

3.42 Definitions of the various terms relevant to this protection are contained in Art 5(1) and Art 5(2) of Regulation 1151/2012. This provides that:

> '1. For the purpose of this Regulation, "designation of origin" is a name which identifies a product:
> (a) originating in a specific place, region or, in exceptional cases, a country;
> (b) whose quality or characteristics are essentially or exclusively due to a particular geographical environment with its inherent natural and human factors; and
> (c) the production steps of which all take place in the defined geographical area.
>
> '2. For the purpose of this Regulation, "geographical indication" is a name which identifies a product:
> (a) originating in a specific place, region or country;
> (b) whose given quality, reputation or other characteristic is essentially attributable to its geographical origin; and
> (c) at least one of the production steps of which take place in the defined geographical area.'

The remainder of Art 5 contains further minor conditions and derogations.

Protected Descriptions—descriptors ineligible for protection

3.43 Article 6 of Regulation 1151/2012 sets out certain types of descriptors that may not become Protected Descriptions. Generic names, or those likely to mislead consumers due to their similarity with animal or plant names, are not eligible for protection.

3.44 Geographical names partly or wholly homonymous with other Protected Descriptions may be registered subject to two factors: (i) traditional usage; and (ii) actual risk of confusion. Thus, for example, where two different and distinct regions share the same name, these provisions will be engaged.

3.45 Where there is conflict with earlier registered trade marks, such that there is a likelihood of consumers being misled, the conflicting geographical name may not be registered.

3.46 Article 54 of Regulation 1151/2012 provides the European Commission with the power to cancel a registration where the criteria for protection are no longer fulfilled. Any person with a legitimate interest may request such a cancellation.

Protected Descriptions—formal requirements for protection

3.47 The procedural requirements are set out in Art 8 of Regulation 1151/2012. Only *groups*, such as local trade groups, may apply for a Protected Description. Applications are made to the European Commission or to Member States' authorities as appropriate to the Protected Description. The application must identify the applicant, set out how the proposed Protected Description fulfils the substantive requirements of Art 5 of Regulation 1151/2012 and provide a specification.

3.48 The contents of the specification are stipulated in Art 7 of Regulation 1151/2012. In essence, the specification must set out the details of the geographical area, the foodstuffs concerned and their specific characteristics, the processes or production methods involved and the connection between the foodstuff and the geographical area. Article 53 of Regulation 1151/2012 contains provisions for amending specifications after registration.

Further details on the formal requirements are contained in Commission Regulation (EC) 664/2014.

3.49 Objections to the proposed Protected Description may be lodged by Member States, third countries, or persons with a legitimate interest in objecting.

Protected Descriptions—use of the protected description

3.50 Under Art 12 of Regulation 1151/2012, the Protected Description may be used by any undertaking *marketing* goods that match the specification registered for that Protected Description.

Article 36 requires Member States to nominate competent authorities to check for compliance; those competent authorities are then responsible for verifying products bearing the Protected Description (Art 37 of Regulation 1151/2012).

3.51 Certain symbols must be used in conjunction with the Protected Description. These symbols are depicted and described in Annex 1 to Regulation 664/2014.

Protected Descriptions—scope of protection

3.52 Protected Descriptions are protected from the following (Art 13 of Regulation 1151/2012):

> '(a) any direct or indirect commercial use of a registered name in respect of products not covered by the registration where those products are comparable to the products registered under that name or where using the name exploits the reputation of the protected name, including when those products are used as an ingredient;
> (b) any misuse, imitation or evocation, even if the true origin of the product or services is indicated or if the protected name is translated or accompanied by an expression such as "style", "type", "method", "as produced in", "imitation" or similar, including when those products are used as an ingredient;
> (c) any other false or misleading indication as to the provenance, origin, nature or essential qualities of the product that is used on the inner or outer packaging, advertising material or documents relating to the product concerned, and the packing of the product in a container liable to convey a false impression as to its origin;
> (d) any other practice liable to mislead the consumer as to the true origin of the product.'

Enforcement of this regulatory system is the responsibility of the competent authorities designated pursuant to Art 36 of Regulation 1151/2012.

Protected Descriptions—relationship with trade marks

3.53 Applications for trade marks the use of which would fall within the scope of protection afforded by Art 13 of Regulation 1151/2012 are to be refused if they relate to the same class of products: see Art 14 of Regulation 1151/2012. Certain older trade marks, registered in good faith, are exempt from this rule: see Art 14(2).

TRADITIONAL SPECIALITY GUARANTEES

3.54 The final category of other rights considered in this chapter is traditional speciality guarantees ('TSGs') which are also governed by Regulation 1151/2012. TSGs are aimed at 'traditional' foodstuffs with recognisable characteristics which are not geographically defined or limited with the aim of safeguarding traditional methods of production and recipes. As with Protected Descriptions (see 3.38), EU TSGs in existence by 31 December 2020 continue to be protected in the UK.

3.55 The framework for the protection of TSGs under Regulation 1151/2012 is similar to that for Protected Descriptions. Article 3 of Regulation 1151/2012 provides that:

> 'For the purposes of this Regulation:
> (3) 'traditional' means proven usage on the domestic market for a period that allows transmission between generations; this period is to be at least 30 years;
> (5) 'specific character' in relation to a product means the characteristic production attributes which distinguish a product clearly from other similar products of the same category;'

3.56 Thus the TSG must be sufficiently well defined and have been in use for a sufficient period of time. Article 18 of Regulation 1151/2012 provides that:

> '1. A name shall be eligible for registration as a traditional speciality guaranteed where it describes a specific product or foodstuff that:
> (a) results from a mode of production, processing or composition corresponding to traditional practice for that product or foodstuff; or
> (b) is produced from raw materials or ingredients that are those traditionally used.
>
> '2. For a name to be registered as a traditional speciality guaranteed, it shall:
> (a) have been traditionally used to refer to the specific product; or
> (b) identify the traditional character or specific character of the product.
>
> '3. If it is demonstrated in the opposition procedure under Article 51 that the name is also used in another Member State or in a third country, in order to distinguish comparable products or products that share an identical or similar name, the decision on registration taken in

accordance with Article 52(3) may provide that the name of the traditional speciality guaranteed is to be accompanied by the claim 'made following the tradition of' immediately followed by the name of a country or a region thereof.

'4. A name may not be registered if it refers only to claims of a general nature used for a set of products, or to claims provided for by particular Union legislation.'

Chapter 4

Absolute grounds for refusal

THE ABSOLUTE GROUNDS FOR A REFUSAL OF REGISTRATION

4.01 A sign that satisfies the criteria for being a trade mark (see **Chapter 2**) is prima facie registrable unless it is specifically excluded from registration. The exclusions are divided into *absolute* grounds for refusal—which are dealt with in this chapter, and *relative* grounds—which are addressed in **Chapter 5**.

4.02 In the UK, the absolute grounds for refusal are contained in s 3 of the Trade Marks Act 1994 ('TMA 1994') under which the following are not registrable:

- signs which do not satisfy the definition of a trade mark;[1]
- trade marks which are devoid of any distinctive character (subject to the proviso mentioned at **4.04** below);
- trade marks which are descriptive (subject to the proviso mentioned below);
- trade marks which have become generic (subject to the proviso mentioned below);
- signs which consist of various specific types of shape;
- trade marks contrary to public policy or morality;
- trade marks which are deceptive;
- trade marks the use of which would be prohibited by law;
- trade marks consisting of specific emblems (as to which, see TMA 1994 s 4);
- trade marks applied for in bad faith.

1 As to which see **Chapter 2**.

4.03 Article 7 of the European Trade Mark Regulation (EU) 2017/1001 ('EUTMR') contains much the same exclusions from registration in respect of EUTMs. However, it also expressly excludes protected geographical marks (see Art 7(1)(g)).

4.04 Both s 3(1) of the TMA 1994 and Art 7(3) of the EUTMR provide that the second, third and fourth of the exclusions listed above will not apply if the trade mark has become distinctive in relation to the goods or services for which it is sought to be registered in consequence of the use which has been made of it.

4.05 Article 7(2) of the EUTMR provides that, for EUTMs, the basis for objection need only arise in part of the Community. This is particularly important in relation to word marks that have a specific meaning in one language which would not necessarily be understood across the rest of the EU.

Signs that do not satisfy the definition of a trade mark—s 3(1)(a); Art 7(1)(a)

4.06 Section 3(1)(a) of the TMA 1994 and Art 7(1)(a) of the EUTMR exclude from registration signs which do not satisfy the definitions of a trade mark contained in s 1(1) of the TMA 1994 and Art 4 of the EUTMR. Those definitions are discussed extensively in **Chapter 2**. In essence, this exclusion contains a restatement that a sign must be capable of suitably clear representation in the register and must be capable of distinguishing goods or services in order to be registrable.

Marks devoid of distinctive character—s 3(1)(b); Art 7(1)(b)

How distinctive?

4.07 Exclusion 1(b) excludes from registration trade marks 'which are devoid of any distinctive character'. In practice, a large proportion of trade mark applications to which objection is made under 1(b) are also at least arguably descriptive and suffer objections under 1(c). Therefore to some extent the case law overlaps and must be read together. Objections under 1(c) are considered in detail below. However, it must be remembered that the grounds of objection are legally separate and need not stand or fall together.

4.08 The use of the words 'devoid' and 'any' in exclusion 1(b) suggests that a low threshold of distinctive character will be sufficient to proceed to registration. The Court of Justice's reasoning, from the early case law such as *BABY-DRY*[1] (primarily a 1(c) case), appears to support this approach since even such a simple 'lexical invention' was registrable. In theory, therefore, the smallest quantity of distinctive character would be sufficient to overcome the 1(b) exclusion. However, since distinctive character is not a quantitatively measurable characteristic, the approach of the Court in later cases suggests that the concept of a threshold of distinctiveness is not the most useful approach and, rather, that one must ask whether the mark under consideration possesses sufficient distinctive character to fulfil its essential function.

1 C-383/99 *Procter & Gamble Co v OHIM* [2002] Ch 82; [2002] ETMR 3.

Distinctive of what?

4.09 In *Philips v Remington*[1] the Court held that a mark that was not excluded under 1(b), 1(c) and 1(d) would not be excluded under 1(a). In other words, a mark which just reached the threshold for sufficient inherent distinctive character would be one capable of acting as a badge of origin. This early decision, whilst focusing mainly on other grounds, emphasises the basic underlying concept of the 1(b) exclusion: to have distinctive character, a mark must be capable of acting as an indicator of commercial origin, literally *distinguishing* the goods or services of one undertaking from those of another.

1 C-299/99 *Koninklijke Philips Electronics v Remington Consumer Products* [2003] Ch 159; [2002] ETMR 81; [2003] RPC 2.

4.10 The concept of distinctiveness as an indicator of origin must be contrasted with the fallacious idea that distinctiveness is to be equated with aesthetic attraction or ornamentation. A trade mark need not be interesting or ornamental in order to be distinctive. By the same token, an appealing mark will not necessarily possess distinctive character. For example:

(a) In *Glaverbel*[1] the CFI (now called the General Court) rejected an appeal from OHIM (now called EUIPO) in relation to an application for a decorative pattern to be applied to glass. The pattern was ornamental but was not memorable and would not, in the Court's view, be perceived by customers as indicating trade origin but rather as simple, attractive decoration.
(b) In *Matratzen* the CJEU ruled that a Spanish national trade mark MATRATZEN, meaning 'mattress' in German and registered for *inter alia* mattresses in Spain, did not lack distinctive character. [2] The relevant public was Spanish-speaking in that situation and would not understand the mark as descriptive or lacking in inherent distinctiveness. Thus, for example, a UK trade mark for CHIEN ('dog' in French) registered for dog food might survive a distinctiveness objection. Of course, when considering an EUTM, languages across the EU must be taken into account.[3]

1 C-445/02 *Glaverbel SA v OHIM* [2005] ETMR 70.
2 C-421/04 *Matratzen Concord AG v Hukla Germany SA* [2006] ETMR 48.
3 This problem was raised in *AS Watson v The Boots Company* Patents County Court, 8 September 2011.

4.11 The requirement that a mark be capable of distinguishing goods or services is the same for any kind of mark[1] (words, devices, 3D marks, etc) though in practice certain types of marks may find it more difficult to satisfy the requirement. For example, in *London Taxi*,[2] shape marks for models of a taxi cab were held to lack distinctive character, and see also the shapes of Land Rover vehicles in *Jaguar Land Rover*.[3] In *Libertel*[4] the CJEU confirmed that a single colour was capable of possessing distinctive character but re-emphasised that it will depend on whether the colour alone can act as an indicator of origin. There is a general public interest in preventing marks of relatively low distinctiveness being too broadly monopolised: thus registrations of low-distinctive marks for a large number of goods and services are less likely to be permitted. It is almost inconceivable that a plain colour could be inherently distinctive; rather, a colour must usually acquire distinctiveness through use (as to which, see below).

1 C-53/01 to C-55/01 *Linde AG, Winward Industries Inc and Rado Uhren AG.*
2 *London Taxi* Corp *Ltd (t/a London Taxi Co) v Fraser-Nash Research Ltd* [2016] EWHC 52 (Ch); [2016] ETMR 18 (upheld on appeal: [2017] EWCA Civ 1729). Shape-mark distinctiveness was also considered in *Mondelez UK Holdings & Services Ltd v EUIPO / Société des produits Nestlé SA*, Case T-112/13 (General Court) [2017] ETMR 13.
3 *Jaguar Land Rover Ltd v Ineos Industries Holdings Ltd* [2020] EWHC 2130 (Ch); [2020] ETMR 56.
4 C-104/01 *Libertel Groep BV v Benelux-Merkenbureau* [2004] Ch 83; [2003] ETMR 63; [2004] FSR 4.

Assessing distinctive character

4.12 Whether or not a particular mark satisfies the requirement of distinctive character must be assessed in relation to the goods or services for which registration is sought and according to the perception of the relevant consumer of those goods or services, ie, the familiar average consumer.[1] Further, the analysis must instead not be made in the abstract but with regard to the actual circumstances of the case including the way the mark is used: see *Libertel*. As usual, the overall impression of the trade mark is what must be examined.[2]

1 C-53/01 to C-55/01 *Linde AG, Winward Industries Inc and Rado Uhren AG.*
2 C-104/00 *DKV v OHIM* and C-472/01 *Procter & Gamble v OHIM.*

4.13 Where a mark is also descriptive, it may be that it is descriptive only for some of the goods and services for which registration is sought. In such a situation, the mark is not necessarily to be taken as inherently distinctive for the remaining goods and services: in *POSTKANTOOR*[1] the Court considered the mark POSTKANTOOR (meaning POST OFFICE in Dutch) to be descriptive for post office services; however, the mark's distinctiveness had to be assessed in the usual way as regards the other goods or services. See also *EUROHYPO*.[2]

1 C-363/99 *Koninklijke KPN Nederland NV v Benelux-Merkenbureau* [2006] Ch 1; [2004] ETMR 57.
2 C-304/06 *Eurohypo AG v OHIM* [2008] ETMR 59.

4.14 A mark may be composed of elements that are not distinctive when taken individually. However, the analysis must as always be of the mark taken as a whole—although where non-distinctive elements are combined in an unsurprising way, it is unlikely that the mark taken as a whole will possess distinctive character. As mentioned above, distinctive character does not depend upon reaching a threshold of linguistic (or artistic, where appropriate) inventiveness but upon the ability of the mark to indicate origin to consumers. Thus in *SAT.2*[1] the CJEU ruled that the mark SAT.2 for satellite broadcasting services was not necessarily devoid of distinctive character since trade marks in the industry frequently consisted of a short word and a number. The rationale appears to be that since other such marks were used, customers would recognise the combination SAT.2 as an identifier of origin, even though it was not particularly distinctive *per se*. Another way in which a mark may fail to be distinctive was identified in the *Scrabble*[2] case. There, the proprietor's 'tile mark' was held to cover an infinite number of different permutations, and combinations of letters and numbers on a tile, as well as a multitude of different possible appearances of the tile, and so lacked any distinctive character.

1 C-329/02 *SAT.1 Satellitenfernsehen GmbH v OHIM* [2005] ETMR 20.
2 *JW Spear & Sons Ltd v Zynga Inc* [2012] EWHC 3345 (Ch); [2013] FSR 28. Upheld on appeal: [2013] EWCA Civ 1175; [2014] 1 All ER 1093.

Packaging and shape marks

4.15 Packaging and other shape marks often suffer from a lack of distinctive character. In *Henkel*[1] the CJEU was asked whether the distinctive character of a 3D mark for the shape of packaging depended on its having capricious features such that the average consumer could recognise it as an indicator of origin. The Court held that a mere departure from the norm was not sufficient to imbue such a mark with distinctive character but that a significant departure from the norm would be. The Court further noted that consumers are not used to looking to packaging shape for indicators of origin and thus the differences must enable a customer to recognise the indicator without the need for too much analysis on his or her part. In *Nestle v Cadbury*[2] the High Court held that the shape of the 'Kit-Kat' chocolate bars was not inherently distinctive in relation to cakes and pastries; just because a shape was outside the norms of a particular sector, that did not automatically imbue it with distinctive character. As to whether the shape had *acquired* distinctiveness, the

Court has referred questions to the CJEU to seek clarification of the law, see para **4.36** below. In similar vein see also *Coca-Cola*, in which the design of a bottle lacked distinctiveness.[3]

1 C-456/01 *Henkel KGaA v OHIM* [2005] ETMR 44.
2 *Societé des Produits Nestle SA v Cadbury UK Ltd* [2014] EWHC 16 (Ch); [2014] FSR 17.
3 *Coca-Cola Co v Office for Harmonisation in the Internal Market (Trade Marks and Designs) (OHIM)* (T-411/14) [2016] ETMR 25.

4.16 Distinctiveness is a matter of fact and degree: where a range of packaging is used for a particular product, a design which falls on the edge of or just outside the usual range will not possess distinctive character, but one which is well outside the usual range may survive a s 3(1)(b) objection. See also *Procter & Gamble*[1] and *Storck.*[2]

1 C-468/01 *Procter & Gamble Company v OHIM* [2004] ETMR 88.
2 C-24/05, C-25/05 *Storck v OHIM* [2006] ECR I-5719.

Slogans

4.17 Slogans have similarly been problematic. After some confused case law, the CJEU in *Audi*[1] has confirmed that whilst slogans and other laudatory expressions were prima facie of lower distinctive character, there was no principle under which they were automatically excluded from registration. Each application must be examined on its merits to see whether the mark could act as an indicator of origin, and of course, in appropriate circumstances evidence of acquired distinctiveness will also be relevant.

1 C-398/08 *Audi AG v OHIM* [2010] ETMR 18.

Comment

4.18 What is to be gleaned from the case law?

(a) The crucial concept of distinctiveness is intimately bound up with the idea of the essential function of a trade mark: acting as an indicator of trade origin. Thus any analysis of whether a mark is objectionable under 1(b) should consider badge of origin as the guiding principle.
(b) The next step is to consider the goods or services for which registration is sought and how the relevant public will view the mark in relation to those goods or services. It is vital to consider these two factors and not to try to assess distinctiveness in the abstract. A device in the shape of a wine bottle, for example, would be lacking distinctive character for alcoholic drinks but might be registrable for pens and pencils.
(c) How the average consumer will assess the mark in terms of a trade mark's essential function becomes increasingly important

when considering more unusual types of marks such as 3D marks, colours and the like. The possibility that a mark will be perceived as decoration, ornamentation or a functional element of a product or packaging is very real where the consumer has not been educated to know better.

(d) With any type of trade mark there is a range of inherent distinctiveness. To take word marks as an example, at the highest end of the distinctiveness spectrum are made-up words like EXXON, XEROX or ASDA which are unique and meaningless. Near the bottom are adjectives relating to the goods or services or which are suggestive of some general desirable property such as TREAT for sugar. In between fall proper nouns such as SAINSBURY'S, nouns like APPLE and adjectives like ORANGE. Each of these latter three is, in fact, a very well-known mark but their inherent distinctiveness depends on both their apparent irrelevance to the goods or services they relate to and their comparative uniqueness of use in the commercial field of interest.

Descriptive marks—s 3(1)(c); Art 7(1)(c)

4.19 The 1(c) exclusion is of trade marks '*which consist exclusively of signs or indications which may serve, in trade, to designate the kind, quality, quantity, intended purpose, value, geographical origin or the time of production of the goods or of rendering of the service, or other characteristics of the goods or service*'.

The last part of this provision makes clear that the 1(c) exclusion applies to trade marks that indicate any characteristic of the goods or services in question; the preceding list of specific characteristics is simply illustrative. The exclusion is generally said to relate to marks that are 'descriptive' of the goods or services to which they relate.

What is to be considered descriptive?

4.20 As with the 1(b) exclusion, the CJEU case law as to what is to be considered descriptive, and thus excluded, and what is considered merely to allude to some characteristic of the goods, has evolved since the harmonisation of EU trade mark law in 1994. The words 'consist exclusively' in the 1(c) exclusion suggest a restrictive interpretation of s 3(1)(c), and marks that include some other meaning should not fall foul of this objection.

4.21 The first 1(c) case to reach the CJEU was *Windsurfing Chiemsee.*[1] Chiemsee is a lake in Bavaria which is popular with windsurfers. The trade mark proprietor had registered a stylised form of CHIEMSEE as a German trade mark for *inter alia* windsurfing products. The Court concluded that 1(c) could operate not only if the word CHIEMSEE already acted as an indication of geographical origin but also if there was a reasonable possibility of its doing so in the future. The Court explained that, similarly to 1(b), the policy underlying the 1(c) exclusion was to prevent monopolisation of terms that should be available for use by other traders (including as collective marks[2]).

1 C-108/97 *Windsurfing Chiemsee Produktions und Vertriebs GmbH v Boots und Segelzubehor Walter Huber* [1999] ETMR 585.

2 For collective marks, see **Chapter 3**.

4.22 Shortly after *Windsurfing Chiemsee,* the CJEU in *The Procter & Gamble Co v OHIM*[1] had to consider whether the mark 'BABY-DRY' used in connection with nappies was descriptive. It held that the mark was sufficiently inventive and unusual to defeat the 1(c) exclusion. It is worth reading the relevant passages in full:

> '40. As regards trade marks composed of words, such as the mark at issue here, descriptiveness must be determined not only in relation to each word taken separately but also in relation to the whole which they form. Any perceptible difference between the combination of words submitted for registration and the terms used in the common parlance of the relevant class of consumers to designate the goods or services or their essential characteristics is apt to confer distinctive character on the word combination enabling it to be registered as a trade mark.
>
> …
>
> 42. In order to assess whether a word combination such as BABY-DRY is capable of distinctiveness, it is therefore necessary to put oneself in the shoes of an English-speaking consumer. From that point of view, and given that the goods concerned in this case are babies' nappies, the determination to be made depends on whether the word combination in question may be viewed as a normal way of referring to the goods or of representing their essential characteristics in common parlance.
>
> 43. As it is, that word combination, whilst it does unquestionably allude to the function which the goods are supposed to fulfil, still does not satisfy the disqualifying criteria set forth in paragraphs 39 to 42 of this judgment. Whilst each of the two words in the combination may form part of expressions used in everyday speech to designate the function of babies' nappies, their syntactically unusual juxtaposition is not a familiar expression in the English language, either for designating babies' nappies or for describing their essential characteristics.

44. Word combinations like BABY-DRY cannot therefore be regarded as exhibiting, as a whole, descriptive character; they are lexical inventions bestowing distinctive power on the mark so formed and may not be refused registration under Article 7(1)(c) of Regulation No 40/94.'

1 C-383/99 *The Procter & Gamble Co v OHIM* [2002] ETMR 3; [2002] Ch 82.

4.23 The Court's decision in *BABY-DRY* therefore construed the 1(c) exclusion very narrowly and opened up the possibility of rather descriptive words and phrases being registered provided that there was some inventive component to them that imbued a level of distinctiveness that overcame the words' otherwise descriptive meaning.

4.24 It did not take long for a more expansive interpretation of 1(c) to emerge from the Court. In *DOUBLEMINT*[1] the CJEU held that the 1(c) exclusion would bite where the mark in question had a descriptive meaning, even if the mark also had other meanings. It said:

'32. In order for OHIM to refuse to register a trade mark under Article 7(1)(c) of Regulation No 40/94, it is not necessary that the signs and indications composing the mark that are referred to in that article actually be in use at the time of the application for registration in a way that is descriptive of goods or services such as those in relation to which the application is filed, or of characteristics of those goods or services. It is sufficient, as the wording of that provision itself indicates, that such signs and indications could be used for such purposes. A sign must therefore be refused registration under that provision if at least one of its possible meanings designates a characteristic of the goods or services concerned.

33. In the present case, the reason given by the Court of First Instance, at paragraph 20 of the contested judgment, for holding that the word at issue could not be refused registration under Article 7(1)(c) was that signs or indications whose meaning goes beyond the merely descriptive are capable of being registered as Community trade marks and, at paragraph 31 of the contested judgment, that that term cannot be characterised as exclusively descriptive. It thus took the view that Article 7(1)(c) of Regulation No 40/94 had to be interpreted as precluding the registration of trade marks which are exclusively descriptive of the goods or services in respect of which registration is sought, or of their characteristics.

34. In so doing, the Court of First Instance applied a test based on whether the mark is exclusively descriptive, which is not the test laid down by Article 7(1)(c) of Regulation No 40/94.

> 35. It thereby failed to ascertain whether the word at issue was capable of being used by other economic operators to designate a characteristic of their goods and services.
>
> 36. It follows that it erred as to the scope of Article 7(1)(c) of Regulation No 40/94.'

1 C-191/01 *Wm Wrigley Jr Co v OHIM* [2004] ETMR 9.

4.25 Whilst the reasoning in *DOUBLEMINT* does not expressly challenge the reasoning of *BABY-DRY*, it is clear that the two decisions do not sit well together: if a phrase which has a possible descriptive meaning must be refused (see *DOUBLEMINT*) it cannot be the case that such a phrase is registrable simply because it is a clever formulation of words (see *BABY-DRY*). *DOUBLEMINT* has been followed in numerous cases and it must be assumed that *BABY-DRY*, at least to the extent of conclusions regarding clever descriptive marks, should no longer be considered to reflect accurately the state of the law. Although *BABY-DRY* is frequently cited in argument by applicants for descriptive marks, the CJEU tends to ignore this and repeat what was said in *DOUBLEMINT* and the following cases discussed below. Any applicant having to rely on *BABY-DRY* is probably in trouble.

4.26 An element of the earlier thinking survives in relation to neologisms formed by a combination of descriptive components. In *BIOMILD*[1] and *POSTKANTOOR* the CJEU held that where a neologism was formed from descriptive components, it was the meaning (if any) of the neologism itself which must be assessed for descriptiveness. It is not correct simply to find a neologism descriptive because each of its components are alone descriptive. In *BIOMILD* it was said:

> '39. As a general rule, the mere combination of elements, each of which is descriptive of characteristics of the goods or services in respect of which registration is sought, itself remains descriptive of those characteristics within the meaning of Article 3(1)(c) of the Directive even if the combination creates a neologism. Merely bringing those elements together without introducing any unusual variations, in particular as to syntax or meaning, cannot result in anything other than a mark consisting exclusively of signs or indications which may serve, in trade, to designate characteristics of the goods or services concerned.
>
> 40. However, such a combination may not be descriptive within the meaning of Article 3(1)(c) of the Directive, provided that it creates an impression which is sufficiently far removed from that produced by the simple combination of those elements. In the case of a word mark, which is intended to be heard as much

as to be read, that condition will have to be satisfied as regards both the aural and the visual impression produced by the mark.

41. Thus, a mark consisting of a neologism composed of elements, each of which is descriptive of characteristics of the goods or services in respect of which registration is sought, is itself descriptive of those characteristics within the meaning of Article 3(1)(c) of the Directive, unless there is a perceptible difference between the neologism and the mere sum of its parts: that assumes that, because of the unusual nature of the combination in relation to the goods or services, the word creates an impression which is sufficiently far removed from that produced by the mere combination of meanings lent by the elements of which it is composed, with the result that the word is more than the sum of its parts.'

1 C-265/00 *Campina Melkunie BV v Benelux-Merkenbureau* [2004] ETMR 58.

4.27 In *POSTKANTOOR* the Court noted that it was not relevant whether there were more usual ways of referring to the goods or services in question: if the mark may describe those goods or services, it will be considered descriptive. Note that there may also be a 'squeeze' between descriptiveness and lack of distinctiveness: in *Starbucks (HK)*[1] it was held that the mark 'NOW TV' was either a characteristic of the television service in question (or else was devoid of distinctive character).

1 *Starbucks (HK) Ltd v British Sky Broadcasting Group Plc* [2012] EWHC 3074 (Ch); [2013] FSR 29.

4.28 The *CELLTECH*[1] case, which closely follows the reasoning in *BIOMILD* and *POSTKANTOOR*, is a helpful illustration of how the 1(c) exclusion should not be taken too far: even if understood as 'cell technology', this was not a precise enough concept to be descriptive of the goods for which registration was sought ('pharmaceutical, veterinary and sanitary preparations, compounds and substances', 'surgical, medical, dental and veterinary apparatus and instruments', and 'research and development services; consultancy services; all relating to the biological, medical and chemical sciences', in Classes 5, 10 and 42 respectively). For further illustrations, see *Fine & Country*[2] in which the mark 'FINE AND COUNTRY' was held not to comprise merely laudatory or descriptive elements in relation to estate agents' services (this was strongly doubted by the Court of Appeal, though ultimately not overturned) whereas in *British Shorinji Kempo*[3] the court decided that the words 'shorinji kempo' were generic identifiers of a particular martial art. As exclusion 1(b) expressly indicates, marks may also be deemed descriptive where they incorporate an element that is commonly used or understood as a geographical identifier of the goods' origin – see *J Portugal Ramos Vinhos*.[4]

1 C-273/05 *Celltech R&D Limited v OHIM* [2007] ETMR 52.
2 *Fine & Country Ltd v Okotoks Ltd* [2013] EWCA Civ 672; [2014] FSR 11.
3 *British Shorinji Kempo Federation's Trade Mark Application* [2014] EWHC 285 (Ch).
4 *J Portugal Ramos Vinhos SA v Adega Cooperativa de Borba CRL* (C-629/17) EU:C:2018:988; [2019] ETMR 14. See also the 'Canary Wharf' mark refused in *Canary Wharf Group Plc v Comptroller General of Patents, Designs and Trade Marks* [2015] EWHC 1588 (Ch); [2015] FSR 34.

Assessing descriptiveness

4.29 As with the 1(b) exclusion, a mark must be assessed under 1(c) by reference to the goods and services for which it is registered and from the point of view of the average consumer: see *POSTKANTOOR*. As noted in relation to exclusion 1(b), the CJEU in *MATRATZEN* held that a national mark which would be descriptive in a language not used in that Member State would not necessarily be descriptive in that country and could be registrable (see para **4.13** above).

Generic marks—s 3(1)(d); Art 7(1)(d)

4.30 The exclusion under 1(d) relates to marks which:

> '… consist exclusively of signs or indications which have become customary in the current language or in the bona fide and established practices of the trade'

—ie trade marks that have become generic. This exclusion relates directly to the essential function of a trade mark: if a sign is used generally in language or trade, it cannot act to identify a particular originator.

4.31 It has already been seen that there is significant overlap between the 1(b) and 1(c) exclusions, and it is apparent that at least some marks that will be objectionable under 1(d) will also be objectionable under 1(b) or 1(c). However, the case law of the CJEU seeks to emphasise the specific characteristics of the 1(d) exclusion.

4.32 In *Merz & Krell*[1] the CJEU had to consider questions relating to an application to register the word BRAVO for use in relation to stationery. The Court accepted that BRAVO was a commonly used word in many languages of the Community but that it was not a work used specifically in relation to stationery. Consistent with the approach to all these exclusions, the Court ruled that the 1(d) exclusion could not be considered in the abstract but only by reference to the specific goods or services applied for. It stated that:

> 'It follows that Article 3(1)(d) of the Directive must be interpreted as only precluding registration of a trade mark where the signs or indications of which the mark is exclusively composed have become customary in the current language or in the bona fide and established practices of the trade to designate the goods or services in respect of which registration of that mark is sought.'

Thus it is not enough for 1(d) that the mark is a bland, non-distinctive word (which might suffice for a 1(b) objection). Rather, the characteristic must actually relate to those goods or services. As to words or signs which describe specific characteristics of the goods or services, the Court in *Merz & Krell* also limited the overlap between 1(c) and 1(d):

> 'It follows that Article 3(1)(d) of the Directive must be interpreted as meaning that it subjects refusal to register a trade mark to the sole condition that the signs or indications of which the trade mark is exclusively composed have become customary in the current language or in the bona fide and established practices of the trade to designate the goods or services in respect of which registration of that mark is sought. It is immaterial, when that provision is applied, whether the signs or indications in question describe the properties or characteristics of those goods or services.'

1 C-517/99 *Merz & Krell GmbH & Co* [2002] ETMR 21.

4.33 So what kind of words fall within 1(d)? It is somewhat difficult to identify hypothetically what kind of words may be generic rather than descriptive (though that is not to say a word cannot be both in certain cases). Some examples from the UK courts assist:

(a) In the *SPORK*[1] case, it was held that the word SPORK in relation to an item of plastic cutlery embodying both a fork and a spoon, had become generic in the catering business such that the trade mark proprietor could no longer protect the term.
(b) By contrast, in *Hormel*[2] the word SPAMBUSTER for email filtering services had not become generic. Here the deputy judge noted that whilst the word would have been understood by the public, it had not become a customarily used expression.

1 *D Green & Co (Stoke Newington) Ltd and Plastico Ltd v Regalzone Ltd* [2002] ETMR 22.
2 *Hormel Foods Corp v Antilles Landscape Investments NV* [2005] ETMR 54.

Acquired distinctiveness—s 3(1); Art 7(3)

4.34 Before moving on to examine the remaining objections, it is convenient at this point to consider the proviso to s 3(1), which makes clear that objections under 1(b), 1(c) or 1(d) can be overcome by proof of acquired distinctiveness.

The idea of acquired distinctiveness is that a mark which may not be inherently registrable may nonetheless, through use, become recognised by the consuming public as a guarantee of origin. If that occurs, the mark is able to fulfil the essential function of a trade mark and so is to be considered distinctive and hence registrable.

4.35 The effect of acquired distinctiveness is set out in the proviso to section 3(1) of the TMA 1994 as follows:

> 'Provided that, a trade mark shall not be refused registration by virtue of paragraph (b), (c) or (d) above if, before the date of application for registration, it has in fact acquired a distinctive character as a result of the use made of it.'

And similarly for the purposes of an EUTM, in Art 7(3) of the EUTMR as follows:

> 'paragraphs 1(b), (c) and (d) shall not apply if the trade ark has become distinctive in relation to the goods or services for which registration is requested in consequence of the use which has been made of it.'

4.36 The CJEU in *Windsurfing Chiemsee* set out in some detail what kind of evidence would be needed to establish acquired distinctiveness and the relevant threshold:

> '51. In assessing the distinctive character of a mark in respect of which registration has been applied for, the following may also be taken into account: the market share held by the mark; how intensive, geographically widespread and long-standing use of the mark has been; the amount invested by the undertaking in promoting the mark; the proportion of the relevant class of persons who, because of the mark, identify goods as originating from a particular undertaking; and statements from chambers of commerce and industry or other trade and professional associations.
>
> 52. If, on the basis of those factors, the competent authority finds that the relevant class of persons, or at least a significant proportion thereof, identify goods as originating from a particular undertaking because of the trade mark, it must hold that the requirement for registering the mark laid down in Article 3(3) of the Directive is satisfied. However, the circumstances in which that requirement may be regarded as satisfied cannot be shown

> to exist solely by reference to general, abstract data such as predetermined percentages.
>
> 53. As regards the method to be used to assess the distinctive character of a mark in respect of which registration is applied for, Community law does not preclude the competent authority, where it has particular difficulty in that connection, from having recourse, under the conditions laid down by its own national law, to an opinion poll as guidance for its judgment (see, to that effect, Case C-210/96 *Gut Springenheide and Tusky* [1998] ECR I-4657, paragraph 37).'

The principles from *Windsurfing Chiemsee* were applied to trade marks generally in *Phillips v Remington.*[1] In *HAVE A BREAK*[2] the CJEU confirmed it was possible for a mark to acquire distinctive character where used together with another mark. In *Nestle v Cadbury*[3] the High Court sought further clarification from the CJEU as to what exactly the applicant needs to show in order to demonstrate acquired distinctiveness. The Court asked whether it is enough for the applicant 'to prove that at the relevant date a significant proportion of the relevant class of persons recognised the mark and associated it with the applicant's goods in the sense that, if they were to be asked who marketed goods bearing that mark, they would identify the applicant', or whether the applicant must instead, 'prove that a significant proportion of the relevant class of persons relied upon the mark (as opposed to any other trade marks which might also be present) as indicating the origin of the goods'. In the Court's own view, the answer is that it ought to be the latter of those two alternatives. In other words, that the test should be about how (or whether) the mark is actually relied upon by consumers as a badge of origin, not simply whether consumers recognise the mark as being associated with a particular maker. See para **4.39** below.

1 C-299/99 *Koninklijke Philips Electronics NV v Remington Consumer Products Ltd* [2002] ETMR 81.
2 C-353/03 *Société des Produits Nestlé SA v Mars UK Ltd* [2005] ETMR 96.
3 *Société des Produits Nestlé SA v Cadbury UK Ltd* [2014] EWHC 16 (Ch); [2014] FSR 17.

Where must distinctiveness be acquired?

4.37 Distinctiveness must be proved in the area where the exclusion is said to operate. Thus for Member States with two language areas, acquired distinctiveness must be proved in the area in which the mark is non-distinctive: *EUROPOLIS.*[1] For EUTMs, a mark that is descriptive in one language will need to be shown to have acquired distinctiveness in the territories in which that language is spoken.

1 C-108/05 *Bovemij Verzekeringen NV v Benelux-Merkenbureau* [2007] ETMR 29.

When must distinctiveness be acquired?

4.38 The language of s 3(1) of the TMA 1994 and the corresponding provisions in Art 7(3) of the EUMTR make clear the distinctiveness must be acquired before the mark is applied for. This was confirmed by the Court of Justice in *PURE DIGITAL.*[1]

1 C-542/07 *Imagination Technologies Limited v OHIM* [2010] ETMR 19.

Particular kinds of marks

4.39 In *Phillips v Remington*, after approving the guidance given in *Windsurfing Chiemsee*, the CJEU confirmed that shape of goods marks could acquire distinctive character, albeit that it would not be easy to prove this. It said:

> '65. In the light of those considerations, the answer to the third question must be that, where a trader has been the only supplier of particular goods to the market, extensive use of a sign which consists of the shape of those goods may be sufficient to give the sign a distinctive character for the purposes of Article 3(3) of the Directive in circumstances where, as a result of that use, a substantial proportion of the relevant class of persons associates that shape with that trader and no other undertaking or believes that goods of that shape come from that trader.
>
> However, it is for the national court to verify that the circumstances in which the requirement under that provision is satisfied are shown to exist on the basis of specific and reliable data, that the presumed expectations of an average consumer of the category of goods or services in question, who is reasonably well-informed and reasonably observant and circumspect, are taken into account and that the identification, by the relevant class of persons, of the product as originating from a given undertaking is as a result of the use of the mark as a trade mark.'

In *Nestlé v Cadbury*[1] the High Court referred questions to the CJEU on the issue of the acquired distinctiveness of the 'Kit-Kat' four-fingered chocolate bar. Following clarification from the CJEU, the Court held that in order to demonstrate acquired distinctiveness, one has to show that a significant proportion of the relevant consumers perceive the goods or services as originating from a particular undertaking because of the shape in question, not just that they recognise the shape and associate it with the undertaking.[2] Even so, a shape mark may acquire distinctiveness in its own right even where it is used alongside a word or figurative mark: see Mondelez.[3]

1 *Societé des Produits Nestle SA v Cadbury UK Ltd* [2014] EWHC 16 (Ch); [2014] FSR 17.

2 *Société des Produits Nestlé SA v Cadbury UK Ltd* [2016] EWHC 50 (Ch); [2016] 4 All ER 1081 (upheld on appeal: [2017] EWCA Civ 358; [2018] 2 All ER 39).
3 *Mondelez UK Holdings & Services Ltd v EUIPO / Société des produits Nestlé SA*, Case T-112/13 (General Court) [2017] ETMR 13.

Marks for the shape of the goods—s 3(2); Art 7(1)(e)

4.40 Under s 1(1) of the TMA 1994 and Art 4 of the EUTMR a sign which consists of the shape of goods and their packaging is prima facie registrable as a trade mark provided it is capable of fulfilling the essential function of identifying the origin of the goods. However, certain shapes are expressly excluded from registration.

Section 3(2) of the TMA 1994 and Art 7(1)(e) of the EUTMR provide that a sign shall not be registered if it consists exclusively of:

> '(a) the shape which results from the nature of the goods themselves,
> (b) the shape of the goods which is necessary to obtain a technical result, or
> (c) the shape which gives substantial value to the goods.'

4.41 The Court of Appeal briefly considered the first of these three 'shape' exclusions in *Philips v Remington.*[1] Philips had attempted to register the shape of its three-headed rotary shaver. Aldous LJ, upholding Jacob J's view that this ground of exclusion was a narrow one, observed that it was difficult to envisage what kind of shapes would be excluded on this ground beyond those occurring naturally. He gave as an example a sign which consisted of the shape of a banana for fruit.

This particular category of shape exclusion has not been considered by the General Court or by the CJEU. However, Aldous LJ's view appears to be correct. If the shape of goods is prima facie registrable as explicitly stated in s 1(1) and Art 4, then this exclusion should be confined to situations in which the shape sought to be registered is the only shape the goods can or will take. Save at a superficial level, it is hard to see how the shape of any manufactured product can be said to result from the nature of the goods as opposed to their design. For example, a simple shape for a bottle could be said to result from the nature of the goods to the extent that it needs to be a hollow solid object with some kind of lid and preferably a flat base, but the better view is that the nature of a bottle, being a container for liquids, need not take any particular shape, and so this exclusion would not apply. Of course, the bottle shape might well not be registrable due to lack of distinctive character, but that is a separate consideration. Note that for all of the 3(2) exclusions, where a sign includes some non-shape element such as colour (eg in red soles for shoes), it will not consist 'exclusively' of a shape and so cannot fall foul of these provisions: see *Louboutin*.[2]

1 [1999] RPC 809.
2 *Louboutin v Van Haren Schoenen BV* (C-163/16) EU:C:2018:423, [2018] ETMR 31.

4.42 The CJEU considered the second of the three 'shape' exclusions (shape necessary for technical result) in *Philips v Remington.*[1] Recalling *Windsurfing Chiemsee,* the Court acknowledged that the scope of the shape exclusions under Art 7 had to be considered in light of their underlying policy. In the case of this particular exclusion, the underlying policy was to prevent the monopolisation via trade mark rights of a technical solution. Thus the Court ruled as follows (referring to the equivalent provisions in the Directive):

> '83. Where the essential functional characteristics of the shape of a product are attributable solely to the technical result, Article 3(1)(e), second indent, precludes registration of a sign consisting of that shape, even if that technical result can be achieved by other shapes.
>
> 84. In the light of those considerations, the answer to the fourth question must be that Article 3(1)(e), second indent, of the Directive must be interpreted to mean that a sign consisting exclusively of the shape of a product is unregistrable by virtue thereof if it is established that the essential functional features of that shape are attributable only to the technical result. Moreover, the ground for refusal or invalidity of registration imposed by that provision cannot be overcome by establishing that there are other shapes which allow the same technical result to be obtained.'

1 [2003] Ch 159; [2002] ETMR 81. This was a preliminary reference on points arising during the English Court of Appeal proceedings.

4.43 The CJEU also considered the shape exclusions in the *Lego*[1] case. The Court held that a shape having a technical function was excluded even though other shapes could be used to achieve the same function. Further, in relation to identification of the essential characteristics the Court held that the perception of the average consumer was not decisive. Other relevant evidence such as patent relating to the product could be taken into account. The shape exclusion came under scrutiny by the CJEU following a reference in *Nestlé v Cadbury.*[2] In that case the High Court asked whether the exclusion takes effect where the shape mark comprises a combination of elements, some of which arise from the nature of the goods themselves (the overall slab shape of a Kit-Kat bar) and some of which are necessary to obtain a technical result (the position, length and depth of the grooves, and their number). The CJEU held that at least one of the grounds for refusal of registration has to be fully applicable to the shape at issue.[3] The Court also held that 'technical result' must be interpreted as referring only to the manner in which the goods function, not the way they are manufactured.

1 C-48/09 *Lego Juris A/S v OHIM* [2010] ETMR 63.
2 *Societé des Produits Nestle SA v Cadbury UK Ltd* [2014] EWHC 16 (Ch); [2014] FSR 17.
3 *Société des Produits Nestlé SA v Cadbury UK Ltd* (C-215/14) [2015] ETMR 50; [2016] FSR 8.

4.44 The third 'shape' exclusion (shape adding substantial value) was considered by Kitchin J in *MAGIC TREE*.[1] The claimant had registered as a trade mark the shape of its 'magic tree' air fresheners, the shape being a representation of a pine tree which was manufactured form cardboard imbued with a particular scent. The defendant began manufacturing similar products and defended itself against the claimant's suit relying *inter alia* on s 3(2)(c). Kitchin J referred to *Philips v Remington*[2] and held that for this exclusion to operate, 'value' must be added by the shape of the goods themselves and not from advertising or marketing that makes the goods attractive. Further, the value added by the shape must be 'substantial value': this will only be the case where the goods with the shape in question have a high value relative to other equivalent goods without the same shape. It is not enough merely that the shape is designed to be attractive to consumers. The defence based on s 3(2)(c) was dismissed. In contrast, in *London Taxi*[3] it was held that the shape of London taxi cabs added substantial value to those goods.

1 *Julius Sämann Ltd v Tetrosyl Ltd* [2006] ETMR 75.
2 Both the ECJ and the Court of Appeal [1999] RPC 809.
3 *London Taxi Corp Ltd (t/a London Taxi Co) v Frazer-Nash Research Ltd* [2017] EWCA Civ 1729; [2018] FSR 7.

Marks contrary to policy or morality—s 3(3)(a); Art 7(1)(f)

4.45 Section 3(3)(a) and Art 7(1)(f) exclude from registration marks which are 'contrary to public policy or to accepted principles of morality'.

The legislative intention behind this exclusion seems clear: if registration of a trade mark would offend the public in some way, it ought to be refused. However, there is little guidance as to the basis on which registration might be refused on this ground: neither the recitals to the EUTMR nor those to the Directive provide any assistance.

4.46 The only case to have reached the CFI (now the General Court) on appeal from OHIM is *INTERTOPS*.[1] The trade mark was registered for sports betting services. The opponent claimed the mark was objectionable under Art 7(1)(f) because the applicant did not have the licence to provide such services (as required in the parties' native Germany) and had, moreover, been banned from offering such services by the German courts. The CFI held that it was the trade mark itself that must be objectionable and not the conduct or anticipated conduct of the applicant in using the mark. The mark itself was not objectionable merely because the applicant would be acting illegally if it used the mark in connection with the services for which it had been applied.

The *INTERTOPS* case is helpful in so far as it confirms that it is the intrinsic qualities of the mark that must be assessed under s 3(3)(a) and Art 7(1)(f). The CJEU has subsequently added that defects in the mark such as failure to specify precisely enough the goods and/or services are not in themselves matters contrary to public policy.[2]

1 T-140/02 *Sportwetten GmbH Gera v OHIM* [2006] ETMR 15.
2 *Sky Plc v SkyKick UK Ltd* (C-371/18) EU:C:2020:45; [2020] ETMR 24.

4.47 In *SCREW YOU*[1] the OHIM Grand Board of Appeal considered an appeal for registration of that mark for a wide range of goods including *inter alia* sunglasses, sporting goods, condoms, sex toys, sporting goods and alcoholic beverages. Noting that rejection of a mark did not mean that the sign could not be used by the applicant, the Grand Board explained that the objection was a balancing exercise between freedom of expression and preventing offence to others. The Grand Board explained that:

> '21 In deciding whether a trade mark should be barred from registration on grounds of public policy or morality, the Office must apply the standards of a reasonable person with normal levels of sensitivity and tolerance. The Office should not refuse to register a trade mark which is only likely to offend a small minority of exceptionally puritanical citizens. Similarly, it should not allow a trade mark on the register simply because it would not offend the equally small minority at the other end of the spectrum who find even gross obscenity acceptable. Some people are easily offended; others are totally unshockable. The Office must assess the mark by reference to the standards and values of ordinary citizens who fall between those two extremes. It is also necessary to consider the context in which the mark is likely to be encountered, assuming normal use of the mark in connection with the goods and services covered by the application. If the goods are of a type that are only sold in licensed sex shops, a more relaxed attitude may be appropriate. If the goods are likely to be advertised on prime-time television or worn in the street with the trade mark prominently displayed, a stricter approach may be justified. It is also necessary to bear in mind that, while broad-minded adults may enjoy bawdy humour in a particular context,

> they might not wish to be exposed to material with explicit sexual content when walking down the street or watching television in the company of their children or elderly parents.'

The mark was rejected for the majority of the goods applied for but permitted for condoms, contraceptives and various goods sold in sex shops on the basis that customers of such goods would be less likely to be offended than the public at large.

1 *Kenneth (trading as Screw You)'s Application* [2007] ETMR 7.

4.48 Further guidance may be gleaned from a number of decisions in the UK by various Appointed Persons. A useful summary of the principles to be derived from a number of English and some European cases is provided by the decision of the Appointed Person in *FCUK*:[1]

> '(1) The applicability of s 3(3)(a) depends on the intrinsic qualities of the mark itself and not on circumstances relating to the conduct of the applicant (*Durferrit*[2] at [76]; *Sportwetten*[3] at [27]–[29]).
> (2) As with any other absolute ground of objection, the applicability of s 3(3)(a) is to be assessed as at the date of application (*Ghazilian*[4] at [44]).
> (3) Section 3(3)(a) should be interpreted and applied consistently with Art 10 ECHR. It follows that registration should be refused only where this is justified by a pressing social need and is proportionate to the legitimate aim pursued. Furthermore, any real doubt as to the applicability of the objection should be resolved by upholding the right to freedom of expression and thus by permitting the registration (*Basic Trademark's Application*[5] at [3]–[6]).
> (4) Section 3(3)(a) must be objectively applied. The personal views of the tribunal are irrelevant (*Ghazilian* at [31]; *Basic Trademark's Application* at [8], [23]; *Stephens v Avery*[6] at 454B).
> (5) While s 3(3)(a) may apply to a mark whose use would not be illegal, the legality or otherwise of use of the mark is a relevant consideration (*Masterman* at 104 11. 16–17, 38–40).
> (6) For s 3(3)(a) to apply, there must be a generally accepted moral principle which use of the mark would plainly contravene (*Ghazilian* at [20]).
> (7) Mere offence to a section of the public, in the sense that that section of the public would consider the mark distasteful, is not enough for s 3(3)(a) to apply (*Masterman* at 103 11. 28–43; *Ghazilian* at [20]).

(8) Section 3(3)(a) does apply if the use of the mark would justifiably cause outrage, or would be the subject of justifiable censure, amongst an identifiable section of the public as being likely significantly to undermine current religious, family or social values (*Ghazilian* at [30]; *Scranage*[7] at [8]).

(9) In the case of a word mark, it is necessary to consider the applicability of s 3(3)(a) on the basis of any usage that the public makes of the word or words of which the mark is comprised. Thus the slang meaning of a word may lead to an objection even if its normal meaning does not (*Dick Lexic*[8] at [8]).

(10) A mark which does not proclaim an opinion, or contain an incitement or convey an insult is less likely to be objectionable than one that does (*Dick Lexic* at [10]; *Basic Trade mark* at [11]).

(11) Different considerations apply to different categories of marks (*Basic Trade mark* at [12]).'

1 *Woodman v French Connection Ltd* [2007] ETMR 8.
2 *Durferrit GmbH v OHIM* (T-224/01) [2003] ECR II-1589.
3 *Sportwetten GmbH Gera* (T-140/02) [2006] ETMR 15.
4 *Ghazilian's Trade Mark Application* [2002] RPC 33.
5 *Basic Trademark's Application* [2006] ETMR 24.
6 *Stephens v Avery* [1988] Ch 449.
7 *Scranage's TM Application* [2008] ETMR 43.
8 *Decision of the Fourth Board of Appeal*, R-111/2002-4, [2005] ETMR 99.

Deceptive trade marks—s 3(3)(b), Art 7(1)(g)

4.49 Section 3(3)(b) and Art 7(1)(g) preclude from registration, marks 'of such a nature as to deceive the public (for instance as to the nature, quality or geographical origin of the goods or services)'.

Once again, the fundamental legislative intention is easily discernible but the precise level of necessary deceit is not plain from the legislation.

4.50 The CJEU considered this exclusion in *ELIZABETH EMANUEL*.[1] Here, the eponymous fashion designer was well known and had sold her business, including the goodwill. When the company running her former business attempted to register her name as a trade mark, Ms Emanuel opposed registration on the grounds that the public would be deceived into believing she was connected with the business. The CJEU ruled that in these kinds of circumstances, the mark was not inherently deceptive because the characteristics and qualities of the clothes produced were unaffected by the change of ownership of the business. The Court noted that the national court could determine that in the circumstances the use of the mark was intended to deceive the public; nevertheless, that would be fraudulent trading rather than the result of the mark itself being deceptive.

The *ELIZABETH EMANUEL* decision provides guidance on how to draw the line between deceptive and non-deceptive marks, noting that there must be 'the existence of actual deceit or a sufficiently serious risk that the consumer will be deceived'. In *W.F. Gozze*[2] the CJEU rejected an allegation of deceptiveness brought on the basis that the proprietor of the mark was failing to ensure, by carrying out periodic quality controls at its licensees, that expectations regarding the quality which the public associates with the mark were being met.

1 C-259/04 *Elizabeth Florence Emanuel v Continental Shelf 128 Ltd* [2006] ETMR 56.
2 *W.F. Gozze Frottierweberei GmbH v Baumwollborse* (Case C-689/15).

4.51 The General Court considered the 1(g) exclusion in *IT@ MANPOWER*[1]—in which the opponent objected to OHIM registering the mark on the basis that it would be deceptive in so far as it was registered for goods and services *not* relating to 'manpower in the sector of information technology'. The mark was registered for a range of goods and services including but not limited to services that could be described as 'manpower in the sector of information technology'. The General Court upheld the OHIM Board of Appeal's finding that the meaning allegedly conveyed by the mark was not specific enough to deceive consumers as to the nature of the goods and services in question. In a sense this is a corollary of the finding that the mark was not descriptive. The focus is the nature of the mark and whether there is a serious risk of deception.

1 T-248/05 *HUP Uslugi Polska*, Court of First Instance, 24 September 2008, upheld by the CJEU in C-520/08, 24 September 2009.

Contrary to law—s 3(4)

4.52 Section 3(4) excludes from registration any mark 'if and to the extent that its use is prohibited in the United Kingdom by any enactment or rule of law or by any provision of Community law'.

This is a specific, narrow exclusion relating to words, phrases or devices the use of which is itself prohibited or restricted. This covers several possible situations:

(a) In relation to EUTMs there are specific exclusions relating to such words as geographical indicators under Art 7(1)(j) and 7(1)(k).
(b) In the UK, marks which contain a false description of the goods or services in question are unlawful under the Trade Descriptions Act 1968. There is a certain amount of overlap here with deceptive marks.

(c) Certain words or phrases are contrary to the wider criminal or civil law, perhaps due to racist or violent connotations.

Emblems—ss 3(5), 4, 57 and 58; Art 7(1)(h) and 7(1)(i)

4.53 By a combination of ss 3(5), 4, 57 and 58, the registration of certain emblems, armorial bearings and the like are restricted. This is a combination of domestic practice and the requirements of article 6*ter* of the Paris Convention. Similar, though less specific restrictions are found in Art 7(1)(h)–(i) of the EUTMR.

4.54 The general principles guiding applications for emblems are discussed by the CJEU in *American Clothing*.[1] The applicant applied to register a mark consisting of a maple leaf with the letters RW written below in a plain font for various goods mostly relating to clothing and luggage. The mark was refused under Art 7(1)(h) on the basis that the mark suggested a link with Canada.

The Court discussed the differing essential functions of State emblems and trade marks, noting that the essential function of the former includes 'identifying a State and … of representing its sovereignty and unity'. State emblems are not registered as such (but rather merely communicated to WIPO by the relevant state) and can not be invalidated.

The Court analysed the position as follows:

> '47 As regards the arguments submitted by American Clothing on the interpretation of the expression 'any imitation from a heraldic point of view' in Article 6ter(1)(a) of the Paris Convention, let me start by observing that that provision prohibits the registration and use of a State emblem not only as a trade mark, but also as an element of a trade mark. The protection granted to emblems is therefore, in this regard, also very broad. Furthermore, the last part of that provision also contributes to guaranteeing broad protection to State emblems, in so far as it prohibits the imitation of the emblem in addition to prohibiting its exact replication.
>
> 48 However, the prohibition of the imitation of an emblem applies only to imitations of it from a heraldic perspective, that is to say, those which contain heraldic connotations which distinguish the emblem from other signs. Thus, the protection against any imitation from a heraldic point of view refers not to the image as such, but to its heraldic expression. It is therefore necessary, in order to determine whether the trade mark contains an imitation from a heraldic point of view, to consider the heraldic description of the emblem at issue.

> 49 It follows that American Clothing's contention that the geometric description of the emblem must be taken into account cannot be accepted. First, such an interpretation runs counter to the approach set out at paragraph 47 of this judgment, according to which emblems benefit from a wide degree of protection, since the inherently precise nature of a graphic description would lead to the emblem being refused protection under Article 6ter(1)(a) of the Paris Convention in the event of any slight discrepancy between the two descriptions. Secondly, the case of graphic conformity with the emblem used by the trade mark is already covered by the first part of that provision, so that the expression 'any imitation from a heraldic point of view' must be different in its scope.
>
> 50 Thus, a trade mark which does not exactly reproduce a State emblem can nevertheless be covered by Article 6ter(1)(a) of the Paris Convention, where it is perceived by the relevant public, in the present case the average consumer, as imitating such an emblem.
>
> …
>
> Lastly, as mentioned in paragraph 47 of this judgment, Article 6ter(1)(a) of the Paris Convention applies not only to trade marks but also to elements of marks which include or imitate State emblems. It is sufficient, therefore, for a single element of the trade mark applied for to represent such an emblem or an imitation thereof for that mark to be refused registration as a Community trade mark. Since the Court of First Instance held that the maple leaf represented on the trade mark applied for is an imitation of the Canadian emblem from the heraldic point of view, it therefore did not need to examine the overall impression produced by the mark, since Article 6ter(1)(a) of the Paris Convention does not require the trade mark as a whole to be taken into account.'

1 C-202/08 *American Clothing Associates NV v OHIM* [2010] ETMR 3.

Bad faith—s 3(6); Art 59(1)(b)

4.55 Section 3(6) of the Act reads as follows:

> 'A trade mark shall not be registered if or to the extent that the application is made in bad faith.'

Bad faith is an absolute ground for refusal of registration. Article 59(1)(b) of the EUTMR appears to have the same effect:

'A Community trade mark shall be declared invalid on application to the Office or on the basis of a counterclaim in infringement proceedings: … b) where the applicant was acting in bad faith when he filed the application for the trade mark.'

The CJEU has made clear that bad faith is to be treated as an autonomous concept of EU law that should have uniform interpretation across the Community.[1]

1 *Malaysia Dairy Industries Pte Ltd v Ankenaevnet for Patenter og Varemaerker* (C-320/12) [2013] ETMR 36.

4.56 The law relating to bad faith was considered by the CJEU, in the 'Chocolate bunnies' case of *Lindt*[1]. The CJEU ruled that:

'In order to determine whether the applicant is acting in bad faith …, the national court must take into consideration all the relevant factors specific to the particular case which pertained at the time of filing the application for registration of the sign as a Community trade mark, in particular:

- the fact that the applicant knows or must know that a third party is using, in at least one Member State, an identical or similar sign for an identical or similar product capable of being confused with the sign for which registration is sought;
- the applicant's intention to prevent that third party from continuing to use such a sign; and
- the degree of legal protection enjoyed by the third party's sign and by the sign for which registration is sought.'

In *Och-Ziff*[2] Arnold J held that the CJEU's analysis in *Lindt* was consistent with his earlier exposition of the law in *Hotel Cipriani*[3] in which he said:

'189. In my judgment it follows from the foregoing considerations that it does not constitute bad faith for a party to apply to register a Community trade mark merely because he knows that third parties are using the same mark in relation to identical goods or services, let alone where the third parties are using similar marks and/or are using them in relation to similar goods or services. The applicant may believe that he has a superior right to registration and use of the mark. For example, it is not uncommon for prospective claimants who intend to sue a prospective defendant for passing off first to file an application for registration to strengthen their position. Even if the applicant does not believe that he has a superior right to registration and use of the mark, he may still believe that he is entitled to registration. The applicant may not intend to seek to enforce the trade mark against the third parties and/or may know or believe that the third parties would have a defence to a claim for infringement on one of the bases discussed above. In particular, the applicant may wish to secure exclusivity in the bulk of the Community while knowing that third parties have local rights in certain areas. An applicant who proceeds on the basis explicitly provided for in Article 107 can hardly be said to be abusing the Community trade mark system.

190. Nor in my judgment does it amount to bad faith if what the applicant seeks to register is not the actual trade mark he himself uses but merely the distinctive part of his trade mark, the other part of which is descriptive or otherwise non-distinctive, and third parties are also using the distinctive part with different non-distinctive elements. It is commonplace for applicants to apply to register the distinctive elements of their trade marks, and with good reason. Moreover, in such a case the applicant would be unlikely to have an Article 9(1)(a) claim against the third parties, yet as noted above counsel for the Defendants accepted that the ability to make an Article 9(1)(b) claim was not enough to constitute bad faith.'

1 C-529/07 *Chocoladenfabriken Lindt & Sprüngli AG v Franz Haüswirth GmbH* [2009] ETMR 56.

2 *Och-Ziff Management Europe Ltd and Oz Management LP v Och Capital LLP, Union Investment Management Ltd and Ochocki* [2011] ETMR 1.

3 *Hotel Cipriani SRL v Cipriani (Grosvenor Street) Ltd* [2009] RPC 9. For Arnold J's later summary of the position under UK law, see *Walton International v Verweij Fashions* [2018] ETMR 34 at [186]–[187].

4.57 Thus it can be seen that in certain circumstances, there is a tension between the 'first to file' system of European trade mark law and preventing legitimate competition from existing users of a certain, distinctive, mark. This is where accusations of bad faith registrations usually become significant. For example, in the *Lindt* case itself, the parties marketed prima facie similar foil-wrapped chocolate Easter rabbits with red bows tied around them. Lindt attempted to register the image of one of these rabbits as a trade mark: it was the first manufacturer to do so, but one can see why this action was arguably an attempt to restrict legitimate competition. In *Lindt* the applicant's knowledge of a possible likelihood of confusion was one of the factors relevant to the assessment of their subjective state of mind for the purposes of considering bad faith. However, in *Koton* the CJEU made clear that likelihood of confusion is a separate concept of trade mark law and is not a necessary (or indeed sufficient) ingredient for a finding of bad faith, even if it may sometimes be relevant to the assessment.[1] In *Koton* the CJEU explained that bad faith is to be assessed objectively, asking whether the applicant's intention was subjectively dishonest taking into account 'all the factual circumstances relevant to the particular case'. The Court considered *Lindt* and other previous cases, and clarified that bad faith applies:

> '…where it is apparent from relevant and consistent indicia that the proprietor of an EU trade mark has filed the application for registration of that mark not with the aim of engaging fairly in competition but with the intention of undermining, in a manner inconsistent with honest practices, the interests of third parties, or with the intention of obtaining, without even targeting a specific third party, an exclusive right for purposes other than those falling within the functions of a trade mark, in particular the essential function of indicating origin recalled in the previous paragraph of this judgment.'

1 *Koton Magazacilik Tekstil Sanayi ve Ticaret v EUIPO* (Case C-104/18 P).

4.58 The Court of Appeal and European jurisprudence on bad faith was applied by Henderson J in *32Red Plc v WHG (International) Ltd.*[1] In that case, the claimant had applied to register certain marks relating to the name 32Red, knowing that the defendant had been using a similar mark. The claimant's aim was to bolster its position in the litigation. The defendant alleged that the UK mark sought by the claimant was invalid for bad faith, The judge rejected that suggestion, saying that the CJEU had been 'at pains' to point out that the claimant's approach did not necessarily constitute bad faith, and adding, 'In my view the application for registration of the UK mark was made for good tactical reasons of this nature'.

1 *32Red Plc v WHG (International) Ltd* [2011] EWHC 62 (Ch); [2011] ETMR 21, (21 January 2011) (and not doubted on appeal). See also *Trump International Ltd v DTTM Operations LLC* [2019] EWHC 769 (Ch); [2019] FSR 28.

4.59 Under UK national law the application for registration must state that the mark either *is* being used by the applicant or with his consent, for the goods and services specified in the application, or that there is a *bona fide* intention that it should be so used.[1] Lack of bona fide intention to use the mark may therefore pave the way for an allegation that the application has been made in bad faith. In contrast, there is no equivalent requirement in the EUTMR, thus the lack of such intention does not on its own amount to bad faith (at least for EUTMs): *Jaguar Land Rover.*[2] Furthermore, on a reference from the UK court in *Skykick*[3] the CJEU has held[4] that s 32(3) TMA 1994 is not incompatible with the Directive, but that while such procedural provisions of national law may be allowable they must not introduce grounds of invalidity not found in the Directive; however, non-compliance can nonetheless constitute evidence of bad faith. By contrast, the CJEU has also indicated that an application for a mark may be found to be made in bad faith if the applicant has no intention of using the mark but simply wants to use it secure a top-level domain name,[5] although in that case the 'bad faith' provision in question was contained in a regulation relating to domain names (Regulation (EC) 874/2004).

1 TMA 1994 s 32(3).
2 *Jaguar Land Rover Ltd v Bombardier Recreational Products Inc* [2016] EWHC 3266 (Ch); [2017] FSR 20.
3 *Sky Plc v Skykick UK Ltd* [2018] EWHC 943 (Ch); [2018] RPC 12.
4 (C-371/18) EU:C:2020:45; [2020] 1 WLUK 242.
5 *Internetportal und Marketing GmbH v Schlicht* (Case C-569/08) [2011] Bus. LR 726; [2010] ETMR 48, CJEU (Second Chamber) 3 June 2010.

Chapter 5

Relative grounds for refusal of registration; trade mark functions; honest concurrent use

INTRODUCTION

5.01 This chapter deals with:

- The relative grounds on which a mark may be refused registration.
- The concept of 'trade mark functions', to which the cases now commonly refer.
- The status of the concept of 'honest concurrent use'.

5.02 As set out below, the relative grounds for a refusal to register a mark are concerned with whether that mark conflicts with an earlier right. That earlier right might be either: (a) an earlier trade mark registration or earlier application for registration of such a mark; or (b) certain other earlier rights. This is a matter of the highest importance. Indeed, in many cases the application of one of the relative grounds for refusal is a more fundamental problem for an applicant than the application of one of the absolute grounds in that a trade mark which conflicts with the absolute grounds can nevertheless be used and can acquire a distinctive character and become registrable. By contrast, a mark which conflicts with an earlier right may be incapable of being used or registered.

Overlap with infringement provisions

5.03 There are a number of similarities in the wording of the provisions dealing with the relative grounds for refusal and of those dealing with infringement.[1] Both sets of provisions require consideration of concepts such as 'identical', 'similar', 'a likelihood of confusion', 'reputation', 'unfair advantage' and 'trade mark functions'. For this reason, many of the cases referred to in this chapter are infringement cases. Infringement itself is considered in **Chapter 14**.

1 In the present context, the court compares the mark of the applicant for registration with the earlier mark. In the infringement context, the court compares the allegedly infringing sign with the registered mark it is said to infringe.

References to legislation

5.04 As has been seen, the law governing UK trade marks and EUTMs is derived from EU Council Directive 2015/2436 ('the Directive'), which updates and replaces the earlier Directive 2008/95/EC. Accordingly, many of the cases dealing with the issues considered in this chapter refer to provisions of the Directive rather than to those of the Trade Marks Act 1994 ('TMA 1994') or of the EU Trade Marks Regulation 2017/1001 ('EUTMR')[1]. This chapter will identify the relevant provisions by reference to each of the Directive, the TMA 1994 and the EUTMR.

1 Replacing Regulation (EU) 207/2009.

CONFLICTS WITH EARLIER REGISTERED TRADE MARKS

Grounds for opposing registration

5.05 The owner of an earlier registered trade mark ('the earlier trade mark') may oppose the registration of a later trade mark ('the later mark') or if the later mark has already been registered may seek to invalidate that registration on four bases[1]—these are where:

- the later mark is identical to the earlier trade mark and the specified goods and services are identical to those of that earlier trade mark;[2] or
- the later mark is identical to the earlier trade mark and the specified goods and services are similar to those of the earlier mark such that there is a likelihood of confusion;[3] or
- the later mark is similar to the earlier trade mark and the goods and services are identical or similar to those of the earlier trade mark such that there exists a likelihood of confusion;[4] or
- the later mark is identical or similar to the earlier mark and the earlier trade mark benefits from a reputation and the use of the later mark without due cause would take unfair advantage of, or be detrimental to, the distinctive character or repute of the earlier registered mark.[5]

1 Under the proposed Draft Regulation 2013/0088(COD) and Draft Directive 2013/0089(COD) there was to be an additional relative ground of opposition. This would be where the mark applied for is liable to be confused with an earlier trade mark protected outside the EU, provided that at the date of the application the earlier mark was still in genuine use, and the applicant was acting in bad faith.

2 Directive Art 5(1)(a); TMA 1994 s 5(1); EUTMR Art 8(1)(a).
3 Directive Art 5(1)(b); TMA 1994 s 5(2)(a); EUTMR Art 8(1)(b).
4 Directive Art 5(1)(b); TMA 1994 s 5(2)(b); EUTMR Art 8(1)(b).
5 Directive Art 5(3); TMA 1994 s 5(3); EUTMR Art 8(5). The reason for the difference in wording between the Directive and EUTMR on the one hand, and the TMA 1994 on the other is discussed at para **5.65** below.

Harm to the trade mark function

5.06 Although it is not expressly referred to in the legislation, CJEU case law has effectively imported an additional consideration. This is whether use of the later mark harms or would be liable to harm one of the 'functions' of the mark (including the essential function of indicating origin).[1] This line of authority appears to represent a retreat from the position that protection is 'absolute' in the case of identical marks and identical goods or services.[2] The meaning and significance of the functions of a trade mark will be considered in greater detail later in this chapter.

1 See the progression through C-2/00 *Michael Hölterhoff v Ulrich Freiesleben*, [2002] ECR I-4187; C-206/01 *Arsenal Football Club v Reed* [2003] ETMR 19; C-48/05 *Adam Opel AG v Autec AG* [2007] ECR I-01017; C-236/08 *Google France Sarl v Louis Vuitton Malletier SA* (and two joined cases) [2010] ETMR 30; C-323/09 *Interflora Inc & anor v Marks & Spencer plc & anor*, 24 March 2011.
2 The 'absolute' protection having previously been thought to be enshrined in the terms of recital 11 to Directive 2008/95/EC, and recital 11 to the EUTMR.

Applications for registration of an earlier mark

5.07 For these purposes, references to an earlier trade mark include *applications* for registration of a mark which would be an earlier trade mark if granted.[1] Hence an applicant for a mark that would be an earlier trade mark may oppose registration of a later mark or, as the case may be, challenge the validity of the registration of a later mark.

1 Directive Art 5(2)(c); TMA 1994 s 6(2); EUTMR Art 8(2)(b).

Issues arising

5.08 In order to assess fully whether one (or more) of the grounds set out above in para **5.05** for challenging registration of a mark applies, it is necessary to examine the meaning of the following terms:

- earlier trade mark;
- identity of marks;
- similarity of marks;
- identity of goods or services;
- similarity of goods or services;

- likelihood of confusion;
- marks with a reputation;
- use with/without due cause;
- taking unfair advantage of the distinctive character or repute; and
- detriment to distinctive character or repute.

5.09 Although, for convenience, these terms are considered separately, they often overlap and need to be considered together. Indeed, the Court of Appeal in *Direct Line* expressly rejected what it referred to as the 'stack' approach—whereby each requirement is considered as if it was a separate watertight compartment to be fulfilled satisfactorily before the next can be considered. It approved instead the 'soup' approach—whereby each of the questions was thrown together in a mix, and were viewed together.[1] This reflects the practice of UKIPO and of the EUIPO.

1 *Direct Line v Esure* [2008] ETMR 77 per Arden LJ at [48].

Earlier trade mark

5.10 The first question to ask is whether there exist any earlier trade marks for the purposes of the TMA 1994 or the EUTMR. As set out below, these are earlier *registered* trade marks (or applications for such marks).

The UK position

5.11 Following Brexit, s 6 of the TMA 1994 identifies the following categories of earlier trade marks:

1 A UK registered trade mark or international trade mark (UK) which has a date of application earlier than that of the opposed mark, taking into account the effect of any claims to priority.
2 A comparable trade mark (EU)[1] or a trade mark registered pursuant to an application made under paragraph 25 of Schedule 2A to the TMA 1994 which has a valid claim to seniority of an earlier registered trade mark or protected international trade mark (UK) even where the earlier trade mark has been surrendered or its registration has expired.
3 A comparable trade mark (IR) or a trade mark registered pursuant to an application made under paragraph 28, 29 or 33 of Schedule 2B to the TMA 1994 which has a valid claim to seniority of an earlier registered trade mark or protected international trade mark (UK), even where the earlier trade mark has been surrendered or its registration has expired.
4 A registered trade mark or international trade mark (UK) which (i) prior to IP completion day has been converted from an EUTM

or international trade mark (EC), which itself had a valid claim to seniority of an earlier registered trade mark or protected international trade mark (UK) even where the earlier trade mark has been surrendered or its registration has expired, and (ii) accordingly has the same claim to seniority.

5 A trade mark that at the application date (or priority date where appropriate) was entitled to protection under the Paris Convention or WTO as a well-known trade mark.

1 Following Brexit (which for these purposes occurred at 11pm on 31 December 2020, known as 'IP completion day'), EUTMs are no longer in force in the UK, but have instead been automatically replaced in the UK by 'comparable trade marks (EU)' on the national register – see TMA 1994 Sch 2A. An equivalent process has occurred for international marks designating the EC, resulting in 'comparable trade marks (IR)' – see TMA 1994 Sch 2B.

The EUTM position

5.12 Article 8(2) of the EUTMR defines 'earlier trade marks' as comprising:

1 EU trade marks;
2 trade marks registered in a Member State (or the Benelux in the case of those countries);
3 trade marks registered under international arrangements (ie, as designations to International Registrations) having effect in a Member State (including the Benelux) or in the Community;
4 applications for any of the marks covered by 1–3 above, subject to their registration; and
5 trade marks that at the application date (or priority date where appropriate) were well known in a Member State in the sense of Article 6*bis* of the Paris Convention.

Identity of marks

5.13 Having identified the earlier (registered) trade mark (or application for such a mark), one must then ask whether it is identical to the mark for which registration is sought.

5.14 In infringement proceedings the equivalent question is whether the 'sign' used by the alleged infringer is identical to the registered mark. In such cases, there can be scope for argument about what the 'sign' actually was. It may be, for example, that features that differ can be treated as part of a separate sign which do not, therefore, detract from the identity which might otherwise exist.[1] By contrast, in the context of proceedings to oppose the registration of a mark (or to invalidate an existing registration) the comparison is more straightforward because both the earlier trade mark and the later mark must be graphically represented on the register. Subject to this, the principles for determining whether marks (or a mark and a sign) are identical or similar are the same in both contexts.

1 See, for example, *Och-Ziff Management Europe Ltd v Och Capital LLP* [2010] EWHC 2599 at [42] et seq and *Samuel Smith Old Brewery (Tadcaster) v Philip Lee* [2011] EWHC 1879, Arnold J at [88]–[91]. For infringement generally, see **Chapter 14** below.

5.15 The test for identity of marks is a strict one. The case law shows that the marks must be identical in the normal sense of the word (ie, without additions or subtractions) or otherwise differ only in 'insignificant' ways that would go unnoticed by the average consumer.[1] For these purposes, the marks should be compared side by side, and small differences that might readily be overlooked if the marks were not alongside each other must nonetheless be taken into account.

An earlier black and white mark is not identical to the same mark in colour unless the differences in colour are insignificant. Similarly, an earlier mark in greyscale is not identical to the same mark in colour, or in black and white, unless the differences in colour or in contrast of shades are insignificant.[2]

1 C-291/00 *LTJ Diffusion SA v Sadas Vertbaudet SA* [2003] ETMR 83 and *Koninklijke Philips NV v Remington Consumer Products Ltd* [2005] FSR 17.

2 See the European Trade Mark and Design Network's *Common Communication on the Common Practice of the Scope of Protection of Black and White ('B&W') Marks*, 15 April 2014, p 2: 'Insignificant' means a difference that only a reasonably observant consumer will perceive on a side-by-side comparison of the marks. For more as regards the use of colour, and of black and white in relation to marks, see para **5.24**, and para **8.06**.

5.16 Equally, even if the only difference in the later mark is the inclusion of merely generic words, these will not be ignored. The comparison is strictly mark for mark. In infringement proceedings it may be possible to argue that the inclusion or omission of generic words is not significant—although such an argument failed in *Och-Ziff* with regard to the addition of the descriptive (or at least non-distinctive) word 'CAPITAL' to the mark 'Och'.[1]

1 *Och-Ziff* at [71].

Similarity of marks

5.17 If the later mark and the earlier trade mark (or, in an infringement case, the mark and the allegedly infringing sign) are not identical, the question will arise whether they are similar.

5.18 If the marks are neither identical nor similar, then registration cannot be refused on the basis of that earlier trade mark (or in the infringement context, there can be no infringement). This is the case regardless of the identity or similarity of the goods and services involved (as to which see below) and regardless of the size and extent of the reputation and distinctiveness of the earlier trade mark or whether it is well known.

5.19 Thus, in order to oppose registration of a later mark (or as the case may be, to obtain a declaration that an existing registration is invalid) the opponent must identify an earlier trade mark that has at least some similarities. The same applies in infringement proceedings.

The test for similarity

5.20 It would seem that the requirement of similarity is not particularly onerous. The Court of Appeal in *Direct Line* took the view that there was no minimum level of required similarity.[1]

1 *Direct Line v Esure* [2008] ETMR 77 per Arden LJ at [49]–[50].

5.21 It should also be borne in mind that the level of similarity which the owner of the earlier trade mark must demonstrate will differ depending on whether they are arguing that the marks are confusingly similar[1] or that the use of the later mark takes advantage of, or is detrimental to, the distinctive character or repute of the earlier mark.[2] In the former case, similarity is tied up with the concept of consumer confusion—the marks must be sufficiently similar that the average consumer will be confused into thinking that the goods or services come from the same undertaking or an economically-linked undertaking.[3] In the latter case the average consumer need only make such an associative link (although other considerations come into play instead – see **5.63** et seq).[4]

1 Ie, that Directive Art 5(1)(b), TMA 1994 s 5(2), EUTMR Art 8(1)(b) applies—see paras **5.36** et seq below.
2 Ie, that Directive Art 5(3)(a), TMA 1994 s 5(3), EUTMR Art 8(5) applies—see paras **5.63** et seq above.
3 C-36/97 *Canon Kabushiki Kaisha v Metro-Golden*-Mayer [1998] ECR I-5507.
4 C-408/01 *Adidas-Salomon AG and others v Fitnessworld Trading Ltd* [2003] ETMR 91.

The factors used to assess similarity

5.22 The main factors to consider are the following:

- the visual similarity of the marks;
- the aural similarity of the marks; and
- the conceptual similarity of the marks.

In considering these three factors, it is important to bear in mind that one cannot simply look at each factor in isolation. Instead, it is the overall impression of the marks that must be considered[1] taking into account the dominant and distinctive elements of the marks.[2] The average consumer is said to perceive a mark as a whole and not to analyse its various details.[3]

1 C–251/95 *Sabel BV v Puma AG* [1998] ETMR 1.
2 C-425/98 *Marca Mode* [2000] ECR I 64861. See also *Samuel Smith Old Brewery (Tadcaster) v Philip Lee* [2011] EWHC 1879, Arnold J at [77(d)], [91] and [105]–[106]. The overall approach to how the average consumer approaches the issues of the similarity between sign and mark and of the likelihood of confusion was summarised by the Court of Appeal in *Comic Enterprises Ltd v Twentieth Century Fox Film Corp* [2016] ETMR 22 at [31], referring in turn to *Specsavers International Healthcare Ltd v Asda Stores Ltd* [2012] FSR 19.
3 C-193/06 *Nestle v OHIM*, 20 September 2007, ECJ, and *Samuel Smith Old Brewery (Tadcaster)* at [77(c)].

5.23 It is also important to bear in mind that in considering the similarity of marks, the court will take into account what is called 'imperfect recollection'. In this regard, it is accepted that consumers rarely have the opportunity to consider marks alongside one another and must instead rely upon their imperfect memory of marks.[1]

1 C-342/97 *Lloyd Schuhfabrik Meyer v Klijsen Handel BV* [1999] ECR I-3819. See also *Samuel Smith Old Brewery (Tadcaster)* at [93].

Visual similarity and the significance of colour

5.24 Determining whether there is a visual similarity between word marks will generally include an assessment of the length of the respective marks, use of prefixes or suffixes, common syllables, and shared elements of shape.

In relation to marks that are devices without the use of text, the relevant points would include the marks' different elements, arrangements or shapes, colours and styles of art.

Where the marks are logos or combinations of words and images, the relevant points to consider are those listed above as relating to words alone and images alone, as well as the arrangement or placement of the text and images around one another.

Following the decision of the CJEU in *Specsavers*[1], UKIPO issued a Tribunal Practice Notice (1/2014) to explain the significance of an earlier mark which is registered in black and white but which has been used in colour. In *Specsavers* the CJEU said that where:

> 'the proprietor has used it extensively in a particular colour or combination of colours with the result that it has become associated in the mind of a significant portion of the public with that colour or combination of colours, the colour or colours which a third party uses in order to represent a sign alleged to infringe that trade mark are relevant in the global assessment of the likelihood of confusion or unfair advantage under that provision'.

Although *Specsavers* was concerned primarily with infringement, the TPN makes clear that the principles set out in that case are also relevant to opposition and cancellation proceedings. So if the registration of the earlier mark includes colour, or the earlier is registered in black and white mark, but has been used in particular colours, the potential or actual use of the later mark in those colours will be relevant to the consideration of visual similarity, and the overall likelihood of confusion.

1 Case C-252/12, *Specsavers International Healthcare Limited and Others v Asda Stores Limited* [2014] FSR 4.

Aural similarity

5.25 Aural similarity turns on similarity where marks are pronounced. Obviously, only those marks that include word elements lend themselves to arguments about aural similarity.

In asking whether two marks sound similar, the factors to consider are the length of the marks, the number of syllables and the pronunciation of the mark, for example, C and K are often used interchangeably (such as CRISPY/KRISPY) as are F and PH (such as in FONE/PHONE). The General Court has held that, for the most part, consumers pay more attention to the first syllable when making an aural comparison,[1] particularly for longer marks, although this is by no means an inflexible rule.

In the context of proceedings before OHIM, it is essential to note that the pronunciation of a mark may differ from one Member State to another. Where an EUTM is used as the basis for opposition or invalidation proceedings, pronunciation can and should be considered from the point of view of all of the Member States; where a national trade mark is used as the basis then pronunciation is considered in the language of that state. However, following Brexit, the position on relying on EUTMs for opposition or invalidation proceedings in the UK has changed: for details see the UKIPO's Tribunal Practice Notice 2/2020.[2]

1 T-146/06 *Sanofi-Aventis* [2008] ECR II-17*.
2 www.gov.uk/government/publications/tribunal-practice-notice-22020-end-of-transition-period-impact-on-tribunal-proceedings

Conceptual similarity

5.26 Certain marks may not look or sound alike but may share a similar concept. This is often the case where the marks are translations, or where the marks are both simple images. In the case of simple images of objects, the consumer will generally recall it by reference to that general type of object, such a depiction of a tree or a bottle. As mentioned above, consumers are generally deemed to have 'imperfect recollection' and so may not remember (or indeed be able to recall perfectly) precisely what an image depicts.

In comparing for conceptual similarity, the relevant point is the overall 'message' of the mark, ie, how the mark would be described. This means that for many comparisons the two marks must be considered conceptually different where one or both do not embody any discernible concept, perhaps by being a made-up word or meaningless sign.

The interrelation of the three aspects

5.27 It is quite conceivable that a mark will only share one type of similarity, yet the marks may still be deemed similar, notwithstanding that they are positively dissimilar in other aspects.[1] The respective weights of the different factors will depend on the type of goods or services involved. In relation to clothing, for example, visual considerations are generally taken to be more important.

Whilst the EUIPO's *Trade Mark Guidelines* (Part C – Oppositions) give some idea as to when marks have been deemed to be similar, such guidelines are without legal force and are not definitive.

1 See in that regard C-251/95 *Sabel BV v Puma AG*, where it was held that mere conceptual similarity may be sufficient, and case C-342/97 *Lloyd Schuhfabrik Meyer v Klijsen Handel BV*, in which phonetic similarity alone sufficed.

Identity of goods or services

5.28 Assuming there are marks that are identical or similar, the question arises whether the goods or services relating to those marks are identical. This is usually a question of fact and it will generally be clear whether or not there is the requisite identity. The requirement is not that the specifications of each mark must be identical but that the specification of the earlier trade mark includes the goods or services specified for the later mark: thus an earlier trade mark registered for 'clothes' will cover a later registration for 'jeans' even though, on a literal view, clothes and jeans are not identical. Following the decision in the *IP TRANSLATOR* case (see para **6.05**) any mark being applied for now ought to indicate clearly exactly which goods and/or services are covered.

5.29 It is essential that an applicant for a later mark or its registered proprietor who faces opposition or invalidation proceedings (as the case may be) responds carefully to any alleged identity of goods and services. A failure to do so may be taken to be an admission of the allegation.

5.30 In this respect it is particularly worth studying the Nice classification system for goods and services.[1] Although the classification system is deemed to be for administrative purposes, in many cases the extent of protection will be limited by the class in which the term is placed. One example of this would be medical dressings, which could fall into classes 5 (plasters, materials for dressings) or 10 (suture materials, bandages). Whilst they are arguably very similar, they are not identical, and the choice of classification may be crucial.

1 See **Chapter 6** below.

5.31 A further consideration in an opposition to registration (or a challenge to the validity of a registration) is whether the terms of the later mark could be amended in order to improve the prospect of obtaining (or keeping) trade mark rights. Where the later mark covers 'clothing' and the earlier trade mark covers 'jeans', the goods of the later mark will be deemed to be identical, notwithstanding the fact that most clothes are not jeans. The specification could, however, be narrowed to more specific types of clothing (for example, 'clothing; sweatshirts; underwear; t-shirts; shorts; jackets; coats'). In practice, such a tactic may be enough to avoid s 5(1) of the TMA 1994 but in most cases the applicant is still likely to fall foul of s 5(2)(a) if the marks are identical and the goods or services very similar.

Similarity of goods and services

5.32 If the goods or services cannot be said to be identical (see above), it is necessary to consider whether they are similar. In theory, there are no limits to the basis on which the *marks* can be seen as similar. In practice, however, the factors that are relevant to the similarity of *goods and services* are as follows:[1]

- the respective users;
- the respective uses through which they reach the market;
- the respective channels;
- the proximity of the goods and services;
- the physical nature of the goods or the nature of the services; and
- whether the goods or services are complementary or are in competition with one another.

1 C-36/97 *Canon*. See also '*Treat*', still referred to by the UKIPO and UK courts: *British Sugar Plc v James Robertson Son Ltd* [1996] RPC 281.

5.33 The relative importance of these factors will differ according to the goods and services being compared. For example, where the goods in question are quite different but are intended for the general public (say pasta on the one hand and leather purses on the other) the fact that the same consumer may purchase both products is unlikely to be a determinative factor. Equally, an industrial food sweetener on the one hand and food products on the other may be deemed similar notwithstanding that the relevant users may be quite different. It may also be relevant to ask whether the goods or services are used at different points in the supply chain: for example, in the EASYHOTEL[1] case, the General Court held that services relating to booking hotels online were not similar to the services relating to the supply of an online hotel booking system: the consumers for the latter services were the service providers of the former (hoteliers) but their customers would not be aware of the latter services.

1 T-316/07 *Commercy AG v OHIM* [2009] ECR II-43.

The meaning of respective users

5.34 The respective users will generally include all users of the relevant goods or services, and all those who may come into contact with those goods or services. They may, therefore, include not only the end user of a product but also the person who purchases that product. For example, a baby food product and a product for adult consumption may have different consumers, but the purchaser may be the same person.

Meaning of 'complementary'

5.35 As set out above, in determining whether goods or services are similar, it is relevant to ask whether they are complementary to each other.

The meaning of the term 'complementary' has somewhat changed over the years. Initially it was taken to mean that the goods may be seen as accessories to one another. Indeed, the General Court suggested that goods or services could only be seen as being complementary where one was necessary for the use of the other and on this basis decided that shoes and handbags were not complementary, nor wine and other beverages.[1] This position was somewhat modified in *Mühlens*[2] where the General Court held that goods[3] could be aesthetically complementary if consumers were used to seeing them sold together under the same mark through the same retail outlets. And in *Kampol* the General Court stated:

> 'It must be borne in mind that complementary goods and services are those which are closely connected in the sense that one is indispensable or important for the use of the other in such a way that consumers may think that the same undertaking is responsible for manufacturing those goods or for providing those services. By definition goods intended for different publics cannot be complementary.'[4]

1 T-169/03 *Sergio Rossi v OHIM* [2005] ECR II-685 and T-175/06; *Coca-Cola Co v OHIM* [2008] ECR II-1055 respectively.
2 T-150/04 *Mülhens v OHIM* [2007] ECR II-2353.
3 In that case luxury goods including perfumes and leather items.
4 *Kampol v OHIM* Case T-382/12, *Official Journal C 253*, 04/08/2014 p 26 at [40]; see further the discussion of this case in *Wasabi Frog v Gulck*, 2014 WL 4423396, Appointed Person (2 September 2014).

Examples of comparisons between goods and services

5.36 Examples of goods and services that are commonly deemed to be similar include:

- telecommunications goods (class 9) and telecommunications services (class 39)—each is carried out using the other;
- retail services for particular goods (class 35) and those goods themselves;
- footwear and clothing;
- handbags and clothing; and
- beers and soft drinks.

Likelihood of confusion

5.37 There is no need to show likelihood of confusion in a case where the marks are identical and the goods and services are identical. In such a case, if some adverse effect on the functions of the trade mark is established, registration of the later mark will be refused or, as the case may be, its registration declared invalid.

If, however, there is:

(a) an identity of marks but only a similarity in goods or services; or
(b) a similarity of marks and an identity or similarity in goods or services;

then registration of the later mark will be refused (or its registration declared invalid) to the extent that it can be shown that there would be a likelihood of confusion.[1] As will be seen, similar provisions apply in relation to the test for infringement.

1 Directive Art 4(1)(b); TMA 1994 s 5(2)(a); EUTMR Art 8(1)(b). If there is no relevant similarity, there can be no confusion even if the other factors are indicative of a likelihood of confusion: C-254/09 *Calvin Klein* [2011] ETMR 5.

What does 'likelihood of confusion' mean?

5.38 For these purposes, the term 'likelihood of confusion' means either:

(1) confusion as to whether the goods or services come from the same person; or
(2) confusion as to whether the owner of the earlier mark was in some way connected with the goods or services of the third party.

And, it has been decided by both the UK courts[1] and the CJEU[2] that, for these purposes, the phrase 'a likelihood of confusion' requires confusion as to the origin of the goods or services, and does not include 'mere' association—ie cases where the later mark merely 'calls to mind' the goods or services of the earlier trade mark owner in circumstances where a consumer would not actually think that they were connected with the earlier trade mark owner. The CJEU's most recent guidance on this issue is found in *Bimbo*:[3] 'the risk that the public might believe that the goods or services in question come from the same undertaking or, as the case may be, from economically-linked undertakings, constitutes a likelihood of confusion'.

1 *Wagamama v City Centre Restaurants* [1995] FSR 713; *British Sugar v James Robertson* [1996] RPC 281.
2 C-251/95 *Sabel BV v Puma AG*; Case C-36/97 *Canon Kabushiki Kaisha v Metro-Golden-Mayer*; C-533/06 *O2 Holdings Ltd v Hutchison* [2008] RPC 33 at [57] and [63].
3 *Bimbo SA v OHIM, Case C-519/12 P; [2014] ETMR 41.*

How to assess the likelihood of confusion

5.39 The fact that there is no evidence of *actual* confusion does not mean that there can be no *likelihood* of confusion. The lack of such evidence could be attributable to the fact that there had been no opportunity for confusion to occur or to be detected.[1]

1 *Samuel Smith Old Brewery (Tadcaster) v Philip Lee* [2011] EWHC 1879, Arnold J at [95]–[97]; [105]–[106].

5.40 Although the meaning of the words 'likelihood of confusion' is the same whether the issue arises in the context of the opposition to the registration of a mark[1] or in the context of the infringement of a mark,[2] there is an important difference between the two contexts in how a court goes about assessing whether there is such a likelihood. In the former context, it is necessary to determine whether there is a likelihood of confusion in all of the circumstances in which the mark applied for *might* be used. In the latter context, it is only necessary to look at the likelihood of confusion in all of the circumstances of the use *actually* made by the alleged infringer.[3]

1 Directive Art 5(1)(b); TMA 1994 s 5(2)(b); EUTMR Art 8(1)(b).
2 Directive Art 10(2)(b); TMA 1994 s 10(2); EUTMR Art 9(1)(b).
3 C-533/06 *O2 Holdings Ltd v Hutchison 3G UK Ltd* [2008] RPC 33 at [66]–[67]. See also *Datacard Corporation v Eagle Technologies Ltd* [2011] EWHC 244; [2011] RPC 17 at [275].

5.41 In theory, there is no limit on the range of factors which may be relevant in trying to demonstrate that there is or is not a likelihood of confusion.[1] The intricacies of the particular market may make any number of factors more or less relevant, or make it more or less likely that confusion would ensue from the use of the mark complained of.

1 C-251/95 *Sabel BV v Puma AG.*

5.42 The generally accepted principles by which a likelihood of confusion is assessed have been summarised as follows:[1]

'(a) the likelihood of confusion must be appreciated globally, taking account of all relevant factors;
(b) the matter must be judged through the eyes of the average consumer of the goods or services in question, who is deemed to be reasonably well informed and reasonably circumspect and observant, but who rarely has the chance to make direct comparisons between marks and must instead rely upon the imperfect picture of them he has kept in his mind, and whose attention varies according to the category of goods or services in question;
(c) the average consumer normally perceives a mark as a whole and does not proceed to analyse its various details;
(d) the visual, aural and conceptual similarities of the marks must normally be assessed by reference to the overall impressions created by the marks bearing in mind their distinctive and dominant components, but it is only when all other components of a complex mark are negligible that it is permissible to make the comparison solely on the basis of the dominant elements;
(e) nevertheless, the overall impression conveyed to the public by a composite trade mark may, in certain circumstances, be dominated by one or more of its components;
(f) and beyond the usual case, where the overall impression created by a mark depends heavily on the dominant features of the mark, it is quite possible that in a particular case an element corresponding to an earlier trade mark may retain an independent distinctive role in a composite mark, without necessarily constituting a dominant element of that mark;
(g) a lesser degree of similarity between the goods or services may be offset by a great degree of similarity between the marks, and vice versa;
(h) there is a greater likelihood of confusion where the earlier mark has a highly distinctive character, either *per se* or because of the use that has been made of it;
(i) mere association, in the strict sense that the later mark brings the earlier mark to mind, is not sufficient;
(j) the reputation of a mark does not give grounds for presuming a likelihood of confusion simply because of a likelihood of association in the strict sense;
(k) if the association between the marks causes the public to wrongly believe that the respective goods [or services]

come from the same or economically-linked undertakings, there is a likelihood of confusion.'

1 See the guidance of UKIPO quoted with approval by Arnold J in *Och-Ziff* at [73] and in *Samuel Smith* at [77]. This list was called 'useful and accurate' in the judgment of Kitchin LJ in *Specsavers* [2012] ETMR 16 at [52] and further endorsed by the Court of Appeal in *Comic Enterprises Ltd v Twentieth Century Fox Film Corp* [2016] ETMR 22 at [31].

5.43 Several of these principles have already been considered when dealing with the similarities of marks. In the present context, the following additional matters are worth considering.

The consumer's level of attention

5.44 The likelihood of confusion must be assessed from the point of view of the 'average consumer', who is deemed to be reasonably well informed and reasonably observant and circumspect.[1] The average consumer is taken to pay differing degrees of attention depending upon the nature of the goods or services involved and the value of those goods (value being generally deemed to mean financial value rather than inherent value arising from the nature of the goods or services).

1 See **5.47** below.

5.45 The level of attention the average consumer pays when selecting a low-value, single-use item (perhaps a snack food) is therefore assumed to be much lower than that afforded to the selection of a high-value item intended to be used for an important purpose over a long period of time (eg, a car[1]). Not only would the consumer of the latter product be likely to be more careful generally, they would also be likely to take more time in making the purchasing decision and the buying process would be likely to involve multiple stages before completion.

1 C-361/04 *Daimler Chrysler (PICASSO/PICARRO)* [2006] ETMR 29.

5.46 A further element would be the nature of the particular consumer. It is generally considered that a professional will take more care in selecting specialist goods or services than the general public would in choosing mass-consumption products. So where goods or services are directed towards professionals *only*, a higher degree of similarity is required, but where the goods or services are directed at *both* professionals and the general public, a likelihood of confusion among only one part of that consumer base will suffice.[1]

1 C-412/05 *Alcon* [2007] ETMR 68.

5.47 The phraseology used by the courts is that the average consumer (ie, the general public) is taken to be 'reasonably well-informed and reasonably observant and circumspect'.[1] It is not enough to ask only whether the 'moron in a hurry' would be confused, despite the relatively low level of attention that consumers are deemed to pay when buying many types of everyday goods.

The concept of the average consumer was considered in detail by the Court of Appeal in *Interflora.*[2] It is not a 'mathematical average' but simply a notional typical consumer. In *Jack Wills* the court discussed the question of the identity of the average consumer where the parties were selling identical goods but targeting rather different markets.[3] If the mark is said to have acquired distinctiveness through use (see **5.56** below) then the relevant consumer must be the average consumer to whom the mark has acquired distinctiveness. In the case of online consumers, the average consumer is taken to be 'a reasonably well-informed and reasonably observant internet user'.[4]

1 C-210/96 *Gut Springenheide and Tusky* [1999] 1 CMLR 1383.
2 *Interflora v Marks & Spencer UK* [2012] EWCA Civ 1501; [2013] FSR 21 at [37]–[44] (the appeal on the survey evidence ruling, not the later appeal from the first trial).
3 *Jack Wills v House of Fraser (Stores)* [2014] ETMR 28.
4 See eg, *Interflora* [2014] EWCA Civ 1403; [2014] ETMR 5 at [12] referring to the CJEU's earlier judgment in the same case; the underlying legal concept is the same as that of the average consumer—[44].

5.48 It is worth noting that while the attentiveness of consumers is taken into account, it is often tempered by other considerations. A classic example of this would be where a brand owner opposes an application by a competitor to protect a lookalike product which bears a somewhat different brand name, but shares aspects of packaging identity. This is often the case in supermarket own-brand cases where it is the packaging and appearance that causes consumers to buy the wrong product. Despite the likelihood that the selection of products may be based on a fleeting view of the shelves (with consumers sometimes shopping on 'autopilot' for the same products each week), courts are often reluctant to accept that the use of visual cues would lead to confusion not least because such features are not commonly registered as trade marks or, if they are, they are of low distinctive character. As a result, in such cases a court is likely to require proof of actual confusion by the consumer.

Timing of the confusion and 'wrong way round' confusion

5.49 In *Och-Ziff* it was decided in the context of infringement proceedings that a likelihood of confusion can arise where use of the mark causes confusion during a consumer's initial interest (so-called 'initial interest confusion') and that it did not matter that that confusion was dispelled later in the transaction or that there was no sale.[1] However, it is clear that a likelihood of confusion can also arise post-sale—such as when goods ordered from a website arrive[2] or where the *ultimate* consumer would be confused even though the initial purchaser would not be.[3] In the context of infringement, it is also now clear that 'wrong way round' confusion suffices to establish a likelihood of confusion, ie where consumers who are familiar with the later mark become confused upon seeing the earlier mark said to be infringed;[4] there appears to be no reason why 'wrong way round' confusion might not be argued as a basis for relative grounds of refusal if it could be shown to be likely on the facts.

1 *Och-Ziff Management Europe Ltd v Och Capital LLP* [2010] EWHC 2599; [2011] ETMR 1 at [97]–[101] and [118]. See also *Datacard* at [276].
2 *Datacard* at [286]–[289].
3 C-206/01 *Arsenal Football Club v Reed* [2003] ETMR 19. *Datacard* at [277]–[280].
4 *Comic Enterprises Ltd v Twentieth Century Fox Film Corp* [2016] ETMR 22.

Significance of the surrounding circumstances

5.50 The question whether there is a likelihood of confusion must be answered on the basis of all the circumstances. Where marks have a high level of visual or phonetic similarity (but perhaps not both), the proprietor of the earlier trade mark will often try to prove that one or other of those similarities plays a leading role in the selection of goods or services and, therefore, that there is an increased likelihood of confusion. Here evidence as to whether such goods are selected by the public with or without the intervention of sales assistants or of other third parties may affect the significance of any phonetic similarity. For example, it has been held that in selecting clothing, consumers are more likely to pick products on the basis of visual elements (although phonetic similarity will not be ignored[1]) but this is, of course, not an absolute rule.

1 T-117/03 *New Look* [2005] ETMR 35.

5.51 As has been indicated above, in the context of opposition or invalidation proceedings, the surrounding circumstances must relate to the goods and services as presented in the specification, and not just to the particular way in which one of the parties markets or intends to market their products. The reason for this is that the comparison is between fair (thus, hypothetical) use of the respective marks. Notwithstanding that one party may have particular intentions, these cannot be taken into account.

5.52 This contrasts with the position in infringement cases where the alleged infringer's actual actions and particular marketing methods will be of immediate relevance.[1] Thus, even where the identity of goods and the distinctive character of the mark might otherwise suggest there is a likelihood of confusion, other factors (such as other differences in the devices used, differences in *other* parts of the signs used on the goods or a clear identification that the goods are from a different supplier) can militate against that conclusion.[2] As the Court of Appeal in *Specsavers*[3] stated:

'In assessing the likelihood of confusion arising from the use of a sign the court must consider the matter from the perspective of the average consumer of the goods or services in question and must take into account all the circumstances of that use that are likely to operate in that average consumer's mind in considering the sign and the impression it is likely to make on him. The sign is not to be considered stripped of its context.'

1 *Samuel Smith Old Brewery (Tadcaster) v Philip Lee* [2011] EWHC 1879, Arnold J at [78].

2 In *Samuel Smith Old Brewery (Tadcaster)* Arnold J concluded at [105]–[106]) that there was no likelihood of confusion in respect of the defendant's 'Yorkshire Bitter' sign but that there was such a likelihood in respect of its 'Yorkshire Warrior' sign. In making his comparison, Arnold J looked beyond just the claimant's mark and defendant's sign and took into account the way in which the defendant had used its sign. This approach is consistent with the approach of the European Court in *O2 Holdings Ltd v Hutchison 3G Ltd* [2008] RPC 33 at [67] and it would seem that the narrower approach adopted by Kitchin J in *Julius Samann Ltd v Tetrosyl* [2006] EWHC 529 at [52] no longer represents the law.

3 *Specsavers International Healthcare v Asda Stores* [2012] EWCA Civ 24; [2012] FSR 19 at [87]. Endorsed by the same court in *Comic Enterprises Ltd v Twentieth Century Fox Film Corp* [2016] ETMR 22 at [33].

Interdependence of assessments of similarity

5.53 In determining whether there is a likelihood of confusion, one factor that is taken into account is the interdependence between the identity or similarity of the marks and the identity or similarity of the goods and services. A greater level of similarity of the marks may outweigh a lower level of similarity of the goods or services.[1]

1 C-36/97 *Canon Kabushiki Kaisha v Metro-Golden-Mayer* [1999] RPC 117.

Distinctiveness or descriptiveness of the earlier trade mark

5.54 The CJEU has made clear that the more distinctive the earlier trade mark, the greater the likelihood of confusion.[1] It has also stated that a mark with a highly distinctive character (whether due to its inherent distinctiveness or to the reputation it enjoys) will enjoy broader protection than a mark with lesser distinctiveness.[2] Conversely, it has also been said that: 'Where descriptive words are included in a registered trade mark, the courts have always and rightly been exceedingly wary of granting a monopoly in their use'.[3]

1 C-251/95 *Sabel BV v Puma AG*. Although as set out above, that likelihood of confusion can be dispelled by the surrounding circumstances—see para **5.50** above and *Samuel Smith Old Brewery (Tadcaster)* at [105]–[106].

2 C-36/97 *Canon.*

3 *British Sky Broadcasting Group v Microsoft Corp* [2013] EWHC 1826 (Ch) at [86], referring to dicta of Millet LJ in *The European* [1998] FSR 283. See also *Planetart LLC v Photobox Ltd* [2020] EWHC 713 at [26]–[29] for a discussion of the issue of a

likelihood of confusion when the similarity between two marks is because they share the same descriptive element or elements.

5.55 As a result, in considering whether a likelihood of confusion exists, the applicant for a later mark will be looking to demonstrate that the earlier trade mark has a low level of inherent distinctiveness. At the same time, the owner of the earlier trade mark will be marshalling any available argument to show the opposite. In this regard, the fact that the earlier trade mark was registered is evidence of its validity[1] and tends to suggest that it had some measure of distinctiveness so its owner is really only concerned with evidence to show that the mark is particularly distinctive or that it has acquired distinctiveness through use (as to which, see below).

1 TMA 1994 s 72; EUTMR Art 99(1).

Distinctiveness of the earlier trade mark through use

5.56 The CJEU has indicated that a mark that has become particularly distinctive through use will be afforded greater protection.[1] It has also indicated[2] that the following factors will be taken into account in ascertaining whether there is 'enhanced' or 'acquired' distinctiveness:

- market share;
- the intensity, geographical spread and length of use of the mark;
- the amount spent on promoting the mark;
- the percentage of the public that identifies goods or services bearing the mark as originating from a particular undertaking; and
- statements from chambers of commerce and industry or other trade and professional associations.

In the UK, the High Court has held that enhanced distinctiveness may arise through use of a mark in a form that is not necessarily identical to its registration, by analogy with the fact that use of a mark in a form that does not alter its distinctive character may be sufficient to avoid revocation for non-use[3] (see **Chapter 14**). It is not sufficient for the trade mark owner to show that a significant proportion of the relevant class of persons recognise and associate the mark with the trade mark owner's goods. They must show that the consumers perceive that the goods designated by the mark originate with a particular undertaking and no other.[4]

1 C-36/97 *Canon*.
2 C- 342/97 *Lloyd Schuhfabrik Meyer v Klijsen Handel* BV [1999] ECR I-3819.
3 *Thomas Pink v Victoria's Secret UK* [2014] EWHC 2631 (Ch); [2014] FSR 40 at [94]–[96].
4 See the Court of Appeal's summary of the law on acquired distinctiveness *in London Taxi Corp Ltd (t/a London Taxi Co) v Frazer-Nash Research Ltd* [2018] FSR 7 starting at [52] (which in that case was in relation to shape marks).

5.57 These factors are not exhaustive, and the EUIPO has suggested that the requirements for a finding of enhanced distinctiveness through use will be stricter where the earlier trade mark is one with limited inherent distinctiveness. This approach would also appear to apply in the UK. In other words, the likelihood of confusion with a weak or non-distinctive earlier trade mark which has benefited from extensive use cannot be equated with the likelihood of confusion with an inherently distinctive mark that has a claim to enhanced distinctiveness due to use. For this reason, owners of earlier trade mark with questionable inherent distinctiveness probably need to do better than merely seek to establish 'average' distinctiveness.

5.58 The evidence ought to show that the mark has enhanced distinctiveness in relation to the relevant goods in the relevant markets. The important consideration in all such cases is the perception and knowledge of the consumer. One example would be a maker of soft drinks seeking to prevent a third party from using a similar mark for retail services for bags, where the drinks maker's earlier rights include registrations for clothing. Although the comparison between soft drinks and bags may well lead to a conclusion that the goods are not similar, a different conclusion may be reached as between bags and clothing. If the drinks maker has produced merchandise in the form of clothing then they may seek to blur the lines of their enhanced distinctiveness to extend it to clothing. In that regard, the person behind the later application or registration should challenge any claims to reputation where appropriate.

To what extent are the common elements of the marks used by various parties?

5.59 In determining the likelihood of confusion, it is the perception of the average consumer that is the essential consideration. If consumers are accustomed to seeing the contentious parts of the marks in wider use by other parties (and so are not used to deciding on origin on the basis of those terms), then there is little likelihood of confusion. Hence owners of later marks often argue that similarities with an earlier mark are in fact similarities shared with a number of other marks.

5.60 This approach will typically take the form of a list of other registrations sharing these similarities. However, decisions in both the UK and the European courts have shown that the mere existence of such registrations is not sufficient for these purposes. There needs to be evidence that these other registrations are in use or at least grounds for arguing that due to the large number of them, it is reasonable to assume that at least some are in use.

5.61 In proceedings at OHIM, the applicant or proprietor of the registration being challenged may need to consider their position in multiple jurisdictions. If the owner of the earlier trade mark has relied upon national rights in Member States then the position should be considered in each of those countries. Where the earlier trade mark is an EUTM then the position in each of the Member States should be considered unless the owner of the EUTM has positively restricted the case to allege that there is a likelihood of confusion in only a subset of Member States. This may arise where, for example, the similarity relies upon languages only known in certain countries, such as the case where one mark is a translation of another but is otherwise visually and phonetically quite different.

Prior decisions; issue estoppel

5.62 In many cases, prior decisions between the same parties will be relevant to the outcome in any subsequent opposition or invalidity proceedings. In particular, the outcome of proceedings before UKIPO, if final and not appealed, can lead to issue estoppel in respect of later proceedings in the High Court. In the *Firecraft*[1] case, an unchallenged finding of invalidity in UKIPO was held to be a final ruling capable of supporting an application for summary judgment when the same issue (passing off) came before the High Court.

1 *Evans (t/a Firecraft) v Focal Point Fires* [2009] EWHC 2784 (Ch). See also *Slater v Anglo Atlantic Media Ltd* [2020] FSR 32.

Marks with a reputation

Relevance of reputation

5.63 As set out in para **5.05** above, another basis on which a mark will be refused registration is if it is identical with or similar to an earlier trade mark which has a reputation[1] and the use of the later mark without due cause would take unfair advantage of, or be detrimental to, the distinctive character or repute of that earlier trade mark.[2] Once again, there is a matching provision relating to when a sign will infringe a registered mark with a reputation.[3]

1 The reputation must be in the UK in respect of a UK trade mark, and in the EU in the case of an EUTM or international registration.
2 Directive Art 5(3)(a); TMA 1994 s 5(3); and EUTMR Art 8(5).
3 Directive Art 10(2)(c); TMA 1994 s 10(3); and EUTMR Art 9(1)(c).

5.64 This section considers when the earlier mark has a 'reputation'. The subsequent sections will consider when the use of the later mark would: (i) take unfair advantage of that reputation; (ii) be detrimental to the distinctive character or repute of the earlier mark; and (iii) be without due cause.

Goods and services may be identical, similar or dissimilar

5.65 Initially s 5(3) of the TMA 1994 stated that the provisions relating to earlier marks with a reputation would only operate where the goods or services for which the later mark was to be registered were 'not similar' to those for which the earlier mark was registered. Similarly, the equivalent infringement provisions in s 10 of the TMA 1994 stated that they only applied where the goods or services for which the allegedly infringing sign had been used were not similar to those of the registered mark. This reflected the wording of Art 4(3) of Directive 2008/95/EC, and Art 8(5) of the version of the EUTMR as it stood at that time. However, it is now established by European case law[1] that these provisions operate whether the relevant goods or services are identical, similar or dissimilar. As a result, the relevant provisions of the TMA 1994 (ie, ss 5(3) and 10(3)) were amended in 2004 to make this clear. The wording of the Directive and EUTMR has also now been updated.

1 C-292/00 *Davidoff & Cie v Gofkid Ltd* [2003] ETMR 42; C-408/01 *Adidas-Salomon AG and others v Fitnessworld Trading Ltd* [2003] ETMR 91.

Evidence required to demonstrate 'reputation'

5.66 In *Och-Ziff* it was commented that the task of showing that a mark has a reputation is not a particularly onerous one.[1]

1 *Och-Ziff Management Europe Ltd v Och Capital LLP* [2010] EWHC 2599; [2011] ETMR 1 at [126]. See also *Coreix v Coretx* [2017] EWHC 1695 (IPEC).

5.67 The leading case on the question of reputation is *General Motors v Yplon.*[1] There, the CJEU indicated that the earlier trade mark must be known by a significant part of the public. In determining whether this condition is fulfilled, the court must take account all of relevant facts, in particular the market share held by the earlier trade mark, the intensity, geographical extent and duration of its use, and the size of the investment made by the undertaking in promoting it.[2] OHIM has indicated that in its view, the *General Motors* case suggests that quantitative criteria are the principal measure and that although the CJEU did not dictate a percentage threshold of knowledge or recognition, there is a limit below which no reputation can be said to subsist. There is no reason to think that the equivalent provisions of the Directive and of TMA 1994 would be viewed any differently. The principles applicable to assessing reputation (in the context of infringement) were considered in *Red Bull.*[3]

1 C-375/97 *General Motors Corporation v Yplon SA* [1999] ETMR 950.
2 At para 27.
3 *Red Bull v Sun Mark* [2012] EWHC 1929 (Ch); [2013] ETMR 53 at [90]–[98]

5.68 The sort of evidence needed to prove that an earlier trade mark has a reputation is largely the same as that required to prove that an earlier trade mark benefits from enhanced distinctiveness as a result of the use made of it. In order to improve their prospects of succeeding, the person opposing registration (or seeking a declaration of invalidity) will often argue that the grounds for refusal which protect against a likelihood of confusion exist in addition to those which protect an earlier mark with reputation.

5.69 It is to be noted that evidence of awareness of the trade mark is only one factor alongside others highlighted by the court in *General Motors*.

5.70 In addition to the factors identified in the *General Motors* case, other evidence that may assist in establishing that the earlier trade mark has a reputation will include unsolicited statements from members of the trade or consumers, survey evidence and official listings from the many impartial listings of 'top brands'. It may also be appropriate to explain the level of exposure that the public may have had to the goods or services. For example, in the case of magazines, the owner of the earlier trade mark may wish to provide readership figures as well as circulation figures in order to demonstrate that exposure to the mark goes beyond merely those that purchase the goods or services. The owner of the earlier trade mark should, wherever possible, seek to provide impartial evidence to support the claim to reputation. For example, whilst 'in-house' evidence will not be ignored, it may not be given much weight unless it is supported by third party evidence.

5.71 One error often made by opponents or applicants for invalidity is to provide evidence of turnover without placing the use in context or giving a market share. In the absence of context, turnover figures are unlikely to be given any weight since their relevance cannot be ascertained.

Relevant public

5.72 The *General Motors* case indicated that the relevant public to be taken into account for the purposes of demonstrating reputation is the public concerned by the earlier trade mark. Where the earlier trade mark covers goods or services for mass consumption, the relevant public will be the public at large. Where the goods or services are more specific, the relevant public will be more limited.

5.73 As a result, it may be in the interests of the owner of the earlier trade mark to amend the coverage of their trade mark to include specific sub-categories. For example, the owner of a trade mark for 'pharmaceutical preparations' may amend it to 'pharmaceutical preparations; pharmaceutical preparations for the treatment of angina'.

By adding the second term, the owner of the earlier trade mark may be able to demonstrate reputation for the narrower goods.

Territory of the evidence

5.74 Any evidence of reputation should be directed at the relevant territory. If evidence is not directed at the relevant territory then the opponent of registration (or, as the case may be, the applicant for invalidity) should seek to extrapolate the evidence to the relevant territory. The applicant or registered proprietor should seek to dissuade the relevant body from accepting such extrapolation.

In the context of EUTMs, the CJEU has held that the owner of the earlier trade mark need not show reputation throughout the Community—it is sufficient that there be reputation in a substantial part of the territory of the Community.[1] For example, reputation in Austria would be deemed to be a substantial part of the Community. Whether a particular territory constitutes a 'substantial part' must presumably be resolved on a case-by-case basis, such as whether reputation in Malta (the smallest EU state by population) would be sufficient. For the purposes of relying on comparable trade marks (EU) for opposition purposes, use of the corresponding EUTM elsewhere in the EU prior to Brexit may be taken into account for the purposes of assessing reputation.[2]

1 C-301/07 *PAGO International GmbH v Tirolmilch registrierte Genossenschaft mbH* [2010] ETMR 5. For the purposes of infringement, the acts complained of need not be in the same territory where the mark has a reputation: *Iron & Smith kft v Unilever NV* (C-125/14) [2015] ETMR 45.

2 UKIPO Tribunal Practice Notice 2/2020.

Taking unfair advantage of the distinctive character or repute of the mark

5.75 The next question is whether the later mark takes or would take *unfair advantage* of the distinctive character or repute of the later mark. This is a question that has been addressed more in the context of infringement than of opposition to registration, but the underlying principles are essentially the same. The meaning of 'unfair advantage' was considered by the CJEU in *L'Oréal v Bellure*, a case about comparative advertising relating to the trade mark proprietor's luxury perfumes and a range of 'smell-alikes' produced by a competitor and advertised by means of a comparison list. The Court considered that an unfair advantage was taken of a mark's reputation where another person seeks to 'free-ride on the coat-tails' of that repute and to benefit from the trade mark proprietor's marketing investment without paying any financial compensation.[1]

1 C-487/07 *L'Oréal and others v Bellure and others* [2009] ETMR 55. The expression 'Free-riding on the coat-tails' comes from the Advocate-General's opinion in C-408/01 *Adidas-Salomon AG and others v Fitnessworld Trading Ltd* [2003] ETMR 91 at

[AG39]. Unfair advantage, as well as dilution and tarnishing (see below), were discussed in some detail in the context of infringement in *Thomas Pink v Victoria's Secret UK* [2014] EWHC 2631 (Ch); [2014] FSR 40 at [183]–[208]. Arnold J also considered unfair advantage in *Enterprise Holdings Inc v Europcar Group UK Ltd* [2015] FSR 22.

5.76 In *VIPA*[1] the General Court referred to unfair advantage in terms of a competitor facilitating its own marketing by means of association with the proprietor's mark. The Advocate-General in *L'Oréal v Bellure* referred to this and went on to suggest that the question of unfairness only arose if the use was arguably with 'due cause' (as to which, see below); where there was no due cause, the use would automatically be unfair.[2] The CJEU in *L'Oréal v Bellure*[3] stated:

> 'As regards the concept of "taking unfair advantage of the distinctive character or the repute of the trade mark", also referred to as "parasitism" or "free-riding", that concept relates not to the detriment caused to the mark but to the advantage taken by the third party as a result of the use of the identical or similar sign. It covers, in particular, cases where, by reason of a transfer of the image of the mark or of the characteristics which it projects to the goods identified by the identical or similar sign, there is clear exploitation on the coat-tails of the mark with a reputation.'

1 C-59/05 *Siemens AG v VIPA Gesellschaft für Visualisierung und Prozessautomatisierung mbH* [2006] ETMR 47—see [40].
2 *L'Oréal v Bellure*—at [AG99].
3 [2010] RPC 1 at [41].

5.77 Subsequently the CJEU in *Interflora*[1] has held that a competitor's use of advertising keywords based on a mark with a reputation could amount to taking an unfair advantage, since the competitor was making commercial gain from the reputation and prestige of the mark without paying any compensation to the proprietor. However, this depended on whether the competitor's goods were 'an imitation' of the proprietor's (unfair) or simply 'an alternative' (which would be legitimate competition, and thus not without 'due cause'—see para **5.87** below). When the case returned to the UK, Kitchin LJ in the Court of Appeal[2] restated the position:

> 'However, if the advertisement offers an alternative to the goods or services of the proprietor and does so without offering a mere imitation of them or causing dilution or tarnishment of the trade mark or adversely affecting the functions of the trade mark, then as a rule the use constitutes fair competition and is not without due cause.'

1 Case 323/09 *Interflora Inc & anor v Marks & Spencer plc & anor* [2012] FSR 3.
2 [2014] EWCA Civ 1403.

5.78 Whether or not an unfair advantage is taken will depend to some measure on the respective goods and services involved. To establish unfair advantage, it is not necessary that the registered mark and the third party's sign be similar enough to result in a likelihood of confusion; nor is it necessary that there be detriment to the registered mark.[1] The infringer must 'ride on the coat-tails' of the mark 'in order to benefit from the power of attraction, the reputation and the prestige of that mark and to exploit, without paying any financial compensation, the marketing effort expended by the proprietor of the mark in order to create and maintain the mark's image'.[2] In the case of a trade mark with a reputation for alcoholic beverages, for example, the use of a similar mark for bar services by a third party may well amount to free riding on the coat tails of that reputation. However, it is worth noting that on many occasions, the trade mark owner who alleges unfair advantage may also be in a position to bring a case that the use is likely to cause confusion, and so will have at least two grounds for objecting to the later mark. The overall position on unfair advantage (albeit in the context of infringement) was reviewed in *Jack Wills*.[3] Notably, the judge held in that case that there was no requirement to prove that the defendant subjectively intended to take advantage of the reputation of the earlier mark. It seems likely that that principle would also be relevant in the context of an application to register a mark, perhaps most obviously where the applicant insists that its intentions are wholly benign.

1 C-487/07 *L'Oréal v Bellure* at [36] and [43].
2 *Red Bull v Sun Mark* [2012] EWHC 1929 (Ch), [2013] ETMR 53 at [94]–[97].
3 *Jack Wills v House of Fraser (Stores)* [2014] EWHC 110 at [69]–[84].

Detriment to distinctive character or repute

5.79 In the alternative to showing that the later mark takes unfair advantage of the reputation of the earlier mark, the opponent of registration of a later mark may seek to show that that mark is detrimental to the distinctive character and/or detrimental to the repute of the earlier mark.[1] For these purposes, the meaning of detriment to distinctive character has been described as being 'blurring' or 'dilution', whilst detriment to repute has been called 'tarnishing'. Each requires proof of a change in the economic behaviour of consumers, or a serious likelihood of such a change.[2]

1 TMA 1994 s 5(3) and EUTMR Art 8(5).
2 C-252/07 *Intel Corporation Inc v CPM United Kingdom Ltd* [2009] ETMR 13. (Whereas unfair advantage does not: *Argos Ltd v Argos Systems Inc* [2019] FSR 3 at [107].)

Detriment to distinctive character—'blurring' or 'dilution'

5.80 Detriment to distinctive character (blurring or dilution), occurs where the use of the later mark would cause the earlier trade mark to be less capable of fulfilling its role to distinguish. Inherently, all marks that share similar elements have the capacity to lessen the distinctive character of each other, since the uniqueness of a mark or an element of a mark is part of what makes it distinctive. In defending such an allegation, the applicant for registration of the later mark should therefore attempt to demonstrate that the mark is used by various companies such that the later mark would not have the effect claimed. However, in the *Intel* case, the CJEU held that the earlier trade mark need not be *unique*, so the mere fact that the mark is used by other undertakings does not necessarily mean that a challenge on this ground is bound to fail.[1]

1 *Intel* C-252/07 [2009] ETMR 13. The Court of Appeal reviewed the law on the 'detriment' provisions in *Comic Enterprises Ltd v Twentieth Century Fox Film Corp* [2016] ETMR 22 at [110].

5.81 The Court in *Intel* also stated that the existence or absence of detriment must be established by reference to the consumers of the goods or services for which the earlier mark is registered: ie, it is not considered purely by reference to the trade mark alone but to the actual (or rather, projected) effect in the market place.

5.82 The CJEU returned to the issue of dilution in *Interflora v Marks & Spencer*.[1] This was a case where Marks & Spencer had bought certain keywords containing the registered mark 'Interflora' so that an internet search using those words would bring up advertising links to its own competing business. In line with previous cases such as *L'Oréal v eBay*[2] the Court said that there is a possibility that dilution will occur if the advertisement does not enable the reasonably well-informed and reasonably observant internet user to tell that the respective undertakings are independent. Dilution may occur if, for example, the use of keyword advertising contributes towards the proprietor's mark coming to be seen as a generic term. Whether or not it does is something for the national court to decide.

1 C-323/09 *Interflora* [76]–[83].
2 C-324/09 *L'Oréal & ors v eBay International & ors* (12 July 2011).

Detriment to repute—'tarnishing'

5.83 Detriment to repute—broadly considered as 'tarnishing'—is deemed to occur when the prestige of the mark is damaged by way of the use of the third party mark in contexts which are inappropriate or otherwise damaging.

Detriment to repute may take two forms:

1 use which is damaging of itself regardless of the particular kind of reputation of the earlier trade mark; and
2 use which is damaging in light of the particular kind of reputation of the earlier trade mark.

5.84 As regards the first form of detriment, the use of a mark that calls to mind the earlier trade mark and is offensive or negative towards the earlier trade mark would probably be detrimental regardless of the goods or services for which the earlier trade mark is used. An example would be to combine the earlier trade mark with an expletive or otherwise general negative reference. For example, in the *VISA*[1] case, the use of the famous mark VISA for condoms was considered objectionable. As regards the second form of detriment, this may occur where the later product is something that is incongruous with the earlier product, for example where the brand has a particular reputation for luxury or quality that will be damaged by association with goods of inferior quality.

1 *IA Sheimer (M) Sdn Bhd's Trade Mark Application* [2000] RPC 484. Detriment was considered more recently in *British Amateur Gymnastics Association v UK Gymnastics Ltd* [2020] EWHC 1678 (IPEC).

5.85 In the context of infringement, the CJEU in *L'Oréal v eBay*[1] considered the question of damage to the reputation of a trade mark. In that case the issue was whether the trade mark proprietor could prevent resale of its luxury perfumes where the products had been unboxed from their original packaging. It was held that as long as the proprietor could show that this damaged the image of the product and, hence, the reputation of the mark, it was entitled to prevent the resale under Art 5(2) of the Directive.

1 C-324/09 *L'Oréal SA & others v eBay International AG & others*, 12 July 2011.

The level of association required in the case of advantage or detriment – a 'link'

5.86 In the case of an allegation that the use of the later mark would take advantage of the distinctive character or repute of the earlier trade mark, the owner of the earlier trade mark must merely show that a 'link' would be formed in the mind of the consumer—that the consumer would make an association without necessarily being confused.[1] Even where the mark has a huge reputation, it cannot be assumed that consumers will connect the two in a relevant manner without some evidence to that effect.[2] Where the earlier trade mark has a reputation then it will often be in the interests of the owner to use both the likelihood of confusion and the unfair advantage/detriment grounds, although this will require a larger amount of supporting evidence since the reputation of the earlier mark must be established. The existence of a link will not necessarily be sufficient to establish injury.[3]

1 C-408/01 *Adidas-Salomon*.
2 C-252/07 *Intel Corp Inc v CPM United Kingdom Ltd* [2009] ETMR 13. For a case where the 'link' was found to be 'tenuous' but just about established, see *Maier v ASOS* [2013] EWHC 283 at [126]–[135]. On appeal, see [2015] EWCA Civ 220 at [143]–[144].
3 *Specsavers* (CA) [2012] EWCA Civ 24 at [123].

Use of the later mark without due cause

5.87 As set out in paras **5.05** and **5.63** above, opposition to the registration of a later mark may be based on an earlier trade mark which has the requisite reputation provided use of the later mark *without due cause* would take unfair advantage of or be detrimental to the distinctive character or repute of the earlier trade mark.

5.88 The TMA 1994 and EUTMR do not provide a definition of 'due cause'. However, the meaning of 'due cause' has been considered by the CJEU in *L'Oréal v Bellure* among other cases.[1] As a result, it now appears that a person who uses a mark as an online keyword or AdWord in order to offer genuine alternative products (rather than mere imitations) is not acting without due cause even where that usage takes advantage of the distinctive character and repute of the mark—but as long as it does not cause detriment to those functions or aspects of the mark. In other words, this is essentially just fair competition.

1 For example, the issue of what constitutes due cause was considered by the Court of Justice on a preliminary reference in *Interflora Inc v Marks & Spencer Plc* (C-323/09) [2012] FSR 3, in the context of keyword advertising. See also *Leidseplein Beheer BV v Red Bull GmbH* (C-65/12) [2014] ETMR 24 at [60] and *Planetart LLC v Photobox Ltd* [2020] EWHC 713 at [43]–[45].

5.89 In *Specsavers* the Court of Appeal reviewed the *L'Oréal* type authorities and summarised the position as follows:

> 'a proprietor of a trade mark with a reputation is not necessarily entitled to prohibit the use by a competitor of his mark in relation to goods for which it is registered even though the mark has been adopted with the intention and for the purpose of taking advantage of its distinctive character and repute, the competitor will derive a real advantage from his use of the mark, and the competitor will not pay any compensation in respect of that use. Consideration must be given to whether the use is without due cause. Specifically, the use of a trade mark as a keyword in order to advertise goods which are an alternative to but not mere imitations of the goods of the proprietor and in a way which does not cause dilution or tarnishment and which does not adversely affect the functions of the trade mark must be regarded as fair competition and cannot be prohibited'.[1]

Where there is use without due cause, that use is almost bound to be unfair. In the context of an application for a mark (rather than infringement proceedings) it will be for the applicant to overcome the presumption that where the use of the mark sought would appear to take advantage of distinctive character or repute of an earlier mark, that use would be without due cause.

1 *Specsavers* (CA) [2012] EWCA Civ 24 at [141].

CONFLICTS WITH OTHER EARLIER RIGHTS

5.90 The registration of a later mark can also be opposed or its registration declared invalid on the basis of earlier rights other than those arising from earlier trade mark applications and registrations. The relevant rights for these purposes fall into a number of categories. This section will begin by considering those rights that apply in the UK before considering those which apply in relation to EUTMs.

UK: rights protecting unregistered trade marks used in the course of trade

5.91 Section 5(4)(a) of the TMA 1994 provides that the registration of a trade mark may be prevented if, and to the extent, that its use may be prevented by any rule of law (particularly the law of passing-off) protecting an unregistered trade mark used in the course of trade.

5.92 The law to be applied in determining whether the earlier unregistered trade mark exists is the same as that applied in a case for passing-off.[1] However, much of the consideration is theoretical because in many cases, there will not have been any use of the later mark, or at least there will not have been any instances of consumers having been misled. In most cases the lack of any examples of consumers having been misled will not be determinative. The reasons for this are twofold:

- even where there has been use of the later trade mark, it will often be for a narrower range of goods and services than the specification; and
- the consideration made by the relevant authority is of the fair use of the later mark, not the specific manner of use to date—any disclaimers, prominent accompanying marks or other distinguishing factors used by the owner of the later mark will only be of relevance if they were incorporated into the mark applied for.

1 See **Chapter 20**.

UK: protection for other unregistered rights (copyright, design right, etc)

5.93 Section 5(4)(b) of the TMA 1994 provides a 'catch-all' for persons who have an earlier right which is not an earlier trade mark as defined by s 6 of the TMA 1994 and which is not a right protected under s 5(4)(a). In most cases the relevant right for these purposes will be a copyright, design right or a registered design. Indeed, such rights are expressly mentioned in s 5(4)(b).

Unregistered rights applicable to EUTMs

5.94 In the case of an EUTM, Art 8(4) of the EUTMR provides that the proprietor of a non-registered trade mark or of another sign used in the course of trade of more than mere local significance can oppose registration of a EUTM if and to the extent that its rights to that sign were acquired prior to the application date of the EUTM (taking into account any claim to priority) and give it the right to prohibit the use of a subsequent trade mark.[1]

1 T-225/06 *Budějovickí Budvar v OHIM, AnheuserBusch (BUDWEISER).*

5.95 It is for the proprietor to prove that the right relied on affords the right to prohibit use of the contested mark or sign by others. However, the opponent is not necessarily required to prove the mark was used in the sense as would be required for a trade mark liable to revocation for non use:[1] whether the mark relied upon gives the right to prohibit subsequent use is a matter for national law. However, the mark must be used in the course of trade to some extent.

1 T-534/08 *Granuband v OHIM,* 30 September 2010, General Court.

5.96 A party who wishes to rely on an earlier sign protected under national law will need to demonstrate the existence of the right relied upon by providing evidence from national legal texts. Where the EUIPO has already recognised the existence of legal protection of a right then evidence on that point will not be required.[1]

1 For a list of the local rights that can be relied upon, see the EUIPO's *Trade Mark Guidelines* (Part C – Oppositions, section 4).

TRADE MARK 'FUNCTIONS'

5.97 In deciding cases on the relative grounds of refusal of registration and also on infringement (see **Chapter 14** below) the courts are increasingly referring to what they call the 'functions' of trade marks, including most prominently:

- the essential (or origin) function;
- the advertising function; and
- the investment function.

These functions can seem confusing and it may help to bear in mind that they are generally invoked where the courts are trying to establish whether or not the proprietor of an earlier mark is entitled to object to the use or registration of a later mark. In each case, the court is asking what is the impact on the operation or usefulness of the earlier trade mark, and whether that impact is a form of harm for which the legislation offers the proprietor protection.

The essential function—origin

5.98 The core function of a trade—its 'essential function'—is undoubtedly the function of indicating origin. This is a notion that can be traced back at least as far as *Terrapin v Terranova*[1], a German reference to the CJEU concerning parallel imports. In that case the Court referred to 'the basic function of the trade mark to guarantee to consumers that the product has the same origin'. Advocate-General Francesco Capotorti later used the phrase 'essential function' in *Hoffmann-la Roche*[2] referring to this function as being 'to guarantee to consumers the identity of the origin of the products'—a definition endorsed by the Court in its judgment.

1 C-119/75 *Terrapin (Overseas) Ltd v Terranova Industrie C. A. Kapferer & Co* [1975] 2 CMLR 482—see [6].
2 *Hoffmann-La Roche & Co AG & Hoffmann-La Roche AG v Centrafarm Vertriebsgesellschaft Pharmazeutischer Erzeugnisse mbH* [1978] FSR 598.

5.99 This origin function was later included in the recitals to the first version of the Directive (21 December 1988), which referred to 'the protection afforded by the registered trade mark, the function of which is in particular to guarantee the trade mark as an indication of origin'.[1] However, the phrase 'essential function' received little attention until the post-harmonisation cases on the meaning of Community legislation, which were decided in the late 1990s and after (see, for example, *Canon*[2] and later significant cases). The concept of the essential function is now a central plank of the European trade mark jurisprudence, and has been adopted by the UK courts.

1 See recital 11 in the codified version of the Directive.
2 C-39/97 *Canon Kabushiki Kaisha v Metro Goldwyn Mayer Inc* [1999] RPC 117.

Other functions—the advertising and investment functions

5.100 The idea that there may be other trade mark functions—functions that are ancillary to the essential (origin) function was already present by the time of *Hag II*[1] in which the Advocate-General referred to the function of 'protecting the proprietor's goodwill'.

1 C-10/89 *SA Cnl-Sucal NV v Hag GF AG* [1990] 3 CMLR 571.

5.101 The issue of ancillary functions was later considered in *Arsenal v Reed.*[1] There replica football merchandise was branded with the registered trade mark of the club but had arguably been sold in such a way that no one who bought the goods could be deceived into thinking they were the genuine goods of the trade mark proprietor. The point was that if the essential function was safeguarded, it was not clear on what basis the proprietor could object to the defendant's use of the sign. To counter this, the Advocate-General suggested that there were various ancillary functions of trade marks that might qualify for protection, including functions as an indicator of repute, a mark of quality, and as a means of advertising (the latter drawing on earlier cases such as *Christian Dior v Evora*[2]). In its judgment, the CJEU held that Art 5(1)(a) of Directive 2008/95/EC (now Directive Art 10(1)(a)) would entitle the proprietor to prevent a third party's use of an identical sign if that use was liable to affect *'the functions of the trade mark, in particular its essential function of guaranteeing to consumers the origin of the goods'*. In other words, damage to the other functions could be relevant, even if only because this ultimately harmed the essential function.[3]

1 C-206/01 *Arsenal Football Club Plc v Reed* [2003] 1 CMLR 12.
2 C-337/95 *Parfums Christian Dior SA and Another v Evora BV* [1998] 1 CMLR 737.
3 This approach to what is now Directive Art 10(1)(a) has been affirmed in cases such as C-245/02 *Anheuser-Busch Inc v Budejovicky Budvar Národni Podnik* [2004] ECR I-10989 and C-17/06 *Céline Sarl v Céline Ltd* [2007] ETMR 80.

5.102 It is now clear that in addition to the essential function, there is an 'advertising function' and also an 'investment function' which may be entitled to protection under trade mark law.

- In *L'Oréal v Bellure*[1] the CJEU stated that what is now Directive Art 10(1)(a) could allow a trade mark proprietor to prevent use of an identical mark even where the essential function was not jeopardised, as long as the use affects or is liable to affect one of the other functions of the mark. The Court referred to 'other functions, in particular that of guaranteeing the quality of the goods or services in question and those of communication, investment or advertising'.
- In *Google France*[2] the CJEU held that 'the proprietor of a trade mark is entitled to prohibit a third party from using, without the proprietor's consent, a sign identical with its trade mark in relation to goods or services which are identical with those for which that trade mark is registered, in the case where that use adversely affects the proprietor's use of its mark as a factor in sales promotion or as an instrument of commercial strategy'. The Court also referred to the advertising function as 'using [the] mark for advertising purposes designed to inform and persuade consumers'.[3] However, the Court concluded that on the facts there was no adverse effect on the advertising function of the proprietors' marks.
- In *Interflora*[4] in the Court went further still and drew a clear distinction between the advertising function and the investment function, a distinction that had not been particularly apparent in the *L'Oréal v Bellure* decision. The Court considered the impact of the alleged infringements on the advertising and investment functions separately, calling those functions 'overlapping but distinct'.[5]

The investment function was described as the use of the mark 'to acquire or preserve a reputation capable of attracting consumers and retaining their loyalty'. By contrast, the Court said that trade marks rights were not supposed to prevent 'practices inherent in competition', and that the defendants' use of the mark in Google's AdWords service did not affect the advertising function, ie, it did not deny the proprietor 'the opportunity of using its mark effectively to inform and win over consumers'. The distinguishing feature of the investment function was said to be that 'when the trade mark is used to acquire or preserve a reputation, not only advertising is employed, but also various commercial techniques'.

1 C-487/07 *L'Oréal SA v Bellure NV* [2009] ETMR 55.
2 C-236/08 *Google France Sarl v Louis Vuitton Malletier SA* (and two joined cases) [2010] ETMR 30.
3 C-236/08; see [91].
4 C-323/09 *Interflora Inc & anor v Marks & Spencer plc & anor* [2012] FSR 3.
5 C-323/09 *Interflora*; see the full discussion at [54]–[66].

5.103 The *Datacard* decision[1] (although it pre-dates *Interflora*) contains a useful discussion of the complex and still emerging law on the ancillary functions of trade marks, and in particular the advertising function. In it, Arnold J said (see [272]):

> 'It seems to me that the key point is that the advertising function of a trade mark is its function of conveying a particular *image* to the average consumer of the goods or services in question. The case law of the CJEU suggests that the advertising function is most likely to be affected when the trade mark has been used by the trade mark proprietor in relation to prestigious goods that have a luxurious image and the third party's use of the signs complained of either takes unfair advantage of that image or adversely affects that image by associating it with down-market goods, marketing methods or advertising.'

The Court of Appeal in *British American Tobacco* referred to the CJEU authorities establishing the various trade mark functions, and added that the way they have been described 'applies equally to the use of an unregistered sign'.[2]

1 *Datacard Corporation v Eagle Technologies Ltd* [2011] EWHC 244; [2011] RPC 17.
2 *R (on the application of British American Tobacco UK Ltd and others) v Secretary of State for Health* [2017] RPC 16.

5.104 However, the Court in *Interflora* was apparently neutral on the question of image in relation to the advertising function. This may suggest that the advertising function is simply about the proprietor's ability to use the trade mark to maintain or enhance its profile with customers, but without necessarily making reference to how customers perceive the proprietor. In that sense, it seems possible in principle that the advertising function of a trade mark could be affected even where consumers had a negative perception of the proprietor. In the *Lush* case, the claimant said the advertising function arose from it having 'built up a strong reputation in the Lush mark', and the judge later referred to the mark's 'quality of attracting custom', which he held was damaged by Amazon's use.[1]

1 *Cosmetic Warriors Ltd v Amazon.co.uk Ltd* [2014] EWHC 181 at [17] and [69].

5.105 By contrast, the investment function described in *Interflora* does place an emphasis on reputation, which indicates something above and beyond merely alerting consumers to the presence of the trade mark proprietor in the marketplace (ie, the basic advertising function). Arnold J said in *Interflora* that where a third party's keyword advertising adversely affects the reputation of a trade mark, as, for example, where the image the trade mark conveys is damaged, then there is an adverse affect on the investment function.[1] In *Lush*, the investment function was tied to the claimant's 'reputation for ethical and environmental-friendly trading'—contrast the advertising function referred to above in **5.104**. The judge in that case accepted that the claimant's ethical reputation; might be damaged by association with Amazon, a company whose attitudes to paying UK tax some might find 'repugnant'.

The overlap of investment with advertising is obvious, in that the effectiveness of adverts often hinges on the proprietor's reputation, but the investment function also appears to encapsulate brand loyalty generally—the proprietor's ability to use the trade mark as a shorthand for everything that consumers value about the goods or services. In that respect, the Court seems to have come full circle to the ideas of 'protecting goodwill' and 'quality or reputation' referred to by the Advocates-General in *Hag II* and *Arsenal v Reed* (see paras **5.99–5.100** above).

1 *Interflora v Marks & Spencer* [2013] FSR 33 at [270]–[274].

CURRENT STATUS OF 'HONEST CONCURRENT USE'

5.106 We turn finally to the issue of 'honest concurrent use'. Under the Trade Marks Act 1938 where two trade marks had co-existed for a period of time, the English courts applied a doctrine of 'honest concurrent use' to prevent the earlier mark's proprietor from preventing the later mark from proceeding to registration. The doctrine was, in effect, a derogation from the first-to-file principle. It recognised that two similar marks could be allowed to coexist, despite a risk of consumer confusion, in order to do justice to the parties who had grown their brands independently. To that extent, it may be seen also as a product of an earlier age of trade mark law where the focus was less on the consumer. The leading UK case on the doctrine being the 1930s House of Lords case of *Pirie.*[1]

1 *Pirie's Application* (1932) 49 RPC 195.

5.107 Section 7 of the TMA 1994 preserved the doctrine (referring to the common law under the 1938 Act). Although this preservation was not based on any provision in the Directive, it was thought to be permitted because the Directive was only a partially harmonising provision.

5.108 However, in the *Budweiser*[1] case, the Advocate-General suggested that the doctrine of honest concurrent use is incompatible with the Directive. In that case the particular issue was whether the defendant should be entitled to invalidate the claimant's later identical mark where the two sides had been trading under the identical brand name 'Budweiser' for many years.[2] It appeared that the claimant's later identical mark might be liable to revocation, despite years of side-by-side use, and even though the Court said consumers were 'well aware of the difference'.

1 C-482/09 *Budějovickí Budvar, národní podnik v Anheuser-Busch Inc*, Advocate-General's Opinion, 3 February 2011.
2 See paras **15.29–15.30** for more details.

5.109 The CJEU in *Budweiser*[1] provided a rather neat answer to this problem while staying within the confines of existing case law. It first endorsed the strict reading of the Directive provisions on acquiescence, noting that a party cannot be said to acquiesce when it has no choice but to put up with another's conduct. It also acknowledged that the time period for acquiescence only begins to run once the later mark is registered (pre-registration use does not count). However, it pointed out that the later mark could only be declared invalid on the relative grounds if the use of the later mark 'has or is liable to have an adverse effect on the essential function of the trade mark'.[2] The Court then gave five separate reasons why in its view there was no such risk of harm to the essential function of the defendant's mark. Each of these reasons was clearly an aspect of the parties' past concurrent use and the fact that, as a result of that use, there was no real danger of affecting the essential function of the mark. When the case returned to the UK, the Court of Appeal held that the proprietor of the earlier mark was not entitled to cancellation of the later mark where there had been a long period of honest concurrent use, and that use had not had (and was not liable to have) an adverse effect on the essential function of the trade mark.[3]

1 C-482/09 *Budějovickí Budvar*, judgment of the CJEU, 22 September 2011.
2 Following the case law mentioned at para **5.06** above.
3 [2012] EWCA Civ 880; [2012] 3 All ER 1405.

5.110 In essence, the approach of the CJEU in *Budweiser* is not inconsistent with the doctrine of honest concurrent use but used the language of modern case law by asking whether (given such past use) the functions of the earlier mark are genuinely jeopardised. It seems that the UK courts, and the UKIPO are now following this approach (as the Court of Appeal in *Budweiser* did).

Even though the CJEU stressed that the circumstances of the case were 'exceptional', similar facts arose in *IPC Media*, in which the mark in dispute was 'Ideal Home'.[1] Since then honest concurrent use has been cited as a defence in a number of cases.[2] The Court of Appeal again found that the long period of honest concurrent use meant that the lower court was entitled to dismiss a claim for infringement. All cases will turn on their own facts, and any party looking to run a defence of honest concurrent use would be wise not only to prove as fully as possible the period, and extent of use alleged, but also to provide convincing support for the claim that there has not been (and is not liable to be) an adverse effect on the essential function of the mark.

1 *IPC Media Ltd v Media 10 Ltd* [2014] EWCA Civ 1439.

2 See eg. *Victoria Plum Ltd v Victorian Plumbing* [2016] FSR 17 and *Easygroup Ltd v Easylife Ltd* [2021] EWHC 1705 (Ch). It has been held that the honesty of concurrent use may change over time: Bentley 1962 *Ltd v* Bentley *Motors Ltd* [2020] ETMR 8.

Chapter 6

Classification

THE REQUIREMENT FOR A CLASSIFICATION SYSTEM

6.01 For the purposes of registration, goods and services must be classified according to a prescribed system of classification.[1]

A classification system allows the efficient searching of trade marks by third parties proposing to use a new trade mark and wanting to establish whether it is available for use, and/or for registration.[2] This function is something to which the registration authorities pay particular regard when considering an application for registration.

The classification system used by UKIPO and EUIPO is the Nice Classification System.[3]

1 See Trade Marks Act 1994 ('TMA 1994') s 34(1) and EU Trade Marks Regulation ('EUTMR') Art 33.
2 Trade Mark Rules ('TMR') r 7 and EU Trade Marks Implementation Regulation ('EUTMIR') Art 7(d).
3 TMR r 7 and UKIPO *Trade Marks Manual, Classification Guide*, Section 2.

NICE CLASSIFICATION SYSTEM

6.02 The Nice Classification System was adopted under the Nice Agreement.[1] Under Art 2(3) of the Nice Agreement, official documents and publications relating to the registration of marks must include the numbers of the classes of the Classification to which the goods or services for which the mark is registered belong.

The system is maintained by the International Bureau of WIPO and is reviewed every year by a committee of experts. In its current edition (eleventh edn, 2021), it comprises 45 classes:

- Classes 1–34 are for goods; and
- Classes 35–45 are for services.

For each class, the Nice Classification System provides:

- Class headings—these contain general indications as to the scope of the class in question. The general indications are the expressions that appear between semicolons in the class heading. For example, the class heading for class 37 ('Construction services; installation and repair services; mining extraction, oil and gas drilling') contains three separate general indications. The class heading for class 4 ('Industrial oils and greases, wax; lubricants; dust absorbing, wetting and binding compositions; fuels and illuminants; candles and wicks for lighting') contains five.
- Explanatory notes—these may include further information as to what each class includes and does not include.
- Alphabetical list of goods/services included in each class. In total around 10,000 types of goods and around 1,000 types of service are listed across the various classes.

Helpful guidance on the system of classification can be found on UKIPO's website.[2]

1 The Nice Agreement was entered into on 15 June 1957. It was revised on 14 July 1967 and amended on 28 September 1979. It was adopted as a 'Special Agreement' in accordance with Art 19 of the Convention for the Protection of Industrial Property 1883.
2 The guidance can be found in the Trade Marks section of UKIPO's website at www.gov.uk/topic/intellectual-property/trade-marks.

THE REQUIREMENT FOR AN APPLICANT TO SPECIFY CLASS(ES) AND THE GOODS, AND/OR SERVICES

6.03 Every application for registration of a mark in UKIPO must contain a statement specifying:

(a) the class(es) in accordance with the Nice Classification to which the application relates; and
(a) the goods and/or services that are appropriate to the class(es).

The specification of goods, and/or services must be done in such a way that indicates clearly the nature of those goods, and/or services and allows them to be classified in the classes of the Nice Classification System.[1]

Similar provisions apply for the registration of EUTMs at EUIPO.[2] The Nice Classification also applies to international registrations under the Madrid Protocol.[3]

The application can be for one or more classes. Further, an applicant may apply for registration in respect of all goods or services included in a class, or in respect of only some of those goods or services.[4]

Pre-filing advice as to how to word a specification can be obtained from UKIPO's Classification Team.[5]

1 See TMA 1994 s 32(2)(c) and TMR r 8(2).
2 See EUTMR Art 33 and EUTMIR Art 7.

3 See Protocol to the Madrid Agreement Art 3(2).
4 C-363/99, *Kjoninklijke KPN Nederland NV v Benelux Merkenbureau (POSTKANTOOR)* [2006] Ch 1 at [112] (CJEU).
5 UKIPO's Classification Team, email: tmclassificationenquiries@ipo.gov.uk.

POINTS FOR THE APPLICANT TO CONSIDER WHEN APPLYING

Requirement for clarity and precision in specifying goods and services

6.04 When applying to register a mark, an applicant must identify the goods and/or services to which the application relates, and must do so with sufficient clarity, and precision to enable the competent authorities, and economic operators (on that basis alone) to determine the extent of the protection being sought.[1] UKIPO or, as the case may be, EUIPO will determine on a case-by-case basis whether the applicant has complied with this requirement. Where appropriate, an examiner will contact the applicant regarding any objections that they have concerning the specification, setting a deadline to respond to such objections.

1 Case C-307/10 *Chartered Institute of Patent Attorneys v Registrar of Trade Marks* (*IP TRANSLATOR*) [2013] RPC 11 at [42]–[49]. EUTMR Art 33(2).

Use of the Class headings to specify goods or services

6.05 On occasions, applicants seek to specify the goods or services by reference only to some, or all of the general indications contained in a class heading from the Nice Classification.[1] This requires some care as such applications can, on occasions, run into difficulties.

First, whilst many of the general indications in the class headings will be sufficiently clear and precise, a few are not. Indeed, some are too general, and/or cover goods or services that are too variable to be compatible with the trade mark's function as an indication of origin.[2] An application which relies on such a specification will not satisfy the requirements of clarity and precision. In a *Common Communication* issued on 28 October 2015 (replacing the previous version issued on 20 February 2014)[3] the various Trade Mark Offices of the EU (including UKIPO and EUIPO) identified five general indications (out of a total of 204) used in the Nice class headings, which they consider to be insufficiently clear and precise. These include, for example, the general indications of 'repair' and of 'installation services' in the class heading for class 37.[4] Those indications are considered to be insufficiently clear, or precise because they do not provide a clear indication of the services being provided, or of the goods in respect of which those services are to be provided. They could, therefore, relate to services carried out by service providers with different levels of technical capabilities, and know-how, and may relate to different market sectors.[5]

Second, it was held by the CJEU in the *IP TRANSLATOR* case that a specification which relies on *all* of the general indications for a particular class heading is ambiguous because it might, or might not be intended to identify less than 100 per cent of the goods or services falling within the relevant class. Prior to *IP TRANSLATOR* there had been a different approach between those (at one point including UKIPO) who took the view that a classification that used the entire wording of a class heading would cover only the goods or services actually referred to in those words and those (such as EUIPO) who took the view that it covered all goods, or services in the class even if not expressly referred to in the heading.[6] Accordingly, an applicant must now specify all goods and services of interest.

In essence, where an applicant relies on the general indications of a class heading, the question is whether that wording allows the goods or services to be identified with sufficient clarity and precision without the need for further details.[7] Disparate types of goods and services should be separately identified rather than being subsumed within indeterminate wording.[8]

1 For example, 'Class 4 Industrial oils and greases, wax; lubricants; dust absorbing, wetting and binding compositions; fuels and illuminants; candles and wicks for lighting'.

2 Case C-307/10 *Chartered Institute of Patent Attorneys v Registrar of Trade Marks (IP TRANSLATOR)* [2013] RPC 11 at [54]–[56].

3 *Common Communication on the Common Practice on the General Indications of the Nice Class Headings* (v1.2) issued by the European Trade Mark and Design Network.

4 The entire class heading reads—'Construction services; installation and repair services; mining extraction, oil and gas drilling'.

5 The five general indications found to be too vague are some (but not all) of the general indications contained in the class headings for four classes, namely 7, 37, 40 and 45 (class 37 contains two of the five vague general indications).

6 See Case C-307/10 *Chartered Institute of Patent Attorneys v Registrar of Trade Marks (IP TRANSLATOR)* [2013] RPC 11 at [57]–[62]. Where a mark was registered before the *IP TRANSLATOR* case solely in respect of the entire heading of a Nice class, the proprietor was able to declare their intention on the date of filing had been to seek protection for goods/services other than those covered by the words of the heading literally construed. Upon such declaration, the registrar amended (provided the relevant services were within the alphabetical list for the relevant class) the register accordingly. In the absence of such a declaration, the registration was deemed to extend only to goods/services covered by the literal meaning of the words.

7 TMR 1994 regs 8(2A)–(2B), EUTMR Art 33(3).

8 See *Re Chartered Institute of Patent Attorney' Trade Mark Application* O-197-13 [2013] RPC 20 at [14]. In this case, a UK application for the mark *IP TRANSLATOR* which relied on the entire class heading of 41 was initially rejected because (following EUIPO *Guidance*) it was held to include *all* of the services to which class 41 applied including services in respect of which the mark would have been descriptive ('translation'). However, on appeal, the Appointed Person (Geoffrey Hobbs QC) following the decision of the CJEU, found that the specification (being of an entire class heading) was ambiguous, and he remitted the matter back to the registrar so that the applicant could be given a chance to confirm that its application was intended to be of a narrower scope than the natural and ordinary meaning of the words used in the application, and to identify the scope of the services intended to be covered.

Specification should cover goods/services in both existing and anticipated future areas of activity

6.06 In deciding on the wording of the specification of goods or services and the relevant class(es), it is important to bear in mind that trade mark protection is provided from the effective date of registration. Moreover, although an applicant can make a further application to gain protection in more classes, that further application may be refused if in the interim a third party has applied to register a conflicting mark in respect of that extended area.

Accordingly, when applying for registration of a mark, it is essential that applicants take care to specify goods and services that cover both their existing and their future anticipated areas of activity.

Difficulties arising when the specification is too broadly stated

6.07 On the other hand, the list of goods and services for which protection is sought should not be unfairly broad or extensive. Applicants often ask for their marks to be registered in respect of *all* classes of goods and services—ie to obtain protection against any use, regardless of the goods or services involved. Such an approach—or any overly broad or extensive list of classes—raises a number of practical and legal difficulties:

- the mark may be descriptive (and, therefore, unregistrable) in respect of some goods or services;[1]
- there may well be a wider range of competing third-party rights (registered and unregistered) which would make registration more difficult;
- the applicant may not be able to make the declaration required under the TMA 1994 that he is using, or has a *bona fide* intention to use, the mark in relation to all such goods or services;[2]
- the application may be seen as being in 'bad faith';[3] and
- the application will be more costly.

The last four of these difficulties are considered below.

1 As was the case before the Registry in *Re Chartered Institute of Patent Attorney' Trade Mark Application (IP TRANSLATOR)* [2013] RPC 20—see above. See also C-363/99, *Koninklijke KPN Nederland NV v Benelux Merkenbureau (POSTKANTOOR)* [2006] Ch 1 at [113].
2 See para **6.09** below.
3 See **Chapter 4**.

1 Competing third-party trade mark rights

6.08 The broader the scope of the application for registration, the more likely it is that an applicant will face difficulties due to existing third-party trade mark rights.

Oppositions by third parties can lead to substantial delay in obtaining a registration. This can be so even if the opposition is against a part of the specification that is of lesser commercial importance to the applicant. Unless the applicant is able to separate the opposed part of the application from the unopposed, the opposition proceedings will delay registration of the application as a whole.

2 Declaration as to use or the intention to use

6.09 For UK trade mark applications, the application for registration must state that the mark either *is* being used by the applicant or with his consent, for the goods and services specified in the application, or that there is a *bona fide* intention that it should be so used.[1] (This requirement does not apply to applications for EUTMs.[2])

Few applications are challenged on this basis, as opponents often take the view that a challenge could be defeated quite simply by the applicant asserting the requisite intention. Nevertheless, the requirement must be borne in mind since an application may fail if and to the extent that the applicant has no honest intention to use the mark on particular goods and services covered by the application (whether such use is direct or by way of a third party).

1 TMA 1994, s 32(3).
2 See case C-53447/1 *Harte-Hanks Data Technologies, Inc v Trillium Digital Systems, Inc TRILLIUM Trade Mark.*
3 See the discussion of the significance of false statements regarding an applicant's intention to use a mark and of the *Skykick* case in **Chapter 4**.

3 Applications made in bad faith

6.10 When considering the breadth of the specification, applicants should also be aware that an application made simply to block third parties using a mark may be considered as falling below the levels of behaviour expected in commercial activities and, therefore, as being made in bad faith.[1]

1 See the discussion of bad faith as a ground for refusal of an application and of the *Skykick* case in **Chapter 4**. See also case C-52907 *Chocoladefabriken Lindt & Sprungli AG v Franz Hauswirth GmbH* [2009] ETMR 56.

4 The cost of protection

6.11 The costs associated with applying for and later defending an over-wide application for registration must also be borne in mind.

The cost of protection depends on the number of classes for which protection is sought. The UK and EU system has a basic fee covering a single class. Clearly, therefore, the more classes for which the registration is sought, the greater the cost.

Exclusions from protection—practice since Postkantoor

6.12 Whilst a specification can contain words limiting protection to a particular description of the goods in question, it cannot use words that purport to limit protection by reference to the goods *not* having a particular quality. In other words, positive words but not negative words must be used to describe the goods.[1]

1 C-363/99, *Koninklijke KPN Nederland NV v Benelux Merkenbureau (POSTKANTOOR)* [2006] Ch 1 at [117]. In *Postkantoor* the issue was whether the mark 'Postkantoor' (Post Office) could be registered for services such as direct mail campaigns, or the issue of postage stamps provided they were not connected with a post office. The CJEU held that that it was not possible to accept a mark for certain goods and services on the basis that they did not possess a particular characteristic as it would lead to uncertainty. In practice, this ruling has subsequently been applied in the somewhat broader way described in the text above.

6.13 It is, however, possible to exclude a sub-category of goods. UKIPO gives the following example of an unacceptable and an acceptable exclusion:

> **Unacceptable**—Trade mark FROG for 'footwear; but not including footwear in the form of frogs'. This is unacceptable because it seeks to exclude by reference to the footwear not having the quality of being in the form of frogs.
> **Acceptable**—Trade mark FROG for 'footwear; but not including novelty footwear'. This is acceptable because it excludes a sub-category of goods.

Retail, wholesale and shopping-centre services

6.14 In the past there was uncertainty surrounding the position of 'retail services'—ie the activities of a trader intended to encourage a customer to conclude a transaction with that trader rather than with a competitor[1]—and, in particular, whether they fell within the concept of 'services' for the purposes of trade mark registration and protection.

The position was definitively clarified in the *Praktiker* case.[2] As a result, where an application for 'retail services' is made before UKIPO or EUIPO, the applicant need not indicate in detail the particular services offered by the trader but must indicate the type of goods to which the services relate. Similar considerations apply in relation to wholesale services.

1 They may include, for example, the selection of an assortment of goods to offer for sale and the offering of a variety of services to customers.
2 C-481/02.

6.15 In relation to shopping centres, there was formerly some doubt as to whether the services offered by shopping centres to consumers—

ie the selection and provision of a location, facilities, information and an attractive ambience—could be protected. However, the High Court ruled in *Land Securities plc*[1] that such services may be protected. As a result, UKIPO has indicated that such services can be protected using the following form of words:

> 'The bringing together for the benefit of others, of a variety of retail outlets, entertainment, restaurant and [other clearly defined related services], enabling customers to conveniently view and purchase goods and make use of and purchase such services in a shopping centre or mall.'

1 [2009] RPC 5.

Amendments to applications—restrictions on widening the scope of an application post-filing

6.16 Under both the TMA 1994 and the EUTMR, an application once filed can be amended to *restrict* the goods or services to which it relates but cannot otherwise be amended—save to correct (a) the name or address of the applicant; (b) errors in the wording or of copying; or (c) obvious mistakes.[1]

Therefore, subject to these limited exceptions, the statement of goods and services to which an application relates cannot be *widened* after the application has been filed. If wider protection is sought, a further application must be made. For this reason, it is essential that proper consideration is given to the specification before the initial application is filed.

1 TMA 1994, s 39(1)–(2); EUTMR, Art 49(1)–(2). See *Re Chartered Institute of Patent Attorney' Trade Mark Application* O-197-13, [2013] RPC 20 at [29]–[31].

6.17 Although the addition of extra goods or services is, in general, not permitted, the applicant may be allowed to amend and add to the *classes* specified in the application. This addition of classes beyond those initially specified is allowed so that the goods or services identified in the application can be placed in their proper classes. The applicant will, of course, have to pay an additional fee for any additional class that is required.

Chapter 7

UK procedure for the registration of a trade mark

INTRODUCTION

7.01 The person entitled to a mark may seek to register it as a UK trade mark. This is done through the UK's Intellectual Property Office ('UKIPO'). It should be borne in mind that the owner of, or an applicant for, a UK trade mark may also apply for international registration under the Madrid International System (considered in **Chapter 9**). The procedure for registering a mark as a European Union trade mark is considered in **Chapter 8.**

7.02 This chapter will consider the UK procedure governing applications for the registration of a trade mark. It will do so under the following headings:

- The application.
- Examination of the application.
- Publication of the application.
- Opposition to the application.

Guidance as regards each of these matters is available on the UKIPO website— https://www.ipo.gov.uk (which now redirects to https://www.gov.uk/government/organisations/intellectual-property-office).

THE APPLICATION

The application form and fees payable

7.03 Applications for registration of a trade mark in the UK should be made by filing an application with UKIPO on Form TM3, or electronically on Form e-TM3[1], accompanied by the requisite fee.

1 See Trade Mark Rules 2008 ('TMR') r 5. The content of Form TM3 reflects the requirements of the Trade Marks Act 1994 ('TMA 1994') s 32 and of the TMR. An

application can be made without using the official Form TM3 provided the applicant either uses a replica of that form or of a form which contains the required information required by the form (r 3(2)).

7.04 On Form TM3 the applicant must give details of the mark (including an illustration), details relating to any claim for priority, a list of the goods or services in respect of which the mark is being used or is intended to be used, a list of any limitations or disclaimers which the applicant wishes to record and details relating to the applicant.

7.05 The application may be filed electronically online or on paper. The applicant may choose between two services:

- standard examination service—this costs £200 plus £50 for each additional class of goods or service specified, but a £30 discount is available for filing online and paying upfront; or
- right start examination service—this is an online service which also costs £200 plus £50 for each additional class, but the applicant only pays 50 per cent of each of these sums upfront. The balance is payable if the applicant decides to proceed after receiving the examination report from UKIPO. The online discount is not available with this service.

7.06 If the application is filed in paper form, the applicant is not entitled to a discount and is limited to the Standard examination service for the standard fee of £200 plus £50 for each additional class of goods or service specified.

7.07 The method of filing can be important in the case of a logo or mark that contains colours. In such cases, where the application is made on paper, there is some possibility that when the representation of the mark is scanned into UKIPO's system, the colours may not be entirely faithful to the original. This is also a consideration for more unusual types of mark such as sound or motion marks. Electronic filing may provide greater accuracy and certainty.

REQUIREMENTS FOR THE FILING OF AN APPLICATION

7.08 Non-compliance with some requirements will result in the application not being given a filing date. Non-compliance with others will not. In either case, however, non-compliance means delay as the application cannot proceed.

Requirements in order to obtain a filing date

7.09 The following are requirements that must be complied with in order to obtain a filing date:

- **A request for registration**—UKIPO deems this to have been made by the simple filing of the relevant form (Form TM3).
- **The applicant's details**—an applicant must give a name and address. In the case of a legal entity, the country and state of incorporation should be given. It should be ensured that the applicant is capable of owning property in its own name. For example, in the case of an unincorporated association, the application may need to be made in the name of certain individuals acting as trustees for the association. In the case of a partnership governed by a partnership agreement, the application can be made in the name of the partnership. The fact that it is a partnership should be indicated.
- **A list of goods and services for which protection is sought**—the applicant must provide a full list of goods and services for which protection is sought. As has been noted, an applicant cannot subsequently broaden the list beyond that provided with the request for registration, and so care should be taken to ensure that the list is complete. By contrast, it is not essential at the time of filing to specify the precise classes into which the listed goods or services fall. This can be resolved subsequently in correspondence with UKIPO. As to how applicants should approach the interpretation and selection of classes, see **Chapter 6**.
- **A representation of the mark**—a representation of the mark or marks must be provided. The question of whether the mark provided is acceptable (whether it is represented in a clear and precise manner) is considered in **Chapter 2**. Note, that the choice of whether to represent the mark in black and white or in colour has important implications, following the decision of the CJEU in *Specsavers.*[1] The position is now set out in a *Common Communication* issued in April 2014[2] that applies equally to UKIPO and EUIPO; the details are explained in **Chapter 8** at para **8.06**. The *Communication* creates an area of uncertainty in relation to UK series marks. If a mark in colour and the black and white equivalent are no longer treated as identical, an attempt to register the same mark in different colours as part of a series may be refused. Until the position is clearer, it may be desirable (where possible) to make separate applications to register colour, and black and white versions of the same mark.

1 Case C-252/12, *Specsavers International Healthcare Ltd and Others v Asda Stores Ltd* [2014] FSR 4.

2 Common Communication on the Common Practice of the Scope of Protection of Black and White ('B&W') Marks (15 April 2014). See also TPN 1/2014.

Requirements not necessary to obtain a filing date

7.10 The requirements that need not be complied with in order to obtain a filing date are:

- **A declaration that the mark is in use or that the applicant has a bona fide intention to use the mark**—Form TM3 contains a declaration to this effect in the signature box so it is unusual for this requirement not to be met where that form is used. Where the applicant does not comply with this requirement, UKIPO is likely to request the declaration at a later date.
- **The payment of the relevant application fee and class fees**—the application is subject to the payment of the application fee (£200 for the first class) and the relevant class fees (£50 for each additional class). It is not essential that the fees accompany the application form. Where fees are missing, UKIPO will contact the applicant.

Deficient applications

7.11 In the case of applications with the deficiencies mentioned above, UKIPO will send a deficiency letter giving the applicant a period of not less than 14 days to remedy any deficiencies. Where a deficiency is not so remedied, the application will be:

- deemed never to have been made if the deficiency was one which was essential to obtain a filing date;[1] or
- treated as abandoned if the deficiency was not one required in order to obtain a filing date.[2]

1 TMR r 13(3)(a).
2 TMR r 13(3)(b).

Further requirements

7.12 **An indication of the class of goods/services**—Rule 8 of the TMR indicates that the relevant class should be given. Where the number of the class is not given, or where multiple classes are used and the class numbers are not given, UKIPO will give a period of not less than one month to resolve the deficiency.[1] If the deficiency is not resolved, the application will be treated as abandoned.[2]

1 TMR r 9(1)–(2).
2 TMR r 9(3)–(4).

7.13 **Address for service**—An applicant must give an address for service in the UK, Gibraltar or Channel Islands.[1] An applicant who is not in one of these countries must give an address or appoint a representative in the UK, Gibraltar or Channel Islands. If such applicant does not, UKIPO will (assuming it has sufficient contact details) contact the applicant to request compliance with this requirement. If no address is given within the set period, or if sufficient contact details are not available, the application will be treated as withdrawn.[2]

1 TMR r 11(1)(a) and (4).
2 TMR r 12. The applicant has one month to comply. Note, that the wording of this and other rules throughout the TMR that relate to time periods has been clarified to use the formula 'a period of × beginning immediately after [the relevant date]' rather than the previous 'beginning on' form of wording. See the Trade Marks and Registered Designs (Amendment) Rules 2013/444.

EXAMINATION OF THE APPLICATION

7.14 Once an application is complete and the appropriate fee has been paid, the application must be examined by UKIPO's examination team to see whether it complies with the requirements of the TMA 1994 and the TMR.[1] The team will examine the application to see if it is caught by any of the absolute or relative grounds for a refusal to register (as to which see **Chapters 4** and **5**).

The examination team aims to provide a report within a month.

1 TMA s 37.

7.15 In its report, the examination team will inform the applicant of UKIPO's objections and requirements regarding the application and will give the applicant the opportunity to address those matters within a period specified by UKIPO in the report. If the applicant cannot satisfy the requirements for registration or fails to respond the application must be refused.[1]

1 TMA s 37(3)–(4). The applicant has the right to ask for an ex parte hearing regarding the refusal.

7.16 The report will also identify any earlier potentially conflicting trade marks[1] and will give the applicant two months to discuss the matter with the examiner and make proposals[2] or to seek to contact the proprietors of those earlier marks, or simply to decide to press on with the application as filed.[3] If no response is received the application should proceed to publication. Importantly, however, the applicant only has one round of correspondence with UKIPO in which to make proposals to deal with the matter of the earlier rights.[4] There is no right to a hearing on the decision to notify.

1 These can be earlier UK trade marks (including comparable marks (EU) reflecting EUTMs in existence as at 11pm on 31 December 2020) or international trade marks that are protected in the UK.
2 One proposal would be to limit the scope of the application so as to remove the potential conflict.
3 The two months period is extendable on showing good reasons—such as a genuine attempt to contact the proprietor of the earlier trade mark.
4 See generally the 'Earlier Rights Fact Sheet' accessible on UKIPO's website.

PUBLICATION OF THE APPLICATION

7.17 Once the examination has been successfully passed, the application will be published in the Trade Marks Journal.[1]

When the application is published, UKIPO will also notify the proprietors of any earlier trade marks which are protected in the UK and which remain in potential conflict with the application. Proprietors of conflicting international trade marks will not be notified.

1 TMR r 16.

OPPOSITION TO THE APPLICATION

7.18 After publication, any person may file a Form TM7 notifying UKIPO of their opposition to the registration and including a statement of the grounds of opposition.[1] The opposition procedure leads ultimately to a decision taken by the Office, either following a hearing or based on the papers, which will determine whether the application should be allowed to proceed to registration. There is also a fast-track opposition procedure available, which is discussed below at para **7.77**.

1 TMA s 38(1)–(2) and TMR r 17(1).

The time for filing opposition to the registration

7.19 The initial period for filing such notification of opposition is two months from the publication[1] although this can be extended by a further month. If the initial period ends on a weekend or on a day when UKIPO is not open, then the opposition may be filed on the next day when UKIPO is open for business.[2]

The one-month extension to the period for filing notice of opposition can be obtained by filing a Form TM7A within the period for the initial opposition.[3] At the time of writing, this Form TM7A must be submitted online[4]—if it is reproduced and sent to UKIPO in any other way it will be ignored, and the would-be opponent risks missing the opportunity to file opposition.[5]

1 TMR r 17(2).
2 TMA s 80(2).
3 TMR r 17(3).
4 TMR r 17(4).
5 Such person may, of course, file an application for a declaration that the resulting registration is invalid.

7.20 When filing Form TM7A seeking an extension of time, the would-be opponent does not have to provide details of any earlier rights. However, the person in whose name the opposition Form TM7 is filed must be the same person in whose name the Form TM7A application for an extension of time was made or (in the case of a company) must be a subsidiary or holding company of that company or any other subsidiary of that holding company.[1] It is, therefore, important to make sure that the Form TM7A is filed in the correct name.

The completed Form TM7A is forwarded to the trade mark applicant as a notification of potential opposition.

1 TMR r 17(3). 'Subsidiary' and 'holding company' have the same meaning as in the Companies Act 2006—see TMR, r 17(9).

The need to contact the applicant for the trade mark before opposing—impact on costs

7.21 As is explained below, there is a cost to filing formal opposition to the registration of a UK application. For this reason, many would-be opponents contact the applicant directly as a matter of course with the hope that the potential dispute can be resolved, avoiding the need for formal opposition. However, this is not always how things play out—time constraints and the unavailability of the appropriate decision-makers often mean that an opposition is filed at the last opportunity without the opponent having first contacted the applicant. If in such cases the applicant was not given sufficient detail about the grounds of the opposition and sufficient time in which to respond to that opposition[1], the hearing officer deciding the opposition may refuse to award the opponent its full costs even if the opposition is successful.

1 Such as by withdrawing the application in full, or in part or by addressing the grounds of opposition.

7.22 In considering whether to penalise a successful opponent in costs, one question that might arise is whether the fact that a Form TM7A was filed, seeking an extension of time, could be said to have given the applicant adequate notice. At the time of writing, this point has not been tested before UKIPO. However, the UKIPO guide *How to complete 'Notice of Opposition and Statement of Grounds (Form TM7)'* states that the date of filing of the TM7A can be inserted into the Form TM7 as the 'Opposition notification date'. Of course, if the matter had previously been the subject of communications or disputes between the parties even before the application to register the mark, there may well be no need for further correspondence. Here a successful opponent is likely to be awarded costs in the opposition proceedings. Such costs are normally on the UKIPO's set scale.

Formalities in the filing of opposition

7.23 As mentioned above, opposition proceedings are formally begun by filing a notice in UKIPO's Form TM7— although it is possible to use a 'home-made' form containing the relevant information. The valid filing of an opposition depends upon the payment of the relevant fee—

(currently £100 if the opposition is based on only s 5(1) and/or s 5(2) of the TMA 1994, but otherwise £200).

7.24 Although the form itself is relatively straightforward, note that the 'Statement of use' section may require some careful consideration. In any case where the ground of opposition is that the mark is identical or similar to an earlier registered mark and is for identical or similar goods or services, the opponent must identify what goods or services from the earlier registration are relied on. However, if the registration procedures of that earlier mark were completed five years or more before the application date (or priority date, where relevant) of the application being opposed, the opponent must also provide a statement detailing whether during that period the earlier mark has been put to genuine use in relation to those goods or services or whether there are proper reasons for non-use.[1] The principles relating to revocation of a mark for non-use are explained in **Chapter 12** and should be referred to in drafting this statement.

1 TMR r 17(5)(d).

7.25 Form TM7 requires the opponent to state for which of the goods and services relied on use is claimed. Therefore, where appropriate, it may be best for the opponent simply to rely on the wording of that registration. For example, an opponent with an earlier UK registration for 'children's clothing; children's footwear' who has only used the mark on coats for children, may have a stronger case on first sight by declaring that use was 'in respect of the following goods of the specification: children's clothing' than if they simply stated 'coats for children'.

7.26 It may also be beneficial to set out the precise goods or services for which there has been use if this would help the applicant understand the nature of the opposition. This is particularly so where the specification is general or where the opponent has covered a class heading for broad terms.

Notification of opposition to applicant

7.27 The TMR provide that the Registrar must send a copy of Form TM7 to the applicant and that the date on which this is done shall be the 'notification date'.[1] The applicant is also sent a covering sheet giving the deadline for it either to file its response in Form TM8, which must include a counterstatement to the opposition, or otherwise to enter into the cooling-off period.

If, after two months from the notification date, the applicant has not filed a Form TM8 or counterstatement and the parties have not entered into the cooling-off period, the application for registration of the mark is treated as abandoned for the opposed goods/services.[2]

1 TMR r 17(8).
2 TMR r 18(2)–(3).

The cooling-off period

7.28 In order to allow the parties to discuss matters, with a view to an amicable resolution (or, at least, a negotiated settlement), the parties can agree to enter into a cooling-off period.[1] In such a case, the applicant's deadline to file the Form TM8 is extended to nine months from the notification date.

The request for a cooling-off period is made by filing Form TM9C, for which there is no fee.[2] This request can be filed by either party, but Form TM9C requires a declaration that the other side has agreed to the entry into the cooling-off period.

1 TMR r 18(4).
2 TMR r 18(4)(b).

Extension of the cooling-off period

7.29 A request can be made to extend the cooling-off period by a further nine months (ie, to 18 months from the notification date) by filing Form TM9E.[1] This form requires a statement that the other side agrees to the further period of time and that the parties are actively seeking to negotiate a settlement.

1 TMR r 18(5).

Termination of the cooling-off period

7.30 Either party can terminate the cooling-off period at any time. The opposition proceedings will then continue.

The applicant can terminate the cooling-off period by filing Form TM8 and counterstatement. The opponent can terminate the cooling-off period by filing Form TM9T, which should be copied to the applicant.[1] In this case, UKIPO will confirm the new deadline for the applicant to file Form TM8 and counterstatement. This new deadline will be the later of either: (a) one month from the filing of Form TM9T by the opponent; or (b) two months from the notification date (ie, the original deadline to file the TM8 and counterstatement).

1 TMR r 18(4)(c).

The applicant's Form TM8 incorporating the counterstatement

7.31 If it does become necessary to file a counterstatement (Form TM8) then, as set out below, there are a number of important elements for the applicant to consider.

THE REQUEST FOR THE OPPONENT TO PROVE USE

7.32 If the opponent is relying on an earlier registered mark whose registration procedures were completed more than five years before the application (or priority) date of the application, then (unless the applicant knows for certain that the opponent will be able to demonstrate the requisite use) the applicant is usually well advised to include in its Form TM8 a request that the opponent prove the content of its statement of use of the earlier mark for the requisite goods or services. The evidence of use should normally relate to the UK only but where the earlier UK registration is a comparable right created post-Brexit,[2] evidence of use in the EU from before 1 January 2021 may be relevant.[3] Failure to prove use means that the earlier registration cannot be taken into account (or at least can only be taken into account insofar as use has been demonstrated), so there is a reasonable argument that the applicant should put the opponent to proof of all assertions of use. Moreover, as all evidence before UKIPO needs to be submitted in a particular format[1] there is always a possibility that the opponent will fail to comply with the formalities, with the result that its evidence is inadmissible. In such case, proof of use is not deemed to have been filed, and the earlier registration is not taken into account in determining the opposition.

1 TMR r 64—the general rule is that evidence must be by way of witness statement unless the Registrar directs otherwise.
2 ie UK marks created to provide continuing protection for EUTMs in existence at 11pm on 31 December 2020. Such marks are identified at UKIPO by a registration number prefixed by UK009 or UK008 where the EUTM had been a designation of an international registration.
3 A number of comparable UK trade marks may correspond to EUTMs that have not been used in the UK. To address a potentially unjust situation created by Brexit, use of the mark in the EU prior to 1 January 2021, inside or outside the UK, will count as use of the comparable UK right. Therefore, where the relevant five-year period for proving use includes time before 1 January 2021, use in the EU will be considered. Where the time period includes time after 1 January 2021, use in the EU within that period will not be taken into account.

THE COUNTERSTATEMENT

7.33 The applicant's counterstatement (Form TM8) should deal with all grounds raised by the opponent—either by admission, or by putting the opponent to proof, or by denial. Where the grounds of opposition are denied, reasons for that denial should be provided.

7.34 The level of detail in the counterstatement will, to some extent, depend upon the level of detail of the opponent's notice of opposition and statement of grounds. For example, where the opponent has simply alleged that the marks are similar and the goods and services are identical or similar, a simple assertion that this is not the case will often suffice from a legal point of view. It is not necessary at this stage to provide all of the legal or factual arguments which will be relied upon in full detail—further opportunity will arise in the course of the evidence to make full submissions and file supporting evidence.

7.35 From a tactical point of view, however, an applicant may wish to consider filing a more substantial counterstatement in order to try to sway any finding in the preliminary indication, insofar as the opposition is based upon s 5(1) or (2). In particular, an applicant may wish to focus on trying to demonstrate that the respective marks are not similar.

PRELIMINARY INDICATIONS

7.36 Previously an opponent or applicant could request a preliminary indication in the TM7 or TM8 respectively. Whilst this is no longer possible, where the grounds of opposition include s 5(1) or (2), the Registrar may issue a preliminary indication after the filing of the TM8 to provide the parties with a prima facie indication as to the likely decision in respect of those grounds of opposition.[1] The Registrar is not obliged to do so and will probably only issue a preliminary indication where one side's case appears to be hopeless or if it believes that an indication is likely to spur the parties to resolve the matter by way of negotiated settlement. A preliminary indication will not be provided if the Registrar takes the view that it would be inappropriate to do so. This will generally be the case, where the case is deemed to be so finely balanced that evidence would be required to come to a decision. This indication is given on the basis of the grounds of opposition and the counterstatement, and not on the basis of any evidence.

1 TMR r 19. (This rule does not apply to fast-track oppositions.)

Implications of a preliminary indication

7.37 Where a preliminary indication is given, the unsuccessful party has no right of appeal.[1] If it disagrees with the preliminary indication, it can proceed to the evidence rounds of the opposition. If it decides not to proceed, then it can allow the preliminary indication to take effect (see below).

1 TMR r 19(7).

7.38 If the matter proceeds to the evidence rounds, the preliminary indication is not binding on the hearing officer—indeed, there is no obligation on UKIPO to provide reasons for the preliminary indication.[1] However, the fact that an adverse preliminary indication was given could affect the costs order made by the hearing officer—particularly if a party which received an adverse preliminary indication opted to proceed to the evidence rounds but then failed to file evidence, before losing at the hearing.

1 TMR r 19(7).

Procedural consequences of a preliminary indication

7.39 Where the preliminary indication is that registration of the mark should not be refused in respect of all or any of the goods or services listed in the application, the opponent has one month from being given this indication in which to file a Form TM53 giving notice of its intention to proceed with the opposition. If no notice is given, its opposition in relation to those goods or services is deemed to have been withdrawn.[1]

1 TMR r 19(4).

7.40 Where the preliminary indication is that registration should be refused in respect of all or any of the goods or services listed in the application, the applicant has one month from being given this indication to file a Form TM53 giving notice of its intention to proceed with the application to register the mark. If no such notice is given, the application to register the mark in respect of the goods or services covered by that preliminary indication is deemed to have been withdrawn.[1]

1 TMR r 19(5).

(a) Where the opposition is based only on s 5(1) or s 5(2)

7.41 The consequences of the 'unsuccessful' party not filing a Form TM53 giving notice of its intention to proceed to the evidence rounds of the opposition procedure are summarised below.

Nature of preliminary indication	Outcome if no Form T53 is filed
Opposition totally rejected	Opposition deemed withdrawn. The application proceeds for all goods/ services covered in the application
Opposition totally upheld	Application deemed to be withdrawn for all opposed goods/services.
Opposition partially upheld	Application deemed refused for some goods/services but accepted for the others. If goods/services for which opposition was upheld are not removed from the application, then the period in which to request entry into the evidence rounds is extended by one-month to permit the applicant to limit the specification for which the mark could be registered. Otherwise all goods/services opposed are refused.

(b) Where the opposition relies upon grounds other than s 5(1) or s 5(2)

7.42 If no Form TM53 is filed with regard to the s 5(1)–(2) grounds of opposition, the evidence rounds of the opposition procedure may have to continue in order to resolve any other grounds of opposition. However, this will not be the case if:

1 the preliminary indication was that registration should be refused on the basis of the s 5(1) or s 5(2) opposition;
2 the applicant did not request entry into the evidence rounds; or
3 the opposition on the other grounds is directed at the same goods/services as those under the s 5(1) or s 5(2) opposition;

In these circumstances registration in respect of the goods or services in question is deemed to have already been refused, and so opposition on the other grounds can fall away.

NOTICE TO PROCEED WITH THE OPPOSITION

7.43 As indicated above, notice to proceed with the opposition—ie to enter the evidence rounds of the opposition procedure—is done by filing Form TM53. No official fee is payable for this form. The form should be sent to the other party as well as to UKIPO.[1]

1 TMR r 19(6).

THE FILING OF EVIDENCE

7.44 If the opposition proceeds to the evidence rounds, the usual procedure is that the first round of evidence is the opponent's evidence to substantiate its opposition. The applicant then files evidence in answer. The opponent can file further evidence—however, this evidence can only be evidence in reply to matters raised in the applicant's evidence. The Registrar has power to allow either party to file further evidence on such terms as the Registrar thinks fit.[1]

1 TMR r 20(4).

7.45 The evidence that will be required in a particular case will depend on many factors. There can be no complete guidance on what exactly an opponent or applicant needs to file in any particular matter. The case law suggests the kinds of evidence that can and should be filed, and this will be set out below. However, the case law is merely illustrative, and it should not be assumed that other evidence is irrelevant or that evidence which was deemed important in one case will have the same impact in another.

7.46 In its first round of evidence, the opponent must (if so required by the applicant's counterstatement) provide evidence of the use of the earlier registered marks as claimed in the statement of use in its Form TM7.[1] The nature of the evidence to be filed and areas of potential difficulty are addressed in **Chapter 12** covering revocation of marks for non-use. It seems clear that the nature of the evidence of non-use in this context is the same as that which would be required in a case of an application for revocation of a registered mark for non-use.

1 This evidence is due at the same time as the opponent's other evidence.

Time limits for the filing of evidence

7.47 The timetable for filing evidence and submissions in the opposition proceedings are set out in the correspondence informing the parties of the entry into the evidential rounds.

This timetable is set by the Registrar.[1] This means that the time limits may be shorter or longer than the typical period of two months, depending on the evidence to be filed. For example, the Registrar may shorten the time limit where less evidence is required or where locating the evidence should not be difficult. On the other hand, where a client relies on long-standing use and reputation in a mark, the evidence-gathering exercise may be somewhat more difficult and a longer time limit may well be appropriate. UKIPO has provided guidance as to the likely time periods to be given.[2]

1 TMR r 20(1). This is a departure from the registry's earlier practice where the time limits were set by the then Rules. As set out in the following paragraph, the time limits can be extended.
2 See TPNs 2/2010 and 3/2008.

Extension of time for filing evidence

7.48 The time limits for filing evidence may be altered by UKIPO either at its own initiative or at the request of a party.[1] The request for such an extension of time is made on a Form TM9. In the context of opposition proceedings, the request is subject to the payment of a fee (£100 at the time of writing).

1 TMR r 77.

7.49 A request for an extension of time should contain detailed information as to the reasons for the extension. In practice, this should include:[1]

- information as to what the party has done to date to try to comply with the existing timetable;

- information regarding what has yet to be done; and
- information as to why it has not been possible to do what has yet to be done.

Whilst a request for an extension of time should usually be made before the expiry of the time limit in question, it can made thereafter. In relation to inter partes proceedings, the overriding objective of UKIPO is to be fair to all parties and so where there has been undue delay then the request may well be refused.

1 See UKIPO *Trade Marks Manual*, Tribunal Section 4.9, underlining the application of *LIQUID FORCE* [1999] RPC 429 and Case No BL 0/481/00 of the Appointed Person.

THE FORM OF EVIDENCE IN OPPOSITION PROCEEDINGS

7.50 Evidence may be given by way of witness statement, affidavit, statutory declaration or any other form which would be permitted before the court.[1] However, unless the Registrar provides otherwise, evidence will generally be by witness statement verified by a statement of truth and containing evidence that the maker of the statement would be allowed to give orally.[2] The correct form of a witness statement, affidavit and statutory declaration can be found within the Civil Procedure Rules, as amended from time to time. In addition, an example of a witness statement can be found in the guidance provided by UKIPO on its website.

In order to be deemed filed, evidence must be sent to the Registrar and to all other parties to the proceedings.[3]

1 TMR r 64(1).
2 TMR r 64(2)–(3) and (5).
3 TMR r 64(6).

Who should give the witness statement

7.51 It is important to bear in mind that a witness can be cross-examined. A witness statement should therefore be given by someone who actually has personal knowledge of the relevant facts, or at least is in a suitable position to obtain and report on the relevant facts. In this regard, it is understood that individuals within organisations do change roles, and access to the relevant records of any company involved may be sufficient for practical purposes. However, evidence from an individual with 'mere' access to the relevant information rather than first-hand experience can seem weak—particularly where the evidence is challenged by the other side.

7.52 One practice that has been used over many years is the submission of 'evidence' from the representatives of the parties. This generally takes two forms:

- Statements by attorneys containing a mixture of evidence and argument. The evidence often includes the results of online searches of the UK register said to be relevant to the issues of similarity or the likelihood of confusion. The argument is usually the witness' own views on those issues.
- Statements by a representative saying that they have access to the records of a party (either directly or by way of requests for information) and filing the evidence as if they were the party.

The first of these approaches is technically acceptable—albeit that the evidence may be of questionable value. In situations where the representative is in the same position as any other member of the public, then evidence in this format would seem appropriate since the attorney is in the same position as the relevant public. The second approach is clearly less acceptable. It is possible that the evidence filed in this manner will be deemed to be hearsay and may be struck out. Alternatively, the Registrar may direct that the evidence be resubmitted by a person who can be cross-examined on the evidence.

Evidence by the opponent regarding the likelihood of confusion—the distinctiveness of the earlier mark

7.53 It is important for an opponent to registration to consider carefully what evidence can be adduced that will help show the earlier mark as being distinctive—either because it is inherently distinctive, or because it has acquired distinctiveness. The greater the distinctiveness of a mark, be it inherent, and/or acquired, the greater the protection afforded to it against third parties when one needs to consider a likelihood of confusion.

(a) The inherent distinctiveness of the mark

7.54 It is generally considered that marks fall into three groups on a sliding scale of inherent distinctiveness.

- First, of all are words with no meaning at all (eg, ROLEX) which have the strongest inherent distinctiveness.
- Second, come words with no particular meaning for the goods or services to which they are applied, such as APPLE in respect of computers (and latterly, all manner of other goods and services).
- Third, (and least inherently distinctive) are those marks that are constructed of terms which are largely or entirely descriptive, such as BRITISH AIRWAYS.

The more inherently distinctive a mark is, the more extensive the protection will be granted against the use of similar marks of third parties.

7.55 In most cases, the inherent distinctiveness of an earlier mark will be clear, particularly where it falls into the ROLEX camp, but at the very least the opponent should make a statement to the effect that the mark falls into that kind of category. Of more importance is the need to point out that a mark has no meaning for particular goods, particular where it could have a meaning for other goods or services. For example, the mark O2 is inherently a much more distinctive mark for telecommunications services than it would be for bottled gases.

(b) The acquired distinctiveness of the mark

7.56 In addition to the inherent distinctiveness of the mark (which is a result of the nature of the mark itself), the mark can be made much distinctive by the use that has actually been made of it. In this regard, whilst the three marks mentioned above (ROLEX, APPLE and BRITISH AIRWAYS) are at different points on the scale of inherent distinctiveness, all three would be likely to be recognised as well-known marks of considerable repute. The kind of evidence that can be filed in support of acquired distinctiveness includes evidence of turnover, market share, spending on advertising and other promotional activities, and survey evidence.

7.57 Where the earlier mark had been accepted for registration on the basis of acquired distinctiveness, the opponent may face an argument that the evidence only establishes the mark as one of 'ordinary' rather than enhanced distinctiveness. In such a case, the opponent should seek to establish that the evidence now goes beyond that which was filed to get the mark accepted for registration, or alternatively that the earlier evidence essentially demonstrated distinctiveness far beyond the level required for registration.

Evidence by the applicant regarding the likelihood of confusion—the distinctiveness of the earlier mark

7.58 For the applicant, the aim in filing evidence as to the likelihood of confusion should be to demonstrate that the earlier mark relied on by the opponent is a weak one and lacks distinctiveness. This may include evidence as to:

(a) The inherent weakness of the earlier mark

7.59 It is worth checking the details of the earlier mark to check whether it was accepted without the need for evidence or whether evidence was required to overcome any objections. If there was a delay between the filing and the registration of a UK registration (more than nine months) this may suggest that some objection was faced. Where the publication date is available, this will help suggest where a problem arose.

If there was a delay between filing and publication, this may indicate some objection regarding the distinctiveness of the mark application before the examiner. A delay between publication and registration would suggest that a third party filed opposition. All of these are worth investigating. In particular, the applicant should consider obtaining a copy of the application file relating to the earlier mark. At the time of writing, the full file can be obtained online on the EUIPO website in respect of EUTMs (which is useful where the earlier mark is a UK comparable trade mark created post-Brexit) and can be ordered from UKIPO in respect of UK registrations. In respect of designations under the Madrid Protocol, the availability of information corresponds with the position for a 'local' filing with the country or organisation involved.

7.60 In these cases, the applicant is looking for any statements that might affect the strength of the mark of the opponent. Where the opponent's mark had been opposed, it may be that it had been registered in the face of opposition on the basis of a mark that is similar to that of the applicant. As a result, the opponent's statements and evidence in attempting to overcome any opposition to registration of their mark(s) may conflict with comments they have subsequently made when opposing the application in question.

Where a mark is weak, small differences may be sufficient to rule out any likelihood of confusion.

(b) The 'acquired weakness' of the mark

7.61 If the longstanding use of a mark on the market can enhance the distinctiveness of the mark in the right circumstances, equally the market conditions can render a mark less distinctive than it might seem on paper. The applicant will therefore be looking for evidence to demonstrate that, because of the market conditions, the marks are less likely to be confused.

7.62 Such evidence may seek to demonstrate that the opponent's mark is similar to other third-party marks with which it has peacefully coexisted without confusion occurring. To show this, many applicants have sought to rely upon evidence of trade marks coexisting on the register. However, as has frequently been said, such 'state of the register' evidence taken by itself is irrelevant.[1] Nonetheless, from the point of view of the applicant, such searches can help to locate third parties who use similar marks.

1 For example, *TREAT, British Sugar Plc v James Robertson & Sons Ltd* [1996] RPC 281 at 305.

7.63 It is important to note that the mere fact that a number of marks similar to the opponent's mark are in use does not of itself suffice. It is likely to be necessary to demonstrate that there has been use of multiple similar marks for the same products. Where an applicant has applied for a range of products, it is easy to fall into the trap of thinking that because a number of similar marks are in use across the range of products, this is sufficient to outweigh any allegations of a likelihood of confusion with the opponent's mark. It is important to verify that the various marks in use are not in different markets. In this regard, it is a particularly easy mistake to assume that just because there are a wide range of registrations with overlapping protection that the use also overlaps on the market.

EVIDENCE REGARDING THE GOODS AND SERVICES

7.64 In relation to the goods and services, the basic points mentioned previously regarding the similarity or otherwise of goods and services apply.[1] It should be remembered that in opposition proceedings the comparison is made on paper. The mere fact that the applicant and the opponent have co-existed on the market does not mean that the opponent is bound to lose an opposition case filed against an application where the specification of goods and services extends beyond the use made of the mark by the applicant. It is essential to look to the full breadth of the opponent's specification and to consider the two marks against each other for the full range of goods or services sought under the application.

1 See **Chapter 5**.

7.65 It is also worth remembering that the sales channels of the respective goods and services used by the parties in reality may not be fully considered. Opposition proceedings consider the paradigm use as described in the specification. One example of this in practice would be where the applicant applies for a trade mark for 'cosmetics and fragrances' which it intends to sell only within its own stores or concessions. The applicant's product may currently be a luxury product and sold subject to substantial intervention by sales staff. Under an opposition, however, all of this will be ignored since UKIPO must take into account the normal sales channels of cosmetics and perfumes. Both can be bought by the general public without assistance and can be sold at a range of prices. The particular sales and marketing strategy of the applicant is irrelevant where that is not reflected by a suitable restriction to the specification of goods and services.

Challenging evidence

7.66 Where a party wishes to challenge the evidence of a witness, this should be made clear in advance of the hearing of the opposition proceedings.[1] In the context of trade mark opposition proceedings, there are three main ways of challenging the evidence of a witness. These are the same three that apply to proceedings in general, namely:

- filing conflicting evidence;
- raising objections to the evidence and seeking clarification of the evidence; and/or
- asking to cross-examine the person giving the evidence.

1 See *Extreme Trade Mark* [2008] RPC 2.

7.67 In the context of opposition proceedings, the parties are given alternate opportunities to prove their case and to file such evidence as they feel relevant to prove their case or disprove that of the other side. As such, it will often be the case that the parties will be deemed to have sufficient opportunity to prove their case or disprove that of the other side simply through the evidence rounds.

Cross-examination

7.68 The TMA 1994 provides the Registrar with the power to allow for the cross-examination of witnesses on the content of their evidence.[1] Under TMR r 62(2) the Registrar has the power to regulate the evidence before it, including the issues on which evidence will be placed and the way in which it will be placed.

In theory, the drafting of this rule gives the Registrar greater powers to refuse a request for cross-examination than under TMR r 55(2) of the preceding rules, which gave the ability to cross-examine unless otherwise directed.

1 TMA s 69; TMR r 65. See also generally the UKIPO *Trade Marks Manual,* Tribunal Section 4.8.9 for guidance on cross-examination before this tribunal.

7.69 The basis for any request for cross-examination is that a party must have the means to challenge relevant evidence. This would suggest that the standard position is that cross-examination should be allowed and should only be refused where the circumstances indicate that it would be inappropriate to do so. UKIPO has indicated that cross-examination will not be allowed where:

- there is nothing to test;
- the contested issues are unimportant to the overall determination;
- the request is unreasonable from a practical point of view (eg, additional hearing time, costs and availability of the witness); or
- where the request is unreasonable in the sense of the overall administration of justice.

7.70 Where a party wishes to cross-examine a witness, the party should give reasonable notice of that fact. UKIPO has indicated that four weeks' notice is generally a reasonable period, but where the witness is based overseas or there are other reasons to believe that the witness' availability to attend would be reduced, a longer notice period is likely to be required.

7.71 It is worth noting that cross-examination may be possible via video conferencing. This will often be an efficient way of dealing with the cross-examination of witnesses based overseas, but the exercise of video conferencing is not without potential pitfalls. Amongst those are the possibility of evidence being filed late, and thus not being available to be presented to the video witness, and the inherent remoteness of that witness from the proceedings. Further issues are addressed in Part 32 of the Civil Procedure Rules, which provides guidance on the use of video conferencing. It is important to note that where video conferencing is used in lieu of attendance of a witness based overseas, it must be ascertained that the government in question allows its nationals or people based within its jurisdiction to be cross-examined before a court in England and Wales by way of video conference, and the party that sets up the video conference will need to inform the Registrar of the enquiries made to ensure that this is permitted.

7.72 A party seeking to cross-examine should, as part of any request for cross-examination, indicate which aspects of the witness' evidence are to be challenged. This information will be taken into account by the Registrar in deciding whether it would be inappropriate to allow cross-examination. Where the issues have been clearly set out, there is also the (albeit uncommon) possibility that the witness may seek to withdraw portions of their evidence. Where a witness is called to be cross-examined, their non-attendance may lead to the evidence being given less weight.

HEARINGS

7.73 Rule 63 makes it clear that the Registrar shall not make an adverse decision against a party without giving the party the opportunity to be heard. The Registrar shall give a period of at least 14 days for the party to be heard. It is possible for the parties to agree for a decision to be made on the papers (ie, on the basis of written submissions alone) or a party that does not wish to appear may simply provide further submissions in lieu of appearing.

SKELETON ARGUMENTS

7.74 Where a party is professionally represented, the Registry requires that party to submit a skeleton argument in advance of the hearing. The practice[1] is that a skeleton argument should be sent to UKIPO by 14:00 two working days before the hearing, with a copy being sent to the other side. Where a party is not professionally represented, there is no requirement on that party to file a skeleton argument,[2] but UKIPO recommend that they file a skeleton argument nonetheless to help prepare for the hearing.

The skeleton arguments should cover the points to be made at the hearing and should indicate any authorities that the party wishes to rely upon.

1 See UKIPO's Tribunal Practice Notice 5/2000. TPN 5/2000 refers to the skeleton argument being received at least 24 hours before the hearing.
2 UKIPO's Tribunal Practice Notice 1/2000.

COSTS

7.75 The Registrar (through a hearing officer) has power to award any party such costs as may be reasonable and to direct how and by what parties they are to be paid.[1] There is also provision for the Registrar to order security for costs.[2]

In preparing for a hearing, it is advisable for the parties to produce a statement of costs and to be prepared to make submissions on the issue of costs. This is because although hearing officers often reserve their decisions on the substance and on costs of the opposition proceedings, they may sometimes decide to make their rulings at the hearing.

1 TMR r 67.
2 TMR r 68.

7.76 Parties should be aware that the level of costs actually recovered under the usual scale of costs allowed by UKIPO can be considerably lower than the actual costs that they have incurred—although in exceptional cases the Registrar may decide to depart from the usual scale of costs that are allowed.[1]

1 For UKIPO *Guidance on Costs*, see TPN 2/2004, TPN 4/2007, and TPN 6/2008.

FAST TRACK OPPOSITIONS

7.77 There is a fast track opposition available to anyone wishing to oppose a published application.[1] The definition of a fast track opposition is found in amended TMR r 2(1). This route is available only for those oppositions which are based solely on s 5(1) and/or s 5(2) of the TMA 1994 (ie, applications which are identical or similar to an earlier trade mark and which cover identical or similar services). A maximum of three earlier registered marks may be relied on, and where proof of use of the earlier mark(s) is required, it must be provided along with the notice of opposition. The fast track is reserved for oppositions that the opponent believes can be resolved without the need for further evidence, or an oral hearing. In other words, all of the evidence is to be submitted with the notice of opposition, and the opposition should be able to be decided 'on paper'.

1 Trade Marks (Fast Track Opposition) (Amendment) Rules 2013/2235.

Fast track procedure

7.78 A notice of fast track opposition is filed on Form TM7F that must be filed electronically.[1] It is forbidden to file both a fast track and standard opposition for the same application concurrently; the two options are mutually exclusive. As with standard oppositions, the notice must be filed within the two months beginning immediately after the date of publication. The opposition period may be extended by one month in the same way as for standard oppositions, by using Form TM7A, which is also filed electronically. The notice of opposition must include (for each earlier mark relied on):

- a representation of the earlier mark;
- details of the authority with which the mark is registered, and the registration number of the mark;
- the goods or services in respect of which the mark is registered, and which are being relied on in the opposition;
- the date of completion of the registration procedure or (as the case may be) the grant of the protection afforded by an international mark; and
- where necessary, a statement dealing with whether the mark has been put to genuine use in the relevant period.

1 This and most other aspects of procedure for fast track oppositions are found in TMR r 17A.

7.79 Where the earlier mark is subject to proof of use, the relevant evidence must be provided along with the Form TM7F. Form TM7F states: 'Please provide a list of examples of the mark in use in the relevant period and indicate against each such entry the goods/services for which you claim it shows use of the mark. Examples of use of the mark could include in price lists, brochures, advertisements, invoices, etc. The documents included in your list should be attached as exhibits, which should be clear and easy to read.' Exhibits must be numbered (for example, 'Exhibit 1', etc) and pages of individual exhibits must also be numbered (for example, 1/7, 2/7, etc). The total number of pages exhibited to Form TM7F must not exceed 100.

7.80 The Registrar will send a copy of the opposition to the applicant, and that event sets the clock running for the TM8 counterstatement in the usual way. Note, that TMR r 19 (preliminary indication by the Registrar) does not apply to fast track oppositions. The evidence rounds set out by TMR r 20 do not apply to fast track oppositions, but the Registrar has a discretion to allow evidence on such terms as he may see fit. If a fast track opposition is consolidated with a standard opposition, the conjoined proceedings will from that point be treated as a standard opposition.[1] Fast track oppositions that fail to satisfy the necessary requirements may be allowed to continue but will be treated as if they had been brought as standard oppositions filed on TM7.[2] Oral proceedings will only be held if the UKIPO requests it, or if either party to the proceedings requests it, and the Registrar considers that oral proceedings are necessary to deal with the case justly, and at proportionate cost.[3] Where no oral hearing is held, the Registrar shall give the parties the opportunity to provide arguments in writing before reaching a decision that is adverse to either party.[4]

1 TMR r 62(1)(g).
2 TMR r 62(1)(j).
3 TMR r 62(5).
4 TMR r 62(6).

APPEALS

7.81 Appeals from a decision in opposition proceedings can be either to the appointed person or to the High Court.[1]

1 See TMA s 76 and TMR r 70.

OBSERVATIONS

7.82 Finally, it should be noted that for a person that wishes to oppose a registration but does not wish to become a party to formal opposition proceedings, TMA 1994 s 38(3) provides for the making of written 'observations' to the Registrar. The Registrar will consider the application to register the mark in the light of these observations.

Chapter 8

Application procedure before EUIPO

INTRODUCTION—EU TRADE MARKS

8.01 An EU Trade Mark ('EUTM') is a trade mark registered through the EU Intellectual Property Office ('EUIPO') in accordance with the EU Trade Mark Regulations ('EUTMR').[1]

Obtaining an EUTM is a cost-effective way of obtaining protection for a mark across the entire EU for, being in the nature of a unitary right, an EUTM has equal effect throughout the European Union. This means that an objection will lead to refusal of the application in its entirety but that, once registered, the EUTM provides a right which can be used to prevent the use of conflicting signs anywhere in the EU[2] even where the owner has only used the mark in part of the EU.

The owner of, or applicant for, an EUTM may also apply for international registration under the Madrid International System (where the owner meets the nationality or domicile requirements) considered in **Chapter 9** below.

Since the UK's withdrawal from the EU became effective at 11pm on 31 December 2020, EUTMs have ceased to be protected in the UK (save as regards causes of action that had accrued before that time). However, where an EUTM was registered on or before that time, a separate UK comparable right was automatically created with effect from that time. Also, in certain limited circumstances, use of a UK comparable right in the UK may support use of an EUTM, but the ability to rely on such use will diminish over the next few years.

1 Regulation (EU) No 2017/1001 of 14 June 2017 on the EU Trade Mark (the 'EUTMR') (as variously amended). See also various EU Regulations dealing with implementation (the EU Trade Mark Implementing Regulation 'EUTMIR') the fees payable and the procedure of EUIPO's Boards of Appeal.

2 See *DHL Express France SAS v Chronopost SA* Case C-235/09—a decision of the Grand Chamber of the CJEU given on 11 April 2011.

EUIPO AND ITS PROCEDURES

8.02 The registration process for a EUTM is administered by EUIPO, based in Alicante, Spain. The aim is to provide, at a reasonable cost, a single registration procedure consisting of a single application, a single language of application, a single administration centre and a single file to be managed.

Guidance as to EUIPO's procedures and copies of relevant materials can be found in the trade marks part of its website—Trade mark and Design guidelines (europa.eu):

- copies of the relevant governing regulations and International Treaties;
- decisions and communications from the President of EUIPO and the President of the Boards of Appeal;
- EUIPO's Guidelines; and
- information on the enforcement of rights in the European Union.

8.03 The registration procedure before EUIPO is as follows:

1. The EUTM applicant files an application for registration of a mark.
2. The EUIPO conducts searches for earlier EUTMs.
3. The application is examined by EUIPO.
4. If accepted, the application is then published to give others the opportunity to oppose registration.
5. If there is no opposition or if an opposition is raised but is rejected, the mark is registered.

THE FILING OF AN APPLICATION FOR A EUTM

8.04 The application for a EUTM can be filed electronically via the EUIPO website or on paper. Filing online has a number of advantages. These include:

- a reduction in fees of €150;
- the ability to pay by credit card;
- receiving immediate confirmation of the relevant EUTM number; and
- online verification to ensure error-free filing and to obtain the earliest filing date.

It is, therefore, in the interests of an applicant to file an application online if possible and the EUIPO encourages electronic means for the filing of all forms and communications.

If the application is filed in paper format it can be made directly by post or by courier service.

The requirements if the application is to be given a filing date.

8.05 In order to be given a filing date, the application must contain the following:[1]

- a request for registration of an EUTM;
- information identifying the applicant;
- a list of the goods, and/or services for which registration is sought;[2] and
- a representation of the mark.[3]

1 EUTMR Art 31(1). See also EUTMIR Art 1. An application which is not given a filing date is of no effect.
2 EUTMIR Art 2(1)(c). An applicant for registration is required to identify the relevant goods and/or services, with clarity and precision so that the relevant authorities and competitors alike can determine the scope of the protection actually being sought. For the law and for the practice in this regard, see **Chapter 6**, paras **6.03–6.13**.
3 See para **8.06** below.

Representation of the mark

8.06 *Requirements under the EUTMR.* As mentioned above, an application for registration of an EUTM must contain a representation of the mark.[1] The rules provide that:

- The mark may be represented in any appropriate form that can be reproduced on the register in a clear, precise, self-contained, easily accessible, intelligible, durable and objective manner.
- If it is not intended to claim any special graphic feature or colour, the mark shall be reproduced in normal script.
- Where registration of a three-dimensional mark is sought, the application must indicate that that is the case and must consist of a photographic or graphic representation of the mark. It may contain up to six different perspectives of the mark.
- Where registration in colour is sought, the application must consist of a colour reproduction of the mark. The colours making up the mark must be indicated in words and a reference to a recognised colour code.
- Where registration of a sound is sought, an audio file may be submitted reproducing the sound or accurate musical notation.
- Position marks, consisting of the way the mark is placed on the goods, requires a reproduction showing the mark with respect to the relevant goods using broken lines to disclaim matter.
- Motion marks and hologram marks may be represented by a video file or graphic reproduction and multimedia marks by an audiovisual file.
- *Use of black and white.* The practice where a mark is shown in black and white is now governed by the terms of a *Common Communication* (issued in April 2014).[2] Prior to this

Communication, EUIPO and the offices of some Member States (including UKIPO) generally regarded a black and white mark as covering all colours. However, this is no longer the case. A mark in black or white (or in greyscale) will no longer be treated as identical to the same mark in colour. As a result, applicants now need carefully to consider the mark that they wish to protect. If a mark will be used in a certain colour, it may now be desirable to file for a version of the mark in that colour.

At the time of writing the practice embodied by the *Communication* has not been tested in the courts, and there is speculation as to its possible effect.

- *Use of colour.*[3] As set out above, where the mark is to be registered in colour, a colour representation must be filed.

  It used to be a requirement to indicate the colour/s appearing within the mark. This is no longer necessary, but colours may still be indicated in the application where this forms an essential part of the description or where required for the purpose of claiming priority in other jurisdictions.[4]

1 EUTMIR Art 2(1)(d) and 3.
2 *Common Communication on the Common Practice of the Scope of Protection of Black and White ('B&W') Marks* (15 April 2014).
3 See generally, *EUIPO Trade Mark Guidelines, Part B, Examination*—section 2 at para 9.
4 The application form contains a specific field for this '*Colour claim for the purpose of claiming priority in other Offices*'.

Further formal requirements

8.07 *Fees*—The filing of an application is subject to the payment of fees.[1] The applicant must ensure that the basic fee is paid within the period of one month of the filing of the application (assuming that the fees were not paid at the time of filing).[2] The fees may be paid by way of bank transfer, credit card or via an account held with EUIPO.[3] It is worth noting that the application does not require all of the appropriate class fees to be paid at the same time as the basic fee in order for the application to be deemed filed. Any deficiency in class fees will be the subject of a later objection. It should be noted that fees will also be due in respect of a request by the applicant that the Office arrange for the national searches to be undertaken.[4]

1 EUTMR Art 31(2). The basic fee is presently €850 if filed electronically or €1,000 if filed on paper. The second class attracts an additional fee of €50 and there is an additional fee of €150 per class beyond this.
2 EUTMR Art 32.
3 Payment details are available online at https://euipo.europa.eu/ohimportal/en/fees-and-payments
4 For further detail regarding the search, see para **8.13** below.

8.08 *Languages*—The applicant must designate two languages for the application. Whilst it is possible to file the application in any of the languages of the EU, the applicant must make one of the languages a language of the Office.[1] The languages of EUIPO are English, French, German, Italian and Spanish. Where the first language is not a language of EUIPO, EUIPO may decide to communicate with the applicant in the second language.

1 EUTMR Art 146.

Claiming priority

8.09 An applicant for an EUTM can sometimes claim an earlier priority date than the date of actual filing. This applies where the applicant had, in the previous six months, filed an application to register the mark in question in a country that is party to the Paris Convention or to the agreement establishing the World Trade Organisation.[1]

The effect of a valid claim to priority is that the EUTM application is deemed to have been filed as at the date of the earlier application for the purposes of establishing which rights take precedence.[2] It is to be noted that the filing date is not deemed to be the earlier date for all purposes—where the applicant seeks to rely upon evidence of acquired distinctiveness, the date will be the actual date of filing of the EUTM application.

A claim to Convention priority is made by filing a declaration of priority with the EUTM application.[3] The evidence required in order to prove the existence of the earlier filing includes copies of the earlier application, filing receipts issued by the relevant office or copies taken from the official databases of the country involved. However, in practice following Decision EX173 of the Executive Director, the EUIPO will check whether the details of the earlier filing are available online from the relevant registry. Only where existence of the earlier filing cannot be located online will the EUIPO request that the applicant provides priority documents.

1 EUTMR Art 34.
2 EUTMR Art 36.
3 EUTMR Art 35. See also EUTMIR Art 4.

Claiming seniority

8.10 An applicant who is the owner of an earlier trade mark registered in a Member State of the EU (or in a state whose registrations have effect in the EU) can claim the seniority of that earlier mark for the EUTM.[1]

The rationale for this is that the EUTM system is intended to promote the free movement of goods by foreseeing and facilitating the replacement of national trade mark rights with EUTMs. Hence the ability to claim seniority based on earlier trade marks recognised in Member States of the EU insofar as the earlier registrations are identical to the EUTM in respect of the mark, the owner and the list of goods and services. EUIPO will only check whether the marks are the same, but a claim will be ineffective where the other aspects prove not to be identical.

Seniority can be claimed at the time of filing of the application or within two months of the filing date.[2] Once claimed, evidence of the earlier registrations must be submitted within three months of the filing date or three months of receipt of the claim if made post-application. In practice, the applicant is not required to submit a copy of the earlier registration where this information is available online. If the EUIPO cannot obtain the relevant information online, a deficiency letter will be sent to the applicant to request documentation.[3]

The required evidence is a copy of the earlier registration certified by the relevant authority. In practice, this may be a copy of the registration certificate, a copy of the journal showing the registration of the claimed national registration or a copy of the official databases of the country involved.

The effect of a claim for seniority is that where the earlier national right is allowed to lapse, the owner of the EUTM is deemed to continue to have the same rights he would have had if the earlier national right had continued to be registered.[4]

1 EUTMR Art 39.
2 EUTMR Art 39(2).
3 EUTMIR Art 6 and 32 and *EUIPO Trade Mark Guidelines, Part B, Examination*—section 2 at para 13.
4 EUTMR Art 39(3).

Withdrawal or amendment of application

8.11 An applicant may at any time withdraw an EUTM application or restrict the list of goods or services contained in the application. Otherwise, the application can only be amended to correct the name or address of the applicant, or errors of wording or of copying or obvious mistakes (provided this does not substantially change the mark or extend the list of goods or services). If the amendments are made after publication, the amended application must be published.[1]

1 EUTMR Art 43.

EXAMINATION OF THE APPLICATION

8.12 The EUTM application will be examined by EUIPO.[1] This involves EUIPO:

- Giving the application a filing date provided the application meets the minimum requirements (ie, it provides the name and address of the applicant, a representation of the mark, a list of goods and services and payment of the fee).

- Conducting a goods and/or services classification check.[2]
- Conducting a formalities examination—checking the signature, languages, owner and/or representative data and any priority and/or seniority claims.
- Accepting or refusing the mark as a sign (ie, considering whether there are absolute grounds for refusing to register the mark).[3]

Applicants are notified of any deficiencies in meeting the formal requirements., The date of such remedying those deficiencies is taken to be the date of filing.[4]

EUIPO does not cite earlier rights in the examination, either as a ground for refusal or for information purposes, but a separate search is undertaken where requested, as discussed at **8.13** below.

1 EUTMR Art 36 and EUTMIR r 9.
2 Further detail regarding the drafting of the specification is contained at **Chapter 6**.
3 In relation to the absolute grounds, see **Chapter 4**.
4 EUTMR Art 32.

The search

8.13 At the time of filing an EUTM, the applicant may request an EU search report (for no additional fee) and/or a national search report (which attracts a fee). Where the applicant opts for an EU search report, then, once EUIPO has given the application a filing date, it will draw up an EU search report setting out earlier registered EUTMs or EUTM applications that might be invoked against the application.[1]

When the applicant has opted for a national search (and has paid the appropriate fee), then once the application has been deemed filed and any specification issues have been resolved, EUIPO will request the production of national search reports from national offices of the Member States of the EU.[2] However, this service is not provided by all Member States and so the results cannot be comprehensive. Currently searches are conducted by the offices in the Czech Republic, Denmark, Hungary, Romania, and Slovakia.

1 EUTMR Art 43(1).
2 EUTMR Art 43(2). The fee is currently €60.

Publication

8.14 Assuming that any and all objections are overcome, the application will be published for opposition purposes.[1]

1 EUTMR Art 44. EUIPO does not inform the applicant of the publication. Users wishing to know when their EUTM application is published can use the EUTM Watch alert e-mail service.

THE OPPOSITION PROCEDURE

8.15 The opposition procedure before EUIPO allows a person to give a notice of opposition opposing the registration of an EUTM Application on the basis of earlier rights.

Notice of opposition must be given to EUIPO within three months of publication ('the opposition period')[1] and there are strict rules as to the proof of those earlier rights on the basis of evidence filed in the appropriate language.

1 EUTMR Art 46(1).

Opposition—the basis for opposing registration

8.16 A notice of opposition may be based on any of the following earlier rights or interests[1]:

1 an earlier trade mark application or registration in a Member State of the EU;[2]
2 an earlier EUTM application or registration;[3]
3 an earlier trade mark registered under the International System (ie, the Madrid Agreement or the Protocol to the Madrid Agreement[4]) which has effect in a Member State or the EU or an application for such a mark;[5]
4 an earlier 'well known' mark under the meaning of Article 6*bis* of the Paris Convention;[6]
5 an earlier non-registered trade mark or earlier sign used in the course of trade of more than mere local significance where the right to the sign or non-registered trade mark were acquired prior to the date of the application, and where the right gives the proprietor the right to prevent the use of a subsequent trade mark.[7]

In all of these instances, the rights relied upon by the opponent must have been acquired prior to the filing date of the application which is opposed. It is important to note that if the owner of the opposed application has claimed priority from an earlier application, then the rights relied on by the opponent must pre-date that priority date.

1 EUTMR Art 46(1).
2 EUTMR Art 8(2)(a)(ii) and 8(2)(b).
3 EUTMR Art 8(2)(a)(i) and 8(2)(b).
4 EUTMR Art 8(2)(iii)–(iv).
5 EUTMR Art 8(2)(b).
6 EUTMR Art 8(2)(c)—see **2.19** above for further details of the definition of a 'well known' mark under the meaning of Art 6*bis*.
7 EUTMR Art 8(4).

8.17 An application for registration of a EUTM cannot be opposed on the basis of other rights (such as a claim to copyright in graphical elements of a mark). Such issues have to be raised by way of invalidity proceedings (see **Chapter 11**).

Opposition—procedural requirements

1 Standing to file a notice of opposition

8.18 The opponent must have standing to oppose registration of the mark.

- In most cases where the earlier right is an application or registration, the person with standing to oppose registration is its proprietor or an authorised licensee.[1]
- Where the earlier right is an unregistered right, the proceedings may be brought by its owner or by a party authorised under the relevant law to exercise that right.[2]
- In the case of a trade mark filed by an agent or representative in his own name in the absence of consent from the trade mark owner, the proceedings must be brought by the trade mark owner.[3]

What this means is that in the case of groups of companies with rights in multiple names, or with national rights in the names of various national subsidiaries, the choice is left as to whether: (a) to file multiple oppositions so that all rights relied on are included (and perhaps ask that the oppositions be joined into a single action); (b) to file fewer oppositions and not include certain rights; or (c) to licence all the rights to one of the companies in the organisation so that only one opposition may be required but covering all rights relied on.[4]

1 EUTMR Art 46(1)(a).
2 EUTMR Art 46(1)(c).
3 EUTMR Art 46(1)(b).
4 EUTMR Art 25.

2 Ability to act before EUIPO

8.19 The rules of EUIPO provide that the notice of opposition should be filed by a party able to act before the Office. Natural or legal persons with a domicile or principal place of business or a real and effective industrial or commercial establishment in the EU, may be represented by an employee or by an employee of a legal person with economic connections with the opposing party.[1] Otherwise a professional representative must be appointed.[2] Further details on representation can be found at **Chapter 10**.

1 EUTMR Art 119(3).
2 EUTMR Art 119(2).

8.20 The meaning of 'real and effective industrial or commercial establishment' appears to be the same as that under the Madrid Agreement and the Protocol to the Madrid Agreement. This would usually be a representative office or a branch.

As regards 'economic connections', EUIPO has indicated that in this context they are deemed to exist where there is an economic dependence such as may exist where the two companies are part of the same group, or where there are management control mechanisms. Such connections may also exist where one company owns the majority of the capital or shares in another, or where it can appoint more than half of the members of the managing body of the other. A mere arrangement or contractual agreement is not sufficient for this purpose.

8.21 It is worth noting that where a party indicates an address that is the location of the 'real and effective establishment' in the EU, correspondence will be sent to that address. As a result, for practical reasons, where a company in the EU would be mentioned as the basis of a claim to establishment in the EU it may be worthwhile appointing an employee of that company as an employee representative before EUIPO so that correspondence is directed to the correct person in the organisation.

8.22 In Opposition proceedings, the failure to appoint a representative (where required) is a deficiency that needs to be remedied. Where an opposition is filed without a representative being appointed where required, the Opposition Division of EUIPO will notify the Opponent that a representative should be appointed and give a deadline in which to appoint a representative. If no representative is appointed within the period then the opposition will be deemed inadmissible.

Where an opponent ceases to be represented during the proceedings (such as where a representative withdraws representation for a party), the Opposition Division will suspend the proceedings and give the opponent a deadline to appoint a representative. If no representative is appointed during that period the opposition will become inadmissible.

Opposition—admissibility of the notice of opposition

8.23 Opposition proceedings are started by the filing of a notice of opposition. Upon receipt of such a notice, EUIPO will:

- send a copy of the notice (and any supporting documentation) to the EUTM applicant;[1] and
- check the notice for admissibility.

As a copy of the notice is sent to the EUTM applicant before the admissibility of the notice has been established, it is important for the applicant regularly to check to see if there has been a ruling on admissibility. If there has been, EUIPO will set a timetable for the determination of the opposition process that will be sent to the applicant.

1 EUTM Delegated Regulation (EUTMDR) (EU) 2018/625 Art 5.

8.24 There are two types of requirement for a notice of operation to be admissible:

- Absolute requirements—ie, where a failure to comply must be remedied before the expiry of the opposition period.[1] In default, the notice of opposition will be rejected as inadmissible;
- Relative requirements—ie, where, if there is a failure to comply, the Opposition Division will raise the matter with the opponent but the failure does not need to be remedied before the expiry of the opposition period. In such cases, the applicant will be given a further period of time to remedy the matters raised.[2] Only after that will a failure to remedy those matters result in the notice of opposition being rejected.

Since the absolute requirements cannot be remedied after the opposition period, and since it is the opponent's sole responsibility to ensure that these requirements are fulfilled, it is essential that the opponent takes particular care to ensure that they are fulfilled.

1 See para **8.25** below.
2 See para **8.32** below (translation of opposition) and para **8.31** below (other relative requirements).

Opposition—the absolute requirements for admissibility

8.25 Under Article 41(3) of the EUTMR, the notice of opposition:

- must be made in writing;
- must specify the grounds on which the opposition is made; and
- is not treated as duly entered until the opposition fees (€320) have been paid.[1]

Further material as to the absolute requirements for admissibility are contained in Art 2 of the EUTMDR.[2] The requirements are that the notice of opposition must:

- be filed within the opposition period;[3]
- clearly identify the application against which opposition is entered;
- clearly identify the earlier mark or the earlier right on which the opposition is based in accordance with Art 2(2) of the EUTMDR[4] and
- contain grounds for opposition in accordance with Art 2(4) of the EUTMDR.[5]

If these absolute requirements are not complied with within the opposition period (ie, the period for filing a notice of opposition) the opposition will be rejected as inadmissible.[4]

1 EUTMR Art 46(3).
2 EUTM Delegated Regulation (EUTMDR) (EU) 2018/625.
3 EUTMR Art 46.
4 As to which, see para **8.27** and paras **8.28–8.29** below.
5 As to which, see para **8.30** below.
6 EUTMDR Art 5.

Opposition—payment of the fees

8.26 The fees must be paid within the opposition period if the opposition is to be deemed filed on time. The payment of the fees may be made by way of a bank transfer, via a current account held with EUIPO or by credit card.

For those who do not regularly file trade mark applications or proceedings against third parties, a current account with EUIPO is less likely to exist. In such cases, a transfer of funds must be made to EUIPO and must be received prior to the opposition deadline. Where the funds do not arrive prior to the opposition deadline, the opposition will be deemed inadmissible unless:

1 the request to make the transfer was made more than 10 days prior to the expiry of the opposition; or
2 the request was made less than 10 days prior to the end of the opposition period and the opponent pays an additional surcharge of 10 per cent of the opposition fee.[1]

1 EUTMR Art 180.

Opposition—more on the absolute requirements for admissibility

1 Identification of the contested application

8.27 Under the EUTMIR, the notice of opposition must contain the file number of the contested EUTM application and the name of the EUTM applicant.[1] If there is some issue in that the name of the applicant does not correspond to that against the application number, the examiner will consider whether the identification of the application can be established without any doubt. If it cannot, the opposition will be deemed inadmissible. The notice of opposition form contains a section for the opponent to indicate the publication date of the application—it is advisable to insert this date to lessen any doubt that may exist as to the EUTM application in question.

1 EUTMDR Art 2(2)(a).

2 Identification of the earlier rights

8.28 The EUTMIR also requires each of the earlier marks or rights on which the opposition is based to be clearly identified.[1] If they are not, they will not be taken into account. If only a single right is relied upon and it is not clearly identified then the opposition will be deemed inadmissible—the opposition fees will not be reimbursed. If multiple rights are relied on and some are clearly identified then those that were not, will simply not be taken into account.

EUIPO's notifications of admissibility often state that a notice of opposition has been deemed admissible at least in relation to one of the rights—ie, there is no positive statement that all of the rights are admissible. In that regard, it is essential for the applicant to check that all rights were in fact identified clearly and to dispute this where it appears they were not.

1 EUTMDR Art 2(2)(b).

8.29 As mentioned above, there are a number of different types of earlier marks or earlier rights on which an opposition can be based. The requisite information required in order to identify them is as follows:

(a) *Earlier trade mark application/registration:* the required information is the application/registration number, an indication whether it has been registered or applied for and an indication of the Member State in which the earlier mark is protected or whether it is a EUTM;[1] EUIPO's guidance indicates that where a copy of the certificate is enclosed, this is sufficient to indicate the country. Where an international registration is relied upon, EUIPO will assume that the opposition is based upon all the countries that are Member States and/or the Benelux countries indicated in the international registration certificate.
(b) *Earlier trade mark application/registration with a reputation:* the required information is the application/ registration number, an indication whether it is registered or applied for, and an indication of Member State or whether a EUTM.[2]
(c) *Agent's mark:* the required information is the application/ registration number, an indication whether it has been registered or applied for, indication of Member State or whether a EUTM. If reliant upon an unregistered right then a representation of the mark must be given.[3]
(d) *Earlier well known mark:* the Member State where the mark is well known; if a registered mark, an indication of the registration number and Member State where registered; if unregistered, a representation of the mark as used and claimed to be well-known.[4]
(e) *Earlier non-registered trade mark or earlier sign used in the course of trade:* indication of the kind or nature of right; the Member State where right is claimed to exist; and a representation of the earlier right.[5]

1 EUTMDR Art 2(2)(b)(i).
2 EUTMDR Art 2(2)(c).
3 EUTMDR Art 2(2)(b)(iii); and EUTMR Art 8(3).
4 EUTMDR Art 2(2)(b)(ii).
5 EUTMDR Art 2(2)(b)(iv).

3 Identification of grounds

8.30 The EUTMIR also require the notice of opposition to state on which of Articles 8(1), (3)–(4); and/or (5) the opposition is based and to give a statement that the requirements are fulfilled.[1] In general, this will be done by completing the official form and if the relevant box or boxes relating to the different grounds are checked then the grounds will be deemed to be properly indicated.

1 EUTMDR Art 2(2)(c).

Opposition—relative admissibility requirements

8.31 In addition to the absolute admissibility requirements considered above, the EUTMDR imposes various other requirements which need to be complied with for the notice of opposition to be admissible. However, these are *relative* admissibility requirements in that, where they are not complied with, EUIPO will contact the opponent and give the opponent a period of time in which to correct or to comply with the relevant requirement(s). It is only if the opponent fails to do this within that period that the opposition will be deemed inadmissible (at least in relation to the earlier right against which there is a deficiency).[1]

1 See paras **8.32–8.36** below.

1 Translation of opposition

8.32 The opposition must be in one of the two languages of the application. Where an opposition is filed in a language of the Office but not one of the application, under the EUTMIR, the opponent must file a translation of the opposition within one month from the expiry of the opposition period. In default, the opposition is rejected as inadmissible. If an incomplete translation is submitted, the parts not translated are not taken into account in determining admissibility.[1]

1 EUTMR Art 146(7) and EUTMDR Art 5.

2 The relevant dates relating to the earlier applications and registrations

8.33 Under the EUTMDR, the notice of opposition should contain the filing date and (where applicable) the registration date and priority date of the earlier mark (unless it is an unregistered well-known trade mark). If these dates are not provided EUIPO will contact the opponent and give the opponent two months in which to provide them. In default of which, the opposition will be deemed inadmissible.[1] EUIPO has indicated that these dates are needed to help eliminate possible errors in identifying earlier rights.

1 EUTMDR Art 2(2)(d).

3 Identification of the earlier mark or sign

8.34 As set out above, under the EUTMDR, it is an absolute requirement in the case of certain unregistered earlier rights that the notice of opposition should contain a representation of the earlier mark.[1] In such cases, therefore, a representation *must* be filed before the expiry of the opposition deadline. However, in relation to any earlier registrations or applications relied on, the EUTMDR also contain a relative admissibility requirement that the notice should contain a representation of the earlier mark as registered or applied for (if the earlier mark was in colour, then the representation should also be in colour). If such a representation is not provided at the time of filing the notice of opposition, EUIPO will contact the opponent and give the opponent two months in which to provide the representation. In default, the opposition will be deemed inadmissible.[2]

In practice, however, this relative requirement has been relaxed by EUIPO. If a representation of the mark of the earlier trade mark application/registration is missing and the earlier right is a national right, EUIPO will set a deadline of two months to supply a representation. If the earlier right is a EUTM then EUIPO will simply make a representation available from its database. If the representation filed is unclear, EUIPO will set a deadline to provide a clear one.[3]

If the deadlines set by EUIPO with regards to the provision of representations (or clear versions) are not complied with then the right in question will be deemed inadmissible.

1 See para **8.29(d)–(e)** above.
2 EUTMDR Art 5(5).
3 *EUIPO Trade Mark guidelines*, Part C, Opposition, 2.4.2.2.

4 Identification of goods and services

8.35 The EUTMDR also provide that the notice of opposition should indicate the goods or services of the earlier right upon which the opposition is based. In default, EUIPO will contact the opponent and give the opponent two months in which to provide the requisite indication. In default, the opposition will be deemed inadmissible.[1]

Where no list is given and a certificate is attached, EUIPO will assume that all goods/services of the earlier registration are relied upon. Similarly, if the opponent indicates that they rely upon all goods and services for which the earlier mark is registered then this is acceptable if the registration certificate is attached. It is worth remembering that in both of these situations, these indications will only be acceptable if the certificate is in the language of the proceedings. If it is not, EUIPO will notify the opponent of this deficiency and give the opponent a deadline to file a translation of the specification.

1 EUTMDR Art 2(2)(g).

5 Scope of reputation

8.36 Where the opponent claims a reputation under their mark, the Member State(s) in which and the goods and services for which reputation is claimed must be specified in the notice of opposition. If the territory for which a reputation is not stated the Office will assume reputation is claimed for where the earlier mark has protection. For example, for an earlier EUTM it will be presumed reputation is claimed for the whole EU.[1] Where the scope is not clear in default, EUIPO will contact the opponent and give the opponent two months in which to provide this information. In default of this, the opposition will be deemed inadmissible.[2]

1 *EUIPO Trade Mark Guidelines*, Part C, Opposition, 2.4.2.4.
2 EUTMDR Art 5.

Opposition—further elements to consider

8.37 As set out below, an opponent should give careful thought to:

- the extent of the opposition, in other words against which goods or services the opposition is to be filed; and
- whether a reasoned statement of grounds should be filed with the notice of opposition.

1 The extent of the opposition

8.38 It is for the opponent to decide and to indicate the extent of the opposition.[1] EUTM applications frequently cover very broad specifications of goods. The reason often being that as there is no requirement that the applicant has a genuine intention to use the mark in respect of the goods or services for which protection has been sought.

The opponent as owner of an earlier trade mark may only be interested in preventing the registration of a mark for a limited list of goods or services, or even a single class of goods or services. It may well be that if the scope of the opposition is so limited and the class in question is of little or limited commercial value to the EUTM applicant, the applicant may deal with that class separately so that the progress of the other classes to registration is not delayed.

1 EUTMDR Art 2(2)(i).

8.39 If an opponent is unsuccessful then the maximum fees to be paid to the applicant are €300—this would be payable whether they opposed one class and lost or opposed all classes and lost on all classes. If the opponent opposes the entirety of the application and only succeeds in relation to some of the classes of goods or services, EUIPO may decide that no award of costs should be made (both parties having had a measure of success). Given that the opponent would not be able to recover the majority of the costs in any event, it may be strategically better to oppose all of the classes.

2 The reasoned statement

8.40 An opponent is not required to file a reasoned statement when filing the notice of opposition. Indeed, the opponent may decide that there is some advantage in not doing so at that time. If the matter proceeds to the evidence stages, the EUTM applicant would have to provide its observations and evidence within two months from the notification and the supply of the opponent's evidence but if the opponent had already given a fully reasoned statement at the filing stage then the EUTM applicant is put on notice of the opponent's case and could begin to anticipate the opponent's evidence and arguments and to prepare accordingly. The opponent may prefer to keep its powder dry not least for the purpose of negotiations.

Alternatively, of course, the opponent may decide that its best course is to file a reasoned statement setting out a full and well-argued case as soon as possible and then look to negotiate with the applicant. This may be preferable if the opposition is a strong one. However, it may also worth considering if the opposition case looks strong on paper but the opponent is aware of practical issues concerning the strength and availability of the evidence to support that case—issues of which the applicant may not be aware at this stage in the procedure.

Opposition—two-month cooling-off period

8.41 Once a notice of opposition has been found admissible, EUIPO will send a communication to the parties informing them that the opposition proceedings will be deemed to commence two months after the receipt of such communication.

This effectively allows the opposition proceedings to enter into a two-month 'cooling-off' period. At the parties' request, this period may be extended to 24 months.[1] It is, however, open to either of the parties to end the cooling-off period at any time once it has been extended.

1 EUTMDR Art 6(1).

Opposition—filing of evidence

8.42 Following the expiry of the cooling-off period, EUIPO must notify the opponent of the opportunity to present facts, evidence and arguments in support of the opposition or to expand on any reasoned statement that has already been filed. Such materials are to be filed by the opponent within a time limit to be specified by EUIPO—being of at least two months after the date when the opposition proceedings are deemed to commence.[1]

Within that same period, the opponent must also file proof of the existence, validity and scope of protection of all earlier rights relied on. This should include proof of any claim to reputation or as to the well-known status of such earlier rights and/or proof of the existence and scope of any earlier non-registered rights or signs relied on. The opponent must also file evidence of its entitlement to file the opposition.[2] If the opponent does not prove the existence, validity and scope of protection within the time allowed, the opposition will be rejected.[3]

1 EUTMDR Art 7(1)—ie, at least two months after the end of the cooling-off period.
2 EUTMDR Art 7(2).
3 EUTMDR Art 8(1).

8.43 All this evidence must be in an appropriate form and in the language of the proceedings or accompanied by a translation (see below).

EUIPO will not take into account any written submissions or documents (or any parts thereof) that have not been submitted or which have not been translated within the time limit it has set.[1]

1 EUTMDR 7(4).

Opposition—proving existence and validity of earlier trade mark applications/registrations

8.44 The nature of the evidence that is required in order to prove the existence and validity of earlier trade mark registrations or applications is set out in Art 7(2) of the EUTMDR.

(a) If the opposition is based on an earlier mark that is a trade mark but not an EUTM then the required evidence is:
- If the mark is not yet registered, a copy of the relevant filing certificate or an equivalent document emanating from the administration where the application has been filed.
- If the mark is registered, a copy of the registration certificate and the latest renewal certificate (if any) showing it is protected.

(b) If the opposition is based on a well-known mark within the meaning of Art 8(2)(c), the required evidence is evidence showing it is well-known in the relevant territory.

(c) If the opposition is based on a mark with a reputation within the meaning of Art 8(5), then in addition to the evidence in: (a) above, evidence must be filed showing it has a reputation and that use of the mark without due cause would take unfair advantage of or be detrimental to its distinctive character or reputation.
(d) If the opposition is based on an earlier right within the meaning of Art 8(4), the required evidence is required of the acquisition, continued existence and the scope of protection of the earlier non-registered mark.
(e) If the opposition is based on Art 8(3), the required evidence is of opponent's proprietorship and the nature of his relationship with the agent or representative.

8.45 For marks that are not EUTMs, EUIPO accepts the following as proof of their existence:

1 Certificates issued by the relevant official body—the applicant may submit copies of the official registration certificate. Where this is not available, an equivalent document such as a certified copy of the official details will suffice.
2 Extracts from official databases—certain intellectual property offices have online access to the official registers. Within the EU, examples are Germany, Spain and Benelux-Merken. The EUIPO also accepts extracts obtained from the Office's TMview portal. It is important to note that extracts from unofficial databases will not be accepted.
3 Extracts from official journals/bulletins—where the opponent is simply trying to demonstrate the existence of an application, this will suffice. Of course, the evidence that a mark has been published for opposition purposes is not sufficient to prove that a mark is registered since the mark may have been subsequently opposed. EUIPO has said that in the case of International Registrations, where the IR has been published and notified to the relevant countries or organisation designated, this will suffice as proof of registration unless the protection in the designated countries or organisation is challenged by the applicant.

8.46 Where the earlier rights expire prior to the deadline to substantiate the opposition, proof of renewal must be filed. This proof must identify all of the details of the renewal, including the fact that the registration was renewed for the full range of the goods or services relied upon.

It is essential that where the opponent claims to be the proprietor of certain earlier rights, those earlier rights are shown to be in the name of the opponent as represented on the notice of opposition. Any divergence between the name of the proprietor of the rights as represented on the proof of the earlier rights and the opponent (should he claim to be the proprietor of the earlier rights) will lead to the rejection of the right.

Opposition—documents to be in the language of the proceedings or translated

8.47 The information and evidence relied on by the opponent to substantiate his claim must be in the language of the proceedings or accompanied by a translation. Whilst in some other situations EUIPO may allow an additional period to provide translations, in this case, the translation must be filed within the same time limit that EUIPO specified for filing the information and evidence itself.[1]

1 EUTMDR Art 7(4) and EUTMIR Art 24.

8.48 Translations of application or registration details should include all information on the certificate. EUIPO has held that where the certificate contains the INID codes, which are the standard codes used on such certificates for identifying the various elements of information, the 'information headers' (eg, 'Filing date') need not be translated. EUIPO has also ruled that irrelevant information or parts having no bearing on the case need not be translated. Of course, the specification must be translated, but it would seem that where only certain classes of the earlier right are relied upon then the remaining classes need not be translated.

There are no formal requirements for the translations. In many cases it is possible to use translations provided to the opponent by the attorneys handling the registration of the earlier rights at the time that those earlier rights were registered (assuming that the opponent is able to use their favoured language as the language of the proceedings).

Opposition—applicant's evidence and observations in reply

8.49 If the opposition is not rejected for a failure to prove the existence, validity or scope of the earlier marks or rights, then EUIPO informs the EUTM applicant of the submission of the opponent and invites the applicant to file observations within a period specified by EUIPO.[1] If no such observations are filed, EUIPO will base its ruling on the evidence filed.[2] If observations are filed by the applicant, EUIPO will (if it thinks it necessary) invite the opponent to reply.[3]

Opponents do not always file evidence and further observations beyond those provided at the time of filing of the original notice of opposition. Accordingly, the EUTM applicant should work to the timetable that EUIPO sets when it informed the applicant of that opposition unless and until that timetable is amended by EUIPO (for example when EUIPO forwards further evidence filed by the opponent).

1 EUTMDR Art 8(2).
2 EUTMDR Art 8(3).
3 EUTMDR Art 8(4).

8.50 On occasions, EUIPO forwards evidence filed by the opponent after the EUTM applicant has submitted its evidence. In such cases, the applicant is of course given the opportunity to file further evidence and observations in light of that evidence. Parties are recommended to monitor the electronic files of EUIPO to check whether evidence has been filed by the other party that has not yet been forwarded. This can give a party a longer period in which to review and respond to that evidence as EUIPO takes, in general, at least two weeks to forward evidence.

8.51 In cases where the opposition is based on a right which was registered more than five years before the filing (or priority) date of the EUTM application in question, the EUTM applicant should before filing its observations, consider whether or not to request that the opponent demonstrates use of that earlier right. This is considered below.

Opposition—applicant's request that opponent proves use

8.52 Where an opposition is based on rights which had been registered for more than five years as at the date of filing (or priority date) of the EUTM application, the EUTM applicant can request that the opponent demonstrate either:

(a) that in that five-year period the earlier EUTM or the earlier national trade mark had been put to genuine use for the goods or services for which it is registered and on which the opponent relies; or alternatively,
(b) that there are proper reasons for non-use.[1]

In the absence of such proof, the opposition is rejected (in whole or in part depending on the extent of the proof of use submitted).[2]

1 EUTMR Art 47(2).
2 EUTMR Art 47(2); and EUTMDR Art 10.

8.53 A request that the opponent proves its use of earlier registrations can be a useful tool for a EUTM applicant because:

- EUIPO deems that there is no need for the applicant to file its evidence and observations in reply until the evidence of use has been submitted.[1]
- The EUTM applicant will be given a further period following the forwarding of the evidence of use to allow it to comment on that evidence (those comments should be submitted with the observations and evidence in reply to that of the Opponent). If one adds together the processing time and granted periods in relation to a request for proof of use (and given that as mentioned EUIPO generally takes at least two weeks to forward evidence), it means that by making such

a request, the Applicant can have a period of around five months beyond that which it would otherwise would have in order to prepare its observations and evidence in reply.

- If (as often happens) the opponent fails to demonstrate use of its earlier registration (or a good reason for non-use), for all or part of the specification, then the earlier registration will not be taken into account, or will only be taken into account in respect of the goods or services for which use can be shown (or non-use justified).

It is important to note that the EUTM applicant's challenge to the proof of use and its observations and evidence in reply will be filed at the same time. It is not unusual for the observations in such cases to be complicated. An applicant may wish to make its submissions based on full specification of the earlier rights relied on by the opponent but to make its further comments and observations based on its view of what EUIPO is likely to deem the opponent's rights to be following its consideration of the evidence of use (but without making any admission in the observations that the applicant accepts that use has been proven).

1 EUTMDR Art 10(5).

Opposition—opponent's proof of 'genuine use'

8.54 Where the opponent has relied on rights that had been registered for more than five years as at the filing (or priority) date of the opposed application, and where the applicant makes the requisite request, the opponent must provide proof of genuine use of the earlier right or proper reasons for its non-use.

As explained in **Chapter 12**, at para **12.06**, the meaning of 'genuine use' has been explained as being use for the purpose of creating or maintaining a market for the goods or services in question. In that regard, in order to be admissible as evidence of genuine use it must be:[1]

- use of the trade mark in question;
- use in relation to the goods or services in question;
- in the relevant time period;
- use in the relevant territory;
- external use;
- use to create or maintain a market for the goods or services, and not be token or sham use.

1 C-40/01 *Ansul BV v Ajax Brandbeveiliging BV* [2005] Ch 97.

8.55 In relation to the requirement that the use of the trade mark must be use of the mark in the form in which it is registered, this includes use in a format that differs in aspects that do not affect the distinctiveness of the mark as registered. Whether or not a particular mark falls within this exception is a matter of degree. The stronger the distinctiveness of a particular aspect of a mark, the more likely it is that the use will be deemed to fall within the exception where the dominant and distinctive element is reproduced. An example would be of a registration consisting of a label for tins of sardines consisting of an image of sardines and a word element DEFISHIOUS used in a format where the word DEFISHIOUS is used, but the sardine image is slightly different.

Opposition—the evidence to prove genuine use

8.56 The evidence to be filed must demonstrate that the use fulfils the requirements set out above. The EUTMIR provide that the evidence shall in principle be confined to the supporting documents and items and sworn or affirmed written statements.[1] That is not to say that written submissions should not be included; rather, such written submissions should seek to identify and clarify the supporting documents and enable the evidence to make sense.

1 EUTMDR Art 10(4).

8.57 The EUTMIR specify that the evidence should demonstrate the time, manner, place and extent of any use.[1] In providing proof of use, all four of these elements must be considered. It is acceptable for documents to corroborate the claimed use, and this will often be required as one type of proof may not be sufficient, particularly where the mark of the earlier registration is not a word mark consisting of the business name or a product name.

1 EUTMDR Art 10(3).

8.58 The EUTMIR list examples of evidence that may used; this includes packages, labels, price lists, catalogues, invoices, photographs and newspaper advertisements. To this one should include invoices. Invoices are generally used to demonstrate use of the mark in question. They are particularly useful in that they will be dated and will have consignor and consignee details so will be useful in showing that sales have occurred at a certain point in particular places. It is worth noting however that this will not of itself demonstrate the way in which the mark was used and upon which goods.

In many cases, invoices will need to be supplemented with copies of catalogues or advertisements so that it can be shown what products were being sold, and the way in which the mark was used on those products. A typical example would be the filing of example invoices showing that sales of goods have been made by reference to the mark X. The mark of the registration may be X as part of a logo and there is a wide specification of goods and services. Evidence limited to examples of invoices is unlikely to suffice in that situation.

Opposition—further evidence and arguments

8.59 Following the period for the applicant to file evidence and observations in support of the application, the opponent will be given a further opportunity to respond, strictly in reply to the evidence and observations of the applicant. This must be filed within the deadline set by EUIPO either initially, or as amended following the filing of evidence by the applicant.

The filing of evidence and observations in reply will generally terminate the proceedings and EUIPO will send a communication informing the parties that the matter will proceed to a decision. The procedure does not generally allow for oral proceedings, and a decision is made based upon the submissions and evidence filed by the parties.

Opposition—formalities for filing evidence

8.60 Documents may be sent to EUIPO by regular mail or private delivery services, or handed in personally at EUIPO's reception desk during official opening hours (8.30–13.30 for personal deliveries). EUIPO prefers online communication. Oppositions may be filed online along with requests for cooling-off periods, evidence and other communications and documents.[1]

1 Full details of the methods of filing (and of notifications by EUIPO) can be found in *EUIPO Trade Mark guidelines*, Part A, General Rules, at section 1, 2—available on EUIPO's website.

8.61 The method of filing can be important. If, for example, colour is important, then filing by fax would show only black and white and a colour copy would also have to be couriered (or posted) so as to arrive with EUIPO within the time limit provided for the filing of the evidence (subject to any extensions of time permitted by EUIPO).

8.62 Evidence submitted by electronic means or by post/courier consisting of paper documents only do not need to be submitted in duplicate. Evidence in the form of data carries and physical items are required to be filed in duplicate, one copy being for the EUTM applicant, the other for EUIPO's Opposition Division.

Opposition—costs

8.63 The Opposition procedure before EUIPO, like that in UKIPO, is not one where the full legal costs will be awarded to the successful party. In fact, the award of costs is even less open to change, with set amounts being awarded on the strict application of a schedule (unlike under UK procedure, where there is some discretion in the award within a scale and discretion to depart from the scale where appropriate).

The costs awarded where the opponent is successful are likely to be the €320 which were the opposition fees[1] as well as €300 in respect of the professional fees incurred.[2] Where the applicant is successful, €300 will be awarded to the applicant in respect of their professional fees.[3] Further costs are available in respect of the actual costs of attending EUIPO in respect of oral proceedings, but these are extremely rare and cannot otherwise be claimed.

1 EUTMR Art 109 and EUTMIR Art 18.
2 EUTMR Art 109(2).
3 EUTMR Art 109(1)-(2).

APPEALS

8.64 Appeals from EUIPO decisions are to the EUIPO Boards of Appeals and from there to the General Court of the European Court of Justice. Such appeals must be brought within two months of the decision to be appealed[1] and take the form of re-hearings. The appellant does not require permission to appeal. Appeals from the General Court are to the full court of the Court of Justice of the European Union on points of law only. Again, such an appeal must be lodged within two months of the decision of the General Court.

1 EUTMR Art 68.

Chapter 9

International conventions—the Madrid System

INTRODUCTION

9.01 There are a number of International Conventions relating to the protection of trade marks. These include:

- The Paris Convention.
- The TRIPS Agreement.
- The Madrid Agreement and Protocol.

Of these, the Paris Convention and the TRIPS Agreement, whilst ratified by the UK (and the EU) are of no direct effect. Consequently, only the Madrid Agreement and Protocol will be considered below.

THE MADRID SYSTEM

9.02 The Madrid System is made up of two treaties: the Madrid Agreement[1] and the Protocol to the Madrid Agreement.[2] Countries that have joined the Madrid System can opt to accede to either one or to both of these treaties.

For the purposes of this Guide, the focus will be on the Protocol to the Madrid Agreement. This is because the United Kingdom and the European Union are members of the Protocol alone. Further, in 2015 all members of the Madrid Union became either Contracting Parties to the Protocol only, or to both the Agreement and the Protocol, and therefore currently the Protocol governs all transactions in respect of all Contracting Parties and users.

1 Concluded in 1891 and periodically revised since.

2 Concluded in 1989 and intended to make the system more flexible and attractive to members.

9.03 The legal framework for the Protocol system is contained in the:

- Protocol Relating to the Madrid Agreement Concerning the International Registration of Marks; ('the Protocol'); and the
- Common Regulations under the Madrid Agreement Concerning the International Registration of Marks and the Protocol Relating to that Agreement ('the Regulations').

Copies of these documents can be found on the website of the World Intellectual Property Organisation ('WIPO') which acts as the administration authority for the Madrid System.[1] WIPO has also produced a Guide to the International Registration of Marks under the Madrid Agreement and the Madrid Protocol.[2]

1 See http://www.wipo.int/madrid/en/legal_texts
2 2021 edn—see http://www.wipo.int/madrid/en/guide/

The Madrid System in outline

9.04 The Madrid International Trademark System of registration provides a simplified (and often cost-effective) means for protecting a mark in a large number of countries. The applicant begins with a national trade mark or EUTM (the 'basic' mark) and then applies for an international registration.

When applying for the international registration, the applicant may designate one or more countries which are members of the Protocol[1] and in which the applicant would like protection. This list of countries (known as 'designations') can subsequently be added to or reduced as required. As the system relies on this central international registration, changes to the international registration (such as changes in ownership) affect the designations.

1 The country may be a member of both the Agreement and the Protocol or of just the Protocol. A country cannot be a member of just the Agreement.

9.05 One significant strength of this international system is that the administration of a multinational trade mark portfolio is much simplified. Rather than having to make changes in multiple countries and to incur the costs of local associates and local official fees, the international system allows for the changes to be made centrally, and for the owner of the registration (called the 'holder' under the Madrid system) to realise savings in the overall cost of such maintenance.

9.06 However, the frailty of the international system is its dependence on the national application or registration (known as the 'basic application' or the 'basic registration'). The international registration relies on the basic application or registration for the first five years following the application for the international trade mark. Any attack on the basic registration (known as 'central attack') threatens the scope and existence of the international registration.

9.07 A further notable element of the international system is that where an application proceeds without objection, notifications of acceptance are simply passed to the applicant. It is only where there are objections that the applicant needs to use local attorneys to handle the designations. This often reduces the initial cost of protection by up to half.

The basic application/registration

9.08 An international registration must be based on a basic application or registration—ie, an application or registration in the office of a Contracting State or (in the case of an EUTM) of a Contracting Organisation with which the applicant has the required connection.[1]

Where the basic application or registration is in the office of a Contracting State, the required connection is that the applicant must be a national of that State, or be domiciled, or have a real and effective industrial or commercial establishment, in that State. If the basic application or registration was in the office of a Contracting Organisation, the applicant must be a national of a State member of that Organisation, or be domiciled, or have a real and effective industrial or commercial establishment, in the territory of that Organisation.

1 Protocol Art 2(1).

9.09 Whether an applicant is a national, or is domiciled or has a 'real and effective establishment' in a particular country is a matter of the law of the country in question. The term 'real and effective establishment' has not been explained definitively. However, it is taken to mean that some commercial or economic activity must occur in that country (as opposed to, say, simple storage facilities).[1] UKIPO has indicated that it would not accept an address with a PO Box number or any indication that an address was only temporary.[2] Following the end of the Brexit transition period (at 11pm on 31 December 2020), a UK national may therefore have difficulty basing a Madrid Protocol application on an EUTM, but they can still rely on a UK basic application or registration filed via the UKIPO.

1 See in that regard the guidance of EUIPO on the meaning of the term in the context of representation before EUIPO (Part A, section 5, para 3.1.1, at https://guidelines.euipo.europa.eu/binary/1922895/2000060000).

2 UKIPO Trade Marks Manual, International Examination Guide, section 2.2.

9.10 It is important to note that the scope of the international registration is determined by the scope of the basic right. Whilst the specification under the international registration can be less extensive than the basic right, it cannot be broader. In that regard, it is important to ensure that, where the various national rights of the applicant differ as to their extent, the most appropriate basic right is used.

Reliance on the basic right

9.11 For the first five years following the filing of the application for an international registration, the international registration is dependent upon the basic right. If the protection of the basic right ceases in total or in part (ie, ceases in the office of the relevant Member State or Organisation), then the international registration will also be restricted or will cease. Although it is possible to transform an international registration under the Madrid Protocol into national rights[1] this is often at substantial additional cost.

On that basis, when choosing a basic right, the applicant should be aware of the possibility of objections to that basic right from the relevant registering office or from third parties. Where possible, it may be prudent to file the Madrid Protocol application once the basic application has passed the opposition period unchallenged.

1 In that regard see para **9.43**.

The application form for an international registration

9.12 The application for an international registration is made by way of the prescribed form—Form MM2.[1] This application form is presented to WIPO by the office of the basic right and therefore must be filed via that office rather than direct to WIPO.[2]

Whilst the application form is largely self-explanatory, it is worth noting that in practice applicants often omit certain information from the form and that this can cause difficulties. In the case of section 2 of the form (which relates to the identification of the applicant) it is important to fill all of the parts of this section, particularly where the United States is designated as one of the countries for which protection is sought. An email address for the applicant must be supplied. Similarly, section 9 (relating to miscellaneous indications relating to the mark) is also often left part completed. Whilst this may not prove fatal to the international registration itself, it may well lead to objections at the stage that the designations are passed to the national offices.

1 Protocol Art 3(1). Form MM2 is available on the WIPO website—http://www.wipo.int
2 Regulations under the Protocol relating to the Madrid Agreement ('Protocol Regulation') r 9.

9.13 When considering how to complete section 10 of the form—which deals with the specification of the international registration—applicants must always bear in mind that this specification should not be broader in its coverage than the specification in the home right. Applicants should also be aware that although many countries allow expansive specifications with reasonably general indications, other countries do not and may well raise objections.

9.14 One country of particular note in this regard is the United States. Where the specification follows the wording of the general class headings (as UK or EUTM applications and registrations will often do) the United States Patent and Trade Mark Office will often raise an objection based upon an overly broad identification of goods or services.

Whilst in many cases the applicant will require as broad a specification as possible (and so may wish simply to await any objections and then to answer them), for applicants with specific interests it may be worth considering providing a restriction under section 10 of the form in relation to the United States. An acceptable list of goods or services can be drawn up by consulting the USPTO's *Identification Manual*.[1]

1 Found at https://idm-tmng.uspto.gov/id-master-list-public.html

9.15 Finally, applicants should note that in the case of a designation of the United States, it will be necessary to file a Form MM18. Where the request to designate the United States is made at the same time as the application for an international registration then the MM18 should either accompany that application or be submitted within a period of two months from when the application is received by the office of origin. If it is not then the designation of the United States is deemed not to have been contained within the application and the designation fee for the United States is reimbursed.

Applications based on a UK trade mark application or registration

9.16 Where the basic right is a UK application or registration then the application is made via UKIPO and is subject to the payment of a transmittal fee of £40. The fee should be remitted with the dedicated fee sheet FS4. UKIPO has produced its own version of the Form MM2 with an integrated fee sheet. Other than the fee sheet and the MM2 Form, no further form is required by UKIPO.

Applications based on an EUTM application or registration

9.17 Where the basic right is an EUTM application or registration then the application shall be filed via EUIPO and is subject to the payment of a transmittal fee of €300. EUIPO has provided its own version of the Form MM2 which can be used which incorporates the payment information in relation to the transmittal fee.

Fees for an international registration

9.18 The fees associated with an international registration under the Madrid System are made up of four elements:

1. *Basic fees*—this is the fee associated with the International Registration before any designations are made. At the time of writing, this fee was 653 or 903 Swiss francs depending on whether or not the reproduction of the mark is in colour.[1]
2. *Supplementary fees*—the fees associated with each additional class of goods or services above three (100 Swiss francs per additional class).
3. *Complementary fees*—the fee per country designated (where that country has elected to receive a complementary fee) (100 Swiss francs for each designated contracting state).
4. *Individual fees*—certain members have individual fees (so note that it is not as simple as paying the complementary fee).

WIPO produces a list of the applicable fees, and also provides a fees calculator[2] so although establishing the correct fees may appear to require some calculation, this is made somewhat easier by the tools provided by WIPO. It is to be noted that the fees on the WIPO site do not include the transmittal fees charged by the office of origin.

1 http://www.wipo.int/madrid/en/fees/sched.html
2 https://madrid.wipo.int/feecalcapp/

Procedure after filing the application

9.19 Following the filing of the application, it is for the office of the basic right to examine the application for the international registration and to ensure that it is acceptable. If it is, the application will be forwarded to the International Bureau of WIPO for examination where it is examined to ensure compliance with the various formal requirements for international registration as a whole, for the requirements particular to any particular designation as well as the specification being considered.

Consideration by WIPO—notification of formal irregularities (irregularities other than as to the classification of goods and services or their indication)

9.20 If WIPO determines that the application for an international registration is irregular then it will send notification of the irregularity.

These may be dealt with in various ways:

- certain irregularities are notified to the office of the basic right for their resolution (often with the applicant providing submissions to the office on how to resolve the deficiency);
- some irregularities are capable of resolution by the applicant directly with WIPO;
- other irregularities are for resolution by the applicant.

Various types of irregularities are considered below. In each case, WIPO will in any event notify the office of origin and the applicant of the irregularity.

9.21 *Irregularities for resolution by the Office of origin*[1]—the irregularities for resolution by the office of origin are that:

(a) The international application was not made on the correct form, was not typed or otherwise printed, or was not signed by the office of origin.
(b) The applicant appears not to be entitled to file the international application.
(c) One or more of the following elements is missing from the application as received by WIPO:
    - indications allowing the identity of the applicant to be established and sufficient to contact the applicant or their representative;
    - indications concerning the applicant's connection with the office of origin;
    - the date and the number of the basic registration or the basic application;
    - a reproduction of the mark;
    - the list of goods and services for which registration of the mark is sought;
    - an indication of the contracting parties designated; or
    - the declaration by the office of origin.

1 Protocol Regulation r 11(4).

9.22 *Irregularities which can be resolved by the Office of Origin or the Applicant*[1]—if the fees forwarded to WIPO are insufficient then a notice of irregularity will be issued providing an indication of the missing sum. This can be paid by the applicant directly to WIPO or to the office of origin, who then forward the sum. This is to be contrasted with a complete failure to pay the international registration fees, which is a irregularity to be remedied by the applicant alone.

1 Protocol Regulation r 11(3).

9.23 *Irregularities to be resolved by the Applicant alone*[1]—all other formal irregularities are to be resolved by the applicant alone.

1 Protocol Regulation r 11(2).

Deadlines for remedying formal irregularities and failure to resolve

9.24 In relation to the formal requirements, a three month period is provided from the notification of the irregularity to remedy it. If the irregularity is not remedied then the international application is deemed abandoned.[1] To the extent that the applicant has paid any fees, these will be refunded less half of the basic fees for an international registration in black and white.[2]

1 Protocol Regulation r 11(2)(b), (3)(b) and (4)(b).
2 Protocol Regulation r 11(5).

Consideration by WIPO—irregularities as the specification of goods and services

9.25 Objections may arise either because WIPO believes that the specification of the international registration does not cover the correct classes or the correct number of classes, or because the specification is unclear.

9.26 *Incorrect classes or number of classes*—if WIPO believes that the incorrect classes have been indicated, or that the result of misclassification means that extra classes are required, then a proposal for reclassification will be sent.[1] This is deemed to be a matter for resolution by the office of origin of the application, and so any comments that the applicant wishes to make should be made to the office of origin. These will then be incorporated into the response of that office.

WIPO provides an initial indication of the classes they believe that the international application should have designated, and will inform the office of origin and applicant of any additional fees which would be incurred if there is a need for additional classes.[2] A period of three months is provided for the comments of the office of origin.[3] If comments are filed then WIPO will provide a final view on the proposal.[4]

1 Protocol Regulation r 12(1)(a).
2 Protocol Regulation r 12(1)(b).
3 Protocol Regulation r 12(2).
4 Protocol Regulation r 12(4)–(6).

9.27 Where WIPO has indicated that additional fees will fall due as a result of the amended specification then the applicant has the choice either to pay the fees thereby adopting WIPO's suggestions or to delete the goods or services which would lead to the additional class or classes.

The relevant deadlines for the payment of these additional fees or for the deletion of the goods or services at issue are as follows:

(a) if no comments are filed against the initial notification—four months from the notification of the proposal;
(b) if comments are filed—three months from the notification of WIPO to confirm or modify its initial proposal.

If any additional fees are not paid or if the goods or services involved are not deleted within the relevant period then the international application is deemed abandoned in its entirety.[1] WIPO will refund any fees minus an amount corresponding to half of the basic fee for an application made in black and white.[2]

1 Protocol Regulation r 12(7).
2 Protocol Regulation r 12(8).

9.28 *The specification is unclear*—if WIPO believes that the specification is unclear (because the goods and services are indicated by a term that is 'too vague for the purposes of classification' or is 'incomprehensible' or 'linguistically incorrect') then it will send notification to the office of origin, sending a copy of the notification to the applicant.[1] The nature of the objection is that a term that has been used is unclear for the purposes of classification because it is unclear in which class the term should be placed, or alternatively because the term used covers goods or services which may fall into multiple classes. In notifying the office of origin and the applicant, WIPO may sometimes make a proposal as to a description which it believes is clear.

1 Protocol Regulation r 13(1).

9.29 A three-month period is allowed for a response, which is to be provided by the office of origin.[1] In the absence of a response which is acceptable to WIPO then if the office of origin has indicated that the term is in the correct class, WIPO will allow the term to remain, but will add an indication that they believe that the term is too vague for classification purposes. If the office of origin has not indicated that the term is in the correct class then that term will be deleted from the specification of the international application.[2]

It is worth noting that the result of a proposal which leads to the addition of classes or movement of goods and services will lead to further objection as to the classification, as discussed above.

1 Protocol Regulation r 13(2)(a).
2 Protocol Regulation r 13(2)(b).

Designations with additional requirements

9.30 In relation to certain designations, particularly in the United States, additional declarations are required. In relation to the United States, a Form MM18 should be filed together with the application for the international application. Where these documents are missing from the application, the applicant has two months from the date that the international application was filed to provide the document. If the document is not provided then the designation of that country will be deemed not to have been made and the fees for that designation will be refunded. The designation of that country can be made as a subsequent designation. When designating the EU a second language must be provided on Form MM2. Additionally, certain designations require the payment of their individual fees in two parts and the second part must be paid once the designation has been accepted for protection.

International registration, notification of the office of origin

9.31 Once any irregularities in the international application have been overcome, WIPO will register the mark in the International Register—with the registration being effective from the date on which the international application was received by the office of origin. A copy of the registration certificate is despatched to the holder.

At this stage, details of the International Registration are notified by WIPO to the offices of any Contracting Party designated for protection by the applicant.1

1 Protocol Art 3(4) and Protocol Regulation r 14(1). The International Registration must contain the data and information specified in r 14(2).

Refusal of protection by a designated office

9.32 Within the rules of the Protocol, any office of a designated Contracting Party can refuse protection for the international mark on the basis of any ground which would preclude registration of a mark deposited directly with that office.[1] On this basis, the offices of the various designated bodies will review the international registration and examine it as against absolute grounds for refusal and (in some countries) against relative grounds. The offices will also consider any oppositions to protection that are filed.

1 Protocol Art 5(1).

9.33 Where a designated office decides to refuse protection for an international registration, notice of that refusal must be given to WIPO within a year of WIPO's notification of the registration unless (as is the case with the UK), the relevant office has declared that the period should be 18 months.[1] The designated office may also declare that a notice of refusal can be given *after* that 18-month period. However a notice of refusal can only be given after the 18-month period if: (i) within that period the designated office in question had given WIPO a notice of provisional refusal;[2] and (ii) where the refusal is based on an opposition, that notification is made within one month of the expiry of any applicable opposition period and, in any case, no more than seven months from the beginning of any opposition period.[3]

1 Protocol Art 5(2)(a)–(b).
2 Ie, notice of the possibility that a refusal would be filed after the 18-month period.
3 Protocol Art 5(2)(c).

9.34 Where an office sends WIPO a refusal of protection, WIPO is obliged to transmit that notice to the holder of the international registration. The holder then has the same remedies as if the mark had been deposited by him direct with that office.[1] However, before an international registration can be found to be invalid in any designated office, the holder must have been given, in good time, an opportunity of defending his rights.[2] It will generally be necessary for the holder to instruct a local attorney to deal with the objection (unless the holder or its representative has the standing to act before the office involved).

1 Protocol Art 5(3).
2 Protocol Art 5(6).

9.35 If the office of a designated Contracting Party gives no notice of refusal (whether final or provisional) within the relevant periods referred to above, then it loses the right to serve a notice refusing protection of the mark.[1] Once all procedures before the office have been completed and there are no grounds for refusing protection, the office must notify WIPO that protection has been granted to the mark.[2]

1 Protocol Art 5(5).
2 Protocol Regulation r 18*ter*(1).

9.36 As set out above, a notice of provisional refusal (where required) must also be served on WIPO and the holder of the international registration must be notified.[1] The holder can then make appropriate representations to the office in question and the relevant office is obliged to notify WIPO whether or not the refusal is withdrawn or is confirmed.[2]

1 Protocol Art 5(3).
2 Protocol Regulation r 18*ter*(2)–(4).

9.37 The Regulations contain specific provisions relating to the contents of such a notice and the consequences of serving an irregular notice.[1] In addition, when the notice is based (in whole or in part) on an opposition, the opponent must be identified and the list of goods or services in respect of which the opposition is raised must be communicated.[2]

1 Protocol Regulation rr 17–18.
2 Protocol Regulation r 17(3).

9.38 Where a notice of provisional refusal is received it is important to note the date of receipt and the deadline for any response. In this regard, there are differences between offices both as to the period allowed for a response and the time from which the period runs. Some are based on the date of the provisional refusal, others on the date the provisional refusal was received by WIPO, and others on the date on which the provisional refusal was received.

9.39 The consequence of failing to respond to the provisional refusal, or failing to overcome the reasons for the provisional refusal, will depend upon the nature of the objection. Some objections, principally those relating to the specification, may simply lead to the refusal of protection for the goods or services involved. Other objections, such as those based upon absolute or relative grounds, may lead to the total refusal of protection.

Validity of international registrations

9.40 A mark once registered at WIPO is effective for ten years and is renewable every ten years upon payment of the appropriate fees.[1]

1 Protocol Arts 6(1) and 7.

Dependence of international registration on the basic right

9.41 As mentioned above, an International application or registration is dependant upon the basic application or registration for the first five years following the filing of the application for the International Registration. If, within that period, the protection under the basic application or registration is amended for whatever reason then the office of origin will notify the International Bureau and the international application or registration will also be amended accordingly. Where the basic application or registration ceases to have effect, the international registration will be cancelled in its entirety.[1]

After the expiry of the five-year period, however, the International registration becomes independent of the basic application or the basic registration.[2]

1 Protocol Art 6(3)–(4).
2 Protocol Art 6(2).

Transformation of international registrations into national/regional rights

9.42 Where the office of origin requests WIPO to cancel the International registration for some or all of the goods or services listed, the Madrid Protocol allows the holder to apply for the mark to be registered in the designated offices.[1] This, in effect, transforms the international registration into a national registration in each of the designated offices. The procedure requires the holder to make separate applications in those countries where protection is sought, and for the holder to include the details of the cancelled International application or registration. The advantage of such a course is that the filing date of the new national right is deemed to be that of the earlier International Application or registration.

In the case of a UK designation, the procedure is that the Form TM4 should be submitted (for which no fees are due). In the case of a designation of the EU, this is by way of a fresh application including the details of the earlier international registration.

1 Protocol Art 9*quinquies*.

9.43 In all cases, the request for transformation must be made within three months of the date of cancellation of the international application or registration (in whole or in part).[1]

1 Protocol Art 9*quinquies*.

Chapter 10

Representation

INTRODUCTION

10.01 The position as regards the appointment of a representative differs depending on whether one is dealing with:

(a) UKIPO,
(b) EUIPO, or
(c) WIPO.

As will be seen, it may be necessary or desirable to appoint a representative—particularly if the applicant is not based in the country or area of the office in question.

REPRESENTATION BEFORE UKIPO

Need for an address in the UK, Gibraltar or Channel Islands

10.02 There is no requirement that applicants be professionally represented before UKIPO.

However, when dealing with UKIPO, an applicant must provide an address for service in the UK, Gibraltar or the Channel Islands.[1] The applicant needs, therefore, an office somewhere within those territories which it can use for the purposes of any correspondence. The UKIPO will also accept the Isle of Man as a valid address for service.[2]

1 Trade Mark Rules 2008, SI 2008/1797 (as amended) ('TMR') r 11.
2 *UK Trade Marks Manual*, Tribunal section 2.1.

Appointment of a representative before the UKIPO

10.03 The Trade Marks Act 1994 ('TMA 1994') provides that any act required to be done by an applicant may also be done by an agent who the applicant has (whether orally or in writing) authorised.[1]

Although UKIPO maintains a register of trade mark attorneys,[2] an applicant need not use such an attorney. Indeed the only restriction on the person who may act as agent for an applicant is that individuals who have committed certain specified offences or misconduct may not be recognised by the Registrar.[3]

The appointment of a representative at the time of filing of an application is made by simply completing the relevant section of the Form TM3. Otherwise, where a representative is appointed for the first time or in substitution for another, the newly appointed agent must file Form TM33 or if appointed in relation to proceedings, Form TM33P.[4] The registrar may require the personal signature or the presence of the agent or the person authorising the agent to act as agent.[5]

1 TMA 1994 s 82.
2 TMA 1994 s 83.
3 TMR r 61.
4 TMR r 60(2)–(3).
5 TMR r 60(1) and (5).

Cancellation of representation

10.04 Representation may be cancelled by way of a simple letter to UKIPO requesting that representation be withdrawn. Where a Form TM33 or TM33P has been filed, and existing representatives had previously been appointed, their ability to act as representatives is cancelled.

REPRESENTATION BEFORE EUIPO

10.05 In relation to proceedings before EUIPO, (other than the filing of an EUTM application), a party which does not have its domicile or its principal place of business or a real and effective industrial or commercial establishment in the European Economic Area ('EEA') must be represented by a legal practitioner or a professional representative.[1]

In other cases, the EU Trade Mark Regulation ('EUTMR') provides that no person shall be compelled to be represented before EUIPO.[2] A person is, of course, free to use a legal practitioner or professional representative. However, a natural or legal person with a domicile or a principal place of business or a real and effective industrial or commercial establishment in the EEA, may be represented by an employee or by an employee of an entity with which it has economic connections.[3]

EUIPO maintains a list of those persons who satisfy its conditions (described below) for acting as legal practitioners and professional representative.

1 EUTMR Art 119(2).
2 EUTMR Art 119(1).
3 EUTMR Art 119(3).

Meaning of 'legal practitioner'

10.06 A legal practitioner is someone who is qualified as a legal practitioner—EUIPO maintains a list of those qualifications which fall within the meaning of 'legal practitioner'.[1] In order to qualify, the legal practitioner must also have a place of business within the EEA and must be entitled to act as a representative in trade mark matters. It is not necessary that the legal representative be based in the country where they are entitled to act, nor that the individual be a national of a Member State of the EEA.

1 According to EUIPO, the term 'legal practitioner' comprises the following professional titles: in Belgium, 'avocat/advocaat/Rechtsanwalt'; in Denmark, 'advokat'; in Germany and Austria, 'Rechtsanwalt'; in Greece, 'Dikhgoroz'; in Spain, 'abogado'; in France and Luxembourg, 'avocat', in Ireland, 'barrister/solicitor'; in Italy, 'avvocato/procuratore legale'; in the Netherlands, 'advocaat'; in Portugal, 'advogado'; in Finland, 'asianajaja/advokat'; in Sweden, 'advokat'.

Meaning of 'professional representative'

10.07 Whilst the term 'legal practitioner' covers qualifications that allow for representation in all matters (and, as a matter of course, trade mark matters), other professionals may be allowed to represent parties. These individuals are deemed professional representatives.

In order to be classed as a professional representative, an individual must be entered on EUIPO's list of professional representatives. To enter that list, the representative must fulfil the national requirements for the EEA Member State involved. In those countries where representation before the national office is dependent upon a particular qualification, professional representatives must hold such qualifications. Where no particular qualifications are required to represent before the appropriate national office, professional representatives must have habitually represented legal or natural persons in trade mark matters before the office concerned for at least five years.[1]

In certain cases those with certain professional qualifications are absolved of the requirement that they have habitually represented parties before their relevant national office for at least five years. The Executive Director of EUIPO is entitled to provide dispensation from the requirement of five years' experience—such a case may arise where the individual was responsible for the trade mark matters of a company without actually acting before the relevant Intellectual Property Office.

1 EUTMR Art 120(2).

10.08 In addition, the professional representative must have a place of business in the EEA[1] and must have a certificate from the relevant national office attesting that the representative has the experience or professional qualification mentioned above.[2] A final requirement is that a professional representative must be a national of a Member State of the EEA.[3] This is a further area in which it is possible to obtain dispensation from the Executive Director of EUIPO and in practice all requests for dispensation from this requirement have been granted. It remains to be seen if this will continue to be the case in respect of UK nationals following the end of the Brexit transition period.[4]

1 EUTMR Art 120(2)(b).
2 EUTMR Art 120(3).
3 EUTMR Art 120(2)(a).
4 See Communication No 2/20 of the Executive Director of EUIPO for further guidance on the changes due to Brexit https://euipo.europa.eu/ohimportal/en/brexit-q-and-a (europa.eu)

REPRESENTATION BEFORE WIPO

10.09 The Regulations governing the Madrid Protocol provide that the applicant for or holder of an international registration may have a representative before WIPO. However, it can only have one representative.[1] This does not need to be the same attorney who is appointed as regards the Office of Origin. Indeed, the representative could be in a different country.

1 Regulations under the Protocol relating to the Madrid Agreement ('Protocol Regulation') r 3(1).

Appointment of a representative

10.10 The appointment of a representative may be made in the international application, or in a subsequent designation or a request for recording a change.[1]

A representative may also be appointed apart from this process by the filing of a letter giving the details of the representative, or by filing a Form MM12. The request needs to include the details of the applicant or holder, the details of the representative and the list of applications or registrations involved. The request can be filed either directly before WIPO or can be filed before the office of the Contracting Party of the holder. The difference between these methods is that if filed directly then the request must be signed by the applicant, or holder; if filed via the national office of the holder then it can be signed by the office instead.[2]

1 Protocol Regulation r 3(2)(a).
2 Protocol Regulation r 3(2)(b).

Cancellation of appointment

10.11 The appointment of a representative may be cancelled by the applicant/holder or by the representative themselves. It will also be cancelled automatically where a new representative is appointed, or where a transfer is recorded (unless the representative is expressly retained by the new proprietor).[1]

1 Protocol Regulation r 3(6)(a).

10.12 Representation may be cancelled by way of a simple letter from the representative or the applicant/holder. Where the applicant/holder cancels the representation, the cancellation takes effect from when the request is received.[1] Where the representative cancels the representation, the cancellation takes effect from when a new representative is appointed or two months from when the request is received (whichever is sooner).[2] The different procedure is due to the need to protect the interests of an applicant/holder whose representative withdraws representation without their knowledge or against their wishes. In the case that the representative applies for cancellation, WIPO will also send the applicant/holder a copy of all communications from the preceding six months and will send them copies of all correspondence from that point on.[3]

1 Protocol Regulation r 3(6)(b).
2 Protocol Regulation r 3(6)(c).
3 Protocol Regulation r 3(6)(d).

Chapter 11

Invalidity

INTRODUCTION

11.01 The Trade Marks Act 1994 ('TMA 1994') and the European Union Trade Mark Regulation ('EUTMR') both provide for the removal from the register of marks that:

(a) ought not to be registered any longer—ie, revocation, which is considered in **Chapter 12**; or
(b) should never have been registered in the first place—ie, invalidation, which is the subject of this **Chapter 11**.

In each case, third parties can challenge the status of a registered mark and, if successful, have it struck from the register. This is a powerful threat to a registered mark, and defendants sued for infringement of a mark will often bring a counterclaim seeking to have the registration of the mark revoked or declared invalid.

As will be seen, invalidation proceedings allow a defendant to rely on earlier marks that might have formed (but did not) the basis of opposition proceedings at the registration stage, as long as the owner of those earlier marks did not consent to the registration.

The grounds for invalidity fall into two broad categories:

1 *relative grounds*—based on the earlier rights of third parties; and
2 *absolute grounds*—based upon the mark's inherent unsuitability for registration.

A INVALIDITY UNDER THE TMA 1994—S 47

The grounds for declaring a trade mark invalid

11.02 Invalidity proceedings in relation to a UK trade mark are governed by s 47 of the TMA 1994. The key subsections of s 47 state:

(1) The registration of a trade mark may be declared invalid on the ground that the trade mark was registered in breach of s 3 or any

of the provisions referred to in that section (absolute grounds for refusal of registration).
Where the trade mark was registered in breach of s 3(1)(b)–(c) or (d), it shall not be declared invalid if, in consequence of the use that has been made of it, it has after registration acquired a distinctive character in relation to the goods or services for which it is registered.

(2) Subject to sections (2A) and (2G) the registration of a trade mark may be declared invalid on the ground:
  (a) that there is an earlier trade mark in relation to which the conditions set out in s 5(1), (2) or (3) obtain; or
  (b) that there is an earlier right in relation to which the condition set out in s 5(4) is satisfied;

unless the proprietor of that earlier trade mark or other earlier right has consented to the registration.

Invalidity due to breach of section 3 (absolute grounds for refusal)

11.03 As to s 47(1), the substantive law and practice as to whether the registration was in breach of any of the absolute grounds for refusal of registration can be found in **Chapter 4.**

Invalidity due to existence of an earlier trade mark or earlier right (relative grounds for refusal)

(i) The substantive law

11.04 The substantive law and practice as to whether there was an earlier trade mark or earlier right that would justify a declaration of invalidity under s 47(2) (ie, the relative grounds of refusal) can be found in **Chapter 5**.

(ii) Consent to registration

11.05 By virtue of s 47(2), a claim for a declaration of invalidity on the basis of an earlier trade mark or an earlier right will not succeed where the proprietor of the earlier trade mark or earlier right has consented to the registration.

No guidance is given as to the meaning of 'consent' for these purposes. However, it would seem appropriate for it to mirror the meaning of 'consent' for the purposes of s 12 of the TMA 1994 (the consent of a proprietor to goods being marketed in the EEA so as to exhaust the proprietor's right to object to the further use of the mark in relation to those goods). On that basis it would need to be shown that the proprietor of the earlier right had unequivocally renounced its right to oppose the registration of the mark.[1] This contrasts with a mere failure to take action or with making a conscious decision to reserve one's position. This approach has been confirmed by the High Court.[2]

1 See C-414/99 *Zino Davidoff SA v A&G Imports Ltd* EU:C:2001:617; [2002] RPC 20. See para **15.41** for a fuller discussion.
2 See *Dalsouple Societe Saumuroise du Caoutchouc v Dalsouple Direct Ltd* [2014] EWHC 3963 (Ch); [2015] ETMR 8.

(iii) Other restrictions on when a mark will be declared invalid on the basis of an earlier trade mark (other than a well-known mark)

11.06 By reason of s 47(2A) of the TMA 1994, a mark will not be declared invalid on the basis of an earlier trade mark unless:

(a) that earlier trade mark had been registered within the period of five years ending with the date of the application for the declaration of invalidity of the mark;
(b) the registration of that earlier trade mark was not completed before that date; or
(c) the use conditions (described below) are met.

Under section 47(2B), the use conditions are met if either:

(a) the earlier trade mark has been put to genuine use in the United Kingdom by the proprietor or with its consent in relation to the goods or services for which it is registered—
  (i) within the period of five years ending with the date of application for the declaration, and
  (ii) within the period of five years ending with the date of filing of the application for registration of the later trade mark or (where applicable) the date of the priority claimed in respect of that application where, at that date, the five year period within which the earlier trade mark should have been put to genuine use as provided in section 46(1)(a) has expired, or
(b) if the earlier trade mark has not been so used, there are proper reasons for that non-use.

Section 47(2A) does not apply where the earlier trade mark is a mark within section 6(1)(c) (ie. a well-known trade mark).[2]

1 For these purposes, 'use' includes use in a form differing in elements which do not alter the distinctive character of the mark in the form in which it was registered and 'use in the United Kingdom' includes affixing the trade mark to goods or to the packaging of goods in the United Kingdom solely for export purposes. In the case of an EUTM or international trade mark (EC), any reference to the United Kingdom is construed as a reference to the EU. Where an earlier trade mark satisfies the use conditions in respect of some only of the goods or services for which it is registered, it shall be treated for the purposes of this section as if it were registered only in respect of those goods or services. See TMA 1994 ss 47(2C)–(2E).
2 TMA 1994 s 47(2F).

(iv) Acquiescence in use of the mark

11.07 Section 48(1) of the TMA 1994 provides that the owner of an earlier trade mark or earlier right will not be entitled (at least not on the basis of its earlier right or registration) to apply to invalidate the registration, or to oppose the ongoing use of the mark for the goods or services for which it has been used, where the owner has acquiesced for a continuous period of five years in the use of the registered trade mark while being aware of such use (unless the application was made in bad faith). Note, that this provision is also discussed at paras **15.27** et seq as it provides a defence to infringement proceedings.

In the context of invalidity proceedings this raises a number of points as follows.

(a) When does the five-year period of acquiescence commence?

11.08 After some uncertainty, it is now clear from the decision of the CJEU in *Budweiser*[1] that the relevant five-year period of acquiescence referred to in s 48 only begins to run from the date of registration, not the filing date—see para **15.29**.

1 C-482/09 *Budějovický Budvar, národní podnik v Anheuser-Busch, Inc.* EU:C:2011:605; [2012] ETMR 2, where the CJEU considered Art 9(1) of Directive 89/104 (now Art 9(1) of Directive 2008/95) to which s 48 gave effect.

(b) For acquiescence, does the applicant for invalidity have to know the mark is registered?

11.09 It is clear from the judgment of the CJEU in *Budweiser*[1] that, in order to found a defence of acquiescence, the proprietor of the mark in question must show that the proprietor of the earlier trade mark or other earlier right had been aware not just of the use of the mark in question, but also that that mark was registered.

In this regard, in ruling on the proper construction of Art 9 of the Directive (to which s 48 gives effect), the CJEU found that there were four prerequisites for the running of the period of limitation in consequence of acquiescence. The fourth of those prerequisites was 'knowledge by the proprietor of the earlier trade mark that the later trade mark has been registered and used after its registration'.

1 C-482/09 *Budějovický Budvar, národní podnik v Anheuser-Busch, Inc.* EU:C:2011:605; [2012] ETMR 2

(c) Does the applicant for invalidity have to be aware of the full use of the later mark, or simply that it is in use for some of the goods or services for which it is registered?

11.10 This question does not appear to have been formally resolved, but it is submitted that the answer would be that where there is use on a broader range of goods and services than those that have come to the attention of the proprietor of the earlier trade mark, s 48(1) will not apply to those additional goods and services.

(d) The effect of a finding of acquiescence

11.11 Where s 48 applies:

(a) there ceases to be any entitlement to challenge the validity of the later mark on the basis of the earlier trade mark or other right; however
(b) the proprietor of the later mark is not entitled to oppose the use of the earlier trade mark or the exploitation of the earlier right, even though the earlier mark or right may no longer be invoked against the later trade mark.[1]

1 TMA 1994 s 48(2).

The procedure for invalidation of UK trade marks under s 47

11.12 An action for invalidity may be by way of counterclaim to an action for infringement by the registered proprietor, or may be a free-standing application to either UKIPO or the court.[1]

1 TMA 1994 s 47(3). Note, that if proceedings are already pending in court, the application must be made to that court. The Registrar also has power to refer applications to the court whether or not proceedings are on foot.

The procedure before UKIPO

(i) Commencement of the invalidity proceedings

11.13 The procedure commences with the filing of an application for a declaration of invalidity.

The application is made by way of the filing of the Form TM26(I), including a statement of the grounds upon which the application is made and a statement of truth[1] and the payment of the relevant fee of £200.

Where the declaration of invalidity is sought on the basis of earlier rights, r 41(2)–(4) set out the details of the earlier rights which the applicant must provide. In relation to a claim to unregistered trade marks (in particular a claim based upon the law of passing off), it is important to specify each of the alleged unregistered rights relied on, including the goods and services said to be covered. For example, where the applicant for declaration of invalidity has used multiple versions of a mark, such as stylised and logo formats, it is important to include claims for each of those marks separately. In the context of the Form TM26(I) this will mean including separate sheets for each of the marks.

Since the decision in *Firecraft*, invalidation proceedings in UKIPO are capable of giving rise to an issue estoppel, cause of action estoppel or abuse of process in later proceedings between the same parties.[2] As a result of this, UKIPO previously stated that in all invalidation actions involving relative grounds under s 5 of the TMA 1994, the parties or their legal representatives must attend a hearing before any decision could be made; this requirement has now been dropped, though the registrar may still direct a hearing.[3]

Where the earlier right is an EUTM for which the applicant for a declaration of invalidity claims a reputation, it is worth considering whether the facts said to give rise to a reputation might also indicate that the proprietor has goodwill in the UK. If so, an additional relative ground of invalidity may be available by virtue of s 5(4)(a) (ie, passing-off). During the post-Brexit period, ongoing applications for invalidity based on an EUTM will continue to be considered by UKIPO. Since 31 December 2020, however, only applications based on UK rights will be admissible. Where an EUTM has been converted to a comparable UK trade mark and an applicant seeks to rely on its reputation, it may be necessary to demonstrate reputation across the EU prior to its conversion.

1 TMR 2008 r 41(1).
2 *Evans t/a Firecraft v Focal Point Fires Plc* [2010] RPC 15. The same is not true as between opposition proceedings and later invalidation proceedings brought on the same grounds: *Special Effects Ltd v L'Oréal SA* [2007] EWCA Civ 1; [2007] RPC 15.
3 TPN 6/2009 and TPN 3/2011; see also TMR 2008 r 62(1).

(ii) The registered proprietor's response

11.14 Where the application for a declaration of invalidity is deemed duly filed, UKIPO will forward a copy of Form TM26(I) to the registered proprietor, who will then have a two month period in which to file Form TM8 and a counterstatement defending the registration against the applicant's claims.[1] Where this is filed, the Registrar will forward a copy to the applicant[2] and the matter will then proceed to the evidence rounds.

1 TMR 2008 r 41(5)–(6).
2 TMR 2008 r 41(7).

11.15 Where the registered proprietor fails to file Form TM8 and counterstatement, the Registrar may treat the registered proprietor as not opposing the application and the registration shall be declared invalid unless the Registrar otherwise directs.[1] In practice, however, UKIPO provides the parties with a period of 14 days to comment on whether the application should be deemed not to be opposed and the registration accordingly deemed invalid. At this point, it will clearly be in the interests of the registered proprietor to argue that the application for a declaration of invalidity should be deemed opposed, thus giving the proprietor the opportunity to try to introduce grounds for opposing to the invalidity claim, despite being late.

Where the registered proprietor wishes to introduce Form TM8 late, there will be a hearing on the question of whether the Registrar should exercise his/her discretion in favour of the proprietor. The factors taken into account in deciding if this discretion should be exercised include:[2]

1 the circumstances relating to the missing of the deadline including reasons why it was missed and the extent to which it was missed;
2 the nature of the applicant's allegations in its statement of grounds;
3 the consequences of treating the proprietor as opposing or not opposing the application;
4 any prejudice to the applicant caused by the delay; and
5 any other relevant considerations, such as the existence of related proceedings between the same parties.

The High Court recently considered these factors and concluded that they applied notwithstanding various amendments to the TMR 2008: it was for the proprietor to show compelling reasons why it should be treated as opposing the application.[3]

1 TMR 2008 r 41(6).
2 *Music Choice Limited v Target Brands Inc* [2006] RPC 13.
3 *Permanent Secretary of the Ministry of Energy, Commerce and Tourism, Republic of Cyprus v John and Pascalis Ltd* [2018] EWHC 3226 (Ch).

(iii) The evidence rounds

11.16 Where the registered proprietor has filed a Form TM8, the Registrar will invite the applicant for a declaration of invalidity to file any evidence or submissions[1] within a specified period.[2]

Evidence will be required in most cases. In particular the applicant is required to file evidence where:[3]

(i) the application is based on an earlier trade mark of a kind falling within s 6(1)(c) of the TMA 1994;[4] or
(ii) the application or part of it is based on grounds other than those set out in s 5(1) or s 5(2); or
(iii) the truth of a matter set out in the statement of use is either denied or not admitted by the proprietor.

If the applicant does not file such evidence, the applicant shall be deemed to have withdrawn the application to the extent that it is based either on the matters in points (i) or (ii) above, or on an earlier trade mark which has been registered and is the subject of the statement of use referred to in point (iii) above.[5]

The Registrar may at any time give leave to either party to file evidence upon such terms as the Registrar thinks fit.[6]

As in all proceedings, evidence must meet the requirements of r 64 of the TMR 2008. This provides that evidence is to be in the form of witness statements unless the Registrar or an enactment provides otherwise. The requirements for a witness statement to be deemed admissible are discussed in relation to opposition proceedings at para **7.32**.

1 TMR 2008 r 42(1).
2 TMR 2008 r 42(2).
3 TMR 2008 r 42(3).
4 'A trade mark … entitled to protection under the Paris Convention or WTO Agreement as a well known trade mark'.
5 TMR 2008 r 42(4).
6 TMR 2008 r 42(5).

(iv) The hearing and appeals

11.17 Following the conclusion of the evidence rounds, the case will proceed to a hearing. As with opposition proceedings, the parties have a choice as to whether they wish for the matter to be decided on the papers alone (ie, without appearing before a hearing officer at UKIPO and providing oral representations). If one of the parties requests an oral hearing then one will be fixed. The other party or parties need not appear—they can simply make written submissions in lieu of appearing. The provisions governing hearings are contained in rr 62–69 of the TMR 2008.

Appeals from any decision of the Registrar lie either to the High Court or to the 'appointed person'.[1] The appointed person means any one of a small number of individuals (typically highly experienced practitioners or academics) appointed by the Lord Chancellor under s 77 of the TMA 1994. Appeals to the appointed person are final[2]—there is no further appeal to the courts, whereas appeals to the High Court may be amenable to further appeal in the usual way. The appointed person has a discretion to refer appeals to the court in any event.[3] Appeals are governed by rr 70–73 of the TMR 2008.

1 TMA 1994 s 76(2).
2 TMA 1994 s 76(4).
3 TMA 1994 s 76(3).

B INVALIDATION PROCEEDINGS AT EUIPO

The basis for invalidation proceedings at EUIPO

11.18 The various grounds on which an EUTM may be declared invalid are found in:

(i) Art 59 of the EUTMR (absolute grounds for invalidity); and
(ii) Art 60 of the EUTMR (relative grounds for invalidity).

(i) Absolute grounds for invalidity—Art 59

11.19 Under Art 52 of the EUTMR, an EUTM may be declared invalid to the extent that:

(a) its registration was contrary to Art 7 of the EUTMR;[1] or
(b) the applicant was acting in bad faith when he filed the application for registration.

Where the registration was made contrary to Arts 7(1)(b), (c) or (d), it may nevertheless not be declared invalid if it can be shown that the mark has become distinctive after registration as a result of the use that has been made of it.[2]

Where the ground(s) of invalidity exist only in respect of some of the goods or services for which the mark is registered, it shall be declared invalid only as regards those goods or services.[3]

1 EUTMR Art 59(1)(a)–(b). For further guidance see **Chapter 4** on absolute grounds for refusing registration.
2 EUTMR Art 59(2).
3 EUTMR Art 59(3).

(ii) Relative grounds for invalidity—Art 60

11.20 Invalidation proceedings before EUIPO allow the applicant for a declaration of invalidity to rely on a broader range of rights than is available in opposition proceedings.

As a result, there will be circumstances where a third party will only be able to launch an attack once the EUTM has actually been registered, by making an application to invalidate the registration rather than opposing during the application stage.

In addition to the grounds available in opposition proceedings[1] an applicant for a declaration of invalidity may also rely upon provisions of Community or national law under which the use of EUTM may be prohibited.[2] The EUTMR highlights the following examples in particular:

- the right to a name;
- a right of personal portrayal;
- copyright; and
- an industrial property right.

In relation to an application for invalidation on the basis of earlier European Union or national trade marks, the relevant case law is the same as that which applies to opposition proceedings—see **Chapter 5**.

1 See EUTMR Art 8 and the discussion in **Chapter 5**.
2 EUTMR Art 60(2).

(iii) Limitations on the ability to bring applications for invalidity

11.21 The EUTMR provides that an EUTM will not be declared invalid where the applicant for invalidation had expressly consented to the registration of the mark prior to submitting the application for invalidity.[1] The Regulation also provides that where an applicant for invalidity has previously applied for a declaration of invalidity or made a counterclaim for invalidity, it may not bring a new application or lodge a new counterclaim on the basis of a right which it could have invoked in support of its first application or counterclaim.[2]

1 EUTMR Art 60(3).
2 EUTMR Art 60(4).

(iv) Acquiescence in relation to EUTM registrations

11.22 The owner of an earlier EUTM who has acquiesced for a period of five successive years in the use of a later EUTM while being aware of such use, is not entitled to apply for a declaration of invalidity against the later mark nor oppose its use for the goods or services for which it has been used unless the registration of the later EUTM was made in bad faith.[1] The same applies to the owner of an earlier national trade mark who has acquiesced for a period of five successive years in the use of the EUTM in that Member State while being aware of such use. As discussed in relation to acquiescence under the TMA 1994, the interpretation of these provisions has been clarified by the decision of the CJEU in *Budweiser.*[2]

Where there is such acquiescence, the owner of the later right shall not be able to oppose the use of the earlier right.[3]

1 EUTMR Art 61(1).
2 C-482/09 *Budějovickí Budvar národní podnik v Anheuser-Busch Inc* EU:C:2011:605; [2012] ETMR 2, a decision of the CJEU concerning the parallel provision, Art 9(1) of the Directive. See paras **11.08–11.09** above, and para **15.29**.
3 EUTMR Art 61(3).

11.23 A final limitation on the ability to bring an application is where an application in relation to the same subject matter, same cause of action and same parties has already been adjudicated by a court in a Member State and has acquired the authority of a final decision.[1]

1 EUTMR Art 62(3).

Procedure for an application for invalidity before EUIPO

(i) The manner of bringing the action before EUIPO

11.24 As well as the option of counterclaiming for a declaration that an EUTM is invalid (ie, in the context of an existing action for trade mark infringement), it is also possible to bring a stand-alone action before EUIPO by filing the appropriate request together with a reasoned statement, and by paying the appropriate official fee, which is €630 as at the time of writing.[1] The application shall not be deemed to have been filed until the fee is paid.[2]

1 EUTMR Art 63(1), Annex 1 para 20; EUTMDR Art 12.
2 EUTMR Art 63(2).

(ii) Who may bring the action

11.25 Any legal or natural person may bring an application for invalidity on the basis of absolute grounds.[1] This includes groups or bodies set up to represent the interests of manufacturers, producers, suppliers of services, traders or consumers which have the capacity under their local law to sue and be sued in their own names.

In relation to an action on the basis of relative grounds, the allowable applicants for invalidation will depend on the ground relied upon.[2] Where the application is based upon relative grounds under Art 60(1) of the EUTMR then the applicant for invalidity may be any of the persons listed in Art 46(1)—the proprietor of the trade mark, a licensee of a registered mark, or the proprietor of an earlier mark or sign referred to in Art 8(4) (or a party authorised under national law to exercise the associated rights). Where the allegation is based on Art 60(2), the application for invalidity must be by the owner or owners of the earlier rights referred to in that provision, or persons authorised under national law to exercise those rights.

It is important to note that a licensee will need to be able to show that the licence provides it with the authority to bring actions.

1 EUTMR Art 63(1)(a).
2 EUTMR Art 63(1)(b)–(c).

(iii) The requirements as at the time of filing of the application for invalidity

11.26 Art 12 of the EUTMDR sets out the information required in the application for invalidity. The information falls into three distinct sections:

(a) Details regarding the EUTM said to be invalid

11.27 The application must contain the registration number of the EUTM in respect of which revocation or a declaration of invalidity is sought and the name of its proprietor.[1]

1 EUTMDR Art 12(1)(a).

(b) Details regarding the extent and basis for the application

11.28 The application must also contain:

(i) the grounds on which the application is based;[1] and
(ii) an indication of the goods or services in respect of which renovation or a declaration of invalidity is sought.[2]

Where the application is based on relative grounds particulars of the right(s) on which the application is based and particulars showing that the applicant is entitled to bring the application.[3]

An application may contain a reasoned statement setting out the facts and arguments on which it is based and supporting evidence.[4]

1 EUTMDR Art 12(1)(b).
2 EUTMDR Art 12(1)(d).
3 EUTMDR Art 12(2).
4 EUTMDR Art 12(4).

(c) The applicant's details

11.29 The application must also contain the following details regarding the applicant:

(i) its name and address in accordance with Art 2(1)(b) of the EUTMIR;[1] and
(ii) if the applicant has appointed a representative, the name and the business address of the representative, in accordance with Art 2(1)(e) of the EUTMDR.[2]

1 EUTMDR Art 12(1)(c)(i).
2 EUTMDR Art 12(1)(c)(ii).

11.30 If the application does not comply with any of the requirements of Art 12 of the EUTMDR, EUIPO will set a period of two months for the deficiencies to be remedied. If they are not remedied within that period then the application will be deemed inadmissible.[1]

1 EUTMDR Art 15(4).

11.31 All evidence upon which the applicant relies must be filed with the application. It should also be noted that the evidence must be filed in the language of the proceedings. An EUTM can be filed in any language of the Union.[1] If that language is not one of the working languages of the Office, the registered proprietor of the EUTM registration must indicate one of those working languages[2] of the Office as the second language. The applicant must either file the application in one of the languages of the Office[3] or one of the languages associated with the EUTM registration.[4] If the language chosen under Art 146(5) is neither of the languages of the EUTM registration, the applicant must translate the application into whichever of those languages is a language of the Office and that language will become the language of the proceedings[5] (subject to any agreement between the parties[6]).

1 EUTMR Art 146(1).
2 Ie, English, French, German, Italian or Spanish—see EUTMR Art 146(2).
3 EUTMR Art 146(5).
4 EUTMR Art 146(6).

5 EUTMR Art 146(7).
6 EUTMR Art 146(8).

Next steps—procedure following an admissible application for a declaration of invalidity

11.32 Assuming the requirements regarding the provision of information (and translations where required) are complied with, EUIPO will notify the registered proprietor of the application and invite it to provide observations and evidence within the specified period.[1] If the proprietor does not file any evidence then EUIPO may simply proceed to make a decision on the basis of what is already before it.[2] After this the matter will generally proceed to a decision, although EUIPO has the ability to allow the parties to file observations (with or without accompanying evidence) as many times as it deems necessary.[3]

1 EUTMDR Art 17(1).
2 EUTMDR Art 17(2).
3 EUTMR Art 64(1).

Proof of use

11.33 To the extent that the application is based upon earlier registered rights which had been registered for over five years as at the date of application for invalidity, the respondent (the proprietor of the later mark) may request that the applicant demonstrate that the earlier registration has been put to genuine use (or that proper reasons for non-use exist).[1] Where in addition the earlier right had been registered for more than five years as at the date of publication of the EUTM, the proprietor of the later mark may request that the applicant demonstrate genuine use within the five years preceding that date, too. To the extent that proof of use is not demonstrated and proper reasons are not provided, the earlier rights will not be taken into account.

1 EUTMR Art 64(2)–(3). As to the details of non-use, see **Chapter 12** in relation to revocation proceedings.

11.34 It is worth noting that, as with the request for proof of use in the context of defending opposition proceedings, the request is made at the time that the response is due. Where a request for proof of use is made, the registered proprietor is not required to file its initial observations at that time, but rather the observations would need to be filed along with any comments on the proof of use filed by the applicant for invalidity.[1] This effectively means that a respondent may obtain a substantially longer period for preparing a response where at least one of the earlier rights relied upon by the applicant for revocation is a registration subject to proof of use.

1 See EUTMDR Art 19(1) and Art 10(5).

Costs and appeals before EUIPO

11.35 The losing party in an application for invalidation will be subject to an award of costs.[1] The costs awarded by EUIPO include 'the fees incurred by the other party as well as all costs … incurred by him essential to the proceedings, including travel and subsistence and the remuneration of an agent, adviser or advocate'.[2] Given that most cases are conducted without recourse to oral proceedings, the costs will generally not exceed the sum of the representation costs and the fee for the action. The costs of representation are capped at €450, which will in most cases be far less than the actual legal fees incurred—there is no mechanism for reclaiming the remainder.

1 EUTMR Art 109.
2 EUTMIR Art 109(1).

11.36 The parties may appeal within two months of the date of notification of the decision; such an appeal has suspensive effect on the decision appealed from.[1] An appeal is subject to the payment of a fee of €720, without which the appeal notice will not be deemed to have been filed.[2] A written statement setting out the grounds of appeal must be filed within four months of the date of notification of the decision appealed from.[3]

In inter partes cases, the Office department which made the contested decision is given an opportunity to rectify the decision if it considers the appeal well founded, provided it notifies the other party and the other party does not object within two months from that notification.[4] Otherwise the appeal will be remitted to the Board of Appeal of EUIPO, which then decides whether the appeal is admissible (see Art 23 of the EUTMDR), and if so whether to allow the appeal. In deciding the appeal, the Board of Appeal will invite the parties to file observations as often as necessary.[5] The Board of Appeal may either remit the case to the department responsible (which will be bound by the reasoning of the Board of Appeal insofar as the facts are the same) or else exercise any power within the competence of that department.

Further appeal is available to the General Court and the CJEU, again within a period of two months from the provision of the decision.[6] The procedural rules relating to actions before the General Court and beyond are not considered in this work.

1 EUTMR Art 66(1).
2 EUTMR Art 68(1), Annex 1 para 21.
3 EUTMR Art 68(1).
4 EUTMR Art 69(1).
5 EUTMR Art 70(2).
6 EUTMR Art 72(1).

Chapter 12

Revocation

INTRODUCTION

12.01 The registration of a trade mark allows the proprietor to prevent others from using an identical or similar mark under certain circumstances. However, the continuing existence of the registration is subject to its timely renewal and to other important requirements. In particular, the mark must be put to genuine use in order to remain on the register, and it must not become misleading or become a term of common usage such that allowing it to be 'owned' by the proprietor would no longer be appropriate. This chapter looks at those requirements, and outlines the actions that can be brought to revoke trade mark rights on the basis of non-use.

This chapter explores the law in this area so far as it is common to UK and European Union trade marks ('EUTMs'), and then considers separately the different actions for revocation of UK and European Union trade marks.

THE ACTION FOR REVOCATION

12.02 Since the UK's withdrawal from the EU, an action for revocation can be brought directly before UKIPO for UKTMs and before EUIPO for EUTMs. Alternatively, the issue of revocation may be raised in an appropriate court by way of a counterclaim to an action by the trade mark owner.[1] In most cases, the action for revocation may focus on all of the goods or services of a registration or just some. In the case of a counterclaim for revocation of an EUTM, however, the counterclaim is limited to the goods and services relied upon in the claim.[2]

1 In proceedings that were commenced prior to the UK's withdrawal from the EU, it appears that the UK courts still have the right to revoke the EUTM as well as the comparable UK mark cloned from it. Save for this, UK courts no longer have power to revoke an EUTM.

2 *Adobe Systems Inc v Netcom Distributors Ltd* [2012] EWHC 1081 (Ch); [2012] ETMR 38.

THE LEGISLATIVE PROVISIONS

12.03 The relevant legislative provisions are found at s 46 of the Trade Marks Act 1994 ('TMA 1994') and Art 58 of the European Union Trade Mark Regulations ('EUTMR'). These provide substantive grounds for the revocation of UK trade marks and EUTMs respectively that can be summarised as follows:

- The registration has not been used for a period of five years from registration (or for the preceding five years where the registration is over five years old).[1]
- The mark has become the common name in the trade for the goods or services involved.[2]
- The mark has become misleading, particularly as to the nature, quality or geographical origin of the goods or services.[3]

These grounds are considered in turn below.

1 TMA 1994 s 46(1)(a)–(b); EUTMR Art 58(1)(a).
2 TMA 1994 s 46(1)(c); EUTMR Art 58(1)(b).
3 TMA 1994 s 46(1)(d); EUTMR Art 58(1)(c).

A REVOCATION FOR NON-USE: S 46(1)(A)–(B); ART 58(1)(A)

12.04 The provisions of the TMA 1994 and the EUTMR in relation to revocation for non-use are essentially identical. In order to consider the question whether a mark is liable to be revoked for non-use it is necessary to look at a number of key phrases within the legislation.

The date to be considered

12.05 In the TMA 1994 it is clear that there are two different periods of non-use that can be considered. The first is the five years following the completion of the registration procedure; the second is a subsequent uninterrupted five-year period beginning at some point after the registration of the mark.

The wording of the EUTMR is not so clear on the point, and does not differentiate between the two scenarios envisaged in the TMA 1994. However, the case law of EUIPO has highlighted that (as with the TMA 1994) the five-year period can begin to run once the registration procedures are complete. In both cases this reflects the position under Art 16(1) of the Directive.

The meaning of 'genuine use'

12.06 In considering whether the proprietor's use of the mark qualifies as 'genuine', the principles that emerge from the cases have been summarised as follows:[1]

- Genuine use means actual use of the trade mark by the proprietor, or by a third party with authority to use the mark.[2]
- The use must be more than merely 'token', which means in this context that it must not serve solely to preserve the rights conferred by the registration.[3]
- The use must be consistent with the essential function of a trade mark, which is to guarantee the identity of the origin of the goods or services to the consumer or end-user by enabling him/her, without any possibility of confusion, to distinguish the goods or services from others which have another origin.[4]
- Affixing of a trade mark on goods as a label of quality is not genuine use unless it guarantees, additionally and simultaneously, to consumers that those goods come from a single undertaking under the control of which the goods are manufactured and which is responsible for their quality.[5]
- The use must be by way of real commercial exploitation of the mark on the market for the relevant goods or services, ie, exploitation that is aimed at maintaining or creating an outlet for the goods or services or a share in that market. An example that meets this criterion would be preparations to put goods or services on the market, such as advertising campaigns. Examples of use that does not meet this criterion would include: (i) internal use by the proprietor; and (ii) the distribution of promotional items as a reward for the purchase of other goods, and to encourage the sale of the latter but use by a non-profit making association can constitute genuine use.[6]
- All the relevant facts and circumstances must be taken into account in determining whether there is real commercial exploitation of the mark, including in particular, the nature of the goods or services at issue, the characteristics of the market concerned, the scale and frequency of use of the mark, whether the mark is used for the purpose of marketing all the goods and services covered by the mark, or just some of them, and the evidence that the proprietor is able to provide.[7]
- Use of the mark need not always be quantitatively significant for it to be deemed genuine. There is no *de minimis* rule. Even minimal use may qualify as genuine use if it is the sort of use that is appropriate in the economic sector concerned for preserving, or creating market share for the relevant goods or services. For example, use of the mark by a single client that imports the relevant goods can be sufficient to demonstrate that such use is genuine, if it appears that the import operation has a genuine commercial justification for the proprietor.[8]
- Not every proven commercial use of the mark will automatically be deemed to constitute genuine use.[9]
- The onus is on the proprietor of the registration to establish use.[10]

The nature of the test for genuine use is considered in more detail in the following paragraphs.

1 *Walton International Ltd v Verweij Fashion BV* [2018] EWHC 1608 (Ch); [2018] ETMR 34 at [115] (Arnold J). See also *'Glee Club'—Comic Enterprises v Twentieth Century Fox Film Corporation* [2014] EWHC 185 (Ch); [2014] FSR 35 at [78] (R Wyand QC) that added the final two principles listed.
2 C-40/01 *Ansul BV v Ajax Brandbeveiliging BV* EU:C:2003:145; [2003] ETMR 45 at [35] and [37].
3 *Ansul* at [36]; C-416/04 P *Sunrider Corp v OHIM* EU:C:2006:310 at [70]; C-442/07 *Verein Radetsky-Order v Bundervsvereinigung Kamaradschaft 'Feldmarschall Radetsky'* EU:C:2008:696; [2009] ETMR 14 at [13]; C-149/11 *Leno Merken BV v Hagelkruis Beheer BV* EU:C:2012:816; [2013] ETMR 16 at [29]; C-609/11 P *Centrotherm Systemtechnik GmbH v Centrotherm Clean Solutions GmbH & Co KG* EU:C:2013:592; [2014] ETMR at [71]; and C-141/13 P *Reber Holding & Co KG v OHIM* EU:C:2014:2089 at [29].
4 *Ansul* at [36]; *Sunrider* at [70]; *Verein* at [13]; C-495/07 *Silberquelle GmbH v Maselli-Strickmode GmbH* EU:C:2009:10; [2009] ETMR 28 at [17]; *Leno* at [29]; and *Centrotherm* at [71].
5 C-689/15 *W.F. Gozze Frottierweberei GmbH v Verein Bremer Baumwollborse* EU:C:2017:434; [2017] Bus LR 1795 at [43]–[51].
6 *Ansul* at [37]–[38]; *Silberquelle* at [18] and [20]–[21]; *Verein* at [14] and [16]–[23]; *Centrotherm* at [71]; and *Reber* at [29].
7 *Ansul* at [38]–[39]; C-259/02 *La Mer Technology Inc v Laboratoires Goemar SA* EU:C:2004:50; [2004] FSR 38 at [22]–[23]; *Sunrider*, [70]–[71] and [76]; *Leno* at [29]–[30] and [56]; *Centrotherm* at [72]–[76]; and *Reber* at [29] and [32]–[34].
8 *Ansul* at [39]; *La Mer* at [21], [24]–[25]; *Sunrider* at [72] and [76]–[77]; and *Leno* at [55].
9 *Reber* at [32].
10 See TMA 1994 s 100.

The level of use required

12.07 For some time, it was thought that in order to defend a claim of non-use, the trade mark proprietor would be required to show more than merely a *de minimis* level of use. However, in the *LA MER* case[1] the Court of Justice ruled that even a small level of sales by the trade mark owner to a UK-based distributor would be sufficient. The same goes for the provision of services.

1 C-259/02 *La Mer Technology Inc v Laboratoires Goemar SA* EU:C:2004:50; [2004] FSR 38.

Nature of activities

12.08 Given that there is no *de minimis* rule, as long as there have been some sales or provision of services, it would at first sight appear relatively easy to defeat a non-use claim. Indeed, it might seem that a trade mark owner could 'rescue' an unused trade mark simply by making a few sales at the appropriate time. However, the Court of Justice made clear in *Ansul*[1] that token use designed to protect the registration would not suffice. Having considered the nature of the use generally, the Court held that the use must be:

- use of the trade mark in question;
- use in relation to the goods or services in question;
- use in the relevant time period;
- use in the relevant territory;
- use on the market, not just relating to 'internal' sales between different departments or sales to an importing agent; and
- use to create or maintain a market for the goods or services, rather than token or sham use.

The Court also took the view that in certain circumstances, using the mark on particular goods or services may in fact serve to maintain a market for *other* goods or services. In that case, the proprietor had used the mark for repair services and replacement chemicals for fire extinguishers, and that was deemed sufficient to maintain a market (and the registration) for fire extinguishers themselves. It is also worth noting that use may consist of affixing the mark for export purposes.

Later, in *Silberquelle*[2] the Court of Justice considered a slightly different problem relating to 'genuine use'. The issue here was whether or not use of the word mark WELLNESS on promotional soft drinks given away free with sales of clothing was genuine use in respect of non-alcoholic drinks (for which the mark was registered). The Court held that affixing the mark to post-contractual products did not create a commercial outlet for the goods, and, as such, the protection conferred by the mark ought not to be maintained where there was no longer any commercial rationale behind the mark.[3] In other words, there had been no genuine use of the mark.

1 C-40/01 *Ansul BV v Ajax Brandbeveiliging BV* EU:C:2003:145; [2003] ETMR 45.

2 C-495/07 *Silberquelle GmbH v Maselli-Strickmode GmbH* EU:C:2009:10; [2009] ETMR 28.

3 See also the similar approach by EUIPO in *ILG Ltd v Crunch International Fitness Inc* [2008] ETMR 17, and compare the Court of Justice's conclusion that not-for-profit use by a charity could still qualify as use: C-442/07 *Verein Radetzky-Orden v Bundesvereinigung Kameradschaft Feldmarschall Radetzky* EU:C:2008:696; [2009] ETMR 14.

12.09 The net result is that an allegation of non-use will be defeated where the trade mark owner has actually realised sales or provided services under the mark, unless the party seeking to revoke the mark can demonstrate that such use was token or sham use, or that it otherwise fell short of use of the mark in the right territory during the relevant period. A proprietor who cannot demonstrate sales or the provision of services under the mark will need to demonstrate that it has at least tried to create or maintain a market (rather than simply protecting its registration). In such circumstances, minimal efforts may not suffice.

Use of the mark as registered

12.10 The use must be of the mark as registered or used in a form which differs only in elements which do not affect the distinctive character of the mark.[1] Clearly this is a question of degree, and there can be no hard-and-fast rules as to what will or will not be classed as affecting the distinctive character. Certain general principles to be aware of are:

- Where a registration consists of mark which has little distinctive character, any differences between the mark as registered and as used may leave the registration vulnerable to an allegation of non-use.
- In considering the marks, the examiner will generally take an overall view as to how the mark would be considered or characterised—a change which affects the way in which the mark would be described is likely to affect the distinctive character.

1 TMA 1994 s 46(2) (in the UK) and EUTMR Art 18(1)(a).

Whether a mark differs in elements that affect its distinctive character

12.11 In the context of revocation proceedings in the UK, the test for whether the mark *as used* would be treated as use of (ie, as validating) the registration of a different mark has been considered in two significant cases.

In the earlier of those two cases[1] the court was called to determine whether the use of the word BUD in a plain script would validate a registration for a script form of the word BUD, and whether a particular stylised version of the mark BUDWEISER BUDBRAU was validated by the use of another form of the same words. In determining that the UKIPO were right to treat the use of the differing forms as being capable of validating the registrations, Lord Walker determined that the questions to answer were:

1 What are the differences between the mark as registered and the mark as used?
2 Do those differences alter the distinctive character of the mark as registered?

1 *Budejovicky Budvar Narodni Podnik v Anheuser Busch Inc* [2002] EWCA Civ 1534; [2003] RPC 25.

12.12 Subsequently, Richard Arnold QC sitting as the Appointed Person at UKIPO[1] restated the test in slightly different terms, namely:

1 What sign was presented as the trade mark on the goods and in the marketing materials during the relevant period?
2 And:
   (a) What is the distinctive character of the registered trade mark?

(b) What are the differences between the mark used and the registered trade mark?
(c) Do the differences identified in (b) alter the distinctive character identified in (a)?

1 In cases O/262/06 *NIRVANA Trade Mark*, and again in case O/061/08 *REMUS Trade Mark*.

12.13 In the course of his judgment, the Appointed Person considered both the European decisions and EUIPO's guidelines on the same subject.[1] Although the European decisions do not set out a methodology, it is suggested that a party seeking to argue the point before EUIPO would be advised to adopt the test as set out above, in order to provide a helpful logical framework. However, it would be wrong to regard the three-stage analysis as tantamount to a statutory code. There are bound to be cases where, whatever the distinctive character of a word mark, the addition of a further word or words would not alter it.[2]

1 O/262/06 *NIRVANA Trade Mark* and O/061/08 *REMUS Trade Mark*.
2 *OAO Alpha-Bank v Alpha Bank AE* [2011] EWHC 2021 (Ch).

12.14 Another aspect of 'use' in variant forms has arisen in *Specsavers*. Following the reference to the CJEU, the Court of Appeal had to consider whether one of the claimant's registered marks was liable to be revoked for non-use.[1] The mark in question consisted simply of two overlapping black ovals. The issue was whether it constituted 'use' of that mark for the claimant to have used one of its other marks, which also comprised two overlapping ovals, but in grey and with the overlap suggested by darker shading, and overlain with the word 'Specsavers' in white. The CJEU had earlier held that where a figurative mark is used in conjunction with a word mark, and where the combination is also a registered mark, that amounts to genuine use of the figurative mark, provided that the distinctive character of the figurative mark has not been altered in the form in which the combination has been used.[2] The Court of Appeal held that, given the evidence showed extensive use of the claimant's figurative mark in a particular colour (green), the figurative mark had genuinely been used in the sense of providing a badge of origin for the goods and services, despite only being used as part of the combination mark.

1 *Specsavers International Healthcare v Asda Stores Ltd* [2014] EWCA Civ 1294; [2015] ETMR 4.
2 C-252/12 *Specsavers International Healthcare v Asda Stores Ltd* EU:C:2013:497; [2014] FSR 4. See also C-12/12 *Colloseum Holding AG v Levi Strauss & Co* EU:C:2013:253; [2013] ETMR 34.

Use for the goods or services of the registration

12.15 The registered proprietor will need to demonstrate that there has been use in relation to the goods or services for which the mark is registered. The Court of Justice has put a slight gloss on this requirement in that the trade mark owner may be deemed to have demonstrated use for products where they have ceased to supply the goods but have continued to supply parts for the product in circumstances where this maintains a market for the product.[1]

1 C-40/01 *Ansul BV v Ajax Brandbeveiliging BV* EU:C:2003:145; [2003] ETMR 45.

Use in the relevant time period

12.16 Where a revocation action has been filed, the registered proprietor must demonstrate that the mark has been put to use during the relevant period. In the case of a claim that the mark has not been used in the period following the completion of the registration procedures, any use must simply be subsequent to the date of completion of the registration procedures. In the case of a claim that the mark has not been used in the preceding period of five years, the relevant period will be the five year period to the day preceding the filing of the application for revocation. Evidence of use of the mark in question must, therefore, be evidence of use within the relevant period. Evidence of use outside that time period is unlikely to be accepted, except where it supports the claim to use within that period. Furthermore, where use is shown in a later period sufficient to avoid revocation, a lack of use in the earlier period will not be fatal.

12.17 Section 46(3) of the TMA 1994 and the latter part of Art 58(1)(a) of the EUTMR provide a potential get-out for proprietors who commence or resume genuine use of the registered mark after the five-year period expires but before any application for revocation is made. In those circumstances, the trade mark may be salvaged from the risk of revocation by putting it back into use. However, the section is subject to a proviso: if the commencement or resumption of use occurs fewer than three months before an application (or counterclaim) for revocation is filed, the use in question will be disregarded unless preparations for the commencement or resumption of use began before the proprietor became aware that an application for revocation might be made.[1]

1 Note that an applicant for revocation is entitled to bring an application immediately after the period of five years ends: *Philosophy Inc v Ferretti Studio Srl* [2002] EWCA Civ 921; [2003] RPC 15.

Use in the relevant territory

12.18 Any use must be in the appropriate territory. In the case of a UK registration, this will generally be use in the UK, although affixing the mark in the UK to goods or their packaging for export purposes is deemed to constitute use of a UK trade mark.[1] In the case of a EUTM registration, use must be shown within the European Union. The territorial borders of the Member States of the European Union are to be disregarded for the purposes of assessing genuine use[2] and provisions of national law are not to be taken into account either.[3]

1 TMA 1994 s 46(2).
2 C-149/11 *Leno Merken BV v Hagelkruis Beheer BV* EU:C:2012:816; [2013] ETMR 16.
3 T-170/11 *Rivella International AG v OHIM* EU:T:2012:374; [2013] ETMR 4; appeal rejected: EU:C:2013:826; [2014] ETMR 20.

Partial revocation

12.19 Where use is demonstrated only in relation to a subset of the goods or services listed in the registration, and where all other requirements are complied with, the focus of attention will then fall upon the breadth of goods or services for which use has been shown. As the relevant provisions state, it is not sufficient that use is shown for just some goods and services, since an application for revocation can be granted to the extent that use has not been shown.[1] As a result, the registered proprietor will generally want to show use for as much of the specification of goods as have been challenged under the application for revocation. Where use is shown only for some of the goods, the specification may be limited to that subset.

1 TMA 1994 s 46(5); EUTMR Art 58(2).

The UK approach to partial revocation on the basis of non-use

12.20 The UK approach was set out by the Court of Appeal in *Norwegian Cruise Line.*[1] In that case, the issue was whether a claim for non-use of a mark would succeed where a mark registered for holidays generally had been used in respect of cruises specifically. It was held that the correct approach was, first, to ask what use had been made of the mark and, second, to ask what would be a fair specification of the relevant goods or services having regard to the use actually made—the example given was for use of a mark for Cox's Orange Pippins; should the registration be for fruit, for apples, for eating apples or for Cox's Orange Pippins?

The Court indicated that the task of determining what was 'a fair specification' was a task which:

> '… should be carried out so as to limit the specification so that it reflects the circumstances of the particular trade and the way that the public would perceive the use. The court, when deciding whether there is confusion under section 10(2), adopts the attitude of the average reasonably informed consumer of the products. If the test of infringement is to be applied by the court

having adopted the attitude of such a person, then I believe it appropriate that the court should do the same when deciding what is the fair way to describe the use that a proprietor has made of his mark. Thus the court should inform itself of the nature of trade and then decide how the notional consumer would describe such use.'

1 *Thomson Holidays Ltd v Norwegian Cruise Line Ltd* [2002] EWCA Civ 1828; [2003] RPC 32, at [31] per Aldous LJ. But see also the Court of Appeal decision in *Maier v Asos* [2015] EWCA Civ 220, in which it was found that where coherent sub-categories exist, it may be permissible to cut down to one of those depending on the evidence of use.

12.21 The result of this exercise is generally not so much a limitation of the specification as a redrafting to reflect whatever use falls within the confines of the original specification (since it is not possible to expand the specification beyond that which it covered at the time of filing).

12.22 Only about six weeks after the *Norwegian Cruise Line* judgment, the Court of Appeal decided the *ESB* case.[1] This concerned the use of the proprietor's 'ESB' mark ('extra special bitter'), which was registered for beer but had only been used in relation to bitter. The Court held that the judge at first instance had been correct to restrict the specification to bitter, taking into account the nature of the relevant trade and a suitable definition of what the relevant goods were.

Attention should also be paid to Tribunal Practice Notice 1/2012. This discusses the UKIPO procedure in relation to partial refusals of applications for registration, but it is also said to be applicable to post-registration invalidation or revocation proceedings. It refers in particular to the judgment of Mann J in *Giorgio Armani*.[2]

More recently in *Redd* the court held that despite the claimant's use of the mark being confined principally to services relating to intellectual property law, it would not be fair to restrict the registration to that area of law rather than legal services generally.[3]

The correct approach to partial revocation has recently been summarised in *Stichting BDO* where in essence, Arnold J stated that the court must look for a specification that reflects the actual use made of the mark, and how the average consumer would fairly describe the goods and services in relation to which that use has been made.[4] A similar approach was adopted in *Glee Club*'.[5]

1 *West (trading as Eastenders) v Fuller Smith & Turner plc* [2003] EWCA Civ 48; [2003] FSR 44.
2 *Giorgio Armani SpA v Sunrich Clothing Ltd* [2010] EWHC 2939 (Ch); [2011] RPC 15.
3 *Redd Solicitors LLP v Red Legal Ltd* [2012] EWPCC 54; [2013] ETMR 13.
4 *Stichting BDO v BDO Unibank Inc* [2013] EWHC 418 (Ch); [2013] FSR 35 at [55].
5 *Comic Enterprises v Twentieth Century Fox Film Corporation* [2014] EWHC 185 (Ch); [2014] FSR 35 at [92]–[94].

The approach to partial revocation on the basis of non-use before EUIPO

12.23 In the case of an action before EUIPO, the approach of the Cancellation Boards is to strike a balance between the wording of Art 58(2), which seems to require partial revocation where the proprietor has not shown the requisite use, and protecting the legitimate interest of the proprietor in being able to extend use of the mark into hitherto unexploited areas covered by the specification.[1]

1 See in that regard T-126/03 *Reckitt Benckiser (España) v OHIM* (ALADIN trade mark) EU:T:2005:288; [2006] ETMR 50, and the EUIPO *Trade Mark Guidelines*, Part C, section 6 at 2.8.

12.24 This balancing exercise was complicated by EUIPO's approach to specifications (see **Chapter 6**, para **6.05** above) where they previously took the view that a classification utilising the entire wording of a class heading would cover all goods or services in the class even if not expressly referred to in the heading. This practice has changed and an applicant must now specify all goods and services of interest. Where an applicant relies on the general indications of a class heading the evidence of use must therefore support the literal meaning of that indication.

Proper reasons for non-use

12.25 Both s 46(1) of the TMA 1994 and Art 58(1) of the EUTMR provide that revocation may be refused where, notwithstanding that the proprietor has failed to demonstrate genuine use, there are 'proper reasons' for non-use.

According to the Court of Appeal in *PHILOSPOPHY*[1] it is for the proprietor of the mark to prove that there are proper reasons for non-use. The Court also highlighted the origin of the 'proper reasons' provision, stating: 'The proprietor is able to show proper reasons by drawing attention to the existence of obstacles to such use arising independently of the will of the proprietor (see Art 19(1) of the TRIPS agreement)'.[2]

1 *Philosophy Inc v Ferretti Studio Srl* [2002] EWCA Civ 921; [2003] RPC 15.
2 *Philosophy* at [25] per Peter Gibson LJ.

Cases where proper reasons have been found

12.26 Proper reasons have been found in the UK where:

- the registered proprietor had intended that the mark be used under licence, but no use had occurred because the licensee was aware of an existing (but ultimately unsuccessful) action against the trade mark in question;[1] and

- due to technical difficulties in manufacturing, it had not been possible to launch the product.[2] Note that such difficulties will generally need to be exceptional, going beyond what is normal or routine.

A variety of further examples may be found in the *EUIPO Guidelines*.[3]

1 O/286/98 *WORTH Trade Marks* [1998] RPC 875.
2 O/084/99 *MAGIC BALL Trade Mark* [2000] RPC 439.
3 Part C, section 6 at 2.11.

12.27 In deciding whether the reasons put forward for non-use are such that the requirement for use in the period should be waived, the tribunal must balance those reasons from a business perspective against the statutory emphasis on the need to use a registration or lose it.[1] In so doing, it is necessary to ascertain whether but for the reasons for non-use, the registered proprietor would, on the balance of probabilities, have used the mark.[2] The difficulties should be matters outside the control of the trade mark owner, and ones for which one would not realistically expect the trade mark holder to plan.[3]

1 *INVERMONT Trade Mark* [1997] RPC 125.
2 See in that regard O/475/01 *CERNIVET* [2002] RPC 30 per Geoffrey Hobbs QC at [51].
3 *INVERMONT Trade Mark* [1997] RPC 125.

B REVOCATION WHERE TRADE MARK HAS BECOME THE COMMON NAME IN THE TRADE FOR A PRODUCT OR SERVICE FOR WHICH IT IS REGISTERED: S 46(1)(C); ART 58(1)(B)

12.28 The registration of a mark may be revoked where the mark has effectively become generic for the goods or services in question.[1] The relevant provisions require that the generic nature of the mark result from the acts or inactivity of the registered proprietor.

There have been few decided cases on these provisions[2] but it seems clear that an applicant for revocation on this ground will need to demonstrate:

1 that the mark has become a common name in the trade for the product or service for which it is registered; and
2 that this has resulted from the acts or inactivity of the registered proprietor.

1 TMA 1994 s 46(1)(c); EUTMR Art 58(1)(b).
2 A few examples: An allegation relying on s 46(1)(c) was roundly dismissed in *32Red Plc v WHG (International) Ltd* [2011] EWHC 62 (Ch); [2011] ETMR 21 at [161] per Henderson J. The provision was also mentioned in *Rousselon Freres ET CIE v Horwood Homewares Limited* [2008] EWHC 881 (Ch); [2008] RPC 30, at [86]. The equivalent provision in the Directive was considered (and the allegation likewise rejected) in *Julius Sämann Ltd v Tetrosyl Ltd* [2006] EWHC 529 (Ch); [2006] ETMR 75 at [111] *et seq*, per Kitchin J.

'The common name' and 'in the trade'

12.29 Although the wording of the legislation suggests that the trade mark must have become the only common name in the trade, the case law indicates that this is not so. For example, in *Hormel Foods*[1] the judge took a purposive view of the legislation, finding that once a mark has become common in the trade it has lost the ability to fulfil its role as an indicator of origin, regardless of whether there are also other common names in the trade. The judge went on to find that the defendant's SPAMBUSTER mark had become a common name in the trade for computing services designed to combat unsolicited email.

It is to be noted that the words 'in the trade', which appear in the TMA 1994 and in the UK translation of the EUTMR, should be read as including consumers and end users as well as those who distribute the product. As mentioned in the *BOSTONGURKA* case[2] the wording in the majority of other language versions of the EUTMR, and the other language versions of the Directive (from which the UK Act is derived) would properly be translated as embracing that wider sense.

The question whether a mark has become a common name is to be assessed by reference to the perception of both trade users and end consumers, but in general it is the end consumer's perception that will be decisive.[3] In the *SCRABBLE* case, at first instance, the mark 'SCRAMBLE' was held to be a common name for word games (as well as being descriptive), but this was reversed on appeal.[4]

1 *Hormel Foods Corp v Antilles Landscape Investments NV* [2005] EWHC 13 (Ch); [2005] RPC 28, per Richard Arnold QC at [167].
2 C-371/02 *Björnekulla Fruktindustrier AB v Procordia Food AB* EU:C:2004:275; [2002] ETMR 42.
3 C-409/12, *Backaldrin Osterreich The Kornspitz Co v Pfahnl Backmittel* EU:C:2014:130; [2014] ETMR 30, applying *Björnekulla*.
4 *JW Spear & Sons v Zynga* [2013] EWHC 3348 (Ch); [2014] FSR 19 and on appeal [2015] EWCA Civ 290; [2015] ETMR 27.

For the product or service for which it is registered

12.30 As discussed above, both the TMA 1994 and the EUTMR provide that where the grounds for revocation exist only in respect of some goods or services, the registration will be revoked only in respect of those goods and services—the finding of grounds for refusal for certain goods or services will not necessarily lead to revocation of the registration as a whole.[1] However, since there have not been many cases on this issue, it is difficult to know how restrictively a court would approach the issue of partial revocation.

1 TMA 1994 s 46(5); EUTMR Art 58(2).

12.31 The Court of Justice has made clear that in the context of evaluating the absolute grounds for refusing registration[1] it is important to take into account the underlying principles for a refusal. In relation to a claim that a mark is descriptive or common in the trade, the underlying principle is that the mark should be kept free so that other traders are not prevented from using what has become the everyday language for the goods or services of their trade. This suggests that the courts would err on the side of the public interest rather than maintaining as much of the proprietor's specification as could be salvaged.

1 TMA 1994 s 3(1); EUTMR Art 7—see **Chapter 4**.

12.32 On this basis, it would seem likely that where this ground for revocation exists, the registration may be revoked not only for the exact goods or services involved, but also for any goods and services which are so closely connected with those for which the mark has become generic that the mark cannot act as a trade mark in that sphere either. An example might be where a registration covers a food product and fast food services. If the name of the food product has become generic, then it may also be appropriate to revoke the registration insofar as it relates to fast food services.

12.33 In considering the extent to which the registration in respect of such 'connected' goods or services should be revoked, it seems likely that the use of the trade mark by the trade mark owner would be relevant. To take the example of the food product and fast food services, it is quite possible that the proprietor's use of the trade mark for those services has in fact rendered the mark distinctive of the proprietor, so that it would be inappropriate to divest the owner of registration for the services. This would mirror the operation of the proviso relating to absolute grounds and distinctiveness acquired through use.[1]

1 TMA 1994 s 3(1); EUTMR Art 7(3).

Resulting from the acts or inactivity of the registered proprietor

12.34 It is not enough that the mark has become the common name for the goods; this situation must result from the registered proprietor's own acts or that person's failure to prevent others from making the mark the common name.[1]

1 Reaffirmed in C-409/12 *Backaldrin Osterreich The Kornspitz Co v Pfahnl Backmittel* EU:C:2014:130; [2014] ETMR 30.

12.35 In relation to the acts of the proprietor, these often involve a failure to adhere to recommended guidelines as to 'good use' of trade marks. 'Good use' generally involves:

(a) Using the mark in capitals, in some other font or with an effect added to the text of the mark to distinguish it from other words in the text.

(b) Using the mark in combination with a generic term for the product in question—the trade mark should not be used to describe the product class itself or goods or services having particular qualities.
(c) Marking the trade mark as being registered[1] by use of the ® symbol, or using the ™ symbol where it is not, to help demonstrate that the sign in question is in fact a trade mark. The ownership of the mark should also be indicated, if possible, to underline that claim.

Clearly this may prove difficult where the product or services in question are strikingly new and different, so that whatever trade mark is chosen runs a real risk of becoming the standard term for those goods or services. Moreover, proprietors of such marks may be under substantial pressure not to use a generic product descriptor alongside their new trade mark, in order to distance the product from the competition for marketing purposes. So long as there is market or legal monopoly over that particular variant, the substantial success of the product may disguise the fact that the mark has in fact come to signify goods or services having particular qualities to the public rather than indicating origin.

1 So long as it is actually registered: under TMA 1994 s 95 it is an offence for a person to represent falsely that a mark is a registered trade mark when he/she knows or has reason to believe that such representation is false. See **Chapter 19**, paras **19.38–19.41**.

12.36 As regards 'inactivity of the registered proprietor', this will require the proprietor's knowledge of and failure to deal with the fact that third parties have been using the trade mark. In the absence of proof that the trade mark owner had actual knowledge and failed to take action, the applicant is likely to need to demonstrate a sufficiently large number of traders using the mark in a generic sense such that knowledge can reasonably be imputed to the registered proprietor.

C REVOCATION WHERE THE TRADE MARK HAS BECOME MISLEADING: S 46(1)(D); ART 58(1)(C)

12.37 Under s 46(1)(d) of the TMA 1994 and Art 58(1)(c) of the EUTMR a registration will be liable for revocation where, in consequence of the use made of it by the proprietor or with his consent, it is liable to mislead the public particularly as to the nature, quality or geographical origin of the goods or services in question. The use of the word 'particularly' suggests that a registration may also be revoked where a mark has become liable to mislead as to other characteristics of the goods or services.

Although there have not been many cases focusing upon this provision[1] it is clear that there is no need to demonstrate that the proprietor intended to mislead—it is sufficient that this has resulted from the use of the mark by the proprietor or with his consent.

1 See, for example, *Nanjing Automobile (Group) Corp v MG Sports and Racing Europe* [2010] EWHC 270 (Ch); and *32Red Plc v WHG (International) Ltd* [2011] EWHC 62 (Ch); [2011] ETMR 21 at [162].

Practice and procedure

Procedure before the UK Registry

12.38 For a UK trade mark an application to revoke a registration on the basis of non-use is made by filing Form TM26(N)[1] from UKIPO and paying the official fee of £200. The application is forwarded to the registered proprietor, who is given an initial period of not more than two months to file Form TM8(N), including a counterstatement.[2] If the registered proprietor intends to assert that the mark has been used, then this should be made clear in the counterstatement. Similarly if the registered proprietor wishes to contend that there were proper reasons for non-use. There is, however, no need to file evidence of use at this point.

1 See the Trade Mark Rules 2008 ('TMR 2008') r 38(1): for grounds other than non-use, use Form TM26(O) (r 39(1)).
2 TMR 2008 r 38(4): for grounds other than non-use, use Form TM8 (r 39(3)).

12.39 If the registered proprietor does not file the Form TM8(N) and counterstatement then the registration will be revoked unless the Registrar directs otherwise.[1] In practice, the Registrar will simply revoke the registration in these circumstances. Before doing so, however, UKIPO will provide the parties with the opportunity to file comments as to whether the Registrar should exercise his/her discretion not to deem the registration revoked.

If the registered proprietor files the Form TM8(N), but does not file evidence with the Form TM8(N) and counterstatement, then UKIPO will set a period of time to file the evidence. UKIPO has indicated[2] that in most cases the period of time will be two months, which corresponds to the minimum period allowed by the Rules.[3] Where the evidence required is more extensive, a greater period may be provided or the registered proprietor may request further time.[4] Following the filing of this evidence, the applicant for revocation will be given the opportunity to file its own evidence and submissions in reply within a two-month period, and further opportunities may be given to file evidence where this appears appropriate.[5] It should be remembered that unless the Registrar directs otherwise, the evidence must be filed by way of witness statements in accordance with r 64(3) of the TMR 2008.

1 TMR 2008 r 38(6): for grounds other than non-use, see r 39(3).
2 Tribunal Practice Note 3/2008 but see also Tribunal Practice Note 2/2010.
3 TMR 2008 r 38(4): for grounds other than non-use, r 40(1) does not set a specific period.
4 For further discussion on extensions of time before the UKIPO see **Chapter 7** relating to UK procedure, specifically the section relating to opposition procedure.
5 TMR 2008 r 38(8): for grounds other than non-use, see r 40(4).

12.40 If the registered proprietor fails to file evidence in support of its case then the Registrar may treat the application for revocation as being unopposed and will deem the registration revoked. As with the failure of the registered proprietor to file the Form TM8(N) (or TM8 for grounds other than non-use) and counterstatement within the relevant period, UKIPO will provide the parties with the opportunity to comment on whether the Registrar should exercise his/her discretion not to deem the registration revoked.

Procedure before EUIPO

12.41 Before EUIPO, the procedure commences with the filing of the application for revocation. The application may be made by way of the form provided by EUIPO or by providing the requisite information identified by Art 12 of the EUTMDR.

12.42 All evidence upon which the applicant relies must be filed with the revocation application. It should also be noted that the evidence must be filed in the language of the proceedings. An EUTM can be filed in any language of the Union.[1] If that language is not one of the working languages of the Office, the registered proprietor of the EUTM registration must indicate one of those working languages[2] of the Office as the second language. The applicant must either file the application in one of the languages of the Office[3] or one of the languages associated with the EUTM registration.[4] If the language chosen under Art 146(5) is neither of the languages of the EUTM registration, the applicant must translate the application into whichever of those languages is a language of the Office and that language will become the language of the proceedings[5] (subject to any agreement between the parties[6]).

1 EUTMR Art 146(1).
2 Ie, English, French, German, Italian or Spanish—see EUTMR Art 146(2).
3 EUTMR Art 146(5).
4 EUTMR Art 146(6).
5 EUTMR Art 146(7).
6 EUTMR Art 146(8).

12.43 The application for revocation is subject to an official fee of €630, which should be paid at the time of filing.[1] If the fee is not paid EUIPO will send the applicant for revocation notification of this deficiency and set a period for the payment.[2] Where the fee is not paid in this period the application for revocation will be deemed inadmissible.

1 EUTMR Annex 1 para 20.
2 EUTMDR Art 15(1).

12.44 If the application for revocation is admissible then the registered proprietor is given the opportunity to file observations and evidence in reply.[1] In the case of an application for revocation on the basis of non-use, if the registered proprietor does not provide proof of use within the period specified by the Office then the EUTM registration will be revoked;[2] in the case of an application for revocation on the basis of grounds other than non-use, the result of the registered proprietor failing to file observations or evidence in support of the registration is that EUIPO may take a decision simply on the basis of the evidence before it.[3] Proceedings at EUIPO are adversarial in nature, meaning that where a party makes an allegation it is imperative for the other side to make a formal challenge if that party does not accept the allegation.

1 EUTMDR Art 17(1).
2 EUTMDR Art 19(1).
3 EUTMDR Art 17(2).

12.45 The observations and evidence of the registered proprietor should likewise be in the language of the proceedings. If a translation is required then this should be filed within one month of the submission of the observations and evidence. In the absence of a translation of observations and evidence into the language of the proceedings, it will not be taken into account. As with the need to translate the observations and evidence in support of the opposition, EUIPO will not notify the registered proprietor of the need to provide a translation.

12.46 The Regulations provide that EUIPO will provide the applicant for revocation with a further opportunity to respond if it wishes.[1]

1 EUTMR Art 64(1).

The effect of revocation

12.47 Where the grounds for revocation are found only to exist in respect of some goods or services, the registration will be revoked in relation to those goods and services only. Where the applicant for revocation believes that the grounds for revocation existed prior to the date of the action for revocation, a specific claim should be made that the grounds for revocation as at this earlier date.

12.48 Where a mark is revoked to any extent, s 46(6) of the TMA 1994 provides that the proprietor's rights shall be deemed to have ceased (to the extent of the revocation) as from the date of the application for revocation or, if the tribunal is satisfied that the relevant grounds of revocation existed at an earlier date, from that date. Under the EUTMR, the registration may be revoked from a date earlier than the application for revocation at the request of one of the parties.[1]

1 EUTMR Art 62(1).

Chapter 13

Ownership of and dealings with trade marks

INTRODUCTION

13.01 This chapter deals with the ownership of trade marks and with dealings such as assignments and licenses.

UK REGISTERED TRADE MARKS

UK trade mark—a property right; legal and beneficial ownership

13.02 A UK registered trade mark is a property right;[1] a form of personal property.[2] As a form of property, normal principles of property law govern issues of title to and dealings with the mark unless the Trade Marks Act 1994 ('TMA 1994') provides otherwise.

There can, therefore, be different legal and beneficial (or equitable) owners of a trade mark. In particular, although the registered proprietor is the legal owner of the trade mark, that person may hold it on trust for another because, for example, of a declaration of trust, or to reflect that person's fiduciary position.[3] As set out in para **13.05** below, there may also be a different beneficial owner where there has been an enforceable contract to assign.

1 TMA 1994 s 2(1).
2 TMA 1994 s 22. This also applies to an application for registration of a mark, see TMA 1994 s 27 and para **13.10** below.
3 No notice of any such trust will be entered on the register—see TMA 1994 s 26.

UK trade mark—co-ownership

13.03 As to legal title to a trade mark, this may be held by co-owners either as tenants in common or as joint tenants. However, the TMA 1994 provides that where a mark is granted to two or more persons jointly, each of them is entitled (subject to any agreement to the contrary) to an equal undivided share in the mark.[1] In other words, unless these persons agree to the contrary, they hold the legal estate as tenants in common rather than as joint tenants.[2]

Subject, again, to any agreement to the contrary, each co-proprietor can do acts that would otherwise be an infringement of the trade mark without needing the consent of the other joint proprietors.[3] However, one co-proprietor cannot grant licences, or assign or charge their share without such consent.[4]

As regards beneficial title to a trade mark, this too can be held either as tenants in common, or as joint tenants.

1 TMA 1994 s 23(1).
2 Where parties hold as tenants in common, they each have a distinct share in the mark, albeit that their shares are undivided. Hence, the share of a deceased tenant in common passes under his or her will or intestacy. By contrast, where parties hold as joint tenants, they have no separate shares and, on the death, of one joint tenant, the property is owned by the surviving joint tenant(s).
3 TMA 1994 s 23(3).
4 TMA 1994 s 23(4). For the distinction between a licence and a mere consent—see below.

UK trade marks—assignments and other transfers

13.04 A UK registered trade mark may be transferred in the same way as other forms of personal or moveable property by:

1 assignment (including an assignment by way of security);
2 testamentary disposition; or
3 operation of law.[1]

Any such transaction may be done with or without the goodwill of a business.[2] It may also be partial—that is limited to some but not all of the goods or services for which the mark is registered or limited in relation to the use of the mark in a particular manner or locality.[3]

1 TMA 1994 s 24(1) and (4).
2 TMA 1994 s 24(1).
3 TMA 1994 s 24(2). Contrast the position for EUTMs—see paras **13.49** and **13.52** below.

13.05 **Assignment**—An assignment is a binding transfer of title—whether under a contract or by gift and includes an assignment by way of a grant of security. In this regard, it is important to bear in mind that trade marks may be used as security for financial transactions in the same way that other personal or moveable property may be used.[1]

The TMA 1994 creates a statutory presumption that a contractual obligation to transfer a business includes an obligation to transfer any registered trade mark, except where there is agreement to the contrary or where it is clear in all the circumstances that this presumption should not apply.[2]

Under the TMA 1994, an assignment of a UK trade mark must be in writing, and must be signed by the assignor. Upon such an assignment, the assignee becomes the proprietor of the relevant mark and registration is not required to complete title although (as set out in **13.47** below) the TMA 1994 provides that a failure to register the assignment will have certain consequences. For this reason, the fact that a person is registered as the proprietor of a mark is merely prima facie evidence as to the identity of the true proprietor.

An assignment that does not comply with the requirements of the TMA 1994 is not effective in law[3]—although it may (provided it is enforceable in equity) confer equitable title on the assignee.

1 TMA 1994 s 24(5) in relation to UK trade marks; see European Union Trade Mark Regulation (EU) 2017/1001 ('EUTMR') Art 22 in relation to European Union Trade Marks.
2 TMA 1994 s 24(1A), added by SI 2018/825, reg 14, with effect from 14 January 2019.
3 TMA 1994 s 24(3)–(4).

13.06 Assignment by testamentary disposition—a UK registered trade mark may be transferred as part of the estate of the deceased proprietor and as part of that person's personal property.[1] The rules as to whether a right has passed by way of any testamentary document are a matter of the law of succession, and guidance on that area is not the subject of this work. The actual transfer to the person entitled is effected by an assent in writing and signed by the deceased's personal representative.[2]

1 TMA 1994 s 24(1).
2 TMA 1994 s 24(3).

13.07 Assignment by way of operation of law—a UK registered trade mark may be assigned by operation of law. Hence, the vesting of a trade mark in the personal representative of a deceased proprietor occurs by operation of law[1] as does the vesting in the trustee in bankruptcy of a proprietor who is made bankrupt.[2] Similarly, there is vesting by operation of law where there is an order of the court or any other competent authority transferring the trade mark (or the application for registration) from the registered proprietor to another person.

1 See *Williams Mortimer & Sunnucks' Executors, Administrators & Probate* twenty-first ednat paras 39–49 et seq.
2 Insolvency Act 1986 s 306.

UK trade marks—registration of assignments and of other transfers

13.08 Certain transactions involving UK registered trade marks are 'registrable transactions'—prescribed particulars of which must be entered in the register.[1] Registrable transactions include (inter alia):

- an assignment of a registered trade mark or any right in it;
- the grant of a security interest;
- an assent;
- a court order transferring a mark or any right in it; and
- any of these transactions in respect of an application for the registration of a trade mark.[2]

As set out at para **13.47** below, a failure to apply to register particulars of these transactions may have serious consequences as regards the protection provided in respect of the mark.

1 TMA 1994 s 25(1).
2 TMA 1994 s 25(2) s 27. The grant of a licence is also a registrable transaction—see further below para **13.13**.

13.09 Applications to register particulars of a registrable transaction are made by filing the forms with the particulars specified below together with a fee of £50:

- *Assignments*[1]—in the case of an assignment of a registered trade mark or any right in it, Form TM16 should be used and should provide:
  (i) the name and address of the assignee;
  (ii) the date of the assignment; and
  (iii) where the assignment is only in respect of any right in the mark, a description of the right assigned.

The Form TM16 should either be signed by both parties to the assignment (or their representative(s)) or be accompanied by documentary proof of the assignment.[2] In general, a simple copy of the assignment document is sufficient; there is no need to file a notarised or certified copy.

- *Security interests*[3]—in the case of a grant of any security interest in a registered trade mark or any right in or under it, Form TM24 should be used and should provide:
  (i) the name and address of the grantee;
  (ii) the nature of the interest (whether fixed or floating); and
  (iii) the extent of the security and the right in or under the mark secured.

The Form TM24 must be signed by or on behalf of the grantor of the security, or be accompanied by documentary evidence of the grant.[4]

- *Assent*[5]—in the case of an assent by personal representatives in relation to a registered trade mark or any right in or under it, Form TM24 should be used and should provide:
  (i) the name and address of the person in whom the mark (or any right) vests by virtue of the assent; and
  (ii) the date of the assent.

The application must be accompanied by such documentary evidence as suffices to establish the assent.[6]

- *Court orders*[7]—in the case of a court or other competent authority transferring a registered trade mark or any right in or under it, Form TM24 should be used and should provide:
  - (i) the name and address of the transferee;
  - (ii) the date of the order; and
  - (iii) where the transfer is only in respect of any right in the mark, a description of the right.

The application must be accompanied by such documentary evidence as suffices to establish the court order.[8]

1 Trade Mark Rules 2008 ('TMR 2008') r 48(1)(a) and r 49(1)(a).
2 TMR 2008 r 49(2)(a).
3 TMR 2008 r 48(1)(c) and r 49(1)(d).
4 TMR 2008 r 49(2)(b).
5 TMR 2008 r 48(1)(d) and r 49(1)(e).
6 TMR 2008 r 49(2).
7 TMR 2008 r 48(1)(e) and r 49(1)(e).
8 TMR 2008 r 49(2).

UK trade marks—title to and dealings with applications for registration

13.10 The provisions of the TMA 1994 described above and relating to ownership and transmission of a registered trade mark apply equally to applications for registration of a mark, subject to certain necessary modifications to the wording of the relevant provisions.[1]

1 TMA 1994 s 27.

UK trade marks—licenses and mere 'consents'

13.11 Normally a licence is merely a permission for the licensee to do something that would otherwise infringe the rights of the licensor. It can but need not arise under a contract; it can arise formally or informally and in writing or orally. Normally, a licence confers no proprietary interest on the licensee nor any right which is enforceable against a third party.

13.12 This position is modified in relation to licences in respect of UK trade marks and applications to register UK trade marks as follows.

13.13 *Licences under the TMA 1994*—for the purposes of the TMA 1994, a licence in relation to a trade mark or in relation to an application to register a trade mark has a special status as a registrable transaction.[1] In contrast to the normal position described above, such a licence is (unless it provides otherwise) binding on the licensor's successors in title.[2] Moreover, licensees are provided with certain rights in relation to infringement actions against third parties (see further below). However, to qualify as a licence for the purposes of the TMA 1994, the licence must be in writing and must be signed by or on behalf of the licensor (the grantor).[3] Moreover, unless and until it is registered it is ineffective against those with conflicting interests, and the licensee will not have the rights and remedies in relation to infringement that are discussed below.[4] Of course, a licensee is only licensed to do those acts which are permitted under the terms of the licence. Other acts may still infringe the proprietor's rights in the trade mark.[5]

1 TMA 1994 ss 25(2)(b) and 27(1).
2 TMA 1994 s 28(3).
3 TMA 1994 s 28(2). Except in Scotland, this requirement may be satisfied in relation to a body corporate by the affixing of its seal.
4 TMA 1994 s 25(3).
5 See para **13.37** below.

13.14 *Mere 'consents'*—a licence (ie, a permission to use the mark) that fails to satisfy the requirements set out above is not a licence for the purposes of the TMA 1994. It may, however, amount to a 'consent' to the use of the mark and, therefore, provide a defence to an infringement action under s 9(1) of the TMA 1994. There is no requirement that a consent be in writing or signed. It can, for example, arise informally and without the need for any contract.

UK trade marks—the terms of a licence

13.15 The TMA 1994 makes no provision for what should be contained in a licence.[1] The policy of the TMA 1994 is that trade mark owners should be free to licence their trade marks with as little or as much control as they see fit. Of course, if a licensee's use of the trade mark results in it becoming generic or misleading to the public, then the registration of the trade mark may be revoked pursuant to s 46(1)(c) or (d) of the TMA 1994.

1 This contrasts with the position in many other countries and also with the old law in the UK.

13.16 The terms of a licence will depend on the requirements, bargaining positions and financial strength of the parties. However, as set out below, there are a number of terms that are either essential or at least advisable in order to ensure clarity and to minimise potential disputes.

1 Non-exclusive, sole or exclusive licence

13.17 The licence should make clear whether it is:

(a) *Non-exclusive* (where the licensor is free to use the mark and to grant further licenses to others); or
(b) *Sole* (where the licensee and the licensor are the only parties that will use the mark); or
(c) *Exclusive* (where only the licensee can use the mark, to the exclusion of all others, including the licensor).

In general, licensees wish for exclusivity to maximise the prospects of a return on their investment. Licensors, however, generally wish to be able to appoint as many licensees as possible in order to ensure the greatest return for themselves. The level of exclusivity that is desirable and sensible will depend on the nature of the market.

13.18 It is worth noting that many licences provide that an exclusive licence will become non-exclusive during the 'notice period' following a notice of termination. This helps ensure that the ongoing 'health' of the brand is not compromised.

13.19 From the point of a licensor, care should be taken when granting an exclusive licence because such a licence will also exclude the trade mark owner from using the mark (and any other licensed IP) for the period of the licence. There have been many cases where a licensor has found that the exclusive licence it has granted covers a wider range of products than it anticipated and it has had to try to renegotiate the licence to make it non-exclusive.

13.20 A licensor granting an exclusive licence may also wish to include a provision which permits termination of the licence or termination of exclusivity if the licence does not generate a certain minimum level of royalty return for the licensor.

2 Territory

13.21 The licence should specify the territory to which it applies. It is open to the licensor to provide a licence for the whole of the UK or for a smaller part of it as they see fit.

3 Goods/services to be licensed

13.22 The parties should specify the goods and/or services covered by the licence. Licensees will generally look for as broad a licence as possible but must take care to ensure that it covers at the least the goods and services for which it anticipates using the mark. Licensors meanwhile will generally look to restrict the scope of the licence and must ensure that it will not restrict either their own trading activities or their ability to license others to use the mark in other areas of commercial activity.

4 Marks to be licensed

13.23 The licence should clearly identify all relevant trade marks to be licensed (and other intellectual property, where appropriate). Where multiple marks are required, these should all be licensed and the manner of their use clarified. In this context, it is common for branding guidelines to be provided and for the licensee's use to be made conditional on being in accordance with those guidelines.

5 Royalties

13.24 There is no requirement that a licence be subject to the payment of a royalty. However, the licensor will generally require some sort of royalty. Licence provisions as to the calculation and payment of royalties are of almost infinite variety. Indeed, entire businesses exist devoted to providing advice and assistance on these matters.

13.25 If it is clear that the licensee will have to make a substantial investment in order to exploit the mark (eg, in terms of upfront or ongoing costs), then the royalty provisions can reflect this and the amount of risk that the licensee is undertaking. Where, however, less investment is required of the licensee, and particularly where the licensor is bearing more of the risk (including, perhaps, marketing costs), the balance would appropriately be weighted more towards the licensor.

13.26 A licence should be drafted so that the way in which the royalty is calculated is clear. It should deal (for example) with what the 'licensed product' is for royalty purposes; with what events (eg, sales) trigger the royalty and with what type of costs (eg, marketing costs, withholding taxes, and the like) can be deducted in calculating the royalty payable.

13.27 A licensor should also consider including a provision allowing verification of the licensee's accounts to ensure that there is no misstatement of the figures used to calculate the royalty. To this end, licences often contain provisions that allow the licensor to audit the licensee's accounts and (if a certain level of under-reporting has occurred) to recover the costs of that audit from the licensee. Clearly, if set at an appropriate level, this can provide a deterrent to under-reporting by the licensee.

6 Sub-licensing

13.28 Some consideration needs to be given as regards sub-licences. Section 28(4) of the TMA 1994 provides that, where the licence so provides, the licensee may grant a sub-licence. It also provides that references in the TMA 1994 to a licence or licensee include a sub-licence or sub-licensee.[1] This suggests that what is said above as regards licenses and mere consents applies equally to sub-licenses. In other words:

- Provided the licence so permits, the licensee can grant a sub-licence which has the special status described in para **13.13** above. Such a sub-licence must be in writing and signed by the licensor and the sub-licence has to be registered.
- Other forms of sub-licence may qualify as mere 'consents'. In other words, they may provide the sub-licensee with a defence to an infringement claim (see para **13.14** above).

1 TMA 1994 s 28(4).

13.29 From the licensor's viewpoint, it is generally advisable to include provisions in the licence that deal expressly with the extent to which the licensee can grant a sub-licence of either type discussed above. Licenses often provide that the licensee can only grant a sub-licence:

- with the consent of the licensor; and
- provided the sub-licensee is bound by the same conditions as the licensee.

The reasons for such provisions are clear. The licensor may have been careful in selecting the licensee and in ensuring that the licensee has the financial means properly to exploit the licence—particularly where the licence is for an extended term or where the termination provisions are not extensive. This care could easily be negated if the licensee could grant a sub-licence over which the licensor has no control.

13.30 It is also worth mentioning that as the parties to the licence are not the same as the parties to the sub-licence, there is often a risk of some 'disconnect' between those parties' rights. For example (depending on the terms of the licence):

- A licensee may well remain liable to pay royalties to the licensor in a case where a sub-licensee has failed to pay the licensee sums due under the sub-licence.
- Similarly, a sub-licensee may find that the sub-licence is terminated because a superior licence has been terminated. In this regard, it should be remembered that the termination of a licence will in general operate to terminate rights (such as sub-licences) created under that licence. As a result, a sub-licensee who has paid everything that is due to the licensee under the sub-licence may find that the sub-licence is determined because the licensee has failed to pay the licensor sums due under the licence.

7 Quality-control provisions

13.31 In many countries, it is necessary to have quality-control provisions in order for a trade mark licence to be valid and for it to be recorded on the register. In the UK there is no such requirement, and the view is that it is the trade mark owner's commercial decision whether they wish to impose requirements over the quality of the goods or services involved.

13.32 The content of such provisions vary enormously, but the basic points are:

(a) What are the qualities to be tested? This will often require verification that the products correspond to a description of the 'product specification' within the licence or to product guidelines that may vary from time to time.
(b) Who will test those qualities? Will this be an employee of the licensor or a third party?
(c) How regularly will the checks be carried out? In the case of clothing or merchandise this may be prior to their introduction; with more technical products this may be on a regular basis.
(d) Will the licensor have the power to request further samples on an ad-hoc basis? If so, will this be simply if the licensee has failed previous checks, and what terms will be set for the licensee's requirement to provide samples in such situations?
(e) Should there be penalties for a failure to comply with the provisions?

8 Period of the agreement and termination provisions

13.33 The licence should contain provisions governing how and when it will come to an end.

13.34 As well as providing for termination at the end of a specified period (the 'term' of the licence), licences often contain provisions allowing early termination in the event of (for example):

- a change in ownership or control of the licensee;
- the insolvency of the licensee; and
- an irremediable breach of the terms of the licence (including, for example, repeated and/or serious breaches of quality-control provisions).

13.35 The termination provisions may also provide for:

- Whether on termination the licensee can sell off remaining branded stock and use existing packaging or marketing materials. In this regard, the termination provisions should take into account that once the licence has been terminated or notice of termination has been given, the licensee may seek to act in ways which are potentially damaging to the trade mark—by, for example, 'dumping' licensed products with inappropriate retailers or selling them at a much reduced price in order to use up their materials or otherwise reduce or eradicate their inventory.

- When the licensor can appoint a new licensee and, if so, when that new licensee can start using the trade mark. It is not uncommon for an exclusive licence to provide that it will become non-exclusive for a period following notice of its termination—thereby allowing the new licensee to commence use of the mark in that period.

9 Rights/obligations regarding infringement

13.36 Finally, the licence may contain provisions regarding the rights and obligations of the parties as regards infringements by third parties. The licensee may, for example, be obliged to inform the licensor of any instances of infringement of the licensed trade marks.

13.37 A licence may also provide an exclusive licensee with the ability to take action in its own name or to compel the licensor to take action in cases of infringement. Licences often specify a period for the licensor to take action against the infringer after which period the licensee will be able to take action.[1]

There may be cases where a licensee can be sued by the proprietor of a registered trade mark for infringement of the trade mark for actions which go beyond what is permitted by the license. Indeed, TMA 1994 s 28(5) expressly provides that a proprietor may invoke the rights conferred by a trade mark against a licensee who contravenes any provision in the licence with regard to: (a) its duration; (b) the form covered by the registration in which the trade mark may be used; (c) the scope or the goods and services for which the licence is granted; (d) the territory in which the trade mark may be affixed; or (e) the quality of the goods manufactured or of the services provided by the licensee.[2]

1 This is particularly important for EUTM licences as the EUTMR (unlike the TMA 1994) does not provide its own period—see paras **13.41** and **13.63** below.
2 TMA 1994 s 28(5), added by SI 2018/825, reg 16 with effect from 14 January 2019. This provision mirrors Art 25(2) of the EUTMR which applies to EUTMs.

UK trade mark—right of licensees to bring infringement proceedings

1 Specific grant of the right of some exclusive licensees to bring action

13.38 Section 31 of the TMA 1994 provides that an exclusive licence *may* provide that the licensee shall have, to such extent as may be provided by the licence, the same rights and remedies in respect of matters occurring after the grant of the licence as if the licence had been an assignment and that such a licensee has the right to bring infringement proceedings against any person other than the proprietor, as if the licensee was the registered proprietor of the trade mark. It is important to note that this right only applies where the licence so provides and so there may well be some exclusive licenses which do not so provide. In the absence of such a provision, a licensee (even an exclusive licensee) must rely upon the general provisions pertaining to the right of a licensee to bring an action for infringement (see paras **13.40** et seq below).

13.39 Where the licence does so provide, the right of the exclusive licensee to bring infringement proceedings is concurrent with the right of the licensor[1] and to the extent that infringement proceedings relate to matters where the parties have concurrent rights then (unless the licence provides otherwise[2]) one party cannot proceed unless the other is joined as a party.[3] Where there are concurrent rights, the damages or account of profits may be apportioned to the licensor and licensee (unless the licence provides otherwise).[4]

1 TMA 1994 s 31(2).
2 TMA 1994 s 31(8).
3 TMA 1994 s 31(4). A person who is joined as a defendant as a result of this provision but who takes no part in the proceedings shall not be made liable in costs—see TMA 1994 s 31(5).
4 TMA 1994 s 31(6) and (8).

2 The general rights of licensees to bring action

13.40 Where the licensee is not an exclusive licensee, or where an exclusive licence does not provide the licensee with the ability to bring proceedings in its own name, s 30 of the TMA 1994 confers on a licensee a more limited right to bring proceedings.

13.41 Under TMA 1994 s 30(1A), except where the licence provides otherwise, a licensee may only bring infringement proceedings with the consent of the proprietor. This is, however, subject to an exception in that the TMA 1994 provides that an exclusive licensee is entitled to call upon its licensor to take infringement proceedings in relation to any activities which affect its interests and, if its licensor refuses to do so or does not take action within two months, is then entitled to bring proceedings in its own name as if it was the proprietor.[1]

Where a licensee brings an infringement action, it may not proceed (save as regards an application for interim relief) without the licensor being formally joined to the proceedings (either as a claimant or as a defendant)[2] (although the licensor will only be liable for costs if they take part in the proceedings[3]). Where damages are awarded to a licensor the pecuniary losses of the licensee may be taken into account and the court may direct that the licensor is to hold such sums on behalf of the licensee.[4] Further, where a proprietor brings infringement proceedings, a licensee who has suffered loss is entitled to intervene in the proceedings for the purpose of obtaining compensation for that loss.[5]

1 TMA 1994 s 30(2) and (3) as amended by SI 2018/82. Previously, the position was that any licensee was entitled to call on the proprietor to bring proceedings and, if the proprietor refused or failed to do so within two months, was entitled to bring proceedings in its own name.
2 TMA 1994 s 30(4).
3 TMA 1994 s 30(5).
4 TMA 1994 s 30(6).
5 TMA 1994 s 30(6A) (added by SI 2018/825, reg 17(6) with effect from 14 January 2019.

13.42 Accordingly, whilst the specific rights to sue provided under TMA 1994 s 31 only arise if they are positively granted, the general rights under TMA 1994 s 30 arise unless and to the extent that they are not positively excluded.

UK trade mark—recordal of licences

13.43 A licence (within the meaning of the TMA 1994) is a registrable transaction within s 25 of the TMA 1994. Whilst registration is not required for the purposes of showing 'genuine use' of the registration nor to establish a defence of consent in infringement proceedings, a failure to apply to register will have serious consequences as regards the protection provided to the licensee. These consequences are considered in para **13.47** below. It is, therefore, very much in the licensee's interest to ensure that the licence is recorded.

13.44 A fee of £50 is payable on an application to UKIPO to record the grant of a trade mark licence. The application is made on the Form TM50 and must be signed by or on behalf of the grantor or be accompanied by documentary evidence that suffices to establish the licence.[1] A single form may relate to all UK trade mark registrations against which the licence is to be recorded so long as they are all in the name of the same registered proprietor.

1 TMR 2008 r 49(1)(b) and (2).

13.45 The information to be provided on the application is:

(i) the name and address of the licensee;
(ii) where the licence is an exclusive licence, that fact;
(iii) where the licence is limited, a description of the limitation; and
(iv) the duration of the licence if the same is 'or is ascertainable' as a definite period.[1]

1 TMR 2008 r 48(1)(b).

13.46 In the case of any amendment to the registered particulars relating to a licence granted under a registered trade mark, particulars reflecting that amendment are provided using Form TM51.[1]

1 TMR 2008 r 48(1)(f) and r 49(1)(c).

UK trade mark—consequences of failure to register a registrable transaction

13.47 Under s 25 of the TMA 1994, there are three direct consequences of failing to register the prescribed particulars of a registrable transaction (eg, an assignment, the grant of a security interest, an assent, a court order or a licence):

- First, until such time as an application has been made for the registration of the relevant prescribed particulars, the transaction will be ineffective against someone who acquires, in ignorance of the registrable transaction, a conflicting interest in or under the registered trade mark.[1]
- Second, and in addition to the above, until such time as an application has been made for the registration of the relevant prescribed particulars, a licensee will not have the rights and remedies in relation to any infringement of the trade mark as would otherwise be available under ss 30 and 31.[2]
- Third, where a person becomes either the subsequent proprietor or licensee of a registered trade mark by virtue of a registrable transaction and the mark is infringed before the prescribed particulars of the transaction are registered, in any proceedings for such an infringement, that person will not be entitled to costs unless: (a) an application for the registration of the prescribed particulars of the transaction is made within six months of the date of the transaction; or (b) the court is satisfied that it was not practicable for such an application to be made within six months and that an application was made as soon as practicable thereafter.[3]

1 TMA 1994 s 25(3)(a).
2 TMA 1994 s 25(3)(b).
3 TMA 1994 s 25(4) (as amended).

13.48 The intention behind s 25 is clearly to try to ensure that the Register records as accurately as possible all interests in or under registered trade marks. The serious consequences that can follow in the event of a failure to register the particulars of a registrable transaction are a strong practical and commercial incentive for assignees and licensees (in particular) to apply for registration of the relevant transaction.

EUROPEAN UNION TRADE MARKS

EUTM—property right to be dealt with in its entirety

13.49 An EUTM, like a UK trade mark, is a property right. However, being a unitary right applying across the EU, some further provision is required as to the law governing dealings with it. In this regard, the

EUTMR provides that an EUTM must be dealt with in its entirety and for the whole area of the Community as a national trade mark registered in the Member State in which:

(a) according to the EUTM register, the proprietor has its seat or domicile on the relevant date;[1] or
(b) if (a) above does not apply, where the proprietor has an establishment; or
(c) if (a) and (b) do not apply, where the EUIPO is situated (ie, Spain).[2]

1 EUTMR Art 19(1).
2 EUTMR Art 19(2).

EUTM—applications for an EUTM

13.50 The provisions discussed below as regards transfers and licences apply equally to applications for a EUTM.[1]

1 EUTMR Art 28.

EUTM—transfers

13.51 Unlike the TMA 1994 (see para **13.04** above) the EUTMR does not specifically list the ways in which an EUTM may be transferred or assigned. However, as an EUTM is clearly personal property, it would seem clear that it may be transmitted on much the same grounds as a UK trade mark. Indeed, assignments by way of succession are mentioned in the EUIPO's *Guidelines on Transfers*. Further, Art 22 expressly states that an EUTM may be charged by way of security independently of the undertaking.

13.52 The position as regards an EUTM contrasts to that for a UK trade mark in several respects:

- In contrast to the position for UK trade marks, an EUTM cannot be divided territorially. As Art 16 makes clear, an EUTM has to be dealt with in its entirety and for the whole of the EU.
- Under the EUTMR, an assignment of an EUTM must (except where it is the result of a judgment) be in writing and signed by both parties to the contract—otherwise it is void. This is somewhat more restrictive than the equivalent requirement in relation to UK trade marks (where only the assignor need sign).[1] Consequently, where a party wishes to assign a portfolio containing rights beyond those covering the UK, it is advisable to ensure that both parties sign the assignment document. As for who may sign the assignment document, this would appear to be a matter of law as to whether a party may, and has, given authorisation to a signatory.

1 Contrast EUTMR Art 20(3) and TMA 1994 s 24(3).

13.53 In other respects, however, the position as regards transfers of EUTMs under the EUTMR is similar to that as regards UK trade marks under the TMA 1994. In particular, an assignment:

- may be independent of any transfer of the undertaking;[1] and
- may be in relation to some or all of the goods and services for which a mark is registered.[2]

1 EUTMR Art 20(1); TMA 1994 s 24(1).
2 EUTMR Art 20(1); TMA 1994 s 24(2)(a).

EUTM—effect vis-à-vis third parties

13.54 A transfer (other than a transfer of the whole undertaking or by any other universal succession) only has effect vis-à-vis a third party after it has been entered on the register—unless the third party acquired title after the transfer and with notice of it.[1] This is broadly similar to the position for UK trade marks.

1 EUTMR Art 27(1)–(2).

EUTM—recordal of transfers

13.55 Where there has been a transfer then, at the request of either of the parties, the transfer must be entered on the register.[1]

1 EUTMR Art 20(4).

13.56 An application for registration of an assignment of an EUTM is made by filing an application for recordal before EUIPO, providing (in accordance with EUTMR r 20(5)) the information set out in r 13(1) of the European Union Trade Mark Implementing Regulation (2018/626) (the 'EUTMIR'), namely:

(a) the registration number of the EUTM;
(b) the full particulars of the new owner;
(c) the details of the goods and services transferred (where the transfer is not for the entire EUTM);
(d) proof of the transfer. This will be satisfied by any of: (a) the application for registration of the transfer being signed by the registered proprietor and the successor in title (or their representative in either case); or (b) the application being submitted by the successor in title (or its representative) and is accompanied by a declaration signed by the registered proprietor (or its representative) that it agrees to the registration of the transfer; or (c) the application being accompanied by a transfer form signed by the registered proprietor and the successor in title (or their representative in either case); or (d) the signing of a completed transfer form or document, as laid down in Art 65(1)(e) of Delegated Regulation EU 2018/625, by the registered

proprietor and the successor in title (or their representative in either case);[1] and

(e) where applicable the name and business address of the representative of the new proprietor.

1 EUTMIR r 13(3).

13.57 Where the representatives will be the same post-transfer (particularly in the case of intra-group transfers) it will often be the case that the recordal will be done by way of the official recordal form so that the documentary evidence need not be filed.

EUTM—licences

13.58 Under Art 25 of the EUTMR, an EUTM licence may be:

- for some or all of the goods or services for which it is registered;
- for the whole or for part of the Community. In other words, even though the EUTM is a single right applying to the whole of the European Union and cannot be transferred other than as a whole (see paras **13.49** and **13.52** above), it is possible to grant licences in respect of an EUTM in relation to parts of the Union; and
- exclusive or non-exclusive.

13.59 In these respects, the position as regards the licensing of EUTMs is broadly similar to that of UK trade marks although, as set out below, there are some differences that are worth noting.

13.60 First, the EUTMR does not specifically require a licence be in writing.[1] However, the rules of the EUTMIR relating to the recordal of licences do mean that proof of the licence may be required and this makes it advisable that the licence be in writing (in addition to all the general reasons to make an agreement in writing).

1 See, for example, the decision in *Jean Christian Perfumes Ltd v Thakrar* [2011] EWHC 1383 (Ch), 27 May 2011, in which an oral licence was held to be a sufficient basis for bringing an action.

13.61 Second, as with UK trade marks, an EUTM licence will bind the parties to it but will not have any effect on a third party unless it is registered or unless that third party knew of it at the time of acquiring its rights in the EUTM.[1] However, the EUTMR also provides that this requirement does not apply in the case of the successor of the entirety of the undertaking, or any other who acquires by way of universal succession.

1 EUTMR Art 27 and TMA 1994 s 25(3).

13.62 Third, under the TMA 1994 in the case of UKTMs, exclusive licensees whose licences permit them to take action in their own names may do so without further ado. By contrast, under Art 25(3) of the EUTMR, in the case of EUTMs an exclusive licensor may only bring an action for infringement if the licensor consents (see para **13.63**) or if (following notification) the licensor does not take action 'within an appropriate period'.[1] The meaning of a 'appropriate period' is not defined by the EUTMR.

1 EUTMR Art 25(3).

13.63 Fourth, until 14 January 2019, under the TMA 1994, non-exclusive licensees were entitled to sue in their own names if their licensors failed to take action within two months of being notified. However, from that date, the position as regards UKTMs changed[1] and reflects that of non-exclusive licensees of EUTMs who can only bring infringement proceedings with the consent of the trade mark proprietors[2]—albeit that the EUTMR does provide that this is without prejudice to the provisions of their licences. Accordingly, it is advisable for a licence to spell out the rights of the licensee to take action and any conditions governing the circumstances and timing in which the licensor may or may not withhold such consent.

1 See para **13.41** above and TMA s 30(1A), (2) and (3) (as amended by SI 2018/825, reg 17).
2 See EUTMR Art 25(3).

13.64 Fifth, until the TMA 1994 was amended to include s 28(5), with effect from 14 January 2019, the TMA 1994 did not contain an equivalent provision to Art 25(2) of the EUTMR which provides that the proprietor of an EUTM may invoke the rights conferred by that trade mark against a licensee who contravenes any provision in the licence contract with regard to:

(a) its duration;
(b) the form covered by the registration in respect of which the trade mark may be used;
(c) the scope of goods or services for which the licence is granted;
(d) the territory in which the trade mark may be affixed; or
(e) the quality of the goods manufactured or the services provided by the licensee.

EUTM—recording of licences at EUIPO

13.65 Under Art 25(5) of the EUTMR, on the request of one of the parties, the grant or transfer of an EUTM licence will be entered in the Register and published. For these purposes, the provisions of Art 13 of the

EUTMIR set out in para **13.56** above apply *mutatis mutandis* (save that the requirement under Art 13(1)(d) of the EUTMIR to provide proof of the transfer will not apply where the request was made by the proprietor of the EUTM).[1]

1 See EUTMR Art 26(1).

13.66 The request for recordal is made by submitting the transfer recordal form and by paying the appropriate fee. This applies where the proprietor and the licensee are identical—ie, several licences can be recorded under a single application.

13.67 The recordal form can be submitted by either of the parties acting alone, or together. If the request is made by the proprietor of the mark or the parties together then the license does not need to be submitted. If the licensee makes the request then the license needs to be provided.

13.68 Whilst it is possible to redact any sensitive clauses (remembering that the files relating to registered trade marks are a matter of public record), it may well be in the interests of the parties for the licensor to file any request for recordal of the licence.

INTERNATIONAL REGISTRATIONS

International registrations—recordal of assignments at WIPO

13.69 The application for recordal of an assignment of an international registration can be made either directly at WIPO or via the appropriate national office. The request can be made by the registered proprietor or by an interested Office made *ex officio* at the request of an interested person. It is important to remember that in order for the assignment to be registrable, the new proprietor must be a person who is entitled to hold the International Registration.[1] If the new owner does not have a real and effective place of business, is not domiciled or is not a national of a country which is a member of the appropriate international system then the assignment will not be recordable to the extent that the assignee fails to qualify.

1 Article 9 to the Protocol relating to the Madrid Agreement.

13.70 In relation to an international registration, there are no particular requirements—the rules applicable to the recordal of the transfer will be those of the office where the request for the recordal is presented (if filed via an office). A fee may be payable.[1]

1 Article 9*ter* to the Protocol.

International registrations—recordal of licences at WIPO

13.71 A licence of an international registration may also be recorded at WIPO.

13.72 Under r 20*bis* of the Common Regulations under the Madrid Agreement, the process for recordal of a licence before WIPO is that an application for recordal must be submitted on the Form MM13 either directly or via the office of the country of the holder of the IR or the office of one of the countries for which the licence is granted and the payment of the appropriate fee (including any fee which may be levied by the office for that purpose). If the request to record the licence is made by the licensee then the request must be made via an office (rather than directly) or the form must be counter-signed by the holder, since the International Board will not record a licence unless it is signed by the holder or an office.

13.73 The request for recordal of the licence must contain the following information:

- the number of the international registration concerned;
- the name of the holder;
- the name and address of the licensee;
- the designated Contracting Parties with respect to which the license is granted; and
- that the license is granted for all the goods and covered by the international registration, or the goods and services for which the license is granted, grouped in the appropriate classes of the International Classification of Goods and Services.

Where appropriate, the recordal can also indicate that the licence is only for a part of a particular territory, whether it is exclusive or sole, and the term of the licence.

Chapter 14

Infringement and parties to infringement actions

INTRODUCTION

14.01 Trade mark law confers a number of exclusive rights on the trade mark proprietor. Subject to exceptions and limitations, certain uses of signs by another person without consent will infringe those rights. This chapter will consider infringement and who may be parties to an infringement action under the following headings:

- A Summary of the infringement provisions.
- B Exclusive rights.
- C Use of identical marks for identical goods or services.
- D Likelihood of confusion.
- E Unfair advantage or detriment to distinctive character or repute.
- F Who may be sued for infringement.
- G Who may sue for infringement.

14.02 Linked issues arising include:

- Limitations and exceptions to infringement—see **Chapter 15**.
- Comparative advertising—see **Chapter 16**.
- Remedies—see **Chapter 17**.
- Threats of registered trade mark infringement proceedings—see **Chapter 18**.

A SUMMARY OF THE INFRINGEMENT PROVISIONS

Relevant legislation

14.03 The law in relation to infringement is contained in ss 9, 10 and 10A of the Trade Marks Act 1994 ('TMA 1994') for UK trade marks and in Art 9 of the EU Trade Mark Regulation[1] ('EUMTR') for EUTMs.

Both are derived from Arts 10 and 11 of the Directive[1]. As many cases refer to the provisions of the Directive (it being the governing legislation prior to Brexit, and being harmonised with the TMA 1994), this chapter will do the same and quote the wording of the Directive. However, the equivalent provisions of the TMA 1994 and the EUTMR will also be identified. Following Brexit, the interpretation and status of retained EU law (including EU case law) are governed by ss 6 and 7 of the European Union (Withdrawal) Act 2018. Retained EU case law still applies unless modified or displaced by UK decisions, or by regulations made under the 2018 Act, but the courts are not bound by post-Brexit decisions of the EU (but may have regard to them). The Supreme Court, and the appellate jurisdiction of the High Court, are not necessarily bound by retained EU case law.

1 Council Regulation (EU) 2017/1001.
2 Directive (EU) 2015/2436 ('the Directive'), which replaces Directive 2008/95/EC, which in turn codified the original harmonising trade mark Directive 89/104.

The infringement provisions

14.04 In summary, under trade mark legislation:

(a) The proprietor of a registered mark has certain exclusive rights in relation to the mark.[1]
(b) Those exclusive rights are infringed by certain acts (the acts as set out in paras (c)–(g) below) where those acts are done by someone *'in the course of trade'* and without the consent of the proprietor.[2]
(c) It is an infringement for a person (in the course of trade and without consent) to use any sign which 'is identical with the trade mark and is used in relation to goods or services which are identical with those for which the trade mark is registered'—Art 10(2)(a) of the Directive; s 10(1) of the TMA 1994; Art 9(2)(a) of the EUTMR.
(d) It is an infringement for a person (in the course of trade and without consent) to use any sign which 'is identical with, or similar to, the trade mark and is used in relation to goods or services which are identical with, or similar to, the goods or services for which the trade mark is registered, if there exists a likelihood of confusion on the part of the public; the likelihood of confusion includes the likelihood of association between the sign and the trade mark'—Art 10(2)(b) of the Directive; s 10(2) of the TMA 1994; Art 9(2)(b) of the EUTMR.
(e) It is an infringement for a person (in the course of trade and without consent) to use any sign which 'is identical with, or similar to, the trade mark irrespective of whether it is used in relation to goods or services which are identical with, similar to, or not similar to, those for which the trade mark is registered, where the latter has a reputation in the Member State and where use of that sign without

due cause takes unfair advantage of, or is detrimental to, the distinctive character or the repute of the trade mark'—Art 10(2)(c) of the Directive; s 10(3) & (3A) TMA 1994; and Art 9(2)(c) of the EUTMR.

(f) The proprietor is entitled (without prejudice to the rights of proprietors acquired before the filing date or the priority date of the registered trade mark) 'to prevent all third parties from bringing goods, in the course of trade, into the Member State [or UK for the TMA 1994] where the trade mark is registered, without being released for free circulation there, where such goods, including the packaging thereof, come from third countries and bear without authorisation a trade mark which is identical with the trade mark registered in respect of such goods, or which cannot be distinguished in its essential aspects from that trade mark'—Art 10(4) of the Directive; s 10A TMA 1994; Art 9(4) of the EUTMR.

(g) The proprietor has the right, 'where the risk exists that the packaging, labels, tags, security or authenticity features or devices, or any other means to which the trade mark is affixed, could be used in relation to goods or services and that use would constitute an infringement of the rights of the proprietor of a trade mark under Article 10(2) and (3) of the Directive … to prohibit the following acts if carried out in the course of trade:
    - (i) affixing a sign identical with, or similar to, the trade mark on packaging, labels, tags, security or authenticity features or devices, or any other means to which the mark may be affixed;
    - (ii) offering or placing on the market, or stocking for those purposes, or importing or exporting, packaging, labels, tags, security or authenticity features or devices, or any other means to which the mark is affixed.'

    —Art 11 of the Directive; s 10(3B) TMA 1994; and Art 10 of the EUTMR.

By far the most commonly cited forms of infringement are (c), (d) and (e) above, so this chapter focuses on those and does not discuss (f) in detail; (g) is dealt with briefly at paras **14.59–14.60** below. The burden of proof is on the claimant to establish each of the elements of infringement.[3]

1 Directive Art 10(1); s 9 TMA 1994; Art 9(1) EUTMR.

2 Directive Art 10(1)–(2); s 9 TMA 1994; Art 9(1) EUTMR. There is a further right to prevent the use of trade marks registered in the name of an agent or representative—see Art 13 of the Directive; s 10B TMA 1994; Art 13 of the EUTMR.

3 After some uncertainty as to whether the CJEU had reversed the burden of proof in the case of online marketplaces such as Amazon (that is, so as to require a third-party advertiser to show that their use of a registered mark as a keyword was sufficiently clear to exclude a risk of confusion) the Court of Appeal in *Interflora v Marks & Spencer* [2015] ETMR 5 has confirmed that it is for the claimant to demonstrate infringement.

Overlap with relative grounds for a refusal to register a mark

14.05 Much of the wording of the infringement provisions is the same as the wording in the provisions governing the relative grounds for a refusal to register a mark. This is hardly surprising. Both involve asking whether a particular sign or mark is or would be too close to another existing mark. For this reason, many of the issues that arise in relation to infringement have already been considered in **Chapter 5** when considering the relative grounds for refusing registration of a mark.

B EXCLUSIVE RIGHTS

14.06 As set out above, the legislation confers 'exclusive rights' on the proprietor. These are the rights to do, and to authorise others to do, those acts which if done by an unauthorised third party would amount to infringements. Other acts cannot infringe.

14.07 The TMA 1994 provides that the exclusive rights of the proprietor take effect from the 'date of registration', which once registration occurs is deemed to be the date of the filing of the application for registration.[1] However, infringement proceedings cannot be commenced before the date on which the trade mark is in fact registered.[2]

1 TMA 1994 s 9(3).
2 TMA 1994 s 9(3)(a).

14.08 The TMA 1994 provides that a UK trade mark can only be infringed by acts in the United Kingdom.[1] The EUTMR by contrast has equal effect throughout the Community and can be infringed by acts occurring in any part of the Community.[2] Following Brexit, EUTMs have no effect in the UK but have been automatically replaced in the UK by a corresponding national mark known as a 'comparable trade mark (EU)' governed by the TMA 1994 and, therefore, only capable of being infringed by acts occurring in the UK. EUTMs remain effective in the remaining Member States of the EU.

1 TMA 1994 s 9(1).
2 EUTMR Art 1(2).

C IDENTICAL MARKS, IDENTICAL GOODS OR SERVICES ('DOUBLE IDENTITY')—DIRECTIVE ART 10(2)(A); TMA 1994 S 10(1); EUTMR ART 9(2)(A)

14.09 It is an infringement for a person (in the course of trade and without consent) to use any sign which is 'identical with the trade mark in relation to goods or services which are identical with those for which it is registered'.[1]

1 Directive Art 10(2)(a); TMA 1994 s 10(1); EUTMR Art 9(2)(a).

14.10 To succeed in an infringement action under this head, six conditions must be satisfied:[1]

(i) there must be use of a sign by a third party;
(ii) the use must be in the course of trade;
(iii) the use must be without the consent of the trade mark proprietor;
(iv) the use must be of a sign that is identical to the mark;
(v) the use must be in relation to goods or services which are identical to those for which the trade mark is registered; and
(vi) the use must affect or be liable to affect the functions of the trade mark.

1 See, for example, C-206/01 *Arsenal Football plc v Reed* [2003] RPC 9; C-245/02 *Anheuser-Busch Inc v Budejovicky Budvar np* [2004] ECR I-10989; C-48/05 *Adam Opel AG v Autec AG* [2007] ETMR 33 and C-17/06 *Céline SARL v Céline SA* [2007] ETMR 80. See also the recent review of the authorities in *Datacard Corporation v Eagle Technologies Ltd* [2011] EWHC 244, [2011] RPC 17. This list was cited in '*Lush*': *Cosmetic Warriors Ltd v Amazon.co.uk Ltd* [2014] EWHC 181 at [28] and in *Cartier International AG & ors v British Sky Broadcasting & ors* [2014] EWHC 3354 at [144].

14.11 These conditions will be considered in turn. Some but not all of them are also relevant to the other types of infringing acts considered later in this chapter.

Condition (i)—use of a sign by a third party

14.12 The first condition is that to infringe, there must have been use of a sign by a third party.

14.13 The meaning of the word 'sign' has already been considered.[1] As will be seen in relation to condition (iv), it is necessary to identify with some precision the particular sign said to have been used.

1 See **Chapter 2**, para **2.03** and **Chapter 5**, para **5.14** above.

14.14 There must have been 'use' of this sign. For these purposes, the legislation provides a non-exhaustive list of the sort of uses that might infringe.[1] They include:

(a) affixing the sign to goods or their packaging;
(b) offering the goods or putting them on the market or stocking them for those purposes under the sign, or offering or supplying services thereunder;
(c) importing or exporting goods under the sign; or
(d) using the sign on business papers and in advertising.

1 Directive Art 10(3), TMA 1994 s 10(4), EUTMR Art 9(3). That this list is non-exhaustive is apparent from the fact that the Directive (and the EUTMR) states that the list is of uses that 'inter alia' may be prohibited. The TMA 1994 uses the words 'in particular' instead of 'inter alia' but the meaning must clearly be the same.

14.15 The concept of 'use' is intended to be very broad. Further, the TMA 1994 provides that the use of the sign may be otherwise than by means of graphic representation.[1] This means that the oral or other non-visual use of a sign may constitute infringement. However, the use must be more than merely incidental or ephemeral, as to which see the comments below concerning the *Trebor Bassett* case[2] where the coincidental appearance of the proprietor's mark was found not to constitute use of the types listed above.

1 TMA 1994 s 103(2). This is in contrast to the position under the 1938 Act which limited the concept of 'use of a mark' to the use of a printed or other visual representation of the mark.
2 *Trebor Bassett Ltd v Football Association* [1997] FSR 211. See para **14.26** below.

14.16 In *L'Oréal SA v eBay International AG*[1] it was noted that for the purposes of what is now Art 10 of the Directive, the operator of an online marketplace (such as eBay) does not itself 'use' a sign which appears on its own website when its customer's offer for sale of goods bearing the mark is displayed, where the marketplace is simply an 'intermediary service provider'.[2] The operator's customer may well be using the sign but the fact that the operator is providing the service which enables its customer to make that display does not mean that the operator is using the sign.

1 C-324–09 *L'Oréal v eBay* at [99]–[105]. See generally *Celine Sarl v Celine SA* (C-17/06) EU:C:2007:497; [2007] ETMR 80, and for a specific example see *Unilever Plc v Griffin* [2010] EWHC 899 (Ch); [2010] FSR 33 (inclusion of 'MARMITE' in a political broadcast).
2 The wording comes from the E-commerce Directive (2000/31/EC) which places limits on the liability of such service providers—see *L'Oréal*.

14.17 The *L'Oréal* case also considered whether there could be 'use' of a sign for the purposes of what is now Directive Art 10(2)(a) when a trader buys and uses an internet search engine keyword corresponding to a trade mark. Such keywords operate so that when an internet user carries out a search on a search engine (eg Google) using that keyword, an advertising link to that trader is displayed. In its judgment, the CJEU made clear that in such a case the trader is indeed 'using' the sign. Accordingly, if that sign corresponds to a trade mark, there is the requisite 'use of a sign' for the purposes of Art 10(2)(a). This is also the case where the keyword is bought for the trader by the operator of an online marketplace such as eBay. Such an operator may well be using the sign both in relation to its own service of providing an online marketplace and also in relation to the goods of its customer. For the purposes of Art 10, the requisite use can be use in relation to the goods or services of another (ie, of eBay's customer).[1]

In *Lush*[2] the judge held that Amazon had 'used' the Lush mark in the relevant sense by bidding on it as a keyword so that Amazon's advertisement would appear in response to a search for Lush. The judge also considered Amazon's use of the Lush mark on its own webpages. When a customer searched for 'lush', the word 'Lush' would appear in drop-down menu options as the customer began to type. The word would also appear on the search results pages over and above the customer's own entry of the term. It was held that this did amount to 'use', and that Amazon was not simply an intermediary service provider. The judge added that the 'right of the public to access technological development does not go so far as to allow a trader such as Amazon to ride rough shod over intellectual property rights, to treat trade marks such as Lush as no more than a generic indication of a class of goods in which the consumer might have an interest'.

1 C-324/09 *L'Oréal v eBay* at [84]–[97]. As seen later in relation to condition (v), eBay's use of the sign in relation to its own services as an online marketplace was not, however, either identical (or similar) to the services for which the mark was registered. So that use could not constitute an infringement under Directive Art 10(2).
2 *Cosmetic Warriors Ltd v Amazon.co.uk Ltd* [2014] EWHC 181.

14.18 The use must, of course, be use in the territory covered by the trade mark—the area for which the proprietor has exclusive rights. Thus, for example, where the server of a website offering goods or services under the trade mark is located in another territory, that offer may constitute use within the territory of the proprietor's exclusive rights[1] provided it is targeted at consumers within that territory. However, the mere fact that the website is accessible to consumers within the territory of the exclusive rights is not of itself enough to show that the offer is targeted at those consumers.[2] Whether an offer is targeted at consumers within the relevant territory is a matter for the national courts to determine on the facts of each case. However, a factor of particular importance is whether the offer is accompanied by details of the geographical areas to which the seller will despatch the product in question.[3] The issue of targeting was considered in detail by Kitchin LJ in Argos,[4] in which he explained that the issue of whether internet use is targeted at the UK is to be considered objectively from the perspective of average consumers in the UK, and that the court must consider all the circumstances of the case (which may also include the subjective intention of the website operator[5]).

1 ie, the UK for a UK national trade mark, and the EU for an EUTM.
2 Case C-324/09 *L'Oréal SA v eBay International AG* at [61]–[64].
3 Case C-324/09 *L'Oréal v eBay* at [65].
4 *Argos Ltd v Argos Systems Inc* [2017] EWHC 231 (Ch) at [160] onwards.
5 *Lifestyle Equities CV v Amazon UK Services Ltd* [2021] EWHC 118 (Ch) at [117] onwards.

14.19 As mentioned above, 'use' can include the importing of goods under the sign. In this regard, trade mark law gives the proprietor the exclusive right to control the initial marketing of goods under the mark in the relevant territory (the EU for EUTMs and the UK for UK trade marks). In other words, the proprietor can prevent importation into that territory of legitimate goods from outside that territory.[1] This is so even though, because the goods are genuine goods, no damage is done to the essential function of the trade mark (of indicating origin).[2] In determining whether goods have been imported, the issue is essentially whether those goods have been introduced into the territory for the purpose of putting them on the market in that territory. Thus, for so long as goods are not released for free circulation in the territory and the requirements of customs-approved treatment and use are satisfied, there has been no importation even though the goods in question are physically in the territory.[3]

1 Case C-414/99 *Zino Davidoff SA v A&G Imports Ltd* [2001] ECRI-8691. It is immaterial that the goods may have been dispatched from outside the EU to consumers in the EU—Case C-98/13, *Blomqvist v Rolex* [2014] ETMR 25.
2 *Eli Lilly & Co v 8PM Chemists Ltd* [2008] EWCA Civ 24 at [20]–[22].
3 See C-405/03 *Class International BV v Colgate Palmolive Co* [2005] ECR I-8735. See also *Eli Lilly* at [23]–[26] where the defendants had used a customs regime known as 'inward processing relief' which was available to a person who intends to send out of the country goods which had been brought by him into the country with the intention of re-exporting them. In *Lifestyle Equities CV v Amazon UK Services Ltd* [2021] EWHC 118 (Ch), the sales took place in the US and there could be no infringement by that alone, prior to importation, and on the facts the principle *in Class International* applied.

Condition (ii)—the use must be use in the course of trade

14.20 An act cannot be an infringement unless it is an act done in the course of trade.[1] Accordingly, use of a sign in a domestic, social or other non-trading manner will not constitute an infringement. For example, where an individual sells a product bearing a trade mark using an online marketplace (eg, eBay) and the transaction does not take place in the context of any wider commercial activity, there is no infringement of that trade mark. Of course, if an individual by reason of the volume, frequency or other characteristic of the sales made goes beyond what may properly be seen as the 'realms of a private activity', then that individual may well be acting in the course of trade.[2]

1 Directive Art 10(2); TMA 1994 s 9; EUTMR Art 9(2).
2 C-324/09 *L'Oréal v eBay* at [55]–[56].

14.21 In the *One in a Million* case[1] it was held that use 'in the course of trade' meant use in the course of a business; it did not require use as a trade mark. Thus use of a trade mark in the course of a business of a professional dealer for the purpose of making domain names more valuable and extracting money from the trade mark owner was a use in the course of a trade. Similarly, in the context of internet advertising, 'where an advertiser purchases from a search engine operator (such as Google) a keyword which is identical to a third party's trade mark in order to display a link to a site on which he offers his goods or services for sale, that advertiser *uses* the third party's trade mark *in the course of trade*'.[2]

1 *Marks & Spencer plc v One in a Million* [1998] FST 265 (Sumption QC) upheld by the Court of Appeal [1999] 1 WLR 903.
2 See *Cosmetic Warriors* [2014] EWHC 181, citing C-238/08 *Google France* at [75]–[98], C-278/08 *BergSpechte* at [18], C-324/09 *L'Oréal v eBay* at [87] and C-323/09 *Interflora Inc v Marks & Spencer plc* at [30]. 'Use in the course of trade' was also considered in the context of websites in *Lifestyle Equities CV v Amazon UK Services Ltd* [2021] EWHC 118 (Ch).

Condition (iii)—the use must be without the consent of the trade mark proprietor

14.22 Whether the trade mark proprietor has consented to the use made of the sign is a question of fact in each case. The meaning of consent is considered later in the context of the concept of exhaustion of rights.[1] Most difficulty arises where it is alleged that a proprietor has impliedly consented to the use in question and, in particular, where the proprietor has stood by and not objected to the use such as to indicate some form of tacit consent to the use in question.[2] It seems, however, that mere inactivity should not be sufficient to constitute consent.

1 See **Chapter 15**, paras **15.31** et seq. and especially at paras **15.39–15.42**.
2 In C-323/09 *Interflora Inc v Marks & Spencer plc* the CJEU commented at [47] that if the referencing service provider (there Google) permitted trade mark proprietors to object to the selection of keywords corresponding to trade marks, then a lack of objection *could* be regarded as 'tacit consent' to the use of the sign.

Condition (iv)—the use must be of a sign that is identical to the mark

14.23 To show infringement under Art 10(2)(a), the sign must be identical to the mark. The meaning of 'identical' here is the same as in Art 5(1) which governs the relative grounds for refusing to register a mark and has been considered in that context—see **Chapter 15**, paras **15.13–15.16**. In summary, having identified the particular sign being used by the third party, the court must ask whether through the eyes of the average consumer that sign is identical to the trade mark in question on a side-by-side comparison.

Condition (v)—the use must be in relation to identical goods or services

14.24 Under this head of infringement, the use must be use in relation to goods or services that are identical to those for which the proprietor's trade mark is registered. Again the meaning of 'identical goods or services' is the same as in the provisions governing the relative grounds for a refusal to register a mark and has been considered in that context—see **Chapter 5**, paras **5.28–5.31** above.

14.25 The requirement that the defendant must have used the sign 'in relation to' the relevant goods or services' can be satisfied even where the defendant has not used his sign upon the goods or services themselves. It may be sufficient that the sign has been used otherwise than by physically affixing or applying it to the goods or services, such as by using a sign as the name of the defendant's shop or on their website.

14.26 However, although there is no requirement that the sign must be physically affixed to the goods, and even though the use does not have to be 'in a trade mark sense', the phrase 'in relation to' does require the use to be other than merely incidental or ephemeral. In the *Trebor Bassett* case[1] the Football Association's three lions trade mark appeared on the defendant's cards because the reproduction of the photograph of an England football player on the cards necessarily incorporated the logo which appeared on the football shirt being worn by that player. Rattee J held that it was not even arguable that such incidental use by the defendant could amount to using the plaintiff's trade mark 'in relation to' the cards.

1 *Trebor Bassett Ltd v Football Association* [1997] FSR 211 at 216.

14.27 In relation to the internet, where a trader uses a keyword that is identical to another's trade mark so that an advertisement for that trader's goods or services is displayed when a search is conducted against that word, then that constitutes use of a sign in relation to that trader's goods or services. This is so even if the sign selected as a keyword does not appear on the face of that advertisement.[1]

1 C-278/08 *BergSpechte* at [19] and Case C-323/09 *Interflora* at [31].

14.28 The decision in *L'Oréal v eBay* is also of interest. In that case, eBay was using signs corresponding to the L'Oreal trade marks as keywords to promote both its own online marketplace and also to promote goods bearing the L'Oréal mark which its customers were offering for sale on that online marketplace. Both uses were uses in relation to goods or services. However, the former did not satisfy this condition because although it was use in relation to eBay's service (its online marketplace), that service was not identical (or even similar) to the goods or services for which the mark was registered.[1] By contrast, the latter use did satisfy the condition. The use was in relation to the goods because it raised the possibility of buying those customers' goods through eBay. There was a clear link between the sign and those goods and those goods were, moreover, identical to those for which the mark was registered.[2] The CJEU made clear that there was no requirement that the goods or services in relation to which the sign was used were those of the person using the mark (ie, of eBay).

1 C-324/09 *L'Oréal v eBay* at [89].
2 *L'Oréal* at [91]–[93].

14.29 The meaning of the words 'in relation to' is also relevant to, and mentioned in, the context of revocation proceedings for non-use in **Chapter 12.**[1]

1 See para **12.15**.

Condition (vi)—the use must affect or be liable to affect the functions of the trade mark

14.30 The CJEU has stressed on a number of occasions that, for the purposes of Art 10(2)(a), use can only infringe the proprietor's exclusive rights if it has an adverse effect on one of the functions of the trade mark. This is despite the fact that the recitals to the Directive state that the protection afforded by a registered trade mark '*should be absolute in the case of identity between the mark and the sign and the goods or services*'.[1]

1 See Recital 16 (formerly recital 11 in Directive 2008/95/EC). See also Recital 11 to the EUTMR.

14.31 Although it has been said that this condition concerns, 'in particular', the essential function (ie, the function of guaranteeing the origin of the goods or services[1]) the CJEU has repeatedly emphasised that for the purposes of Art 10(2)(a), the adverse effect can be in respect of any of the trade mark functions—the function of indicating origin, the function of guaranteeing quality, or the functions of communication, investment or advertising.[2]

1 See C-206/01 *Arsenal Football Club* at [51].
2 See C-487/07 *L'Oréal and others* at [60]–[65] and C-323/09 *Interflora* at [37]–[40]. By contrast, under Art 10(2)(b), a likelihood of confusion (ie, an adverse effect on the essential function) is an essential requirement for liability. Trade mark 'functions' are discussed at **5.97–5.110**.

Adverse effect on the function of indicating origin (the 'essential' function)

14.32 In *Google France*[1] the CJEU stated that there is an adverse effect on the essential function where the advertising does not enable reasonably well informed and observant internet users, or enables them only with difficulty, to ascertain whether the goods in question emanate from the trade mark proprietor or from a third party not linked to that proprietor. This conclusion was the subject of criticism by, amongst others, Arnold J in *Datacard*[2] on the basis that it introduces a sort of 'confusion' test (with a reversed onus on the third party) which is not apparent from the wording of Art 10(2)(a). However, it is now clear from the Court of Appeal's judgment in *Interflora* that the burden is in fact on the claimant to show a likelihood of confusion.[3]

In *Cartier* it was held that the essential function may be damaged by the online sale of counterfeits even where it is made clear that the goods are only replica, since such a disclaimer does not exclude the risk of post-sale confusion.[4]

1 C-238/08 *Google France* at [99].
2 [2011] EWHC 244 at [260]–[267].
3 *Interflora v Marks & Spencer* [2014] EWCA Civ 1403.
4 *Cartier International AG & ors v British Sky Broadcasting & ors* [2014] EWHC 3354.

14.33 In *Interflora*[1] the issue concerned Marks & Spencer's use of 'Interflora' as a keyword so that an advertisement for its own goods and services was displayed when an internet user carried a Google search using that word. The CJEU stated that:[2]

(a) The question whether there was an adverse effect on the function of indicating origin depends on the manner in which the advertisement is presented. In this regard, the fact that the advertisement was displayed on screen immediately after a user had used the relevant keyword and that the keyword also continued to be displayed on the screen as the search term used, was relevant to whether the user might be mistaken as to the origin of the goods or services advertised.
(b) If the advertisement suggested an economic link between the advertiser and the trade mark proprietor, then that must have an adverse effect on that mark's function of indicating the origin of the relevant goods or services.
(c) The question whether there was the requisite adverse effect was a matter for the national court to assess on the basis of the particular facts.
(d) The fact that the referencing service provider (Google) had not permitted trade mark proprietors to prevent others selecting signs as keywords that were identical to the trade mark was irrelevant. Although *if* the referencing service provider had permitted trade mark proprietors to object to such a selection, a lack of objection *could* be regarded as 'tacit consent' to the use of the sign.
(e) If the presentation of the advertisement would lead a reasonably well-informed and reasonably observant user of the internet to conclude that Marks & Spencer was a part of Interflora's commercial network, then the function of indicating origin would have been adversely affected.

(f) In examining the facts, the national court may look at: (i) whether a reasonably well-informed and reasonably observant user of the internet would be aware, on the basis of general knowledge, that there was no commercial connection between the advertiser and the trade mark proprietor; and (ii) if this was not generally known, whether the advertisement itself would have made the user aware of the lack of such a connection.

(g) On the facts of *Interflora*, the fact that the Interflora network contained a large number of retailers of varying sizes and commercial profiles would make it very difficult for even a reasonably well-informed and observant user to determine whether or not Marks & Spencer was or was not a part of that network.

(h) In the absence of any general knowledge that there was no commercial link between Marks & Spencer and Interflora, the issue was whether the fact that the advertisement stated 'M&S Flowers' would have indicated that there was no such link.

1 C-323/09 *Interflora Inc v Marks & Spencer plc* [2012] ETMR 1.
2 See [44]–[53].

Adverse effect on the advertising function

14.34 In relation to the advertising function, in *Interflora* the CJEU made it very clear that the use by a competitor in an internet referencing service (such as Google's 'AdWords') of a sign identical to a trade mark does not have an adverse effect on the advertising function of the trade mark.[1] This is so, even though such use might have repercussions on the advertising use of the mark—by for example, causing the proprietor to pay more in order to ensure that when an internet user carries out a search using that sign, the proprietor's advertisement would be displayed more prominently than that of its competitor. The mere fact that a proprietor may have to pay more to maintain or to enhance its profile with consumers does not constitute an adverse effect on the advertising function. It is, rather, the effect of competition. The Court concluded that internet advertising on the basis of keywords corresponding to trade marks is legitimate competition in that it ensures that consumers are offered alternatives.[2]

However, in *Lush* the use of the mark by Amazon was rather different, and was found to damage the advertising function: 'The evidence establishes that they rely on the reputation of the mark to attract custom. That quality of attracting custom, in my judgment, is bound to be damaged by the use by Amazon of the Lush mark to attract the attention of consumers to and attempt to sell to them the goods of third parties whilst at the same time making no effort at all to inform the consumer that the goods being offered are not in fact the goods of Lush'.[3]

1 C-323/09 *Interflora Inc v Marks & Spencer plc* at [54].

2 *Interflora* at [56]–[59].
3 *Cosmetic Warriors Ltd v Amazon.co.uk Ltd* [2014] EWHC 181.

14.35 It should be remembered, however, that other trade mark functions might be adversely affected even when the advertising function is not.

Adverse effect on the investment function

14.36 The investment function was described by the Court in *Interflora*, as the use of a trade mark to acquire or preserve a reputation capable of attracting consumers and retaining their loyalty. Although this function overlaps with the advertising function, it has its own distinct purpose in that a trader may use a variety of techniques to acquire or preserve a reputation—only one of which is advertising.[1] Hence, when use by a third party of a sign identical to a trade mark substantially interferes with the proprietor's use of its mark to acquire or preserve a reputation capable of attracting customers or retaining their loyalty, the investment function has been adversely affected.[2]

1 C-323/09 *Interflora Inc v Marks & Spencer plc* at [60]–[61].
2 *Interflora* at [62]–[63].

14.37 In *Interflora* the CJEU referred[1] to its earlier decision in *L'Oréal v eBay* as an example of damage to the investment function. In *L'Oréal* the Court had ruled[2] that a person who resells goods (in that case perfumes, cosmetics and hair care products) having removed those goods from their original packaging, might be infringing the trade mark under Art 10(2) if the removal from the packaging damaged the image and therefore the reputation of the trade mark.

1 C-323/09 *Interflora Inc v Marks & Spencer plc* at [63].
2 C-324/09 *L'Oréal v eBay* at [83].

14.38 In *Interflora* itself, the Court reiterated what it had said in relation to the advertising function, namely that the proprietor could not object to fair competition. The mere fact that the competitor's actions meant that the proprietor had to adapt its efforts in order to acquire or maintain a reputation was not sufficient to show the requisite adverse effect. Nor was the fact that some consumers might switch to the competitor's goods or services.[1] The investment function was held to have been adversely affected in *Lush*, since the brand had built up an 'ethical' image that could be tarnished by association with Amazon's tax practices in the UK, which Amazon's witness accepted would be repugnant to some.[2]

1 C-323/09 *Interflora Inc v Marks & Spencer plc* at [64].
2 *Cosmetic Warriors Ltd v Amazon.co.uk Ltd* [2014] EWHC 181 at [70]–[71].

D LIKELIHOOD OF CONFUSION – DIRECTIVE ART 10(2)(B); TMA 1994 S 10(2); EUTMR ART 9(2)(B)

14.39 It is an infringement for a person (in the course of trade and without consent) to use any sign which 'is identical with, or similar to, the trade mark and is used in relation to goods or services which are identical with, or similar to, the goods or services for which the trade mark is registered, if there exists a likelihood of confusion on the part of the public; the likelihood of confusion includes the likelihood of association between the sign and the trade mark'.[1]

1 Directive Art 10(2)(b); TMA 1994 s 10(2); EUTMR Art 9(2)(b).

14.40 To succeed in an infringement action under this head, six conditions must be satisfied:

(i) There must be use of a sign by a third party.
(ii) The use must be in the course of trade.
(iii) The use must be without the consent of the trade mark proprietor.
(iv) The use must be of a sign that is identical or similar to the mark.
(v) The use must be in relation to goods or services that are identical or similar to those for which the trade mark is registered.
(vi) There must be, because of the above identity or similarities, a likelihood of confusion on the part of the public (the likelihood of confusion includes the likelihood of association between the sign and the trade mark).

Conditions (i), (ii) and (iii)

14.41 These conditions are the same as those that apply in relation to double identity infringements under Art 5(1)(a) and are dealt with above:

(a) For condition (i) (use of a sign by a third party) see paras **14.12–14.19** above.
(b) For condition (ii) (use in the course of trade) see paras **14.20–14.21** above.
(c) For condition (iii) (use without the consent of the trade mark proprietor) see para **14.22** above.

Condition (iv)—use of a sign that is identical or similar to the mark

14.42 The test as to when a sign is identical to a mark is considered at paras **5.13–5.16** above. Whether a sign is similar to a mark is discussed at paras **5.17–5.27** above.

Condition (v)—use in relation to identical or similar goods or services

14.43 Whether goods or services are identical is considered at paras **5.28–5.31** above. Whether they are similar is considered at paras **5.32–5.36** above. The meaning of the words 'in relation to' is considered at paras **14.24–14.26** above.

Condition (vi)—likelihood of confusion

14.44 The test for establishing whether or not there is the requisite likelihood of confusion is considered in detail at paras **5.37–5.62** above.

E UNFAIR ADVANTAGE OF OR DETRIMENT TO THE DISTINCTIVE CHARACTER OR REPUTE OF A MARK—DIRECTIVE ART 10(2)(C), TMA 1994 S 10(3), EUTMR ART 9(2)(C)

14.45 It is an infringement for a person (in the course of trade and without consent) to use any sign which 'is identical with, or similar to, the trade mark irrespective of whether it is used in relation to goods or services which are identical with, similar to, or not similar to, those for which the trade mark is registered, where the latter has a reputation in the Member State and where use of that sign without due cause takes unfair advantage of, or is detrimental to, the distinctive character or the repute of the trade mark'.[1]

1 Directive Art 10(2)(c); TMA 1994 s 10(3); EUTMR Art 9(2)(c).

14.46 As set out in *Comic Enterprises Ltd v Twentieth Century Fox Film Corp,* to succeed in an infringement action under this head, nine conditions must be satisfied:

(i) the mark must have a reputation in the relevant territory;
(ii) there must be use of a sign by a third party in the relevant territory;
(iii) the use must be in the course of trade;
(iv) the use must be without the consent of the trade mark proprietor;
(v) the use must be of a sign that is identical or similar to the mark;
(vi) the use must be in relation to goods or services;
(vii) the use of the sign must give rise to a 'link' with the mark in the mind of the average consumer;
(viii) there must be one of three types of injury:
  (a) detriment to the distinctive character of the mark ('dilution' or 'blurring');
  (b) detriment to the repute of the mark ('tarnishing'); or
  (c) unfair advantage taken of the distinctive character or repute of the mark ('free-riding'); and
(ix) the use must be 'without due cause'.

1 [2016] EWCA Civ 41 per Kitchin LJ at [111].

Condition (i)—mark must have a reputation

14.47 This condition has been considered in detail in paras **5.66–5.74** above. In summary, it is not a particularly onerous requirement.[1] A mark has a 'reputation' if it is known either by the public at large or by a significant part of the public concerned by the product or services covered by that mark. It need not have a reputation throughout the territory.[2]

1 *Datacard Corporation v Eagle Technologies Ltd* [2011] EWHC 244 at [291] (Arnold J.) citing C-375/97 *General Motors Corp v Yplon SA*.
2 C-375/97 *General Motors Corp v Yplon SA* at [24]–[28]. See also C-301/07 *PAGO International GmbH v Tirolmilch Registrierte Genossenschaft mbH*.

Conditions (ii)–(v)

14.48 Conditions (ii)–(v) are the same as those that apply to infringement cases under Art 5(1)(b) (s 10(2) TMA 1994) and have been considered above (see paras.**14.41–14.42** above.

Condition (vi)

14.49 Condition (vi) is simply that the use must be in relation to goods or services. As has already been noted,[1] the earlier wording of the European legislation stated that this type of infringement depended on the requisite use being in relation to goods or services 'which are not similar'); it is now clearly established that this type of infringement can occur whether the goods or services in question are identical, similar or dissimilar to those for which the mark is registered, and the updated Directive and EUTMR make this clear. Section 10(3A) of the TMA 1994 also now reflects this.

1 See para **5.65**.

Condition (vii)—link with the mark

14.50 In relation to this condition, the CJEU has stated[1] that:

> 'The infringements referred to in Art 5(2) … where they occur, are the consequence of a certain degree of similarity between the mark and the sign, by virtue of which the relevant section of the public makes a connection between the sign and the mark, that is to say, establishes a link between them even though it does not confuse them. The existence of such a link must, just like a likelihood of confusion in the context of Art 5(1)(b) … be appreciated globally, taking into account all factors relevant to the circumstances of the case …'.

And that:

> 'The fact that for the average consumer, who is reasonably well informed and reasonably observant and circumspect, the later mark calls the earlier mark with a reputation to mind is tantamount to the existence of such a link … between the conflicting marks. The fact that:
>
> > the earlier mark has a huge reputation for certain specific types of goods or services, and
> >
> > those goods or services and the goods or services for which the later mark is registered are dissimilar or dissimilar to a substantial degree, and
> >
> > the earlier mark is unique in respect of any goods or services,
>
> does not necessarily imply that there is a link … between the conflicting marks[2]'.

1 See C-408/01 *Adidas Salomon AG and Adidas Benelux v Fitnessworld Trading Ltd.*

2 C-252/07 *Intel Corporation Inc v CPM United Kingdom Ltd* at [63]. The guidance provided in the *Adidas* and *Intel* cases was quoted by the Court of Appeal in *Specsavers International Healthcare Ltd v Asda Stores Ltd* [2012] EWCA Civ 24 at [120]–[121]. See also *Datacard* at [292] (Arnold J).

Condition (viii)—injury: causing detriment to or taking unfair advantage of distinctive character or repute

14.51 Condition (viii) is that the use made by the defendant is such as to cause one of three types of injury:

(a) detriment to the distinctive character of the mark ('dilution' or 'blurring')—this has already been considered at **Chapter 5**, paras **5.80–5.82** above; or
(b) detriment to the repute of the mark ('tarnishing')—considered at paras **5.83–5.86** above; or
(c) unfair advantage taken of the distinctive character or repute of the mark ('free-riding')—considered at paras **5.75–5.78** above.

The meaning of each of these has already been considered.

14.52 If the use of the sign does not satisfy condition (vii) (ie, if it does not create in the mind of the average consumer a link with the mark) then it is unlikely that condition (viii) will be satisfied. Indeed, it has been said that the more immediately and strongly the earlier mark is brought to mind by the later mark, the greater the likelihood that the current or future use of the later mark is taking unfair advantage of, or is detrimental to, the distinctive character or the repute of the earlier mark. However, the existence of a link in the mind of the average consumer between the sign and the mark is not sufficient, in itself, to show that condition (viii) is satisfied.[1]

1 C-252/07 *Intel Corporation Inc* at [31]–[32] and [67].

Condition (ix)—use was without due cause

14.53 The condition that, to infringe, the use must have been without due cause has been considered at paras **5.87–5.89** above.

F WHO MAY BE SUED FOR INFRINGEMENT

14.54 The parties who may be sued for infringement may include:

(a) those who use the mark in the ways set out above;
(b) joint tortfeasors, including in some cases directors and shareholders of companies; and
(c) those who apply the mark to materials in the ways set out in s 10(5) of the TMA 1994.

Those using the mark

14.55 Obviously, a person who actually uses a trade mark in one of the ways discussed above can be sued for infringement.

Joint tortfeasors

14.56 In English law, accessories to trade mark infringement can also be sued on the basis that they are joint tortfeasors. The relevant authorities were reviewed by Arnold J in *L'Oreal v eBay.*[1] A joint tortfeasor is someone who did not necessarily carry out the actual act of infringement but in some way combined with another to secure that the act was carried out;[2] or who had been so involved in the act or who had in some way made the act of infringement his own such that he should be held liable for it.[3] It is usually someone who had been party to a common design to carry out or who had procured the relevant act.[4] Mere assistance (even knowing assistance) is not enough, nor is the fact that a person had had the means (but not the duty) to prevent the infringement.[5]

1 [2009] RPC 21 at [346]–[352].
2 *Fabio Perini SPA v LPC Group plc* [2010] EWCA Civ. 525 at [104]–[105].
3 *Sabaf SPA v MFI Furniture Centres* [2002] EWCA Civ. 976.
4 The words 'common design' should not be used as if they formed part of a statute; words such as 'concerted action' or 'agreed on common action' could equally be used—see *Unilever plc v Gillette (UK) Ltd* [1989] RPC 583 at 609.
5 *L'Oreal v eBay* [2009] EWHC 1094 (Ch) at [380]–[382]. See also *CBS Songs Ltd v Amstrad Consumer Electronics plc* [1988] AC 1013.

14.57 A director or shareholder of a company that infringes trade mark may be liable as a joint tortfeasor. To be jointly liable with the company, a director must have done more than merely carrying out his constitutional role in the governance of the company (ie, voting at board meetings). Similarly, a shareholder must have done more than merely vote at general meetings and appoint directors. The question remains whether such person intends and procures and shares a common design that the infringement should take place.[1] In this regard, the court will ask by whom the decision to carry out the act was made and who gave the instructions. It is clearly easier to show that the director or shareholder in a small company is liable on this basis.[2] Joint tortfeasance was also considered in *Lush*, where the first defendant was a UK company responsible for fulfilling orders, while the second was a Luxembourg company that operated the website amazon.co.uk. The court held that on the facts of that case, both were liable.[3] However, an individual joint tortfeasor's liability does not necessarily extend to liability for the profits of a company with which they are jointly liable.[4]

1 *MCA Records Inc v Charly Records Ltd* [2002] FSR 26 at [48]–[52].
2 See, for example, *Boegli-Gravures SA v Darsail-ASP Ltd* [2009] EWHC 2690 (Pat) at [134]–[137].
3 *Cosmetic Warriors Ltd v Amazon.co.uk Ltd* [2014] EWHC 181 at [79]–[85].
4 *Lifestyle Equities CV v Santa Monica Polo Club Ltd* [2020] EWHC 68 (Ch).

14.58 It appears that the imposition of liability on joint tortfeasors under English law is not contrary to the Directive. However, the position in relation to EUTMs prior to Brexit was unclear. In such a case, it could be said that the effect of the EUTM is governed solely by the provisions of the EUTMR whilst, in other respects, infringement is governed by the law of the relevant Member State.[1] It might, therefore, have been argued that there was no jurisdiction to impose liability on an accessory as it would amount to an extension of the effect of the EUTM beyond what is provided in Arts 9–14 of the EUTMR.[2] Following the automatic replacement of EUTMs in the UK by 'comparable trade marks (EU)', those rights are now subject to national law in the usual way.

1 EUTMR Art 17.
2 See the discussion in *L'Oréal v eBay* [2009] EWHC 1094 (Ch) at [344]–[345].

Affixing a sign to materials—Directive Art 11; TMA 1994 s 10(3B); EUTMR Art 10

14.59 This provision concerns infringement by doing 'preparatory acts in relation to packaging or other means'. It replaces similar provisions found in s 10(5) of the TMA 1994 (and the European legislation). It provides that a person infringes the right of the trade mark proprietor by:

(a) affixing a sign identical with, or similar to, the trade mark on packaging, labels, tags, security or authenticity features or devices, or any other means to which the mark may be affixed; or
(b) offering or placing on the market, or stocking for those purposes, or importing or exporting, packaging, labels, tags, security or authenticity features or devices, or any other means to which the mark is affixed.

in circumstances where the risk exists that the packaging, labels, tags, security or authenticity features or devices, or any other means to which the trade mark is affixed, could be used in relation to goods or services and that use would constitute an infringement of the rights of the proprietor of a trade mark under Article 10(2) and (3) of the Directive.

14.60 Previously TMA 1994 s 10(5) only applied to those who knew or had reason to believe that the application of the mark was not duly authorised. However, on its current wording it simply requires the objective existence of the risk that the materials to which the mark has been applied could be used in such a way that would constitute an infringement. Thus, there is no longer any defence of innocence to this form of infringement – persons affixing signs to materials may be liable even if they did not realise that the risk existed.

G WHO MAY SUE FOR INFRINGEMENT?

Proprietors

14.61 The exclusive rights are conferred on the proprietor, who may, therefore, sue for the infringement of those rights.

Co-proprietors

14.62 Under s 23(5) of the TMA 1994, infringement proceedings may be brought by any co-proprietor of a registered trade mark. However, one co-proprietor may not without the leave of the court proceed with that action unless each other co-proprietor is either joined as a claimant or added as a defendant, except in the case of an application for interlocutory relief. Where a co-proprietor is added as a defendant, he will not be liable for any costs in the action unless he takes part in the proceedings.[1]

1 TMA 1994 s 23(5); in the event that the co-proprietor has rights and obligations as a trustee or a personal representative, such rights and obligations are not affected: s 23(6).

Licensees

14.63 The position of trade mark licensees in relation to infringement proceedings has already been considered—in relation to UK trade marks at paras **13.38–13.42** above, and in relation to EUTMs at paras **13.62–13.63** above.

Chapter 15

Defences, disclaimers and limitations

INTRODUCTION

15.01 The previous chapter dealt with a proprietor's exclusive rights and with acts that can amount to an infringement. However, in order to assess whether the proprietor can prevent such acts, it is necessary to consider whether any of the defences to infringement apply or whether the allegedly infringing act falls within the scope of a disclaimer or limitation in respect of the proprietor's rights.

15.02 *The UK position*—The TMA 1994 contains provisions stating that a registered trade mark *'is not infringed'* by certain specified acts. The Act also provides for disclaimers and limitations on the scope of registered rights. These defences, disclaimers and limitations include:

1 The three defences arising from limitations on the effect of a registered trade mark—s 11.
2 Non-use as a defence—s 11A.
3 Acquiescence—s 48.
4 Exhaustion of rights—s 12.
5 Disclaimers and limitations to the registrations—s 13.
6 Rights conferred on co-proprietors—s 23.

Of course, the question whether any of these defences, disclaimers or limitations apply is irrelevant if the defendant can show that the act complained of was not capable of being an infringement or that the trade mark was not validly registered.

15.03 *The EU position*—the EU Trade Mark Regulation ('EUTMR') speaks of *limitation* on the effects of a trade mark registration. However, the substantive provisions of the EUTMR broadly correspond to those of the TMA 1994 referred to above, but this correspondence is not always exact, so exercise caution. Broadly speaking the EUTMR provides for:

1 Defences—Arts 14, 16 and 138.
2 Acquiescence—Art 61.
3 Exhaustion of rights—Art 15.

Note that EUTMR Art 37 used to include a provision for the use of disclaimers, as in TMA 1994 s 13, but this has been removed. In what follows, the correspondence between the 1994 Act and the EUTMR will be made clear where appropriate.

15.04 *Is there also a competition defence?*—An issue that was considered by the Supreme Court in *Oracle* is whether there is also a competition defence—ie, that the assertion of a trade mark would amount to an anti-competitive practice.[1] The issue arose because the defendant had argued that the claimant's exclusive right to first marketing of its goods in the EEA must be subject to some qualification where the claimant had a practice of making it as difficult as possible to tell whether goods had already been so marketed, thereby stifling the resale market. It was said that such a practice was contrary to Arts 34–36 TFEU. However, the Supreme Court rejected that argument and overturned the Court of Appeal's earlier ruling that such a defence to infringement might exist.

1 *Oracle America Inc (formerly Sun Microsystems Inc) v M-Tech Data Ltd* [2012] UKSC 27.

DEFENCES UNDER S 11/ARTS 14, 16 AND 138

15.05 The defences under s 11 of the TMA 1994 fall into three broad categories:

- the defence that the mark complained of is a registered trade mark where that mark would not be declared invalid pursuant to s 47(2A), (2G) or s 48(1);
- so-called descriptive use (itself comprising three sub-divisions); and
- the use of earlier unregistered rights in a particular locality.

It is worth noting that s 11 was amended as from 14 January 2019 to implement Directive 2015/2436, including some provisions relating to EUTMs that have subsequently been deleted with effect from 31 December 2020, ie following Brexit; these are mentioned at **15.08** below. Any practitioner considering s 11 defences ought to check the legislation as it stood at each relevant time period.

Note that only the second of these three categories is mirrored by Art 14 of the EUTMR. The first is replicated in Art 16, while the third is found in Art 138.

Use of a registered trade mark where that mark is not liable to be declared invalid—s 11(1)/Art 16

15.06 Under s 11(1) of the TMA 1994, a registered trade mark cannot be infringed by the use of another registered trade mark where that later mark would be spared from a declaration of invalidity (based on the earlier mark) pursuant to any of the three named provisions of the TMA 1994, ie s 47(2A), (2G) or s 48(1). The provisions referred to in s 47 limit the ability of the earlier mark to invalidate the later mark where the earlier mark is itself liable to be revoked or declared invalid (such as for non-use, or failure to meet the absolute grounds for registration), while s 48(1) provides a defence to a declaration of invalidity where the proprietor of the earlier mark has acquiesced in the use of the registered mark for a continuous period of five years in the UK. Those provisions are considered in more detail in **Chapter 11**.

15.07 Where a claimant with a passing off claim but no registered mark is faced with a defendant with a registered mark, the claimant may first seek to invalidate that registration via UKIPO. The High Court has held that where a party has successfully applied for invalidity before UKIPO and that decision has become final (ie, the owner of the invalidated registration has not appealed) then the claimant will be able to obtain summary judgment in proceedings for passing off.[1] The reason for this is that the defendant is estopped from arguing that passing off would not occur. Proceedings before UKIPO followed by a prompt request for summary judgment will often be much less expensive than proceedings for passing off which go to a full trial, although this route does depend on the decision of the UKIPO becoming final and not subject to any appeal.

1 *Evans t/a Firecraft v Focal Point Fires Plc* [2010] ETMR 29. See also *Slater v Anglo Atlantic Media Ltd* [2020] FSR 32.

15.08 Further, it is to be noted that references in the Act to a registered trade mark appear to be limited to a trade mark registration under the TMA 1994, or a registered collective mark or certification mark[1]. The version of s 11 in force between 14 January 2019 and 30 December 2020 included sub-s (1A), which expressly extended the same defence to registered EUTMs (ie the defence found in Art 16 of the EUTMR). Although s 11(1A) is now repealed and EUTMs have no force in the UK, the owner of an EUTM will instead also have the automatically generated replacement national registration, the 'comparable trade mark (EU)', to which the s 11 defence may apply.

1 Sections 1(2), 2(1) and 104 of the TMA 1994.

Descriptive use—s 11(2)/Art 14

15.09 Section 11(2) of the TMA 1994 and Art 14 of the EUTMR provide that a trade mark is not infringed by the use of:

(a) an individual's own name or address;
(b) non-distinctive indications, or indications of characteristics of goods or services; or
(c) the use of the trade mark to indicate the intended purpose of the goods or service.

However, the use may still infringe if it is not in accordance with honest practices in industrial or commercial matters. This section is important in the arena of comparative advertising, as to which see **Chapter 16**.

Use of one's own name—s 11(2)(a)/Art 14(1)(a)

15.10 A trade mark is not infringed by the use of an individual's own name or address provided such use is in accordance with honest practices in industrial or commercial matters.[1]

1 TMA 1994 s 11(2)(a) and EUTMR Art 14(a).

15.11 This defence covers use of a person's personal name or their address. Following amendment of this section on 14 January 2019 to comply with Directive 2015/2436, the own-name defence is available only for natural persons, but prior to that date it was also available to companies.[1] In the case of a company, the company was able to omit corporate suffixes such as 'Ltd' or 'Plc' and still benefit from this defence, but needed to be careful not to over-abbreviate its name in use or else risk the use no longer counting as its 'own name'.[2]

1 C-17/*06 Céline Sàrl v Céline SA* [2007] ECR I-7041 at [31]. Under the proposed Draft Regulation 2013/0088(COD) and Draft Directive 2013/0089(COD) the own-name defence would apply to personal names only.
2 *Premier Luggage & Bags Ltd v Premier Co (UK) Ltd* [2003] FSR 5.

15.12 When the defence was available to companies, the 'honest practices' proviso (considered further below) meant that it could rarely apply to the names of newly formed companies, or in other words to names only newly selected.[1] In *Cipriani* the own-name defence failed in respect of the company called Cipriani (Grosvenor Street) Ltd because the marks in question ('Cipriani' and 'Cipriani London') were not the defendant's actual name, notwithstanding the omission of stylings such as 'Ltd' (see *Celine*). The defence also failed in respect of another defendant, Mr Cipriani, because it was not him who was doing the acts complained of in relation to the marks.[2]

1 *Asprey & Garrard Ltd v WRA (Guns) Ltd* [2002] FSR 31.
2 *Hotel Cipriani Srl v Cipriani (Grosvenor Street) Ltd* [2008] EWHC 3032 (Ch) at [129]–[141].

Use of indications of characteristics—s 11(2)(b)/Art 14(1)(b)

15.13 Subject to the 'honest practices' proviso considered below, a registered trade mark is not infringed by the use of non-distinctive indications or of indications concerning characteristics of the goods or services in question. The TMA 1994 gives a non-exhaustive list of the kinds of characteristics that may be relevant—namely *'the kind, quality, quantity, intended purpose, value, geographical origin or time of production of goods or of rendering of services'*.

15.14 In many situations where this defence is relied upon, defendants may also be able to argue that there is no infringement because the registered trade mark is descriptive or non-distinctive such that there is no likelihood of confusion (see **Chapter 14**). In most such instances be necessary (or at least highly advisable) to challenge the validity of the registration via invalidation or revocation proceedings (see **Chapter 11**).

15.15 It is also important to consider whether the defendant is in fact using the 'indication' in question as a trade mark rather than a mere descriptor. In *British Sugar*[1] Jacob J held that if the defendant was using the indication as a trade mark, then even if it was potentially descriptive, it was not actually being used in a descriptive manner and so the s 11(2)(b) defence would not operate. However, the Court of Appeal in *Fine & Country*[2] clarified that this is not correct, in view of the CJEU's 2004 decision in *Gerolsteiner.*[3] In *Fine & Country*, the court pointed out that the mere fact that the word 'FINE' had been used as a brand or *quasi*-trade mark did not preclude the operation of this defence. In *Adam Opel*[4] the CJEU held that the defence did not apply in a case where the reproduction of the claimant's mark on replica cars was due to the replicas being faithful to the original and not so as to indicate to consumers a characteristic of them.

1 *British Sugar Plc v James Robertson & Sons Limited* [1997] ETMR 118.
2 *Fine & Country Ltd v Ototoks (formerly Spicerhaart Ltd)* [2013] EWCA Civ 672 at [116]–[119].
3 Case C-100/02 *Gerolsteiner Brunnen GmbH & Co v Putsch GmbH* [2004] RPC 39.
4 C-48/05 *Adam Opel AG v Autec AG* [2007] ETMR 33.

15.16 In the case of a claimant relying upon a registration comprising distinctive and non-distinctive elements, a defendant may again find it advisable to attack the registration. The claimant will be faced with the prospect of having to defend its registration and may have to adopt positions that will be prejudicial to its infringement claim. In addition, a defendant may also seek to rely on an obiter statement that was made in the *Whirlpool* case.[1] This questioned the validity of a registration consisting of descriptive and non-descriptive elements where no disclaimer was given of (exclusive) rights in the descriptive elements. As a result, the extent and nature of the rights provided by the registration were not clear.

1 *Whirlpool Corporation v Kenwood Limited* [2008] EWHC 1930 (Ch) per Geoffrey Hobbs QC.

15.17 In the *WET WET WET* case[1] the court found that the s 11(2)(b) defence operated where the defendant had used the registered trade mark WET WET WET as part of the title of a book—namely *A Sweet Little Mystery—Wet Wet Wet—The Inside Story*. This may suggest that the defence is available where the mark is used to describe the content of the goods. However, this will not always be the case—the classic example being the use of the name of a musical band or the name of a film for an audiovisual recording. If the defence were always available in such cases then the trade mark owner could not prevent the use of a trade mark to describe the content of counterfeit goods. It would appear that the question is very much dependant on the requirement that the use be in accordance with honest business practices, which is explained later in this chapter.

In *Betty Boop*[2] the court rejected the defendant's argument that its use of pictures of the well-known cartoon character in relation to unofficial products was simply descriptive—not least because the swing tags on the product also said 'officially licensed' or words to that effect. The judge also held that the use was not in accordance with honest practices.

A section 11(2)(b) defence also failed in *Glee Club*, as the word 'glee' was held not to be descriptive of the defendant's TV series.[3] In *Samuel Smith*[4] however, the court accepted that the use of a white rose was intended to be (and would be perceived by the average consumer as) an indication that the beers were brewed in, or associated with Yorkshire, namely the white rose was an indication concerning the geographical, UK county, origin of the goods.

1 *Bravado Merchandising Services Ltd v Mainstram Publishing (Edinburgh) Ltd* [1996] FSR 205.
2 *Hearst Holdings v AVELA* [2014] EWHC 439 (Ch) at [179]–[189].
3 *Comic Enterprises Ltd v Twentieth Century Fox Film Corporation* [2014] EWHC 185 (Ch) at [142]–[145].
4 *Samuel Smith Old Brewery (Tadcaster) v Philip Lee (trading as Cropton Brewery)* [2011] EWHC 1879 (Ch) at [111].

15.18 A good example of the importance of the 'honest practices' proviso (discussed further below) is *Hasbro Inc v 123 Nahrmittel GmbH*.[1] In that case Floyd J held that the defendant had taken unfair advantage of the claimant's PLAY-DOH mark by marketing its product as 'play dough', which was said to be merely descriptive. As such, the defendant had not complied with a duty to act fairly in relation to the trade mark owner, and, therefore, could not claim that the use was in accordance with honest commercial practices.

1 *Hasbro Inc v 123 Nahrmittel GmbH* [2011] EWHC 199 (Ch); [2011] ETMR 25 (11 February 2011).

Use to indicate intended purpose—s 11(2)(c)/Art 14(1)(c)

15.19 Subject again to the 'honest practice' proviso considered below, a registered trade mark is not infringed by the use of that trade mark to indicate the intended purpose of the goods (in particular as accessories or spare parts).[1] This provision seeks to preserve the public interest in competition in the provision of accessories and spare parts, but is of broader application than that.

1 TMA 1994 s 11(2)(c) and EUTMR Art 14(1)(c).

15.20 This defence requires the defendant to demonstrate that the use is 'necessary to indicate the intended purpose'.

Clearly, the meaning of 'necessary' determines the effectiveness of this provision. It was held in *Gillette* that the meaning of 'necessary' is not restricted to cases where the mark is required in order for the product to enter the market but also extends to cases where the mark is required in order for the product to be effectively marketed.[1] However, the mark must not be used in a way that suggests a commercial connection between the user of the mark and the mark's proprietor.[2] The principles were set out again by Arnold J in *DataCard*, citing the CJEU in *Gillette*:

- This provision merely requires that the use of the trade mark be necessary to indicate a given purpose of the product.
- The provision cites accessories or spare parts only an example, but it not limited to those categories.
- This defence covers the use of a trade mark to inform the public that the advertiser carries out the repair or maintenance of products bearing that trade mark that have been marketed under that mark by its owner, or with that owner's consent. Such use is necessary to preserve undistorted competition in the market for that product or service.
- The same applies to compatibility with the trade mark proprietor's products (in that case, razor blade handles).
- 'Necessity' entails that the use of the trade mark is, in practice, the only effective way of providing the relevant information. Only if there are other norms or standards that provide a full and comprehensible way of communicating the information will the use of the trade mark be deemed not necessary.

1 C-228/03 *Gillette Co v LA Laboratories OY* [2005] ETMR 67.
2 C-63/97 *Bayerische Motorenwerke AG v Deenik* [1999] ETMR 339.

15.21 An example would be the marketing of replacement razor blades to fit a branded product, as in the *Gillette* case. Assuming that no other intellectual property rights apply to the razor (particularly its handle) then a competitor may want to market replacement blades that fit the handle of a competitor. The competitor should be free to use the third-party trade mark to indicate that their blades fit the third-party handle.

15.22 Understandably, the freedom of the competitor to use another trader's trade mark is not absolute. There is substance in the argument that a defendant may not need to go beyond the mere word mark to indicate the intended purpose of the goods—for example, if the defendant uses the logo or stylised version of the trade mark which the trade mark owner has protected then the defence may not be available either because the use of the logo or stylised version is not necessary—the use of the word mark alone would suffice—or because the use is no longer in accordance with honest business practices.

The 'honest practices' proviso to s 11(2)/Art 14

15.23 Each of the defences available under s 11(2)/Art 14—ie, (a) use of an individual's own name or address; (b) descriptive uses; and (c) use to indicate the intended purpose of goods or services—is subject to the proviso that such use is *'in accordance with honest practices in industrial or commercial matters'*. This proviso is intended to provide a fair balance between the monopoly rights of trade mark registrations and the need to allow legitimate competition.

15.24 The meaning of the proviso has been considered by the CJEU in a number of cases including *Gillette*, where it described its purpose as encapsulating a 'duty to act fairly in relation to the legitimate interests of the trade mark proprietor'. For the application of these principles in the English courts, see *Hotel Cipriani,*[1] *Och-Ziff*[2] and *Samuel Smith,*[3] all decisions of Arnold J. The latter case considered the 'honest practices' provision in the context of a purported indicator of geographical origins, as opposed to the own-name defences raised in the earlier cases. The judge summarised the principles as follows:

- The requirement to act in accordance with honest practices in industrial or commercial matters constitutes in substance the expression of a duty to act fairly in relation to the legitimate interests of the trade mark proprietor.
- The court should carry out an overall assessment of all the relevant circumstances, and in particular should assess whether the defendant can be regarded as unfairly competing with the proprietor of the trade mark.

- An important factor is whether the use of the sign complained of either gives rise to consumer deception or takes unfair advantage of, or is detrimental to, the distinctive character, or repute of the trade mark. If it does, it is unlikely to qualify as being in accordance with honest practices.
- A mere likelihood of confusion will not disqualify the use from being in accordance with honest practices if there is a good reason why such a likelihood of confusion should be tolerated.

The court must balance the defendant's fair use of the mark against the legitimate interests of the mark's proprietor.[4] Arnold J set out a 'non-exhaustive' list of relevant factors at [118] of *Samuel Smith*, and went on to hold that the use of the sign ceased to be fair once the defendant knew that the Ministry of Defence (whose permission had been required to use the sign) had withdrawn permission in order to respect the claimant's trade mark rights. The Court of Appeal has since followed the same approach as Arnold J and in *Maier* described the test as requiring the court to 'carry out an overall assessment of all the circumstances and determine whether the defendant is competing fairly'.[5]

1 *Hotel Cipriani SRL and others v Cipriani (Grosvenor Street) Limited and others* [2009] RPC 9.
2 *Och-Ziff Management Europe Limited and another v Och Capital LLP and others* [2011] ETMR 1.
3 *Samuel Smith Old Brewery (Tadcaster) v Philip Lee (trading as Cropton Brewery)* [2011] EWHC 1879 (Ch) at [114]–[117].
4 C-245/02 *Anheuser-Busch Inc v Budejovicky Budvar Narodni Podnik* [2005] ETMR 27. See also *Hasbro Inc v 123 Nahrmittel GmbH* [2011] EWHC 199 (Ch); [2011] ETMR 25 (11 February 2011).
5 *Maier v ASOS Plc* [2015] ETMR 26.

15.25 In *Gerolsteiner* the Court stated that the mere fact that the use may cause confusion is not enough to conclude that the use is not in accordance with honest commercial practices. However, as explained in the *Gillette* case, the fact that there has been consumer confusion or damage to a mark or that advantage has been taken of a mark's reputation is relevant; use would not be in accordance with honest practices if:

- it is done in such a manner as to give the impression that there is a commercial connection between the third party and the trade mark owner;
- it affects the value of the trade mark by taking unfair advantage of its distinctive character or repute;
- it entails the discrediting or denigration of that mark; or
- the third party presents its product as an imitation or replica of the product bearing the trade mark of which it is not the owner.

Indeed, the courts now seem to treat a likelihood of confusion as incompatible with honest practices.[1] The defendant's knowledge is also relevant to the question of honesty, including the reasons for use of the mark.[2] In some circumstances, the court will take the view that the defendant should have known about the claimant's mark. Such was the case in *Betty Boop*, where the court held that the use was not in accordance with honest practices, because (among the various reasons given) the defendant knew of the claimant's marks and their reputation, and had also tried, and failed to object to registration of one of the claimant's EUTMs.[3] In contrast, an allegation of acting outside honest practices was rejected in *Evegate Publishing*.[4] Likewise in *Maier v ASOS*[5] the defendant had built up its business and good will prior to becoming aware of the claimant and it had never intended to confuse the public, so the own-name defence succeeded.

1 *Bayerischen Motoren Werke AG v Round & Metal Ltd* [2012] EWHC 2099 (Pat) at [113].
2 See C-245/02 *Anheuser-Busch Inc v Budejovicky Budvar Narodni Podnik* [2005] ETMR 27 and C-17/06 *Celine Sarl v Celine SA* [2007] ETMR 80.
3 *Hearst Holdings v AVELA* [2014] EWHC 439 (Ch) at [181]–[183].
4 *Evegate Publishing Limited v Newsquest Media (Southern) Limited* [2013] EWHC 1975 (Ch) at [209]–[223].
5 *Maier v ASOS* [2015] ETMR 26.

Use of earlier rights in a particular locality—s 11(3)/Art 138

15.26 Under s 11(3) TMA 1994 a registered trade mark is not infringed by the use in the course of trade in a particular locality of an earlier right that applies only in that locality. The equivalent provision in relation to EUTMs is Art 138 of the EUTMR. 'Earlier right' means any unregistered mark, or other sign used continuously in relation to goods or services, as long as that use began earlier than either of: first, the use of the registered trade mark, or second, the registration of the registered trade mark in respect of the relevant goods and services. Earlier rights only apply under this section to the extent that they would enable the unregistered mark or sign to be protected in that locality by virtue of any rule of law—in particular, passing off. As such, this defence is usually a question of applying the principles of passing off (as to which see **Chapter 20**) to the facts of the case. Such a defence was tested and found not to succeed in *Boxing Brands*[1] on the basis that the necessary goodwill was absent (at least in relation to the goods in question). In contrast, the court allowed a s 11(3) defence in *Redd* in relation to use of the sign 'Red' within the county of Northamptonshire.[2]

1 *Boxing Brands Ltd v Sports Direct International Plc* [2013] EWHC 2200 (Ch) at [81]–[96].
2 *Redd Solicitors v Red Legal* [2012] EWPCC 54 at [120]–[122].

ACQUIESCENCE—S 48/ART 61

15.27 Acquiescence can provide a complete bar to an infringement action. The TMA 1994 and EUTMR both provide that where the owner of the earlier trade mark or earlier right has acquiesced for a continuous period of five years in the use of a registered trade mark (ie use in the UK for the TMA 1994, and use 'in the Union' for the EUTMR), being aware of such use, there shall no longer be an entitlement on the basis of that earlier trade mark or earlier right to invalidate or oppose the use of the later trade mark in relation to the goods and services in relation to which it has been used.[1]

1 TMA 1994 s 48(1)(b) and EUTMR Art 61.

15.28 It should be noted that the existence of this statutory defence, derived from the Directive, does not extinguish or alter the possible availability of common law estoppel defences where circumstances permit.[1] Note, also that s 48(1) of the TMA 1994 and Art 61(1) specify that the defence of acquiescence is unavailable where the registration of the later mark was applied for in bad faith.

1 *Budějovickí Budvar, Národní Podnik v Anheuser-Busch, Inc* [2008] RPC 21.

15.29 The issue of whether a proprietor has 'acquiesced' where it knew of the other party's use but was unable to prevent it was considered by the CJEU in *Budweiser*.[1] In that case the particular issue was whether the defendant should be entitled to invalidate the claimant's later identical mark where the two sides, Budvar and Anheuser-Busch, had been trading under the identical brand name 'Budweiser' for many years. It happened that Anheuser's registration pre-dated that of Budvar, so it qualified as an earlier mark for invalidation purposes. Anheuser brought its invalidation action just a single day before the date five years from the registration of Budvar's mark, after which the action would have been debarred by acquiescence[2] so Budvar wanted to rely on the fact that Anheuser had put up with the use before the registration as well as after. Anheuser argued that the period of acquiescence could only begin to run from the date of registration, and that in any event Anheuser could not be said to have acquiesced when it had had no legal means of preventing Budvar's use, such avenues having been exhausted long previously.

1 See *Budějovickí Budvar, Národní Podnik v Anheuser-Busch, Inc* [2010] RPC 7.
2 Directive Art 9.

15.30 The CJEU took a strict view of the Directive's provisions on acquiescence, finding that on the ordinary meaning of the words, it could not be said that Anheuser had acquiesced in the use of the later mark where it had been unable to prevent that use.[1] It also held that the relevant period for acquiescence did only begin to run once the mark was registered. Significantly, however, whilst the CJEU rejected the acquiescence defence, it went on to hold that there were five clear factors (essentially all a direct result of the parties' many years of side-by-side use of the mark) which meant that the use of later mark was not liable to affect the essential function of Anheuser's identical mark, so that Anheuser's claim to invalidate Budvar's mark should not succeed (see the discussion on 'honest concurrent use' in **Chapter 5**).

1 C-482/09 *Budějovickí Budvar, Národní Podnik v Anheuser-Busch, Inc*, judgment of the CJEU, 22 September 2011.

EXHAUSTION OF RIGHTS—S 12/ART 15

15.31 Section 12 of the TMA 1994 provides that a registered trade mark is not infringed by the use of the trade mark in relation to goods that have been put on the market in the UK or the European Economic Area under that trade mark by the proprietor or with his consent, while Art 15 EUTMR provides the same for EUTMs but in relation to goods put on the market in the EEA only. In such a scenario, the proprietor's rights are said to have been 'exhausted' in respect of those goods. These provisions seek to reconcile the ability of a trade mark owner to control the use of his trade mark with the concept of free movement of goods within the Community (now the European Economic Area—the European Community plus Norway, Iceland and Liechtenstein). It can be seen that there is a degree of asymmetry as between the UK and EU provisions post-Brexit, so that for goods put on the market in the UK any EUTM rights are not deemed exhausted, but UK national rights are exhausted in relation to goods marketed outside the UK but within the EEA.

15.32 The provisions make an exception to the principle of exhaustion where there exist 'legitimate reasons for the proprietor to oppose further dealings with the goods', such as where the condition of the goods has been changed or impaired (see further below).

15.33 Part of the 'control' provided by trade mark rights is the ability to control the price at which products are sold, either directly via sales straight to the consumer, or indirectly via the sale price to wholesalers and distributors. This is often referred to as control of *first marketing* of the goods, following which the proprietor's control is exhausted and can no longer be exercised.[1] However, the price of goods in one country may differ substantially from that in another because of a number of factors, not least the perception of the product on different markets, and the differing financial means of consumers. For third parties, the existence of this differential in price presents an opportunity to profit by purchasing goods in a country where the sale price is low and reselling them in a country where the product has a higher. The differential is something exploited not only by smaller enterprising companies but also by very large multinationals with procurement departments seeking savings.

1 This fundamental point emerges from the CJEU in C-414/99 *Zino Davidoff* [2002] ETMR 9.

Exhaustion in Europe and beyond

15.34 As noted above, where goods have been placed on the market in the UK or EEA by the proprietor or with his consent then any UK rights are deemed exhausted, but the converse is not true for EUTM rights. Exhaustion of EUTM rights is confined to cases where goods have been placed on the market in the EEA, maintaining the European concept of free movement of goods within the EEA. Accordingly, marketing in the UK will not give rise to an exhaustion defence to EUTM rights. Any exhaustion defence is subject to the 'legitimate reasons' proviso considered at para **15.43** below.

15.35 What then if the goods have been placed on the market by the proprietor or with his consent, but in a country outside the UK and EEA? Many may feel that it is unfair that such goods should become subject to the full rights of the trade mark owner if they subsequently enter the UK or EEA. The question of whether such goods are subject to some kind of concept of 'international exhaustion' in relation to the EEA was considered in the *Silhouette* case.[1] The CJEU found that although the Directive did not provide guidance as to whether international exhaustion applies, the matter could not be left to the individual members to make their own provisions. Instead, the Court held that the principle of exhaustion did not operate and that it was confined to cases where the trade mark proprietor had consented to the importation into the EEA.

1 C-355/96 *Silhouette International Schmied GmbH & Co KG v Hartlauer Handelsgesellschaft mbH* [1998] ETMR 539.

15.36 Since the rules relating to exhaustion depend on whether or not the goods were put on the market in the UK or EEA by or with the consent of the trade mark proprietor, this is one of the first questions of fact which a defendant must address. Given that exhaustion constitutes a defence to a claim of infringement, the burden of proof is generally on the defendant.[1] In the *Van Doren* case, however, it was underlined that the burden of proof may be reversed (ie, the proprietor has to prove that the first marketing was in fact outside the EEA) where it might otherwise enable the trade mark owner to partition the internal market by putting pressure on the defendant.

1 C-244/00 *Van Doren + Q GmbH v Lifestyle sports + sportswear Handelsgesellschaft mbH* [2003] ETMR 75. See also *Honda Motor Co Ltd v David Silver Spares Ltd* [2010] FSR 40.

Acts amounting to first marketing

15.37 For the defence to apply, it must be shown that goods have been put on the market. This not always straightforward. For example:

- Even where the products are for eventual export (and even where the contract specifically states that the products are for export only), sales in the EEA to a purchaser constitute 'putting the goods onto the market'.[1]
- By contrast, where goods have been placed in the EEA-based stores of the trade mark owner but remained unsold, or where they are imported into the EEA by the trade mark owner with the mere intention of sales, the goods are deemed not to have been placed on the market.[2]

Note, also the decision of the Supreme Court in *Oracle v M-Tech* in relation to first marketing—see para **15.04** above.

1 C-16/03 *Peak Holdings v Axolin-Elinor AB* [2005] ETMR 28.
2 C-16/03 *Peak Holdings v Axolin-Elinor AB* [2005] ETMR 28.

15.38 In *L'Oréal v eBay*, questions about unboxed and tester products in the cosmetics industry were referred by Arnold J to the CJEU.[1] The response of the court was that:

- tester products and sampling bottles of cosmetics or perfumes marked 'demonstration' or 'not for sale' were, perhaps unsurprisingly, not put on the market simply by being supplied free of charge to authorised distributors for their intended purpose;[2] and
- unboxed cosmetics goods could not be said to have been put on the market where Community directives required that they be marketed in boxed condition with appropriate labelling, or where removing the packaging could be shown to damage the image of the product.

1 C-324/09 *L'Oréal SA v eBay International AG* [2009] EWHC 1094 (Ch); [2009] RPC 21.
2 See also C-127/09 *Coty Prestige Lancaster Group GmbH v Simex Trading AG* [2010] FSR 38.

By or with the consent of the proprietor

15.39 Assuming that a defendant can establish that the goods were first marketed inside the EEA, the defendant must also show that this was done by or with the consent of the proprietor. In *Sebago*[1] the Court found that consent must be shown in relation to the particular batch of products in question and could not be inferred from the fact that the proprietor had previously consented to the first marketing of the same or a similar type of goods.

1 C-173/98 *Sebago Inc. and Ancienne Maison Dubois et Fils SA v GB-Unic SA* [1999] ETMR 681.

Demonstrating consent

15.40 Consent falls into two types—express consent, and consent implied from actions or indirect comments. The former is clearly easier to establish.

15.41 The issue of consent arose in *Davidoff*[1] where the European Court found that:

- it was conceivable that implied consent could constitute sufficient consent;
- mere silence by the trade mark proprietor would not constitute implied consent;
- the lack of conditions placed upon the marketing of the goods initially marketed outside the EEA does not necessarily mean that there was any implied consent to their importation into the EEA;
- consent may be implied '*where it follows from facts and circumstances prior to, simultaneous with or subsequent to the placing of the goods on the market outside the EEA which ... unequivocally demonstrate that the proprietor has renounced his right to oppose placing of the goods on the market within the EEA*'; and
- consent cannot be implied from the fact that the trade mark owner has not communicated to all subsequent purchasers his opposition to the marketing and sale of the products in the EEA, nor from the absence of a warning on the product against their being placed on the market in the EEA.

1 C-414/99 *Zino Davidoff* [2002] RPC 20.

15.42 As a result, an importer wishing to demonstrate consent to the importation of non-EEA goods must show that there was unequivocal consent to the importation of the batch or batches in question. Such consent must usually originate from the proprietor, but in suitable cases may come from the proprietor's licensees.[1]

1 C-59/08 *Copad SA v Christian Dior Couture SA* [2009] FSR 22.

LEGITIMATE REASONS TO OPPOSE THE FURTHER DEALINGS IN THE GOODS

15.43 Section 12(2) of the TMA 1994 and Art 15(2) of the EUTMR provide that the exhaustion principle does not apply where 'legitimate reasons' exist to oppose further dealings in the goods. Examples given in s 12 of such legitimate reasons include a change in or impairment to the condition of the goods since their first marketing.

15.44 The majority of cases relating to exhaustion in the EEA have concerned pharmaceuticals or luxury branded goods. In the pharmaceuticals context, parallel importers have sometimes attempted to go beyond the 'mere' importation of the products by altering the goods themselves. For example, different countries may have different pack sizes, and so the importer has sought to repackage the original product according to these consumer expectations. In others, the importer has sought to apply the trade mark used for the product in the target country, rather than that used for the same product in other countries—sometimes that may be done by way of putting a label over the old trade mark ('overstickering') and in other cases by repackaging the goods entirely. Such activity has the potential to affect the essential function of the trade mark as a badge of origin and, therefore, has come under the scrutiny of the courts, which have examined what alteration of the goods may be permissible or justified.

15.45 In *Bristol-Myers Squibb*[1] the CJEU held that the trade mark owner has the right to prevent the repackaging of products under the 'legitimate reasons' principle. An importer must give the trade mark proprietor notice of their activities, but will be able to import without consent where:

- the use of the trade mark rights to prevent parallel imports would contribute to the artificial partitioning of markets between Member States;
- the repackaging does not adversely affect the original condition of the product;
- the presentation of the repackaged product is not such as to be liable to damage the reputation of the trade mark and of its owner—the packaging must not be defective, of poor quality, or untidy; and
- the parallel importer complies with certain obligations regarding labelling, notification and the provision of samples.

1 Joined cases C-427/93, C-429/93 and C-436/93 *Bristol-Myers Squibb v Paranova* [1996] ETMR 1.

The meaning of artificial partitioning

15.46 The law relating to parallel imports reflects a balance between the competing aims of respecting trade mark rights and the principle of free movement of goods in the UK/EEA. The court in *Bristol-Myers Squibb* underlined that it is not necessary that the trade mark owner intends to partition the market—the question is whether the enforcement of trade mark rights would have that effect. In considering whether artificial partitioning would result, the court must also consider whether the assertion of trade mark rights is necessary to protect the 'essential function' of the trade mark, namely to guarantee the source of the goods, and to ensure it is not subject to any third-party interference.

15.47 According to *Bristol-Myers Squibb*, where the proposed actions of the importer are not necessary to enable the goods to be marketed, the trade mark owner's attempts to prevent those actions will not contribute to the artificial partitioning of the market. However, the CJEU has subsequently underlined that 'necessary' is not limited to those acts *strictly* necessary for the products to be marketed, but also includes actions which are objectively required for effective access to the market. An example of this would be the repackaging of imported products rather than merely overstickering the appropriate trade mark. Whilst attaching the correct trade mark is all that is strictly necessary, if it is shown that consumers are particularly likely to reject overstickered products then repackaging may be necessary in order to access the market.[1]

1 C-443/99 *Merck, Sharp & Dohme GmbH v Paranova Pharmazeutika Handels GmbH* [2002] ETMR 80.

Adversely affecting the original condition of the product

15.48 In the case of repackaged goods, the trade mark owner will be entitled to oppose the use of the trade mark if the goods are taken out of packaging or are otherwise subject to steps that may affect the safety of the product. For example, that might be the omission of important accompanying information, or alternatively repackaging the products in poor-quality packets such that the goods will not be preserved properly or may become damaged.[1]

1 C-71/94 *Eurim-Pharm* [1997] 1 CMLR 1222.

Presentation not to affect the reputation of the trade mark or of its owner

15.49 It has been suggested that the trade mark owner may only oppose steps which are contrary to the usual presentation of the mark where the reputation would be 'seriously damaged'.[1] It has also been held that the use of a mark may be infringing where the goods are sold contrary to contractual conditions preventing their sale to certain types of stores, which is commonly done in order to preserve the exclusive nature of certain goods.[2] However, such an action may only succeed where the resale damages the reputation of the mark, so there may well be no claim if the brand in question does not benefit from a reputation sufficiently luxurious to be capable of sustaining damage through sales to low-end retailers. Of course, an action for breach of contract may still exist.

1 C-337/95 *Parfums Christian Dior SA and Parfums Christian Dior BV v Evora BV* [1998] ETMR 26.
2 C-59/08 *Copad SA v Christian Dior Couture SA* [2009] FSR 22.

15.50 In the case of pharmaceutical products, the issue has often been whether or not the parallel importer is entitled to design their own box, give prominence to their own mark, de-brand the product (ie, take off the original trade mark) or fail to make any reference to the trade mark owner. The CJEU has held that whether or not the importer's actions affect the reputation of the trade mark is a matter of fact for the national court to consider in each case.[1] The UK High Court in *Speciality European Pharma* held that an importer had infringed the mark 'REGURIN' where it had used the mark to rebrand the imported product but it was not objectively necessary to do so in order to gain access to the UK market.[2]

1 C-348/04 *Boehringer Ingelheim KG v Swingward Ltd* [2007] ETMR 71.
2 *Speciality European Pharma Limited v Doncaster Pharmaceuticals Group Ltd* [2013] EWHC 3624 (Ch).

Requirement to label, provide notice and provide samples

15.51 It was held in *Bristol-Myers Squibb* that the parallel importer must state who repackaged any product and the manufacturer of the product. He must also notify the trade mark owner before the product is put on sale[1] and, on demand, provide a specimen of the packaging. This applies in the case of overstickering, too, where there must be a clear reference to who overstickered the product.[2] However, in *Orifarm* the CJEU held that a trade mark proprietor could not object to remarketing merely on the ground that the new packaging did not indicate the actual repackager, but only the entity that had ordered the repackaging and taken responsibility for it.[3]

1 For a consideration of the remedies available where a party fails to notify, see *Hollister Inc v Medik Ostomy Supplies Ltd*, [2012] EWCA Civ 1419.
2 C-348/04 *Boehringer Ingelheim KG v Swingward Ltd* [2007] ETMR 71.
3 C-400/09 *Orifarm A/S v Merck Sharp & Dohme Corp* [2011] ETMR 59.

Disclaimers—s 13(1)(a)

15.52 The TMA 1994 s 13(1)(a) provides that the applicant for, or proprietor of, a registration may disclaim the rights to exclusive use of an element of the trade mark or agree a limitation to their rights (see para **15.57** below).

15.53 The purpose of a disclaimer is to exclude the ability to rely on a particular element in the absence of the other elements. An example might be a registration of the words ACME TRADE MARKS for 'legal services'. If the applicant accepted a disclaimer on the words TRADE MARKS then he or she could not prevent a third party using the words TRADE MARKS in their mark (or as their mark), but could nonetheless take action against the use of ACME or ACME TRADE MARKS by third parties.

15.54 The use of disclaimers has been limited substantially in recent times. Under the Trade Marks Act 1938 it was reasonably common to be asked to include a disclaimer of exclusive rights in elements of a mark. In overseas territories whose law is based upon the 1938 Act it is still common to face such requests.

15.55 Under the TMA 1994, the practice is typically to explore the registrability of the various elements in greater detail at the point at which they are relied upon. The requirement that there be a likelihood of confusion in order to prevent the use or registration of a similar mark will generally mean that where a trade mark has non-distinctive or descriptive elements, it will not be possible to challenge successfully the use of the non-distinctive or descriptive elements on their own, or to prevent the registration of a mark simply because it includes those non-distinctive elements.

15.56 It was suggested in *Whirlpool* that the use of disclaimers is important where a party obtains a registration of a mark comprising a non-distinctive shape in combination with a word or logo element.[1] This type of registration is liable to give rise to doubts about whether the owner is entitled to prevent the use of the shape on its own, not just in combination with the logo, and owners will often seek to take advantage of that uncertainty. The court in *Whirlpool* suggested that where a shape has been registered in combination with verbal or figurative elements, and where rights in the shape alone are not claimed, a disclaimer should be entered against the registration voluntarily by the proprietor of the mark under threat of cancellation of the registration.

1 *Whirlpool Corporation v Kenwood Limited* [2008] EWHC 1930 (Ch).

LIMITATIONS—S 13(1)(B)

15.57 Section 13(1)(b) of the TMA 1994 allows for applicants to agree to territorial or other limitations on their rights. The inclusion of such limitations generally indicates a compromise designed to reconcile a competing claim to rights in the mark. For example, this might be because a third party has unregistered rights in the mark in a specific locality part of the country, such that they would in theory be able to oppose the mark on the grounds of passing off. The effect of a limitation is that a proprietor's registration does not afford any rights beyond the specified limits. Limitations may not be expressed as a negative, ie, the goods or services not having a particular characteristic. An application to add a limitation is likely to be refused where it amounts to a modification of the mark itself rather than a limitation on the rights conferred by the mark.[1]

1 *Fromageries Bel v J Sainsbury plc* [2020] Bus LR 440 at [88]–[92].

THE RIGHTS OF CO-PROPRIETORS UNDER UK LAW

15.58 Whilst it may seem a somewhat strange way to view the effect of joint ownership, co-proprietors of a trade mark registration may be said to have a defence against each other in respect of any claim to infringement brought by the others.

The rights of co-owners are set out in s 23 of the TMA 1994, which provides that, subject to agreement between the co-owners, any of them is entitled to do anything which would otherwise amount to an infringement of the jointly-owned mark without permission of the other co-owners. However, permission of each co-owner is required in order to license, assign or charge the mark or any share in it.

Chapter 16

Comparative and misleading advertising, and malicious falsehood

INTRODUCTION

16.01 Comparative and misleading advertising is addressed by Directive 2006/114/EC (usually known as the Comparative Advertising Directive—or 'CAD'). The CAD is a codification of the law contained the earlier version, Directive 84/450/EEC, and the subsequent amendments to that Directive.

The CAD is implemented in the UK principally by the Business Protection from Misleading Marketing Regulations 2008 ('the BPMMR').[1] However, some aspects are implemented by the Consumer Protection from Unfair Trading Regulations 2008 (as amended).[2] Enforcement is shared between local trading standards authorities and the Office of Fair Trading.

1 SI 2008/1276. The CAD was formerly implemented by the Control of Misleading Advertising Regulations 1988, SI 1988/915. As of 14 November 2013 the BPMMR are subject to minor amendments relating to the Gas and Electricity Markets Authority, but these do not have any significant bearing on the general content of this chapter.

2 SI 2008/1277.

16.02 This chapter focuses on the use of trade marks in comparative advertising, rather than attempting to cover all aspects of misleading and comparative advertising. Although the CAD does not have direct effect in the UK, the BPMMR transliterates the important concepts directly from the CAD, and must be construed in light of that directive. Accordingly, it is generally most convenient to refer to the original language of the CAD.

16.03 In so far as it relates to trade marks, the law of comparative advertising typically comes into play when one provider of goods or services uses the registered mark or marks of another provider in order to make claims about the relative merits or qualities of their respective goods or services. If the trade mark proprietor claims that this constitutes an infringement, the party using the trade mark for comparative purposes will wish to show that such use is permissible or justified under the relevant legislation.

16.04 There is a series of UK cases that focused on the (now repealed) s 10(6) of the Trade Marks Act 1994 ('TMA 1994'), which for a time was treated as the relevant provision governing comparative advertising.[1] However, s 10(6) has no specific equivalent in the Directive. After it was criticised by the Court of Appeal in *O2 v Hutchinson*[2] as being 'an unnecessary distraction in an already complicated branch of the law', it appeared to be otiose. It was repealed in 2018.

1 See eg, *British Airways Plc v Ryanair Ltd* [2001] FSR 32 (which concerned Ryanair advertisements referring *inter alia* to 'EXPENSIVE BA … DS!'). In that case Jacob J made the generally applicable point that the courts will not suppress honest comparative adverts where a competitor does not like the adverts precisely because they are true.

2 *O2 Holdings Ltd v Hutchison 3G UK Ltd* [2006] EWCA Civ 1656; [2007] ETMR 19.

16.05 It is clear from *O2 v Hutchison* and from the decision of the CJEU[1] that the relevant legislation (in addition to the CAD) is Art 6(1) of the Directive, as enacted in s 11(2)(b) of the TMA 1994. This provides a defence where comparative use of a registered mark is 'in accordance with honest practices in business and commercial matters'. For these purposes, use of another party's trade mark will be in accordance with the 'honest practices' requirement of s 11(2)(b) if that use complies with the CAD.

1 *O2 Holdings Ltd v Hutchison 3G UK Ltd* [2006] EWCA Civ 1656; [2007] ETMR 19 and C-533/06 *O2 Holdings Ltd v Hutchison 3G UK Ltd* EU:C:2008:339; [2008] ETMR 55.

16.06 It should be noted that there is no specific tort of misleading advertising created under the CAD regime. However, prior to the advent of European influence in this area, traders often used the tort of malicious falsehood or trade libel to complain of comparative or misleading advertising that affected them. This tort will be examined in brief in the latter part of this chapter. The tort is still frequently referred to but its utility in comparative advertising situations has reduced since the advent of the European legislation and subsequent case law.

GENERAL SCHEME OF THE CAD

16.07 Leaving aside the later provisions of the CAD dealing with implementation and enforcement, the scheme of the directive is fairly simple.

- Article 4 provides that comparative advertising is permitted as long as eight conditions (a)–(h) are met, the first of which is the important requirement that the advertising is not misleading.
- Article 2 contains certain key definitions, such as 'comparative advertising' and 'misleading advertising'.
- Article 3 provides a supplementary list of factors that must be taken into account when weighing up whether or not advertising is misleading.

The definitions in Article 2

16.08 Article 2 of the CAD contains the following five core definitions:[1]

(a) Advertising:

> 'the making of a representation in any form in connection with a trade, business, craft or profession in order to promote the supply of goods or services …'

(b) Misleading advertising:

> 'any advertising which in any way, including its presentation, deceives or is likely to deceive the persons to whom it is addressed or whom it reaches and which, by reason of its deceptive nature, is likely to affect their economic behaviour or which, for those reasons, injures or is likely to injure a competitor.'

(c) Comparative advertising:

> 'any advertising which explicitly or by implication identifies a competitor or goods or services offered by a competitor'

(d) Trader:

> 'any natural or legal person who is acting for purposes related to his trade, craft, business or profession and anyone acting in the name of or on behalf of a trader'

(e) Code owner:

> 'any entity, including a trade or group of traders, which is responsible for the formulation and revision of a code of conduct and/or for monitoring compliance with the code by those who have undertaken to be bound by it'.

In *Toshiba Europe*[2] and subsequent cases, the CJEU has held that these provisions should be interpreted in a liberal manner most favourable to permitting such advertisements, with the aim of encouraging legitimate competition.

In *Belgian Electronic Sorting Technology* the CJEU held that 'advertising' could include the use of a domain name and metatags within a website's metadata, but not the mere registration of the domain name; that was just a formal act rather than a form of commercial representation.[3]

1 See BPMMR regs 2 and 3(2). The definitions under the CAD and the BPMMR are materially the same.
2 C-112/99 *Toshiba Europe GmbH v Katun Germany GmbH* EU:C:2001:566; [2002] FSR 39.
3 C-657/11 *Belgian Electronic Sorting Technology NV v Peelaers* EU:C:2013:516; [2013] ETMR 45.

16.09 One obvious question that arises from the definition of 'comparative advertising' is who is a 'competitor'? If the advertising has no effect on a competitor, on the face of it the CAD provisions are irrelevant. The CJEU in *Landtsheer*[1] identified a number of different factors to be considered when deciding whether two undertakings have the status of competitors:

- the nature of the goods or services, particularly whether one can be substituted for the other;
- the current and possible future development of the market for those goods or services;
- the geographical extent of the advertising; and
- the characteristics of the product which are promoted and the image the advertiser is attempting to impart.

1 C-381/05 *De Landtsheer Emmanuel SA v Comite Interprofessionel du Vin de Champagne* EU:C:2007:230; [2007] ETMR 69.

16.10 The CJEU also held that, in principle, reference to a type of competitor product (rather than a specific competitor) will fall within the ambit of the CAD. The reason is that such advertising effectively makes a comparison with all competitors who make that particular product, even though none of those competitors have been referred to by name or brand. Comparative advertising may also entail using identifiers other than a competitor's trade mark, such as a logo or an image of a shop front, but such use is subject to the same requirements as use of trade marks.[1]

1 C-44/01 *Pippig Augenoptik GmbH & Co KG v Hartlauer Hendelsgesellschaft mbH* EU:C:2003:205; [2004] ETMR 5.

Misleading advertising—Article 3

16.11 Although a comprehensive treatment of misleading advertising is outside the scope of this book, it is important to understand a little about what may constitute misleading advertising since, as already noted, comparative advertising is only permitted where it is not misleading. Article 3 of the CAD states that in deciding whether advertising is misleading[1] account shall be taken of all the features of the advertisement and goes on, helpfully, to list particular features to be considered it states (with emphasis added) that:

'account shall be taken of all [the advertisement's] features, and in particular of any information it contains concerning:

(a) **the characteristics of goods or services**, such as their availability, nature, execution, composition, method and date of manufacture or provision, fitness for purpose, uses, quantity, specification, geographical or commercial origin or the results to be expected form their use, or the results and material features of tests or checks carried out on the goods or services;

(b) **the price** or the manner in which the price is calculated, and the **conditions** on which the goods are supplied or the services provided;

(c) **the nature, attributes and rights of the advertiser**, such as his identity and assets, his qualifications and ownership of industrial, commercial or intellectual property rights or his awards and distinctions.'

1 See BPMMR reg 3(3)–(5).

16.12 Note, that in some circumstances it may be misleading to leave out the brand name of a better-known brand in comparative advertising.[1]

1 C-44/01 *Pippig Augenoptik GmbH & Co KG v Hartlauer Hendelsgesellschaft mbH* EU:C:2003:205; [2004] ETMR 5.

Allowable comparative advertising—Article 4

16.13 Under Art 4 of the CAD[1] comparative advertising (ie, advertising identifying a competitor or their goods or services) is permitted provided the following eight conditions are met (again with emphasis added):

'(a) it is **not misleading**…;[2]

(b) it compares goods or services **meeting the same needs or intended for the same purpose**;[3]

(c) it **objectively compares** one or more material, relevant, verifiable and representative **features** of those goods and services, which may include price;[4]

(d) it **does not discredit or denigrate** the trade marks, trade names, other distinguishing marks, goods, services, activities or circumstances of a competitor;

(e) for products with designation of origin, it relates in each case to products with the **same designation**;

(f) it **does not take unfair advantage of the reputation of a trade mark**, trade name or other distinguishing marks of a competitor or of the designation of origin of competing products;

(g) it **does not present goods or services as imitations or replicas** of goods or services bearing a protected mark or trade name;

(h) it **does not create confusion among traders**, between the advertiser and a competitor or between the advertiser's trade marks, trade names, other distinguishing marks, goods or services and those of a competitor.'

1 See BPMMR reg 4.
2 In the sense of CAD Articles 2(b), 3 and 8(1), and/or by reference to Directive 2005/29/EC of 11 May 2005 concerning unfair business-to-consumer commercial practices.
3 This is not to be equated with the test for whether there is a competitive relationship between the undertakings such as to engage CAD: see C-381/05 *De Landtsheer Emmanuel SA v Comite Interprofessionel du Vin de Champagne* EU:C:2007:230; [2007] ETMR 69.
4 See, for example, C-112/99 *Toshiba Europe GmbH v Katun Germany GmbH* EU:C:2001:566; [2002] FSR 39.

16.14 Note, that Member States are not free to apply their own stricter standards: the lawfulness of comparative advertising must be determined solely by reference to the CAD—see *Pippig Augenoptik*[1] and *Lidl SNC*.[2] The CJEU in *Pippig* stated that it may be legitimate to compare products sold through different distribution channels even if that comparison suggests a larger price difference than was average for those products. The use of test purchases in assembling comparative advertising information was also held to be permissible. The Court found that making a price comparison, even an unfavourable one, does not in itself amount to denigration within the meaning of what is now Art 4(d) of the CAD.

1 C-44/01 *Pippig Augenoptik GmbH & Co KG v Hartlauer Hendelsgesellschaft mbH* EU:C:2003:205; [2004] ETMR 5.
2 C-159/09 *Lidl SNC v Vierzon Distribution SA* EU:C:2010:696; [2011] ETMR 6.

16.15 As regards Art 4(e) of the CAD, where the product being advertised does not benefit from a designation of origin, it is not automatically impermissible to refer to the designation of origin of the products being compared. However, in assessing whether such comparisons are lawful, the court should look at whether the aim of the advertisement 'is solely to distinguish between the differences between the products of the advertiser and those of his competitor and thus to highlight differences objectively'.[1]

1 C-381/05 *De Landtsheer Emmanuel SA v Comite Interprofessionel du Vin de Champagne* EU:C:2007:230; [2007] ETMR 69.

16.16 In *Lidl Belgium*[1] the CJEU considered advertising comparing two 'sample baskets' of products. The Court held that such advertising was permissible in principle, provided the condition of objective comparison was satisfied. In such a situation, fulfilment of the objective comparison condition does not require each and every product to be exhaustively listed in the advertisement. However, a general claim to be cheaper overall may be misleading if the advertisement does not make clear that the comparison is based on a limited selection of products, or does not give some details of that selection.

1 C-356/04 *Lidl Belgium GmbH & Co KG v Etablissementen Franz Colruyt NV* EU:C:2006:585; [2007] ETMR 28.

16.17 The CJEU held in *Toshiba Europe*[1] that the use of a manufacturer's product numbers in a competitor's catalogue that listed spare parts could in principle constitute legitimate comparative advertising. However, if the persons at whom the catalogue was directed would associate the original manufacturer's reputation with the competitor's products, an unfair advantage was taken. Account has to be taken of the overall presentation of the advertising and the type of persons for whom it is intended. In contrast, the CJEU said in the case of *Siemens* that no unfair advantage is taken of the reputation of a distinguishing mark merely by using it in a catalogue where the goods were for sale to specialists who would not be confused between the two companies.[2]

1 C-112/99 *Toshiba Europe GmbH v Katun Germany GmbH* EU:C:2001:566; [2002] FSR 39.
2 C-59/05 *Siemens AG v VIPA Gesellschaft für Visualisierung und Prozeßautomatisierung mbH* EU:C:2006:147; [2006] ETMR 47.

16.18 Unfair advantage was explored further in *L'Oreal v Bellure*,[1] in which the CJEU looked at the scenario where a competitor had used trade marks of L'Oréal's premium brands in a comparison list to draw attention to 'smell-alike' perfumes made by the competitor. The Court was asked whether a likelihood of confusion was a necessary ingredient of 'unfair advantage', and whether comparative advertising could be stopped even where it did not jeopardise the 'essential function' of the mark (ie, the mark as a badge of origin). The Court was also asked whether presenting imitation products fell within Art 4(f)–(g) of the CAD.[2]

1 C-487/07 *L'Oreal SA v Bellure NV* EU:C:2009:378; [2009] ETMR 55.
2 In fact the Court referred to the pre-codification version of the legislation, but the differences are not material for these purposes.

16.19 The Court held that such lists were capable of amounting to comparative advertising, and that the use of the comparison list had certain specific effects. However, the Court also said that the comparison may not be permitted even if there was no likelihood of confusion among the relevant public and no detriment to the mark—merely to take unfair advantage of the mark's repute would suffice for the advertising to be objectionable. Furthermore, the use of the trade marks in this way *was* taking an advantage of the mark with the reputation, and that this advantage *was* unfair within the meaning of Art 4(f) of the CAD since the advertiser sought to 'ride on the coat tails' of the mark with the reputation without paying any compensation for the proprietor's marketing efforts. The Court also said that if the conditions of Art 4 of the CAD are not fulfilled, the use of the trade marks on the comparison list may constitute infringement under Art 5(1)(a) even though the essential function of the trade mark is unaffected, since the trade mark's other functions, in particular the advertising function, may be affected. Lastly the Court ruled that implied statements that the perfumes were imitations or replicas of some sort did not satisfy the condition set out in Art 4(g) of the CAD.

16.20 The condition included in Art 4(h)[1] was analysed by the CJEU in *O2 v Hutchison*.[2] In that case, the Court was asked to look at the interaction between the CAD and trade mark infringement, particularly the likelihood of confusion under Art 5(1)(b) of the Trade Marks Directive (s 10(2) of the TMA 1994). The Court ruled that the word 'confusion' is to be interpreted in the same way in both the Directive and in Art 4(h) of the CAD. Consequently, an advertiser who uses a competitor's trade marks in such as way as to infringe under Art 5(1)(b) will not fulfil condition (h) and thus the advertising will not be permitted under CAD.[3] If, however, the use is such that there is no likelihood of confusion, then condition (h) will be satisfied. Thus, the facts of each case must be examined to see whether there is the requisite confusion and in particular whether there is relevant use of the mark in those specific circumstances so as to affect its essential function. Note also that the use must also not succumb to the pitfalls identified in *L'Oréal v Bellure*.[4] In *O2* itself, the CJEU came to the view that the advertisement as a whole was not misleading and did not suggest a commercial link between O2 and Hutchinson. Thus there was no likelihood of confusion within the meaning of Art 5(1)(b).

1 The pre-codification wording was as follows: 'it does not create confusion in the market place between the advertiser and a competitor or between the advertiser's trade marks, trade names, other distinguishing marks, goods or services and those of a competitor'.
2 C-533/06 *O2 Holdings Ltd v Hutchison 3G UK Ltd* EU:C:2008:339; [2008] ETMR 55.
3 See, for example, *Hasbro Inc v 123 Nahrmittel GmbH* [2011] EWHC 199 (Ch); [2011] ETMR 25 at [224] per Floyd J.
4 C-487/07 *L'Oreal SA v Bellure NV* EU:C:2009:378; [2009] ETMR 55.

16.21 The European jurisprudence was considered by an English court in *Rockwool v Kingspan*.[1] In that case, the defendant had made a promotional video of a dramatic fire-safety demonstration, purporting to show the relative inferiority of the claimant's fire-retarding products. Kitchin J held that the video was misleading and failed to make an objective comparison of material, verifiable and representative features of the parties' products. However, the claimant lost its claim for malicious falsehood—as to which, see below.

1 *Kingspan Group Plc v Rockwool Ltd* [2011] EWHC 250 (Ch).

MALICIOUS FALSEHOOD

16.22 Malicious falsehood is a cause of action arising under the common law. It encompasses a number of acts, and is variously referred to as trade libel, injurious falsehood, slander of title and slander of goods. The usual starting point is where a claimant says that some third party has published an untrue and harmful statement about the claimant's goods. The claimant must then prove that:[1]

- the statement was published to someone other than the claimant, and was untrue;
- the statement was made maliciously; and
- the claimant has suffered special damage as a result.[2]

The limitation period for claims in malicious falsehood is 12 months, but this is subject to the court's discretion to extend the time if it is thought equitable to do so.[3]

1 See, for example, *Kaye v Robertson* [1991] FSR 62, in which Glidewell LJ also considered the more familiar causes of action of libel and passing off. For an example of a claim that failed to meet the various elements of the tort, see *C v T BC* [2014] EWHC 2482 (QB); [2015] ELR 1.
2 However, s 3(1) of the Defamation Act 1952 provides that no special damage need be proved where (*inter alia*) the statement is in the form of words published in writing or some other permanent form and is calculated to case pecuniary damage to the claimant.
3 Limitation Act 1980, ss 4A and 32A (as amended by the Defamation Act 1996 s 5).

16.23 Malicious falsehood may well be committed in a case involving comparative advertising and/or groundless threats, where untrue statements about third-party goods or services or the behaviour of third parties may be made with malice and with the aim of causing the third party's business to suffer. The tort may also be committed in passing off cases, where a party passes off its own inferior goods as being the goods of the claimant.[1]

In *Niche Products* the question arose whether a statement could constitute an objectionable statement for the purposes of the tort where it comprised a letter sent by the defendant to various customers, stating the claimant had issued a 'misleading' and 'erroneous' report about a change in the composition of the defendant's goods.[2] The defendant argued that the statement had to be about the claimant's goods or business. The court disagreed and refused to strike out the claim, on the basis that the statement amounted to a comment on something emanating from the claimant, and as such was addressing what that competitor's business was doing.

1 *Wilts UDL v Thomas Robinson Sons & Co Ltd* [1957] RPC 220, where old stock was passed off as being new, harming the plaintiff.
2 *Niche Products Ltd v MacDermid Offshore Solutions LLC* [2013] EWHC 3540 (IPEC); [2014] EMLR 9.

Definition of malice

16.24 Malice is taken to mean a dishonest or improper motive. It has been said that it is not malicious to make in good faith a statement that turns out to be incorrect, even if the statement is made by the defendant in its own interest.[1] It has also been said that 'negligence is quite different from malice'.[2] This contrasts with the following two instances, which have been said to constitute malicious misrepresentations:[3]

1 a statement which is false and published with the intention of injuring the claimant even if the defendant thought the statement to be true; and
2 a statement which is false, and which the defendant knew to be false, regardless of whether it was intended to injure.

1 *Balden v Shorter* [1933] Ch 427. See also *Greers Ltd v Pearman and Corder Ltd* (1922) 39 RPC 406.
2 *Khader v Aziz* [2009] EWHC 2027 (QB), 31 July 2009.
3 *Wilts UDL v Thomas Robinson Sons & Co Ltd* [1957] RPC 220.

16.25 Further, malice may be found where the defendant was reckless as to the truth of the statement—ie, where the defendant did not consider or care whether or not the statement was true.[1] This is a subjective concept, so the defendant will not be found reckless (and therefore malicious) if they can show that they really did believe the statement, even if the belief is irrational. In *Niche Products* the court rejected the defendant's suggestion that the pleading of malice was 'speculative' and should be struck out.[2] In *Cruddas* a claim of malice was upheld where two journalists had known that their articles were false in the meanings that the journalists knew that those articles bore, and they had a dominant intention to injure the claimant.[3] In that case, the publisher of the newspapers was also vicariously liable for the articles. On appeal the court upheld findings of malicious falsehood in respect of the secondary meanings of the articles.[4]

1 *Kaye v Robertson* [1991] FSR 62. See also *Tesla Motors Ltd v BBC* [2011] EWHC 2760 (QB).
2 *Niche Products Ltd v MacDermid Offshore Solutions LLC* [2013] EWHC 3540 (IPEC); [2014] EMLR 9.
3 *Cruddas v Calvert* [2013] EWHC 2298 (QB).
4 [2015] EWCA Civ 171; [2015] EMLR 16.

The meaning of the statement

16.26 Standard defamation cases involve what is often called the 'one-meaning rule'—that is, the claimant must identify the 'natural and ordinary meaning' of the words and show that the meaning is defamatory. Many libel cases focus on attempts to strike out the claim on the basis that the words complained of do not support the alleged defamatory meaning.

16.27 The one-meaning rule used also to be applied in malicious falsehood cases. Indeed, in *Vodafone*[1] both parties agreed that that rule applied—although Jacob J expressed his sympathy for an alternative approach whereby the claimant need only show that a substantial number of people would give the words complained of the meaning alleged by the claimant. Subsequently, however, the application of the one-meaning rule to malicious falsehood cases has been comprehensively rejected. In *Ajinomoto Sweeteners Europe SAS v Asda Stores Ltd*[2] the Court of Appeal held that the rule was 'anomalous, frequently otiose and, where not otiose, unjust'. It found instead that a court should consider what meaning or meanings the words complained of would really have borne to relevant customers and if, when viewed in this way, there was a damaging meaning to the words, the court should go on to consider whether there was proof of malice in relation to that damaging meaning. In the course of the *Cruddas* litigation the Court of Appeal has restated this principle, saying that:[3] 'In malicious falsehood every reasonably available meaning, damaging or not, has to be considered.'.

1 *Vodafone Group plc v Orange Personal Communications Services Ltd* [1997] FSR 34.
2 *Ajinomoto Sweeteners Europe SAS v Asda Stores Ltd* [2010] EWCA Civ 609; [2010] FSR 30.
3 *Cruddas v Calvert* [2013] EWCA Civ 748; [2014] EMLR 5 at [32]. See also [2015] EWCA Civ 171; [2015] EMLR 16.

Damage

16.28 Aside from the statutory provisions making it unnecessary to show special damage in some cases (see **16.22** above), the claimant must generally show that it has suffered some actual loss. This must be the direct result of the statements made by the defendant. It might, for example, comprise loss of custom, or perhaps the one-off loss of a particular contract.

Hyperbole and puffery

16.29 In deciding whether a statement is malicious, account will be taken of puffery, hyperbole and the general nature of the market for the products involved.[1] There is a difference between unlawful disparagement and legitimately advancing one's own products at the expense of others, or publicising the strong points of one's products without mentioning other aspects in which the competitors' products may be better.

1 *Vodafone Group plc v Orange Personal Communications Services Ltd* [1997] FSR 34, per Jacob J at [3].

16.30 The difference between sharp advertising practice and unacceptable falsehood is something of a moving target, and much will depend on the products involved. In the case of pharmaceuticals there may be very little room for overblown claims because of the public's expectation of accuracy[1] whereas mobile telephone tariffs may be less transparent.[2] In the latter case, the judge pointed out that the more precise the claim, the more likely it is that the public would expect it to be accurate. This balancing act has interesting implications for the toiletries and cosmetics industry, which has increasingly focused on advertising products with extraordinary claims about their functional benefits. At the same time, the public is clearly aware to some extent that much of this is vague puffery and relies on *faux*-scientific research, such as the use of surveys with statistically insignificant numbers of participants. It would seem that these products are closer to mobile phone tariffs. As such, producers would do well to keep their claims vague in nature and avoid referring to competitors.

1 *Ciba-Geigy v Parke Davis & Co Ltd* [1994] FSR 8.
2 *Vodafone Group plc v Orange Personal Communications Services Ltd* [1997] FSR 34, per Jacob J at [39].

Malicious falsehood and comparative advertising

16.31 A claim for malicious falsehood may often be pleaded alongside a claim for trade mark infringement in a situation where there has been comparative advertising. However, it usually adds little to the claimant's prospects of success in such cases.[1] As has been seen, the use of third-party trade marks is acceptable in comparative advertising where the use meets the requirements of the CAD, so it would be strange if an advert were found not to infringe a registered trade mark but nevertheless to constitute a malicious falsehood. Pleading malicious falsehood is more likely to assist where the advertiser has not used the claimant's trade marks, but has made the reference clear through other means.

1 A parallel claim for malicious falsehood failed in *Kingspan Group Plc v Rockwool Ltd* [2011] EWHC 250 (Ch).

Relief

16.32 The usual remedies of damages and final injunctions are available. Claimants may recover their pecuniary losses and may also, following the decision of the Court of Appeal in *Khodaparast v Shad*[1] be awarded aggravated damages for distress and injury to feelings.

1 *Khodaparast v Shad* [2000] 1 WLR 618.

16.33 Interim injunctions are also available. However, in *Boehringer v VetPlus*[1] the Court of Appeal held that, although essentially a commercial dispute, interim injunction applications relating to comparative advertising must be treated as involving issues of freedom of expression. As such, an application for an interim injunction will not be assessed purely by reference to the familiar *American Cyanamid* principles;[2] the claimant must satisfy the court that it is 'likely' to receive a final injunction at trial (ie, adopting the rule set out in *Bonnard v Perryman*[3] in relation to defamation). An interim injunction in a claim for malicious falsehood was granted in *Francotyp-Postalia.*[4]

1 *Boehringer Ingelheim Ltd v Vetplus Ltd* [2007] EWCA Civ 583; [2007] FSR 29.
2 *American Cyanamid Co v Ethicon Ltd* [1975] AC 396 (UKHL)
3 [1891] 2 Ch 269.
4 *Francotyp-Postalia v Mailing Room* [2014] EWHC 4521 (QB). The extent of the injunctive relief was limited on appeal: [2015] EWCA Civ 1167.

Chapter 17

Remedies

INTRODUCTION

17.01 This chapter looks at the remedies for:

(a) Infringement of a registered trade mark.
(b) Infringement of marks entitled to protection under the Paris Convention ('well-known trade marks')—s 56(2) of the Trade Marks Act 1994 ('TMA 1994').
(c) Unauthorised application for the registration of the mark made by an agent or representative of the proprietor of a mark—s 60 of the TMA 1994.
(d) Unauthorised use of the Royal Arms, etc—s 99(4) of the TMA 1994.

It will also consider the position regarding co-proprietors and licensees, and the jurisdiction of the various courts.

REMEDIES FOR INFRINGEMENT OF REGISTERED TRADE MARKS

Remedies—UK trade marks

17.02 Where a registered UK trade mark has been infringed, there are a number of possible remedies available to the proprietor or exclusive licensee[1], namely:

(a) Damages—s 14(2) of the TMA 1994.
(b) Account (of profits)—s 14(2) of the TMA 1994.
(c) Injunction—s 14(2) of the TMA 1994.
(d) Any other relief which would be available in respect of the infringement of any other property right—s 14(2) of the TMA 1994.
(e) Erasure, removal or obliteration of an 'offending sign'—s 15(1) of the TMA 1994.
(f) Destruction of infringing goods—s 15(2) of the TMA 1994.
(g) Delivery up of infringing goods, material or articles—s 16 of the TMA 1994.

(h) Destruction or forfeiture of infringing goods, material or articles—s 19(1) of the TMA 1994.
(i) Prohibition on the importation of infringing goods, material or articles where notice is given to the relevant Customs—s 89 of the TMA 1994 and, more importantly, Regulation (EU) No 608/2013.[2]

1 TMA 1994 ss 2(1), 14 and 31(1)–(2).
2 As amended by The Customs (Enforcement of Intellectual Property Rights) (Amendment) (EU Exit) Regulations 2019, SI 2019/514 with effect from 11pm on 31 December 2020 when the UK's withdrawal from the EU became effective.

Remedies—the effect of Brexit; comparable trade marks (EU)

17.03 Since the UK's withdrawal from the EU became effective at 11pm on 31 December 2020, EU trade marks ('EUTMs') have been of no effect in the UK and actions in respect of them can no longer be brought before the UK courts. However, a EUTM that was in existence at that date is treated as having been registered under the TMA 1994. Such marks are referred to as comparable trade marks (EU) and, unless otherwise provided in Sch 2A of the TMA 1994, the provisions of the TMA 1994 apply to them.[1] Accordingly, the remedies referred to above will apply to a claim for infringement of such a mark.

Where proceedings in respect of an EUTM commenced before 11pm on 31 December 2020, Sch 2A of the TMA 1994 provides that the provisions of the EU Trade Mark Regulation 2017 governing jurisdiction and procedure[2] continue to apply (subject to certain exceptions).[3] Thus, a UK court hearing such proceedings may still grant the remedies applicable in respect of these marks as EUTMs (as to which see below), including an injunction covering the EU in respect of the mark as an EUTM. However, Sch 2A also gives the UK court power to grant an injunction in the UK in respect of the comparable trade mark (EU) that replaced the EUTM in the UK on 31 December 2020, or to revoke such a mark.[4]

1 TMA 1994 Sch 2A as amended by The Trade Marks (Amendment etc) (EU Exit) Regulations 2019, SI 2019/269 and the Intellectual Property (Amendment etc) (EU Exit) Regulations 2020, SI 2020/1050. Such a mark is referred to as a 'comparable trade mark' (EU).
2 Ie Chapter X of the EU Trade Mark Regulation (EU 2017/1001). Chapter X consists of EUTMR Arts 122–135. In the case of comparable trade marks (EU), the application of Art 128(2), (4), (6) and (7) and Art 132 are excluded.
3 See TMA 1994 Sch 2A para 20(1) and (2).
4 See TMA 1994 Sch 2A para 20(3) and (4).

Remedies—EUTMs

17.04 EUTMs remain of effect in the continuing countries of the EU. Where a court in a continuing Member State of the EU has jurisdiction in relation to EUTMs, Art 17 of the European Union Trade Marks Regulation

('EUTMR') provides that the *effects* of an EUTM are governed solely by the provisions of the EUTMR but that, in other respects, infringement of an EUTM is governed by the national law relating to infringement of a national trade mark in accordance with the provisions of Chapter X of the EUTMR.[1] Those provisions refer to the granting of injunctions and to provisional and protective measures, but make clear that in other respects, EU trade mark courts shall apply the law of the Member State in which the acts of infringement or threatened infringement are committed.[2]

1 Chapter X consists of EUTMR Arts 122–135.
2 EUTMR Arts 129–131.

Pecuniary remedies—election between damages or an account of profits

17.05 Under s 14(2) of the TMA 1994, the proprietor of a registered trade mark may be entitled to certain pecuniary remedies—namely an award of damages or an account of profits. As set out below, an award of damages is made by reference to the loss caused to the proprietor and is a remedy to which the proprietor is entitled as of right. By contrast, an account of profits is measured by reference to the benefit derived by the infringer but its availability is subject to equitable principles.

17.06 A claimant can plead a claim to damages for the loss suffered and a claim to an account of the defendant's profits as alternatives. However, the claimant cannot recover both damages and an account in respect of any particular act of infringement. The claimant must elect between the two remedies.[1] This election is usually made after liability has been established and, once made, cannot be reversed. Where the defendant has been found to have infringed under s 10(3), the proprietor's decision on election may well depend on whether the defendant's use had taken unfair advantage of the distinctive character or repute of the proprietor's mark or whether it had been detrimental to that character or repute. In the former case, an account of the defendant's profits may be more favourable to the claimant; in the latter case, damages may well be the better remedy.

1 This is the case notwithstanding the terms of the Enforcement Directive (2004/48/EC) Art 13(1). See *Hollister Inc v Medik Ostomy Supplies Ltd* [2012] EWCA Civ 1419 at [56].

17.07 The courts often direct that the issue of quantum (ie, determining the measure of damages or the amount payable on the account of profits) be stayed until after liability has been established. In such cases, assuming the claimant succeeds on the issue of liability, the court will usually order the defendant to disclose documents relating to quantum to help the claimant to decide how to exercise its election[1] and will give other directions—such as for the filing of statements of case—for the future conduct of the proceedings to resolve the issue of quantum.

1 *Island Records Ltd v Tring International plc* [1995] FSR 560.

Damages

17.08 A proprietor or exclusive licensee is entitled as of right to recover damages in respect of any infringement of the trade mark.

The EU Enforcement Directive

17.09 Art 13 of the EU Enforcement Directive[1] draws a distinction between damages in the case of an infringer who knowingly or with reasonable grounds to know engages in infringing activity and damages in the case of a person without such knowledge or grounds of knowledge (respectively, a 'non-innocent infringer' and an 'innocent infringer'). In the case of a non-innocent infringer, Art 13(1) requires that when the judicial authorities set the damages:

> '(a) they shall take into account all appropriate aspects, such as the negative economic consequences, including lost profits, which the injured party has suffered, any unfair profits made by the infringer and, in appropriate cases, elements other than economic factors, such as the moral prejudice caused to the rightholder by the infringement;
> or
> (b) as an alternative to (a), they may, in appropriate cases, set the damages as a lump sum on the basis of elements such as at least the amount of royalties or fees which would have been due if the infringer had requested authorization to use the intellectual property right in question.'

By contrast, in the case of an innocent infringer, Art 13(2) leaves it to Member States to determine what remedies may be provided by way of the recovery of profits or the payment of damages.

1 Directive 2004/48/EC on the Enforcement of Intellectual Property Rights ('the Enforcement Directive'). From 11pm on 31 December 2020, when the UK's withdrawal from the EU became effective, directives then in force became part of 'retained EU law' in the UK. Accordingly, the terms of the Enforcement Directive remain relevant when construing the UK domestic legislation (discussed in para **17.10** below) passed to implement its requirements.

17.10 The UK implemented the Enforcement Directive by means of the Intellectual Property (Enforcement etc) Regulations 2006.[1] Regulation 3(1) and (2) of those regulations adopt the wording of Art 13(1) of the Directive (set out above) without substantive amendment. However, regulation 3(3) preserves '*the operation of any enactment or rule of law relating to remedies for the* infringement *of intellectual property rights except to the extent that it is inconsistent with the provisions of this regulation*'. It would seem, therefore, that existing UK law is preserved in relation to, for example, innocent infringers.

1 SI 2006/1028.

17.11 It is not clear that Art 13(1) has made a great deal of difference in cases concerning non-innocent infringers, primarily because so few trade mark cases reach the stage where the Court is required to assess damages or an account of profits. It might be thought that an award of damages under Art 13(1)(a) should be more generous than would normally be the case under English law because of the need to take into account factors such as '*any unfair profits made by the infringer*' and (in appropriate cases) '*elements other than economic factors, such as the moral prejudice caused to the rightholder*'. Usually under English law these factors are not relevant as the emphasis is on compensating the claimant for its losses rather than on punishing the defendant. However, the terms of Art 13(1) suggest that where it applies, damages could be somewhat more generous to a claimant.

In *Experience Hendrix LLC v Times Newspapers Limited*[1] Art 13(1) applied because the defendant had had reasonable grounds for knowing that it was engaging in infringing activities. However, because the infringer had not been indifferent let alone recklessly indifferent, the court declined to award additional damages. The court's approach suggests that the damages might have been increased if the defendant had been more culpable.[2] In general, however, the court in *Experience Hendrix* followed the ordinary principles of English law concerning the assessment of damages (as to which, see para **17.12** et seq below).[3]

In *Henderson v All Around the World Recording Ltd*,[4] it was held that the reference to 'unfair profits' did not permit an award of profits to include an account of profits but did permit an award of damages to be related to the defendant's profit from a knowing infringement where the claimant would not otherwise be compensated in damages assessed on the normal bases or by a strict account of profits. It was also stated that the fact that 'moral prejudice' could be taken in to account could allow damages for mental distress, injury to feelings and humiliation provided the compensation otherwise available would be non-existent or disproportionate to the moral prejudice suffered (an example being a defendant's publication on the internet for not profit of a photograph showing private grief).

1 [2010] EWHC 1986 (Sir William Blackburne).
2 [2010] EWHC 1986 at [76].
3 [2010] EWHC 1986 at [133].
4 [2014] EWHC 3087 (IPEC).

The general rules

17.12 Infringement of a trade mark is a statutory tort and the assessment of the damages recoverable is governed by the same rules that apply to other torts, namely that:

(a) The burden is on the claimant to prove the loss claimed.[1]
(b) The guiding principle is not to punish the defendant. Rather, it is to compensate the claimant, to restore the claimant to the position in which the claimant would have been had the infringement not occurred.[2]
(c) Nevertheless, because the defendant is an infringer, damages should be liberally assessed.[3]
(d) The proprietor can only recover losses that are:
    (i) foreseeable (ie, not too remote); and
    (ii) caused by the infringement; and
    (iii) not excluded from recovery by public or social policy.[4]

1 *General Tire and Rubber Company v Firestone Tyre and Rubber Company Limited* [1976] RPC 197 per Lord Wilberforce at 212.
2 *General Tire* at 212. As mentioned above, it is possible that for non-innocent infringers Art 13(1) of the Enforcement Directive now permits the court to increase the measure of damages to reflect factors such as the 'unfair profits made by the infringer' and the 'moral prejudice suffered by the rightholder'.
3 *General Tire* at 212.
4 *Gerber Garment Technology Inc v Lectra Systems Ltd* [1997] RPC 443 per Staughton LJ at 452.

Ways of calculating damages

17.13 The House of Lords in *General Tire & Rubber Co v Firestone Type & Rubber Co Ltd* (a patent case) identified three ways of calculating the damages recoverable by a claimant.[1]

> '(a) The first way is where the rightholder is in the business of exploiting its rights. In such cases, the rightholder can be compensated for its lost sales – the measure of damage being its lost profit. Determining what profit the claimant might have made but for the infringement can pose formidable evidential difficulties.[2] However, it must be borne in mind that the claim is for lost *profits* and not the lost receipts. One must, therefore, deduct the expenses which would have been incurred in order for the claimant to earn its profit. However, it has been confirmed in the *Gerber* case[3] that if only the marginal costs of production and sale have been saved, then the remainder of the lost income will be recoverable in full without deducting a proportion of general overheads. It should also be borne in mind that it is very unlikely that every infringing sale

by the defendant represents a lost sale to the claimant, although, in *Gerber*, Jacob J concluded that the patentee had lost a chance of making sales and went on to evaluate the lost chances as a whole rather than separately in relation to individual infringing sales.

(b) The second way is where the rightholder is in the business of licensing its rights for others to exploit. In such cases, the rightholder can be compensated for the opportunity which it has lost to grant a licence. In such a case, the starting point for the damages is the licensor's usual royalty rate. Such damages can be claimed even though the claimant has not lost any sales of goods.[4]

(c) The third way is where the right holder does not exploit the rights commercially. Here the usual "loss-sustained" approach does not operate and the courts will instead adopt the "notional licence" approach. In other words, the court will award damages based on what it believes would have been payable in a hypothetical transaction between a hypothetical willing licensor and a hypothetical willing licensee. It will do so even if the real parties would never have entered into such a transaction.[5] It will also do so even if there is no comparables for such a transaction to assist the court. In such a case a court will have to adopt a rough and ready approach – albeit erring on the side of under-compensation'.[6]

1 See also *Blayney v Clogau St David's Gold Mines Ltd* [2003] FSR 19 (a copyright case) and *National Guild of Removers & Storers Ltd v Silveria* [2010] EWPCC 015 (a trade mark case).

2 As is apparent from the very lengthy discussion on the subject in *Experience Hendrix LLC v Times Newspapers Limited* [2010] EWHC 1986 at [143]–[221].

3 [1997] RPC 443.

4 An example is *National Guild of Removers & Storers Ltd v Silveria* [2010] EWPCC 015.

5 See *Experience Hendrix LLC v Times Newspapers Limited* [2010] EWHC 1986 at [134].

6 *Blayney v Clogau St David's Gold Mines Ltd* [2003] FSR 19 at [31]–[34].

17.14 A claimant may be entitled to recover damages for sales which he can show he has lost but also a royalty to cover sales which the claimant would have been able to make.[1] In *National Guild of Removers & Storers* the claimant was awarded damages on the 'user' principle identified above, ie, the loss of royalty which the defendant should have paid in order to use the mark.[2] The user principle also formed the basis for assessing damages in *32Red*.[3] Damages may also be awarded where the defendant's infringing goods are of an inferior quality to those of the proprietor. Damages are therefore awarded to compensate the proprietor for the injury to the goodwill or reputation attaching to his trade mark.

1 *Blayney v Clogau St David's Gold Mines Ltd* [2003] FSR 19 at [20]–[21].
2 *National Guild of Removers & Storers Ltd v Silveria & ors* [2010] EWPCC 15; [2011] FSR 9.
3 *32Red Plc v WHG (International) Ltd* [2013] EWHC 815 (Ch).

Secondary loss

17.15 In addition to claiming its direct loss of sales, a claimant may also claim for what may be referred to as 'secondary loss', that is:

(a) the lost prospect of making follow-on sales (eg, of spare parts) and servicing the goods; and
(b) the defendant may be in a better position to compete generally with the plaintiff by establishing a bridgehead or springboard to enter the market.

The question whether secondary loss of this nature is recoverable was considered in the *Gerber* case (a patent case). There, the Court of Appeal looked at the overall objective of the Patents Act 1977 and concluded that its aim is to protect patentees from commercial loss resulting from the wrongful infringement of their rights. Accordingly, by reference to s 61 of the Patents Act 1977 and viewing the cases as a whole, the Court of Appeal held that no rule of law could be found which restricts the scope of recovery of damages by way of loss of profits to activities of the defendant which themselves constituted infringement of the patent. Thus, provided that the secondary loss is both foreseeable (ie, not too remote) and is, in fact, caused by the infringement, it will be recoverable. There is no reason in principle why this reasoning should not apply in trade mark cases.

Losses by a subsidiary

17.16 Although an infringement action is brought by the registered proprietor (or by a licensee under ss 30 or 31) loss may in fact be suffered by another company in which the proprietor has a shareholding (eg, a subsidiary or a sister company). In such circumstances, the company suffering the loss may not have a cause of action against the infringer. However, the proprietor can recover damages for any reduction in the value of its interest in that subsidiary/sister company (whether that is an income or a capital loss) which is caused by the loss suffered by that other company. This is likely to be the reduction in the value of the proprietor's shareholding in that other company caused by the defendant's infringement. However, in the *Gerber* case, the Court of Appeal rejected the argument that every dollar lost to the subsidiary reduced the value of the parent's shareholding by a like amount. Instead, the Court of Appeal treated each company as a separate legal entity and required the plaintiff to prove and quantify its own financial loss to its own pocket. Thus, although a parent company will, in principle, be able to recover damages by reason of the loss suffered by its subsidiary, it is the reduction in the value of the parent's shareholding which must be quantified, not the actual loss suffered by the subsidiary as such.

Account of profits, s 14(2)

17.17 As mentioned above, an account of profits is an alternative remedy to damages. It is an equitable remedy and its availability is subject to the usual equitable principles. In particular, the court has a discretion whether or not to order an account. For example, the defendant's knowledge of the proprietor's registration may affect the making of an order for an account of profits. The court will also have regard to any delay by the proprietor in bringing the proceedings and/or any acquiescence in relation to the defendant's conduct.

17.18 The rationale for ordering an account of profits is not to punish the defendant, but to prevent unjust enrichment by them. It is therefore inappropriate for the plaintiff to receive more than the profit made by the defendant which is attributable to the infringement in question. If the defendant can establish that any element of the profit is attributable to factors other than the use of the infringing mark, then this should be reflected in the account of profits awarded.

17.19 Proprietors electing for an account of the defendant's profits should bear in mind the problem of defining accurately the defendant's profit. There is always a risk that the 'profit' which is attributable to the defendant's infringing acts can be reduced by 'creative accountancy' and claimants are often better advised to seek to recover damages because, notwithstanding the difficulties associated with trying to prove what might have been, at least the claimant is in control of the evidence upon which the calculation is to be based and the onus is then on the defendant to rebut that evidence. The burden is also on the defendant to show what costs are properly attributable to the infringing activities—it is not acceptable just to apportion a percentage of general overheads.[1] For an example of how the court will conduct an account of profits, see the *HENLEYS* case.[2]

1 *Hollister Inc v Medik Ostomy Supplies Ltd* [2012] EWCA Civ 1419; [2013] FSR 24.
2 *Woolley v UP Global Sourcing UK Ltd* [2014] EWHC 493 (Ch); [2014] FSR 37.

Injunctions, s 14(2)

17.20 Section 14(2) of the TMA 1994 and Arts 9 and 11 of the Enforcement Directive make clear that an injunction can be granted in respect of a trade mark infringement. An injunction is 'a court order prohibiting a person from doing something or requiring a person to do something'[1] and can be on an interim or a permanent basis. It is an equitable remedy and so (like an account of profits) the decision whether to grant an injunction is subject to the usual equitable principles, including delay and acquiescence.

1 See the Glossary attached to the Civil Procedure Rules (the CPR).

17.21 An injunction can be granted to prevent a contemplated act that would infringe trade mark (a *quia timet* injunction) or it could prevent the continuation or repetition of acts said to constitute an infringement. There must, of course, be some evidence to show that the act in question is threatened or is likely to be continued or repeated. Injunctions may also extend to 'blocking injunctions' against websites (and the internet service providers hosting them) that are being used to infringe trade marks.[1]

1 *Cartier International AG v British Sky Broadcasting Ltd & ors* [2014] EWHC 3765 (Ch).

Interim injunctions

17.22 An interim injunction (formerly known as an interlocutory injunction) is an injunction granted pending final resolution of the main claim—ie, pre-trial. It is granted, therefore, at a stage before the parties' rights have been determined. For a more detailed discussion of the principles which govern the court's power to grant such an injunction reference should be made to the relevant books on civil procedure. However, in exercising those powers, a court must have regard to Art 9 of the Enforcement Directive which, as mentioned above, continues to be of effect in the UK as part of retained EU law. Thus, under Art 9:

(1) Member States must ensure that their courts can grant "an interlocutory injunction intended to prevent any imminent infringement of an intellectual property right, or to forbid … The continuation of the alleged infringements of that right, or to make such continuation subject to the lodging of guarantees intended to ensure the compensation of the right holder …";
(2) Member States must ensure that the courts have power to order the precautionary seizure of movable and immovable property of the alleged infringer – including the blocking of his bank account and other assets. In England, this requirement is met by the court's power to grant freezing orders (formerly known as "Mareva orders");
(3) The courts may require the applicant for such an injunction to provide "reasonably available evidence" to allow the court to satisfy itself with a reasonable degree of certainty that the applicant is the rightholder and that that right is being infringed or that infringement is imminent;

(4) Member States must ensure that in appropriate cases (and in particular where delay would cause irreparable harm) the measures in (1) and (2) above can be taken without the defendants having been heard (i.e. at a "without notice" hearing) – provided the parties are informed without delay after execution of the measures at the latest and provided that, within a reasonable time after notification of those measures, a review (including a right to be heard) shall take place at the request of the defendant to decide whether those measures should be modified, revoked or confirmed;
(5) Member States must ensure that such interim measures will be revoked or cease to have effect if the rightholder fails within a reasonable period to institute proceedings leading to a decision on the merits of the case;
(6) The courts may require the claimant to provide adequate security or an assurance intended to ensure compensation for any prejudice suffered by the defendant; and
(7) The courts shall have power to order the claimant to compensate the defendant where the interim measures are revoked or lapse due to any act or omission of the claimant or where it is subsequently found that there was no infringement of threat of infringement of an intellectual property right.

17.23 In English law, the test for in determining whether to grant an interim injunction was laid down by the House of Lords in *American Cyanamid Co v Ethicon Ltd.*[1] The test is to ask the following questions:

(1) Has the claimant shown a serious issue to be tried?
(2) If so, would an award of damages at trial adequately compensate the claimant for the loss suffered before trial?
(3) If damages would not adequately compensate the claimant, would the claimant's cross undertaking in damages adequately compensate the defendant if it emerged at trial that the interim relief should not have been granted?
(4) If there is doubt as to the adequacy of damages for either party, does the balance of convenience favour the grant of interim relief?

1 [1975] AC 396.

17.24 In the context of intellectual property cases, the application of these questions tends to be somewhat modified. In *Series 5 Software Ltd v Clarke*[1] Laddie J concluded that there was nothing in *American Cyanamid* which prevented a court from taking into account its view of the strength of each party's case. He gave the following guidance:

'(1) The grant of an interim injunction is a matter of discretion and depends on all the facts of the case;

(2) There are no fixed rules;
(3) The court should rarely attempt to resolve complex issues of disputed fact or law; and
(4) Major factors the court should bear in mind are:
    (i) the extent to which damages are likely to be an adequate remedy and the ability of the other party to pay;
    (ii) the balance of convenience;
    (iii) the maintenance of the status quo; and
    (iv) any clear view the court may reach as to the relative strength of the parties' cases. This is particularly important when the decision whether or not to grant the interim injunction would effectively determine the outcome of the entire case.'.

1 [1996] FSR 273.

17.25 Delay in seeking interim relief is often fatal to an application unless it is explained and justified.

Further, a claimant seeking an interim injunction will have to give the usual cross-undertaking as to damages. This is an undertaking that, if the interim injunction is subsequently discharged, the claimant will (if so ordered by the court) compensate the defendant for losses suffered by the defendant caused by the injunction. As the grant of an interim injunction often causes a defendant serious inconvenience and can sometimes put a defendant out of business, the potential losses can be very substantial and the claimant's potential liability under this cross-undertaking can be a serious matter. The claimant's ability to satisfy such a cross-undertaking will, therefore, be a matter of concern to the court and in some cases, the claimant will be required to fortify a cross-undertaking by putting up security in respect of the damages which defendant may suffer.

17.26 The wording of any injunction should make clear what exactly it is that the defendant should not do. In the case of an interim injunction, it is best to avoid seeking an order which prohibits the defendant 'infringing the claimant's trade mark'. This is because, at that stage in the proceedings issues of validity and infringement have yet to be resolved and it will not be clear whether the defendant has breached the order until those issues have been resolved. It is better, therefore, to specific particular acts which are prohibited—eg, acts promoting an animated character known as 'Lady Goo Goo'.[1]

1 See *Ate My Heart Inc v Mind Candy Ltd* [2011] EWHC 2741.

Final injunction

17.27 A final injunction will only be granted if the defendant is found to have infringed the proprietor's trade mark following the hearing of all the evidence at the full trial.[1] Of course, the issue of balance of convenience is irrelevant in issuing a final injunction, but other relevant factors which affect the grant of equitable relief will be applicable. A final injunction can be granted whether or not the court also awards damages or an account of profits. In the *Glee* case, the court granted an injunction requiring the defendant to rename its well-known television program, although the injunction did allow the defendant to make clear that it 'previously known as Glee' or words to that effect.[2] Injunctive relief was also granted in the *Lush* case brought against Amazon.co.uk in relation to the sale of the cosmetics, and bath products on the online marketplace.[3]

1 In addition to TMA 1994 s 14(2), see also Enforcement Directive Art 11.
2 *Comic Enterprise Ltd v Twentieth Century Fox Film Corp* [2014] EWHC 2286 (Ch); [2014] ETMR 51. The court expressly stated its view that such an injunction was not inconsistent with the Enforcement Directive.
3 *Cosmetic Warriors Ltd v Amazon.co.uk Ltd* [2014] EWHC 1316 (Ch).

Any other relief, s 14(2)

17.28 The TMA 1994, although expressly referring to damages, injunctions and an account of profits, does not limit the available remedies, and states that the proprietor is entitled to all such other relief as is available in respect of the infringement of any other property right. This is clearly intended to be a 'catch-all' provision, although the most frequently sought and certainly the most practical remedies are those which have already been mentioned, namely damages, an account of profits and an injunction. However, special mention should be made of search orders (formerly known as an 'Anton Piller' order[1]) and orders for the disclosure of information regarding infringing activity—both of which are specifically provided for in the Enforcement Directive.[2]

1 Named after one of the early cases in which such an order was granted: *Anton Piller KG v Manufacturing Processes Ltd* [1976] FSR 129.
2 Enforcement Directive Arts 7–8.

Search Orders ('Anton Piller' Orders) and Imaging Orders

17.29 A search order is an order which enables a team (usually including the claimant's solicitors, a forensic computer expert and an independent supervising solicitor) to enter the defendant's premises in order to search for and seize goods bearing infringing trade marks or other evidence of the alleged acts of infringement.

Because of the invasive nature of search orders, applications for and the enforcement of such orders are subject to a number of requirements and, for detailed guidance, reference should be made to up-to-date books on civil procedure.[1] However, in outline, a claimant must show a strong *prima facie* case of infringement; clear evidence that the defendant is in possession of incriminating documents or materials; a real possibility of a risk that such documents or materials will be destroyed or removed and that the defendant would not abide by an injunction ordering their preservation; and that the damage caused by the order will not be excessive.[2] The practical importance of a search order is that the claimant can seek an order contemporaneously with or even before commencing proceedings for trade mark infringement. This gives a proprietor the element of surprise and will reduce the chances that the defendant will have concealed infringing goods or other evidence of infringement.

Search orders can involve a wide-ranging, time-consuming and often very expensive search. They also require members of the team to review the defendant's documents, which can lead to issues of privilege and confidentiality. Accordingly, before seeking a search order, a claimant should consider whether its objectives would be better served by obtaining an imaging order. An imaging order requires a defendant to permit the imaging of its electronic storage devices (ie computers and mobile phones) and are usually far cheaper, less intrusive and more appropriate than search orders. As Arnold LJ commented in *TBD (Owen Holland) v Simons*:

> 'It has become increasingly common for claimants in cases like the present one to make without notice applications seeking both a traditional search order and an imaging order. In my view, any court confronted with such an application should first consider whether to grant an imaging order. If the court is prepared to grant an imaging order, then it should be presumed unless the contrary is shown that a traditional search order is unnecessary. Even if the court is prepared to grant a search order at all, careful consideration should be given as to the scope of the order having regard to the imaging order.'[3]

1 For an illustration of the problems that can arise and a detailed exploration of the development of the law as regards search orders and the difficulties that can arise, see *TBD (Owen Holland) Ltd v Simons* [2020] EWCA Civ 1182.
2 *Indichii Salus Ltd v Chandrasekaran* [2006] EWHC 521.
3 [2020] EWCA Civ 1182 at [180]

17.30 Due to the draconian nature of the search order remedy, the standard-form order contains a number of provisions designed to safeguard the position of the defendant.[1] These include:

(a) the need for the search to be overseen by an independent supervising solicitor who is experienced in relation to search orders;
(b) the requirement to warn the defendant of the defendant's right to assert any privilege against self-incrimination;
(c) provisions to preserve legal professional privilege and confidentiality; and

(d) the giving of undertakings restricting the use that can be made of material seized in the search.

There is at present, no standard form imaging order, but clearly any imaging order must also contain appropriate safeguards. In this regard, the Court of Appeal in *TBD (Owen Holland) v Simons* stated that:

> 'the basic safeguard required in imaging orders is that, save in exceptional cases, the images should be kept in the safekeeping of the forensic computer expert, and not searched or inspected by anyone, until the return date. If there is to be any departure from this, it will require a very high degree of justification, and must be specifically and explicitly approved by the court.'[2]

In the case of both search orders and imaging orders, it must be borne in mind that their purpose is the preservation of documents or materials. They are not intended to provide a claimant with an early means of obtaining disclosure from a defendant, let alone with the opportunity to conduct its own inspection of the defendant's documents and materials. The question whether the claimant should be allowed access to the documents or materials preserved by such orders is a separate question and requires separate consideration at a return date before the court. In the context of imaging orders, the Court of Appeal in *TBD (Owen Holland)* said:

> 'On the return date, consideration must be given to the timing and methodology of disclosure and inspection of documents captured in the images. The presumption should be that it will be for the defendant to give disclosure of such documents in the normal way, but this presumption may be departed from where there is sufficient justification. Even if the presumption is departed from, there should be no unilateral searching of the images by or on behalf of the claimant: the methodology of the search must be either agreed between the parties or approved by the court.'[3]

The same will apply to documents and materials preserved under a search order.

1 See CPR Practice Direction 25A—Interim Injunctions and see *TBD (Owen Holland) Ltd v Simons* [2020] EWCA Civ 1182.
2 [2020] EWCA Civ 1182 at [193].
3 [2020] EWCA Civ 1182 at [193].

Orders for the disclosure of information about infringing activity

17.31 The courts have power to order a defendant to provide the claimant with information concerning the suppliers and purchasers of infringing materials. Such information can include the names and addresses of such persons and the dates and details of relevant transactions. The order is justified on the basis that the person providing the information is either a wrongdoer or comes within the *Norwich Pharmacal* principles.[1] To obtain such an order, the claimant must show that there is a good indication of wrongdoing, [2] that the information is needed for a legitimate purpose (which purpose must be identified[3]) and, where the order is sought against an innocent party, that that party is the only practicable source of the information. The remedy in such cases is not only one of last resort; its essential purpose is to do justice and it requires the exercise of a discretion after weighing all relevant factors including (for example) the competing public interests in allowing an applicant to vindicate its rights, in protecting a party's privacy and in protecting journalistic sources.[4]

1 *Norwich Pharmacal Co v Customs and Excise Commissioners* [1974] AC 133—where the House of Lords recognised that a person who is innocently involved in wrongdoing may have a duty to assist the victim of that wrongdoing by providing disclosure and information.
2 *Mitsui & Co Ltd v Nexen Petroleum UK Ltd* [2005] EWHC 625; [2005] 3 All ER 511.
3 *Ashworth Hospital Authority v MGN Ltd* [2002] UKHL 29; [2002] 1 WLR 2033 at [60]. 'The use of the material will then be restricted expressly or implicitly to the disclosed purposes unless and until the court permits it to be used for another purpose'.
4 *The Rugby Football Union v Consolidated Information Services Ltd* [2012] UKSC 55 at [17].

17.32 The availability of disclosure orders is consistent with Art 8(1) of the Enforcement Directive which provides that Members States must ensure that courts can make an order:

> 'that information on the origin and distribution networks of the goods or services which infringe an intellectual property right be provided by the infringer and/or any other person who:
> (a) was found in possession of the infringing goods on a commercial scale;
> (b) was found to be using the infringing services on a commercial scale;
> (c) was found to be providing on a commercial scale services used in infringing activities; or
> (d) was indicated by the person referred to in point (a), (b) or (c) as being involved in the production, manufacture or distribution of the goods or the provision of the services.'

17.33 Under Art 8(2) of the Directive, the information required shall, as appropriate, comprise:

> '(a) the names and addresses of the producers, manufacturers, distributors, suppliers and other previous holders of the goods or services, as well as the intended wholesalers and retailers;

(b) Information on the quantities produced, manufactured, delivered, received or ordered, as well as the price obtained for the goods or services in question.'

The making of such order is subject to other statutory provisions governing (inter alia) the use or misuse of such information or the protection of confidential information of the processing of personal data.[1]

1 Enforcement Directive Art 8(3). As mentioned above (see para **17.09**) the provisions of the Enforcement Directive are part of 'retained EU law' in the UK notwithstanding the UK's withdrawal from the EU.

Remedies in respect of infringing goods, material and articles

17.34 As mentioned above, there are a number of remedies in relation to infringing goods, materials or articles in the possession, custody or control of the defendant. These remedies include:

(1) Erasure, removal or obliteration of an 'offending sign'—s 15(1) of the TMA 1994.
(2) Destruction of infringing goods—s 15(2) of the TMA 1994.
(3) Delivery up of infringing goods, material or articles—s 16 of the TMA 1994.
(4) Destruction or forfeiture of infringing goods, material or articles—s 19(1) of the TMA 1994.
(5) The giving of notice to Customs and Excise—s 89 of the TMA 1994[1] or Regulation (EU) No 608/2013.[2]

1 A notice under TMA 1994 s 89 must be in respect of goods, material or articles but they need not be in the possession, custody or control of the defendant.
2 As amended by The Customs (Enforcement of Intellectual Property Rights) (Amendment) (EU Exit) Regulations 2019, SI 2019/514 with effect from 11pm on 31 December 2020 when the UK's withdrawal from the EU became effective.

17.35 As has been mentioned, for cases commenced after 11pm on 31 December 2020, the UK courts no longer have any jurisdiction in a claim relating to a EUTM. However, before that time (and for actions commenced before that time), the remedies provided by ss 14–19 of the TMA 1994 applied equally to EUTMs[1] and were in line with Art 10 of the Enforcement Directive, which requires Member States to ensure that their courts are able to take appropriate measures in respect of goods that have been found to infringe an intellectual property right (and materials and implements used in their creation) including measures such as:

(a) recall from the channels of commerce;
(b) definitive removal from the channels of commerce; or
(c) destruction.

1 Community Trade Mark Regulations 2006, SI 2006/1027 reg 5(3).

Meaning of 'infringing goods'—TMA 1994 s 17(2)

17.36 The above remedies relate to infringing goods. Under s 17(2) of the TMA 1994, goods are 'infringing goods' if they (or their packaging) bear a sign which is identical with or similar to a registered trade mark and either:

(a) the application of the sign to the goods or to their packaging was itself an infringement of the trade mark; or
(b) the goods are proposed to be imported into the United Kingdom and the application of the sign to the goods or to their packaging would have been an infringement of the trade mark if the application had occurred in the United Kingdom; or
(c) the use of the sign otherwise constitutes an infringement of the trade mark.

Meaning of 'infringing material'—TMA 1994 s 17(4)

17.37 Under s 17(4) of the TMA 1994, material is 'infringing material' if it bears a sign which is identical with or similar to a registered trade mark and either:

(a) the material is used:
    (i) for labelling or packaging goods;
    (ii) as a business paper; or
    (iii) for advertising goods or services,

  provided that the material is used in such a way as to infringe the trade mark; or
(b) the material is intended to be so used and such use would infringe the registered trade mark.

Meaning of 'infringing articles'—TMA 1994 s 17(5)

17.38 Under s 17(5) of the TMA 1994, articles are 'infringing articles' if they:

(a) are specifically designed or adapted for making copies of a sign which is identical with or similar to a registered trade mark; and
(b) are in the possession, custody or control of a person who knows or has reason to believe that such articles either have been or are to be used to produce infringing goods or material.

The requirement that the article be 'specifically designed or adapted' for the purpose of making copies of a sign will be too onerous for many trade mark owners. For example, the tools of trade of a counterfeiter may have many uses other than the copying of trade marks and it may, therefore, be difficult to establish that the article was 'specifically' designed or adapted, albeit that this requirement does not mean that the article be 'exclusively' designed or adapted for the purposes of making copies of the sign.

Erasure, removal or obliteration of an 'offending sign'—TMA 1994 s 15

17.39 Under s 15(1)(a) of the TMA 1994, the court may make an order requiring the defendant to cause an offending sign to be erased, removed or obliterated from any infringing goods, material or articles which are in the defendant's possession, custody or control.

17.40 Under s 15(2) of the TMA 1994, if (but only if) an order for erasure, removal or obliteration has not been complied with by the defendant, or if it appears to the court that it is likely that such an order will not be complied with by the defendant, the court may instead order that the infringing goods, material or articles be delivered up to a person nominated by the court for that person to erase, remove or obliterate the sign.

Destruction of infringing goods—TMA 1994 s 15

17.41 If the remedy of erasure, removal or obliteration referred to above is not reasonably practicable, then s 15(1)(b) of the TMA 1994 permits the court instead to order the defendant to arrange for the destruction of the infringing goods, material or articles in question. If such an order is not complied with or if it appears likely that it would not be complied with, s 15(2) empowers the court to order that the infringing goods, material or articles be delivered up to another person for destruction.

17.42 This will be a useful (if not essential) remedy where the mark is integral to the goods, for example, where the mark consists of the shape of the goods themselves.

Delivery up of infringing goods, material or articles—TMA 1994 s 16

17.43 Under s 16 of the TMA 1994, a proprietor can apply to the court for an order for the delivery up of infringing goods, material or articles. There are, however, a number of conditions to be satisfied before the court can make such an order:

(a) the order may only be granted in respect of infringing goods, material or articles which a person has in his possession, custody or control in the course of business;[1]
(b) the application for such an order must be made before the end of a six-year period as specified in s 18 of the TMA 1994;[2] and
(c) no order shall be made unless the court also makes or there are grounds for making an order under s 19 of the TMA 1994 (ie, an order for the disposal of the infringing goods, material or articles).[3]

1 TMA 1994 s 16(1).
2 TMA 1994 s 16(2)—see below.
3 TMA 1994 s 16(2). The grounds for making an order under s 19 are considered below.

17.44 The order for delivery up can be made against someone other than the person who has infringed the proprietor's trade mark, provided that person has infringing goods, material or articles in his possession, custody or control in the course of a business.

17.45 It seems that an order for delivery up can only be made pursuant to a specific application made by the proprietor.[1] However, the court may order that the actual delivery up be made to the proprietor or to any other person and, indeed, applications are often made for an order for delivery up to the claimant or to 'such other person as the court may direct'. The person to whom the infringing goods, material or articles are delivered up must, if no order for their disposal has been made under s 19, retain them pending the making of such an order or a decision not to make an order under that section.[2] An order for either delivery up, or re-labelling of infringing goods held by the defendant was made in the *Glee* case, but the court said that any order relating to goods held by third parties would require a separate application.[3]

1 Compare the words of s 16(1) ('*the proprietor may apply* ...') with the words of s 15(1) ('*the court may make an order* ...'). Presumably, a claimant who omits such a claim can seek permission to amend its claim.
2 TMA 1994 s 16(3).
3 *Comic Enterprise Ltd v Twentieth Century Fox Film Corp* [2014] EWHC 2286 (Ch); [2014] ETMR 51.

17.46 An application for an order for delivery up under s 16 must be made within a statutory limitation period. Subject to the exceptions discussed below, this is a period of six years calculated from a date that varies depending upon whether one is seeking the delivery up of goods or material or articles.[1]

Goods—In the case of infringing goods, the six-year period commences on the date on which the trade mark was applied to the goods or their packaging.

Material—In the case of infringing material, the six-year period commences on the date on which the trade mark was applied to the material.

Articles—In the case of infringing articles, the six-year period commences on the date on which they were made.

1 TMA 1994 s 18(1)(a)–(c).

17.47 The exceptions[1] apply where the proprietor of the registered trade mark, during the whole or part of the limitation period is either:

(a) under a disability;[2] or
(b) prevented from discovering the facts entitling him to apply for an order for delivery up as the result of fraud or concealment.

In either of these circumstances an application for delivery up may be made at any time before the end of the six-year period calculated from the date on which the proprietor:

(a) ceased to be under the disability; or (as the case may be);
(b) could with reasonable diligence have discovered the facts entitling him to apply for an order for delivery up.[3]

1 See TMA 1994 s 18(2).
2 For the meaning of 'disability', see TMA 1994 s 18(3).
3 TMA 1994 s 18(2).

Destruction or forfeiture of infringing goods, material or articles—TMA 1994 s 19(1)

17.48 Section 19(1) of the TMA 1994 provides that:

> 'Where infringing goods, material or articles have been delivered up in pursuance of an order under section 16, an application may be made to the court for –
> (a) an order that they be destroyed or forfeited to such person as the court may think fit, or
> (b) a formal decision that no such order should be made.'

17.49 On a literal construction, the opening words of s 19(1) would suggest that an application for an order under s 19 could not be made until after goods, materials or articles had been delivered up under an order made under s 16. However, it has been held that this literal construction is wrong and that when s 19 is read together with s 16 and in the light of 'commercial common sense', the correct position is that an application under s 19 can be made at the same time as an application under s 16 or sequentially.[1]

1 *Miller Brewing Co v Ruhi Enterprises Ltd* [2003] EWHC 1606; [2004] FSR 5.

17.50 The wording of s 19(1) clearly envisages that it could be the defendant who applies to the court for a decision that no order for destruction or forfeiture is made. In deciding whether to make an order for the destruction or forfeiture of goods, materials or articles, the court will have regard to whether other remedies are available which would be adequate to compensate and to protect the interests of the proprietor (and any licensee). If the court considers damages to be an adequate remedy, then it may decide to make no order for destruction or forfeiture provided that the proprietor's interests are or will otherwise be protected. In such event, the person in whose possession, custody or control the goods, material or articles were before being delivered up (usually the defendant) will be entitled to their return.[1]

1 TMA 1994 s 19(5).

17.51 Under s 19(3), provision must be made by rules of court for the service of notice on persons having an interest in the infringing goods, material or articles and for such persons to be entitled to appear in proceedings under s 19 and appeals therefrom. Section 19(3) also provides that an order under s 19 will not take effect until the end of the period within which the person interested is entitled to appeal and, if an appeal is made, the order will not take effect until the appeal is finally disposed of.

17.52 If more than one person is interested in the relevant goods, material or articles, then the court will make an order as it thinks just.[1]

1 TMA 1994 s 19(4).

Notice to Customs—Regulation (EU) No 608/2013 and TMA 1994 s 89

17.53 In order to try to stop the importation of infringing goods into the United Kingdom, the proprietor of a registered trade mark (or his licensee) may notify the Commissioners of Customs and Excise ('Customs') of the expected arrival of such goods. The idea being that Customs will then detain the goods.

There are two bases on which such a notification can be made, one is under Regulation (EU) No. 608/2013 ('the 2013 Regulation') as amended to apply in the UK after the UK's withdrawal from the EU,[1] the other is s 89 of the TMA 1994. However, these two bases are mutually exclusive; a notice cannot be given under s 89 in respect of goods placed in or expected to be placed in one of the situations to which the 2013 Regulation applies.[2]

1 The amendments were made by The Customs (Enforcement of Intellectual Property Rights) (Amendment) (EU Exit) Regulations 2019, SI 2019/514 with effect from 11pm on 31 December 2020 when the UK's withdrawal from the EU became effective.
2 TMA 1994 s 89(3). For those situations, see para **17.54** below.

Regulation (EU) No 608/2013 (as amended)

17.54 The 2013 Regulation (as amended) applies to goods which are 'suspected of infringing an intellectual property right' and particularly goods which are in one of the following situations, namely:

(a) when declared for release for free circulation, export or re-export;
(b) when entering or leaving the customs territory of the UK; or
(c) when placed under a suspensive procedure or in a free zone or free warehouse.[1]

1 See the 2013 Regulation Art 1(1) (as amended).

17.55 For these purposes, 'intellectual property right' includes (inter alia) a trade mark (meaning a trade mark registered in the UK or under international arrangements which has effect in the UK but not, since the UK's withdrawal from the EU, an EUTM)[1] and goods are suspected of infringing such rights if there are reasonable indications that in the UK they are prima facie the subject of an act infringing an intellectual property right.[2]

However, certain goods are excluded from the operation of the Regulation (as amended), namely:

(a) goods which have been released for free circulation under the end-use regime;
(b) goods of a non-commercial nature contained in a traveller's personal luggage; and
(c) goods that have been manufactured with the consent of the right holder or goods manufactured by a person duly authorised by the right holder to manufacture a certain quantity of goods, in excess of such quantities agreed.[3]

1 The 2013 Regulation Arts 2(1)(a) and 2(2) as amended.
2 The 2013 Regulation Art 2(7) as amended.
3 The 2013 Regulation Art 1(3)–(5) as amended.

17.56 Where the 2013 Regulation (as amended) applies, a trade mark proprietor or any person or entity authorised formally by a trade mark proprietor to initiate infringement proceedings is entitled to submit an application to the customs authorities for action to be taken.[1]

1 The 2013 Regulation Art 3 (as amended). For the relevant actions, see para **17.58** below.

17.57 Under Art 6 of the 2013 Regulation, the application must contain certain specified information including (but not limited to) the following:

- details concerning the applicant;
- the status of the applicant;
- documents to satisfy Customs that the applicant is entitled to submit the application;
- if using a representative, details of that representative and evidence of that person's power to act as representative in the UK;
- the intellectual property right to be enforced;
- specific and technical data on the authentic goods (including bar codes and images where appropriate);
- information needed to enable the Customs Authority to readily identify the goods in question;
- information relevant to the Customs Authority's analysis and assessment of the risk of infringement;
- undertakings by the applicant (i) to comply with the notification requirements of Art 15, (ii) to forward and update any information

relevant to the Custom's Authority's analysis and assessment of the risk of infringement, (iii) to assume liability under the conditions laid down in Art 28, and (iv) to bear the costs referred to in Art 29;
- an agreement that data may be processed by the UK; and
- whether the applicant requests use of the Art 26 procedure and, where requested, agrees to cover the costs related to destruction of goods under that procedure.

17.58 If the relevant customs authority grants the application, it must specify the period (of up to one year but extendable) during which it will take action.[1]

Having taken a decision on the application, where the authority identifies goods suspected of infringing an intellectual property right covered by that decision, it must suspend release of these goods or detain them.[2] Before doing so, the authority may require the holder of the decision to provide it with any relevant information with respect to the goods and it may provide that person with information as to the quantity and nature of the goods (and with images) as appropriate.[3] Within one working day of any suspension or detention, the authority must give the declarant or holder of the goods and the holder of the decision notice of the suspension or detention and must inform them of the quantity and nature of the goods involved.[4]

1 The 2013 Regulation Arts 11 and 12.
2 The 2013 Regulation Art 17(1).
3 The 2013 Regulation Art 17(2).
4 The 2013 Regulation Art 17(3)–(4).

17.59 Where goods are suspected of infringing an intellectual property right but are not covered by a decision granting an application, the authorities are also empowered (except in the case of perishable goods) to detain or suspend the release of such goods.[1]

Before taking such action, the customs authorities may (without disclosing any information other than the quantity and nature of the goods) request any person potentially entitled to submit an application to provide relevant information.[2] Further, within one working day of such a suspension or detention, the authorities must inform both the declarant or holder of the goods and persons entitled to submit an application in respect of those goods of the suspension or detention.[3] Where the authority has not identified any person entitled to make an application within one day of such suspension or detention, or where such a person has been notified but has not submitted an application within four working days of such notification, then the customs authorities must grant release of the goods or end their detention immediately after completion of all customs formalities.[4]

1 The 2013 Regulation Art 18(1).
2 The 2013 Regulation Art 18(2).
3 The 2013 Regulation Art 18(3).
4 The 2013 Regulation Art 18(4).

17.60 Article 23(1) of the Regulation (as amended) provides a simplified procedure whereby goods suspected of infringing an intellectual property right may be destroyed under customs control with the agreement (or deemed agreement) of the interested parties and without any need to determine whether they actually infringe. This destruction by consent can be done provided, within ten days of being notified (or three days in the case of perishable goods):

(1) the holder of the decision has given written confirmation that, in its conviction, the goods infringed an intellectual property right and that it agrees to their destruction; and
(2) the holder or declarant of the goods has given written confirmation of its agreement to such destruction. However, if, within the relevant period, the holder or declarant of the goods has not provided such confirmation and has not objected to the destruction of the goods, the authority is able to deem that it has confirmed its agreement.

If the holder of the decision does not provide the necessary confirmation, then (unless the Authority has been duly informed of the initiation of proceedings to determine the issue of infringement), the Authority is obliged to release the goods or to end their detention.

Under Art 23(3), where the holder or declarant of the goods has not confirmed its agreement to the destruction of the goods and is not deemed to have agreed, the Authority must immediately notify the holder of the decision who then has ten days of the notification (three days in the case of perishable goods) to initiate proceedings to determine whether an intellectual property right has been infringed. The Authority may extend that ten-day period in appropriate cases but, if proceedings are not initiated, the goods must be released or their detention ended.[1]

An alternative route to the destruction of goods is provided by Art 26 of the Regulation. This applies to goods where (a) the goods are suspected of being counterfeit or pirated, (b) the goods are not perishable, (c) the goods are covered by a decision granting an application, (d) the holder of the decision has requested the use of the Art 26 procedure and (e) the goods are transported in small consignments.[2] In such a case, within one working day of a suspension of release or detention, the Customs Authority will notify the declarant or holder of the goods of this and of the Authority's intention to destroy the goods.[3] The declarant or holder of the goods then has ten working days to 'express his point of view'.[4] If that person agrees to the destruction or does not notify its opposition to destruction within the ten-day period, the destruction may be carried out under the Authority's control.[5] If the declarant or holder of the goods has not agreed (or is not deemed to have agreed) to destruction of the goods, the Authority must notify the holder of the decision and, unless that person initiates proceedings within ten working days of such notification, must release the goods or put an end to their detention after completion of all customs formalities.[6]

For guidance as to the sort of evidence that will be relevant in the event that the holder of the decision does initiate proceedings to show that an intellectual property right has been infringed, see *Koninklijke Philips Electronics NV v Lucheng Meijing Industrial Co Ltd.*[7] See also *Blomqvist v Rolex SA* where the CJEU ruled that the authorities have power to seize goods simply by virtue of the fact that they have been acquired into the relevant state—there is no need for them to have been targeted at that state by advertising or other means.[8]

1 See the 2013 Regulation Art 23(4) and (5).
2 See the 2013 Regulation Art 26(1). A 'small consignment' means a postal or express courier consignment which (a) contains three units or less; or (b) has a gross weight of less than 2kg and 'units' are goods classified under the Harmonised Commodity Description and Coding System provided for under the International Convention on Harmonised System as done in Brussels on 14 June 1983 if unpackaged or the package of such goods intended for retail sale to the ultimate consumer, see the 2013 Regulation Art 2(19) (as amended).
3 See the 2013 Regulation Art 26(3).
4 See the 2013 Regulation Art 26(4).
5 See the 2013 Regulation Art 26(5)–(7).
6 See the 2013 Regulation Art 26(8)–(9).
7 Case C-446/09 and Case C-495/09.
8 Case C-98/13.

17.61 The Regulation provides that the Customs Authority shall not be liable for granting an application even if no goods suspected of infringing an intellectual property right are detected or no action is taken to detain them.[1] However, the holder of the decision can be liable for damage caused to the holder of the goods or declarant where (i) a procedure initiated under the Regulation is discontinued due to an act or omission of the holder of the decision, (ii) samples taken under Art 19(2) are not returned or are damaged and beyond use due to an act or omission of the holder of the decision, or (iii) goods are subsequently found nit to infringe.[2] The holder of the decision can also be asked by the Authority to reimburse the costs incurred by the Authority including the costs of storage or detention and destruction.[3]

1 See the 2013 Regulation Art 27.
2 See the 2013 Regulation Art 28.
3 See the 2013 Regulation Art 29.

TMA 1994 s 89

17.62 As mentioned above, s 89 of the TMA 1994 only applies where the 2013 Regulation discussed above does not apply.[1] Under s 89(1) the proprietor (or licensee) may give Customs notice in writing:[2]

(a) that he is the proprietor (or, as the case may be, a licensee) of the trade mark;[3]
(b) specifying the time and place that goods, materials or articles infringing that trade mark are expected to arrive in the UK:
  (i) from outside the European Economic Area (EEA); or
  (ii) from within the EEA but not having been in free circulation in the EEA.
(c) requesting Customs to treat the infringing goods, material or articles as 'prohibited goods'.

1 TMA 1994 s 89(3).
2 The notice is in the form set out in the Schedule to the Trade Marks (Customs) Regulations 1994, SI 1994/2625. See Trade Marks (Customs) Regulations 1994, SI 1994/2625 reg 2.
3 In contrast to the position as regards notifications under the 2013 Regulation (where, upon the UK's withdrawal from the EU, the definition of a trade mark in Art 2(2) was amended so as not to include EUTMs), Community Trade Mark Regulations 2006, SI 2006/1027 Art 7 appears still to provide that s 89 applies to an EUTM as well as to a UK trade mark.

17.63 Whilst a notice is in force, the importation of the goods to which the notice relates (otherwise than by a person for his private and domestic use) is prohibited. Thus the goods may not be imported into the United Kingdom and are liable to forfeiture.[1]

1 TMA 1994 s 89(2). No other remedy arises by reason of the prohibition.

17.64 Under s 90 of the TMA 1994, Customs have power to make regulations as to the giving of a s 89 notice. The relevant regulations are the Trade Marks (Customs) Regulations 1994.[1] Regulation 2 of these regulations provides that a s 89 notice should be in the form set out in the Schedule to the regulations and that a separate form has to be used in respect of each arrival of goods. The regulations also deal with matters such as:

(a) the fees to be paid by the proprietor for lodging the notice;[2]
(b) the giving of security by the proprietor to cover Customs' potential liability or expenses;[3] and
(c) the giving of an indemnity by the proprietor.[4]

1 SI 1994/2625.
2 £30—SI 1994/2625 reg 3.
3 SI 1994/2625 reg 4.
4 SI 1994/2625 reg 5.

REMEDIES FOR INFRINGEMENT OF WELL-KNOWN MARKS

17.65 The law relating to the protection of well-known trade marks is considered in **Chapter 2** above.

17.66 *Entitlement to an injunction*—if a well-known trade mark is registered under the 1994 Act, the proprietor will be entitled to the usual remedies discussed above. However, the proprietor may be entitled to an injunction even if the well-known mark is not registered. This is because s 56(2) of the TMA 1994 provides that the proprietor of a well-known mark is entitled to an injunction to restrain the use in the United Kingdom of a trade mark[1] which or the essential part of which:

(a) is either identical with or similar to the proprietor's well-known trade mark; and
(b) is used in respect of identical or similar goods or services to those for which the proprietor's trade mark is well known;

provided the defendant's use of the trade mark is likely to cause confusion.

As pointed out by the Supreme Court in *Starbucks (HK) Ltd v British Sky Broadcasting Group*, this means that, where a mark is used abroad and has a reputation in this country, it still can be protected if it satisfies s 56(1), even if the proprietor of the mark cannot establish any customers or sufficient goodwill in this jurisdiction.[2]

1 Interestingly s 56(2) refers to the grant of an injunction against the use of 'a trade mark'. This contrasts with s 10 that defines infringement of registered trade marks by the use of 'a sign'.
2 [2015] UKSC 31 at [64].

17.67 *Essential part of a trade mark*—as set out above, an injunction may be granted under s 56(2) if the 'essential part' of the defendant's trade mark is either identical with or similar to the well-known trade mark. Presumably, the 'essential part' of the defendant's mark will be the distinctive element(s) of the mark which distinguish the goods or services to which it is applied. It is, then, those elements that must be compared with the well-known trade mark in order to determine whether there is the requisite identity or similarity.

17.68 *The need to prove confusion*—importantly, the availability of an injunction under s 56(2) is not dependent upon establishing infringement as such (although it involves establishing conduct that would constitute infringement under s 10(1)–(2) of the TMA 1994). However, unlike an action for infringement under s 10(1) (ie, where the sign in question is identical with the registered trade mark and is used in respect of identical goods or services), to be entitled to an injunction under s 56(2), the proprietor of the well-known mark always has to establish that the defendant's use of the mark is likely to cause confusion. This is so even where the defendant is using an identical mark on identical goods or services (although in such cases this should not present the proprietor with any great difficulty).

17.69 The words 'likely to cause confusion' are similar but not identical to the words used in s 10(2) where, in order to constitute an infringement of a registered trade mark, the use of the defendant's sign must give rise to 'a likelihood of confusion on the part of the public …'. The different wording is because the latter phrase was derived from the Directive, whereas s 56(2) was based on Article 6*bis* of the Paris Convention. However, it is likely that the phrases will be construed and applied consistently.

17.70 *Limitations on the right to an injunction*—the right to an injunction under s 56(2) can be defeated in a number of other ways.

(a) *Acquiescence*—an injunction will not be granted if s 48 of the TMA 1994 applies—ie, if the defendant's use was of a registered trade mark and the proprietor of the well-known mark had acquiesced in that use in the United Kingdom for a continuous period of five years being aware of that use. As an exception to this exception, s 48 will not provide a defence if the original registration of the trade mark was applied for in bad faith.
(b) *Saving for bona fide use*—an injunction will not be granted under s 56(2) to prevent the continuation of any bona fide use of a mark (whether registered or unregistered) which commenced prior to 31 October 1994 (the date on which s 56 came into force).[1] This contrasts with the requirement under s 11(3) where, in order to constitute a defence to infringement use must be of an earlier right which is 'protected by virtue of any rule of law (in particular, the law of passing-off)'.
(c) *Nationals of a Convention Country*—it is important to remember that s 56(2) only provides a remedy to proprietors of well-known marks who are nationals of or domiciled (etc) in a Convention country which, by virtue of the definition of 'Convention country' in s 55(1)(b), does not include the United Kingdom.

1 TMA 1994 s 56(3).

17.71 *Priority of well-known marks over registered trade marks*—because the injunction under s 56(2) is against use *'of a trade mark'* (which necessarily includes registered trade marks), the proprietor of a well-known trade mark can enjoin the use of a registered trade mark if such use otherwise falls within s 56(2). It seems, therefore, that the well-known trade mark takes priority over a registered trade mark in the event that there is a conflict. This conclusion is confirmed by the proviso at the end of the s 56(2) which provides that the right to the injunction is subject to s 48—ie, to any acquiescence by the proprietor in '*the use of a registered trade mark*'. The proprietor of the trade mark cannot, therefore, rely on his registration to defeat an application for an injunction based on a well-known trade mark. Nor can he rely on the defence contained in s 11(1) of the TMA 1994 because that defence is only available in an action for the infringement of a registered trade mark—and an injunction under s 56(2) is not founded on such an action. Indeed, none of the statutory defences available to a defendant in an action for infringement are available to defeat such an application, except for acquiescence and bona fide prior use.[1]

1 As expressly provided for in TMA 1994 s 56(2)–(3).

17.72 *Comparison with passing off*—Given that an injunction under s 56(2) will often be sought in conjunction with a claim in tort for passing-off, it is worth contrasting the two actions. It is likely that the injunction under s 56(2) may be more readily available for two reasons:

(a) insofar as it may be easier to establish that the defendant's use is likely to cause confusion (for the purposes of s 56(2)) than it is to establish misrepresentation and deception (for the purposes of passing off); and
(b) since the plaintiff does not need to have goodwill as such in the United Kingdom; in order to rely on s 56(2)—on the other hand, the plaintiff in a passing off action does not, as a matter of law, need to establish that his mark is 'well known' although the notoriety of his mark will be a factor in the case.

UNAUTHORISED APPLICATION FOR REGISTRATION BY AN AGENT OR REPRESENTATIVE

17.73 Another statutory remedy is that contained in TMA 1994 s 10B. This is available where a trade mark is registered in the name of an agent or representative (eg, a distributor) of the person who is the proprietor of that trade mark and without the consent of that person.

17.74 Under s 10B of the TMA 1994, unless the agent or representative justifies its registration, the proprietor can do either or both of (a) preventing use of the trade mark by the agent or representative and (b) applying for rectification of the register to substitute its name for that of the agent or representative.[1]

1 TMA 1994 s 10B(2), which was added to the TMA by SI 2018/825, reg 11. This effectively replaced TMA 1994 s 60 which was repealed by SI 2018/825, reg 28, subject to transitional provisions in SI 2018/825, regs 53 and 54.

17.75 *Justification*—as set out above, the remedies contained in s 10B are not available if, or to the extent that, the agent or representative justifies its action. What is it, though, that the agent or representative must 'justify'? In the context of s 10B, it is its action in registering the trade mark in its name. Obvious ways in which the agent or representative could seek to justify his action would be to rely on either an express or implied authorisation (whether contractual or otherwise) or to assert that it truly is the proprietor.

UNAUTHORISED USE OF ROYAL ARMS

17.76 The TMA 1994 creates certain criminal offences relating to the unauthorised use, in connection with any business, of the royal arms (or arms which so closely resemble the royal arms as to be calculated to deceive) or any other device, emblem or title in such a manner as to be calculated to lead to the belief that:

(a) in the case of the royal arms, he is authorised by Her Majesty to use the royal arms; or
(b) in the case of other relevant devices, emblems or titles, that he is employed by or supplies goods or services to Her Majesty or other members of the royal family.[1]

1 See TMA 1994 s 99(1)–(3).

17.77 In addition to constituting a criminal offence, the TMA 1994 also provides that the unauthorised use, in connection with any business, of the royal arms (or closely resembling arms) may be restrained by injunction in proceedings brought by:

(a) any person who is authorised to use the arms; or
(b) any person authorised by the Lord Chamberlain to take such proceedings.[1]

1 TMA 1994 s 99(4).

17.78 Similarly, the unauthorised use, in connection with any business, of any device, emblem or title in such a manner as to be calculated to lead to the belief that the person using the mark is employed by, or supplies goods or services to, Her Majesty or other members of the royal family may also be restrained by injunction in proceedings brought by:

(a) any person who is authorised to use the device, emblem or title in question; or
(b) any person authorised by the Lord Chamberlain to take such proceedings.

17.79 There is a defence to a claim for such injunction in s 99(5) of the TMA 1994 which provides that:

> 'Nothing in [s 99] affects any right of the proprietor of a trade mark containing any such arms, device, emblem or title to use that trade mark.'

It would seem, therefore, that as long as the defendant to such proceedings can establish that the arms etc are contained in a mark which is a 'trade mark' (as defined in s 1(1)) and that he is the proprietor of that trade mark, then his use of that trade mark cannot be enjoined pursuant to s 99(4).

CO-PROPRIETORS

17.80 Subject to any agreement between them to the contrary, co-proprietors of a trade mark are entitled to an equal undivided share in the registered trade mark.[1] Accordingly, any pecuniary remedy which co-proprietors may be awarded in respect of the infringement of their trade mark will be shared equally.

1 TMA 1994 s 23.

17.81 It will, therefore, be advisable for a co-proprietor who brings infringement proceedings by himself[1] to reach an agreement in advance with his co-proprietor(s) as to the apportionment of any pecuniary remedy which may be awarded in respect of the infringement.

1 In accordance with TMA 1994 s 23(5).

LICENSEES

17.82 *Introduction, ss 30 and 31*—as has already been discussed in **Chapter 13**, the circumstances in which a licensee can sue for relief will depend upon the nature and terms of the licence.

17.83 *Where the claimant is an exclusive licensees with right to sue,* where an exclusive licence provides that the licensee shall have the same rights and remedies in respect of matters occurring after the grant of the licence as if the licence had been an assignment, then the licensee may bring infringement proceedings against any person (other than the proprietor) in its own name[2] and its rights and remedies are deemed to be concurrent with those of the proprietor.[3] Some of the effects of 'concurrency' are that, in an action for infringement:

(a) the court, in assessing damages, will take into account:
    (i) the terms of the licence; and

    (ii) any pecuniary remedy already awarded or available to either the proprietor or the licensee in respect of the infringement;[4]
(b) no account of profits will be directed by the court if either:
    (i) an award of damages has been made; or
    (ii) an account of profits has been directed, in favour of the other of them in respect of the same infringement;[5] and
(c) the court will, if an account of profits is directed, apportion those profits between the proprietor and the exclusive licensee as the court considers just.[6]

These conditions apply to any action for infringement in respect of which the proprietor and an exclusive licensee have or had concurrent rights, regardless of whether they are both parties to the proceedings. If not, the court will make directions as it thinks fit as to how the party to the proceedings is to hold the proceeds of any pecuniary remedy on behalf of the other.

1 For the definitions of exclusive licensee and exclusive licence see TMA 1994 s 29(1).
2 TMA 1994 s 31(1); the proprietor himself will need to be joined as a plaintiff or added as a defendant: s 31(4), but not in the case of an application for interlocutory relief which can be made by the licensee alone: TMA 1994 s 31(4). By reason of the words 'other than the proprietor', the exclusive licensee's rights against the proprietor will arise, if at all, under contract; see *Northern & Shell plc v Condé Nast and National Magazines Distributers Ltd* [1995] RPC 117.
3 TMA 1994 s 31(2).
4 TMA 1994 s 31(6)(a).
5 TMA 1994 s 31(6)(b).
6 TMA 1994 s 31(6)(c) subject to any agreement between the proprietor and the licensee: TMA 1994 s 31(6)(c) and (8).

17.84 *Where the claimant is another type of licensee*—other licensees have more limited rights of action. First, under s 30(2) and (3) of the TMA 1994, other types of exclusive licensee (ie exclusive licensees whose licences do not provide that the licensee shall have the same rights and remedies as if the licence had been an assignment) can, subject to the terms of the licence, bring proceedings in their own names as if they were proprietor in circumstances where the proprietor has refused or failed to do so within two months of being called upon by his licensee. It appears, therefore, that such licensees will be entitled to the same rights and remedies to which the proprietor would have been entitled had the proprietor commenced the proceedings. This does not mean, of course, that the licensee can recover damages suffered by the proprietor: the licensee will only be able to recover those damages which he himself has suffered.[1] Subject to this, under s 30(1A) of the TMA 1994, other licences can only bring proceedings for infringement if the licence so provides or if the proprietor consents. As s 30(1A) does not contain the words 'as if he were the proprietor', it is not entirely clear on what basis such licensees sue but it appears to be envisaged that such licensees can sue for their own damages.

In every case under s 30, the licensee is required (except when seeking interim relief) to join the proprietor as a party (either as a co-claimant or defendant).[2]

1 *Northern & Shell plc v Condé Nast and National Magazines Distributers Ltd* [1995] RPC 117.
2 TMA 1994 s 30(4). Such a proprietor shall not be made liable in costs unless it takes part in the proceedings – see TMA 1994 s 30(5).

17.85 *Where the claimant is the proprietor*—where infringement proceedings are brought by the proprietor, the position of a licensee will again depend on whether or not they are exclusive licensees with the rights and remedies of an assignee. If they are, then the position is that if the proprietor and the exclusive licensee are not both parties to the proceedings, the court will give directions as it thinks fit as to the extent to which the party to the proceedings is to hold the proceeds of any pecuniary remedy on behalf of the other.[1] In the case of other licensees, the position in infringement proceedings brought by the proprietor, is that any loss suffered or likely to be suffered by licensees[2] will be taken into account and the court will give directions as it thinks fit as to the extent to which the proprietor is to hold the proceeds of any pecuniary remedy on behalf of licensees.[3]

1 TMA 1994 s 31(6).
2 Including exclusive licensees not having the rights and remedies of an assignee under s 31(1), as well as sub-licensees in the case of an exclusive licensee having the rights and remedies of an assignee: s 30(7).
3 TMA 1994 s 30(6).

JURISDICTION OF THE COURTS

17.86 Under the Civil Procedure Rules[1] claims relating to UK trade marks and (in cases commenced before 11pm on 31 December 2020 when the UK's withdrawal from the EU became effective) EUTMs must be started in one of:

(a) the Chancery Division of the High Court;
(b) the Intellectual Property Enterprise Court ('IPEC');[2] or
(c) (save as set out in the practice direction to Part 63 CPR) a county court hearing centre where there is also a Chancery District Registry—currently Birmingham, Bristol, Cardiff, Leeds, Liverpool, Manchester, and Newcastle-upon-Tyne.[3]

1 CPR 63.13 and PD 63 para 16.1(14).
2 Formerly, the Patents County Court. This court is now a specialist list of the Chancery Division of the High Court—see r 26 Civil Procedure (Amendment No 7) Rules 2013/1974. The *IPEC Guide* is readily available online and provides a very useful aide to proceedings in this court. See also *Intellectual Property Enterprise Court: Practice and Procedure* 2nd edn by Angela Fox, Sweet & Maxwell (June 2016).
3 CPR PD 63, paras 16.1(14) and 16.2–16.3. The County Courts at Caernarfon, Mold and Preston (at which there are Chancery registries) are said by CPR PD 63, para 16.3, to be excluded.

17.87 The High Court has unlimited jurisdiction to grant the remedies contained in the TMA 1994 in respect of UK trade marks.[1] For cases commenced before 11pm on 31 December 2020 (when the UK's withdrawal from the EU became effective), the High Court was also a designated Community trade mark court and so had jurisdiction also to grant those remedies in respect of EUTMs.[2]

1 The definition of 'The Court' in TMA 1994 s 75 expressly refers to the High Court. Hence, the High Court can also hear revocation proceedings.
2 Community Trade Mark Regulations 2006, SI 2006/1027 reg 12.

17.88 As regards IPEC, this has the jurisdiction conferred on all county courts to hear tort cases.[1] Accordingly it has jurisdiction to hear infringement cases—although its jurisdiction in relation to a claim for damages or an account of profits is limited to £500,000.[2] In addition, as IPEC is a part of the High Court, it is able to grant other remedies including, for example, those contained in TMA 1994 ss 15 (erasure, removal, obliteration, destruction), 16 (delivery up), 19 (destruction or forfeiture), 23(5) (co-proprietors), 25(4)(b), 46 (revocation), 47 (declaration of invalidity), 64 (rectification of registration), 73 (certificate of validity) and 74 (direction to registrar to appear) and also in para 12 of Sch 1 (infringement of collective marks) and para 14 of Sch 2 ((infringement of certification marks). Save in its small track, IPEC also has power to grant interim injunctions and to make search and imaging orders.[3] For cases commenced before 11pm on 31 December 2020 IPEC was also a designated Community trade mark court and so had jurisdiction also to grant all such remedies in respect of EUTMs[4] (subject to the above financial limit).

1 County Courts Act 1984 s 15.
2 CPR 63.17A(1). See also Patents County Court (Financial Limits) (No 2) Order 2011, SI 2011/2222 Art 3.
3 CPR r 63.27(4).
4 Community Trade Mark Regulations 2006, SI 2006/1027 reg 12(1).

17.89 The county courts in Birmingham, Bristol, Cardiff, Leeds, Liverpool, Manchester and Newcastle upon Tyne have jurisdiction in relation to UK trade marks and (for cases brought before 11pm on 31 December 2020) EUTMs[1]—save that there is no limitation on the value of the claim.[2]

1 CPR r 63.13 and PD 63, paras 16.2 and 16.3 and Community Trade Mark Regulations 2006 reg 12(1)–(2).
2 County Courts Act 1984 s 15, and High Court and County Court Jurisdiction Order 1991 (as amended) Art 2(1)(l).

17.90 Theoretically other County Courts have jurisdiction to hear claims for infringement of UK trade marks as a statutory tort—although given CPR 63.13, such proceedings are likely to be transferred or struck out.[1] Such courts have no jurisdiction in relation to the other remedies under the TMA 1994 (ss 15–16, etc).[2] Nor were they designated EUTM courts.

1 County Courts Act 1984 s 15. As mentioned in the footnotes to **17.87**, it is possible that the county courts at Caernarfon, Mold, and Preston have jurisdiction in relation to infringement proceedings where the only remedies sought are those provided for in TMA 1994 s 14 (damages, account, and injunctions).

2 This is because they are not included in the definition of 'the Court' in TMA 1994 s 75. See *Minsterstone Ltd v Be Modern Ltd* [2002] FSR 53.

17.91 For matters of jurisdiction involving the country in which proceedings should be commenced and which country's law the courts should apply, readers are referred to the specialist books on the subject.

Chapter 18

Groundless threats

INTRODUCTION

18.01 To allege infringement of a registered trade mark is a serious matter. It may well cause the recipient of the allegation to fear that court proceedings will be brought, potentially leading to injunctions in respect of alleged infringements (often involving a core part of the recipient's business) as well as exposure to costs and an award of damages. It may also cause third parties to stop dealing with the recipient of the threat. Accordingly, recipients often cease the acts complained of for purely commercial reasons and to avoid unnecessary risk, even when they strenuously deny that "any infringement has occurred.

18.02 For this reason, where a person threatens another with proceedings for infringement of a registered trade mark, the law allows "any person aggrieved" to bring proceedings for relief:[1]

- For UK trade marks, this is pursuant to ss 21–21F of the Trade Marks 1994 ('TMA 1994').[2] The same applies to comparable trade marks (EU).[3]
- For EUTMs in respect of proceedings commenced before 31 December 2020, this is pursuant to the Community Trade Mark Regulations 2006 (by which the provisions of ss 21–21D and s 21F of the TMA 1994 also apply to EUTMs and to protected designations of the EUTM under an international registration).[4]
- For protected designations of the UK under an International Registration, this is pursuant to the Trade Marks (International Registration) Order 2008.[5]

1 For the policy underlying the threats provisions, see *Best Buy Co Inc v Worldwide Sales Corp Espana SL* [2011] EWCA Civ 618 at [14] and [21] where the Court of Appeal approved the comment of Lightman J in *L'Oréal (UK) Ltd v Johnson & Johnson* [2000] FSR 686 at [12] that: 'The policy represented by the first statutory threats provision … was clearly to stop patentees who were (in Pope's words about Addison) "willing to wound but afraid to strike" from holding the sword of Damocles above another's head …'.

2 TMA 1994 ss 21–21F were substituted for the former s 21 by pursuant to the Intellectual Property (Unjustified Threats) Act 2017 with effect from 1 October 2017. The same Act also similarly amended the threats provisions relating to designs.

3 Ie, UK marks created to reflect EUTMs in existence as at 31 December 2020—see TMA 1994 Sch 2A para 1(3).

4 SI 2006/1027 reg 6(1)–(2) (as amended by the Intellectual Property (Unjustified Threats) Act 2017).

5 SI 2008/2206 reg 3(3). The position under the 2008 Regulations is slightly less clear than it was under the 1996 Regulations that they replaced (SI 1996/714). Under the 1996 Regulations, art 4(6) expressly provided for the application of TMA 1994 s 21 to protected international trade marks (UK). By contrast, reg 3(3) of the 2008 Regulations provides that (save for certain provisions listed in Part 1 of Sch 1 to the Regulations) the provisions of the TMA 1994 apply to international trade marks (UK).

THREATS OF INFRINGEMENT PROCEEDINGS

18.03 Under the threats provisions of the TMA 1994, a cause of action can arise where a person makes a communication which contains a threat of infringement proceedings. In the case of threats made on or after 1 October 2017, a communication contains such a threat if a reasonable person in the position of a recipient would understand from the communication that:

(a) a registered trade mark exists; and
(b) a person intends to bring proceedings (whether in a court in the United Kingdom or elsewhere) against another person for infringement of that trade mark by (i) an act done in the United Kingdom, or (ii) an act which, if done, would be done in the United Kingdom.[1]

The threat, therefore, must relate to acts or prospective acts to be done in the UK. However, the threatened infringement proceedings could be in the UK or elsewhere.

As to what may constitute a threat for these purposes, as is clear from the reference to 'a reasonable person in the position of the recipient', the test is objective. It requires the court to have regard to all of the relevant circumstances as at the date the communication and to take the communication as a whole and in context.[2] A communication may not be seen as a threat to bring infringement proceedings when looked at in isolation, but may be when seen in the context of the whole course of dealing[3] and a threat may be implied, even where the letter specifically states proceedings are not contemplated.[4] It does not matter that at the time of the threat and unknown to the recipient, proceedings had in fact been issued.[5] In the context of the analogous threats provisions relating to Community design rights, the High Court has held that the use of eBay's VeRo programme to take down alleged infringements of a design constituted an actionable threat of proceedings.[6] As the test is objective, evidence of how a communication was subjectively understood by the recipient is not strictly admissible nor is evidence of subsequent correspondence likely to be of much assistance.[7] However, if a reasonable recipient would have sought specialist legal advice as to the meaning of a communication, then the question whether objectively it constituted a threat would have been answered in the light of that advice.[8]

1 TMA 1994, s 21(1) (as amended). For threats made before 1 October 2017, see the previous edition of this work.
2 See, *Lifestyle Equities CV v Royal County of Berkshire Polo Club Limited* [2018] EWHC 3552 (Ch) at [91]. See also *Samsung Electronics (UK) Ltd v Apple Inc* [2012] EWHC 889 at [35(i)], *C and P Development Co (London) Ltd v Sisabro Novelty Co Ltd* (1953) 70 RPC 277 at 280 (a patent case) and *Best Buy Co Inc v Worldwide Sales Corporation Espana SL* [2011] EWCA Civ 618 at [18] where the fact that the letter proposed a settlement supported the argument that it constituted a threat of proceedings.
3 See *Brain v Ingledew Brown Bennison & Garrett* [1997] FSR 511 at 521. See also *L'Oreal (UK) Ltd v Johnson & Johnson* [2000] FSR 686 where a solicitor's letter (said to be the work of a master of Delphic utterances) arguably constituted a threat even though it disclaimed making any threat. The threat might have been veiled and muffled but it was sufficient to unsettle a recipient. See also *EC Medica Group UK Ltd v Dearnley-Davison* [2018] EWHC 1952 at [124]–[127] where the claimant's email to the defendant's customer stated that the claimant had no current intention of suing the defendant's customers but was nevertheless held to constitute a threat.
4 *Grimme Landmaschinenfabrik GmbH & Co KG v Scott* [2010] FSR 11.
5 *Lifestyle Equities CV v Royal County of Berkshire Polo Club Limited* [2018] EWHC 3552 (Ch) at [99]–[101].
6 *Quads 4 Kids Ltd v Campbell* [2006] EWHC 2482 (Ch).
7 *Best Buy Co Inc v Worldwide Sales Corp Espana SL* [2011] EWCA Civ 618 at [19]. See also *Prince v Prince* [1998] FSR 21.
8 *Tech 21 UK Ltd v Logitech Europe SA* [2015] EWHC 2614 at [69].

FORM OF THREAT

18.04 The TMA 1994 does not set any criteria as regards the form or nature of the communication. It may be oral or written and the threat it contains may be express or implied, veiled and covert, conditional or future. It may be made in response to an enquiry from the person threatened,[1] made as part of a semi-formal complaints procedure[2] or made in a private letter.[3] Moreover, as appears from s 21(2) of the TMA 1994, the threat could be contained in a communication directed at the public or a section of the public (eg in a press release or circular), provided that communication could be seen as being directed at a person. It is enough that the words or deeds in question, viewed objectively, show an intention to bring infringement proceedings.[4] At present, it is unclear whether a threats action can be brought on the basis of a without prejudice communication.[5]

1 *Samsung Electronics (UK) Ltd v Apple Inc* [2012] EWHC 889 at [35(iii)] and *L'Oreal (UK) Ltd v Johnson & Johnson* [2000] FSR 686 at [12] (approved by Lord Neuberger MR in *Best Buy Co Inc v Worldwide Sales Corporation Espana SL* [2011] EWCA Civ 618 at [20]–[23]).
2 See *Quads 4 Kids v Campbell* [2006] EWHC 2482.
3 *Skinner v Perry* (1893) 10 RPC 1.
4 *Samsung Electronics (UK) Ltd v Apple Inc.* [2012] EWHC 889 at [35(ii)].

5 Contrast *Unilever Plc v The Proctor & Gamble Co* [2000] 1 WLR 2436 (CA) with *Best Buy Co Inc v Worldwide Sales Corporation Espana SL* [2011] EWCA Civ 618 at [42]–[45].

EXCLUDED THREATS

18.05 Under s 21A(2)–(5) of the TMA 1994, certain threats are not actionable. They are:

(1) A threat of infringement proceedings where the infringement is alleged to consist of:
   (a) applying, or causing another person to apply, a sign to goods or their packaging;
   (b) importing, for disposal, goods to which, or to the packaging of which, a sign has been applied; or
   (c) supplying services under a sign.[1]

   This exclusion reflects the fact that the evil against which the threats provisions guards is the making of threats to customers and traders and is not the making of threats against those primarily responsible for putting infringing goods on the market.

(2) A threat of proceedings in respect of acts which, if done, would fall within the exclusion in (1) above.[2]

(3) A threat of proceedings if the threat:
   (a) is made against a person who has done, or intends to do, an act mentioned in (1)(a) or (1)(b) above in relation to goods or their packaging; and
   (b) is a threat of proceedings for infringement alleged to consist of doing anything else in relation to those goods or their packaging.[3]

(4) A threat of proceedings if the threat: (a) is made against a person who has done, or intends to do, an act mentioned in (1)(c) above in relation to services, and (b) is a threat for infringement alleged to consist of doing anything else in relation to those services.[4]

(5) Threats which are not express threats and which are contained in a permitted communication as defined in s 21B of the TMA 1994,[5] as to which, see further below.

1 TMA 1994 s 21A(2).
2 TMA 1994 s 21A(3).
3 TMA 1994 s 21A(4).
4 TMA 1994 s 21A(5).
5 TMA 1994 s 21A(6).

THE PERMITTED COMMUNICATIONS EXCLUSION

18.06 As indicated above, under s 21B(1)(6) of the TMA 1994, a threat of infringement proceedings which is not an express threat is not actionable if it is contained in a permitted communication.

Not an 'express threat'

18.07 The permitted communication exclusion only applies if the threat contained in a communication is not an express threat of infringement proceedings. The exclusion will not, therefore, apply to a letter before action sent in accordance with the CPR which, by definition, will contain an express threat of infringement proceedings. It may, however, apply to a letter which merely seeks information and in which any threat is merely implied.

A permitted communication

18.08 To be excluded the (implied) threat of infringement proceedings must be contained in a permitted communication. For these purposes, a communication is a permitted communication if:

(a) so far as it contains information that relates to the threat, it is made for a permitted purpose; and
(b) all of the information relating to the threat is information that:
   (i) is necessary for that purpose; and
   (ii) the person making the communication reasonably believes is true.[1]

Information that is 'necessary'

18.09 The TMA 1994 provides some examples of the sort of information that would be necessary for a permitted purpose,[2] namely:

(a) a statement that a registered trade mark exists and is in force or that an application for registration of a trade mark has been made;
(b) details of the registered trade mark or of a right in or under a registered trade mark which:
   (i) are accurate in all material respects; and
   (ii) are not misleading in any material respect; and
(c) information enabling the identification of articles that are alleged to be infringing articles in relation to the design.

A permitted purpose

18.10 To be excluded the communication must also be for a permitted purpose. Under s 21B(2) of the TMA 1994, each of the following is a permitted purpose:[3]

(a) giving notice that a registered trade mark exists;
(b) discovering whether, or by whom, a registered trade mark has been infringed by an act mentioned in s 21A(2)(a), (b) or (c);[4]
(c) giving notice that a person has a right in or under the registered trade mark, where another person's awareness of the right is relevant to

any proceedings that may be brought in respect of the registered trade mark.

Again, this is not a closed list and the court may, having regard to the purposes permitted under (a)–(c) above, treat any other purpose as 'a permitted purpose' if it considers that it is in the interests of justice to do so.[5]

Purposes that are not permitted

18.11 Some purposes are expressly stated to be not permitted,[6] namely:

(a) requesting a person to cease using in the course of trade, a sign in relation to goods or services;
(b) requesting a person to deliver up or destroy goods; or
(c) requesting a person to give an undertaking relating to the use of a sign in relation to goods or services.

1 TMA 1994 s 21B(1).
2 TMA 1994 s 21B(5). It is clear from the wording of TMA 1994 s 21B(1)(b) that these are examples and not an exhaustive list.
3 CDPA 1988 s 253B(2).
4 For such acts, see para **18.05(1)** above.
5 TMA 1994 s 21B(3).
6 TMA 1994 s 21B(4).

PERSON AGGRIEVED

18.12 Assuming the threat is actionable, the person entitled to bring an action in respect of it is a 'person aggrieved by the threat'.[1] The TMA 1994 does not provide a definition of such a person but, on the basis of the pre-2017 authorities, it would seem that a person aggrieved is a person with a real, as opposed to a fanciful, commercial, interest with which the threat interferes.[2] In patent cases, it has been held that persons aggrieved must be able to show non-trivial damage to themselves arising from the threat[3] and these cases were referred to with apparent approval in *Samuel Smith Old Brewery (Tadcaster) v Lee*[4] (a trade mark case). Despite this, the courts have been willing to infer damage in appropriate cases despite the lack of direct evidence of damage.[5] However, given the authorities, it seems clear that if the circumstances are such that the court could not properly infer damage, a threats action would not lie.

The 'person aggrieved' will often be the recipient of the threats. However, a third party may also be a person aggrieved—for example, where a threat causes the recipient of the threat to withdraw orders from that third party or otherwise disrupts the course of business between the recipient and that third party. Whether a person has suffered damage is a matter of fact to be demonstrated by the person bringing the action for unjustified threats. Clearly, much will depend on the need to show a causal link between the threat and the damage.

1 TMA 1994 s 21A(1)
2 See *Brain v Ingledew Brown Bennison & Garrett* [1997] FSR 511 at 519. A director of or a shareholder in a company may have sufficient personal interest in the company that he or she would be a person aggrieved by threats made against that company (see 524). Where a threat is made against a retailer of allegedly infringing articles, the supplier of those goods may be a person aggrieved—see *Carflow Products (UK) Ltd v Linwood Securities (Birmingham) Ltd* [1996] FSR 424. In *Generics (UK) Ltd v Warner-Lambert Co LLC* [2015] EWHC 2548 (Pat) a patentee wrote to the Department of Health seeking to persuade it to issue guidance with respect to a drug. As the letter was not intended for dissemination to pharmacists, a rival pharmaceutical company was not a person aggrieved by the letter. By contrast, where the same patentee wrote to a pharmacy seeking to persuade it not to stock that rival's product, the rival was a person aggrieved (see [718]–[719]).
3 *Dimplex (UK) Ltd v De Longhi* Ltd [1996] FSR 622 and *Brain v Ingeldew Brown Bennington & Garrett (No 3)* [1997] FSR 511 at 516–520.
4 [2011] EWHC 1879 (Ch).
5 See *Data Marketing & Secretarial Ltd v S & S Enterprises Ltd* [2014] EWHC 1499 (IPEC) at [47] where HHJ Hacon suggested (obiter) that the person at whom the threat was directed will be a person aggrieved even if no evidence of damage, or of the likelihood of damage is adduced, as damage will be inferred. See also *Best Buy Co Inc v Worldwide Sales Corp España SL* [2011] EWCA Civ 618 at [49]–[51].

PERSON LIABLE IN RESPECT OF AN ACTIONABLE THREAT

18.13 Subject to the professional adviser exception considered below, the person against whom a threats action can be brought is the person who makes the threat. There is no requirement that that person should have an interest in the registered trade mark in question.[1]

1 TMA 1994 s 21C(1).

THREATS BY PROFESSIONAL ADVISER

18.14 In the case of threats made on or after 1 October 2017, a professional adviser (or any person vicariously liable for the actions of that professional adviser) is excluded from liability for making an actionable threat provided certain conditions are met.[1] For these purposes, it is for the person seeking to be excluded from liability to show that he or she was acting as a professional adviser and that the relevant conditions (see below) were met.[2] The fact that a professional adviser (or the person vicariously liable) is covered by the exclusion does not affect the liability of the person on whose instructions that person was acting.[3]

1 TMA 1994 s 21D(1).
2 TMA 1994 s 21D(5).
3 TMA 1994 s 21D(4).

Professional adviser

18.15 For the purposes of this exclusion, a 'professional adviser' is a person who, in relation to the making of the communication containing the threat: (a) is acting in a professional capacity in providing legal services or the services of a trade mark attorney or a patent attorney, and (b) is regulated in the provision of legal services, or the services of a trade mark attorney or a patent attorney, by one or more regulatory bodies (whether through membership of a regulatory body, the issue of a licence to practise or any other means).[1]

1 TMA 1994 s 21D(2).

The conditions to be satisfied

18.16 The conditions to be satisfied if a professional adviser (or any person vicariously liable for the actions of a professional adviser) is to fall within the exclusion are that: (a) in making the communication the professional adviser was acting on the instructions of another person; and (b) when the communication was made the professional adviser identifies the person on whose instructions the adviser is acting.[1]

1 TMA 1994 s 21D(3).

DEFENCES

18.17 If it is proved that an actionable threat has been made, then a person aggrieved is entitled to relief unless the maker of the threat can establish one of two defences.

The first defence is that the threat had been justified, ie that the acts in respect of which proceedings were threatened did constitute (or if done would have constituted) an infringement of the registered trade mark.[1]

The second defence is where the maker of the threat shows that (a) despite having taken reasonable steps, that person has not identified anyone who has done an act mentioned TMA 1994 s 21A(2)(a), (b) or (c) in relation to the goods or their packaging or the services which were the subject of the threat; and (b) that person notified the recipient of the threat, before or at the time of making the threat, of the steps taken.[2]

1 TMA 1994 s 21C(2).
2 TMA 1994 s 21C(3).

REMEDIES

18.18 Where a threats action succeeds, a court may:[1]

(a) make a declaration that the threat was unjustifiable;
(b) grant an injunction against the continuance of such threats; or
(c) award damages in respect of any loss sustained by the aggrieved person by reason of the threat.

Where damages are claimed, it is necessary to show actual damage, and that this damage was caused by the threat. This would typically be the lost trade caused by being forced to withdraw the product, or the withdrawal of orders by customers due to the existence of the threats.[2]

1 TMA 1994 s 21C(1).
2 *LB Europe Ltd (t/a DuPont Liquid Packaging Systems) v Smurfit Bag in Box SA* [2008] EWHC 1231 (Ch).

Chapter 19

Criminal offences

INTRODUCTION

19.01 Offences under the TMA 1994 fall into two categories: those relating to the unauthorised use of a trade mark and those relating to the trade mark register and other offences. The former category is generally more important than the latter and will occupy the bulk of this chapter.

UNAUTHORISED USE OF A TRADE MARK: COUNTERFEITING

19.02 Counterfeiting is dealt with by s 92 of the Trade Marks Act 1994 ('TMA 1994'). There are three types of offences, set out under subsections (1), (2) and (3) respectively, all of which have a large number of similar components. It should be noted that in this chapter, the word 'counterfeit' is used to mean both 'true' counterfeit goods (ie goods which have not been manufactured by or under licence from the trade mark proprietor) and also 'grey market' goods (ie goods which were made by or under licence from the trade mark proprietor but whose sale has not been authorised by that person for some reason). The offences created by s 92(1) to (3) can apply in respect of dealings with both types of goods.[1]

A specific defence to liability under s 92(1) is provided by s 92(5) and is discussed further below.

1 *R v M* [2017] UKSC 58.

19.03 Most criminal offences require a particular mental element (*mens rea*) and a given set of actions or circumstances (*actus reus*). The mental elements of the s 92 offences present a low threshold by comparison to crimes such as theft or murder. The *actus reus* components are discussed further below.

The mental element

19.04 The mental element required under each of the three s 92 offences is the same—namely:

> 'A person commits an offence who with a view to gain for himself or another, or with intent to cause loss to another …'.

There is then a common requirement that the act be *'without the consent of the proprietor'*.

19.05 The common mental element of each of the three s 92 offences is therefore that the person acts either 'with a view to gain' or 'with intent to cause loss', depending on the circumstances. It is important to note that there is a distinction between 'with a view' and 'with intent'.

19.06 As regards 'with a view', the Court of Appeal in *Zaman*[1] approved a formulation given by the trial judge in that case that 'with a view' means to have something in contemplation, not necessarily as something desired or intended but as something that might realistically occur.

1 *R v Zaman* [2002] EWCA Crim 1862; [2003] FSR 13.

19.07 'With intent', on the other hand, is a well-recognised concept in criminal law with an astonishing array of judicial analysis—including that of the House of Lords in *Woollin.*[1] In essence, a person intends to do something if he or she foresees the outcome as a virtually certain consequence (barring some intervening act) whether or not that outcome is desired by that person. However, the jury in a counterfeiting case will normally not need to be given such a complex direction on this point by the judge, since whether the defendant intended to cause loss is likely to be fairly obvious.

1 *R v Woollin* [1999] 1 AC 82 (HL).

Without consent

19.08 For an offence to be committed, the act complained of must have been done without the proprietor's consent. This is stated explicitly in s 92. The onus of proving this lies on the prosecution. However, a defendant may well assert that his or her use was not without consent, for example, by suggesting that the sign was applied with the proprietor's consent and the goods are simply being resold.

19.09 The prosecution in counterfeiting cases will frequently adduce expert evidence in order to prove that the goods in relation to which the defendant has been charged are not goods that have been manufactured with consent. The courts have consistently upheld the use of appropriate expert evidence, whilst emphasising that the expert evidence must not replace the independent judgment of the jury or magistrates.[1]

1 See, for example, *Akhtar v Grout* (1998) 162 JP 714 (CA).

Infringing signs

19.10 The offences all require some form of use of a sign. In each case s 92 requires that sign to be *'identical to, or likely to be mistaken for, a registered trade mark'*. Identity is a concept familiar from civil infringement (see **Chapters 5** and **14**) and there is no reason to suspect its meaning here is any different, but 'likely to be mistaken for' is a formula of words only used in s 92.

Use of the infringing sign

19.11 In *Johnstone*[1] the House of Lords held that an offence is only committed under s 92 where the trade mark is *used* in the sense of affecting its function of origin. This is a question of fact in every case, but the court should look beyond the facts of the initial transaction and consider whether the mark is being used if for example the goods were to be sold on later.[2] Their Lordships were somewhat equivocal as to whether an offence could be committed in a situation where there was no civil infringement.

1 *R v Johnstone* [2003] UKHL 28; [2003] FSR 42; [2004] ETMR 2.
2 *CPS v Morgan* [2006] EWCA Crim 1742, 14 July 2006. This is consistent with the approach to civil infringement.

19.12 There is very little case law on this concept of use. In *Boulter*[1] the Court of Appeal held that a defendant was 'using' the mark where his signs were identical to registered marks but very poor quality reproductions; however, the Court did not analyse the ambit of 'identical or likely to be mistaken for'.

1 *R v Boulter* [2008] EWCA Crim 2375; [2009] ETMR 6.

19.13 Although there are parallels with civil infringement, there is not a complete overlap between civil infringement and criminal liability. Even if one ignores the differences between 'likely to be mistaken for' and 'likelihood of confusion', s 92(4) provides that:

> 'A person does not commit an offence under this section unless –
> (a) the goods are goods in respect of which the trade mark is registered, or
> (b) the trade mark has a reputation in the United Kingdom and the use of the sign takes or would take unfair advantage of,

or is detrimental to, the distinctive character or repute of the trade mark.'

Therefore, there is apparently no criminal liability for using a sign likely to be mistaken for a registered trade mark on goods *similar to* the goods in respect of which the trade mark is registered, unless the avenue of reputation and unfair advantage or detriment is available to the prosecution.

19.14 Further, there is no criminal liability for use of a sign likely to be mistaken for a registered trade mark in relation to *services*. This is suggested throughout s 92 by the frequent reference to activity in relation to 'goods'. Moreover, s 92(4) makes it explicit that signs used for services are not covered by the s 92 offences at all.

19.15 Lastly in the way of limitation on the scope of the offences, it is all too often overlooked (even by the prosecution) that no offence is committed in relation to activity carried out before the date of publication of the registration.[1]

1 TMA 1994 s 9(3).

Section 92(1)—goods bearing the sign

19.16 Subject to the points made above, under s 92(1) an offence may be committed by: a person who, without the consent of the proprietor:

> '(a) applies to goods or their packaging a sign identical to, or likely to be mistaken for, a registered trade mark; or
> (b) sells or lets for hire, offers or exposes for sale or hire or distributes goods which bear or the packaging of which bears, such a sign; or
> (c) has in his possession, custody or control in the course of a business any such goods with a view to the doing of anything, by himself or another, which would be an offence under paragraph (b).'

These are all separate, standalone offences. It is not necessary that there has been an offence under (a) in order for there to be an offence under (b). In other words, (b) and (c) can apply to 'grey market' goods as well as to true counterfeit goods.[1]

1 *R v M* [2017] UKSC 58 at [7]–[12].

19.17 Thus s 92(1) catches each link in the chain of production and sale (or hire) of counterfeit goods which bear an infringing sign:

- paragraph (a) deals with the manufacturer;
- paragraph (b) covers the vendor; and

- paragraph (c) serves to catch persons who are involved in the trade of counterfeit goods but against whom none of the specific activities under paragraph (b) can be proved. It may apply, for example, to someone who has not yet commenced trading in counterfeit goods but has obtained them for that purpose, or perhaps to someone who is storing the goods for another person who will act as vendor.

19.18 As regards paragraph (c), the Court of Appeal in *Kousar*[1] allowed the defendant's appeal where the goods in question were kept in their house by her husband. She had no role in running her husband's business and the Court concluded that she was not in possession of the goods in the course of business. Also, her mere *ability to control* what was kept in the house (in the sense of her ability to demand its removal) was not to be equated with 'control' as required by s 92(1). Her knowledge of the goods' presence and her acquiescence thereto was not sufficient to constitute an offence. The Court referred to authorities relating to the concept of possession in relation to drugs offences, but did not specifically opine on whether the concept was the same for offences under s 92.

1 *R v Kousar* [2009] EWCA Crim 139; [2009] 2 CrAppR 5.

19.19 Paragraph (c) introduces an additional mental element for offences under that paragraph—namely that it be done '*with a view to the doing of anything, by himself or another, which would be an offence under paragraph (b)*'. The test for 'with a view to' is the same as in the rest of s 92.[1]

1 *R v Zaman* [2002] EWCA Crim 1862; [2003] FSR 13.

Section 92(2)—materials bearing the sign

19.20 Subject, again, to the general points considered at paras **19.02–19.15** above, the second type of offence is that set out in s 92(2). This provides that an offence may be committed by a person who:

> '(a) applies a sign identical to, or likely to be mistaken for, a registered trade mark to material intended to be used –
> (i) for labelling or packaging goods,
> (ii) as a business paper in relation to goods, or
> (iii) for advertising goods, or
> (b) uses in the course of a business material bearing such a sign for labelling or packaging goods, as a business paper in relation to goods, or for advertising goods, or
> (c) has in his possession, custody or control in the course of a business any such material with a view to the doing of anything, by himself or another, which would be an offence under paragraph (b).'

19.21 The structure of s 92(2) clearly mirrors that of s 92(1) but it is concerned with the application of signs to business materials rather than to goods themselves. There is a certain overlap between s 92(1) and (2) when it comes to signs on packaging.

19.22 Again, the activities listed in s 92(2)(a)–(c) are intended to catch every step in the process. The types of activities described in (a) and (c) (ie, 'applies' and 'possession, custody or control') are identical to those in the equivalent paragraphs of s 92(1). Paragraph (b) prohibits the 'use' of business materials bearing the sign. This is potentially wider than the formulation in s 92(1)(b) but in practice it is difficult to envisage much 'use' that is not at least related to selling, letting, offering or exposing for sale or hire or distributing the goods, other than use on business papers or use in advertising, but those latter activities are themselves specifically listed in s 92(2)(b).

Section 92(3)—articles for making signs

19.23 The final type of offence under s 92 is that provided for in s 92(3), which is concerned with the production and potential use of articles for making copies of registered marks. Subject, once again, to the general points considered above, s 92(3) provides that an offence may be committed by a person who:

> '(a) makes an article specifically designed or adapted for making copies of a sign identical to, or likely to be mistaken for, a registered trade mark, or
> (b) has such an article in his possession, custody or control in the course of a business,
>
> knowing or having reason to believe that it has been, or is to be, used to produce goods, or material for labelling or packaging goods, as a business paper in relation to goods, or for advertising goods.'

19.24 The offences under s 92(3) are therefore similar to those of the preceding subsections but fall into only two paragraphs. The article in question must have been 'specifically designed or adapted' for making infringing signs. As such, ordinary copying equipment does not normally fall within the scope of the offence, but things like moulds for casting trade marks on counterfeit watches would be covered.

19.25 Like s 92(2), s 92(3) adds an additional mental element to this offence—ie, *'knowing or having reason to believe …'* (etc). There is no case law on this point, but the concept of knowledge is widely used in the criminal law, even if its precise ambit varies from offence to offence.

Section 92(5) defence—reasonable belief of non-infringement

19.26 As has been discussed above, the mental element for the main offences is one of gain or causing loss and does not relate to the infringement as such. In order to avoid criminalising people who might well have innocent motives, Parliament provided in s 92(5) a defence to the offences created under s 92(1)–(3). Section 92(5) states that:

> 'It is a defence for a person charged with an offence under this section to show that he believed on reasonable grounds that the use of the sign in the manner in which it was used, or was to be used, was not an infringement of the registered trade mark.'

19.27 The defence consists of two parts: subjective belief on the part of the person charged and objectively reasonable grounds for that belief.[1] The defence places a legal burden on the defendant to prove (on the balance of probabilities) that he or she held the relevant belief.[2] There is no general defence of good faith.[3] Further, the courts have held on various occasions that this defence is not made out where, as happens quite commonly, the defendant has bought the goods at low prices from an unknown person without paperwork.[4] In such circumstances it is considered unreasonable for the defendant to assume that the goods are genuine.

1 See *R v Malik (Ashok Kumar)* [2011] EWCA Crim 1107 at [15].
2 See *R v Johnstone* [2003] UKHL 28; [2003] FSR 42; [2004] ETMR 2 at [53].
3 See *R v McCrudden* [2005] EWCA Crim 466, 21 February 2005 at [10].
4 See *West Sussex County Council v Kahraman* [2006] EWHC 1703 (Admin); *Essex Trading Standards v Singh* [2009] EWHC 520 (Admin), 3 March 2009; *R v Pettit* [2009] EWCA Crim 2573, 17 November 2009 and *Stockton-on-Tees Borough Council v Frost* [2010] EWHC 1304 (Admin), 27 April 2010.

19.28 Defendants relying on s 92(5) usually focus on the defendant's own belief that the goods were genuine. However, the defence may not be limited to that situation. In *Rhodes* the Court of Appeal suggested[1] that if the defendant had employed a trade mark agent to search the register prior to commencing trading, and the agent had failed to spot a registered mark and advised there was no such mark, this could found a reasonable belief that 'the use of the sign … was not an infringement of the registered trade mark'. This construction was supported by the House of Lords in *Johnstone*, rejecting earlier case law[2] that had suggested that the definite article in '*the* registered mark' in s 92(5) introduced a supposition that the defendant would be taken to know of the registered mark. However, the Court of Appeal in *Malik* quashed a conviction where the defence was raised and the judge did not leave the question for the jury to decide.[3]

1 *R v Rhodes* [2003] FSR 9 at [21]–[22].
2 *Torbay District Council v Singh* [2000] FSR 158 (CA).
3 *R v Malik (Ashok Kumar)* [2011] EWCA 1107.

19.29 Of course, many defendants will be unable to rely on the s 92(5) defence as contemplated in *Rhodes* for one simple reason: in practice most counterfeit goods bear famous or well-known marks, and trade mark agents are unlikely to make such an error in any case.

Partnerships and bodies corporate

19.30 Where it is alleged that a partnership or a body corporate (such as a limited company) is guilty of an offence, s 101 of the TMA 1994 sets out certain natural persons who may also be liable. In essence, partners are guilty of the same offence as the partnership unless they can prove they were ignorant of or attempted to stop the commission of the offence.[1] Where a body corporate has committed an offence with the 'consent or connivance' of a director, manager, secretary or other similar officer (or any other person purporting to act in any such capacity) that person is also guilty of that offence.[2]

1 TMA 1994 s 101(4). It is not necessary for the partnership to have been convicted but only to show it would have been guilty of the offence: see *R v Wakefield* [2004] EWCA Crim 2278, where the partnership had been wound up before trial.
2 TMA 1994 s 101(5).

Enforcement

19.31 Trading standards officers[1] and the police[2] have powers to obtain a warrant to search premises and seize goods. Forfeiture is governed by s 97, which allows goods, materials or articles[3] to be retained and destroyed provided an offence has been committed. The application of s 97 was considered by the Court of Appeal in *R v Drain*[4] which noted that:

(i) Under s 97(1) the fact that goods have come into possession of a person in connection with the investigation of an offence is sufficient to give that person standing to make an application for forfeiture. There is no requirement that a prosecution be brought.
(ii) If a prosecution is brought, s 97(2) makes clear that an application for forfeiture may be made in any court where a prosecution relating to some or all of the goods has been brought. There is no requirement for a conviction.
(iii) Section 97(3) makes clear that, on such an application, the court shall not make an order for forfeiture unless it is satisfied that a relevant offence has been committed in relation to the goods in question. However, there is nothing in s 97 to prevent an order for forfeiture being made even where there has been an acquittal, provided the court is satisfied on the balance of probabilities that a relevant offence has been committed.

Note also that there are various wide powers for customs seizure and disposal of infringing goods under Council Regulation (EU) 608/2013 (as amended to apply in the UK since the UK's withdrawal from the EU), and under TMA 1994 ss 89–91—see **Chapter 17**.

1 Under TMA 1994 s 93.
2 Under TMA 1994 s 92A.
3 Goods which (or the packaging of which) bears an identical sign or one likely to be mistaken for a registered trade mark, materials bearing such a sign and intended to be used for labelling or packaging, as a business paper, or for advertising goods and articles specifically designed or adapted for making copies of such a sign—see TMA 1994 s 97(1).
4 *R v Drain* [2018] EWCA Crim at [18].

Penalties

19.32 The maximum penalties for offences under s 92 are set by s 92(6) as:

> '(a) on summary conviction … imprisonment for a term not exceeding six months or a fine not exceeding the statutory maximum, or both;
> (b) on conviction on indictment to a fine or imprisonment for a term not exceeding ten years, or both.'

19.33 At present, the maximum fine that may be imposed on summary conviction is £5,000.[1] Following conviction, a defendant may also be subjected to a confiscation order under the Proceeds of Crime Act 2002 to recover the profit he or she has made from a criminal lifestyle. The details of this process are outside the scope of this book, but for an illustration see the use of a confiscation order in *R v Ghori*;[2] the Court of Appeal in a separate case rejected the submission that such an order was oppressive.[3]

1 Magistrates' Courts Act 1980 s 32(9) as amended.
2 *R v Ghori* [2012] EWCA Crim 1115.
3 *R v Beazley* [2013] EWCA Crim 567; [2013] 1 WLR 3331.

OFFENCES RELATING TO THE REGISTER

19.34 There are five offences relating to the register. These are contained in ss 94–95 of the TMA 1994.

Section 94—Falsification of the register

19.35 Three offences are provided under this section:

> '(1) It is an offence for a person to make, or cause to be made, a false entry in the register of trade marks, knowing or having reason to believe that it is false.

(2) It is an offence for a person –
(a) to make or cause to be made anything falsely purporting to be a copy of an entry in the register, or
(b) to produce or tender or cause to be produced or tendered in evidence any such thing,
knowing or having reason to believe it is false.'

19.36 The courts do not appear to have had an opportunity to explore the interpretation of these offences. The mental element of each offence is 'knowing or having reason to believe it is false'. The first offence, in s 94(1), appears to be directed to persons changing the content of the actual register, presumably both employees of the registrar and persons making representations to those employees. The second and third offences, in s 94(2), appear to be directed to use of fake entries on the register, including in relation to court proceedings.

19.37 Offences under s 94 carry a maximum penalty of six months' imprisonment, and/or a fine on summary conviction, or two years imprisonment or a fine on conviction on indictment.[1]

1 TMA 1994 s 94(3).

Section 95—Falsely representing a mark as registered

19.38 Section 95(1) provides for two offences relating to falsely representing a mark as registered:

'(1) It is an offence for a person –
(a) falsely to represent that a mark is a registered trade mark, or
(b) to make a false representation as to the goods or services for which a trade mark is registered knowing or having reason to believe that the representation is false.'

19.39 Both offences relate to pretending that a sign is a registered trade mark, presumably with the intention of preventing other traders from adopting the same or a similar sign in their branding. Helpfully, s 95(2) sets out two specific types of this pretence—namely using the word 'registered' or using 'any other word or symbol importing a reference … to registration': presumably in particular the ® symbol.

19.40 Section 95(2) also contains a defence where the defendant can show that 'the reference is to registration elsewhere than in the United Kingdom and that the trade mark is in fact so registered for the goods and services in question.' In *Second Sight*[1] Lightman J held that there was no need for there to be an indication that the trade mark was registered somewhere other than in the UK, as long as the mark really was registered elsewhere and the use of the mark was consistent with that registration.

1 *Second Sight Ltd v Novell UK Ltd* [1995] RPC 423, 437.

19.41 The offences are triable summarily only, and carry a maximum penalty of a fine not exceeding level 3.

OTHER OFFENCES

Section 99—Unauthorised use of royal arms

19.42 Two offences relating to royal arms and patronage are found in s 99 of the TMA 1994. Section 99(1) relates to unauthorised use of the royal arms, while s 99(2) contains an offence relating to use of a device, emblem or title calculated to lead to the belief that the user is employed by or supplies goods to the royal family (unless such use is specifically authorised). The offences are triable summarily only, and carry a maximum penalty of a fine not exceeding level 2.

Chapter 20

Passing off

> 'For myself, I believe the principle of law may be very plainly stated, and that is that nobody has any right to represent his goods as the goods of somebody else. How far the use of particular words, signs, or pictures does or does not come up to the proposition ... must always be a question of evidence.'

INTRODUCTION

20.01 Lord Halsbury's concise statement of the tort of passing off in the case of *Reddaway v Banham* remains as valid today as it was well over a century ago.[1] Of course, the law has embellished and refined the tort in the intervening years, but the basic principle set out in that case remains the same. The purpose of this chapter is to see where the law of passing off has got to today.[2]

1 *Frank Reddaway & Co Ltd v George Banham & Co Ltd* (1896) 13 RPC 218 at [224]; described by Jacob J as 'the classic exposition' of the tort: [1995] FSR 169 at [175].

2 Necessarily a book such as this can only attempt an overview. For a detailed exposition of the law, see Professor Christopher Wadlow *Wadlow on The Law of Passing-Off* (sixth edn, Sweet & Maxwell, 2021).

20.02 As a business grows, it is likely (and certainly it will be the intention of the business) that customers will become loyal to its particular products or services, and will choose them over those of competitors. It can therefore be very tempting for competitors, instead of offering a better alternative or marketing more effectively, to hold out or dress up their own products or services in such a way as to mislead or deceive customers into thinking that they are purchasing the products or services of the first business. This is what is known as 'passing off', and the law has accorded it the status of a tort in order to prevent unfair competition by such means.

THE BOUNDARIES OF PASSING OFF—NEED FOR DECEPTION AND GOODWILL

20.03 The first sentence of Lord Halsbury's dictum encapsulates the simple rationale of the tort, while the second sentence identifies the very difficult problem of defining its boundaries—when is the relevant act actually committed? Those boundaries have appeared to expand and contract over time, as different judges have applied the same basic principle to the facts in a variety of commercial climates. Harman J summed up the situation as follows in *Fortnum & Mason*:[1]

> '… in the end the trouble with passing off cases is that they all turn upon their curiosities of individual fact. The principles may be clear enough…. But the application of those principles to the facts of individual cases is extremely anxious for those judges who have to try and decide them.'

1 *Fortnum & Mason plc v Fortnam Ltd* [1994] FSR 438 at [443].

20.04 Before turning to consider the law of passing off as it stands today, there is merit in following the approach of Jacob J in the *Roho* case and identifying what is *not* the law.[1] In that case, Jacob J reminded us that:

- there is no tort of copying a product or idea;
- there is no tort of taking a man's market or customers;
- neither the market nor the customers are anyone's to own;
- there is no tort of making use of another's goodwill as such; and
- there is no tort of competition.

1 *Hodgkinson and Corby Ltd v Wards Mobility Services Ltd* [1995] FSR 169.

20.05 Thus, the mere fact that a competitor copies some aspect of the claimant's business, the mere fact that it may profit from a market created and established by the claimant, and the mere fact that it may take the claimant's customers does not necessarily amount to passing off. At the heart of passing off lies deception (or a likelihood of deception), typically deception of the ultimate consumer. As we shall see, such deception can only occur where the claimant has established the necessary 'goodwill' among consumers, and where the defendant's conduct amounts to a misrepresentation. Note that it is not necessary that there be any *intention* to deceive the customer, though in many cases there will of course be such an intention, however much the defendant protests otherwise.

The rationale behind the common law tort of passing off is two-fold:

(1) to protect the goodwill of a business; and
(2) to prevent a competitor from unjustly benefiting from that goodwill.

CONTRAST WITH TRADE MARK LAW

20.06 Although passing off will often involve the defendant using the claimant's trade mark (whether registered or unregistered), the tort of passing off does not protect trade marks as a form of property. Unlike the Directive and the Trade Marks Act 1994 ('TMA 1994'), the common law does not recognise any breach of proprietary rights in a trade mark. However, in some respects the tort of passing off is wider than an action for trade mark infringement. A claimant can only bring a trade mark infringement action if it owns a registered mark (whether a national mark or an EUTM), whereas passing off requires no registered right and is founded on a misrepresentation by the defendant (usually that its goods or services are those of the claimant). As already mentioned, the misrepresentation will often take the form of the defendant using the claimant's trade mark, but in principle there is no limit to the category of signs, representation and indicators of trade origin that may give rise to a misrepresentation.[1]

1 This approach is consistent with the comment of Lord Scarman in the *Pub Squash* case: 'The tort is no longer anchored, as in its nineteenth century formulation, to the name or trade mark of a product or business. It is wide enough to encompass other descriptive material, such as slogans or visual images, which radio, television or newspaper advertising campaigns can lead the market to associate with a claimant's product, provided always that such descriptive material has become part of the goodwill of the product'—see [1981] RPC 429 at [490].

WHO CAN SUE

20.07 Although the tort of passing off is based on customers being deceived, it is not those customers who can sue for passing off (although there may be other remedies open to such customers under consumer protection or trading standards laws, for example). Instead, a passing off action can only be brought by the person or class of persons whose goodwill is being injured by the misrepresentation. However, the net effect of a successful passing-off action is that the public will, in practice, be protected from being deceived as to the origin of goods or services or as to their quality. As with trade mark infringement, this consumer protection is an ancillary effect of the tort rather than its underlying purpose.

'EXTENDED' AND 'REVERSE' PASSING OFF

20.08 One interesting feature of passing off is that there are certain variations on the tort which are qualitatively slightly distinct from the 'classic' form (although the classic form is by far the most common). These are:

(a) 'Extended' passing off[1]—this usually refers to the situation where the defendant passes off its products or services not necessarily as those of another, but as belonging to a wide category in which goodwill exists and collectively benefits everyone in the trade (eg, champagne producers or vodka manufacturers[2]) rather than being owned by any particular person or business.

(b) 'Reverse' passing off—where the misrepresentation is not that the defendant's goods are those of the claimant, but rather that the claimant's goods are somehow associated with the defendant, thereby inducing customers to transact with the defendant.[3] This is really just a different flavour of misrepresentation, rather than an entirely different species of tort.

1 See the speech of Lord Fraser in 'Advocaat': *Erven Warnink BV v J Townend & Sons (Hull) Ltd (No.1)* [1980] RPC 31. The central issue was whether the claimant as a producer of a liqueur generically known as advocaat was entitled to prevent others from marketing drinks that did not meet the standard which the public had come to expect from 'true' advocaat. It was held that there was goodwill in the collective business of making advocaat, the claimant had an interest in that goodwill, and the defendant's acts were damaging the claimant's interest.

2 See the '*Vodkat*' case: *Diageo North America Inc v Intercontinental Brands (ICB) Ltd* [2010] EWHC 17 (Ch); [2010] RPC 12. See also 'Greek yoghurt'—see *Fage UK v Chobani UK* [2013] EWHC 630 (Ch); [2013] FSR 32 (upheld on appeal) in which the claimant was held to be entitled to restrain the defendant from selling as 'Greek yoghurt' a product that had in fact been made in the US, and was not produced in the same way as yoghurt that the public had come to know as true Greek yoghurt.

3 Reverse passing off was considered in the context of a summary judgment application in *Devonshire Pine v Day* [2013] EWHC 2619 (Ch).

SIGNIFICANCE OF CASE LAW

20.09 There is an enormous body of case law that has defined and refined the scope and requirements of the tort of passing off over the years. However, note that many of those cases were decided very much on their own particular facts and are merely illustrative of the numerous ways in which the courts have applied the generally accepted principles. Furthermore, many of the decisions arise out of applications for interim injunctions, and are therefore of limited value even on their own particular facts (except in terms of what will suffice for the grant of such an injunction). It is not within the scope of this type of guide to review all of the historical developments of passing off;[1] instead, the remainder of this chapter simply aims to describe the scope and requirements of the tort as they appear to us to stand as at the middle of 2021.

1 For further discussion on the history of passing-off, see *Singer Machine Manufacturers v Wilson* (1876) 2 Ch D 434 at [452]; *GE Trade Mark* [1973] RPC 297 at [325]–[327] and *Harrods Ltd v Harrodian School Ltd* [1996] RPC 697 at [706]–[709] and [712]–[715].

ELEMENTS OF THE CLASSIC FORM OF PASSING OFF

20.10 The necessary ingredients of an action in passing off were authoritatively stated by the House of Lords in the *Jif Lemon* case, in which the defendants were accused of passing off their lemon juice as that of the claimant by virtue of the distinctive lemon-like packaging employed.[1] In that case, Lord Oliver and Lord Jauncey each identified three elements of a passing off action, which are frequently referred to as the 'classical trinity'.[2] Lord Oliver expressed them in these terms:[3]

> 'First, he must establish a goodwill or reputation attached to the goods or services which he supplies in the mind of the purchasing public by association with the identifying "get-up" (whether it consists simply as a brand name or a trade description, or the individual features of labelling or packaging) under which his particular goods or services are offered to the public, such that the get-up is recognised by the public as distinctive specifically of the claimant's goods or services. Secondly, he must demonstrate a misrepresentation by the defendant to the public (whether or not intentional) leading or likely to lead the public to believe that goods or services offered by him are the goods or services of the claimant. Whether the public is aware of the claimant's identity as manufacturer or supplier of the goods or services is immaterial, as long as they are identified with a particular source which is in fact the claimant.... Thirdly, he must demonstrate that he suffers, or in a *quia timet* action, that he is likely to suffer, damage by reason of the erroneous belief engendered by the defendant's misrepresentation that the source of the defendant's goods or services is the same as the source of those offered by the claimant.'

1 *Reckitt & Colman Products Ltd v Borden Inc* [1990] RPC 341.
2 Following the description of the same by Nourse LJ in the Parma Ham case: *Consorzio del Prosciutto di Parma v Marks & Spencer plc* [1991] RPC 351.
3 *Reckitt & Colman Products Ltd v Borden Inc* [1990] RPC 341 at [406].

20.11 Lord Jauncey too identified three elements in the tort of passing off:[1]

> 'It is a prerequisite of any successful passing off action that the plaintiff's goods have acquired a reputation in the market and are known by some distinguishing feature. It is also a prerequisite that the misrepresentation has deceived or is likely to deceive and that the plaintiff is likely to suffer damage by such deception. Mere confusion which does not lead to a sale is not sufficient. ... In a case such as the present where what is in issue is whether the goods of A are likely to be passed off as those of B, a plaintiff,

to succeed, must establish (1) that his goods have acquired a particular reputation among the public; (2) that persons wishing to buy his goods are likely to be misled into buying the goods of the defendant; and (3) that he is likely to suffer damage thereby.'.

1 *Reckitt & Colman Products Ltd v Borden Inc* [1990] RPC 341 at [417].

20.12 Lord Jauncey also referred to Lord Diplock's speech in the classic case of *Advocaat* (concerning extended-form passing off), where it had been said that for there to be a valid cause of action in passing off, five characteristics must be present[1]:

(1) a misrepresentation;
(2) made by a trader in the course of trade;
(3) to prospective customers of its or ultimate consumers of goods or services supplied by it;
(4) which is calculated to injure the business or goodwill of another trader (in the sense that this is a reasonably foreseeable consequence); and
(5) which causes actual damage to the business or goodwill of the trader by whom the action is brought or (in a *quia timet* action) will probably do so.

1 *Erven Warnink BV v J Townend & Sons (Hull) Ltd* [1980] RPC 31 at [93].

20.13 The classical trinity is the preferred formulation today, but however one expresses or defines the elements or characteristics of a passing off action, there is no avoiding the fact that the outcome of each case will depend very much on the quality of the evidence put to the court. The claimant in each case will have to establish the following matters:

(1) sufficient goodwill associated with the claimant's business, goods or services;
(2) the defendant's conduct amounts to a misrepresentation to customers (or potential customers), which deceives those customers into believing that the defendant's business or its goods or services are those of, or connected in a relevant way with, the claimant; and
(3) the misrepresentation causes or is likely to cause damage to the claimant's business or goodwill.

20.14 What is likely to give rise to a 'sufficient goodwill' will be a combination of several factors, including:

(i) the inherent distinctiveness (or otherwise) of the trade mark or sign used by the claimant;
(ii) the quality of the claimant's goods or services in question;
(iii) the nature and extent of the use of the trade mark by the claimant, in terms of the period of use, the geographic extent of such use and the

quantity, volume or value of sales of the goods or services in relation to which the mark has been used; and
(iv) the nature and extent of the advertising and other promotion of the goods or services in question.

20.15 The question whether the defendant's use of the claimant's trade mark constitutes a misrepresentation will also depend upon a combination of several factors, including:

(i) the origin of the goods or services;
(ii) the nature of the market place, the trade channels used for putting the goods or services on the market, the activities of competitors and their use of their own trade marks and other signs;
(iii) the nature of the goods or services themselves;
(iv) the nature of the customers in question; and
(v) the use by the defendant of any distinguishing features (or 'disavowals') which, when looked at as a whole, may negate the operative effect of what may otherwise have been a misrepresentation.

20.16 For the purposes of the final element, the claimant may suffer damage directly or indirectly in the following ways:

(i) loss of sales;
(ii) a diminution of the value of the goodwill associated with the claimant's products or services, ie, the dilution of its reputation amongst the claimant's customers and potential customers;
(iii) a diminution in the value of the claimant's trade mark as a licensable asset; and
(iv) loss of opportunity to expand the claimant's business into other (usually related) goods or services, ie, a limitation or restriction on the claimant's ability to exploit and develop its brand.

STRUCTURE OF THIS CHAPTER

20.17 Although it is relatively easy to state the law of passing off as a collection of three (or perhaps five) elements, the difficulty lies in trying to say with confidence whether any particular activity falls within those elements. The remaining paragraphs of this chapter attempt to bring together some of the many cases in a way which will enable the reader to appreciate the scope and requirements of a passing off action. Accordingly, we will consider the various issues in separate sections as follows:

A The nature of the requisite goodwill.
B Embodiment of goodwill—the range of trade marks, signs, get-ups, images and other features of the claimant's business in which goodwill may be vested.

C The subject matter of an operative misrepresentation.
D Factors negating what might otherwise be a misrepresentation.
E The relevance of a common field of activity as between the claimant's and the defendant's businesses.
F The type of damage or loss that may be suffered by the claimant.
G The evidence that the claimant may need to present to the court, and the ways of obtaining that evidence.
H Defences.
I Remedies.
J Practical matters for trade mark owners and practitioners alike.

A NATURE OF GOODWILL

20.18 The first issue to consider is the nature of the goodwill that the claimant must have built up, because without sufficient, and relevant goodwill there may be no operative misrepresentation, and/or no damage or loss suffered (or likely to be suffered) by the claimant. In other words, if the claimant has no trading reputation of any description, it can hardly be the victim of others pretending to sell its wares.

Definition of goodwill

20.19 The concept of goodwill is very broad. Lord Macnaghten is credited with the classic definition of goodwill (one that is said not to have been improved upon in more than a century) when he stated:

> 'It is a thing very easy to describe, very difficult to define. It is the benefit and advantage of the good name, reputation and connection of a business. It is the attractive force which brings in custom.'.[1]

The 'attractive force' normally derives from the quality of the goods or services in question, with reference to all the relevant features including functionality, aesthetic appearance, value for money, performance, reliability, inherent quality, and the purpose for which the product is intended to be used. However, there is no requirement that the claimant's products be somehow superior to others on the market—cheap-and-cheerful or even downright lousy goods can be just as much the subject of brand loyalty as any high-end product. Over time, customers' loyalty to those goods or services will become embodied in the form of goodwill towards whatever particular trade mark or branding has been used by the claimant in establishing that custom or trade (the subject of the next section). It is this attractive force, however it manifests itself in relation to the particular goods or services in question, that the common law seeks to protect: the ability of the mark to denote a particular quality or character of the goods or services.[2] Note that it goes beyond mere reputation—

it depends for existence on an associated business or trade. Although goodwill usually attaches to commercial organisations, it can in the right circumstances also accrue to other bodies, such as political groups,[3] charities, Government departments, and unincorporated associations.[4]

1 *IRC v Muller & Co's Margarine Ltd* [1901] AC 217 at [223].
2 *Powell v Birmingham Vinegar Brewery Co* [1897] 14 RPC 721.
3 *Burge v Haycock* [2001] EWCA Civ 900; [2002] RPC 28.
4 See para **20.23** below.

Ownership of goodwill

20.20 The ownership of goodwill is not always a straightforward or obvious matter, such as where, for example, goods are made by one party but distributed or retailed by a second. A useful starting point is to note that goodwill depends on the fact that consumers care that there is a specific entity behind the goods, but they do not need to know (or even care) who or what that entity is. Very often the customer will only know or recognise the trade mark which is used in relation to the particular goods or services and for this reason the goodwill (or attractive force) is embodied in that trade mark. It is sufficient that the goodwill attaches to the trade mark and not necessarily to the identity of the manufacturer or supplier, provided that customers understand the trade mark to indicate a particular (albeit unidentified) origin.[1] The ownership of that goodwill is then largely a question of fact, involving considerations such as who consumers perceive to be responsible for the quality of the goods bearing the mark. Note that the ownership of goodwill may also be determined by operation of law, such as where a distributor contractually agrees that all goodwill will accrue to the manufacturer.

1 There are numerous authorities for this proposition, see for example: *T. Oertli AG v E. J. Bowman (London) Ltd* [1959] RPC 1, per Lord Simmons at [4].

20.21 In the *Penguin/Puffin* case it was confirmed that to establish passing off it was unnecessary to prove that the customer knew or cared about the name of the manufacturer who owned the goodwill, provided that the customer knew that there was such a person and cared that the goods which he/she bought were made by that person.[1] In that case, Walker J was satisfied that although the majority of customers would not know who manufactured Penguin biscuits as such, they would be concerned about the taste, quality and cost of the product which the PENGUIN trade mark had come to represent. This finding of fact may be contrasted with the *Spice Girls* case[2] in which Lightman J thought that the defendants, in supplying a sticker collection featuring the Spice Girls, were doing no more than catering for a popular demand for 'effigies and quotes of today's idols' and that such popular demand was not concerned about the origin of the goods in question. In other words, customers would not know who manufactured the sticker collection and would not care whether the collection was being published either with or without the consent of the Spice Girls.

1 *United Biscuits (UK) Ltd v Asda Stores Ltd* [1997] RPC 513 at [533].
2 *Halliwell v Panini* (6 June 1997, unreported); see also *Elvis Presley Trade Marks* [1997] RPC 543.

20.22 Goodwill may be shared in appropriate circumstances, such as in *Gromax*, where the supplier-distributor relationship was such as to lead the court to conclude the goodwill was shared between them.[1] In *Sir Robert McAlpine* Mann J held that where goodwill was co-owned, neither co-owner had more right to the name than the other and one party could not begin use of the name which suggested exclusion of the other.[2] As between connected or related companies, in *Scandecor* the Court of Appeal reversed the trial judge's decision that the relevant goodwill was shared, and found instead that it all belonged to the defendant.[3] However, note that *Scandecor* turned on a particularly complicated set of facts. In general, a claimant will not be permitted to restrain a defendant's use of a confusingly similar mark where the defendant can justify the use on the basis of independent generation of goodwill, or so-called 'common ancestor' goodwill, of which *Dent v Turpin*[4] is a classic example. Such a situation was considered (and relief refused) in *TFC Croydon*.[5]

1 *Gromax Plasticulture Ltd v Don & Low Nonwovens Ltd* [1999] RPC 367.
2 *Sir Robert McAlpine Ltd v Alfred McAlpine Plc* [2004] EWHC 630 (Ch); [2004] RPC 36.
3 *Scandecor Development AB v Scandecor Marketing AV* [1999] FSR 26.
4 *Dent v Turpin* (1861) 70 ER 1003.
5 *TFC Croydon Ltd v Foodland UK Ltd* O-443-14 (an appeal to the Appointed Person on conjoined opposition/invalidity proceedings at UKIPO). See also *WS Foster & Son Ltd v Brooks Brothers UK Ltd* [2013] EWPCC 18.

20.23 The one certainty is that the goodwill must actually accrue to the claimant in order to found a cause of action. In *Rugby Football Union v Cotton Traders Ltd*, Lloyd J held that the claimant's action failed because the public associated the rose devise with the England rugby team, not with the RFU.[1] An unincorporated association may accrue goodwill provided that its constitution or rules of governance allow for it to own property.[2] In *Fine & Country* the Court of Appeal rejected an argument that goodwill could not attach to the claimant companies since they were dormant.[3] It was relevant that the brand in question allowed the other claimant, the non-dormant parent company, to franchise the brand, and attract licence fees.

1 *Rugby Football Union v Cotton Traders Ltd* [2002] EWHC 467 (Ch); [2002] ETMR 76.
2 *Artistic Upholstery Ltd v Art Forma (Furniture) Ltd* [2000] FSR 311.
3 *Fine & Country Ltd v Okotoks Ltd (formerly Spicerhaart Ltd)* [2013] EWCA Civ 672; [2014] FSR 11.

Scope and extent of goodwill

20.24 It is always important to identify the scope and extent of the relevant goodwill. Initially, a trader's goodwill is likely to extend only as far as its actual business and will only relate to the goods or services actually sold or supplied. However, over time the goodwill may grow to the point where using the branding which embodies that goodwill in relation to other goods or services may also amount to a misrepresentation, even though those particular goods or services are not sold or supplied by the claimant. Thus, although it is very important for the claimant to establish the scope of its business and the range of goods and services which it sells or supplies that does not necessarily predefine or limit the nature of the business or the goods or services sold or supplied by the defendant which may be passed off as those of the claimant. Goodwill is often geographically limited in scope to a local area where the case concerns a local business (see, for example, *Bignell v Just Employment Law Ltd*[1]) but can also widen substantially over time as the trader's reputation spreads. A trading name alone, absent trade, will not be enough to generate goodwill.[2]

1 *Bignell (t/a Just Employment) v Just Employment Law Ltd* [2008] FSR 6 and also *Caspian Pizza Ltd v Shah* [2017] EWCA Civ 1874; [2018] ECC 18.
2 *Media Agency Group Ltd v Space Media Agency Ltd* [2019] EWCA Civ 712; [2019] FSR 27.

20.25 One must, therefore, distinguish the enquiry that relates to the scope and the extent of the goodwill in the claimant's actual business from the separate enquiry as to whether the defendant has made a misrepresentation to the public. In **20.64–20.67** below, we examine the relevance of the fields of activity of the claimant and the defendant and the extent to which a lack of a common field of activity may either negate the existence of an operative misrepresentation and/or result in the representation causing no damage to the claimant.

Time of assessment

20.26 The relevant time at which to assess the claimant's goodwill is the commencement of the acts or course of conduct said to amount to actual or threatened passing off. This is a potentially important point. If a defendant has begun a course of conduct before the claimant has accrued any, or sufficient, goodwill, it is unlikely that continuance of the same course of conduct will amount to passing off—see for example *Daimler Chrysler AG v Alavi (t/a Merc).*[1]

1 *Daimler Chrysler AG v Alavi (t/a Merc)* [2001] RPC 42.

Goodwill in 'extended' passing off

20.27 The requisite goodwill may not be exclusive to one particular business, but may vest in an open-ended class of persons or businesses who together share the benefit of that goodwill without actually owning it. Examples include:

- producers who carry on business in a particular geographic area, such as champagne producers in the Champagne district of France;[1] sherry producers in the Jerez district of Spain;[2] whisky producers in Scotland;[3] chocolate manufacturers in Switzerland;[4] and yogurt producers in Greece;[5]
- producers who manufacture goods to a common and defined specification or standard such as in accordance with the recipe for advocaat[6] or in accordance with industry standards and regulations, such as vodka producers[7] or manufacturers of lenses for safety helmets;[8] or
- suppliers of services who operate under a code of practice or in accordance with rules or guidelines.

In such cases the action may be brought either by the trade association established to represent its members and/or by one or more individual members of the relevant class, although the Court of Appeal in *Chocosuisse* stated that for a claimant to have adequate 'standing' to bring an extended-form passing off claim, they must have a legitimate business interest in their own right, not purely as a representative group acting on behalf of manufacturers.[9] For a review of this category of passing off cases see Arnold J's decision in *Vodkat.*[10]

1 *J Bollinger v Costa Brava Wine Co Ltd* [1960] RPC 16 and [1961] RPC 116, and *Taittinger SA v Allbev Ltd* [1993] FSR 641 and Court of Appeal at 659.
2 *Vine Products Ltd v MacKenzie & Co Ltd* [1969] RPC 1.
3 *John Walker & Sons Ltd v Henry Ost & Co Ltd* [1970] RPC 489.
4 *Chocosuisse Union Des Fabricants Suisses de Chocolat v Cadbury Ltd* [1998] RPC 117.
5 *Fage UK v Chobani UK* [2013] EWHC 630 (Ch); [2013] FSR 32 (upheld on appeal—[2014] EWCA Civ 5; [2014] FSR 29).
6 *Erven Warnink BV v J Townend & Sons (Hull) Ltd* [1980] RPC 85.
7 *Diageo North America Inc v Intercontinental Brands (ICB) Ltd* [2010] EWHC 17 (Ch); [2010] RPC 12; [2010] EWCA Civ 920; [2011] RPC 2.
8 *Hodge Clemco Ltd v Airblast Ltd* [1995] FSR 806.
9 *Chocosuisse Union Des Fabricants Suisses de Chocolat v Cadbury Ltd* [1999] RPC 826 (CA). See also *Scotch Whisky Association v JD Vintners Ltd* [1997] Eu.LR 446.
10 *Diageo North America Inc v Intercontinental Brands (ICB) Ltd* [2010] EWHC 17 (Ch); [2010] RPC 12, at [4]–[35].

20.28 Extended passing off protects the accuracy and exclusivity of the descriptive term, which in the *Vodkat* case[1] (vodka) indicated both the familiar qualities of vodka itself, and also compliance with European regulations on spirit drinks. Importantly, it should be noted that shared ownership of goodwill in a descriptive term such as champagne or Swiss chocolate does not entitle the corresponding class of traders to prevent a new competitor from manufacturing and selling goods to which the term can accurately be applied. In that sense the class of co-owners of the goodwill is open-ended; even so, new competitors would be wise to ensure they meet the requirements of the descriptive term if they want to use it. Note that prior to *Vodkat* it was not clear whether the descriptive term had to have some sort of special connotation of quality or prestige, which is something that seemed to be present in the champagne and whisky[2] cases. This 'cachet' point was argued by the defendants at the Court of Appeal.[3] The Court held that there was no such requirement that the descriptor must denote a superior or luxury brand, and on the facts there was significant goodwill in vodka as a clear, colourless, tasteless, high-strength spirit.

1 *Diageo North America Inc v Intercontinental Brands (ICB) Ltd* [2010] EWHC 17 (Ch); [2010] RPC 12,
2 See, for example, *Scotch Whisky Association v Glen Kella Distillers Ltd (No 2)* [1997] EuLR 455.
3 *Diageo North America Inc v Intercontinental Brands (ICB) Ltd* [2010] EWCA Civ 920; [2011] RPC 2.

International goodwill

20.29 Care needs to be taken to distinguish between reputation and goodwill. A trader may have a reputation in the United Kingdom because of its advertising overseas and/or its sales to UK customers who have travelled abroad, but it may have no goodwill as such in the United Kingdom because it does not trade or carry on business in this country. In such a case reputation alone is not sufficient to establish a passing off action. Although business or trading activity in the United Kingdom is necessary in order to establish the requisite goodwill (the attractive force), it is not necessary that the claimant should have an actual place of business in the United Kingdom, provided that it does business there. Examples include the following:

- in *Sheraton* the court found that goodwill had been established in the United Kingdom, as the claimant received bookings at an office in the United Kingdom for its hotels, albeit that the hotels themselves were located in the United States;[1]
- in contrast in *Crazy Horse* the court ruled against the owner of the Crazy Horse Saloon in Paris and allowed the defendant to set up a bar/club of the same name in London because the claimant could only establish a mere reputation in this country (through advertising and through British tourists visiting the Crazy Horse Saloon in Paris), but could not establish any actual sales, bookings or other business in the United Kingdom;[2]

- similarly in *Budweiser* the Court of Appeal held that reputation 'spilling over' into the United Kingdom from advertising in American magazines was insufficient and that the availability of the American Budweiser beer to American servicemen on American military bases in the United Kingdom did not give rise to goodwill in this country;[3] and
- Knox J confirmed, after considering the history of the case law on this subject, that if a claimant has no customers in this jurisdiction it will not succeed in attempting to restrain passing off;[4] and
- in *Starbucks (HK) Ltd*[5] a claim was dismissed where the claimant had established goodwill in Hong Kong but not in the UK (the preparatory steps it had taken in the UK being, on the facts, insufficient). The Court of Appeal affirmed that goodwill in the UK is an indispensable ingredient of passing off.

1 *Sheraton Corpn of America v Sheraton Motels Ltd* [1964] RPC 202; see also *Anciens Établissements Panhard et Levassor SA v Panhard-Levassor Motor Co Ltd* [1901] 2 Ch 513, where the importation of cars from France into England was sufficient notwithstanding that the claimant did not have a place of business or an agent here.

2 *Alain Bernardin et Cie v Pavilion Properties Ltd* [1967] RPC 581.

3 *Anheuser-Busch Inc v Budejovicky Budvar NP* [1984] FSR 413.

4 *Jian Tools for Sales Inc v Roderick Manhattan Group Ltd* [1995] FSR 924 at [935]–[937].

5 *Starbucks (HK) Ltd v British Sky Broadcasting Group Plc* [2013] EWCA Civ 1465; [2014] FSR 20 at [103] (upheld on appeal – [2015] UKSC 31; [2015] FSR 29). In *Starbucks* it was held that the fact that people in the UK could, via the internet, gain access to the programmes emanating from the claimant's operation in Hong Kong was not sufficient to establish goodwill in the UK. However, the Court of Appeal did recognize that it would be possible to establish goodwill in the supply of a service in the UK even if it was made without charge or profit and even if supplied only to a foreign speaking ethnic minority section of the public (see [106]).

20.30 The position may be even more uncertain where the trader is providing services rather than goods, highlighting what Sir Nicolas Browne-Wilkinson VC in *The Hit Factory*[1] referred to as 'the challenge thrown up by trading patterns which cross national and jurisdictional boundaries'. The leading authority on such situations is now the Court of Appeal decision in *Hotel Cipriani*[2] which followed the requirement in *Budweiser* that the claimant must have actual customers in the UK.

1 *Pete Waterman Ltd v CBS United Kingdom Ltd* [1993] EMLR 27, which concerned UK goodwill in the name 'The Hit Factory' arising from a New York studio trading under that name.

2 *Hotel Cipriani Srl v Cipriani (Grosvenor Street) Ltd* [2010] EWCA Civ 110; [2010] RPC 16.

20.31 Thus with the law as it stands, a foreign organisation with substantial reputation but nothing in the way of trade may find its reputation parasitised by a third party which sets up business in the UK. Such was the case in *NASA*[1] in which a clothing manufacturer used the mark NASA and thereby established sufficient goodwill to create an arguable case in passing off, even against a defendant licensed by the famous US space administration to use the same mark in the UK. Some question whether this should be so, and the courts in other common law jurisdictions have been prepared to recognise and to protect international reputation without local goodwill.[2] Of course, claimants who do not carry on business in the UK are likely to find it much more difficult to establish an operative misrepresentation and/or damage.

1 *Nice and Safe Attitude Ltd v Piers Flook (T/A 'Slaam Clothing Co')* [1997] FSR 14.
2 In Hong Kong: *Tan-Ichi Co v Jancar Ltd* [1990] FSR 151; in India: *Calvin Klein Inc v International Apparel Syndicate* [1995] FSR 515; in Australia: *Fletcher Challenge v Fletcher Challenge Pty Ltd* [1982] FSR 1; and in Ireland: *C&A Modes v C&A (Waterford) Ltd* [1978] FSR 126.

'Anticipatory' goodwill

20.32 Goodwill is normally built up over the medium to long term and will result from, in broad terms:

(a) substantial sales of the goods or services in question; and
(b) substantial advertising/marketing of the goods or services.

The general rule is that the pre-trading period (even if it includes preparations for trading) does not give rise to goodwill. However, it is possible to establish goodwill in the UK by sufficient advertising or advance promotional activities even though the advertised or promoted goods or services are not yet available for purchase or acquisition.[1] Further, there are cases where sufficient goodwill has been established literally overnight and prior to the commencement of actual trade. Two important cases are:

- *Fletcher Challenge*[2] an Australian case in which advance publicity of the merger of two companies to form a new company was sufficient to establish sufficient goodwill in the name of the newly merged company; and
- *Glaxo Wellcome*[3] a more recent decision of the UK High Court on similar facts to *Fletcher Challenge*, where the court accepted that the claimant owned the goodwill in the name Glaxo Wellcome notwithstanding that it had only very recently been formed as a result of the merger between Glaxo and Wellcome.

1 *Starbucks (HK) Ltd v British Sky Broadcasting Group Plc* [2013] EWCA Civ 1465; [2014] FSR 20 at [106] (approving [2012] EWHC 3074; [2013] FSR 29 at [135] and as approved by [2015] UKSC 31; [2015] FSR 29).

2 *Fletcher Challenge Ltd v Fletcher Challenge Pty Ltd* [1981] 1 NSWLR 196; [1982] FSR 1.

3 *Glaxo plc and Wellcome plc v Glaxo Wellcome Ltd* [1996] FSR 388. This case may be contrasted with the *Ben & Jerry's* case (19 January 1995, IPD 18051) where the well known manufacturer of BEN & JERRY'S ice cream was not granted an injunction against Ben & Jerry's Ice Cream Ltd because the defendant had not traded and had stated positively that it had no present intention to do so. Ferris J held that the claimant had to show more than the mere existence of the defendant company bearing its corporate name.

Residual goodwill

20.33 Where a trader ceases or suspends the use of a particular trade mark, and/or trade or business altogether, what effect does such a cessation/suspension have on the existence of any previously established goodwill? The answer is that residual goodwill may subsist for a considerable period of time after the claimant has ceased or suspended carrying on business, particularly where the goodwill was very substantial to begin with, or where the claimant has taken steps to keep the goodwill alive. The law was reviewed by Arnold J in *Maslyukov v Diageo*[1] in which he stated the correct test as regards residual goodwill was whether the business had been abandoned, inconsistent with any possibility of revival, such as to destroy the goodwill; mere cessation of business is not enough. Examples of residual goodwill cases include:

- *Ad-Lib Club*[2] where four years' suspension of use did not extinguish the claimant's residual goodwill because there was advance publicity concerning the claimant's return to business;
- *Thermawear*[3] where the claimant's residual goodwill lasted for five years after the cessation of business;
- the 'Liberty X' case[4] where Laddie J described as 'borderline' his finding of residual goodwill where a band with only modest sales and a limited following had ceased functioning six years prior to the conduct complained of;
- *Mary Wilson Enterprises Inc*, which looked at the goodwill in the music group name 'THE SUPREMES';[5] and
- in *WS Foster & Son* it was said that the goodwill in that instance could not be expected to survive 40 years with no use following a public and high-profile abandonment.[6]

1 *Maslyukov v Diageo Distilling Ltd* [2010] EWHC 443 (Ch); [2010] RPC 21 at [73]–[75].

2 *Ad-Lib Club v Granville* [1971] FSR1.

3 *Thermawear Ltd v Vedonis Ltd* [1982] RPC 44.

4 *Sutherland v V2 Music Limited* [2002] EWHC 14 (Ch); [2002] EMLR 28.

5 *Mary Wilson Enterprises Inc's Trade Mark Application* [2003] EMLR 14. More recently, goodwill in the band name 'The Animals' formed the basis of a passing-off objection to a trade mark: *Burdon v Steel* O-369-13 (Appointed Person).

6 *WS Foster & Son Ltd v Brooks Brothers UK Ltd* [2013] EWPCC 18.

An alternative to goodwill—s 56(2) of the Trade Marks Act 1994

20.34 In the absence of actual goodwill in the United Kingdom, the proprietor of a trade mark may still have a remedy if its mark is 'well-known' for the purposes of s 56(2) of the TMA 1994, ie, well known within the meaning of the Paris Convention or the WTO Agreement. An injunction is available under s 56(2) to protect marks that are either registered or unregistered, provided that they are, in fact, well known.[1]

1 See **Chapter 2** for the definition of 'well known', and **Chapter 17** for a commentary on the injunction available under s 56(2).

B EMBODIMENT OF GOODWILL

20.35 As already stated, the claimant must establish sufficient goodwill relating to its goods or services or business. By its nature, invoking that goodwill in order to attract custom depends on customers recognising the claimant's goods or services, and this is usually done by means of a trade mark or other aspects of packaging or marketing. So what kinds of features may serve this function of embodying the goodwill? The answer is that there is essentially no limit to the sorts of trade marks, signs, get-ups or other outward traits that may embody the claimant's goodwill, the use of which by a third party may constitute an actionable misrepresentation. The following paragraphs explore some of the many different ways in which goodwill may be embodied.

Inherently distinctive trade marks

20.36 Goodwill is normally embodied in or attaches to a trade mark, particularly where the trade mark is inherently distinctive (such as made-up like Xerox, or words which have no obvious connection with the goods—a classic example being 'north pole bananas'). The courts have referred to inherently distinctive trade marks as 'fancy' or 'newly coined' because they have no meaning when originally applied to the claimant's goods or services or, at most, merely contain an indirect reference or skilful allusion to some character or quality of the claimant's goods or services. In such cases, the courts will readily assume that there can be no conceivable legitimate use of such trade marks by another person and that, in employing such a mark in connection with its own goods or services, the defendant is likely to deceive customers (or potential customers). In the *Penguin/Puffin* case[1] Walker J stated that:

> 'There is a good deal of authority for the proposition that long use of a particularly distinctive get-up does (without creating a monopoly) place on a new competitor (minded to use a similar get-up) a special obligation to avoid confusion.'.

1 *United Biscuits (UK) Ltd v Asda Stores Ltd* [1997] RPC 513.

20.37 Of course, it must be stressed that what is inherently distinctive for one category of goods or services may not be distinctive if used in relation to another category, and the defendant's use of the claimant's inherently distinctive trade mark may nonetheless not constitute an actionable misrepresentation if, for example, in the circumstances of the case:

(a) the defendant's use is in relation to dissimilar goods or services; and/or
(b) the defendant otherwise distinguishes its goods or services.

Other signs, get-ups, images and features

20.38 In addition to inherently distinctive trade marks, any other trade mark (using that word broadly, to include any sign, feature, indication, image or get-up) may embody the claimant's goodwill, and could be used by the defendant in such a way as to constitute a misrepresentation. Examples of trade marks which may embody (if not constitute) the necessary goodwill capable of protection, include the following:

(a) the distinctive packaging or get-up of the goods, such as the lemon-shaped, lemon-coloured and lemon-sized container in the *Jif Lemon* case;[1]
(b) slogans;[2]
(c) visual images;[3]
(d) radio, TV or newspaper advertising campaigns;[4]
(e) trading styles;[5]
(f) names of businesses, companies and unincorporated associations;[6] and
(g) any other sign which enables a customer to distinguish one proprietor's goods or services from competing goods or services, or (in the words of Lord Jauncey in the *Jif Lemon* case) any sign which 'is the badge of the claimant's goodwill, that which associates the goods with the claimant in the mind of the public'.

1 *Reckitt & Coleman Products Ltd v Borden Inc* [1990] RPC 341.
2 Although this has proved difficult in practice, with the exception of the Penguin/Puffin case (*United Biscuits (UK) Ltd v Asda Stores Ltd* [1997] RPC 513), in which the defendant was found to have infringed the claimant's registered mark 'P … P … P … Pick up a Penguin'; it was held that this would probably have amounted to passing off as well.
3 For example, *Jacobson (D) & Sons v Globe* [2008] EWHC 88 (Ch); [2008] FSR 21.
4 The features of the 'pub squash man', a fictional character developed by the claimant to advertise its product: *Cadbury-Schweppes Pty Ltd v Pub Squash Co Ltd* [1981] 1 WLR 193. See also *RHM Foods v Bovril* [1983] RPC 275 (CA).
5 *Cadbury-Schweppes Pty Ltd v Pub Squash Co Ltd* [1981] 1 WLR 193.
6 *Law Society of England and Wales v Society of Lawyers* [1996] FSR 739.

20.39 In the *Roho* cushion case[1] Jacob J had to consider whether the distinctive appearance of a cushion could be 'passed-off'. In that case the defendant used a different name for its cushion and, on all the facts, it was held that by virtue of the way in which the goods were sold and reached customers, the likelihood of actual deception was non-existent. However, the judgment is instructive in that Jacob J reviewed numerous cases and made clear that there is no difference in law whether a misrepresentation arises by the defendant's use of a trade mark or sign, or whether it results from the very appearance of the goods themselves. The appearance of goods can therefore itself embody or represent the requisite goodwill for passing off purposes—indeed this was recognised and anticipated by Lord Herschell over one hundred years ago in the *Camel hair belting* case[2] when he said:

> 'It is a fundamental rule which governs all cases, whatever be the particular mode adopted by any man for putting off his goods as those of a rival trader, whether it is done by the use of mark which become his Trade Mark, or in *any other way* …'.

The relevant question identified by Jacob J was whether the claimant had proved that the shape of its cushion was the 'crucial point of reference' for those who specifically wanted a Roho cushion.

1 *Hodgkinson and Corby Ltd v Wards Mobility Services Ltd* [1995] FSR 169.
2 *Frank Reddaway & Co Ltd v George Banham & Co Ltd* (1896) 13 RPC 218 at [231]; see also *Singer Manufacturing Co v Loog* (1880) 18 Ch D 395 per James LJ at [412].

20.40 In general terms, the claimant in a passing off action has to show that customers are 'moved to buy by source' and, if that is the case, the claimant will have to identify the feature or features of its goods by which the public identify the source of the goods in question. A claimant who relies on a feature which is not a trade mark in the traditional sense may have difficulty in establishing that the public are 'moved to buy' by reference to that particular feature, no matter how well recognised it may be. If the feature is not regarded as a trade mark (ie, it is not regarded by customers as a badge of trade origin) then the use of that feature by a third party will generally not amount to a misrepresentation because customers will not be deceived. Put another way, if customers are likely to buy the article in question because of what it is, and not in reliance upon any belief that the feature indicates any particular trade origin, then the claimant will have failed to establish any, or sufficient, goodwill in the feature because it does not exert any 'attractive force which brings in custom'. One, therefore, has to draw a distinction between:

(a) features which merely make the product attractive to customers (eg, its aesthetic appeal or its functionality), but which do not, of themselves, embody any goodwill for a passing off action; and

(b) features which also indicate a particular trade origin or source such that customers are moved to buy the article because of its source and not just because they like the look of it or like what it does.

The hurdle for the claimant to overcome was described by Learned Hand J in an American case concerning the physical appearance of an adjustable wrench as follows:

> 'The claimant [must] show that the appearance of his wares has in fact come to mean that some particular person … makes them, and the public cares who does make them, and not merely for their appearance and structure.'.[1]

A similar point was made by Jacob J in the *Roho* case: motivation to buy a product due to its shape would not be passing off if that shape was desirable for functional reasons.[2] See also *Numatic v Qualtex* for an example in which goodwill subsisted in a product's appearance.[3]

1 *Crescent Tool Co v Kilborn & Bishop Co* 247 F 299 (1917).
2 *Hodgkinson and Corby Ltd v Wards Mobility Services Ltd* [1995] FSR 169.
3 *Numatic International Ltd v Qualtex UK Ltd* [2010] EWHC 1237 (Ch); [2010] RPC 25.

Descriptive names—secondary meaning

20.41 Obviously it will be easier to establish that the claimant has acquired the necessary goodwill in a particular trade mark if the trade mark in question is inherently distinctive. A non-distinctive mark or sign which merely describes the goods, services or business of the claimant will usually not be sufficient because such a mark or sign does not of itself embody any special attractive force or distinguish the claimant's goods or services from those of its competitors. The courts also show a very real reluctance to afford quasi-monopolistic protection to ordinary English words.[1] However, a mark or sign which would at first sight appear to be descriptive or non-distinctive may be shown by evidence of use and recognition in the marketplace to have acquired a 'secondary meaning'—that is, a second *distinctive* meaning apart from its primary descriptive meaning. Examples of such marks and signs include the following:

- the words 'camel hair belting', the term used to describe belting made of camel hair, was nonetheless held to have acquired a secondary meaning;[2]
- the lemon-coloured, lemon-sized, lemon-shaped container for Jif lemon juice was held to signify to customers not just any lemon juice but that of the claimant in particular;[3]
- the phrase 'farm fluid', although intrinsically non-distinctive, was not in common use and was therefore capable of distinguishing the claimant's goods;[4]

- the publisher of the *Daily Mail* and *Mail on Sunday* was granted an interim injunction against use of the proposed names *Evening Mail* or *London Evening Mail*;[5] and
- the trading name 'Phones4u' used to sell mobile phones.[6]

1 As to which, see *William Stephens Ltd v Cassell* (1913) 30 RPC 199, where Neville J spoke of protecting 'all His Majesty's subjects in their right to use the King's English'.
2 *Frank Reddaway & Co Ltd v George Banham & Co Ltd* (1896) 13 RPC 218; [1896] AC 199.
3 *Reckitt & Colman Products Ltd v Borden Inc* [1990] RPC 341. Notwithstanding the apparent descriptiveness of the container, the court held that the evidence showed that the container had acquired a secondary distinctive meaning.
4 *Antec International v South Western Chicks (Warren) Ltd* [1998] FSR 738.
5 *Associated Newspapers Ltd v Express Newspapers* [2003] EWHC 1322 (Ch); [2003] FSR 51.
6 *Phones 4U Ltd v Phone4u.co.uk Internet Ltd* [2006] EWCA Civ 244; [2007] RPC 5 allowing the claimant's appeal in part.

20.42 On the other hand, there are cases where a descriptive/non-distinctive mark was held not to have acquired the requisite secondary meaning, such as:

- The term 'slip-on' was used by the claimant to describe its shoes but was held by the court not to have acquired a secondary meaning.[1]
- The name 'Office Cleaning Services' was so descriptive that the claimant had to accept the risk of confusion, and the defendant's 'Office Cleaning Association' was sufficiently different.[2]
- The name 'Radio Taxis', in which where the court referred to *One in a Million and* concluded that the defendant's lack of intention to pass off meant that registering the domain name www.radiotaxis.com did not amount to passing off.[3]
- The claimant failed to show that it had the requisite goodwill in the name 'Cranford College', in running a state secondary school in a town called Cranford.[4]

In *Evegate Publishing*, although it was not the only factor in the case, the descriptive nature of the magazine titles in question ('South East Farmer' *vs* 'The Southern Farmer') was held to point to only a low level of confusion between the titles.[5]

1 *Burberrys v Cording & Co Ltd* (1909) 26 RPC 693; but see the discussion of the issues by Parker J at [701].
2 *Office Cleaning Services Ltd v Westminster Office Cleaning Association* (1946) 63 RPC 39; see also *British Diabetic Association v Diabetic Society* [1996] FSR 1.
3 *Radio Taxicabs v Owner Drivers Radio Taxi Services* [2004] RPC 19; and *BT & Ors v One in a Million Ltd* [1999] FSR 1.
4 *Cranford Community College v Cranford College Ltd* [2014] EWHC 2999 (IPEC); [2015] ETMR 7.
5 *Evegate Publishing Ltd v Newsquest Media (Southern) Ltd* [2013] EWHC 1975 (Ch).

20.43 It has always been recognised that this is a difficult line to draw. Lord Scarman in the *Pub Squash* case, delivering the opinion of the Privy Council, stated:

> '… [the tort of passing off] is wide enough to encompass other descriptive material such as slogans or visual images … provided always that such descriptive material has become part of the goodwill of the product. And the test is whether the product has derived from the advertising a distinctive character which the market recognises.'[1]

Thus, a claimant relying on a descriptive name will have to show that that name is not merely well known but has become associated in the mind of the public with the claimant as manufacturer or as the source of the product. Only then is the defendant's use of the name capable of causing the public to believe that the defendant's goods are those of the claimant. Once again, the test adopted by Jacob J is whether the public is moved to buy by source and, if so, what are the features of the claimant's product that enable the public to identify its product. It will be a matter of evidence whether a common or descriptive name has acquired the necessary 'secondary meaning'.

1 *Cadbury-Schweppes Pty Ltd v Pub Squash Co Ltd* [1981] 1 WLR 193 at [200].

C THE SUBJECT MATTER OF THE MISREPRESENTATION

20.44 In broad terms, any misrepresentation that deceives customers as to the origin of the goods or services in question may give rise to passing off (but note that mere confusion is not enough[1]). A misrepresentation as to origin is probably the archetypal form of passing off, but the cases show that misrepresentations may take a number of forms.

1 See *HFC Bank PLC v HSBC Bank plc* [2000] FSR 176.

Misrepresentation as to origin

20.45 It is so well established that a misrepresentation by the defendant that its goods or services are those of the claimant amounts to passing off (as long as it results in damage) that we can move on immediately to look at the wider variations on this form of the tort.

Misrepresentation as to association, sponsorship, endorsement or other trade connection

20.46 In many cases the alleged misrepresentation is said to arise out of a false suggestion or implication of some form of association, sponsorship, approval or other trade connection with the claimant. Issues arise here because:

(a) passing off does not protect the claimant's trade mark *per se*: it protects the claimant's goodwill which the trade mark may come to represent and embody. As we have seen, the goodwill may be limited to a particular category of goods or services; and
(b) the use of the claimant's likeness or image may not in fact amount to a representation of any association, sponsorship, approval or other connection with the claimant.

20.47 The cases show not only that the facts can vary enormously but also that the reasoning of the courts has not been consistent in this area:

- In *Kojak*[1] the defendant's use of the name KOJAKPOPS for its lollipops drew inspiration from and clearly referred to the then well-known television character Kojak. However, this was held not to amount to passing off, despite the fact that a feature of the television character was his habit of sucking lollipops.
- In *Teenage Mutant Ninja Turtles*[2] the defendant's use of drawings based on the famous turtle cartoon characters amounted to passing-off because it was accepted that by that time a substantial percentage of the buying public expected and knew that where a famous cartoon or television character is reproduced on goods, that reproduction is a result of a licence granted by the owner of the intellectual property rights (or other rights) in the character. The case represents something of a high-water mark for claimants' rights in passing off.
- In the *Spice Girls* case[3] the use of images of the pop group was held not to amount to a misrepresentation. Lightman J felt that the public would not take the use of their images in a sticker collection as amounting to a representation that they were responsible for licensing, endorsing, approving or in any other way associating themselves with the stickers. Instead, the defendant was simply 'catering for the popular demand for effigies and quotes of today's idols', and that was something which took no account of the origin or provenance of the goods themselves.
- In *Irvine v Talksport*[4] Laddie J upheld a claim by racing driver Eddie Irvine where the defendant radio station had advertised by using (without Irvine's authorisation) a photograph of Irvine doctored to show him holding a radio tuned to Talksport.
- In *Harrods*[5] the judges in the Court of Appeal were agreed on the essential ingredients of the tort of passing off, but differed as to what misrepresentation is relevant to the tort. Millet LJ (with Beldam LJ concurring) thought that it had to be one where the claimant would be taken by the public to have made itself responsible for the quality of

the defendant's goods or services, and that a belief that the claimant had sponsored or given financial support to the defendant would not suffice. Sir Michael Kerr (dissenting, citing and adopting the words of Cozens-Hardy MR in the *Buttercup* case[6]) was satisfied that a trader might be injured if the defendant misrepresented that it was simply 'connected' or 'in some way mixed up' with the claimant.

- In the *Law Society* case[7] Rimer J was satisfied that there was an arguable case that the use of the defendant's name ('Society of Lawyers') involved misrepresenting to the public the status of those to whom it issued its certificates and would mislead the public into believing that the defendant's members had legal qualifications or were solicitors.
- In *Penguin/Puffin*[8] Walker J felt that it was sufficient for the general public to be led to suppose, assume or guess that the claimant was in some way responsible for the defendant's goods or services. In that case, although the defendant's PUFFIN packaging was considered to be sufficiently different from the claimant's PENGUIN packaging that it was unlikely that a significant proportion of shoppers would fail to distinguish the two products, it was held that the public would nonetheless suppose, assume or guess that there was a 'connection' between the PUFFIN and PENGUIN biscuits, in that the two biscuits were made by the same manufacturer, when in fact they were not. (It is worth noting that Walker J expressly relied upon the *Buttercup* case, which was also relied upon by Sir Michael Kerr in his dissenting judgment in the *Harrods* case—see above).
- In *Primark*[9] the fact that the defendant's clothing was made by the same supplier as the claimant's did not afford the defendant a defence to passing off. The claimant was not responsible for, for example, the quality of those items of clothing, and to suggest the defendant's clothing was associated with the claimant was misleading.
- In *Polo*[10] in the Court of Appeal, Aldous LJ drew the fine but important distinction between a representation by the defendant which could lead members of the public to 'make an association' with the claimant's product (not actionable), and a representation that the claimant *is actually associated with or is* the manufacturer of the defendant's product (actionable). His Lordship thought that the former type of association would not amount to a misrepresentation because, at most, it would be a representation as to the shape and taste of the defendant's Lifesaver sweets and that they were the same type of sweets as Polo mints. Such an 'association' with the claimant's product was not sufficient to establish passing off because it did not amount to a misrepresentation that the defendant's Lifesavers were in fact Polos or that they came from the claimant.

- Similarly, the clear allusion to (even parody of) the well-known Baywatch television series by the producers of the adult satellite programme 'Babewatch' was held not to amount to passing off.[11] The similarity of the names, and even the subject matter of the two programmes (beach scenes, red swimming costumes and red life-floats etc), was not sufficient to amount to an operative misrepresentation because of the distinguishing features of the mode of transmission, mode of reception and content.
- In the *Rihanna* case, the Court of Appeal upheld a finding that high-street retailer Topshop had committed passing off by using an image of the singer Rihanna on some of its t-shirts.[12] The Court of Appeal agreed with Birss J that the use of the image amounted to a representation that Rihanna had endorsed the t-shirts, particularly as the image resonated with one that she had used on her most recent album. Although Rihanna accepted that she had no general right to prevent the use of her image, that did not mean that such usage would never give rise to a misrepresentation about the origin of goods. On the facts, consumers would be misled into buying t-shirts, and the claimant was seeking to take advantage of Rihanna's position as a style icon to her fans.

1 *Tavener Rutledge Ltd v Trexapalm Ltd* [1977] RPC 275, see also *Wombles Ltd v Womble Skips Ltd* [1977] RPC 99 and *Lyngstad v Anabas Products Ltd* [1977] FSR 62 (the '*Abba*' case).
2 *Mirage Studios v Counter-Feat Clothing Co Ltd* [1991] FSR 145.
3 *Halliwell v Panini*, 6 June 1997, unreported (Lightman J); see also similar comments by Laddie J in *Elvis Presley Trade Marks* [1997] RPC 543.
4 *Irvine v Talksport Ltd* [2002] EWHC 367 (Ch); [2002] FSR 60.
5 *Harrods Ltd v Harrodian School Ltd* [1996] RPC 697.
6 *Ewing (t/a Buttercup Dairy Co) v Buttercup Margarine Co Ltd* (1917) 34 RPC 232.
7 *Law Society of England and Wales v Society of Lawyers* [1997] FSR 739.
8 *United Biscuits (UK) Ltd v Asda Stores Ltd* [1997] RPC 513.
9 *Primark Stores Ltd v Lollypop Clothing* [2001] ETMR 30.
10 *Nestlé (UK) Ltd v Trustin the Food Finders Ltd* (22 August 1996, unreported), CA.
11 *Baywatch Productions Co Inc v Home Video Channel* [1997] FSR 22.
12 *Fenty v Arcadia Group Brands (t/a Topshop)* [2013] EWHC 2310 (Ch); [2014] FSR 5; on appeal [2015] EWCA Civ 3; [2015] FSR 14. See also *Hearst Holdings v Avela* [2014] EWHC 439 (Ch); [2014] FSR 36, where the defendant's use of the image of the 'Betty Boop' cartoon character was held to amount to passing off.

20.48 The *Baywatch* and *Polo* decisions (despite being based on very different facts) underscore the fact that it is not enough for a claimant to show that customers may make some form of mere association with the claimant's product. This was reiterated recently in *Moroccanoil.*[1] The association must be far more precise—that is, the notion that the claimant is actually associated or connected in a relevant way with the defendant's goods.

1 *Moroccanoil Israel Ltd v Aldi Stores Ltd* [2014] EWHC 1686 (IPEC); [2015] FSR 4 at [32].

Other misrepresentations: the key element of deception, and the notion of 'initial interest' confusion

20.49 Other examples of operative misrepresentations reflect the central premise that 'at the heart of passing off lies deception or its likelihood, deception of the ultimate consumer in particular'.[1] Thus, in addition to the archetypal case of the defendant selling its goods as those of the claimant, the tort of passing off now recognises other heads of misrepresentation, including:

- Representing that the defendant's goods are the same as those of the claimant (in terms of quality, performance or functionality), when they are not.[2]
- Representing that the defendant's goods are the same as goods sold by a class of persons of which the claimant is a member, when they are not.[3] This is the 'extended' form of passing off.
- Deliberately inviting confusion. In another case involving The Law Society[4] Aldous J granted an interlocutory injunction against the defendant because, by selecting a telephone number confusingly similar to the claimant's, the defendant may well have represented that it was the claimant, either by saying so or by failing to take steps to disabuse anyone mistakenly calling its number (ie, misrepresentation by silence).
- A misrepresentation to the effect that the defendant's goods would 'suit' the claimant's goods, albeit that this has been described as being at the outer limits of passing off. In *Hodge Clemco v Airblast*[5] although the defendant's lenses would have fitted into the claimant's helmets, the helmets when fitted with the defendant's lenses would not have complied with the relevant safety regulations.
- 'Reverse' passing off, whereby the defendant makes a misrepresentation, not as to its own goods, but as to the claimant's goods. This may include selling the claimant's lower quality goods as those of the claimant's higher-quality goods[6] or using the claimant's goods by way of advertisement to induce a purchase of the defendant's goods.[7] It is important to note that so-called 'initial interest' confusion may suffice for passing off—that is, an initial confusion on the part of the consumer, even where that deception is corrected by the time of purchase. However, the Court of Appeal has also said that, 'The misrepresentation must be more than transitory: it is not sufficient that purchasers are initially misled but their misunderstanding is dispelled before any material step is taken'.[8]

1 Per Jacob J in *Hodgkinson and Corby Ltd v Wards Mobility Services Ltd* [1995] FSR 169 at [175]; cited by Walker J in the *NASA* case where he states that: 'it is deception, and nothing else, that lies at the heart of passing off'; [1997] FSR 14 at [20].

2 *Combe International Ltd v Scholl (UK) Ltd* [1980] RPC 1.

3 *Erven Warnink BV v J Townend & Sons (Hull) Ltd* [1980] RPC 31 (the *Advocaat* case).

4 *Law Society of England and Wales v Griffiths* [1995] RPC 16.
5 *Hodge Clemco Ltd v Airblast Ltd* [1995] FSR 806. See also *LEEC Ltd v Morquip Ltd* (unreported, noted in [1996] 6 EIPR D-176) where Laddie J held that the use by the defendant of photographs or other illustrations of the claimant's products, to demonstrate that its products were equivalent to or a substitute for the claimant's, was not passing off per se unless the claimant could prove some actual deception through such use (ie, a misrepresentation). On the evidence there was no such deception.
6 *AG Spalding & Bros v AW Gamage Ltd* (1915) 32 RPC 273.
7 *Bristol Conservatories Ltd v Conservatories Custom Built Ltd* [1989] RPC 455.
8 *Och-Ziff Management Europe Ltd v Och Capital LLP* [2010] EWHC 2599 (Ch); [2011] FSR 11 at [79]–[101] (discussing initial interest confusion in the context of trade mark infringement) and then at [155]–[160] in relation to passing off; *Woolley v Ultimate Products* [2012] EWCA Civ 1038 at [4]. These two authorities were considered and contrasted in *Moroccanoil Israel Ltd v Aldi Stores Ltd* [2014] EWHC 1686 (IPEC); [2015] FSR 4 in which the court concluded the fact that initial interest confusion has been dispelled may mean there is no relevant damage.

20.50 It is important to note that a defendant may also commit a tort by putting a means of misrepresentation into the hands of another person. For example, a manufacturer who supplies goods to a retailer may be liable in passing off even though it is the retailer who actually makes the misrepresentation to the ultimate customers.[1] In such a case the court will look to see whether the manufacturer has supplied a 'badge of fraud' so as to enable the passing off.[2] In the *One in a Million* case[3] it was held that the mere creation of an 'instrument of deception' (such as the registration of a deceptive company name or domain name) without either using it or putting it into the hands of someone else to do so, is not passing off per se. Use of the domain name minigearbox.co.uk was found to amount to an operative misrepresentation in relation to a claimant's 'MINI' trade mark for cars.[4]

However, a *quia timet* injunction is available where the defendant's conduct amounts to a threat of passing off or is calculated to infringe the claimant's rights. Thus, the Court of Appeal in *One in a Million*[5] held that the defendant's purpose in registering certain 'cybersquatting' domain names was to extract money by the threat of misusing the claimants' goodwill, and so an injunction was appropriate. By contrast, a passing off claim failed in *L'Oréal v Bellure*[6] where the Court of Appeal held that smell-alike perfume products did not by themselves amount to instruments of deception, since they did not 'inherently tell a lie'. The Court also held that there was nothing wrong in creating a smell-alike competitor to a well-known perfume, and there was (on the facts) no evidence that anyone had been misled by the similarity of the fragrances.[7]

1 *Sykes v Sykes* (1824) 3 B&C 541.
2 See, for example, *Cadbury Ltd v Ulmer GmbH* [1988] FSR 385.
3 *BT & Ors v One in a Million* [1998] FSR 265 (Jonathan Sumption QC).
4 *Bayerische Motoren Werke AG v Shaun Coley (t/a BMW Mini Gearbox Centre)* [2014] EWHC 3053 (IPEC). See also *Vertical Leisure Ltd v Poleplus Ltd*

[2014] EWHC 2077 (IPEC) in which the defendant had registered domain names that included the claimant's brand names for its pole-dancing products.
5 *British Telecommunications Plc v One in a Million Ltd* [1999] FSR 1.
6 *L'Oréal SA v Bellure NV* [2007] EWCA Civ 968; [2008] RPC 9.
7 The trade mark claim in *L'Oreal v Bellure*, however, was ultimately successful. See [2010] EWCA Civ 535; [2010] RPC 23.

Who must be deceived by the misrepresentation?

20.51 The misrepresentation must in general be made to actual or potential customers of the claimant, as otherwise the claimant's goodwill will not be injured. This is usually a very wide class of persons. However, the judges in the Court of Appeal in *Harrods*[1] appeared divided as to how this principle should be applied. In that case the famous Knightsbridge store was suing the 'Harrodian School' for passing itself off as being connected with Harrods. Millett LJ seemed to take a narrow view, stating that the relevant public was the common customers of the parties (that is, affluent members of the middle class who live in London, shop at Harrods and wish to send their children to a fee-paying school). Sir Michael Kerr on the other hand was prepared to consider the effect of the misrepresentation on anyone who was aware of the retailer and who was at least a potential customer of it, but who may never have heard of the defendant's school. It is suggested that the wider approach is correct: such people are potentially relevant because, when they do hear of the defendant's school, the relevant question will be whether they are deceived into thinking that the school is connected or associated in a material sense with the retailer.

1 *Harrods Ltd v Harrodian School Ltd* [1996] RPC 697.

20.52 Although deception is a key requirement for passing off (see above), the leading cases make clear that it is sufficient for the claimant to demonstrate a *likelihood* of deception[1] so it is not strictly necessarily to produce evidence of actual confusion.[2] However, in practice it is almost always desirable to do so where possible.

1 *Reckitt & Colman Products Ltd v Borden Inc* [1990] RPC 341 (per Lord Oliver).
2 *Mont Blanc Simplo GmbH v Sepia Products Inc* (2000) 23(3) IPD 23021; *Times*, 2 February 2000. See also *Diageo North America Inc v Intercontinental Brands (ICB) Ltd* [2010] EWCA Civ 920; [2011] RPC 2 at [37]: 'Evidence of actual confusion is of assistance, but is not conclusive'.

D FACTORS WHICH MAY NEGATE A 'MISREPRESENTATION'

20.53 There are a number of ways in which the defendant may be able to avoid or negate what would otherwise be a misrepresentation. This is because the courts will generally look at all the relevant evidence in order to decide the case.

Does intent matter?

20.54 It is well established that the claimant does not need to show that the defendant had any intent to pass-off, let alone any malicious intent. Accordingly, lack of intent is normally no defence. Nonetheless, the question why the defendant chose to adopt a particular name, trade mark or get-up is always highly relevant—indeed, it has been called 'a question which falls to be asked and answered'.[1] Where there is clear evidence to suggest that the defendant's conduct was undertaken with a view to diverting business from the claimant, then the court will be likely to conclude that the defendant will (or is likely to) succeed in its aim.[2]

1 Kerr LJ in *Sodastream Ltd v Thorn Cascade Co Ltd* [1982] RPC 459.
2 See the comment to this effect by Aldous J in *Law Society of England and Wales v Griffiths* [1995] RPC 16 at 21; and see also Lindley LJ in *Slazenger & Sons v Feltham & Co* (1889) 6 RPC 531, whose comments were cited by both Millett LJ in *Harrods Ltd v Harrodian School Ltd* [1996] RPC 697 at 706, and Walker J in *United Biscuits (UK) Ltd v Asda Stores Ltd* [1997] RPC 513.

20.55 In *Penguin/Puffin*, Walker J clearly thought that the defendants were acting on legal advice as to how they might make only just enough changes to their packaging to avoid what they judged to be an unacceptable risk of being sued. In the circumstances, the defendants were said to be 'taking a conscious decision to live dangerously', and it was held that that was not a matter which the court could disregard.[1] Similarly, in the *One in a Million* case[2] the judge observed that a defendant who deliberately registers a domain name on account of its similarity to the name, brand name or trade mark of an unconnected business must expect to find itself on the receiving end of an injunction to restrain the threat of passing off. However, the flip side of this was seen in the later case of *Radiotaxis*, where the lack of any ill will or intent in registering the domain name www.radiotaxis.com formed a crucial part of the judge's reasoning that there had not been any passing off.

An 'innocent' defendant (ie, one who lacks any intent to pass off) may be liable in damages in addition to being injuncted.[3]

1 *United Biscuits (UK) Ltd v Asda Stores Ltd* [1997] RPC 513.
2 *BT & Ors v One in a Million* [1998] FSR 265.
3 *Gillette UK Ltd v Edenwest Ltd* [1994] RPC 279 at [291]–[294], in which Blackburne J reviewed the conflicting (sometimes obiter) decisions on this point and concluded that the relief available where passing off is established should not be governed by considerations which may have been applicable to the cause of action at an earlier stage of its development.

Use of own name

20.56 It is questionable whether it amounts to a defence to an allegation of misrepresentation to say that the defendant was using its own name.

It has been suggested that, provided the defendant is using its own name honestly, then it must be allowed to trade in its own name and, if some confusion results, that is considered to be a lesser evil than depriving it of its 'natural and inherent right'.[1] However, such a defence was rejected in *Asprey Garrard* since the name in question was of the individual behind the company, not of the company itself.[2] Moreover, the defence will not apply to newly adopted or changed company names. If any such defence is to succeed, it seems clear that the name must be the defendant's actual name (not an abbreviation or nickname), the defendant must use the name honestly, and it must do nothing to cause confusion deliberately. The court will look carefully to see whether, in fact, the defendant is indeed passing off its business, goods or services. The following cases illustrate the approach:

- An injunction was granted where the defendant deliberately adopted a name to benefit from the claimant's goodwill.[3]
- A qualified injunction was granted forbidding the defendant from using a surname without further clearly distinguishing its business.[4]
- Some cases have drawn a rather fine distinction between the defendant *carrying on business* under its own name and, on the other hand, using the name *in respect of its goods.*[5] However, since a business name will often become the brand name for goods, this may be a distinction without a difference.
- Ultimately, where the defendant is in fact representing its goods as those of the claimant, it is no defence to say that it is doing so only by using its own name.[6]
- Where the defendant has traded under its own name and then sold the business (including the goodwill) to the claimant, it cannot rely on the own-name defence to re-commence trading under the same or a highly similar name.[7]

The own-name defence was considered in some detail in the *Hotel Cipriani* judgments, albeit in relation to registered trade marks rather than in the sphere of passing off.[8] The Court of Appeal held that a trading name could give rise to the defence as well as a corporate name (referring to *Asprey & Garrard* and *Premier Luggage*[9]) but affirmed that a newly adopted name would not do. In *Och-Ziff*[10] the own-name defence failed for want of compliance with honest practices in industrial and commercial matters.

1 *Marengo v Daily Sketch and Sunday Graphic Ltd* (1948) 65 RPC 242 per Lord Simonds at 251.
2 *Asprey & Garrard Ltd v WRA Guns Ltd (t/a William R Asprey Esq)* [2001] EWCA Civ 1499; [2002] FSR 31.
3 *Joseph Rodgers & Sons v W N Rodgers & Co* (1924) 41 RPC 277.
4 *Wright, Layman & Umney Ltd v Wright* (1949) 66 RPC 149.

5 The distinction was made by Romer J in the *Rodgers v Rodgers* case. *Joseph Rodgers & Sons v W N Rodgers & Co* (1924) 41 RPC 277.
6 *NAD Electronics Inc v NAD Computer Systems Ltd* [1997] FSR 380.
7 *IN Newman Ltd v Adlem* [2005] EWCA Civ 741; [2006] FSR 16.
8 *Hotel Cipriani Srl v Cipriani (Grosvenor Street) Ltd* [2008] EWHC 3032 (Ch); [2009] RPC 9; [2010] EWCA Civ 110; [2010] RPC 16.
9 *Asprey & Garrard Ltd v WRA Guns Ltd (t/a William R Asprey Esq)* [2001] EWCA Civ 1499; [2002] FSR 31; *Premier Luggage & Bags Ltd v Premier Co (UK) Ltd* [2002] EWCA Civ 387; [2003] FSR 5.
10 *Och-Ziff Management Europe Ltd v Och Capital LLP* [2010] EWHC 2599 (Ch); [2011] FSR 11.

Acts outside the United Kingdom

20.57 The relevant trade for the purpose of passing off is the claimant's trade within this jurisdiction and not any trade carried on overseas. For example, in *Fortnum & Mason*[1] the well-known English retailer was unable to prevent the defendant from using the name FORTNAM because the claimant's trade was in top-end merchandise in England, whereas the defendants sold cheap, wholesale goods abroad. Accordingly, Harman J could find no basis on which to conclude that any customers would buy the defendant's goods in the belief that they were acquiring the goods of the claimant.

1 *Fortnum & Mason plc v Fortnam Ltd* [1994] FSR 438.

20.58 However, the situation will be different where the defendant's activities will necessarily stray into the jurisdiction (whether by design or by accident): in *Internet World*[1] Jacob J restrained the German defendant from passing off its INTERNET WORLD trade show and exhibitions, which were intended to be held in Germany but which were advertised in the UK through the internet (albeit via a website based on a server in Germany).

1 *Mecklermedia Corpn v D C Congress GmbH* [1998] Ch 40.

Descriptive use of terms or names

20.59 A defendant will often assert that it is merely using a term or name to describe some aspect of the nature, quality, composition, geographic origin or purpose of its business, goods or services. Such a defence is based not so much on negating the misrepresentation as on asserting that there is no misrepresentation in the first place. It will be a question of fact whether a descriptive term or name used by the defendant has acquired a 'secondary meaning' that has become distinctive of the claimant's business, goods or services and, if so, the defendant may still be passing off through the use of that term or name.

20.60 The circumstances in which a claimant can succeed in a passing off action based on a descriptive name, and the significance of the length of use of that name, have been considered in numerous cases.[1] The starting principle is that the courts will not readily assume that where the defendant uses descriptive words which are already used by the claimant this is likely to cause deception, and the courts will tend to accept small differences as adequate to avoid such deception. As in the context of the use of one's own name (see above), the cases again suggest that there may be a distinction to be drawn where the descriptive term or name is used in relation to the actual article or product, rather than as the trading name of a business. In the latter case, the nature of the business, its goods or services and the way in which the business is carried on may either negate or add to the likelihood of deception.

1 Significant cases include: *McCain International v Country Fayre Foods* [1981] RPC 69 (especially at 73/80); *My Kinda Town Ltd v Soll and Grunts Investments* [1983] RPC 407 (especially at 415 and 424–426); *Reckitt & Coleman Products Ltd v Borden Inc* [1990] RPC 341 (especially at 412); and *County Sound plc v Ocean Sound Ltd* [1991] FSR 367 (especially at 373–376). See also the detailed and helpful analysis in *Planetart LLC v Photobox Free Prints Ltd* [2020] EWHC 713; [2020] FSR 26 at [59]–[77].

Use of other distinguishing material, including disclaimers

20.61 We have already noted that the court will look at all the circumstances of the case to determine whether the defendant's activities amount to an operative misrepresentation. It is not sufficient for the claimant simply to show that the defendant is using a similar (or even identical) trade mark, which is the approximate equivalent ingredient for trade mark infringement under the TMA 1994. This is because the tort of passing off (unlike the TMA 1994) seeks to protect goodwill rather than enforce trade mark rights as such, so the overall features of the defendant's business, goods or services may mean that there is no operative misrepresentation despite the existence of similarities. For example:

- In the *Polo* case[1] (see above in relation to misrepresentation), despite the similarity of the shape of the defendant's Lifesavers sweets to the claimant's Polo mints, both Walker J and Aldous LJ thought that the packaging as a whole of the defendant's product and the fact that it bore the trade mark Lifesavers meant that consumers would not be led to believe that Lifesavers were the product of the claimant. Aldous LJ observed that the situation might have been different if Lifesavers had been marketed in an unmarked plastic bag, because in such circumstances the representation to consumers conveyed by the shape of LIFESAVERS alone may have been such as to suggest that they were either POLOS or manufactured by the claimant.

- In *Fortnum & Mason*[2] the similarity of the defendant's name (FORTNAM) was on its own insufficient to establish passing off because of:
  - (a) the differing nature of the trade channels—the claimant being a retailer and the defendant a wholesaler; and
  - (b) the differing quality and cost of the goods and hence the nature of the ultimate consumer—the claimant selling high-class, relatively expensive goods and the defendant selling relatively cheap goods.
- On the other hand, in *Penguin/Puffin* Walker J thought that even though the PENGUIN *trade mark* was not infringed by the defendant's PUFFIN sign, nonetheless, the overall look of the PUFFIN packaging would cause a substantial number of customers to suppose that there was a connection between the PUFFIN biscuit and the claimant.[3] Thus, the misrepresentation conveyed by the similar packaging as a whole was not negated by the use of a different trade mark.
- In *Roho*[4] Jacob J thought that the near-identical shape and appearance of the defendant's wheelchair cushions did not amount to a misrepresentation because the shape itself was not a feature by reference to which customers bought the cushion. In effect, the shape and appearance of the parties' respective cushions conveyed no representation as to the origin of the goods and, instead, other features of the two products clearly distinguished them, such as:
  - (a) the manner in which they were bought (ie, because they were expensive, they were not bought casually);
  - (b) the process of supply, which inevitably involved health care professionals (who were described as caring and careful people);
  - (c) the process of ordering the goods by reference to a precise model number; and
  - (d) the use by the defendant of a dissimilar trade mark.
- In *Blu-Tack* the misrepresentation (if any) was made too late.[5] The feature of the defendant's product complained of (the blue colour of the adhesive) was not visible at the point of sale because the adhesive itself was packaged inside a wallet which was not in any way to be confused with the wallet in which the claimant's BLU-TACK was sold.
- Compare the facts of *Blu-Tack* with *Sodastream*[6] in which the defendant's fizzy drink cylinders were substantially identical to the claimant's cylinders. The only significant difference was an attached label, but this did not sufficiently distinguish the two products, and, therefore, did not negate the misrepresentation conveyed by the substantially identical features.
- Similarly, in *Jif Lemon*[7] the fact that the defendant used distinguishing labels attached to the neck of its lemon-shaped

containers did not negate the misrepresentation (caused by the similarity of the containers themselves), because the trial judge found that those purchasing lemon juice did not read the labels and would simply assume that all lemon-shaped containers contained Jif lemon juice.

- In *Specsavers*[8] Mann J held that there was no misrepresentation in the defendant's use of a green and white logo featuring two ovals and the words 'Be a real spec saver at Asda'. The judge held that there was simply not enough, even in the combined effect, to amount to a misrepresentation, since the context in which the sign was used was enough to ensure no confusion: it was in an Asda store, with an Asda logo, and used Asda's name in the strapline.
- In *MOROCCANOIL*[9] an 'initial interest' confusion that might have arisen (see para **20.49** above) had been dispelled by the time of purchase.

1 *Nestlé (UK) Ltd v Trustin the Food Finders Ltd* (19 August 1996, unreported) (Walker J) (22 August 1996, unreported), CA.
2 *Fortnum & Mason plc v Fortnam Ltd* [1994] FSR 438.
3 *United Biscuits (UK) Ltd v Asda Stores Ltd* [1997] RPC 513.
4 *Hodgkinson and Corby Ltd v Wards Mobility Services Ltd* [1995] FSR 169.
5 *Bostik Ltd v Sellotape GB Ltd* [1994] RPC 556.
6 *Sodastream Ltd v Thorn Cascade Co Ltd* [1982] RPC 459.
7 *Reckitt & Colman Products Ltd v Borden Inc* [1990] RPC 341.
8 *Specsavers International Healthcare Ltd v Asda Stores Ltd (No. 2)* [2010] EWHC 2035 (Ch); [2011] FSR 1; see [191]–[194].
9 *Moroccanoil Israel Ltd v Aldi Stores Ltd* [2014] EWHC 1686 (IPEC); [2015] FSR 4.

20.62 As that last example makes clear, it may be possible to adopt certain features of a competitor's product or branding (even if those features are distinctive of the competitor) provided that some other aspect of one's business, goods or services sufficiently distinguishes them from those of the competitor. One needs to tread carefully however: Walker J in *Penguin/Puffin* was clearly influenced by the fact that the defendant had chosen to 'live dangerously' by adopting as much as it thought it could of the PENGUIN packaging. In contrast, Mann J in *Specsavers* found for the defendant despite noting that it had chosen to live dangerously.

Comparative advertising, spares and accessories

20.63 The use of the claimant's trade mark or name in a comparative advertisement will not on its own amount to passing off because there is generally no misrepresentation as such: usually quite the opposite—the defendant is deliberately distinguishing its goods or services from those of the claimant by comparing them in some way. Similarly, a statement by the defendant that its goods are spares or accessories for the claimant's goods conveys no relevant misrepresentation for passing-off purposes. However, there may still be trade mark infringement issues if the defendant is taking unfair advantage of the distinctiveness or repute of any registered mark belonging to the claimant (see **Chapter 14**) and the law of malicious falsehood may also be relevant (see **Chapter 16**).

E COMMON FIELD OF ACTIVITY

20.64 The significance or otherwise of a 'common field of activity' as between the claimant's and the defendant's businesses has long been a topic of much discussion. The issue in a nutshell is whether there must be, as a matter of law, a 'common field of activity' in order to be able to succeed in a passing off claim. In the *Harrods* case[1] Millett LJ reviewed the history of this issue, commencing with *Uncle Mac*[2] in which Wynn-Parry J coined the phrase and dismissed the claimant's claim for want of a common field of activity. Suffice it to say that it is now well settled that there is no threshold requirement of overlap in fields of activity, but the respective fields of activity of the parties remains a relevant (but not determinative) consideration in assessing the likelihood of deception and the likelihood of damage.

1 *Harrods Ltd v Harrodian School Ltd* [1996] RPC 697.
2 *McCulloch v Lewis A May (Produce Distributors) Ltd* (1948) 65 RPC 58. In the Abba case (*Lyngstad v Anabas Products Ltd* [1977] FSR 62) Oliver J explained that Wynn-Parry J was not adding a new element to the tort of passing off: instead, he said that the expression 'common field of activity' is merely a convenient shorthand term for the need for a real possibility of confusion.

Relevance to deception or likelihood of deception

20.65 The proximity or overlap of the parties' respective fields of activity is a factor to be taken into account when deciding whether the defendant's conduct will (or is likely to) deceive the relevant public. It is clearly possible to conceive of a situation where the defendant's use of even a very well-known trade mark will convey no misrepresentation to the relevant customers because the defendant's business, goods or services are wholly different from those sold or supplied by the claimant. The following cases illustrate the issues:

- *Annabel's*[1] is an early case in which the Court of Appeal found that there *was* a common field of activity (to a certain degree) between the claimant nightclub and the defendant escort agency, but it was implied that this was not strictly a necessary ingredient: it simply went to the overall question of likelihood of confusion.
- In *Stringfellows*[2] the nature of the claimant's business (a nightclub) was so remote from the defendant's products (oven chips) that the Court of Appeal refused to grant an injunction to the claimant

notwithstanding that the defendant was clearly making use of the claimant's reputation in its advertising. However, such use did not amount to passing off because there was no suggestion that customers would be deceived into thinking that the claimant had anything to do with the manufacture and/or supply of the oven chips.

- In *Harrods*[3] Millett LJ recognised that where the claimant's business name is a household name, the degree of overlap between the fields of activity of the parties' respective business may be less relevant in assessing whether there is likely to be deception, although it must still be considered. On the facts of the case, the Court of Appeal (by a majority of two to one) held that parents would not send their children to the Harrodian School wrongly thinking that it was connected or associated with the Harrods department store.
- In another case involving a famous English retailer, Harman J held in *Fortnum & Mason* that despite the claimant's very great goodwill in the name FORTNUMS which was 'long established and beyond question in its particular field', the defendant's use of FORTNAMS did not amount to passing off, having regard to the nature of the goods in which the respective parties dealt and the nature of their respective trade channels.[4] Although Harman J cited *Stringfellows* (and others dealing with this issue), it is clear that his decision is based not on the lack of a common field of activity per se, but on the fact that, having looked at all of the evidence, there was no real likelihood of deception.
- Contrast those cases with *Lego*[5] where the claimant manufacturer of children's plastic building blocks succeeded in its passing off action against the manufacturer of plastic irrigation equipment. The fact that both products were made out of plastic may have been influential in this decision.
- In *Teenage Mutant Ninja Turtles*[6] Sir Nicholas Browne-Wilkinson VC specifically refused to follow the stricter approach typified in the English cases of *Wombles*, *Kojak* and *Abba*[7] and instead approved the less onerous assessment of two Australian cases, namely *Muppets* and *Fido Dido*.[8] He held that the fact that there was no common field of activity as such between the first claimant (the proprietor of four reptilian cartoon characters) and the defendants (distributors of goods in relation to which an image of similar characters was used) was irrelevant, because the public would still be deceived, not into thinking that the claimants were in fact the manufacturers or suppliers of the goods, but into believing or expecting that the claimants had granted a licence to the defendants to sell the goods. This was based on evidence that showed that the public believed that the turtle characters would not appear on a product without the licence of the claimant and, in the absence of such a licence, the public had therefore been

deceived into a wrongful belief. It may be that *Turtles* will only be relevant in the context of character merchandising, but even so, it is suggested it will trump the contrary approach taken by Lightman J in the *Spice Girls* case.[9]

- In *Nike*[10] the owners of the well known NIKE clothing and sports brand succeeded in a passing off action where the defendants were engaged in the distribution of toiletries and cosmetics. Jacob J accepted the evidence which showed that the marketing and sale of the defendant's goods would lead to actual deception, notwithstanding that the parties traded in entirely different fields of activity and even though the claimant had no present intention to move into toiletries/cosmetics.
- In the *NASA* case[11] Walker J observed that the *Lego* and *Turtles* cases illustrate a 'relaxation' of the common field of activity concept, but do not mark its extinction.
- Arnold J held in *Och-Ziff* held that an absence of direct competition between the parties did not prevent the defendant's activities from creating a likelihood of association, nor from doing damage to the claimant's goodwill.[12]
- Another factor to bear in mind is the ever-changing nature of the marketplace; in *NAD* Ferris J noted that the fields of audio hi-fi and computers were converging and were no longer sufficiently distinct to prevent confusion.[13] Well over a decade later, we can see that his observation about convergence was rather astute.

1 *Annabel's (Berkeley Square) Ltd v G. Schock (t/a Annabel's Escort Agency)* [1972] FSR 261.
2 *Stringfellow v McCain Foods (GB) Ltd* [1984] RPC 501.
3 *Harrods Ltd v Harrodian School Ltd* [1996] RPC 697.
4 *Fortnum & Mason plc v Fortnam Ltd* [1994] FSR 438.
5 *Lego System A/S v Lego M Lemelstritch Ltd* [1983] FSR 155.
6 *Mirage Studios v Counter-Feat Clothing Co Ltd* [1991] FSR 145.
7 *Wombles Ltd v Womble Skips Ltd* [1977] RPC 99; *Tavener Rutledge Ltd v Trexapalm Ltd* [1977] RPC 275; *Lyngstad v Anabas Products Ltd* [1977] FSR 62.
8 *Children's Television Workshop Inc v Woolworths (NSW) Ltd* [1981] 1 NSWLR 273; *Fido Dido Inc v Venture Stores (Retailers) Pty Ltd* (1988) 16 IPR 365.
9 *Halliwell v Panini* (6 June 1997, unreported).
10 *Nike (Ireland) Ltd v Network Management Ltd* (22 July 1994, unreported).
11 *Nice and Safe Attitude Ltd v Piers Flook* [1997] FSR 14.
12 *Och-Ziff Management Europe Ltd v Och Capital LLP* [2010] EWHC 2599 (Ch); [2011] FSR 11.
13 *NAD Electronics Inc v NAD Computer Systems Ltd* [1997] FSR 380.

20.66 It is also worth noting that, while a lack of a common field of activity will not necessarily deprive the claimant of a remedy, nor does the existence of a common field of activity guarantee a finding of passing off. For example, in *Roho* there was found to be no passing off despite the fact that the defendant copied certain features of the claimant's cushions and sold in direct competition with the claimant.[1] On the facts it was held that the features in question were not indicative of the claimant.

1 *Hodgkinson and Corby Ltd v Wards Mobility Services Ltd* [1995] FSR 169.

Relationship with damage

20.67 There is also the question whether the claimant can suffer any direct loss (in terms of sales) if there is no common field of activity with the defendant. The answer may be that there is no damage in these circumstances (at least not directly, but see below as to damage to goodwill). For example, in *Stringfellows*[1] Slade LJ cautioned that even if there is a risk of confusion, the court should not too readily go on to infer a likelihood of resulting damage; in such a case, a heavy onus falls on the claimant to show that its business is likely to suffer damage and more than minimal loss. The requirement of damage is explored more fully in the next section. In ASSOS/ASOS it was held that the fact that the defendant had almost nothing to do with the claimant's field of business (primarily specialist cycling clothing) meant that there could be no damage to the claimant's goodwill.[2]

1 *Stringfellow v McCain Foods (GB) Ltd* [1984] RPC 501.
2 *Maier v Asos Plc* [2013] EWHC 2831 (Ch); [2014] FSR 16; see [169]–[173].

F DAMAGE TO OR LOSS OF GOODWILL

20.68 Damage is the final fundamental requirement of the tort of passing off, and in particular damage to the claimant's goodwill. Lord Fraser stated in *Advocaat* that the claimant must show 'that he has suffered, or is really likely to suffer, substantial damage to its property in the goodwill'.[1] Without damage, there is no tort of passing off. As mentioned in the introduction to this chapter, there is no tort of merely making use of another's goodwill: the goodwill itself must be damaged. The following paragraphs explore the various forms that such damage may take.

1 *Erven Warnink BV v J Townend & Sons (Hull) Ltd* [1980] RPC 31.

Loss of sales, damage by substitution

20.69 In the classic case of passing off, where the defendant represents its business, goods or services as those of the claimant, there is an obvious risk that the claimant will lose customers and potential customers who transfer their custom to the defendant in the erroneous belief that they are dealing with the claimant. However, note that the damage must be of the right sort: in *Glee Club*[1] it was said that, 'The damage suffered by the claimant is caused by its venues being confused with the defendant's TV show and its potential customers being put off. That is not passing off'.

1 *Comic Enterprises Ltd v Twentieth Century Fox Film Corporation* [2014] EWHC 185 (Ch); [2014] FSR 35 at [147].

Dilution of the value of the goodwill

20.70 Where the parties are not in direct competition with each other there will be no sales that are 'lost' by the claimant to the defendant. However, a number of cases have identified other ways in which the claimant's goodwill can be damaged in this scenario:

- In the *Lego* case[1] it was accepted that a customer who was dissatisfied with the defendant's LEGO plastic irrigation equipment might be dissuaded from buying one of the claimant's LEGO plastic toy construction kits.
- Also in *Lego*, Falconer J recognised that one way in which a claimant may commercialise its goodwill is to license or franchise another trader to use its trade mark and its attractive force (ie, its goodwill) in another field of activity. The defendant's continuing use of LEGO in relation to its irrigation equipment therefore negated the claimant's opportunity to commercialise its goodwill in the market for such equipment, and this was held to damage that goodwill.
- Compare *Lego* with *Stringfellow*[2] where the evidence did not support a finding that the defendant's sales of STRINGFELLOWS oven chips had deprived the claimant of an opportunity to merchandise his name in relation to other products (let alone oven chips). Nor did the court accept that the claimant's nightclub would suffer a fall in membership or attendance.
- In the *Elderflower Champagne* case[3] the Court of Appeal accepted as relevant damage the 'blurring or erosion of the uniqueness' that attached to the mark CHAMPAGNE, and this was said to 'debase' the exclusive reputation of the Champagne houses.
- *Elderflower Champagne* may be contrasted with the decision in *Harrods*[4] where Millett LJ accepted that the application of the claimant's trade mark to inferior goods was likely to injure the claimant's goodwill if customers assumed the inferior goods to be those of the claimant, but he confessed to an 'intellectual difficulty' in accepting the concept that the law could recognise a head of damage (for the purposes of passing off) which did not depend on confusion.[5]
- These difficulties do not seem to have concerned judges in subsequent cases. Laddie J in *Chocosuisse* took the view that the claimant would inevitably suffer actionable damage if the exclusivity of the designation 'Swiss chocolate' were diminished.[6] Quoting the

Master of the Rolls in *Elderflower Champagne* case, he described the damage as 'insidious'.

- Likewise, Arnold J in *Vodkat* had no hesitation in finding that even where there had been no loss of sales, there was damage in the erosion of distinctiveness of the term vodka by products that did not fairly merit that description.[7] The erosion type of damage was also found in *Och-Ziff*.[8]

1 *Lego System A/S v Lego M Lemelstrich Ltd* [1983] FSR 155.
2 *Stringfellow v McCain Foods (GB) Ltd* [1984] RPC 501.
3 *Taittinger SA v Allbev Ltd* [1993] FSR 641.
4 *Harrods Ltd v Harrodian School Ltd* [1996] RPC 697.
5 For further commentary on this issue, see Carty, 'Passing Off at the Crossroads' [1996] 11 EIPR 629.
6 *Chocosuisse Union des Fabricants Suisses de Chocolat v Cadbury Ltd* [1998] RPC 117.
7 *Diageo North America Inc v Intercontinental Brands (ICB) Ltd* [2010] EWHC 17 (Ch); [2010] RPC 12, at [235].
8 *Och-Ziff Management Europe Ltd v Och Capital LLP* [2010] EWHC 2599 (Ch); [2011] FSR 11.

G EVIDENCE

20.71 As we have already emphasised, the outcome of a passing off case will typically depend on the court's findings of fact, which in turn depend on the quality of the evidence submitted to the court by the parties. The type of information or statistics, and the way in which this evidence can be obtained, will depend on the parties' respective businesses, and the way in which the defendant is alleged to be making the relevant misrepresentation. Furthermore, different types of evidence will be required in establishing the three elements of the 'classical trinity' of goodwill, misrepresentation, and damage. The following paragraphs examine in broad terms the type of evidence required in order to establish each of these elements and the ways in which that evidence might be obtained.

Evidence of reputation/goodwill

20.72 The claimant needs to establish, in the first place, sufficient goodwill in the United Kingdom. The following evidence is therefore likely to be relevant:

1 The length of time that the claimant has been in business and, more specifically, the length of time that the claimant has sold or supplied the goods or services in question.
2 The turnover of the claimant's business and, in particular, the turnover in the goods or services in question.
3 The nature and extent of the claimant's activities in advertising/marketing its business, goods or services.

4 The individual and collective awareness and opinions of members of the relevant trade, business or profession.
5 The awareness and opinions of members of the relevant sector of the public, ie, the likely consumers/customers of the goods or services in question.

20.73 The purpose of this evidence is to establish, in the words of Jacob J in the *Roho* case[1] that customers are 'moved to buy by source'. That is, the trade mark of the claimant's product must have acquired a sufficient 'attractive force' such that customers will want the goods of that particular brand rather than the goods of any brand. If consumers do not know of the trade mark or brand, or do not realise that it indicates the source of the goods or services in question, then the claimant will not have established a sufficient goodwill. In marketing terms, the claimant must establish 'brand loyalty'.

1 *Hodgkinson and Corby Ltd v Wards Mobility Services Ltd* [1995] FSR 169.

Evidence of misrepresentation

20.74 The second element of the classical trinity (a misrepresentation) will often be established by showing that people are at least confused, if not deceived, by the defendant's conduct. Thus, the claimant proves the misrepresentation by submitting evidence of confusion or deception. Accordingly, the most relevant evidence will be independent evidence from members of the relevant trade, business or profession, and also from members of the relevant public. However, the decision is ultimately one for the judge. In *Spalding v Gamage*[1] Lord Parker made it clear that the question whether the defendant's conduct amounts to a misrepresentation is 'a matter for the judge, who, looking at the documents and evidence before him/her, comes to his/her own conclusion'.

1 *AG Spalding & Bros v AW Gamage Ltd* (1915) 32 RPC 273.

20.75 There is, however, one exception, acknowledged by Lord Parker: where the goods in question are of a kind not normally sold to the general public but in a specialised market. In such cases, evidence from persons accustomed to dealing in that specialised market as to the likelihood of deception or confusion will be essential. In the *Sodastream* case[1] the judge was particularly welcoming of evidence from the relevant trade, saying that 'it is perfectly proper and admissible for someone in the trade to express opinions about the likely reaction of others in relation to matters which are within his or her sphere of work'.

1 *Sodastream Ltd v Thorn Cascade Co Ltd* [1982] RPC 459.

20.76 Furthermore, judges will sometimes accept the evidence of the public in preference to or in substitution for their own subjective views. In *Jif Lemon*, even though Lord Bridge felt surprised by the finding that a lemon-coloured, lemon-shaped container had become distinctive of the claimant's goods, he agreed (reluctantly) that the trial judge was right as a matter of law to find in favour of the claimant.[1] In *Chocosuisse*[2] Laddie J confessed that he would not have taken the defendant's SWISS CHALET product to be Swiss chocolate, but he was concerned not to allow his personal view to influence his decision for two reasons (the latter of which was said to be especially significant):

(a) he thought that it would not be right to assume automatically that his view would be shared even by a substantial minority of the public at large; and
(b) he only came to hear of the defendant's product knowing that it was the subject of passing off proceedings, which made it difficult to assess what his reaction might have been in a genuine point-of-sale situation.

1 *Reckitt & Colman Products Ltd v Borden Inc* [1990] RPC 341.
2 *Chocosuisse Union des Fabricants Suisses de Chocolat v Cadbury Ltd* [1998] RPC 117.

20.77 It is suggested that this must be right, because the test is not whether any one individual is or is not confused or deceived, even if that individual is a judge; the test is whether a relevant section of the public is (or is likely to be) confused or deceived. The point was clearly illustrated in that same case, where Laddie J found on the evidence that the majority of consumers would not be confused or deceived into thinking that the defendant's SWISS CHALET chocolate came from Switzerland. Nonetheless, he was satisfied that 'a substantial number of the public' would be confused as to whether SWISS CHALET is Swiss chocolate or not. In contrast, the courts will reject evidence of the now famous 'moron in a hurry'—ie, the member of the public who is confused or deceived simply because he or she does not pay reasonable attention to protect his or her own interests.[1]

1 *Star Industrial Co Ltd v Yap Kwee Kor* [1976] FSR 256.

20.78 Many passing off cases are commenced before the defendant has begun trading or, at least, before it has undertaken the activities of which the claimant complains. In such cases, it is impossible to obtain evidence of actual confusion or deception, but this is not of itself an insurmountable obstacle. In *Sodastream*[1] Kerr LJ stated that in interlocutory proceedings, it is not a justifiable criticism to say that the claimant has not adduced any evidence of actual confusion among the general public, especially where the product with which the claimant takes issue is not yet on the market. Thus, evidence of the likely reactions of customers to the proposed activities of the defendant was admitted. In *One in a Million*[2] Jonathan Sumption QC issued a final injunction in a *quia timet* action despite the absence of proof of damage, on the basis that the defendant's conduct was calculated to infringe the claimant's rights.

1 *Sodastream Ltd v Thorn Cascade Co Ltd* [1982] RPC 459.
2 *BT & Ors v One in a Million Ltd* [1999] FSR 1.

20.79 However, where the defendant has already commenced selling or supplying the goods or services in question, then the lack of any evidence of actual confusion or deception may pose much greater problems, and may even sink the claimant's case. This is because the courts are entitled to infer that the relevant section of the public simply is not confused or deceived, and therefore there has been no misrepresentation. The inference will be drawn all the more readily where the parties have been trading for some time, for example:

- In *City Link v Lakin*[1] the parties had been trading side by side for a number of years and, in that time, despite both using CITY LINK as part of their business name, the only evidence of confusion was a few misdirected cheques or invoices.
- In the *Fortnum & Mason* case[2] Harman J thought that the fact that the defendant had been trading under the name FORTNAM for around five years without anybody at any time bringing its existence to the notice of the claimant went 'some way' to supporting his conclusion that people were not likely to confuse the two businesses.
- In *Harrods*[3] Millett LJ (with Beldam LJ concurring) thought that the lapse of time between the publication of the defendant's brochure and the trial was such that, had confusion really arisen, the claimant would have been in a position to call evidence that some of its customers had at least asked for a brochure of the school, or enquired about whether the store supplied the school's uniforms or that its customers had otherwise 'manifested an impression that the school was connected with the store'.

1 *City Link Travel Holdings Ltd v Lakin* [1979] FSR 653.
2 *Fortnum & Mason plc v Fortnam Ltd* [1994] FSR 438.
3 *Harrods Ltd v Harrodian School Ltd* [1996] RPC 697.

20.80 Sometimes the claimant may have difficulty in getting members of the public to admit to being confused or deceived because they may feel foolish. However, the claimant may instead be able to rely on other hallmarks of confusion or deception, which may in fact be more persuasive than a testifying witness, and certainly may be of greater probative value than surveys and questionnaires. A good example is evidence of complaints or enquiries intended to be directed to or about the claimant, which have in fact been made to or about the defendant (or vice versa). In the *Neutrogena* case[1] Jacob J (affirmed on appeal by the Court of Appeal) accepted the likelihood of deception and confusion based on evidence of letters of complaint about NEUTROGENA which were sent to the Independent Television Commission concerning an advertisement on television which was in fact for the defendant's product NEUTRALIA. Likewise it will generally be very persuasive to produce evidence of orders, invoices or returned goods being misdirected.

1 *Neutrogena Corpn v Golden Ltd* [1996] RPC 473 CA.

20.81 The courts will, however, make allowances where the circumstances may be such that it is inherently unlikely that the claimant will ever hear of the confusion or deception, even where it is widespread. In *Andrex/Nouvelle*[1] which concerned toilet tissue, Laddie J accepted that this was the case because tissue is a low-cost item and customers may either never realise that they had been deceived or would not complain even if they did realise.

1 *Kimberly-Clark Ltd v Fort Sterling Ltd* [1997] FSR 877.

Evidence of damage to goodwill

20.82 We have already seen that the defendant's misrepresentation may cause different types of damage or injury, including lost sales, loss of franchising opportunities and loss of the exclusivity in the trade mark. Although many claimants may be focused on obtaining an injunction to bring the defendant's conduct to a halt, financial damages can also be a substantial part of the relief. The court will normally order an inquiry as to damages (except where it appears that the claimant has suffered only nominal damage) or an account of profits, and it is at this stage that evidence again comes into play.

20.83 At the inquiry, which will generally be conducted by a Master, the object is not so much to carry out a precise calculation based on a minute examination of the evidence, but to award a sum which fairly compensates for the damage to the claimant's goodwill—damage which, because the goodwill is intangible, can never be the subject of precise calculation. The general statement of principle is that the claimant is entitled to recover the damages that are the natural and direct consequence of the unlawful acts of the defendant, including:

> 'any loss of trade actually suffered by the claimants, either directly from the acts complained of, or properly attributable to injury to the claimant's reputation, business, goodwill and trade and business connection caused by the acts complained of; in other words, such damages as flow directly and in the

usual course of things, from the wrongful acts, excluding any speculative and unproven damage'[1].

1 *AG Spalding & Bros v AW Gamage Ltd* (1918) 35 RPC 101, per Swinfen Eady LJ at 117.

20.84 As always, each case will depend on its own facts. Evidence of sales made by the defendant will be relevant, and may be taken to indicate sales lost by the claimant. However, not all sales by the defendant will necessarily result from the misrepresentation—they may occur due to some other aspect of the goods or simply because the individual customer likes the defendant's product.[1]

1 See, for example, *Dormeuil Frères v Feraglow Ltd* [1990] RPC 449, where Knox J refused to award damages on a royalty basis for each sale by the defendant.

20.85 In contrast to evidence of sales, the effects of dilution (loss of exclusivity and reputation) will always be difficult to demonstrate explicitly. The judge will usually have to form an opinion based on the degree of the claimant's goodwill and its reputation in the marketplace; and the quality of the defendant's goods or services. In *Chocosuisse*[1] Laddie J accepted as a general proposition, without the need for specific evidence on the subject, that in the extended passing off cases if there is likely to be confusion then it must follow that the exclusivity of the designation (in that case 'Swiss chocolate') will suffer, causing damage to the claimants and those whom they represent.

1 *Chocosuisse Union des Fabricants Suisses de Chocolat v Cadbury Ltd* [1998] RPC 117.

20.86 Likewise, it may be difficult to produce evidence of the claimant's potential to expand its market or to license (franchise/merchandise) third parties in another market sector, let alone evidence that the defendant has actually limited or negated that potential. In *Lego* the court accepted that the capacity existed for the manufacturer of LEGO children's plastic building blocks to expand, either itself or by licensing third parties, to manufacture plastic irrigation equipment and sell it under the trade mark LEGO.[1] The court accepted this proposition based on two factors:

(a) the overwhelming evidence of the strength (and hence value) of the goodwill attaching to the mark LEGO such that it was a 'household word'; and
(b) the testimony of a marketing expert, in whose opinion the claimant had a clear opportunity for licensing or franchising the mark LEGO in other fields, particularly the 'plastics area'. It was said that garden implements would have been an 'ideal market'.

1 *Lego System A/S v Lego M Lemelstritch Ltd* [1983] FSR 155. Falconer J in *Lego* relied in particular on the Australian case of *Henderson v Radio Corpn Pty Ltd* [1969] RPC 218

where the Supreme Court of New South Wales equated the appropriation of another's reputation as an injury no less than the appropriation of goods or money.

20.87 Conversely, in *Stringfellows*[1] the court was not prepared to accept, in the absence of any evidence, that the owner of a nightclub had the capacity to expand into making oven chips, and, therefore, there was no damage to the claimant's business.

1 *Stringfellow v McCain Foods (GB) Ltd* [1984] RPC 501.

Methods of obtaining evidence

20.88 Evidence concerning a claimant's own business should be readily accessible. However, a claimant may also need to obtain supplementary evidence from various other sources such as:

(a) the public in general, or from the relevant section of the public;
(b) members of the trade;
(c) the defendant, in relation to its business; and
(d) experts.

Survey evidence

20.89 One type of evidence that remains perennially popular despite its many problems is survey evidence—statistical or other data obtained by conducting surveys or using questionnaires. It has always been usual to seek the permission of the court before conducting a full-scale survey. However, in view of the strict guidance on survey evidence provided by the Court of Appeal in *Interflora* (in the context of likelihood of confusion in trade mark disputes),[1] it seems clear that any party wishing to adduce survey evidence (other than a pilot survey) in a passing off case, must now seek permission, and will need to persuade the court that the evidence will be of 'real value'. Even then, permission will only be given if the value justifies the cost. Principles drawn from pre-*Interflora* cases must now be read in the light of the *Interflora* guidance.

There have been many cases in which one or both sides have sought to deploy such evidence. In some cases, it has been admitted and relied upon, but in others it has been wholly rejected as being either irrelevant or because of the way in which the survey was conducted. Whitford J in *John Player Special*[2] stated the requirements that, in his opinion, were necessary in order for survey evidence to be both admissible and of probative value:

(i) the survey must be done fairly and by a method such that a relevant cross-section of the public is interviewed;
(ii) it must be of a sufficient size to produce a statistically significant result;

(iii) where several surveys are carried out, full disclosure must be given to the other side of their number, the methodology and the numbers of persons involved;
(iv) the totality of all answers given to all surveys must be disclosed and made available to the other side;
(v) the questions should neither be leading, nor should they direct the interviewee into a field of speculation upon which he would never otherwise have embarked;
(vi) the exact answers must be recorded, not an abbreviation or digest;
(vii) the instructions given to those carrying out the interviews, and to those who subsequently code the answers if computer coding is used, must be disclosed.

Survey evidence has been rejected (or at least given little weight) in certain cases for various reasons:

(i) The issue as to the likelihood of confusion or deception is ultimately one for the courts to decide, not to be settled by surveys.[3] Even so, it should always be remembered that the question is not whether the judge is likely to be confused or deceived, but whether the judge is satisfied that a relevant section of the public would be confused or deceived.
(ii) The methodology used to conduct the survey was flawed. For example, in *Vodkat*[4] Arnold J held that the questions were not well drafted, and the sample of respondents did not represent a good cross-section.
(iii) The conditions of the survey did not reflect those of the point of sale; for example, in the *Polo* case the claimant adduced evidence of customers' reactions on seeing the defendant's sweets contained loose in a plastic bag, whereas they were actually sold wrapped in distinctive packaging with the defendant's trade mark/brand name.[5] Compare this with the survey in *Chocosuisse*[6] where the claimant's solicitors set up a display stand to mimic an actual in-store confectionary display.
(iv) Respondents were asked to speculate about an issue that would not normally arise in their minds at the point of sale. For example, asking 'What does this trade mark mean to you?' may be a leading question, since the trade mark may not 'mean' anything until the person is asked to speculate. Again, in *Chocosuisse* the members of the public were never asked 'What does the trade mark SWISS CHALET mean to you?'. Instead, the solicitors asked respondents to choose the cheapest Swiss chocolate from a wide selection of confectionery—the fact that certain people then chose the defendant's SWISS CHALET chocolate was accepted as evidence that that trade mark conveyed a misrepresentation that the product was Swiss chocolate.

1 The traditional approach may be seen in, eg, *Diageo North America Inc v Intercontinental Brands (ICB) Ltd* [2010] EWHC 17 (Ch); [2010] RPC 12 at [159]. For

the Court of Appeal's guidance see *Interflora v Marks & Spencer* [2013] EWCA Civ 319; [2013] FSR 26. Note that the Court of Appeal has subsequently explained that the 'real value' test was not intended to oblige courts to perform an interim evaluation of the likely outcome, it is simply about scrutinising the value of a survey as evidence: *Zee Entertainment Enterprises Ltd v Zeebox Ltd* [2014] EWCA Civ 82; [2014] FSR 26. An application to adduce the results of a survey was considered and refused in *Cosmetic Warriors Ltd v Amazon.co.uk Ltd* [2013] EWHC 2470 (Ch); [2014] FSR 15; contrast *Fage UK Ltd v Chobani UK Ltd* [2013] EWHC 298 (Ch) in which permission was granted.

2 *Imperial Group v Philip Morris* [1984] RPC 293 at [302]–[303].

3 See the comments of Dillon LJ in *Mothercare UK Ltd v Penguin Books Ltd* [1988] RPC 113; see also *Parker-Knoll Ltd v Knoll International Ltd* [1962] RPC 265, per Lord Hodson, and *Financial Times Ltd v Evening Standard Ltd* [1991] FSR 7, per Aldous J.

4 *Diageo North America Inc v Intercontinental Brands (ICB) Ltd* [2010] EWHC 17 (Ch); [2010] RPC 12 at [162] and [164]. See also *Nationwide Building Society v Nationwide Estate Agents* [1987] FSR 579 at [588].

5 *Nestlé (UK) Ltd v Trustin the Food Finders Ltd* (22 August 1996, unreported), CA.

6 *Chocosuisse Union des Fabricants Suisses de Chocolat v Cadbury Ltd* [1998] RPC 117.

20.90 Despite the mixed success of surveys, and the inevitable criticisms that will be made by each party against the other's survey, it is suggested that such evidence will continue to be an important part of the claimant's case. That is especially so in interim proceedings, where claimants must establish that there is a serious issue to be tried in terms of the likelihood of confusion or deception:

- In *Andrex/Nouvelle*[1] Laddie J accepted that the claimant's survey evidence had qualitative value and, even though it did not prove that all interviewees would have been deceived had they seen the defendant's packaging, the evidence was consistent with a 'considerable number' of them being so deceived. The same judge later took the same approach in *Chocosuisse*.
- In the *Pot Noodle* case[2] Blackburne J felt that the affidavit evidence obtained from a survey of members of the public was open to criticism (in relation to the way in which it was obtained and the pro forma nature of the affidavits) but did not feel able to disregard it. He went on to find that there was therefore a serious issue to be tried.
- The Court of Appeal in *Neutrogena*[3] was not able to arrive at any quantitative or qualitative measure of the confusion caused by the defendant's use of NEUTRALIA, but Morritt LJ still concluded that the confusion was 'substantial' and that the effect on the goodwill of NEUTROGENA was 'real'.

The defendant has a rather more difficult task in rebutting such evidence, because simply bringing along witnesses who say that they were not confused or deceived does not, of course, prove that no one was misled. It may be possible, however, to provide evidence from witnesses who, from online reviews, appear to have been confused but, when challenged are able to negate that assumption, albeit it may be difficult to establish exactly what they were thinking at the point of an apparent act of confusion.[4]

1 *Kimberly-Clark Ltd v Fort Sterling Ltd* [1997] FSR 877.
2 *Dalgety Spillers Foods Ltd v Food Brokers Ltd* [1994] FSR 504.
3 *Neutrogena Corp v Golden Ltd (t/a Garnier)* [1996] RPC 473.
4 *Easygroup Ltd v Easylife Ltd* [2021] EWHC 1705 (Ch).

Witness collection programmes

20.91 Overlapping with the gathering of survey evidence is the use of 'witness collection programmes', whereby one or both parties will approach ordinary, independent members of the public, selected at random, and ask various questions relating to the goods or services in question. There are various possible purposes in doing so:

(a) to obtain individual affidavits from those who are willing to participate;
(b) as the basis of a survey which can then be the subject of expert opinion from the person responsible for the survey as to the likely or actual state of mind of the relevant section of the public as a whole; or
(c) as the basis of a survey which can then be used to establish or support a wider conclusion.

20.92 These programmes can be useful in establishing either the reputation of the claimant and/or the likelihood of confusion or deception (for the purposes of proving a misrepresentation). However, one should bear in mind the observations of Jacob J in *Neutrogena*[1] to the effect that surveys or witness collection programmes of the type in which questionnaires are filled in and the results subjected to statistical analysis are unnecessarily elaborate. Further, he described pure questionnaire evidence as 'seldom helpful'. Instead, he thought that 'the best evidence is the oral evidence of those alleged to have been deceived or confused'—that is, witnesses giving oral evidence-in-chief rather than simply confirming their witness statements.

1 *Neutrogena Corp v Golden Ltd (t/a Garnier)* [1996] RPC 473.

Expert evidence

20.93 Another important source of evidence is experts. Such evidence will be admissible in relation to a variety of different aspects of the case, but only with the court's permission:[1]

(a) the superiority/inferiority of the goods or services in question;
(b) the circumstances and the places in which the goods are sold, the kind of persons who bought them, and the manner in which the public were accustomed to ask for those goods;

(c) whether the relevant section of the public would be confused or deceived—though this may be deemed inadmissible where the experience of the judge as an ordinary shopper or consumer will put him/her in as good a position as anyone to assess the likelihood of confusion; and
(d) what the survey evidence (if any) 'proves', ie, whether the statistics obtained can be extrapolated and used to come to a finding that a substantial number of the relevant section of the public are likely to be confused or deceived.

1 See, for example, *Fenty v Arcadia Group Brands Ltd (t/a Topshop)* [2013] EWHC 1945 (Ch); [2013] FSR 37. Evidence of facts about a particular trade from someone in that trade is not expert evidence.

Trap-purchases

20.94 As an alternative (or in addition) to a survey, the claimant may seek to obtain evidence by making 'trap purchases'. For example, the claimant (or someone on its behalf) places an order with the defendant for the claimant's goods, in expectation that the defendant will substitute its goods for those of the claimant. Alternatively, trap purchases may be used to demonstrate that third-party retailers are confused as to the nature of the defendant's goods.[1] There are a number of general propositions that can be stated in relation to trap orders. They must be:

(a) clear and unambiguous;
(b) fair, in the sense of not calculated to induce the defendant or third party to fall into the trap;
(c) carried out in circumstances analogous to the conditions under which a 'genuine' order would be placed, and such as to avoid the defendant simply making a bona fide mistake;[2] and
(d) once carried out, the defendant should be advised without delay in order to allow it to investigate.[3]

1 For example, in *Vodkat* the claimant's representatives asked for vodka, and were instead sold the Vodkat product: *Diageo North America Inc v Intercontinental Brands (ICB) Ltd* [2010] EWHC 17 (Ch); [2010] RPC 12.
2 See the warnings to this effect of Roxburgh J in *Procea Products Ltd v Evans & Sons Ltd* (1951) 68 RPC 210 at [211].
3 Harman J held a trap order to be unsatisfactory in *Cellular Clothing Co Ltd v G White & Co Ltd* (1952) 70 RPC 9 at [14], because no notice was given to the defendant.

20.95 Arnold J reviewed the law on trap purchases in *Vodkat*[1] and indicated that where trap purchases are used to demonstrate confusion, it may be appropriate to inform those said to have been confused to obtain their explanation. However, the judge held that on the facts of the case, the trap purchases did still have probative value.[2]

1 *Diageo North America Inc v Intercontinental Brands (ICB) Ltd* [2010] EWHC 17 (Ch); [2010] RPC 12 at [39]–[45].
2 *Diageo* at [190].

H DEFENCES

20.96 The approach of a defendant in defending a passing off case is generally to argue that the claimant has not demonstrated one or more of the elements that make up the tort of passing off. In this respect the factual investigation will once again be paramount, and the defendant will want to look at all the hurdles that the claimant has to jump over and to see which ones are most likely to trip it up, or to see where the claimant's evidence is weakest. The defendant will also want to consider relying on its own evidence of matters such as factors negating the alleged misrepresentation (see above), or expert evidence on the nature of the parties' respective markets or the (un)reliability of the survey evidence. A defendant may also seek to rely on equitable defences such as delay or acquiescence.

20.97 Concurrent use of a trade mark similar to that of the claimant may also afford a defence. This defence generally comes good where the use has gone on for a considerable time, such that one or more of the following (potentially overlapping) factors may apply:

- the distinctiveness of the claimant's mark(s) may have been eroded to the point of being unenforceable;
- goodwill is in fact shared between the two parties (common where a business has split into two parts); or
- what may originally have been an actionable passing off ceases to be so once the public learns to distinguish the competing enterprises.

20.98 There is clearly also some overlap here with the defence of delay or acquiescence, whereby the claimant's failure to take action in good time eventually debars them from an action. Once again, it will be a question of fact in each case as to whether one party's use is genuinely actionable by another. A good example of where one party was allowed to continue its earlier and long-standing use is *Merc*[1] in which Mercedes-Benz objected to a trader who had used the mark 'Merc' in relation to clothing for many years. He was found to have his own independent goodwill and reputation. In that case Pumfrey J also noted: 'There must come a time after which the court would not interfere with a continued course of trading which might have involved passing off at its inception but no longer did so'. He explained that the logical point at which this would occur would be six years after the time at which it could safely be said that the defendant was no longer committing an actionable tort (ie, after the end of the limitation period).

1 *Daimler Chrysler v Alavi (t/a Merc)* [2001] RPC 42.

20.99 Certain specific defences relating to rebutting an alleged misrepresentation are dealt with in Section D at para **20.53** above, including the question of whether there is an 'own-name defence'. Note that innocence is not a defence to passing off, though it may affect the remedies that the court will award (see below).

I REMEDIES

20.100 Passing off is a tort, and therefore the common law principles apply as they do to all other torts. In broad terms, the remedies available for passing off are the same as those that are available for the infringement of a registered trade mark (as to which, see **Chapter 8**). Thus, the remedies fall under the following headings:

(a) damages or an account of profit;
(b) an injunction to restrain passing off;
(c) delivery up of goods and materials; and
(d) a mandatory injunction requiring the defendant to change its name (including its corporate, business or domain name).

As stated, the principles set out in **Chapter 17** are directly applicable, and, therefore, the comments that follow merely address certain issues that are peculiar to passing off cases.

Damages

20.101 A successful claimant may elect either to have an inquiry as to its own damages or an account of the profits made by the defendant. The general principle in passing off cases for the award of damages is to compensate the claimant for the natural and direct consequences of the unlawful acts of the defendant. The specific heads of damage which are recoverable in a passing off action have already been discussed above because, unlike in trade mark infringement, the existence of damage is a necessary component of the cause of action. In *Irvine v Talksport*[1] the damages to be assessed were for an image that implied that the claimant racing driver had endorsed the defendant's products. In that situation, the Court of Appeal decided that the correct approach to damages was a licence fee taking account of the claimant's evidence of what he was accustomed to charging for such endorsements. The damages were increased by the court from £2,000 to £25,000 on that basis. Damages were also assessed on a licence fee basis in *National Guild of Removers and Storers*, taking into account the nature of the right that had been infringed, and the length of the period of infringement.[2]

1 *Irvine v Talksport Ltd* [2003] FSR 35.
2 *National Guild of Removers and Storers v Statham* [2014] EWHC 3572 (IPEC).

20.102 It is also worth noting that an 'innocent' defendant (eg, one who deals in goods which it has no reason to believe are counterfeit) is in no better position as regards damages. Blackburne J in *Gillette*[1] reviewed the cases and concluded that innocent passing off should be treated in the same way as innocent trade mark infringement and, as such, damages are recoverable whether or not the defendant knew what it was doing.

1 *Gillette UK Ltd v Edenwest Ltd* [1994] RPC 279 at [291].

Account of profits

20.103 As with trade mark infringement, it is important when considering an account of profits to identify those profits made by the defendant that were actually attributable to the operative misrepresentation. In *My Kinda Town*[1] Slade J refused to order the defendant to account to the claimant for *all* its profits. He stated:

> 'It is necessary to ascertain how much of the profits made by the defendants over the relevant period are properly attributable to the use of the name Chicago Pizza Co. Clearly, profits made by the defendants by the sale of meals to customers who are *not* confused by this name are not attributable to this use.'

Obviously, this calculation cannot be carried out with scientific or mathematical precision, and, therefore, the Master in charge will have to come to a reasonable apportionment based on the evidence at the trial. For a recent detailed example of an account of profits see *Woolley*.[2]

1 *My Kinda Town v Soll and Grunts Investments* [1983] RPC 15.
2 *Woolley v UP Global Sourcing UK Ltd* [2014] EWHC 493 (Ch); [2014] FSR 37.

20.104 The innocence of the defendant does not affect the claimant's entitlement to damages (see above), but because an account of profits is an equitable remedy, innocence will be relevant to the exercise of the judge's discretion. Thus the claimant may well be wise to opt for an inquiry as to damages rather than an account of the defendant's profits, if the judge finds that the defendant's passing off was innocent.

Injunctions

20.105 An injunction is an equitable remedy, and, therefore, general equitable principles will apply. This can work both for and against the claimant. On the one hand, the terms of the injunction can be tailored to do that which is necessary to do justice in the particular circumstances of the case, but on the other, the court may decide that an injunction is impossible to frame fairly, or is inappropriate in light of the claimant's conduct (such as delay or inequitable behaviour).[1] The court in *Vodkat*, despite finding that there had been passing off, refused to grant an unqualified injunction against the use of the name VODKAT, since it was held that there remained a theoretical possibility that the name could be used without confusion.[2]

1 See, for example, *Microsoft Corp v Plato Technology Ltd* [1999] FSR 834.
2 *Diageo North America Inc v Intercontinental Brands (ICB) Ltd* [2010] EWHC 173 (Pat).

Interim injunctions

20.106 In terms of interim injunctions (as opposed to final injunctions granted after judgment), the following is a non-exhaustive list of issues that are likely to be relevant in passing off cases:

1 The fundamental principle which the courts are seeking to apply is to take whichever course of action appears to carry the lower risk of injustice if it should turn out to be 'wrong' (in the sense that, at the full trial, the decision goes the other way).[1] For helpful illustrations of this balancing process see *Cowshed* (in the context of trade marks; injunction refused) and *Fage* (extended passing off; injunction granted).[2]

2 The *American Cyanamid*[3] principles will apply (as to which, see **Chapter 17**). In particular, the claimant must establish that there is a serious question to be tried. For example, if there is no goodwill established at this stage, an interim injunction is not appropriate: *BBC v Talksport Ltd.*[4]

3 In *Antec International*[5] Laddie J stated that it was correct to make some assessment of the parties' respective prospects of success at the interlocutory stage, and that this was 'particularly so' in a passing off case, where the merits bear on the likelihood of damage, which is a factor to be taken into account in assessing the balance of convenience.

4 An interim injunction will not usually be granted if the claimant can adequately be compensated for the injury to its goodwill by the defendant paying the claimant's damages.[6] However, the ability of the defendant to pay the claimant's damages will be relevant.

5 The court will also consider the ability of the claimant to give and make good on an undertaking as to damages (that is, an undertaking to compensate the defendant for the effect of the injunction if the claimant is ultimately is unsuccessful at trial).

6 The desirability of maintaining the status quo existing immediately preceding the issue of the application will generally be relevant, especially where the defendant has not yet commenced trading. However this may be unimportant if neither party has commenced significant trading activities, as was the case in *Barnsley Brewery*.[7]

7 Any delay by the claimant in bringing the proceedings which has resulted in the defendant incurring additional expenditure will militate against the grant of an injunction. For example, in the *Pot Noodles* case[8] the defendant had written to the claimant one year before the launch of its product. The fact that the claimant chose to ignore the warning, and in the meantime allowed the defendant to expend time, trouble and money in launching its product, was a factor that 'weighed heavily' in Blackburne J's refusal to grant an injunction. Delay was the factor that meant that an interim injunction was refused in an otherwise fairly evenly balanced case, in *Ukelele Orchestra*.[9]

8 So-called 'unclean hands' on the part of the claimant will often be incompatible with an equitable remedy such as injunction. For example, where the claimant itself has used the trade mark or name in a way that is deceptive, the court may decide it will not uphold its request to stop others from doing so. In *Chocosuisse*[10] Laddie J considered this issue and concluded that a claimant should only fail where the court concludes that, in all the circumstances of the case, it is unconscionable for it to be given the relief to which it would otherwise be entitled.

9 A claimant may also struggle where it has failed to take all reasonable steps to police the use of its trade marks by third parties and, generally, to secure the continued exclusive connotation of the trade mark as a 'badge of origin'. However, in *Chocosuisse* Laddie J stated that the exclusivity of the mark is a question of fact, and if that exclusivity exists, then the claimant's contribution (positive or negative) is irrelevant. Conversely, the fact that the claimant has taken all reasonable steps to police the use of its trade mark does not help its case if, in fact, the exclusivity has been lost.

10 The fact that an interim injunction may, in practice, be decisive of the outcome of the case (in the sense that, if an interim injunction is granted, the defendant will often not bother to contest a final hearing) will be relevant, since it will go to assessing the risk of injustice.[11]

1 *Films Rover International Ltd v Cannon Film Sales Ltd* [1987] 1 WLR 670 at 680.
2 *Cowshed Products Ltd v Island Origins Ltd* [2010] EWHC 3357 (Ch); [2011] ETMR 42; and *Fage UK Ltd v Danone Ltd* [2013] EWHC 133 (Ch) and [2013] EWHC 202 (Ch).
3 *American Cyanamid Co v Ethicon Ltd* [1975] AC 396.
4 *BBC v Talksport Ltd (No 1)* [2001] FSR 6.
5 *Antec International Ltd v South Western Chicks (Warren) Ltd* [1997] FSR 278.
6 See *Cowshed Products Ltd v Island Origins Ltd* [2010] EWHC 3357 (Ch); [2011] ETMR 42.
7 *Barnsley Brewery Co Ltd v RBNB* [1997] FSR 462.
8 *Dalgety Spillers Foods Ltd v Food Brokers Ltd* [1994] FSR 504.
9 *Ukelele Orchestra of Great Britain (A firm) v Clausen* [2014] EWHC 3789 (IPEC).
10 *Chocosuisse Union des Fabricants Suisses de Chocolat v Cadbury Ltd* [1998] RPC 117.
11 *Barnsley Brewery Co Ltd v RBNB* [1997] FSR 462.

Comment on interim injunctions

20.107 Lord Diplock in the House of Lords in *American Cyanamid* noted that it would be unwise to attempt even to list the various matters which may need to be taken into consideration in deciding where the balance of convenience lies, let alone to suggest the relative weight to be attached to these matters, as this will vary from case to case. This is undoubtedly correct. A list derived from cases decided during the past decade alone would take up many pages. This makes it difficult for practitioners to advise on the prospects of obtaining interim relief because the balance of convenience issue will need to be considered in almost every passing off case, if only because there will normally be doubt as to the adequacy of damages. Indeed, some cases have suggested that damages cannot be adequate simply because the loss or injury suffered by the claimant is, of its nature, not capable of precise quantification. Therefore, the consideration of the factors relevant to the balance of convenience is often the major task of the court in such cases.

20.108 Finally, the successful claimant who is awarded an interim injunction should also consider making an application for an immediate lump sum order for its costs to be paid by the defendant. For an example of a case where this was considered to be appropriate, see *Direct Line*, where the defendant chose to represent itself in court.[1]

1 *Direct Line Group Ltd v Direct Line Estate Agency Ltd* [1997] FSR 374 at [377]–[379].

Delivery up

20.109 A practical remedy that claimants will often seek is an order requiring the defendant to deliver up to the claimant (or to destroy) the offending goods. Such an order will only be made, however, if the goods cannot be rendered benign—that is, by the removal, obliteration or obviation of the offending misrepresentation, or by repackaging the goods, or otherwise through the use of disclaimers and the like.

Order to change name

20.110 Another practical remedy for a claimant to consider is a mandatory injunction requiring the defendant to change its own corporate, business or Internet domain name. See, for example, *Glaxo*, *Law Society*, *Harrods* and *One in a Million.*[1] In the *One in a Million* case Jonathan Sumption QC likened the order to an order for the delivery-up of infringing goods.

1 *Glaxo plc v GlaxoWellcome Ltd* [1996] FSR 388; *Law Society of England and Wales v Society of Lawyers* [1996] FSR 739; *Harrods Ltd v UK Network Services Ltd*, Ch 1996 No 5453, unreported; and *BT v One in a Million* [1998] FSR 265.

J PRACTICAL MATTERS

Pre-emptive measures to consider

20.111 Although it is always worth considering registration of trade marks in order to gain the generally stronger protection afforded by trade mark legislation (see earlier chapters), passing off actions do still provide a valuable alternative for the well-prepared claimant. Given the importance of the evidence in passing off cases, users of unregistered trade marks should strongly consider taking pre-emptive measures so that they are in the best position possible to submit strong evidence to the court, whether in full proceedings or in support of an application for an interim injunction. The following steps can assist in preparing for any future dispute (which may be won without the need to go to court):

- Keeping records of sales and turnover.
- Keeping records of advertising and marketing expenditure.
- Establishing a system to record incidents of actual confusion, such as enquiries, complaints, letters, invoices, phone calls etc being directed to the proprietor when they were intended for the other party.
- Subscribing to a trade mark watching service and maintaining market awareness generally, including by educating employees and agents as to the issues and importance of maintaining the exclusivity of any trade marks.
- Policing any licensees' use of trade marks to ensure that quality-control mechanisms are in place and enforced.
- Adhering to best-practice guidelines relating to the use of one's trade marks.
- Keeping copies of letters of recommendation, gratitude or endorsement.
- Keeping copies of articles and other publications (in print or other media) written or broadcast by independent third parties concerning the business, goods or services.
- If necessary, taking professional advice and (where appropriate) swift action to deal with third parties who may be passing off.

20.112 Such measures will greatly improve a claimant's prospects of success, as well as assisting its legal advisers and thereby reducing costs. Of course, a claimant will also need certain additional information or evidence that can only be obtained once the activities of the other party have commenced (or have been threatened), namely:

(a) evidence of actual confusion or deception (or evidence of the likelihood of confusion or deception); and

(b) the relevant facts relating to the other party itself and its goods or services, including the length of time that it has been on the market, its sales figures and its advertising and marketing expenditure.

All of the above will also be relevant in assessing whether the elements of passing off can be established.

Other matters

20.113 Another reason for a potential claimant to seek professional advice is the need to consider seeking court orders such as search orders and/or freezing injunctions, which may help protect the claimant's position. Readers should also have regard to the sanctions for groundless threats of trade mark infringement proceedings, discussed in **Chapter 18**. These may be relevant in that a threat of passing off proceedings, in conjunction with notifying the other party of the existence of a separate registered trade mark, may constitute such a groundless threat, even if the two points are not mentioned in the same communication.

Chapter 21

Olympic symbols

INTRODUCTION

21.01 This chapter deals with the protection provided by the Olympic Symbol, etc (Protection) Act 1995 ('the 1995 Act') for certain symbols connected with the Olympics.

For symbols connected with the London Olympics of 2012 further protection was provided by the London Olympic Games and Paralympic Games Act 2006 ('the 2006 Act'). However, the relevant provisions of the 2006 Act ceased to have effect at the end of 31 December 2012.

21.02 The 1995 Act (and the 2006 Act) reflect the fact that the Olympic and Paralympic Games are hugely significant commercial ventures in which the branding of goods and services plays a vital part—not least in the raising of money to fund the staging of the events. This suggests a need for legislation to protect the Olympic brand.

THE OLYMPICS ASSOCIATION RIGHT

21.03 The 1995 Act creates rights known as the Olympics Association Right and the Paralympics Association Right (collectively the 'OAR').[1]

During the period of the London Olympics, the rights and remedies associated with the OAR were exercisable jointly or concurrently by the British Olympic Association and the London Organising Committee ('LOCOG').[2] However, since 30 September 2012, the right to consent to acts occurring after 31 December 2012 that would otherwise infringe the OAR has been exercisable solely by the British Olympic Association.[3]

1 Olympic Symbol, etc (Protection) Act 1995 ss 1(1) and 5A.

2 Olympic Symbol, etc (Protection) Act 1995 s 1(2) and Olympics and Paralympics Association Rights (Appointment of Proprietors) Order 2006, SI 2006/1119 art 4.

3 Olympics and Paralympics Association Rights (Appointment of Proprietors) Order 2006, SI 2006/1119 art 6(2)(b).

21.04 The London Olympic Games and Paralympic Games Act 2006 created the London Olympics Association Right (the 'LOAR'). The rights and remedies associated with the LOAR were exercisable by LOCOG.[1] However, they ceased to have effect at the end of 31 December 2012.[2]

1 London Olympic Games and Paralympic Games Act 2006 Sch 4 para 10(2)(b).
2 London Olympic Games and Paralympic Games Act 2006 s 40(8).

INFRINGEMENT

21.05 The OAR provides protection against certain uses of certain 'representations'. Under s 3(1) of the 1995 Act, a person will infringe the OAR:

> '… if in the course of trade he uses
> (a) a representation of the Olympic symbol, the Olympic motto[1] or a protected word, or
> (b) a representation of something so similar to the Olympic symbol or the Olympic motto as to be likely to create in the public mind an association with it or a word so similar to a protected word as to be likely to create in the public mind an association with the Olympic Games or the Olympic movement,
>
> (in this Act referred to as "a controlled representation").'

However, s 4(3) of the 1995 Act also provides that:

> 'A person does not infringe the [OAR] by using a controlled representation in a context which is not likely to suggest an association between a person, product or service and the Olympic Games or the Olympic movement …'.

1 'Citius, altius, fortius'—see Olympic Symbol, etc (Protection) Act 1995 s 18(1).

21.06 The 1995 Act provides[1] a non-exhaustive list of the sort of uses of representations that are capable of infringing the OAR. These include:

(1) affixing the sign to goods or their packaging;
(2) incorporating it in a flag or banner;
(3) offering or exposing for sale, putting on the market or stocks for those purposes goods which bear it or whose packaging bears it;
(4) importing or exporting goods which bear it or whose packaging bears it;
(5) offers or supplies services under a sign which consists of or contains it; or
(6) using the sign on business papers and in advertising.

Similar provisions apply in relation to the infringement of a trade mark and have been considered in that context.[2]

1 Olympic Symbol, etc (Protection) Act 1995 s 3(2).
2 See paras **14.14–14.19**.

RELEVANT REPRESENTATIONS

21.07 As set out above, s 3(1) of the 1995 Act specifies certain 'controlled representations' whose use can infringe the OAR—namely:

(a) the Olympic symbol, Olympic motto, or a protected word;[1] or
(b) something so similar to the Olympic symbol or motto as to be likely to create in the public mind an association with it or a word so similar to a protected word as to be likely to create in the public mind an association with the Olympic Games or movement.

1 Ie, the words 'Olympiad', 'Olympiads', 'Olympian', 'Olympians', 'Olympic' or 'Olympics'—see 1995 Act s 18(2)(a). Note, also the corresponding words for the Paralympics association right in s 18(2)(b): 'Paralympiad', etc. For the slightly different definition of the representations that might have infringed the LOAR (pre-31 December 2012) see Sch 4 para 3 of the 2006 Act, and the third edn of this *User's Guide* at para 21.09.

21.08 It will be noted that the 1995 Act does not specify any particular form for the way in which the required representation is used. It would seem, therefore, that the representation could be in writing or oral.

SUGGESTING AN ASSOCIATION

21.09 There mere use of one of the representations listed above will not automatically infringe the OAR. As is clear from s 4(3) of the 1995 Act, the issue is always whether the use complained of is '*likely to suggest an association*' with the Olympic Games or the Olympic movement.

21.10 There is no direct equivalent in other areas of intellectual property law to this concept of 'an association'. However, the 1995 Act provides another non-exhaustive definition in relation to this requirement. It states that '*the concept of association*' between a person, goods or a service and the Olympic Games or the Olympic movement:

'… includes in particular –
(i) any kind of contractual relationship;
(ii) any kind of commercial relationship;
(iii) any kind of corporate or structural connection; and
(iv) the provision by a person of financial or other support for

or in connection with the Olympic Games or Olympic movement …'[1].

1 Olympic Symbol, etc (Protection) Act 1995 s 4(3)(a).

21.11 This clearly shows that it is the commercial value of the Olympic brands that is being protected. However, the fact that infringement is defined by reference to the likelihood of 'an association' and that the use must be 'in the course of trade' (as discussed below) suggests that there is some degree of flexibility for the courts in determining whether or not a particular act infringes the OAR.

USE IN COURSE OF TRADE, IN THE UK, WITHOUT CONSENT

21.12 Under the 1995 Act, use can only infringe the OAR if it is done:

(a) 'in the course of trade';[1]
(b) in the United Kingdom;[2] and
(c) without the requisite consent.[3]

The meanings of these phrases have already been considered in the context of trade mark infringement—see paras **14.20–14.22** above.

1 Olympic Symbol, etc (Protection) Act 1995 s 3(1).
2 Olympic Symbol, etc (Protection) Act 1995 s 2(2).
3 Olympic Symbol, etc (Protection) Act 1995 s 2(2)(b).

DEFENCES

21.13 The 1995 Act provides a number of defences. Thus, the OAR is not infringed by:

(a) certain publishing or broadcasting involving the games in question;[1]
(b) the use of a representation in relation to goods put on the market in the EEA by the proprietor or with his consent provided it was used at the time that those goods were put on the market and the proprietor does not oppose further dealings with the goods;[2]
(c) the use in relation to certain pre-existing rights or names.[3]

1 Olympic Symbol, etc (Protection) Act 1995 s 4(1).
2 Olympic Symbol, etc (Protection) Act 1995 s 4(5).
3 Olympic Symbol, etc (Protection) Act 1995 s 4(11)–(14).

21.14 There is a further statutory defence.[1] This is that:

'a person does not suggest an association with the Olympic Games or Olympic Movement only by making a statement which–
(i) accords with honest practices in industrial or commercial matters, and

(ii) does not make promotional or other commercial use of a protected word by incorporating it in a context to which the Olympic Games and the Olympic movement are substantively irrelevant.'

1 Olympic Symbol, etc (Protection) Act 1995 s 4(3)(b).

21.15 This is not an easy provision to construe. However, it seems that provided the context is one in which the Games *are* substantively irrelevant, the defence will operate provided the use made is not promotional (or commercial) but that it will not operate if the use is promotional. If the Games are substantively relevant, the defence cannot apply regardless of whether the use was or was not promotional (or commercial).

REMEDIES

21.16 An infringement of the OAR is actionable by the proprietor, who has available 'all such relief by way of damages, injunctions, accounts or otherwise … as is available in respect of the infringement of a property right'.[1] The Secretary of State is also empowered to make regulations as to further remedies such as erasure, delivery up and disposal.[2]

1 Olympic Symbol, etc (Protection) Act 1995 s 6.
2 Olympic Symbol, etc (Protection) Act 1995 s 7.

Appendix 1

Trade Marks Act 1994

PART 1 REGISTERED TRADE MARKS

Introductory

1 Trade marks

[(1) In this Act "trade mark" means any sign which is capable—

(a) of being represented in the register in a manner which enables the registrar and other competent authorities and the public to determine the clear and precise subject matter of the protection afforded to the proprietor, and
(b) of distinguishing goods or services of one undertaking from those of other undertakings.

A trade mark may, in particular, consist of words (including personal names), designs, letters, numerals, colours, sounds or the shape of goods or their packaging.][1]

(2) References in this Act to a trade mark include, unless the context otherwise requires, references to a collective mark (see section 49) or certification mark (see section 50).

NOTES

1 Substituted by Trade Marks Regulations 2018, SI 2018/825, regs 2, 3 (14 January 2019).

2 Registered trade marks

(1) A registered trade mark is a property right obtained by the registration of the trade mark under this Act and the proprietor of a registered trade mark has the rights and remedies provided by this Act.

(2) No proceedings lie to prevent or recover damages for the infringement of an unregistered trade mark as such; but nothing in this Act affects the law relating to passing off.

Grounds for refusal of registration

3 Absolute grounds for refusal of registration

(1) The following shall not be registered—

(a) signs which do not satisfy the requirements of section 1(1).
(b) trade marks which are devoid of any distinctive character.
(c) trade marks which consist exclusively of signs or indications which may serve, in trade, to designate the kind, quality, quantity, intended purpose, value, geographical origin, the time of production of goods or of rendering of services, or other characteristics of goods or services,
(d) trade marks which consist exclusively of signs or indications which have become customary in the current language or in the bona fide and established practices of the trade:

Provided that, a trade mark shall not be refused registration by virtue of paragraph (b), (c) or (d) above if, before the date of application for registration, it has in fact acquired a distinctive character as a result of the use made of it.

(2) A sign shall not be registered as a trade mark if it consists exclusively of—

(a) the shape[, or another characteristic,][1] which results from the nature of the goods themselves,
(b) the shape[, or another characteristic,][1] of goods which is necessary to obtain a technical result, or
(c) the shape[, or another characteristic,][1] which gives substantial value to the goods.

(3) A trade mark shall not be registered if it is—

(a) contrary to public policy or to accepted principles of morality, or
(b) of such a nature as to deceive the public (for instance as to the nature, quality or geographical origin of the goods or service).

(4) A trade mark shall not be registered if or to the extent that its use is prohibited in the United Kingdom by any enactment or rule of law […][2] [other than law relating to trade marks][1].

[(4A) A trade mark is not to be registered if its registration is prohibited by or under—

(a) any enactment or rule of law, [or][3]
(b) […][2]
(c) any international agreement to which the United Kingdom […][2] is a party,

providing for the protection of designations of origin or geographical indications.

(4B) A trade mark is not to be registered if its registration is prohibited by or under—

(a) any [enactment or rule of law][4], or
(b) any international agreement to which the [United Kingdom][4] is a party,

providing for the protection of traditional terms for wine or traditional specialities guaranteed.

(4C) A trade mark is not to be registered if it—

(a) consists of, or reproduces in its essential elements, an earlier plant variety denomination registered as mentioned in subsection (4D), and
(b) is in respect of plant varieties of the same or closely related species.

(4D) Subsection (4C)(a) refers to registration in accordance with any—

(a) enactment or rule of law, [or][3]
(b) [...][2]
(c) international agreement to which the United Kingdom [...][2] is a party,

providing for the protection of plant variety rights.][1]

(5) A trade mark shall not be registered in the cases specified, or referred to, in section 4 (specially protected emblems).

(6) A trade mark shall not be registered if or to the extent that the application is made in bad faith.

NOTES

1 Inserted by Trade Marks Regulations 2018, SI 2018/825, regs 2, 4 (14 January 2019).
2 Repealed by Trademarks (Amendment etc.) (EU Exit) Regulations 2019, SI 2019/269, reg 4, Sch 3, paras 1, 2(1), (2), (3)(b), (c), (5)(b), (c) (31 January 2020).
3 Inserted by Trade Marks (Amendment etc.) (EU Exit) Regulations 2019, SI 2019/269, reg 4, Sch 3, paras 1, 2(1), (3)(a), (5)(a) (31 January 2020).
4 Substituted by Trade Marks (Amendment etc.) (EU Exit) Regulations 2019, SI 2019/269, reg 4, Sch 3, paras 1, 2(1), (4) (31 January 2020) (as substituted by Intellectual Property (Amendment etc.) (EU Exit) Regulations 2020, SI 2020/1050, regs 7, 10(a) (31 December 2020)).

4 *Specially protected emblems*

(1) A trade mark which consists of or contains—

(a) the Royal arms, or any of the principal armorial bearings of the Royal arms, or any insignia or device so nearly resembling the Royal arms or any such armorial bearing as to be likely to be mistaken for them or it,
(b) a representation of the Royal crown or any of the Royal flags,
(c) a representation of Her Majesty or any member of the Royal family, or any colourable imitation thereof, or
(d) words, letters or devices likely to lead persons to think that the applicant either has or recently has had Royal patronage or authorisation,

shall not be registered unless it appears to the registrar that consent has been given by or on behalf of Her Majesty or, as the case may be, the relevant member of the Royal family.

(2) A trade mark which consists of or contains a representation of—

(a) the national flag of the United Kingdom (commonly known as the Union Jack), or
(b) the flag of England, Wales, Scotland, Northern Ireland or the Isle of Man,

shall not be registered if it appears to the registrar that the use of the trade mark would be misleading or grossly offensive.

Provision may be made by rules identifying the flags to which paragraph (b) applies.

(3) A trade mark shall not be registered in the cases specified in—

section 57 (national emblems, &c. of Convention countries), or section 58 (emblems, &c. of certain international organisations).

(4) Provision may be made by rules prohibiting in such cases as may be prescribed the registration of a trade mark which consists of or contains—

(a) arms to which a person is entitled by virtue of a grant of arms by the Crown, or
(b) insignia so nearly resembling such arms as to be likely to be mistaken for them,

unless it appears to the registrar that consent has been given by or on behalf of that person.

Where such a mark is registered, nothing in this Act shall be construed as authorising its use in any way contrary to the laws of arms.

[(5) A trade mark which consists of or contains a controlled representation within the meaning of the Olympic Symbol etc. (Protection) Act 1995 shall not be registered unless it appears to the registrar—

(a) that the application is made by the person for the time being appointed under section 1(2) of the Olympic Symbol etc. (Protection) Act 1995 (power of Secretary of State to appoint a person as the proprietor of the Olympics association right), or
(b) that consent has been given by or on behalf of the person mentioned in paragraph (a) above.][1]

NOTES

1 Inserted by Olympic Symbol etc. (Protection) Act 1995, s 13(2) (20 September 1995).

5 *Relative grounds for refusal of registration*

(1) A trade mark shall not be registered if it is identical with an earlier trade mark and the goods or services for which the trade mark is applied for are identical with the goods or services for which the earlier trade mark is protected.

(2) A trade mark shall not be registered if because—

(a) it is identical with an earlier trade mark and is to be registered for goods or services similar to those for which the earlier trade mark is protected, or
(b) it is similar to an earlier trade mark and is to be registered for goods or services identical with or similar to those for which the earlier trade mark is protected,

there exists a likelihood of confusion of the part of the public, which includes the likelihood of association with the earlier trade mark.

(3) A trade mark which—

(a) is identical with or similar to an earlier trade mark, [...][1]

[...][1]

shall not be registered if, or to the extent that, the earlier trade mark has a reputation in the United Kingdom [...][2] and the use of the later mark without due cause would take unfair advantage of, or be detrimental to, the distinctive character or the repute of the earlier trade mark.

[(3A) Subsection (3) applies irrespective of whether the goods and services for which the trade mark is to be registered are identical with, similar to or not similar to those for which the earlier trade mark is protected.][3]

(4) A trade mark shall not be registered if, or to the extent that, its use in the United Kingdom is liable to be prevented—

(a) by virtue of any rule of law (in particular, the law of passing off) protecting an unregistered trade mark or other sign used in the course of [trade, where the condition in subsection (4A) is met,][4]

[(aa) by virtue of [...][2] any enactment or rule of law, providing for protection of designations of origin or geographical indications, where the condition in subsection (4B) is met, or][3]

(b) by virtue of an earlier right other than those referred to in subsections (1) to (3) or paragraph (a) [or (aa)][3] above, in particular by virtue of the law of copyright [or the law relating to industrial property rights][4].

A person thus entitled to prevent the use of a trade mark is referred to in this Act as the proprietor of an "earlier right" in relation to the trade mark.

[(4A) The condition mentioned in subsection (4)(a) is that the rights to the unregistered trade mark or other sign were acquired prior to the date of application for registration of the trade mark or date of the priority claimed for that application.

(4B) The condition mentioned in subsection 4(aa) is that—

(a) an application for a designation of origin or a geographical indication has been submitted prior to the date of application for registration of the trade mark or the date of the priority claimed for that application, and

(b) the designation of origin or (as the case may be) geographical indication is subsequently registered.][3]

(5) Nothing in this section prevents the registration of a trade mark where the proprietor of the earlier trade mark or other earlier right consents to the registration.

[(6) Where an agent or representative ("R") of the proprietor of a trade mark applies, without the proprietor's consent, for the registration of the trade mark in R's own name, the application is to be refused unless R justifies that action.][3]

NOTES

1 Repealed by Trade Marks (Proof of Use, etc.) Regulations 2004, SI 2004/946, reg 7(1) (5 May 2004).

2 Repealed by Trade Marks (Amendment etc.) (EU Exit) Regulations 2019, SI 2019/269, reg 4, Sch 3, paras 1, 3 (31 January 2020).

3 Inserted by Trade Marks Regulations 2018, SI 2018/825, regs 2, 5(1), (2), (4), (5)(a), (6), (7) (14 January 2019).

4 Substituted by Trade Marks Regulations 2018, SI 2018/825, regs 2, 5(1), (3), (5)(b) (14 January 2019).

[5A Grounds for refusal relating to only some of the goods or services

Where grounds for refusal of an application for registration of a trade mark exist in respect of only some of the goods or services in respect of which the trade mark is applied for, the application is to be refused in relation to those goods and services only.][1]

NOTES

1 Inserted by Trade Marks Regulations 2018, SI 2018/825, regs 2, 6 (14 January 2019).

6 *Meaning of "earlier trade mark"*

(1) In this Act an "earlier trade mark" means —

(a) a registered trade mark [...][1] [or][2] international trade mark (UK)[, [...][1]][3] which has a date of application for registration earlier than that of the trade mark in question, taking account (where appropriate) of the priorities claimed in respect of the trade marks,

[(aa) a comparable trade mark (EU) or a trade mark registered pursuant to an application made under paragraph 25 of Schedule 2A which has a valid claim to seniority of an earlier registered trade mark or protected international trade mark (UK) even where the earlier trade mark has been surrendered or its registration has expired;][2]

[(ab) a comparable trade mark (IR) or a trade mark registered pursuant to an application made under paragraph 28, 29 or 33 of Schedule 2B which has a valid claim to seniority of an earlier registered trade mark or protected international trade mark (UK) even where the earlier trade mark has been surrendered or its registration has expired;][4]

[(b) [...][1]

(ba) a registered trade mark or international trade mark (UK) which–

(i) [prior to [IP completion day][5]][2] has been converted from a [European Union][6] trade mark or international trade mark (EC) which itself had a valid claim to seniority [of an earlier registered trade mark or protected international trade mark (UK) even where the earlier trade mark has been surrendered or its registration has expired][7], and

(ii) accordingly has the same claim to seniority, or][3]

(c) a trade mark which, at the date of application for registration of the trade mark in question or (where appropriate) of the priority claimed in respect of the application, was entitled to protection under the Parts Convention [or the WTO agreement][8] as a well known trade mark.

[(1A) In subsection (1), "protected international trade mark (UK)" has the same meaning as in the Trade Marks (International Registration) Order 2008.][2]

(2) References in this Act to an earlier trade mark include a trade mark in respect of which an application for registration has been made and which, if registered, would be an earlier trade mark by virtue of subsection (1)(a) [...][1], subject to its being so registered [(taking account of subsection (2C))][4].

[(2A) References in this Act to an earlier trade mark include a trade mark in respect of which an application for registration has been made pursuant to paragraph 25 of Schedule 2A and which if registered would be an earlier trade mark by virtue of subsection (1)(aa), subject to its being so registered.][2]

[(2B) References in this Act to an earlier trade mark include a trade mark in respect of which an application for registration has been made pursuant to paragraph 28, 29 or 33 of Schedule 2B and which if registered would be an earlier trade mark by virtue of subsection (1)(ab), subject to its being so registered.

(2C) Where an application for registration of a trade mark has been made pursuant to paragraph 25 of Schedule 2A or paragraph 28, 29 or 33 of Schedule 2B, subsection (l)(a) is to apply as if the date of application for registration of the trade mark were—

(a) in the case of an application made pursuant to paragraph 25 of Schedule 2A, the relevant date referred to in paragraph 25(2) in respect of that application;
(b) in the case of an application made pursuant to paragraph 28 of Schedule 2B, the relevant date referred to in paragraph 28(2) in respect of that application (taking account of paragraph 28(5));
(c) in the case of an application made pursuant to paragraph 29 of Schedule 2B, the relevant date referred to in paragraph 29(2) in respect of that application (taking account of paragraph 29(4));
(d) in the case of an application made pursuant to paragraph 33 of Schedule 2B, the relevant date referred to in paragraph 33(2) or (3) (as the case may be) in respect of that application (taking account of paragraph 33(4)).][4]

(3) [...][9]

NOTES

1 Repealed by Trade Marks (Amendment etc.) (EU Exit) Regulations 2019, SI 2019/269, reg 4, Sch 3, paras 1, 4(1), (2), (4), (7) (31 January 2020).
2 Inserted by Trade Marks (Amendment etc.) (EU Exit) Regulations 2019, SI 2019/269, reg 4, Sch 3, paras 1, 4(1), (2)(a), (3), (5)(a), (6), (8) (31 January 2020).
3 Substituted by Trade Marks (International Registrations Designating the European Community, etc.) Regulations 2004, SI 2004/2332, reg 4 (1 October 2004).
4 Inserted by Designs and International Trade Marks (Amendment etc.) (EU Exit) Regulations 2019, SI 2019/638, reg 10(1), Sch 8, paras 16, 17 (31 December 2020).
5 Substituted by Intellectual Property (Amendment etc.) (EU Exit) Regulations 2020, SI 2020/1050, regs 7, 10(b) (31 December 2020).
6 Substituted by European Union Trade Mark Regulations 2016, SI 2016/299, reg 15, Schedule, para 1 (6 April 2016).
7 Substituted by Trade Marks (Amendment etc.) (EU Exit) Regulations 2019, SI 2019/269, reg 4, Sch 3, paras 1, 4(1), (5)(b) (31 January 2020).
8 Inserted by Patents and Trade Marks (World Trade Organisation) Regulations 1999, SI 1999/1899, reg 13(1) (29 July 1999).
9 Repealed by Trade Marks Regulations 2018, SI 2018/825, regs 2, 7(1), (3) (14 January 2019).

[6A Raising of relative grounds in opposition proceedings in case of non-use

(1) This section applies where–

(a) an application for registration of a trade mark has been published,
(b) there is an earlier trade mark [of a kind falling within section 6(1)(a), [(aa)][1] or (ba)][2] in relation to which the conditions set out in section 5(1), (2) or (3) obtain, and
(c) the registration procedure for the earlier trade mark was completed before the start of the [relevant period][3].

[(1A) In this section "the relevant period" means the period of 5 years ending with the date of the application for registration mentioned in subsection (1)(a) or (where applicable) the date of the priority claimed for that application.][4]

(2) In opposition proceedings, the registrar shall not refuse to register the trade mark by reason of the earlier trade mark unless the use conditions are met.

(3) The use conditions are met if–

(a) within the [relevant period][3] the earlier trade mark has been put to genuine use in the United Kingdom by the proprietor or with his consent in relation to the goods or services for which it is registered, or

(b) the earlier trade mark has not been so used, but there are proper reasons for non-use.

(4) For these purposes–

(a) use of a trade mark includes use in a form [(the "variant form")][4] differing in elements which do not alter the distinctive character of the mark in the form in which it was registered [(regardless of whether or not the trade mark in the variant form is also registered in the name of the proprietor)][4], and

(b) use in the United Kingdom includes affixing the trade mark to goods or to the packaging of goods in the United Kingdom solely for export purposes.

(5) [...][5]

(6) Where an earlier trade mark satisfies the use conditions in respect of some only of the goods or services for which it is registered, it shall be treated for the purposes of this section as if it were registered only in respect of those goods or services.

(7) Nothing in this section affects–

(a) the refusal of registration on the grounds mentioned in section 3 (absolute grounds for refusal) or section 5(4) (relative grounds of refusal on the basis of an earlier right), or

(b) the making of an application for a declaration of invalidity under section 47(2) (application on relative grounds where no consent to registration).][6]

NOTES

1 Substituted by Trade Marks (Amendment etc.) (EU Exit) Regulations 2019, SI 2019/269, reg 4, Sch 3, paras 1, 5(1), (2) (31 January 2020).

2 Inserted by Trade Marks (Earlier Trade Marks) Regulations 2008, SI 2008/1067, reg 4(1), (2) (10 May 2008: insertion has effect subject to transitional provisions specified in SI 2008/1067, reg 6).

3 Substituted by Trade Marks Regulations 2018, SI 2018/825, regs 2, 8(1), (2), (4) (14 January 2019).

4 Inserted by Trade Marks Regulations 2018, SI 2018/825, regs 2, 8(1), (3), (5) (14 January 2019).

5 Repealed by Trade Marks (Amendment etc.) (EU Exit) Regulations 2019, SI 2019/269, reg 4, Sch 3, paras 1, 5(1), (3) (31 January 2020).

6 Inserted by Trade Marks (Proof of Use, etc.) Regulations 2004, SI 2004/946, reg 4 (5 May 2004).

7 *Raising of relative grounds in case of honest concurrent use*

(1) This section applies where on an application for the registration of a trade mark it appears to the registrar—

(a) that there is an earlier trade mark in relation to which the conditions set out in section 5(1), (2) or (3) obtain, or

(b) that there is an earlier right in relation to which the condition set out in section 5(4) is satisfied,

but the applicant shows to the satisfaction of the registrar that there has been honest concurrent use of the trade mark for which registration is sought.

(2) In that case the registrar shall not refuse the application by reason of the earlier trade mark or other earlier right unless objection on that ground is raised in opposition proceedings by the proprietor of that earlier trade mark or other earlier right.

(3) For the purposes of this section "honest concurrent use" means such use in the United Kingdom, by the applicant or with his consent, as would formerly have amounted to honest concurrent use for the purposes of section 12(2) of the Trade Marks Act 1938.

(4) Nothing in this section affects—

(a) the refusal of registration on the grounds mentioned in section 3 (absolute grounds for refusal), or
(b) the making of an application for a declaration of invalidity under section 47(2) (application on relative grounds where no consent to registration).

(5) This section does not apply when there is an order in force under section 8 below.

8 Power to require that relative grounds be raised in opposition proceedings

(1) The Secretary of State may by order provide that in any case a trade mark shall not be refused registration on a ground mentioned in section 5 (relative grounds for refusal) unless objection on that ground is raised in opposition proceedings by the proprietor of the earlier trade mark or other earlier right.

(2) The order may make such consequential provision as appears to the Secretary of State appropriate—

(a) with respect to the carrying out by the registrar of searches of earlier trade marks, and
(b) as to the persons by whom an application for a declaration of invalidity may be made on the grounds specified in section 47(2) (relative grounds).

(3) An order making such provision as is mentioned in subsection (2)(a) may direct that so much of section 37 (examination of application) as requires a search to be carried out shall cease to have effect.

(4) An order making such provision as is mentioned in subsection (2)(b) may provide that so much of section 47(3) as provides that any person may make an application for a declaration of invalidity shall have effect subject to the provisions of the order.

(5) An order under this section shall be made by statutory instrument, and no order shall be made unless a draft of it has been laid before and approved by a resolution of each House of Parliament.

No such draft of an order making such provision as is mentioned in subsection (1) shall be laid before Parliament until after the end of the period of ten years beginning with the day on which applications for Community trade marks may first be filed in pursuance of [Council Regulation (EC) No 40/94 of 20th December 1993 on the Community Trade Mark][1].

(6) An order under this section may contain such transitional provisions as appear to the Secretary of State to be appropriate.

NOTES

1 Substituted by European Union Trade Mark Regulations 2016, SI 2016/299, reg 15, Schedule, para 2 (6 April 2016).

Effects of registered trade mark

9 Rights conferred by registered trade mark

(1) The proprietor of a registered trade mark has exclusive rights in the trade mark which are infringed by use of the trade mark in the United Kingdom without his consent.

The acts amounting to infringement, if done without the consent of the proprietor, are specified in [subsections (1) to (3) of][1] section 10.

[(1A) See subsection (3B) of section 10 for provision about certain other acts amounting to infringement of a registered trade mark.

(1B) Subsection (1) is without prejudice to the rights of proprietors acquired before the date of filing of the application for registration or (where applicable) the date of the priority claimed in respect of that application.][1]

(2) References in this Act to the infringement of a registered trade mark are to any [...][2] infringement of the rights of the proprietor [such as is mentioned in subsection (1) or (1A)][1].

(3) The rights of the proprietor have effect from the date of registration (which in accordance with section 40(3) is the date of filing of the application for registration):

Provided that—

- (a) no infringement proceedings may be begun before the date on which the trade mark is in fact registered; and
- (b) no offence under section 92 (unauthorised use of trade mark, &c. in relation to goods) is committed by anything done before the date of publication of the registration.

NOTES

1 Inserted by Trade Marks Regulations 2018, SI 2018/825, regs 2, 9(1), (2), (3), (4)(b) (14 January 2019).

2 Repealed by Trade Marks Regulations 2018, SI 2018/825, regs 2, 9(1), (4)(a) (14 January 2019).

10 Infringement of registered trade mark

(1) A person infringes a registered trade mark if he uses in the course of trade a sign which is identical with the trade mark in relation to goods or services which are identical with those for which it is registered.

(2) A person infringes a registered trade mark if he uses in the course of trade a sign where because—

(a) the sign is identical with the trade mark and is used in relation to goods or services similar to those for which the trade mark is registered, or
(b) the sign is similar to the trade mark and is used in relation to goods or services identical with or similar to those for which the trade mark is registered,

there exists a likelihood of confusion on the part of the public, which includes the likelihood of association with the trade mark.

(3) A person infringes a registered trade mark if he uses in the course of trade[, in relation to goods or services,][1] a sign which—

(a) is identical with or similar to the trade mark, […][2]

[…][2]

where the trade mark has a reputation in the United Kingdom and the use of the sign, being without due cause, takes unfair advantage of, or is detrimental to, the distinctive character or the repute of the trade mark.

[(3A) Subsection (3) applies irrespective of whether the goods and services in relation to which the sign is used are identical with, similar to or not similar to those for which the trade mark is registered.

(3B) Where the risk exists that the packaging, labels, tags, security or authenticity features or devices, or any other means to which the trade mark is affixed could be used in relation to goods or services and that use would constitute an infringement of the rights of the proprietor of the trade mark, a person infringes a registered trade mark if the person carries out in the course of trade any of the following acts—

(a) affixing a sign identical with, or similar to, the trade mark on packaging, labels, tags, security or authenticity features or devices, or any other means to which the mark may be affixed; or
(b) offering or placing on the market, or stocking for those purposes, or importing or exporting, packaging, labels, tags, security or authenticity features or devices, or any other means to which the mark is affixed.][3]

(4) For the purposes of this section a person uses a sign if, in particular, he—

(a) affixes it to goods or the packaging thereof;
(b) offers or exposes goods for sale, puts them on the market or stocks them for those purposes under the sign, or offers or supplies services under the sign;
(c) imports or exports goods under the sign; […][4]
[(ca) uses the sign as a trade or company name or part of a trade or company name;][3]
(d) uses the sign on business papers [and][5] in advertising[; or][3]
[(e) uses the sign in comparative advertising in a manner that is contrary to the Business Protection from Misleading Marketing Regulations 2008.][3]

(5) […][4]

(6) […][4]

NOTES

1 Inserted by Trade Marks (Proof of Use, etc.) Regulations 2004, SI 2004/946, reg 7(2)(a) (5 May 2004).
2 Repealed by Trade Marks (Proof of Use, etc.) Regulations 2004, SI 2004/946, reg 7(2)(b) (5 May 2004).
3 Inserted by Trade Marks Regulations 2018, SI 2018/825, regs 2, 10(1), (2), (4), (5)(b), (6) (14 January 2019).
4 Repealed by Trade Marks Regulations 2018, SI 2018/825, regs 2, 10(1), (3), (7) (14 January 2019).
5 Substituted by Trade Marks Regulations 2018, SI 2018/825, regs 2, 10(1), (5)(a) (14 January 2019).

[10A Right to prevent goods entering the UK without being released for free circulation

(1) The proprietor of a registered trade mark is entitled to prevent third parties from bringing goods into the United Kingdom in the course of trade without being released for free circulation if they are goods for which the trade mark is registered which—

(a) come from outside the customs territory of the [United Kingdom][1]; and
(b) bear without authorisation a sign which is identical with the trade mark or cannot be distinguished in its essential aspects from the trade mark.

(2) In subsection (1) the reference to goods for which the trade mark is registered includes a reference to the packaging of goods for which the trade mark is registered.

(3) Subsection (1) is without prejudice to the rights of proprietors acquired before the date of application for registration of the trade mark, or (where applicable) the date of the priority claimed in respect of that application.

(4) The entitlement of the proprietor under subsection (1) is to lapse if—

(a) proceedings are initiated in accordance with the European Customs Enforcement Regulation to determine whether the trade mark has been infringed; and
(b) during those proceedings evidence is provided by the declarant or the holder of the goods that the proprietor of the trade mark is not entitled to prohibit the placing of the goods on the market in the country of final destination.

(5) References in this Act to the "European Customs Enforcement Regulation" are references to Regulation (EU) No 608/2013 of the European Parliament and of the Council of 12 June 2013 concerning customs enforcement of intellectual property rights [as amended from time to time][2].][3]

NOTES

1 Substituted by Trade Marks (Amendment etc.) (EU Exit) Regulations 2019, SI 2019/269, reg 4, Sch 3, paras 1, 6(1), (2) (31 January 2020).
2 Inserted by Trade Marks (Amendment etc.) (EU Exit) Regulations 2019, SI 2019/269, reg 4, Sch 3, paras 1, 6(1), (3) (31 January 2020).
3 Inserted by Trade Marks Regulations 2018, SI 2018/825, regs 2, 11 (14 January 2019).

[10B Prohibition on the use of a trade mark registered in the name of an agent or representative

(1) Subsection (2) applies where a trade mark is registered in the name of an agent or representative of a person ("P") who is the proprietor of the trade mark, without P's consent.

(2) Unless the agent or representative justifies the action mentioned in subsection (1), P may do either or both of the following—

(a) prevent the use of the trade mark by the agent or representative (notwithstanding the rights conferred by this Act in relation to a registered trade mark);
(b) apply for the rectification of the register so as to substitute P's name as the proprietor of the registered trade mark.][1]

NOTES

1 Inserted by Trade Marks Regulations 2018, SI 2018/825, regs 2, 11 (14 January 2019).

11 Limits on effect of registered trade mark

(1) A registered trade mark is not infringed by the use of [a later registered trade mark where that later registered trade mark would not be declared invalid pursuant to section 47(2A) or (2G) or section 48(1)][1].

[(1A) [...][2]

(1B) Where subsection (1) [...][2] applies, the later registered trade mark is not infringed by the use of the earlier trade mark even though the earlier trade mark may no longer be invoked against the later registered trade mark.][3]

(2) A registered trade mark is not infringed by—

(a) the use by [an individual][1] of his own name or address,
(b) the use of [signs or indications which are not distinctive or which concern][1] the kind, quality, quantity, intended purpose, value, geographical origin, the time of production of goods or of rendering of services, or other characteristics of goods or services, or
(c) the use of the trade mark [for the purpose of identifying or referring to goods or services as those of the proprietor of that trade mark, in particular where that use][1] is necessary to indicate the intended purpose of a product or service (in particular, as accessories or spare parts),

provided the use is in accordance with honest practices in industrial or commercial matters.

(3) A registered trade mark is not infringed by the use in the course of trade in a particular locality of an earlier right which applies only in that locality.

For this purpose an "earlier right" means an unregistered trade mark or other sign continuously used in relation to goods or services by a person or a predecessor in title of his from a date prior to whichever is the earlier of—

(a) the use of the first-mentioned trade mark in relation to those goods or services by the proprietor or a predecessor in title of his, or

(b) the registration of the first-mentioned trade mark in respect of those goods or services in the name of the proprietor or a predecessor in title of his;

and an earlier right shall be regarded as applying in a locality if, or to the extent that, its use in that locality is protected by virtue of any rule of law (in particular, the law of passing off).

NOTES

1 Substituted by Trade Marks Regulations 2018, SI 2018/825, regs 2, 12(1), (2), (4), (5), (6) (14 January 2019).
2 Repealed by Trade Marks (Amendment etc.) (EU Exit) Regulations 2019, SI 2019/269, reg 4, Sch 3, paras 1, 7 (31 January 2020).
3 Inserted by Trade Marks Regulations 2018, SI 2018/825, regs 2, 12(1), (3) (14 January 2019).

[11A Non-use as defence in infringement proceedings

(1) The proprietor of a trade mark is entitled to prohibit the use of a sign only to the extent that the registration of the trade mark is not liable to be revoked pursuant to section 46(1)(a) or (b) (revocation on basis of non-use) at the date the action for infringement is brought.

(2) Subsection (3) applies in relation to an action for infringement of a registered trade mark where the registration procedure for the trade mark was completed before the start of the period of five years ending with the date the action is brought.

(3) If the defendant so requests, the proprietor of the trade mark must furnish proof—

(a) that during the five-year period preceding the date the action for infringement is brought, the trade mark has been put to genuine use in the United Kingdom by or with the consent of the proprietor in relation to the goods and services for which it is registered and which are cited as justification for the action, or
(b) that there are proper reasons for non-use.

(4) Nothing in subsections (2) and (3) overrides any provision of section 46, as applied by subsection (1) (including the words from "Provided that" to the end of subsection (3)).][1]

NOTES
1 Inserted by Trade Marks Regulations 2018, SI 2018/825, regs 2, 13 (14 January 2019).

12 Exhaustion of rights conferred by registered trade mark

(1) A registered trade mark is not infringed by the use of the trade mark in relation to goods which have been put on the market in the European Economic Area under that trade mark by the proprietor or with his consent.

(2) Subsection (1) does not apply where there exist legitimate reasons for the proprietor to oppose further dealings in the goods (in particular, where the condition of the goods has been changed or impaired after they have been put on the market).

13 Registration subject to disclaimer or limitation

(1) An applicant for registration of a trade mark, or the proprietor of a registered trade mark, may—

(a) disclaim any right to the exclusive use of any specified element of the trade mark, or
(b) agree that the rights conferred by the registration shall be subject to a specified territorial or other limitation;

and where the registration of a trade mark is subject to a disclaimer or limitation, the rights conferred by section 9 (rights conferred by registered trade mark) are restricted accordingly.

(2) Provision shall be made by rules as to the publication and entry in the register of a disclaimer or limitation.

Infringement proceedings

14 Action for infringement

(1) An infringement of a registered trade mark is actionable by the proprietor of the trade mark.

(2) In an action for infringement all such relief by way of damages, injunctions, accounts or otherwise is available to him as is available in respect of the infringement of any other property right.

15 Order for erasure &c. of offending sign

(1) Where a person is found to have infringed a registered trade mark, the court may make an order requiring him—

(a) to cause the offending sign to be erased, removed or obliterated from any infringing goods, material or articles in his possession, custody or control, or
(b) if it is not reasonably practicable for the offending sign to be erased, removed or obliterated, to secure the destruction of the infringing goods, material or articles in question.

(2) If an order under subsection (1) is not complied with, or it appears to the court likely that such an order would not be complied with, the court may order that the infringing goods, material or articles be delivered to such person as the court may direct for erasure, removal or obliteration of the sign, or for destruction, as the case may be.

16 Order for delivery up of infringing goods, material or articles

(1) The proprietor of a registered trade mark may apply to the court for an order for the delivery up to him, or such other person as the court may direct, of any infringing goods, material or articles which a person has in his possession, custody or control in the course of a business.

(2) An application shall not be made after the end of the period specified in section 18 (period after which remedy of delivery up not available), and no order shall be made unless the court also makes, or it appears to the court that there are grounds for making, an order under section 19 (order as to disposal of infringing goods, &c.).

(3) A person to whom any infringing goods, material or articles are delivered up in pursuance of an order under this section shall, if an order under section 19 is not made, retain them pending the making of an order, or the decision not to make an order, under that section.

(4) Nothing in this section affects any other power of the court.

17 Meaning of "infringing goods, material or articles"

(1) In this Act the expressions "infringing goods", "infringing material" and "infringing articles" shall be construed as follows

(2) Goods are "infringing goods", in relation to a registered trade mark, if they or their packaging bear a sign identical or similar to that mark and—

(a) the application of the sign to the goods or their packaging was an infringement of the registered trade mark, or
(b) the goods are proposed to be imported into the United Kingdom and the application of the sign in the United Kingdom to them or their packaging would be an infringement of the registered trade mark, or
(c) the sign has otherwise been used in relation to the goods in such a way as to infringe the registered trade mark.

(3) Nothing in subsection (2) shall be construed as affecting the importation of goods which may lawfully be imported into the United Kingdom by virtue of an enforceable [EU][1] right.

(4) Material is "infringing material", in relation to a registered trade mark if it bears a sign identical or similar to that mark and either—

(a) it is used for labelling or packaging goods, as a business paper, or for advertising goods or services, in such a way as to infringe the registered trade mark, or
(b) it is intended to be so used and such use would infringe the registered trade mark.

(5) "Infringing articles", in relation to a registered trade mark, means articles—

(a) which are specifically designed or adapted for making copies of a sign identical or similar to that mark, and
(b) which a person has in his possession, custody or control, knowing or having reason to believe that they have been or are to be used to produce infringing goods or material.

NOTES

1 Substituted by Treaty of Lisbon (Changes in Terminology) Order 2011, SI 2011/1043, art 6(1)(f) (22 April 2011)

18 Period after which remedy of delivery up not available

(1) An application for an order under section 16 (order for delivery up of infringing goods, material or articles) may not be made after the end of the period of six years from—

(a) in the case of infringing goods, the date on which the trade mark was applied to the goods or their packaging,
(b) in the case of infringing material, the date on which the trade mark was applied to the material, or
(c) in the case of infringing articles, the date on which they were made,

except as mentioned in the following provisions.

(2) If during the whole or part of that period the proprietor of the registered trade mark—

(a) is under a disability, or
(b) is prevented by fraud or concealment from discovering the facts entitling him to apply for an order.

an application may be made at any time before the end of the period of six years from the date on which he ceased to be under a disability or, as the case may be, could with reasonable diligence have discovered those facts.

(3) In subsection (2) "disability"—

(a) in England and Wales, has the same meaning as in the Limitation Act 1980;
(b) in Scotland, means legal disability within the meaning of the Prescription and Limitation (Scotland) Act 1973,
(c) in Northern Ireland, has the same meaning as in the Limitation (Northern Ireland) Order 1989.

19 Order as to disposal of infringing goods, material or articles

(1) Where infringing goods, material or articles have been delivered up in pursuance of an order under section 16, an application may be made to the court—

(a) for an order that they be destroyed or forfeited to such person as the court may think fit, or
(b) for a decision that no such order should be made.

(2) In considering what order (if any) should be made, the court shall consider whether other remedies available in an action for infringement of the registered trade mark would be adequate to compensate the proprietor and any licensee and protect their interests.

(3) Provision shall be made by rules of court as to the service of notice on persons having an interest in the goods, material or articles, and any such person is entitled—

(a) to appear in proceedings for an order under this section, whether or not he was served with notice, and
(b) to appeal against any order made, whether or not he appeared;

and an order shall not take effect until the end of the period within which notice of an appeal may be given or, if before the end of that period notice of appeal is duly given, until the final determination or abandonment of the proceedings on the appeal.

(4) Where there is more than one person interested in the goods, material or articles, the court shall make such order as it thinks just.

(5) If the court decides that no order should be made under this section, the person in whose possession, custody or control the goods, material or articles were before being delivered up is entitled to their return.

(6) References in this section to a person having an interest in goods, material or articles include any person in whose favour an order could be made

[(a) under this section [...][1];
(b) under section 24D of the Registered Designs Act 1949;
(c) under section 114, 204 or 231 of the Copyright, Designs and Patents Act 1988; or
(d) under regulation 1C of the Community Design Regulations 2005 (SI 2005/2339).][2]

NOTES

1 Repealed by Trade Marks (Amendment etc.) (EU Exit) Regulations 2019, SI 2019/269, reg 4, Sch 3, paras 1, 8 (31 January 2020).

2 Substituted by Intellectual Property (Enforcement, etc.) Regulations 2006, SI 2006/1028, reg 2(2), Sch 2, paras 15, 16 (29 April 2006).

20 Jurisdiction of sheriff court or county court in Northern Ireland

Proceedings for an order under section 16 (order for delivery up of infringing goods, material or articles) or section 19 (order as to disposal of infringing goods, &c.) may be brought—

(a) in the sheriff court in Scotland, or
(b) in a county court in Northern Ireland.

This does not affect the jurisdiction of the Court of Session or the High Court in Northern Ireland.

[Unjustified threats

21 Threats of infringement proceedings

(1) A communication contains a "threat of infringement proceedings" if a reasonable person in the position of a recipient would understand from the communication that—

(a) a registered trade mark exists, and
(b) a person intends to bring proceedings (whether in a court in the United Kingdom or elsewhere) against another person for infringement of the registered trade mark by—
   (i) an act done in the United Kingdom, or
   (ii) an act which, if done, would be done in the United Kingdom.

(2) References in this section and in section 21C to a "recipient" include, in the case of a communication directed to the public or a section of the public, references to a person to whom the communication is directed.][1]

NOTES

1 Inserted by Intellectual Property (Unjustified Threats) Act 2017, s 2(1), (2) (1 October 2017).

[21A *Actionable threats*

(1) Subject to subsections (2) to (6), a threat of infringement proceedings made by any person is actionable by any person aggrieved by the threat.

(2) A threat of infringement proceedings is not actionable if the infringement is alleged to consist of—

(a) applying, or causing another person to apply, a sign to goods or their packaging,
(b) importing, for disposal, goods to which, or to the packaging of which, a sign has been applied, or
(c) supplying services under a sign.

(3) A threat of infringement proceedings is not actionable if the infringement is alleged to consist of an act which, if done, would constitute an infringement of a kind mentioned in subsection (2)(a), (b) or (c).

(4) A threat of infringement proceedings is not actionable if the threat—

(a) is made to a person who has done, or intends to do, an act mentioned in subsection (2)(a) or (b) in relation to goods or their packaging, and
(b) is a threat of proceedings for an infringement alleged to consist of doing anything else in relation to those goods or their packaging.

(5) A threat of infringement proceedings is not actionable if the threat—

(a) is made to a person who has done, or intends to do, an act mentioned in subsection (2)(c) in relation to services, and
(b) is a threat of proceedings for an infringement alleged to consist of doing anything else in relation to those services.

(6) A threat of infringement proceedings which is not an express threat is not actionable if it is contained in a permitted communication.

(7) In sections 21C and 21D "an actionable threat" means a threat of infringement proceedings that is actionable in accordance with this section.][1]

NOTES

1 Inserted by Intellectual Property (Unjustified Threats) Act 2017, s 2(1), (2) (1 October 2017).

[21B *Permitted communications*

(1) For the purposes of section 21A(6), a communication containing a threat of infringement proceedings is a "permitted communication" if—

(a) the communication, so far as it contains information that relates to the threat, is made for a permitted purpose;

(b) all of the information that relates to the threat is information that—
   (i) is necessary for that purpose (see subsection (5)(a) to (c) for some examples of necessary information), and
   (ii) the person making the communication reasonably believes is true.

(2) Each of the following is a "permitted purpose"—

(a) giving notice that a registered trade mark exists;
(b) discovering whether, or by whom, a registered trade mark has been infringed by an act mentioned in section 21A(2)(a), (b) or (c);
(c) giving notice that a person has a right in or under a registered trade mark, where another person's awareness of the right is relevant to any proceedings that may be brought in respect of the registered trade mark.

(3) The court may, having regard to the nature of the purposes listed in subsection (2)(a) to (c), treat any other purpose as a "permitted purpose" if it considers that it is in the interests of justice to do so.

(4) But the following may not be treated as a "permitted purpose"—

(a) requesting a person to cease using, in the course of trade, a sign in relation to goods or services,
(b) requesting a person to deliver up or destroy goods, or
(c) requesting a person to give an undertaking relating to the use of a sign in relation to goods or services.

(5) If any of the following information is included in a communication made for a permitted purpose, it is information that is "necessary for that purpose" (see subsection (1)(b)(i))—

(a) a statement that a registered trade mark exists and is in force or that an application for the registration of a trade mark has been made;
(b) details of the registered trade mark, or of a right in or under the registered trade mark, which—
   (i) are accurate in all material respects, and
   (ii) are not misleading in any material respect; and
(c) information enabling the identification of the goods or their packaging, or the services, in relation to which it is alleged that the use of a sign constitutes an infringement of the registered trade mark.][1]

NOTES

1 Inserted by Intellectual Property (Unjustified Threats) Act 2017, s 2(1), (2) (1 October 2017).

[21C Remedies and defences

(1) Proceedings in respect of an actionable threat may be brought against the person who made the threat for—

(a) a declaration that the threat is unjustified;
(b) an injunction against the continuance of the threat;
(c) damages in respect of any loss sustained by the aggrieved person by reason of the threat.

(2) It is a defence for the person who made the threat to show that the act in respect of which proceedings were threatened constitutes (or if done would constitute) an infringement of the registered trade mark.

(3) It is a defence for the person who made the threat to show—

(a) that, despite having taken reasonable steps, the person has not identified anyone who has done an act mentioned in section 21A(2)(a), (b) or (c) in relation to the goods or their packaging or the services which are the subject of the threat, and
(b) that the person notified the recipient, before or at the time of making the threat, of the steps taken.][1]

NOTES

1 Inserted by Intellectual Property (Unjustified Threats) Act 2017, s 2(1), (2) (1 October 2017).

[21D Professional advisers

(1) Proceedings in respect of an actionable threat may not be brought against a professional adviser (or any person vicariously liable for the actions of that professional adviser) if the conditions in subsection (3) are met.

(2) In this section "professional adviser" means a person who, in relation to the making of the communication containing the threat—

(a) is acting in a professional capacity in providing legal services or the services of a trade mark attorney or a patent attorney, and
(b) is regulated in the provision of legal services, or the services of a trade mark attorney or a patent attorney, by one or more regulatory bodies (whether through membership of a regulatory body, the issue of a licence to practise or any other means).

(3) The conditions are that—

(a) in making the communication the professional adviser is acting on the instructions of another person, and
(b) when the communication is made the professional adviser identifies the person on whose instructions the adviser is acting.

(4) This section does not affect any liability of the person on whose instructions the professional adviser is acting.

(5) It is for a person asserting that subsection (1) applies to prove (if required) that at the material time—

(a) the person concerned was acting as a professional adviser, and
(b) the conditions in subsection (3) were met.][1]

NOTES

1 Inserted by Intellectual Property (Unjustified Threats) Act 2017, s 2(1), (2) (1 October 2017).

[21E Supplementary: pending registration

(1) In sections 21 and 21B references to a registered trade mark include references to a trade mark in respect of which an application for registration has been published under section 38.

(2) Where the threat of infringement proceedings is made after an application for registration has been published (but before registration) the reference in section 21C(2) to "the registered trade mark" is to be treated as a reference to the trade mark registered in pursuance of that application.][1]

NOTES

1 Inserted by Intellectual Property (Unjustified Threats) Act 2017, s 2(1), (2) (1 October 2017).

[21F Supplementary: proceedings for delivery up etc.

In section 21(1)(b) the reference to proceedings for infringement of a registered trade mark includes a reference to—

(a) proceedings for an order under section 16 (order for delivery up of infringing goods, material or articles), and
(b) proceedings for an order under section 19 (order as to disposal of infringing goods, material or articles).][1]

NOTES

1 Inserted by Intellectual Property (Unjustified Threats) Act 2017, s 2(1), (2) (1 October 2017).

Registered trade mark as object of property

22 Nature of registered trade mark

A registered trade mark is personal property (in Scotland, incorporeal moveable property).

23 Co-ownership of registered trade mark

(1) Where a registered trade mark is granted to two or more persons jointly, each of them is entitled, subject to an agreement to the contrary, to an equal undivided share in the registered trade mark.

(2) The following provisions apply where two or more persons are co-proprietors of a registered trade mark, by virtue of subsection (1) or otherwise.

(3) Subject to any agreement to the contrary, each co-proprietor is entitled, by himself or his agents, to do for his own benefit and without the consent of or the need to account to the other or others, any act which would otherwise amount to an infringement of the registered trade mark

(4) One co-proprietor may not without the consent of the other or others—

(a) grant a licence to use the registered trade mark, or
(b) assign or charge his share in the registered trade mark (or, in Scotland, cause or permit security to be granted over it).

(5) Infringement proceedings may be brought by any co-proprietor, but he may not, without the leave of the court, proceed with the action unless the other, or each of the others, is either joined as a plaintiff or added as a defendant.

A co-proprietor who is thus added as a defendant shall not be made liable for any costs in the action unless he takes part in the proceedings.

Nothing in this subsection affects the granting of interlocutory relief on the application of a single co-proprietor.

(6) Nothing in this section affects the mutual rights and obligations of trustees or personal representatives, or their rights and obligations as such.

24 *Assignment, &c. of registered trade mark*

(1) A registered trade mark is transmissible by assignment, testamentary disposition or operation of law in the same way as other personal or moveable property.

It is so transmissible either in connection with the goodwill of a business or independently.

[(1A) A contractual obligation to transfer a business is to be taken to include an obligation to transfer any registered trade mark, except where there is agreement to the contrary or it is clear in all the circumstances that this presumption should not apply.][1]

(2) An assignment or other transmission of a registered trade mark may be partial, that is, limited so as to apply—

(a) in relation to some but not all of the goods or services for which the trade mark is registered, or
(b) in relation to use of the trade mark in a particular manner or a particular locality.

(3) An assignment of a registered trade mark, or an assent relating to a registered trade mark, is not effective unless it is in writing signed by or on behalf of the assignor or, as the case may be, a personal representative.

Except in Scotland, this requirement may be satisfied in a case where the assignor or personal representative is a body corporate by the affixing of its seal.

(4) The above provisions apply to assignment by way of security as in relation to any other assignment.

(5) A registered trade mark may be the subject of a charge (in Scotland, security) in the same way as other personal or moveable property.

(6) Nothing in this Act shall be construed as affecting the assignment or other transmission of an unregistered trade mark as part of the goodwill of a business.

NOTES

1 Inserted by Trade Marks Regulations 2018, SI 2018/825, regs 2, 14 (14 January 2019).

25 *Registration of transactions affecting registered trade mark*

(1) On application being made to the registrar by—

(a) a person claiming to be entitled to an interest in or under a registered trade mark by virtue of a registrable transaction, or
(b) any other person claiming to be affected by such a transaction,

the prescribed particulars of the transaction shall be entered in the register.

(2) The following are registrable transactions—

(a) an assignment of a registered trade mark or any right in it;
(b) the grant of a licence under a registered trade mark;
(c) the granting of any security interest (whether fixed or floating) over a registered trade mark or any right in or under it;
(d) the making by personal representatives of an assent in relation to a registered trade mark or any right in or under it;
(e) an order of a court or other competent authority transferring a registered trade mark or any right in or under it.

(3) Until an application has been made for registration of the prescribed particulars of a registrable transaction—

(a) the transaction is ineffective as against a person acquiring a conflicting interest in or under the registered trade mark in ignorance of it, and
(b) a person claiming to be a licensee by virtue of the transaction does not have the protection of section 30 or 31 (rights and remedies of licensee in relation to infringement).

(4) Where a person becomes the proprietor or a licensee of a registered trade mark by virtue of a registrable transaction [and the mark is infringed before the prescribed particulars of the transaction are registered, in proceedings for such an infringement, the court shall not award him costs unless—][1]

[(a) an application for registration of the prescribed particulars of the transaction is made before the end of the period of six months beginning with its date, or
(b) the court is satisfied that it was not practicable for such an application to be made before the end of that period and that an application was made as soon as practicable thereafter.][1]

(5) Provision may be made by rules as to—

(a) the amendment of registered particulars relating to a licence so as to reflect any alteration of the terms of the licence, and
(b) the removal of such particulars from the register—
    (i) where it appears from the registered particulars that the licence was granted for a fixed period and that period has expired, or
    (ii) where no such period is indicated and, after such period as may be prescribed, the registrar has notified the parties of his intention to remove the particulars from the register.

(6) Provision may also be made by rules as to the amendment or removal from the register of particulars relating to a security interest on the application of, or with the consent of, the person entitled to the benefit of that interest.

NOTES

1 Substituted by Intellectual Property (Enforcement, etc.) Regulations 2006, SI 2006/1028, reg 2(2), Sch 2, paras 15, 17 (29 April 2006).

26 *Trusts and equities*

(1) No notice of any trust (express, implied or constructive) shall be entered in the register; and the registrar shall not be affected by any such notice.

(2) Subject to the provisions of this Act, equities (in Scotland, rights) in respect of a registered trade mark may be enforced in like manner as in respect of other personal or moveable property.

27 *Application for registration of trade mark as an object of property*

(1) The provisions of sections 22 to 26 (which relate to a registered trade mark as an object of property) [and sections 28 to 31 (which related to licensing)][1] apply, with the necessary modifications, in relation to an application for the registration of a trade mark as in relation to a registered trade mark.

(2) In section 23 (co-ownership of registered trade mark) as it applies in relation to an application for registration the reference in subsection (1) to the granting of the registration shall be construed as a reference to the making of the application.

(3) In section 25 (registration of transactions affecting registered trade marks) as it applies in relation to a transaction affecting an application for the registration of a trade mark, the references to the entry of particulars in the register, and to the making of an application to register particulars, shall be construed as references to the giving of notice to the registrar of those particulars.

NOTES

1 Inserted by Trade Marks Regulations 2018, SI 2018/825, regs 2, 15 (14 January 2019).

Licensing

28 *Licensing of registered trade mark*

(1) A licence to use a registered trade mark may be general or limited.

A limited licence may, in particular, apply—

(a) in relation to some but not all of the goods or services for which the trade mark is registered, or
(b) in relation to use of the trade mark in a particular manner or a particular locality.

(2) A licence is not effective unless it is in writing signed by or on behalf of the grantor.

Except in Scotland, this requirement may be satisfied in a case where the grantor is a body corporate by the affixing of its seal.

(3) Unless the licence provides otherwise, it is binding on a successor in title to the grantor's interest.

References in this Act to doing anything with, or without, the consent of the proprietor of a registered trade mark shall be construed accordingly.

(4) Where the licence so provides, a sub-licence may be granted by the licensee; and references in this Act to a licence or licensee include a sub-licence or sub-licensee.

[(5) The proprietor of a registered trade mark may invoke the rights conferred by that trade mark against a licensee who contravenes any provision in the licence with regard to—

(a) its duration,
(b) the form covered by the registration in which the trade mark may be used,
(c) the scope of the goods or services for which the licence is granted,
(d) the territory in which the trade mark may be affixed, or
(e) the quality of the goods manufactured or of the services provided by the licensee.][1]

NOTES

1 Inserted by Trade Marks Regulations 2018, SI 2018/825, regs 2, 16 (14 January 2019).

29 Exclusive licences

(1) In this Act an "exclusive licence" means a licence (whether general or limited) authorising the licensee to the exclusion of all other persons, including the person granting the licence, to use a registered trade mark in the manner authorised by the licence.

The expression "exclusive licensee" shall be construed accordingly

(2) An exclusive licensee has the same rights against a successor in title who is bound by the licence as he has against the person granting the licence.

30 General provisions as to rights of licensees in case of infringement

(1) This section has effect with respect to the rights of a licensee in relation to infringement of a registered trade mark.

The provisions of this section do not apply where or to the extent that, by virtue of section 31(1) below (exclusive licensee having rights and remedies of assignee), the licensee has a right to bring proceedings in his own name.

[(1A) Except so far as the licence provides otherwise a licensee may only bring proceedings for infringement of the registered trade mark with the consent of the proprietor (but see subsections (2) and (3)).][1]

(2) [An exclusive licensee may][2] call on the proprietor of the registered trade mark to take infringement proceedings in respect of any matter which affects his interests.

(3) If the proprietor [mentioned in subsection (2)][1]—

(a) refuses to do so, or
(b) fails to do so within two months after being called upon.

The [exclusive][1] licensee may bring the proceedings in his own name as if he were the proprietor.

(4) Where infringement proceedings are brought by a licensee by virtue of this section [or with the consent of the proprietor or pursuant to the licence][1] the licensee may not, without the leave of the court, proceed with the action unless the proprietor is either joined as a plaintiff or added as a defendant.

This does not affect the granting of interlocutory relief on an application by a licensee alone.

(5) A proprietor who is added as a defendant as mentioned in subsection (4) shall not be made liable for any costs in the action unless he takes part in the proceedings.

(6) In infringement proceedings brought by the proprietor of a registered trade mark any loss suffered or likely to be suffered by licensees shall be taken into account; and the court may give such directions as it thinks fit as to the extent to which the plaintiff is to hold the proceeds of any pecuniary remedy on behalf of licensees.

[(6A) Where the proprietor of a registered trade mark brings infringement proceedings, a licensee who has suffered loss is entitled to intervene in the proceedings for the purpose of obtaining compensation for that loss.][1]

(7) The provisions of this section apply in relation to an exclusive licensee if or to the extent that he has, by virtue of section 31(1), the rights and remedies of an assignee as if he were the proprietor of the registered trade mark.

NOTES

1 Inserted by Trade Marks Regulations 2018, SI 2018/825, regs 2, 17(1), (2), (4)–(6) (14 January 2019).

2 Substituted by Trade Marks Regulations 2018, SI 2018/825, regs 2, 17(1), (3) (14 January 2019).

31 Exclusive licensee having rights and remedies of assignee

(1) An exclusive licence may provide that the licensee shall have, to such extent as may be provided by the licence, the same rights and remedies in respect of matters occurring after the grant of the licence as if the licence had been an assignment.

Where or to the extent that such provision is made, the licensee is entitled, subject to the provisions of the licence and to the following provisions of this section, to bring infringement proceedings, against any person other than the proprietor, in his own name.

(2) Any such rights and remedies of an exclusive licensee are concurrent with those of the proprietor of the registered trade mark, and references to the proprietor of a registered trade mark in the provisions of this Act relating to infringement shall be construed accordingly.

(3) In an action brought by an exclusive licensee by virtue of this section a defendant may avail himself of any defence which would have been available to him if the action had been brought by the proprietor of the registered trade mark.

(4) Where proceedings for infringement of a registered trade mark brought by the proprietor or an exclusive licensee relate wholly or partly to an infringement in respect of which they have concurrent rights of action, the proprietor or, as the case may be, the exclusive licensee may not, without the leave of the court, proceed with the action unless the other is either joined as a plaintiff or added as a defendant.

This does not affect the granting of interlocutory relief on an application by a proprietor or exclusive licensee alone.

(5) A person who is added as a defendant as mentioned in subsection (4) shall not be made liable for any costs in the action unless he takes part in the proceedings.

(6) Where an action for infringement of a registered trade mark is brought which relates wholly or partly to an infringement in respect of which the proprietor and an exclusive licensee have or had concurrent rights of action—

(a) the court shall in assessing damages take into account—
  (i) the terms of the licence, and
  (ii) any pecuniary remedy already awarded or available to either of them in respect of the infringement;
(b) no account of profits shall be directed if an award of damages has been made, or an account of profits has been directed, in favour of the other of them in respect of the infringement; and
(c) the court shall if an account of profits is directed apportion the profits between them as the court considers just, subject to any agreement between them.

The provisions of this subsection apply whether or not the proprietor and the exclusive licensee are both parties to the action, and if they are not both parties the court may give such directions as it thinks fit as to the extent to which the party to the proceedings is to hold the proceeds of any pecuniary remedy on behalf of the other.

(7) The proprietor of a registered trade mark shall notify any exclusive licensee who has a concurrent right of action before applying for an order under section 16 (order for delivery up), and the court may on the application of the licensee make such order under that section as it thinks fit having regard to the terms of the licence.

(8) The provisions of subsections (4) to (7) above have effect subject to any agreement to the contrary between the exclusive licensee and the proprietor.

APPLICATION FOR REGISTERED TRADE MARK

32 Application for registration

(1) An application for registration of a trade mark shall be made to the registrar.

(2) The application shall contain—

(a) a request for registration of a trade mark,
(b) the name and address of the applicant,
(c) a statement of the goods or services in relation to which it is sought to register the trade mark, and
(d) a representation of the trade mark[, which is capable of being represented in the register in a manner which enables the registrar and other competent authorities and the public to determine the clear and precise subject matter of the protection afforded to the proprietor][1].

(3) The application shall state that the trade mark is being used, by the applicant or with his consent, in relation to those goods or services, or that he has a bona fide intention that it should be so used.

(4) The application shall be subject to the payment of the application fee and such class fees as may be appropriate

NOTES

1 Inserted by Trade Marks Regulations 2018, SI 2018/825, regs 2, 18 (14 January 2019).

33 *Date of filing*

(1) The date of filing of an application for registration of a trade mark is the date on which documents containing everything required by section 32(2) are furnished to the registrar by the applicant.

If the documents are furnished on different days, the date of filing is the last of those days.

(2) References in this Act to the date of application for registration are to the date of filing of the application.

34 *Classification of trade marks*

(1) Goods and services shall be classified for the purposes of the registration of trade marks according to a prescribed system of classification.

(2) Any question arising as to the class within which any goods or services fall shall be determined by the registrar, whose decision shall be final.

Priority

35 *Claim to priority of Convention application*

(1) A person who has duly filed an application for protection of a trade mark in a Convention country (a "Convention application"), or his successor in title, has a right to priority, for the purposes of registering the same trade mark under this Act for some or all of the same goods or services, for a period of six months from the date of filing of the first such application.

(2) If the application for registration under this Act is made within that six-month period—

(a) the relevant date for the purposes of establishing which rights take precedence shall be the date of filing of the first Convention application, and

(b) the registrability of the trade mark shall not be affected by any use of the mark in the United Kingdom in the period between that date and the date of the application under this Act.

(3) Any filing which in a Convention country is equivalent to a regular national filing, under its domestic legislation or an international agreement, shall be treated as giving rise to the right of priority.

A "regular national filing" means a filing which is adequate to establish the date on which the application was filed in that country, whatever may be the subsequent fate of the application.

(4) A subsequent application concerning the same subject as the first Convention application, filed in the same Convention country, shall be considered the first

Convention application (of which the filing date is the starting date of the period of priority), if at the time of the subsequent application—

(a) the previous application has been withdrawn, abandoned or refused, without having been laid open to public inspection and without leaving any rights outstanding, and
(b) it has not yet served as a basis for claiming a right of priority.

The previous application may not thereafter serve as a basis for claiming a right of priority.

(5) Provision may be made by rules as to the manner of claiming a right to priority on the basis of a Convention application.

(6) A right to priority arising as a result of a Convention application may be assigned or otherwise transmitted, either with the application or independently.
The reference in subsection (1) to the applicant's "successor in title" shall be construed accordingly.

36 Claim to priority from other relevant overseas application

(1) Her Majesty may by Order in Council make provision for conferring on a person who has duly filed an application for protection of a trade mark in—

(a) any of the Channel Islands or a colony, or
(b) a country or territory in relation to which Her Majesty's Government in the United Kingdom have entered into a treaty, convention, arrangement or engagement for the reciprocal protection of trade marks,

a right to priority, for the purpose of registering the same trade mark under this Act for some or all of the same goods or services, for a specified period from the date of filing of that application.

(2) An Order in Council under this section may make provision corresponding to that made by section 35 in relation to Convention countries or such other provision as appears to Her Majesty to be appropriate.

(3) A statutory instrument containing an Order in Council under this section shall be subject to annulment in pursuance of a resolution of either House of Parliament.

Registration procedure

37 Examination of application

(1) The registrar shall examine whether an application for registration of a trade mark satisfies the requirements of this Act (including any requirements imposed by rules)

[…][1]

(3) If it appears to the registrar that the requirements for registration are not met, he shall inform the applicant and give him an opportunity, within such period as the registrar may specify, to make representations or to amend the application.

(4) If the applicant fails to satisfy the registrar that those requirements are met, or to amend the application so as to meet them, or fails to respond before the end of the specified period, the registrar shall refuse to accept the application.

(5) If it appears to the registrar that the requirements for registration are met, he shall accept the application.

NOTES

1 Repealed by Trade Marks (Relative Grounds) Order 2007, SI 2007/1976, art 3 (1 October 2007: repeal has effect subject to transitional provisions specified in SI 2007/1976 art 6(1)).

38 Publication, opposition proceedings and observations

(1) When an application for registration has been accepted, the registrar shall cause the application to be published in the prescribed manner

(2) Any person may, within the prescribed time from the date of the publication of the application, give notice to the registrar of opposition to the registration.

The notice shall be given in writing in the prescribed manner, and shall include a statement of the grounds of opposition.

[(2A) Where a notice of opposition is filed on the basis of one or more earlier trade marks or other earlier rights—

(a) the rights (if plural) must all belong to the same proprietor;
(b) the notice may be filed on the basis of part, or the totality, of the goods or services in respect of which the earlier right is protected or applied for.

(2B) A notice of opposition may be directed against part or the totality of the goods or services in respect of which the contested mark is applied for.][1]

(3) Where an application has been published, any person may, at any time before the registration of the trade mark, make observations in writing to the registrar as to whether the trade mark should be registered; and the registrar shall inform the applicant of any such observations.

A person who makes observations does not thereby become a party to the proceedings on the application.

NOTES

1 Inserted by Trade Marks Regulations 2018, SI 2018/825, regs 2, 19 (14 January 2019).

39 Withdrawal, restriction or amendment of application

(1) The applicant may at any time withdraw his application or restrict the goods or services covered by the application.

If the application has been published, the withdrawal or restriction shall also be published.

(2) In other respects, an application may be amended, at the request of the applicant, only by correcting—

(a) the name or address of the applicant,
(b) errors of wording or of copying, or
(c) obvious mistakes,

and then only where the correction does not substantially affect the identity of the trade mark or extend the goods or services covered by the application

(3) Provision shall be made by rules for the publication of any amendment which affects the representation of the trade mark, or the goods or services covered by the application, and for the making of objections by any person claiming to be affected by it.

40 Registration

(1) Where an application has been accepted and—

(a) no notice of opposition is given within the period referred to in section 38(2), or
(b) all opposition proceedings are withdrawn or decided in favour of the applicant,

the registrar shall register the trade mark, unless it appears to him having regard to matters coming to his notice [since the application was accepted that the registration requirements (other than those mentioned in section 5(1), (2) or (3)) were not met at that time.][1]

(2) A trade mark shall not be registered unless any fee prescribed for the registration is paid within the prescribed period.

If the fee is not paid within that period, the application shall be deemed to be withdrawn.

(3) A trade mark when registered shall be registered as of the date of filing of the application for registration, and that date shall be deemed for the purposes of this Act to be the date of registration.

(4) On the registration of a trade mark the registrar shall publish the registration in the prescribed manner and issue to the applicant a certificate of registration.

NOTES

1 Substituted by Trade Marks (Proof of Use, etc.) Regulations 2004, SI 2004/946, reg 5 (5 May 2004).

41 Registration: supplementary provisions

(1) Provision may be made by rules as to—

(a) the division of an application for the registration of a trade mark into several applications;
[(aa) the division of a registration of a trade mark into several registrations;][1]
(b) the merging of separate applications or registrations;
(c) the registration of a series of trade marks.

(2) A series of trade marks means a number of trade marks which resemble each other as to their material particulars and differ only as to matters of a non-distinctive character not substantially affecting the identity of the trade mark.

(3) Rules under this section may include provision as to—

(a) the circumstances in which, and conditions subject to which, division, merger or registration of a series is permitted, and
(b) the purposes for which an application [or registration][1] to which the rules apply is to be treated as a single application [or registration][1] and those for which it is to be treated as a number of separate applications [or registrations][1].

NOTES
1 Inserted by Trade Marks Regulations 2018, SI 2018/825, regs 2, 20 (14 January 2019).

Duration, renewal and alteration of registered trade mark

42 Duration of registration

(1) A trade mark shall be registered for a period of ten years from the date of registration.

(2) Registration may be renewed in accordance with section 43 for further periods of ten years.

43 Renewal of registration

(1) The registration of a trade mark may be renewed at the request of the proprietor, subject to payment of a renewal fee.

(2) Provision shall be made by rules for the registrar to inform the proprietor of a registered trade mark, before the expiry of the registration, of the date of expiry and the manner in which the registration may be renewed.

(3) A request for renewal must be made, and the renewal fee paid, before the expiry of the registration.

Failing this, the request may be made and the fee paid within such further period (of not less than six months) as may be prescribed, in which case an additional renewal fee must also be paid within that period.

[(3A) If a request for renewal is made or the renewal fee is paid in respect of only some of the goods or services for which the trade mark is registered, the registration is to be renewed for those goods or services only.][1]

(4) Renewal shall take effect from the expiry of the previous registration.

(5) If the registration is not renewed in accordance with the above provisions, the registrar shall remove the trade mark from the register.

Provision may be made by rules for the restoration of the registration of a trade mark which has been removed from the register, subject to such condition (if any) as may be prescribed.

(6) The renewal or restoration of the registration of a trade mark shall be published in the prescribed manner.

NOTES
1 Inserted by Trade Marks Regulations 2018, SI 2018/825, regs 2, 21 (14 January 2019).

44 Alteration of registered trade mark

(1) A registered trade mark shall not be altered in the register, during the period of registration or on renewal.

(2) Nevertheless, the registrar may, at the request of the proprietor, allow the alteration of a registered trade mark where the mark includes the proprietor's name or address and the alteration is limited to alteration of that name or address and does not substantially affect the identity of the mark.

(3) Provision shall be made by rules for the publication of any such alteration and the making of objections by any person claiming to be affected by it.

Surrender, revocation and invalidity

45 Surrender of registered trade mark

(1) A registered trade mark may be surrendered by the proprietor in respect of some or all of the goods or services for which it is registered.

(2) Provision may be made by rules—

(a) as to the manner and effect of a surrender, and
(b) for protecting the interests of other persons having a right in the registered trade mark.

46 Revocation of registration

(1) The registration of a trade mark may be revoked on any of the following grounds—

(a) that within the period of five years following the date of completion of the registration procedure it has not been put to genuine use in the United Kingdom, by the proprietor or with his consent, in relation to the goods or services for which it is registered, and there are no proper reasons for non-use;
(b) that such use has been suspended for an uninterrupted period of five years, and there are no proper reasons for non-use;
(c) that, in consequence of acts or inactivity of the proprietor, it has become the common name in the trade for a product or service for which it is registered;
(d) that in consequence of the use made of it by the proprietor or with his consent in relation to the goods or services for which it is registered, it is liable to mislead the public, particularly as to the nature, quality or geographical origin of those goods or services.

(2) For the purposes of subsection (1) use of a trade mark includes use in a form [(the "variant form")][1] differing in elements which do not alter the distinctive character of the mark in the form in which it was registered [(regardless of whether or not the trade mark in the variant form is also registered in the name of the proprietor)][1], and use in the United Kingdom includes affixing the trade mark to goods or to the packaging of goods in the United Kingdom solely for export purposes.

(3) The registration of a trade mark shall not be revoked on the ground mentioned in subsection (1)(a) or (b) if such use as is referred to in that paragraph

is commenced or resumed after the expiry of the five year period and before the application for revocation is made:

Provided that, any such commencement or resumption of use after the expiry of the five year period but within the period of three months before the making of the application shall be disregarded unless preparation for the commencement or resumption began before the proprietor became aware that the application might be made.

(4) An application for revocation may be made by any person, and may be made either to the registrar or to the court, except that—

(a) if proceedings concerning the trade mark in question are pending in the court, the application must be made to the court; and
(b) if in any other case the application is made to the registrar, he may at any stage of the proceedings refer the application to the court.

(5) Where grounds for revocation exist in respect of only some of the goods or services for which the trade mark is registered, revocation shall relate to those goods or services only.

(6) Where the registration of a trade mark is revoked to any extent, the rights of the proprietor shall be deemed to have ceased to that extent as from—

(a) the date of the application for revocation, or
(b) if the registrar or court is satisfied that the grounds for revocation existed at an earlier date, that date.

NOTES

1 Inserted by Trade Marks Regulations 2018, SI 2018/825, regs 2, 22 (14 January 2019).

47 Grounds for invalidity of registration

(1) The registration of a trade mark may be declared invalid on the ground that the trade mark was registered in breach of section 3 or any of the provisions referred to in that section (absolute grounds for refusal of registration).

Where the trade mark was registered in breach of subsection (1)(b), (c) or (d) of that section, it shall not be declared invalid if, in consequence of the use which has been made of it, it has after registration acquired a distinctive character in relation to the goods or services for which it is registered.

(2) [Subject to subsections (2A) and (2G),][1] the registration of a trade mark may be declared invalid on the ground—

(a) that there is an earlier trade mark in relation to which the conditions set out in section 5(1), (2) or (3) obtain, or
(b) that there is an earlier right in relation to which the condition set out in section 5(4) is satisfied,

unless the proprietor of that earlier trade mark or other earlier right has consented to the registration.

[(2ZA) The registration of a trade mark may be declared invalid on the ground that the trade mark was registered in breach of section 5(6).][1]

[(2A) [...][2] The registration of a trade mark may not be declared invalid on the ground that there is an earlier trade mark unless–

(a) the registration procedure for the earlier trade mark was completed within the period of five years ending with the date of the application for the declaration,
(b) the registration procedure for the earlier trade mark was not completed before that date, or
(c) the use conditions are met.

(2B) The use conditions are met if–

[(a) the earlier trade mark has been put to genuine use in the United Kingdom by the proprietor or with their consent in relation to the goods or services for which it is registered—
  (i) within the period of 5 years ending with the date of application for the declaration, and
  (ii) within the period of 5 years endingwith the date of filing of the application for registration of the later trade mark or (where applicable) the date of the priority claimed in respect of that application where, at that date, the five year period within which the earlier trade mark should have been put to genuine use as provided in section 46(1)(a) has expired, or][3]
(b) it has not been so used, but there are proper reasons for non-use.

(2C) For these purposes–

(a) use of a trade mark includes use in a form [(the "variant form")][1] differing in elements which do not alter the distinctive character of the mark in the form in which it was registered [(regardless of whether or not the trade mark in the variant form is also registered in the name of the proprietor)][1], and
(b) use in the United Kingdom includes affixing the trade mark to goods or to the packaging of goods in the United Kingdom solely for export purposes.

(2D) [...][4]

(2E) Where an earlier trade mark satisfies the use conditions in respect of some only of the goods or services for which it is registered, it shall be treated for the purposes of this section as if it were registered only in respect of those goods or services.][5]

[(2F) Subsection (2A) does not apply where the earlier trade mark is a trade mark within section 6(1)(c).][6]

[(2G) An application for a declaration of invalidity on the basis of an earlier trade mark must be refused if it would have been refused, for any of the reasons set out in subsection (2H), had the application for the declaration been made on the date of filing of the application for registration of the later trade mark or (where applicable) the date of the priority claimed in respect of that application.

(2H) The reasons referred to in subsection (2G) are—

(a) that on the date in question the earlier trade mark was liable to be declared invalid by virtue of section 3(1)(b), (c) or (d), (and had not yet acquired a distinctive character as mentioned in the words after paragraph (d) in section 3(1));

(b) that the application for a declaration of invalidity is based on section 5(2) and the earlier trade mark had not yet become sufficiently distinctive to support a finding of likelihood of confusion within the meaning of section 5(2);

(c) that the application for a declaration of invalidity is based on section 5(3)(a) and the earlier trade mark had not yet acquired a reputation within the meaning of section 5(3).][1]

(3) An application for a declaration of invalidity may be made by any person, and may be made either to the registrar or to the court, except that—

(a) if proceedings concerning the trade mark in question are pending in the court, the application must be made to the court; and

(b) if in any other case the application is made to the registrar, he may at any stage of the proceedings refer the application to the court.

(4) In the case of bad faith in the registration of a trade mark, the registrar himself may apply to the court for a declaration of the invalidity of the registration.

(5) Where the grounds of invalidity exist in respect of only some of the goods or services for which the trade mark is registered, the trade mark shall be declared invalid as regards those goods or services only.

[(5A) An application for a declaration of invalidity may be filed on the basis of one or more earlier trade marks or other earlier rights provided they all belong to the same proprietor.][1]

(6) Where the registration of a trade mark is declared invalid to any extent, the registration shall to that extent be deemed never to have been made.

Provided that this shall not affect transactions past and closed.

NOTES

1 Inserted by Trade Marks Regulations 2018, SI 2018/825, regs 2, 23(1)–(3), (6), (8), (9) (14 January 2019).

2 Repealed by Trade Marks Regulations 2018, SI 2018/825, regs 2, 23(1), (4) (14 January 2019).

3 Substituted by Trade Marks Regulations 2018, SI 2018/825, regs 2, 23(1), (5) (14 January 2019).

4 Repealed by Trade Marks (Amendment etc.) (EU Exit) Regulations 2019, SI 2019/269, reg 4, Sch 3, paras 1, 9 (31 January 2020).

5 Inserted by Trade Marks (Proof of Use, etc.) Regulations 2004, SI 2004/946, reg 6 (5 May 2004).

6 Inserted by Trade Marks (Earlier Trade Marks) Regulations 2008, SI 2008/1067, reg 5(1), (3) (10 May 2008: insertion has effect subject to transitional provisions specified in SI 2008/1067 regs 7 and 8).

48 *Effect of acquiescence*

(1) Where the proprietor of an earlier trade mark or other earlier right has acquiesced for a continuous period of five years in the use of a registered trade mark in

the United Kingdom, being aware of that use, there shall cease to be any entitlement on the basis of that earlier trade mark or other right—

(a) to apply for a declaration that the registration of the later trade mark is invalid, or
(b) to oppose the use of the later trade mark in relation to the goods or services in relation to which it has been so used.

unless the registration of the later trade mark was applied for in bad faith.

(2) Where subsection (1) applies, the proprietor of the later trade mark is not entitled to oppose the use of the earlier trade mark or, as the case may be, the exploitation of the earlier right, notwithstanding that the earlier trade mark or right may no longer be invoked against his later trade mark.

Collective marks

49 Collective marks

[(1) A collective mark is a mark which is described as such when it is applied for and is capable of distinguishing the goods and services of members of the association which is the proprietor of the mark from those of other undertakings.

(1A) The following may be registered as the proprietor of a collective mark—

(a) an association of manufacturers, producers, suppliers of services or traders which has the capacity in its own name to enter into contracts and to sue or be sued; and
(b) a legal person governed by public law.][1]

(2) The provisions of this Act apply to collective marks subject to the provisions of Schedule 1.

NOTES

1 Substituted by Trade Marks Regulations 2018, SI 2018/825, regs 2, 24 (14 January 2019).

Certification marks

50 Certification marks

(1) A certification mark is a mark [which is described as such when the mark is applied for and indicates][1] that the goods or services in connection with which it is used are certified by the proprietor of the mark in respect of origin, material, mode of manufacture of goods or performance of services, quality, accuracy or other characteristics.

(2) The provisions of this Act apply to certification marks subject to the provisions of Schedule 2.

NOTES

1 Substituted by Trade Marks Regulations 2018, SI 2018/825, regs 2, 25 (14 January 2019).

PART II [EUROPEAN UNION][1] TRADE MARKS AND INTERNATIONAL MATTERS

[European Union][1] trade marks

[51 Meaning of "European Union trade mark"

In this Act—

"European Union trade mark" has the meaning given by Article 1(1) of the European Union Trade Mark Regulation; and

"the European Union Trade Mark Regulation" means [Regulation (EU) 2017/1001 of the European Parliament and of the Council of 14 June 2017 on the European Union Trade Mark][2] [(as it had effect immediately before [IP completion day][3])][4].][1]

NOTES

1 Substituted by European Union Trade Mark Regulations 2016, SI 2016/299, regs 2–4 (6 April 2016).
2 Substituted by Trade Marks Regulations 2018, SI 2018/825, regs 2, 26 (14 January 2019).
3 Substituted by Intellectual Property (Amendment etc.) (EU Exit) Regulations 2020, SI 2020/1050, regs 7, 10(c) (31 December 2020).
4 Inserted by Trade Marks (Amendment etc.) (EU Exit) Regulations 2019, SI 2019/269, reg 4, Sch 3, paras 1, 10 (31 January 2020).

52 […]1

[…][1]

NOTES

1 Repealed by Trade Marks (Amendment etc.) (EU Exit) Regulations 2019, SI 2019/269, reg 4, Sch 3, paras 1, 11 (31 January 2020).

[52A Certain trade marks registered as European Union trade marks to be treated as registered trade marks

Schedule 2A makes provision for European Union trade marks (including certain expired and removed marks) to be treated as registered trade marks with effect from [IP completion day][1] and about certain applications for a European Union trade mark made before [IP completion day][1].][2]

NOTES

1 Substituted by Intellectual Property (Amendment etc.) (EU Exit) Regulations 2020, SI 2020/1050, regs 7, 9(a) (31 December 2020).
2 Inserted by Trade Marks (Amendment etc.) (EU Exit) Regulations 2019, SI 2019/269, reg 2, Sch 1, paras 1, 2 (31 January 2020).

The Madrid Protocol international registration

53 The Madrid Protocol

In this Act—

"the Madrid Protocol" means the Protocol relating to the Madrid Agreement concerning the International Registration of Marks, adopted at Madrid on 27th June 1989;

"the International Bureau" has the meaning given by Article 2(1) of that Protocol, and

[[...][1]][2]

"international trade mark (UK)" means a trade mark which is entitled to protection in the United Kingdom under that Protocol.

NOTES

1 Repealed by Designs and International Trade Marks (Amendment etc.) (EU Exit) Regulations 2019, SI 2019/638, reg 10(1), Sch 8, paras 16, 18 (31 December 2020).

2 Inserted by Trade Marks (International Registrations Designating the European Community, etc.) Regulations 2004, SI 2004/2332, reg 5 (1 October 2004).

54 Power to make provision giving effect to Madrid Protocol

(1) The Secretary of State may by order make such provision as he thinks fit for giving effect in the United Kingdom to the provisions of the Madrid Protocol.

(2) Provision may, in particular, be made with respect to—

(a) the making of application for international registrations by way of the Patent Office as office of origin;
(b) the procedures to be followed where the basic United Kingdom application or registration fails or ceases to be in force;
(c) the procedures to be followed where the Patent Office receives from the International Bureau a request for extension of protection to the United Kingdom;
(d) the effects of a successful request for extension of protection to the United Kingdom;
(e) the transformation of an application for an international registration, or an international registration, into a national application for registration,
(f) the communication of information to the International Bureau.
(g) the payment of fees and amounts prescribed in respect of application for international registrations, extensions of protection and renewals.

(3) Without prejudice to the generality of subsection (1), provision may be made by regulations under this section applying in relation to an international trade mark (UK) the provisions of—

[(a) sections 21 to 21F (unjustified threats);][1]
(b) sections 89 to 91 (importation of infringing goods, material or articles); and
(c) sections 92, 93, 95 and 96 (offences).

(4) An order under this section shall be made by statutory instrument which shall be subject to annulment in pursuance of a resolution of either House of Parliament.

NOTES

1 Substituted by Intellectual Property (Unjustified Threats) Act 2017, s 2(1), (4) (1 October 2017).

[54A Certain international trade marks protected in the European Union to be treated as registered trade marks

Schedule 2B makes provision for international trade marks protected in the European Union (including certain expired marks) to be treated as registered trade marks with effect from [IP completion day][1] and about certain applications for the protection of an international trade mark in the European Union and transformation applications made before [IP completion day][1].][2]

NOTES

1 Substituted by Intellectual Property (Amendment etc.) (EU Exit) Regulations 2020, SI 2020/1050, regs 13, 22(a) (31 December 2020).
2 Inserted by Designs and International Trade Marks (Amendment etc.) (EU Exit) Regulations 2019, SI 2019/638, reg 6, Sch 4, paras 1, 2 (31 January 2020).

The Paris Convention: supplementary provisions

55 The Paris Convention

(1) In this Act—

(a) "the Paris Convention" means the Paris Convention for the Protection of Industrial Property of March 20th 1883, as revised or amended from time to time , [...][1]
[(aa) "the WTO agreement" means the Agreement establishing the World Trade Organisation signed at Marrakesh on 15th April 1994, and][2]
(b) a "Convention country" means a country, other than the United Kingdom, which is a party to that Convention[or to that Agreement][3].

(2) The Secretary of State may by order make such amendments of this Act, and rules made under this Act, as appear to him appropriate in consequence of any revision or amendment of the Parts Convention [or the WTO agreement][4] after the passing of this Act.

(3) Any such order shall be made by statutory instrument which shall be subject to annulment in pursuance of a resolution of either House of Parliament.

NOTES

1 Repealed by Patents and Trade Marks (World Trade Organisation) Regulations 1999, SI 1999/1899, reg 13(2) (29 July 1999).
2 Inserted by Patents and Trade Marks (World Trade Organisation) Regulations 1999, SI 1999/1899, reg 13(2) (29 July 1999).
3 Inserted by Intellectual Property (Enforcement, etc.) Regulations 2006, SI 2006/1028, reg 2(2), Sch 2, paras 15, 18 (29 April 2006).
4 Inserted by Patents and Trade Marks (World Trade Organisation) Regulations 1999, SI 1999/1899, reg 13(3) (29 July 1999).

56 Protection of well-known trade marks Article 6bis

(1) References in this Act to a trade mark which is entitled to protection under the Paris Convention [or the WTO agreement][1] as a well known trade mark are to a mark which is well-known in the United Kingdom as being the mark of a person who—

(a) is a national of a Convention country, or
(b) is domiciled in, or has a real and effective industrial or commercial establishment in, a Convention country.

whether or not that person carries on business, or has any goodwill, in the United Kingdom.

References to the proprietor of such a mark shall be construed accordingly.

(2) The proprietor of a trade mark which is entitled to protection under the Paris Convention [or the WTO agreement][1] as a well known trade mark is entitled to restrain by injunction the use in the United Kingdom of a trade mark which, or the essential part of which, is identical or similar to his mark, in relation to identical or similar goods or services, where the use is likely to cause confusion.

This right is subject to section 48 (effect of acquiescence by proprietor of earlier trade mark).

(3) Nothing in subsection (2) affects the continuation of any bona fide use of a trade mark begun before the commencement of this section

NOTES

1 Inserted by Patents and Trade Marks (World Trade Organisation) Regulations 1999, SI 1999/1899, reg 13(4) (29 July 1999).

57 National emblems, &c. of Convention countries: Article 6ter

(1) A trade mark which consists of or contains the flag of a Convention country shall not be registered without the authorisation of the competent authorities of that country, unless it appears to the registrar that use of the flag in the manner proposed is permitted without such authorisation.

(2) A trade mark which consists of or contains the armorial bearings or any other state emblem of a Convention country which is protected under the Paris Convention [or the WTO agreement][1] shall not be registered without the authorisation of the competent authorities of that country.

(3) A trade mark which consists of or contains an official sign or hallmark adopted by a Convention country and indicating control and warranty shall not, where the sign or hallmark is protected under the Paris Convention [or the WTO agreement][1], be registered in relation to goods or services of the same, or a similar kind, as those in relation to which it indicates control and warranty, without the authorisation of the competent authorities of the country concerned.

(4) The provisions of this section as to national flags and other state emblems, and official signs or hallmarks, apply equally to anything which from a heraldic point of view imitates any such flag or other emblem, or sign or hallmark.

(5) Nothing in this section prevents the registration of a trade mark on the application of a national of a country who is authorised to make use of a state emblem, or official sign or hallmark, of that country, notwithstanding that it is similar to that of another country.

(6) Where by virtue of this section the authorisation of the competent authorities of a Convention country is or would be required for the registration of a trade mark, those authorities are entitled to restrain by injunction any use of the mark in the United Kingdom without their authorisation.

NOTES

1 Inserted by Patents and Trade Marks (World Trade Organisation) Regulations 1999, SI 1999/1899, reg 13(5) (29 July 1999).

58 Emblems, &c. of certain international organisations: Article 6ter

(1) This section applies to—

(a) the armorial bearings, flags or other emblems, and
(b) the abbreviations and names,

of international intergovernmental organisations of which one or more Convention countries are members.

(2) A trade mark which consists of or contains any such emblem, abbreviation or name which is protected under the Paris Convention [or the WTO agreement][1] shall not be registered without the authorisation of the international organisation concerned, unless it appears to the registrar that the use of the emblem, abbreviation or name in the manner proposed—

(a) is not such as to suggest to the public that a connection exists between the organisation and the trade mark, or
(b) is not likely to mislead the public as to the existence of a connection between the user and the organisation.

(3) The provisions of this section as to emblems of an international organisation apply equally to anything which from a heraldic point of view imitates any such emblem.

(4) Where by virtue of this section the authorisation of an international organisation is or would be required for the registration of a trade mark, that organisation is entitled to restrain by injunction any use of the mark in the United Kingdom without its authorisation.

(5) Nothing in this section affects the rights of a person whose bona fide use of the trade mark in question began before 4th January 1962 (when the relevant provisions of the Paris Convention entered into force in relation to the United Kingdom).

NOTES

1 Inserted by Patents and Trade Marks (World Trade Organisation) Regulations 1999, SI 1999/1899, reg 13(6) (29 July 1999).

59 Notification under Article 6ter of the Convention

(1) For the purposes of section 57 state emblems of a Convention country (other than the national flag), and official signs or hallmarks, shall be regarded as protected under the Paris Convention only if, or to the extent that—

(a) the country in question has notified the United Kingdom in accordance with Article 6ter(3) of the Convention that it desires to protect that emblem, sign or hallmark,
(b) the notification remains in force, and
(c) the United Kingdom has not objected to it in accordance with Article 6ter(4) or any such objection has been withdrawn.

(2) For the purposes of section 58 the emblems, abbreviations and names of an international organisation shall be regarded as protected under the Paris Convention only if, or to the extent that—

(a) the organisation in question has notified the United Kingdom in accordance with Article 6ter(3) of the Convention that it desires to protect that emblem, abbreviation or name,
(b) the notification remains in force, and
(c) the United Kingdom has not objected to it in accordance with Article 6ter(4) or any such objection has been withdrawn.

(3) Notification under Article 6ter(3) of the Paris Convention shall have effect only in relation to applications for registration made more than two months after the receipt of the notification.

(4) The registrar shall keep and make available for public inspection by any person, at all reasonable hours and free of charge, a list of—

(a) the state emblems and official signs or hallmarks, and
(b) the emblems, abbreviations and names of international organisations,

which are for the time being protected under the Paris Convention by virtue of notification under Article 6ter(3).

[(5) Any reference in this section to Article 6ter of the Paris Convention shall be construed as including a reference to that Article as applied by the WTO agreement.][1]

NOTES

1 Inserted by Patents and Trade Marks (World Trade Organisation) Regulations 1999, SI 1999/1899, reg 13(7) (29 July 1999).

60 [...][1]

[...][1]

NOTES

1 Repealed by Trade Marks Regulations 2018, SI 2018/825, regs 2, 28 (14 January 2019).

[Nice Classification

60A Similarity of goods and services

(1) For the purposes of this Act goods and services—

(a) are not to be regarded as being similar to each other on the ground that they appear in the same class under the Nice Classification;
(b) are not to be regarded as being dissimilar from each other on the ground that they appear in different classes under the Nice Classification.

(2) In subsection (1), the "Nice Classification" means the system of classification under the Nice Agreement Concerning the International Classification of Goods and Services for the Purposes of the Registration of Marks of 15 June 1957, which was last amended on 28 September 1979.][1]

NOTES

1 Inserted by Trade Marks Regulations 2018, SI 2018/825, regs 2, 29 (14 January 2019).

61 [...]1

[...][1]

NOTES

1 Repealed by Finance Act 2000, s 156(1), Sch 40, Pt III (28 July 2000).

PART III ADMINISTRATIVE AND OTHER SUPPLEMENTARY PROVISIONS

The registrar

62 The register

In this Act "the registrar" means the Comptroller-General of Patents, Designs and Trade Marks.

63 The register

(1) The registrar shall maintain a register of trade marks.

References in this Act to "the register" are to that register; and references to registration (in particular, in the expression "registered trade mark") are, unless the context otherwise requires, to registration in that register.

(2) There shall be entered in the register in accordance with this Act—

(a) registered trade marks.
(b) such particulars as may be prescribed of registrable transactions affecting a registered trade mark, and
(c) such other matters relating to registered trade marks as may be prescribed.

(3) The register shall be kept in such manner as may be prescribed, and provision shall in particular be made for—

(a) public inspection of the register, and
(b) the supply of certified or uncertified copies, or extracts, of entries in the register.

64 Rectification or correction of the register

(1) Any person having a sufficient interest may apply for the rectification of an error or omission in the register.

Provided that an application for rectification may not be made in respect of a matter affecting the validity of the registration of a trade mark.

(2) An application for rectification may be made either to the registrar or to the court, except that—

(a) if proceedings concerning the trade mark in question are pending in the court, the application must be made to the court; and
(b) if in any other case the application is made to the registrar, he may at any stage of the proceedings refer the application to the court.

(3) Except where the registrar or the court directs otherwise, the effect of rectification of the register is that the error or omission in question shall be deemed never to have been made.

(4) The registrar may, on request made in the prescribed manner by the proprietor of a registered trade mark, or a licensee, enter any change in his name or address as recorded in the register.

(5) The registrar may remove from the register matter appearing to him to have ceased to have effect.

65 *Adaptation of entries to new classification*

(1) Provision may be made by rules empowering the registrar to do such things as he considers necessary to implement any amended or substituted classification of goods or services for the purposes of the registration of trade marks.

(2) Provision may in particular be made for the amendment of existing entries on the register so as to accord with the new classification.

(3) Any such power of amendment shall not be exercised so as to extend the rights conferred by the registration, except where it appears to the registrar that compliance with this requirement would involve undue complexity and that any extension would not be substantial and would not adversely affect the rights of any person.

(4) The rules may empower the registrar—

(a) to require the proprietor of a registered trade mark, within such time as may be prescribed, to file a proposal for amendment of the register, and
(b) to cancel or refuse to renew the registration of the trade mark in the event of his failing to do so.

(5) Any such proposal shall be advertised, and may be opposed, in such manner as may be prescribed.

Powers and duties of the registrar

66 *Power to require use of forms*

(1) The registrar may require the use of such forms as he may direct for any purpose relating to the registration of a trade mark or any other proceeding before him under this Act.

(2) The forms, and any directions of the registrar with respect to their use, shall be published in the prescribed manner.

67 *Information about applications and registered trade marks*

(1) After publication of an application for registration of a trade mark, the registrar shall on request provide a person with such information and permit him to inspect such documents relating to the application, or to any registered trade

mark resulting from it, as may be specified in the request, subject, however, to any prescribed restrictions.

Any request must be made in the prescribed manner and be accompanied by the appropriate fee (if any).

(2) Before publication of an application for registration of a trade mark, documents or information constituting or relating to the application shall not be published by the registrar or communicated by him to any person except—

(a) in such cases and to such extent as may be prescribed, or
(b) with the consent of the applicant;

but subject as follows.

(3) Where a person has been notified that an application for registration of a trade mark has been made, and that the applicant will if the application is granted bring proceedings against him in respect of acts done after publication of the application, he may make a request under subsection (1) notwithstanding that the application has not been published and that subsection shall apply accordingly.

68 Costs and security for costs

(1) Provision may be made by rules empowering the registrar, in any proceedings before him under this Act

(a) to award any party such costs as he may consider reasonable, and
(b) to direct how and by what parties they are to be paid.

(2) Any such order of the registrar may be enforced—

(a) in England and Wales or Northern Ireland, in the same way as an order of the High Court;
(b) in Scotland, in the same way as a decree for expenses granted by the Court of Session.

(3) Provision may be made by rules empowering the registrar, in such cases as may be prescribed, to require a party to proceedings before him to give security for costs, in relation to those proceedings or to proceedings on appeal, and as to the consequences if security is not given.

69 Evidence before registrar

Provision may be made by rules—

(a) as to the giving of evidence in proceedings before the registrar under this Act by affidavit or statutory declaration,
(b) conferring on the registrar the powers of an official referee of the [Senior Courts or of the Court of Judicature][1] as regards the examination of witnesses on oath and the discovery and production of documents; and
(c) applying in relation to the attendance of witnesses in proceedings before the registrar the rules applicable to the attendance of witnesses before such a referee.

NOTES

1 Substituted by Constitutional Reform Act 2005, s 59(5), Sch 11, para 31 (1 October 2009).

70 Exclusion of liability in respect of official acts

(1) The registrar shall not be taken to warrant the validity of the registration of a trade mark under this Act or under any treaty, convention, arrangement or engagement to which the United Kingdom is a party.

(2) The registrar is not subject to any liability by reason of, or in connection with, any examination required or authorised by this Act, or any such treaty, convention, arrangement or engagement, or any report or other proceedings consequent on such examination.

(3) No proceedings lie against an officer of the registrar in respect of any matter for which, by virtue of this section, the registrar is not liable.

71 Registrar's annual report

(1) The Comptroller-General of Patents, Designs and Trade Marks shall in his annual report under section 121 of the Patents Act 1977 include a report on the execution of this Act, including the discharge of his functions under the Madrid protocol.

(2) The report shall include an account of all money received and paid by him under or by virtue of this Act.

Legal proceedings and appeals

72 Registration to be prima facie evidence of validity

In all legal proceedings relating to a registered trade mark (including proceedings for rectification of the register) the registration of a person as proprietor of a trade mark shall be prima facie evidence of the validity of the original registration and of any subsequent assignment or other transmission of it.

73 Certificate of validity of contested registration

(1) If in proceedings before the court the validity of the registration of a trade mark is contested and it is found by the court that the trade mark is validly registered, the court may give a certificate to that effect.

(2) If the court gives such a certificate and in subsequent proceedings—

(a) the validity of the registration is again questioned, and
(b) the proprietor obtains a final order or judgment in his favour,

he is entitled to his costs as between solicitor and client unless the court directs otherwise.

This subsection does not extend to the costs of an appeal in any such proceedings.

74 *Registrar's appearance in proceedings involving the register*

(1) In proceedings before the court involving an application for—

(a) the revocation of the registration of a trade mark,
(b) a declaration of the invalidity of the registration of a trade mark, or
(c) the rectification of the register,

the registrar is entitled to appear and be heard, and shall appear if so directed by the court.

(2) Unless otherwise directed by the court, the registrar may instead of appearing submit to the court a statement in writing signed by him, giving particulars of

(a) any proceedings before him in relation to the matter in issue,
(b) the grounds of any decision given by him affecting it,
(c) the practice of the Patent Office in like cases, or
(d) such matters relevant to the issues and within his knowledge as registrar as he thinks fit;

and the statement shall be deemed to form part of the evidence in the proceedings.

(3) Anything which the registrar is or may be authorised or required to do under this section may be done on his behalf by a duly authorised officer.

75 *The court*

In this Act, unless the context otherwise requires, "the court" means —

(a) in England and Wales[, the High Court[, or the county court where it has][1] jurisdiction by virtue of an order made under section 1 of the Courts and Legal Services Act 1990,][2]
[(aa) in Northern Ireland, the High Court, and][2]
(b) in Scotland, the Court of Session.

NOTES

1 Substituted by Crime and Courts Act 2013, s 17(6), Sch 9, para 134 (22 April 2014).
2 Substituted by High Court and County Courts Jurisdiction (Amendment) Order 2005, SI 2005/587, art 4(1), (2) (1 April 2005).

76 *Appeals from the registrar*

(1) An appeal lies from any decision of the registrar under this Act, except as otherwise expressly provided by rules.

For this purpose "decision"includes any act of the registrar in exercise of a discretion vested in him by or under this Act.

(2) Any such appeal may be brought either to an appointed person or to the court

(3) Where an appeal is made to an appointed person, he may refer the appeal to the court if—

(a) it appears to him that a point of general legal importance is involved.
(b) the registrar requests that it be so referred, or
(c) such a request is made by any party to the proceedings before the registrar in which the decision appealed against was made.

Before doing so the appointed person shall give the appellant and any other party to the appeal an opportunity to make representations as to whether the appeal should be referred to the court.

(4) Where an appeal is made to an appointed person and he does not refer it to the court, he shall hear and determine the appeal and his decision shall be final.

(5) The provisions of sections 68 and 69 (costs and security for costs; evidence) apply in relation to proceedings before an appointed person as in relation to proceedings before the registrar.

[(6) In the application of this section to England and Wales, "the court" means the High Court.][1]

NOTES

1 Added by High Court and County Courts Jurisdiction (Amendment) Order 2005, SI 2005/587, art 4(1), (3) (1 April 2005).

77 *Persons appointed to hear and determine appeals*

(1) For the purposes of section 76 an "appointed person" means a person appointed by the Lord Chancellor to hear and decide appeals under this Act.

(2) A person is not eligible for such appointment unless—

[(a) he satisfies the judicial-appointment eligibility condition on a 5-year basis;][1]
(b) he is an advocate or solicitor in Scotland of at least [5][2] years' standing;
(c) he is a member of the Bar of Northern Ireland or [solicitor of the Court of Judicature of Northern Ireland][3] of at least [5][2] years' standing; or
(d) he has held judicial office.

(3) An appointed person shall hold and vacate office in accordance with his terms of appointment, subject to the following provisions—

(a) there shall be paid to him such remuneration (whether by way of salary or fees), and such allowances, as the Secretary of State with the approval of the Treasury may determine;
(b) he may resign his office by notice in writing to the Lord Chancellor;
(c) the Lord Chancellor may by notice in writing remove him from office if—
  (i) he has become bankrupt or [a debt relief order (under Part 7A of the Insolvency Act 1986) has been made in respect of him or he has][4] made an arrangement with his creditors or, in Scotland, his estate has been sequestrated or he has executed a trust deed for his creditors or entered into a composition contract, or
  (ii) he is incapacitated by physical or mental illness,

or if he is in the opinion of the Lord Chancellor otherwise unable or unfit to perform his duties as an appointed person.

(4) The Lord Chancellor shall consult the Lord Advocate before exercising his powers under this section

[(5) The Lord Chancellor may remove a person from office under subsection (3)(c) only with the concurrence of the appropriate senior judge.

(6) The appropriate senior judge is the Lord Chief Justice of England and Wales, unless–

(a) the person to be removed exercises functions wholly or mainly in Scotland, in which case it is the Lord President of the Court of Session, or
(b) the person to be removed exercises functions wholly or mainly in Northern Ireland, in which case it is the Lord Chief Justice of Northern Ireland.][5]

NOTES

1 Substituted by Tribunals, Courts and Enforcement Act 2007, s 50(6), Sch 10, para 25(1), (2) (21 July 2008: substitution has effect subject to transitional provisions specified in SI 2008/1653 art 3).
2 Substituted by Tribunals, Courts and Enforcement Act 2007, s 50(6), Sch 10, para 25(1), (3) (21 July 2008: substitution has effect subject to transitional provisions specified in SI 2008/1653 art 3)
3 Substituted by Constitutional Reform Act 2005, s 59(5), Sch 11, para 5 (1 October 2009).
4 Inserted by Tribunals, Courts and Enforcement Act 2007 (Consequential Amendments) Order 2012, SI 2012/2404, art 3(2), Sch 2, para 31 (1 October 2012).
5 Inserted by Constitutional Reform Act 2005, s 15(1), Sch 4, para 238 (3 April 2006).

Rules, fees, hours of business, &c.

78 Power of Secretary of State to make rules

(1) The Secretary of State may make rules—

(a) for the purposes of any provision of this Act authorising the making of rules with respect to any matter, and
(b) for prescribing anything authorised or required by any provision of this Act to be prescribed,

and generally for regulating practice and procedure under this Act.

(2) Provision may, in particular, be made—

(a) as to the manner of filing of applications and other documents;
(b) requiring and regulating the translation of documents and the filing and authentication of any translation;
(c) as to the service of documents;
(d) authorising the rectification of irregularities of procedure;
(e) prescribing time limits for anything required to be done in connection with any proceeding under this Act;
(f) providing for the extension of any time limit so prescribed, or specified by the registrar, whether or not it has already expired.

(3) Rules under this Act shall be made by statutory instrument which shall be subject to annulment in pursuance of a resolution of either House of Parliament.

79 Fees

(1) There shall be paid in respect of applications and registration and other matters under this Act such fees as may be prescribed.

(2) Provision may be made by rules as to—

(a) the payment of a single fee in respect of two or more matters, and
(b) the circumstances (if any) in which a fee may be repaid or remitted.

80 Hours of business and business days

(1) The registrar may give directions specifying the hours of business of the Patent Office for the purpose of the transaction by the public of business under this Act, and the days which are business days for that purpose.

(2) Business done on any day after the specified hours of business, or on a day which is not a business day, shall be deemed to have been done on the next business day; and where the time for doing anything under this Act expires on a day which is not a business day, that time shall be extended to the next business day.

(3) Directions under this section may make different provision for different classes of business and shall be published in the prescribed manner.

81 The trade marks journal

Provision shall be made by rules for the publication by the registrar of a journal containing particulars of any application for the registration of a trade mark (including a representation of the mark) and such other information relating to trade marks as the registrar thinks fit.

Trade mark agents

82 Recognition of agents

Except as otherwise provided by rules [and subject to the Legal Services Act 2007][1], any act required or authorised by this Act to be done by or to a person in connection with the registration of a trade mark, or any procedure relating to a registered trade mark, may be done by or to an agent authorised by that person orally or in writing.

NOTES

1 Inserted by Legal Services Act 2007, s 184(1), (2) (1 January 2010).

[83 The register of trade mark attorneys

(1) There is to continue to be a register of persons who act as agent for others for the purpose of applying for or obtaining the registration of trade marks.

(2) In this Act a registered trade mark attorney means an individual whose name is entered on the register kept under this section.

(3) The register is to be kept by the Institute of Trade Mark Attorneys.

(4) The Secretary of State may, by order, amend subsection (3) so as to require the register to be kept by the person specified in the order.

(5) Before making an order under subsection (4), the Secretary of State must consult the Legal Services Board.

(6) An order under this section must be made by statutory instrument.

(7) An order under this section may not be made unless a draft of it has been laid before, and approved by a resolution of, each House of Parliament.][1]

NOTES

1 Sections 83-83A substituted for s 83 as amended by SI 2009/3339 art 2 by Legal Services Act 2007, s 184(1), (3) (1 January 2010: insertion came into force on 16 December 2009 but could not take effect until the commencement of Legal Services Act 2007, s 184 on 1 January 2010).

[83A Regulation of trade mark attorneys

(1) The person who keeps the register under section 83 may make regulations which regulate–

(a) the keeping of the register and the registration of persons;
(b) the carrying on of trade mark agency work by registered persons.

(2) Those regulations may, amongst other things, make–

(a) provision as to the educational and training qualifications, and other requirements, which must be satisfied before an individual may be registered or for an individual to remain registered;
(b) provision as to the requirements which must be met by a body (corporate or unincorporate) before it may be registered or for it to remain registered, including provision as to the management and control of the body;
(c) provision as to the educational, training or other requirements to be met by regulated persons;
(d) provision regulating the practice, conduct and discipline of registered persons or regulated persons;
(e) provision authorising in such cases as may be specified in the regulations the erasure from the register of the name of any person registered in it, or the suspension of a person's registration;
(f) provision requiring the payment of such fees as may be specified in or determined in accordance with the regulations;
(g) provision about the provision to be made by registered persons in respect of complaints made against them;
(h) provision about the keeping of records and accounts by registered persons or regulated persons;
(i) provision for reviews of or appeals against decisions made under the regulations;
(j) provision as to the indemnification of registered persons or regulated persons against losses arising from claims in respect of civil liability incurred by them.

(3) Regulations under this section may make different provision for different purposes.

(4) Regulations under this section which are not regulatory arrangements within the meaning of the Legal Services Act 2007 are to be treated as such arrangements for the purposes of that Act.

(5) Before the appointed day, regulations under this section may be made only with the approval of the Secretary of State.

(6) The powers conferred to make regulations under this section are not to be taken to prejudice–

(a) any other power which the person who keeps the register may have to make rules or regulations (however they may be described and whether they are made under an enactment or otherwise);
(b) any rules or regulations made by that person under any such power.

(7) In this section–

"appointed day" means the day appointed for the coming into force of paragraph 1 of Schedule 4 to the Legal Services Act 2007;
"manager", in relation to a body, has the same meaning as in the Legal Services Act 2007 (see section 207);
"registered person" means–
(a) a registered trade mark attorney, or
(b) a body (corporate or unincorporate) registered in the register kept under section 83;
"regulated person" means a person who is not a registered person but is a manager or employee of a body which is a registered person;
"trade mark agency work" means work done in the course of carrying on the business of acting as agent for others for the purpose of–
(a) applying for or obtaining the registration of trade marks in the United Kingdom or elsewhere, or
(b) conducting proceedings before the Comptroller relating to applications for or otherwise in connection with the registration of trade marks.][1]

NOTES

1 Sections 83-83A substituted for s 83 as amended by SI 2009/3339 art 2 by Legal Services Act 2007, s 184(1), (3) (1 January 2010: insertion came into force on 16 December 2009 but could not take effect until the commencement of Legal Services Act 2007, s 184 on 1 January 2010).

84 Unregistered persons not to be described as registered trade mark agents

(1) An individual who is not a registered trade mark [attorney][1] shall not—

(a) carry on a business (otherwise than in partnership) under any name or other description which contains the words "registered trade mark agent" [or registered trade mark attorney][2]; or
(b) in the course of a business otherwise describe or hold himself out, or permit himself to be described or held out, as a registered trade mark agent [or a registered trade mark attorney][2].

(2) A partnership [or other unincorporated body][3] shall not—

(a) carry on a business under any name or other description which contains the words "registered trade mark agent" [or registered trade mark attorney][2]; or
(b) in the course of a business otherwise describe or hold itself out, or permit itself to be described or held out, as a firm of registered trade mark agents [or registered trade mark attorneys][2],

unless [the partnership or other body is registered in the register kept under section 83.][4]

(3) A body corporate shall not—

(a) carry on a business (otherwise than in partnership) under any name or other description which contains the words "registered trade mark agent" [or registered trade mark attorney][2]; or
(b) in the course of a business otherwise describe or hold itself out, or permit itself to be described or held out, as a registered trade mark agent [or a registered trade mark attorney][2],

unless [the body corporate is registered in the register kept under section 83.][4]

(4) A person who contravenes this section commits an offence and is liable on summary conviction to a fine not exceeding level 5 on the standard scale; and proceedings for such an offence may be begun at any time within a year from the date of the offence.

NOTES

1 Substituted by Legal Services Act 2007, s 208(1), Sch 21, paras 109, 111(a)(i) (1 January 2010).
2 Inserted by Legal Services Act 2007, s 208(1), Sch 21, paras 109, 111(a)(ii), (iii), (b), (c) (1 January 2010).
3 Inserted by Legal Services Act 2007, s 184(1), (4)(a)(i) (1 January 2010).
4 Substituted by Legal Services Act 2007, s 184(1), (4)(a)(ii), (b) (1 January 2010).

85 *[…]*[1]

[…][1]

NOTES

1 Repealed by Legal Services Act 2007, Sch 23, para 1.

86 *Use of the term "trade mark attorney"*

(1) No offence is committed under the enactments restricting the use of certain expressions in reference to persons not qualified to act as solicitors by the use of the term "trade mark attorney" in reference to a registered trade mark [attorney][1].

(2) The enactments referred to in subsection (1) are section 21 of the Solicitors Act 1974, section 31 of the Solicitors (Scotland) Act 1980 and Article 22 of the Solicitors (Northern Ireland) Order 1976.

NOTES

1 Substituted by Legal Services Act 2007, s 208(1), Sch 21, paras 109, 112 (1 January 2010).

87 *Privilege for communications with registered trade mark agents*

(1) This section applies to[–][1]

[(a)][1] communications as toany matter relating to the protection of any design or trade mark, or as to any matter involving passing off[, and][1]
[(b) documents, material or information relating to any matter mentioned in paragraph (a).][1]

[(2) Where a trade mark attorney acts for a client in relation to a matter mentioned in subsection (1), any communication, document, material or information to which this section applies is privileged from disclosure in like manner as if the trade mark attorney had at all material times been acting as the client's solicitor.][2]

(3) In subsection (2) ["trade mark attorney"][2] means —

(a) a registered trade mark [attorney][2], or
(b) a partnership entitled to describe itself as a firm of registered trade mark [attorneys][2], or
(c) [any other unincorporated body or][3] a body corporate entitled to describe itself as a registered trade mark [attorney][2] [or][4]
[(d) a person whose name appears on the list of professional representatives for trade mark matters maintained by the European Union Intellectual Property Office referred to in Article 120 of the European Union Trade Mark Regulation.][4]

[(4) Where a trade mark attorney is a person falling within subsection (3)(d), subsection (2) applies as if the reference to a matter mentioned in subsection (1) were a reference to a matter relating to the protection of a trade mark.][4]

NOTES

1 Inserted by Legal Services Act 2007, s 208(1), Sch 21, paras 109, 113(a), (b) (1 January 2010).
2 Substituted by Legal Services Act 2007, s 208(1), Sch 21, paras 109, 113(c), (d) (1 January 2010).
3 Inserted by Legal Services Act 2007, s 184(1), (6) (1 January 2010).
4 Inserted by Trade Marks (Amendment etc.) (EU Exit) Regulations 2019, SI 2019/269, reg 4, Sch 3, paras 1, 12 (31 January 2020).

88 Power of registrar to refuse to deal with certain agents

(1) The Secretary of State may make rules authorising the registrar to refuse to recognise as agent in respect of any business under this Act—

(a) a person who has been convicted of an offence under section 84 (unregistered persons describing themselves as registered trade mark agents);
(b) [a person][1] whose name has been erased from and not restored to, or who is suspended from, the register of trade mark [attorneys][2] on the ground of misconduct;
(c) a person who is found by the Secretary of State to have been guilty of such conduct as would, in the case of [a person][1] registered in the register of trade mark [attorneys][2], render [the person][1] liable to have [the person's][1] name erased from the register on the ground of misconduct;
(d) a partnership or body corporate of which one of the partners or directors is a person whom the registrar could refuse to recognise under paragraph (a), (b) or (c) above.

(2) The rules may contain such incidental and supplementary provisions as appear to the Secretary of State to be appropriate and may, in particular, prescribe circumstances in which a person is or is not to be taken to have been guilty of misconduct.

NOTES

1 Substituted by Legal Services Act 2007 (Consequential Amendments) Order 2009, SI 2009/3348, art 5 (1 January 2010 being the day on which Legal Services Act 2007, s 13 comes into force).
2 Substituted by Legal Services Act 2007, s 208(1), Sch 21, paras 109, 114 (1 January 2010).

Importation of infringing goods, material or articles

89 Infringing goods, material or articles may be treated as prohibited goods

(1) The proprietor of a registered trade mark, or a licensee, may give notice in writing to the Commissioners of Customs and Excise—

(a) that he is the proprietor or, as the case may be, a licensee of the registered trade mark,
(b) that, at a time and place specified in the notice, goods which are, in relation to that registered trade mark, infringing goods, material or articles are expected to arrive in the United Kingdom—
  (i) from outside the European Economic Area, or
  (ii) from within that Area but not having been entered for free circulation, and
(c) that he requests the Commissioners to treat them as prohibited goods.

(2) When a notice is in force under this section the importation of the goods to which the notice relates, otherwise than by a person for his private and domestic use, is prohibited; but a person is not by reason of the prohibition liable to any penalty other than forfeiture of the goods.

[(3) This section does not apply to goods placed in, or expected to be placed in, one of the situations referred to in Article 1(1), in respect of which an application may be made under [Article 3 of the European Customs Enforcement Regulation][1].][2]

NOTES

1 Substituted by Trade Marks Regulations 2018, SI 2018/825, regs 2, 3 (14 January 2019).

2 Substituted by Goods Infringing Intellectual Property Rights (Customs) Regulations 2004, SI 2004/1473, reg 13 (1 July 2004).

90 Power of Commissioners of Customs and Excise to make regulations

(1) The Commissioners of Customs and Excise may make regulations prescribing the form in which notice is to be given under section 89 and requiring a person giving notice—

(a) to furnish the Commissioners with such evidence as may be specified in the regulations, either on giving notice or when the goods are imported, or at both those times, and
(b) to comply with such other conditions as may be specified in the regulations

(2) The regulations may, in particular, require a person giving such a notice

(a) to pay such fees in respect of the notice as may be specified by the regulations;
(b) to give such security as may be so specified in respect of any liability or expense which the Commissioners may incurring consequence of the notice by reason of the detention of any goods or anything done to goods detained;
(c) to indemnify the Commissioners against any such liability or expense, whether security has been given or not.

(3) The regulations may make different provision as respects different classes of case to which they apply and may include such incidental and supplementary provisions as the Commissioners consider expedient.

(4) Regulations under this section shall be made by statutory instrument which shall be subject to annulment in pursuance of a resolution of either House of Parliament.

[...][1]

NOTES

1 Repealed by Commissioners for Revenue and Customs Act 2005, ss 50(6), 52(2), Sch 4, para 57, Sch 5 (18 April 2005).

91 [Power of Commissioners for Revenue and Customs to disclose information]1

Where information relating to infringing goods, material or articles had been obtained [or is held][2] by [the Commissioners for her Majesty's Revenue and Customs][1] for the purposes of, or in connection with, the exercise of [functions of Her Majesty's Revenue and Customs][1] in relation to imported goods, the Commissioners may authorise the disclosure of that information for the purpose of facilitating the exercise by any person of any function in connection with the investigation or prosecution of [an offence under—

(a) section 92 below (unauthorised use of trade mark, &c in relation to goods),
(b) the Trade Descriptions Act 1968,
(c) the Business Protection from Misleading Marketing Regulations 2008, or
(d) the Consumer Protection from Unfair Trading Regulations 2008.][3]

NOTES

1 Substituted by Commissioners for Revenue and Customs Act 2005, s 50(6), Sch 4, para 58(1)(a), (c), (2) (18 April 2005).
2 Inserted by Commissioners for Revenue and Customs Act 2005, s 50(6), Sch 4, para 58(1)(b) (18 April 2005).
3 Substituted by Consumer Protection from Unfair Trading Regulations 2008, SI 2008/1277, s 30(1), Sch 2, paras 53, 54 (26 May 2008).

Offences

92 Unauthorised use of trade mark, &c. in relation to goods

(1) A person commits an offence who with a view to gain for himself or another, or with intent to cause loss to another, and without the consent of the proprietor—

(a) applies to goods or their packaging a sign identical to, or likely to be mistaken for, a registered trade mark, or
(b) sells or lets for hire, offers or exposes for sale or hire or distributes goods which bear, or the packaging of which bears, such a sign, or
(c) has in his possession, custody or control in the course of a business any such goods with a view to the doing of anything, by himself or another, which would be an offence under paragraph (b).

(2) A person commits an offence who with a view to gain for himself or another, or with intent to cause loss to another, and without the consent of the proprietor—

(a) applies a sign identical to, or likely to be mistaken for, a registered trade mark to material intended to be used—
   (i) for labelling or packaging goods,
   (ii) as a business paper in relation to goods, or
   (iii) for advertising goods, or
(b) uses in the course of a business material bearing such a sign for labelling or packaging goods, as a business paper in relation to goods, or for advertising goods, or
(c) has in his possession, custody or control in the course of a business any such material with a view to the doing of anything, by himself or another, which would be an offence under paragraph (b).

(3) A person commits an offence who with a view to gain for himself or another, or with intent to cause loss to another, and without the consent of the proprietor—

(a) makes an article specifically designed or adapted for making copies of a sign identical to, or likely to be mistaken for, a registered trade mark, or
(b) has such an article in his possession, custody or control in the course of a business,

knowing or having reason to believe that it has been, or is to be, used to produce goods, or material for labelling or packaging goods, as a business paper in relation to goods, or for advertising goods.

(4) A person does not commit an offence under this section unless—

(a) the goods are goods in respect of which the trade mark is registered, or
(b) the trade mark has a reputation in the United Kingdom and the use of the sign takes or would take unfair advantage of, or is or would be detrimental to, the distinctive character or the repute of the trade mark.

(5) It is a defence for a person charged with an offence under this section to show that he believed on reasonable grounds that the use of the sign in the manner in which it was used, or was to be used, was not an infringement of the registered trade mark.

(6) A person guilty of an offence under this section is liable—

(a) on summary conviction to imprisonment for a term not exceeding six months or a fine not exceeding the statutory maximum, or both;
(b) on conviction on indictment to a fine or imprisonment for a term not exceeding ten years, or both.

[92A Search warrants

(1) Where a justice of the peace (in Scotland, a sheriff or justice of the peace) is satisfied by information on oath given by a constable (in Scotland, by evidence on oath) that there are reasonable grounds for believing—

(a) that an offence under section 92 (unauthorised use of trade mark, etc. in relation to goods) has been or is about to be committed in any premises, and
(b) that evidence that such an offence has been or is about to be committed is in those premises,

he may issue a warrant authorising a constable to enter and search the premises, using such reasonable force as is necessary.

(2) The power conferred by subsection (1) does not, in England and Wales, extend to authorising a search for material of the kinds mentioned in section 9(2) of the Police and Criminal Evidence Act 1984 (c. 60) (certain classes of personal or confidential material).

(3) A warrant under subsection (1)—

(a) may authorise persons to accompany any constable executing the warrant, and

(b) remains in force for [three months][1] from the date of its issue.

(4) In executing a warrant issued under subsection (1) a constable may seize an article if he reasonably believes that it is evidence that any offence under section 92 has been or is about to be committed.

(5) In this section "premises"includes land, buildings, fixed or moveable structures, vehicles, vessels, aircraft and hovercraft.][2]

NOTES

1 Substituted by Serious Organised Crime and Police Act 2005, s 174(1), Sch 16, para 8 (1 January 2006 subject to transitory provisions specified in SI 2005/3495, art 2(2)).

2 Inserted by Copyright, etc. and Trade Marks (Offences and Enforcement) Act 2002, s 6 (20 November 2002).

93 Enforcement function of local weights and measures authority

(1) It is the duty of every local weights and measures authority to enforce within their area the provisions of section 92 (unauthorised use of trade mark, &c. in relation to goods).

(2) [...][1]

(3) Subsection (1) above does not apply in relation to the enforcement of section 92 in Northern Ireland, but it is the duty of the Department of Economic Development to enforce that section in Northern Ireland.

[...][2]

[(3A) For the investigatory powers available to a local weights and measures authority or the Department of Enterprise, Trade and Investment in Northern Ireland for the purposes of the duties in this section, see Schedule 5 to the Consumer Rights Act 2015.][2]

(4) Any enactment which authorises the disclosure of information for the purpose of facilitating the enforcement of the Trade Descriptions Act 1968 shall apply as if section 92 above were contained in that Act and as if the functions of any person in relation to the enforcement of that section were functions under that Act.

(5) Nothing in this section shall be construed as authorising a local weights and measures authority to bring proceedings in Scotland for an offence.

NOTES

1 Repealed by Consumer Rights Act 2015, s 77(2), Sch 6, para 59(1)–(3) (1 October 2015).

2 Inserted by Consumer Rights Act 2015, s 77(2), Sch 6, para 59(1), (4) (1 October 2015).

94 *Falsification of register, &c*

(1) It is an offence for a person to make, or cause to be made, a false entry in the register of trade marks, knowing or having reason to believe that it is false.

(2) It is an offence for a person—

(a) to make or cause to be made anything falsely purporting to be a copy of an entry in the register, or
(b) to produce or tender or cause to be produced or tendered in evidence any such thing,

knowing or having reason to believe that it is false.

(3) A person guilty of an offence under this section is liable—

(a) on conviction on indictment, to imprisonment for a term not exceeding two years or a fine, or both;
(b) on summary conviction, to imprisonment for a term not exceeding six months or a fine not exceeding the statutory maximum, or both.

95 *Falsely representing trade mark as registered*

(1) It is an offence for a person—

(a) falsely to represent that a mark is a registered trade mark, or
(b) to make a false representation as to the goods or services for which a trade mark is registered

knowing or having reason to believe that the representation is false.

(2) For the purposes of this section, the use in the United Kingdom in relation to a trade mark—

(a) of the word "registered", or
(b) of any other word or symbol importing a reference (express or implied) to registration,

shall be deemed to be a representation as to registration under this Act unless it is shown that the reference is to registration elsewhere than in the United Kingdom and that the trade mark is in fact so registered for the goods or services in question.

(3) A person guilty of an offence under this section is liable on summary conviction to a fine not exceeding level 3 on the standard scale.

96 *Supplementary provisions as to summary proceedings in Scotland*

(1) Notwithstanding anything in [section 136 of the Criminal Procedure (Scotland) Act 1995][1], summary proceedings in Scotland for an offence under this Act may be begun at any time within six months after the date on which evidence sufficient in the Lord Advocate's opinion to justify the proceedings came to his knowledge.

For this purpose a certificate of the Lord Advocate as to the date on which such evidence came to his knowledge is conclusive evidence.

(2) For the purposes of subsection (1) and of any other provision of this Act as to the time within which summary proceedings for an offence may be brought, proceedings in Scotland shall be deemed to be begun on the date on which a warrant to apprehend or to cite the accused is granted, if such warrant is executed without undue delay.

NOTES

1 Substituted by Criminal Procedure (Consequential Provisions) (Scotland) Act 1995, s 5, Sch 4, para 92(1), (2) (1 April 1996 subject to transitional provisions, transitory modifications and savings specified in Criminal Procedure (Consequential Provisions) (Scotland) Act 1995, Sch 3).

Forfeiture of counterfeit goods, &c.

97 *Forfeiture; England and Wales or Northern Ireland*

(1) In England and Wales or Northern Ireland where there has come into the possession of any person in connection with the investigation or prosecution of a relevant offence—

(a) goods which, or the packaging of which, bears a sign identical to or likely to be mistaken for a registered trade mark,
(b) material bearing such a sign and intended to be used for labelling or packaging goods, as a business paper in relation to goods, or for advertising goods, or
(c) articles specifically designed or adapted for making copies of such a sign,

that person may apply under this section for an order for the forfeiture of the goods, material or articles.

(2) An application under this section may be made—

(a) where proceedings have been brought in any court for a relevant offence relating to some or all of the goods, material or articles, to that court;
(b) where no application for the forfeiture of the goods, material or articles has been made under paragraph (a), by way of complaint to a magistrates' court.

(3) On an application under this section the court shall make an order for the forfeiture of any goods, material or articles only if it is satisfied that a relevant offence has been committed in relation to the goods, material or articles.

(4) A court may infer for the purposes of this section that such an offence has been committed in relation to any goods, material or articles if it is satisfied that such an offence has been committed in relation to goods, material or articles which are representative of them (whether by reason of being of the same design or part of the same consignment or batch or otherwise).

(5) Any person aggrieved by an order made under this section by a magistrates court, or by a decision of such a court not to make such an order, may appeal against that order or decision—

(a) in England and Wales, to the Crown Court;
(b) in Northern Ireland, to the county court,

and an order so made may contain such provision as appears to the court to be appropriate for delaying the coming into force of the order pending the making and determination of any appeal (including any application under section 111 of the Magistrates' Courts Act 1980 or Article 146 of the Magistrates' Courts (Northern Ireland) Order 1981 (statement of case))

(6) Subject to subsection (7), where any goods, material or articles are forfeited under this section they shall be destroyed in accordance with such directions as the court may give.

(7) On making an order under this section the court may, if it considers it appropriate to do so, direct that the goods, material or articles to which the order relates shall (instead of being destroyed) be released, to such person as the court may specify, on condition that that person—

(a) causes the offending sign to be erased, removed or obliterated, and
(b) complies with any order to pay costs which has been made against him in the proceedings for the order for forfeiture.

(8) For the purposes of this section a "relevant offence" means

[(a) an offence under section 92 above (unauthorised use of trade mark, &c in relation to goods),
(b) an offence under the Trade Descriptions Act 1968,
(c) an offence under the Business Protection from Misleading Marketing Regulations 2008,
(d) an offence under the Consumer Protection from Unfair Trading Regulations 2008, or
(e) any offence involving dishonesty or deception.][1]

NOTES

1 Substituted by Consumer Protection from Unfair Trading Regulations 2008, SI 2008/1277, s 30(1), Sch 2, paras 53, 55 (26 May 2008).

98 *Forfeiture; Scotland*

(1) In Scotland the court may make an order for the forfeiture of any—

(a) goods which bear, or the packaging of which bears, a sign identical to or likely to be mistaken for a registered trade mark,
(b) material bearing such a sign and intended to be used for labelling or packaging goods, as a business paper in relation to goods, or for advertising goods, or
(c) articles specifically designed or adapted for making copies of such a sign.

(2) An order under this section may be made—

(a) on an application by the procurator-fiscal made in the manner specified in [section 134 of the Criminal Procedure (Scotland) Act 1995][1], or
(b) where a person is convicted of a relevant offence, in addition to any other penalty which the court may impose.

(3) On an application under subsection (2)(a), the court shall make an order for the forfeiture of any goods, material or articles only if it is satisfied that a relevant offence has been committed in relation to the goods, material or articles.

(4) The court may infer for the purposes of this section that such an offence has been committed in relation to any goods, material or articles if it is satisfied that

such an offence has been committed in relation to goods, material or articles which are representative of them (whether by reason of being of the same design or part of the same consignment or batch or otherwise).

(5) The procurator-fiscal making the application under subsection (2)(a) shall serve on any person appearing to him to be the owner of, or otherwise to have an interest in, the goods, material or articles to which the application relates a copy of the application, together with a notice giving him the opportunity to appear at the hearing of the application to show cause why the goods, material or articles should not be forfeited.

(6) Service under subsection (5) shall be carried out, and such service may be proved, in the manner specified for citation of an accused in summary proceedings under the [Criminal Procedure (Scotland) Act 1995][1].

(7) Any person upon whom notice is served under subsection (5) and any other person claiming to be the owner of, or otherwise to have an interest in, goods, material or articles to which an application under this section relates shall be entitled to appear at the hearing of the application to show cause why the goods, material or articles should not be forfeited.

(8) The court shall not make an order following an application under subsection (2)(a)—

(a) if any person on whom notice is served under subsection (5) does not appear, unless service of the notice on that person is proved; or
(b) if no notice under subsection (5) has been served, unless the court is satisfied that in the circumstances it was reasonable not to serve such notice.

(9) Where an order for the forfeiture of any goods, material or articles is made following an application under subsection (2)(a) any person who appeared, or was entitled to appear, to show cause why goods, material or articles should not be forfeited may, within 21 days of the making of the order, appeal to the High Court by Bill of suspension; and [section 182(5)(a) to (e) of the Criminal Procedure (Scotland) Act 1995][1] shall apply to an appeal under this subsection as it applies to a stated case under Part II of that Act.

(10) An order following an application under subsection (2)(a) shall not take effect—

(a) until the end of the period of 21 days beginning with the day after the day on which the order is made; or
(b) if an appeal is made under subsection (9) above within that period, until the appeal is determined or abandoned

(11) An order under subsection (2)(b) shall not take effect—

(a) until the end of the period within which an appeal against the order could be brought under the [Criminal Procedure (Scotland) Act 1995][1]; or
(b) if an appeal is made within that period, until the appeal is determined or abandoned.

(12) Subject to subsection (13), goods, material or articles forfeited under this section shall be destroyed in accordance with such directions as the court may give.

(13) On making an order under this section the court may if it considers it appropriate to do so, direct that the goods, material or articles to which the order relates shall (instead of being destroyed) be released, to such person as the court may specify, on condition that that person causes the offending sign to be erased, removed or obliterated

(14) For the purposes of this section—

"relevant offence" means

- [(a) an offence under section 92 above (unauthorised use of trade mark, &c in relation to goods),
- (b) an offence under the Trade Descriptions Act 1968,
- (c) an offence under the Business Protection from Misleading Marketing Regulations 2008,
- (d) an offence under the Consumer Protection from Unfair Trading Regulations 2008, or
- (e) any offence involving dishonesty or deception;][2]

"the court" means —

- (a) in relation to an order made on an application under subsection (2)(a), the sheriff, and
- (b) in relation to an order made unless subsection (2)(b), the court which imposed the penalty.

NOTES

1 Substituted by Criminal Procedure (Consequential Provisions) (Scotland) Act 1995, s 5, Sch 4, para 92(1), (3) (1 April 1996 subject to transitional provisions, transitory modifications and savings specified in Criminal Procedure (Consequential Provisions) (Scotland) Act 1995, Sch 3).

2 Substituted by Consumer Protection from Unfair Trading Regulations 2008, SI 2008/1277, s 30(1), Sch 2, paras 53, 56 (26 May 2008).

PART IV MISCELLANEOUS AND GENERAL PROVISIONS

Miscellaneous

99 Unauthorised use of Royal arms. &c

(1) A person shall not without the authority of Her Majesty use in connection with any business the Royal arms (or arms so closely resembling the Royal arms as to be calculated to deceive) in such manner as to be calculated to lead to the belief that he is duly authorised to use the Royal arms.

(2) A person shall not without the authority of Her Majesty or of a member of the Royal family use in connection with any business any device, emblem or title in such a manner as to be calculated to lead to the belief that he is employed by, or supplies goods or services to Her Majesty or that member of the Royal family.

(3) A person who contravenes subsection (1) commits an offence and is liable on summary conviction to a fine not exceeding level 2 on the standard scale.

(4) Contravention of subsection (1) or (2) may be restrained by injunction in proceedings brought by—

(a) any person who is authorised to use the arms, device, emblem or title in question, or
(b) any person authorised by the Lord Chamberlain to take such proceedings

(5) Nothing in this section affects any right of the proprietor of a trade mark containing any such arms, device, emblem or title to use that trade mark.

[99A Reproduction of trade marks in dictionaries, encyclopaedias etc.

(1) Subsection (2) applies if the reproduction of a trade mark in a dictionary, encyclopaedia or similar reference work, in print or electronic form, gives the impression that it constitutes the generic name of the goods or services for which the trade mark is registered.

(2) The publisher of the work must, at the request in writing of the proprietor of the trade mark, ensure that the reproduction of the trade mark is accompanied by an indication that it is a registered trade mark.

(3) The action required by subsection (2) must be taken—

(a) without delay, and
(b) in the case of works in printed form, at the latest in the next edition of the publication.

(4) If the publisher fails to take any action required by subsection (2) the court may, on an application by the proprietor—

(a) order the publisher to take the action concerned;
(b) if the work is in printed form, order the publisher to erase or amend the reproduction of the trade mark or secure the destruction of copies of the work in the publisher's possession, custody or control; or
(c) grant such other order as the court in the circumstances considers appropriate.][1]

NOTES

1 Inserted by Trade Marks Regulations 2018, SI 2018/825, regs 2, 31 (14 January 2019).

100 Burden of proving use of trade mark

If in any civil proceedings under this Act a question arises as to the use to which a registered trade mark has been put, if is for the proprietor to show what use has been made of it.

101 Offences committed by partnerships and bodies corporate

(1) Proceedings for an offence under this Act alleged to have been committed by a partnership shall be brought against the partnership in the name of the firm and not in that of the partners; but without prejudice to any liability of the partners under subsection (4) below.

(2) The following provisions apply for the purposes of such proceedings as in relation to a body corporate—

(a) any rules of court relating to the service of documents,

(b) in England and Wales or Northern Ireland, Schedule 3 to the Magistrates' Courts Act 1980 or Schedule 4 to the Magistrates' Courts (Northern Ireland) Order 1981 (procedure on charge of offence).

(3) A fine imposed on a partnership on its conviction in such proceedings shall be paid out of the partnership assets.

(4) Where a partnership is guilty of an offence under this Act, every partner, other than a partner who is proved to have been ignorant of or to have attempted to prevent the commission of the offence, is also guilty of the offence and liable to be proceeded against and punished accordingly.

(5) Where an offence under this Act committed by a body corporate is proved to have been committed with the consent or connivance of a director, manager, secretary or other similar officer of the body, or a person purporting to act in any such capacity, he as well as the body corporate is guilty of the offence and liable to be proceeded against and punished accordingly.

Interpretation

102 Adaptation of expressions for Scotland

In the application of this Act to Scotland—

"account of profits" means accounting and payment of profits.
"accounts" means count, reckoning and payment.
"assignment" means assignation;
"costs" means expenses;
"declaration" means declarator;
"defendant" means defender;
"delivery up" means delivery;
"injunction" means interdict;
"interlocutory relief" means interim remedy; and
"plaintiff" means pursuer.

103 Minor definitions

(1) In this Act—

"business" includes a trade or profession;
"director", in relation to a body corporate whose affairs are managed by its members, means any member of the body;
"infringement proceedings", in relation to a registered trade mark, includes proceedings under section 16 (order for delivery up of infringing goods, &c.);
"publish" means make available to the public, and references to publication—
(a) in relation to an application for registration, are to publication under section 38(1), and
(b) in relation to registration, are to publication under section 40(4);
"statutory provisions" includes provisions of subordinate legislation within the meaning of the Interpretation Act 1978;
"trade" includes any business or profession..

(2) References in this Act to use (or any particular description of use) of a trade mark, or of a sign identical with, similar to, or likely to be mistaken for a trade mark, include use (or that description of use) otherwise than by means of a graphic representation.

(3) […][1]

NOTES

1 Repealed by Trade Marks (Amendment etc.) (EU Exit) Regulations 2019, SI 2019/269, reg 4, Sch 3, paras 1, 13 (31 January 2020).

104 Index of defined expressions

In this Act the expressions listed below are defined by or otherwise fall to be construed in accordance with the provisions indicated—

account of profits and accounts (in Scotland)	section 102
appointed person (for purposes of section 76)	section 77
assignment (in Scotland)	section 102
business	section 103(1)
certification mark	section 50(1)
collective mark	section 49(1)
commencement (of this Act)	section 109(2)
[…][1]	[…][1]
[…][1]	[…][1]
[comparable trade mark (EU)	Schedule 2A, paragraph 1(2)][2]
[comparable trade mark (IR)	Schedule 2B, paragraph 1(4)][3]
Convention country	section 55(1)(b)
costs (in Scotland)	section 102
the court	section 75
date of application	section 33(2)
[date of application (comparable trade mark (EU))	Schedule 2A, paragraph 1(8)(b)][2]
[date of application (comparable trade mark (IR))	Schedule 2B, paragraph 1(10)(b)][3]
date of filing	section 33(1)
[date of filing (comparable trade mark (EU))	Schedule 2A, paragraph 1(8)(a)][2]
[date of filing (comparable trade mark (IR))	Schedule 2B, paragraph 1(10)(a)][3]
date of registration	section 40(3)
[date of registration (comparable trade mark (EU))	Schedule 2A, paragraph 1(4)][2]
[date of registration (comparable trade mark (IR))	Schedule 2B, paragraph 1(6)][3]
defendant (in Scotland)	section 102
delivery up (in Scotland)	section 102
Director	section 103(1)

earlier right	section 5(4)
earlier trade mark	section 6
[European Customs Enforcement Regulation	section 10A][4]
[European Union trade mark	section 51][5]
[European Union Trade Mark Regulation	section 51][5]
exclusive licence and licensee	section 29(1)
infringement (of registered trade mark)	section 9(1) and (2) and 10
infringement proceedings	section 103(1)
infringing articles	section 17
infringing goods	section 17
infringing material	section 17
injunction (in Scotland)	section 102
interlocutory relief (in Scotland)	section 102
the International Bureau	section 53
[[…][6]	[…][6]][7]
International trade mark (UK)	section 53
Madrid Protocol	section 53
Paris Convention	section 55(1)(a)
plaintiff (in Scotland)	section 102
Prescribed	section 78(1)(b)
protected under the Paris Convention	
—well-known trade marks	section 56(1)
—state emblems and official signs or hallmarks	section 57(1)
—emblems, &c. of international organisations	section 58(2)
publish and references to publication	section 103(1)
register, registered (and related expressions)	section 63(1)
registered trade mark [attorney][8]	[section 83(2)][8]
registrable transaction	section 25(2)
the registrar	section 62
Rules	section 78
statutory provisions	section 103(1)
Trade	section 103(1)
trade mark	
—generally	section 1(1)
—includes collective mark or certification mark	section 1(2)
United Kingdom (references include Isle of Man)	section 108(2)
use (of trade mark or sign)	section 103(2)
well-known trade mark (under Paris Convention)	section 56(1)

NOTES

1. Repealed by European Union Trade Mark Regulations 2016, SI 2016/299, reg 15, Schedule, para 3 (6 April 2016).
2. Inserted by Trade Marks (Amendment etc.) (EU Exit) Regulations 2019, SI 2019/269, reg 4, Sch 3, paras 1, 14 (31 January 2020).
3. Inserted by Designs and International Trade Marks (Amendment etc.) (EU Exit) Regulations 2019, SI 2019/638, reg 10(1), Sch 8, paras 16, 19(1)–(5) (31 December 2020).
4. Inserted by Trade Marks Regulations 2018, SI 2018/825, regs 2, 32 (14 January 2019).
5. Inserted by European Union Trade Mark Regulations 2016, SI 2016/299, reg 15, Schedule, para 3 (6 April 2016).

6 Repealed by Designs and International Trade Marks (Amendment etc.) (EU Exit) Regulations 2019, SI 2019/638, reg 10(1), Sch 8, paras 16, 19(1), (6) (31 December 2020).
7 Inserted by Trade Marks (International Registrations Designating the European Community, etc.) Regulations 2004, SI 2004/2332, reg 6 (1 October 2004).
8 Substituted by Legal Services Act 2007, s 208(1), Sch 21, paras 109, 115 (1 January 2010).

Other general provisions

105 Transitional provisions

The provisions of Schedule 3 have effect with respect to transitional matters, including the treatment of marks registered under the Trade Marks Act 1938, and applications for registration and other proceedings pending under that Act, on the commencement of this Act.

106 Consequential amendments and repeals

(1) The enactments specified in Schedule 4 are amended in accordance with that Schedule, the amendments being consequential on the provisions of this Act.

(2) The enactments specified in Schedule 5 are repealed to the extent specified

107 Territorial waters and the continental shelf

(1) For the purposes of this Act the territorial waters of the United Kingdom shall be treated as part of the United Kingdom.

(2) This Act applies to things done in the United Kingdom sector of the continental shelf on a structure or vessel which is present there for purposes directly connected with the exploration of the sea bed or subsoil or the exploitation of their natural resources as it applies to things done in the United Kingdom.

(3) The United Kingdom sector of the continental shelf means the areas designated by order under section 1(7) of the Continental Shelf Act 1964.

108 Extent

(1) This Act extends to England and Wales, Scotland and Northern Ireland.

(2) This Act also extends to the Isle of Man, subject to such exceptions and modifications as Her Majesty may specify by Order in Council, and subject to any such Order references in this Act to the United Kingdom shall be construed as including the Isle of Man.

109 Commencement

(1) The provisions of this Act come into force on such day as the Secretary of State may appoint by order made by statutory instrument.

Different days may be appointed for different provisions and different purposes.

(2) The references to the commencement of this Act in Schedules 3 and 4 (transitional provisions and consequential amendments) are to the commencement of the main substantive provisions of Parts I and III of this Act and the consequential repeal of the Trade Marks Act 1938.

Provision may be made by order under this section identifying the date of that commencement

110 Short title

This Act may be cited as the Trade Marks Act 1994.

Schedule 1 Collective marks

Section 49

GENERAL

1 The provisions of this Act apply to collective marks subject to the following provisions.

SIGNS OF WHICH A COLLECTIVE MARK MAY CONSIST

2 In relation to a collective mark the reference in section 1(1) (signs of which a trade mark may consist) to distinguishing goods or services of one undertaking from those of other undertakings shall be construed as a reference to distinguishing goods or services of members of the association which is the proprietor of the mark from those of other undertakings.

INDICATION OF GEOGRAPHICAL ORIGIN

3 (1) Notwithstanding section 3(1)(c), a collective mark may be registered which consists of signs or indications which may serve, in trade, to designate the geographical origin of the goods or services.

(2) However, the proprietor of such a mark is not entitled to prohibit the use of the signs or indications in accordance with honest practices in industrial or commercial matters (in particular, by a person who is entitled to use a geographical name).

MARK NOT TO BE MISLEADING AS TO CHARACTER OR SIGNIFICANCE

4 (1) A collective mark shall not be registered if the public is liable to be misled as regards the character or significance of the mark, in particular if it is likely to be taken to be something other than a collective mark.

(2) The registrar may accordingly require that a mark in respect of which application is made for registration include some indication that it is a collective mark.

Notwithstanding section 39(2), an application may be amended so as to comply with any such requirement.

REGULATIONS GOVERNING USE OF COLLECTIVE MARK

5 (1) An applicant for registration of a collective mark must fine with the registrar regulations governing the use of the mark.

(2) The regulations must specify the persons authorised to use the mark, the conditions of membership of the association and [...][1] the conditions of use of the mark, including any sanctions against misuse.

[(3) Where the regulations govern use of a mark referred to in paragraph 3(1), they must authorise any person whose goods or services originate in the geographical area concerned to become a member of the association which is the proprietor of the mark, provided that the person fulfils all the other conditions of the regulations.][2]

[(4)][2] Further requirements with which the regulations have to comply may be imposed by rules.

NOTES

1 Repealed by Trade Marks Regulations 2018, SI 2018/825, regs 2, 33(1), (2)(a) (14 January 2019).

2 Inserted by Trade Marks Regulations 2018, SI 2018/825, regs 2, 33(1), (2)(b), (c) (14 January 2019).

APPROVAL OF REGULATIONS BY REGISTRAR

6 (1) A collective mark shall not be registered unless the regulations governing the use of the mark—

(a) comply with paragraph 5(2) [and (3)][1] and any further requirements imposed by rules, and

(b) are not contrary to public policy or to accepted principles of morality

(2) Before the end of the prescribed period after the date of the application for registration of a collective mark, the applicant must file the regulations with the registrar and pay the prescribed fee.

If he does not do so, the application shall be deemed to be withdrawn.

NOTES

1 Inserted by Trade Marks Regulations 2018, SI 2018/825, regs 2, 33(1), (3) (14 January 2019).

7 (1) The registrar shall consider whether the requirements mentioned in paragraph 6(1) are met.

(2) If it appears to the registrar that those requirements are not met, he shall the applicant and give him an opportunity, within such period as the registrar may specify, to make representations or to file amended regulations.

(3) If the applicant fails to satisfy the registrar that those requirements are not, or to file regulations amended so as to meet them, or fails to respond before the end of the specified period, the registrar shall refuse the application.

(4) If it appears to the registrar that those requirements, and the other requirements for registration, are met, he shall accept the application and shall proceed

in accordance with section 38 (publication, opposition proceedings and observations).

8 The regulations shall be published and notice of opposition may be given, and observations may be made, relating to the matters mentioned in paragraph 6(1).

This is in addition to any other grounds on which the application may be opposed or observations made.

REGULATIONS TO BE OPEN TO INSPECTION

9 The regulations governing the use of a registered collective mark shall be open to public inspection in the same way as the register.

AMENDMENT OF REGULATIONS

10 (1) An amendment of the regulations governing the use of a registered collective mark is not effective unless and until the amended regulations are filed with the registrar and accepted by him.

(2) Before accepting any amended regulations the registrar may in any case where it appears to him expedient to do so cause them to be published.

(3) If he does so, notice of opposition may be given, and observations may be made, relating to the matters mentioned in paragraph 6(1).

INFRINGEMENT RIGHTS OF AUTHORISED USERS

11 The following provisions apply in relation to an authorised user of a registered collective mark as in relation to a licensee of a trade mark—

(a) section 10(5) (definition of infringement: unauthorised application of mark to certain material);
(b) section 19(2) (order as to disposal of infringing goods, material or articles adequacy of other remedies);
(c) section 89 (prohibition of importation of infringing goods, material or articles request to Commissioners of Customs and Excise).

INFRINGEMENT RIGHTS OF AUTHORISED USERS

12 (1) The following provisions (which correspond to the provisions of section 30 general provisions as to rights of licensees in case of infringement) have effect as regards the rights of an authorised user in relation to infringement of a registered collective mark.

[(2) Subject to any agreement to the contrary between the authorised user and the proprietor, an authorised user may only bring proceedings for infringement of a registered collective mark with the consent of the proprietor.][1]

(3) […][2]

(4) [Where proceedings are brought by an authorised user for infringement of a registered collective mark (with the consent of the proprietor or pursuant to any agreement referred to in sub-paragraph (2))][1], the authorised user may not, without the leave of the court, proceed with the action unless the proprietor is either joined as a plaintiff or added as a defendant.

This does not affect the granting of interlocutory relief on an application by an authorised user alone.

(5) A proprietor who is added as a defendant as mentioned in sub-paragraph (4) shall not be made liable for any costs in the action unless he takes part in the proceedings.

(6) In infringement proceedings brought by the proprietor of a registered collective mark any loss suffered or likely to be suffered by authorised users shall be taken into account; and the court may give such directions as it thinks fit as to the extent to which the plaintiff is to hold the proceeds of any pecuniary remedy on behalf of such users.

[(7) Where the proprietor of a registered collective mark brings infringement proceedings, an authorised user who has suffered loss is entitled to intervene in the proceedings for the purpose of obtaining compensation for that loss.][3]

NOTES

1 Substituted by Trade Marks Regulations 2018, SI 2018/825, regs 2, 33(1), (4)(a), (c) (14 January 2019).

2 Repealed by Trade Marks Regulations 2018, SI 2018/825, regs 2, 33(1), (4)(b) (14 January 2019).

3 Inserted by Trade Marks Regulations 2018, SI 2018/825, regs 2, 33(1), (4)(d) (14 January 2019).

GROUNDS FOR REVOCATION OF REGISTRATION

13 Apart from the grounds of revocation provided for in section 46, the registration of a collective mark may be revoked on the ground

(a) that the manner in which the mark has been used by the [persons authorised to use it][1] has caused it to become liable to mislead the public in the manner referred to in paragraph 4(1); or

(b) that the proprietor [has not taken reasonable steps to prevent the mark being used in a manner that is incompatible with the conditions of use laid down in][1] the regulations governing the use of the mark [(as amended from time to time)][2], or

(c) that an amendment of the regulations has been made so that the regulations

  (i) no longer comply with paragraph 5(2) [and (3)][2] and any further conditions imposed by rules, or

  (ii) are contrary to public policy or to accepted principles of morality.

NOTES

1 Substituted by Trade Marks Regulations 2018, SI 2018/825, regs 2, 33(1), (5)(a), (b)(i) (14 January 2019).

2 Inserted by Trade Marks Regulations 2018, SI 2018/825, regs 2, 33(1), (5)(b)(ii), (c) (14 January 2019).

GROUNDS FOR INVALIDITY OF REGISTRATION

14 Apart from the grounds of invalidity provided for in section 47, the registration of a collective mark [shall][1] be declared invalid on the ground that the mark was registered in breach of the provisions of [section 49(1A) (definition of who may be registered as the proprietor of a certification mark) or][2] paragraph 4(1) or 6(1) [unless the breach was only of paragraph 6(1) and the proprietor of the mark, by amending the regulations governing use, complies with the requirements of paragraph 6(1)][2].

NOTES

1 Substituted by Trade Marks Regulations 2018, SI 2018/825, regs 2, 33(1), (6)(a) (14 January 2019).

2 Inserted by Trade Marks Regulations 2018, SI 2018/825, regs 2, 33(1), (6)(b), (c) (14 January 2019).

Schedule 2 Certification marks

Section 50

GENERAL

1 The provisions of this Act apply to certification marks subject to the following provisions.

SIGNS OF WHICH A CERTIFICATION MARK MAY CONSIST

2 In relation to a certification mark the reference in section 1(1) (signs of which a trade mark may consist) to distinguishing goods or services of one undertaking from those of other undertakings shall be construed as a reference to distinguishing goods or services which are certified from those which are not.

INDICATION OF GEOGRAPHICAL ORIGIN

3 (1) Notwithstanding section 3(1)(c) a certification mark may be registered which consists of signs or indications which may serve, in trade, to designate the geographical origin of the goods or services.

(2) However, the proprietor of such a mark is not entitled to prohibit the use of the signs or indications in accordance with honest practices in industrial or commercial matters (in particular, by a person who is entitled to use a geographical name).

NATURE OF PROPRIETOR'S BUSINESS

4 A certification mark shall not be registered if the proprietor carries on a business involving the supply of goods or services of the kind certified.

MARK NOT TO BE MISLEADING AS TO CHARACTER OR SIGNIFICANCE

5 (1) A certification mark shall not be registered if the public is liable to be misled as regards the character or significance of the mark, in particular if it is likely to be taken to be something other than a certification mark.

(2) The registrar may accordingly require that a mark in respect of which application is made for registration include some indication that it is a certification mark.

Notwithstanding section 39(2); an application may be amended so as to comply with any such requirement.

REGULATIONS GOVERNING USE OF CERTIFICATION MARK

6 (1) An applicant for registration of a certification mark must file with the registrar regulations governing the use of the mark.

(2) The regulations must indicate who is authorised to use the mark, the characteristics to be certified by the mark, how the certifying body is to test those characteristics and to supervise the use of the mark, the fees (if any) to be paid in connection with the operation of the mark and the procedures for resolving disputes.

Further requirements with which the regulations have to comply may be imposed by rules.

APPROVAL OF REGULATIONS, &C.

7 (1) A certification mark shall not be registered unless—

(a) the regulations governing the use of the mark—
  (i) comply with paragraph 6(2) and any further requirements imposed by rules, and
  (ii) are not contrary to public policy or to accepted principles of morality, and

(b) the applicant is competent to certify the goods or services for which the mark is to be registered.

(2) Before the end of the prescribed period after the date of the application for registration of a certification mark, the applicant must file the regulations with the registrar and pay the prescribed fee.

If he does not do so, the application shall be deemed to be withdrawn.

8 (1) The registrar shall consider whether the requirements mentioned in paragraph 7(1) are met.

(2) If it appears to the registrar that those requirements are not met, he shall inform the applicant and give him an opportunity, within such period as the registrar may specify, to make representations or to file amended regulations.

(3) If the applicant fails to satisfy the registrar that those requirements are met, or to file regulations amended so as to meet them, or fails to respond before the end of the specified period, the registrar shall refuse the application.

(4) If it appears to the registrar that those requirements, and the other requirements for registration, are met, he shall accept the application and shall proceed in accordance with section 38 (publication, opposition proceedings and observations).

9 The regulations shall be published and notice of opposition may be given, and observations may be made, relating to the matters mentioned in paragraph 7(1)

This is in addition to any other grounds on which the application may be opposed or observations made.

REGULATIONS TO BE OPEN TO INSPECTION

10 The regulations governing the use of a registered certification mark shall be open to public inspection in the same way as the register.

AMENDMENT OF REGULATIONS

11 (1) An amendment of the regulations governing the use of a registered certification mark is not effective unless and until the amended regulations art filed with the registrar and accepted by him.

(2) Before accepting any amended regulations the registrar may in any case where it appears to him expedient to do so cause them to be published.

(3) If he does so, notice of opposition may be given, and observations may be made, relating to the matters mentioned in paragraph 7(1).

CONSENT TO ASSIGNMENT OF REGISTERED CERTIFICATION MARK

12 The assignment or other transmission of a registered certification mark is not effective without the consent of the registrar.

INFRINGEMENT RIGHTS OF AUTHORISED USERS

13 The following provisions apply in relation to an authorised user of a registered certification mark as in relation to a licensee of a trade mark—

(a) section 10(5) (definition of infringement unauthorised application of mark to certain material);
(b) section 19(2) (order as to disposal of infringing goods, material or articles: adequacy of other remedies);
(c) section 89 (prohibition of importation of infringing goods, material or articles request to Commissioners of Customs and Excise).

14 In infringement proceedings brought by the proprietor of a registered certification mark any loss suffered or likely to be suffered by authorised users shall be taken into account, and the court may give such directions as it thinks fit as to the extent to which the plaintiff is to told the proceeds of any pecuniary remedy on behalf of such users.

GROUNDS FOR REVOCATION OF REGISTRATION

15 Apart from the grounds of revocation provided for in section 46, the registration of a certification mark may be revoked on the ground—

(a) that the proprietor has begun to carry on such a business as is mentioned in paragraph 4.
(b) that the manner in which the mark has been used by the proprietor has caused it to become liable to mislead the public in the manner referred to in paragraph 5(1),
(c) that the proprietor has failed to observe, or to secure the observance of, the regulations governing the use of the mark,
(d) that an amendment of the regulations has been made so that the regulations—
    (i) no longer comply with paragraph 6(2) and any further conditions imposed by rules, or
    (ii) are contrary to public policy or to accepted principles of morality, or
(e) that the proprietor is no longer competent to certify the goods or services for which the mark is registered.

GROUNDS FOR INVALIDITY OF REGISTRATION

16 Apart from the grounds of invalidity provided for in section 47, the registration of a certification mark may be declared invalid on the ground that the mark was registered in breach of the provisions of paragraph 4, 5(1) or 7(1)

[Schedule 2A European Union trade marks

Section 52A

PART 1 EXISTING EUROPEAN UNION TRADE MARKS

1 A trade mark registered as an existing EUTM to be treated as registered under this Act

(1) A trade mark which is registered in the EUTM Register immediately before [IP completion day][1] (an "existing EUTM") is to be treated on and after [IP completion day][1] as if an application had been made, and the trade mark had been registered, under this Act in respect of the same goods or services as the existing EUTM is registered in the EUTM Register.

(2) A registered trade mark which comes into being by virtue of sub-paragraph (1) is referred to in this Act as a comparable trade mark (EU).

(3) This Act applies to a comparable trade mark (EU) as it applies to other registered trade marks except as otherwise provided in this Schedule.

(4) A comparable trade mark (EU) is deemed for the purposes of this Act to be registered as of the filing date accorded pursuant to Article 32 to the application which resulted in the registration of the corresponding EUTM and that date is deemed for the purposes of this Act to be the date of registration.

(5) Section 40(3) and (4) does not apply to the registration of a comparable trade mark (EU) under this Part.

(6) Section 67(1) applies in relation to the provision of information and the inspection of documents relating to a comparable trade mark (EU) notwithstand-

ing that there will have been no application under this Act for the registration of the trade mark (and so no publication of an application).

(7) Nothing in this Act authorises the imposition of a fee, or the making of provision by rules or regulations which authorises the imposition of a fee, in respect of any matter relating to a comparable trade mark (EU) (see instead provision made by regulations under Schedule 4 to the European Union (Withdrawal) Act 2018).

(8) For the purposes of this Act—

(a) the date of filing of an application for registration of a comparable trade mark (EU) is the filing date accorded pursuant to Article 32 to the application which resulted in the registration of the corresponding EUTM;
(b) references to the date of application for registration of a comparable trade mark (EU) are to the date of filing of the application;
(c) where an earlier trade mark is a comparable trade mark (EU), references to the completion of the registration procedure for the earlier trade mark are to the completion of the registration procedure in respect of the corresponding EUTM.

(9) In this Schedule—

(a) "corresponding EUTM", in relation to a comparable trade mark (EU), means the existing EUTM from which the comparable trade mark (EU) derives;
(b) "the EUTM Register" means the register of European Union trade marks maintained by the European Union Intellectual Property Office.][2]

NOTES

1 Substituted by Intellectual Property (Amendment etc.) (EU Exit) Regulations 2020, SI 2020/1050, regs 7, 9(b)(i) (31 December 2020).

2 Inserted by Trade Marks (Amendment etc.) (EU Exit) Regulations 2019, SI 2019/269, reg 2, Sch 1, paras 1, 3 (31 January 2020).

[2 Opt out

(1) Subject to sub-paragraph (2), the proprietor of an existing EUTM may, at any time on or after [IP completion day][1], serve notice on the registrar that the trade mark is not to be treated as if the trade mark had been registered under this Act (an "opt out notice").

(2) An opt out notice may not be served where on or after [IP completion day][1]—

(a) the comparable trade mark (EU) has been put to use in the United Kingdom by the proprietor or with the proprietor's consent (which use includes affixing the trade mark to goods or to the packaging of goods in the United Kingdom solely for export purposes);
(b) the comparable trade mark (EU) (or any right in or under it) has been made the subject of an assignment, licence, security interest or any other agreement or document except for an assent by personal representatives in relation to the comparable trade mark (EU); or
(c) proceedings based on the comparable trade mark (EU) have been initiated by the proprietor or with the proprietor's consent.

(3) An opt out notice must—

(a) identify the existing EUTM; and
(b) include the name and address of any person having an interest in the existing EUTM which had effect before [IP completion day][1] in the United Kingdom, and in respect of which an entry was recorded in the EUTM Register.

(4) An opt out notice is of no effect unless the proprietor in that notice certifies that any such person—

(a) has been given not less than three months' notice of the proprietor's intention to serve an opt out notice; or
(b) is not affected or if affected, consents to the opt out.

(5) Where a notice has been served in accordance with this paragraph—

(a) the comparable trade mark (EU) which derives from the existing EUTM ceases with effect from [IP completion day][1] to be treated as if it had been registered under this Act; and
(b) the registrar must, where particulars of the comparable trade mark (EU) have been entered in the register, remove the comparable trade mark (EU) from the register.][2]

NOTES

1 Substituted by Intellectual Property (Amendment etc.) (EU Exit) Regulations 2020, SI 2020/1050, regs 7, 9(b)(i) (31 December 2020).
2 Inserted by Trade Marks (Amendment etc.) (EU Exit) Regulations 2019, SI 2019/269, reg 2, Sch 1, paras 1, 3 (31 January 2020).

[3 Entries to be made in the register in relation to a comparable trade mark (EU)

(1) The registrar must as soon as reasonably practicable after [IP completion day][1] enter a comparable trade mark (EU) in the register.

(2) The particulars of the goods or services in respect of which the comparable trade mark (EU) is treated as if it had been registered must be taken from the English language version of the entry for the corresponding EUTM in the EUTM Register.

(3) Where—

(a) the application for registration of the corresponding EUTM was not filed in English; or
(b) the second language indicated by the applicant pursuant to Article 146(3) was a language other than English,

a person having a sufficient interest who considers that the English language version is inaccurate may apply to the registrar for rectification of the register by the substitution of an English translation of the relevant authentic text (as determined in accordance with Article 147(3)) verified to the satisfaction of the registrar as corresponding to the authentic text.][2]

NOTES

1 Substituted by Intellectual Property (Amendment etc.) (EU Exit) Regulations 2020, SI 2020/1050, regs 7, 9(b)(i) (31 December 2020).
2 Inserted by Trade Marks (Amendment etc.) (EU Exit) Regulations 2019, SI 2019/269, reg 2, Sch 1, paras 1, 3 (31 January 2020).

[4 Comparable trade mark (EU) which derives from an EU Collective Mark or EU Certification Mark

(1) This paragraph applies where the European Union trade mark from which a comparable trade mark (EU) derives is an EU collective mark or an EU certification mark.

(2) The comparable trade mark (EU) is to be treated as either a collective mark or a certification mark, as the case may be.

(3) The proprietor of the comparable trade mark (EU) must, following notice from the registrar, file with the registrar regulations governing the use of the European Union trade mark, submitted pursuant to the European Union Trade Mark Regulation, which had effect immediately before [IP completion day][1].

(4) Where the regulations referred to in sub-paragraph (3) are in a language other than English they must be filed together with a translation into English verified to the satisfaction of the registrar as corresponding to the original text.

(5) Paragraph 9 of Schedule 1 and paragraph 10 of Schedule 2 apply in relation to the translation referred to in sub-paragraph (4) as they apply in relation to the regulations referred to in sub-paragraph (3).

(6) Where the regulations or any translation are not filed in accordance with the above provisions—

(a) the registrar must remove the comparable trade mark (EU) from the register; and

(b) the rights of the proprietor shall be deemed to have ceased as from the date of removal.][2]

NOTES

1 Substituted by Intellectual Property (Amendment etc.) (EU Exit) Regulations 2020, SI 2020/1050, regs 7, 9(b)(i) (31 December 2020).

2 Inserted by Trade Marks (Amendment etc.) (EU Exit) Regulations 2019, SI 2019/269, reg 2, Sch 1, paras 1, 3 (31 January 2020).

[5 Renewal of a comparable trade mark (EU) which expires within six months after [IP completion day] 1

(1) This paragraph applies to the renewal of the registration of a comparable trade mark (EU) which expires within the period beginning with [IP completion day][1] and ending with the end of the relevant period (and accordingly section 43(1) to (3A) does not apply).

(2) The registration of the comparable trade mark (EU) may be renewed at the request of the proprietor before the expiry of the registration.

(3) Where the registration of the comparable trade mark (EU) is not renewed in accordance with sub-paragraph (2)—

(a) on, or as soon as reasonably practicable after, the expiry of the registration, the registrar must notify the proprietor that the registration has expired and of the manner in which the registration may be renewed; and

(b) a request for renewal must be made within the period of six months beginning with the date of the notice.

(4) If a request for renewal is made in respect of only some of the goods or services for which the comparable trade mark (EU) is registered, the registration is to be renewed for those goods or services only.

(5) If the registration is not renewed in accordance with the above provisions, the registrar must remove the comparable trade mark (EU) from the register.

(6) Section 43(4) and (6) applies to the registration of a comparable trade mark (EU) which is renewed in accordance with the above provisions.

(7) In paragraph (1), the "relevant period" means the period of six months beginning with the day after that on which [IP completion day][1] falls.][2]

NOTES

1 Substituted by Intellectual Property (Amendment etc.) (EU Exit) Regulations 2020, SI 2020/1050, regs 7, 9(b)(i) (31 December 2020).

2 Inserted by Trade Marks (Amendment etc.) (EU Exit) Regulations 2019, SI 2019/269, reg 2, Sch 1, paras 1, 3 (31 January 2020).

[6 Restoration of a comparable trade mark (EU)

Where a comparable trade mark (EU) is removed from the register pursuant to paragraph 5, the rules relating to the restoration of the registration of a trade mark (referred to in section 43(5)) apply in relation to the restoration of the comparable trade mark (EU) to the register.][1]

NOTES

1 Inserted by Trade Marks (Amendment etc.) (EU Exit) Regulations 2019, SI 2019/269, reg 2, Sch 1, paras 1, 3 (31 January 2020).

[7 Raising of relative grounds in opposition proceedings in case of non-use

(1) Section 6A applies where an earlier trade mark is a comparable trade mark (EU), subject to the modifications set out below.

(2) Where the relevant period referred to in section 6A(3)(a) (the "five-year period") has expired before [IP completion day][1]—

(a) the references in section 6A(3) and (6) to the earlier trade mark are to be treated as references to the corresponding EUTM; and

(b) the references in section 6A(3) and (4) to the United Kingdom include the European Union.

(3) Where [IP completion day][1] falls within the five-year period, in respect of that part of the five-year period which falls before [IP completion day][1]—

(a) the references in section 6A(3) and (6) to the earlier trade mark are to be treated as references to the corresponding EUTM ; and

(b) the references in section 6A to the United Kingdom include the European Union.][2]

NOTES

1 Substituted by Intellectual Property (Amendment etc.) (EU Exit) Regulations 2020, SI 2020/1050, regs 7, 9(b)(i) (31 December 2020).

2 Inserted by Trade Marks (Amendment etc.) (EU Exit) Regulations 2019, SI 2019/269, reg 2, Sch 1, paras 1, 3 (31 January 2020).

[8 Non-use as defence in infringement proceedings and revocation of registration of a comparable trade mark (EU)

(1) Sections 11A and 46 apply in relation to a comparable trade mark (EU), subject to the modifications set out below.

(2) Where the period of five years referred to in sections 11A(3)(a) and 46(1)(a) or (b) (the "five-year period") has expired before [IP completion day][1]—

(a) the references in sections 11A(3) and (insofar as they relate to use of a trade mark) 46 to a trade mark are to be treated as references to the corresponding EUTM; and

(b) the references in sections 11A and 46 to the United Kingdom include the European Union.

(3) Where [IP completion day][1] falls within the five-year period, in respect of that part of the five-year period which falls before [IP completion day][1]—

(a) the references in sections 11A(3) and (insofar as they relate to use of a trade mark) 46 to a trade mark, are to be treated as references to the corresponding EUTM ; and

(b) the references in sections 11A and 46 to the United Kingdom include the European Union.][2]

NOTES

1 Substituted by Intellectual Property (Amendment etc.) (EU Exit) Regulations 2020, SI 2020/1050, regs 7, 9(b)(i) (31 December 2020).

2 Inserted by Trade Marks (Amendment etc.) (EU Exit) Regulations 2019, SI 2019/269, reg 2, Sch 1, paras 1, 3 (31 January 2020).

[9 Grounds for invalidity of registration of a trade mark based upon an earlier comparable trade mark (EU)

(1) Section 47 applies where an earlier trade mark is a comparable trade mark (EU), subject to the modifications set out below.

(2) Where the period of five years referred to in sections 47(2A)(a) and 47(2B) (the "five-year period") has expired before [IP completion day][1]—

(a) the references in section 47(2B) and (2E) to the earlier trade mark are to be treated as references to the corresponding EUTM ; and

(b) the references in section 47 to the United Kingdom include the European Union.

(3) Where [IP completion day][1] falls within the five-year period, in respect of that part of the five-year period which falls before [IP completion day][1]—

(a) the references in section 47(2B) and (2E) to the earlier trade mark are to be treated as references to the corresponding EUTM ; and

(b) the references in section 47 to the United Kingdom include the European Union.][2]

NOTES

1 Substituted by Intellectual Property (Amendment etc.) (EU Exit) Regulations 2020, SI 2020/1050, regs 7, 9(b)(i) (31 December 2020).

2 Inserted by Trade Marks (Amendment etc.) (EU Exit) Regulations 2019, SI 2019/269, reg 2, Sch 1, paras 1, 3 (31 January 2020).

[10 Reputation of a comparable trade mark (EU)

(1) Sections 5 and 10 apply in relation to a comparable trade mark (EU), subject to the modifications set out below.

(2) Where the reputation of a comparable trade mark (EU) falls to be considered in respect of any time before [IP completion day][1], references in sections 5(3) and 10(3) to—

(a) the reputation of the mark are to be treated as references to the reputation of the corresponding EUTM; and
(b) the United Kingdom include the European Union.][2]

NOTES
1 Substituted by Intellectual Property (Amendment etc.) (EU Exit) Regulations 2020, SI 2020/1050, regs 7, 9(b)(i) (31 December 2020).
2 Inserted by Trade Marks (Amendment etc.) (EU Exit) Regulations 2019, SI 2019/269, reg 2, Sch 1, paras 1, 3 (31 January 2020).

[11 Rights conferred by registered trade mark

Section 9 applies in relation to a comparable trade mark (EU) but as if—

(a) the words in brackets in subsection (3) referring to section 40(3) were replaced with a reference to paragraph 1(4) of this Schedule; and
(b) the proviso in subsection (3) were omitted.][1]

NOTES
1 Inserted by Trade Marks (Amendment etc.) (EU Exit) Regulations 2019, SI 2019/269, reg 2, Sch 1, paras 1, 3 (31 January 2020).

[12 Effect of claim of priority

(1) This paragraph applies where—

(a) the proprietor of an existing EUTM has claimed a right of priority in accordance with Article 35; and
(b) immediately before [IP completion day][1] there is an entry in the EUTM Register containing particulars of that claim of priority (a "claim of priority").

(2) The proprietor of the comparable trade mark (EU) which derives from the existing EUTM is to be treated on and after [IP completion day][1] as having the same claim of priority.

(3) Accordingly, the relevant date for the purposes of establishing, in relation to the comparable trade mark (EU), which rights take precedence is the date of filing of the application for a trade mark in a Convention country which formed the basis for the claim of priority.][2]

NOTES
1 Substituted by Intellectual Property (Amendment etc.) (EU Exit) Regulations 2020, SI 2020/1050, regs 7, 9(b)(i) (31 December 2020).
2 Inserted by Trade Marks (Amendment etc.) (EU Exit) Regulations 2019, SI 2019/269, reg 2, Sch 1, paras 1, 3 (31 January 2020).

[13 Effect of seniority claim

(1) This paragraph applies where immediately before [IP completion day][1] an existing EUTM has a valid claim to seniority of a trade mark which trade mark (the "senior mark") is a registered trade mark or a protected international trade mark (UK).

(2) The comparable trade mark (EU) which derives from the existing EUTM is to be treated on and after [IP completion day][1] as if it had a valid claim to seniority of the senior mark.

(3) Accordingly, where the proprietor of the comparable trade mark (EU) surrenders the senior mark or allows it to lapse (whether wholly or partially), subject to paragraph 14, the proprietor of the comparable trade mark (EU) is deemed to continue to have the same rights as the proprietor would have had if the senior mark had continued to be registered in respect of all the goods or services for which it was registered prior to the surrender or lapse.

(4) An existing EUTM has a valid claim to seniority of a trade mark where—

(a) a claim has been filed in accordance with Article 39 or 40; and
(b) the seniority claimed for the existing EUTM has not lapsed in the circumstances referred to in Article 39.][2]

NOTES

1 Substituted by Intellectual Property (Amendment etc.) (EU Exit) Regulations 2020, SI 2020/1050, regs 7, 9(b)(i) (31 December 2020).
2 Inserted by Trade Marks (Amendment etc.) (EU Exit) Regulations 2019, SI 2019/269, reg 2, Sch 1, paras 1, 3 (31 January 2020).

[14 Determination of invalidity and liability to revocation in relation to claims of seniority

(1) Where pursuant to paragraph 13 a comparable trade mark (EU) is treated as if it had a valid claim to seniority of a registered trade mark which has been—

(a) removed from the register under section 43; or
(b) surrendered under section 45,

any person may apply to the registrar or to the court for the declaration set out in sub-paragraph (2).

(2) The declaration is that if the trade mark had not been so removed or surrendered, the registration of the trade mark would have been liable to be revoked under section 46 with effect from a date specified in the declaration or declared invalid under section 47.

(3) Where the declaration is that had the trade mark not been so removed or surrendered the registration of it would have been liable to be—

(a) revoked under section 46 with effect from a date prior to—
    (i) the filing date accorded pursuant to Article 32 to the application which resulted in the registration of the existing EUTM from which the comparable trade mark (EU) derives where there has been no claim of priority; or

(ii) the priority date (if any) accorded pursuant to a right of priority claimed pursuant to Article 35 in respect of the existing EUTM from which the comparable trade mark (EU) derives where there has been a claim of priority; or

(b) declared invalid under section 47,

the seniority claimed for the comparable trade mark (EU) is to be treated as if it never had effect.

(4) Where pursuant to paragraph 13 a comparable trade mark (EU) is treated as if it had a valid claim to seniority of a protected international trade mark (UK) which has been—

(a) removed from the register of trade marks maintained by the International Bureau for the purposes of the Madrid Protocol; or
(b) surrendered under the Madrid Protocol,

any person may apply to the registrar or to the court for the declaration set out in sub-paragraph (5).

(5) The declaration is that, if the trade mark had not been so removed or surrendered, the protection of the mark in the United Kingdom would have been liable to be revoked under section 46 with effect from a date specified in the declaration or declared invalid under section 47.

(6) Where the declaration is that had the trade mark not been so removed or surrendered the protection of the mark in the United Kingdom would have been liable to be—

(a) revoked under section 46 with effect from a date prior to—
  (i) the filing date accorded pursuant to Article 32 to the application which resulted in the registration of the existing EUTM from which the comparable trade mark (EU) derives where there has been no claim of priority; or
  (ii) the priority date (if any) accorded pursuant to a right of priority claimed pursuant to Article 35 in respect of the existing EUTM from which the comparable trade mark (EU) derives where there has been a claim of priority; or
(b) declared invalid under section 47,

the seniority claimed for the comparable trade mark (EU) is to be treated as if it never had effect.

(7) References in sub-paragraphs (5) and (6) to sections 46 and 47 are to those sections as they apply to a protected international trade mark (UK) under an order made pursuant to section 54.

(8) Where a trade mark has been surrendered or allowed to lapse in respect of some only of the goods or services for which it is registered, the declaration in sub-paragraphs (2) and (5) is that if the goods or services had not been removed from the registration, the registration of the trade mark would have been liable to be revoked under section 46 with effect from a date specified in the declaration or declared invalid under section 47 and sub-paragraphs (3) and (6) shall be construed accordingly.][1]

NOTES

1 Inserted by Trade Marks (Amendment etc.) (EU Exit) Regulations 2019, SI 2019/269, reg 2, Sch 1, paras 1, 3 (31 January 2020).

[15 Procedure for declaration that trade mark would have been liable to be revoked or declared invalid

(1) In the case of proceedings on an application under paragraph 14 before the registrar, the rules relating to applications for and proceedings relating to the revocation or invalidation of a trade mark apply, with necessary modifications.

(2) In the case of proceedings on an application under paragraph 14 before the court, section 74 applies to the proceedings as it applies to proceedings involving an application of the type referred to in section 74(1)(a) to (c).][1]

NOTES

1 Inserted by Trade Marks (Amendment etc.) (EU Exit) Regulations 2019, SI 2019/269, reg 2, Sch 1, paras 1, 3 (31 January 2020).

[16 Assignment of an existing EUTM not registered on [IP completion day]1

(1) This paragraph applies where before [IP completion day][1] an existing EUTM (or any right in it) is the subject of an assignment (a "relevant assignment") which immediately before [IP completion day][1] is not recorded in the EUTM Register.

(2) Section 25 applies in relation to a relevant assignment as if it were a registrable transaction affecting a comparable trade mark (EU), subject to the modification set out below.

(3) An application under section 25(1) may only be made by—

(a) a person claiming to be entitled to an interest in or under a comparable trade mark (EU) by virtue of a relevant assignment of the corresponding EUTM; or

(b) the proprietor of the comparable trade mark (EU).][2]

NOTES

1 Substituted by Intellectual Property (Amendment etc.) (EU Exit) Regulations 2020, SI 2020/1050, regs 7, 9(b)(i) (31 December 2020).

2 Inserted by Trade Marks (Amendment etc.) (EU Exit) Regulations 2019, SI 2019/269, reg 2, Sch 1, paras 1, 3 (31 January 2020).

[17 Effect of a licence of an existing EUTM

(1) This paragraph applies where immediately before [IP completion day][1] an existing EUTM is the subject of a licence (a "relevant licence") which—

(a) authorises the doing of acts in the United Kingdom which would otherwise infringe the European Union trade mark; and

(b) does not expire on [IP completion day][1].

(2) Subject to any agreement to the contrary between the licensee and the licensor, a relevant licence continues to authorise the doing of acts in the United Kingdom which would otherwise infringe the comparable trade mark (EU) which derives from the existing EUTM.

(3) Sub-paragraph (2) is subject to—

(a) the terms on which the relevant licence was granted; and
(b) such modifications to the terms referred to in paragraph (a) as are necessary for their application in the United Kingdom.

(4) Section 25 applies in relation to a relevant licence as if it were a registrable transaction affecting a comparable trade mark (EU), subject to the modifications set out below.

(5) An application under section 25(1) may only be made by—

(a) a person claiming to be a licensee by virtue of the relevant licence; or
(b) the proprietor of the comparable trade mark (EU).

(6) Where immediately before [IP completion day][1] there is an entry in the EUTM Register relating to a relevant licence—

(a) section 25(3) and (4) does not apply until after the expiry of the relevant period; and
(b) section 25(4)(a) applies after the expiry of the relevant period but as if the reference to six months beginning with the date of the transaction were a reference to eighteen months beginning with [IP completion day][1].

(7) In paragraph (6)(a), the "relevant period" means the period of twelve months beginning with the day after that on which [IP completion day][1] falls.][2]

NOTES

1 Substituted by Intellectual Property (Amendment etc.) (EU Exit) Regulations 2020, SI 2020/1050, regs 7, 9(b)(i) (31 December 2020).
2 Inserted by Trade Marks (Amendment etc.) (EU Exit) Regulations 2019, SI 2019/269, reg 2, Sch 1, paras 1, 3 (31 January 2020).

[18 Effect of a security interest in an existing EUTM

(1) This paragraph applies where immediately before [IP completion day][1] an existing EUTM (or any right in or under it) is the subject of a security interest (a "relevant security interest") which does not terminate on [IP completion day][1].

(2) References to the existing EUTM in any document which grants or refers to the relevant security interest are to be read as including references to the comparable trade mark (EU) which derives from the existing EUTM.

(3) Section 25 applies in relation to a relevant security interest as if it were a registrable transaction affecting a comparable trade mark (EU), subject to the modifications set out below.

(4) An application under section 25(1) may only be made by—

(a) a person claiming to be entitled to an interest in or under a comparable trade mark (EU) by virtue of the relevant security interest; or
(b) the proprietor of the comparable trade mark (EU).

(5) Where immediately before [IP completion day][1] there is an entry in the EUTM Register relating to a relevant security interest—

(a) section 25(3) and (4) do not apply until after the expiry of the relevant period; and
(b) section 25(4)(a) applies after the expiry of the relevant period but as if the reference to six months beginning with the date of the transaction were a reference to eighteen months beginning with [IP completion day][1].

(6) In paragraph (5)(a), the "relevant period" means the period of twelve months beginning with the day after that on which [IP completion day][1] falls.][2]

NOTES

1 Substituted by Intellectual Property (Amendment etc.) (EU Exit) Regulations 2020, SI 2020/1050, regs 7, 9(b)(i) (31 December 2020).

2 Inserted by Trade Marks (Amendment etc.) (EU Exit) Regulations 2019, SI 2019/269, reg 2, Sch 1, paras 1, 3 (31 January 2020).

[19 Continuity of rights in relation to a comparable trade mark (EU)

(1) References to an existing EUTM or the registration of an existing EUTM in any document made before [IP completion day][1] shall, unless there is evidence that the document was not intended to have effect in the United Kingdom, be read on and after [IP completion day][1] as including references to the comparable trade mark (EU) or the registration of the comparable trade mark (EU) which derives from the existing EUTM.

(2) Subject to any agreement to the contrary, a consent granted before [IP completion day][1] by the proprietor of an existing EUTM to the doing on or after [IP completion day][1] of an act in the United Kingdom which would otherwise infringe the comparable trade mark (EU) which derives from the existing EUTM is to be treated for the purposes of section 9 as a consent to the doing of that act.][2]

NOTES

1 Substituted by Intellectual Property (Amendment etc.) (EU Exit) Regulations 2020, SI 2020/1050, regs 7, 9(b)(i) (31 December 2020).

2 Inserted by Trade Marks (Amendment etc.) (EU Exit) Regulations 2019, SI 2019/269, reg 2, Sch 1, paras 1, 3 (31 January 2020).

[20 Existing EUTM: pending proceedings

(1) This paragraph applies where on [IP completion day][1] an existing EUTM is the subject of proceedings which are pending ("pending proceedings") before a court in the United Kingdom designated for the purposes of Article 123 ("EU trade mark court").

(2) Subject to sub-paragraphs (3) and (4), the provisions contained or referred to in Chapter 10 of the European Union Trade Mark Regulation (with the exception of Articles 128(2), (4), (6) and (7) and 132) continue to apply to the pending proceedings as if the United Kingdom were still a Member State with effect from [IP completion day][1].

(3) Where the pending proceedings involve a claim for infringement of an existing EUTM, without prejudice to any other relief by way of damages, accounts or otherwise available to the proprietor of the existing EUTM, the EU trade mark

court may grant an injunction to prohibit unauthorised use of the comparable trade mark (EU) which derives from the existing EUTM.

(4) Where the pending proceedings involve a counterclaim for the revocation of, or a declaration of invalidity in relation to, an existing EUTM, the EU trade mark court may revoke the registration of the comparable trade mark (EU) which derives from the existing EUTM or declare the registration of the comparable trade mark (EU) which derives from the existing EUTM to be invalid.

(5) Where the grounds for revocation or invalidity exist in respect of only some of the goods or services for which the existing EUTM is registered, the revocation or declaration of invalidity in respect of the registration of the comparable trade mark (EU) which derives from the existing EUTM relates to those goods or services only.

(6) Where (by virtue of sub-paragraph (4)) the registration of a comparable trade mark (EU) is revoked to any extent, the rights of the proprietor are deemed to have ceased to that extent as from—

(a) the date of the counterclaim for revocation, or
(b) if the court is satisfied that the grounds for revocation existed at an earlier date, that date.

(7) Where (by virtue of sub-paragraph (4)) the registration of a comparable trade mark (EU) is declared invalid to any extent, the registration is to that extent to be deemed never to have been made, provided that this does not affect transactions past and closed.

(8) For the purposes of this paragraph proceedings are treated as pending on [IP completion day][1] if they were instituted but not finally determined before [IP completion day][1].][2]

NOTES

1 Substituted by Intellectual Property (Amendment etc.) (EU Exit) Regulations 2020, SI 2020/1050, regs 7, 9(b)(i) (31 December 2020).
2 Inserted by Trade Marks (Amendment etc.) (EU Exit) Regulations 2019, SI 2019/269, reg 2, Sch 1, paras 1, 3 (31 January 2020).

[21 Existing EUTM: effect of injunction

(1) This paragraph applies where immediately before [IP completion day][1] an injunction is in force prohibiting the performance of acts in the United Kingdom which infringe or would infringe an existing EUTM (a "relevant injunction").

(2) Subject to any order of the court to the contrary, a relevant injunction will have effect and be enforceable to prohibit the performance of acts which infringe or would infringe a comparable trade mark (EU) to the same extent as in relation to the European Union trade mark from which the comparable trade mark (EU) derives as if it were an injunction granted by the court.][2]

NOTES

1 Substituted by Intellectual Property (Amendment etc.) (EU Exit) Regulations 2020, SI 2020/1050, regs 7, 9(b)(i) (31 December 2020).
2 Inserted by Trade Marks (Amendment etc.) (EU Exit) Regulations 2019, SI 2019/269, reg 2, Sch 1, paras 1, 3 (31 January 2020).

[21A Existing EUTM: effect of invalidity or revocation

(1) This paragraph applies where, on IP completion day, an existing EUTM is the subject of proceedings under Article 58 (Grounds for revocation), 59 (Absolute grounds for invalidity) or 60 (Relative grounds for invalidity) which have been instituted but not finally determined before IP completion day ("cancellation proceedings").

(2) Subject to sub-paragraph (4), where—

(a) the existing EUTM is revoked or declared invalid (whether wholly or partially) pursuant to a decision in the cancellation proceedings which is finally determined, and
(b) the registrar has—
    (i) received notice of the situation referred to in paragraph (a) ("a cancellation notice"), or
    (ii) otherwise become aware of the situation referred to in paragraph (a),

the registration of the comparable trade mark (EU) which derives from the existing EUTM must be revoked or declared invalid to the same extent as the existing EUTM.

(3) Where (by virtue of sub-paragraph (2)) the registration of a comparable trade mark (EU) is revoked or declared invalid to any extent, the registrar must—

(a) remove the comparable trade mark (EU) from the register (where the revocation or declaration of invalidity relates to all the goods or services for which the existing EUTM was registered); or
(b) amend the entry in the register listing the goods or services for which the comparable trade mark (EU) is registered (where the revocation or declaration of invalidity relates to only some of the goods or services for which the existing EUTM was registered).

(4) The registration of a comparable trade mark (EU) must not be revoked or declared invalid under sub-paragraph (2) where the grounds on which the existing EUTM was revoked or declared invalid (whether wholly or partially) would not apply or would not have been satisfied in relation to the comparable trade mark (EU)—

(a) if the comparable trade mark (EU) had existed as at the date the cancellation proceedings were instituted, and
(b) an application for the revocation or a declaration of invalidity of the comparable trade mark (EU) based on those grounds had been made on that date under section 46 or 47 (as the case may be).

(5) Where a comparable trade mark (EU) is revoked or declared invalid to any extent pursuant to this paragraph—

(a) the rights of the proprietor are deemed to have ceased to that extent as from the date on which the rights of the proprietor of the existing EUTM are deemed to have ceased under the EUTM Regulation;
(b) subject to any claim for compensation for damage caused by negligence or lack of good faith on the part of the proprietor or a claim for restitution based upon the unjust enrichment of the proprietor, the revocation or invalidity of the comparable trade mark (EU) does not affect—

(i) a decision arising from infringement proceedings which has been finally determined and which has been enforced prior to the date on which the entry in the register of the comparable trade mark (EU) has been removed or amended pursuant to sub-paragraph (3) ("the decision date");
(ii) any contract entered into prior to the decision date to the extent that it has been performed prior to the decision date, subject to the right of a party to the contract to claim the repayment of any consideration paid under the contract where, having regard to the circumstances, it is fair and equitable for such repayment to be made.

(6) A cancellation notice may be submitted to the registrar by any person.

(7) For the purposes of this paragraph—

(a) proceedings are instituted if an application or counterclaim for revocation or for a declaration of invalidity—
(i) has been filed (and not subsequently withdrawn) with the European Union Intellectual Property Office or a court designated for the purposes of Article 123, and
(ii) meets the requirements for being accorded a filing date under the European Union Trade Mark Regulation and Commission Delegated Regulation (EU) 2018/625 of 5th March 2018;
(b) a decision is finally determined when—
(i) it has been determined, and
(ii) there is no further possibility of the determination being varied or set aside (disregarding any power to grant permission to appeal out of time).][1]

NOTES

1 Inserted by Intellectual Property (Amendment etc.) (EU Exit) Regulations 2020, SI 2020/1050, regs 7, 9(b)(ii) (31 December 2020).

[PART 2 TREATMENT OF EUROPEAN UNION TRADE MARKS WHICH EXPIRE DURING THE PERIOD OF SIX MONTHS ENDING ON [IP COMPLETION DAY][1]

22 Registration of certain expired European Union trade marks

(1) This Part applies to a trade mark which was registered in the EUTM Register immediately before the transitional period but which, as a result of the expiry of the registration of the European Union trade mark during the transitional period, does not fall within paragraph 1(1) (an "expired EUTM").

(2) An expired EUTM is to be treated as if it were an existing EUTM.

(3) The provisions of Part 1 of this Schedule apply to an expired EUTM as they apply to an existing EUTM subject to the provisions of this Part of the Schedule.

(4) Notwithstanding the entry in the register (under paragraph 3, as applied by sub-paragraph (3)) of a comparable trade mark (EU) which derives from an expired EUTM, the registration of the comparable trade mark (EU) is expired

until it is renewed in accordance with paragraph 23 (or the comparable trade mark (EU) is removed from the register in accordance with paragraph 23(4)).

(5) In this paragraph, "transitional period" means the period of six months ending with [IP completion day][1].][2]

NOTES

1 Substituted by Intellectual Property (Amendment etc.) (EU Exit) Regulations 2020, SI 2020/1050, regs 7, 9(b)(i) (31 December 2020).
2 Inserted by Trade Marks (Amendment etc.) (EU Exit) Regulations 2019, SI 2019/269, reg 2, Sch 1, paras 1, 3 (31 January 2020).

[23 Renewal of an expired EUTM

(1) Where the registration of an expired EUTM is renewed in accordance with Article 53 of the Continuing EUTM Regulation the registrar must, as soon as reasonably practicable after the date of such renewal, renew the registration of the comparable trade mark (EU) which derives from the expired EUTM.

(2) A comparable trade mark (EU) which is renewed under sub-paragraph (1) shall be renewed for a period of ten years from the expiry of the registration of the expired EUTM.

(3) If the registration of an expired EUTM is renewed in respect of only some of the goods or services in respect of which the expired EUTM was registered before its registration expired, the registration of the comparable trade mark (EU) under sub-paragraph (1) is to be renewed for those goods or services only.

(4) If the registration of an expired EUTM is not renewed within the time period permitted by Article 53 of the Continuing EUTM Regulation—

(a) the registrar must remove from the register the comparable trade mark (EU) which derives from the expired EUTM; and
(b) the comparable trade mark (EU) ceases with effect from [IP completion day][1] to be treated as if it had been registered under this Act.

(5) In this Schedule, the "Continuing EUTM Regulation" means Regulation (EU) 2017/1001 of the European Parliament and of the Council of 14 June 2017 on the European Union Trade Mark F5 as it has effect in EU law.][2]

NOTES

1 Substituted by Intellectual Property (Amendment etc.) (EU Exit) Regulations 2020, SI 2020/1050, regs 7, 9(b)(i) (31 December 2020).
2 Inserted by Trade Marks (Amendment etc.) (EU Exit) Regulations 2019, SI 2019/269, reg 2, Sch 1, paras 1, 3 (31 January 2020).

[PART 3 APPLICATIONS FOR EUROPEAN UNION TRADE MARKS WHICH ARE PENDING ON [IP COMPLETION DAY][1]

24 Application of Part

(1) This Part applies to an application for registration of a trade mark under the EUTM Regulation in respect of which the conditions in sub-paragraph (2) are satisfied (an "existing EUTM application").

(2) The conditions referred to in sub-paragraph (1) are—

(a) the application has been accorded a filing date pursuant to Article 32; and
(b) as at the time immediately before [IP completion day][1], the application has been neither granted nor refused by the European Union Intellectual Property Office.][2]

NOTES

1 Substituted by Intellectual Property (Amendment etc.) (EU Exit) Regulations 2020, SI 2020/1050, regs 7, 9(b)(i) (31 December 2020).
2 Inserted by Trade Marks (Amendment etc.) (EU Exit) Regulations 2019, SI 2019/269, reg 2, Sch 1, paras 1, 3 (31 January 2020).

[25 Application for registration under this Act based upon an existing EUTM application

(1) This paragraph applies where a person who has filed an existing EUTM application or a successor in title of that person applies for registration of the same trade mark under this Act for some or all of the same goods or services.

(2) Where an application for registration referred to in sub-paragraph (1) is made within a period beginning with [IP completion day][1] and ending with the end of the relevant period—

(a) the relevant date for the purposes of establishing which rights take precedence is the earliest of—
   (i) the filing date accorded pursuant to Article 32 to the existing EUTM application;
   (ii) the date of priority (if any) accorded pursuant to a right of priority claimed pursuant to Article 35 in respect of the existing EUTM application; and
(b) the registrability of the trade mark shall not be affected by any use of the mark in the United Kingdom which commenced in the period between the date referred to in paragraph (a) and the date of the application under this Act.

(3) In paragraph (2), the "relevant period" means the period of nine months beginning with the day after that on which [IP completion day][1] falls.][2]

NOTES

1 Substituted by Intellectual Property (Amendment etc.) (EU Exit) Regulations 2020, SI 2020/1050, regs 7, 9(b)(i) (31 December 2020).
2 Inserted by Trade Marks (Amendment etc.) (EU Exit) Regulations 2019, SI 2019/269, reg 2, Sch 1, paras 1, 3 (31 January 2020).

[26 Right to claim seniority where seniority has been claimed by an existing EUTM application

(1) Where an existing EUTM application claims seniority of a trade mark which trade mark ("the senior mark") is a registered trade mark or a protected international trade mark (UK), the applicant may claim seniority of the senior mark in an application for registration of a trade mark ("a relevant mark") pursuant to this Part.

(2) The effect of a seniority claim made pursuant to sub-paragraph (1) is that where following the registration of the relevant mark the proprietor of that mark surrenders the senior mark or allows it to lapse (wholly or partially), subject to paragraph 27, the proprietor of the relevant mark is deemed to continue to have the same rights as the proprietor would have had if the senior mark had continued to be registered in respect of all the goods or services for which it was registered prior to the surrender or lapse.

(3) Provision may be made by rules as to the manner of claiming seniority pursuant to this paragraph.][1]

NOTES

1 Inserted by Trade Marks (Amendment etc.) (EU Exit) Regulations 2019, SI 2019/269, reg 2, Sch 1, paras 1, 3 (31 January 2020).

[27 Determination of invalidity and liability to revocation in relation to claim of seniority under paragraph 26

(1) Where a relevant mark has claimed seniority of a registered trade mark which has been—

(a) removed from the register under section 43; or
(b) surrendered under section 45,

any person may apply to the registrar or to the court for the declaration set out in sub-paragraph (2).

(2) The declaration is that, if the trade mark had not been so removed or surrendered, the registration of the trade mark would have been liable to be revoked under section 46 with effect from a date specified in the declaration or declared invalid under section 47.

(3) Where the declaration is that had the trade mark not been so removed or surrendered, the registration of it would have been liable to be—

(a) revoked under section 46 with effect from a date prior to—
 (i) the filing date accorded pursuant to Article 32 to the existing EUTM application on which the application for registration of a relevant mark is based where there has been no claim of priority; or
 (ii) the priority date (if any) accorded pursuant to a right of priority claimed pursuant to Article 35 in respect of the existing EUTM application on which the registration of a relevant mark is based where there has been a claim of priority; or
(b) declared invalid under section 47,

the seniority claimed for the relevant mark is to be treated as if it never had effect.

(4) Where a relevant mark has claimed seniority of a protected international trade mark (UK) which has been—

(a) removed from the register of trade marks maintained by the International Bureau for the purposes of the Madrid Protocol; or
(b) surrendered under the Madrid Protocol,

any person may apply to the registrar or to the court for the declaration set out in sub-paragraph (5).

(5) The declaration is that, if the trade mark had not been so removed or surrendered, the protection of the trade mark in the United Kingdom would have been liable to be revoked under section 46 with effect from a date specified in the declaration or declared invalid under section 47.

(6) Where the declaration is that had the trade mark not been so removed or surrendered, the registration of it would have been liable to be—

(a) revoked under section 46 with effect from a date prior to—
  (i) the filing date accorded pursuant to Article 32 to the existing EUTM application on which the application for registration of a relevant mark is based where there has been no claim of priority; or
  (ii) the priority date (if any) accorded pursuant to a right of priority claimed pursuant to Article 35 in respect of the existing EUTM application on which the registration of a relevant mark is based where there has been a claim of priority; or
(b) declared invalid under section 47,

the seniority claimed for the relevant mark is to be treated as if it never had effect.

(7) References in sub-paragraphs (5) and (6) to sections 46 and 47 are to those sections as they apply to a protected international trade mark (UK) under an order made pursuant to section 54.

(8) Where a trade mark has been surrendered or allowed to lapse in respect of only some of the goods or services for which it is registered, the declaration in sub-paragraphs (2) and (5) is that if the goods or services had not been removed from the registration, the registration of the trade mark would have been liable to be revoked under section 46 with effect from a date specified in the declaration or declared invalid under section 47 and sub-paragraphs (3) and (6) shall be construed accordingly.

(9) The provisions of paragraph 15 apply in relation to an application under this paragraph as they apply to an application under paragraph 14.][1]

NOTES

1 Inserted by Trade Marks (Amendment etc.) (EU Exit) Regulations 2019, SI 2019/269, reg 2, Sch 1, paras 1, 3 (31 January 2020).

[PART 4 RESTORATION OF EUROPEAN UNION TRADE MARK REGISTRATIONS AND APPLICATIONS

28 Restoration of a European Union trade mark to the EUTM Register

(1) This paragraph applies where—

(a) before [IP completion day][1] a trade mark is removed from the EUTM Register pursuant to the European Union Trade Mark Regulation; and
(b) on or after [IP completion day][1] the trade mark is restored to the EUTM Register pursuant to the Continuing EUTM Regulation.

(2) Where the proprietor of a European Union trade mark referred to in sub-paragraph (1)(b) files a request with the registrar within the period of six months beginning with the date of such restoration—

(a) the trade mark will be treated as if it was an existing EUTM on [IP completion day][1]; and
(b) the provisions of Part 1 apply to the comparable trade mark (EU) which derives from the existing EUTM.][2]

NOTES

1 Substituted by Intellectual Property (Amendment etc.) (EU Exit) Regulations 2020, SI 2020/1050, regs 7, 9(b)(i) (31 December 2020).
2 Inserted by Trade Marks (Amendment etc.) (EU Exit) Regulations 2019, SI 2019/269, reg 2, Sch 1, paras 1, 3 (31 January 2020).

[29 Restoration of an application for a European Union trade mark

(1) This paragraph applies where—

(a) before [IP completion day][1] an application for a European Union trade mark is refused pursuant to the European Union Trade Mark Regulation; and
(b) on or after [IP completion day][1] the application (a "relevant application") is restored pursuant to the Continuing EUTM Regulation.

(2) Where a person who has filed a relevant application or a successor in title of that person applies for registration of the same trade mark under this Act for some or all of the same goods or services, the provisions of paragraphs 25, 26 and 27 apply to the relevant application as if it were an existing EUTM application but as if the "relevant period" in paragraph 25(2) meant the period of nine months beginning with the date on which the relevant application is restored as referred to in sub-paragraph (1)(b).][2]

NOTES

1 Substituted by Intellectual Property (Amendment etc.) (EU Exit) Regulations 2020, SI 2020/1050, regs 7, 9(b)(i) (31 December 2020).
2 Inserted by Trade Marks (Amendment etc.) (EU Exit) Regulations 2019, SI 2019/269, reg 2, Sch 1, paras 1, 3 (31 January 2020).

[PART 5 INTERPRETATION

30 Interpretation

(1) In this Schedule—

"comparable trade mark (EU)" has the meaning given by paragraph 1(2);
"the Continuing EUTM Regulation" has the meaning given by paragraph 23(5);
"corresponding EUTM" has the meaning given by paragraph 1(9)(a);
"the EUTM Register" has the meaning given by paragraph 1(9)(b);
"existing EUTM" has the meaning given by paragraph 1(1);
"existing EUTM application" has the meaning given by paragraph 24(1);
"expired EUTM" has the meaning given by paragraph 22(1);
"the previous EUTM Regulations" means Council Regulation (EC) No 207/2009 of 26th February 2009 on the European Union trade mark and

Council Regulation (EC) No 40/94 of 20th December 1993 on the Community trade mark;

"protected international trade mark (UK)" has the same meaning as in the Trade Marks (International Registration) Order 2008.

(2) References in this Schedule to—

(a) an "Article" are to an Article of the European Union Trade Mark Regulation and include references to any equivalent Article contained in the previous EUTM Regulations;

(b) the European Union Trade Mark Regulation include references to the previous EUTM Regulations;

(c) a European Union trade mark include references to an EU collective mark and an EU certification mark as defined in Articles 74 and 83.][1]

NOTES

1 Inserted by Trade Marks (Amendment etc.) (EU Exit) Regulations 2019, SI 2019/269, reg 2, Sch 1, paras 1, 3 (31 January 2020).

[Schedule 2B International trade marks protected in the European Union

Section 54A

PART 1 EXISTING INTERNATIONAL TRADE MARKS PROTECTED IN THE EUROPEAN UNION

1 An international trade mark protected in the European Union to be treated as registered under this Act

(1) A trade mark which, immediately before [IP completion day][1], is an international trade mark which is protected in the European Union in accordance with Article 189(2) of the European Union Trade Mark Regulation (an "existing IR(EU)") is to be treated on and after [IP completion day][1] as if an application had been made, and the trade mark had been registered, under this Act in respect of the same goods or services in respect of which the international trade mark is protected in the European Union.

(2) Where the international registration to which an international trade mark is subject is sub-divided to reflect the making of more than one request for territorial extension to the European Union under Article 3ter there is to be deemed for the purposes of sub-paragraph (1) to be a separate trade mark in respect of the goods or services covered by each sub-division of the registration.

(3) Where the international registration to which an international trade mark is subject has been created by virtue of Rule 27(2) (recording of partial change in ownership) (a "separate international registration"), it is irrelevant for the purposes of the application of sub-paragraph (2) to that separate international registration that the requests for territorial extension were made before the separate international registration was created.

(4) A registered trade mark which comes into being by virtue of sub-paragraph (1) is referred to in this Act as a comparable trade mark (IR).

(5) This Act applies to a comparable trade mark (IR) as it applies to other registered trade marks except as otherwise provided in this Schedule.

(6) A comparable trade mark (IR) is deemed for the purposes of this Act to be registered as of—

(a) where the protection in the European Union of the existing IR(EU) from which the comparable trade mark (IR) derives resulted from a request for territorial extension under Article 3ter(1) (request mentioned in original application), the date of registration of the existing IR(EU) accorded pursuant to Article 3(4); or
(b) where the protection in the European Union of the existing IR(EU) from which the comparable trade mark (IR) derives resulted from a request for territorial extension under Article 3ter(2) (subsequent request), the date on which the request was recorded in the International Register,

and that date is deemed for the purposes of this Act to be the date of registration.

(7) Section 40(3) and (4) does not apply to the registration of a comparable trade mark (IR) under this Part.

(8) Section 67(1) applies in relation to the provision of information and the inspection of documents relating to a comparable trade mark (IR) notwithstanding that there will have been no application under this Act for the registration of the trade mark (and so no publication of an application).

(9) Nothing in this Act authorises the imposition of a fee, or the making of provision by rules or regulations which authorises the imposition of a fee, in respect of any matter relating to a comparable trade mark (IR) (see instead provision made by regulations under Schedule 4 to the European Union (Withdrawal) Act 2018).

(10) For the purposes of this Act—

(a) the date of filing of an application for registration of a comparable trade mark (IR) is the same date as the deemed date of registration of the comparable trade mark (IR) under sub-paragraph (6);
(b) references to the date of application for registration of a comparable trade mark (IR) are to the date of filing of the application;
(c) where an earlier trade mark is a comparable trade mark (IR), references to the completion of the registration procedure for the earlier trade mark are to publication by the European Union Intellectual Property Office of the matters referred to in Article 190(2) of the European Union Trade Mark Regulation in respect of the existing IR(EU) from which the comparable trade mark (IR) derives.

(11) In this Schedule—

(a) "the International Register" means the register of trade marks maintained by the International Bureau for the purposes of the Madrid Protocol;
(b) "international registration" means a registration made in the International Register in accordance with the Madrid Protocol;
(c) "international trade mark" means a trade mark which is the subject of an international registration.][2]

NOTES

1 Substituted by Intellectual Property (Amendment etc.) (EU Exit) Regulations 2020, SI 2020/1050, regs 13, 22(b) (31 December 2020).

2 Inserted by Designs and International Trade Marks (Amendment etc.) (EU Exit) Regulations 2019, SI 2019/638, reg 6, Sch 4, paras 1, 3 (31 January 2020).

[2 *Opt out*

(1) Subject to sub-paragraphs (2) and (6), the proprietor of an existing IR(EU) may, at any time on or after [IP completion day][1], serve notice on the registrar that the trade mark is not to be treated as if the trade mark had been registered under this Act (an "opt out notice").

(2) An opt out notice may not be served where on or after [IP completion day][1]—

(a) the comparable trade mark (IR) has been put to use in the United Kingdom by the proprietor or with the proprietor's consent (which use includes affixing the trade mark to goods or to the packaging of goods in the United Kingdom solely for export purposes);

(b) the comparable trade mark (IR) (or any right in or under it) has been made the subject of an assignment, licence, security interest or any other agreement or document except for an assent by personal representatives in relation to the comparable trade mark (IR); or

(c) proceedings based on the comparable trade mark (IR) have been initiated by the proprietor or with the proprietor's consent.

(3) An opt out notice must—

(a) identify the number of the international registration to which the existing IR(EU) to which the notice relates is subject; and

(b) include the name and address of any person having an interest in the existing IR(EU) which had effect before [IP completion day][1] in the United Kingdom, and in respect of which an entry was recorded in the International Register.

(4) An opt out notice is of no effect unless the proprietor in that notice certifies that any such person—

(a) has been given not less than three months' notice of the proprietor's intention to serve an opt out notice; or

(b) is not affected or if affected, consents to the opt out.

(5) Where a notice has been served in accordance with this paragraph—

(a) the comparable trade mark (IR) which derives from the existing IR(EU) ceases with effect from [IP completion day][1] to be treated as if it had been registered under this Act; and

(b) the registrar must, where particulars of the comparable trade mark (IR) have been entered in the register, remove the comparable trade mark (IR) from the register.

(6) Where an international trade mark which is protected in the European Union is treated as being more than one trade mark by virtue of paragraph 1(2)—

(a) an opt out notice must relate to all of the existing IR(EU)s which (by virtue of paragraph 1(2)) derive from the international trade mark;

(b) the references in sub-paragraph (2) to the comparable trade mark (IR) are to be read as references to any of the comparable trade marks (IR) which derive from the existing IR(EU)s to which the opt out notice relates; and
(c) the references in sub-paragraph (5) to the comparable trade mark (IR) are to be read as references to all of the comparable trade marks (IR) which derive from the existing IR(EU)s to which the notice relates.][2]

NOTES

1 Substituted by Intellectual Property (Amendment etc.) (EU Exit) Regulations 2020, SI 2020/1050, regs 13, 22(b) (31 December 2020).
2 Inserted by Designs and International Trade Marks (Amendment etc.) (EU Exit) Regulations 2019, SI 2019/638, reg 6, Sch 4, paras 1, 3 (31 January 2020).

[3 Entries to be made in the register in relation to a comparable trade mark (IR)

(1) The registrar must as soon as reasonably practicable after [IP completion day][1] enter a comparable trade mark (IR) in the register.

(2) The particulars of the goods or services in respect of which the comparable trade mark (IR) is treated as if it had been registered must be taken from the English language version of the entry in the International Register for the corresponding (IR).

(3) Where on or after [IP completion day][1] the entry in the International Register containing the particulars referred to in sub-paragraph (2) is modified to correct an error pursuant to Rule 28, a person having a sufficient interest may apply to the registrar for rectification of the register by the substitution of the English language version of the entry for the corresponding (IR) in the International Register as modified.

(4) In this Schedule, the "corresponding (IR)", in relation to a comparable trade mark (IR), means the existing IR(EU) from which the comparable trade mark (IR) derives.][2]

NOTES

1 Substituted by Intellectual Property (Amendment etc.) (EU Exit) Regulations 2020, SI 2020/1050, regs 13, 22(b) (31 December 2020).
2 Inserted by Designs and International Trade Marks (Amendment etc.) (EU Exit) Regulations 2019, SI 2019/638, reg 6, Sch 4, paras 1, 3 (31 January 2020).

[4 Comparable trade mark (IR) which derives from a mark treated as an EU Collective Mark or EU Certification Mark

(1) This paragraph applies where the existing IR(EU) from which a comparable trade mark (IR) derives is dealt with for the purposes of the European Union Trade Mark Regulation as an EU collective mark or an EU certification mark.

(2) The comparable trade mark (IR) is to be treated as either a collective mark or a certification mark, as the case may be.

(3) The proprietor of the comparable trade mark (IR) must, following notice from the registrar, file with the registrar regulations governing the use of the international trade mark, submitted pursuant to the European Union Trade Mark Regulation, which had effect immediately before [IP completion day][1].

(4) Where the regulations referred to in sub-paragraph (3) are in a language other than English they must be filed together with a translation into English verified to the satisfaction of the registrar as corresponding to the original text.

(5) Paragraph 9 of Schedule 1 and paragraph 10 of Schedule 2 apply in relation to the translation referred to in sub-paragraph (4) as they apply in relation to the regulations referred to in sub-paragraph (3).

(6) Where the regulations or any translation are not filed in accordance with the above provisions—

(a) the registrar must remove the comparable trade mark (IR) from the register; and
(b) the rights of the proprietor shall be deemed to have ceased as from the date of removal.][2]

NOTES

1 Substituted by Intellectual Property (Amendment etc.) (EU Exit) Regulations 2020, SI 2020/1050, regs 13, 22(b) (31 December 2020).
2 Inserted by Designs and International Trade Marks (Amendment etc.) (EU Exit) Regulations 2019, SI 2019/638, reg 6, Sch 4, paras 1, 3 (31 January 2020).

[5 Renewal of a comparable trade mark (IR) which expires within six months after [IP completion day] 1

(1) This paragraph applies to the renewal of the registration of a comparable trade mark (IR) which expires within the period beginning with [IP completion day][1] and ending with the end of the relevant period (and accordingly section 43(1) to (3A) does not apply).

(2) The registration of the comparable trade mark (IR) may be renewed at the request of the proprietor before the expiry of the registration.

(3) Where the registration of the comparable trade mark (IR) is not renewed in accordance with sub-paragraph (2)—

(a) on, or as soon as reasonably practicable after, the expiry of the registration, the registrar must notify the proprietor that the registration has expired and of the manner in which the registration may be renewed; and
(b) a request for renewal must be made within the period of six months beginning with the date of the notice.

(4) If a request for renewal is made in respect of only some of the goods or services for which the comparable trade mark (IR) is registered, the registration is to be renewed for those goods or services only.

(5) If the registration is not renewed in accordance with the above provisions, the registrar must remove the comparable trade mark (IR) from the register.

(6) Section 43(4) and (6) applies to the registration of a comparable trade mark (IR) which is renewed in accordance with the above provisions.

(7) In sub-paragraph (1), the "relevant period" means the period of six months beginning with the day after that on which [IP completion day][1] falls.][2]

NOTES

1 Substituted by Intellectual Property (Amendment etc.) (EU Exit) Regulations 2020, SI 2020/1050, regs 13, 22(b) (31 December 2020).

2 Inserted by Designs and International Trade Marks (Amendment etc.) (EU Exit) Regulations 2019, SI 2019/638, reg 6, Sch 4, paras 1, 3 (31 January 2020).

[6 Restoration of a comparable trade mark (IR)

Where a comparable trade mark (IR) is removed from the register pursuant to paragraph 5, the rules relating to the restoration of the registration of a trade mark (referred to in section 43(5)) apply in relation to the restoration of the comparable trade mark (IR) to the register.][1]

NOTES

1 Inserted by Designs and International Trade Marks (Amendment etc.) (EU Exit) Regulations 2019, SI 2019/638, reg 6, Sch 4, paras 1, 3 (31 January 2020).

[7 Raising of relative grounds in opposition proceedings in case of non-use

(1) Section 6A applies where an earlier trade mark is a comparable trade mark (IR), subject to the modifications set out below.

(2) Where the relevant period referred to in section 6A(3)(a) (the "five-year period") has expired before [IP completion day][1]—

(a) the references in section 6A(3) and (6) to the earlier trade mark are to be treated as references to the corresponding (IR); and

(b) the references in section 6A(3) and (4) to the United Kingdom include the European Union.

(3) Where [IP completion day][1] falls within the five-year period, in respect of that part of the five-year period which falls before [IP completion day][1]—

(a) the references in section 6A(3) and (6) to the earlier trade mark are to be treated as references to the corresponding (IR); and

(b) the references in section 6A to the United Kingdom include the European Union.][2]

NOTES

1 Substituted by Intellectual Property (Amendment etc.) (EU Exit) Regulations 2020, SI 2020/1050, regs 13, 22(b) (31 December 2020).

2 Inserted by Designs and International Trade Marks (Amendment etc.) (EU Exit) Regulations 2019, SI 2019/638, reg 6, Sch 4, paras 1, 3 (31 January 2020).

[8 Non-use as defence in infringement proceedings and revocation of registration of a comparable trade mark (IR)

(1) Sections 11A and 46 apply in relation to a comparable trade mark (IR), subject to the modifications set out below.

(2) Where the period of five years referred to in sections 11A(3)(a) and 46(1)(a) or (b) (the "five-year period") has expired before [IP completion day][1]—

(a) the references in sections 11A(3) and (insofar as they relate to use of a trade mark) 46 to a trade mark are to be treated as references to the corresponding (IR); and

(b) the references in sections 11A and 46 to the United Kingdom include the European Union.

(3) Where [IP completion day][1] falls within the five-year period, in respect of that part of the five-year period which falls before [IP completion day][1]—

(a) the references in sections 11A(3) and (insofar as they relate to use of a trade mark) 46 to a trade mark, are to be treated as references to the corresponding (IR); and
(b) the references in sections 11A and 46 to the United Kingdom include the European Union.][2]

NOTES

1 Substituted by Intellectual Property (Amendment etc.) (EU Exit) Regulations 2020, SI 2020/1050, regs 13, 22(b) (31 December 2020).
2 Inserted by Designs and International Trade Marks (Amendment etc.) (EU Exit) Regulations 2019, SI 2019/638, reg 6, Sch 4, paras 1, 3 (31 January 2020).

[9 Grounds for invalidity of registration of a trade mark based upon an earlier comparable trade mark (IR)

(1) Section 47 applies where an earlier trade mark is a comparable trade mark (IR), subject to the modifications set out below.

(2) Where the period of five years referred to in sections 47(2A)(a) and 47(2B) (the "five-year period") has expired before [IP completion day][1]—

(a) the references in section 47(2B) and (2E) to the earlier trade mark are to be treated as references to the corresponding (IR); and
(b) the references in section 47 to the United Kingdom include the European Union.

(3) Where [IP completion day][1] falls within the five-year period, in respect of that part of the five-year period which falls before [IP completion day][1]—

(a) the references in section 47(2B) and (2E) to the earlier trade mark are to be treated as references to the corresponding (IR); and
(b) the references in section 47 to the United Kingdom include the European Union.][2]

NOTES

1 Substituted by Intellectual Property (Amendment etc.) (EU Exit) Regulations 2020, SI 2020/1050, regs 13, 22(b) (31 December 2020).
2 Inserted by Designs and International Trade Marks (Amendment etc.) (EU Exit) Regulations 2019, SI 2019/638, reg 6, Sch 4, paras 1, 3 (31 January 2020).

[10 Reputation of a comparable trade mark (IR)

(1) Sections 5 and 10 apply in relation to a comparable trade mark (IR), subject to the modifications set out below.

(2) Where the reputation of a comparable trade mark (IR) falls to be considered in respect of any time before [IP completion day][1], references in sections 5(3) and 10(3) to—

(a) the reputation of the mark are to be treated as references to the reputation of the corresponding (IR); and
(b) the United Kingdom include the European Union.][2]

NOTES

1 Substituted by Intellectual Property (Amendment etc.) (EU Exit) Regulations 2020, SI 2020/1050, regs 13, 22(b) (31 December 2020).
2 Inserted by Designs and International Trade Marks (Amendment etc.) (EU Exit) Regulations 2019, SI 2019/638, reg 6, Sch 4, paras 1, 3 (31 January 2020).

[11 Rights conferred by registered trade mark

Section 9 applies in relation to a comparable trade mark (IR) but as if—

(a) the words in brackets in subsection (3) referring to section 40(3) were replaced with a reference to paragraph 1(6) of this Schedule; and
(b) the proviso in subsection (3) were omitted.][1]

NOTES

1 Inserted by Designs and International Trade Marks (Amendment etc.) (EU Exit) Regulations 2019, SI 2019/638, reg 6, Sch 4, paras 1, 3 (31 January 2020).

[12 Effect of disclaimer

Where, immediately before [IP completion day][1], the protection in the European Union of an existing IR(EU) is subject to a disclaimer recorded in the International Register, the registration of the comparable trade mark (IR) which derives from the existing IR(EU) is to be treated on and after [IP completion day][1] as subject to the same disclaimer (and section 13 applies accordingly but as if the reference to "publication" in subsection (2) was omitted).][2]

NOTES

1 Substituted by Intellectual Property (Amendment etc.) (EU Exit) Regulations 2020, SI 2020/1050, regs 13, 22(b) (31 December 2020).
2 Inserted by Designs and International Trade Marks (Amendment etc.) (EU Exit) Regulations 2019, SI 2019/638, reg 6, Sch 4, paras 1, 3 (31 January 2020).

[13 Effect of claim of priority

(1) This paragraph applies where—

(a) a right of priority was claimed in respect of an international application for protection of a trade mark in accordance with Rule 9(4)(iv);
(b) immediately before [IP completion day][1] there is an entry in the International Register in respect of that trade mark containing particulars of that claim of priority (a "claim of priority");
(c) the trade mark is an existing IR(EU).

(2) Subject to sub-paragraph (4), the proprietor of the comparable trade mark (IR) which derives from the existing IR(EU) is to be treated on and after [IP completion day][1] as having the same claim of priority.

(3) Accordingly, the relevant date for the purposes of establishing, in relation to the comparable trade mark (IR), which rights take precedence is the date of filing of the application for a trade mark in a Convention country which formed the basis for the claim of priority.

(4) Where the protection in the European Union of the existing IR(EU) resulted from a request for territorial extension under Article 3ter(2), the proprietor of the comparable trade mark (IR) which derives from the existing IR(EU) is to be treated on and after [IP completion day][1] as having the same claim of priority only where the request for territorial extension was recorded in the International Register within a period of six months beginning with the day after the priority date recorded in the International Register in respect of the international application referred to in sub-paragraph (1)(a).][2]

NOTES

1 Substituted by Intellectual Property (Amendment etc.) (EU Exit) Regulations 2020, SI 2020/1050, regs 13, 22(b) (31 December 2020).

2 Inserted by Designs and International Trade Marks (Amendment etc.) (EU Exit) Regulations 2019, SI 2019/638, reg 6, Sch 4, paras 1, 3 (31 January 2020).

[14 Effect of seniority claim

(1) This paragraph applies where immediately before [IP completion day][1] an existing IR(EU) has a valid claim to seniority of a trade mark which trade mark (the "senior mark") is a registered trade mark or a protected international trade mark (UK).

(2) The comparable trade mark (IR) which derives from the existing IR(EU) is to be treated on and after [IP completion day][1] as if it had a valid claim to seniority of the senior mark.

(3) Accordingly, where the proprietor of the comparable trade mark (IR) surrenders the senior mark or allows it to lapse (whether wholly or partially), subject to paragraph 15, the proprietor of the comparable trade mark (IR) is deemed to continue to have the same rights as the proprietor would have had if the senior mark had continued to be registered in respect of all the goods or services for which it was registered prior to the surrender or lapse.

(4) An existing IR(EU) has a valid claim to seniority of a trade mark where—

(a) a claim has been filed in accordance with Article 191 or 192 of the European Union Trade Mark Regulation in respect of the international registration to which the existing IR(EU) is subject; and

(b) the seniority so claimed has not lapsed in the circumstances referred to in Article 39 of that Regulation (as it applies to international registrations under Article 182 of that Regulation).][2]

NOTES

1 Substituted by Intellectual Property (Amendment etc.) (EU Exit) Regulations 2020, SI 2020/1050, regs 13, 22(b) (31 December 2020).

2 Inserted by Designs and International Trade Marks (Amendment etc.) (EU Exit) Regulations 2019, SI 2019/638, reg 6, Sch 4, paras 1, 3 (31 January 2020).

[15 Determination of invalidity and liability to revocation in relation to claims of seniority

(1) Where pursuant to paragraph 14 a comparable trade mark (IR) is treated as if it had a valid claim to seniority of a registered trade mark which has been—

(a) removed from the register under section 43; or
(b) surrendered under section 45,

any person may apply to the registrar or to the court for the declaration set out in sub-paragraph (2).

(2) The declaration is that if the trade mark had not been so removed or surrendered, the registration of the trade mark would have been liable to be revoked under section 46 with effect from a date specified in the declaration or declared invalid under section 47.

(3) Where the declaration is that had the trade mark not been so removed or surrendered the registration of it would have been liable to be—

(a) revoked under section 46 with effect from a date prior to—
    (i) where there has been no claim of priority pursuant to Article 35 of the European Union Trade Mark Regulation (as it applies to international registrations under Article 182 of that Regulation) in respect of the existing IR(EU) from which the comparable trade mark (IR) derives, the deemed date of registration of the comparable trade mark (IR); or
    (ii) where there has been a claim of priority, the priority date accorded pursuant to a right of priority claimed pursuant to Article 35 of the European Union Trade Mark Regulation in respect of the existing IR(EU) from which the comparable trade mark (IR) derives; or
(b) declared invalid under section 47,

the seniority claimed for the comparable trade mark (IR) is to be treated as if it never had effect.

(4) Where pursuant to paragraph 14 a comparable trade mark (IR) is treated as if it had a valid claim to seniority of a protected international trade mark (UK) which has been—

(a) removed from the International Register; or
(b) surrendered under the Madrid Protocol,

any person may apply to the registrar or to the court for the declaration set out in sub-paragraph (5).

(5) The declaration is that, if the trade mark had not been so removed or surrendered, the protection of the mark in the United Kingdom would have been liable to be revoked under section 46 with effect from a date specified in the declaration or declared invalid under section 47.

(6) Where the declaration is that had the trade mark not been so removed or surrendered the protection of the mark in the United Kingdom would have been liable to be—

(a) revoked under section 46 with effect from a date prior to—
    (i) where there has been no claim of priority pursuant to Article 35 of the European Union Trade Mark Regulation (as it applies to international registrations under Article 182 of that Regulation) in respect of the existing IR(EU) from which the comparable trade mark (IR) derives, the deemed date of registration of the comparable trade mark (IR); or

(ii) where there has been a claim of priority, the priority date accorded pursuant to a right of priority claimed pursuant to Article 35 of the European Union Trade Mark Regulation in respect of the existing IR(EU) from which the comparable trade mark (IR) derives; or

(b) declared invalid under section 47,

the seniority claimed for the comparable trade mark (IR) is to be treated as if it never had effect.

(7) Where the protection in the European Union of an existing IR(EU) resulted from a request for territorial extension under Article 3ter(2), a right of priority claimed pursuant to Article 35 of the European Union Trade Mark Regulation in respect of the existing IR(EU) is to be disregarded for the purposes of sub-paragraphs (3)(a)(ii) and (6)(a)(ii) unless the request for territorial extension was recorded in the International Register within a period of six months beginning with the day after the priority date recorded in the International Register in respect of the international application for protection of the trade mark which is the same as the one in respect of which the request for territorial extension was filed.

(8) References in sub-paragraphs (5) and (6) to sections 46 and 47 are to those sections as they apply to a protected international trade mark (UK) under an order made pursuant to section 54.

(9) Where a trade mark has been surrendered or allowed to lapse in respect of some only of the goods or services for which it is registered, the declaration in sub-paragraphs (2) and (5) is that if the goods or services had not been removed from the registration, the registration of the trade mark would have been liable to be revoked under section 46 with effect from a date specified in the declaration or declared invalid under section 47 and sub-paragraphs (3) and (6) shall be construed accordingly.][1]

NOTES

1 Inserted by Designs and International Trade Marks (Amendment etc.) (EU Exit) Regulations 2019, SI 2019/638, reg 6, Sch 4, paras 1, 3 (31 January 2020).

[16 Procedure for declaration that trade mark would have been liable to be revoked or declared invalid

(1) In the case of proceedings on an application under paragraph 15 before the registrar, the rules relating to applications for and proceedings relating to the revocation or invalidation of a trade mark apply, with necessary modifications.

(2) In the case of proceedings on an application under paragraph 15 before the court, section 74 applies to the proceedings as it applies to proceedings involving an application of the type referred to in section 74(1)(a) to (c).][1]

NOTES

1 Inserted by Designs and International Trade Marks (Amendment etc.) (EU Exit) Regulations 2019, SI 2019/638, reg 6, Sch 4, paras 1, 3 (31 January 2020).

[17 Assignment of an existing IR(EU) not registered on [IP completion day] 1

(1) This paragraph applies where before [IP completion day][1] an existing IR(EU) (or any right in it) is the subject of an assignment (a "relevant assignment") which

immediately before [IP completion day][1] is not recorded in the International Register.

(2) Section 25 applies in relation to a relevant assignment as if it were a registrable transaction affecting a comparable trade mark (IR), subject to the modification set out below.

(3) An application under section 25(1) may only be made by—

(a) a person claiming to be entitled to an interest in or under a comparable trade mark (IR) by virtue of a relevant assignment of the corresponding (IR); or
(b) the proprietor of the comparable trade mark (IR).][2]

NOTES

1 Substituted by Intellectual Property (Amendment etc.) (EU Exit) Regulations 2020, SI 2020/1050, regs 13, 22(b) (31 December 2020).
2 Inserted by Designs and International Trade Marks (Amendment etc.) (EU Exit) Regulations 2019, SI 2019/638, reg 6, Sch 4, paras 1, 3 (31 January 2020).

[18 Effect of a licence of an existing IR(EU)

(1) This paragraph applies where immediately before [IP completion day][1] an existing IR(EU) is the subject of a licence (a "relevant licence") which—

(a) authorises the doing of acts in the United Kingdom which would otherwise infringe the international trade mark; and
(b) does not expire on [IP completion day][1].

(2) Subject to any agreement to the contrary between the licensee and the licensor, a relevant licence continues to authorise the doing of acts in the United Kingdom which would otherwise infringe the comparable trade mark (IR) which derives from the existing IR(EU).

(3) Sub-paragraph (2) is subject to—

(a) the terms on which the relevant licence was granted; and
(b) such modifications to the terms referred to in paragraph (a) as are necessary for their application in the United Kingdom.

(4) Section 25 applies in relation to a relevant licence as if it were a registrable transaction affecting a comparable trade mark (IR), subject to the modifications set out below.

(5) An application under section 25(1) may only be made by—

(a) a person claiming to be a licensee by virtue of the relevant licence; or
(b) the proprietor of the comparable trade mark (IR).

(6) Where immediately before [IP completion day][1] there is an entry in the International Register relating to a relevant licence—

(a) section 25(3) and (4) does not apply until after the expiry of the relevant period; and
(b) section 25(4)(a) applies after the expiry of the relevant period but as if the reference to six months beginning with the date of the transaction were a reference to eighteen months beginning with [IP completion day][1].

(7) In sub-paragraph (6)(a), the "relevant period" means the period of twelve months beginning with the day after that on which [IP completion day][1] falls.][2]

NOTES

1 Substituted by Intellectual Property (Amendment etc.) (EU Exit) Regulations 2020, SI 2020/1050, regs 13, 22(b) (31 December 2020).

2 Inserted by Designs and International Trade Marks (Amendment etc.) (EU Exit) Regulations 2019, SI 2019/638, reg 6, Sch 4, paras 1, 3 (31 January 2020).

[19 Effect of a security interest in an existing IR(EU)

(1) This paragraph applies where immediately before [IP completion day][1] an existing IR(EU) (or any right in or under it) is the subject of a security interest (a "relevant security interest") which—

(a) restricts the proprietor's right to dispose in the European Union of the existing IR(EU); and

(b) does not terminate on [IP completion day][1].

(2) References to the existing IR(EU), or the international registration to which the existing IR(EU) is subject, in any document which grants or refers to the relevant security interest are to be read as including references to the comparable trade mark (IR) which derives from the existing IR(EU).

(3) Section 25 applies in relation to a relevant security interest as if it were a registrable transaction affecting a comparable trade mark (IR), subject to the modifications set out below.

(4) An application under section 25(1) may only be made by—

(a) a person claiming to be entitled to an interest in or under a comparable trade mark (IR) by virtue of the relevant security interest; or

(b) the proprietor of the comparable trade mark (IR).

(5) Where immediately before [IP completion day][1] there is an entry in the International Register relating to a relevant security interest—

(a) section 25(3) and (4) do not apply until after the expiry of the relevant period; and

(b) section 25(4)(a) applies after the expiry of the relevant period but as if the reference to six months beginning with the date of the transaction were a reference to eighteen months beginning with [IP completion day][1].

(6) In sub-paragraph (5)(a), the "relevant period" means the period of twelve months beginning with the day after that on which [IP completion day][1] falls.][2]

NOTES

1 Substituted by Intellectual Property (Amendment etc.) (EU Exit) Regulations 2020, SI 2020/1050, regs 13, 22(b) (31 December 2020).

2 Inserted by Designs and International Trade Marks (Amendment etc.) (EU Exit) Regulations 2019, SI 2019/638, reg 6, Sch 4, paras 1, 3 (31 January 2020).

[20 Continuity of rights in relation to a comparable trade mark (IR)

(1) References to an existing IR(EU), or the international registration to which an existing IR(EU) is subject, in any document made before [IP completion day][1]

shall, unless there is evidence that the document was not intended to have effect in the United Kingdom, be read on and after [IP completion day][1] as including references to the comparable trade mark (IR) or the registration of the comparable trade mark (IR) which derives from the existing IR(EU).

(2) Subject to any agreement to the contrary, a consent granted before [IP completion day][1] by the proprietor of an existing IR(EU) to the doing on or after [IP completion day][1] of an act in the United Kingdom which would otherwise infringe the comparable trade mark (IR) which derives from the existing IR(EU) is to be treated for the purposes of section 9 as a consent to the doing of that act.][2]

NOTES

1 Substituted by Intellectual Property (Amendment etc.) (EU Exit) Regulations 2020, SI 2020/1050, regs 13, 22(b) (31 December 2020).

2 Inserted by Designs and International Trade Marks (Amendment etc.) (EU Exit) Regulations 2019, SI 2019/638, reg 6, Sch 4, paras 1, 3 (31 January 2020).

[21 Existing IR(EU): pending proceedings

(1) This paragraph applies where on [IP completion day][1] an existing IR(EU) is the subject of proceedings which are pending ("pending proceedings") before a court in the United Kingdom designated for the purposes of Article 123 of the European Union Trade Mark Regulation ("EU trade mark court").

(2) Subject to sub-paragraphs (3) and (4), the provisions contained or referred to in Chapter 10 of the European Union Trade Mark Regulation (with the exception of Articles 128(2), (4), (6) and (7) and 132) continue to apply to the pending proceedings as if the United Kingdom were still a Member State with effect from [IP completion day][1].

(3) Where the pending proceedings involve a claim for infringement of an existing IR(EU), without prejudice to any other relief by way of damages, accounts or otherwise available to the proprietor of the existing IR(EU), the EU trade mark court may grant an injunction to prohibit unauthorised use of the comparable trade mark (IR) which derives from the existing IR(EU).

(4) Where the pending proceedings involve a counterclaim for the revocation of, or a declaration of invalidity in relation to, an existing IR(EU), the EU trade mark court may revoke the registration of the comparable trade mark (IR) which derives from the existing IR(EU) or declare the registration of the comparable trade mark (IR) which derives from the existing IR(EU) to be invalid.

(5) Where the grounds for revocation or invalidity exist in respect of only some of the goods or services for which the existing IR(EU) is registered, the revocation or declaration of invalidity in respect of the registration of the comparable trade mark (IR) which derives from the existing IR(EU) relates to those goods or services only.

(6) Where (by virtue of sub-paragraph (4)) the registration of a comparable trade mark (IR) is revoked to any extent, the rights of the proprietor are deemed to have ceased to that extent as from—

(a) the date of the counterclaim for revocation, or

(b) if the court is satisfied that the grounds for revocation existed at an earlier date, that date.

(7) Where (by virtue of sub-paragraph (4)) the registration of a comparable trade mark (IR) is declared invalid to any extent, the registration is to that extent to be deemed never to have been made, provided that this does not affect transactions past and closed.

(8) For the purposes of this paragraph proceedings are treated as pending on [IP completion day][1] if they were instituted but not finally determined before [IP completion day][1].][2]

NOTES

1 Substituted by Intellectual Property (Amendment etc.) (EU Exit) Regulations 2020, SI 2020/1050, regs 13, 22(b) (31 December 2020).

2 Inserted by Designs and International Trade Marks (Amendment etc.) (EU Exit) Regulations 2019, SI 2019/638, reg 6, Sch 4, paras 1, 3 (31 January 2020).

[22 Existing IR(EU): effect of injunction

(1) This paragraph applies where immediately before [IP completion day][1] an injunction is in force prohibiting the performance of acts in the United Kingdom which infringe or would infringe an existing IR(EU) (a "relevant injunction").

(2) Subject to any order of the court to the contrary, a relevant injunction will have effect and be enforceable to prohibit the performance of acts which infringe or would infringe a comparable trade mark (IR) to the same extent as in relation to the existing IR(EU) from which the comparable trade mark (IR) derives as if it were an injunction granted by the court.][2]

NOTES

1 Substituted by Intellectual Property (Amendment etc.) (EU Exit) Regulations 2020, SI 2020/1050, regs 13, 22(b) (31 December 2020).

2 Inserted by Designs and International Trade Marks (Amendment etc.) (EU Exit) Regulations 2019, SI 2019/638, reg 6, Sch 4, paras 1, 3 (31 January 2020).

[PART 2 TREATMENT OF INTERNATIONAL TRADE MARKS PROTECTED IN THE EUROPEAN UNION WHICH EXPIRE DURING THE PERIOD OF SIX MONTHS ENDING ON [IP COMPLETION DAY][1]

23 Registration of certain expired international trade marks

(1) This Part applies to an international trade mark which, immediately before the transitional period, was protected in the European Union in accordance with Article 189(2) of the European Union Trade Mark Regulation but which, as a result of the expiry of the registration of the international trade mark during the transitional period, does not fall within paragraph 1(1) (an "expired IR(EU)").

(2) Where the international registration to which an international trade mark is subject has been sub-divided as referred to in paragraph 1(2), there is to be deemed for the purposes of sub-paragraph (1) to be a separate expired trade mark in respect of the goods or services covered by each sub-division of the registration.

(3) An expired IR(EU) is to be treated as if it were an existing IR(EU).

(4) The provisions of Part 1 of this Schedule apply to an expired IR(EU) as they apply to an existing IR(EU) subject to the provisions of this Part of the Schedule.

(5) Notwithstanding the entry in the register (under paragraph 3, as applied by sub-paragraph (4)) of a comparable trade mark (IR) which derives from an expired IR(EU), the registration of the comparable trade mark (IR) is expired until the proprietor gives notice to the registrar in accordance with paragraph 24(1)(b) (or the comparable trade mark (IR) is removed from the register in accordance with paragraph 24(2)).

(6) In this paragraph, "transitional period" means the period of six months ending with [IP completion day][1].][2]

NOTES

1 Substituted by Intellectual Property (Amendment etc.) (EU Exit) Regulations 2020, SI 2020/1050, regs 13, 22(b) (31 December 2020).

2 Inserted by Designs and International Trade Marks (Amendment etc.) (EU Exit) Regulations 2019, SI 2019/638, reg 6, Sch 4, paras 1, 3 (31 January 2020).

[24 Renewal of an expired IR(EU)

(1) Where within the period beginning with [IP completion day][1] and ending with the end of the relevant period—

(a) the international registration to which an expired IR(EU) is subject is renewed in accordance with Article 7; and

(b) the proprietor of the expired IR(EU) notifies the registrar of such renewal (a "renewal notice"),

paragraphs 25 and 26 apply to the renewal of the registration of the comparable trade mark (IR) which derives from the expired IR(EU).

(2) If within the period referred to in sub-paragraph (1) the proprietor fails to notify the registrar in accordance with sub-paragraph (1)(b)—

(a) the registrar must remove from the register the comparable trade mark (IR) which derives from the expired IR(EU); and

(b) the comparable trade mark (IR) ceases with effect from [IP completion day][1] to be treated as if it had been registered under this Act.

(3) In sub-paragraph (1), the "relevant period" means the period of nine months beginning with the day after that on which [IP completion day][1] falls.][2]

NOTES

1 Substituted by Intellectual Property (Amendment etc.) (EU Exit) Regulations 2020, SI 2020/1050, regs 13, 22(b) (31 December 2020).

2 Inserted by Designs and International Trade Marks (Amendment etc.) (EU Exit) Regulations 2019, SI 2019/638, reg 6, Sch 4, paras 1, 3 (31 January 2020).

[25 Renewal of an expired IR(EU): territorial extension under Article 3ter(1)

(1) Where the protection in the European Union of an expired IR(EU) resulted from a request for territorial extension under Article 3ter(1), the registrar must,

as soon as reasonably practicable following receipt of the renewal notice, renew the registration of the comparable trade mark (IR) which derives from the expired IR(EU).

(2) A comparable trade mark (IR) which is renewed under sub-paragraph (1) shall be renewed for a period of ten years from the expiry of the international registration to which the expired IR(EU) is subject.

(3) Section 43(6) applies to the registration of a comparable trade mark (IR) which is renewed in accordance with this paragraph.][1]

NOTES

1 Inserted by Designs and International Trade Marks (Amendment etc.) (EU Exit) Regulations 2019, SI 2019/638, reg 6, Sch 4, paras 1, 3 (31 January 2020).

[26 Renewal of an expired IR(EU): territorial extension under Article 3ter(2)

(1) This paragraph applies where the protection in the European Union of an expired IR(EU) resulted from a request for territorial extension under Article 3ter(2).

(2) The relevant date for the purposes of determining the date of renewal of the registration of the comparable trade mark (IR) which derives from the expired IR(EU) (the "relevant renewal date") shall be—

(a) the date of expiry of the period of ten years from the date on which the request for territorial extension was recorded in the International Register; or

(b) where the international registration to which the expired IR(EU) is subject has been renewed since the date referred to in paragraph (a), the anniversary of that date, computed by reference to periods of ten years, following the last renewal of the registration prior to the date of the renewal notice (the "notice date").

(3) Where the relevant renewal date of a comparable trade mark (IR) falls prior to the notice date, the registrar must, as soon as reasonably practicable following receipt of a renewal notice, renew the registration of the comparable trade mark (IR) which derives from the expired IR(EU).

(4) Where the relevant renewal date of a comparable trade mark (IR) falls before the expiry of the period of six months beginning with the notice date, sub-paragraphs (5) and (6) apply (and accordingly section 43(1) to (3A) does not apply).

(5) The registration of the comparable trade mark (IR) may be renewed at the request of the proprietor before the relevant renewal date.

(6) Where the registration of the comparable trade mark (IR) is not renewed in accordance with sub-paragraph (5)—

(a) on, or as soon as reasonably practicable after, the relevant renewal date, the registrar must notify the proprietor that the registration of the comparable trade mark (IR) has expired and of the manner in which registration may be renewed; and

(b) a request for renewal must be made within a period of six months beginning with the date of the notice.

(7) If a request for renewal is made in respect of only some of the goods or services for which the comparable trade mark (IR) is registered, the registration is to be renewed for those goods or services only.

(8) A comparable trade mark (IR) which is renewed under sub-paragraph (3) or pursuant to a request for renewal in accordance with sub-paragraph (5) or (6) shall be renewed for a period of ten years from the relevant renewal date (and accordingly, section 43(4) does not apply).

(9) Where sub-paragraphs (5) and (6) apply to the renewal of the registration of a comparable trade mark (IR) and the registration is not renewed in accordance with those provisions, the registrar must remove the comparable trade mark (IR) from the register.

(10) Section 43(6) applies to the registration of a comparable trade mark (IR) which is renewed in accordance with this paragraph.

(11) Where a comparable trade mark (IR) is removed from the register pursuant to sub-paragraph (9), the rules relating to the restoration of the registration of a trade mark (referred to in section 43(5)) apply in relation to the restoration of the comparable trade mark (IR) to the register.

(12) Where the relevant renewal date of a comparable trade mark (IR) falls on or after the expiry of the period of six months beginning with the notice date, section 43 applies to the renewal of the registration of the comparable trade mark (IR) and references to the expiry of the registration are to be treated as references to the relevant renewal date of the comparable trade mark (IR).][1]

NOTES

1 Inserted by Designs and International Trade Marks (Amendment etc.) (EU Exit) Regulations 2019, SI 2019/638, reg 6, Sch 4, paras 1, 3 (31 January 2020).

[PART 3 APPLICATIONS FOR THE EXTENSION OF PROTECTION OF INTERNATIONAL REGISTRATIONS TO THE EUROPEAN UNION WHICH ARE PENDING ON [IP COMPLETION DAY][1]

27 *Interpretation*

(1) In this Part—

(a) references to an "existing ITM application" are to an international application which contains a request for extension of the protection resulting from an international registration to the European Union under Article 3ter(1) in respect of which the conditions in sub-paragraph (2) are satisfied;

(b) references to an "existing request for EU extension" are to a request for extension to the European Union of the protection resulting from an international registration made subsequent to the international registration pursuant to Article 3ter(2) in respect of which the conditions in sub-paragraph (3) are satisfied;

(c) references to an "international application" are to an application to the International Bureau under Article 2(2) for the registration of a trade mark in the International Register.

(2) The conditions referred to in sub-paragraph (1)(a) are—

(a) the international application was filed before [IP completion day][1] with the Office of origin in accordance with Article 2(2); and
(b) as at the time immediately before [IP completion day][1], the request for extension of protection to the European Union mentioned in the international application has been neither granted nor refused by the European Union Intellectual Property Office.

(3) The conditions referred to in sub-paragraph (1)(b) are—

(a) the request for extension of protection to the European Union was filed before [IP completion day][1] with the Office of origin or the International Bureau (as the case may be) in accordance with Rule 24(2); and
(b) as at the time immediately before [IP completion day][1], the request for extension of protection to the European Union has been neither granted nor refused by the European Union Intellectual Property Office under the European Union Trade Mark Regulation.

(4) In sub-paragraphs (2)(b) and (3)(b) —

(a) the reference to the request for extension of protection to the European Union being "granted" means the European Union Intellectual Property Office having sent to the International Bureau a statement to the effect that protection is granted to the mark in the European Union in accordance with Rule 18ter; and
(b) the reference to the request for extension of protection to the European Union being "refused" means the European Union Intellectual Property Office having sent to the International Bureau a notification of refusal in accordance with Article 5(1) or (2) which refusal has not been subsequently `withdrawn.][2]

NOTES

1 Substituted by Intellectual Property (Amendment etc.) (EU Exit) Regulations 2020, SI 2020/1050, regs 13, 22(b) (31 December 2020).

2 Inserted by Designs and International Trade Marks (Amendment etc.) (EU Exit) Regulations 2019, SI 2019/638, reg 6, Sch 4, paras 1, 3 (31 January 2020).

[28 Application for registration under this Act based upon an existing ITM application or an existing request for EU extension recorded in the International Register prior to [IP completion day] 1

(1) This paragraph applies where—

(a) either—
  (i) an existing ITM application has been filed with the International Bureau in respect of a trade mark and the date accorded to the international registration of the trade mark pursuant to Article 3(4) is a date prior to [IP completion day][1]; or

(ii) an existing request for EU extension in respect of a trade mark has been filed with the International Bureau and the date on which it was recorded in the International Register pursuant to Article 3ter(2) is a date prior to [IP completion day][1];

(b) the person who filed the existing ITM application or (as the case may be) the existing request for EU extension, or a successor in title of that person, applies for registration of the same trade mark under this Act for some or all of the same goods or services, and

(c) the application under this Act is made within a period beginning with [IP completion day][1] and ending with the end of the period referred to in sub-paragraph (4).

(2) Where this paragraph applies, the relevant date for the purposes of establishing which rights take precedence is the earliest of—

(a) the date accorded to the international trade mark the subject of the existing ITM application pursuant to Article 3(4) or, in the case of an existing request for EU extension, the date on which the request was recorded in the International Register pursuant to Article 3ter(2);

(b) the date of priority (if any) accorded pursuant to a right of priority claimed pursuant to Article 4 of the Paris Convention in respect of the existing ITM application or the existing request for EU extension (as the case may be).

(3) The registrability of the trade mark the subject of an application under this Act of the type mentioned in sub-paragraph (1)(b) and made within the period mentioned in sub-paragraph (1)(c) shall not be affected by any use of the mark in the United Kingdom which commenced in the period between the date referred to in sub-paragraph (2) and the date of the application under this Act.

(4) In sub-paragraph (1)(c), the period referred to is the period of nine months beginning with the day after that on which [IP completion day][1] falls.

(5) A right of priority claimed pursuant to Article 4 of the Paris Convention in respect of an existing request for EU extension is to be disregarded for the purposes of sub-paragraph (2)(b) unless the existing request for EU extension was recorded in the International Register within a period of six months beginning with the day after the priority date recorded in the International Register in respect of the international application for protection of the trade mark which is the same as the one in respect of which the existing request for EU extension was filed.][2]

NOTES

1 Substituted by Intellectual Property (Amendment etc.) (EU Exit) Regulations 2020, SI 2020/1050, regs 13, 22(b) (31 December 2020).

2 Inserted by Designs and International Trade Marks (Amendment etc.) (EU Exit) Regulations 2019, SI 2019/638, reg 6, Sch 4, paras 1, 3 (31 January 2020).

[29 Application for registration under this Act based upon an existing ITM application or an existing request for EU extension recorded in the International Register on or after [IP completion day] I

(1) This paragraph applies where—

(a) either—
   (i) an existing ITM application has been filed with the International Bureau in respect of a trade mark and the date accorded to the international registration of the trade mark pursuant to Article 3(4) is a date on or after [IP completion day][1]; or
   (ii) an existing request for EU extension in respect of a trade mark has been filed with the International Bureau and the date on which it was recorded in the International Register pursuant to Article 3ter(2) is a date on or after [IP completion day][1];
(b) the person who filed the existing ITM application or (as the case may be) the existing request for EU extension, or a successor in title of that person, applies for registration of the same trade mark under this Act for some or all of the same goods or services; and
(c) the application under this Act is made within the period of nine months beginning with the date referred to in sub-paragraph (a)(i) or (ii) (as the case may be).

(2) Where this paragraph applies, the relevant date for the purposes of establishing which rights take precedence is the earliest of—

(a) the date accorded to the international trade mark the subject of the existing ITM application pursuant to Article 3(4) or, in the case of an existing request for EU extension, the date on which the request was recorded in the International Register pursuant to Article 3ter(2);
(b) the date of priority (if any) accorded pursuant to a right of priority claimed pursuant to Article 4 of the Paris Convention in respect of the existing ITM application or the existing request for EU extension (as the case may be).

(3) The registrability of the trade mark the subject of an application under this Act of the type mentioned in sub-paragraph (1)(b) and made within the period mentioned in sub-paragraph (1)(c) shall not be affected by any use of the mark in the United Kingdom which commenced in the period between the date referred to in sub-paragraph (2) and the date of the application under this Act.

(4) A right of priority claimed pursuant to Article 4 of the Paris Convention in respect of an existing request for EU extension is to be disregarded for the purposes of sub-paragraph (2)(b) unless the existing request for EU extension was recorded in the International Register within a period of six months beginning with the day after the priority date recorded in the International Register in respect of the international application for protection of the trade mark which is the same as the one in respect of which the existing request for EU extension was filed.][2]

NOTES

1 Substituted by Intellectual Property (Amendment etc.) (EU Exit) Regulations 2020, SI 2020/1050, regs 13, 22(b) (31 December 2020).

2 Inserted by Designs and International Trade Marks (Amendment etc.) (EU Exit) Regulations 2019, SI 2019/638, reg 6, Sch 4, paras 1, 3 (31 January 2020).

[30 Right to claim seniority where seniority has been claimed by an existing ITM application or an existing request for EU extension

(1) Where an existing ITM application or an existing request for EU extension claims seniority of a trade mark which trade mark ("the senior mark") is a regis-

tered trade mark or a protected international trade mark (UK), the applicant may claim seniority of the senior mark in an application for registration of a trade mark (a "relevant mark") pursuant to this Part.

(2) The effect of a seniority claim made pursuant to sub-paragraph (1) is that where following the registration of the relevant mark the proprietor of that mark surrenders the senior mark or allows it to lapse (wholly or partially), subject to paragraph 31, the proprietor of the relevant mark is deemed to continue to have the same rights as the proprietor would have had if the senior mark had continued to be registered in respect of all the goods or services for which it was registered prior to the surrender or lapse.

(3) Provision may be made by rules as to the manner of claiming seniority pursuant to this paragraph.

(4) In sub-paragraph (1), an application for registration of a trade mark "pursuant to this Part" means an application that is of the type mentioned in paragraph 28(1)(b) or 29(1)(b) and that is made within the period mentioned in paragraph 28(1)(c) or 29(1)(c) (as the case may be).][1]

NOTES

1 Inserted by Designs and International Trade Marks (Amendment etc.) (EU Exit) Regulations 2019, SI 2019/638, reg 6, Sch 4, paras 1, 3 (31 January 2020).

[31 Determination of invalidity and liability to revocation in relation to claim of seniority under paragraph 30

(1) Where a relevant mark has claimed seniority of a registered trade mark which has been—

(a) removed from the register under section 43; or
(b) surrendered under section 45,

any person may apply to the registrar or to the court for the declaration set out in sub-paragraph (2).

(2) The declaration is that, if the trade mark had not been so removed or surrendered, the registration of the trade mark would have been liable to be revoked under section 46 with effect from a date specified in the declaration or declared invalid under section 47.

(3) Where the declaration is that had the trade mark not been so removed or surrendered, the registration of it would have been liable to be—

(a) revoked under section 46 with effect from a date prior to—
  (i) where the application for registration of the relevant mark was based on an existing ITM application and there has been no claim of priority, the date of registration accorded pursuant to Article 3(4) to the international trade mark the subject of the existing ITM application;
  (ii) where the application for registration of the relevant mark was based on an existing request for EU extension and there has been no claim of priority, the date on which the request was recorded in the International Register pursuant to Article 3ter(2);

(iii) where the application for registration of the relevant mark was based on an existing ITM application or an existing request for EU extension and there has been a claim of priority, the priority date accorded pursuant to a right of priority claimed pursuant to Article 4 of the Paris Convention; or

(b) declared invalid under section 47,

the seniority claimed for the relevant mark is to be treated as if it never had effect.

(4) Where a relevant mark has claimed seniority of a protected international trade mark (UK) which has been—

(a) removed from the International Register; or
(b) surrendered under the Madrid Protocol,

any person may apply to the registrar or to the court for the declaration set out in sub-paragraph (5).

(5) The declaration is that, if the trade mark had not been so removed or surrendered, the protection of the trade mark in the United Kingdom would have been liable to be revoked under section 46 with effect from a date specified in the declaration or declared invalid under section 47.

(6) Where the declaration is that had the trade mark not been so removed or surrendered, the registration of it would have been liable to be—

(a) revoked under section 46 with effect from a date prior to—
  (i) where the application for registration of the relevant mark was based on an existing ITM application and there has been no claim of priority, the date of registration accorded pursuant to Article 3(4) to the international trade mark the subject of the existing ITM application;
  (ii) where the application for registration of the relevant mark was based on an existing request for EU extension and there has been no claim of priority, the date on which the request was recorded in the International Register pursuant to Article 3ter(2);
  (iii) where the application for registration of the relevant mark was based on an existing ITM application or an existing request for EU extension and there has been a claim of priority, the priority date accorded pursuant to a right of priority claimed pursuant to Article 4 of the Paris Convention; or
(b) declared invalid under section 47,

the seniority claimed for the relevant mark is to be treated as if it never had effect.

(7) Where the application for registration of the relevant mark was based on an existing request for EU extension a right of priority claimed pursuant to Article 35 of the European Union Trade Mark Regulation in respect of the request for EU extension is to be disregarded for the purposes of sub-paragraphs (3)(a)(iii) and (6)(a)(iii) unless the request for territorial extension was recorded in the International Register within a period of six months beginning with the day after the priority date recorded in the International Register in respect of the international application for protection of the trade mark which is the same as the one in respect of which the request for EU extension was filed.

(8) References in sub-paragraphs (5) and (6) to sections 46 and 47 are to those sections as they apply to a protected international trade mark (UK) under an order made pursuant to section 54.

(9) Where a trade mark has been surrendered or allowed to lapse in respect of only some of the goods or services for which it is registered, the declaration in sub-paragraphs (2) and (5) is that if the goods or services had not been removed from the registration, the registration of the trade mark would have been liable to be revoked under section 46 with effect from a date specified in the declaration or declared invalid under section 47 and sub-paragraphs (3) and (6) shall be construed accordingly.

(10) The provisions of paragraph 16 apply in relation to an application under this paragraph as they apply to an application under paragraph 15.][1]

NOTES

1 Inserted by Designs and International Trade Marks (Amendment etc.) (EU Exit) Regulations 2019, SI 2019/638, reg 6, Sch 4, paras 1, 3 (31 January 2020).

[PART 4 TRANSFORMATION APPLICATIONS WHICH ARE PENDING ON [IP COMPLETION DAY][1]

32 *Transformation applications*

(1) In this Part, references to a "transformation application" are to an application for transformation of an international registration which has been cancelled (a "cancelled international registration") into an application for registration of a European Union trade mark filed under Article 204 of the European Union Trade Mark Regulation in respect of which the conditions in sub-paragraph (2) are satisfied.

(2) The conditions referred to in sub-paragraph (1) are—

(a) the transformation application was filed before [IP completion day][1] with the European Union Intellectual Property Office;

(b) as at the time immediately before [IP completion day][1] the transformation application has neither been granted nor refused by the European Union Intellectual Property Office under the European Union Trade Mark Regulation; and

(c) the international registration was not cancelled at the request of the Patent Office as Office of origin for the international registration of the trade mark.

(3) In sub-paragraph (2)(b)—

(a) the reference to the transformation application being "granted" means a European Union trade mark being registered under the European Union Trade Mark Regulation pursuant to the transformation application; and

(b) the reference to the transformation application being "refused" means the transformation application being subject to the provisions in Article 204(5) of the European Union Trade Mark Regulation.][2]

NOTES

1 Substituted by Intellectual Property (Amendment etc.) (EU Exit) Regulations 2020, SI 2020/1050, regs 13, 22(b) (31 December 2020).

2 Inserted by Designs and International Trade Marks (Amendment etc.) (EU Exit) Regulations 2019, SI 2019/638, reg 6, Sch 4, paras 1, 3 (31 January 2020).

[33 Application for registration based upon a cancelled international registration

(1) This paragraph applies where—

(a) a person who has filed a transformation application in respect of a cancelled international registration, or a successor in title of that person, applies for registration under this Act of a trade mark which is the same as the trade mark which was the subject of the cancelled international registration and in respect of some or all of the same goods or services included in the international registration;

(b) the application for registration under this Act is made within the period beginning with [IP completion day][1] and ending with the end of the relevant period; and

(c) on or before the date of the transformation application on which the application for registration under this Act is based the trade mark that was the subject of the cancelled international registration—

   (i) was protected in the European Union in accordance with Article 189(2) of the European Union Trade Mark Regulation; or

   (ii) was the subject of an existing ITM application or an existing request for EU extension which, as at that date, had neither been granted nor refused by the European Union Intellectual Property Office (the references to "granted" and "refused" having the same meaning as given by paragraph 27(4)).

(2) Where this paragraph applies by virtue of sub-paragraph (1)(c)(i), the relevant date for the purposes of establishing which rights take precedence is the earliest of—

(a) where—

   (i) the protection in the European Union of the trade mark that was the subject of the cancelled international registration resulted from a request for territorial extension under Article 3ter(1), the date of registration accorded to the international registration pursuant to Article 3(4); or

   (ii) the protection in the European Union of the trade mark that was the subject of the cancelled international registration resulted from a request for territorial extension under Article 3ter(2), the date on which the request was recorded in the International Register; and

(b) the date of priority (if any) accorded pursuant to a right of priority claimed pursuant to Article 4 of the Paris Convention in respect of the request referred to in paragraph (a)(i) or (ii).

(3) Where this paragraph applies by virtue of sub-paragraph (1)(c)(ii), the relevant date for the purposes of establishing which rights take precedence is the earliest of—

(a) the date accorded to the trade mark that was the subject of the existing ITM application pursuant to Article 3(4) or, in the case of an existing request for EU extension, the date on which the request was recorded in the International Register pursuant to Article 3ter(2); and

(b) the date of priority (if any) accorded pursuant to a right of priority claimed pursuant to Article 4 of the Paris Convention in respect of the request referred to in paragraph (a).

(4) A right of priority claimed pursuant to Article 4 of the Paris Convention in respect of a request for territorial extension to the European Union made under Article 3ter(2) is to be disregarded for the purposes of sub-paragraphs (2)(b) and (3)(b) unless the request for extension was recorded in the International Register within a period of six months beginning with the day after the priority date recorded in the International Register in respect of the international application for protection of the trade mark which is the same as the one in respect of which the request for extension was filed.

(5) The registrability of the trade mark the subject of an application under this Act of the type mentioned in sub-paragraph (1)(a) and made within the period mentioned in sub-paragraph (1)(b) shall not be affected by any use of the mark in the United Kingdom which commenced in the period between the date referred to in sub-paragraph (2) or (3) (as the case may be) and the date of the application for registration of the trade mark under this Act.

(6) Paragraphs 30 and 31 apply in relation to an application for a trade mark under this Act of the type mentioned in sub-paragraph (1)(a) and made within the period mentioned in sub-paragraph (1)(b), as they apply in relation to an application for registration of a trade mark pursuant to Part 3, but as if—

(a) the references to an existing ITM application or an existing request for EU extension and an existing ITM application and an existing request for EU extension had the same meaning as they have in this paragraph; and
(b) the references to an existing ITM application included references to a "protected EU designation".

(7) In this paragraph—

(a) an "existing ITM application" means an international application which contains a request for extension of the protection resulting from an international registration to the European Union under Article 3ter(1) which has been filed with the Office of origin in accordance with Article 2(2);
(b) an "existing request for EU extension" means a request for extension to the European Union of the protection resulting from an international registration made subsequent to the international registration pursuant to Article 3ter(2) which has been filed with the Office of origin or the International Bureau (as the case may be) in accordance with Rule 24(2);
(c) the "relevant period" means the period of nine months beginning with the day after that on which [IP completion day][1] falls;
(d) a "protected EU designation" means an international registration which prior to its cancellation was protected in the European Union in accordance with Article 189(2) of the European Union Trade Mark Regulation.][2]

NOTES

1 Substituted by Intellectual Property (Amendment etc.) (EU Exit) Regulations 2020, SI 2020/1050, regs 13, 22(b) (31 December 2020).

2 Inserted by Designs and International Trade Marks (Amendment etc.) (EU Exit) Regulations 2019, SI 2019/638, reg 6, Sch 4, paras 1, 3 (31 January 2020).

[PART 5 INTERPRETATION

34 Interpretation

(1) In this Schedule—

"comparable trade mark (IR)" has the meaning given by paragraph 1(4);
"the Common Regulations" means the Common Regulations under the Madrid Agreement concerning the international registration of marks and the Madrid Protocol in force on 1st November 2017;
"corresponding (IR)" has the meaning given by paragraph 3(4);
"existing IR(EU)" has the meaning given by paragraph 1(1);
"expired IR(EU)" has the meaning given by paragraph 23(1);
"international application" has the meaning given by paragraph 27(1)(c);
"the International Register" has the meaning given by paragraph 1(11)(a);
"international registration" has the meaning given by paragraph 1(11)(b);
"international trade mark" has the meaning given by paragraph 1(11)(c);
"Office of origin" has the meaning given by Article 2(2);
"the previous EUTM Regulations" means Council Regulation (EC) No 207/2009 of 26th February 2009 on the European Union trade mark and Council Regulation (EC) No 40/94 of 20th December 1993 on the Community trade mark;
"protected international trade mark (UK)" has the same meaning as in the Trade Marks (International Registration) Order 2008;

(2) References in this Schedule to—

(a) an "Article" are to an Article of the Madrid Protocol;
(b) an Article of the European Union Trade mark Regulation include references to any equivalent Article contained in the previous EUTM Regulations;
(c) the European Union Trade Mark Regulation include references to the previous EUTM Regulations;
(d) an international trade mark include references to an international trade mark which is dealt with for the purposes of the European Union Trade Mark Regulation as an EU collective mark or an EU certification mark;
(e) a "Rule" are to a Rule of the Common Regulations.

(3) In this Schedule, references to a request for territorial extension, in relation to an existing IR(EU) which is the subject of a separate international registration within the meaning of paragraph 1(3), are to the request made before the separate international registration was created.][1]

NOTES

1 Inserted by Designs and International Trade Marks (Amendment etc.) (EU Exit) Regulations 2019, SI 2019/638, reg 6, Sch 4, paras 1, 3 (31 January 2020).

Schedule 3 Transitional provisions

Section 105

INTRODUCTORY

1 (1) In this Schedule—

"existing registered mark" means a trade mark, certification trade mark or service mark registered under the 1938 Act immediately before the commencement of this Act;

"the 1938 Act" means the Trade Marks Act 1938; and
"the old law" means that Act and any other enactment or rule of law applying to existing registered marks immediately before the commencement of this Act.

(2) For the purposes of this Schedule—

(a) an application shall be treated as pending on the commencement of this Act if it was made but not finally determined before commencement, and
(b) the date on which it was made shall be taken to be the date of filing under the 1938 Act.

EXISTING REGISTERED MARKS

2 (1) Existing registered marks (whether registered in Part A or B of the register kept under the 1938 Act shall be transferred on the commencement of this Act to the register kept under this Act and have effect, subject to the provisions of this Schedule, as if registered under this Act.

(2) Existing registered marks registered as a series under section 21(2) of the 1938 Act shall be similarly registered in the new register.

Provision may be made by rules for putting such entries in the same form as is required for entries under this Act.

(3) In any other case notes indicating that existing registered marks are associated with other marks shall cease to have effect on the commencement of this Act.

3 (1) A condition entered on the former register in relation to an existing registered mark immediately before the commencement of this Act shall cease to have effect on commencement.

Proceedings under section 33 of the 1938 Act (application to expunge or vary registration for breach of condition) which are pending on the commencement of this Act shall be dealt with under the old law and any necessary alteration made to the new register.

(2) A disclaimer or limitation entered on the former register in relation to an existing registered mark immediately before the commencement of this Act shall be transferred to the new register and have effect as if entered on the register in pursuance of section 13 of this Act.

EFFECTS OF REGISTRATION: INFRINGEMENT

4 (1) Sections 9 to 12 of this Act (effects of registration) apply in relation to an existing registered mark as from the commencement of this Act and section 14 of this Act (action for infringement) applies in relation to infringement of an existing registered mark committed after the commencement of this Act, subject to sub-paragraph (2) below.

The old law continues to apply in relation to infringements committed before commencement

(2) It is not an infringement of—

(a) an existing registered mark, or

(b) a registered trade mark of which the distinctive elements are the same or substantially the same as those of an existing registered mark and which is registered for the same goods or services.

to continue after commencement any use which did not amount to infringement of the existing registered mark under the old law.

INFRINGING GOODS, MATERIAL OR ARTICLES

5 Section 16 of this Act(order for delivery up of infringing goods, material or articles) applies to infringing goods, material or articles whether made before or after the commencement of this Act.

RIGHTS AND REMEDIES OF LICENSEE OR AUTHORISED USER

6 (1) Section 30 (general provisions as to rights of licensees in case of infringement) of this Act applies to licences granted before the commencement of this Act, but only in relation to infringements committed after commencement

(2) Paragraph 14 of Schedule 2 of this Act(court to take into account loss suffered by authorised users, &c) applies only in relation to infringements committed after commencement.

CO-OWNERSHIP OF REGISTERED MARK

7 The provisions of section 23 of this Act (co-ownership of registered mark) apply as from the commencement of this Act to an existing registered mark of which two or more persons were immediately before commencement registered as joint proprietors.

But so long as the relations between the joint proprietors remain such as are described in section 63 of the 1938 Act (joint ownership) there shall be taken to be an agreement to exclude the operation of subsections (1) and (3) of section 23 of this Act (ownership in undivided shares and right of co-proprietor to make separate use of the mark).

ASSIGNMENT. &C. OF REGISTERED MARK

8 (1) Section 24 of this Act (assignment or other transmission of registered mark) applies to transactions and events occurring after the commencement of this Act in relation to an existing registered mark, and the old law continues to apply in relation to transactions and events occurring before commencement.

(2) Existing entries under section 25 of the 1938 Act (registration of assignments and transmissions) shall be transferred on the commencement of this Act to the register kept under this Act and have effect as if made under section 25 of this Act.

Provision may be made by rules for putting such entries in the same form as is required for entries made under this Act.

(3) An application for registration under section 25 of the 1938 Act which is pending before the registrar on the commencement of this Act shall be treated as an application for registration under section 25 of this Act and shall proceed accordingly.

The registrar may require the applicant to amend his application so as to conform with the requirements of this Act.

(4) An application for registration under section 25 of the 1938 Act which has been determined by the registrar but not finally determined before the commencement of this Act shall be dealt with under the old law; and sub-paragraph (2) above shall apply in relation to any resulting entry in the register.

(5) Where before the commencement of this Act a person has become entitled by assignment or transmission to an existing registered mark but has not registered his title, any application for registration after commencement shall be made under section 25 of this Act.

(6) In cases to which sub-paragraph (3) or (5) applies section 25(3) of the 1938 Act continues to apply (and section 25(3) and (4) of this Act do not apply as regards the consequences of failing to register.

LICENSING OF REGISTERED MARK

9 (1) Sections 28 and 29(2) of this Act (licensing of registered trade mark; rights of exclusive license against grantor's successor in title) apply only in relation to licences granted after the commencement of this Act; and the old law continues to apply in relation to licences granted before commencement.

(2) Existing entries under section 28 of the 1938 Act (registered users) shall be transferred on the commencement of this Act to the register kept under this Act and have effect as if made under section 25 of this Act.

Provision may be made by rules for putting such entries in the same form as it required for entries made under this Act.

(3) An application for registration as a registered user which is pending before the registrar on the commencement of this Act shall be treated as an application for registration of a licence under section 25(1) of this Act and shall proceed accordingly.

The registrar may require the applicant to amend his application so as to conform with the requirements of this Act.

(4) An application for registration as a registered user which has been determined by the registrar but not finally determined before the commencement of this Act shall be dealt with under the old law; and sub-paragraph (2) above shall apply in relation to any resulting entry in the register.

(5) Any proceedings pending on the commencement of this Act under section 28(8) or (10) of the 1938 Act (variation or cancellation of registration of registered user) shall be dealt with under the old law and any necessary alteration made to the new register.

PENDING APPLICATIONS FOR REGISTRATION

10 (1) An application for registration of a mark under the 1938 Act which is pending on the commencement of this Act shall be dealt with under the old law, subject as mentioned below, and if registered the mark shall be treated for the purposes of this Schedule as an existing registered mark.

(2) The power of the Secretary of State under section 78 of this Act to make rules regulating practice and procedure, and as to the matters mentioned in subsection (2) of that section, is exercisable in relation to such an application, and different provision may be made for such applications from that made for other applications.

(3) Section 23 of the 1938 Act (provisions as to associated trade marks) shall be disregarded in dealing after the commencement of this Act with an application for registration.

CONVERSION OF PENDING APPLICATION

11 (1) In the case of a pending application for registration which has not been advertised under section 18 of the 1938 Act before the commencement of this Act, the applicant may give notice to the registrar claiming to have the registrability of the mark determined in accordance with the provisions of this Act.

(2) The notice must be in the prescribed form, be accompanied by the appropriate fee and be given no later than six months after the commencement of this Act.

(3) Notice duly given is irrevocable and has the effect that the application shall be treated as if made immediately after the commencement of this Act.

TRADE MARKS REGISTERED ACCORDING TO OLD CLASSIFICATION

12 The registrar may exercise the powers conferred by rules under section 65 of this Act (adaptation of entries to new classification) to secure that any existing registered marks which do not conform to the system of classification prescribed under section 34 of this Act are brought into conformity with that system.

This applies, in particular, to existing registered marks classified according to the pre-1938 classification set out in Schedule 3 to the Trade Marks Rules 1986.

CLAIM TO PRIORITY FROM OVERSEAS APPLICATION

13 Section 35 of this Act claim to priority of Convention application) applies to an application for registration under this Act made after the commencement of this Act notwithstanding that the Convention application was made before commencement.

14 (1) Where before the commencement of this Act a person has duly filed an application for protection of a trade mark in a relevant country within the meaning of section 39A of the 1938 Act which is not a Convention country (a "relevant overseas application"), he, or his successor in title, has a right to priority, for the purposes of registering the same trade mark under this Act for some or all of the same goods or services, for a period of six months from the date of filing of the relevant overseas application.

(2) If the application for registration under this Act is made within that six-month period—

(a) the relevant date for the purposes of establishing which rights take precedence shall be the date of filing of the relevant overseas application, and
(b) the registrability of the trade mark shall not be affected by any use of the mark in the United Kingdom in the period between that date and the date of the application under this Act.

(3) Any filing which in a relevant country is equivalent to a regular national filing, under its domestic legislation or an international agreement, shall be treated as giving rise to the right of priority.

A "regular national filing" means a filing which is adequate to establish the date on which the application was filed in that country, whatever may be the subsequent fate of the application.

(4) A subsequent application concerning the same subject as the relevant overseas application, filed in the same country, shall be considered the relevant overseas application (of which the filing date is the starting date of the period of priority), if at the time of the subsequent application—

(a) the previous application has been withdrawn, abandoned or refused, without having been laid open to public inspection and without leaving any rights outstanding, and
(b) it has not yet served as a basis for claiming a right of priority.

The previous application may not thereafter serve as a basis for claiming a right of priority.

(5) Provision may be made by rules as to the manner of claiming a right to priority on the basis of a relevant overseas application.

(6) A right to priority arising as a result of a relevant overseas application may be assigned or otherwise transmitted, either with the application or independently.

The reference in sub-paragraph (1) to the applicant's "successor in title"shall be construed accordingly.

(7) Nothing in this paragraph affects proceedings on an application for registration under the 1938 Act made before the commencement of this Act (see paragraph 10 above).

DURATION AND RENEWAL OF REGISTRATION

15 (1) Section 42(1) of this Act (duration of original period of registration) applies in relation to the registration of a mark in pursuance of an application made after the commencement of this Act; and the old law applies in any other case.

(2) Sections 42(2) and 43 of this Act (renewal) apply where the renewal falls due on or after the commencement of this Act; and the old law continues to apply in any other case.

(3) In either case it is immaterial when the fee is paid.

PENDING APPLICATION FOR ALTERATION OF REGISTERED MARK

16 An application under section 35 of the 1938 Act (alternation of registered trade mark) which is pending on the commencement of this Act shall be dealt with under the old law and any necessary alteration made to the new register.

REVOCATION FOR NON-USE

17 (1) An application under section 26 of the 1938 Act (removal from register or imposition of limitation on ground of non-use) which is pending on the commencement of this Act shall be dealt with under the old law and any necessary alteration made to the new register.

(2) An application under section 46(1)(a) or (b) of this Act (revocation for non-use) may be made in relation to an existing registered mark at any time after the commencement of this Act.

Provided that no such application for the revocation of the registration of an existing registered mark registered by virtue of section 27 of the 1938 Act (defensive registration of well-known trade marks) may be made until more than five years after the commencement of this Act.

APPLICATION FOR RECTIFICATION, &C.

18 (1) An application under section 32 or 34 of the 1938 Act (rectification or correction of the register) which is pending on the commencement of this Act shall be dealt with under the old law and any necessary alteration made to the new register.

(2) For the purposes of proceedings under section 47 of this Act (grounds for invalidity of registration) as it applies in relation to an existing registered mark, the provisions of this Act shall be deemed to have been in force at all material times.

Provided that no objection to the validity of the registration of an existing registered mark may be taken on the ground specified in subsection (3) of section 5 of this Act (relative grounds for refusal of registration conflict with earlier mark registered for different goods or services).

REGULATIONS AS TO USE OF CERTIFICATION MARK

19 (1) Regulations governing the use of an existing registered certification mark deposited at the Patent Office in pursuance of section 37 of the 1938 Act shall be treated after the commencement of this Act as if filed under paragraph 6 of Schedule 2 to this Act.

(2) Any request for amendment of the regulations which was pending on the commencement of this Act shall be dealt with under the old law.

SHEFFIELD MARKS

20 (1) For the purposes of this Schedule the Sheffield register kept under Schedule 2 to the 1938 Act shall be treated as part of the register of trade marks kept under that Act.

(2) Applications made to the Cutlers' Company in accordance with that Schedule which are pending on the commencement of this Act shall proceed after commencement as if they had been made to the registrar.

CERTIFICATE OF VALIDITY OF CONTESTED REGISTRATION

21 A certificate given before the commencement of this Act under section 47 of the 1938 Act (certificate of validity of contested registration) shall have effect as if given under section 73(1) of this Act.

TRADE MARK AGENTS

22 (1) Rules in force immediately before the commencement of this Act under section 282 or 283 of the Copyright, Designs and Patents Act 1988 (register of trade mark agents; persons entitled to described themselves as registered) shall continue in force and have effect as if made under section 83 or 85 of this Act.

(2) Rules in force immediately before the commencement of this Act under section 40 of the 1938 Act as to the persons whom the registrar may refuse to recognise as agents for the purposes of business under that Act shall continue in force and have effect as if made under section 88 of this Act.

(3) Rules continued in force under this paragraph may be varied or revoked by further rules made under the relevant provisions of this Act.

Schedule 4 Consequential amendments

Section 106(1)

GENERAL ADAPTATION OF EXISTING REFERENCES

1 (1) References in statutory provisions passed or made before the commencement of this Act to trade marks or registered trade marks within the meaning of the Trade Marks Act 1938 shall, unless the context otherwise requires, be construed after the commencement of this Act as references to trade marks or registered trade marks within the meaning of this Act.

(2) Sub-paragraph (1) applies, in particular, to the references in the following provisions—

Industrial Organisation and Development Act 1947	Schedule 1, paragraph 7
Crown Proceedings Act 1947	section 3(1)(b)
[...][1]	
Printer's Imprint Act 1961	section 1(1)(b)
[...][2]	
[...][3]	
Patents Act 1977	section 19(2) section 27(4) section 123(7)
Unfair Contract Terms Act 1977	Schedule 1, paragraph 1(c)
Judicature (Northern Ireland) Act 1978	section 94A(5)
State Immunity Act 1978	section 7(a) and (b).
[Senior Courts Act 1981][4]	section 72(5)
	Schedule 1, paragraph 1(i)
Civil Jurisdiction and Judgments Act 1982	Schedule 5, paragraph 2 Schedule 8, paragraph 2(14) and 4(2)
Value Added Tax Act 1983	Schedule 3, paragraph 1
[...][5]	
Law Reform (Miscellaneous Provisions) (Scotland) Act 1985	section 15(5)
Atomic Energy Authority Act 1986	section 8(2)
[...][6]	
Consumer Protection Act 1987	section 2(2)(b)
Consumer Protection (Northern Ireland) Order 1987.	article 5(2)(b)
Income and Corporation Taxes Act 1988	section 83(a)
Taxation of Chargeable Gains Act 1992	section 275(h)
Tribunals and Inquiries Act 1992	Schedule 1, paragraph 34.

NOTES

1 Repealed by Statute Law (Repeals) Act 2004, s 1(1), Sch 1, Pt 2, Ch (1) (22 July 2004).
2 Repealed by Plant Varieties Act 1997, s 52, Sch 4 (8 May 1998).
3 Repealed by Northern Ireland Act 1998, s 100(2), Sch 15 (2 December 1999: repeal has effect as SI 1999/3209 subject to savings and transitional provisions specified in Northern Ireland Act 1998, Sch 15, paras 21-23).
4 Substituted by Constitutional Reform Act 2005, s 59(5), Sch 11, para 1(2) (1 October 2009).

5 Repealed by Companies Act 2006, s 1295, Sch 16 (1 October 2009 as SI 2008/2860).
6 Repealed by Companies Act 2006 (Consequential Amendments, Transitional Provisions and Savings) Order 2009, SI 2009/1941, art 2(2), Sch 2 (1 October 2009).

PATENTS AND DESIGNS ACT 1907 (C.29)

2 (1) The Patents and Designs Act 1907 is amended as follows.

(2) In section 62 (the Patent Office)—

(a) in subsection (1) for ""this Act and the Trade Marks Act 1905"" substitute ""the Patents Act 1977 the Registered Designs Act 1949 and the Trade Marks Act 1994"", and
(b) In subsections (2) and (3) for ""the Board of Trade"" substitute ""the Secretary of State"".

(3) In section 63 (officers and clerks of the Patent Office)—

(a) for ""the Board of Trade"" in each place where it occurs substitute ""the Secretary of State""; and
(b) in subsection (2) omit the words from ""and those salaries"" to the end.

(4) The repeal by the Patents Act 1949 and the Registered Designs Act 1949 of the whole of the 1907 Act, except certain provisions, shall be deemed not to have extended to the long title, date of enactment or enacting words or to so much of section 99 as provides the Act with its short title.

PATENTS, DESIGNS, COPYRIGHT AND TRADE MARKS (EMERGENCY) ACT 1939 (C.107)

3 (1) The Patents, Designs, Copyright and Trade Marks (Emergency) Act 1939 is amended as follows.

(2) For section 3 (power of comptroller to suspend rights of enemy or enemy subject) substitute—

"3 Power of comptroller to suspend trade mark rights of enemy or enemy subject

(1) Where on application made by a person proposing to supply goods or services of any description it is made to appear to the comptroller

(a) that it is difficult or impracticable to describe or refer to the goods or services without the use of a registered trade mark, and
(b) that the proprietor of the registered trade mark (whether alone or jointly with another) is an enemy or an enemy subject,

the comptroller may make an order suspending the rights given by the registered trade mark.

(2) An order under this section shall suspend those rights as regards the use of the trade mark—

(a) by the applicant, and
(b) by any person authorised by the applicant to do, for the purposes of or in connection with the supply by the applicant of the goods or services, things which would otherwise infringe the registered trade mark,

to such extent and for such period as the comptroller considers necessary to enable the applicant to render well-known and established some other means of describing or referring to the goods or services in question which does not involves the use of the trade mark.

(3) Where an order has been made under this section; no action for passing off lies on the part of any person interested in the registered trade mark in respect of any use of it which by virtue of the order is not an infringement of the right conferred by it.

(4) An order under this section may be varied or revoked by a subsequent order made by the comptroller".

(3) In each of the following provisions—

(a) section 4(1)(c) (effect of war on registration of trade marks),
(b) section 6(1) (power of comptroller to extend time limits),
(c) section 7(1)(a) (evidence as to nationality, &c.), and
(d) the definition of ""the trade comptroller"" in section 10(1) (interpretation),

for ""the Trade Marks Act 1938"" substitute ""the Trade Marks Act 1994"".

TRADE DESCRIPTIONS ACT 1968 (C.29)

4 In the Trade Descriptions Act 1968, in section 34 (exemption of trade description contained in pre-1968 trade mark)—

(a) in the opening words, omit ""within the meaning of the Trade Marks Act 1938""; and
(b) in paragraph (c) for ""a person registered under section 28 of the Trade Marks Act 1938 as a registered user of the trade mark"" substitute "", in the case of a registered trade mark, a person licensed to use it"".

SOLICITORS ACT 1974 (C.47)

5 […][1]

NOTES

1 Repealed by Legal Services Act 2007, s 210, Sch 23 (1 January 2010 as SI 2009/3250).

HOUSE OF COMMONS DISQUALIFICATION ACT 1975 (C.24)

6 In Part III of Schedule 1 to the House of Commons Disqualification Act 1975 (other disqualifying offices), for the entry relating to persons appointed to hear and determine appeals under the Trade Marks Act 1938 substitute—

"Person appointed to hear and determine appeals under the Trade Marks Act 1994.".

RESTRICTIVE TRADE PRACTICES ACT 1976 (C. 34)

7 In Schedule 3 to the Restrictive Trade Practices Act 1976 (excepted agreements), for paragraph 4 (agreements relating to trade marks) substitute—

"4 (1) This Act does not apply to an agreement authorising the use of a registered trade mark (other than a collective mark or certification mark) if no such restrictions as are described in section 6(1) or 11(2) above are accepted, and no such information provisions as are described in section 7(1) or 12(2) above are made, except in respect of—

(a) the descriptions of goods bearing the mark which are to be produced or supplied, or the processes of manufacture to be applied to such goods or to goods to which the mark is to be applied, or
(b) the kinds of services in relation to which the mark as to be used which are to be made available or supplied, or the form or manner in which such services are to be made available or supplied, or
(c) the descriptions of goods which are to be produced or supplied in connection with the supply of services in relation to which the mark is to be used, or the process of manufacture to be applied to such goods.

(2) This Act does not apply to an agreement authorising the use of a registered collective mark or certification mark if—

(a) the agreement is made in accordance with regulations approved by the registrar under Schedule 1 or 2 to the Trade Marks Act 1994 and
(b) no such restrictions as are described in section 6(1) or 11(2) above are accepted, and no such information provisions as are described in section 7(1) or 12(2) above are made, except as permitted by those regulations".

COPYRIGHT, DESIGNS AND PATENTS ACT 1988 (C.48)

8 (1) The Copyright, Designs and Patents Act 1988 is amended as follows.

(2) In section 114(6), 204(6) and 231(6) (persons regarded as having an interest in infringing copies, &c.), for ""section 58C of the Trade Marks Act 1938"" substitute ""section 19 of the Trade Marks Act 1994"".

(3) In section 280(1) (privilege for communications with patent agents), for ""trade mark or service mark"" substitute ""or trade mark"".

TRIBUNALS AND INQUIRIES ACT 1992 (C.53)

9 In Part 1 of Schedule 1 to the Tribunals and Inquiries Act 1992 (tribunals under direct supervision of Council on Tribunals), for ""Patents, designs, trade marks and service marks"" substitute ""Patents, designs and trade marks"".

Schedule 5 Repeals and revocations

Section 106(2)

Chapter or number	*Short title*	*Extent of repeal or revocation*
1891 c. 50.	Commissioners for Oaths Act 1891.	In section 1, the words ""or the Patents, Designs and Trade Marks Acts 1883 to 1888"".
1907 c. 29.	Patents and Designs Act 1907.	In section 63(2), the words from ""and those salaries"" to the end.
1938 c. 22.	Trade Marks Act 1938.	The whole Act.
1947 c. 44.	Crown Proceedings Act 1947.	In section 3(1)(b), the words ""or registered services mark"".
1949 c. 87.	Patents Act 1949.	Section 92(2).
1964 c. 14.	Plant Varieties and Seeds Act 1964.	In section 5A(4), the words ""under the Trade Marks Act 1938"".
1967 c. 80.	Criminal Justice Act 1967.	In Schedule 3, in Parts I and IV, the entries relating to the Trade Marks Act 1938.
1978 c. 23.	Judicature (Northern Ireland) Act 1978.	In Schedule 5, in Part II, the paragraphs amending the Trade Marks Act 1938.
1984 c. 19.	Trade Marks (Amendment) Act 1984.	The whole Act.
1985 c. 6.	Companies Act 1985.	In section 396 – (a) in subsection (3A)(a), and (b) in subsection (2)(d)(i) as inserted by the Companies Act 1989, the words ""service mark,"".
1986 c. 12.	Statute Law (Repeals) Act 1986.	In Schedule 2, paragraph 2.
1986 c. 39.	Patents, Designs and Marks Act 1986.	Section 2. Section 4(4). In Schedule 1, paragraphs 1 and 2. Schedule 2.

Chapter or number	*Short title*	*Extent of repeal or revocation*
S.I. 1986/1032.	Companies (Northern Ireland) Order 1986.	In article 403 – (a) in paragraph (3A)(a), and (b) in paragraph (2)(d)(i) as inserted by the Companies (No.2) (Northern Ireland) Order 1990, the words "“service mark,”".
1987 c. 43.	Consumer Protection Act 1987.	In section 45 – (a) in subsection (1), the definition of "mark" and "trade mark"; (b) subsection (4).
S.I. 1987/2049.	Consumer Protection (Northern Ireland) Order 1987.	In article 2 – (a) in paragraph (2) the definitions of "mark" and "trade mark", (b) paragraph (3).
1988 c. 1.	Income and Corporation Taxes Act 1988.	In section 83, the words from "“References in this section”" to the end.
1988 c. 48.	Copyright, Designs and Patents Act 1988.	Sections 282 to 284. In section 286, the definition of "registered trade mark agent". Section 300.
1992 c. 12.	Taxation of Chargeable Gains Act 1992.	In section 275(h), the words "“service marks”" and "“service mark”".

Appendix 2

Regulation (EU) 2017/1001 of the European Parliament and of the Council

of 14 June 2017

on the European Union trade mark (codification)

The European Parliament and the Council of the European Union,

Having regard to the Treaty on the Functioning of the European Union, and in particular the first paragraph of Article 118 thereof,

Having regard to the proposal from the European Commission,

After transmission of the draft legislative act to the national parliaments,

Acting in accordance with the ordinary legislative procedure,

Whereas:

(1) Council Regulation (EC) No 207/2009 has been substantially amended several times. In the interests of clarity and rationality, that Regulation should be codified.

(2) Council Regulation (EC) No 40/94, which was codified in 2009 as Regulation (EC) No 207/2009, created a system of trade mark protection specific to the Union which provided for the protection of trade marks at the level of the Union, in parallel to the protection of trade marks available at the level of the Member States in accordance with the national trade mark systems, harmonised by Council Directive 89/104/EEC, which was codified as Directive 2008/95/EC of the European Parliament and of the Council.

(3) It is desirable to promote throughout the Union a harmonious development of economic activities and a continuous and balanced expansion by completing an internal market which functions properly and offers conditions which are similar to those obtaining in a national market. In order to establish a market of this kind and make it increasingly a single market, not only should barriers to free movement of goods and services be removed and arrangements be instituted which

ensure that competition is not distorted, but, in addition, legal conditions should be laid down which enable undertakings to adapt their activities to the scale of the Union, whether in manufacturing and distributing goods or in providing services. For those purposes, trade marks enabling the products and services of undertakings to be distinguished by identical means throughout the entire Union, regardless of frontiers, should feature amongst the legal instruments which undertakings have at their disposal.

(4) For the purpose of pursuing the Union's said objectives it would appear necessary to provide for Union arrangements for trade marks whereby undertakings can by means of one procedural system obtain EU trade marks to which uniform protection is given and which produce their effects throughout the entire area of the Union. The principle of the unitary character of the EU trade mark thus stated should apply unless otherwise provided for in this Regulation.

(5) The barrier of territoriality of the rights conferred on proprietors of trade marks by the laws of the Member States cannot be removed by approximation of laws. In order to open up unrestricted economic activity in the whole of the internal market for the benefit of undertakings, it should be possible to register trade marks which are governed by a uniform Union law directly applicable in all Member States.

(6) The experience acquired since the establishment of the Community trade mark system has shown that undertakings from within the Union and from third countries have accepted the system which has become a successful and viable complement and alternative to the protection of trade marks at the level of the Member States.

(7) The Union law relating to trade marks nevertheless does not replace the laws of the Member States on trade marks. It would not in fact appear to be justified to require undertakings to apply for registration of their trade marks as EU trade marks.

(8) National trade marks continue to be necessary for those undertakings which do not want protection of their trade marks at Union level, or which are unable to obtain Union-wide protection while national protection does not face any obstacles. It should be left to each person seeking trade mark protection to decide whether the protection is sought only as a national trade mark in one or more Member States, or only as an EU trade mark, or both.

(9) The rights in an EU trade mark should not be obtained otherwise than by registration, and registration should be refused in particular if the trade mark is not distinctive, if it is unlawful or if it conflicts with earlier rights.

(10) A sign should be permitted to be represented in any appropriate form using generally available technology, and thus not necessarily by graphic means, as long as the representation is clear, precise, self-contained, easily accessible, intelligible, durable and objective.

(11) The protection afforded by an EU trade mark, the function of which is in particular to guarantee the trade mark as an indication of origin, should be absolute in the case of identity between the mark and the sign and the goods or services. The protection should apply also in cases of similarity between the mark and the

sign and the goods or services. An interpretation should be given for the concept of similarity in relation to the likelihood of confusion. The likelihood of confusion, the appreciation of which depends on numerous elements and, in particular, on the recognition of the trade mark on the market, the association which can be made with the used or registered sign, the degree of similarity between the trade mark and the sign and between the goods or services identified, should constitute the specific condition for such protection.

(12) In order to ensure legal certainty and full consistency with the principle of priority, under which a registered earlier trade mark takes precedence over later registered trade marks, it is necessary to provide that the enforcement of rights conferred by an EU trade mark should be without prejudice to the rights of proprietors acquired prior to the filing or priority date of the EU trade mark. This is in conformity with Article 16(1) of the Agreement on trade-related aspects of intellectual property rights of 15 April 1994.

(13) Confusion as to the commercial source from which the goods or services emanate may occur when a company uses the same or a similar sign as a trade name in such a way that a link is established between the company bearing the name and the goods or services coming from that company. Infringement of an EU trade mark should therefore also comprise the use of the sign as a trade name or similar designation as long as the use is made for the purposes of distinguishing goods or services.

(14) In order to ensure legal certainty and full consistency with specific Union legislation, it is appropriate to provide that the proprietor of an EU trade mark should be entitled to prohibit a third party from using a sign in comparative advertising where such comparative advertising is contrary to Directive 2006/114/EC of the European Parliament and of the Council.

(15) In order to ensure trade mark protection and combat counterfeiting effectively, and in line with international obligations of the Union under the framework of the World Trade Organisation (WTO), in particular Article V of the General Agreement on Tariffs and Trade (GATT) on freedom of transit and, as regards generic medicines, the 'Declaration on the TRIPS Agreement and public health' adopted by the Doha WTO Ministerial Conference on 14 November 2001, the proprietor of an EU trade mark should be entitled to prevent third parties from bringing goods, in the course of trade, into the Union without being released for free circulation there, where such goods come from third countries and bear without authorisation a trade mark which is identical or essentially identical with the EU trade mark registered in respect of such goods.

(16) To this effect, it should be permissible for EU trade mark proprietors to prevent the entry of infringing goods and their placement in all customs situations, including transit, transhipment, warehousing, free zones, temporary storage, inward processing or temporary admission, also when such goods are not intended to be placed on the market of the Union. In performing customs controls, the customs authorities should make use of the powers and procedures laid down in Regulation (EU) No 608/2013 of the European Parliament and the Council, also at the request of the right holders. In particular, the customs authorities should carry out the relevant controls on the basis of risk analysis criteria.

(17) In order to reconcile the need to ensure the effective enforcement of trade mark rights with the necessity to avoid hampering the free flow of trade in legitimate goods, the entitlement of the proprietor of the EU trade mark should lapse where, during the subsequent proceedings initiated before the European Union trade mark court ('EU trade mark court') competent to take a substantive decision on whether the EU trade mark has been infringed, the declarant or the holder of the goods is able to prove that the proprietor of the EU trade mark is not entitled to prohibit the placing of the goods on the market in the country of final destination.

(18) Article 28 of Regulation (EU) No 608/2013 provides that a right holder is to be liable for damages towards the holder of the goods where, inter alia, the goods in question are subsequently found not to infringe an intellectual property right.

(19) Appropriate measures should be taken with a view to ensuring the smooth transit of generic medicines. With respect to international non-proprietary names (INN) as globally recognised generic names for active substances in pharmaceutical preparations, it is vital to take due account of the existing limitations on the effect of EU trade mark rights. Consequently, the proprietor of an EU trade mark should not have the right to prevent a third party from bringing goods into the Union without being released for free circulation there, based upon similarities between the INN for the active ingredient in the medicines and the trade mark.

(20) In order to enable proprietors of EU trade marks to combat counterfeiting effectively, they should be entitled to prohibit the affixing of an infringing mark to goods and preparatory acts carried out prior to the affixing.

(21) The exclusive rights conferred by an EU trade mark should not entitle the proprietor to prohibit the use of signs or indications by third parties which are used fairly and thus in accordance with honest practices in industrial and commercial matters. In order to ensure equal conditions for trade names and EU trade marks in the event of conflicts, given that trade names are regularly granted unrestricted protection against later trade marks, such use should be only considered to include the use of the personal name of the third party. It should further permit the use of descriptive or non-distinctive signs or indications in general. Furthermore, the proprietor should not be entitled to prevent the fair and honest use of the EU trade mark for the purpose of identifying or referring to the goods or services as those of the proprietor. Use of a trade mark by third parties to draw the consumer's attention to the resale of genuine goods that were originally sold by or with the consent of the proprietor of the EU trade mark in the Union should be considered as being fair as long as it is at the same time in accordance with honest practices in industrial and commercial matters. Use of a trade mark by third parties for the purpose of artistic expression should be considered as being fair as long as it is at the same time in accordance with honest practices in industrial and commercial matters. Furthermore, this Regulation should be applied in a way that ensures full respect for fundamental rights and freedoms, and in particular the freedom of expression.

(22) It follows from the principle of free movement of goods that it is essential that the proprietor of an EU trade mark not be entitled to prohibit its use by a third party in relation to goods which have been put into circulation in the European Economic Area, under the trade mark, by him or with his consent, save where

there exist legitimate reasons for the proprietor to oppose further commercialisation of the goods.

(23) In order to ensure legal certainty and safeguard legitimately acquired trade mark rights, it is appropriate and necessary to lay down, without prejudice to the principle that the later trade mark cannot be enforced against the earlier trade mark, that proprietors of EU trade marks should not be entitled to oppose the use of a later trade mark if the later trade mark was acquired at a time when the earlier trade mark could not be enforced against the later trade mark.

(24) There is no justification for protecting EU trade marks or, as against them, any trade mark which has been registered before them, except where the trade marks are actually used.

(25) For reasons of equity and legal certainty, the use of an EU trade mark in a form that differs in elements which do not alter the distinctive character of that mark in the form in which it is registered should be sufficient to preserve the rights conferred regardless of whether the trade mark in the form as used is also registered.

(26) An EU trade mark is to be regarded as an object of property which exists separately from the undertakings whose goods or services are designated by it. Accordingly, it should be capable of being transferred, of being charged as security in favour of a third party and of being the subject matter of licences.

(27) Administrative measures are necessary at Union level for implementing in relation to every trade mark the trade mark law laid down by this Regulation. It is therefore essential, while retaining the Union's existing institutional structure and balance of powers, to provide for a European Union Intellectual Property Office ('the Office') which is independent in relation to technical matters and has legal, administrative and financial autonomy. To this end it is necessary and appropriate that the Office should be a body of the Union having legal personality and exercising the powers which are conferred on it by this Regulation, and that it should operate within the framework of Union law without detracting from the competences exercised by the Union institutions.

(28) EU trade mark protection is granted in relation to specific goods or services whose nature and number determine the extent of protection afforded to the trade mark proprietor. It is therefore essential to lay down rules for the designation and classification of goods and services in this Regulation and to ensure legal certainty and sound administration by requiring that the goods and services for which trade mark protection is sought are identified by the applicant with sufficient clarity and precision to enable the competent authorities and economic operators, on the basis of the application alone, to determine the extent of the protection applied for. The use of general terms should be interpreted as only including all goods and services clearly covered by the literal meaning of the term. Proprietors of EU trade marks, which because of the practice of the Office prior to 22 June 2012 were registered in respect of the entire heading of a class of the system of classification established by the Nice Agreement Concerning the International Classification of Goods and Services for the Purposes of the Registration of Marks of 15 June 1957, should be given the possibility to adapt their lists of goods and services in order to ensure that the content of the Register

meets the requisite standard of clarity and precision in accordance with the case law of the Court of Justice of the European Union.

(29) In order to avoid unnecessary delays in registering an EU trade mark, it is appropriate to lay down a regime of optional EU and national trade mark searches that should be flexible in terms of user needs and preferences. The optional EU and national trade mark searches should be complemented by the making available of all-encompassing, fast and powerful search engines for the use of the public free of charge within the context of cooperation between the Office and the central industrial property offices of the Member States, including the Benelux Office for Intellectual Property.

(30) It is necessary to ensure that parties who are affected by decisions made by the Office are protected by the law in a manner which is suited to the special character of trade mark law. To that end, provision should be made for an appeal to lie from decisions of the various decision-making instances of the Office. A Board of Appeal of the Office should decide on the appeal. Decisions of the Boards of Appeal should, in turn, be amenable to actions before the General Court, which has jurisdiction to annul or to alter the contested decision.

(31) In order to ensure the protection of EU trade marks the Member States should designate, having regard to their own national system, as limited a number as possible of national courts of first and second instance having jurisdiction in matters of infringement and validity of EU trade marks.

(32) It is essential that decisions regarding the validity and infringement of EU trade marks have effect and cover the entire area of the Union, as this is the only way of preventing inconsistent decisions on the part of the courts and the Office and of ensuring that the unitary character of EU trade marks is not undermined. The provisions of Regulation (EU) No 1215/2012 of the European Parliament and of the Council should apply to all actions at law relating to EU trade marks, save where this Regulation derogates from those rules.

(33) Contradictory judgments should be avoided in actions which involve the same acts and the same parties and which are brought on the basis of an EU trade mark and parallel national trade marks. For this purpose, when the actions are brought in the same Member State, the way in which this is to be achieved is a matter for national procedural rules, which are not prejudiced by this Regulation, whilst when the actions are brought in different Member States, provisions modelled on the rules on lis pendens and related actions of Regulation (EU) No 1215/2012 appear appropriate.

(34) With the aim of promoting convergence of practices and of developing common tools, it is necessary to establish an appropriate framework for cooperation between the Office and the industrial property offices of the Member States, including the Benelux Office for Intellectual Property, defining key areas of cooperation and enabling the Office to coordinate relevant common projects of interest to the Union and the Member States and to finance, up to a maximum amount, those projects. Those cooperation activities should be beneficial for undertakings using trade mark systems in Europe. For users of the Union regime laid down in this Regulation, the projects, particularly the databases for search and consultation purposes, should provide additional, inclusive, efficient tools

that are free of charge to comply with the specific requirements arising from the unitary character of the EU trade mark.

(35) It is desirable to facilitate friendly, expeditious and efficient dispute resolution by entrusting the Office with the establishment of a mediation centre the services of which could be used by any person with the aim of achieving a friendly settlement of disputes relating to EU trade marks and Community designs by mutual agreement.

(36) The setting up of the EU trade mark system has resulted in increased financial burdens for the central industrial property offices and other authorities of the Member States. The additional costs are related to the handling of a higher number of opposition and invalidity proceedings involving EU trade marks or brought by proprietors of such trade marks; to the awareness-raising activities linked to the EU trade mark system; as well as to activities intended to ensure the enforcement of EU trade mark rights. It is, therefore, appropriate to ensure that the Office offset part of the costs incurred by Member States for the role they play in ensuring the smooth functioning of the EU trade mark system. The payment of such offsetting should be subject to the submission, by Member States, of relevant statistical data. The offsetting of costs should not be of such an extent that it would cause a budgetary deficit for the Office.

(37) In order to guarantee the full autonomy and independence of the Office, it is considered necessary to grant it an autonomous budget whose revenue comes principally from fees paid by the users of the system. However, the Union budgetary procedure remains applicable as far as any subsidies chargeable to the general budget of the Union are concerned. Moreover, the auditing of accounts should be undertaken by the Court of Auditors.

(38) In the interest of sound financial management, the accumulation by the Office of significant budgetary surpluses should be avoided. This should be without prejudice to the Office maintaining a financial reserve covering one year of its operational expenditure to ensure the continuity of its operations and the performance of its tasks. That reserve should only be used to ensure the continuity of the tasks of the Office as specified in this Regulation.

(39) Given the essential importance of the amounts of fees payable to the Office for the functioning of the EU trade mark system and its complementary relationship as regards national trade mark systems, it is necessary to set those fee amounts directly in this Regulation in the form of an annex. The amounts of the fees should be fixed at a level which ensures that: first, the revenue they produce is in principle sufficient for the budget of the Office to be balanced; second, there is coexistence and complementarity between the EU trade mark and the national trade mark systems, also taking into account the size of the market covered by the EU trade mark and the needs of small and medium-sized enterprises; and third, the rights of proprietors of an EU trade mark are enforced efficiently in the Member States.

(40) In order to ensure an effective, efficient and expeditious examination and registration of EU trade mark applications by the Office using procedures which are transparent, thorough, fair and equitable, the power to adopt acts in accordance with Article 290 of the Treaty on the Functioning of the European Union

(TFEU) should be delegated to the Commission in respect of specifying the details on the procedures for filing and examining an opposition and on the procedures governing the amendment of the application.

(41) In order to ensure that an EU trade mark can be revoked or declared invalid in an effective and efficient way by means of transparent, thorough, fair and equitable procedures, the power to adopt acts in accordance with Article 290 TFEU should be delegated to the Commission in respect of specifying the procedures for revocation and declaration of invalidity.

(42) In order to allow for an effective, efficient and complete review of decisions of the Office by the Boards of Appeal by means of a transparent, thorough, fair and equitable procedure which takes into account the principles laid down in this Regulation, the power to adopt acts in accordance with Article 290 TFEU should be delegated to the Commission in respect of specifying the formal content of the notice of appeal, the procedure for the filing and examination of an appeal, the formal content and form of the Board of Appeal's decisions, and the reimbursement of the appeal fees.

(43) In order to ensure a smooth, effective and efficient operation of the EU trade mark system, the power to adopt acts in accordance with Article 290 TFEU should be delegated to the Commission in respect of specifying the requirements as to the details on oral proceedings and the detailed arrangements for taking of evidence, the detailed arrangements for notification, the means of communication and the forms to be used by the parties to proceedings, the rules governing the calculation and duration of time limits, the procedures for the revocation of a decision or for cancellation of an entry in the Register, the detailed arrangements for the resumption of proceedings, and the details on representation before the Office.

(44) In order to ensure an effective and efficient organisation of the Boards of Appeal, the power to adopt acts in accordance with Article 290 TFEU should be delegated to the Commission in respect of specifying the details on the organisation of the Boards of Appeal.

(45) In order to ensure the effective and efficient registration of international trade marks in a manner that is fully consistent with the rules of the Protocol relating to the Madrid Agreement concerning the international registration of marks, adopted at Madrid on 27 June 1989 ('Madrid Protocol'), the power to adopt acts in accordance with Article 290 TFEU should be delegated to the Commission in respect of specifying the details on the procedures concerning the filing and examination of an opposition, including the necessary communications to be made to the World Intellectual Property Organisation (WIPO), and the details of the procedure concerning international registrations based on a basic application or basic registration relating to a collective mark, certification mark or guarantee mark.

(46) It is of particular importance that the Commission carry out appropriate consultations during its preparatory work, including at expert level, and that those consultations be conducted in accordance with the principles laid down in the Interinstitutional Agreement of 13 April 2016 on Better Law-Making. In particular, to ensure equal participation in the preparation of delegated acts, the European Parliament and the Council receive all documents at the same time as

Member States' experts, and their experts systematically have access to meetings of Commission expert groups dealing with the preparation of delegated acts.

(47) In order to ensure uniform conditions for the implementation of this Regulation, implementing powers should be conferred on the Commission in respect of specifying the details concerning applications, requests, certificates, claims, regulations, notifications and any other document under the relevant procedural requirements established by this Regulation, as well as in respect of maximum rates for costs essential to the proceedings and actually incurred, details concerning publications in the European Union Trade Marks Bulletin and the Official Journal of the Office, the detailed arrangements for exchange of information between the Office and national authorities, detailed arrangements concerning translations of supporting documents in written proceedings, exact types of decisions to be taken by a single member of the opposition or cancellation divisions, details of the notification obligation pursuant to the Madrid Protocol, and detailed requirements regarding the request for territorial extension subsequent to international registration. Those powers should be exercised in accordance with Regulation (EU) No 182/2011 of the European Parliament and of the Council.

(48) Since the objectives of this Regulation cannot be sufficiently achieved by the Member States but can rather, by reason of its scale and effects, be better achieved at Union level, the Union may adopt measures, in accordance with the principle of subsidiarity as set out in Article 5 of the Treaty on European Union. In accordance with the principle of proportionality as set out in that Article, this Regulation does not go beyond what is necessary in order to achieve those objectives,

Have adopted this Regulation:

CHAPTER I GENERAL PROVISIONS

Article 1
EU trade mark

1. A trade mark for goods or services which is registered in accordance with the conditions contained in this Regulation and in the manner herein provided is hereinafter referred to as a 'European Union trade mark ("EU trade mark")'.

2. An EU trade mark shall have a unitary character. It shall have equal effect throughout the Union: it shall not be registered, transferred or surrendered or be the subject of a decision revoking the rights of the proprietor or declaring it invalid, nor shall its use be prohibited, save in respect of the whole Union. This principle shall apply unless otherwise provided for in this Regulation.

Article 2
Office

1. A European Union Intellectual Property Office ('the Office') is established.

2. All references in Union law to the Office for Harmonization in the Internal Market (Trade Marks and Designs) shall be read as references to the Office.

Article 3
Capacity to act

For the purpose of implementing this Regulation, companies or firms and other legal bodies shall be regarded as legal persons if, under the terms of the law governing them, they have the capacity in their own name to have rights and obligations of all kinds, to make contracts or accomplish other legal acts, and to sue and be sued.

CHAPTER II THE LAW RELATING TO TRADE MARKS

Section 1 Definition of an EU trade mark and obtaining an EU trade mark

Article 4
Signs of which an EU trade mark may consist

An EU trade mark may consist of any signs, in particular words, including personal names, or designs, letters, numerals, colours, the shape of goods or of the packaging of goods, or sounds, provided that such signs are capable of:

(a) distinguishing the goods or services of one undertaking from those of other undertakings; and
(b) being represented on the Register of European Union trade marks ('the Register'), in a manner which enables the competent authorities and the public to determine the clear and precise subject matter of the protection afforded to its proprietor.

Article 5
Persons who can be proprietors of EU trade marks

Any natural or legal person, including authorities established under public law, may be the proprietor of an EU trade mark.

Article 6
Means whereby an EU trade mark is obtained

An EU trade mark shall be obtained by registration.

Article 7
Absolute grounds for refusal

1. The following shall not be registered:

(a) signs which do not conform to the requirements of Article 4;
(b) trade marks which are devoid of any distinctive character;
(c) trade marks which consist exclusively of signs or indications which may serve, in trade, to designate the kind, quality, quantity, intended purpose, value, geographical origin or the time of production of the goods or of rendering of the service, or other characteristics of the goods or service;

(d) trade marks which consist exclusively of signs or indications which have become customary in the current language or in the bona fide and established practices of the trade;
(e) signs which consist exclusively of:
  (i) the shape, or another characteristic, which results from the nature of the goods themselves;
  (ii) the shape, or another characteristic, of goods which is necessary to obtain a technical result;
  (iii) the shape, or another characteristic, which gives substantial value to the goods;
(f) trade marks which are contrary to public policy or to accepted principles of morality;
(g) trade marks which are of such a nature as to deceive the public, for instance as to the nature, quality or geographical origin of the goods or service;
(h) trade marks which have not been authorised by the competent authorities and are to be refused pursuant to Article 6ter of the Paris Convention for the Protection of Industrial Property ('Paris Convention');
(i) trade marks which include badges, emblems or escutcheons other than those covered by Article 6ter of the Paris Convention and which are of particular public interest, unless the consent of the competent authority to their registration has been given;
(j) trade marks which are excluded from registration, pursuant to Union legislation or national law or to international agreements to which the Union or the Member State concerned is party, providing for protection of designations of origin and geographical indications;
(k) trade marks which are excluded from registration pursuant to Union legislation or international agreements to which the Union is party, providing for protection of traditional terms for wine;
(l) trade marks which are excluded from registration pursuant to Union legislation or international agreements to which the Union is party, providing for protection of traditional specialities guaranteed;
(m) trade marks which consist of, or reproduce in their essential elements, an earlier plant variety denomination registered in accordance with Union legislation or national law, or international agreements to which the Union or the Member State concerned is a party, providing for protection of plant variety rights, and which are in respect of plant varieties of the same or closely related species.

2. Paragraph 1 shall apply notwithstanding that the grounds of non-registrability obtain in only part of the Union.

3. Paragraph 1(b), (c) and (d) shall not apply if the trade mark has become distinctive in relation to the goods or services for which registration is requested as a consequence of the use which has been made of it.

Article 8
Relative grounds for refusal

1. Upon opposition by the proprietor of an earlier trade mark, the trade mark applied for shall not be registered:

(a) if it is identical with the earlier trade mark and the goods or services for which registration is applied for are identical with the goods or services for which the earlier trade mark is protected;
(b) if, because of its identity with, or similarity to, the earlier trade mark and the identity or similarity of the goods or services covered by the trade marks there exists a likelihood of confusion on the part of the public in the territory in which the earlier trade mark is protected; the likelihood of confusion includes the likelihood of association with the earlier trade mark.

2. For the purposes of paragraph 1, 'earlier trade mark' means:

(a) trade marks of the following kinds with a date of application for registration which is earlier than the date of application for registration of the EU trade mark, taking account, where appropriate, of the priorities claimed in respect of those trade marks:
  (i) EU trade marks;
  (ii) trade marks registered in a Member State, or, in the case of Belgium, the Netherlands or Luxembourg, at the Benelux Office for Intellectual Property;
  (iii) trade marks registered under international arrangements which have effect in a Member State;
  (iv) trade marks registered under international arrangements which have effect in the Union;
(b) applications for the trade marks referred to in point (a), subject to their registration;
(c) trade marks which, on the date of application for registration of the EU trade mark, or, where appropriate, of the priority claimed in respect of the application for registration of the EU trade mark, are well known in a Member State, in the sense in which the words 'well known' are used in Article 6bis of the Paris Convention.

3. Upon opposition by the proprietor of the trade mark, a trade mark shall not be registered where an agent or representative of the proprietor of the trade mark applies for registration thereof in his own name without the proprietor's consent, unless the agent or representative justifies his action.

4. Upon opposition by the proprietor of a non-registered trade mark or of another sign used in the course of trade of more than mere local significance, the trade mark applied for shall not be registered where and to the extent that, pursuant to Union legislation or the law of the Member State governing that sign:

(a) rights to that sign were acquired prior to the date of application for registration of the EU trade mark, or the date of the priority claimed for the application for registration of the EU trade mark;
(b) that sign confers on its proprietor the right to prohibit the use of a subsequent trade mark.

5. Upon opposition by the proprietor of a registered earlier trade mark within the meaning of paragraph 2, the trade mark applied for shall not be registered where it is identical with, or similar to, an earlier trade mark, irrespective of whether the goods or services for which it is applied are identical with, similar to or not similar to those for which the earlier trade mark is registered, where, in the case

of an earlier EU trade mark, the trade mark has a reputation in the Union or, in the case of an earlier national trade mark, the trade mark has a reputation in the Member State concerned, and where the use without due cause of the trade mark applied for would take unfair advantage of, or be detrimental to, the distinctive character or the repute of the earlier trade mark.

6. Upon opposition by any person authorised under the relevant law to exercise the rights arising from a designation of origin or a geographical indication, the trade mark applied for shall not be registered where and to the extent that, pursuant to the Union legislation or national law providing for the protection of designations of origin or geographical indications:

(i) an application for a designation of origin or a geographical indication had already been submitted, in accordance with Union legislation or national law, prior to the date of application for registration of the EU trade mark or the date of the priority claimed for the application, subject to its subsequent registration;
(ii) that designation of origin or geographical indication confers the right to prohibit the use of a subsequent trade mark.

Section 2 Effects of an EU trade mark

Article 9

Rights conferred by an EU trade mark

1. The registration of an EU trade mark shall confer on the proprietor exclusive rights therein.

2. Without prejudice to the rights of proprietors acquired before the filing date or the priority date of the EU trade mark, the proprietor of that EU trade mark shall be entitled to prevent all third parties not having his consent from using in the course of trade, in relation to goods or services, any sign where:

(a) the sign is identical with the EU trade mark and is used in relation to goods or services which are identical with those for which the EU trade mark is registered;
(b) the sign is identical with, or similar to, the EU trade mark and is used in relation to goods or services which are identical with, or similar to, the goods or services for which the EU trade mark is registered, if there exists a likelihood of confusion on the part of the public; the likelihood of confusion includes the likelihood of association between the sign and the trade mark;
(c) the sign is identical with, or similar to, the EU trade mark irrespective of whether it is used in relation to goods or services which are identical with, similar to or not similar to those for which the EU trade mark is registered, where the latter has a reputation in the Union and where use of that sign without due cause takes unfair advantage of, or is detrimental to, the distinctive character or the repute of the EU trade mark.

3. The following, in particular, may be prohibited under paragraph 2:

(a) affixing the sign to the goods or to the packaging of those goods;
(b) offering the goods, putting them on the market, or stocking them for those purposes under the sign, or offering or supplying services thereunder;

(c) importing or exporting the goods under the sign;
(d) using the sign as a trade or company name or part of a trade or company name;
(e) using the sign on business papers and in advertising;
(f) using the sign in comparative advertising in a manner that is contrary to Directive 2006/114/EC.

4. Without prejudice to the rights of proprietors acquired before the filing date or the priority date of the EU trade mark, the proprietor of that EU trade mark shall also be entitled to prevent all third parties from bringing goods, in the course of trade, into the Union without being released for free circulation there, where such goods, including packaging, come from third countries and bear without authorisation a trade mark which is identical with the EU trade mark registered in respect of such goods, or which cannot be distinguished in its essential aspects from that trade mark.

The entitlement of the proprietor of an EU trade mark pursuant to the first subparagraph shall lapse if, during the proceedings to determine whether the EU trade mark has been infringed, initiated in accordance with Regulation (EU) No 608/2013, evidence is provided by the declarant or the holder of the goods that the proprietor of the EU trade mark is not entitled to prohibit the placing of the goods on the market in the country of final destination.

Article 10

Right to prohibit preparatory acts in relation to the use of packaging or other means

Where the risk exists that the packaging, labels, tags, security or authenticity features or devices or any other means to which the mark is affixed could be used in relation to goods or services and such use would constitute an infringement of the rights of the proprietor of an EU trade mark under Article 9(2) and (3), the proprietor of that trade mark shall have the right to prohibit the following acts if carried out in the course of trade:

(a) affixing a sign identical with, or similar to, the EU trade mark on packaging, labels, tags, security or authenticity features or devices or any other means to which the mark may be affixed;
(b) offering or placing on the market, or stocking for those purposes, or importing or exporting, packaging, labels, tags, security or authenticity features or devices or any other means to which the mark is affixed.

Article 11

Date from which rights against third parties prevail

1. The rights conferred by an EU trade mark shall prevail against third parties from the date of publication of the registration of the trade mark.

2. Reasonable compensation may be claimed in respect of acts occurring after the date of publication of an EU trade mark application, where those acts would, after publication of the registration of the trade mark, be prohibited by virtue of that publication.

3. A court seised of a case shall not decide upon the merits of that case until the registration has been published.

Article 12
Reproduction of an EU trade mark in a dictionary

If the reproduction of an EU trade mark in a dictionary, encyclopaedia or similar reference work gives the impression that it constitutes the generic name of the goods or services for which the trade mark is registered, the publisher of the work shall, at the request of the proprietor of the EU trade mark, ensure that the reproduction of the trade mark at the latest in the next edition of the publication is accompanied by an indication that it is a registered trade mark.

Article 13
Prohibition of the use of an EU trade mark registered in the name of an agent or representative

Where an EU trade mark is registered in the name of the agent or representative of a person who is the proprietor of that trade mark, without the proprietor's authorisation, the latter shall be entitled to oppose the use of his mark by his agent or representative if he has not authorised such use, unless the agent or representative justifies his action.

Article 14
Limitation of the effects of an EU trade mark

1. An EU trade mark shall not entitle the proprietor to prohibit a third party from using, in the course of trade:

(a) the name or address of the third party, where that third party is a natural person;
(b) signs or indications which are not distinctive or which concern the kind, quality, quantity, intended purpose, value, geographical origin, the time of production of goods or of rendering of the service, or other characteristics of the goods or services;
(c) the EU trade mark for the purpose of identifying or referring to goods or services as those of the proprietor of that trade mark, in particular, where the use of that trade mark is necessary to indicate the intended purpose of a product or service, in particular as accessories or spare parts.

2. Paragraph 1 shall only apply where the use made by the third party is in accordance with honest practices in industrial or commercial matters.

Article 15
Exhaustion of the rights conferred by an EU trade mark

1. An EU trade mark shall not entitle the proprietor to prohibit its use in relation to goods which have been put on the market in the European Economic Area under that trade mark by the proprietor or with his consent.

2. Paragraph 1 shall not apply where there exist legitimate reasons for the proprietor to oppose further commercialisation of the goods, especially where the condition of the goods is changed or impaired after they have been put on the market.

Article 16

Intervening right of the proprietor of a later registered trade mark as a defence in infringement proceedings

1. In infringement proceedings, the proprietor of an EU trade mark shall not be entitled to prohibit the use of a later registered EU trade mark where that later trade mark would not be declared invalid pursuant to Article 60(1), (3) or (4), Article 61(1) or (2), or Article 64(2) of this Regulation.

2. In infringement proceedings, the proprietor of an EU trade mark shall not be entitled to prohibit the use of a later registered national trade mark where that later registered national trade mark would not be declared invalid pursuant to Article 8 or Article 9(1) or (2), or Article 46(3) of Directive (EU) 2015/2436 of the European Parliament and of the Council.

3. Where the proprietor of an EU trade mark is not entitled to prohibit the use of a later registered trade mark pursuant to paragraph 1 or 2, the proprietor of that later registered trade mark shall not be entitled to prohibit the use of that earlier EU trade mark in infringement proceedings.

Article 17

Complementary application of national law relating to infringement

1. The effects of EU trade marks shall be governed solely by the provisions of this Regulation. In other respects, infringement of an EU trade mark shall be governed by the national law relating to infringement of a national trade mark in accordance with the provisions of Chapter X.

2. This Regulation shall not prevent actions concerning an EU trade mark being brought under the law of Member States relating in particular to civil liability and unfair competition.

3. The rules of procedure to be applied shall be determined in accordance with the provisions of Chapter X.

Section 3 Use of an EU trade mark

Article 18

Use of an EU trade mark

1. If, within a period of five years following registration, the proprietor has not put the EU trade mark to genuine use in the Union in connection with the goods or services in respect of which it is registered, or if such use has been suspended during an uninterrupted period of five years, the EU trade mark shall be subject to the sanctions provided for in this Regulation, unless there are proper reasons for non-use.

The following shall also constitute use within the meaning of the first subparagraph:

(a) use of the EU trade mark in a form differing in elements which do not alter the distinctive character of the mark in the form in which it was registered, regardless of whether or not the trade mark in the form as used is also registered in the name of the proprietor;
(b) affixing of the EU trade mark to goods or to the packaging thereof in the Union solely for export purposes.

2. Use of the EU trade mark with the consent of the proprietor shall be deemed to constitute use by the proprietor.

Section 4 EU trade marks as objects of property

Article 19

Dealing with EU trade marks as national trade marks

1. Unless Articles 20 to 28 provide otherwise, an EU trade mark as an object of property shall be dealt with in its entirety, and for the whole area of the Union, as a national trade mark registered in the Member State in which, according to the Register:

(a) the proprietor has his seat or his domicile on the relevant date;
(b) where point (a) does not apply, the proprietor has an establishment on the relevant date.

2. In cases which are not provided for by paragraph 1, the Member State referred to in that paragraph shall be the Member State in which the seat of the Office is situated.

3. If two or more persons are mentioned in the Register as joint proprietors, paragraph 1 shall apply to the joint proprietor first mentioned; failing this, it shall apply to the subsequent joint proprietors in the order in which they are mentioned. Where paragraph 1 does not apply to any of the joint proprietors, paragraph 2 shall apply.

Article 20

Transfer

1. An EU trade mark may be transferred, separately from any transfer of the undertaking, in respect of some or all of the goods or services for which it is registered.

2. A transfer of the whole of the undertaking shall include the transfer of the EU trade mark except where, in accordance with the law governing the transfer, there is agreement to the contrary or circumstances clearly dictate otherwise. This provision shall apply to the contractual obligation to transfer the undertaking.

3. Without prejudice to paragraph 2, an assignment of the EU trade mark shall be made in writing and shall require the signature of the parties to the contract, except when it is a result of a judgment; otherwise it shall be void.

4. On request of one of the parties a transfer shall be entered in the Register and published.

5. An application for registration of a transfer shall contain information to identify the EU trade mark, the new proprietor, the goods and services to which the transfer relates, as well as documents duly establishing the transfer in accordance with paragraphs 2 and 3. The application may further contain, where applicable, information to identify the representative of the new proprietor.

6. The Commission shall adopt implementing acts specifying:

(a) the details to be contained in the application for registration of a transfer;
(b) the kind of documentation required to establish a transfer, taking account of the agreements given by the registered proprietor and the successor in title;
(c) the details of how to process applications for partial transfers, ensuring that the goods and services in the remaining registration and the new registration do not overlap and that a separate file, including a new registration number, is established for the new registration.

Those implementing acts shall be adopted in accordance with the examination procedure referred to in Article 207(2).

7. Where the conditions applicable to the registration of a transfer, as laid down in paragraphs 1, 2 and 3, or in the implementing acts referred to in paragraph 6, are not fulfilled, the Office shall notify the applicant of the deficiencies. If the deficiencies are not remedied within a period to be specified by the Office, it shall reject the application for registration of the transfer.

8. A single application for registration of a transfer may be submitted for two or more trade marks, provided that the registered proprietor and the successor in title are the same in each case.

9. Paragraphs 5 to 8 shall also apply to applications for EU trade marks.

10. In the case of a partial transfer, any application made by the original proprietor pending with regard to the original registration shall be deemed to be pending with regard to the remaining registration and the new registration. Where such application is subject to the payment of fees and those fees have been paid by the original proprietor, the new proprietor shall not be liable to pay any additional fees with regard to such application.

11. As long as the transfer has not been entered in the Register, the successor in title may not invoke the rights arising from the registration of the EU trade mark.

12. Where there are time limits to be observed vis-à-vis the Office, the successor in title may make the corresponding statements to the Office once the request for registration of the transfer has been received by the Office.

13. All documents which require notification to the proprietor of the EU trade mark in accordance with Article 98 shall be addressed to the person registered as proprietor.

Article 21
Transfer of a trade mark registered in the name of an agent

1. Where an EU trade mark is registered in the name of the agent or representative of a person who is the proprietor of that trade mark, without the proprietor's

authorisation, the latter shall be entitled to demand the assignment of the EU trade mark in his favour, unless such agent or representative justifies his action.

2. The proprietor may submit a request for assignment pursuant to paragraph 1 of this Article to the following:

(a) the Office, pursuant to Article 60(1)(b), instead of an application for a declaration of invalidity;
(b) a European Union trade mark court ('EU trade mark court') as referred to in Article 123, instead of a counterclaim for a declaration of invalidity based on Article 128(1).

Article 22
Rights in rem

1. An EU trade mark may, independently of the undertaking, be given as security or be the subject of rights in rem.

2. At the request of one of the parties, the rights referred to in paragraph 1 or the transfer of those rights shall be entered in the Register and published.

3. An entry in the Register effected pursuant to paragraph 2 shall be cancelled or modified at the request of one of the parties.

Article 23
Levy of execution

1. An EU trade mark may be levied in execution.

2. As regards the procedure for levy of execution in respect of an EU trade mark, the courts and authorities of the Member States determined in accordance with Article 19 shall have exclusive jurisdiction.

3. On request of one the parties, the levy of execution shall be entered in the Register and published.

4. An entry in the Register effected pursuant to paragraph 3 shall be cancelled or modified at the request of one of the parties.

Article 24
Insolvency proceedings

1. The only insolvency proceedings in which an EU trade mark may be involved are those opened in the Member State in the territory of which the debtor has his centre of main interests.

However, where the debtor is an insurance undertaking or a credit institution as defined in Directive 2009/138/EC of the European Parliament and of the Council and Directive 2001/24/EC of the European Parliament and of the Council, respectively, the only insolvency proceedings in which an EU trade mark may be involved are those opened in the Member State where that undertaking or institution has been authorised.

2. In the case of joint proprietorship of an EU trade mark, paragraph 1 shall apply to the share of the joint proprietor.

3. Where an EU trade mark is involved in insolvency proceedings, on request of the competent national authority an entry to this effect shall be made in the Register and published in the European Union Trade Marks Bulletin referred to in Article 116.

Article 25
Licensing

1. An EU trade mark may be licensed for some or all of the goods or services for which it is registered and for the whole or part of the Union. A licence may be exclusive or non-exclusive.

2. The proprietor of an EU trade mark may invoke the rights conferred by that trade mark against a licensee who contravenes any provision in his licensing contract with regard to:

(a) its duration;
(b) the form covered by the registration in which the trade mark may be used;
(c) the scope of the goods or services for which the licence is granted;
(d) the territory in which the trade mark may be affixed; or
(e) the quality of the goods manufactured or of the services provided by the licensee.

3. Without prejudice to the provisions of the licensing contract, the licensee may bring proceedings for infringement of an EU trade mark only if its proprietor consents thereto. However, the holder of an exclusive licence may bring such proceedings if the proprietor of the trade mark, after formal notice, does not himself bring infringement proceedings within an appropriate period.

4. A licensee shall, for the purpose of obtaining compensation for damage suffered by him, be entitled to intervene in infringement proceedings brought by the proprietor of the EU trade mark.

5. On request of one of the parties the grant or transfer of a licence in respect of an EU trade mark shall be entered in the Register and published.

6. An entry in the Register effected pursuant to paragraph 5 shall be cancelled or modified at the request of one of the parties.

Article 26
Procedure for entering licences and other rights in the Register

1. Article 20(5) and (6) and the rules adopted pursuant to it and Article 20(8) shall apply mutatis mutandis to the registration of a right in rem or transfer of a right in rem as referred to in Article 22(2), the levy of execution as referred to in Article 23(3), the involvement in insolvency proceedings as referred to in Article 24(3), as well as to the registration of a licence or transfer of a licence as referred to in Article 25(5), subject to the following:

(a) the requirement relating to the identification of goods and services to which the transfer relates shall not apply in respect of a request for registration of a right in rem, of a levy of execution or of insolvency proceedings;
(b) the requirement relating to the documents proving the transfer shall not apply where the request is made by the proprietor of the EU trade mark.

2. The application for registration of the rights referred to in paragraph 1 shall not be deemed to have been filed until the required fee has been paid.

3. The application for registration of a licence may contain a request to record a licence in the Register as one or more of the following:

(a) an exclusive licence;
(b) a sub-licence in the event that the licence is granted by a licensee whose licence is recorded in the Register;
(c) a licence limited to only part of the goods or services for which the mark is registered;
(d) a licence limited to part of the Union;
(e) a temporary licence.

Where a request is made to record the licence as a licence listed in points (c), (d) and (e) of the first subparagraph, the application for registration of a licence shall indicate the goods and services, the part of the Union and the time period for which the licence is granted.

4. Where the conditions applicable to registration, as laid down in Articles 22 to 25, in paragraphs 1 and 3 of this Article and in the other applicable rules adopted pursuant to this Regulation, are not fulfilled, the Office shall notify the applicant of the deficiency. If the deficiency is not corrected within a period specified by the Office, it shall reject the application for registration.

5. Paragraphs 1 and 3 shall apply mutatis mutandis to applications for EU trade marks.

Article 27
Effects vis-à-vis third parties

1. Legal acts referred to in Articles 20, 22 and 25 concerning an EU trade mark shall have effects vis-à-vis third parties in all the Member States only after entry in the Register. Nevertheless, such an act, before it is so entered, shall have effect vis-à-vis third parties who have acquired rights in the trade mark after the date of that act but who knew of the act at the date on which the rights were acquired.

2. Paragraph 1 shall not apply in the case of a person who acquires the EU trade mark or a right concerning the EU trade mark by way of transfer of the whole of the undertaking or by any other universal succession.

3. The effects vis-à-vis third parties of the legal acts referred to in Article 23 shall be governed by the law of the Member State determined in accordance with Article 19.

4. Until such time as common rules for the Member States in the field of bankruptcy enter into force, the effects vis-à-vis third parties of bankruptcy or similar

proceedings shall be governed by the law of the Member State in which such proceedings are first brought within the meaning of national law or of conventions applicable in this field.

Article 28
The application for an EU trade mark as an object of property

Articles 19 to 27 shall apply to applications for EU trade marks.

Article 29
Procedure for cancelling or modifying the entry in the Register of licences and other rights

1. A registration effected under Article 26(1) shall be cancelled or modified at the request of one of the persons concerned.

2. The application shall contain the registration number of the EU trade mark concerned and the particulars of the right for which registration is requested to be cancelled or modified.

3. The application for cancellation of a licence, a right in rem or an enforcement measure shall not be deemed to have been filed until the required fee has been paid.

4. The application shall be accompanied by documents showing that the registered right no longer exists or that the licensee or the holder of another right consents to the cancellation or modification of the registration.

5. Where the requirements for cancellation or modification of the registration are not satisfied, the Office shall notify the applicant of the deficiency. If the deficiency is not corrected within a period to be specified by the Office, it shall reject the application for cancellation or modification of the registration.

6. Paragraphs 1 to 5 of this Article shall apply mutatis mutandis to entries made in the files pursuant to Article 26(5).

CHAPTER II APPLICATION FOR EU TRADE MARKS

Section 1 Filing of applications and the conditions which govern them

Article 30
Filing of applications

1. An application for an EU trade mark shall be filed at the Office.

2. The Office shall issue to the applicant, without delay, a receipt which shall include at least the file number, a representation, description or other identification of the mark, the nature and the number of the documents and the date of their receipt. That receipt may be issued by electronic means.

Article 31

Conditions with which applications must comply

1. An application for an EU trade mark shall contain:

(a) a request for the registration of an EU trade mark;
(b) information identifying the applicant;
(c) a list of the goods or services in respect of which the registration is requested;
(d) a representation of the mark, which satisfies the requirements set out in Article 4(b).

2. The application for an EU trade mark shall be subject to the payment of the application fee covering one class of goods or services and, where appropriate, of one or more class fees for each class of goods and services exceeding the first class and, where applicable, the search fee.

3. In addition to the requirements referred to in paragraphs 1 and 2, an application for an EU trade mark shall comply with the formal requirements laid down in this Regulation and in the implementing acts adopted pursuant to it. If those conditions provide for the trade mark to be represented electronically, the Executive Director may determine the formats and maximum size of such an electronic file.

4. The Commission shall adopt implementing acts specifying the details to be contained in the application. Those implementing acts shall be adopted in accordance with the examination procedure referred to in Article 207(2).

Article 32

Date of filing

The date of filing of an EU trade mark application shall be the date on which the documents containing the information specified in Article 31(1) are filed with the Office by the applicant, subject to payment of the application fee within one month of filing those documents.

Article 33

Designation and classification of goods and services

1. Goods and services in respect of which trade mark registration is applied for shall be classified in conformity with the system of classification established by the Nice Agreement Concerning the International Classification of Goods and Services for the Purposes of the Registration of Marks of 15 June 1957 ('the Nice Classification').

2. The goods and services for which the protection of the trade mark is sought shall be identified by the applicant with sufficient clarity and precision to enable the competent authorities and economic operators, on that sole basis, to determine the extent of the protection sought.

3. For the purposes of paragraph 2, the general indications included in the class headings of the Nice Classification or other general terms may be used, provided that they comply with the requisite standards of clarity and precision set out in this Article.

4. The Office shall reject an application in respect of indications or terms which are unclear or imprecise, where the applicant does not suggest an acceptable wording within a period set by the Office to that effect.

5. The use of general terms, including the general indications of the class headings of the Nice Classification, shall be interpreted as including all the goods or services clearly covered by the literal meaning of the indication or term. The use of such terms or indications shall not be interpreted as comprising a claim to goods or services which cannot be so understood.

6. Where the applicant requests registration for more than one class, the applicant shall group the goods and services according to the classes of the Nice Classification, each group being preceded by the number of the class to which that group of goods or services belongs, and shall present them in the order of the classes.

7. Goods and services shall not be regarded as being similar to each other on the ground that they appear in the same class under the Nice Classification. Goods and services shall not be regarded as being dissimilar from each other on the ground that they appear in different classes under the Nice Classification.

8. Proprietors of EU trade marks applied for before 22 June 2012 which are registered in respect of the entire heading of a Nice class may declare that their intention on the date of filing had been to seek protection in respect of goods or services beyond those covered by the literal meaning of the heading of that class, provided that the goods or services so designated are included in the alphabetical list for that class in the edition of the Nice Classification in force at the date of filing.

The declaration shall be filed at the Office by 24 September 2016, and shall indicate, in a clear, precise and specific manner, the goods and services, other than those clearly covered by the literal meaning of the indications of the class heading, originally covered by the proprietor's intention. The Office shall take appropriate measures to amend the Register accordingly. The possibility to make a declaration in accordance with the first subparagraph of this paragraph shall be without prejudice to the application of Article 18, Article 47(2), Article 58(1)(a), and Article 64(2).

EU trade marks for which no declaration is filed within the period referred to in the second subparagraph shall be deemed to extend, as from the expiry of that period, only to goods or services clearly covered by the literal meaning of the indications included in the heading of the relevant class.

9. Where the register is amended, the exclusive rights conferred by the EU trade mark under Article 9 shall not prevent a third party from continuing to use a trade mark in relation to goods or services where and to the extent that the use of the trade mark for those goods or services:

(a) commenced before the register was amended; and
(b) did not infringe the proprietor's rights based on the literal meaning of the record of the goods and services in the register at that time.

In addition, the amendment of the list of goods or services recorded in the register shall not give the proprietor of the EU trade mark the right to oppose or to apply for a declaration of invalidity of a later trade mark where and to the extent that:

(a) the later trade mark was either in use, or an application had been made to register the trade mark, for goods or services before the register was amended; and
(b) the use of the trade mark in relation to those goods or services did not infringe, or would not have infringed, the proprietor's rights based on the literal meaning of the record of the goods and services in the register at that time.

Section 2 Priority

Article 34
Right of priority

1. A person who has duly filed an application for a trade mark in or in respect of any State party to the Paris Convention or to the Agreement establishing the World Trade Organisation, or his successors in title, shall enjoy, for the purpose of filing an EU trade mark application for the same trade mark in respect of goods or services which are identical with or contained within those for which the application has been filed, a right of priority during a period of six months from the date of filing of the first application.

2. Every filing that is equivalent to a regular national filing under the national law of the State where it was made or under bilateral or multilateral agreements shall be recognised as giving rise to a right of priority.

3. By a regular national filing is meant any filing that is sufficient to establish the date on which the application was filed, whatever may be the outcome of the application.

4. A subsequent application for a trade mark which was the subject of a previous first application in respect of the same goods or services and which is filed in or in respect of the same State shall be considered as the first application for the purposes of determining priority, provided that, at the date of filing of the subsequent application, the previous application has been withdrawn, abandoned or refused, without being open to public inspection and without leaving any rights outstanding, and has not served as a basis for claiming a right of priority. The previous application may not thereafter serve as a basis for claiming a right of priority.

5. If the first filing has been made in a State which is not a party to the Paris Convention or to the Agreement establishing the World Trade Organisation, paragraphs 1 to 4 shall apply only in so far as that State, according to published findings, grants, on the basis of the first filing made at the Office and subject to conditions equivalent to those laid down in this Regulation, a right of priority having equivalent effect. The Executive Director shall, where necessary, request the Commission to consider enquiring as to whether a State within the meaning of the first sentence accords that reciprocal treatment. If the Commission determines that reciprocal treatment in accordance with the first sentence is accorded, it shall publish a communication to that effect in the Official Journal of the European Union.

6. Paragraph 5 shall apply from the date of publication in the Official Journal of the European Union of the communication determining that reciprocal treatment is accorded, unless the communication states an earlier date from which it

is applicable. It shall cease to apply from the date of publication in the Official Journal of the European Union of a communication of the Commission to the effect that reciprocal treatment is no longer accorded, unless the communication states an earlier date from which it is applicable.

7. Communications as referred to in paragraphs 5 and 6 shall also be published in the Official Journal of the Office.

Article 35
Claiming priority

1. Priority claims shall be filed together with the EU trade mark application and shall include the date, number and country of the previous application. The documentation in support of priority claims shall be filed within three months of the filing date.

2. The Commission shall adopt implementing acts specifying the kind of documentation to be filed for claiming the priority of a previous application in accordance with paragraph 1 of this Article. Those implementing acts shall be adopted in accordance with the examination procedure referred to in Article 207(2).

3. The Executive Director may determine that the documentation to be provided by the applicant in support of the priority claim may consist of less than what is required under the specifications adopted in accordance with paragraph 2, provided that the information required is available to the Office from other sources.

Article 36
Effect of priority right

The right of priority shall have the effect that the date of priority shall count as the date of filing of the EU trade mark application for the purposes of establishing which rights take precedence.

Article 37
Equivalence of Union filing with national filing

An EU trade mark application which has been accorded a date of filing shall, in the Member States, be equivalent to a regular national filing, where appropriate with the priority claimed for the EU trade mark application.

Section 3 Exhibition priority

Article 38
Exhibition priority

1. If an applicant for an EU trade mark has displayed goods or services under the mark applied for, at an official or officially recognised international exhibition falling within the terms of the Convention relating to international exhibitions signed at Paris on 22 November 1928 and last revised on 30 November 1972, he may, if he files the application within a period of six months of the date of the

first display of the goods or services under the mark applied for, claim a right of priority from that date within the meaning of Article 36. The priority claim shall be filed together with the EU trade mark application.

2. An applicant who wishes to claim priority pursuant to paragraph 1 shall file evidence of the display of goods or services under the mark applied for within three months of the filing date.

3. An exhibition priority granted in a Member State or in a third country shall not extend the period of priority laid down in Article 34.

4. The Commission shall adopt implementing acts specifying the type and details of evidence to be filed for claiming an exhibition priority in accordance with paragraph 2 of this Article. Those implementing acts shall be adopted in accordance with the examination procedure referred to in Article 207(2).

Section 4 Seniority of a national trade mark

Article 39

Claiming seniority of a national trade mark in an application for an EU trade mark or subsequent to the filing of the application

1. The proprietor of an earlier trade mark registered in a Member State, including a trade mark registered in the Benelux countries, or registered under international arrangements having effect in a Member State, who applies for an identical trade mark for registration as an EU trade mark for goods or services which are identical with or contained within those for which the earlier trade mark has been registered, may claim for the EU trade mark the seniority of the earlier trade mark in respect of the Member State in or for which it is registered.

2. Seniority claims shall either be filed together with the EU trade mark application or within two months of the filing date of the application, and shall include the Member State or Member States in or for which the mark is registered, the number and the filing date of the relevant registration, and the goods and services for which the mark is registered. Where the seniority of one or more registered earlier trade marks is claimed in the application, the documentation in support of the seniority claim shall be filed within three months of the filing date. Where the applicant wishes to claim the seniority subsequent to the filing of the application, the documentation in support of the seniority claim shall be submitted to the Office within three months of receipt of the seniority claim.

3. Seniority shall have the sole effect under this Regulation that, where the proprietor of the EU trade mark surrenders the earlier trade mark or allows it to lapse, he shall be deemed to continue to have the same rights as he would have had if the earlier trade mark had continued to be registered.

4. The seniority claimed for the EU trade mark shall lapse where the earlier trade mark the seniority of which is claimed is declared to be invalid or revoked. Where the earlier trade mark is revoked, the seniority shall lapse provided that the revocation takes effect prior to the filing date or priority date of that EU trade mark.

5. The Office shall inform the Benelux Office for Intellectual Property or the central industrial property office of the Member State concerned of the effective claiming of seniority.

6. The Commission shall adopt implementing acts specifying the kind of documentation to be filed for claiming the seniority of a national trade mark or a trade mark registered under international agreements having effect in a Member State in accordance with paragraph 2 of this Article. Those implementing acts shall be adopted in accordance with the examination procedure referred to in Article 207(2).

7. The Executive Director may determine that the documentation to be provided by the applicant in support of the seniority claim may consist of less than what is required under the specifications adopted in accordance with paragraph 6, provided that the information required is available to the Office from other sources.

Article 40

Claiming seniority of a national trade mark after registration of an EU trade mark

1. The proprietor of an EU trade mark who is the proprietor of an earlier identical trade mark registered in a Member State, including a trade mark registered in the Benelux countries or of an earlier identical trade mark, with an international registration effective in a Member State, for goods or services which are identical to those for which the earlier trade mark has been registered, or contained within them, may claim the seniority of the earlier trade mark in respect of the Member State in or for which it was registered.

2. Seniority claims filed pursuant to paragraph 1 of this Article shall include the registration number of the EU trade mark, the name and address of its proprietor, the Member State or Member States in or for which the earlier mark is registered, the number and the filing date of the relevant registration, the goods and services for which the mark is registered and those in respect of which seniority is claimed, and supporting documentation as provided for in the rules adopted pursuant to Article 39(6).

3. If the requirements governing the claiming of seniority are not fulfilled, the Office shall communicate the deficiency to the proprietor of the EU trade mark. If the deficiency is not remedied within a period to be specified by the Office, the Office shall reject the claim.

4. Article 39(3), (4), (5) and (7) shall apply.

CHAPTER IV REGISTRATION PROCEDURE

Section 1 Examination of applications

Article 41

Examination of the conditions of filing

1. The Office shall examine whether:

(a) the EU trade mark application satisfies the requirements for the accordance of a date of filing in accordance with Article 32;
(b) the EU trade mark application complies with the conditions and requirements referred to in Article 31(3);
(c) where appropriate, the class fees have been paid within the prescribed period.

2. Where the EU trade mark application does not satisfy the requirements referred to in paragraph 1, the Office shall request the applicant to remedy the deficiencies or the default on payment within two months of the receipt of the notification.

3. If the deficiencies or the default on payment established pursuant to paragraph 1(a) are not remedied within this period, the application shall not be dealt with as an EU trade mark application. If the applicant complies with the Office's request, the Office shall accord as the date of filing of the application the date on which the deficiencies or the default on payment established are remedied.

4. If the deficiencies established pursuant to paragraph 1(b) are not remedied within the prescribed period, the Office shall refuse the application.

5. If the default on payment established pursuant to paragraph 1(c) is not remedied within the prescribed period, the application shall be deemed to be withdrawn unless it is clear which categories of goods or services the amount paid is intended to cover. In the absence of other criteria to determine which classes are intended to be covered, the Office shall take the classes in the order of the classification. The application shall be deemed to have been withdrawn with regard to those classes for which the class fees have not been paid or have not been paid in full.

6. Failure to satisfy the requirements concerning the claim to priority shall result in loss of the right of priority for the application.

7. Failure to satisfy the requirements concerning the claiming of seniority of a national trade mark shall result in loss of that right for the application.

8. Where failure to satisfy the requirements referred to in paragraph 1(b) and (c) concerns only some of the goods or services, the Office shall refuse the application, or the right of priority or the right of seniority shall be lost, only in so far as those goods and services are concerned.

Article 42
Examination as to absolute grounds for refusal

1. Where, under Article 7, a trade mark is ineligible for registration in respect of some or all of the goods or services covered by the EU trade mark application, the application shall be refused as regards those goods or services.

2. The application shall not be refused before the applicant has been allowed the opportunity to withdraw or amend the application or to submit his observations. To this effect, the Office shall notify the applicant of the grounds for refusing registration and shall specify a period within which he may withdraw or amend the application or submit his observations. Where the applicant fails to overcome the grounds for refusing registration, the Office shall refuse registration in whole or in part.

Section 2 Search

Article 43
Search report

1. The Office shall, at the request of the applicant for the EU trade mark when filing the application, draw up a European Union search report ('EU search report') citing those earlier EU trade marks or EU trade mark applications discovered which may be invoked under Article 8 against the registration of the EU trade mark applied for.

2. Where, at the time of filing an EU trade mark application, the applicant requests that a search report be prepared by the central industrial property offices of the Member States and where the appropriate search fee has been paid within the time limit for the payment of the filing fee, the Office shall transmit without delay a copy of the EU trade mark application to the central industrial property office of each Member State which has informed the Office of its decision to operate a search in its own register of trade marks in respect of EU trade mark applications.

3. Each of the central industrial property offices of the Member States referred to in paragraph 2 shall communicate a search report which shall either cite any earlier national trade marks, national trade mark applications or trade marks registered under international agreements, having effect in the Member State or Member States concerned, which have been discovered and which may be invoked under Article 8 against the registration of the EU trade mark applied for, or state that the search has revealed no such rights.

4. The Office, after consulting the Management Board provided for in Article 153 ('the Management Board'), shall establish the contents and modalities for the reports.

5. The Office shall pay an amount to each central industrial property office for each search report provided in accordance with paragraph 3. The amount, which shall be the same for each office, shall be fixed by the Budget Committee by means of a decision adopted by a majority of three quarters of the representatives of the Member States.

6. The Office shall transmit to the applicant for the EU trade mark the EU search report requested and any requested national search reports received.

7. Upon publication of the EU trade mark application, the Office shall inform the proprietors of any earlier EU trade marks or EU trade mark applications cited in the EU search report of the publication of the EU trade mark application. The latter shall apply irrespective of whether the applicant has requested to receive the EU search report, unless the proprietor of an earlier registration or application requests not to receive the notification.

Section 3 Publication of the application

Article 44
Publication of the application

1. If the conditions which the application for an EU trade mark is required to satisfy have been fulfilled, the application shall be published for the purposes of

Article 46 to the extent that it has not been refused pursuant to Article 42. The publication of the application shall be without prejudice to information already made available to the public otherwise in accordance with this Regulation or acts adopted pursuant to this Regulation.

2. Where, after publication, the application is refused pursuant to Article 42, the decision that it has been refused shall be published upon becoming final.

3. Where the publication of the application contains an error attributable to the Office, the Office shall of its own motion or at the request of the applicant correct the error and publish the correction.

The rules adopted pursuant to Article 49(3) shall apply mutatis mutandis where a correction is requested by the applicant.

4. Article 46(2) shall also apply where the correction concerns the list of goods or services or the representation of the mark.

5. The Commission shall adopt implementing acts laying down the details to be contained in the publication of the application. Those implementing acts shall be adopted in accordance with the examination procedure referred to in Article 207(2).

Section 4 Observations by third parties and opposition

Article 45

Observations by third parties

1. Any natural or legal person and any group or body representing manufacturers, producers, suppliers of services, traders or consumers may submit to the Office written observations, explaining on which grounds, under Articles 5 and 7, the trade mark should not be registered ex officio.

Persons and groups or bodies as referred to in the first subparagraph shall not be parties to the proceedings before the Office.

2. Third party observations shall be submitted before the end of the opposition period or, where an opposition against the trade mark has been filed, before the final decision on the opposition is taken.

3. The submission referred to in paragraph 1 shall be without prejudice to the right of the Office to re-open the examination of absolute grounds on its own initiative at any time before registration, where appropriate.

4. The observations referred to in paragraph 1 shall be communicated to the applicant who may comment on them.

Article 46

Opposition

1. Within a period of three months following the publication of an EU trade mark application, notice of opposition to registration of the trade mark may be given on the grounds that it may not be registered under Article 8:

(a) by the proprietors of earlier trade marks referred to in Article 8(2) as well as licensees authorised by the proprietors of those trade marks, in respect of Article 8(1) and (5);
(b) by the proprietors of trade marks referred to in Article 8(3);
(c) by the proprietors of earlier marks or signs referred to in Article 8(4) and by persons authorised under the relevant national law to exercise these rights;
(d) by the persons authorised under the relevant Union legislation or national law to exercise the rights referred to in Article 8(6).

2. Notice of opposition to registration of the trade mark may also be given, subject to the conditions laid down in paragraph 1, in the event of the publication of an amended application in accordance with the second sentence of Article 49(2).

3. Opposition shall be expressed in writing, and shall specify the grounds on which it is made. It shall not be considered as duly entered until the opposition fee has been paid.

4. Within a period to be fixed by the Office, the opponent may submit facts, evidence and arguments in support of his case.

Article 47
Examination of opposition

1. In the examination of the opposition the Office shall invite the parties, as often as necessary, to file observations, within a period set by the Office, on communications from the other parties or issued by itself.

2. If the applicant so requests, the proprietor of an earlier EU trade mark who has given notice of opposition shall furnish proof that, during the five-year period preceding the date of filing or the date of priority of the EU trade mark application, the earlier EU trade mark has been put to genuine use in the Union in connection with the goods or services in respect of which it is registered and which he cites as justification for his opposition, or that there are proper reasons for non-use, provided that the earlier EU trade mark has at that date been registered for not less than five years. In the absence of proof to this effect, the opposition shall be rejected. If the earlier EU trade mark has been used in relation to only part of the goods or services for which it is registered it shall, for the purposes of the examination of the opposition, be deemed to be registered in respect only of that part of the goods or services.

3. Paragraph 2 shall apply to earlier national trade marks referred to in Article 8(2)(a), by substituting use in the Member State in which the earlier national trade mark is protected for use in the Union.

4. The Office may, if it thinks fit, invite the parties to make a friendly settlement.

5. If examination of the opposition reveals that the trade mark may not be registered in respect of some or all of the goods or services for which the EU trade mark application has been made, the application shall be refused in respect of those goods or services. Otherwise the opposition shall be rejected.

6. The decision refusing the application shall be published upon becoming final.

Article 48
Delegation of powers

The Commission is empowered to adopt delegated acts in accordance with Article 208 specifying the details of the procedure for filing and examining an opposition set out in Articles 46 and 47.

Section 5 Withdrawal, restriction, amendment and division of the application

Article 49
Withdrawal, restriction and amendment of the application

1. The applicant may at any time withdraw his EU trade mark application or restrict the list of goods or services contained therein. Where the application has already been published, the withdrawal or restriction shall also be published.

2. In other respects, an EU trade mark application may be amended, upon request of the applicant, only by correcting the name and address of the applicant, errors of wording or of copying, or obvious mistakes, provided that such correction does not substantially change the trade mark or extend the list of goods or services. Where the amendments affect the representation of the trade mark or the list of goods or services and are made after publication of the application, the trade mark application shall be published as amended.

3. The Commission is empowered to adopt delegated acts in accordance with Article 208 specifying the details of the procedure governing the amendment of the application.

Article 50
Division of the application

1. The applicant may divide the application by declaring that some of the goods or services included in the original application will be the subject of one or more divisional applications. The goods or services in the divisional application shall not overlap with the goods or services which remain in the original application or those which are included in other divisional applications.

2. The declaration of division shall not be admissible:

(a) if, where an opposition has been entered against the original application, such a divisional application has the effect of introducing a division amongst the goods or services against which the opposition has been directed, until the decision of the Opposition Division has become final or the opposition proceedings are finally terminated otherwise;
(b) before the date of filing referred to in Article 32 has been accorded by the Office and during the opposition period provided for in Article 46(1).

3. The declaration of division shall be subject to a fee. The declaration shall be deemed not to have been made until the fee has been paid.

4. Where the Office finds that the requirements laid down in paragraph 1 and in the rules adopted pursuant to paragraph 9(a) are not fulfilled, it shall invite the

applicant to remedy the deficiencies within a period to be specified by the Office. If the deficiencies are not remedied before the time limit expires, the Office shall refuse the declaration of division.

5. The division shall take effect on the date on which it is recorded in the files kept by the Office concerning the original application.

6. All requests and applications submitted and all fees paid with regard to the original application prior to the date on which the Office receives the declaration of division are deemed also to have been submitted or paid with regard to the divisional application or applications. The fees for the original application which have been duly paid prior to the date on which the declaration of division is received shall not be refunded.

7. The divisional application shall preserve the filing date and any priority date and seniority date of the original application.

8. Where the declaration of division relates to an application which has already been published pursuant to Article 44, the division shall be published. The divisional application shall be published. The publication shall not open a new period for the filing of oppositions.

9. The Commission shall adopt implementing acts specifying:

(a) the details to be contained in a declaration of the division of an application made pursuant to paragraph 1;
(b) the details as to how to process a declaration of the division of an application, ensuring that a separate file, including a new application number, is established for the divisional application;
(c) the details to be contained in the publication of the divisional application pursuant to paragraph 8.

Those implementing acts shall be adopted in accordance with the examination procedure referred to in Article 207(2).

Section 6 Registration

Article 51
Registration

1. Where an application meets the requirements set out in this Regulation and where no notice of opposition has been given within the period referred to in Article 46(1) or where any opposition entered has been finally disposed of by withdrawal, rejection or other disposition, the trade mark and the particulars referred to in Article 111(2) shall be recorded in the Register. The registration shall be published.

2. The Office shall issue a certificate of registration. That certificate may be issued by electronic means. The Office shall provide certified or uncertified copies of the certificate subject to the payment of a fee, where those copies are issued other than by electronic means.

3. The Commission shall adopt implementing acts specifying the details to be contained in and the form of the certificate of registration referred to in para-

graph 2 of this Article. Those implementing acts shall be adopted in accordance with the examination procedure referred to in Article 207(2).

CHAPTER V DURATION, RENEWAL, ALTERATION AND DIVISION OF EU TRADE MARKS

Article 52
Duration of registration

EU trade marks shall be registered for a period of 10 years from the date of filing of the application. Registration may be renewed in accordance with Article 53 for further periods of 10 years.

Article 53
Renewal

1. Registration of the EU trade mark shall be renewed at the request of the proprietor of the EU trade mark or any person expressly authorised by him, provided that the fees have been paid.

2. The Office shall inform the proprietor of the EU trade mark, and any person having a registered right in respect of the EU trade mark, of the expiry of the registration at least six months before the said expiry. Failure to give such information shall not involve the responsibility of the Office and shall not affect the expiry of the registration.

3. The request for renewal shall be submitted in the six-month period prior to the expiry of the registration. The basic fee for the renewal and, where appropriate, one or more class fees for each class of goods or services exceeding the first one shall also be paid within this period. Failing this, the request may be submitted and the fees paid within a further period of six months following the expiry of registration, provided that an additional fee for late payment of the renewal fee or late submission of the request for renewal is paid within this further period.

4. The request for renewal shall include:

(a) the name of the person requesting renewal;
(b) the registration number of the EU trade mark to be renewed;
(c) if the renewal is requested for only part of the registered goods and services, an indication of those classes or those goods and services for which renewal is requested, or those classes or those goods and services for which renewal is not requested, grouped according to the classes of the Nice classification, each group being preceded by the number of the class of that classification to which that group of goods or services belongs, and presented in the order of classes of that classification.

If the payment referred to in paragraph 3 is made, it shall be deemed to constitute a request for renewal provided that it contains all necessary indications to establish the purpose of the payment.

5. Where the request is submitted or the fees paid in respect of only some of the goods or services for which the EU trade mark is registered, registration shall be

renewed for those goods or services only. Where the fees paid are insufficient to cover all the classes of goods and services for which renewal is requested, registration shall be renewed if it is clear which class or classes are to be covered. In the absence of other criteria, the Office shall take the classes into account in the order of classification.

6. Renewal shall take effect from the day following the date on which the existing registration expires. The renewal shall be registered.

7. Where the request for renewal is filed within the periods provided for in paragraph 3, but the other conditions governing renewal provided for in this Article are not satisfied, the Office shall inform the applicant of the deficiencies found.

8. Where a request for renewal is not submitted or is submitted after the expiry of the period provided for in paragraph 3, or where the fees are not paid or are paid only after the period in question has expired, or where the deficiencies referred to in paragraph 7 are not remedied within that period, the Office shall determine that the registration has expired and shall notify the proprietor of the EU trade mark accordingly. Where the determination has become final, the Office shall cancel the mark from the register. The cancellation shall take effect from the day following the date on which the existing registration expired. Where the renewal fees have been paid but the registration is not renewed, those fees shall be refunded.

9. A single request for renewal may be submitted for two or more marks, upon payment of the required fees for each of the marks, provided that the proprietors or the representatives are the same in each case.

Article 54
Alteration

1. The EU trade mark shall not be altered in the Register during the period of registration or on renewal thereof.

2. Nevertheless, where the EU trademark includes the name and address of the proprietor, any alteration thereof not substantially affecting the identity of the trade mark as originally registered may be registered at the request of the proprietor.

3. The request for alteration shall include the element of the mark to be altered and that element in its altered version.

The Commission shall adopt implementing acts specifying the details to be contained in the request for alteration. Those implementing acts shall be adopted in accordance with the examination procedure referred to in Article 207(2).

4. The request shall be deemed not to have been filed until the required fee has been paid. If the fee has not been paid or has not been paid in full, the Office shall inform the applicant accordingly. A single request may be made for the alteration of the same element in two or more registrations of the same proprietor. The required fee shall be paid in respect of each registration to be altered. If the requirements governing the alteration of the registration are not fulfilled, the Office shall communicate the deficiency to the applicant. If the deficiency is not remedied within a period to be specified by the Office, the Office shall reject the request.

5. The publication of the registration of the alteration shall contain a representation of the EU trade mark as altered. Third parties whose rights may be affected by the alteration may challenge the registration thereof within the period of three months following publication. Articles 46 and 47 and rules adopted pursuant to Article 48 shall apply to the publication of the registration of the alteration.

Article 55
Change of the name or address

1. A change of the name or address of the proprietor of the EU trade mark which is not an alteration of the EU trade mark pursuant to Article 54(2) and which is not the consequence of a whole or partial transfer of the EU trade mark shall, at the request of the proprietor, be recorded in the Register.

The Commission shall adopt implementing acts specifying the details to be contained in a request for the change of name or address pursuant to the first subparagraph of this paragraph. Those implementing acts shall be adopted in accordance with the examination procedure referred to in Article 207(2).

2. A single request may be made for the change of the name or address in respect of two or more registrations of the same proprietor.

3. If the requirements governing the recording of a change are not fulfilled, the Office shall communicate the deficiency to the proprietor of the EU trade mark. If the deficiency is not remedied within a period to be specified by the Office, the Office shall reject the request.

4. Paragraphs 1, 2 and 3 shall also apply to a change of the name or address of the registered representative.

5. Paragraphs 1 to 4 shall apply to applications for EU trade marks. The change shall be recorded in the files kept by the Office on the EU trade mark application.

Article 56
Division of the registration

1. The proprietor of the EU trade mark may divide the registration by declaring that some of the goods or services included in the original registration will be the subject of one or more divisional registrations. The goods or services in the divisional registration shall not overlap with the goods or services which remain in the original registration or those which are included in other divisional registrations.

2. The declaration of division shall not be admissible:

(a) if, where an application for revocation of rights or for a declaration of invalidity has been entered at the Office against the original registration, such a divisional declaration has the effect of introducing a division amongst the goods or services against which the application for revocation of rights or for a declaration of invalidity is directed, until the decision of the Cancellation Division has become final or the proceedings are finally terminated otherwise;

(b) if, where a counterclaim for revocation or for a declaration of invalidity has been entered in a case before an EU trade mark court, such a divisional declaration has the effect of introducing a division amongst the goods or services against which the counterclaim is directed, until the mention of the EU trade mark court's judgment is recorded in the Register pursuant to Article 128(6).

3. If the requirements laid down in paragraph 1 and pursuant to the implementing acts referred to in paragraph 8 are not fulfilled, or the list of goods and services which form the divisional registration overlap with the goods and services which remain in the original registration, the Office shall invite the proprietor of the EU trade mark to remedy the deficiencies within such period as it may specify. If the deficiencies are not remedied before the period expires, the Office shall refuse the declaration of division.

4. The declaration of division shall be subject to a fee. The declaration shall be deemed not to have been made until the fee has been paid.

5. The division shall take effect on the date on which it is entered in the Register.

6. All requests and applications submitted and all fees paid with regard to the original registration prior to the date on which the Office receives the declaration of division shall be deemed also to have been submitted or paid with regard to the divisional registration or registrations. The fees for the original registration which have been duly paid prior to the date on which the declaration of division is received shall not be refunded.

7. The divisional registration shall preserve the filing date and any priority date and seniority date of the original registration.

8. The Commission shall adopt implementing acts specifying:

(a) the details to be contained in a declaration of the division of a registration pursuant to paragraph 1;
(b) the details as how to process a declaration of the division of a registration, ensuring that a separate file, including a new registration number, is established for the divisional registration.

Those implementing acts shall be adopted in accordance with the examination procedure referred to in Article 207(2).

CHAPTER VI SURRENDER, REVOCATION AND INVALIDITY

Section 1 Surrender

Article 57
Surrender

1. An EU trade mark may be surrendered in respect of some or all of the goods or services for which it is registered.

2. The surrender shall be declared to the Office in writing by the proprietor of the trade mark. It shall not have effect until it has been entered in the Register.

The validity of the surrender of an EU trade mark which is declared to the Office subsequent to the submission of an application for revocation of that trade mark pursuant to Article 63(1) shall be conditional upon the final rejection or withdrawal of the application for revocation.

3. Surrender shall be entered only with the agreement of the proprietor of a right relating to the EU trade mark and which is entered in the Register. If a licence has been registered, surrender shall be entered in the Register only if the proprietor of the EU trade mark proves that he has informed the licensee of his intention to surrender. The entry of the surrender shall be made on expiry of the three-month period after the date on which the proprietor satisfies the Office that he has informed the licensee of his intention to surrender, or before the expiry of that period, as soon as he proves that the licensee has given his consent.

4. If the requirements governing surrender are not fulfilled, the Office shall communicate the deficiencies to the declarant. If the deficiencies are not remedied within a period to be specified by the Office, the Office shall reject the entry of surrender in the Register.

5. The Commission shall adopt implementing acts specifying the details to be contained in a declaration of surrender pursuant to paragraph 2 of this Article and the kind of documentation required to establish a third party's agreement pursuant to paragraph 3 of this Article. Those implementing acts shall be adopted in accordance with the examination procedure referred to in Article 207(2).

Section 2 Grounds for revocation

Article 58

Grounds for revocation

1. The rights of the proprietor of the EU trade mark shall be declared to be revoked on application to the Office or on the basis of a counterclaim in infringement proceedings:

(a) if, within a continuous period of five years, the trade mark has not been put to genuine use in the Union in connection with the goods or services in respect of which it is registered, and there are no proper reasons for non-use; however, no person may claim that the proprietor's rights in an EU trade mark should be revoked where, during the interval between expiry of the five-year period and filing of the application or counterclaim, genuine use of the trade mark has been started or resumed; the commencement or resumption of use within a period of three months preceding the filing of the application or counterclaim which began at the earliest on expiry of the continuous period of five years of non-use shall, however, be disregarded where preparations for the commencement or resumption occur only after the proprietor becomes aware that the application or counterclaim may be filed;

(b) if, in consequence of acts or inactivity of the proprietor, the trade mark has become the common name in the trade for a product or service in respect of which it is registered;

(c) if, in consequence of the use made of the trade mark by the proprietor of the trade mark or with his consent in respect of the goods or services for which it is registered, the trade mark is liable to mislead the public, particularly as to the nature, quality or geographical origin of those goods or services.

2. Where the grounds for revocation of rights exist in respect of only some of the goods or services for which the EU trade mark is registered, the rights of the proprietor shall be declared to be revoked in respect of those goods or services only.

Section 3 Grounds for invalidity

Article 59
Absolute grounds for invalidity

1. An EU trade mark shall be declared invalid on application to the Office or on the basis of a counterclaim in infringement proceedings:

(a) where the EU trade mark has been registered contrary to the provisions of Article 7;
(b) where the applicant was acting in bad faith when he filed the application for the trade mark.

2. Where the EU trade mark has been registered in breach of the provisions of Article 7(1)(b), (c) or (d), it may nevertheless not be declared invalid if, in consequence of the use which has been made of it, it has after registration acquired a distinctive character in relation to the goods or services for which it is registered.

3. Where the ground for invalidity exists in respect of only some of the goods or services for which the EU trade mark is registered, the trade mark shall be declared invalid as regards those goods or services only.

Article 60
Relative grounds for invalidity

1. An EU trade mark shall be declared invalid on application to the Office or on the basis of a counterclaim in infringement proceedings:

(a) where there is an earlier trade mark as referred to in Article 8(2) and the conditions set out in paragraph 1 or 5 of that Article are fulfilled;
(b) where there is a trade mark as referred to in Article 8(3) and the conditions set out in that paragraph are fulfilled;
(c) where there is an earlier right as referred to in Article 8(4) and the conditions set out in that paragraph are fulfilled;
(d) where there is an earlier designation of origin or geographical indication as referred to in Article 8(6) and the conditions set out in that paragraph are fulfilled.

All the conditions referred to in the first subparagraph shall be fulfilled at the filing date or the priority date of the EU trade mark.

2. An EU trade mark shall also be declared invalid on application to the Office or on the basis of a counterclaim in infringement proceedings where the use of such trade mark may be prohibited pursuant to another earlier right under the Union legislation or national law governing its protection, and in particular:

(a) a right to a name;
(b) a right of personal portrayal;
(c) a copyright;
(d) an industrial property right.

3. An EU trade mark may not be declared invalid where the proprietor of a right referred to in paragraph 1 or 2 consents expressly to the registration of the EU trade mark before submission of the application for a declaration of invalidity or the counterclaim.

4. Where the proprietor of one of the rights referred to in paragraph 1 or 2 has previously applied for a declaration that an EU trade mark is invalid or made a counterclaim in infringement proceedings, he may not submit a new application for a declaration of invalidity or lodge a counterclaim on the basis of another of the said rights which he could have invoked in support of his first application or counterclaim.

5. Article 59(3) shall apply.

Article 61
Limitation in consequence of acquiescence

1. Where the proprietor of an EU trade mark has acquiesced, for a period of five successive years, in the use of a later EU trade mark in the Union while being aware of such use, he shall no longer be entitled on the basis of the earlier trade mark to apply for a declaration that the later trade mark is invalid in respect of the goods or services for which the later trade mark has been used, unless registration of the later EU trade mark was applied for in bad faith.

2. Where the proprietor of an earlier national trade mark as referred to in Article 8(2) or of another earlier sign referred to in Article 8(4) has acquiesced, for a period of five successive years, in the use of a later EU trade mark in the Member State in which the earlier trade mark or the other earlier sign is protected while being aware of such use, he shall no longer be entitled on the basis of the earlier trade mark or of the other earlier sign to apply for a declaration that the later trade mark is invalid in respect of the goods or services for which the later trade mark has been used, unless registration of the later EU trade mark was applied for in bad faith.

3. In the cases referred to in paragraphs 1 and 2, the proprietor of a later EU trade mark shall not be entitled to oppose the use of the earlier right, even though that right may no longer be invoked against the later EU trade mark.

Section 4 Consequences of revocation and invalidity

Article 62
Consequences of revocation and invalidity

1. The EU trade mark shall be deemed not to have had, as from the date of the application for revocation or of the counterclaim, the effects specified in this Regulation, to the extent that the rights of the proprietor have been revoked. An earlier date, on which one of the grounds for revocation occurred, may be fixed in the decision at the request of one of the parties.

2. The EU trade mark shall be deemed not to have had, as from the outset, the effects specified in this Regulation, to the extent that the trade mark has been declared invalid.

3. Subject to the national provisions relating either to claims for compensation for damage caused by negligence or lack of good faith on the part of the proprietor of the trade mark, or to unjust enrichment, the retroactive effect of revocation or invalidity of the trade mark shall not affect:

(a) any decision on infringement which has acquired the authority of a final decision and been enforced prior to the revocation or invalidity decision;
(b) any contract concluded prior to the revocation or invalidity decision, in so far as it has been performed before that decision; however, repayment, to an extent justified by the circumstances, of sums paid under the relevant contract may be claimed on grounds of equity.

Section 5 Proceedings in the office in relation to revocation or invalidity

Article 63
Application for revocation or for a declaration of invalidity

1. An application for revocation of the rights of the proprietor of an EU trade mark or for a declaration that the trade mark is invalid may be submitted to the Office:

(a) where Articles 58 and 59 apply, by any natural or legal person and any group or body set up for the purpose of representing the interests of manufacturers, producers, suppliers of services, traders or consumers, which, under the terms of the law governing it, has the capacity in its own name to sue and be sued;
(b) where Article 60(1) applies, by the persons referred to in Article 46(1);
(c) where Article 60(2) applies, by the owners of the earlier rights referred to in that provision or by the persons who are entitled under Union legislation or the law of the Member State concerned to exercise the rights in question.

2. The application shall be filed in a written reasoned statement. It shall not be deemed to have been filed until the fee has been paid.

3. An application for revocation or for a declaration of invalidity shall be inadmissible where an application relating to the same subject matter and cause of action, and involving the same parties, has been adjudicated on its merits, either by the Office or by an EU trade mark court as referred to in Article 123, and the decision of the Office or that court on that application has acquired the authority of a final decision.

Article 64
Examination of the application

1. On the examination of the application for revocation of rights or for a declaration of invalidity, the Office shall invite the parties, as often as necessary, to file observations, within a period to be fixed by the Office, on communications from the other parties or issued by itself.

2. If the proprietor of the EU trade mark so requests, the proprietor of an earlier EU trade mark, being a party to the invalidity proceedings, shall furnish proof that, during the period of five years preceding the date of the application for a declaration of invalidity, the earlier EU trade mark has been put to genuine use in the Union in connection with the goods or services in respect of which it is registered and which the proprietor of that earlier trade mark cites as justification for his application, or that there are proper reasons for non-use, provided that the earlier EU trade mark has at that date been registered for not less than five years. If, at the date on which the EU trade mark application was filed or at the priority date of the EU trade mark application, the earlier EU trade mark had been registered for not less than five years, the proprietor of the earlier EU trade mark shall furnish proof that, in addition, the conditions set out in Article 47(2) were satisfied at that date. In the absence of proof to this effect, the application for a declaration of invalidity shall be rejected. If the earlier EU trade mark has been used only in relation to part of the goods or services for which it is registered, it shall, for the purpose of the examination of the application for a declaration of invalidity, be deemed to be registered in respect of that part of the goods or services only.

3. Paragraph 2 shall apply to earlier national trade marks referred to in Article 8(2)(a), by substituting use in the Member State in which the earlier national trade mark is protected for use in the Union.

4. The Office may, if it thinks fit, invite the parties to make a friendly settlement.

5. If the examination of the application for revocation of rights or for a declaration of invalidity reveals that the trade mark should not have been registered in respect of some or all of the goods or services for which it is registered, the rights of the proprietor of the EU trade mark shall be revoked or it shall be declared invalid in respect of those goods or services. Otherwise the application for revocation of rights or for a declaration of invalidity shall be rejected.

6. A record of the Office's decision on the application for revocation of rights or for a declaration of invalidity shall be entered in the Register once it has become final.

Article 65
Delegation of powers

The Commission is empowered to adopt delegated acts in accordance with Article 208 specifying the details of the procedures governing the revocation and declaration of invalidity of an EU trade mark as referred to in Articles 63 and 64, as well as the transfer of an EU trade mark registered in the name of an agent as referred to in Article 21.

CHAPTER VII APPEALS

Article 66
Decisions subject to appeal

1. An appeal shall lie from decisions of any of the decision-making instances of the Office listed in points (a) to (d) of Article 159, and, where appropriate,

point (f) of that Article. Those decisions shall take effect only as from the date of expiration of the appeal period referred to in Article 68. The filing of the appeal shall have suspensive effect.

2. A decision which does not terminate proceedings as regards one of the parties can only be appealed together with the final decision, unless the decision allows separate appeal.

Article 67

Persons entitled to appeal and to be parties to appeal proceedings

Any party to proceedings adversely affected by a decision may appeal. Any other parties to the proceedings shall be parties to the appeal proceedings as of right.

Article 68

Time limit and form of appeal

1. Notice of appeal shall be filed in writing at the Office within two months of the date of notification of the decision. The notice shall be deemed to have been filed only when the fee for appeal has been paid. It shall be filed in the language of the proceedings in which the decision subject to appeal was taken. Within four months of the date of notification of the decision, a written statement setting out the grounds of appeal shall be filed.

2. In inter partes proceedings, the defendant may, in his response, seek a decision annulling or altering the contested decision on a point not raised in the appeal. Such submissions shall cease to have effect should the appellant discontinue the proceedings.

Article 69

Revision of decisions in ex parte cases

1. If the party which has lodged the appeal is the sole party to the procedure, and if the department whose decision is contested considers the appeal to be admissible and well founded, the department shall rectify its decision.

2. If the decision is not rectified within one month of receipt of the statement of grounds, the appeal shall be remitted to the Board of Appeal without delay, and without comment as to its merit.

Article 70

Examination of appeals

1. If the appeal is admissible, the Board of Appeal shall examine whether the appeal is allowable.

2. In the examination of the appeal, the Board of Appeal shall invite the parties, as often as necessary, to file observations, within a period to be fixed by the Board of Appeal, on communications from the other parties or issued by itself.

Article 71

Decisions in respect of appeals

1. Following the examination as to the allowability of the appeal, the Board of Appeal shall decide on the appeal. The Board of Appeal may either exercise any power within the competence of the department which was responsible for the decision appealed or remit the case to that department for further prosecution.

2. If the Board of Appeal remits the case for further prosecution to the department whose decision was appealed, that department shall be bound by the ratio decidendi of the Board of Appeal, in so far as the facts are the same.

3. The decisions of the Board of Appeal shall take effect only as from the date of expiry of the period referred to in Article 72(5) or, if an action has been brought before the General Court within that period, as from the date of dismissal of such action or of any appeal filed with the Court of Justice against the decision of the General Court.

Article 72

Actions before the Court of Justice

1. Actions may be brought before the General Court against decisions of the Boards of Appeal in relation to appeals.

2. The action may be brought on grounds of lack of competence, infringement of an essential procedural requirement, infringement of the TFEU, infringement of this Regulation or of any rule of law relating to their application or misuse of power.

3. The General Court shall have jurisdiction to annul or to alter the contested decision.

4. The action shall be open to any party to proceedings before the Board of Appeal adversely affected by its decision.

5. The action shall be brought before the General Court within two months of the date of notification of the decision of the Board of Appeal.

6. The Office shall take the necessary measures to comply with the judgment of the General Court or, in the event of an appeal against that judgment, the Court of Justice.

Article 73

Delegation of powers

The Commission is empowered to adopt delegated acts in accordance with Article 208 specifying:

(a) the formal content of the notice of appeal referred to in Article 68 and the procedure for the filing and the examination of an appeal;
(b) the formal content and form of the Board of Appeal's decisions as referred to in Article 71;
(c) the reimbursement of the appeal fee referred to in Article 68.

CHAPTER VIII SPECIFIC PROVISIONS ON EUROPEAN UNION COLLECTIVE MARKS AND CERTIFICATION MARKS

Section 1 EU collective marks

Article 74
EU collective marks

1. A European Union collective mark ('EU collective mark') shall be an EU trade mark which is described as such when the mark is applied for and is capable of distinguishing the goods or services of the members of the association which is the proprietor of the mark from those of other undertakings. Associations of manufacturers, producers, suppliers of services, or traders which, under the terms of the law governing them, have the capacity in their own name to have rights and obligations of all kinds, to make contracts or accomplish other legal acts, and to sue and be sued, as well as legal persons governed by public law, may apply for EU collective marks.

2. By way of derogation from Article 7(1)(c), signs or indications which may serve, in trade, to designate the geographical origin of the goods or services may constitute EU collective marks within the meaning of paragraph 1. An EU collective mark shall not entitle the proprietor to prohibit a third party from using in the course of trade such signs or indications, provided that he uses them in accordance with honest practices in industrial or commercial matters; in particular, such a mark shall not be invoked against a third party who is entitled to use a geographical name.

3. Chapters I to VII and IX to XIV shall apply to EU collective marks to the extent that this section does not provide otherwise.

Article 75
Regulations governing use of an EU collective mark

1. An applicant for an EU collective mark shall submit regulations governing use within two months of the date of filing.

2. The regulations governing use shall specify the persons authorised to use the mark, the conditions of membership of the association and, where they exist, the conditions of use of the mark, including sanctions. The regulations governing use of a mark referred to in Article 74(2) shall authorise any person whose goods or services originate in the geographical area concerned to become a member of the association which is the proprietor of the mark.

3. The Commission shall adopt implementing acts specifying the details to be contained in the regulations referred to in paragraph 2 of this Article. Those implementing acts shall be adopted in accordance with the examination procedure referred to in Article 207(2).

Article 76
Refusal of the application

1. In addition to the grounds for refusal of an EU trade mark application provided for in Articles 41 and 42, an application for an EU collective mark shall be refused where the provisions of Articles 74 or 75 are not satisfied, or where the

regulations governing use are contrary to public policy or to accepted principles of morality.

2. An application for an EU collective mark shall also be refused if the public is liable to be misled as regards the character or the significance of the mark, in particular if it is likely to be taken to be something other than a collective mark.

3. An application shall not be refused if the applicant, as a result of amendment of the regulations governing use, meets the requirements of paragraphs 1 and 2.

Article 77

Observations by third parties

Where written observations on an EU collective mark are submitted to the Office pursuant to Article 45, those observations may also be based on the particular grounds on which the application for an EU collective mark should be refused pursuant to Article 76.

Article 78

Use of marks

Use of an EU collective mark by any person who has authority to use it shall satisfy the requirements of this Regulation, provided that the other conditions which this Regulation imposes with regard to the use of EU trade marks are fulfilled.

Article 79

Amendment of the regulations governing use of the EU collective mark

1. The proprietor of an EU collective mark shall submit to the Office any amended regulations governing use.

2. The amendment shall not be mentioned in the Register if the amended regulations do not satisfy the requirements of Article 75 or involve one of the grounds for refusal referred to in Article 76.

3. Written observations made in accordance with Article 77 may also be submitted with regard to amended regulations governing use.

4. For the purposes of applying this Regulation, amendments to the regulations governing use shall take effect only from the date of entry of the mention of the amendment in the Register.

Article 80

Persons who are entitled to bring an action for infringement

1. The provisions of Article 25(3) and (4) concerning the rights of licensees shall apply to every person who has authority to use an EU collective mark.

2. The proprietor of an EU collective mark shall be entitled to claim compensation on behalf of persons who have authority to use the mark where they have sustained damage in consequence of unauthorised use of the mark.

Article 81
Grounds for revocation

Apart from the grounds for revocation provided for in Article 58, the rights of the proprietor of an EU collective mark shall be revoked on application to the Office or on the basis of a counterclaim in infringement proceedings, if:

(a) the proprietor does not take reasonable steps to prevent the mark being used in a manner incompatible with the conditions of use, where these exist, laid down in the regulations governing use, amendments to which have, where appropriate, been mentioned in the Register;
(b) the manner in which the mark has been used by the proprietor has caused it to become liable to mislead the public in the manner referred to in Article 76(2);
(c) an amendment to the regulations governing use of the mark has been mentioned in the Register in breach of the provisions of Article 79(2), unless the proprietor of the mark, by further amending the regulations governing use, complies with the requirements of those provisions.

Article 82
Grounds for invalidity

Apart from the grounds for invalidity provided for in Articles 59 and 60, an EU collective mark which is registered in breach of the provisions of Article 76 shall be declared invalid on application to the Office or on the basis of a counterclaim in infringement proceedings, unless the proprietor of the mark, by amending the regulations governing use, complies with the requirements of those provisions.

Section 2 EU certification marks

Article 83
EU certification marks

1. An EU certification mark shall be an EU trade mark which is described as such when the mark is applied for and is capable of distinguishing goods or services which are certified by the proprietor of the mark in respect of material, mode of manufacture of goods or performance of services, quality, accuracy or other characteristics, with the exception of geographical origin, from goods and services which are not so certified.

2. Any natural or legal person, including institutions, authorities and bodies governed by public law, may apply for EU certification marks provided that such person does not carry on a business involving the supply of goods or services of the kind certified.

3. Chapters I to VII and IX to XIV shall apply to EU certification marks to the extent that this Section does not provide otherwise.

Article 84
Regulations governing use of an EU certification mark

1. An applicant for an EU certification mark shall submit regulations governing the use of the EU certification mark within two months of the date of filing.

2. The regulations governing use shall specify the persons authorised to use the mark, the characteristics to be certified by the mark, how the certifying body is to test those characteristics and to supervise the use of the mark. Those regulations shall also specify the conditions of use of the mark, including sanctions.

3. The Commission shall adopt implementing acts specifying the details to be contained in the regulations referred to in paragraph 2 of this Article. Those implementing acts shall be adopted in accordance with the examination procedure referred to in Article 207(2).

Article 85
Refusal of the application

1. In addition to the grounds for refusal of an EU trade mark application provided for in Articles 41 and 42, an application for an EU certification mark shall be refused where the conditions set out in Articles 83 and 84 are not satisfied, or where the regulations governing use are contrary to public policy or to accepted principles of morality.

2. An application for an EU certification mark shall also be refused if the public is liable to be misled as regards the character or the significance of the mark, in particular if it is likely to be taken to be something other than a certification mark.

3. An application shall not be refused if the applicant, as a result of an amendment of the regulations governing use, meets the requirements of paragraphs 1 and 2.

Article 86
Observations by third parties

Where written observations on an EU certification mark are submitted to the Office pursuant to Article 45, those observations may also be based on the particular grounds on which the application for an EU certification mark should be refused pursuant to Article 85.

Article 87
Use of the EU certification mark

Use of an EU certification mark by any person who has authority to use it pursuant to the regulations governing use referred to in Article 84 shall satisfy the requirements of this Regulation, provided that the other conditions laid down in this Regulation with regard to the use of EU trade marks are fulfilled.

Article 88
Amendment of the regulations governing use of the EU certification mark

1. The proprietor of an EU certification mark shall submit to the Office any amended regulations governing use.

2. Amendments shall not be mentioned in the Register where the regulations as amended do not satisfy the requirements of Article 84 or involve one of the grounds for refusal referred to in Article 85.

3. Written observations in accordance with Article 86 may also be submitted with regard to amended regulations governing use.

4. For the purposes of this Regulation, amendments to the regulations governing use shall take effect only as from the date of entry of the mention of the amendment in the Register.

Article 89
Transfer

By way of derogation from Article 20(1), an EU certification mark may only be transferred to a person who meets the requirements of Article 83(2).

Article 90
Persons who are entitled to bring an action for infringement

1. Only the proprietor of an EU certification mark, or any person specifically authorised by him to that effect, shall be entitled to bring an action for infringement.

2. The proprietor of an EU certification mark shall be entitled to claim compensation on behalf of persons who have authority to use the mark where they have sustained damage as a consequence of unauthorised use of the mark.

Article 91
Grounds for revocation

In addition to the grounds for revocation provided for in Article 58, the rights of the proprietor of an EU certification mark shall be revoked on application to the Office or on the basis of a counterclaim in infringement proceedings, where any of the following conditions is fulfilled:

(a) the proprietor no longer complies with the requirements set out in Article 83(2);
(b) the proprietor does not take reasonable steps to prevent the EU certification mark being used in a manner that is incompatible with the conditions of use laid down in the regulations governing use, amendments to which have, where appropriate, been mentioned in the Register;
(c) the manner in which the EU certification mark has been used by the proprietor has caused it to become liable to mislead the public in the manner referred to in Article 85(2);
(d) an amendment to the regulations governing use of the EU certification mark has been mentioned in the Register in breach of Article 88(2), unless the proprietor of the mark, by further amending the regulations governing use, complies with the requirements of that Article.

Article 92
Grounds for invalidity

In addition to the grounds for invalidity provided for in Articles 59 and 60, an EU certification mark which is registered in breach of Article 85 shall be declared invalid on application to the Office or on the basis of a counterclaim in infringement proceedings, unless the proprietor of the EU certification mark, by amending the regulations governing use, complies with the requirements of Article 85.

Article 93
Conversion

Without prejudice to Article 139(2), conversion of an application for an EU certification mark or of a registered EU certification mark shall not take place where the national law of the Member State concerned does not provide for the registration of guarantee or certification marks pursuant to Article 28 of Directive (EU) 2015/2436.

CHAPTER IX PROCEDURE

Section I General provisions

Article 94
Decisions and communications of the Office

1. Decisions of the Office shall state the reasons on which they are based. They shall be based only on reasons or evidence on which the parties concerned have had an opportunity to present their comments. Where oral proceedings are held before the Office, the decision may be given orally. Subsequently, the decision shall be notified in writing to the parties.

2. Any decision, communication or notice from the Office shall indicate the department or division of the Office as well as the name or the names of the official or officials responsible. They shall be signed by that official or those officials, or, instead of a signature, carry a printed or stamped seal of the Office. The Executive Director may determine that other means of identifying the department or division of the Office and the name of the official or officials responsible, or an identification other than a seal, may be used where decisions, communications or notices from the Office are transmitted by telecopier or any other technical means of communication.

3. Decisions of the Office which are open to appeal shall be accompanied by a written communication indicating that any notice of appeal is to be filed in writing at the Office within two months of the date of notification of the decision in question. The communications shall also draw the attention of the parties to the provisions laid down in Articles 66, 67 and 68. The parties may not plead any failure on the part of the Office to communicate the availability of appeal proceedings.

Article 95
Examination of the facts by the Office of its own motion

1. In proceedings before it the Office shall examine the facts of its own motion; however, in proceedings relating to relative grounds for refusal of registration, the Office shall be restricted in this examination to the facts, evidence and arguments provided by the parties and the relief sought. In invalidity proceedings pursuant to Article 59, the Office shall limit its examination to the grounds and arguments submitted by the parties.

2. The Office may disregard facts or evidence which are not submitted in due time by the parties concerned.

Article 96
Oral proceedings

1. If the Office considers that oral proceedings would be expedient they shall be held either at the instance of the Office or at the request of any party to the proceedings.

2. Oral proceedings before the examiners, the Opposition Division and the Department in charge of the Register shall not be public.

3. Oral proceedings, including delivery of the decision, shall be public before the Cancellation Division and the Boards of Appeal, in so far as the department before which the proceedings are taking place does not decide otherwise in cases where admission of the public could have serious and unjustified disadvantages, in particular for a party to the proceedings.

4. The Commission is empowered to adopt delegated acts in accordance with Article 208 specifying the detailed arrangements for oral proceedings, including the detailed arrangements for the use of languages in accordance with Article 146.

Article 97
Taking of evidence

1. In any proceedings before the Office, the means of giving or obtaining evidence shall include the following:

(a) hearing the parties;
(b) requests for information;
(c) the production of documents and items of evidence;
(d) hearing witnesses;
(e) opinions by experts;
(f) statements in writing sworn or affirmed or having a similar effect under the law of the State in which the statement is drawn up.

2. The relevant department may commission one of its members to examine the evidence adduced.

3. If the Office considers it necessary for a party, witness or expert to give evidence orally, it shall issue a summons to the person concerned to appear before it. The period of notice provided in such summons shall be at least one month, unless they agree to a shorter period.

4. The parties shall be informed of the hearing of a witness or expert before the Office. They shall have the right to be present and to put questions to the witness or expert.

5. The Executive Director shall determine the amounts of expenses to be paid, including advances, as regards the costs of taking of evidence as referred to in this Article.

6. The Commission is empowered to adopt delegated acts in accordance with Article 208 specifying the detailed arrangements for the taking of evidence.

Article 98

Notification

1. The Office shall, as a matter of course, notify those concerned of decisions and summonses and of any notice or other communication from which a time limit is reckoned, or of which those concerned are to be notified under other provisions of this Regulation or of acts adopted pursuant to this Regulation, or of which notification has been ordered by the Executive Director.

2. The Executive Director may determine which documents other than decisions subject to a time limit for appeal and summonses shall be notified by registered letter with proof of delivery.

3. Notification may be effected by different means, including by electronic means. The details regarding electronic means shall be determined by the Executive Director.

4. Where notification is to be effected by public notice, the Executive Director shall determine how the public notice is to be given and shall fix the beginning of the one-month period on the expiry of which the document shall be deemed to have been notified.

5. The Commission is empowered to adopt delegated acts in accordance with Article 208 specifying the detailed arrangements for notification.

Article 99

Notification of loss of rights

Where the Office finds that the loss of any rights results from this Regulation or acts adopted pursuant to this Regulation, without any decision having been taken, it shall communicate this to the person concerned in accordance with Article 98. The latter may apply for a decision on the matter within two months of notification of the communication, if he considers that the finding of the Office is incorrect. The Office shall adopt such a decision only where it disagrees with the person requesting it; otherwise the Office shall amend its finding and inform the person requesting the decision.

Article 100

Communications to the Office

1. Communications addressed to the Office may be effected by electronic means. The Executive Director shall determine to what extent and under which technical conditions those communications may be submitted electronically.

2. The Commission is empowered to adopt delegated acts in accordance with Article 208 specifying the rules on the means of communication, including the electronic means of communication, to be used by the parties to proceedings before the Office and the forms to be made available by the Office.

Article 101
Time limits

1. Time limits shall be laid down in terms of full years, months, weeks or days. Calculation shall start on the day following the day on which the relevant event occurred. The duration of time limits shall be no less than one month and no more than six months.

2. The Executive Director shall determine, before the commencement of each calendar year, the days on which the Office is not open for receipt of documents or on which ordinary post is not delivered in the locality in which the Office is located.

3. The Executive Director shall determine the duration of the period of interruption in the case of a general interruption in the delivery of post in the Member State where the Office is located or, in the case of an actual interruption of the Office's connection to admitted electronic means of communication.

4. If an exceptional occurrence, such as a natural disaster or strike, interrupts or interferes with proper communication from the parties to the proceedings to the Office or vice-versa, the Executive Director may determine that for parties to the proceedings having their residence or registered office in the Member State concerned or who have appointed a representative with a place of business in the Member State concerned all time limits that otherwise would expire on or after the date of commencement of such occurrence, as determined by him, shall extend until a date to be determined by him. When determining that date, he shall assess when the exceptional occurrence comes to an end. If the occurrence affects the seat of the Office, such determination of the Executive Director shall specify that it applies in respect of all parties to the proceedings.

5. The Commission is empowered to adopt delegated acts in accordance with Article 208 specifying the details regarding the calculation and duration of time limits.

Article 102
Correction of errors and manifest oversights

1. The Office shall correct any linguistic errors or errors of transcription and manifest oversights in its decisions, or technical errors attributable to it in registering an EU trade mark or in publishing the registration of its own motion or at the request of a party.

2. Where the correction of errors in the registration of an EU trade mark or the publication of the registration is requested by the proprietor, Article 55 shall apply mutatis mutandis.

3. Corrections of errors in the registration of an EU trade mark and in the publication of the registration shall be published by the Office.

Article 103
Revocation of decisions

1. Where the Office has made an entry in the Register or taken a decision which contains an obvious error attributable to the Office, it shall ensure that the entry is cancelled or the decision is revoked. Where there is only one party to the proceedings and the entry or the act affects its rights, cancellation or revocation shall be determined even if the error was not evident to the party.

2. Cancellation or revocation as referred to in paragraph 1 shall be determined, ex officio or at the request of one of the parties to the proceedings, by the department which made the entry or took the decision. The cancellation of the entry in the Register or the revocation of the decision shall be effected within one year of the date on which the entry was made in the Register or that decision was taken, after consultation with the parties to the proceedings and any proprietor of rights to the EU trade mark in question that are entered in the Register. The Office shall keep records of any such cancellation or revocation.

3. The Commission is empowered to adopt delegated acts in accordance with Article 208 specifying the procedure for the revocation of a decision or for the cancellation of an entry in the Register.

4. This Article shall be without prejudice to the right of the parties to submit an appeal under Articles 66 and 72, or to the possibility of correcting errors and manifest oversights under Article 102. Where an appeal has been filed against a decision of the Office containing an error, the appeal proceedings shall become devoid of purpose upon revocation by the Office of its decision pursuant to paragraph 1 of this Article. In the latter case, the appeal fee shall be reimbursed to the appellant.

Article 104
Restitutio in integrum

1. The applicant for or proprietor of an EU trade mark or any other party to proceedings before the Office who, in spite of all due care required by the circumstances having been taken, was unable to comply with a time limit vis-à-vis the Office shall, upon application, have his rights re-established if the obstacle to compliance has the direct consequence, by virtue of the provisions of this Regulation, of causing the loss of any right or means of redress.

2. The application shall be filed in writing within two months of the removal of the obstacle to compliance with the time limit. The omitted act shall be completed within this period. The application shall only be admissible within the year immediately following the expiry of the unobserved time limit. In the case of non-submission of the request for renewal of registration or of non-payment of a renewal fee, the further period of six months provided in the third sentence of Article 53(3) shall be deducted from the period of one year.

3. The application shall state the grounds on which it is based and shall set out the facts on which it relies. It shall not be deemed to be filed until the fee for re-establishment of rights has been paid.

4. The department competent to decide on the omitted act shall decide upon the application.

5. This Article shall not be applicable to the time limits referred to in paragraph 2 of this Article, Article 46(1) and (3) and Article 105.

6. Where the applicant for or proprietor of an EU trade mark has his rights re-established, he may not invoke his rights vis-à-vis a third party who, in good faith, has put goods on the market or supplied services under a sign which is identical with, or similar to, the EU trade mark in the course of the period between the loss of rights in the application or in the EU trade mark and publication of the mention of re-establishment of those rights.

7. A third party who may avail himself of the provisions of paragraph 6 may bring third party proceedings against the decision re-establishing the rights of the applicant for or proprietor of an EU trade mark within a period of two months as from the date of publication of the mention of re-establishment of those rights.

8. Nothing in this Article shall limit the right of a Member State to grant restitutio in integrum in respect of time limits provided for in this Regulation and to be observed vis-à-vis the authorities of such State.

Article 105
Continuation of proceedings

1. An applicant for or proprietor of an EU trade mark or any other party to proceedings before the Office who has omitted to observe a time limit vis-à-vis the Office may, upon request, obtain the continuation of proceedings, provided that at the time the request is made the omitted act has been carried out. The request for continuation of proceedings shall be admissible only if it is submitted within two months of the expiry of the unobserved time limit. The request shall not be deemed to have been filed until the fee for continuation of the proceedings has been paid.

2. This Article shall not apply to the time limits laid down in Article 32, Article 34(1), Article 38(1), Article 41(2), Article 46(1) and (3), Article 53(3), Article 68, Article 72(5), Article 104(2) and Article 139, or to the time limits laid down in paragraph 1 of this Article or the time limit for claiming seniority pursuant to Article 39 after the application has been filed.

3. The department competent to decide on the omitted act shall decide upon the application.

4. If the Office accepts the application, the consequences of having failed to observe the time limit shall be deemed not to have occurred. If a decision has been taken between the expiry of that time limit and the request for the continuation of proceedings, the department competent to decide on the omitted act shall review the decision and, where completion of the omitted act itself is sufficient, take a different decision. If, following the review, the Office concludes that the original decision does not require to be altered, it shall confirm that decision in writing.

5. If the Office rejects the application, the fee shall be refunded.

Article 106
Interruption of proceedings

1. Proceedings before the Office shall be interrupted:

(a) in the event of the death or legal incapacity of the applicant for, or proprietor of, an EU trade mark or of the person authorised by national law to act on his behalf. To the extent that that death or incapacity does not affect the authorisation of a representative appointed under Article 120, proceedings shall be interrupted only on application by such representative;

(b) in the event of the applicant for, or proprietor of, an EU trade mark being prevented, for legal reasons resulting from action taken against his property, from continuing the proceedings before the Office;

(c) in the event of the death or legal incapacity of the representative of an applicant for, or proprietor of, an EU trade mark, or of that representative being prevented, for legal reasons resulting from action taken against his property, from continuing the proceedings before the Office.

2. Proceedings before the Office shall be resumed as soon as the identity of the person authorised to continue them has been established.

3. The Commission is empowered to adopt delegated acts in accordance with Article 208 specifying the detailed arrangements for the resumption of proceedings before the Office.

Article 107
Reference to general principles

In the absence of procedural provisions in this Regulation or in acts adopted pursuant to this Regulation, the Office shall take into account the principles of procedural law generally recognised in the Member States.

Article 108
Termination of financial obligations

1. Rights of the Office to the payment of a fee shall be extinguished after four years from the end of the calendar year in which the fee fell due.

2. Rights against the Office for the refunding of fees or sums of money paid in excess of a fee shall be extinguished after four years from the end of the calendar year in which the right arose.

3. The period laid down in paragraphs 1 and 2 shall be interrupted, in the case covered by paragraph 1, by a request for payment of the fee, and in the case covered by paragraph 2, by a reasoned claim in writing. On interruption it shall begin again immediately and shall end at the latest six years after the end of the year in which it originally began, unless, in the meantime, judicial proceedings to enforce the right have begun; in this case the period shall end at the earliest one year after the judgment has acquired the authority of a final decision.

Section 2 Costs

Article 109

Costs

1. The losing party in opposition proceedings, proceedings for revocation, proceedings for a declaration of invalidity or appeal proceedings shall bear the fees paid by the other party. Without prejudice to Article 146(7), the losing party shall also bear all costs incurred by the other party that are essential to the proceedings, including travel and subsistence and the remuneration of a representative within the meaning of Article 120(1), within the limits of the scales set for each category of costs in the implementing act to be adopted in accordance with paragraph 2 of this Article. The fees to be borne by the losing party shall be limited to the fees paid by the other party for opposition, for an application for revocation or for a declaration of invalidity of the EU trade mark and for appeal.

2. The Commission shall adopt implementing acts specifying the maximum rates for costs essential to the proceedings and actually incurred by the successful party. Those implementing acts shall be adopted in accordance with the examination procedure referred to in Article 207(2).

When specifying such amounts with respect to travel and subsistence costs, the Commission shall take into account the distance between the place of residence or business of the party, representative or witness or expert and the place where the oral proceedings are held, the procedural stage at which the costs have been incurred, and, as far as costs of representation within the meaning of Article 120(1) are concerned, the need to ensure that the obligation to bear the costs may not be misused for tactical reasons by the other party. Subsistence expenses shall be calculated in accordance with the Staff Regulations of Officials of the Union and the Conditions of Employment of Other Servants of the Union, laid down in Council Regulation (EEC, Euratom, ECSC) No 259/68 ('the Staff Regulations' and 'Conditions of Employment' respectively).

The losing party shall bear the costs for one opposing party only and, where applicable, one representative only.

3. However, where each party succeeds on some and fails on other heads, or if reasons of equity so dictate, the Opposition Division, Cancellation Division or Board of Appeal shall decide a different apportionment of costs.

4. The party who terminates the proceedings by withdrawing the EU trade mark application, the opposition, the application for revocation of rights, the application for a declaration of invalidity or the appeal, or by not renewing registration of the EU trade mark or by surrendering the EU trade mark, shall bear the fees and the costs incurred by the other party as stipulated in paragraphs 1 and 3.

5. Where a case does not proceed to judgment the costs shall be at the discretion of the Opposition Division, Cancellation Division or Board of Appeal.

6. Where the parties conclude before the Opposition Division, Cancellation Division or Board of Appeal a settlement of costs differing from that provided for in paragraphs 1 to 5, the department concerned shall take note of that agreement.

7. The Opposition Division or Cancellation Division or Board of Appeal shall fix the amount of the costs to be paid pursuant to paragraphs 1 to 6 of this Article when the costs to be paid are limited to the fees paid to the Office and the representation costs. In all other cases, the registry of the Board of Appeal or a member of the staff of the Opposition Division or Cancellation Division shall fix, on request, the amount of the costs to be reimbursed. The request shall be admissible only for the period of two months following the date on which the decision for which an application was made for the costs to be fixed becomes final and shall be accompanied by a bill and supporting evidence. For the costs of representation pursuant to Article 120(1), an assurance by the representative that the costs have been incurred shall be sufficient. For other costs, it shall be sufficient if their plausibility is established. Where the amount of the costs is fixed pursuant to the first sentence of this paragraph, representation costs shall be awarded at the level laid down in the implementing act adopted pursuant to paragraph 2 of this Article and irrespective of whether they have been actually incurred.

8. The decision on the fixing of costs, stating the reasons on which it is based, may be reviewed by a decision of the Opposition Division or Cancellation Division or Board of Appeal on a request filed within one month of the date of notification of the awarding of costs. It shall not be deemed to be filed until the fee for reviewing the amount of the costs has been paid. The Opposition Division, the Cancellation Division or the Board of Appeal, as the case may be, shall take a decision on the request for a review of the decision on the fixing of costs without oral proceedings.

Article 110
Enforcement of decisions fixing the amount of costs

1. Any final decision of the Office fixing the amount of costs shall be enforceable.

2. Enforcement shall be governed by the rules of civil procedure in force in the State in the territory of which it is carried out. Each Member State shall designate a single authority responsible for verifying the authenticity of the decision referred to in paragraph 1 and shall communicate its contact details to the Office, the Court of Justice and the Commission. The order for the enforcement of the decision shall be appended to the decision by that authority, with the verification of the authenticity of the decision as the sole formality.

3. When these formalities have been completed on application by the party concerned, the latter may proceed to enforcement in accordance with the national law, by bringing the matter directly before the competent authority.

4. Enforcement may be suspended only by a decision of the Court of Justice. However, the courts of the country concerned shall have jurisdiction over complaints that enforcement is being carried out in an irregular manner.

Section 3 Information which may be made available to the public and to the authorities of the Member States

Article 111
Register of EU trade marks

1. The Office shall keep a Register of EU trade marks which it shall keep up to date.

2. The Register shall contain the following entries relating to EU trade mark applications and registrations:

(a) the date of filing the application;
(b) the file number of the application;
(c) the date of the publication of the application;
(d) the name and address of the applicant;
(e) the name and business address of the representative, other than a representative as referred to in the first sentence of Article 119(3);
(f) the representation of the mark, with indications as to its nature; and, where applicable, a description of the mark;
(g) an indication of the goods and services by their names;
(h) particulars of claims of priority pursuant to Article 35;
(i) particulars of claims of exhibition priority pursuant to Article 38;
(j) particulars of claims of seniority of a registered earlier trade mark as referred to in Article 39;
(k) a statement that the mark has become distinctive in consequence of the use which has been made of it, pursuant to Article 7(3);
(l) an indication that the mark is a collective mark;
(m) an indication that the mark is a certification mark;
(n) the language in which the application was filed and the second language which the applicant has indicated in his application, pursuant to Article 146(3);
(o) the date of registration of the mark in the Register and the registration number;
(p) a statement that the application is the result of a transformation of an international registration designating the Union, pursuant to Article 204 of this Regulation, together with the date of the international registration pursuant to Article 3(4) of the Madrid Protocol or the date on which the territorial extension to the Union made subsequent to the international registration pursuant to Article 3ter(2) of the Madrid Protocol was recorded and, where applicable, the date of priority of the international registration.

3. The Register shall also contain the following entries, each accompanied by the date of recording of such entry:

(a) changes in the name, address or nationality of the proprietor of an EU trade mark or a change in the State in which he is domiciled or has his seat or establishment;
(b) changes in the name or business address of the representative, other than a representative as referred to in the first sentence of Article 119(3);
(c) where a new representative is appointed, the name and business address of that representative;
(d) amendments and alterations of the mark, pursuant to Articles 49 and 54, and corrections of errors;
(e) notice of amendments to the regulations governing the use of the collective mark pursuant to Article 79;
(f) particulars of claims of seniority of a registered earlier trade mark as referred to in Article 39, pursuant to Article 40;
(g) total or partial transfers pursuant to Article 20;

(h) creation or transfer of a right in rem pursuant to Article 22, and the nature of the right in rem;
(i) levy of execution pursuant to Article 23 and insolvency proceedings pursuant to Article 24;
(j) the grant or transfer of a licence pursuant to Article 25 and, where applicable, the type of licence;
(k) renewal of a registration pursuant to Article 53, the date from which it takes effect and any restrictions pursuant to Article 53(4);
(l) a record of a determination of the expiry of a registration pursuant to Article 53;
(m) declarations of withdrawal or surrender by the proprietor of the mark pursuant to Articles 49 and 57 respectively;
(n) the date of submission and the particulars of an opposition pursuant to Article 46, of an application pursuant to Article 63, or a counterclaim pursuant to Article 128(4) for revocation or for a declaration of invalidity, or of an appeal pursuant to Article 68;
(o) the date and content of a decision on an opposition, on an application or counterclaim pursuant to Article 64(6) or the third sentence of Article 128(6), or on an appeal pursuant to Article 71;
(p) a record of the receipt of a request for conversion pursuant to Article 140(2);
(q) the cancellation of the representative recorded pursuant to point (e) of paragraph 2 of this Article;
(r) the cancellation of the seniority of a national mark;
(s) the modification to or cancellation from the Register of the items referred to in points (h), (i) and (j) of this paragraph;
(t) the replacement of the EU trade mark by an international registration pursuant to Article 197;
(u) the date and number of international registrations based on the EU trade mark application which has been registered as an EU trade mark pursuant to Article 185(1);
(v) the date and number of international registrations based on the EU trade mark pursuant to Article 185(2);
(w) the division of an application pursuant to Article 50 and the division of a registration pursuant to Article 56, together with the items referred to in paragraph 2 of this Article in respect of the divisional registration, as well as the list of goods and services of the original registration as amended;
(x) the revocation of a decision or an entry in the Register pursuant to Article 103, where the revocation concerns a decision or entry which has been published;
(y) notice of amendments to the regulations governing the use of the EU certification mark pursuant to Article 88.

4. The Executive Director may determine that items other than those referred to in paragraphs 2 and 3 of this Article are to be entered in the Register, subject to Article 149(4).

5. The Register may be maintained in electronic form. The Office shall collect, organise, make public and store the items referred to in paragraphs 2 and 3, including any personal data, for the purposes laid down in paragraph 8. The Office shall keep the register easily accessible for public inspection.

6. The proprietor of an EU trade mark shall be notified of any change in the Register.

7. The Office shall provide certified or uncertified extracts from the Register on request and on payment of a fee.

8. The processing of the data concerning the entries set out in paragraphs 2 and 3, including any personal data, shall take place for the purposes of:

(a) administering the applications and/or registrations as described in this Regulation and acts adopted pursuant to it;
(b) maintaining a public register for inspection by, and the information of, public authorities and economic operators, in order to enable them to exercise the rights conferred on them by this Regulation and be informed about the existence of prior rights belonging to third parties; and
(c) producing reports and statistics enabling the Office to optimise its operations and improve the functioning of the system.

9. All the data, including personal data, concerning the entries in paragraphs 2 and 3 shall be considered to be of public interest and may be accessed by any third party. For reasons of legal certainty, the entries in the Register shall be kept for an indefinite period of time.

Article 112
Database

1. In addition to the obligation to keep a Register within the meaning of Article 111, the Office shall collect and store in an electronic database all the particulars provided by applicants or any other party to the proceedings pursuant to this Regulation or acts adopted pursuant to it.

2. The electronic database may include personal data, beyond those included in the Register pursuant to Article 111, to the extent that such particulars are required by this Regulation or by acts adopted pursuant to it. The collection, storage and processing of such data shall serve the purposes of:

(a) administering the applications and/or registrations as described in this Regulation and in acts adopted pursuant to it;
(b) accessing the information necessary for conducting the relevant proceedings more easily and efficiently;
(c) communicating with the applicants and other parties to the proceedings;
(d) producing reports and statistics enabling the Office to optimise its operations and improve the functioning of the system.

3. The Executive Director shall determine the conditions of access to the electronic database and the manner in which its contents, other than the personal data referred to in paragraph 2 of this Article but including those listed in Article 111, may be made available in machine-readable form, including the charge for such access.

4. Access to the personal data referred to in paragraph 2 shall be restricted and such data shall not be made publicly available unless the party concerned has given his express consent.

5. All data shall be kept indefinitely. However, the party concerned may request the removal of any personal data from the database after 18 months from the expiry of the EU trade mark or the closure of the relevant inter partes procedure. The party concerned shall have the right to obtain the correction of inaccurate or erroneous data at any time.

Article 113
Online access to decisions

1. The decisions of the Office shall be made available online for the information and consultation of the general public in the interest of transparency and predictability. Any party to the proceedings that led to the adoption of the decision may request the removal of any personal data included in the decision.

2. The Office may provide online access to judgments of national and Union courts related to its tasks in order to raise public awareness of intellectual property matters and promote convergence of practices. The Office shall respect the conditions of the initial publication with regard to personal data.

Article 114
Inspection of files

1. The files relating to EU trade mark applications which have not yet been published shall not be made available for inspection without the consent of the applicant.

2. Any person who can prove that the applicant for an EU trade mark has stated that after the trade mark has been registered he will invoke the rights under it against him may obtain inspection of the files prior to the publication of that application and without the consent of the applicant.

3. Subsequent to the publication of the EU trade mark application, the files relating to such application and the resulting trade mark may be inspected on request.

4. Where the files are inspected pursuant to paragraph 2 or 3 of this Article, documents relating to exclusion or objection pursuant to Article 169, draft decisions and opinions, and all other internal documents used for the preparation of decisions and opinions, as well as parts of the file which the party concerned showed a special interest in keeping confidential before the request for inspection of the files was made, unless inspection of such parts of the file is justified by overriding, legitimate interests of the party seeking inspection, may be withheld from inspection.

5. Inspection of the files of EU trade mark applications and of registered EU trade marks shall be of the original document, or of copies thereof, or of technical means of storage if the files are stored in this way. The Executive Director shall determine the means of inspection.

6. Where inspection of files takes place as provided for in paragraph 7, the request for inspection of the files shall not be deemed to have been made until the required fee has been paid. No fee shall be payable if inspection of technical means of storage takes place online.

7. Inspection of the files shall take place at the premises of the Office. On request, inspection of the files shall be effected by means of issuing copies of file documents. The issuing of such copies shall be conditional on the payment of a fee. The Office shall also issue on request certified or uncertified copies of the application for an EU trade mark upon payment of a fee.

8. The files kept by the Office relating to international registrations designating the Union may be inspected on request as from the date of publication referred to in Article 190(1), in accordance with the conditions laid down in paragraphs 1, 3 and 4 of this Article.

9. Subject to the restrictions provided for in paragraph 4, the Office may, on request, communicate information from any file of an EU trade mark applied for or of a registered EU trade mark, subject to payment of a fee. However, the Office may require the exercise of the option to obtain inspection of the file itself should it deem this to be appropriate in view of the quantity of information to be supplied.

Article 115
Keeping of files

1. The Office shall keep the files of any procedure relating to an EU trade mark application or EU trade mark registration. The Executive Director shall determine the form in which those files shall be kept.

2. Where the files are kept in electronic format, the electronic files, or back-up copies thereof, shall be kept indefinitely. The original documents filed by parties to the proceedings, and forming the basis of such electronic files, shall be disposed of after a period following their reception by the Office, which shall be determined by the Executive Director.

3. Where and to the extent that files or parts of the files are kept in any form other than electronically, documents or items of evidence constituting part of such files shall be kept for at least five years from the end of the year in which the application is rejected or withdrawn or is deemed to be withdrawn, the registration of the EU trade mark expires completely pursuant to Article 53, the complete surrender of the EU trade mark is registered pursuant to Article 57, or the EU trade mark is completely removed from the Register pursuant to Article 64(6) or 128(6).

Article 116
Periodical publications

1. The Office shall periodically publish:

(a) a European Union Trade Marks Bulletin containing publications of applications and of entries made in the Register as well as other particulars relating to applications or registrations of EU trade marks the publication of which is required under this Regulation or by acts adopted pursuant to it;

(b) an Official Journal of the Office containing notices and information of a general character issued by the Executive Director, as well as any other information relevant to this Regulation or its implementation.

The publications referred to in points (a) and (b) of the first subparagraph may be effected by electronic means.

2. The European Union Trade Marks Bulletin shall be published in a manner and at a frequency to be determined by the Executive Director.

3. The Official Journal of the Office shall be published in the languages of the Office. However, the Executive Director may determine that certain items shall be published in the Official Journal of the Office in the official languages of the Union.

4. The Commission shall adopt implementing acts specifying:

(a) the date to be taken as the date of publication in the European Union Trade Marks Bulletin;
(b) the manner of publication of entries regarding the registration of a trade mark which do not contain changes as compared to the publication of the application;
(c) the forms in which editions of the Official Journal of the Office may be made available to the public.

Those implementing acts shall be adopted in accordance with the examination procedure referred to in Article 207(2).

Article 117

Administrative cooperation

1. Unless otherwise provided in this Regulation or in national laws, the Office and the courts or authorities of the Member States shall on request give assistance to each other by communicating information or opening files for inspection. Where the Office lays files open to inspection by courts, Public Prosecutors' Offices or central industrial property offices, the inspection shall not be subject to the restrictions laid down in Article 114.

2. The Office shall not charge fees for the communication of information or the opening of files for inspection.

3. The Commission shall adopt implementing acts specifying the detailed arrangements as to how the Office and the authorities of the Member States are to exchange information between each other and open files for inspection, taking into account the restrictions to which the inspection of files relating to EU trade mark applications or registrations is subject, pursuant to Article 114, when it is opened to third parties. Those implementing acts shall be adopted in accordance with the examination procedure referred to in Article 207(2).

Article 118

Exchange of publications

1. The Office and the central industrial property offices of the Member States shall despatch to each other on request and for their own use one or more copies of their respective publications free of charge.

2. The Office may conclude agreements relating to the exchange or supply of publications.

Section 4 Representation

Article 119
General principles of representation

1. Subject to the provisions of paragraph 2, no person shall be compelled to be represented before the Office.

2. Without prejudice to the second sentence of paragraph 3 of this Article, natural or legal persons having neither their domicile nor their principal place of business or a real and effective industrial or commercial establishment in the European Economic Area shall be represented before the Office in accordance with Article 120(1) in all proceedings provided for by this Regulation, other than the filing of an application for an EU trade mark.

3. Natural or legal persons having their domicile or principal place of business or a real and effective industrial or commercial establishment in the European Economic Area may be represented before the Office by an employee. An employee of a legal person to which this paragraph applies may also represent other legal persons which have economic connections with the first legal person, even if those other legal persons have neither their domicile nor their principal place of business nor a real and effective industrial or commercial establishment within the European Economic Area. Employees who represent persons, within the meaning of this paragraph, shall, at the request of the Office or, where appropriate, of the party to the proceedings, file with it a signed authorisation for insertion in the files.

4. Where there is more than one applicant or more than one third party acting in common, a common representative shall be appointed.

Article 120
Professional representatives

1. Representation of natural or legal persons before the Office may only be undertaken by:

(a) a legal practitioner qualified in one of the Member States of the European Economic Area and having his place of business within the European Economic Area, to the extent that he is entitled, within the said Member State, to act as a representative in trade mark matters;
(b) professional representatives whose names appear on the list maintained for this purpose by the Office.

Representatives acting before the Office shall, at the request of the Office or, where appropriate, of the other party to the proceedings, file with it a signed authorisation for insertion on the files.

2. Any natural person who fulfils the following conditions may be entered on the list of professional representatives:

(a) being a national of one of the Member States of the European Economic Area;
(b) having his place of business or employment in the European Economic Area;
(c) being entitled to represent natural or legal persons in trade mark matters before the Benelux Office for Intellectual Property or before the central industrial

property office of a Member State of the European Economic Area. Where, in the State concerned, the entitlement is not conditional upon the requirement of special professional qualifications, persons applying to be entered on the list who act in trade mark matters before the Benelux Office for Intellectual Property or those central industrial property offices shall have habitually so acted for at least five years. However, persons whose professional qualification to represent natural or legal persons in trade mark matters before the Benelux Office for Intellectual Property or those central industrial property offices is officially recognised in accordance with the regulations laid down by the State concerned shall not be required to have exercised the profession.

3. Entry shall be effected upon request, accompanied by a certificate furnished by the central industrial property office of the Member State concerned, indicating that the conditions laid down in paragraph 2 are fulfilled.

4. The Executive Director may grant an exemption from:

(a) the requirement in the second sentence of paragraph 2(c), if the applicant furnishes proof that he has acquired the requisite qualification in another way;
(b) the requirement set out in paragraph 2(a) in the case of highly qualified professionals, provided that the requirements set out in paragraph 2(b) and (c) are fulfilled.

5. A person may be removed from the list of professional representatives at his request or when no longer in a capacity to represent. The amendments of the list of professional representatives shall be published in the Official Journal of the Office.

Article 121

Delegation of powers

The Commission is empowered to adopt delegated acts in accordance with Article 208 specifying:

(a) the conditions and the procedure for the appointment of a common representative as referred to in Article 119(4);
(b) the conditions under which employees referred to in Article 119(3) and professional representatives referred to in Article 120(1) shall file with the Office a signed authorisation in order to undertake representation, and the content of that authorisation;
(c) the circumstances in which a person may be removed from the list of professional representatives referred to in Article 120(5).

CHAPTER X JURISDICTION AND PROCEDURE IN LEGAL ACTIONS RELATING TO EU TRADE MARKS

Section 1 Application of Union rules on jurisdiction and the recognition and enforcement of judgments in civil and commercial matters

Article 122

Application of Union rules on jurisdiction and the recognition and enforcement of judgments in civil and commercial matters

1. Unless otherwise specified in this Regulation, the Union rules on jurisdiction and the recognition and enforcement of judgments in civil and commercial mat-

ters shall apply to proceedings relating to EU trade marks and applications for EU trade marks, as well as to proceedings relating to simultaneous and successive actions on the basis of EU trade marks and national trade marks.

2. In the case of proceedings in respect of the actions and claims referred to in Article 124:

(a) Articles 4 and 6, points 1, 2, 3 and 5 of Article 7 and Article 35 of Regulation (EU) No 1215/2012 shall not apply;
(b) Articles 25 and 26 of Regulation (EU) No 1215/2012 shall apply subject to the limitations in Article 125(4) of this Regulation;
(c) the provisions of Chapter II of Regulation (EU) No 1215/2012 which are applicable to persons domiciled in a Member State shall also be applicable to persons who do not have a domicile in any Member State but have an establishment therein.

3. References in this Regulation to Regulation (EU) No 1215/2012 shall include, where appropriate, the Agreement between the European Community and the Kingdom of Denmark on jurisdiction and the recognition and enforcement of judgments in civil and commercial matters done on 19 October 2005.

Section 2 Disputes concerning the infringement and validity of EU trade marks

Article 123
EU trade mark courts

1. The Member States shall designate in their territories as limited a number as possible of national courts and tribunals of first and second instance, which shall perform the functions assigned to them by this Regulation.

2. Any change made in the number, names or territorial jurisdiction of the courts included in the list of EU trade mark courts communicated by a Member State to the Commission in accordance with Article 95(2) of Regulation (EC) No 207/2009 shall be notified without delay by the Member State concerned to the Commission.

3. The information referred to in paragraph 2 shall be notified by the Commission to the Member States and published in the Official Journal of the European Union.

Article 124
Jurisdiction over infringement and validity

The EU trade mark courts shall have exclusive jurisdiction:

(a) for all infringement actions and — if they are permitted under national law — actions in respect of threatened infringement relating to EU trade marks;
(b) for actions for declaration of non-infringement, if they are permitted under national law;
(c) for all actions brought as a result of acts referred to in Article 11(2);
(d) for counterclaims for revocation or for a declaration of invalidity of the EU trade mark pursuant to Article 128.

Article 125
International jurisdiction

1. Subject to the provisions of this Regulation as well as to any provisions of Regulation (EU) No 1215/2012 applicable by virtue of Article 122, proceedings in respect of the actions and claims referred to in Article 124 shall be brought in the courts of the Member State in which the defendant is domiciled or, if he is not domiciled in any of the Member States, in which he has an establishment.

2. If the defendant is neither domiciled nor has an establishment in any of the Member States, such proceedings shall be brought in the courts of the Member State in which the plaintiff is domiciled or, if he is not domiciled in any of the Member States, in which he has an establishment.

3. If neither the defendant nor the plaintiff is so domiciled or has such an establishment, such proceedings shall be brought in the courts of the Member State where the Office has its seat.

4. Notwithstanding the provisions of paragraphs 1, 2 and 3:

(a) Article 25 of Regulation (EU) No 1215/2012 shall apply if the parties agree that a different EU trade mark court shall have jurisdiction;
(b) Article 26 of Regulation (EU) No 1215/2012 shall apply if the defendant enters an appearance before a different EU trade mark court.

5. Proceedings in respect of the actions and claims referred to in Article 124, with the exception of actions for a declaration of non-infringement of an EU trade mark, may also be brought in the courts of the Member State in which the act of infringement has been committed or threatened, or in which an act referred to in Article 11(2) has been committed.

Article 126
Extent of jurisdiction

1. An EU trade mark court whose jurisdiction is based on Article 125(1) to (4) shall have jurisdiction in respect of:

(a) acts of infringement committed or threatened within the territory of any of the Member States;
(b) acts referred to in Article 11(2) committed within the territory of any of the Member States.

2. An EU trade mark court whose jurisdiction is based on Article 125(5) shall have jurisdiction only in respect of acts committed or threatened within the territory of the Member State in which that court is situated.

Article 127
Presumption of validity — Defence as to the merits

1. The EU trade mark courts shall treat the EU trade mark as valid unless its validity is put in issue by the defendant with a counterclaim for revocation or for a declaration of invalidity.

2. The validity of an EU trade mark may not be put in issue in an action for a declaration of non-infringement.

3. In the actions referred to in points (a) and (c) of Article 124, a plea relating to revocation of the EU trade mark submitted otherwise than by way of a counterclaim shall be admissible where the defendant claims that the EU trade mark could be revoked for lack of genuine use at the time the infringement action was brought.

Article 128
Counterclaims

1. A counterclaim for revocation or for a declaration of invalidity may only be based on the grounds for revocation or invalidity mentioned in this Regulation.

2. An EU trade mark court shall reject a counterclaim for revocation or for a declaration of invalidity if a decision taken by the Office relating to the same subject matter and cause of action and involving the same parties has already become final.

3. If the counterclaim is brought in a legal action to which the proprietor of the trade mark is not already a party, he shall be informed thereof and may be joined as a party to the action in accordance with the conditions set out in national law.

4. The EU trade mark court with which a counterclaim for revocation or for a declaration of invalidity of the EU trade mark has been filed shall not proceed with the examination of the counterclaim, until either the interested party or the court has informed the Office of the date on which the counterclaim was filed. The Office shall record that information in the Register. If an application for revocation or for a declaration of invalidity of the EU trade mark had already been filed before the Office before the counterclaim was filed, the court shall be informed thereof by the Office and stay the proceedings in accordance with Article 132(1) until the decision on the application is final or the application is withdrawn.

5. Article 64(2) to (5) shall apply.

6. Where an EU trade mark court has given a judgment which has become final on a counterclaim for revocation or for a declaration of invalidity of an EU trade mark, a copy of the judgment shall be sent to the Office without delay, either by the court or by any of the parties to the national proceedings. The Office or any other interested party may request information about such transmission. The Office shall mention the judgment in the Register and shall take the necessary measures to comply with its operative part.

7. The EU trade mark court hearing a counterclaim for revocation or for a declaration of invalidity may stay the proceedings on application by the proprietor of the EU trade mark and after hearing the other parties and may request the defendant to submit an application for revocation or for a declaration of invalidity to the Office within a time limit which it shall determine. If the application is not made within the time limit, the proceedings shall continue; the counterclaim shall be deemed withdrawn. Article 132(3) shall apply.

Article 129
Applicable law

1. The EU trade mark courts shall apply the provisions of this Regulation.

2. On all trade mark matters not covered by this Regulation, the relevant EU trade mark court shall apply the applicable national law.

3. Unless otherwise provided for in this Regulation, an EU trade mark court shall apply the rules of procedure governing the same type of action relating to a national trade mark in the Member State in which the court is located.

Article 130
Sanctions

1. Where an EU trade mark court finds that the defendant has infringed or threatened to infringe an EU trade mark, it shall, unless there are special reasons for not doing so, issue an order prohibiting the defendant from proceeding with the acts which infringed or would infringe the EU trade mark. It shall also take such measures in accordance with its national law as are aimed at ensuring that this prohibition is complied with.

2. The EU trade mark court may also apply measures or orders available under the applicable law which it deems appropriate in the circumstances of the case.

Article 131
Provisional and protective measures

1. Application may be made to the courts of a Member State, including EU trade mark courts, for such provisional, including protective, measures in respect of an EU trade mark or EU trade mark application as may be available under the law of that State in respect of a national trade mark, even if, under this Regulation, an EU trade mark court of another Member State has jurisdiction as to the substance of the matter.

2. An EU trade mark court whose jurisdiction is based on Article 125(1), (2), (3) or (4) shall have jurisdiction to grant provisional and protective measures which, subject to any necessary procedure for recognition and enforcement pursuant to Chapter III of Regulation (EU) No 1215/2012, are applicable in the territory of any Member State. No other court shall have such jurisdiction.

Article 132
Specific rules on related actions

1. An EU trade mark court hearing an action referred to in Article 124 other than an action for a declaration of non-infringement shall, unless there are special grounds for continuing the hearing, of its own motion after hearing the parties or at the request of one of the parties and after hearing the other parties, stay the proceedings where the validity of the EU trade mark is already in issue before another EU trade mark court on account of a counterclaim or where an application for revocation or for a declaration of invalidity has already been filed at the Office.

2. The Office, when hearing an application for revocation or for a declaration of invalidity shall, unless there are special grounds for continuing the hearing, of its own motion after hearing the parties or at the request of one of the parties and after hearing the other parties, stay the proceedings where the validity of the EU trade mark is already in issue on account of a counterclaim before an EU trade mark court. However, if one of the parties to the proceedings before the EU trade mark court so requests, the court may, after hearing the other parties to these proceedings, stay the proceedings. The Office shall in this instance continue the proceedings pending before it.

3. Where the EU trade mark court stays the proceedings it may order provisional and protective measures for the duration of the stay.

Article 133

Jurisdiction of EU trade mark courts of second instance — Further appeal

1. An appeal to the EU trade mark courts of second instance shall lie from judgments of the EU trade mark courts of first instance in respect of proceedings arising from the actions and claims referred to in Article 124.

2. The conditions under which an appeal may be lodged with an EU trade mark court of second instance shall be determined by the national law of the Member State in which that court is located.

3. The national rules concerning further appeal shall be applicable in respect of judgments of EU trade mark courts of second instance.

Section 3 Other disputes concerning EU trade marks

Article 134

Supplementary provisions on the jurisdiction of national courts other than EU trade mark courts

1. Within the Member State whose courts have jurisdiction under Article 122(1) those courts shall have jurisdiction for actions other than those referred to in Article 124, which would have jurisdiction ratione loci and ratione materiae in the case of actions relating to a national trade mark registered in that State.

2. Actions relating to an EU trade mark, other than those referred to in Article 124, for which no court has jurisdiction under Article 122(1) and paragraph 1 of this Article may be heard before the courts of the Member State in which the Office has its seat.

Article 135

Obligation of the national court

A national court which is dealing with an action relating to an EU trade mark, other than the action referred to in Article 124, shall treat the EU trade mark as valid.

CHAPTER XI EFFECTS ON THE LAWS OF THE MEMBER STATES

Section 1 Civil actions on the basis of more than one trade mark

Article 136

Simultaneous and successive civil actions on the basis of EU trade marks and national trade marks

1. Where actions for infringement involving the same cause of action and between the same parties are brought in the courts of different Member States, one seised on the basis of an EU trade mark and the other seised on the basis of a national trade mark:

(a) the court other than the court first seised shall of its own motion decline jurisdiction in favour of that court where the trade marks concerned are identical and valid for identical goods or services. The court which would be required to decline jurisdiction may stay its proceedings if the jurisdiction of the other court is contested;

(b) the court other than the court first seised may stay its proceedings where the trade marks concerned are identical and valid for similar goods or services and where the trade marks concerned are similar and valid for identical or similar goods or services.

2. The court hearing an action for infringement on the basis of an EU trade mark shall reject the action if a final judgment on the merits has been given on the same cause of action and between the same parties on the basis of an identical national trade mark valid for identical goods or services.

3. The court hearing an action for infringement on the basis of a national trade mark shall reject the action if a final judgment on the merits has been given on the same cause of action and between the same parties on the basis of an identical EU trade mark valid for identical goods or services.

4. Paragraphs 1, 2 and 3 shall not apply in respect of provisional, including protective, measures.

Section 2 Application of national laws for the purpose of prohibiting the use of EU trade marks

Article 137

Prohibition of use of EU trade marks

1. This Regulation shall, unless otherwise provided for, not affect the right existing under the laws of the Member States to invoke claims for infringement of earlier rights within the meaning of Article 8 or Article 60(2) in relation to the use of a later EU trade mark. Claims for infringement of earlier rights within the meaning of Article 8(2) and (4) may, however, no longer be invoked if the proprietor of the earlier right may no longer apply for a declaration that the EU trade mark is invalid in accordance with Article 61(2).

2. This Regulation shall, unless otherwise provided for, not affect the right to bring proceedings under the civil, administrative or criminal law of a Member State or under provisions of Union law for the purpose of prohibiting the use of an

EU trade mark to the extent that the use of a national trade mark may be prohibited under the law of that Member State or under Union law.

Article 138
Prior rights applicable to particular localities

1. The proprietor of an earlier right which only applies to a particular locality may oppose the use of the EU trade mark in the territory where his right is protected in so far as the law of the Member State concerned so permits.

2. Paragraph 1 shall cease to apply if the proprietor of the earlier right has acquiesced in the use of the EU trade mark in the territory where his right is protected for a period of five successive years, being aware of such use, unless the EU trade mark was applied for in bad faith.

3. The proprietor of the EU trade mark shall not be entitled to oppose use of the right referred to in paragraph 1 even though that right may no longer be invoked against the EU trade mark.

Section 3 Conversion into a national trade mark application

Article 139
Request for the application of national procedure

1. The applicant for or proprietor of an EU trade mark may request the conversion of his EU trade mark application or EU trade mark into a national trade mark application:

(a) to the extent that the EU trade mark application is refused, withdrawn, or deemed to be withdrawn;
(b) to the extent that the EU trade mark ceases to have effect.

2. Conversion shall not take place:

(a) where the rights of the proprietor of the EU trade mark have been revoked on the grounds of non-use, unless in the Member State for which conversion is requested the EU trade mark has been put to use which would be considered to be genuine use under the laws of that Member State;
(b) for the purpose of protection in a Member State in which, in accordance with the decision of the Office or of the national court, grounds for refusal of registration or grounds for revocation or invalidity apply to the EU trade mark application or EU trade mark.

3. The national trade mark application resulting from the conversion of an EU trade mark application or an EU trade mark shall enjoy in respect of the Member State concerned the date of filing or the date of priority of that application or trade mark and, where appropriate, the seniority of a trade mark of that State claimed under Articles 39 or 40.

4. In cases where an EU trade mark application is deemed to be withdrawn, the Office shall send to the applicant a communication fixing a period of three months from the date of that communication in which a request for conversion may be filed.

5. Where the EU trade mark application is withdrawn or the EU trade mark ceases to have effect as a result of a surrender being recorded or of failure to renew the registration, the request for conversion shall be filed within three months of the date on which the EU trade mark application has been withdrawn or on which the EU trade mark ceases to have effect.

6. Where the EU trade mark application is refused by decision of the Office or where the EU trade mark ceases to have effect as a result of a decision of the Office or of an EU trade mark court, the request for conversion shall be filed within three months of the date on which that decision acquired the authority of a final decision.

7. The effect referred to in Article 37 shall lapse if the request is not filed in due time.

Article 140

Submission, publication and transmission of the request for conversion

1. A request for conversion shall be filed with the Office within the relevant period pursuant to Article 139(4), (5) or (6), and shall include an indication of the grounds for conversion in accordance with Article 139(1)(a) or (b), the Member States in respect of which conversion is requested, and the goods and services subject to conversion. Where conversion is requested following a failure to renew the registration, the period of three months provided for in Article 139(5) shall begin to run on the day following the last day on which the request for renewal can be presented pursuant to Article 53(3). The request for conversion shall not be deemed to be filed until the conversion fee has been paid.

2. Where the request for conversion relates to an EU trade mark application which has already been published or where the request for conversion relates to an EU trade mark, receipt of any such request shall be recorded in the Register and the request for conversion shall be published.

3. The Office shall check whether the conversion requested fulfils the conditions set out in this Regulation, in particular Article 139(1), (2), (4), (5) and (6), and paragraph 1 of this Article, together with the formal conditions specified in the implementing act adopted pursuant to paragraph 6 of this Article. If the conditions governing the request are not fulfilled, the Office shall notify the applicant of the deficiencies. If the deficiencies are not remedied within a period to be specified by the Office, the Office shall reject the request for conversion. Where Article 139(2) applies, the Office shall reject the request for conversion as inadmissible only with respect to those Member States for which conversion is excluded under that provision. Where the conversion fee has not been paid within the relevant period of three months pursuant to Article 139(4), (5) or (6), the Office shall inform the applicant that the request for conversion is deemed not to have been filed.

4. If the Office or an EU trade mark court has refused the EU trade mark application or has declared the EU trade mark invalid on absolute grounds by reference to the language of a Member State, conversion shall be excluded under Article 139(2) for all the Member States in which that language is one of the official languages. If the Office or an EU trade mark court has refused the EU trade mark

application or has declared the EU trade mark invalid on absolute grounds which are found to apply throughout the Union or on account of an earlier EU trade mark or other Union industrial property right, conversion shall be excluded under Article 139(2) for all Member States.

5. Where the request for conversion complies with the requirements referred to in paragraph 3 of this Article, the Office shall transmit the request for conversion and the data referred to in Article 111(2) to the central industrial property offices of the Member States, including the Benelux Office for Intellectual Property, for which the request has been found admissible. The Office shall inform the applicant of the date of transmission.

6. The Commission shall adopt implementing acts specifying:

(a) the details to be contained in a request for conversion of an EU trade mark application or a registered EU trade mark into a national trade mark application pursuant to paragraph 1;
(b) the details which are to be contained in the publication of the request for conversion pursuant to paragraph 2.

Those implementing acts shall be adopted in accordance with the examination procedure referred to in Article 207(2).

Article 141
Formal requirements for conversion

1. Any central industrial property office to which the request for conversion is transmitted may obtain from the Office any additional information concerning the request enabling that office to make a decision regarding the national trade mark resulting from the conversion.

2. An EU trade mark application or an EU trade mark transmitted in accordance with Article 140 shall not be subject to formal requirements of national law which are different from or additional to those provided for in this Regulation or in acts adopted pursuant to this Regulation.

3. Any central industrial property office to which the request is transmitted may require that the applicant shall, within not less than two months:

(a) pay the national application fee;
(b) file a translation in one of the official languages of the State in question of the request and of the documents accompanying it;
(c) indicate an address for service in the State in question;
(d) supply a representation of the trade mark in the number of copies specified by the State in question.

CHAPTER XII THE OFFICE

Section 1 General provisions

Article 142
Legal status

1. The Office shall be an agency of the Union. It shall have legal personality.

2. In each of the Member States the Office shall enjoy the most extensive legal capacity accorded to legal persons under their laws; it may, in particular, acquire or dispose of movable and immovable property and may be a party to legal proceedings.

3. The Office shall be represented by its Executive Director.

Article 143
Staff

1. The Staff Regulations, the Conditions of Employment and the rules adopted by agreement between the institutions of the Union for giving effect to those Staff Regulations and Conditions of Employment shall apply to the staff of the Office, without prejudice to the application of Article 166 of this Regulation to the members of the Boards of Appeal.

2. Without prejudice to paragraph 1, the Office may make use of seconded national experts or other staff not employed by the Office. The Management Board shall adopt a decision laying down rules on the secondment to the Office of national experts.

Article 144
Privileges and immunities

The Protocol on the Privileges and Immunities of the Union shall apply to the Office and its staff.

Article 145
Liability

1. The contractual liability of the Office shall be governed by the law applicable to the contract in question.

2. The Court of Justice shall be competent to give judgment pursuant to any arbitration clause contained in a contract concluded by the Office.

3. In the case of non-contractual liability, the Office shall, in accordance with the general principles common to the laws of the Member States, make good any damage caused by its departments or by its servants in the performance of their duties.

4. The Court of Justice shall have jurisdiction in disputes relating to compensation for the damage referred to in paragraph 3.

5. The personal liability of its servants towards the Office shall be governed by the provisions laid down in the Staff Regulations or in the Conditions of Employment applicable to them.

Article 146
Languages

1. The application for an EU trade mark shall be filed in one of the official languages of the Union.

2. The languages of the Office shall be English, French, German, Italian and Spanish.

3. The applicant shall indicate a second language which shall be a language of the Office the use of which he accepts as a possible language of proceedings for opposition, revocation or invalidity proceedings.

If the application was filed in a language which is not one of the languages of the Office, the Office shall arrange to have the application, as described in Article 31(1), translated into the language indicated by the applicant.

4. Where the applicant for an EU trade mark is the sole party to proceedings before the Office, the language of proceedings shall be the language used for filing the application for an EU trade mark. If the application was made in a language other than the languages of the Office, the Office may send written communications to the applicant in the second language indicated by the applicant in his application.

5. The notice of opposition and an application for revocation or a declaration of invalidity shall be filed in one of the languages of the Office.

6. Without prejudice to paragraph 5:

(a) any application or declaration relating to an EU trade mark application may be filed in the language used for filing the application for that EU trade mark or in the second language indicated by the applicant in his application;
(b) any application or declaration relating to a registered EU trade mark may be filed in one of the languages of the Office.

However, when the application is filed by using any form provided by the Office as referred to in Article 100(2), such forms may be used in any of the official languages of the Union, provided that the form is completed in one of the languages of the Office, as far as textual elements are concerned.

7. If the language chosen, in accordance with paragraph 5, for the notice of opposition or the application for revocation or invalidity is the language of the application for a trade mark or the second language indicated when the application was filed, that language shall be the language of the proceedings.

If the language chosen, in accordance with paragraph 5, for the notice of opposition or the application for revocation or invalidity is neither the language of the application for a trade mark nor the second language indicated when the application was filed, the opposing party or the party seeking revocation or invalidity shall be required to produce, at his own expense, a translation of his application either into the language of the application for a trade mark, provided that it is a language of the Office, or into the second language indicated when the application was filed. The translation shall be produced within one month of the expiry of the opposition period or of the date of filing an application for revocation or a declaration of invalidity. The language into which the application has been translated shall then become the language of the proceedings.

8. Parties to opposition, revocation, invalidity or appeal proceedings may agree that a different official language of the Union is to be the language of the proceedings.

9. Without prejudice to paragraphs 4 and 8, and unless provided otherwise, in written proceedings before the Office any party may use any language of the Office. If the language chosen is not the language of the proceedings, the party shall supply a translation into that language within one month of the date of the submission of the original document. Where the applicant for an EU trade mark is the sole party to proceedings before the Office and the language used for the filing of the application for the EU trade mark is not one of the languages of the Office, the translation may also be filed in the second language indicated by the applicant in his application.

10. The Executive Director shall determine the manner in which translations are to be certified.

11. The Commission shall adopt implementing acts specifying:

(a) the extent to which supporting documents to be used in written proceedings before the Office may be filed in any language of the Union, and the need to supply a translation;
(b) the requisite standards of translations to be filed with the Office.

Those implementing acts shall be adopted in accordance with the examination procedure referred to Article 207(2).

Article 147
Publication and entries in the Register

1. An application for an EU trade mark, as described in Article 31(1), and all other information the publication of which is prescribed by this Regulation or an act adopted pursuant to this Regulation, shall be published in all the official languages of the Union.

2. All entries in the Register shall be made in all the official languages of the Union.

3. In cases of doubt, the text in the language of the Office in which the application for the EU trade mark was filed shall be authentic. If the application was filed in an official language of the Union other than one of the languages of the Office, the text in the second language indicated by the applicant shall be authentic.

Article 148
Translation services

The translation services required for the functioning of the Office shall be provided by the Translation Centre for the Bodies of the European Union.

Article 149
Transparency

1. Regulation (EC) No 1049/2001 of the European Parliament and of the Council shall apply to documents held by the Office.

2. The Management Board shall adopt detailed rules for applying Regulation (EC) No 1049/2001.

3. Decisions taken by the Office under Article 8 of Regulation (EC) No 1049/2001 may be challenged through the European Ombudsman or form the subject of an action before the Court of Justice of the European Union, under the conditions laid down in Articles 228 and 263 TFEU respectively.

4. The processing of personal data by the Office shall be subject to Regulation (EC) No 45/2001 of the European Parliament and of the Council.

Article 150

Security rules on the protection of classified and sensitive non-classified information

The Office shall apply the security principles contained in the Commission's security rules for protecting European Union Classified Information (EUCI) and sensitive non-classified information, as set out in Commission Decisions (EU, Euratom) 2015/443 and 2015/444. The security principles shall cover, inter alia, provisions for the exchange, processing and storage of such information.

Section 2 Tasks of the office and cooperation to promote convergence

Article 151

Tasks of the Office

1. The Office shall have the following tasks:

(a) administration and promotion of the EU trade mark system established in this Regulation;
(b) administration and promotion of the European Union design system established in Council Regulation (EC) No 6/2002;
(c) promoting convergence of practices and tools in the fields of trade marks and designs, in cooperation with the central industrial property offices in the Member States, including the Benelux Office for Intellectual Property;
(d) the tasks referred to in Regulation (EU) No 386/2012 of the European Parliament and of the Council;
(e) the tasks conferred on it under Directive 2012/28/EU of the European Parliament and of the Council.

2. The Office shall cooperate with institutions, authorities, bodies, industrial property offices, international and non-governmental organisations in relation to the tasks conferred on it in paragraph 1.

3. The Office may provide voluntary mediation services for the purpose of assisting parties in reaching a friendly settlement.

Article 152

Cooperation to promote convergence of practices and tools

1. The Office and the central industrial property offices of the Member States and the Benelux Office for Intellectual Property shall cooperate with each other

to promote convergence of practices and tools in the field of trade marks and designs.

Without prejudice to paragraph 3, this cooperation shall in particular cover the following areas of activity:

(a) the development of common examination standards;
(b) the creation of common or connected databases and portals for Union-wide consultation, search and classification purposes;
(c) the continuous provision and exchange of data and information, including for the purposes of feeding of the databases and portals referred to in point (b);
(d) the establishment of common standards and practices, with a view to ensuring interoperability between procedures and systems throughout the Union and enhancing their consistency, efficiency and effectiveness;
(e) the sharing of information on industrial property rights and procedures, including mutual support to helpdesks and information centres;
(f) the exchange of technical expertise and assistance in relation to the areas referred to in points (a) to (e).

2. On the basis of a proposal by the Executive Director, the Management Board shall define and coordinate projects of interest to the Union and the Member States with regard to the areas referred to in paragraphs 1 and 6, and shall invite the central industrial property offices of the Member States and the Benelux Office for Intellectual Property to participate in those projects.

The project definition shall contain the specific obligations and responsibilities of each participating industrial property office of the Member States, the Benelux Office for Intellectual Property and the Office. The Office shall consult with user representatives in particular in the phases of definition of the projects and evaluation of their results.

3. The central industrial property offices of the Member States and the Benelux Office for Intellectual Property may opt out of, restrict or temporarily suspend their cooperation in the projects referred to in the first subparagraph of paragraph 2.

When making use of the possibilities provided for in the first subparagraph, the central industrial property offices of the Member States and the Benelux Office for Intellectual Property shall provide the Office with a written statement explaining the reasons for their decision.

4. Once having committed to participate in certain projects, the central industrial property offices of the Member States and the Benelux Office for Intellectual Property shall, without prejudice to paragraph 3, participate effectively in the projects referred to in paragraph 2 with a view to ensuring that they are developed, function, are interoperable and kept up to date.

5. The Office shall provide financial support to the projects referred to in paragraph 2 to the extent that is necessary in order to ensure, for the purposes of paragraph 4, the effective participation of the central industrial property offices of the Member States and the Benelux Office for Intellectual Property in those projects. That financial support may take the form of grants and in-kind contributions.

The total amount of funding shall not exceed 15 % of the yearly revenue of the Office. The beneficiaries of grants shall be the central industrial property offices of the Member States and the Benelux Office for Intellectual Property. Grants may be awarded without calls for proposals in accordance with the financial rules applicable to the Office and with the principles of grant procedures contained in Regulation (EU, Euratom) No 966/2012 of the European Parliament and of the Council and in Commission Delegated Regulation (EU) No 1268/2012.

6. The Office and the relevant competent authorities of the Member States shall cooperate with each other on a voluntary basis to promote the raising of awareness concerning the trade mark system and the fight against counterfeiting. Such cooperation shall include projects aiming, in particular, at the implementation of established standards and practices as well as at organising education and training activities. The financial support for those projects shall be part of the total amount of funding referred to in paragraph 5. Paragraphs 2 to 5 shall apply mutatis mutandis.

Section 3 Management Board

Article 153
Functions of the Management Board

1. Without prejudice to the functions attributed to the Budget Committee in Section 6, the Management Board shall have the following functions:

(a) on the basis of a draft submitted by the Executive Director in accordance with Article 157(4)(c), adopting the annual work programme of the Office for the coming year, taking into account the opinion of the Commission, and forwarding the adopted annual work programme to the European Parliament, to the Council and to the Commission;
(b) on the basis of a draft submitted by the Executive Director in accordance with Article 157(4)(e) and taking into account the opinion of the Commission, adopting a multiannual strategic programme for the Office, including the Office's strategy for international cooperation, following an exchange of views between the Executive Director and the relevant committee in the European Parliament, and forwarding the adopted multiannual strategic programme to the European Parliament, to the Council and to the Commission;
(c) on the basis of a draft submitted by the Executive Director in accordance with Article 157(4)(g), adopting the annual report and forwarding the adopted annual report to the European Parliament, to the Council, to the Commission and to the Court of Auditors;
(d) on the basis of a draft submitted by the Executive Director in accordance with Article 157(4)(h), adopting the multiannual staff policy plan;
(e) exercising the powers conferred on it under Article 152(2);
(f) exercising the powers conferred on it under Article 172(5);
(g) adopting rules on the prevention and management of conflicts of interest in the Office;
(h) in accordance with paragraph 2, exercising, with respect to the staff of the Office, the powers conferred by the Staff Regulations on the Appointing Authority and by the Conditions of Employment on the Authority Empow-

ered to Conclude Contracts of Employment ('the appointing authority powers');

(i) adopting appropriate implementing rules to give effect to the Staff Regulations and the Conditions of Employment in accordance with Article 110 of the Staff Regulations;

(j) drawing up the list of candidates provided for in Article 158(2);

(k) ensuring adequate follow-up to the findings and recommendations stemming from the internal or external audit reports and evaluations referred to in Article 210, as well as from investigations of the European Anti-fraud Office (OLAF);

(l) being consulted before adoption of the guidelines for examination in the Office and in the other cases provided for in this Regulation;

(m) providing opinions and requests for information to the Executive Director and to the Commission where it considers it necessary.

2. The Management Board shall adopt, in accordance with Article 110 of the Staff Regulations and Article 142 of the Conditions of Employment, a decision based on Article 2(1) of the Staff Regulations and on Article 6 of the Conditions of Employment, delegating the relevant appointing authority powers to the Executive Director and defining the conditions under which that delegation of appointing authority powers can be suspended.

The Executive Director shall be authorised to sub-delegate those powers.

Where exceptional circumstances so require, the Management Board may, by way of a decision, temporarily suspend the delegation of the appointing authority powers to the Executive Director and those sub-delegated by the latter, and exercise them itself or delegate them to one of its members or to a staff member other than the Executive Director.

Article 154
Composition of the Management Board

1. The Management Board shall be composed of one representative of each Member State, two representatives of the Commission and one representative of the European Parliament, and their respective alternates.

2. The members of the Management Board may, subject to its rules of procedure, be assisted by advisers or experts.

Article 155
Chairperson of the Management Board

1. The Management Board shall elect a chairperson and a deputy chairperson from among its members. The deputy chairperson shall ex officio replace the chairperson in the event of his being prevented from attending to his duties.

2. The duration of the terms of office of the chairperson and the deputy chairperson shall be four years. The terms of office shall be renewable once. If, however, their membership of the Management Board ends at any time during their term of office, their term of office shall automatically expire on that date also.

Article 156
Meetings

1. Meetings of the Management Board shall be convened by its chairperson.

2. The Executive Director shall take part in the deliberations, unless the Management Board decides otherwise.

3. The Management Board shall hold an ordinary meeting at least once a year. In addition, it shall meet on the initiative of its chairperson or at the request of the Commission or of one-third of the Member States.

4. The Management Board shall adopt rules of procedure.

5. The Management Board shall take its decisions by an absolute majority of its members. However, a majority of two-thirds of its members shall be required for the decisions which the Management Board is empowered to take under Article 153(1)(a) and (b), Article 155(1) and Article 158(2) and (4). In both cases each member shall have one vote.

6. The Management Board may invite observers to attend its meetings.

7. The secretariat for the Management Board shall be provided by the Office.

Section 4 Executive Director

Article 157
Functions of the Executive Director

1. The Office shall be managed by the Executive Director. The Executive Director shall be accountable to the Management Board.

2. Without prejudice to the powers of the Commission, the Management Board, and the Budget Committee, the Executive Director shall be independent in the performance of his duties and shall neither seek nor take instructions from a government or from any other body.

3. The Executive Director shall be the legal representative of the Office.

4. The Executive Director shall have in particular the following functions, which may be delegated:

(a) taking all necessary steps, including the adoption of internal administrative instructions and the publication of notices, to ensure the functioning of the Office;
(b) implementing the decisions adopted by the Management Board;
(c) preparing a draft annual work programme indicating estimated human and financial resources for each activity, and submitting it to the Management Board after consultation of the Commission;
(d) submitting to the Management Board proposals pursuant to Article 152(2);
(e) preparing a draft multiannual strategic programme, including the Office's strategy for international cooperation, and submitting it to the Management Board after consultation of the Commission and following an exchange of views with the relevant committee in the European Parliament;

(f) implementing the annual work programme and the multiannual strategic programme and reporting to the Management Board on their implementation;
(g) preparing the annual report on the Office's activities and presenting it to the Management Board for approval;
(h) preparing a draft multiannual staff policy plan and submitting it to the Management Board after consultation of the Commission;
(i) preparing an action plan following-up on the conclusions of the internal or external audit reports and evaluations, as well as following up on the investigations of the OLAF, and reporting on progress twice a year to the Commission and to the Management Board;
(j) protecting the financial interests of the Union by the application of preventive measures against fraud, corruption and any other illegal activities, by effective checks and, if irregularities are detected, by recovering amounts wrongly paid and, where appropriate, by imposing effective, proportionate and dissuasive administrative and financial penalties;
(k) preparing an anti-fraud strategy for the Office and presenting it to the Budget Committee for approval;
(l) in order to ensure uniform application of the Regulation, referring, where appropriate, to the enlarged Board of Appeal ('the Grand Board') questions on a point of law, in particular if the Boards of Appeal have issued diverging decisions on the point;
(m) drawing up estimates of the revenue and expenditure of the Office and implementing the budget;
(n) exercising the powers entrusted to him in respect of staff by the Management Board under Article 153(1)(h);
(o) exercising the powers conferred on him under Articles 31(3), 34(5), 35(3), 94(2), 97(5), Articles 98, 100, 101, Articles 111(4), 112(3), 114(5), Articles 115, 116, Articles 120(4), 146(10), Article 178, Articles 179(1) and 180(2), and Article 181 in accordance with the criteria set out in this Regulation and in the acts adopted pursuant to this Regulation.

5. The Executive Director shall be assisted by one or more Deputy Executive Directors. If the Executive Director is absent or indisposed, the Deputy Executive Director or one of the Deputy Executive Directors shall replace him in accordance with the procedure laid down by the Management Board.

Article 158

Appointment and removal of the Executive Director and extension of term of office

1. The Executive Director shall be engaged as a temporary agent of the Office under Article 2(a) of the Conditions of Employment.

2. The Executive Director shall be appointed by the Council by simple majority, from a list of candidates proposed by the Management Board, following an open and transparent selection procedure. Before being appointed, the candidate selected by the Management Board may be invited to make a statement before any competent European Parliament committee and to answer questions put by its members. For the purpose of concluding the contract with the Executive Director, the Office shall be represented by the chairperson of the Management Board.

The Executive Director may be removed from office only upon a decision of the Council acting on a proposal from the Management Board.

3. The term of office of the Executive Director shall be five years. By the end of that period, the Management Board shall undertake an assessment which takes into account an evaluation of the performance of the Executive Director and the Office's future tasks and challenges.

4. The Council, taking into account the assessment referred to in paragraph 3, may extend the term of office of the Executive Director once and for no more than five years.

5. An Executive Director whose term of office has been extended may not participate in another selection procedure for the same post at the end of his overall term of office.

6. The Deputy Executive Director or Deputy Executive Directors shall be appointed or removed from office as provided for in paragraph 2, after consultation of the Executive Director and, where applicable, the Executive Director-elect. The term of office of the Deputy Executive Director shall be five years. It may be extended once and for no more than five years by the Council, after consultation of the Executive Director.

Section 5 Implementation of procedures

Article 159
Competence

For taking decisions in connection with the procedures laid down in this Regulation, the following shall be competent:

(a) examiners;
(b) Opposition Divisions;
(c) a department in charge of the Register;
(d) Cancellation Divisions;
(e) Boards of Appeal;
(f) any other unit or person appointed by the Executive Director to that effect.

Article 160
Examiners

An examiner shall be responsible for taking decisions on behalf of the Office in relation to an application for registration of an EU trade mark, including the matters referred to in Articles 41, 42, 76 and 85, except in so far as an Opposition Division is responsible.

Article 161
Opposition Divisions

1. An Opposition Division shall be responsible for taking decisions on an opposition to an application to register an EU trade mark.

2. The decisions of the Opposition Divisions shall be taken by three-member groups. At least one member shall be legally qualified. Decisions relating to costs or to procedures shall be taken by a single member.

The Commission shall adopt implementing acts specifying the exact types of decisions that are to be taken by a single member. Those implementing acts shall be adopted in accordance with the examination procedure referred to in Article 207(2).

Article 162
Department in charge of the Register

1. The Department in charge of the Register shall be responsible for taking decisions in respect of entries in the Register.

2. It shall also be responsible for keeping the list of professional representatives referred to in Article 120(2).

3. The decisions of the Department shall be taken by a single member.

Article 163
Cancellation Divisions

1. A Cancellation Division shall be responsible for taking decisions in relation to:

(a) applications for the revocation or a declaration of invalidity of an EU trade mark;
(b) requests for the assignment of an EU trade mark as provided for in Article 21.

2. The decisions of the Cancellation Divisions shall be taken by three-member groups. At least one member shall be legally qualified. Decisions relating to costs or to procedures as specified in the acts adopted pursuant to Article 161(2) shall be taken by a single member.

Article 164
General Competence

Decisions required under this Regulation which do not fall within the competence of an examiner, an Opposition Division, a Cancellation Division or the Department in charge of the Register, shall be taken by any official or unit appointed by the Executive Director for that purpose.

Article 165
Boards of Appeal

1. The Boards of Appeal shall be responsible for deciding on appeals from decisions taken pursuant to Articles 160 to 164.

2. The decisions of the Boards of Appeal shall be taken by three members, at least two of whom are legally qualified. In certain specific cases, decisions shall

be taken by the Grand Board chaired by the President of the Boards of Appeal or by a single member, who shall be legally qualified.

3. In order to determine the special cases which fall under the jurisdiction of the Grand Board, account should be taken of the legal difficulty or the importance of the case or of special circumstances which justify it. Such cases may be referred to the Grand Board:

(a) by the authority of the Boards of Appeal referred to in Article 166(4)(a); or
(b) by the Board handling the case.

4. The Grand Board shall also be responsible for giving reasoned opinions on questions of law referred to it by the Executive Director pursuant to Article 157(4)(l).

5. To determine which specific cases fall under the authority of a single member, account should be taken of the lack of difficulty of the legal or factual matters raised, the limited importance of the individual case or the absence of other specific circumstances. The decision to confer a case on one member in the cases referred to shall be adopted by the Board handling the case.

Article 166

Independence of the members of the Boards of Appeal

1. The President of the Boards of Appeal and the chairpersons of the Boards shall be appointed, in accordance with the procedure laid down in Article 158 for the appointment of the Executive Director, for a term of five years. They shall not be removed from office during this term, unless there are serious grounds for such removal and the Court of Justice, on application by the institution which appointed them, takes a decision to this effect.

2. The term of office of the President of the Boards of Appeal may be extended once for one additional five-year period, or until retirement age if this age is reached during the new term of office, after a prior positive evaluation of his performance by the Management Board.

3. The term of office of the chairpersons of the Boards may be extended for additional five-year periods, or until retirement age if this age is reached during the new term of office, after a prior positive evaluation of their performance by the Management Board, and after consulting the President of the Boards of Appeal.

4. The President of the Boards of Appeal shall have the following managerial and organisational functions:

(a) chairing the Presidium of the Boards of Appeal ('the Presidium'), responsible for laying down the rules and organising the work of the Boards;
(b) ensuring the implementation of the decisions of the Presidium;
(c) allocating cases to a Board on the basis of objective criteria determined by the Presidium;
(d) forwarding to the Executive Director the Boards' expenditure requirements, with a view to drawing up the expenditure estimates.

The President of the Boards of Appeal shall chair the Grand Board.

5. The members of the Boards of Appeal shall be appointed by the Management Board for a term of five years. Their term of office may be extended for additional five-year periods, or until retirement age if that age is reached during the new term of office after a prior positive evaluation of their performance by the Management Board, and after consulting the President of the Boards of Appeal.

6. The members of the Boards of Appeal shall not be removed from office unless there are serious grounds for such removal and the Court of Justice, after the case has been referred to it by the Management Board on the recommendation of the President of the Boards of Appeal, and after consulting the chairperson of the Board to which the member concerned belongs, takes a decision to this effect.

7. The President of the Boards of Appeal and the chairpersons and members of the Boards of Appeal shall be independent. In their decisions, they shall not be bound by any instructions.

8. Decisions taken by the Grand Board on appeals or opinions on questions of law referred to it by the Executive Director pursuant to Article 165 shall be binding on the decision-making instances of the Office listed in Article 159.

9. The President of the Boards of Appeal and the chairpersons and members of the Boards of Appeal shall not be examiners or members of the Opposition Divisions, the Department in charge of the Register or Cancellation Divisions.

Article 167
Presidium of the Boards of Appeal and Grand Board

1. The Presidium shall comprise the President of the Boards of Appeal, who shall chair it, the chairmen of the Boards and Board members elected for each calendar year by and from among all the members of the Boards other than the President of the Boards of Appeal and the chairmen of the Boards. The number of Board members so elected shall constitute a quarter of the number of Board members, other than the President of the Boards of Appeal and the chairmen of the Boards, and that number shall be rounded up if necessary.

2. The Grand Board referred to in Article 165(2) shall comprise nine members, including the President of the Boards of Appeal, the chairmen of the Boards, the rapporteur designated prior to referral to the Grand Board, if applicable, and members drawn in rotation from a list comprising the names of all members of the Boards of Appeal other than the President of the Boards of Appeal and the chairmen of the Boards.

Article 168
Delegation of powers

The Commission is empowered to adopt delegated acts in accordance with Article 208 specifying the details concerning the organisation of the Boards of Appeal, including the setting up and the role of the Presidium, the composition of the Grand Board and the rules on referrals to it, and the conditions under which decisions are to be taken by a single member in accordance with Article 165(2) and (5).

Article 169
Exclusion and objection

1. Examiners and members of the Divisions set up within the Office or of the Boards of Appeal may not take part in any proceedings if they have any personal interest therein, or if they have previously been involved as representatives of one of the parties. Two of the three members of an Opposition Division shall not have taken part in examining the application. Members of the Cancellation Divisions may not take part in any proceedings if they have participated in the final decision on the case in the proceedings for registration or opposition proceedings. Members of the Boards of Appeal may not take part in appeal proceedings if they participated in the decision under appeal.

2. If, for one of the reasons mentioned in paragraph 1 or for any other reason, a member of a Division or of a Board of Appeal considers that he should not take part in any proceedings, he shall inform the Division or Board accordingly.

3. Examiners and members of the Divisions or of a Board of Appeal may be objected to by any party for one of the reasons mentioned in paragraph 1, or if suspected of partiality. An objection shall not be admissible if, while being aware of a reason for objection, the party has taken a procedural step. No objection may be based upon the nationality of examiners or members.

4. The Divisions and the Boards of Appeal shall decide as to the action to be taken in the cases specified in paragraphs 2 and 3 without the participation of the member concerned. For the purposes of taking this decision the member who withdraws or has been objected to shall be replaced in the Division or Board of Appeal by his alternate.

Article 170
Mediation centre

1. For the purposes of Article 151(3), the Office may establish a Mediation Centre ('the Centre').

2. Any natural or legal person may use the Centre's services on a voluntary basis with the aim of reaching a friendly settlement of disputes, based on this Regulation or Regulation (EC) No 6/2002, by mutual agreement.

3. The parties shall have recourse to mediation by means of a joint request. The request shall not be deemed to have been filed until the corresponding charge has been paid. The Executive Director shall fix the amount to be charged in accordance with Article 178(1).

4. In the case of disputes subject to the proceedings pending before the Opposition Divisions, Cancellation Divisions or before the Boards of Appeal of the Office a joint request for mediation may be presented at any time after the lodging of a notice of opposition, an application for revocation or an application for a declaration of invalidity or a notice of appeal against decisions of the Opposition or Cancellation Divisions.

5. The proceedings in question shall be suspended and the time periods, other than the time periods for the payment of the applicable fee, shall be interrupted as from the date of the filing of a joint request for mediation. The time periods shall continue as from the day on which the proceedings are resumed.

6. The parties shall be invited to jointly appoint, from the list referred to in paragraph 12, a mediator who has declared that he has a command of the language of the mediation in question. Where the parties do not appoint a mediator within 20 days of the invitation to do so, the mediation shall be deemed to have failed.

7. The parties shall agree together with the mediator on the detailed arrangements for the mediation in a mediation agreement.

8. The mediator shall conclude the mediation proceedings as soon as the parties reach a settlement agreement, or one of the parties declares that it wishes to end the mediation or the mediator establishes that the parties have failed to reach such an agreement.

9. The mediator shall inform the parties as well as the relevant instance of the Office as soon as the mediation proceedings have been concluded.

10. The discussions and negotiations conducted within the framework of mediation shall be confidential for all persons involved in the mediation, in particular for the mediator, the parties and their representatives. All documents and information submitted during the mediation shall be kept separately from, and shall not be part of, the file of any other proceedings before the Office.

11. The mediation shall be conducted in one of the official languages of the Union to be agreed upon by the parties. Where the mediation relates to disputes pending before the Office, the mediation shall be conducted in the language of the Office proceedings, unless otherwise agreed by the parties.

12. The Office shall establish a list of mediators who shall support parties in resolving disputes. The mediators shall be independent and possess relevant skills and experience. The list may include mediators who are employed by the Office, and mediators who are not so employed.

13. Mediators shall be impartial in the exercise of their duties and shall declare any real or perceived conflict of interest upon their designation. Members of the decision-making instances of the Office listed in Article 159 shall not take part in mediation concerning a case in which they have:

(a) had any prior involvement in the proceedings referred to mediation;
(b) any personal interest in those proceedings; or
(c) been previously involved as a representative of one of the parties.

14. Mediators shall not take part as members of the decision-making instances of the Office listed in Article 159 in proceedings resumed as a consequence of a mediation failure.

15. The Office may cooperate with other recognised national or international bodies dealing with mediation.

Section 6 Budget and financial control

Article 171
Budget Committee

1. The Budget Committee shall have the functions assigned to it in this Section.

2. Articles 154 and 155, Article 156(1) to (4), and (5), in so far as it relates to the election of the chairperson and deputy chairperson, and Article 156(6) and (7) shall apply to the Budget Committee, mutatis mutandis.

3. The Budget Committee shall take its decisions by an absolute majority of its members. However, a majority of two-thirds of its members shall be required for the decisions which the Budget Committee is empowered to take under Article 173(3) and Article 177. In both cases each member shall have one vote.

Article 172
Budget

1. Estimates of all the Office's revenue and expenditure shall be prepared for each financial year and shall be shown in the Office's budget. Each financial year shall correspond to the calendar year.

2. The revenue and expenditure shown in the budget shall be in balance.

3. Revenue shall comprise, without prejudice to other types of income, total fees payable under Annex I to this Regulation, total fees as provided for in Regulation (EC) No 6/2002, total fees payable, under the Madrid Protocol, for an international registration designating the Union, and other payments made to Contracting Parties to the Madrid Protocol, total fees payable, under the Geneva Act referred to in Article 106c of Regulation (EC) No 6/2002, for an international registration designating the Union and other payments made to Contracting Parties to the Geneva Act, and, to the extent necessary, a subsidy entered against a specific heading of the Commission section of the general budget of the Union.

4. Every year the Office shall offset the costs incurred by the central industrial property offices of the Member States, by the Benelux Office for Intellectual Property and by any other relevant authority to be nominated by a Member State, as the result of the specific tasks which they carry out as functional parts of the EU trade mark system in the context of the following services and procedures:

(a) opposition and invalidity proceedings before the central industrial property offices of the Member States and the Benelux Office for Intellectual Property involving EU trade marks;
(b) provision of information on the functioning of the EU trade mark system through helpdesks and information centres;
(c) enforcement of EU trade marks, including action taken pursuant to Article 9(4).

5. The overall offsetting of the costs identified in paragraph 4 shall correspond to 5 % of the yearly revenue of the Office. Without prejudice to the third subparagraph of this paragraph, on a proposal by the Office and after having consulted the Budget Committee, the Management Board shall determine the distribution key on the basis of the following fair, equitable and relevant indicators:

(a) the annual number of EU trade mark applications originating from applicants in each Member State;
(b) the annual number of national trade mark applications in each Member State;

(c) the annual number of oppositions and applications for a declaration of invalidity submitted by proprietors of EU trade marks in each Member State;
(d) the annual number of cases brought before the EU trade mark courts designated by each Member State in accordance with Article 123.

For the purpose of substantiating the costs referred to in paragraph 4, Member States shall submit to the Office by 31 March of each year, statistical data demonstrating the figures referred to in points (a) to (d) of the first subparagraph of this paragraph for the preceding year, which shall be included in the proposal to be made to the Management Board.

On grounds of equity, the costs incurred by the bodies referred to in paragraph 4 in each Member State shall be deemed to correspond to at least 2 % of the total offsetting provided for under this paragraph.

6. The obligation by the Office to offset the costs referred to in paragraph 4 and incurred in a given year shall only apply to the extent that no budgetary deficit occurs in that year.

7. In the event of a budgetary surplus, and without prejudice to paragraph 10, on a proposal by the Office and after having consulted the Budget Committee, the Management Board may increase the percentage laid down in paragraph 5 to a maximum of 10 % of the yearly revenue of the Office.

8. Without prejudice to paragraphs 4 to 7 and paragraph 10 of this Article and to Articles 151 and 152, where a substantive surplus is generated over five consecutive years, the Budget Committee, upon a proposal from the Office and in accordance with the annual work programme and multiannual strategic programme referred to in Article 153(1)(a) and (b), shall decide by a two-thirds majority on the transfer to the budget of the Union of a surplus generated from 23 March 2016.

9. The Office shall prepare on a biannual basis a report for the European Parliament, the Council and the Commission on its financial situation, including on the financial operations performed under Article 152(5) and (6), and paragraphs 5 and 7 of this Article. On the basis of that report, the Commission shall review the financial situation of the Office.

10. The Office shall provide for a reserve fund covering one year of its operational expenditure to ensure the continuity of its operations and the execution of its tasks.

Article 173
Preparation of the budget

1. The Executive Director shall draw up each year an estimate of the Office's revenue and expenditure for the following year and shall send it to the Budget Committee not later than 31 March in each year, together with a list of posts.

2. Should the budget estimates provide for a Union subsidy, the Budget Committee shall immediately forward the estimate to the Commission, which shall forward it to the budget authority of the Union. The Commission may attach an opinion on the estimate along with an alternative estimate.

3. The Budget Committee shall adopt the budget, which shall include the Office's list of posts. Should the budget estimates contain a subsidy from the general budget of the Union, the Office's budget shall, if necessary, be adjusted.

Article 174
Audit and control

1. An internal audit function shall be set up within the Office, to be performed in compliance with the relevant international standards. The internal auditor, appointed by the Executive Director, shall be responsible to him for verifying the proper operation of budget implementation systems and procedures of the Office.

2. The internal auditor shall advise the Executive Director on dealing with risks, by issuing independent opinions on the quality of management and control systems and by issuing recommendations for improving the conditions of implementation of operations and promoting sound financial management.

3. The responsibility for putting in place internal control systems and procedures suitable for carrying out his tasks shall lie with the authorising officer.

Article 175
Combating fraud

1. In order to facilitate combating fraud, corruption and other unlawful activities under Regulation (EU, Euratom) No 883/2013 of the European Parliament and of the Council, the Office shall accede to the Inter-institutional Agreement of 25 May 1999 concerning internal investigations by OLAF, and adopt the appropriate provisions applicable to all the employees of the Office using the template set out in the Annex to that Agreement.

2. The Court of Auditors shall have the power of audit, on the basis of documents and on the spot, over all grant beneficiaries, contractors and subcontractors who have received Union funds from the Office.

3. OLAF may carry out investigations, including on-the-spot checks and inspections, in accordance with the provisions and procedures laid down in Regulation (EU, Euratom) No 883/2013 and Council Regulation (Euratom, EC) No 2185/96 with a view to establishing whether there has been fraud, corruption or any other illegal activity affecting the financial interests of the Union in connection with a grant or a contract funded by the Office.

4. Without prejudice to paragraphs 1, 2 and 3, cooperation agreements with third countries and international organisations, contracts, grant agreements and grant decisions of the Office shall contain provisions expressly empowering the Court of Auditors and OLAF to conduct such audits and investigations, in accordance with their respective competences.

5. The Budget Committee shall adopt an anti-fraud strategy which is proportionate to the fraud risks having regard to the cost-benefit of the measures to be implemented.

Article 176
Auditing of accounts

1. Not later than 31 March in each year the Executive Director shall transmit to the Commission, the European Parliament, the Budget Committee and the Court of Auditors accounts of the Office's total revenue and expenditure for the preceding financial year. The Court of Auditors shall examine them in accordance with Article 287 TFEU.

2. The Budget Committee shall give a discharge to the Executive Director in respect of the implementation of the budget.

Article 177
Financial provisions

The Budget Committee shall, after consulting the Court of Auditors and the Commission, adopt internal financial provisions specifying, in particular, the procedure for establishing and implementing the Office's budget. As far as is compatible with the particular nature of the Office, the financial provisions shall be based on the financial regulations adopted for other bodies set up by the Union.

Article 178
Fees and charges and due date

1. The Executive Director shall lay down the amount to be charged for any services rendered by the Office other than those set out in Annex I, as well as the amount to be charged for the European Union Trade Marks Bulletin, the Official Journal of the Office and any other publications issued by the Office. The amounts of charges shall be set in euros and shall be published in the Official Journal of the Office. The amount of each charge shall not exceed what is necessary to cover the costs of the specific service rendered by the Office.

2. Fees and charges in respect of which the due date is not specified in this Regulation shall be due on the date of receipt of the request for the service for which the fee or the charge is incurred.

With the consent of the Budget Committee, the Executive Director may determine which of the services mentioned in the first subparagraph are not to be dependent upon the advance payment of the corresponding fees or charges.

Article 179
Payment of fees and charges

1. Fees and charges due to the Office shall be paid by payment or transfer to a bank account held by the Office.

With the consent of the Budget Committee, the Executive Director may establish which specific methods of payment other than those set out in the first subparagraph, in particular by means of deposits in current accounts held with the Office, may be used.

Determinations made pursuant to the second subparagraph shall be published in the Official Journal of the Office.

All payments, including by any other method of payment established pursuant to the second subparagraph, shall be made in euros.

2. Every payment shall indicate the name of the person making the payment and shall contain the necessary information to enable the Office to establish immediately the purpose of the payment. In particular, the following information shall be provided:

(a) when the application fee is paid, the purpose of the payment, namely 'application fee';
(b) when the opposition fee is paid, the file number of the application and the name of the applicant for the EU trade mark against which opposition is entered, and the purpose of the payment, namely 'opposition fee';
(c) when the revocation fee and the invalidity fee are paid, the registration number and the name of the proprietor of the EU trade mark against which the application is directed, and the purpose of the payment, namely 'revocation fee' or 'invalidity fee'.

3. If the purpose of the payment referred to in paragraph 2 cannot immediately be established, the Office shall require the person making the payment to notify it in writing of this purpose within such period as it may specify. If the person does not comply with this request in due time, the payment shall be considered not to have been made. The amount which has been paid shall be refunded.

Article 180
Deemed date of payment

1. In the cases referred to in the first subparagraph of Article 179(1), the date on which the payment shall be considered to have been made to the Office shall be the date on which the amount of the payment or of the transfer is actually entered in a bank account held by the Office.

2. Where the methods of payment referred to in the second subparagraph of Article 179(1) may be used, the Executive Director shall establish the date on which such payments are to be considered to have been made.

3. Where, under paragraphs 1 and 2, payment of a fee is not considered to have been made until after the expiry of the period in which it was due, it shall be considered that this period has been observed if evidence is provided to the Office that the persons who made the payment in a Member State, within the period within which the payment should have been made, duly gave an order to a banking establishment to transfer the amount of the payment, and paid a surcharge of 10 % of the relevant fee or fees, but not exceeding EUR 200. No surcharge shall be payable if the relevant order to the banking establishment has been given not later than 10 days before the expiry of the period for payment.

4. The Office may request the person who made the payment to produce evidence as to the date on which the order to the banking establishment as referred

to in paragraph 3 was given and, where required, to pay the relevant surcharge within a period to be specified by it. If the person fails to comply with that request or if the evidence is insufficient, or if the required surcharge is not paid in due time, the period for payment shall be considered not to have been observed.

Article 181

Insufficient payments and refund of insignificant amounts

1. A time limit for payment shall, in principle, be considered to have been observed only if the full amount of the fee has been paid in due time. If the fee is not paid in full, the amount which has been paid shall be refunded after the period for payment has expired.

2. The Office may, however, in so far as is possible within the time remaining before the end of the period, give the person making the payment the opportunity to pay the amount lacking or, where this is considered justified, overlook any small amounts lacking, without prejudice to the rights of the person making the payment.

3. With the consent of the Budget Committee, the Executive Director may waive action for the enforced recovery of any sum due where the sum to be recovered is minimal or where such recovery is too uncertain.

4. Where an excessive sum is paid to cover a fee or a charge, the excess shall not be refunded if the amount is insignificant and the party concerned has not expressly requested a refund.

With the consent of the Budget Committee the Executive Director may determine the amount below which an excessive sum paid to cover a fee or a charge shall not be refunded.

Determinations pursuant to the second subparagraph shall be published in the Official Journal of the Office.

CHAPTER XIII INTERNATIONAL REGISTRATION OF MARKS

Section 1 General provisions

Article 182

Application of provisions

Unless otherwise specified in this chapter, this Regulation and the acts adopted pursuant to this Regulation shall apply to applications for international registrations under the Madrid Protocol ('international applications'), based on an application for an EU trade mark or on an EU trade mark and to registrations of marks in the international register maintained by the International Bureau of the World Intellectual Property Organisation ('international registrations' and 'the International Bureau', respectively) designating the Union.

Section 2 International registration on the basis of applications for an EU trade mark and of EU trade marks

Article 183
Filing of an international application

1. International applications pursuant to Article 3 of the Madrid Protocol based on an application for an EU trade mark or on an EU trade mark shall be filed at the Office.

2. Where an international application is filed before the mark on which the international registration is to be based has been registered as an EU trade mark, the applicant for the international registration shall indicate whether the international registration is to be based on an EU trade mark application or registration. Where the international registration is to be based on an EU trade mark once it is registered, the international application shall be deemed to have been received at the Office on the date of registration of the EU trade mark.

Article 184
Form and contents of the international application

1. The international application shall be filed in one of the official languages of the Union, using a form provided by the Office. The Office shall inform the applicant filing the international application of the date on which the documents making up the international application are received by the Office. Unless otherwise specified by the applicant on form when he files the international application, the Office shall correspond with the applicant in the language of filing in a standard form.

2. If the international application is filed in a language which is not one of the languages allowed under the Madrid Protocol, the applicant shall indicate a second language from among those languages. This shall be the language in which the Office submits the international application to the International Bureau.

3. Where the international application is filed in a language other than one of the languages allowed under the Madrid Protocol for the filing of international applications, the applicant may provide a translation of the list of goods or services and of any other textual elements forming part of the international application in the language in which the international application is to be submitted to the International Bureau pursuant to paragraph 2. If the application is not accompanied by such translation, the applicant shall authorise the Office to include that translation in the international application. Where the translation has not yet been established in the course of the registration procedure for the EU trade mark application on which the international application is based, the Office shall, without delay, arrange for the translation.

4. The filing of an international application shall be subject to the payment of a fee to the Office. Where the international registration is to be based on an EU trade mark once it is registered, the fee shall be due on the date of registration of the EU trade mark. The application shall be deemed not to have been filed until the required fee has been paid. Where the fee has not been paid, the Office shall inform the applicant accordingly. In the event of electronic filing, the Office may authorise the International Bureau to collect the fee on its behalf.

5. Where the examination of the international application reveals any of the following deficiencies, the Office shall invite the applicant to remedy those deficiencies within such period as it may specify:

(a) the international application has not been filed using the form referred to in paragraph 1, and does not contain all the indications and information required by that form;
(b) the list of goods and services contained in the international application is not covered by the list of goods and services appearing in the basic EU trade mark application or basic EU trade mark;
(c) the mark which is subject to the international application is not identical with the mark as it appears in the basic EU trade mark application or basic EU trade mark;
(d) an indication in the international application as to the trade mark, other than a disclaimer or a colour claim, does not also appear in the basic EU trade mark application or basic EU trade mark;
(e) where colour is claimed in the international application as a distinctive feature of the mark, the basic EU trade mark application or basic EU trade mark is not in the same colour or colours; or
(f) according to the indications made in the international form, the applicant is not eligible to file an international application through the Office in accordance with Article 2(1)(ii) of the Madrid Protocol.

6. Where the applicant has failed to authorise the Office to include a translation as provided for in paragraph 3, or where it is otherwise unclear on which list of goods and services the international application is to be based, the Office shall invite the applicant to make the required indications within such period as it may specify.

7. If the deficiencies referred to in paragraph 5 are not remedied or the required indications referred to in paragraph 6 are not given within the period fixed by the Office, the Office shall refuse to forward the international application to the International Bureau.

8. The Office shall forward the international application to the International Bureau along with the certification provided for under Article 3(1) of the Madrid Protocol as soon as the international application meets the requirements laid down in this Article, the implementing act adopted pursuant to paragraph 9 of this Article, and in Article 183 of this Regulation.

9. The Commission shall adopt implementing acts specifying the exact form, including the elements thereof, to be used for the filing of an international application pursuant to paragraph 1. Those implementing acts shall be adopted in accordance with the examination procedure referred to in Article 207(2).

Article 185
Recordal in the files and in the Register

1. The date and number of an international registration based on an EU trade mark application shall be recorded in the files of that application. When the application results in an EU trade mark, the date and number of the international registration shall be entered in the Register.

2. The date and number of an international registration based on an EU trade mark shall be entered in the Register.

Article 186

Notification of the invalidity of the basic application or registration

1. Within a period of five years of the date of the international registration, the Office shall notify the International Bureau of any facts and decisions affecting the validity of the EU trade mark application or the EU trade mark registration on which the international registration was based.

2. The Commission shall adopt implementing acts specifying the individual facts and decisions subject to the notification obligation in accordance with Article 6(3) of the Madrid Protocol as well as the relevant point in time of such notifications. Those implementing acts shall be adopted in accordance with the examination procedure referred to in Article 207(2) of this Regulation.

Article 187

Request for territorial extension subsequent to international registration

1. A request for territorial extension made subsequent to an international registration pursuant to Article 3ter(2) of the Madrid Protocol may be filed through the intermediary of the Office. The request shall be filed in the language in which the international application was filed pursuant to Article 184 of this Regulation. It shall include indications to substantiate the entitlement to make a designation in accordance with Article 2(1)(ii) and Article 3ter(2) of the Madrid Protocol. The Office shall inform the applicant requesting the territorial extension of the date on which the request for territorial extension was received.

2. The Commission shall adopt implementing acts specifying the detailed requirements regarding the request for territorial extension pursuant to paragraph 1 of this Article. Those implementing acts shall be adopted in accordance with the examination procedure referred to in Article 207(2).

3. Where the request for territorial extension made subsequent to the international registration does not comply with the requirements set out in paragraph 1 and in the implementing act adopted pursuant to paragraph 2, the Office shall invite the applicant to remedy the deficiencies found within such time limit as it may specify. If the deficiencies are not remedied within the time limit fixed by the Office, the Office shall refuse to forward the request to the International Bureau. The Office shall not refuse to forward the request to the International Bureau before the applicant has had the opportunity to correct any deficiency detected in the request.

4. The Office shall forward the request for territorial extension made subsequent to the international registration to the International Bureau as soon as the requirements referred to in paragraph 3 are complied with.

Article 188

International fees

Any fees payable to the International Bureau under the Madrid Protocol shall be paid direct to the International Bureau.

Section 3 International registrations designating the Union

Article 189

Effects of international registrations designating the Union

1. An international registration designating the Union shall, from the date of its registration pursuant to Article 3(4) of the Madrid Protocol or from the date of the subsequent designation of the Union pursuant to Article 3ter(2) of the Madrid Protocol, have the same effect as an application for an EU trade mark.

2. If no refusal has been notified in accordance with Article 5(1) and (2) of the Madrid Protocol or if any such refusal has been withdrawn, the international registration of a mark designating the Union shall, from the date referred to in paragraph 1, have the same effect as the registration of a mark as an EU trade mark.

3. For the purposes of applying Article 11 of this Regulation, publication of the particulars of the international registration designating the Union pursuant to Article 190(1) shall take the place of publication of an EU trade mark application, and publication pursuant to Article 190(2) shall take the place of publication of the registration of an EU trade mark.

Article 190

Publication

1. The Office shall publish the date of registration of a mark designating the Union pursuant to Article 3(4) of the Madrid Protocol or the date of the subsequent designation of the Union pursuant to Article 3ter(2) of the Madrid Protocol, the language of filing of the international application and the second language indicated by the applicant, the number of the international registration and the date of publication of such registration in the Gazette published by the International Bureau, a reproduction of the mark and the numbers of the classes of the goods or services in respect of which protection is claimed.

2. If no refusal of protection of an international registration designating the Union has been notified in accordance with Article 5(1) and (2) of the Madrid Protocol or if any such refusal has been withdrawn, the Office shall publish this fact, together with the number of the international registration and, where applicable, the date of publication of such registration in the Gazette published by the International Bureau.

Article 191

Seniority claimed in an international application

1. The applicant for an international registration designating the Union may claim, in the international application, the seniority of an earlier trade mark registered in a Member State, including a trade mark registered in the Benelux countries, or registered under international arrangements having effect in a Member State, as provided for in Article 39.

2. The documentation, as specified in the implementing act adopted pursuant to Article 39(6), in support of the seniority claim shall be submitted within three

months of the date on which the International Bureau notifies the international registration to the Office. In this regard, Article 39(7) shall apply.

3. Where the holder of the international registration is obliged to be represented before the Office pursuant to Article 119(2), the communication as referred to in paragraph 2 of this Article shall contain the appointment of a representative within the meaning of Article 120(1).

4. Where the Office finds that the seniority claim under paragraph 1 of this Article does not comply with Article 39, or does not comply with the other requirements laid down in this Article, it shall invite the applicant to remedy the deficiencies. If the requirements referred to in the first sentence are not satisfied within the time limit specified by the Office, the right of seniority in respect of that international registration shall be lost. If the deficiencies concern only some of the goods and services, the right of seniority shall be lost only in so far as those goods and services are concerned.

5. The Office shall inform the International Bureau of any declaration of a loss of the right of seniority pursuant to paragraph 4. It shall also inform the International Bureau of any withdrawal or restriction of the seniority claim.

6. Article 39(5) shall apply, unless the right of seniority is declared lost pursuant to paragraph 4 of this Article.

Article 192
Seniority claimed before the Office

1. The holder of an international registration designating the Union may, as from the date of publication of the effects of such registration pursuant to Article 190(2), claim at the Office the seniority of an earlier trade mark registered in a Member State, including a trade mark registered in the Benelux countries, or registered under international arrangements having effect in a Member State, as provided for in Article 40.

2. When the seniority is claimed before the date referred to in paragraph 1, the seniority claim shall be deemed to have been received by the Office on that date.

3. A seniority claim under paragraph 1 of this Article shall fulfil the requirements referred to in Article 40 and shall contain information to enable its examination against those requirements.

4. If the requirements governing the claiming of seniority referred to in paragraph 3 and specified in the implementing act adopted pursuant to paragraph 6 are not fulfilled, the Office shall invite the holder of the international registration to remedy the deficiencies. If the deficiencies are not remedied within a period to be specified by the Office, the Office shall reject the claim.

5. Where the Office has accepted the seniority claim, or where a seniority claim has been withdrawn or cancelled by the Office, the Office shall inform the International Bureau accordingly.

6. The Commission shall adopt implementing acts specifying the details to be contained in a seniority claim under paragraph 1 of this Article and the details

of the information to be notified pursuant to paragraph 5 of this Article. Those implementing acts shall be adopted in accordance with the examination procedure referred to in Article 207(2).

Article 193

Designation of goods and services and examination as to absolute grounds for refusal

1. International registrations designating the Union shall be subject to examination as to their conformity with Article 33(2), (3) and (4) and to absolute grounds for refusal in the same way as applications for EU trade marks.

2. Where an international registration designating the Union is found to be ineligible for protection pursuant to Article 33(4) or Article 42(1) of this Regulation for all or any part of the goods and services for which it has been registered by the International Bureau, the Office shall issue an ex officio provisional notification of refusal to the International Bureau, in accordance with Article 5(1) and (2) of the Madrid Protocol.

3. Where the holder of an international registration is obliged to be represented before the Office pursuant to Article 119(2), the notification referred to in paragraph 2 of this Article shall contain an invitation to appoint a representative within the meaning of Article 120(1).

4. The notification of provisional refusal shall state the reasons on which it is based, and shall specify a time period by which the holder of the international registration may submit his observations and, if appropriate, shall appoint a representative. The time period shall start on the day on which the Office issues the provisional refusal.

5. Where the Office finds that the international application designating the Union does not contain the indication of a second language pursuant to Article 206 of this Regulation, the Office shall issue an ex officio provisional notification of refusal to the International Bureau pursuant to Article 5(1) and (2) of the Madrid Protocol.

6. Where the holder of an international registration fails to overcome the ground for refusing protection within the time limit or, if appropriate, to appoint a representative or to indicate a second language, the Office shall refuse the protection in whole or for part of the goods and services for which the international registration is registered. The refusal of protection shall take the place of a refusal of an EU trade mark application. The decision shall be subject to appeal in accordance with Articles 66 to 72.

7. Where, as of the start of the opposition period referred to in Article 196(2), the Office has not issued an ex officio provisional notification of refusal pursuant to paragraph 2 of this Article, it shall send a statement to the International Bureau, indicating that the examination of absolute grounds of refusal pursuant to Article 42 has been completed but that the international registration is still subject to oppositions or observations of third parties. This interim statement shall be without prejudice to the right of the Office to re-open the examination of

absolute grounds on its own initiative any time before the final statement of grant of protection has been issued.

8. The Commission shall adopt implementing acts specifying the details to be contained in the notification of ex officio provisional refusal of protection to be sent to the International Bureau and in the final communications to be sent to the International Bureau on the final grant or refusal of protection. Those implementing acts shall be adopted in accordance with the examination procedure referred to in Article 207(2).

Article 194
Collective and certification marks

1. Where an international registration is based on a basic application or basic registration relating to a collective mark, certification mark or guarantee mark, the international registration designating the Union shall be dealt with as an EU collective mark or as an EU certification mark, whichever is applicable.

2. The holder of the international registration shall submit the regulations governing the use of the mark, as provided for in Articles 75 and 84, directly to the Office within two months of the date on which the International Bureau notifies the international registration to the Office.

3. The Commission is empowered to adopt delegated acts in accordance with Article 208 specifying the details of the procedure concerning international registrations based on a basic application or basic registration relating to a collective mark, certification mark or guarantee mark.

Article 195
Search

1. Once the Office has received a notification of an international registration designating the Union, it shall draw up a Union search report as provided for in Article 43(1) provided that a request for a search report, pursuant to Article 43(1), is made to the Office within one month of the date of notification.

2. As soon as the Office has received a notification of an international registration designating the Union, the Office shall transmit a copy thereof to the central industrial property office of each Member State which has informed the Office of its decision to operate a search in its own register of trade marks as provided for in Article 43(2) provided that a request for a search report, pursuant to Article 43(2), is made to the Office within one month of the date of notification and the search fee is paid within the same period.

3. Article 43(3) to (6) shall apply mutatis mutandis.

4. The Office shall inform the proprietors of any earlier EU trade marks or EU trade mark applications cited in the Union search report of the publication of the international registration designating the Union as provided for in Article 190(1). This shall apply whether or not the holder of the international registration has requested to receive the EU search report, unless the proprietor of an earlier registration or application requests not to receive the notification.

Article 196
Opposition

1. International registration designating the Union shall be subject to opposition in the same way as published EU trade mark applications.

2. Notice of opposition shall be filed within a period of three months which shall begin one month following the date of the publication pursuant to Article 190(1). The opposition shall not be considered as duly entered until the opposition fee has been paid.

3. Refusal of protection shall take the place of refusal of an EU trade mark application.

4. The Commission is empowered to adopt delegated acts in accordance with Article 208 specifying the procedure for the filing and examination of an opposition, including the necessary communications to be made to the International Bureau.

Article 197
Replacement of an EU trade mark by an international registration

The Office shall, upon request, enter a notice in the Register that an EU trade mark is deemed to have been replaced by an international registration in accordance with Article 4bis of the Madrid Protocol.

Article 198
Invalidation of the effects of an international registration

1. The effects of an international registration designating the Union may be declared invalid.

2. The application for invalidation of the effects of an international registration designating the Union shall take the place of an application for a declaration of revocation as provided for in Article 58 or for a declaration of invalidity as provided for in Article 59 or Article 60.

3. Where pursuant to Article 64 or Article 128 of this Regulation and this Article, the effects of an international registration designating the Union have been declared invalid by means of a final decision, the Office shall notify the International Bureau in accordance with Article 5(6) of the Madrid Protocol.

4. The Commission shall adopt implementing acts specifying the details to be contained in the notification to be made to the International Bureau pursuant to paragraph 3 of this Article. Those implementing acts shall be adopted in accordance with the examination procedure referred to in Article 207(2).

Article 199
Legal effect of registration of transfers

The recordal of a change in the ownership of an international registration on the International Register shall have the same effect as the entry of a transfer in the Register pursuant to Article 20.

Article 200

Legal effect of registration of licences and other rights

The recordal of a licence or a restriction of the holder's right of disposal in respect of an international registration in the International Register shall have the same effect as the registration of a right in rem, a levy of execution, insolvency proceedings or a licence in the Register pursuant to Articles 22, 23, 24 and 25 respectively.

Article 201

Examination of requests for registration of transfers, licences or restrictions of a holder's right of disposal

The Office shall transmit requests to register a change in ownership, a licence or a restriction of the holder's right of disposal, the amendment or cancellation of a licence or the removal of a restriction of the holder's right of disposal which have been filed with it to the International Bureau, if accompanied by appropriate proof of the transfer, licence, or the restriction of the right of disposal, or by proof that the licence no longer exists or that it has been amended, or that the restriction of the right of disposal has been removed.

Article 202

Conversion of a designation of the Union through an international registration into a national trade mark application or into a designation of Member States

1. Where a designation of the Union through an international registration has been refused or ceases to have effect, the holder of the international registration may request the conversion of the designation of the Union:

(a) into a national trade mark application pursuant to Articles 139, 140 and 141;
(b) into a designation of a Member State party to the Madrid Protocol, provided that on the date when conversion was requested it was possible to have designated that Member State directly under the Madrid Protocol. Articles 139, 140 and 141 of this Regulation shall apply.

2. The national trade mark application or the designation of a Member State party to the Madrid Protocol resulting from the conversion of the designation of the Union through an international registration shall enjoy, in respect of the Member State concerned, the date of the international registration pursuant to Article 3(4) of the Madrid Protocol or the date of the extension to the Union pursuant to Article 3ter(2) of the Madrid Protocol, if the latter was made subsequent to the international registration, or the date of priority of that registration and, where appropriate, the seniority of a trade mark of that State claimed under Article 191 of this Regulation.

3. The request for conversion shall be published.

4. The request for conversion of an international registration designating the Union into a national trade mark application shall include the information and indications referred to in Article 140(1).

5. Where conversion is requested pursuant to this Article and Article 139(5) of this Regulation following a failure to renew the international registration, the request referred to in paragraph 4 of this Article shall contain an indication to that effect and the date on which the protection expired. The period of three months provided for in Article 139(5) of this Regulation shall begin to run on the day following the last day on which the renewal may still be effected pursuant to Article 7(4) of the Madrid Protocol.

6. Article 140(3) and (5) shall apply to the request for conversion referred to in paragraph 4 of this Article mutatis mutandis.

7. The request for conversion of an international registration designating the Union into a designation of a Member State party to the Madrid Protocol shall include the indications and elements referred to in paragraphs 4 and 5.

8. Article 140(3) shall apply to the request for conversion referred to in paragraph 7 of this Article mutatis mutandis. The Office shall also reject the request for conversion where the conditions to designate the Member State which is a party to the Madrid Protocol or to the Madrid Agreement were fulfilled neither on the date of the designation of the Union nor on the date on which the application for conversion was received or, pursuant to the last sentence of Article 140(1), is deemed to have been received by the Office.

9. Where the request for conversion referred to in paragraph 7 complies with the requirements of this Regulation and rules adopted pursuant to it, the Office shall transmit the request without delay to the International Bureau. The Office shall inform the holder of the international registration of the date of transmission.

10. The Commission shall adopt implementing acts specifying:

(a) the details to be contained in the requests for conversion referred to in paragraphs 4 and 7;
(b) the details to be contained in the publication of the requests for conversion pursuant to paragraph 3.

Those implementing acts shall be adopted in accordance with the examination procedure referred to in Article 207(2).

Article 203
Use of a mark subject of an international registration

For the purposes of applying Article 18(1), Article 47(2), Article 58(1)(a) and Article 64(2), the date of publication pursuant to Article 190(2) shall take the place of the date of registration for the purpose of establishing the date as from which the mark which is the subject of an international registration designating the Union shall be put to genuine use in the Union.

Article 204
Transformation

1. Subject to paragraph 2, the provisions applicable to EU trade mark applications shall apply mutatis mutandis to applications for transformation of an international registration into an EU trade mark application pursuant to Article 9quinquies of the Madrid Protocol.

2. When the application for transformation relates to an international registration designating the Union the particulars of which have been published pursuant to Article 190(2), Articles 42 to 47 shall not apply.

3. In order to be considered a transformation of an international registration which has been cancelled at the request of the office of origin by the International Bureau pursuant to Article 9quinquies of the Madrid Protocol, an EU trade mark application shall contain an indication to that effect. That indication shall be made when filing the application.

4. Where, in the course of the examination in accordance with Article 41(1)(b), the Office finds that the application was not filed within three months of the date on which the international registration was cancelled by the International Bureau, or the goods and services for which the EU trade mark is to be registered are not contained in the list of goods and services for which the international registration was registered in respect of the Union, the Office shall invite the applicant to remedy the deficiencies.

5. If the deficiencies referred to in paragraph 4 are not remedied within the time period specified by the Office, the right to the date of the international registration or the territorial extension and, if any, of the priority of the international registration shall be lost.

6. The Commission shall adopt implementing acts specifying the details to be contained in an application for transformation pursuant to paragraph 3 of this Article. Those implementing acts shall be adopted in accordance with the examination procedure referred to in Article 207(2).

Article 205
Communication with the International Bureau

Communication with the International Bureau shall be in a manner and format agreed on between the International Bureau and the Office, and preferably be by electronic means. Any reference to forms shall be construed as including forms made available in electronic format.

Article 206
Use of languages

For the purpose of applying this Regulation, and rules adopted pursuant to it, to international registrations designating the Union, the language of filing of the international application shall be the language of the proceedings within the meaning of Article 146(4), and the second language indicated in the international application shall be the second language within the meaning of Article 146(3).

CHAPTER XIV FINAL PROVISIONS

Article 207
Committee Procedure

1. The Commission shall be assisted by a Committee on Implementation Rules. That committee shall be a committee within the meaning of Regulation (EU) No 182/2011.

2. Where reference is made to this paragraph, Article 5 of Regulation (EU) No 182/2011 shall apply.

Article 208
Exercise of the delegation

1. The power to adopt delegated acts is conferred on the Commission subject to the conditions laid down in this Article.

2. The power to adopt delegated acts referred to in Article 48, Article 49(3), Articles 65 and 73, Articles 96(4), 97(6), 98(5), 100(2), 101(5), 103(3), and 106(3), Articles 121 and 168, and Articles 194(3) and 196(4) shall be conferred on the Commission for an indeterminate period of time from 23 March 2016.

3. The delegation of power referred to in Article 48, Article 49(3), Articles 65 and 73, Articles 96(4), 97(6), 98(5), 100(2), 101(5), 103(3), and 106(3), Articles 121 and 168, and Articles 194(3) and 196(4) may be revoked at any time by the European Parliament or by the Council. A decision to revoke shall put an end to the delegation of the power specified in that decision. It shall take effect the day following the publication of the decision in the Official Journal of the European Union or at a later date specified therein. It shall not affect the validity of any delegated acts already in force.

4. Before adopting a delegated act, the Commission shall carry out consultations with experts, including experts designated by each Member State in accordance with the principles laid down in the Interinstitutional Agreement of 13 April 2016 on Better Law-Making.

5. As soon as it adopts a delegated act, the Commission shall notify it simultaneously to the European Parliament and to the Council.

6. A delegated act adopted pursuant to Article 48, Article 49(3), Articles 65 and 73, Articles 96(4), 97(6), 98(5), 100(2), 101(5), 103(3), and 106(3), Articles 121 and 168, and Articles 194(3) and 196(4) shall enter into force only if no objection has been expressed either by the European Parliament or by the Council within a period of two months of notification of that act to the European Parliament and the Council or if, before the expiry of that period, the European Parliament and the Council have both informed the Commission that they will not object. That period shall be extended by two months at the initiative of the European Parliament or of the Council.

Article 209
Provisions relating to the enlargement of the Union

1. As of the date of accession of Bulgaria, the Czech Republic, Estonia, Croatia, Cyprus, Latvia, Lithuania, Hungary, Malta, Poland, Romania, Slovenia and Slovakia ('new Member State(s)'), an EU trade mark registered or applied for pursuant to this Regulation before their respective date of accession shall be extended to the territory of those Member States in order to have equal effect throughout the Union.

2. The registration of an EU trade mark which was under application at the date of accession may not be refused on the basis of any of the absolute grounds for

refusal listed in Article 7(1), if these grounds became applicable merely because of the accession of a new Member State.

3. Where an application for the registration of an EU trade mark has been filed during the six months prior to the date of accession, notice of opposition may be given pursuant to Article 46 where an earlier trade mark or another earlier right within the meaning of Article 8 was acquired in a new Member State prior to accession, provided that it was acquired in good faith and that the filing date or, where applicable, the priority date or the date of acquisition in the new Member State of the earlier trade mark or other earlier right precedes the filing date or, where applicable, the priority date of the EU trade mark applied for.

4. An EU trade mark as referred to in paragraph 1 may not be declared invalid:

(a) pursuant to Article 59 if the grounds for invalidity became applicable merely because of the accession of a new Member State;
(b) pursuant to Article 60(1) and (2) if the earlier national right was registered, applied for or acquired in a new Member State prior to the date of accession.

5. The use of an EU trade mark as referred to in paragraph 1 may be prohibited pursuant to Articles 137 and 138, if the earlier trade mark or other earlier right was registered, applied for or acquired in good faith in the new Member State prior to the date of accession of that State; or, where applicable, has a priority date prior to the date of accession of that State.

Article 210
Evaluation and review

1. By 24 March 2021, and every five years thereafter, the Commission shall evaluate the implementation of this Regulation.

2. The evaluation shall review the legal framework for cooperation between the Office and the central industrial property offices of the Member States and the Benelux Office for Intellectual Property, paying particular attention to the financing mechanism laid down in Article 152. The evaluation shall further assess the impact, effectiveness and efficiency of the Office and its working practices. The evaluation shall, in particular, address the possible need to modify the mandate of the Office, and the financial implications of any such modification.

3. The Commission shall forward the evaluation report together with its conclusions drawn on the basis of that report to the European Parliament, the Council and the Management Board. The findings of the evaluation shall be made public.

4. On the occasion of every second evaluation, there shall be an assessment of the results achieved by the Office having regard to its objectives, mandate and tasks.

Article 211
Repeal

Regulation (EC) No 207/2009 is repealed.

References to the repealed Regulation shall be construed as references to this Regulation and shall be read in accordance with the correlation table in Annex III.

Article 212

Entry into force

This Regulation shall enter into force on the twentieth day following that of its publication in the Official Journal of the European Union.

It shall apply from 1 October 2017.

This Regulation shall be binding in its entirety and directly applicable in all Member States.

Done at Strasbourg, 14 June 2017.

For the European Parliament

The President

A. TAJANI

For the Council

The President

H. DALLI

ANNEX I AMOUNT OF FEES

A. The fees to be paid to the Office under this Regulation shall be as follows (in EUR):

1. Basic fee for the application for an individual EU trade mark (Article 31(2)):
EUR 1 000
2. Basic fee for the application for an individual EU trade mark by electronic means (Article 31(2)):
EUR 850
3. Fee for the second class of goods and services for an individual EU trade mark (Article 31(2)):
EUR 50
4. Fee for each class of goods and services exceeding two for an individual EU trade mark (Article 31(2)):
EUR 150
5. Basic fee for the application for an EU collective mark or an EU certification mark (Article 31(2) and Article 74(3) or Article 83(3)):
EUR 1 800
6. Basic fee for the application for an EU collective mark or an EU certification mark by electronic means (Article 31(2) and Article 74(3) or Article 83(3)):
EUR 1 500
7. Fee for the second class of goods and services for an EU collective mark or an EU certification mark: (Article 31(2) and Article 74(3) or Article 83(3)):
EUR 50

8. Fee for each class of goods and services exceeding two for an EU collective mark or an EU certification mark (Article 31(2) and 74(3) or Article 83(3)): EUR 150
9. Search fee for an EU trade mark application (Article 43(2)) or for an international registration designating the Union (Article 43(2) and Article 195(2)): EUR 12 multiplied by the number of central industrial property offices referred to in Article 43(2); that amount, and the subsequent changes, shall be published by the Office in the Official Journal of the Office.
10. Opposition fee (Article 46(3)): EUR 320
11. Basic fee for the renewal of an individual EU trade mark (Article 53(3)): EUR 1 000
12. Basic fee for the renewal of an individual EU trade mark by electronic means (Article 53(3)): EUR 850
13. Fee for the renewal of the second class of goods and services for an individual EU trade mark (Article 53(3)): EUR 50
14. Fee for the renewal of each class of goods and services exceeding two for an individual EU trade mark (Article 53(3)): EUR 150
15. Basic fee for the renewal of an EU collective mark or an EU certification mark (Article 53(3) and Article 74(3) or Article 83(3): EUR 1 800
16. Basic fee for the renewal of an EU collective mark or an EU certification mark by electronic means (Article 53(3) and Article 74(3) or Article 83(3)): EUR 1 500
17. Fee for the renewal of the second class of goods and services for an EU collective mark or an EU certification mark (Article 53(3) and Article 74(3) or Article 83(3)): EUR 50
18. Fee for the renewal of each class of goods and services exceeding two for an EU collective mark or an EU certification mark (Article 53(3) and Article 74(3) or Article 83(3)): EUR 150
19. Additional fee for the late payment of the renewal fee or the late submission of the request for renewal (Article 53(3)): 25 % of the belated renewal fee, subject to a maximum of EUR 1 500
20. Fee for the application for revocation or for a declaration of invalidity (Article 63(2)): EUR 630
21. Appeal fee (Article 68(1)): EUR 720

22. Fee for the application of restitutio in integrum (Article 104(3)):
EUR 200

23. Fee for the application for the conversion of an EU trade mark application or an EU trade mark (Article 140(1), also in conjunction with Article 202(1)):
(a) into a national trade mark application;
(b) into a designation of Member States under the Madrid Protocol:
EUR 200

24. Fee for continuation of proceedings (Article 105(1)):
EUR 400

25. Fee for the declaration of division of a registered EU trade mark (Article 56(4) or an application for an EU trade mark (Article 50(3)):
EUR 250

26. Fee for the application for the registration of a licence or another right in respect of a registered EU trade mark (Article 26(2)) or an application for an EU trade mark (Article 26(2)):

(a) grant of a licence;
(b) transfer of a licence;
(c) creation of a right in rem;
(d) transfer of a right in rem;
(e) levy of execution:

EUR 200 per registration, but where multiple requests are submitted in the same application or at the same time, not to exceed a total of EUR 1 000

27. Fee for the cancellation of the registration of a licence or other right (Article 29(3)):
EUR 200 per cancellation, but where multiple requests are submitted in the same application or at the same time, not to exceed a total of EUR 1 000

28. Fee for the alteration of a registered EU trade mark (Article 54(4)):
EUR 200

29. Fee for the issue of a copy of the application for an EU trade mark (Article 114(7)), a copy of the certificate of registration (Article 51(2)), or an extract from the register (Article 111(7)):

(a) uncertified copy or extract:
EUR 10
(b) certified copy or extract:
EUR 30

30. Fee for the inspection of the files (Article 114(6)):
EUR 30

31. Fee for the issue of copies of file documents (Article 114(7)):
(a) uncertified copy:
EUR 10
(b) certified copy:
EUR 30
plus per page, exceeding 10
EUR 1

32. Fee for the communication of information in a file (Article 114(9)):
    EUR 10

33. Fee for the review of the determination of the procedural costs to be refunded (Article 109(8)):
    EUR 100

34. Fee for the filing of an international application at the Office (Article 184(4)):
    EUR 300

B. Fees to be paid to the International Bureau

I. Individual fee for an international registration designating the Union

1. The applicant for an international registration designating the Union shall be required to pay to the International Bureau an individual fee for the designation of the Union in accordance with Article 8(7) of the Madrid Protocol.

2. The holder of an international registration who files a request for territorial extension designating the Union made subsequent to the international registration shall be required to pay to the International Bureau an individual fee for the designation of the Union in accordance with Article 8(7) of the Madrid Protocol.

3. The amount of the fee under points B.I.1 or B.I.2 shall be the equivalent in Swiss Francs, as established by the Director-General of the WIPO pursuant to Rule 35(2) of the Common Regulations under the Madrid Agreement and Protocol, of the following amounts:

(a) for an individual trade mark: EUR 820 plus, where applicable, EUR 50 for the second class of goods and services and EUR 150 for each class of goods and services contained in the international registration exceeding two;
(b) for a collective mark or a certification mark: EUR 1 400 plus, where applicable, EUR 50 for the second class of goods and services and EUR 150 for each class of goods or services exceeding two.

II. Individual fee for a renewal of an international registration designating the Union

1. The holder of an international registration designating the Union shall be required to pay to the International Bureau, as a part of the fees for a renewal of the international registration, an individual fee for the designation of the Union in accordance with Article 8(7) of the Madrid Protocol.

2. The amount of the fee referred to in point B.II.1 shall be the equivalent in Swiss Francs, as established by the Director-General of the WIPO pursuant to Rule 35(2) of the Common Regulations under the Madrid Agreement and Protocol, of the following amounts:

(a) for an individual trade mark: EUR 820 plus, where applicable, EUR 50 for the second class of goods and services and EUR 150 for each class of goods and services contained in the international registration exceeding two;
(b) for a collective mark or a certification mark: EUR 1 400 plus, where applicable, EUR 50 for the second class of goods and services and EUR 150 for each class of goods and services contained in the international registration exceeding two.

ANNEX II REPEALED REGULATION WITH LIST OF ITS SUCCESSIVE AMENDMENTS

Council Regulation (EC) No 207/2009 (OJ L 78, 24.3.2009, p. 1)	
Act of Accession of 2012, Annex III, point 2(I)	
Regulation (EU) 2015/2424 of the European Parliament and of the Council (OJ L 341, 24.12.2015, p. 21)	Only Article 1

ANNEX III CORRELATION TABLE

Regulation (EC) No 207/2009	This Regulation
Articles 1 to 7	Articles 1 to 7
Article 8(1) to (4)	Article 8(1) to (4)
Article 8(4a)	Article 8(6)
Article 8(5)	Article 8(5)
Article 9	Article 9
Article 9a	Article 10
Article 9b	Article 11
Article 10	Article 12
Article 11	Article 13
Article 12	Article 14
Article 13	Article 15
Article 13a	Article 16
Article 14	Article 17
Article 15	Article 18
Article 16	Article 19
Article 17(1), (2) and (3)	Article 20(1), (2) and (3)
Article 17(5)	Article 20(4)
Article 17(5a)	Article 20(5)
Article 17(5b)	Article 20(6)
Article 17(5c)	Article 20(7)
Article 17(5d)	Article 20(8)
Article 17(5e)	Article 20(9)
Article 17(5f)	Article 20(10)
Article 17(6)	Article 20(11)
Article 17(7)	Article 20(12)
Article 17(8)	Article 20(13)

Regulation (EC) No 207/2009	This Regulation
Article 18	Article 21
Article 19	Article 22
Article 20	Article 23
Article 21	Article 24
Article 22	Article 25
Article 22a	Article 26
Article 23	Article 27
Article 24	Article 28
Article 24a	Article 29
Article 25	Article 30
Article 26	Article 31
Article 27	Article 32
Article 28	Article 33
Article 29	Article 34
Article 30	Article 35
Article 31	Article 36
Article 32	Article 37
Article 33	Article 38
Article 34(1)	Article 39(1)
Article 34(1a)	Article 39(2)
Article 34(2)	Article 39(3)
Article 34(3)	Article 39(4)
Article 34(4)	Article 39(5)
Article 34(5)	Article 39(6)
Article 34(6)	Article 39(7)
Article 35	Article 40
Article 36	Article 41
Article 37(1)	Article 42(1)
Article 37(3)	Article 42(2)
Article 38	Article 43
Article 39	Article 44
Article 40	Article 45
Article 41	Article 46
Article 42	Article 47
Article 42a	Article 48
Article 43	Article 49
Article 44(1) and (2)	Article 50(1) and (2)
Article 44(4)	Article 50(3)
Article 44(4a)	Article 50(4)

Regulation (EC) No 207/2009	This Regulation
Article 44(5) to (9)	Article 50(5) to (9)
Article 45	Article 51
Article 46	Article 52
Article 47	Article 53
Article 48	Article 54
Article 48a	Article 55
Article 49	Article 56
Article 50	Article 57
Article 51	Article 58
Article 52	Article 59
Article 53	Article 60
Article 54	Article 61
Article 55	Article 62
Article 56	Article 63
Article 57	Article 64
Article 57a	Article 65
Article 58	Article 66
Article 59	Article 67
Article 60	Article 68
Article 61	Article 69
Article 63	Article 70
Article 64	Article 71
Article 65	Article 72
Article 65a	Article 73
Article 66	Article 74
Article 67	Article 75
Article 68	Article 76
Article 69	Article 77
Article 70	Article 78
Article 71	Article 79
Article 72	Article 80
Article 73	Article 81
Article 74	Article 82
Article 74a	Article 83
Article 74b	Article 84
Article 74c	Article 85
Article 74d	Article 86
Article 74e	Article 87
Article 74f	Article 88

Regulation (EC) No 207/2009	This Regulation
Article 74g	Article 89
Article 74h	Article 90
Article 74i	Article 91
Article 74j	Article 92
Article 74k	Article 93
Article 75	Article 94
Article 76	Article 95
Article 77	Article 96
Article 78	Article 97
Article 79	Article 98
Article 79a	Article 99
Article 79b	Article 100
Article 79c	Article 101
Article 79d	Article 102
Article 80	Article 103
Article 81	Article 104
Article 82	Article 105
Article 82a	Article 106
Article 83	Article 107
Article 84	Article 108
Article 85(1)	Article 109(1)
Article 85(1a)	Article 109(2)
Article 85(2)	Article 109(3)
Article 85(3)	Article 109(4)
Article 85(4)	Article 109(5)
Article 85(5)	Article 109(6)
Article 85(6)	Article 109(7)
Article 85(7)	Article 109(8)
Article 86	Article 110
Article 87	Article 111
Article 87a	Article 112
Article 87b	Article 113
Article 88	Article 114
Article 88a	Article 115
Article 89	Article 116
Article 90	Article 117
Article 91	Article 118
Article 92	Article 119
Article 93	Article 120

Regulation (EC) No 207/2009	This Regulation
Article 93a	Article 121
Article 94	Article 122
Article 95(1)	Article 123(1)
Article 95(2)	—
Article 95(3)	Article 123(2)
Article 95(4)	Article 123(3)
Article 95(5)	—
Article 96	Article 124
Article 97	Article 125
Article 98	Article 126
Article 99	Article 127
Article 100	Article 128
Article 101	Article 129
Article 102	Article 130
Article 103	Article 131
Article 104	Article 132
Article 105	Article 133
Article 106	Article 134
Article 107	Article 135
Article 109	Article 136
Article 110	Article 137
Article 111	Article 138
Article 112	Article 139
Article 113	Article 140
Article 114	Article 141
Article 115	Article 142
Article 116	Article 143
Article 117	Article 144
Article 118	Article 145
Article 119(1) to (5)	Article 146(1) to (5)
Article 119(5a)	Article 146(6)
Article 119(6)	Article 146(7)
Article 119(7)	Article 146(8)
Article 119(8)	Article 146(9)
Article 119(9)	Article 146(10)
Article 119(10)	Article 146(11)
Article 120	Article 147
Article 121	Article 148
Article 123	Article 149

Regulation (EC) No 207/2009	This Regulation
Article 123a	Article 150
Article 123b	Article 151
Article 123c	Article 152
Article 124	Article 153
Article 125	Article 154
Article 126	Article 155
Article 127	Article 156
Article 128	Article 157
Article 129	Article 158
Article 130	Article 159
Article 131	Article 160
Article 132	Article 161
Article 133	Article 162
Article 134	Article 163
Article 134a	Article 164
Article 135	Article 165
Article 136	Article 166
Article 136a	Article 167
Article 136b	Article 168
Article 137	Article 169
Article 137a	Article 170
Article 138	Article 171
Article 139	Article 172
Article 140	Article 173
Article 141	Article 174
Article 141a	Article 175
Article 142	Article 176
Article 143	Article 177
Article 144	Article 178
Article 144a	Article 179
Article 144b	Article 180
Article 144c	Article 181
Article 145	Article 182
Article 146	Article 183
Article 147	Article 184
Article 148	Article 185
Article 148a	Article 186
Article 149	Article 187
Article 150	Article 188

Regulation (EC) No 207/2009	This Regulation
Article 151	Article 189
Article 152	Article 190
Article 153	Article 191
Article 153a	Article 192
Article 154	Article 193
Article 154a	Article 194
Article 155	Article 195
Article 156	Article 196
Article 157	Article 197
Article 158	Article 198
Article 158a	Article 199
Article 158b	Article 200
Article 158c	Article 201
Article 159	Article 202
Article 160	Article 203
Article 161	Article 204
Article 161a	Article 205
Article 161b	Article 206
Article 163	Article 207
Article 163a(1)	Article 208(1)
Article 163a(2), first sentence	Article 208(2)
Article 163a(2), second sentence	Article 208(4)
Article 163a(3)	Article 208(3)
Article 163a(4)	Article 208(5)
Article 163a(5)	Article 208(6)
Article 165	Article 209
Article 165a	Article 210
Article 166	Article 211
Article 167	Article 212
Annex -I	Annex I
Annex I	Annex II
Annex II	Annex III

Appendix 3

Directive (EU) 2015/2436 of the European Parliament and of the Council

of 16 December 2015

to approximate the laws of the Member States relating to trade marks

The European Parliament and the Council of the European Union,

Having regard to the Treaty on the Functioning of the European Union, and in particular Article 114(1) thereof,

Having regard to the proposal from the European Commission,

After transmission of the draft legislative act to the national parliaments,

Having regard to the opinion of the European Economic and Social Committee,

Acting in accordance with the ordinary legislative procedure,

Whereas:

(1) A number of amendments should be made to Directive 2008/95/EC of the European Parliament and of the Council. In the interests of clarity, that Directive should be recast.

(2) Directive 2008/95/EC has harmonised central provisions of substantive trade mark law which at the time of adoption were considered as most directly affecting the functioning of the internal market by impeding the free movement of goods and the freedom to provide services in the Union.

(3) Trade mark protection in the Member States coexists with protection available at Union level through European Union trade marks ('EU trade marks') which are unitary in character and valid throughout the Union as laid down in Council Regulation (EC) No 207/2009. The coexistence and balance of trade mark systems at national and Union level in fact constitutes a cornerstone of the Union's approach to intellectual property protection.

(4) Further to the Commission's communication of 16 July 2008 on an industrial property rights strategy for Europe, the Commission carried out a comprehensive evaluation of the overall functioning of the trade mark system in Europe as a whole, covering Union and national levels and the interrelation between the two.

(5) In its conclusions of 25 May 2010 on the future revision of the trade mark system in the European Union, the Council called on the Commission to present proposals for the revision of Regulation (EC) No 207/2009 and Directive 2008/95/EC. The revision of that Directive should include measures to make it more consistent with Regulation (EC) No 207/2009, which would thus reduce the areas of divergence within the trade mark system in Europe as a whole, while maintaining national trade mark protection as an attractive option for applicants. In this context, the complementary relationship between the EU trade mark system and national trade mark systems should be ensured.

(6) The Commission concluded in its communication of 24 May 2011 entitled 'A single market for intellectual property rights' that in order to meet increased demands from stakeholders for faster, higher quality, more streamlined trade mark registration systems, which are also more consistent, user friendly, publicly accessible and technologically up to date, there is a necessity to modernise the trade mark system in the Union as a whole and adapt it to the internet era.

(7) Consultation and evaluation for the purpose of this Directive has revealed that, in spite of the previous partial harmonisation of national laws, there remain areas where further harmonisation could have a positive impact on competitiveness and growth.

(8) In order to serve the objective of fostering and creating a well-functioning internal market and to facilitate acquiring and protecting trade marks in the Union, to the benefit of the growth and the competitiveness of European businesses, in particular small and medium-sized enterprises, it is necessary to go beyond the limited scope of approximation achieved by Directive 2008/95/EC and extend approximation to other aspects of substantive trade mark law governing trade marks protected through registration pursuant to Regulation (EC) No 207/2009.

(9) For the purpose of making trade mark registrations throughout the Union easier to obtain and administer, it is essential to approximate not only provisions of substantive law but also procedural rules. Therefore, the principal procedural rules in the area of trade mark registration in the Member States and in the EU trade mark system should be aligned. As regards procedures under national law, it is sufficient to lay down general principles, leaving the Member States free to establish more specific rules.

(10) It is essential to ensure that registered trade marks enjoy the same protection under the legal systems of all the Member States. In line with the extensive protection granted to EU trade marks which have a reputation in the Union, extensive protection should also be granted at national level to all registered trade marks which have a reputation in the Member State concerned.

(11) This Directive should not deprive the Member States of the right to continue to protect trade marks acquired through use but should take them into account only with regard to their relationship with trade marks acquired by registration.

(12) Attainment of the objectives of this approximation of laws requires that the conditions for obtaining and continuing to hold a registered trade mark be, in general, identical in all Member States.

(13) To this end, it is necessary to list examples of signs which are capable of constituting a trade mark, provided that such signs are capable of distinguishing the goods or services of one undertaking from those of other undertakings. In order to fulfil the objectives of the registration system for trade marks, namely to ensure legal certainty and sound administration, it is also essential to require that the sign is capable of being represented in a manner which is clear, precise, self-contained, easily accessible, intelligible, durable and objective. A sign should therefore be permitted to be represented in any appropriate form using generally available technology, and thus not necessarily by graphic means, as long as the representation offers satisfactory guarantees to that effect.

(14) Furthermore, the grounds for refusal or invalidity concerning the trade mark itself, including the absence of any distinctive character, or concerning conflicts between the trade mark and earlier rights, should be listed in an exhaustive manner, even if some of those grounds are listed as an option for the Member States which should therefore be able to maintain or introduce them in their legislation.

(15) In order to ensure that the levels of protection afforded to geographical indications by Union legislation and national law are applied in a uniform and exhaustive manner in the examination of absolute and relative grounds for refusal throughout the Union, this Directive should include the same provisions in relation to geographical indications as contained in Regulation (EC) No 207/2009. Furthermore, it is appropriate to ensure that the scope of absolute grounds is extended to also cover protected traditional terms for wine and traditional specialties guaranteed.

(16) The protection afforded by the registered trade mark, the function of which is in particular to guarantee the trade mark as an indication of origin, should be absolute in the event of there being identity between the mark and the corresponding sign and the goods or services. The protection should apply also in the case of similarity between the mark and the sign and the goods or services. It is indispensable to give an interpretation of the concept of similarity in relation to the likelihood of confusion. The likelihood of confusion, the appreciation of which depends on numerous elements and, in particular, on the recognition of the trade mark on the market, the association which can be made with the used or registered sign, the degree of similarity between the trade mark and the sign and between the goods or services identified, should constitute the specific condition for such protection. The ways in which a likelihood of confusion can be established, and in particular the onus of proof in that regard, should be a matter for national procedural rules which should not be prejudiced by this Directive.

(17) In order to ensure legal certainty and full consistency with the principle of priority, under which a registered earlier trade mark takes precedence over later

registered trade marks, it is necessary to provide that the enforcement of rights which are conferred by a trade mark should be without prejudice to the rights of proprietors acquired prior to the filing or priority date of the trade mark. Such an approach is in conformity with Article 16(1) of the Agreement on trade-related aspects of intellectual property rights of 15 April 1994 ('TRIPS Agreement').

(18) It is appropriate to provide that an infringement of a trade mark can only be established if there is a finding that the infringing mark or sign is used in the course of trade for the purposes of distinguishing goods or services. Use of the sign for purposes other than for distinguishing goods or services should be subject to the provisions of national law.

(19) The concept of infringement of a trade mark should also comprise the use of the sign as a trade name or similar designation, as long as such use is made for the purposes of distinguishing goods or services.

(20) In order to ensure legal certainty and full consistency with specific Union legislation, it is appropriate to provide that the proprietor of a trade mark should be entitled to prohibit a third party from using a sign in comparative advertising where such comparative advertising is contrary to Directive 2006/114/EC of the European Parliament and of the Council.

(21) In order to strengthen trade mark protection and combat counterfeiting more effectively, and in line with international obligations of the Member States under the World Trade Organisation (WTO) framework, in particular Article V of the General Agreement on Tariffs and Trade on freedom of transit and, as regards generic medicines, the 'Declaration on the TRIPS Agreement and public health' adopted by the Doha WTO Ministerial Conference on 14 November 2001, the proprietor of a trade mark should be entitled to prevent third parties from bringing goods, in the course of trade, into the Member State where the trade mark is registered without being released for free circulation there, where such goods come from third countries and bear without authorisation a trade mark which is identical or essentially identical with the trade mark registered in respect of such goods.

(22) To this effect, it should be permissible for trade mark proprietors to prevent the entry of infringing goods and their placement in all customs situations, including, in particular transit, transhipment, warehousing, free zones, temporary storage, inward processing or temporary admission, also when such goods are not intended to be placed on the market of the Member State concerned. In performing customs controls, the customs authorities should make use of the powers and procedures laid down in Regulation (EU) No 608/2013 of the European Parliament and of the Council, also at the request of the right holders. In particular, the customs authorities should carry out the relevant controls on the basis of risk analysis criteria.

(23) In order to reconcile the need to ensure the effective enforcement of trade mark rights with the necessity to avoid hampering the free flow of trade in legitimate goods, the entitlement of the proprietor of the trade mark should lapse where, during the subsequent proceedings initiated before the judicial or other authority competent to take a substantive decision on whether the registered trade mark has been infringed, the declarant or the holder of the goods is able to prove

that the proprietor of the registered trade mark is not entitled to prohibit the placing of the goods on the market in the country of final destination.

(24) Article 28 of Regulation (EU) No 608/2013 provides that a right holder is to be liable for damages towards the holder of the goods where, inter alia, the goods in question are subsequently found not to infringe an intellectual property right.

(25) Appropriate measures should be taken with a view to ensuring the smooth transit of generic medicines. With respect to international non-proprietary names (INN) as globally recognised generic names for active substances in pharmaceutical preparations, it is vital to take due account of the existing limitations on the effect of trade mark rights. Consequently, the proprietor of a trade mark should not have the right to prevent a third party from bringing goods into a Member State where the trade mark is registered without being released for free circulation there based upon similarities between the INN for the active ingredient in the medicines and the trade mark.

(26) In order to enable proprietors of registered trade marks to combat counterfeiting more effectively, they should be entitled to prohibit the affixing of an infringing trade mark to goods, and certain preparatory acts carried out prior to such affixing.

(27) The exclusive rights conferred by a trade mark should not entitle the proprietor to prohibit the use of signs or indications by third parties which are used fairly and thus in accordance with honest practices in industrial and commercial matters. In order to create equal conditions for trade names and trade marks against the background that trade names are regularly granted unrestricted protection against later trade marks, such use should only be considered to include the use of the personal name of the third party. Such use should further permit the use of descriptive or non-distinctive signs or indications in general. Furthermore, the proprietor should not be entitled to prevent the fair and honest use of the mark for the purpose of identifying or referring to the goods or services as those of the proprietor. Use of a trade mark by third parties to draw the consumer`s attention to the resale of genuine goods that were originally sold by, or with the consent of, the proprietor of the trade mark in the Union should be considered as being fair as long as it is at the same time in accordance with honest practices in industrial and commercial matters. Use of a trade mark by third parties for the purpose of artistic expression should be considered as being fair as long as it is at the same time in accordance with honest practices in industrial and commercial matters. Furthermore, this Directive should be applied in a way that ensures full respect for fundamental rights and freedoms, and in particular the freedom of expression.

(28) It follows from the principle of free movement of goods that the proprietor of a trade mark should not be entitled to prohibit its use by a third party in relation to goods which have been put into circulation in the Union, under the trade mark, by him or with his consent, unless the proprietor has legitimate reasons to oppose further commercialisation of the goods.

(29) It is important, for reasons of legal certainty to provide that, without prejudice to his interests as a proprietor of an earlier trade mark, the latter may no longer request a declaration of invalidity or oppose the use of a trade mark subsequent to his own trade mark, of which he has knowingly tolerated the use for

a substantial length of time, unless the application for the subsequent trade mark was made in bad faith.

(30) In order to ensure legal certainty and safeguard legitimately acquired trade mark rights, it is appropriate and necessary to provide that, without prejudice to the principle that the later trade mark cannot be enforced against the earlier trade mark, proprietors of earlier trade marks should not be entitled to obtain refusal or invalidation or to oppose the use of a later trade mark if the later trade mark was acquired at a time when the earlier trade mark was liable to be declared invalid or revoked, for example because it had not yet acquired distinctiveness through use, or if the earlier trade mark could not be enforced against the later trade mark because the necessary conditions were not applicable, for example when the earlier mark had not yet obtained a reputation.

(31) Trade marks fulfil their purpose of distinguishing goods or services and allowing consumers to make informed choices only when they are actually used on the market. A requirement of use is also necessary in order to reduce the total number of trade marks registered and protected in the Union and, consequently, the number of conflicts which arise between them. It is therefore essential to require that registered trade marks actually be used in connection with the goods or services for which they are registered, or, if not used in that connection within five years of the date of the completion of the registration procedure, be liable to be revoked.

(32) Consequently, a registered trade mark should only be protected in so far as it is actually used and a registered earlier trade mark should not enable its proprietor to oppose or invalidate a later trade mark if that proprietor has not put his trade mark to genuine use. Furthermore, Member States should provide that a trade mark may not be successfully invoked in infringement proceedings if it is established, as a result of a plea, that the trade mark could be revoked or, when the action is brought against a later right, could have been revoked at the time when the later right was acquired.

(33) It is appropriate to provide that, where the seniority of a national mark or a trade mark registered under international arrangements having effect in the Member State has been claimed for an EU trade mark and the mark providing the basis for the seniority claim has thereafter been surrendered or allowed to lapse, the validity of that mark can still be challenged. Such a challenge should be limited to situations where the mark could have been declared invalid or revoked at the time it was removed from the register.

(34) For reasons of coherence and in order to facilitate the commercial exploitation of trade marks in the Union, the rules applicable to trade marks as objects of property should be aligned to the extent appropriate with those already in place for EU trade marks, and should include rules on assignment and transfer, licensing, rights in rem and levy of execution.

(35) Collective trade marks have proven a useful instrument for promoting goods or services with specific common properties. It is therefore appropriate to subject national collective trade marks to rules similar to the rules applicable to European Union collective marks.

(36) In order to improve and facilitate access to trade mark protection and to increase legal certainty and predictability, the procedure for the registration of trade marks in the Member States should be efficient and transparent and should follow rules similar to those applicable to EU trade marks.

(37) In order to ensure legal certainty with regard to the scope of trade mark rights and to facilitate access to trade mark protection, the designation and classification of goods and services covered by a trade mark application should follow the same rules in all Member States and should be aligned to those applicable to EU trade marks. In order to enable the competent authorities and economic operators to determine the extent of the trade mark protection sought on the basis of the application alone, the designation of goods and services should be sufficiently clear and precise. The use of general terms should be interpreted as including only goods and services clearly covered by the literal meaning of a term. In the interest of clarity and legal certainty, the Member States' central industrial property offices and the Benelux Office for Intellectual Property should, in cooperation with each other, endeavour to compile a list reflecting their respective administrative practices with regard to the classification of goods and services.

(38) For the purpose of ensuring effective trade mark protection, Member States should make available an efficient administrative opposition procedure, allowing at least the proprietor of earlier trade mark rights and any person authorised under the relevant law to exercise the rights arising from a protected designation of origin or a geographical indication to oppose the registration of a trade mark application. Furthermore, in order to offer efficient means of revoking trademarks or declaring them invalid, Member States should provide for an administrative procedure for revocation or declaration of invalidity within the longer transposition period of seven years, after the entry into force of this Directive.

(39) It is desirable that Member States' central industrial property offices and the Benelux Office for Intellectual Property cooperate with each other and with the European Union Intellectual Property Office in all fields of trade mark registration and administration in order to promote convergence of practices and tools, such as the creation and updating of common or connected databases and portals for consultation and search purposes. The Member States should further ensure that their offices cooperate with each other and with the European Union Intellectual Property Office in all other areas of their activities which are relevant for the protection of trade marks in the Union.

(40) This Directive should not exclude the application to trade marks of provisions of law of the Member States other than trade mark law, such as provisions relating to unfair competition, civil liability or consumer protection.

(41) Member States are bound by the Paris Convention for the Protection of Industrial Property ('the Paris Convention') and the TRIPS Agreement. It is necessary that this Directive be entirely consistent with that Convention and that Agreement. The obligations of the Member States resulting from that Convention and that Agreement should not be affected by this Directive. Where appropriate, the second paragraph of Article 351 of the Treaty on the Functioning of the European Union should apply.

(42) Since the objectives of this Directive, namely to foster and create a well-functioning internal market and to facilitate the registration, administration and protection of trade marks in the Union to the benefit of growth and competitiveness, cannot be sufficiently achieved by the Member States but can rather, by reason of its scale and effects, be better achieved at Union level, the Union may adopt measures, in accordance with the principle of subsidiarity as set out in Article 5 of the Treaty on European Union. In accordance with the principle of proportionality as set out in that Article, this Directive does not go beyond what is necessary in order to achieve those objectives.

(43) Directive 95/46/EC of the European Parliament and of the Council governs the processing of personal data carried out in the Member States in the context of this Directive.

(44) The European Data Protection Supervisor was consulted in accordance with Article 28(2) of Regulation (EC) No 45/2001 of the European Parliament and of the Council and delivered an opinion on 11 July 2013.

(45) The obligation to transpose this Directive into national law should be confined to those provisions which represent a substantive amendment as compared with the earlier Directive. The obligation to transpose the provisions which are unchanged arises under the earlier Directive.

(46) This Directive should be without prejudice to the obligations of the Member States under Directive 2008/95/EC relating to the time limit for transposition of Council Directive 89/104/EEC into national law as set out in Part B of Annex I to Directive 2008/95/EC,

Have adopted this Directive:

CHAPTER 1 GENERAL PROVISIONS

Article 1
Scope

This Directive applies to every trade mark in respect of goods or services which is the subject of registration or of an application for registration in a Member State as an individual trade mark, a guarantee or certification mark or a collective mark, or which is the subject of a registration or an application for registration in the Benelux Office for Intellectual Property or of an international registration having effect in a Member State.

Article 2
Definitions

For the purpose of this Directive, the following definitions apply:

(a) 'office' means the central industrial property office of the Member State or the Benelux Office for Intellectual Property, entrusted with the registration of trade marks;
(b) 'register' means the register of trade marks kept by an office.

CHAPTER 2 SUBSTANTIVE LAW ON TRADE MARKS

Section 1 Signs of which a trade mark may consist

Article 3

Signs of which a trade mark may consist

A trade mark may consist of any signs, in particular words, including personal names, or designs, letters, numerals, colours, the shape of goods or of the packaging of goods, or sounds, provided that such signs are capable of:

(a) distinguishing the goods or services of one undertaking from those of other undertakings; and
(b) being represented on the register in a manner which enables the competent authorities and the public to determine the clear and precise subject matter of the protection afforded to its proprietor.

Section 2 Grounds for refusal or invalidity

Article 4

Absolute grounds for refusal or invalidity

1. The following shall not be registered or, if registered, shall be liable to be declared invalid:

(a) signs which cannot constitute a trade mark;
(b) trade marks which are devoid of any distinctive character;
(c) trade marks which consist exclusively of signs or indications which may serve, in trade, to designate the kind, quality, quantity, intended purpose, value, geographical origin, or the time of production of the goods or of rendering of the service, or other characteristics of the goods or services;
(d) trade marks which consist exclusively of signs or indications which have become customary in the current language or in the bona fide and established practices of the trade;
(e) signs which consist exclusively of:
    (i) the shape, or another characteristic, which results from the nature of the goods themselves;
    (ii) the shape, or another characteristic, of goods which is necessary to obtain a technical result;
    (iii) the shape, or another characteristic, which gives substantial value to the goods;
(f) trade marks which are contrary to public policy or to accepted principles of morality;
(g) trade marks which are of such a nature as to deceive the public, for instance, as to the nature, quality or geographical origin of the goods or service;
(h) trade marks which have not been authorised by the competent authorities and are to be refused or invalidated pursuant to Article 6ter of the Paris Convention;
(i) trade marks which are excluded from registration pursuant to Union legislation or the national law of the Member State concerned, or to international agreements to which the Union or the Member State concerned is party, providing for protection of designations of origin and geographical indications;

(j) trade marks which are excluded from registration pursuant to Union legislation or international agreements to which the Union is party, providing for protection of traditional terms for wine;
(k) trade marks which are excluded from registration pursuant to Union legislation or international agreements to which the Union is party, providing for protection of traditional specialities guaranteed;
(l) trade marks which consist of, or reproduce in their essential elements, an earlier plant variety denomination registered in accordance with Union legislation or the national law of the Member State concerned, or international agreements to which the Union or the Member State concerned is party, providing protection for plant variety rights, and which are in respect of plant varieties of the same or closely related species.

2. A trade mark shall be liable to be declared invalid where the application for registration of the trade mark was made in bad faith by the applicant. Any Member State may also provide that such a trade mark is not to be registered.

3. Any Member State may provide that a trade mark is not to be registered or, if registered, is liable to be declared invalid where and to the extent that:

(a) the use of that trade mark may be prohibited pursuant to provisions of law other than trade mark law of the Member State concerned or of the Union;
(b) the trade mark includes a sign of high symbolic value, in particular a religious symbol;
(c) the trade mark includes badges, emblems and escutcheons other than those covered by Article 6ter of the Paris Convention and which are of public interest, unless the consent of the competent authority to their registration has been given in conformity with the law of the Member State.

4. A trade mark shall not be refused registration in accordance with paragraph 1(b), (c) or (d) if, before the date of application for registration, following the use which has been made of it, it has acquired a distinctive character. A trade mark shall not be declared invalid for the same reasons if, before the date of application for a declaration of invalidity, following the use which has been made of it, it has acquired a distinctive character.

5. Any Member State may provide that paragraph 4 is also to apply where the distinctive character was acquired after the date of application for registration but before the date of registration.

Article 5
Relative grounds for refusal or invalidity

1. A trade mark shall not be registered or, if registered, shall be liable to be declared invalid where:

(a) it is identical with an earlier trade mark, and the goods or services for which the trade mark is applied for or is registered are identical with the goods or services for which the earlier trade mark is protected;
(b) because of its identity with, or similarity to, the earlier trade mark and the identity or similarity of the goods or services covered by the trade marks, there exists a likelihood of confusion on the part of the public; the likeli-

hood of confusion includes the likelihood of association with the earlier trade mark.

2. 'Earlier trade marks' within the meaning of paragraph 1 means:

(a) trade marks of the following kinds with a date of application for registration which is earlier than the date of application for registration of the trade mark, taking account, where appropriate, of the priorities claimed in respect of those trade marks:
   (i) EU trade marks;
   (ii) trade marks registered in the Member State concerned or, in the case of Belgium, Luxembourg or the Netherlands, at the Benelux Office for Intellectual Property;
   (iii) trade marks registered under international arrangements which have effect in the Member State concerned;
(b) EU trade marks which validly claim seniority, in accordance with Regulation (EC) No 207/2009, of a trade mark referred to in points (a)(ii) and (iii), even when the latter trade mark has been surrendered or allowed to lapse;
(c) applications for the trade marks referred to in points (a) and (b), subject to their registration;
(d) trade marks which, on the date of application for registration of the trade mark, or, where appropriate, of the priority claimed in respect of the application for registration of the trade mark, are well known in the Member State concerned, in the sense in which the words 'well-known' are used in Article 6bis of the Paris Convention.

3. Furthermore, a trade mark shall not be registered or, if registered, shall be liable to be declared invalid where:

(a) it is identical with, or similar to, an earlier trade mark irrespective of whether the goods or services for which it is applied or registered are identical with, similar to or not similar to those for which the earlier trade mark is registered, where the earlier trade mark has a reputation in the Member State in respect of which registration is applied for or in which the trade mark is registered or, in the case of an EU trade mark, has a reputation in the Union and the use of the later trade mark without due cause would take unfair advantage of, or be detrimental to, the distinctive character or the repute of the earlier trade mark;
(b) an agent or representative of the proprietor of the trade mark applies for registration thereof in his own name without the proprietor's authorisation, unless the agent or representative justifies his action;
(c) and to the extent that, pursuant to Union legislation or the law of the Member State concerned providing for protection of designations of origin and geographical indications:
   (i) an application for a designation of origin or a geographical indication had already been submitted in accordance with Union legislation or the law of the Member State concerned prior to the date of application for registration of the trade mark or the date of the priority claimed for the application, subject to its subsequent registration;
   (ii) that designation of origin or geographical indication confers on the person authorised under the relevant law to exercise the rights arising therefrom the right to prohibit the use of a subsequent trade mark.

4. Any Member State may provide that a trade mark is not to be registered or, if registered, is liable to be declared invalid where, and to the extent that:

(a) rights to a non-registered trade mark or to another sign used in the course of trade were acquired prior to the date of application for registration of the subsequent trade mark, or the date of the priority claimed for the application for registration of the subsequent trade mark, and that non-registered trade mark or other sign confers on its proprietor the right to prohibit the use of a subsequent trade mark;
(b) the use of the trade mark may be prohibited by virtue of an earlier right, other than the rights referred to in paragraph 2 and point (a) of this paragraph, and in particular:
    (i) a right to a name;
    (ii) a right of personal portrayal;
    (iii) a copyright;
    (iv) an industrial property right;
(c) the trade mark is liable to be confused with an earlier trade mark protected abroad, provided that, at the date of the application, the applicant was acting in bad faith.

5. The Member States shall ensure that in appropriate circumstances there is no obligation to refuse registration or to declare a trade mark invalid where the proprietor of the earlier trade mark or other earlier right consents to the registration of the later trade mark.

6. Any Member State may provide that, by way of derogation from paragraphs 1 to 5, the grounds for refusal of registration or invalidity in force in that Member State prior to the date of the entry into force of the provisions necessary to comply with Directive 89/104/EEC are to apply to trade marks for which an application has been made prior to that date.

Article 6

Establishment a posteriori of invalidity or revocation of a trade mark

Where the seniority of a national trade mark or of a trade mark registered under international arrangements having effect in the Member State, which has been surrendered or allowed to lapse, is claimed for an EU trade mark, the invalidity or revocation of the trade mark providing the basis for the seniority claim may be established a posteriori, provided that the invalidity or revocation could have been declared at the time the mark was surrendered or allowed to lapse. In such a case, the seniority shall cease to produce its effects.

Article 7

Grounds for refusal or invalidity relating to only some of the goods or services

Where grounds for refusal of registration or for invalidity of a trade mark exist in respect of only some of the goods or services for which that trade mark has been applied or registered, refusal of registration or invalidity shall cover those goods or services only.

Article 8

Lack of distinctive character or of reputation of an earlier trade mark precluding a declaration of invalidity of a registered trade mark

An application for a declaration of invalidity on the basis of an earlier trade mark shall not succeed at the date of application for invalidation if it would not have been successful at the filing date or the priority date of the later trade mark for any of the following reasons:

(a) the earlier trade mark, liable to be declared invalid pursuant to Article 4(1)(b), (c) or (d), had not yet acquired a distinctive character as referred to in Article 4(4);
(b) the application for a declaration of invalidity is based on Article 5(1)(b) and the earlier trade mark had not yet become sufficiently distinctive to support a finding of likelihood of confusion within the meaning of Article 5(1)(b);
(c) the application for a declaration of invalidity is based on Article 5(3)(a) and the earlier trade mark had not yet acquired a reputation within the meaning of Article 5(3)(a).

Article 9

Preclusion of a declaration of invalidity due to acquiescence

1. Where, in a Member State, the proprietor of an earlier trade mark as referred to in Article 5(2) or Article 5(3)(a) has acquiesced, for a period of five successive years, in the use of a later trade mark registered in that Member State while being aware of such use, that proprietor shall no longer be entitled on the basis of the earlier trade mark to apply for a declaration that the later trade mark is invalid in respect of the goods or services for which the later trade mark has been used, unless registration of the later trade mark was applied for in bad faith.

2. Member States may provide that paragraph 1 of this Article is to apply to the proprietor of any other earlier right referred to in Article 5(4)(a) or (b).

3. In the cases referred to in paragraphs 1 and 2, the proprietor of a later registered trade mark shall not be entitled to oppose the use of the earlier right, even though that right may no longer be invoked against the later trade mark.

Section 3 Rights conferred and limitations

Article 10

Rights conferred by a trade mark

1. The registration of a trade mark shall confer on the proprietor exclusive rights therein.

2. Without prejudice to the rights of proprietors acquired before the filing date or the priority date of the registered trade mark, the proprietor of that registered trade mark shall be entitled to prevent all third parties not having his consent from using in the course of trade, in relation to goods or services, any sign where:

(a) the sign is identical with the trade mark and is used in relation to goods or services which are identical with those for which the trade mark is registered;

(b) the sign is identical with, or similar to, the trade mark and is used in relation to goods or services which are identical with, or similar to, the goods or services for which the trade mark is registered, if there exists a likelihood of confusion on the part of the public; the likelihood of confusion includes the likelihood of association between the sign and the trade mark;
(c) the sign is identical with, or similar to, the trade mark irrespective of whether it is used in relation to goods or services which are identical with, similar to, or not similar to, those for which the trade mark is registered, where the latter has a reputation in the Member State and where use of that sign without due cause takes unfair advantage of, or is detrimental to, the distinctive character or the repute of the trade mark.

3. The following, in particular, may be prohibited under paragraph 2:

(a) affixing the sign to the goods or to the packaging thereof;
(b) offering the goods or putting them on the market, or stocking them for those purposes, under the sign, or offering or supplying services thereunder;
(c) importing or exporting the goods under the sign;
(d) using the sign as a trade or company name or part of a trade or company name;
(e) using the sign on business papers and in advertising;
(f) using the sign in comparative advertising in a manner that is contrary to Directive 2006/114/EC.

4. Without prejudice to the rights of proprietors acquired before the filing date or the priority date of the registered trade mark, the proprietor of that registered trade mark shall also be entitled to prevent all third parties from bringing goods, in the course of trade, into the Member State where the trade mark is registered, without being released for free circulation there, where such goods, including the packaging thereof, come from third countries and bear without authorisation a trade mark which is identical with the trade mark registered in respect of such goods, or which cannot be distinguished in its essential aspects from that trade mark.

The entitlement of the trade mark proprietor pursuant to the first subparagraph shall lapse if, during the proceedings to determine whether the registered trade mark has been infringed, initiated in accordance with Regulation (EU) No 608/2013, evidence is provided by the declarant or the holder of the goods that the proprietor of the registered trade mark is not entitled to prohibit the placing of the goods on the market in the country of final destination.

5. Where, under the law of a Member State, the use of a sign under the conditions referred to in paragraph 2 (b) or (c) could not be prohibited before the date of entry into force of the provisions necessary to comply with Directive 89/104/EEC in the Member State concerned, the rights conferred by the trade mark may not be relied on to prevent the continued use of the sign.

6. Paragraphs 1, 2, 3 and 5 shall not affect provisions in any Member State relating to the protection against the use of a sign other than use for the purposes of distinguishing goods or services, where use of that sign without due cause takes unfair advantage of, or is detrimental to, the distinctive character or the repute of the trade mark.

Article 11

The right to prohibit preparatory acts in relation to the use of packaging or other means

Where the risk exists that the packaging, labels, tags, security or authenticity features or devices, or any other means to which the trade mark is affixed, could be used in relation to goods or services and that use would constitute an infringement of the rights of the proprietor of a trade mark under Article 10(2) and (3), the proprietor of that trade mark shall have the right to prohibit the following acts if carried out in the course of trade:

(a) affixing a sign identical with, or similar to, the trade mark on packaging, labels, tags, security or authenticity features or devices, or any other means to which the mark may be affixed;
(b) offering or placing on the market, or stocking for those purposes, or importing or exporting, packaging, labels, tags, security or authenticity features or devices, or any other means to which the mark is affixed.

Article 12

Reproduction of trade marks in dictionaries

If the reproduction of a trade mark in a dictionary, encyclopaedia or similar reference work, in print or electronic form, gives the impression that it constitutes the generic name of the goods or services for which the trade mark is registered, the publisher of the work shall, at the request of the proprietor of the trade mark, ensure that the reproduction of the trade mark is, without delay, and in the case of works in printed form at the latest in the next edition of the publication, accompanied by an indication that it is a registered trade mark.

Article 13

Prohibition of the use of a trade mark registered in the name of an agent or representative

1. Where a trade mark is registered in the name of the agent or representative of a person who is the proprietor of that trade mark, without the proprietor's consent, the latter shall be entitled to do either or both of the following:

(a) oppose the use of the trade mark by his agent or representative;
(b) demand the assignment of the trade mark in his favour.

2. Paragraph 1 shall not apply where the agent or representative justifies his action.

Article 14

Limitation of the effects of a trade mark

1. A trade mark shall not entitle the proprietor to prohibit a third party from using, in the course of trade:

(a) the name or address of the third party, where that third party is a natural person;

(b) signs or indications which are not distinctive or which concern the kind, quality, quantity, intended purpose, value, geographical origin, the time of production of goods or of rendering of the service, or other characteristics of goods or services;
(c) the trade mark for the purpose of identifying or referring to goods or services as those of the proprietor of that trade mark, in particular, where the use of the trade mark is necessary to indicate the intended purpose of a product or service, in particular as accessories or spare parts.

2. Paragraph 1 shall only apply where the use made by the third party is in accordance with honest practices in industrial or commercial matters.

3. A trade mark shall not entitle the proprietor to prohibit a third party from using, in the course of trade, an earlier right which only applies in a particular locality, if that right is recognised by the law of the Member State in question and the use of that right is within the limits of the territory in which it is recognised.

Article 15
Exhaustion of the rights conferred by a trade mark

1. A trade mark shall not entitle the proprietor to prohibit its use in relation to goods which have been put on the market in the Union under that trade mark by the proprietor or with the proprietor's consent.

2. Paragraph 1 shall not apply where there exist legitimate reasons for the proprietor to oppose further commercialisation of the goods, especially where the condition of the goods is changed or impaired after they have been put on the market.

Article 16
Use of trade marks

1. If, within a period of five years following the date of the completion of the registration procedure, the proprietor has not put the trade mark to genuine use in the Member State in connection with the goods or services in respect of which it is registered, or if such use has been suspended during a continuous five-year period, the trade mark shall be subject to the limits and sanctions provided for in Article 17, Article 19(1), Article 44(1) and (2), and Article 46(3) and (4), unless there are proper reasons for non-use.

2. Where a Member State provides for opposition proceedings following registration, the five-year period referred to in paragraph 1 shall be calculated from the date when the mark can no longer be opposed or, in the event that an opposition has been lodged, from the date when a decision terminating the opposition proceedings became final or the opposition was withdrawn.

3. With regard to trade marks registered under international arrangements and having effect in the Member State, the five-year period referred to in paragraph 1 shall be calculated from the date when the mark can no longer be rejected or opposed. Where an opposition has been lodged or when an objection on absolute or relative grounds has been notified, the period shall be calculated from the date

when a decision terminating the opposition proceedings or a ruling on absolute or relative grounds for refusal became final or the opposition was withdrawn.

4. The date of commencement of the five-year period, as referred to in paragraphs 1 and 2, shall be entered in the register.

5. The following shall also constitute use within the meaning of paragraph 1:

(a) use of the trade mark in a form differing in elements which do not alter the distinctive character of the mark in the form in which it was registered, regardless of whether or not the trade mark in the form as used is also registered in the name of the proprietor;
(b) affixing of the trade mark to goods or to the packaging thereof in the Member State concerned solely for export purposes.

6. Use of the trade mark with the consent of the proprietor shall be deemed to constitute use by the proprietor.

Article 17
Non-use as defence in infringement proceedings

The proprietor of a trade mark shall be entitled to prohibit the use of a sign only to the extent that the proprietor's rights are not liable to be revoked pursuant to Article 19 at the time the infringement action is brought. If the defendant so requests, the proprietor of the trade mark shall furnish proof that, during the five-year period preceding the date of bringing the action, the trade mark has been put to genuine use as provided in Article 16 in connection with the goods or services in respect of which it is registered and which are cited as justification for the action, or that there are proper reasons for non-use, provided that the registration procedure of the trade mark has at the date of bringing the action been completed for not less than five years.

Article 18
Intervening right of the proprietor of a later registered trade mark as defence in infringement proceedings

1. In infringement proceedings, the proprietor of a trade mark shall not be entitled to prohibit the use of a later registered mark where that later trade mark would not be declared invalid pursuant to Article 8, Article 9(1) or (2) or Article 46(3).

2. In infringement proceedings, the proprietor of a trade mark shall not be entitled to prohibit the use of a later registered EU trade mark where that later trade mark would not be declared invalid pursuant to Article 53(1), (3) or (4), 54(1) or (2) or 57(2) of Regulation (EC) No 207/2009.

3. Where the proprietor of a trade mark is not entitled to prohibit the use of a later registered trade mark pursuant to paragraph 1 or 2, the proprietor of that later registered trade mark shall not be entitled to prohibit the use of the earlier trade mark in infringement proceedings, even though that earlier right may no longer be invoked against the later trade mark.

Section 4 Revocation of trade mark rights

Article 19

Absence of genuine use as ground for revocation

1. A trade mark shall be liable to revocation if, within a continuous five-year period, it has not been put to genuine use in the Member State in connection with the goods or services in respect of which it is registered, and there are no proper reasons for non-use.

2. No person may claim that the proprietor's rights in a trade mark should be revoked where, during the interval between expiry of the five-year period and filing of the application for revocation, genuine use of the trade mark has been started or resumed.

3. The commencement or resumption of use within the three-month period preceding the filing of the application for revocation which began at the earliest on expiry of the continuous five-year period of non-use shall be disregarded where preparations for the commencement or resumption occur only after the proprietor becomes aware that the application for revocation may be filed.

Article 20

Trade mark having become generic or misleading indication as grounds for revocation

A trade mark shall be liable to revocation if, after the date on which it was registered:

(a) as a result of acts or inactivity of the proprietor, it has become the common name in the trade for a product or service in respect of which it is registered;

(b) as a result of the use made of it by the proprietor of the trade mark or with the proprietor's consent in respect of the goods or services for which it is registered, it is liable to mislead the public, particularly as to the nature, quality or geographical origin of those goods or services.

Article 21

Revocation relating to only some of the goods or services

Where grounds for revocation of a trade mark exist in respect of only some of the goods or services for which that trade mark has been registered, revocation shall cover those goods or services only.

Section 5 Trade marks as objects of property

Article 22

Transfer of registered trade marks

1. A trade mark may be transferred, separately from any transfer of the undertaking, in respect of some or all of the goods or services for which it is registered.

2. A transfer of the whole of the undertaking shall include the transfer of the trade mark except where there is agreement to the contrary or circumstances

clearly dictate otherwise. This provision shall apply to the contractual obligation to transfer the undertaking.

3. Member States shall have procedures in place to allow for the recordal of transfers in their registers.

Article 23
Rights in rem

1. A trade mark may, independently of the undertaking, be given as security or be the subject of rights in rem.

2. Member States shall have procedures in place to allow for the recordal of rights in rem in their registers.

Article 24
Levy of execution

1. A trade mark may be levied in execution.

2. Member States shall have procedures in place to allow for the recordal of levy of execution in their registers.

Article 25
Licensing

1. A trade mark may be licensed for some or all of the goods or services for which it is registered and for the whole or part of the Member State concerned. A licence may be exclusive or non-exclusive.

2. The proprietor of a trade mark may invoke the rights conferred by that trade mark against a licensee who contravenes any provision in his licensing contract with regard to:

(a) its duration;
(b) the form covered by the registration in which the trade mark may be used;
(c) the scope of the goods or services for which the licence is granted;
(d) the territory in which the trade mark may be affixed; or
(e) the quality of the goods manufactured or of the services provided by the licensee.

3. Without prejudice to the provisions of the licensing contract, the licensee may bring proceedings for infringement of a trade mark only if its proprietor consents thereto. However, the holder of an exclusive licence may bring such proceedings if the proprietor of the trade mark, after formal notice, does not himself bring infringement proceedings within an appropriate period.

4. A licensee shall, for the purpose of obtaining compensation for damage suffered by him, be entitled to intervene in infringement proceedings brought by the proprietor of the trade mark.

5. Member States shall have procedures in place to allow for the recordal of licences in their registers.

Article 26
Applications for a trade mark as an object of property

Articles 22 to 25 shall apply to applications for trade marks.

Section 6 Guarantee or certification marks and collective marks

Article 27
Definitions

For the purposes of this Directive, the following definitions apply:

(a) 'guarantee or certification mark' means a trade mark which is described as such when the mark is applied for and is capable of distinguishing goods or services which are certified by the proprietor of the mark in respect of material, mode of manufacture of goods or performance of services, quality, accuracy or other characteristics, from goods and services which are not so certified;

(b) 'collective mark' means a trade mark which is described as such when the mark is applied for and is capable of distinguishing the goods or services of the members of an association which is the proprietor of the mark from the goods or services of other undertakings.

Article 28
Guarantee or certification marks

1. Member States may provide for the registration of guarantee or certification marks.

2. Any natural or legal person, including institutions, authorities and bodies governed by public law, may apply for guarantee or certification marks provided that such person does not carry on a business involving the supply of goods or services of the kind certified.

Member States may provide that a guarantee or certification mark is not to be registered unless the applicant is competent to certify the goods or services for which the mark is to be registered.

3. Member States may provide that guarantee or certification marks are not to be registered, or are to be revoked or declared invalid, on grounds other than those specified in Articles 4, 19 and 20, where the function of those marks so requires.

4. By way of derogation from Article 4(1)(c), Member States may provide that signs or indications which may serve, in trade, to designate the geographical origin of the goods or services may constitute guarantee or certification marks. Such a guarantee or certification mark shall not entitle the proprietor to prohibit a third party from using in the course of trade such signs or indications, provided that third party uses them in accordance with honest practices in industrial or commercial matters. In particular, such a mark may not be invoked against a third party who is entitled to use a geographical name.

5. The requirements laid down in Article 16 shall be satisfied where genuine use of a guarantee or certification mark in accordance with Article 16 is made by any person who has the authority to use it.

Article 29
Collective marks

1. Member States shall provide for the registration of collective marks.

2. Associations of manufacturers, producers, suppliers of services or traders, which, under the terms of the law governing them, have the capacity in their own name to have rights and obligations, to make contracts or accomplish other legal acts, and to sue and be sued, as well as legal persons governed by public law, may apply for collective marks.

3. By way of derogation from Article 4(1)(c), Member States may provide that signs or indications which may serve, in trade, to designate the geographical origin of the goods or services may constitute collective marks. Such a collective mark shall not entitle the proprietor to prohibit a third party from using, in the course of trade, such signs or indications, provided that third party uses them in accordance with honest practices in industrial or commercial matters. In particular, such a mark may not be invoked against a third party who is entitled to use a geographical name.

Article 30
Regulations governing use of a collective mark

1. An applicant for a collective mark shall submit the regulations governing its use to the office.

2. The regulations governing use shall specify at least the persons authorised to use the mark, the conditions of membership of the association and the conditions of use of the mark, including sanctions. The regulations governing use of a mark referred to in Article 29(3) shall authorise any person whose goods or services originate in the geographical area concerned to become a member of the association which is the proprietor of the mark, provided that the person fulfils all the other conditions of the regulations.

Article 31
Refusal of an application

1. In addition to the grounds for refusal of a trade mark application provided for in Article 4, where appropriate with the exception of Article 4(1)(c) concerning signs or indications which may serve, in trade, to designate the geographical origin of the goods or services, and Article 5,and without prejudice to the right of an office not to undertake examination ex officio of relative grounds, an application for a collective mark shall be refused where the provisions of point (b) of Article 27, Article 29 or Article 30 are not satisfied, or where the regulations governing use of that collective mark are contrary to public policy or to accepted principles of morality.

2. An application for a collective mark shall also be refused if the public is liable to be misled as regards the character or the significance of the mark, in particular if it is likely to be taken to be something other than a collective mark.

3. An application shall not be refused if the applicant, as a result of amendment of the regulations governing use of the collective mark, meets the requirements referred to in paragraphs 1 and 2.

Article 32
Use of collective marks

The requirements of Article 16 shall be satisfied where genuine use of a collective mark in accordance with that Article is made by any person who has authority to use it.

Article 33
Amendments to the regulations governing use of a collective mark

1. The proprietor of a collective mark shall submit to the office any amended regulations governing use.

2. Amendments to the regulations governing use shall be mentioned in the register unless the amended regulations do not satisfy the requirements of Article 30 or involve one of the grounds for refusal referred to in Article 31.

3. For the purposes of this Directive, amendments to the regulations governing use shall take effect only from the date of entry of the mention of those amendments in the register.

Article 34
Persons entitled to bring an action for infringement

1. Article 25(3) and (4) shall apply to every person who has the authority to use a collective mark.

2. The proprietor of a collective mark shall be entitled to claim compensation on behalf of persons who have authority to use the mark where those persons have sustained damage as a result of unauthorised use of the mark.

Article 35
Additional grounds for revocation

In addition to the grounds for revocation provided for in Articles 19 and 20, the rights of the proprietor of a collective mark shall be revoked on the following grounds:

(a) the proprietor does not take reasonable steps to prevent the mark being used in a manner that is incompatible with the conditions of use laid down in the regulations governing use, including any amendments thereto mentioned in the register;

(b) the manner in which the mark has been used by authorised persons has caused it to become liable to mislead the public in the manner referred to in Article 31(2);

(c) an amendment to the regulations governing use of the mark has been mentioned in the register in breach of Article 33(2), unless the proprietor of the mark, by further amending the regulations governing use, complies with the requirements of that Article.

Article 36

Additional grounds for invalidity

In addition to the grounds for invalidity provided for in Article 4, where appropriate with the exception of Article 4(1)(c) concerning signs or indications which may serve, in trade, to designate the geographical origin of the goods or services, and Article 5, a collective mark which is registered in breach of Article 31 shall be declared invalid unless the proprietor of the mark, by amending the regulations governing use, complies with the requirements of Article 31.

CHAPTER 3 PROCEDURES

Section 1 Application and registration

Article 37

Application requirements

1. An application for registration of a trade mark shall contain at least all of the following:

(a) a request for registration;
(b) information identifying the applicant;
(c) a list of the goods or services in respect of which the registration is requested;
(d) a representation of the trade mark, which satisfies the requirements set out in point (b) of Article 3.

2. The application for a trade mark shall be subject to the payment of a fee determined by the Member State concerned.

Article 38

Date of filing

1. The date of filing of a trade mark application shall be the date on which the documents containing the information specified in Article 37(1) are filed with the office by the applicant.

2. Member States may, in addition, provide that the accordance of the date of filing is to be subject to the payment of a fee as referred to in Article 37(2).

Article 39

Designation and classification of goods and services

1. The goods and services in respect of which trade mark registration is applied for shall be classified in conformity with the system of classification established by the Nice Agreement Concerning the International Classification of Goods and

Services for the Purposes of the Registration of Marks of 15 June 1957 ('the Nice Classification').

2. The goods and services for which protection is sought shall be identified by the applicant with sufficient clarity and precision to enable the competent authorities and economic operators, on that sole basis, to determine the extent of the protection sought.

3. For the purposes of paragraph 2, the general indications included in the class headings of the Nice Classification or other general terms may be used, provided that they comply with the requisite standards of clarity and precision set out in this Article.

4. The office shall reject an application in respect of indications or terms which are unclear or imprecise, where the applicant does not suggest an acceptable wording within a period set by the office to that effect.

5. The use of general terms, including the general indications of the class headings of the Nice Classification, shall be interpreted as including all the goods or services clearly covered by the literal meaning of the indication or term. The use of such terms or indications shall not be interpreted as comprising a claim to goods or services which cannot be so understood.

6. Where the applicant requests registration for more than one class, the applicant shall group the goods and services according to the classes of the Nice Classification, each group being preceded by the number of the class to which that group of goods or services belongs, and shall present them in the order of the classes.

7. Goods and services shall not be regarded as being similar to each other on the ground that they appear in the same class under the Nice Classification. Goods and services shall not be regarded as being dissimilar from each other on the ground that they appear in different classes under the Nice Classification.

Article 40
Observations by third parties

1. Member States may provide that prior to registration of a trade mark, any natural or legal person and any group or body representing manufacturers, producers, suppliers of services, traders or consumers may submit to the office written observations, explaining on which grounds the trade mark should not be registered ex officio.

Persons and groups or bodies, as referred to in the first subparagraph, shall not be parties to the proceedings before the office.

2. In addition to the grounds referred to in paragraph 1 of this Article, any natural or legal person and any group or body representing manufacturers, producers, suppliers of services, traders or consumers may submit to the office written observations based on the particular grounds on which the application for a collective mark should be refused under Article 31(1) and (2). This provision may be extended to cover certification and guarantee marks where regulated in Member States.

Article 41

Division of applications and registrations

The applicant or proprietor may divide a national trade mark application or registration into two or more separate applications or registrations by sending a declaration to the office and indicating for each divisional application or registration the goods or services covered by the original application or registration which are to be covered by the divisional applications or registrations.

Article 42

Class fees

Member States may provide that the application and renewal of a trade mark is to be subject to an additional fee for each class of goods and services beyond the first class.

Section 2 Procedures for opposition, revocation and invalidity

Article 43

Opposition procedure

1. Member States shall provide for an efficient and expeditious administrative procedure before their offices for opposing the registration of a trade mark application on the grounds provided for in Article 5.

2. The administrative procedure referred to in paragraph 1 of this Article shall at least provide that the proprietor of an earlier trade mark as referred to in Article 5(2) and Article 5(3)(a), and the person authorised under the relevant law to exercise the rights arising from a protected designation of origin or geographical indication as referred to in Article 5(3)(c) shall be entitled to file a notice of opposition. A notice of opposition may be filed on the basis of one or more earlier rights, provided that they all belong to the same proprietor, and on the basis of part or the totality of the goods or services in respect of which the earlier right is protected or applied for, and may be directed against part or the totality of the goods or services in respect of which the contested mark is applied for.

3. The parties shall be granted, at their joint request, a minimum of two months in the opposition proceedings in order to allow for the possibility of a friendly settlement between the opposing party and the applicant.

Article 44

Non-use as defence in opposition proceedings

1. In opposition proceedings pursuant to Article 43, where at the filing date or date of priority of the later trade mark, the five-year period within which the earlier trade mark must have been put to genuine use as provided for in Article 16 had expired, at the request of the applicant, the proprietor of the earlier trade mark who has given notice of opposition shall furnish proof that the earlier trade mark has been put to genuine use as provided for in Article 16 during the five-year period preceding the filing date or date of priority of the later trade mark, or that proper reasons for non-use existed. In the absence of proof to this effect, the opposition shall be rejected.

2. If the earlier trade mark has been used in relation to only part of the goods or services for which it is registered, it shall, for the purpose of the examination of the opposition as provided for in paragraph 1, be deemed to be registered in respect of that part of the goods or services only.

3. Paragraphs 1 and 2 of this Article shall also apply where the earlier trade mark is an EU trade mark. In such a case, the genuine use of the EU trade mark shall be determined in accordance with Article 15 of Regulation (EC) No 207/2009.

Article 45

Procedure for revocation or declaration of invalidity

1. Without prejudice to the right of the parties to appeal to the courts, Member States shall provide for an efficient and expeditious administrative procedure before their offices for the revocation or declaration of invalidity of a trade mark.

2. The administrative procedure for revocation shall provide that the trade mark is to be revoked on the grounds provided for in Articles 19 and 20.

3. The administrative procedure for invalidity shall provide that the trade mark is to be declared invalid at least on the following grounds:

(a) the trade mark should not have been registered because it does not comply with the requirements provided for in Article 4;
(b) the trade mark should not have been registered because of the existence of an earlier right within the meaning of Article 5(1) to (3).

4. The administrative procedure shall provide that at least the following are to be entitled to file an application for revocation or for a declaration of invalidity:

(a) in the case of paragraph 2 and paragraph 3(a), any natural or legal person and any group or body set up for the purpose of representing the interests of manufacturers, producers, suppliers of services, traders or consumers, and which, under the terms of the law governing it, has the capacity to sue in its own name and to be sued;
(b) in the case of paragraph 3(b) of this Article, the proprietor of an earlier trade mark as referred to in Article 5(2) and Article 5(3)(a), and the person authorised under the relevant law to exercise the rights arising from a protected designation of origin or geographical indication as referred to in Article 5(3)(c).

5. An application for revocation or for a declaration of invalidity may be directed against a part or the totality of the goods or services in respect of which the contested mark is registered.

6. An application for a declaration of invalidity may be filed on the basis of one or more earlier rights, provided they all belong to the same proprietor.

Article 46

Non-use as a defence in proceedings seeking a declaration of invalidity

1. In proceedings for a declaration of invalidity based on a registered trade mark with an earlier filing date or priority date, if the proprietor of the later trade mark

so requests, the proprietor of the earlier trade mark shall furnish proof that, during the five-year period preceding the date of the application for a declaration of invalidity, the earlier trade mark has been put to genuine use, as provided for in Article 16, in connection with the goods or services in respect of which it is registered and which are cited as justification for the application, or that there are proper reasons for non-use, provided that the registration process of the earlier trade mark has at the date of the application for a declaration of invalidity been completed for not less than five years.

2. Where, at the filing date or date of priority of the later trade mark, the five-year period within which the earlier trade mark was to have been put to genuine use, as provided for in Article 16, had expired, the proprietor of the earlier trade mark shall, in addition to the proof required under paragraph 1 of this Article, furnish proof that the trade mark was put to genuine use during the five-year period preceding the filing date or date of priority, or that proper reasons for non-use existed.

3. In the absence of the proof referred to in paragraphs 1 and 2, an application for a declaration of invalidity on the basis of an earlier trade mark shall be rejected.

4. If the earlier trade mark has been used in accordance with Article 16 in relation to only part of the goods or services for which it is registered, it shall, for the purpose of the examination of the application for a declaration of invalidity, be deemed to be registered in respect of that part of the goods or services only.

5. Paragraphs 1 to 4 of this Article shall also apply where the earlier trade mark is an EU trade mark. In such a case, genuine use of the EU trade mark shall be determined in accordance with Article 15 of Regulation (EC) No 207/2009.

Article 47
Consequences of revocation and invalidity

1. A registered trade mark shall be deemed not to have had, as from the date of the application for revocation, the effects specified in this Directive, to the extent that the rights of the proprietor have been revoked. An earlier date, on which one of the grounds for revocation occurred, may be fixed in the decision on the application for revocation, at the request of one of the parties.

2. A registered trade mark shall be deemed not to have had, as from the outset, the effects specified in this Directive, to the extent that the trade mark has been declared invalid.

Section 3 Duration and renewal of registration

Article 48
Duration of registration

1. Trade marks shall be registered for a period of 10 years from the date of filing of the application.

2. Registration may be renewed in accordance with Article 49 for further 10-year periods.

Article 49
Renewal

1. Registration of a trade mark shall be renewed at the request of the proprietor of the trade mark or any person authorised to do so by law or by contract, provided that the renewal fees have been paid. Member States may provide that receipt of payment of the renewal fees is to be deemed to constitute such a request.

2. The office shall inform the proprietor of the trade mark of the expiry of the registration at least six months before the said expiry. The office shall not be held liable if it fails to give such information.

3. The request for renewal shall be submitted and the renewal fees shall be paid within a period of at least six months immediately preceding the expiry of the registration. Failing that, the request may be submitted within a further period of six months immediately following the expiry of the registration or of the subsequent renewal thereof. The renewal fees and an additional fee shall be paid within that further period.

4. Where the request is submitted or the fees paid in respect of only some of the goods or services for which the trade mark is registered, registration shall be renewed for those goods or services only.

5. Renewal shall take effect from the day following the date on which the existing registration expires. The renewal shall be recorded in the register.

Section 4 Communication with the office

Article 50
Communication with the office

Parties to the proceedings or, where appointed, their representatives, shall designate an official address for all official communication with the office. Member States shall have the right to require that such an official address be situated in the European Economic Area.

CHAPTER 4 ADMINISTRATIVE COOPERATION

Article 51
Cooperation in the area of trade mark registration and administration

The offices shall be free to cooperate effectively with each other and with the European Union Intellectual Property Office in order to promote convergence of practices and tools in relation to the examination and registration of trade marks.

Article 52
Cooperation in other areas

The offices shall be free to cooperate effectively with each other and with the European Union Intellectual Property Office in all areas of their activities other than those referred to in Article 51 which are of relevance for the protection of trade marks in the Union.

CHAPTER 5 FINAL PROVISIONS

Article 53
Data protection

The processing of any personal data carried out in the Member States in the framework of this Directive shall be subject to national law implementing Directive 95/46/EC.

Article 54
Transposition

1. Member States shall bring into force the laws, regulations and administrative provisions necessary to comply with Articles 3 to 6, Articles 8 to 14, Articles 16, 17 and 18, Articles 22 to 39, Article 41, Articles 43 to 50 by 14 January 2019. Member States shall bring into force the laws, regulations and administrative provisions to comply with Article 45 by 14 January 2023. They shall immediately communicate the text of those measures to the Commission.

When Member States adopt those measures, they shall contain a reference to this Directive or be accompanied by such a reference on the occasion of their official publication. They shall also include a statement that references in existing laws, regulations and administrative provisions to the Directive repealed by this Directive shall be construed as references to this Directive. Member States shall determine how such reference is to be made and how that statement is to be formulated.

2. Member States shall communicate to the Commission the text of the main provisions of national law which they adopt in the field covered by this Directive.

Article 55
Repeal

Directive 2008/95/EC is repealed with effect from 15 January 2019, without prejudice to the obligations of the Member States relating to the time limit for the transposition into national law of Directive 89/104/EEC set out in Part B of Annex I to Directive 2008/95/EC.

References to the repealed Directive shall be construed as references to this Directive and shall be read in accordance with the correlation table in the Annex.

Article 56
Entry into Force

This Directive shall enter into force on the twentieth day following that of its publication in the Official Journal of the European Union.

Articles 1, 7, 15, 19, 20, 21 and 54 to 57 shall apply from 15 January 2019.

Article 57
Addressees

This Directive is addressed to the Member States.

Done at Strasbourg, 16 December 2015.

For the European Parliament

The President

M. SCHULZ

For the Council

The President

N. SCHMIT

ANNEX CORRELATION TABLE

Directive 2008/95/EC	This Directive
Article 1	Article 1
—	Article 2
Article 2	Article 3
Article 3(1)(a) to (h)	Article 4(1)(a) to (h)
—	Article 4(1)(i) to (l)
Article 3(2)(a) to (c)	Article 4(3)(a) to (c)
Article 3(2)(d)	Article 4(2)
Article 3(3), first sentence	Article 4(4), first sentence
—	Article 4(4), second sentence
Article 3(3), second sentence	Article 4(5)
Article 3(4)	—
Article 4(1) and (2)	Article 5(1) and (2)
Article 4(3) and (4)(a)	Article 5(3)(a)
—	Article 5(3)(b)
—	Article 5(3)(c)
Article 4(4)(b) and (c)	Article 5(4)(a) and (b)
Article 4(4)(d) to (f)	—
Article 4(4)(g)	Article 5(4)(c)
Article 4(5) and (6)	Article 5(5) and (6)
—	Article 8
Article 5(1), first sentence	Article 10(1)
Article 5(1), second sentence, introductory part	Article 10(2), introductory part of the sentence
Article 5(1)(a) and (b)	Article 10(2)(a) and (b)

Directive 2008/95/EC	This Directive
Article 5(2)	Article 10(2)(c)
Article 5(3)(a) to (c)	Article 10(3)(a) to (c)
—	Article 10(3)(d)
Article 5(3)(d)	Article 10(3)(e)
—	Article 10(3)(f)
—	Article 10(4)
Article 5(4) and (5)	Article 10(5) and (6)
—	Article 11
—	Article 12
—	Article 13
Article 6(1)(a) to (c)	Article 14(1)(a) to (c), and (2)
Article 6(2)	Article 14(3)
Article 7	Article 15
Article 8(1) and (2)	Article 25(1) and (2)
—	Article 25(3) to (5)
Article 9	Article 9
Article 10(1), first subparagraph	Article 16(1)
—	Article 16(2) to (4)
Article 10(1), second subparagraph	Article 16(5)
Article 10(2)	Article 16(6)
Article 10(3)	—
Article 11(1)	Article 46(1) to (3)
Article 11(2)	Article 44(1)
Article 11(3)	Article 17
Article 11(4)	Articles 17, 44(2) and Article 46(4)
—	Article 18
Article 12(1), first subparagraph	Article 19(1)
Article 12(1), second subparagraph	Article 19(2)
Article 12(1), third subparagraph	Article 19(3)
Article 12(2)	Article 20
Article 13	Article 7 and Article 21
Article 14	Article 6
—	Articles 22 to 24
—	Article 26
—	Article 27
Article 15(1)	Article 28(1) and (3)
Article 15(2)	Article 28(4)
—	Article 28(2) and (5)
—	Articles 29 to 54(1)

Directive 2008/95/EC	This Directive
Article 16	Article 54(2)
Article 17	Article 55
Article 18	Article 56
Article 19	Article 57

Index

[all references are to paragraph number]

Absolute grounds for refusal of registration
acquired distinctiveness – s 3(1); Art 7(3), 4.34–4.39
bad faith registration – s 3(6); Art 59(1)(b), 4.55–4.59
collective marks, and, 3.13–3.15
contrary to law – s 3(4), 4.52
contrary to policy or morality – s 3(3)(a); Art 7(1)(f), 4.45–4.48
deceptive trade marks – s 3(3)(b); Art 7(1)(g), 4.49–4.51
descriptive marks – s 3(1)(c); Art 7(1)(c), 4.19–4.29
devoid of distinctive character – s 3(1)(b); Art 7(1)(b), 4.07–4.18
emblems – ss 3(5), 4, 57 and 58; Arts 7(1)(h) and 7(1)(i), 4.53–4.54
generally, 4.01–4.05
generic marks – s 3(1)(c); Art 7(1)(c), 4.30–4.33
shape of goods – s 3(2); Art 7(1)(e), 4.40–4.44
signs which do not satisfy requirements of s 1(1) – s 3(1)(a); Art 7(1)(a), 4.06

Account of profits
election, 17.05–17.07
generally, 17.17–17.19
Olympic symbols rights, and, 21.16
passing off, and, 20.103–20.104

Acquiescence
defences to infringement, and, 15.27–15.30

Acquiescence – *contd*
invalidity proceedings, and
awareness of full use of later mark, 11.10
commencement of relevant period, 11.08
effect of finding, 11.11
EUTM registrations, 11.22–11.23
generally, 11.07
knowledge of registration of mark, 11.09

Acquired distinctiveness
absolute grounds of refusal, and, 4.34–4.39
evidence of likelihood of confusion in opposition to registration in UK, and, 7.56–7.57

Address for service
applications for registration in UK, and, 7.13

Advertising
comparative and misleading *see* **Comparative advertising**

Advertising functions
generally, 5.100–5.105
infringement, and, 14.34–14.35

Affixing sign to materials
infringement proceedings, and, 14.59–14.60

Agents
remedies for unauthorised application for registration, and
generally, 17.73–17.74
justification, 17.75

Amendment of applications
classification system, and, 6.16–6.17
filing of application for EUTM, and, 8.11
Amendment of regulations
collective and certification marks, and
European Union, 3.35
United Kingdom, 3.25
'Anton Piller' orders
generally, 17.29–17.30
Appeals
invalidity proceedings and
EUIPO, before, 11.36
UKIPO, before, 11.17
opposition to registration in UK, and, 7.81
registration of marks before EUIPO, and, 8.64
Applications for registration
absolute grounds for refusal
acquired distinctiveness – s 3(1); Art 7(3), 4.34–4.39
bad faith registration – s 3(6); Art 59(1)(b), 4.55–4.59
collective marks, and, 3.13–3.15
contrary to law – s 3(4), 4.52
contrary to policy or morality – s 3(3)(a); Art 7(1)(f), 4.45–4.48
deceptive trade marks – s 3(3)(b); Art 7(1)(g), 4.49–4.51
descriptive marks – s 3(1)(c); Art 7(1)(c), 4.19–4.29
devoid of distinctive character – s 3(1)(b); Art 7(1)(b), 4.07–4.18
emblems – ss 3(5), 4, 57 and 58; Arts 7(1)(h) and 7(1)(i), 4.53–4.54
generally, 4.01–4.05
generic marks – s 3(1)(c); Art 7(1)(c), 4.30–4.33
shape of goods – s 3(2); Art 7(1)(e), 4.40–4.44
signs which do not satisfy requirements of s 1(1) – s 3(1)(a); Art 7(1)(a), 4.06
Applications for registration – *contd*
certification marks, and
absolute grounds for refusal, 3.13–3.15
applicants, 3.08–3.11
generally, 3.06–3.07
invalidity, 3.27–3.29
misleading marks, 3.17–3.18
post-registration amendment of regulations, 3.24
post-registration transfer of ownership, 3.25–3.26
process, 3.12
revocation, 3.27–3.29
earlier marks, and, 5.07
EUIPO, before
see also **Applications for registration (EUIPO)**
appeals, 8.64
examination, 8.12–8.13
filing, 8.04–8.11
generally, 8.02–8.03
introduction, 8.01
opposition, 8.15–8.63
procedures, 8.02–8.03
publication, 8.14
international trade marks, and
see also **Applications for registration (WIPO)**
application form, 9.12–9.19
basic application, 9.08–9.11
consideration by WIPO, 9.20–9.29
designations with additional requirements, 9.30
introduction, 9.02
legal framework, 9.03
notification of office of origin, 9.31–9.43
outline, in, 9.04–9.07
WIPO, and, 9.03
relative grounds for refusal
applications for registration of earlier marks, and, 5.07
copyright, and, 5.93
design right, and, 5.93
detriment to distinctive character, 5.79–5.82
detriment to repute, 5.83–5.86

Applications for registration – *contd*
relative grounds for refusal – *contd*
distinctiveness of earlier mark through use, 5.56–5.58
'earlier trade mark', 5.10–5.12
extent of use of common elements of marks as used by parties, 5.59–5.61
harm to trade mark function, 5.06
identity of goods and services, 5.28–5.31
identity of marks, 5.13–5.16
interdependence of assessments of similarity, 5.53–5.55
introduction, 5.05
issues arising, 5.08–5.09
likelihood of confusion, 5.37–5.52
prior decisions, 5.62
reputation, 5.63–5.74
similarity of goods and services, 5.32–5.36
similarity of marks, 5.17–5.27
unfair advantage of distinctive character or repute, 5.75–5.78
unregistered marks used in course of trade, and, 5.91–5.92
use of later mark without due cause, 5.87–5.89
UKIPO, to
see also **Applications for registration (UK)**
address for service, 7.13
deficient, 7.11
examination, 7.14–7.16
fees, 7.06
filing, 7.07–7.10
form, 7.04–7.05
further requirements, 7.12–7.13
indication of class of goods or services, 7.12
introduction, 7.03
opposition, 7.18–7.82
publication, 7.17
Applications for registration (EUIPO)
amendment, 8.11
Applications for registration (EUIPO) – *contd*
applicant's details, 8.05
claiming priority, 8.09
claiming seniority, 8.10
contents, 8.05
examination, 8.12–8.13
fees, 8.07
filing
amendment of application, 8.11
applicant's details, 8.05
claiming priority, 8.09
claiming seniority, 8.10
further formalities, 8.07
introduction, 8.04
languages, 8.08
list of goods and services for which protection is sought, 8.05
payment of fees, 8.07
representation of mark, 8.06
request for registration, 8.05
requirements if application to be given filing date, 8.05
withdrawal of application, 8.11
generally, 8.02–8.03
guidance, 8.02
introduction, 8.01
list of goods and services for which protection is sought, 8.05
opposition
ability to act before EUIPO, 8.19–8.22
absolute admissibility requirements, 8.25–8.30
admissibility of notice of opposition, 8.23–8.24
applicant's evidence, 8.49–8.51
basis, 8.16–8.17
cooling-off period, 8.41
costs, 8.63
dates relating to earlier applications and registrations, 8.33
extent of opposition, 8.38–8.39
filing evidence, 8.42–8.43, 8.60–8.62
further elements, 8.37–8.40

Applications for registration (EUIPO) – *contd*
opposition – *contd*
further evidence and arguments, 8.59
generally, 8.15
genuine use, 8.52–8.58
identification of contested application, 8.27
identification of earlier mark or sign, 8.34
identification of earlier rights, 8.28–8.29
identification of goods and services, 8.35
identification of grounds, 8.30
language of documents, 8.47–8.48
notice, 8.15
observations in reply, 8.49–8.51
opponent's proof of genuine use, 8.54–8.55
payment of fees, 8.26
procedural requirements, 8.18–8.22
proof of existence and validity of earlier applications and registrations, 8.44–8.46
proof of genuine use, 8.54–8.58
reasoned statement, 8.40
relative admissibility requirements, 8.31–8.36
request that opponent proves use, 8.52–8.53
scope of reputation, 8.36
standing to file notice, 8.18
translation, 8.32
payment of fees, 8.07
priority, 8.09
procedures, 8.02–8.03
publication, 8.14
representation of mark, 8.06
request for registration, 8.05
search, 8.13
seniority, 8.10
withdrawal of application, 8.11
Applications for registration (UK)
address for service, 7.13
applicant's details, 7.09
Applications for registration (UK) – *contd*
dealings, and, 13.10
declaration that mark in use, 7.10
deficient application, 7.11
examination, 7.14–7.16
fees, 7.06
filing
applicant's details, 7.09
declaration that mark in use, 7.10
list of goods and services for which protection is sought, 7.09
method, 7.07
obtaining filing date, 7.09–7.10
payment of fees, 7.10
representation of mark, 7.09
request for registration, 7.09
requirements, 7.08
form, 7.04–7.05
indication of class of goods or services, 7.12
introduction, 7.01–7.02
list of goods and services for which protection is sought, 7.09
obtaining filing date, 7.09–7.10
opposition
appeals, 7.81
applicant's form, 7.31
challenging evidence, 7.66–7.67
cooling-off period, 7.28–7.30
costs, 7.75–7.76
counterstatement, 7.33–7.35
cross-examination, 7.68–7.72
evidence as to goods and services, 7.64–7.72
extension of cooling-off period, 7.29
extension of time for filing evidence, 7.48–7.49
fast-track oppositions, 7.77–7.80
filing evidence, 7.44–7.49
filing formalities, 7.23–7.26
form of evidence, 7.50–7.63
hearings, 7.73
introduction, 7.18
notice to proceed, 7.43
notification to applicant for mark, 7.27

Applications for registration (UK) – *contd*
opposition – *contd*
observations, 7.82
preliminary indications, 7.36–7.42
pre-opposition contact to applicant for mark, 7.21–7.22
request for opponent to prove use, 7.32
skeleton arguments, 7.74
statement of use of rights over five years old, 7.24–7.26
termination of cooling-off period, 7.30
time for filing, 7.19–7.20
time limits for filing evidence, 7.47
witness statements, 7.50–7.63
payment of fees, 7.10
preliminary indications
consequences, 7.39–7.42
implications, 7.37–7.38
introduction, 7.36
opposition based on other than s 5(1) or (2), 7.42
opposition based only on s 5(1) or (2), 7.41
publication, 7.17
representation of mark, 7.09
request for registration, 7.09
UKIPO, and, 7.01
Applications for registration (WIPO)
based on EUTM application or registration, 9.17
based on UKTM application or registration, 9.16
'basic' application
generally, 9.08–9.11
initial reliance on basic right, 9.11
introduction, 9.06
'basic' marks, 9.04
'central attack', 9.06
consideration by WIPO
formal irregularities, 9.20–9.24
Applications for registration (WIPO) – *contd*
consideration by WIPO – *contd*
irregularities as to specification of goods and services, 9.25–9.29
designation of countries, 9.04
designations with additional requirements, 9.30
EU trade marks (EUTMs), and, 9.04
examination, 9.19
fees, 9.18
formal irregularities
deadlines for resolution, 9.24
generally, 9.20
resolution by applicant, for, 9.22–9.23
resolution by Office of origin, for, 9.21–9.22
generally, 9.12–9.19
introduction, 9.02
irregularities as to specification of goods and services
generally, 9.25
incorrect classes or numbers of classes, 9.26–9.27
specification is unclear, 9.28–9.29
legal framework, 9.03
national marks, and, 9.04
notification of office of origin, 9.31–9.43
outline, in, 9.04–9.07
'real and effective establishment', 9.08–9.09
refusal of protection by designated office, 9.32–9.39
registration, 9.31
reliance on basic right, 9.11
strength of system, 9.05
WIPO, and, 9.03
Assents
UK trade marks (UKTMs), and, 13.08–13.09
Assignments
EU trade marks (EUTMs), and
effect vis-à-vis third parties, 13.54
generally, 13.51–13.53
recordal, 13.55–13.57

Assignments – *contd*
international marks, and 13.69–13.70
UK trade marks (UKTMs), and
generally, 13.05
introduction, 13.04
operation of law, by, 13.07
registration, 13.08–13.09
testamentary disposition, by, 13.06
Aural similarity
relative grounds for refusal, and, 5.25

Bad faith
absolute grounds of refusal, and, 4.55–4.59
classification system, and
generally, 6.10
introduction, 6.07
'Blurring'
infringement, and, 14.51–14.52
relative grounds for refusal, and, 5.80–5.82
Burden of proof
infringement proceedings, and, 14.04

Capable of being represented clearly and precisely
colours, 2.05
designs, 2.08
generally, 2.04
phrases, 2.09
shape of goods or packaging, 2.08
slogans, 2.09
smells, 2.07
sounds, 2.06
Capable of distinguishing goods or services
generally, 2.10
Certification marks *see* **Collective and certification marks**
Challenging evidence
opposition to registration in UK, and, 7.66–7.67
Claimants
co-proprietors, 14.62
licensees, 14.63
passing off, and, 20.07
proprietors, 14.61
Classification system
amendments to applications, 6.16–6.17
anticipated future areas of activity, 6.06
bad faith, and
generally, 6.10
introduction, 6.07
clarity, 6.04
competing third-party trade mark rights, 6.08
cost of protection, 6.11
declaration as to use or intention to use, 6.09
exclusions from protection, 6.12–6.13
existing future areas of activity, 6.06
general requirement, 6.01
headings, 6.05
intention to use, 6.09
Nice Classification, 6.02
post-Postkantoor practice, 6.12–6.13
precision, 6.04
requirement to specify class(es) and goods and/or services, 6.03
retail services, 6.14–6.15
shopping-centre services, 6.14–6.15
specifying goods and services
clarity, 6.04
existing and anticipated future areas of activity, 6.06
precision, 6.04
use of class headings, 6.05
UKIPO guidance, 6.02
use, 6.09
wholesale services, 6.14–6.15
widening scope of application after filing, 6.16–6.17
Collective and certification marks
see also **European Union collective and certification marks**
applications for registration
absolute grounds for refusal, 3.13–3.15
applicants, 3.08–3.11
generally, 3.06–3.07

Collective and certification marks – *contd*
applications for registration – *contd*
invalidity, 3.27–3.29
misleading marks, 3.17–3.18
post-registration amendment of regulations, 3.24
post-registration transfer of ownership, 3.25–3.26
process, 3.12
revocation, 3.27–3.29
generally, 3.02–3.04
infringement, 3.30
introduction, 1.10
invalidity, 3.27–3.29
misleading marks, 3.17–3.18
post-registration amendment of regulations, 3.24
post-registration transfer of ownership, 3.25–3.26
regulations
generally, 3.22
introduction, 3.19–3.20
time for filing, 3.21
revocation, 3.27–3.29
Colours
capable of being represented clearly and precisely, 2.05
relative grounds for refusal, and, 5.24
Common field of activity
damage, and, 20.67
deception, and, 20.65–20.66
generally, 20 64
likelihood of deception, and, 20.65–20.66
Common name in the trade for the product or service for which registered
'common name', 12.29
'for the product or service for which it is registered', 12.30–12.33
generally, 12.28
'in the trade', 12.29
resulting from acts or inactivity of registered proprietor, 12.34–12.36
Community trade marks (CTMs) *see* **European Union trade marks (EUTMs)**
Company names
choice, 2.29
compulsory change, 2.31
domain names, 2.36–2.39
generally, 2.28
overview, 2.27
passing off, 2.33–2.34
publicity to be given to, 2.32
trade mark infringement, 2.33–2.34
unincorporated businesses and partnerships, 2.35
voluntary change, 2.30
Comparative advertising
'advertising', 16.08
allowable, 16.13–16.21
'code owner', 16.08
Comparative Advertising Directive (CAD)
general scheme of, 16.07–16.21
generally, 16.01
conditions, 16.13
definitions, 16.08–16.10
generally, 16.01–16.06
legislative framework, 16.01
malicious falsehood *see* **Malicious falsehood**
misleading advertising
definition, 16.08
generally, 16.11–16.12
'trader', 16.08
Competition
defences to infringement, and, 15.04
Conceptual similarity
relative grounds for refusal, and, 5.26
Contrary to law
absolute grounds of refusal, and, 4.52
Contrary to policy or morality
absolute grounds of refusal, and, 4.45–4.48
Cooling-off period
opposition to registration before EUIPO, and, 8.41

Cooling-off period – *contd*
opposition to registration in UK, and
extension, 7.29
generally, 7.28
termination, 7.30
Co-ownership
UK trade marks (UKTMs), and, 13.03
Co-proprietors
infringement proceedings, and
defences, 15.58
generally, 14.62
remedies, and, 17.80–17.81
Copyright
relative grounds for refusal, and, 5.93
Costs
invalidation proceedings before EUIPO, and, 11.35
opposition to registration before EUIPO, and, 8.63
opposition to registration in UK, and
generally, 7.75–7.76
notification to applicant for mark, 7.27
Counterfeiting
articles for making signs, 19.23–19.25
bodies corporate, 19.30
defence, 19.26–19.29
enforcement, 19.31
generally, 19.02–19.03
goods bearing sign, 19.16–19.19
infringing signs, 19.10–19.15
materials bearing sign, 19.20–19.22
mental element, 19.04–19.07
partnerships, 19.30
penalties, 19.32–19.33
reasonable belief of non-infringement, 19.26–19.29
types of offence, 19.02
use of infringing sign, 19.11–19.15
'with a view', 19.06
'with intent', 19.07
without consent, 19.08–19.09
Counterstatement
opposition to registration in UK, and
generally, 7.33–7.35
introduction, 7.32
Court orders
UK trade marks (UKTMs), and, 13.08–13.09
Criminal offences
counterfeiting
articles for making signs, 19.23–19.25
bodies corporate, 19.30
defence, 19.26–19.29
enforcement, 19.31
generally, 19.02–19.03
goods bearing sign, 19.16–19.19
infringing signs, 19.10–19.15
materials bearing sign, 19.20–19.22
mental element, 19.04–19.07
partnerships, 19.30
penalties, 19.32–19.33
reasonable belief of non-infringement, 19.26–19.29
types of offence, 19.02
use of infringing sign, 19.11–19.15
'with a view', 19.06
'with intent', 19.07
without consent, 19.08–19.09
falsely representing mark as registered, 19.38–19.41
falsification of registers, 19.35–19.37
introduction, 19.01
register, and
falsely representing mark as registered, 19.38–19.41
falsification, 19.35–19.37
introduction, 19.34
unauthorised use of a trade mark
articles for making signs, 19.23–19.25
bodies corporate, 19.30
defence, 19.26–19.29
enforcement, 19.31
generally, 19.02–19.03
goods bearing sign, 19.16–19.19

Criminal offences – *contd*
unauthorised use of a trade mark – *contd*
infringing signs, 19.10–19.15
materials bearing sign, 19.20–19.22
mental element, 19.04–19.07
partnerships, 19.30
penalties, 19.32–19.33
reasonable belief of non-infringement, 19.26–19.29
types of offence, 19.02
use of infringing sign, 19.11–19.15
'with a view', 19.06
'with intent', 19.07
without consent, 19.08–19.09
unauthorised use of Royal Arms, 19.42
Cross-examination
opposition to registration in UK, and, 7.68–7.72

Damage
malicious falsehood, and, 16.28
goodwill, and
dilution of value of goodwill, 20.70
introduction, 20.68
loss of sales, 20.69
Damages
election, 17.05–17.07
Enforcement Directive, 17.09–17.11
general rules, 17.12
generally, 17.08–17.16
losses by subsidiary, 17.16
malicious falsehood, and, 16.32
methods of calculation, 17.13–17.14
Olympic symbols rights, and, 21.16
passing off, and, 20.101–20.102
secondary loss, 17.15
Dealings with European Union trade marks (EUTMs)
applications for registration, and, 13.50
assignment
effect vis-à-vis third parties, 13.54
Dealings with European Union trade marks (EUTMs) – *contd*
assignment – *contd*
generally, 13.51–13.53
recordal, 13.55–13.57
effect vis-à-vis third parties, 13.54
licences
generally, 13.58–13.64
recordal, 13.65–13.68
types, 13.58
property right, as, 13.49
Dealings with UK trade marks (UKTMs)
applications for registration, and, 13.10
assent, 13.08–13.09
assignment
generally, 13.05
introduction, 13.04
operation of law, by, 13.07
registration, 13.08–13.09
testamentary disposition, by, 13.06
co-ownership, 13.03
court orders, 13.08–13.09
dealings with UK applications for registration, 13.10
dealings with UK registered marks
assignment, 13.05
generally, 13.04
operation of law, 13.07
registration, 13.08–13.09
security, 13.04, 13.05
testamentary disposition, 13.06
introduction, 13.01
licences
consequences of failure to register, 13.47–13.48
duration, 13.33–13.35
exclusive, 13.17–13.20
generally, 13.11–13.13
goods to be licensed, 13.22
infringement, and, 13.36–13.42
marks to be licensed, 13.23
non-exclusive, 13.17–13.20
quality control, 13.21–13.22
recordal, 13.43–13.46
royalties, 13.24–13.27
services to be licensed, 13.22

Dealings with UK trade marks (UKTMs) – *contd*
licences – *contd*
sole, 13.17–13.20
sub-licensing, 13.28–13.30
termination, 13.33–13.35
terms, 13.15–13.37
territory, 13.21
types, 13.17
'mere' consents, 13.14
security interests
introduction, 13.04, 13.05
registration, 13.08–13.09
UK registered marks, of
assignment, 13.05
co-ownership, 13.03
dealings, 13.04–13.07
licences, 13.11–13.46
'mere' consents, 13.14
operation of law, 13.07
property right, as, 13.02
registration, 13.08–13.09
security, 13.04, 13.05
testamentary disposition, 13.06
title to applications for registration, 13.10

Deception
passing off, and
common field of activity, 20.65–20.66
generally, 20.03–20.05
misrepresentation, 20.49–20.50

Deceptive trade marks
absolute grounds of refusal, and, 4.49–4.51

Defences
groundless threats, and, 18.17
Olympic symbols rights, and, 21.13–21.15
passing off, and, 20.96–20.99
unauthorised use of a trade mark, and, 19.26–19.29

Defences to infringement
acquiescence, 15.27–15.30
Art 14 EUTMR, under, 15.05, 15.09–15.25
Art 15 EUTMR, under, 15.31–15.51

Defences to infringement – *contd*
Art 16 EUTMR, under, 15.05–15.08
Art 61 EUTMR, under, 15.27–15.30
Art 138 EUTMR, under, 15.05, 15.26
competition, 15.04
co-proprietors' rights, 15.58
descriptive use
'honest practices' proviso, 15.23–15.25
introduction, 15.09
use of earlier rights in particular locality, 15.26
use of indications of characteristics, 15.13–15.18
use of one's own name, 15.10–15.12
use to indicate intended purpose, 15.19–15.22
disclaimers to registration, 15.52–15.56
EU position, 15.03
exhaustion of rights
acts amounting to first marketing, 15.37–15.37
adversely affecting original condition of product, 15.48
artificial partitioning, 15.46–15.47
by or with consent of proprietor, 15.39–15.42
Europe and beyond, 15.34–15.36
generally, 15.31–15.33
legitimate reasons to oppose further dealings in goods, 15.43–15.45
presentation not to affect reputation of trade mark owner, 15.49–15.50
requirement to label, provide notice and samples, 15.51
'honest practices' proviso, 15.23–15.25
introduction, 15.01–15.04
limitations to registration, 15.57
s 11 TMA 1994, under, 15.05–15.26

Defences to infringement – *contd*
s 12 TMA 1994, under, 15.31–15.51
s 13 TMA 1994, under
disclaimers to registration, 15.52–15.56
limitations to registration, 15.57
s 23 TMA 1994, under, 15.58
s 48 TMA 1994, under, 15.27–15.30
UK position, 15.02
unregistered trade marks, 2.16
use of earlier rights in particular locality, 15.26
use of indications of characteristics
generally, 15.13–15.18
'honest practices' proviso, 15.23–15.25
introduction, 15.09
use of one's own name
generally, 15.10–15.12
'honest practices' proviso, 15.23–15.25
introduction, 15.09
use of registered trade mark where mark not declared invalid, 15.06–15.08
use to indicate intended purpose of goods and services
generally, 15.19–15.22
'honest practices' proviso, 15.23–15.25
introduction, 15.09
well-known trade marks, 2.24–2.25
Defendants
affixing sign to materials, 14.59–14.60
introduction, 14.54
joint tortfeasors, 14.56–14.58
persons using mark, 14.55
Deficient applications
registration of marks in UK, and, 7.11
Delivery up
infringing goods, material and articles, and, 17.43–17.47
Olympic symbols rights, and, 21.16
passing off, and, 20.109
Descriptive marks
absolute grounds of refusal, and, 4.19–4.29
Descriptive names
passing off, and, 20.41–20.43
Descriptive use
'honest practices' proviso, 15.23–15.25
introduction, 15.09
use of indications of characteristics, 15.13–15.18
use of one's own name, 15.10–15.12
use to indicate intended purpose, 15.19–15.22
Descriptiveness
earlier trade mark, 5.54
Design right
relative grounds for refusal, and, 5.93
Designations of origin (PDOs) *see* **Protected descriptions**
Designs
capable of being represented clearly and precisely, 2.08
Destruction
infringing goods, and, 17.41–17.42
infringing goods, material and articles, and, 17.48–17.52
Olympic symbols rights, and, 21.16
Detriment
distinctive character, to
'blurring' or 'dilution', 5.80–5.82
generally, 5.79
level of association, 5.86
repute, to
generally, 5.83–5.85
level of association, 5.86
Devoid of distinctive character
absolute grounds of refusal, and, 4.07–4.18
Dilution
infringement, and, 14.51–14.52
relative grounds for refusal, and, 5.80–5.82
passing off, and, 20.70
Disclaimers to registration
defences to infringement, and, 15.52–15.56

Distinctiveness
absolute grounds of refusal, and, 4.07–4.18
earlier mark through use, of
generally, 5.56–5.58
likelihood of confusion, and, 5.54–5.55
Domain names
company names, and, 2.36–2.39

Earlier rights
opposition procedure before EUIPO and identification requirements, 8.28–8.29
relative grounds for refusal, and
copyright, protection, 5.93
design right, protection, 5.93
introduction, 5.90
protection for other unregistered rights, 5.93
unregistered marks used in course of trade, 5.91–5.92
unregistered rights applicable to EUTMs, 5.94–5.96
use in particular locality, defence to infringement, 15.26
Earlier trade marks
applications for registration, and, 5.07
definition
EU position, 5.12
generally, 5.10–5.12
UK position, 5.11
introduction, 5.02
opposition to registration before EUIPO, and
dates relating to, 8.33
generally, 8.34
proof of existence and validity, 8.44–8.46
relative grounds for refusal, and
applications for registration of earlier marks, and, 5.07
detriment to distinctive character, 5.79–5.82
detriment to repute, 5.83–5.86
distinctiveness of earlier mark through use, 5.56–5.58
'earlier trade mark', 5.10–5.12

Earlier trade marks – *contd*
relative grounds for refusal, and – *contd*
extent of use of common elements of marks as used by parties, 5.59–5.61
harm to trade mark function, 5.06
identity of goods and services, 5.28–5.31
identity of marks, 5.13–5.16
interdependence of assessments of similarity, 5.53–5.55
introduction, 5.05
issues arising, 5.08–5.09
likelihood of confusion, 5.37–5.52
prior decisions, 5.62
reputation, 5.63–5.74
similarity of goods and services, 5.32–5.36
similarity of marks, 5.17–5.27
unfair advantage of distinctive character or repute, 5.75–5.78
use of later mark without due cause, 5.87–5.89
Emblems
absolute grounds of refusal, and, 4.53–4.54
Erasure of offending sign
generally, 17.39–17.40
Essential function
generally, 5.98–5.99
infringement, and, 14.32–14.33
European Union collective and certification marks
amendment of regulations, 3.35
application process, 3.32
examination, 3.34
generally, 3.31
infringement, 3.37
invalidity, 3.36
regulations, 3.33
revocation, 3.36
European Union Intellectual Property Office (EUIPO)
applications for registration of marks, and
see also **Applications for registration (EUIPO)**

European Union Intellectual Property Office (EUIPO) – *contd*
applications for registration of marks, and – *contd*
appeals, 8.64
examination, 8.12–8.13
filing, 8.04–8.11
generally, 8.02–8.03
introduction, 8.01
opposition, 8.15–8.63
procedures, 8.02–8.03
publication, 8.14
invalidation proceedings, at
absolute grounds, 11.19
acquiescence, 11.22–11.23
appeals, 11.36
applicants, 11.25
applicant's details, 11.29–11.31
basis for proceedings, 11.18–11.23
costs, 11.35
details of extent and basis for application, 11.28
details of right against which declaration is requested, 11.27
filing requirements, 11.26–11.31
limitations on ability to bring applications, 11.21
manner of bringing action, 11.24
observations and evidence, 11.32
procedure, 11.24–11.31
proof of use, 11.33–11.34
relative grounds, 11.20
recording of licences, at 13.65–13.68
registered trade marks, 1.02
representation, before
generally, 10.05
'legal practitioner', 10.06
'professional representative', 10.07–10.08
European Union trade marks (EUTMs)
application for registration, and *see also* **Applications for registration (EUIPO)**
appeals, 8.64
examination, 8.12–8.13
filing, 8.04–8.11
generally, 8.02–8.03
introduction, 8.01
opposition, 8.15–8.63
procedures, 8.02–8.03
publication, 8.14
common principles and effect of Brexit, 1.05
dealings with *see* **Dealings with European Union trade marks (EUTMs)**
interpretation of law, determination, 1.05
invalidation proceedings at EUIPO, and
absolute grounds, 11.19
acquiescence, 11.22–11.23
appeals, 11.36
applicants, 11.25
applicant's details, 11.29–11.31
basis for proceedings, 11.18–11.23
costs, 11.35
details of extent and basis for application, 11.28
details of right against which declaration is requested, 11.27
filing requirements, 11.26–11.31
limitations on ability to bring applications, 11.21
manner of bringing action, 11.24
observations and evidence, 11.32
procedure, 11.24–11.31
proof of use, 11.33–11.34
relative grounds, 11.20
ownership *see* **Ownership of European Union trade marks (EUTMs)**
protection
EU Regulation (EUTMR), under, 1.04
UK, in, 1.02, 1.04

European Union trade marks (EUTMs) – *contd*
remedies for infringement
effect of Brexit, 17.03
generally, 17.04
unregistered rights, opposition to registration, 5.94–5.96
European Union Trade Marks Regulation (EUTMR)
grounds for refusal of registration, and, 5.04
infringement, and 14.03
registered trade marks, and
common principles and effect of Brexit, 1.05
generally, 1.02, 1.04
revocation of marks, and, 12.03
Examination of applications
EU collective and certification marks, and, 3.34
registration of marks before EUIPO, and, 8.12–8.13
registration of marks before WIPO, and, 9.19
registration of marks in UK, and, 7.14–7.16
Exclusive licensees
remedies for infringement, and
damages, 17.08–17.16
generally, 17.02, 17.83–17.84
Exclusive rights
infringement proceedings, and, 14.06–14.08
Exhaustion of rights
acts amounting to first marketing, 15.37–15.37
adversely affecting original condition of product, 15.48
artificial partitioning, 15.46–15.47
by or with consent of proprietor, 15.39–15.42
Europe and beyond, 15.34–15.36
generally, 15.31–15.33
legitimate reasons to oppose further dealings in goods, 15.43–15.45
presentation not to affect reputation of trade mark owner, 15.49–15.50
Exhaustion of rights – *contd*
requirement to label, provide notice and samples, 15.51
Expert evidence
passing off, and, 20.93

Falsely representing mark as registered
generally, 19.38–19.41
Falsification of registers
generally, 19.35–19.37
Fast-track oppositions
registration in UK, and, 7.77–7.80
Fees
applications for registration before EUIPO, and, 8.07
applications for registration before WIPO, and, 9.18
applications for registration in UK, and, 7.06
opposition to registration before EUIPO, and, 8.26
opposition to registration in UK, and, 7.23
Filing applications
opposition to registration in UK, and
evidence, 7.44–7.49
generally, 7.23
statement of use of rights over five years old, 7.24–7.26
registration of marks before EUIPO, and
amendment of application, 8.11
applicant's details, 8.05
claiming priority, 8.09
claiming seniority, 8.10
further formalities, 8.07
introduction, 8.04
languages, 8.08
list of goods and services for which protection is sought, 8.05
payment of fees, 8.07
representation of mark, 8.06
request for registration, 8.05
requirements if application to be given filing date, 8.05
withdrawal of application, 8.11

Filing applications – *contd*
registration of marks in UK, and
applicant's details, 7.09
declaration that mark in use, 7.10
list of goods and services for which protection is sought, 7.09
method, 7.07
obtaining filing date, 7.09–7.10
payment of fees, 7.10
representation of mark, 7.09
request for registration, 7.09
requirements, 7.08
Filing evidence
opposition to registration in UK, and
extension of time, 7.48–7.49
generally, 7.44–7.46
time limits, 7.47
'First to file' principle
honest concurrent use, and, 5.106
Forfeiture of infringing goods, material and articles
generally, 17.48–17.52
Free-riding
infringement proceedings, and, 14.51–14.52
Freezing injunctions
passing off, and, 20.113
'Functions'
advertising functions, 5.100–5.105
essential function, 5.98–5.99
generally, 5.97
harm, and, 5.06
investment functions, 5.100–5.105
origin function, 5.98–5.99
relative grounds for refusal, and, 5.06

Generic marks
absolute grounds of refusal, and, 4.30–4.33
revocation, and
'common name', 12.29
'for the product or service for which it is registered', 12.30–12.33
generally, 12.28
'in the trade', 12.29
Generic marks – *contd*
revocation, and – *contd*
resulting from acts or inactivity of registered proprietor, 12.34–12.36
Genuine use
opposition to registration before EUIPO, and, 8.52–8.58
Geographical indications (PGIs) *see* **Protected descriptions**
Get-ups
passing off, and, 20.38–20.40
Goods and services
definition of 'trade mark', and, 2.11
opposition to registration before EUIPO, and, 8.35
opposition to registration in UK, and, 7.64–7.72
Goodwill
anticipatory goodwill, 20.32
definition, 20.19
descriptive names, 20.41–20.43
embodiment, 20.35–20.43
evidence, 20.72–20.73
'extended' passing off, in, 20.27–20.28
extent, 20.24–20.25
features, 20.38–20.40
generally, 20.03–20.05
get-ups, 20.38–20.40
images, 20.38–20.40
inherently distinctive trade marks, 20.36–20.37
international goodwill, 20.29–20.31
introduction, 20.18
nature, 20.18–20.34
ownership, 20.20–20.23
residual goodwill, 20.33
s 56(2) TMA, and, 20.34
scope, 20.24–20.25
secondary meaning, 20.41–20.43
signs, 20.38–20.40
time of assessment, 20.26
Groundless threats
defences, 18.17
excluded threats, 18.05
form of threat, 18.04
introduction, 18.01–18.02

Groundless threats – *contd*
permitted communications exclusion
generally, 18.06
information that is 'necessary', 18.09
not an 'express threat', 18.07
permitted communication, 18.08
permitted purpose, 18.10
purposes not permitted, 18.11
person aggrieved, 18.12
person liable in respect of actionable threat, 18.13
remedies, 18.18
'threat of infringement proceedings', 18.03
threats by professional adviser
conditions to be satisfied, 18.16
generally, 18.14
'professional adviser', 18.15
Grounds for refusal
absolute grounds
acquired distinctiveness – s 3(1); Art 7(3), 4.34–4.39
bad faith registration – s 3(6); Art 59(1)(b), 4.55–4.59
collective marks, and, 3.13–3.15
contrary to law – s 3(4), 4.52
contrary to policy or morality – s 3(3)(a); Art 7(1)(f), 4.45–4.48
deceptive trade marks – s 3(3)(b); Art 7(1)(g), 4.49–4.51
descriptive marks – s 3(1)(c); Art 7(1)(c), 4.19–4.29
devoid of distinctive character – s 3(1)(b); Art 7(1)(b), 4.07–4.18
emblems – ss 3(5), 4, 57 and 58; Arts 7(1)(h) and 7(1)(i), 4.53–4.54
generally, 4.01–4.05
generic marks – s 3(1)(c); Art 7(1)(c), 4.30–4.33
shape of goods – s 3(2); Art 7(1)(e), 4.40–4.44
signs which do not satisfy requirements of s 1(1) – s 3(1)(a); Art 7(1)(a), 4.06
Grounds for refusal – *contd*
conflicts with earlier rights
copyright, protection, 5.93
design right, protection, 5.93
introduction, 5.90
protection of other unregistered rights, 5.93
unregistered marks used in course of trade, 5.91–5.92
unregistered rights applicable to EUTMs, 5.94–5.96
conflicts with earlier trade marks
applications for registration of earlier marks, and, 5.07
detriment to distinctive character, 5.79–5.82
detriment to repute, 5.83–5.86
distinctiveness of earlier mark through use, 5.56–5.58
'earlier trade mark', 5.10–5.12
extent of use of common elements of marks as used by parties, 5.59–5.61
harm to trade mark function, 5.06
identity of goods and services, 5.28–5.31
identity of marks, 5.13–5.16
interdependence of assessments of similarity, 5.53–5.55
introduction, 5.05
issues arising, 5.08–5.09
likelihood of confusion, 5.37–5.52
prior decisions, 5.62
reputation, 5.63–5.74
similarity of goods and services, 5.32–5.36
similarity of marks, 5.17–5.27
unfair advantage of distinctive character or repute, 5.75–5.78
use of later mark without due cause, 5.87–5.89
relative grounds
applications for registration of earlier marks, and, 5.07
copyright, and, 5.93
design right, and, 5.93

Grounds for refusal – *contd*
relative grounds – *contd*
detriment to distinctive character, 5.79–5.82
detriment to repute, 5.83–5.86
distinctiveness of earlier mark through use, 5.56–5.58
'earlier trade mark', 5.10–5.12
extent of use of common elements of marks as used by parties, 5.59–5.61
harm to trade mark function, 5.06
identity of goods and services, 5.28–5.31
identity of marks, 5.13–5.16
interdependence of assessments of similarity, 5.53–5.55
introduction, 5.05
issues arising, 5.08–5.09
likelihood of confusion, 5.37–5.52
prior decisions, 5.62
reputation, 5.63–5.74
similarity of goods and services, 5.32–5.36
similarity of marks, 5.17–5.27
unfair advantage of distinctive character or repute, 5.75–5.78
unregistered marks used in course of trade, and, 5.91–5.92
use of later mark without due cause, 5.87–5.89

Harm to trade mark function
relative grounds for refusal, and, 5.06
Hearings
opposition to registration in UK, and, 7.73
Honest concurrent use
generally, 5.106–5.110
'Honest practices' proviso
defences to infringement, and, 15.23–15.25
Hyperbole
malicious falsehood, and, 16.29–16.30
Identical marks, identical goods or services
see also **Infringement**
conditions, 14.10
generally, 14.09–14.11
use affect or be liable to affect functions of mark
advertising function, 14.34–14.35
essential function, 14.32–14.33
generally, 14.30–14.31
investment function, 14.36–14.38
origin function, 14.32–14.33
use in course of trade, 14.20–14.21
use in relation to identical goods or services, 14.24–14.29
use of a sign by a third party, 14.12–14.19
use of a sign identical to mark, 14.23
use without consent of trade mark proprietor, 14.22
Identity of goods and services
relative grounds for refusal, and, 5.28–5.31
Identity of marks
relative grounds for refusal, and, 5.13–5.16
Images
passing off, and, 20.38–20.40
Imaging orders
generally, 17.29–17.30
Indication of class of goods or services
applications for registration before EUIPO, and, 8.05
applications for registration in UK, and, 7.12
Indication of intended purpose of goods and services
generally, 15.19–15.22
'honest practices' proviso, 15.23–15.25
introduction, 15.09
Indications of characteristics
generally, 15.13–15.18
'honest practices' proviso, 15.23–15.25
introduction, 15.09

Infringement
affixing sign to materials, 14.59–14.60
burden of proof, 14.04
claimants
co-proprietors, 14.62
licensees, 14.63
proprietors, 14.61
collective and certification marks, and
European Union, 3.37
United Kingdom, 3.30
company names, and, 2.33–2.34
defences
see also **Defences to infringement**
acquiescence, 15.27–15.30
Art 14 EUTMR, under, 15.05, 15.09–15.25
Art 15 EUTMR, under, 15.31–15.51
Art 16 EUTMR, under, 15.05–15.08
Art 61 EUTMR, under, 15.27–15.30
Art 138 EUTMR, under, 15.05, 15.26
co-proprietors' rights, 15.58
descriptive use, 15.09
disclaimers, 15.52–15.56
exhaustion of rights, 15.31–15.51
'honest practice' proviso, 15.23–15.25
introduction, 15.01–15.04
limitations, 15.57
s 11 TMA 1994, under, 15.05–15.26
s 12 TMA 1994, under, 15.31–15.51
s 13 TMA 1994, under 15.52–15.57
s 23 TMA 1994, under, 15.58
s 48 TMA 1994, under, 15.27–15.30
unregistered trade marks, 2.16
use of indications of characteristics, 15.13–15.18
use of one's own name, 15.10–15.12

Infringement – *contd*
defences – *contd*
use of registered trade mark where mark not declared invalid, 15.06–15.08
use to indicate intended purpose, 15.19–15.22
well-known trade marks, 2.24–2.25
defendants to proceedings
affixing sign to materials, 14.59–14.60
introduction, 14.54
joint tortfeasors, 14.56–14.58
persons using mark, 14.55
detriment to distinctive character or repute of mark
blurring, 14.51–14.52
conditions, 14.46–14.53
dilution, 14.51–14.52
generally, 14.45–14.46
injury, 14.51–14.52
mark must have a reputation, 14.47
tarnishing, 14.51–14.52
use has link with mark, 14.50
use without due cause, 14.53
exclusive rights, 14.06–14.08
groundless threats *see* **Groundless threats**
identical marks, identical goods or services
conditions, 14.10
generally, 14.09–14.11
use affect or be liable to affect functions of mark, 14.30–14.38
use in course of trade, 14.20–14.21
use in relation to identical goods or services, 14.24–14.29
use of a sign by a third party, 14.12–14.19
use of a sign identical to mark, 14.23
use without consent of trade mark proprietor, 14.22
introduction, 14.01–14.01
invalidity proceedings, and, 11.01

Infringement – *contd*
labelling, and affixing sign to materials, 14.59–14.60
legislative framework, 14.03
likelihood of confusion
conditions, 14.40
generally, 14.39–14.40
likelihood of confusion, 14.44
use in course of trade, 14.41
use in relation to identical or similar goods or services, 14.43
use of a sign by a third party, 14.41
use of a sign identical or similar to mark, 14.42
use without consent of trade mark proprietor, 14.41
Olympic symbols rights, and, 21.05–21.06
packaging, and affixing sign to materials, 14.59–14.60
parties to proceedings
claimants, 14.61–14.63
defendants, 14.54–14.60
relative grounds for refusal, and
generally, 5.03
introduction, 14.05
remedies
see also **Remedies**
account of profits, 17.17–17.19
'Anton Piller' orders, 17.29–17.30
Brexit, effect on comparable trade marks (EU), 17.03
co-proprietors, and, 17.80–17.81
damages, 17.05–17.16
delivery up, 17.43–17.47
destruction, 17.41–17.42, 17.48–17.52
election between damages and account, 17.05–17.07
erasure of offending sign, 17.39–17.40
EU trade marks (EUTMs), and, 17.03–17.04
forfeiture of infringing goods, material and articles, 17.48–17.52

Infringement – *contd*
remedies – *contd*
imaging orders, 17.29–17.30
infringing goods, material and articles, and, 17.34–17.52
injunctions, 17.20–17.27
introduction, 17.01
jurisdiction of courts, 17.86–17.91
licensees, and, 17.82–17.85
notice to Customs, 17.53–17.64
obliteration of offending sign, 17.39–17.40
orders for disclosure of information about infringing activity, 17.31–17.33
removal of offending sign, 17.39–17.40
search orders, 17.29–17.30
UK registered trade marks, and, 17.02, 17.05–17.52
well-known marks, and, 17.65–17.72
summary of provisions, 14.04
threats of infringement proceedings *see* **Groundless threats**
trade mark 'functions'
advertising functions, 5.100–5.105
essential function, 5.98–5.99
generally, 5.97
harm, and, 5.06
investment functions, 5.100–5.105
origin function, 5.98–5.99
unfair advantage of distinctive character or repute of mark
conditions, 14.46–14.53
free-riding, 14.51–14.52
generally, 14.45–14.46
injury, 14.51–14.52
mark must have a reputation, 14.47
use has link with mark, 14.50
use without due cause, 14.53
unregistered trade marks, and, 2.16
well-known trade marks, and, 2.24–2.25

Infringing goods, material and articles
delivery up of infringing goods, material and articles, 17.43–17.47
destruction of infringing goods, 17.41–17.42
destruction of infringing goods, material and articles, 17.48–17.52
erasure of offending sign, 17.39–17.40
forfeiture of infringing goods, material and articles, 17.48–17.52
generally, 17.34–17.35
'infringing articles', 17.38
'infringing goods', 17.36
'infringing material', 17.37
notice to Customs
generally, 17.53
Regulation (EU) No. 608/2013 (as amended), 17.54–17.61
TMA 1994, s 89, 17.62–17.64
obliteration of offending sign, 17.39–17.40
removal of offending sign, 17.39–17.40
Injunctions
final injunctions, 17.27
generally, 17.20–17.21
interim injunctions, 17.22–17.26
malicious falsehood, and, 16.32–16.33
Olympic symbols rights, and, 21.16
passing off, and
generally, 20.105
interim injunctions, 20.106–20.108
unauthorised application for registration by agent or representative, and
generally, 17.73–17.74
justification, 17.75
well-known marks, and
acquiescence, 17.70
bona fide use, 17.70
entitlement, 17.66
essential part of trade mark, 17.67
Injunctions – *contd*
well-known marks, and – *contd*
limitations on right, 17.70
priority over registered trade marks, 17.71
proof of confusion, 17.68–17.69
Injury
infringement, and, 14.51–14.52
Intention to use
classification system, and, 6.09
International conventions
generally, 1.12
introduction, 9.01
Madrid system
see also **International trade marks**
application form, 9.12–9.19
basic application, 9.08–9.11
consideration by WIPO, 9.20–9.29
designations with additional requirements, 9.30
introduction, 9.02
legal framework, 9.03
notification of office of origin, 9.31–9.43
outline, in, 9.04–9.07
WIPO, and, 9.03
Paris Convention, 9.01
TRIPS Agreement, 9.01
International trade marks
application for registration
based on EUTM application or registration, 9.17
based on UKTM application or registration, 9.16
consideration by WIPO, 9.20–9.29
examination, 9.19
fees, 9.18
generally, 9.12–9.19
'basic' application or registration
generally, 9.08–9.11
initial reliance on basic right, 9.11
introduction, 9.06
'basic' marks, 9.04
'central attack', 9.06

International trade marks – *contd*
consideration by WIPO
formal irregularities, 9.20–9.24
irregularities as to specification of goods and services, 9.25–9.29
conversion of registration into national/regional rights, 9.42–9.43
dealings
assignment, 13.69–13.70
licences, 13.71–13.73
royalties, 13.24–13.27
services to be licensed, 13.22
sole, 13.17–13.20
sub-licensing, 13.28–13.30
termination, 13.33–13.35
terms, 13.15–13.37
territory, 13.21
types, 13.17
dependence of registration on basic right, 9.41
designation of countries, 9.04
designations with additional requirements, 9.30
EU trade marks (EUTMs), and, 9.04
examination, 9.19
fees, 9.18
formal irregularities
deadlines for resolution, 9.24
generally, 9.20
resolution by applicant, for, 9.22–9.23
resolution by Office of origin, for, 9.21–9.22
introduction, 9.02
irregularities as to specification of goods and services
generally, 9.25
incorrect classes or numbers of classes, 9.26–9.27
specification is unclear, 9.28–9.29
legal framework, 9.03
national marks, and, 9.04
notification of office of origin, 9.31–9.43
outline, in, 9.04–9.07

International trade marks – *contd*
'real and effective establishment', 9.08–9.09
refusal of protection by designated office, 9.32–9.39
registration, 9.31
reliance on basic right, 9.11
strength of system, 9.05
transformation of registration into national/regional rights, 9.42–9.43
validity of registration, 9.40
WIPO, and, 9.03

Invalidity
acquiescence, and
awareness of full use of later mark, 11.10
commencement of relevant period, 11.08
effect of finding, 11.11
EUTM registrations, 11.22–11.23
generally, 11.07
knowledge of registration of mark, 11.09
collective and certification marks, and
European Union, 3.36
United Kingdom, 3.27–3.29
earlier rights of third parties, and, 11.01
EUIPO, before
absolute grounds, 11.19
acquiescence, 11.22–11.23
appeals, 11.36
applicants, 11.25
applicant's details, 11.29–11.31
basis for proceedings, 11.18–11.23
costs, 11.35
details of extent and basis for application, 11.28
details of right against which declaration is requested, 11.27
filing requirements, 11.26–11.31
limitations on ability to bring applications, 11.21
manner of bringing action, 11.24

Invalidity – *contd*
EUIPO, before – *contd*
observations and evidence, 11.32
procedure, 11.24–11.31
proof of use, 11.33–11.34
relative grounds, 11.20
grounds, 11.01
infringement proceedings, and, 11.01
international trade marks, and, 9.40
introduction, 11.01
TMA 1994, under
absolute grounds for refusal, and, 11.03
acquiescence, and, 11.07–11.11
appeals, 11.17
breach of s 3, 11.03
commencement of proceedings, 11.13
consent to registration, 11.05
evidence and submissions, 11.16
existence of earlier trade mark, 11.04–11.06
grounds for declaration, 11.02–11.06
hearings, 11.17
procedure, 11.12–11.17
relative grounds for refusal, and, 11.04–11.05
response of registered proprietor to proceedings, 11.14–11.15
unsuitability of mark for registration, and, 11.01
Investment functions
infringement, and, 14.36–14.38
generally, 5.100–5.105
Issue estoppel
relative grounds for refusal, and, 5.62

Joint tortfeasors
infringement proceedings, and, 14.56–14.58
Jurisdiction of courts
remedies for infringement, and, 17.86–17.91

Labelling
infringement proceedings, affixing sign to materials and, 14.59–14.60
Language
applications for registration before EUIPO, and, 8.08
opposition to registration before EUIPO, and, 8.47–8.48
Licensees
infringement proceedings, and, 14.63
remedies for infringement, and 17.82–17.85
Licences
EU trade marks (EUTMs), and
generally, 13.58–13.64
recordal, 13.65–13.68
types, 13.58
international marks, and, 13.71–13.73
UK trade marks (UKTMs), and
consequences of failure to register, 13.47–13.48
duration, 13.33–13.35
exclusive, 13.17–13.20
generally, 13.11–13.13
goods to be licensed, 13.22
infringement, and, 13.36–13.42
marks to be licensed, 13.23
non-exclusive, 13.17–13.20
quality control, 13.21–13.22
recordal, 13.43–13.46
royalties, 13.24–13.27
services to be licensed, 13.22
sole, 13.17–13.20
sub-licensing, 13.28–13.30
termination, 13.33–13.35
terms, 13.15–13.37
territory, 13.21
types, 13.17
Likelihood of confusion
assessment, 5.39–5.43
consumer's level of attention, 5.44–5.48
distinctiveness/descriptiveness of earlier mark, 5.54–5.55
generally, 5.37
infringement, and
conditions, 14.40
generally, 14.39–14.40
likelihood of confusion, 14.44
use in course of trade, 14.41

Likelihood of confusion – *contd*
infringement, and – *contd*
use in relation to identical or similar goods or services, 14.43
use of a sign by a third party, 14.41
use of a sign identical or similar to mark, 14.42
use without consent of trade mark proprietor, 14.41
interdependence of assessments, 5.54–5.55
meaning, 5.38
opposition to registration in UK, and
acquired distinctiveness of mark, 7.56–7.57
generally, 7.53
inherent distinctiveness of mark, 7.54–7.55
significance of surrounding circumstances, 5.50–5.52
timing of confusion/'wrong way round' confusion, 5.49
Limitations to registration
defences to infringement, and, 15.57
London Olympics Association Right
generally, 21.04

Madrid Agreement and Protocol
see also **International trade marks**
application form, 9.12–9.19
basic application, 9.08–9.11
consideration by WIPO, 9.20–9.29
designations with additional requirements, 9.30
introduction, 9.02
legal framework, 9.03
notification of office of origin, 9.31–9.43
outline, in, 9.04–9.07
WIPO, and, 9.03
Malicious falsehood
comparative advertising, and, 16.31
damages, 16.32
generally, 16.22–16.23
Malicious falsehood – *contd*
hyperbole, 16.29–16.30
injunctions, 16.32–16.33
malice, 16.24–16.25
meaning of statement, 16.26–16.27
'one-meaning rule', 16.26
puffery, 16.29–16.30
relief, 16.32–16.33
remedies, 16.32–16.33
special damage, 16.28
'Mere' consents
UK trade marks (UKTMs), and, 13.14
Misleading advertising *see* **Comparative advertising**
Misleading marks
collective marks, and, 3.17–3.18
revocation, and
generally, 12.37
procedure before EUIPO, 12.41–12.46
procedure before UKIPO, 12.38–12.40
Misrepresentation
acts outside UK, 20.57–20.58
association, as to, 20.46–20.48
comparative advertising, 20.63
deception, and, 20.49–20.50
descriptive use of terms or names, 20.59–20.60
endorsement, as to, 20.46–20.48
evidence, 20.74–20.81
factors which may negate, 20.53–20.63
introduction, 20.44
origin, as to, 20.45
persons deceived, 20.51–20.52
spares and accessories, 20.63
sponsorship, as to, 20.46–20.48
trade connection, as to, 20.46–20.48
use of other distinguishing material, 20.61–20.62
use of own name, 20.56

Nice Classification *see also* **Classification system**
generally, 6.02

Non-use
date to be considered, 12.05
generally, 12.04
'genuine use', 12.06
legitimate reasons, 12.26–12.27
level of use required, 12.07
mark differing in elements affecting distinctive character, 12.11–12.14
nature of activities, 12.08–12.09
partial revocation
action before EUIPO, 12.23–12.24
generally, 12.19
UK approach, 12.20–12.22
proper reasons, 12.25–12.27
use for goods or services of the registration, 12.15
use in relevant territory, 12.18
use in relevant time period, 12.16–12.17
use of mark as registered, 12.10
Notice of opposition
absolute admissibility requirements
generally, 8.25
payment of fees, 8.26
translation, 8.32
admissibility
absolute requirements, 8.25–8.30
dates relating to earlier applications and registrations, 8.33
generally, 8.23–8.24
identification of contested application, 8.27
identification of earlier mark or sign, 8.34
identification of earlier rights, 8.28–8.29
identification of goods and services, 8.35
identification of grounds, 8.30
payment of fees, 8.26
relative requirements, 8.31–8.36
scope of reputation, 8.36
translation, 8.32
grounds, 8.16–8.17
introduction, 8.15
standing to file, 8.18
Notice to Customs
remedies for infringing goods, material and articles, and
generally, 17.53
Regulation (EU) No. 608/2013 (as amended), 17.54–17.61
TMA 1994, s 89, 17.62–17.64
Notice to proceed
opposition to registration in UK, and, 7.43
Notification to applicant for mark
opposition to registration in UK, and, 7.27

Obliteration of offending sign
generally, 17.39–17.40
Observations
opposition to registration in UK, and, 7.82
Olympics Association Right
accounts of profits, 21.16
damages, 21.16
defences, 21.13–21.15
delivery up, 21.16
erasure, 21.16
generally, 21.03
infringement, 21.05–21.06
injunctions, 21.16
introduction, 21.01–21.02
LOCOG, and, 21.03
London Olympics Association Right, 21.04
overview, 1.14
Paralympics Association Right, 21.03
relevant rights, 21.03–21.04
remedies, 21.16
representations
generally, 21.07–21.08
introduction, 21.05–21.06
suggesting an association, 21.09–21.11
use in course of trade, in UK, without consent, 21.12
Opposition to registration (EUIPO)
ability to act before EUIPO, 8.19–8.22
absolute admissibility requirements
generally, 8.25

Opposition to registration (EUIPO) – *contd*
absolute admissibility requirements – *contd*
identification of contested application, 8.27
identification of earlier rights, 8.28–8.29
identification of grounds, 8.30
payment of fees, 8.26
admissibility of notice of opposition
absolute requirements, 8.25–8.30
dates relating to earlier applications and registrations, 8.33
generally, 8.23–8.24
identification of contested application, 8.27
identification of earlier mark or sign, 8.34
identification of earlier rights, 8.28–8.29
identification of goods and services, 8.35
identification of grounds, 8.30
payment of fees, 8.26
relative requirements, 8.31–8.36
scope of reputation, 8.36
translation, 8.32
applicant's evidence, 8.49–8.51
basis, 8.16–8.17
contested application, 8.27
cooling-off period, 8.41
costs, 8.63
dates relating to earlier applications and registrations, 8.33
earlier applications and registrations
dates relating to, 8.33
proof of existence and validity, 8.44–8.46
earlier mark or sign, 8.34
earlier rights, 8.28–8.29
evidence
applicant, by, 8.49–8.51
filing, 8.42–8.43
formalities for filing, 8.60–8.62
further arguments, 8.59

Opposition to registration (EUIPO) – *contd*
evidence – *contd*
language of documents, 8.47–8.48
observations in reply, 8.49–8.51
proof of existence and validity of earlier applications and registrations, 8.44–8.46
proof of genuine use, 8.54–8.58
request that opponent proves use, 8.52–8.53
extent of opposition, 8.38–8.39
fees, 8.26
filing evidence
formalities, 8.60–8.62
generally, 8.42–8.43
further elements, 8.37–8.40
further evidence and arguments, 8.59
generally, 8.15
genuine use, 8.52–8.58
goods and services, 8.35
grounds, 8.16–8.17
identification of contested application, 8.27
identification of earlier mark or sign, 8.34
identification of earlier rights, 8.28–8.29
identification of goods and services, 8.35
identification of grounds, 8.30
language of documents, 8.47–8.48
notice
admissibility, 8.23–8.36
grounds, 8.16–8.17
introduction, 8.15
standing to file, 8.18
observations in reply, 8.49–8.51
opponent's proof of genuine use, 8.54–8.55
payment of fees, 8.26
procedural requirements
ability to act before EUIPO, 8.19–8.22
standing to file notice, 8.18
proof of existence and validity of earlier applications and registrations, 8.44–8.46

Opposition to registration (EUIPO) – *contd*
proof of genuine use
generally, 8.54–8.58
request, 8.52–8.53
reasoned statement, 8.40
relative admissibility requirements
dates relating to earlier applications and registrations, 8.33
generally, 8.31
identification of earlier mark or sign, 8.34
identification of goods and services, 8.35
scope of reputation, 8.36
translation, 8.32
request that opponent proves use, 8.52–8.53
scope of reputation, 8.36
standing to file notice, 8.18
translation, 8.32
Opposition to registration (UK)
appeals, 7.81
applicant's form, 7.31
challenging evidence, 7.66–7.67
cooling-off period
extension, 7.29
generally, 7.28
termination, 7.30
costs
generally, 7.75–7.76
notification to applicant for mark, 7.27
counterstatement
generally, 7.33–7.35
introduction, 7.32
cross-examination, 7.68–7.72
evidence as to goods and services, 7.64–7.72
evidence as to likelihood of confusion by applicant
acquired weakness of mark, 7.61–7.63
generally, 7.58
inherent weakness of mark, 7.59–7.60
Opposition to registration (UK) – *contd*
evidence as to likelihood of confusion by opponent
acquired distinctiveness of mark, 7.56–7.57
generally, 7.53
inherent distinctiveness of mark, 7.54–7.55
extension of cooling-off period, 7.29
extension of time for filing evidence, 7.48–7.49
fast-track oppositions
generally, 7.77
procedure, 7.78—7.80
filing evidence
extension of time, 7.48–7.49
generally, 7.44–7.46
time limits, 7.47
filing formalities
generally, 7.23
statement of use of rights over five years old, 7.24–7.26
form, 7.18
form of evidence
generally, 7.50
goods and services, 7.64–7.72
likelihood of confusion, 7.53–7.63
persons making witness statement, 7.51–7.52
hearings, 7.73
introduction, 7.18
notice to proceed, 7.43
notification to applicant for mark, 7.27
observations, 7.82
preliminary indications
consequences, 7.39–7.42
implications, 7.37–7.38
introduction, 7.36
opposition based on other than s 5(1) or (2), 7.42
opposition based only on s 5(1) or (2), 7.41
pre-opposition contact to applicant for mark, 7.21–7.22
request for opponent to prove use, 7.32

Opposition to registration (UK) – *contd*
skeleton arguments, 7.74
statement of use of rights over five years old, 7.24–7.26
termination of cooling-off period, 7.30
time for filing, 7.19–7.20
time limits for filing evidence, 7.47
witness statements
generally, 7.50
goods and services, 7.64–7.72
likelihood of confusion, 7.53–7.63
persons making, 7.51–7.52
Order to change name
passing off, and, 20.110
Orders for disclosure of information about infringing activity
generally, 17.31–17.33
Origin function
infringement, and, 14.32–14.33
generally, 5.98–5.99
Own name
generally, 15.10–15.12
'honest practices' proviso, 15.23–15.25
introduction, 15.09
passing off, and, 20.56
Ownership of European Union trade marks (EUTMs)
applications for registration, and, 13.50
assignment
effect vis-à-vis third parties, 13.54
generally, 13.51–13.53
recordal, 13.55–13.57
effect vis-à-vis third parties, 13.54
licences
generally, 13.58–13.64
recordal, 13.65–13.68
types, 13.58
property right, as, 13.49
Ownership of UK trade marks (UKTMs)
applications for registration, and, 13.10
Ownership of UK trade marks (UKTMs) – *contd*
assent, 13.08–13.09
assignment
generally, 13.05
introduction, 13.04
operation of law, by, 13.07
registration, 13.08–13.09
testamentary disposition, by, 13.06
co-ownership, 13.03
court orders, 13.08–13.09
dealings with UK applications for registration, 13.10
dealings with UK registered marks
assignment, 13.05
generally, 13.04
operation of law, 13.07
registration, 13.08–13.09
security, 13.04, 13.05
testamentary disposition, 13.06
introduction, 13.01
licences
consequences of failure to register, 13.47–13.48
duration, 13.33–13.35
exclusive, 13.17–13.20
generally, 13.11–13.13
goods to be licensed, 13.22
infringement, and, 13.36–13.42
marks to be licensed, 13.23
non-exclusive, 13.17–13.20
quality control, 13.21–13.22
recordal, 13.43–13.46
royalties, 13.24–13.27
services to be licensed, 13.22
sole, 13.17–13.20
sub-licensing, 13.28–13.30
termination, 13.33–13.35
terms, 13.15–13.37
territory, 13.21
types, 13.17
'mere' consents, 13.14
security interests
introduction, 13.04, 13.05
registration, 13.08–13.09
UK registered marks, of
assignment, 13.05
co-ownership, 13.03

Ownership of UK trade marks (UKTMs) – *contd*
UK registered marks, of – *contd*
dealings, 13.04–13.07
licences, 13.11–13.46
'mere' consents, 13.14
operation of law, 13.07
property right, as, 13.02
registration, 13.08–13.09
security, 13.04, 13.05
testamentary disposition, 13.06
title to applications for registration, 13.10

Packaging
capable of being represented clearly and precisely, 2.08
infringement proceedings, affixing sign to materials and, 14.59–14.60
Paralympics Association Right *see also* **Olympics Association Right**
generally, 21.03
Paris Convention
international trade marks, and, 9.01
Parties to infringement proceedings
claimants
co-proprietors, 14.62
licensees, 14.63
proprietors, 14.61
defendants
affixing sign to materials, 14.59–14.60
introduction, 14.54
joint tortfeasors, 14.56–14.58
persons using mark, 14.55
Partnerships
company names, and, 2.35
unauthorised use of a trade mark, 19.30
Passing off
account of profits, 20.103–20.104
anticipatory goodwill, 20.32
case law, 20.09
claimants, 20.07
common field of activity
damage, and, 20.67
deception, and, 20.65–20.66

Passing off – *contd*
common field of activity – *contd*
generally, 20 64
likelihood of deception, and, 20.65–20.66
company names, and, 2.33–2.34
damage to or loss of goodwill
dilution of value of goodwill, 20.70
introduction, 20.68
loss of sales, 20.69
damages, 20.101–20.102
deception, 20.03–20.05
defences, 20.96–20.99
delivery up, 20.109
descriptive names, 20.41–20.43
dilution of value of goodwill, 20.70
elements, 20.10–20.16
evidence
damage to goodwill, of, 20.82–20.87
expert evidence, 20.93
generally, 20.71
goodwill, of, 20.72–20.73
methods of obtaining, 20.88–20.95
misrepresentation, of, 20.74–20.81
reputation, of, 20.72–20.73
survey evidence, 20.89–20.90
trap-purchases, 20.94–20.95
witness collection programmes, 20.91–20.92
expert evidence, 20.93
'extended' passing off
generally, 20.08
goodwill, 20.27–20.28
freezing injunctions, 20.113
generally, 1.13
get-ups, 20.38–20.40
goodwill
anticipatory goodwill, 20.32
definition, 20.19
descriptive names, 20.41–20.43
embodiment, 20.35–20.43
evidence, 20.72–20.73
'extended' passing off, in, 20.27–20.28
extent, 20.24–20.25

Passing off – *contd*
goodwill – *contd*
features, 20.38–20.40
generally, 20.03–20.05
get-ups, 20.38–20.40
images, 20.38–20.40
inherently distinctive trade marks, 20.36–20.37
international goodwill, 20.29–20.31
introduction, 20.18
nature, 20.18–20.34
ownership, 20.20–20.23
residual goodwill, 20.33
s 56(2) TMA, and, 20.34
scope, 20.24–20.25
secondary meaning, 20.41–20.43
signs, 20.38–20.40
time of assessment, 20.26
images, 20.38–20.40
inherently distinctive trade marks, 20.36–20.37
injunctions
generally, 20.105
interim injunctions, 20.106–20.108
international goodwill, 20.29–20.31
introduction, 20.01–20.02
loss of sales, 20.69
misrepresentation
acts outside UK, 20.57–20.58
association, as to, 20.46–20.48
comparative advertising, 20.63
deception, and, 20.49–20.50
descriptive use of terms or names, 20.59–20.60
endorsement, as to, 20.46–20.48
evidence, 20.74–20.81
factors which may negate, 20.53–20.63
introduction, 20.44
origin, as to, 20.45
persons deceived, 20.51–20.52
spares and accessories, 20.63
sponsorship, as to, 20.46–20.48
trade connection, as to, 20.46–20.48
use of other distinguishing material, 20.61–20.62
use of own name, 20.56

Passing off – *contd*
order to change name, 20.110
pre-emptive measures, 20.111–20.112
records, 20.111
remedies
account of profits, 20.103–20.104
damages, 20.101–20.102
delivery up, 20.109
generally, 20.100
injunctions, 20.105–20.108
order to change name, 20.110
reputation, 20.72–20.73
residual goodwill, 20.33
'reverse' passing off, 20.08
search orders, 20.113
survey evidence, 20.89–20.90
trade mark law, and, 20.06
trap-purchases, 20.94–20.95
unregistered trade marks, and, 2.14
use of own name, 20.56
well-known marks, and
generally, 20.34
introduction, 17.72
witness collection programmes, 20.91–20.92
Phrases
capable of being represented clearly and precisely, 2.09
Pre-emptive measures
passing off, and, 20.111–20.112
Preliminary indications of opposition
consequences, 7.39–7.42
implications, 7.37–7.38
introduction, 7.36
opposition based on other than s 5(1) or (2), 7.42
opposition based only on s 5(1) or (2), 7.41
Prior decisions
relative grounds for refusal, and, 5.62
Priority
claiming and filing application for EUTM, 8.09

Professional advisers
threats by
conditions to be satisfied, 18.16
generally, 18.14
'professional adviser', 18.15
Property rights
EU trade marks (EUTMs), and, 13.49
UK trade marks (UKTMs), and, 13.10
Proprietors
infringement proceedings, and, 14.61
Protected descriptions
definitions, 3.42
descriptors ineligible, 3.43–3.46
designations of origin (PDOs)
definition, 3.42
introduction, 3.38
foodstuffs, 3.40
formal requirements, 3.47–3.49
generally, 3.05, 3.38
geographical indications (PGIs)
definition, 3.42
introduction, 3.38
ineligible descriptors, 3.43–3.46
introduction, 1.11
purpose, 3.39
relationship with trade marks, 3.53
scope of protection, 3.52
subject matter, 3.39–3.42
traditional speciality guarantees (TSGs), 3.54–3.56
use, 3.50–3.51
Publication of applications
registration of marks before EUIPO, and, 8.14
registration of marks in UK, and, 7.17
Puffery
malicious falsehood, and, 16.29–16.30

Registered trade marks
defences to infringement, and, 15.06–15.08
generally, 1.02–1.08
Registration of trade marks
EUIPO, before
see also **Registration of trade marks (EUIPO)**
appeals, 8.64
examination, 8.12–8.13
filing, 8.04–8.11
generally, 8.02–8.03
introduction, 8.01
opposition, 8.15–8.63
procedures, 8.02–8.03
publication, 8.14
international trade marks, and
see also **Registration of trade marks (WIPO)**
application form, 9.12–9.19
basic application, 9.08–9.11
consideration by WIPO, 9.20–9.29
designations with additional requirements, 9.30
introduction, 9.02
legal framework, 9.03
notification of office of origin, 9.31–9.43
outline, in, 9.04–9.07
WIPO, and, 9.03
UKIPO, to
see also **Registration of trade marks (UK)**
address for service, 7.13
deficient, 7.11
examination, 7.14–7.16
fees, 7.06
filing, 7.07–7.10
form, 7.04–7.05
further requirements, 7.12–7.13
indication of class of goods or services, 7.12
introduction, 7.03
opposition, 7.18–7.82
publication, 7.17
Registration of trade marks (EUIPO)
appeals, 8.64
applicant's details, 8.05
applications
amendment, 8.11
contents, 8.05

Registration of trade marks (EUIPO) – *contd*
applications – *contd*
examination, 8.12
filing, 8.04–8.11
generally, 8.02–8.03
introduction, 8.01
opposition, 8.15–8.63
procedures, 8.02–8.03
publication, 8.14
search, 8.13
withdrawal, 8.11
claiming priority, 8.09
claiming seniority, 8.10
examination, 8.12–8.13
fees, 8.07
filing
amendment of application, 8.11
applicant's details, 8.05
claiming priority, 8.09
claiming seniority, 8.10
further formalities, 8.07
introduction, 8.04
languages, 8.08
list of goods and services for which protection is sought, 8.05
payment of fees, 8.07
representation of mark, 8.06
request for registration, 8.05
requirements if application to be given filing date, 8.05
withdrawal of application, 8.11
generally, 8.02–8.03
guidance, 8.02
introduction, 8.01
list of goods and services for which protection is sought, 8.05
opposition
ability to act before EUIPO, 8.19–8.22
absolute admissibility requirements, 8.25–8.30
admissibility of notice of opposition, 8.23–8.24
applicant's evidence, 8.49–8.51
basis, 8.16–8.17
cooling-off period, 8.41
costs, 8.63

Registration of trade marks (EUIPO) – *contd*
opposition – *contd*
dates relating to earlier applications and registrations, 8.33
extent of opposition, 8.38–8.39
filing evidence, 8.42–8.43, 8.60–8.62
further elements, 8.37–8.40
further evidence and arguments, 8.59
generally, 8.15
genuine use, 8.52–8.58
identification of contested application, 8.27
identification of earlier mark or sign, 8.34
identification of earlier rights, 8.28–8.29
identification of goods and services, 8.35
identification of grounds, 8.30
language of documents, 8.47–8.48
notice, 8.15
observations in reply, 8.49–8.51
opponent's proof of genuine use, 8.54–8.55
payment of fees, 8.26
procedural requirements, 8.18–8.22
proof of existence and validity of earlier applications and registrations, 8.44–8.46
proof of genuine use, 8.54–8.58
reasoned statement, 8.40
relative admissibility requirements, 8.31–8.36
request that opponent proves use, 8.52–8.53
scope of reputation, 8.36
standing to file notice, 8.18
translation, 8.32
payment of fees, 8.07
priority, 8.09
procedures, 8.02–8.03
publication, 8.14
representation of mark, 8.06

Registration of trade marks (EUIPO) – *contd*
request for registration, 8.05
search, 8.13
seniority, 8.10
withdrawal of application, 8.11
Registration of trade marks (UK)
address for service, 7.13
applicant's details, 7.09
application
address for service, 7.13
deficient, 7.11
examination, 7.14–7.16
fees, 7.06
filing, 7.07–7.10
form, 7.04–7.05
further requirements, 7.12–7.13
indication of class of goods or services, 7.12
introduction, 7.03
opposition, 7.18–7.82
publication, 7.17
declaration that mark in use, 7.10
deficient application, 7.11
examination, 7.14–7.16
fees, 7.06
filing application
applicant's details, 7.09
declaration that mark in use, 7.10
list of goods and services for which protection is sought, 7.09
method, 7.07
obtaining filing date, 7.09–7.10
payment of fees, 7.10
representation of mark, 7.09
request for registration, 7.09
requirements, 7.08
form for application, 7.04–7.05
indication of class of goods or services, 7.12
introduction, 7.01–7.02
list of goods and services for which protection is sought, 7.09
obtaining filing date, 7.09–7.10
opposition to application
appeals, 7.81
applicant's form, 7.31
challenging evidence, 7.66–7.67
Registration of trade marks (UK) – *contd*
opposition to application – *contd*
cooling-off period, 7.28–7.30
costs, 7.75–7.76
counterstatement, 7.33–7.35
cross-examination, 7.68–7.72
evidence as to goods and services, 7.64–7.72
extension of cooling-off period, 7.29
extension of time for filing evidence, 7.48–7.49
fast-track oppositions, 7.77—7.80
filing evidence, 7.44–7.49
filing formalities, 7.23–7.26
form of evidence, 7.50–7.63
hearings, 7.73
introduction, 7.18
notice to proceed, 7.43
notification to applicant for mark, 7.27
observations, 7.82
preliminary indications, 7.36–7.42
pre-opposition contact to applicant for mark, 7.21–7.22
request for opponent to prove use, 7.32
skeleton arguments, 7.74
statement of use of rights over five years old, 7.24–7.26
termination of cooling-off period, 7.30
time for filing, 7.19–7.20
time limits for filing evidence, 7.47
witness statements, 7.50–7.63
payment of fees, 7.10
preliminary indications
consequences, 7.39–7.42
implications, 7.37–7.38
introduction, 7.36
opposition based on other than s 5(1) or (2), 7.42
opposition based only on s 5(1) or (2), 7.41

Registration of trade marks (UK) – *contd*
publication of application, 7.17
representation of mark, 7.09
request for registration, 7.09
UKIPO, and, 7.01
Registration of trade marks (WIPO)
application
based on EUTM application or registration, 9.17
based on UKTM application or registration, 9.16
consideration by WIPO, 9.20–9.29
examination, 9.19
fees, 9.18
generally, 9.12–9.19
'basic' application
generally, 9.08–9.11
initial reliance on basic right, 9.11
introduction, 9.06
'basic' marks, 9.04
'central attack', 9.06
consideration by WIPO
formal irregularities, 9.20–9.24
irregularities as to specification of goods and services, 9.25–9.29
conversion of registration into national/regional rights, 9.42–9.43
dependence on basic right, 9.41
designation of countries, 9.04
designations with additional requirements, 9.30
EU trade marks (EUTMs), and, 9.04
examination, 9.19
fees, 9.18
formal irregularities
deadlines for resolution, 9.24
generally, 9.20
resolution by applicant, for, 9.22–9.23
resolution by Office of origin, for, 9.21–9.22
introduction, 9.02
Registration of trade marks (WIPO) – *contd*
irregularities as to specification of goods and services
generally, 9.25
incorrect classes or numbers of classes, 9.26–9.27
specification is unclear, 9.28–9.29
legal framework, 9.03
national marks, and, 9.04
notification of office of origin, 9.31–9.43
outline, in, 9.04–9.07
'real and effective establishment', 9.08–9.09
refusal of protection by designated office, 9.32–9.39
reliance on basic right, 9.11
strength of system, 9.05
transformation of registration into national/regional rights, 9.42–9.43
validity, 9.40
Relative grounds for refusal of registration
applications for registration of earlier marks, and, 5.07
aural similarity, 5.25
'blurring', 5.80–5.82
colour, 5.24
conceptual similarity, 5.26
conflicts with earlier rights
copyright, protection, 5.93
design right, protection, 5.93
introduction, 5.90
protection for other unregistered rights, 5.93
unregistered marks used in course of trade, 5.91–5.92
unregistered rights applicable to EUTMs, 5.94–5.96
conflicts with earlier trade marks
applications for registration of earlier marks, and, 5.07
detriment to distinctive character, 5.79–5.82
detriment to repute, 5.83–5.86
distinctiveness of earlier mark through use, 5.56–5.58

Relative grounds for refusal of registration – *contd*
conflicts with earlier trade marks – *contd*
'earlier trade mark', 5.10–5.12
extent of use of common elements of marks as used by parties, 5.59–5.61
harm to trade mark function, 5.06
identity of goods and services, 5.28–5.31
identity of marks, 5.13–5.16
interdependence of assessments of similarity, 5.53–5.55
introduction, 5.05
issues arising, 5.08–5.09
likelihood of confusion, 5.37–5.52
prior decisions, 5.62
reputation, 5.63–5.74
similarity of goods and services, 5.32–5.36
similarity of marks, 5.17–5.27
unfair advantage of distinctive character or repute, 5.75–5.78
use of later mark without due cause, 5.87–5.89
copyright, and, 5.93
descriptiveness of earlier trade mark, 5.54–5.55
design right, and, 5.93
detriment to distinctive character
'blurring' or 'dilution', 5.80–5.82
generally, 5.79
level of association, 5.86
detriment to repute
generally, 5.83–5.85
level of association, 5.86
'dilution', 5.80–5.82
distinctiveness of earlier mark through use
generally, 5.56–5.58
likelihood of confusion, and, 5.54–5.55
earlier trade marks, and
applications for registration, and, 5.07

Relative grounds for refusal of registration – *contd*
earlier trade marks, and – *contd*
definition, 5.10–5.12
descriptiveness, 5.54–5.55
distinctiveness, 5.54–5.58
EU position, 5.12
introduction, 5.02
UK position, 5.11
extent of use of common elements of marks as used by parties
generally, 5.59–5.61
issue estoppel, 5.62
harm to trade mark function, 5.06
identity of goods and services, 5.28–5.31
identity of marks, 5.13–5.16
infringement, and, 5.03
interdependence of assessments of similarity, 5.53–5.55
introduction, 5.01–5.02
issue estoppel, 5.62
legislative references, 5.04
likelihood of confusion
assessment, 5.39–5.43
consumer's level of attention, 5.44–5.48
distinctiveness/descriptiveness of earlier mark, 5.54–5.55
generally, 5.37
interdependence of assessments, 5.53–5.55
meaning, 5.38
significance of surrounding circumstances, 5.50–5.52
timing of confusion/'wrong way round' confusion, 5.49
prior decisions, 5.62
relative grounds for refusal, and, 5.06
reputation
detriment, and, 5.83–5.86
evidence required, 5.66–5.71
goods and services may be identical, similar or dissimilar, 5.65
relevance, 5.63–5.64
relevant public, 5.72–5.73
taking unfair advantage, and, 5.75–5.78

Relative grounds for refusal of registration – *contd*
reputation – *contd*
territory of evidence, 5.74
similarity of goods and services
'complementary', 5.35
examples of comparisons between goods and services, 5.36
generally, 5.32–5.33
respective users, 5.34
similarity of marks
aural similarity, 5.25
colour, 5.24
conceptual similarity, 5.26
factors used to assess, 5.22–5.23
generally, 5.17–5.19
interrelation of three aspects, 5.27
test, 5.20–5.21
visual similarity, 5.24
'tarnishing', 5.83–5.85
trade mark 'functions'
advertising functions, 5.100–5.105
essential function, 5.98–5.99
generally, 5.97
harm, and, 5.06
investment functions, 5.100–5.105
origin function, 5.98–5.99
unfair advantage of distinctive character or repute
generally, 5.75–5.78
level of association, 5.86
unregistered marks used in course of trade, and, 5.91–5.92
use of later mark without due cause, 5.87–5.89
visual similarity, 5.24

Remedies
account of profits
election, 17.05–17.07
generally, 17.17–17.19
'Anton Piller' orders, 17.29–17.30
co-proprietors, and, 17.80–17.81
damages
election, 17.05–17.07

Remedies – *contd*
damages – *contd*
Enforcement Directive, 17.09–17.11
general rules, 17.12
generally, 17.08–17.16
losses by subsidiary, 17.16
methods of calculation, 17.13–17.14
secondary loss, 17.15
delivery up of infringing goods, material and articles, 17.43–17.47
destruction of infringing goods, 17.41–17.42
destruction of infringing goods, material and articles, 17.48–17.52
election between damages and account, 17.05–17.07
erasure of offending sign, 17.39–17.40
forfeiture of infringing goods, material and articles, 17.48–17.52
groundless threats, 18.18
imaging orders, 17.29–17.30
infringement of EU trade marks (EUTMs)
effect of Brexit, 17.03
generally, 17.04
infringement of UK registered trade marks (UKTMs), for
account of profits, 17.17–17.19
'Anton Piller' orders, 17.29–17.30
damages, 17.08–17.16
delivery up of infringing goods, material and articles, 17.43–17.47
destruction of infringing goods, 17.41–17.42
destruction of infringing goods, material and articles, 17.48–17.52
effect of Brexit on comparable trade marks (EU), 17.03
election between damages and account, 17.05–17.07

Remedies – *contd*
infringement of UK registered trade marks (UKTMs), for – *contd*
erasure of offending sign, 17.39–17.40
forfeiture of infringing goods, material and articles, 17.48–17.52
generally, 17.02
imaging orders, 17.29–17.30
injunctions, 17.20–17.27
obliteration of offending sign, 17.39–17.40
orders for disclosure of information about infringing activity, 17.31–17.33
other relief, 17.28
removal of offending sign, 17.39–17.40
search orders, 17.29–17.30
infringement of well-known marks
generally, 2.26; 17.65–17.72
injunctions, 17.66–17.71
passing off, and, 17.72
infringing goods, material and articles, and
delivery up of infringing goods, material and articles, 17.43–17.47
destruction of infringing goods, 17.41–17.42
destruction of infringing goods, material and articles, 17.48–17.52
erasure of offending sign, 17.39–17.40
forfeiture of infringing goods, material and articles, 17.48–17.52
generally, 17.34–17.35
'infringing articles', 17.38
'infringing goods', 17.36
'infringing material', 17.37
notice to Customs, 17.53–17.64
obliteration of offending sign, 17.39–17.40
removal of offending sign, 17.39–17.40

Remedies – *contd*
injunctions
final injunctions, 17.27
generally, 17.20–17.21
interim injunctions, 17.22–17.26
unauthorised application for registration by agent or representative, and, 17.73–17.75
well-known marks, and, 17.66–17.71
introduction, 17.01
jurisdiction of courts, 17.86–17.91
licensees, and 17.82–17.85
malicious falsehood, and, 16.32–16.33
notice to Customs
generally, 17.53
Regulation (EU) No. 608/2013 (as amended), 17.54–17.61
TMA 1994, s 89, 17.62–17.64
obliteration of offending sign, 17.39–17.40
Olympic symbols rights, and, 21.16
orders for disclosure of information about infringing activity, 17.31–17.33
passing off, and
account of profits, 20.103–20.104
damages, 20.101–20.102
delivery up, 20.109
generally, 20.100
injunctions, 20.105–20.108
order to change name, 20.110
removal of offending sign, 17.39–17.40
search orders, 17.29–17.30
unauthorised application for registration by agent or representative, for
generally, 17.73–17.74
justification, 17.75
unauthorised use of Royal Arms, 17.76–17.79
well-known trade marks, and, 2.26

Removal of offending sign
generally, 17.39–17.40

Representation of mark
registration of marks before EUIPO, and, 8.06
registration of marks in UK, and, 7.09
withdrawal of application, 8.11
Representatives
EUIPO, before
generally, 10.05
'legal practitioner', 10.06
'professional representative', 10.07–10.08
introduction, 10.01
remedies for unauthorised application for registration, and
generally, 17.73–17.74
justification, 17.75
UKIPO, before
appointment, 10.03
cancellation, 10.04
need for address in UK, Gibraltar or CI, 10.02
WIPO, before
appointment, 10.10
cancellation, 10.11–10.12
generally, 10.09
Reputation
detriment, and, 5.83–5.86
evidence required, 5.66–5.71
goods and services may be identical, similar or dissimilar, 5.65
infringement proceedings, and, 14.47
passing off, and, 20.72–20.73
relevance, 5.63–5.64
relevant public, 5.72–5.73
taking unfair advantage, and, 5.75–5.78
territory of evidence, 5.74
Request for opponent to prove use
opposition to registration in UK, and, 7.32
Retail services
classification system, and, 6.14–6.15
Revocation
collective and certification marks, and
European Union, 3.36
United Kingdom, 3.27–3.29
common name in the trade for the product or service for which registered – s 46(1)(c); Art 58(1)(b)
'common name', 12.29
'for the product or service for which it is registered', 12.30–12.33
generally, 12.28
'in the trade', 12.29
resulting from acts or inactivity of registered proprietor, 12.34–12.36
effect, 12.47–12.48
generally, 12.02
generic names – s 46(1)(c); Art 58(1)(b)
'common name', 12.29
'for the product or service for which it is registered', 12.30–12.33
generally, 12.28
'in the trade', 12.29
resulting from acts or inactivity of registered proprietor, 12.34–12.36
introduction, 12.01
legislative framework, 12.03
non-use, for – s 46(1)(a)–(b); Art 58(1)(a)
date to be considered, 12.05
generally, 12.04
'genuine use', 12.06
legitimate reasons, 12.26–12.27
level of use required, 12.07
mark differing in elements affecting distinctive character, 12.11–12.14
nature of activities, 12.08–12.09
partial revocation, 12.19–12.24
proper reasons, 12.25–12.27
use for goods or services of the registration, 12.15
use in relevant territory, 12.18

Revocation – *contd*
non-use, for – s 46(1)(a)–(b); Art 58(1)(a) – *contd*
use in relevant time period, 12.16–12.17
use of mark as registered, 12.10
partial revocation for non-use
action before EUIPO, 12.23–12.24
generally, 12.19
UK approach, 12.20–12.22
trade mark has become misleading, where – s 46(1)(d); Art 58(1)(c)
generally, 12.37
procedure before EUIPO, 12.41–12.46
procedure before UKIPO, 12.38–12.40
Royal Arms
remedies for unauthorised use, and, 17.76–17.79

Search
registration of marks before EUIPO, and, 8.13
Search orders
generally, 17.29–17.30
passing off, and, 20.113
Security interests
UK trade marks (UKTMs), and
introduction, 13.04, 13.05
registration, 13.08–13.09
Seniority
claiming at time of filing application for EUTM, 8.10
Shape of goods
absolute grounds of refusal, and, 4.40–4.44
capable of being represented clearly and precisely, 2.08
Shape of packaging
capable of being represented clearly and precisely, 2.08
Shopping-centre services
classification system, and, 6.14–6.15
Sign
generally, 2.03
Sign – *contd*
infringement, and
affixing sign to materials, 14.59–14.60
use of sign by third party, 14.12–14.19, 14.41
use of sign identical to mark, 14.23, 14.42
not satisfying statutory requirements, absolute grounds of refusal, 4.06
Similarity of goods and services
'complementary', 5.35
examples of comparisons between goods and services, 5.36
generally, 5.32–5.33
respective users, 5.34
Similarity of marks
aural similarity, 5.25
colour, 5.24
conceptual similarity, 5.26
factors used to assess, 5.22–5.23
generally, 5.17–5.19
interrelation of three aspects, 5.27
test, 5.20–5.21
visual similarity, 5.24
Skeleton arguments
opposition to registration in UK, and, 7.74
Slogans
capable of being represented clearly and precisely, 2.09
Smells
capable of being represented clearly and precisely, 2.07
Sounds
capable of being represented clearly and precisely, 2.06
Statement of use of rights over five years old
opposition to registration in UK, and, 7.24–7.26
Survey evidence
passing off, and, 20.89–20.90

'Tarnishing'
infringement, and, 14.51–14.52
relative grounds for refusal, and, 5.83–5.86

Threats actions *see* **Groundless threats**
Time limits
opposition to registration in UK, and
filing applications, 7.19–7.20
filing evidence, 7.47
Trade Marks Act 1994
grounds for refusal of registration, and, 5.04
infringement, and 14.03
registered trade marks, and
common principles and effect of Brexit, 1.05
generally, 1.02–1.04
revocation of marks, and, 12.03
Trade mark 'functions'
advertising functions, 5.100–5.105
essential function, 5.98–5.99
generally, 5.97
harm, and, 5.06
investment functions, 5.100–5.105
origin function, 5.98–5.99
relative grounds for refusal, and, 5.06
Trade marks *see also* **European Union trade marks (EUTMs); UK trade marks (UKTMs)**
capable of being represented clearly and precisely
colours, 2.05
designs, 2.08
generally, 2.04
phrases, 2.09
shape of goods or packaging, 2.08
slogans, 2.09
smells, 2.07
sounds, 2.06
capable of distinguishing goods or services, 2.10
colours, 2.05
company names
choice, 2.29
compulsory change, 2.31
domain names, 2.36–2.39
generally, 2.28
overview, 2.27
passing off, 2.33–2.34
Trade Marks– *contd*
company names – *contd*
publicity to be given to, 2.32
trade mark infringement, 2.33–2.34
unincorporated businesses and partnerships, 2.35
voluntary change, 2.30
definition
capable of being represented clearly and precisely, 2.04–2.09
capable of distinguishing goods or services, 2.10
generally, 2.01–2.02
goods and services, 2.11
'sign', 2.03
undertakings, 2.13
designs, 2.08
goods and services, 2.11
packaging, 2.08
phrases, 2.09
shape of goods or packaging, 2.08
'sign', 2.03
slogans, 2.09
smells, 2.07
sounds, 2.06
undertakings, 2.13
unregistered trade marks
defence to infringement, 2.16
impediment to registration, 2.15
introduction, 2.13
passing off, 2.14
well-known trade marks, 2.17
well-known trade marks
basis for opposing registration of later marks, 2.23
'Convention country', 2.19
defence to infringement of later marks, 2.24–2.25
generally, 2.18
meaning of 'well known', 2.20–2.22
remedies for infringement, 2.26
unregistered trade marks, and, 2.17
Traditional speciality guarantees (TSGs)
generally, 3.54–3.56
introduction, 1.11

Transfer of ownership
certification marks, and, 3.25–3.26
collective marks, and, 3.25–3.26
Translation
opposition to registration before EUIPO, and, 8.32
Trap-purchases
passing off, and, 20.94–20.95
TRIPS Agreement
international trade marks, and, 9.01

UK Intellectual Property Office (UKIPO)
applications for registration of marks, and
see also **Applications for registration (UK)**
address for service, 7.13
deficient, 7.11
examination, 7.14–7.16
fees, 7.06
filing, 7.07–7.10
form, 7.04–7.05
further requirements, 7.12–7.13
indication of class of goods or services, 7.12
introduction, 7.01–7.03
opposition, 7.18–7.82
publication, 7.17
invalidity, and
absolute grounds for refusal, and, 11.03
acquiescence, and, 11.07–11.11
appeals, 11.17
breach of s 3, 11.03
commencement of proceedings, 11.13
consent to registration, 11.05
evidence and submissions, 11.16
existence of earlier trade mark, 11.04–11.06
grounds for declaration, 11.02–11.06
hearings, 11.17
procedure, 11.12–11.17
relative grounds for refusal, and, 11.04–11.05
response of registered proprietor to proceedings, 11.14–11.15
UK Intellectual Property Office (UKIPO) – *contd*
registered trade marks, 1.02
representation, and
appointment, 10.03
cancellation, 10.04
need for address in UK, Gibraltar or CI, 10.02
UK trade marks (UKTMs)
common principles and effect of Brexit, 1.05
dealings with *see* **Dealings with UK trade marks (UKTMs)**
interpretation of law, determination, 1.05
ownership *see* **Ownership of UK trade marks (UKTMs)**
protection
registered trade marks, and, 1.02
Trade Marks Act 1994, under, 1.03
registered trade marks
dealings with *see* **Dealings with UK trade marks (UKTMs)**
protection, 1.02
Unauthorised application for registration by agent or representative
generally, 17.73–17.74
justification, 17.75
Unauthorised use of a trade mark
articles for making signs, 19.23–19.25
bodies corporate, 19.30
defence, 19.26–19.29
enforcement, 19.31
generally, 19.02–19.03
goods bearing sign, 19.16–19.19
infringing signs, 19.10–19.15
materials bearing sign, 19.20–19.22
mental element, 19.04–19.07
partnerships, 19.30
penalties, 19.32–19.33
reasonable belief of non-infringement, 19.26–19.29
types of offence, 19.02
use of infringing sign, 19.11–19.15
'with a view', 19.06
'with intent', 19.07
without consent, 19.08–19.09

Unauthorised use of Royal Arms
generally, 19.42
remedies for infringement, and, 17.76–17.79
Undertakings
generally, 2.13
Unfair advantage
distinctive character or repute, and
generally, 5.75–5.78
level of association, 5.86
Unincorporated businesses
company names, and, 2.35
Unregistered marks used in course of trade
relative grounds for refusal, and, 5.91–5.92
Unregistered trade marks
defence to infringement, 2.16
impediment to registration, 2.15
introduction, 2.13
passing off, 2.14
use in course of trade, and, 5.91–5.92
well-known trade marks, 2.17
Use of later mark without due cause
relative grounds for refusal, and, 5.87–5.89
Use of own name
generally, 15.10–15.12
'honest practices' proviso, 15.23–15.25
introduction, 15.09
passing off, and, 20.56
User of a mark
infringement proceedings, and, 14.55

Visual similarity
relative grounds for refusal, and, 5.24

Well-known trade marks
basis for opposing registration of later marks, 2.23
'Convention country', 2.19
defence to infringement of later marks, 2.24–2.25
generally, 2.18

Well-known trade marks – *contd*
injunctions
acquiescence, 17.70
bona fide use, 17.70
entitlement, 17.66
essential part of trade mark, 17.67
limitations on right, 17.70
priority over registered trade marks, 17.71
proof of confusion, 17.68–17.69
introduction, 1.09
meaning of 'well known', 2.20–2.22
passing off, and
generally, 20.34
introduction, 17.72
remedies for infringement
generally, 2.26; 17.65–17.72
injunctions, 17.66–17.71
passing off, and, 17.72
unregistered trade marks, and, 2.17
Wholesale services
classification system, and, 6.14–6.15
Witness statements
applicant as to likelihood of confusion, by
acquired weakness of mark, 7.61–7.63
generally, 7.58
inherent weakness of mark, 7.59–7.60
opponent as to likelihood of confusion, by
acquired distinctiveness of mark, 7.56–7.57
generally, 7.53
inherent distinctiveness of mark, 7.54–7.55
opposition to registration in UK, and
generally, 7.50
goods and services, 7.64–7.72
likelihood of confusion, 7.53–7.63
persons making, 7.51–7.52

World Intellectual Property Organisation (WIPO)
applications for registration, and *see also* **Applications for registration (WIPO)**
application form, 9.12–9.19
basic application, 9.08–9.11
consideration by WIPO, 9.20–9.29
designations with additional requirements, 9.30
introduction, 9.02
legal framework, 9.03

World Intellectual Property Organisation (WIPO) – *contd*
applications for registration, and – *contd*
notification of office of origin, 9.31–9.43
outline, in, 9.04–9.07
generally, 9.03
registered trade marks, 1.02
representation, and
appointment, 10.10
cancellation, 10.11–10.12
generally, 10.09

www.ingramcontent.com/pod-product-compliance
Ingram Content Group UK Ltd.
Pitfield, Milton Keynes, MK11 3LW, UK
UKHW020122290926
15471UKWH00003B/225

9 781526 511553